# FUNK

## by Dave Thompson

Backbeat
Books

San Francisco

Published by Backbeat Books
600 Harrison Street, San Francisco, CA 94105
An imprint of the Music Player Network
United Entertainment Media

Distributed to the book trade in the U.S. and Canada by
Publishers Group West 1700 Fourth Street, Berkeley, CA 94710

Distributed to the music trade in the U.S. and Canada by
Hal Leonard Publishing P.O. Box 13819, Milwaukee, WI 53213

Cover Design by Richard Leeds
Text Composition by Impressions Book and Journal Services, Inc.
Front Cover Photo of George Clinton: Robb D. Cohen
Back Cover Photo of James Brown: © Raeburn Flerlage/Chansley Entertainment Archives

Library of Congress Cataloging-in-Publication Data

Thompson, Dave
    Funk / by Dave Thompson
        p. cm. — (Third Ear)
    Includes bibliographical references (p. ), discographies, and index.
    ISBN 0–87930–629–7 (alk. Paper)
        1. Funk (Music)—History and criticism. 2. Funk (Music)—Discography. I. Title. II. Series.

ML3527.8 .T56 2001
781.64—dc21                                2001025189

Printed in the United States of America

01 02 03 04 05      5 4 3 2 1

# TABLE OF CONTENTS

*Acknowledgments*  v
*Introduction*  vii

**PART ONE: PRE-FUNK**
Vicki Anderson  1
Autumn Records  2
Beau Dollar & the Dapps  2
Archie Bell & the Drells  3
Booker T. & the MGs  4
James Brown  8
Bobby Byrd  27
Dyke & the Blazers  29
Isley Brothers  30
Fela Ransome Kuti  36
The Last Poets  41
The Mar-Keys  43
Stax/Volt Records  45
Sly Stone  47
Watts Prophets  53

**Essays**
Frontiers of Funk: Gumbo and the Groove  55
Frontiers of Funk: The Psyche-Funka-Delic
    Experience  59
Frontiers of Funk: Motown Gets With It  64

**PART TWO: CLASSIC FUNK**
Act One  69
Average White Band  69
Baby Huey and the Babysitters  73
The Bar-Kays  73
Black Nazty  77
Hamilton Bohannon  77
Brother to Brother  79
Donald Byrd and the Blackbyrds  80
Jimmy Castor  82
George Clinton  84
Bootsy Collins  103
Lyn Collins  109
The Commodores  110
Ruth Copeland  114
The Counts  115
Curtom Records  116
Carl Douglas  117
Earth Wind & Fire  118

Enterprise Records  124
Funk Inc.  124
Gonzalez  126
Larry Graham  126
Herbie Hancock  129
Fuzzy Haskins  133
Isaac Hayes  134
Eddie Hazel  139
Hot Chocolate  141
Hot City Bump Band  142
Invictus Records  143
The JBs  145
Kokomo  148
Kool & the Gang  149
Lafayette Afro Rock Band  156
Malo  157
Curtis Mayfield  158
The Meters  164
Zigaboo Modeliste  169
New Birth  169
The Ohio Players  171
Maceo Parker  176
People Records  179
Rufus  181
Tower of Power  183
Undisputed Truth  188
War  189
Fred Wesley  193
Westbound Records  195
Barry White  196
Norman Whitfield  202
Charles Wright and the Watts 103rd Street Rhythm
    Band  203

**Essays**
Blaxploitaion: Funk Goes to the Movies  207
The British Rock Funk Connection  214

**PART THREE: DISCO FUNK**
Aurra  219
Roy Ayers  220
Taka Boom  222
Brass Construction  223
Brick  226
The Brides of Funkenstein  226

The Brothers Johnson  228
B.T. Express  230
Cameo  231
Rafael Cameron  234
Chocolate Milk  235
The Clarke-Duke Project  236
Con Funk Shun  239
Crown Heights Affair  242
Dazz Band  243
The Fatback Band  245
Fat Larry's Band  249
Faze-O  250
The Gap Band  250
Heatwave  254
Hi Tension  256
Instant Funk  256
Rick James  259
KC & the Sunshine Band  262
Chaka Khan  265
Lakeside  268
LTD  270
Maze  271
Midnight Star  272
Mutiny  274
Parlet  275
Praxis  276
Rose Royce  276
Skyy  278
Slave  279
S.O.S. Band  282
Stuff  283
Stylus  284
Sun  285
Wild Cherry  285

## Essays

Disco and the Death of Funk  287
Hot Grooves: Cold Storage  291

## PART FOUR: THE NEW SCHOOL

Acid Jazz Records  293
Adu  295
Beggar and Co.  295
Brand New Heavies  296
Brooklyn Funk Essentials  297
Chuck Brown and the Soul Searchers  297
Defunkt  299
Digital Underground  300

Fishbone  302
Freeez  303
Galactic  304
Imagination  305
Incognito  306
Incorporated Thang Band  308
Jamiroquai  308
Chaz Jankel  310
Kashif  311
Kiddo  312
Bill Laswell  313
Light of the World  314
Linx  315
Power Station  315
Prince  316
The Red Hot Chili Peppers  323
Roogalator  326
Shakatak  327
Skunkhour  328
The Time  329
Trouble Funk  330
24–7 Spyz  331
Bernie Worrell  332
Zapp  333

## Essays

P-Funk Meets the F-Punk  337
The Birth of Go-Go  342
Rap: The Sons of the P  346
Funkin' Up a Storm: Essential Funk Compilations  350

## ESSENTIAL FUNK—THE TOP 24  356

*General Bibliography*  357
*Photo Credits*  358
*Index*  359

**FUNK**

# ACKNOWLEDGMENTS

Any book this size necessarily demands the help and dedication of an army of people. I'd like to thank everybody who threw something into the pot, but most especially Amy Hanson, tireless research assistant and occasional co-author; Jo-Ann Greene, for fearlessly proofreading beyond the call of duty; Danny Adler and John DeBlaiso, for pointing me in the direction of so many obscure and unknown records; and Miles and Arthur at Holy Cow Records of Seattle, for having so many of them.

Thanks also to everybody else who helped bring the beast to life: my agent, Sherrill Chidiac; Dorothy Cox, Nancy Tabor and all at Backbeat Books; Anchorite Man, Back Ears (whose ears are apparently still on backwards), Jennifer Ballantine, Bateerz and family (not forgetting the Crab), Blind Pew, Barb East, Ella, the Gremlins, who probably live in the furnace, K-Mart (not the store), Geoff Monmouth, the late Mrs. Spider, Nutkin, Rita & Eric, Snarleyyowl, Sprocket, Squidge, a lot of Thompsons, Michael Veal and Neville Viking. Finally, my gratitude to the many researchers who took this journey before me.

# INTRODUCTION

Funk is the sound of James Brown colliding with Thelonious Monk, of Fela Kuti jamming with the Jefferson Airplane, of Santana impacting with the Family Stone. It is the ruthless discipline of rhythm and the awesome expansion of improvisation; it is the righteousness of social comment and the rebelliousness of political action; it is the febrile joy of Mardi Gras and the supercharged slam of Kwanza.

There is more: a Stax label single spinning in an inner-city juke joint, Funkenstein's flashlight, Sly Stone's sex machine, papa's brand new bag. "Funk" is a slang word for smell and a euphemism for sex. But most of all, it is one of the basic building blocks of music, the moment when two, four, any number of musicians stop playing *with* one another and begin playing as one, driven by the beat, working inside the rhythm. Funk is the sound of the absolute organic purity that existed before there were words to mould the moment and it will still be there long after they are gone.

Funk is the sound of human instinct, where forms as culturally and musically remote as the space jams of the psychedelic age, the mantric miasma of Afro-beat, and the electronic pulsing of modern synthesizers merge in the movements of the dancer; this is why the best funk will have you dancing before you're even aware it's playing, and the worst will leave you cold as ice. You cannot fake the funk.

Few great funk songs ever started life on paper; they began in rehearsal studios or concert halls, with the musicians playing, improvising, feeding and feeling one another until they hit a groove and the groove took over. Maybe later they would edit it down, trim the fat around the heart, lop off an excess 5, 15, 30 minutes, whatever, but only if they could do so without excising the feeling. War spent two years with "Me and Baby Brother" before they were confident enough to slice an eight-minute live jam down to a three-minute single. Other bands, great bands among them, never released a single 45 that truly did them justice.

There is, musicologists will tell you, a distinct formula to it, hitting the downbeat at the beginning of a bar, that magical moment that James Brown called "the one." Most musicians—even those who were themselves gravitating toward funk—played around that downbeat. Brown emphasized it, directing everything to it and making sure everybody hit it hard. But a cat with no ears could tell you, a band can be funky without playing funk . . . and a band can play funk without sounding in the slightest bit funky." Funk is a state of mind and a state of body. One—the One—cannot exist without the other.

Why would it even want to?

## HOW TO USE THIS BOOK

Alongside the earlier soul and later rap/hip-hop, funk is the most enduring musical form to emerge out of the American Black community, yet it is also the most misunderstood. The term itself has been pirated to accompany any number of musical sins, few of which have anything to do with the music in its purest form—although a large part of the problem rests in funk's own refusal to tie itself down to any singular set of rules, and its development, accordingly, along so many different paths. This book attempts to follow, and illustrate, that development by dividing the history into four parts, as follows:

**PART ONE: PRE-FUNK.** This section indexes the artists whose work during the 1950s and 1960s unquestionably laid the groundwork for what was to come.

James Brown, of course, became the undisputed Godfather of Funk. His revolutionary marriage of syncopation and rhythmic rhythm guitar establishing, as early as 1962 ("Limbo Jimbo"), a musical formula that he continued refining through the early-mid-'60s before, by his own admission, he finally got it right with "Papa's Got a Brand New Bag" in 1965. But other acts were working in a similar arena—instrumental acts, like the Stax Records houseband, Booker T. & the MGs, Motown stars Junior Walker and the All-Stars, and vocal groups, like Archie Bell & the Drells.

As the decade progressed, these acts' messages became more political—a brand new bag indeed. But it was with the emergence of San Francisco's Sly Stone, in 1967, that the sound became a crescendo. Unafraid to blend his musical preferences with the experimental commentary emerging from elsewhere on the American scene (primarily, but not exclusively, within his own Bay Area homeland), Stone's example and influence percolated into the hearts of both mainstream rock and R&B.

The resulting cataclysm, which history today terms psychedelia, shocked popular music, then shaped it. Disparate themes slammed together, then exploded out again. For every artist who emerged in the unabashed shadow of conventional R&B, there was another whose musical prerogatives were drawn from the disciplines of jazz, another from rich, but largely untapped African and Latin sources, and another still whose roots lay alongside Stone. But not one of the musical forms that came together in the psychedelic potpourri emerged unchanged. Pop groups became rock bands (even the terminology changed), modern jazz turned to fusion, traditional music was suddenly folk rock, and vast swathes of R&B were now funk.

**PART TWO: CLASSIC FUNK.** The heart of the book, this section deals with what is now designated the golden age of funk, the late '60s and early-mid-'70s. Many of the bands in this section were unashamedly, and unabashedly, forged within the musical melting pot of psychedelia. But it is no coincidence that politics, too, should enflame and inform much of what would take place, the ghastly dichotomy of an entire generation being sent overseas to fight for the freedoms that many of them couldn't even enjoy in their homeland. The Vietnam War was almost three years old before America finally, consciously, began to embrace the concept of true civil liberty as a cause, as opposed to a theory; as a right, not a rhetoric; as a reality to embrace, not a Utopia to export. Funk was on the frontline of the ensuing struggles—both those that had been won, and those that were still to come.

Amid this seething ferment, George Clinton, War, Isaac Hayes, the Bar-Kays, Ohio Express, Kool & the Gang, Earth Wind & Fire, Curtis Mayfield and so many more stepped out of the shadows of their '60s soul and R&B endeavors and donned robes as the Ambassadors of the Funk. And as they did so, they adopted musical ideas, forms and structures, which had never (or rarely) played a part in their earlier works, and made them their own.

DJ and writer Rickey Vincent, author of the funk narrative *Funk: the Music, the People and the Rhythm of the One* (St Martin's Griffin, NY, 1995) isolates three separate (if mutually compatible) streams of funk as dominating the music's own early-mid-'70s peak: the "Funky Soul" of Curtis Mayfield, Barry White, Stevie Wonder (and, curiously absent from Vincent's categorization, Isaac Hayes); the multi-racial, multi-genre "United Funk/Funk Rock" of George Clinton, War, Kool & the Gang, Graham Central Station and so forth; and "Jazz Funk," the hybrid fusion sound of Herbie Hancock, Donald Byrd, Grover Washington, Jr., and company. Subject though they were to continued refinement and cross fertilization, these three formats remained in play through to the end of the decade. They would not, however, stand alone.

Even at its mid-'70s height, the funk family was tiny. Other musical genres attract practitioners and hangers-on like dead meat attracts flies (often, very like . . .). Funk, however, remained a closed shop, one that might attract a fleeting visit from sundry passers-by, but rarely encouraged any of them to take up permanent residence.

They could still make their presence felt, though. A number of traditional rock 'n' rollers—David Bowie, Jeff Beck, the Rolling Stones—pitched their tents in the garden for a while; others took out a lease on the guest house. Whether deliberately or otherwise, rock subverted many of funk's rhythmic characteristics (not to mention much of its language), and occasionally did it well.

**PART THREE: DISCO FUNK.** The advent of disco is considered by many commentators (and many bands, too) to have spelled the end of funk in its purest form, a doomsday evidenced by the decline in the powers of many of the music's most potent perpetrators. In fact, disco repurified funk, brought an end to a period of increasing self-reference and forced the music, if not the musicians, to again look beyond its own confines.

In the early '70s, psychedelic rock had provided funk with its most immediate impetus. In the late '70s, disco did the same thing, not only in the form of the new instruments and technology, which disco's patronage was nudging into the mainstream, but also in terms of musical ethics (or, detractors say, the lack thereof). Although the boundaries do occasionally become extraordinarily muddled, the bands in this section are those who did the most to keep funk alive in the face of everything.

Like the funk that, as James Brown once said, it closely aped, disco is defined musically within fairly rigid guidelines. It needed a thumping beat—and the faster the better. It oozed strings and howling horns, and, even at its most innocent, it sweated hot sex from every pore.

It was also totally genuine; even after electronics swept onto the scene, there were few machines even remotely capable of providing the lush and sweeping body assault of an orchestra of violins. There were, however, a lot of would-be arrangers and orchestrators who saw the success of Barry White's Love Unlimited Orchestra, the Salsoul Orchestra and Gamble and Huff's MFSB (Mothers, Fathers, Sisters, Brothers), and fancied grabbing a piece of the string-driven action for themselves.

Neither was there any shortage of established artists who, whether searching for a pick-me-up for a fading career, or looking for a challenge for other reasons entirely, were willing to throw themselves onto the disco dance floor: Patti Labelle, Donna Summer, the Rolling Stones, Thelma Houston, Diana Ross, Rod Stewart . . . . Hamilton Bohannon cut a single called "Disco Stomp" a full year before the music truly took off, and it was funk with an eye for the ease with which a catchy phrase could capture the mood.

James Brown released "Disco Man" a few years after, and even he admitted it was horrible. But it was a determined soul indeed who could stand outside the gates of disco and continue to look the other way. Some musical forms had more meaning; others had more sophistication. But even the brightest butterfly is drawn into the flame eventually. And only the smartest ones wear asbestos underwear.

First generation funk juggernauts P-Funk, War, the Ohio Players, Kool & the Gang, Barry White, and Earth Wind & Fire scored some of their biggest-ever hits during the disco era (so did hitherto uncompromising rock iconoclasts Rod Stewart and the Rolling Stones). Second wave superheroes Brass Construction, BT Express, Slave and Crown Heights Affair were forged just on the cusp of the new age. And as for the popularly argued notion that disco was somehow inferior—because, as both James Brown and author Rickey Vincent put it, its "bands" tended to be mere masks for one canny studio wizard—where does that leave the JBs, the Last Word, the First Family, Vicki Anderson, Lyn Collins (all James Brown written/produced/arranged and often co-performed), the Brides of Funkenstein, the Horny Horns, Bootsy's Rubber Band, Parlet (all George Clinton-powered projects), Brass Construction, BT Express, Skyy, and Rafael Cameron (all Randy Muller)? If you don't like disco music, that's your prerogative. But don't try to justify your disdain with facts and intellectual purity. It doesn't work.

**PART FOUR: THE NEW SCHOOL.** Nevertheless, no matter how one breaks down its components, few musical forms have been so universally despised as disco. The critical assault commenced immediately; the musical backlash followed with the most pronounced attack emerging out of the UK—a land that had hitherto done little more than follow the American lead.

Led off by the studiously eclectic (and, not at all coincidentally, Anglo-American) Roogalator, this new funk's most noticeable departure was its insistence that dance music no longer needed to be danceable. From Britain's post-punk ferment, the Pop Group, the Gang of Four and Public Image Ltd.; from New York's No Wave scene, James Chance and Defunkt all came shuffling in on seismic bass lines and scratching rhythms, rewriting rock's familiar signatures in precisely the same fashion as the likes of George Clinton had a decade before.

The difference was, whereas the mainstream music press had never addressed funk's absorption of rock'n'roll with anything more than tokenist condescension (the shaming consequence being that the majority of white fans have still never heard Funkadelic's "Maggot Brain"), they readily recognized rock's absorption of funk as the breaching of a vast new frontier—a tokenism of a different kind, of course, but one that this time provoked rebellion.

The New Yorkers went their own way entirely, allying rhythm with dissonance to forge a new music, which owed a greater debt to Stockhausen than Stone, but still touched home base occasionally, via the maneuverings of producer Bill Laswell. In the London nightclubs of the late '70s, however, Parliament was all powerful, up there alongside Kraftwerk and David Bowie and ripe, therefore, for assimilation into the music made by the kids who danced there.

Shakatak, Linx, Beggar and Co. and Level 42 all sprang into the "classic" funk void, which the naivety of punk amateurs left empty. And, shortlived though it might have been, the Britfunk movement of 1980–82 almost singlehandedly paved the way for the acid jazz scene of the late decade. Likewise, the similarly underground, equally rebellious, hip-hop parties of contemporary Black America took their own brands from the fires of funk and ultimately ignited rap.

These developments did not occur in isolated incompatibility. The Red Hot Chili Peppers, arguably the single most influential white funk band of all time, recorded their first album with Andy Gill of the Gang of Four, and their second with George Clinton. Both records possess their own unique flavoring, but both are bound together by their devotion to the funk.

That same devotion is the thread that binds the bands in this book. The edges blur in places; though certain inclusions and omissions alike may seem arbitrary, it should be remembered that many acts came to (or, contrarily, departed from) funk into other musical genres in which their impact was just as vast—if not immeasurable. From the world of rock 'n' roll, Jimi Hendrix, Rare Earth, David Bowie, Jeff Beck, Fishbone and the Gang of Four; from the world of jazz, Miles Davis, Chick Corea, John Coltrane, Sun Ra, the Crusaders, and Ramsey Lewis; from that of soul and R&B, Otis Redding, Marvin Gaye, Joe Tex, Bobby Womack, Stevie Wonder . . . the lists are endless, but in each and every instance the same question produced the same answer.

For what will the artist be remembered? A few minutes of sometimes-superlative funk cut at a specific juncture in a lifelong career? Or for a body of equally exemplary work, unleashed in another genre altogether? In other words, if you went shopping for a copy of Public Enemy's *It Takes a Nation of Millions to Hold Us Back*, an album whose very essence is rooted in funk, where would you expect to find it? Alongside all their other albums, filed neatly under Rap? Or somewhere else in the store entirely, peeking out between Praxis and Rose Royce?

Many of these artists are featured in this book, within the retelling of other bands' careers, or within the essays, which attempt to document further the history, development and the often staggering scope of funk. Purists will argue, doubtless, against the significance given to disco (and the lack of attention paid to jazz) and bemoan the attention afforded to certain periods of a band's career, at the expense of other, equally successful eras. Simultaneously, anybody who remembers only the string of anodyne ballads that enshrined Spandau Ballet in pop history, may find it difficult to believe that there was ever a time when that band was feted among Britain's first truly subversive funk acts.

Others will notice that, in telling the story of funk, there is no concerted attempt made to describe what the music sounds like, and no dissertation on language and lyrics, politics and meaning. This is deliberate. It has been said that writing about music is like dancing to architecture, an expression coined with funk fully in mind. No words on earth can truly capture the sound of the JBs in full flow, of War when they lock into a solid good-time groove, of Herbie Hancock making you dance til you're dizzy. So why even try?

This book is about the events, the people and the records. For at the end of the day, it is not what the musicians play that matters, nor how the music is played. It is why it is played, and what happens when the musicians stop playing and start feeling that truly counts. George Clinton once said, "Funk is whatever it needs to be at the time that it is." And, as is so often the case, nobody ever put it better.

## THE ENCYCLOPEDIA

**ENTRY STYLE:** Each individual entry adheres to the same format, opening with the original, or earliest-documented lineup of the band profiled. Birthdates/places (where known) and instruments (abbreviated, see below) played follow. Thereafter, full career synopses include subsequent lineup changes and major career events. LPs, TV programs, movies, newspapers, magazines, and stage plays are noted in *italics*. Artists cross-referenced to separate entries appear in **bold**. Song titles appear in double quotes. Rock 'n' roll is spelled thus; rhythm and blues is abbreviated to R&B.

**ABBREVIATIONS:** Abbreviations are used for the following instruments: vcls = vocals; gtr = guitar; bs = bass; kybds = keyboards; orgn = organ; pno = piano; sax = saxophone; trom = trombone; trum = trumpet; hrns = horns; flglhrn = flugelhorn; hrmnca = harmonica; perc = percussion; cngs = congas; prod = producer. In addition, country names and state names appear as their most familiar abbreviation: UK = United Kingdom; US = United States; CA = California; NY = New York, etc.

**DISCOGRAPHIES:** Full single/45 discographies are supplied for key performers; other entries feature "chartlogs," noting all R&B and pop chart hits. Reissues and repressings are generally not considered unless they are chart hits.

Full LP discographies are included for every band, noting year of release and original record label. Except where noted, LP/CD listings are as complete as possible. All are US releases unless otherwise stated: UK, Germany (Ger), Australia (Aus), Japan (Jap), etc. In those instances where an album appeared internationally in a prior year to the US release, this original release is given, with the domestic issue generally listed only where the title and/or contents differ. The availability of releases is not addressed. (As labels dig deeper into the vault in search of fresh material for reissue, even albums that were once considered unsalable are now returning to the racks, often disappearing again soon after). Neither are formats (vinyl, tape, CD, etc.) considered. In general, pre-1986 releases were originally available on vinyl and cassette only; post 1986, CDs came to dominate, although many releases continued to appear on vinyl (some exclusively). The discographies strive to differentiate between albums intended to showcase fresh material—a group's "new album"—and those (SELECTED COMPILATIONS AND ARCHIVE RELEASES) that collect previously unreleased material from earlier in a band's career, rare and unavailable cuts, or greatest hits/best of selections. These listings are generally complete, but do omit titles that either duplicate or supersede other collections. Where relevant, solo, side project and other related releases follow the main band discography.

**CHART DATA:** Where applicable, both US R&B and pop chart positions have been provided. On occasions where both sides of a single merit a chart entry, the label and chart positions is inserted following the A-Side; the B-side is followed by its chart data only.

**NOTE:** *Billboard*'s R&B charts have undergone several changes in name during the period covered in this book, usually incorporating the phrase R&B/Rhythm & Blues (Top Selling, Best Selling, Most Played, etc.). However, the chart has also been titled "Best Selling/Hot Soul (1969–82)" and "[Hot/Top] Black Singles (1982–90)." For ease of reference, all are termed R&B in this book.

**SAMPLES AND REPLAYED ELEMENTS:** Where possible, selected listings of samples and replayed elements have been included, under the overall heading SELECTED SAMPLES. These note original song, sampling artist and title of song featuring sample. Compiled from a multitude of sources, both printed and Internet (see Bibliography), this information has been double-checked wherever possible; however, we acknowledge that errors may have crept in and apologize in advance for any mistaken identifications. Similarly, while every effort has been made to supply complete listings, the entries should not be considered comprehensive.

**REVIEWS AND RATINGS:** Reviews of selected albums are included as a general guide to the band's music and impact. All reviews were written by Amy Hanson and Dave Thompson. Albums are rated on a scale of **1**–**9**, with **1** representing a very poor release, and **9** the best in the band's catalog. It should be noted that these ratings apply only within an individual band's discography—a rating of **7** in one band's catalog does not necessarily imply it is superior to a **5** in another's. A rating of **1** is not, therefore, intended to suggest that an album is one of the worst ever made (although it probably is), simply that it is the worst the band in question has ever made. The majority of releases are rated between **5** and **7**, indicating that while the band may not have attained its (potential) peak, the album is definitely worthy. In addition, a rating of **10** has been awarded to those albums that can be considered essential listening, not only for their content, but also for their historical and/or cultural impact. A full listing of these follows.

**NOTE:** Appended to the essays included in this book, "Recommended Listening" lists are NOT rated. Neither are "Various Artist" compilation albums.

**ACCURACY:** Every attempt has been made to guarantee the accuracy of the information included. Of course it is inevitable that some screaming errors will leap out at the informed reader, and for these we apologize. However, unlike other music encyclopedias, we do not even pretend that they are deliberate errors, designed to spotlight instances of plagiarism. Perhaps naively, we believe that all information contained within an encyclopedia should be presumed to be reliable, and not necessitate double-checking every fact elsewhere, on the off chance that it is a booby trap.

# PART ONE: PRE-FUNK

## TONY ALLEN, see FELA RANSOME KUTI

## VICKI ANDERSON

**BORN:** *Myra Barnes, Houston, TX*

One of James Brown's greatest funky divas (he himself has described her as *the* greatest), Vicki Anderson joined his live Revue in spring 1965. She had already cut a solo single for Fontana the previous year. Anderson's manager met Brown (while the Godfather was gigging in Anderson's Houston hometown) and played him her tape. Brown said, in his autobiography, "I bought the tape from him with the idea of recording her myself."

He got the chance a few months later, when current leading lady Anna King left the Revue. Brown asked Anderson to join the act in Miami. She arrived at the studio while they were recording (and Bobby Byrd was still writing lyrics for) a new song, "Baby I Love You." Anderson's "audition" for the Revue was to sing the finished song; that same performance became her next single, released on Smash in June 1965. "She was not just the best singer I ever had with the Revue," Brown wrote, "she was the best singer, period. She could out-sing anybody I know. Any day. Standing flat-footed."

Anderson remained with Brown's Revue for the next two years, turning down the lead role in the Broadway show *Hallelujah Baby* during that period. She also maintained her recording career, cutting eight further singles under Brown's aegis. She quit the group in 1967, shortly after her marriage to organist Byrd. (The pair duetted on 1968's "Here Is My Everything" single.)

Retiring to Houston to raise her family (Anderson's daughter from a previous relationship, Carleen, had been living with her grandparents), she nevertheless continued recording. And, in January 1970, she returned to the Revue following the departure of Marva Whitney.

Anderson remained on board for another 18 months, during which time she cut the moving "Let It Be Me" duet with Brown and also released two singles ("Message from the Soul Sisters" and "Super Good") with the Bootsy Collins-era JBs under her given name, Myra Barnes.

After one final Brown-produced single, "Don't Throw Your Love in the Garbage Can," Anderson retired again. She has since released just two 45s, "You're Welcome" (as Momie-O) in 1975, and "You and Me Together" in 1980. She appeared on several of her husband's equally sporadic

recordings and the pair joined several "Funky People" tours during the '80s and '90s, alongside fellow Brown alumni Lyn Collins, Marva Whitney, and the JB Horns. They rejoined Brown's own All Stars live show in 1988. In 1993, Anderson and Byrd released a reworked "Don't Throw Your Love" under the name "Bobby Byrd & Pfunk-ness featuring Vicki Anderson."

### VICKI ANDERSON COMPLETE DISCOGRAPHY

#### SINGLES

1964 My Man/I Won't Be Back (Fontana)
1965 Baby I Love You/Nobody Cares (Smash)
1965 Never Never Never Let You Go (part one)/(part two) (Fontana)
1966 I Can't Let You Go (part one)/(part two) (New Breed)
1966 Wide Awake in a Dream/Nobody Cares (Deluxe)
1966 You Send Me/Within My Heart (King)
1967 I Got a Good Man/I Can't Stop Loving (Tuff)
1967 If You Want, Give Me What I Want/Tears of Joy (King)
1967 Baby Don't You Know/The Feeling Is Real (King)
1968 I'll Work It Out/What the World Needs Now (King)
1969 Answer to Mother Popcorn/I'll Work It Out (King)
1969 I Want To Be in the Land of Milk and Honey/Wide Awake in a Dream (King)
1970 No More Heartaches/Never Find a Love like Mine (King)
1970 Yesterday (live)/Message from the Soul Sisters (King)
1971 I'm Too Tough for Mr. Big Stuff/I Want To Be in the Land of Milk and Honey (People)
1971 I'm Too Tough for Mr. Big Stuff/Sound Funky (Brownstone)
1971 I'll Work It Out/I Want To Be in the Land of Milk and Honey (Brownstone)
1972 Don't Throw Your Love in the Garbage Can/I Want To Be in the Land of Milk and Honey (Brownstone)
1980 You and Me Together (rap) (Dash)

#### VICKI ANDERSON AND JAMES BROWN

1967 Think/Nobody Cares (King)
1968 You Got the Power/What the World Needs Now (King)
1970 Let It Be Me/Baby Don't You Know (King)

#### VICKI ANDERSON WITH BOBBY BYRD

1968 Here Is My Everything/Loving You (ABC)
1993 I'm on the Move/Don't Throw Your Love in the Garbage Can (Soulciety)

#### AS MYRA BARNES

1970 Message from the Soul Sisters (part one)/(part two) (King)
1970 Super Good (part one)/(part two) (King)

#### AS MOMIE-O

1975 You're Welcome, Stop on By/Once You Get Started (Identify)

I Want To Be in the Land of Milk and Honey — Main Source: Live at the Barbecue (1991)

I Want To Be in the Land of Milk and Honey — Naughty by Nature: Penetration (1999)

Message from the Soul Sisters — Above the Law: Freedom of Speech (1990)

Message from the Soul Sisters — Big Daddy Kane: Calling Mr. Welfare (1989)

Message from the Soul Sisters — Black Moon: Son Get Wrec (remix) (1993)

Message from the Soul Sisters — Gang Starr: No More Mr. Nice Guy (1990)

Message from the Soul Sisters — Geto Boys: City Under Siege (1990)

Message from the Soul Sisters — Lil' Kim: No Time (1996)

Massage from the Soul Sisters — Main Source: Vamos a Rapiar (1991)

Super Good — Biz Markie: Family Tree (1993)

## AUTUMN RECORDS

Autumn Records was launched, in 1964, by San Francisco disc jockeys Bobby Mitchell and Tom Donahue, but is best remembered for employing the young and unknown Sylvester Stewart—the future Sly Stone—as in-house writer and producer. Introduced to the duo following a gig at an American Legion Hall, Stewart swiftly impressed the DJs with his vision and abilities, confirming his talent when he launched singer Bobby Freeman's career with the novelty "C'mon and Swim," a self-composed exhortation to do the dance of the same name.

The Top Five "C'mon and Swim" was followed with the Top 60 hit "S-W- I-M"; then, before the world grew tired of this latest dance craze, Stewart himself leaped into the waters with his own "I Just Learned How To Swim." It sank.

With Autumn's own output impossible to confine to any one genre, Stewart spent the next three years blithely traveling from gritty garage hopefuls like the Chosen Few, the Mojo Men and the Spearmints, to the breezy folk rock of the Beau Brummels, while cutting three singles of his own. He was also at least partially influential in Autumn's decision to sign a new folk rock act, the Great!! Society!! (The group later dropped the extraneous exclamation points.)

Released in March 1966, the Great Society's debut single, guitarist Darby Slick's "Somebody To Love," was the first release on Autumn's newly launched Northbeach subsidiary and was produced by Stewart. According to legend, he ran the Society through 50 takes before he was satisfied. Of course a later version of the song, re-recorded by vocalist Grace Slick after she joined Jefferson Airplane, became one of the best-loved recordings of the entire era.

Stewart and Autumn parted company during 1967; Stewart left behind him a wealth of his own material, subsequently released across a long series of (possibly mislead-ingly titled) compilations. But he took with him three years of invaluable studio experience, which he was soon putting to very good use indeed.

### AUTUMN RECORDS/SLY STONE PRODUCTIONS 1964–67

1 Bobby Freeman: Let's Surf Again/Come to Me
2 Bobby Freeman: C'mon and Swim (part one)/(part two)
3 Sly Stewart: I Just Learned How To Swim/Scat Swim
5 Bobby Freeman: SWIM/That Little Old Heartbreaker Me
7 Spearmints: Little One/Jo-Ann
8 Beau Brummels: Laugh Laugh/Still in Love with You Baby
9 Bobby Freeman: I'll Never Fall in Love Again/Friends
10 Beau Brummels: Just a Little/They'll Make You Cry
11 Mojo Men: Off the Hook/Mama's Little Baby
14 Sly: Buttermilk (part one)/(part two)
15 The Vejtables: I Still Love You/Anything
16 Beau Brummels: You Tell Me Why/I Want You
17 Chosen Few: Nobody but Me/I Think It's Time
19 Mojo Men: Dance with Me/Loneliest Boy in Town
20 Beau Brummels: Don't Talk to Strangers/In Good Time
24 Beau Brummels: Good Time Music/Sad Little Girl*
25 Bobby Freeman: The Duck/Cross My Heart
26 Sly: Temptation Walk (part one)/(part two)
27 Mojo Men: She's My Baby/Fire in My Heart

### NORTHBEACH RECORDS

1001 Great!! Society!! — Someone To Love/Free Advice

## BAND OF GYPSIES, see FRONTIERS OF FUNK: THE PSYCHE-FUNKA-DELIA EXPERIENCE

## MYRA BARNES, see VICKI ANDERSON

## BEAU DOLLAR & THE DAPPS

**FORMED:** *1965, Cincinnati, OH*

**ORIGINAL LINE-UP:** *Eddie Setser (gtr), Charles Summers (bs), Tim Hedding (kybds), Ron Geisman (trum), Ken Tibbets (trum), Les Asch (sax), David Parkinson (sax), Beau Dollar (b.William Bowman—drms)*

Beau Dollar & the Dapps were a Cincinnati R&B combo and residents at the city's famed Living Room nightclub when they were discovered by James Brown during 1965. He took the group into the studio that same year to cut the two-part "It's a Gas" single, intended for release on King under the name the James Brown Dancers.

Brown's then ongoing dispute with the label saw the single go unissued, but Brown kept tabs on the Dapps and, in late 1967, paired them with his own musical director, Arthur "Pee Wee" Ellis, for two singles released over the next six months, "Bringing Up the Guitar" and "There Was a Time." Another session saw the Dapps accompany Brown himself on the mammoth "I Can't Stand Myself (When You Touch Me)."

The following year, the Dapps fronted their own "I'll Be Sweeter Tomorrow" single, and backed the Soul Believers on "Nobody Knows the Trouble I've Seen." Drummer/vocalist Beau Dollar alone was credited on another classic Brown production, 1968's "Who Knows?" (released 1970).

Brown also paired the Dapps with R&B veteran Hank Ballard, one of the singer's own formative influences and idols (Brown had been producing sporadic releases for Ballard since 1963's "It's Love, Baby"). This new partnership cut "How You Gonna Get Respect" in fall 1968. "You're So Sexy" followed in early 1969.

The Dapps broke up later that year; Brown promptly located another Cincinnati outfit, the Pacesetters, featuring bassist Bootsy Collins. He toyed briefly with launching them as the New Dapps before taking them as his own backing musicians and renaming them the JBs.

### BEAU DOLLAR & THE DAPPS COMPLETE DISCOGRAPHY
#### SINGLES
#### BEAU DOLLAR & THE DAPPS
1969 I'll Be Sweeter Tomorrow/A Woman, a Friend, a Lover (King)

#### THE SOUL BELIEVERS & THE DAPPS
1968 Nobody Knows the Trouble I've Seen/I'm with You (King)

#### THE DAPPS, FEATURING ARTHUR "PEE WEE" ELLIS
1968 Bringing Up the Guitar/Gittin' a Little Hipper (King)
1968 There was a Time/The Rabbit Got the Gun (King)

#### HANK BALLARD & THE DAPPS
1968 How You Gonna Get Respect/Teardrops on Your Letter (King)
1969 You're So Sexy/Thrill on the Hill (King)

#### BEAU DOLLAR
1970 Who Knows?/I Wanna Go Where the Soul Trees Grow (King)

#### SELECTED SAMPLES
Who Knows? — Soul II Soul: Jazzie's Groove (1989)

## ARCHIE BELL & THE DRELLS
**FORMED:** 1966, Houston, TX
**ORIGINAL LINE-UP:** *Archie Bell (b. 9/1/44, Henderson, TX—vcls), James Wise (b. 5/1/48, Houston TX—vcls), Willie Parnell (b. 4/12/45, Houston TX—vcls), Cornelius Fuller (vcls), LC Watts (vcls)*

The brother of all-American footballer Ricky Bell, Archie Bell, formed the Drells in 1966, with four school friends from Leo Smith Junior High in Houston. Anxious for the group's name to rhyme with his own, he christened them the Drells, because another act from Harvey, IL, had already made a splash as the Dells.

Early lineup changes saw the lineup finally settle down as Bell, James Wise, Joe Cross and Huey "Billy" Butler, and Bell & the Drells became a regular sight on the local talent show circuit. It was at one such event that they were spotted by KCOH disc jockey Skipper Lee Frazier, who signed them to his own Ovid label.

Although the group members were vocalists only, backed by an array of studio musicians, Bell had already determined that the Drells would not become synonymous with lightweight harmonizing and sweet singing, the fate of many combos of that ilk. Rather, he turned his own writing skills toward a hard-nosed political angle, all the more so after the group's early progress—a small regional success with "She's My Woman, She's My Girl" (released on the East West label)—was interrupted by the draft board.

Bell was sent to Vietnam in early 1967; home for a short period of leave, the Drells cut their next single, the deliriously vamping "Tighten Up" ("we dance as good as we walk"). An immediate local hit following its December 1967 release by Ovid, the song was picked up for distribution by Atlantic Records and entered the R&B chart in early April. By mid-May, it was #1 on both the R&B and pop charts, and heading toward sales of three million plus, while an album comprising further songs recorded at that same session followed it into the R&B Top 20.

Still in the army, Bell was in hospital in West Germany, recovering after being shot in the leg in Vietnam, and missed the entire experience. The Drells toured briefly without him, with James Wise taking lead vocals and Charles Gibbs recruited as backing singer. Bell performed only as his army leave periods permitted, and it was simply good fortune that the next step in the Drells' development was taken during one of these brief visits.

Performing in New Jersey, Bell and company were introduced to freelance Philadelphia-based producers Leon Huff and Kenneth Gamble. They promptly took Bell & the Drells into the Atlantic Studios in New York to cut more material, including three further singles, the jagged "I Can't Stop Dancing," "Do the Choo Choo" and January 1969's presciently ominous "There's Gonna Be a Showdown." All three reached the R&B Top 30.

Bell was discharged from the military on April 19, 1969, and returned to his group; the Drells' first full album with Gamble and Huff, *I Can't Stop Dancing*, made the Top 30 in mid-1969. Diminishing chart returns over the next year, however, saw the group break with their mentors and link instead with producer David Crawford; he produced their final Atlantic label chart entry, a cover of Sam & Dave's "Wrap It Up."

Over the next two years, Archie Bell & the Drells existed in the shadows somewhat, but regular UK live appearances paid off when a reissue of the 1969 B-side "Here I Go Again" gave them a British #11 in October 1972. A similarly revitalized "Showdown" followed in January 1973 and, with their Atlantic contract finally lapsing, the group resurfaced in the US on the Glades label. That same year brought further success with "Dancing to Your Music" and "Ain't Nothing for a Man in Love," but when "Girls Grow Up Faster than Boys" flopped in late 1973, Bell & the Drells reunited with Gamble and Huff and joined the TSOP label roster.

Paired with the Philly house musicians Instant Funk, a mid-1975 hit with Bunny Sigler's "I Could Dance All Night" relaunched the band's chart career; "The Soul City Walk" and "Let's Groove" followed, while the Drells' latest album, *Dance Your Troubles Away*, amazingly became an even bigger smash than *Tighten Up*. Absent from the Drells' next album, Instant Funk's immediately recognizable sound was back for 1979's *Strategy*. That proved the group's final chart entry; they broke up in 1980, and the following year Bell launched a short-lived solo career with Becket Records.

## ARCHIE BELL & THE DRELLS
### CHART LOG
1968 Tighten Up (part one)/(part two) (Atlantic—#1 R&B/#1 pop)

1968 I Can't Stop Dancing/You're Such a Beautiful Child (Atlantic—#5 R&B/#9 pop)

1968 Do the Choo Choo (Atlantic—#17 R&B/#44 pop)/Love Will Rain on You (#25 R&B)

1969 There's Gonna Be a Showdown/Go for What You Know (Atlantic—#6 R&B/#21 pop)

1969 I Love My Baby (Atlantic—#40 R&B/#94 pop)/Just a Little Closer (#128 pop)

1969 Girl You're Too Young/Do the Hand Jive (Atlantic—#13 R&B/#59 pop)

1969 My Balloon's Going Up/Giving Up Dancing (Atlantic—No. 36 R&B/#87 pop)

1970 A World Without Music (Atlantic—#46 R&B/#90 pop)/Here I Go Again (#112 pop)

1970 Wrap It Up/Deal with Him (Atlantic—#33 R&B/#93 pop)

1973 Dancing to Your Music/Count the Ways (Glades—#11 R&B/#61 pop)

1973 Ain't Nothing for a Man in Love/You Never Know What's on a Woman's Mind (Glades—#36 R&B)

1975 I Could Dance All Night/King of the Castle (TSOP—#25 R&B)

1975 The Soul City Walk/King of the Castle (TSOP—#42 R&B)

1976 Let's Groove (part one)/(part two) (TSOP—#7 R&B)

1977 Everybody Have a Good Time/I Bet I Can Do That Dance You're Doin' (Philadelphia I—#68 R&B)

1977 Glad You Could Make It/There's No Other Like You (Philadelphia I—#63 R&B)

1978 I've Been Missing You/It's Hard Not To Like You (Philadelphia I—#56 R&B)

1979 Strategy/We Got 'Em Dancin' (Philadelphia I—#21 R&B)

### LPs
**9** 1968 Tighten Up (Atlantic - #15 R&B/#142 pop)
The two part title track leads the way, a jumping potpourri of styles and grooves capped by Bell's plaintive "Soldier's Prayer, 1967" and a brutal "In the Midnight Hour."

**7** 1968 I Can't Stop Dancing (Atlantic—#28 R&B)

**7** 1969 There's Gonna Be a Showdown (Atlantic)
The brooding "Showdown" sets the stage for an album firmly locked into the politics of the time—even if some of the moods are a little sweet.

**6** 1975 Dance Your Troubles Away (TSOP—#11 R&B/#95 pop)
Lushly orchestrated, maybe even a little over-produced, with the TV friendly "I Could Dance All Night"—a deceptive winner.

**6** 1976 Where Will You Go When the Party's Over (Philadelphia I, #47 R&B)
Despite their Philly affiliations and the company's preference for sweet vocal groups, the Drells never relinquished their earlier vision; "Don't Let Love Get You Down" emerges as one of the hardest hitting funk tracks in the TSOP/Philly International label's history.

**6** 1977 Hard Not To Like It (Philadelphia I)

**6** 1979 Strategy (Philadelphia I—#37 R&B)

### SELECTED COMPILATIONS AND ARCHIVE RELEASES
**8** 1994 Tightening It Up: The Best of. . . (Rhino)
Sensible drive through the Atlantic years, emphasizing the hits

**7** 1999 Disco Showdown (Music Club)

### SELECTED SAMPLES
Don't Let Love Get You Down — Big Daddy Kane: DJs Get No Credit (1991)

Don't Let Love Get You Down — Ed OG: Bug a Boo (1991)

Tighten Up — 2nd II None: Ain't Nothin' Wrong (1991)

Tighten Up — Janet Jackson: FreeXone (1997)

## BOOKER T. & THE MGs
**FORMED:** *1962, Memphis, TN*
**ORIGINAL LINE-UP:** *Booker T. Jones (b. 11/12/44, Memphis, TN—kybds), Steve Cropper (b. 10/21/41, Willow Spring,*

**Dunn, Jones, Cropper, and Jackson (l-r): Booker T. & the MGs.**

MO—gtr), *Lewis Steinberg (bs), Al Jackson (b. 11/27/ 35, d.10/1/75—drms)*

The original MGs formed in 1962, as the houseband at Volt Records, the newly formed subsidiary of Stax. Originally cast as subordinate to the better-established Mar-Keys, that situation changed dramatically when the core of Booker T. Jones and Lewis Steinberg was augmented by guitarist Steve Cropper, following his departure from the Mar-Keys, and drummer Al Jackson. Booker T. & the MGs were born.

The MGs' vinyl debut came about completely by accident. Jones, Cropper, Steinberg and Jackson (playing his first full session for Stax) were jamming while waiting for singer Billy Lee Riley to arrive to cut a radio jingle. The tapes were rolling and, when the jam was over, with Cropper himself insisting it was the "best damn instrumental I've heard in I don't know when," the only question was, What it should be titled?

They settled on "Green Onions"—"green" at label co-

owner Estelle Axton's suggestion and "onions" after Steinberg said they were the funkiest things he could think of. Of course, Cropper later remarked, "To him they were funky because they were stinky." But the term soon took on a completely different meaning.

Originally released on Volt as the B-side to "Behave Yourself," but flipped and switched to Stax as soon as it became apparent that a monster was on the way, "Green Onions" topped the R&B chart in fall 1962, and made #3 on the pop listings. It also, alongside the Mar-Keys' "Last Night," set the pace for the future—at Stax, across the country at Motown (Junior Walker & the All Stars were formed in direct emulation of the MGs) and anywhere else that the fractured guitar, driving organ, thumping drums and walking bass found fertile ground.

It was those instruments, particularly the organ, that most obviously set the MGs aside from other combos and became their signature sound. Indeed, investigate the Stax catalog of the 1960s and the MGs' imprimatur is everywhere, from Booker T.'s writing partnership with singer William Bell and Steve Cropper's increasingly pronounced contributions as composer, musician and producer to their combined duties in the studio.

Meanwhile, the MGs' own chart career had stalled for a most peculiar reason: *Billboard* magazine's decision to abandon separate soul/R&B charts in November 1963, on the grounds that the music was now crossing over in such vast quantities that there was no longer a need for one. It was late January 1965 before the publishers saw the error of their ways, by which time six new MGs singles had passed by, with just two scratching the pop 100, "Mo' Onions" and "Soul Dressing." Others (including the restrained "Home Grown" and the horn-laden "Chinese Checkers") simply vanished.

Former Mar-Key Duck Dunn (b. 11/24/41, Memphis, TN) replaced Steinberg in mid-1964. Earlier in the year, Cropper produced a version of Roosevelt Sykes' "The Honeydripper" with another Dunn outfit, the Van-Dells, then joined the bassist as members of the ad-hoc Cobras, for a reprise of a song Cropper had written for the high school combo, which they both started out in, "Restless." Dunn's first recording as an MG was "Boot-Leg," their first major 45 since "Green Onions" and their first release not to feature Booker T. himself; he was combining his career with music studies at the Indiana University and was away there at the time of the session. Isaac Hayes took his place.

Jones was back for 1965's "Be My Lady," a record that, with the benefit of hindsight, can be seen as the launchpad for much of the MGs' late-'60s output. A genuinely funk-sodden slow jam that, like "Green Onions," emerged out of the musicians simply playing around in the studio, the record also marked the end of the MGs' initial phase. "My Sweet Potato" in July 1966 signified the dawn of the next, as Jones moved from organ to acoustic piano. Writing in the booklet accompanying the Stax Records *Complete Singles Collection 1959–68*, journalist Rob Bowman describes the song as initiating a new trademark, establishing "grooves that were fraught with tension and would serve as a basis to build climactic wave by climactic wave."

This process peaked with the immortal "Time Is Tight" three years later. In the meantime, the MGs honed it to within a shade of perfection with "Hip Hug Her," a lithesome cover of the Young Rascals' "Groovin'," and "Winter Snow," recorded with the song's composer, Isaac Hayes, joining Jones on keyboards and credited to Booker T. & the MGs, featuring Isaac Hayes.

Having accompanied Otis Redding at the June 1967 Monterey Pop Festival, the MGs landed another of their sporadic hits during the summer 1968, as "Soul Limbo" climbed to #7. Over the next year, their next two successes were both Hollywood scores, the title song to Clint Eastwood's *Hang 'Em High* and "Time Is Tight," from Ruby Dee's *Uptight*.

Their biggest single since "Green Onions," "Time Is Tight" marked the end of the MGs' most innovative period, as they settled into a rut of simply creating MG-ified versions of the day's biggest songs. The 1969 album *Booker T. Set* featured versions of recent classics by the Doors, the Beatles, Herb Alpert and Simon & Garfunkel ("Mrs. Robinson"). The following year, *McLemore Avenue* drew much attention for its funky recreation of the Beatles' *Abbey Road* LP (the Avenue, of course, was the site of the Stax studios, just as Abbey Road housed the Beatles' favorite studios). But it was the audacity and imagination of the project that impressed, as much as the music.

Furthermore, with Cropper now an in-demand sessionman and Jones still completing his music studies in Indiana, it was becoming increasingly difficult for the quartet to actually get together. Following one further hit, an abrupt edit of the eight-minute title track to 1971's *Melting Pot* album, the original MGs broke up.

Jones formed a new partnership with his wife, vocalist Priscilla Coolidge (sister of singer Rita), cutting four albums under his own name over the next four years; Cropper relocated to Los Angeles, where he cut his own superstar-studded solo album, *With a Little Help from My Friends*. Dunn and Jackson then formed a new MGs lineup with Bobby Manuel (gtr) and Carson Whitsett (kybds), scoring with "Sugarcane," in 1973, but achieving little else.

In 1975, Cropper, Dunn and Jackson reunited under the aegis of producer Tom Dowd and English rocker Rod Stewart to record the latter's *Atlantic Crossing* album. They regrouped with Jones soon after, but the reunion was short-lived. On October 1, 1975, Jackson was shot and killed by a burglar at his Memphis home. Among his final recordings was a version of the Bee Gees' "To Love Somebody," again backing Rod Stewart (and included in his *Story Teller* box set). "I believe it to be my great pleasure and honor to be the last to sing with the MGs as a unit," Stewart confirmed in the accompanying booklet.

With Willie Hall filling the void, the MGs recorded their comeback album, *Universal Language*, but again broke up as Jones returned to his solo work—he later formed the Booker T. Trio—and the others joined Cropper as sessionmen. Cropper and Dunn together appeared as the backing musicians in the *Blues Brothers* movie, among numerous other projects.

In 1992, the surviving MGs reformed again, this time with drummer Steve Jordan, to perform as the backing ensemble at the Bob Dylan tribute concert at Madison Square Garden. (They were also inducted into the Rock & Roll Hall of Fame.) The following year the same quartet toured the US with fellow rock legend Neil Young, before Jordan was succeeded by Steve Potts, Al Jackson's nephew, and the MGs recorded a new album, *That's the Way It Should Be*.

## BOOKER T. & THE MGS COMPLETE DISCOGRAPHY
### SINGLES/CHART LOG

1962 Behave Yourself/Green Onions (Volt)
1962 Green Onions/Behave Yourself (Stax—#1 R&B/#3 pop)
1963 Jelly Bread/Aw' Mercy (Stax)
1963 Home Grown/Big Train (Stax)
1963 Chinese Checkers/Plum Nellie (Stax)
1964 Mo' Onions/Tic-Tac-Toe (Stax—#97 pop)
1964 Soul Dressing/MG Party (Stax—#95 pop)
1964 Can't Be Still/Terrible Thing (Stax)
1965 Boot-Leg/Outrage (Stax—#10 R&B/#58 pop)
1966 Be My Lady/Red Beans and Rice (Stax)
1966 My Sweet Potato (Stax—#18 R&B/#85 pop)/Booker Loo (#37 R&B)
1966 Jingle Bells/Winter Wonderland (Stax)
1967 Hip Hug-Her/Summertime (Stax—#6 R&B/#37 pop)
1967 Groovin' (Stax—#10 R&B/#21 pop)/Slim Jenkins' Place (#70 pop)
1967 Hip Hug-Her/Summertime (Stax—#6 R&B/# 37 pop)
1968 Hang 'Em High/Over Easy (Stax—#35 R&B/#9 pop)
1969 Time Is Tight/Johnny I Love You (Stax—#7 R&B/#6 pop)
1969 Mrs. Robinson/Soul Clap 69 (Stax—#35 R&B/#37 pop)
1969 Slum Baby/Meditation (Stax—#46 R&B/#88 pop)
1970 Something/Sunday Sermon (Stax)
1971 Melting Pot/Kinda Easy Like (Stax—#21 R&B/#45 pop)
1971 Fuquawi/Jamaica This Morning (Stax)
1973 Sugarcane/Black Ride (Stax—#67 R&B)
1977 Sticky Stuff/Tie Stick (Asylum—#68 R&B)
1977 Grab Bag/Reincarnation (Asylum)

### LPs

**8** **1962 Green Onions (Stax—#33 pop)**
Okay, so no one needs to hear the lounge Stax take on "Stranger on the Shore," and most of the songs are way too short. But few all-instrumental albums of the era are so captivating.

**6** **1964 Soul Dressing (Stax)**
"Night Owl Walk," "Jelly Bread" and "Plum Nellie" are the highlights on an album that *may* indeed be very much the son of its father, but it has a good time regardless.

**5** **1965 And Now! (Stax—#18 R&B)**
"In the Midnight Hour" gets the MG treatment; nothing else really comes close.

**5** **1966 In the Christmas Spirit (Stax)**
**6** **1967 Hip Hug-Her (Stax—#4 R&B/#35 pop)**
**4** **1968 Doin' Our Thing (Stax—#17 R&B/#176 pop)**
Embracing current pop, Staxified takes on "You Keep Me Hanging On" and "Ode to Billy Joe," sees the MGs moving dangerously close to supermarket music territory.

**8** **1968 Soul Limbo (Stax—#14 R&B/#127 pop)**
And then it all comes right again, with the magnificent, calypso-flavored title track, the seismic funk "Heads or Tails" and the spaghetti soul groove of "Hang 'Em High." Hendrix's "Foxy Lady" isn't bad either.

**7** **1969 Uptight (original soundtrack) (Stax—#7 R&B/#98 pop)**
Imagine a soundtrack with one killer single on board. This is it.

**6** **1969 The Booker T. Set (Stax—#10 R&B/#53 pop)**
Too much of this album lurches toward easy listening territory, with little more than Booker's standard funky organ sound to distinguish them from another day in another hip supermarket. "Love Child" is oddly pleasurable, though, while "Sing a Simple Song" has an in-yer-face guitar and the Isleys' "It's Your Thing" simply refuses to let things sink too low.

**6** **1970 McLemore Avenue (Stax—#19 R&B/#107 pop)**
The Beatles' *Abbey Road*, funkified. Some excellent moments clouded by a few fairly unimaginative ones, with the already overwrought "Something" containing a bit of both.

**6** **1971 Melting Pot (Stax—#2 R&B/#43 pop)**
The super-funky title track notwithstanding, it's all very slick, very produced, very smooth and awash with cheesy choral harmonies. But there's a hint of Isaac Hayes in there, and some archetypal MGs breaks.

**5** **1973 The MGs (Stax—#56 R&B)**
**5** **1977 Universal Language (Asylum—#59 R&B/#209 pop)**
**4** **1993 That's the Way It Should Be (Sony)**

### SELECTED COMPILATIONS AND ARCHIVE RELEASES

**6** **1967 Back to Back (split LP with the Mar-Keys) (Stax)**
**7** **1968 The Best Of (Stax)**
**7** **1970 Greatest Hits (Stax—#18 R&B/#132 pop)**
**8** **1993 The Very Best Of (Rhino)**
Excellent digest of the MGs' better-known (Stax/Atlantic) hit period.

**8** **1998 The Best of (Ace, UK)**
Picking up in 1968, tracing the band through the exhilarating highs and depressingly workmanlike lows of the next

four years, but topped off by a phenomenal live (France, 1967) "Green Onions."

## SELECTED SAMPLES

Bootleg — Boogie Down Production: Sex and Violence (1992)
Bootleg — Cypress Hill: Born To Get Busy (1991)
Chicken Pox — Show & AG: Silence of the Lambs (1992)
Children, Don't Get Weary — Lo Fidelity Allstars: How To Operate with a Blown Mind (1998)
Children, Don't Get Weary — Raekwon: Glaciers of Ice (1995)
Green Onions — MC Lyte: I Am the Lyte (1989)
Hip Hug-Her — Mary J. Blige: Everything (remix) (1998)
Hip Hug-Her — Das EFX: Losseys (1992)
Hip Hug-Her — Heavy D: Don't Curse (1991)
Hip Hug-Her — Ice Cube: Givin' Up the Nappy Dug Out (1991)
Hip Hug-Her — Lord Finesse: I Like My Girls with a Boom (1991)
Hip Hug-Her — Ol' Dirty Bastard: Shimmy Shammy Ya (1995)
Melting Pot — Big Daddy Kane: Another Victory (1989)
Sing a Simple Song — Brand Nubian: Love Me or Leave Me Alone (1993)

## JAMES BROWN

**BORN:** 5/3/33, Barnwell, SC

"Soul Brother #1," "the Hardest Working Man in Show Business," "Mr. Dynamite," James Brown has been given a lot of titles over the years (usually by himself). But few are so appropriate as that conferred upon him as recently as 1997, for another in the multitude of reissues and repackagings that have dominated his catalog (and bedeviled his collectors) over the past decade, the budget-priced live compilation *Grandmaster of Funk* itself was not an essential purchase for any fan. But its title summed up 40 plus years of Brown's music and impact as accurately as any, and more tellingly than most. To many people, the otherwise peerless George Clinton and Sly Stone included, James Brown IS funk. And a lot more besides.

### EARLY YEARS

As a child in Barnwell, SC, Brown was a promising sportsman, adept at both boxing and baseball. But from the moment he won a junior talent contest around the age of 11, performing a song called "So Long," his attention was geared toward music as well. In his autobiography, *The Godfather of Soul*, Brown pinpoints two other crucial encounters: the circuses, which came through town and taught him the value of showmanship; and a short film about of Louis Jordan and his Tympany Five, which proved the importance of performance.

A vibrant R&B/jazz quintet shot through with a broad sense of theatrical humor, the Tympany Five's showstopper was "Caldonia, What Makes Your Big Head So Hard"—a song, which Brown recalled, "you could really put on a show with." He learned to sing and play it and soon was hamming up his own version at every opportunity. Reflecting upon how his own act utilized many of the tricks, which the Tympany Five developed, Brown admitted, "I guess that Louis Jordan short is what first started me thinking along those lines."

Brown formed his first band, the Cremona Trio in 1945 (despite their name, the band often boasted up to five members). Having already won a succession of talent nights at both the local Lenox and Harlem Theaters, Brown developed a strong local following and the Trio were soon gigging around high schools and the local army base.

Brown's dreams were curtailed in 1949, shortly after his 16th birthday, when he was sentenced to eight-to-16 years imprisonment for grand theft auto. The music continued, however, when he and fellow inmates Johnny Terry, "Hucklebuck" Davis and the singularly named "Shag" first formed a gospel quartet, then began adding homemade instruments—a comb and paper, a washtub bass, a drum kit made from lard tubs and for Brown, what he calls, "a sort of mandolin [made] out of a wooden box."

Serving time at the jail in Toccoa, GA, Brown was also on the prison basketball team, visiting neighboring schools to play. It was during one of these outings that he first encountered pianist Bobby Byrd and, when Brown was paroled in June 1952, having served three years, Byrd's family put him up for a time, while he sorted himself out.

Brown joined a new group, the Ever Ready Gospel Singers, and cut his first record, an acetate of Ethel Waters' "His Eye Is on the Sparrow." He lost heart, however, after the Singers drove as far afield as Nashville in search of a DJ to play it and couldn't interest one. He returned to Toccoa, where Byrd invited him to join the Avons, a vocal group he was trying to get off the ground, but whose hopes had been seriously dashed after their best vocalist, Troy Collins, died in a car crash.

Modeling themselves after the top R&B groups of the day—the Orioles, the Five Keys, Billy Ward & the Dominoes (featuring Clyde McPhatter) and so forth—the Avons featured vocalists Byrd, Sylvester Keels, Doyle Oglesby, Fred Pulliam, Nash Knox and Roy Scott, plus Brown and his prison-mate Johnny Terry. Gigging throughout Georgia and into South Carolina, the Avons were just one of dozens of similar acts playing the local juke joints; indeed, it transpired that they were also one of at least two other outfits

The Godfather of Soul: the inimitable James Brown in action.

called the Avons. To avoid confusion, they became the Toccoa Band.

Brown was constantly on the look out for ways to improve the Toccoa Band's standing and reputation. He recruited a guitarist, Nafloyd Smith, complete with a cheap Sears guitar and amplifier, and inadvertently the group took the first step toward their destiny as they learned to increase the volume of their vocals to drown the little amp's incessant feedback. When their newly acquired manager, local undertaker Barry Trimier, suggested adding percussion to the troupe—rather than try and keep the beat by stamping their feet—Brown fashioned a cymbal from a piece of metal and contributed that to the lineup. With a tom-tom and a field drum, which somebody found in storage at a nearby high school, plus any other instruments that came to hand, the Toccoa Band sounded like nothing else on earth. ✗

By 1954, the group was gigging as the Flames, becoming the Famous Flames after a Macon promotor thought it might help draw more people into his club. They performed their own material, too; Brown's "Goin' Back to Rome" and Brown/Terry's "Please Please Please"—an impassioned shouter based around the Orioles' "Baby Please Don't Go"—were early additions to the repertoire. The Famous Flames also launched their recording career, cutting tracks at local radio stations, then handing them to various labels to be pressed. Brown himself apparently remembers only one of them, "So Long," cut for the NRC label in Greenville.

The Macon gig became a regular highlight of the band's routine. It was promoted by one Clint Brantley, a local entrepreneur whose roster also featured the then-unknown (but quickly rising) Little Richard. When Richard split town in 1955, following his first national success "Tutti Frutti," the Famous Flames took over every venue he had ever ruled and, shortly before Christmas, Brantley had them cut a demo of "Please Please Please."

Local radio loved the song and aired the acetate constantly. Not one label, however, was interested in releasing it. Even in the wake of the screaming shock of Little Richard, the Famous Flames' brutal bellowing was simply too unorthodox. Only one industry figure sided with them, Ralph Bass, an A&R man at King Records in Cincinnati. He signed the Famous Flames, but their very first recording session, on February 4, 1956, almost ended in disaster. Label head Syd Nathan had hated the demo of "Please Please Please"; he hated the re-recording even more.

For a time, it looked as though the record would not even be released; King's standard practice was to ship a record within a few days of recording. "Please Please Please" sat for a month before Nathan finally announced that "against his better judgement," as Brown put it, he would release it on the low-key Federal subsidiary at the beginning of March 1956.

With the band touring tirelessly behind it, "Please Please Please" became the label's biggest 45 ever. Despite the success, however, the Famous Flames' own position was unstable. In keeping with the traditions of the time, the next single, June's "I Don't Know," was more or less a direct descendent of its predecessor, and the record buying public stayed away in droves.

"No No No," "Just Won't Do Right," "Chonnie-On-Chon" followed it into oblivion and, as the first anniversary of their first hit rolled around, the Famous Flames themselves broke up following a dispute over their future billing. They had recently recruited a new manager, Universal Attractions agency chief Ben Bart, who insisted on renaming them James Brown & the Famous Flames. On top of the disappointments of the past few singles, that was the final straw for Brown's bandmates. They quit en masse.

Brown spent much of 1957 working with pickup musicians, while King maintained a barrage of further unsuccessful releases. Brown consoles himself with the knowledge that, "you can hear a lot of where soul music came from by listening to some of those tunes." But with King refusing to allow him back into the studio, Brown knew he'd been as good as dropped.

The turning point came following Little Richard's retirement from rock 'n' roll in October 1957. Brown was recruited to replace him at a string of shows, then followed through with a tour in his own right, backed by a new generation of Famous Flames: Bill Hollings, Louis Madison and J.W. Archer. Impressed by the success of his concerts, King called Brown back to the studio to try and break what had now become an eight-single losing streak. "That Dood It" fared no better than its predecessors, but Brown persuaded the label to give him one last chance, joining with producer Andy Gibson for "Try Me," a yearning, passionate ballad that could not have been further removed from "Please Please Please." It soared to #1 on the R&B chart in October 1958.

Brown built a new band comprising Byrd, JC Davis (tnr sax), Bobby Roach (gtr), Bernard Odum (bs), Roscoe Patrick (trum), Albert Corley (sax) and Nat Kendrick (drms). This group debuted on Brown's next single, the Top 20 entry "I Want You So Bad."

Brown debuted at the Harlem Apollo on April 24, 1959 (opening for labelmate Little Willie John nine years later, the subject of Brown's *Thinking About. . .* album), accompanied by yet another generation of singing Flames, including Byrd, returning founder Terry, plus Baby Lloyd Stallworth and Bobby Bennett.

The gig preceded a period of absolute chart domination for Brown and the Famous Flames, both in their own right and, initiating what subsequently became a common practice for Brown, under an unexpected pseudonym. In early 1960, Brown achieved a massive hit with "(Do The) Mashed Potatoes," a novelty dance song released on Henry Stone's Dade label under the name of drummer Nat Kendrick and the Swans. Brown wrote, produced and, alongside his bandmates, performed on the record, behind Miami DJ King Coleman. The song rose to #8 on the R&B chart and, responding to Brown's increasing ambition, Sid Nathan finally transferred the singer from Federal to the higher profile King label in 1961.

The music continued changing as Brown's success grew. He was incorporating more jazz into the brew. "'I'll Go Crazy' is blues," he explained, "but it's a different kind of blues, up-tempo, a kind of jazz blues." His cover of the Five Royales' "Think," he continued, "is a combination of gospel and jazz, a rhythm hold is what we used to call it. When people talk about soul music, they talk only about gospel and R&B coming together. But . . . you have to remember the jazz."

In 1960, Brown cut his first full album, *Think* (two previous LPs had simply compiled singles, B-sides and unused session outtakes); two further sets, divided between vocal and instrumental performances, followed before Brown released his first live album, the classic *Live at the Apollo*, in January 1963. He also launched his own Try Me label, cutting singles by Tammi Montgomery (aka Tammi Terrill), Johnny & Bill (fronted by Pigmeat Markham) and the Poets, all members of the massive Revue show that Brown first built around his own performance in 1960, and continued to expand as the decade progressed.

Indeed, the coterie of musicians at Brown's disposal could turn their hand to anything, either backing existing artists or assuming the identities of new "stars." But the steady turn-over of musicians did not affect Brown's performance, rather it only encouraged him to further heights, refining his vision as he encountered ever-different players.

By 1960, guitarist Roach had been succeeded by Les Buie, and bassist Odum by Hubert Perry; J.C. Davis left in 1961 to join Etta James, to be replaced as bandleader by one of Brown's former schoolfriends, St. Clair Pinckney. Although he remained in the Famous Flames, Pinckney then stepped aside in summer 1962, for arranger Lewis Hamlin (d. 1991), a brilliant musician who Pinckney himself later described as "the forgotten man in setting the musical course of the band."

In 1964, believing his King contract to be at an end, Brown formed his own production company, Fair Deal, and linked his entire operation to a new record label, the Mercury subsidiary Smash. King, however, disputed the arrangement and was granted an injunction against Brown releasing any further vocal recordings for Smash.

The injunction was upheld when the case came to court, and Brown was forced to record instrumentals alone for Smash, while ignoring King's demands for vocal performances. It was only after some months of stalemate that Brown realized that there was more to the dispute than the rights to his own work—Mercury seemed to be actively trying to close King down.

Immediately, Brown swung back into vocal action, recording a new song and handing it over to the embattled Syd Nathan. Working with Nat Jones, Brown redeveloped a rhythm first worked up for summer 1964's "Out of Sight," and created "Papa's Got a Brand New Bag," a yelping, insistent tour de force, which King gratefully released in July 1965.

It became Brown's first R&B chart-topper since "Try Me"; it saved King from extinction (Brown was rewarded with a new, infinitely improved contract) and, while Brown himself considered the record to be simply the next stage in his own creative development, for other listeners it was the birth of a new musical genre altogether.

"'Papa's Bag' was years ahead of its time," Brown wrote. "I was still called a soul singer, but . . . I had gone off in a different direction. I had discovered that my strength was not in the horns, it was in the rhythm. I was hearing everything, even the guitars, like they were drums. Later on, they said it was the beginning of funk. I just thought of it as where my music was going. The title told it all: I had a new bag."

### 1964–70

The Famous Flames were gone. Now Brown alone handled the vocals (their final session with him was for "Out of Sight"). "Papa's Bag" was recorded with ex-Johnny Otis Band guitarist Jimmy Nolen (d. 12/18/83) and trumpeters Ron Tooley, Joe Dupars and Levi Rasbury augmenting the "Out of Sight" lineup of Sam Thomas (bs); organist Jones; tenor saxophonists Pinckney, Eldee Williams and Al Clark; baritone wizard Maceo Parker; and his brother, drummer Melvin Parker.

Over the next two years, an even more powerful unit came into being, christened by Brown "the New Breed." Alfred "Pee Wee" Ellis replaced Jones as bandleader in January 1967. Alphonso Kellum joined Nolen on guitar; Tim Drummond and later, Charles Sherrell, replaced bassist Thomas; jazz trumpeter Waymon Reed was brought in, and twin drummers John "Jabo" Starks (ex-Bobby Bland) and Clyde Stubblefield moved into position. But still, the lineup, which created "Papa's Bag," can truly be described as one of the most innovative groups Brown ever led.

"Papa's Bag" was massive, not only in the US but also across Europe. (British comedians Peter Cook and Dudley Moore even recorded a parody version in which Moore, as "Bo Duddley," attempts to explain the lyrics to a bemused interviewer, Cook). It was followed up the chart by "I Got You (I Feel Good)," which peaked just as "Papa's Bag" won Brown a Grammy for Best R&B Performance. The grandiose "It's a Man's Man's Man's World," coincided with Brown's first appearance on *The Ed Sullivan Show*. With both the *Man's Man's World* and the all-instrumental *James Brown Plays New Breed* albums, it was clear that Brown and his band weren't content with simply developing a whole new form of musical expression. They wanted to take it as far as they could as well.

The music, however, represented only a portion of the change in Brown's approach. He was also becoming increasingly politicized, presenting American youth with the salutary "Don't Be a Drop-Out" and personally delivering the first copy of the record to Vice President Hubert Humphrey. The pair discussed Brown's own dream of launching a Stay at School campaign, which, following its launch in 1966, saw Brown spend time and money visiting the nation's high schools. He also bought the first in a chain of radio stations, WGYW in Knoxville, TN, renaming it WJBE and initiating programming devoted wholly to the Black community.

He eschewed involvement with more radical groups and action, however. Throughout the riot-torn summer of 1967, Brown was touring Europe. But he contributed to activist H. Rap Brown's defense fund and, amid the turmoil following the assassination of Martin Luther King, Brown broadcast appeals for calm on both WJBE and WEBB, his station in Baltimore, before hurriedly arranging a live TV broadcast of his scheduled show at the Boston Garden. All three cities subsequently reported considerably less civil unrest than they had anticipated.

Brown continued his stream of genre-defining 45s. A ferocious spring-1967 jam developed into Brown's next R&B chart-topper, "Cold Sweat." It set the pace for a stream of future records—by Brown and others—that followed its lead of recapturing the mood of a live performance, seeking out a groove and running with it.

Often the musicians would already be jamming when Brown arrived at the studio; he would listen for a moment, then leap aboard, improvising lyrics around whatever they were playing, then calling it a take. It was a spontaneous, seemingly magical process, music at its most organic and, when the mood was right, its funkiest.

"I Got the Feelin'" followed "Cold Sweat" to the top of the R&B chart; "Licking Stick" (debuting Brown's first White band member, bassist Tim Hammond) and the double A-side "I Can't Stand Myself"/"There Was a Time" were Top Five. The much misunderstood "America Is My Home," released while Brown toured US army bases in Vietnam, made the Top 20; and August 1968's "Say It Loud, I'm Black and Proud" (Brown's first with trombone master Fred Wesley) emerged another #1, turning up the funk heat even higher. But in its wake, Brown found himself riding a further firestorm of conflicting emotions from within his audience.

Although there was little about the song to precipitate such a response, White America could not help but regard "Say It Loud" as an anthem of angry militancy (ironically, "America Is My Home" had alienated many Blacks). Nor could Brown himself halt the snowball, once it started rolling.

Under a banner headline reiterating the song's title, Brown took out a full-page ad in the New York press insisting, "James Brown is totally committed to Black power—the kind that is achieved not through the muzzle of a rifle, but through education and economic leverage." It made no difference. Across the country, "Say It Loud" (and, by extension, much of Brown's other music) was being quietly dropped by White Top 40 radio stations. Meanwhile, fresh furor broke out when a Brown gig at the Washington DC Armory ended in two days of rioting after the rumor circulated that a White sniper had assassinated the singer.

Throughout this tumultuous period, Brown continued gigging. In July 1969, a triumphant sequence of shows saw him fill Madison Square Garden in his own right, and co-headline the Newport Jazz Festival alongside Sly & the Family Stone, Jeff Beck and Led Zeppelin. He burst into living rooms across America as co-host of the *Mike Douglas Show*; and recorded the *Sex Machine* live album, the greatest testament of all to his live power.

He attempted broadening his appeal even further, throwing himself into work with a three-piece lounge act, an orchestra, even a rock group, led by arranger/organist Dave Matthews and featuring the ever-loyal Byrd, Kenny Poole (gtr), Michael Moore (bs) and Jimmy Madison (drms). This latter outfit recorded the album *Sho Is Funky Down Here*; the lineup was also responsible for a stunning rock version of "Talkin' Loud and Sayin' Nothin'," scheduled as a single in 1970, but eventually cancelled in subsequent favor of a more traditional funk-based rendition.

But the pressures were closing in on him, although when the final straw snapped, it was broken from an utterly unexpected quarter. First, Brown learned that the IRS was demanding close to $2 million in unpaid back taxes; then he was slapped with a paternity suit. At the end of his tether, Brown closed a show in Memphis, TN on September 6, 1969, by announcing he was retiring from live performances as of July 4, 1970.

He reversed the decision just weeks later, but the clouds of unrest did not drift away. Brown opened the new decade with a short residency at the Las Vegas International Hotel; weeks later, however, on March 9, 1970, Brown's band announced they were quitting en masse, the final shot in a long simmering dispute over wages.

## 1970–75

The departure was not a bolt from the blue; indeed, Brown had been preparing for just such an eventuality for some months, quietly grooming a young Cincinnati outfit called the Pacesetters to step into the breach at a moment's notice—and that is what they got. On the day of the next show, in Columbus, GA, Brown called Bobby Byrd back in Cincinnati and told him to round up the Pacesetters and put them on the next plane. They were whisked from the airport to the venue; their gear was set up under the noses of Brown's own, now ex-band. Scant hours later, they were onstage in front of the biggest audience of their lives.

Lining-up as Bootsy Collins (bs), his brother Phelps (gtr), Robert McCullough (sax), Clayton Gunnels (trum) and Frank Waddy (drms), the Pacesetters became what Brown described as "the nucleus of a very good band." The group was completed, over the next few months, by the return of Stubblefield, Starks (for a total of three available drummers) and guitarist Hearlon Martin from the old group, plus the loyal Byrd and trumpeter Daryl Jamison.

Brown and the newly named JBs spent much of 1970 on the road, both at home and touring Europe and Africa. In Nigeria, the party met local superstar Fela Ransome Kuti, widely regarded as the African James Brown; in Zambia, Brown was astonished to learn that President Kenneth Kaunda was a knowledgeable soul fan for whom the worst part of his job was that he now had to listen to music secretly. And in Europe, particularly in Germany, Brown was mortified to discover a new form of dance music, "disco," taking the place of live concerts in the nightclubs. He consoled himself with the belief that such a pernicious evil could never take root in the US.

Another of the departed musicians, trombonist Fred Wesley, returned to Brown's side around Christmas 1970. His first session with the JBs, cutting "Soul Power" in January 1971, became the Collins' lineup's last—less than two months later, history repeated itself when the Pacesetters confronted Brown over wages, then quit when nothing more than half-pay was forthcoming. They had played with him for precisely 381 days.

Brown immediately set about rebuilding the group. Wesley, Byrd, Starks, Martin and Pinckney remained or were recalled; then, with Robert Coleman (gtr), Jimmy Parker (sax), Russell Crimes and Jerome Sanford (trum), Fred Thomas (bs), John Morgan (drms) and Johnny Griffin (kybds), Brown relaunched the JBs, fronted both onstage and on their own records by Wesley.

The King label had folded by now. After ailing for years, with Brown its only reliable source of income, the company was tottering even before Brown announced he intended leaving when his contract was up in mid-1971. He signed to Polydor, securing a distribution deal for the People label at the same time and launching into a period of unparalleled activity.

Over the next five years, Brown produced releases by the JBs, longtime associates Bobby Byrd and his wife, Vicki Anderson; Marva Whitney (who replaced Anderson in the Revue in 1967 and cut Brown's answer to the Isley Brothers' "It's Your Thing" and "It's My Thing") and her eventual successor, Lyn Collins; Hank Ballard and the newly returned Maceo Parker. The JBs themselves also recorded under such pseudonyms as the Last Word, the First Family, the Believers and, under Parker's leadership, Maceo & the Macks. Brown also launched the short-lived Brownstone label in partnership with Henry Stone—he previously headed up Dade, home of the long-ago "Do the Mashed Potatoes" project.

Several of these releases were hits and People remained active until as late as 1976. (Previous Brown-led labels Try Me (1963), Dynamite (1965) and New Breed (1966) had barely lasted a year, and Brownstone, too, was to prove seriously short-lived.) But, of course, the main action was at the heart of the hurricane, with the seemingly effortless stream of singles, which the self-ordained "Minister of New Super Heavy Funk" was unleashing almost on a weekly basis.

The brooding neo-rap "Escape-ism," the fashion-craze conscious "Hot Pants (She Got To Use What She Got To Get What She Wants)," the four part, 12-minute "Make It Funky," "Get On the Good Foot" and "I Got a Bag of My Own" were major hits. A duet with Collins, "What My Baby Needs Now Is a Little More Lovin'," and a stream of tight

JBs instrumentals followed. Indeed, the JBs seemed set at times to challenge Brown's own chart domination, as the latest incarnations of the group established themselves as one of the hottest, tightest instrumental acts around—with Brown a similarly influential producer.

So much chart success did not go unnoticed in Hollywood. Following the massive success of Isaac Hayes' score for *Shaft* and Curtis Mayfield's *Superfly*, Brown was recruited to compose a soundtrack for *Black Caesar*, director Larry Cohen's 1973 recreation of the old 1930s-style gangster movies now haunting late-night TV.

Brown did not take the commission too seriously, apparently informing Wesley that he intended simply digging through his archive and finding old songs to match the movie. Wesley disagreed and did conjure up some more appropriate music, but neither *Black Caesar* nor *Slaughter's Big Rip-Off*, a second soundtrack the next year, were especially successful examples of the soundtrack-writer's art. It is ironic, then, that when Brown did finally put his mind to the job, for the *Black Caesar* sequel, *Hell up in Harlem*, director Cohen rejected his offerings because they weren't funky enough. Brown promptly pieced together the material as a concept album, *The Payback*, and wound up with his most successful record of the entire decade.

Yet, even as he instated an even more dramatic groove to his funk (and *The Payback* was an especially powerful record), there was also a sense that in terms of innovation, Brown had taken his bag as far as he could go. Wesley told Alan Leeds, "James started copying people. I thought he was losing his mind. I used to tell him, you're copying people, who are copying you." Once, Brown's competitors had looked to him for musical guidance—Wesley himself claimed George Clinton connected with Bootsy Collins "because he had been affiliated with James. Even though it was a short affiliation . . . George wanted some of that. It all comes from wanting to have a piece of James Brown." But now, Clinton had streaked ahead. There was a new King on the throne.

The mid-'70s grew darker. Another damaging round of battles with the IRS loomed. Brown's radio stations were in trouble over nonpayment of mechanical royalties, while Brown himself was dragged publicly into a messy payola trial. Equally damaging, his relationship with his label, Polydor, was moving toward its own crisis. Despite his success, Brown had never been convinced about Polydor's ability to market and promote his music. This was no problem while his records were selling as a matter of course, but it became increasingly worrisome as his commercial appeal began to slip in the face of the musical movement he once believed would never take root in America, the dreaded disco.

Almost imperceptibly, Brown drifted into semiretirement. He continued playing live, but concentrated on major shows in Europe, Africa and the Far East. The days of crisscrossing the US were over. The JBs began to crumble around him—Bobby Byrd had already left the fold, launching a solo career and touring with the Bootsy-era JBs. When they moved onto P-Funk, Wesley and Parker were swift to join them there. With a new band built around Jimmy Nolen and drummer Tony Cook, March 1977's "Body Heat" became Brown's last Hot 100 entry of the decade.

Brown settled in Augusta with his second wife, Deedee Jenkins (his first marriage, to Velma Warren, ended in divorce in 1969; this second one ended in 1978) and, between 1974–76, ran his own syndicated TV dance show, *Future Shock* from a local studio. (Production later shifted to Atlanta.) In terms of a major public profile, however, Brown had all but slipped off the radar and might have remained there, he later admitted, were it not for the death of Elvis Presley in 1977. "For some reason his death hit me very hard," Brown wrote. "We were a lot alike in many ways— both poor boys from the country, raised on gospel and R&B. 'Hound Dog' and 'Please' both came out the same year."

Suddenly Brown knew what he had to do. "I had been stopped, but I was not finished." He determined to throw himself back into his work with all the enthusiasm and energy it deserved. Brown returned to the road for a triumphant European tour in June 1978, then headed to New York for the reopening of the Apollo on July 12—a high profile engagement that could not fail to catapult him back into the limelight.

Unfortunately, he had reckoned without his old adversary, the legal system. The European tour coincided with a trial connected with one of Brown's radio stations and, though Brown had attempted to inform the court of his commitments, his failure to appear led to a charge of contempt. Brown was arrested and jailed five nights into the Apollo run.

He posted his bond and was released, but there was no freedom outside. Work on his next album was stalled while Brown and Polydor argued over its direction. He wanted to make a new funk monster; they envisaged (and eventually got) a Brad Shapiro-produced slice of slickness and soullessness titled *The Original Disco Man*. A second Shapiro set, *People*, followed in 1979. Brown disliked them both, but at least they pushed him into making a major decision. He had *come* back, now he had to *fight* back as well.

In November 1979, Brown called a press conference to announce he was suing Polydor over royalties. A new album-by-album deal was negotiated, but within a year, the two parties separated. Brown signed to Henry Stone's new label, TK, and celebrated a new decade with a new hit, *Soul Syndrome*.

## RAPP PAYBACK 1980–2000

Brown resolved to begin rebuilding from the ground up, touring smaller clubs; then he received a remarkable fillip when he was recruited for the *Blues Brothers* movie and was promptly catapulted into the attention of an entire new generation. He acknowledged the impact and importance of a new wave of music, too, when he revamped "Payback" for the 14-minute long UK success "Rapp Payback (Where Iz Moses)," and visibility begat visibility.

On December 13, 1980, Brown headlined *Saturday Night Live*. On February 2, 1982, he starred on *Solid Gold* (and, equally importantly, met his third wife, Adrianne Rodriguez); in between times, he toured constantly. He contributed to Blues Brother Dan Ackroyd's next movie, *Dr. Detroit*, and was briefly signed to Island Records, which despatched him to Nassau to record with reggae/dub giants Sly Dunbar and Robbie Shakespeare. For whatever reason, the sessions were never completed and Island released Brown soon after. But the very act of recording a high-profile, big-budget album had rejuvenated him even further, which, Brown suspected, was the point all along. Island label chief Chris Blackwell simply wanted to help him out.

In 1984, Brown joined forces with Afrika Bambaataa for the magnificent "Unity," a seething blend of classic Brown and archetypal Bambaataa. In 1985, he was recruited for *Rocky IV*, performing Dan Hartman and Charlie Midnight's "Living in America." A Best Male R&B Performance Grammy-winner, the track also became Brown's biggest 45 since "The Payback," over a decade before.

A new record contract with Scotti Brothers ensured Brown's rise continued. The *Gravity* album saw Brown surround himself with the cream of mid-'80s talent, including blues guitarist Stevie Ray Vaughan, vocalists Stevie Winwood and Alison Moyet, and musical director Dan Hartman. Maceo Parker rejoined him once more, and Brown's live shows were again a wonder to behold. At the Beverley Theater in Los Angeles, Brown was joined onstage by Michael Jackson and Prince, two more disciples who may have eclipsed him commercially, but who admitted they still had a lot to learn. "When I was in California later," Brown recalled, "[Prince] came to a show and lay on the floor backstage and watched my feet. Afterward he asked me if I had roller skates on my feet."

In January 1986, Brown was inducted into the Rock & Roll Hall of Fame, although 1988's ferociously contemporary *I'm Real*, recorded with the Full Force production team, proved he wasn't ready to be fossilized just yet. Months later, however, everything he had worked toward over the past eight years collapsed.

In the space of ten months, Brown was arrested five times. This sorry spell culminated in May 1988 when he discovered somebody had used the private bathroom at his office in Atlanta. Armed with a shotgun he burst into the building next door, where a delegation of insurance salesmen were meeting, demanding to know who had done it; of course somebody called the police, at which point Brown fled in his pickup truck. The ensuing high-speed chase ended only when the police shot out his front tires and Brown crashed into a ditch—23 bullet holes riddled the vehicle. Brown surrendered and was charged with failure to stop for the police, a so-called blue light violation.

He was released on bail, but 24 hours later was arrested again, this time for driving under the influence of PCP and marijuana. Again he was released, before going to trial in October to face the two existing charges, plus a third of aggravated assault. He was convicted and sentenced to six months imprisonment on the assault charge—and a staggering five-and-one-half years for the blue light violation. Neither the DUI charge nor (though the media made much of them) recently raised allegations that Brown frequently beat his wife, were taken into consideration by the court.

That was not the end of it, either. The trial accounted only for the portion of the chase that took place in South Carolina. It had carried into Georgia and, several weeks later, that court, too, exacted its pound of flesh, a second six-year term to run concurrent with the South Carolina ruling. Writing in 1990, journalist Dave Marsh described it as "perhaps the longest sentence ever given in the United States for a traffic charge."

Brown was released on parole in February 1991, and immediately announced a full return to action. (He continued to brush with the law, on charges ranging from domestic assault in 1995, to illegal discharge of a firearm in 1998.) In June 1991, the TV special *Living in America* paired Brown with the then-cream of the R&B scene, MC Hammer, En Vogue and Bell Biv Devoe; while an increasing schedule of live and TV appearances set about re-establishing his reputation as the hardest working man in showbusiness.

The industry flocked to honor his return: at the American Music Awards in January 1992, he received the Award of Merit; the following month at the Grammys, he received a Lifetime Achievement Award. The next year, both the R&B Foundation Pioneer Awards and the National Association of Black Owned Broadcasters granted him their own Lifetime Achievement Awards. Also in 1993, his hometown, Augusta, renamed part of Ninth Street in his honor, James Brown Boulevard. He received a star on the Hollywood Walk of Fame in 1997.

At the same time, Polydor commenced an archive release program that returned much of Brown's '60s and '70s canon to the stores, via some genuinely imaginative, and oftentimes thematic, collections of both familiar and rare material. The first of these, the *Star Time* box set, won the Best Album Notes category at the Grammys; others were simply content with the gratitude of a still loyal audience of collectors.

Meantime, Brown was busy in his own regard. He completed his first new albums since 1988's *I'm Real*, the patchy *Love Overdue* and the stronger *Universal James*. A triumphant return to the Apollo yielded the *Live at the Apollo 1995* album, while his touring schedule settled down to include regular birthday celebrations in Augusta and such highprofile shows as the Concert for the Rock & Roll Hall of Fame in September 1995, the Centennial Olympic Games in Atlanta in 1996, the MacWorld Convention in Boston in 1997 and the opening of the Experience Music Museum in Seattle in June, 2000, where he was backed by Wesley, Parker and Bootsy Collins, among others.

## FURTHER READING
*James Brown: The Godfather of Soul*, by James Brown with Bruce Tucker (revised edition: Thunder's Mouth Press, 1997)

## JAMES BROWN COMPLETE DISCOGRAPHY
### SINGLES/CHART LOG
1956 Please Please Please/Why Do You Do Me? (Federal—#6 R&B/#106 pop)
1956 I Don't Know/I Feel That Old Feeling Coming On (Federal)
1956 No No No/Hold My Baby's Hand (Federal)
1956 Just Won't Do Right/Let's Make It (Federal)
1957 Chonnie-On-Chon/I Won't Plead No More (Federal)
1957 Can't Be the Same/Gonna Try (Federal)
1957 Love or a Game/Messing with the Blues (Federal)
1957 You're Mine You're Mine/I Walked Alone (Federal)
1957 That Dood It/Baby Cries over the Ocean (Federal)

1958 Begging Begging/That's When I Lost My Heart (Federal)
1958 Try Me/Tell Me What I Did Wrong (Federal—#1 R&B/#48 pop)
1959 I Want You So Bad/There Must Be a Reason (Federal—#20 R&B)
1959 I've Got To Change/It Hurts To Tell You (Federal)
1959 Good Good Lovin'/Don't Let It Happen to Me (Federal)
1959 Got To Cry/It Was You (Federal)
1960 I'll Go Crazy/I Know It's True (Federal—#15 R&B)
1960 Think (Federal - #7 R&B/#33 pop)/You've Got the Power (#14 R&B/#86 pop)
1960 This Old Heart/Wonder when You're Coming Home (Federal—#20 R&B/#79 pop)
1960 The Bells/And I Do Just What I Want (King—#68 pop)
1961 Hold It/The Scratch (King)
1961 Bewildered/If You Want Me (King—#8 R&B/#40 pop)
1961 I Don't Mind/Love Don't Love Nobody (King—#4 R&B/#47 pop)
1961 Suds/Sticky (King)
1961 Cross Firing/Night Flying (King)
1961 Baby You're Right/I'll Never Never Let You Go (King—#2 R&B/#49 pop)
1961 Just You and Me Darling/I Love You, Yes I Do (King—#17 R&B)
1961 Lost Someone/Cross Firing (King—#2 R&B/#48 pop)
1962 Night Train/Why Does Everything Happen to Me (King—#5 R&B/#35 pop)
1962 Shout and Shimmy/Come over Here (King—#16 R&B/#61 pop)
1962 Mashed Potatoes USA/You Don't Have To Go (King—#21 R&B/#82 pop)
1962 I've Got Money (King—#93 pop)/Three Hearts in aTangle (#18 R&B)
1963 Every Beat of My Heart (King—#99 pop)/Like a Baby (#24 R&B)
1963 Prisoner of Love/Choo Choo Locomotion (King—#6 R&B/#18 pop)
1963 These Foolish Things/Feel It (part one) (King—#25 R&B/#55 pop)
1963 Signed Sealed and Delivered/Waiting in Vain (King—#77 pop)
1963 I've Got To Change/The Bells (King)
1964 Oh Baby Don't You Weep (part one)/(part two) (King—#23 pop)
1964 Please Please Please/In the Wee Wee Hours (King—#95 pop)
1964 Caldonia/Evil (Smash—#95 pop)
1964 Again/How Long Darling (King)
1964 So Long/Dancing Little Thing (King)
1964 The Things I Used To Do/Out of the Blue (Smash—#99 pop)
1964 Out of Sight/Maybe the Last Time (Smash—#24 pop)
1964 Tell Me What You're Gonna Do/I Don't Care (King)
1964 Think/Try Me (King)
1964 Fine Old Foxy Self/medley (King)
1964 Have Mercy, Baby/Just Won't Do Right (King—#92 pop)
1965 Devil's Hideaway/Who's Afraid of Virginia Woolf (Smash)
1965 I Got You/Only You (Smash—unissued)
1965 This Old Heart/It Was You (King)
1965 Papa's Got a Brand New Bag (part one)/(part two) (King—#1 R&B/#8 pop)
1965 Try Me/Papa's Got a Brand New Bag (Smash—#34 R&B/#63 pop)
1965 I Got You (I Feel Good)/I Can't Help It (King—#1 R&B/#3 pop)
1966 Lost Someone (King—#94 pop)/I'll Go Crazy (#38 R&B/#73 pop)
1966 Ain't That a Groove (part one)/(part two) (King—#6 R&B/#42 pop)

1966 Prisoner of Love/I've Got To Change (King)

1966 New Breed (part one)/(part two) (Smash)

1966 Come over Here/Tell Me What You're Gonna Do (King)

1966 It's a Man's Man's Man's World/Is It Yes or Is It No? (King—#1 R&B/#8 pop)

1966 Just Won't Do Right/I've Got Money (King)

1966 James Brown's Boo-Ga-Loo/Lost in a Mood of Changes (Smash)

1966 It Was You/I Don't Care (King)

1966 This Old Heart/How Long Darling? (King)

1966 Money Won't Change You (part one)/(part two) (King—#11 R&B/#53 pop)

1966 Don't Be a Drop Out/Tell Me That You Love Me (King—#4 R&B/#50 pop)

1966 The Christmas Song (version one)/(version two) (King)

1966 Sweet Little Baby Boy (part one)/(part two) (King)

1966 Let's Make Christmas Mean Something This Year (part one)/(part two) (King)

1967 Bring It Up/Nobody Knows (King—#7 R&B/#29 pop)

1967 Let's Go Get Stoned/Our Day Will Come (Smash)

1967 Let Yourself Go/Stone Fox (King—withdrawn)

1967 Kansas City/Stone Fox (King—#21 R&B/#55 pop)

1967 Let Yourself Go/Good Rockin' Tonight (King—#5 R&B/#46 pop)

1967 Jimmy Mack/What Do You Like (Smash)

1967 I Love You, Porgy/Yours and Mine (Bethlehem)

1967 Cold Sweat (part one)/(part two) (King—#1 R&B/#7 pop)

1967 It Won't Be Me/Mona Lisa (King—withdrawn)

1967 Get It Together (part one)/(part two) (King—#11 R&B/#40 pop)

1967 Funky Soul #1/The Soul of JB (King)

1967 I Can't Stand Myself (King—#4 R&B/#28 pop)/There Was a Time (#3 R&B/#36 pop)

1968 I Got the Feelin'/If I Ruled the World (King—#1 R&B/#6 pop)

1968 Maybe Good Maybe Bad (part one)/(part two) (King)

1968 Shhhhhhhh/Here I Go (King)

1968 Licking Stick (part one)/(part two) (King—#2 R&B/#14 pop)

1968 America Is My Home (part one)/(part two) (King—#13 R&B/#52 pop)

1968 I Guess I'll Have to Cry Cry Cry/Just Plain Funk (King—#15 R&B/#55 pop)

1968 Say It Loud, I'm Black and I'm Proud (part one)/(part two) (King—#1 R&B/#10 pop)

1968 I Love You/Maybe I'll Understand (King/Colgate)

1968 Goodbye My Love/Shades of Brown (King—#9 R&B/#31 pop)

1968 Santa Claus Goes Straight to the Ghetto/You Know It (King)

1968 Tit for Tat/Believers Shall Enjoy (King—#86 pop)

1968 Let's Unite the Whole World at Christmas/In the Middle (part one) (King)

1969 Give it up or Turnit a Loose/I'll Lose My Mind (King—#1 R&B/#15 pop)

1969 Steve Soul a Talk with the News/Shades of Brown (part two) (King)

1969 Soul Pride (part one)/(part two) (King—#33 R&B/#117 pop)

1969 You Got To Have a Mother for Me (part one)/(part two) (King—unissued)

1969 I Don't Want Nobody To Give Me Nothing (part one)/(part two) (King—#3 R&B/#20 pop)

1969 The Little Groove Maker Me (part one)/(part two) (King—unissued)

1969 The Popcorn/The Chicken (King—#11 R&B/#30 pop)

1969 Mother Popcorn (part one)/(part two) (King—#1 R&B/11 pop)

1969 Lowdown Popcorn/Top of the Stack (King—#16 R&B/#41 pop)

1969 World (part one)/(part two) (King—#8 R&B/#37 pop)

1969 Let a Man Come in and Do the Popcorn (part one)/Sometime (King—#2 R&B/#21 pop)

1969 I'm Not Demanding (part one)/(part two) (King—unissued)

1969 Ain't It Funky Now (part one)/(part two) (King—#3 R&B/#24 pop)

1969 Let a Man Come in and Do the Popcorn (part two)/Gittin' a Little Hipper (part two) (King—#6 R&B/#40 pop)

1969 It's Christmas Time (part one)/(part two) (King)

1970 Steve Soul Soul President/Popcorn with a Feeling (Federal)

1970 Brother Rapp (part one)/(part two) (King—unissued)

1970 Funky Drummer (part one)/(part two) (King—#20 R&B/#51 pop)

1970 It's a New Day/Georgia on My Mind (King—#3 R&B/#32 pop)

1970 Talkin' Loud and Sayin' Nothing (part one)/(part two) (King)

1970 Brother Rapp/Bewildered (King—#2 R&B/#32 pop)

1970 Get Up, I Feel Like Being a Sex Machine (part one)/(part two) (King—#2 R&B/#15 pop)

1970 A Man Has To Go Back to the Crossroads/The Drunk (Bethlehem)

1970 I'm Not Demanding (part one)/(part two) (King)

1970 Super Bad (parts one/two)/(part three) (King—#1 R&B/#13 pop)

1970 Hey America/(instrumental) (King)

1970 Santa Claus Is Definitely Here To Stay/(instrumental) (King)

1970 Get up, Get into It and Get Involved (part one)/(part two) (King—#4 R&B/#34 pop)

1970 Talkin' Loud and Sayin' Nothing (part one)/(part two) (King)

1971 Spinning Wheel (part one)/(part two) (King—#90 pop)

1971 Soul Power (part one)/(part two) (King—#3 R&B/#29 pop)

1971 I Cried/World (part two) (King—#15 R&B/#50 pop)

1971 Escape-ism (part one)/(part two) (People—#6 R&B/#35 pop)

1971 Hot Pants (part one)/(part two) (People—#1 R&B/#15 pop)

1971 Make It Funky (part one)/(part two) (Polydor—#1 R&B/#22 pop)

1971 My Part-Make It Funky (part three)/(part four) (Polydor—#68 pop)

1971 I'm a Greedy Man (part one)/(part two) (Polydor—#7 R&B/#35 pop)

1972 Talkin' Loud and Sayin' Nothing (part one)/(part two) (Polydor—#1 R&B/#27 pop)

1972 King Heroin/Theme from King Heroin (Polydor—#6 R&B/#40 pop)

1972 There It Is (part one)/(part two) (Polydor—#4 R&B/#43 pop)

1972 Honky Tonk (part one)/(part two) (Polydor—#7 R&B/#44 pop)

1972 Get Oon the Good Foot (part one)/(part two) (Polydor—#1 R&B/18 pop)

1972 I Got a Bag of My Own/Public Enemy #1 (part one) (Polydor—#3 R&B/#44 pop)

1973 I Got Ants in My Pants (part one)/(parts 15/16) (Polydor—#4 R&B/#27 pop)

1973 Down and out in New York City/Mama's Dead (Polydor—#13 R&B/#50 pop)

1973 The Boss/Like It Is, Like It Was (Polydor—unissued)

1973 Think/Something (Polydor—#15 R&B/#77 pop)

1973 Think (alternate)/Something (Polydor—#37 R&B/#80 pop)

1973 Woman (part one)/(part two) (Polydor—unissued)

1973 Sexy Sexy Sexy/Slaughter Theme (Polydor—#6 R&B/#50 pop)

1973 Stone to the Bone (part one)/(part two) (Polydor—#4 R&B/#58 pop)

1974 The Payback (part one)/(part two) (Polydor—#1 R&B/#26 pop)

1974 My Thang/Public Enemy #1 (part one) (Polydor—#1 R&B/#29 pop)

1974 Papa Don't Take No Mess (part one)/(part two) (Polydor—#1 R&B/#31 pop)

1974 Funky President (Polydor—#4 R&B/#44 pop)/Cold Blooded (#99 pop)

1975 Reality/I Need Your Love So Bad (Polydor—#19 R&B/#80 pop)

1975 Sex Machine (part one)/(part two) (Polydor—#16 R&B/#61 pop)

1975 Dead on It (part one)/(part two) (Polydor—withdrawn)

1975 Hustle (Dead on It)/(Dead on It (part two) (Polydor—#11 R&B)

1975 Superbad Superslick (part one)/(part two) (Polydor—#28 R&B)

1975 Hot/Superbad Superslick (Polydor—#31 R&B)

1976 Dooley's Junkyard Dogs (long)/(short) (Polydor)

1976 For Sentimental Reasons/Goodnight My Love (Polydor—#70 R&B)

1976 Get Up Offa That Thing/Release the Pressure (Polydor—#4 R&B/#45 pop)

1976 I Refuse To Lose/Home Again (Polydor—#47 R&B)

1976 Bodyheat (part one)/(part two) (Polydor—#13 R&B/#91 pop)

1977 Kiss in 77/Woman (Polydor—#35 R&B)

1977 Give Me Some Skin/People Wake Up and Live (Polydor—#20 R&B)

1977 Take Me Higher and Groove Me/Summertime (Polydor)

1977 People Who Criticize/If You Don't Give a Doggone About It (Polydor—#45 R&B)

1978 Love Me Tender/Have a Happy Day (Polydor)

1978 Eyesight/I Never Never Never Will Forget (Polydor—#38 R&B)

1978 The Spank/Love Me Tender (Polydor—#26 R&B)

1978 Nature (part one)/(part two) (Polydor)

1978 For Goodness Sakes, Look at Those Cakes (part one)/(part two) (Polydor—#52 R&B)

1979 Someone To Talk To (part one)/(part two) (Polydor)

1979 It's Too Funky in Here/Are We Really Dancing (Polydor—#15 R&B)

1979 Star Generation/Women Are Something Else (Polydor—#63 R&B)

1979 Let the Boogie Do the Rest/The Original Disco Man (Polydor)

1980 Regrets/Stone Cold Drag (Polydor—#53 R&B)

1980 Let the Funk Flow/Sometimes That's All There Is (Polydor)

1980 Get Up Offa That Thing/It's Too Funky in Here (Polydor)

1980 Rapp Payback (part one)/(part two) (TK—#46 R&B)

1981 Stay with Me/Smokin' and Drinkin' (TK—#80 R&B)

1983 Bring It On/Night Time Is the Right Time (Augusta Sound—#73 R&B)

1983 As Long as I Love You/For Your Precious Love (Augusta Sound—unissued)

1983 King of Soul/(cut by Devo) (Backstreet)

1985 Living in America/(cut by Vinci Di Cola) (Scotti Bros—#10 R&B/#4 pop)

1986 Gravity/(dub mix) (Scotti Bros—#26 R&B/#93 pop)

1987 How Do You Stop/House of Rock (Scotti Bros—#10 R&B)

1988 I'm Real/Tribute (Scotti Bros—#2 R&B)

1988 Static/Godfather Runnin' the Joint (Scotti Bros—#5 R&B)

1988 Time To Get Busy/Busy JB (Scotti Bros)

1989 It's Your Money/You and Me (Scotti Bros)

1991 Move On (remix) (Scotti Bros—#48 R&B)

1993 Can't Get Any Harder (remix) (Scotti Bros—#76 R&B)

## JAMES BROWN/YVONNE FAIR

1962 Tell Me Why/Say So Long (King)

1962 It Hurts To Be in Love/You Can Make It if You Try (King)

## JAMES BROWN/VICKI ANDERSON

1967 Think/(Vicki Anderson cut) (King—#100 pop)

1968 You've Got the Power/(Vicki Anderson cut) (King)

1970 Let It Be Me/(Vicki Anderson cut) (King)

## JAMES BROWN/BOBBY BYRD

1968 You've Got To Change Your Mind/(Bobby Byrd cut) (King—#47 R&B)

## JAMES BROWN/MARVA WHITNEY

1969 You've Got To Have a Job/(Marva Whitney cut) (King)

## JAMES BROWN/LYN COLLINS

1972 What My Baby Needs Now/This Guy's in Love (Polydor—#17 R&B/#56 pop)

1973 Let It Be Me/It's All Right (Polydor—unissued)

## JAMES BROWN/REV. AL SHARPTON AND THE GOSPEL ENERGIES

1981 God Has Smiled on Me (part one)/(part two) (Royal King)

## JAMES BROWN/AFRIKA BAMBAATAA

1983 Unity (parts one-three)/(parts four-six) (Tommy Boy—#87 R&B)

## JAMES BROWN/ARETHA FRANKLIN

1989 Gimme Your Love/Think (Arista—#48 R&B)

## JAMES BROWN

### LPs

(note: [L] denotes live album, [Ld] denotes studio recordings with dubbed audience effects, [I] denotes all instrumental)

**7** **1960 Think (King)**

Nonstop primal Brown, 12 cuts recorded over the previous 18 months, with an immediacy that defies description.

**6** **1961 The Amazing James Brown (King)**

**5** **1961 Presents His Band/Night Train [I] )(King)**

Brown's first instrumental album, tightly wound but more jazz inflected than his later work.

**6** **1962 James Brown and His Famous Flames (King)**

**10** **1963 Live at the Apollo [L] (King)**

Recorded 10/24/62, an incredible 40-minute performance comes screaming through the deficiencies of period recordingtechnology, as dynamic and dangerous as everyone always says Brown could be.

**7** **1963 Prisoner of Love (King)**

**7** **1964 Pure Dynamite: Live at the Royal [L] (King)**

**7** **1964 Showtime [Ld] (Smash)**

Overdubbed audience sounds detract from a strong studio performance.

**6** **1964 Grits and Soul [I] (Smash—#9 R&B/#124 pop)**

**6** **1966 James Brown Plays James Brown Today and Yesterday [I] (King—#3 R&B/#42 pop)**

**7** **1966 Mighty Instrumentals [I] (King)**

**8** **1966 James Brown Plays New Breed (The Boo-Ga-Loo) [I] (King—#11 R&B/#101 pop)**

One of the best Brown instrumental albums, highlighted by the aptly named "Fat Bag" and the tight "New Breed."

**7** **1966 The James Brown Christmas Album (King)**

**6** **1966 Handful of Soul [I] (Smash—#24 R&B/#135 pop)**

**9** **1967 The James Brown Show [L] (Smash)**

Various artists live album, capturing the sheer majesty of the Brown Revue.

**7** **1967 Raw Soul (King)**

**7** **1967 Live at the Garden [L] (King—#5 R&B/#41 pop)**

**6** **1967 James Brown Plays the Real Thing [I] (Smash—#27 R&B/#164 pop)**

**6** **1967 Cold Sweat (King—#5 R&B/#135 pop)**

**8** **1968 James Brown Presents His Show of Tomorrow (King)**

A companion to the *James Brown Show*, isolating recent and favored additions to the Revue, including two Brown cuts.

**9** **1968 I Can't Stand Myself (When You Touch Me) (King—#4 R&B/#17 pop)**

A thunderous collection captures Brown at the peak of his late '60s powers, topped off by the instrumental "Soul of JB" and the Dapps-fired title track.

**6** **1968 I Got the Feelin' (King—#8 R&B/#135 pop)**

**7** **1968 James Brown Plays Nothing but Soul [I] (King—#20 R&B/#150 pop)**

**7** **1968 Live at the Apollo Vol. II [L] (King—#2 R&B/#32 pop)**

**6** **1968 Thinking About Little Willie John and a Few Nice Things (King)**

**6** **1968 A Soulful Christmas (King)**

**9** **1969 Say It Loud—I'm Black and I'm Proud (King—#6 R&B/#53 pop)**

"Licking Stick," "Cry Cry Cry" and "Shades of Brown," the title track . . . what more do you need to know?

**4** **1969 Gettin' Down to It (King—#14 R&B/#99 pop)**

One of Brown's less satisfactory outings, combining with the Dee Felice Trio for a look inside the world of lounge-funk.

**7** **1969 James Brown Plays and Directs the Popcorn [I] (King—#4 R&B/#40 pop)**

Not, sadly, a collection of all the popcorn-titled tracks in Brown's contemporary repertoire, but a worthy set of eminently danceable instrumentals all the same.

**7** **1969 It's a Mother (King—#2 R&B/#26 pop)**

**7** **1970 Ain't It Funky [I] (King—#5 R&B/#43 pop)**

**5** **1970 Soul on Top (King—#12 R&B/#125 pop)**

Another one to shock the expectations—Brown fronts the Louie Bellson Orchestra.

**6** **1970 It's a New Day So Let a Man Come In (King—#11 R&B/#121 pop)**

**8** **1970 Sex Machine [L/Ld] (King—#4 R&B/#29 pop)**

Old and new bands collide across an album that single-handedly defines funk for the new decade. Not quite Brown's greatest album, but certainly one of the most influential.

**7** **1970 Hey America (King)**

**7** **1971 Superbad [Ld] (King—#4 R&B/#61 pop)**

**7** **1971 Sho Is Funky Down Here [I] (King—#26 R&B/#137 pop)**

No matter how fashionable it is to condemn Brown's attempt to corner the market in underground rock, there's no doubting the effectiveness of his efforts. Some vocals might have helped, though.

**8** **1971 Hot Pants (Polydor—#4 R&B/#22 pop)**

Lengthy versions of "Hot Pants" and "Escape-ism" dominate an apparently hurried, but effortlessly loose-limbed label debut.

**7** **1971 Revolution of the Mind—Live at the Apollo Vol. 3 [L] (Polydor—#7 R&B/#39 pop)**

**9** **1972 There It Is (Polydor—#10 R&B/#60 pop)**

"Pick up on this!" Seven driving minutes of "I'm a Greedy Man," the ruthless ballad-paced "King Heroin" and the fierce "Talkin' Loud" make up Brown's most dramatic '70s album.

**8** **1972 Get on the Good Foot (Polydor—#8 R&B/#68 pop)**

**5** **1973 Black Caesar- (original soundtrack) (Polydor—#2 R&B/#31 pop)**

**6** **1973 Slaughter's Big Rip-Off OST (Polydor—#15 R&B/#92 pop)**

**10** **1974 The Payback (Polydor—#1 R&B/#34 pop)**

Double album dominated by the superlative title track, but also the musical (and lyrical) culmination of the past five years.

**8** **1974 Hell (Polydor—#2 R&B/#35 pop)**

**7** 1975 Reality (Polydor—#5 R&B/#56 pop)

**8** 1975 Sex Machine Today (Polydor—#10 R&B/#103 pop)

**7** 1975 Everybody's Doin' the Hustle and Dead on the Double Bump (Polydor—#22 R&B/#193 pop)

**7** 1976 Hot (Polydor—#25 R&B)

The last essential Brown album of the 1970s features an updated "Please Please Please" alongside archetypal funk shouters of more recent vintage.

**6** 1976 Get Up Offa That Thing (Polydor—#14 R&B/#147 pop)

**6** 1977 Body Heat (Polydor—#20 R&B/#126 pop)

**6** 1977 Mutha's Nature (Polydor—#31 R&B)

**7** 1978 Jam 1980s (Polydor—#30 R&B/121 pop)

**5** 1979 Take a Look at Those Cakes (Polydor—#58 R&B)

**6** 1979 The Original Disco Man (Polydor—#37 R&B/#152 pop)

**4** 1980 People (Polydor—#68 R&B)

**6** 1980 Hot on the One (L) (Polydor)

**8** 1980 Soul Syndrome (TK)

Like *The Payback* before it, "Rapp Payback" was one of those moments when time stood still. The remainder of the album pales alongside it, but at least the Godfather was back.

**5** 1981 Nonstop! (Polydor)

**7** 1981 Live in NYC [L] (Audio Fidelity)

He hated disco, but it embraced him—the Godfather shakes up Studio 54 in fine fashion.

**6** 1983 Bring It On (Augusta)

**6** 1986 Live in Concert [L] (Sugar Hill)

**7** 1986 Gravity (Scotti Bros—#39 R&B/#156 pop)

**6** 1988 I'm Real (Scotti Bros—#15 R&B/#96 pop)

**6** 1989 Soul Session Live [L] (Scotti Bros)

**6** 1991 Love Overdue (Scotti Bros—#51 R&B)

**7** 1992 Universal James (RCA)

**7** 1993 Can't Get Any Harder (RCA)

**6** 1998 I'm Back (Polygram)

**5** 1999 Merry Christmas Album (Waxworks)

Less musically intense than Brown's 1960s' festive offerings, social comment ("Don't Forget the Poor") blends with timeliness ("Merry Christmas Millennium") for an album of thoughtful fun.

### SELECTED COMPILATIONS AND ARCHIVE RELEASES

There are more James Brown compilations on the retail and collectors' markets than there are regular albums. The following highly selective discography is divided into two parts: the first details albums one might encounter on the collectors' circuit; the second features currently available CDs documenting specific periods of Brown's career—above and beyond the *Star Time* box set.

### ORIGINAL RELEASES

**7** 1959 Please, Please, Please (King)

Vivid sound is the promise emblazoned on the cover, and that's what you're gonna get, spread across 16 classic early 45 sides.

**7** 1959 Try Me (aka The Unbeatable James Brown) (King)

**7** 1962 Shout and Shimmy (King)

**8** 1965 Papa's Got a Brand New Bag (King—#2 R&B/#26 pop)

The jacket alone is a work of art, notably the somewhat literal interpretation of the title. Within, the near-segue between the two part "Papa's Bag" and the ska-inflected "Mashed Potatoes USA" is seamlessly honking

**8** 1966 I Got You (King—#2 R&B/#36 pop)

Another killer King jacket and, again, a record to match. Soundtracking the *Ski Party* movie with the energizing title track, "Good Good Lovin'," "You've Got the Power". . . the thing with early Brown is, you know precisely what it's going to sound like, but it still stuns with its strength and audacity.

**8** 1966 It's a Man's, Man's, Man's World (King—#11 R&B/#90 pop)

NB: Each of the above LPs originally appeared in the immediate aftermath of the title hit, generally compiling recent singles, B-sides and studio sessions.

### ANTHOLOGIES

**8** 1972 Soul Classics (Polydor—#13 R&B/#83 pop)

**8** 1973 Soul Classics, Vol. 2 (Polydor—#30 R&B/#202 pop)

**8** 1975 Soul Classics, Vol. 3 (Polydor)

The story so far, mid-'70s style.

**7** 1984 Roots of a Revolution (Polydor)

Two CD set concentrating on the 1956–64 era, as Brown's music stepped away from doo wop and into the proto-Funk arena.

**9** 1984 The Federal Years, part one (Solid Smoke)

**9** 1984 The Federal Years part two (Solid Smoke)

Exactly what they say, a well-compiled primer to the best of the '50s/early-'60s material.

**9** 1984 Ain't That a Groove 1966–69 (Polydor)

**8** 1984 Doing It to Death 1970–73 (Polydor)

**8** 1985 Dead on the Heavy Funk 1974–76 (Polydor)

Worthy collections concentrating on the best of Brown's most crucial decade. Excellent booklets and annotation add to the thrill.

**8** 1986 James Brown's Funky People (Polydor)

**7** 1988 James Brown's Funky People, Vol. 2 (Polydor)

The first two volumes (#3 appeared in 2000) detailing the development and origins of the People label, via rare and unreleased material.

**8** 1991 Messing with the Blues (Polydor)

Fine two CD collection of Brown's exploration of one of his most profound formative influences.

**9** **1991 Star Time (Polydor—#89 R&B)**

Career spanning box set whets the appetite for more, much more . . . .

**8** **1992 Love Power Peace (Polydor)**

Recorded at the Paris Olympia, the only official live recording featuring the Collins-era JBs.

**7** **1992 Greatest Hits of the Fourth Decade (Scotti Bros)**

The pickings are slim, but the results bear scrutiny.

**8** **1993 Soul Pride (The Instrumentals) (PolyGram)**

Two CD set tracing the roots of Brown's later funk from a shockingly under-appreciated direction.

**6** **1995 Funky Christmas (Polydor)**

The best of Brown's jingle bell excursions.

**9** **1996 Foundations of Funk: A Brand New Bag 1964–69 (Polydor)**

**8** **1996 Funk Power—1970: A Brand New Thang (Polydor)**

**9** **1996 Make It Funky: The Big Payback 1971–75 (Polydor)**

Essential companions to the 1984/85 packages, concentrating on rare, alternate and unreleased versions of the period's best material.

**7** **1997 Funky Men (P-Vine—Jap)**

Near-essential round-up of TK-era Brown and related (JBs, Bobby Byrd) material, including rare singles and both the full (14 minute) and remixed "Rapp Payback."

**7** **1998 Say It Live and Loud (Polydor)**

Fiery 1968 recording from Dallas. Arguably, this represents one of Brown's all-time peaks as a live performer and the CD captures every last drop of sweat.

*SELECTED SAMPLES*

A Blind Man Could See It — Blackstreet: No Diggity (remix) (1996)

A Blind Man Could See It — Coolio: Sticky Fingers (1994)

A Blind Man Could See It — Das EFX: They Want EFX (1992)

A Blind Man Could See It — Lord Finesse: Funky Techincian (1990)

A Blind Man Could See It — Punch & Words: Da Cipher (1998)

A Blind Man Could See It — Snoop Doggy Dogg: Vapors (1996)

A Blind Man Could See It — Steady B: Use Me Again (1989)

A Blind Man Could See It — Sting, featuring Puff Daddy and Pras: Roxanne '97 (1997)

Ain't It Funky — Beastie Boys: Hey Ladies (1989)

Ain't It Funky — Mysterme: Unsolved Mysterme (1993)

Baby, Here I Come — EPMD: Big Payback (1989)

Baby, Here I Come — Insane Poetry: Angel of Death (1992)

Baby, Here I Come — Red Hot Lover Tone: I Like (1992)

Blues and Pants — Cypress Hill: The Phunky Feel One (1992)

Blues and Pants — DJ Jazzy Jeff & the Fresh Prince: Too Damn Hype (1989)

Blues and Pants — Geto Boys: Scarface (1990)

Blues and Pants — Ice-T: New Jack Hustler (Nino's Theme) (1991)

Blues and Pants — Masta Ace Incorporated: Ain't U Da Masta (1993)

Blues and Pants — Pete Rock & CL Smooth: If It Ain't Rough, It Ain't Right (1992)

Blues and Pants — Soul for Real: Love You So (1996)

Blues and Pants — Soul II Soul: Get a Life (1990)

Blues and Pants — Steady B: Anyway U Want It (1989)

Blues and Pants — Supercat: Ghetto Red Hot (video mix) (1992)

The Boss — Big Daddy Kane: Niggaz Never Learn (1993)

The Boss — Das EFX: Undaground Rappa (1993)

The Boss — Ice-T: You Played Yourself (1989)

The Boss — Lord Finesse: Bad Mutha (1990)

The Boss — Da Youngsta's: Who's the Mic Wrecka? (1993)

Bring It Up (Hipster's Avenue) — Brothers Like Outlaws: Kickin' Jazz (1992)

Bring It Up (Hipster's Avenue) — Gang Starr: Manifest (1989)

Bring It Up (Hipster's Avenue) — Kid 'N Play: Gittin' Funky (1988)

Bring It Up (Hipster's Avenue) — UMC: See the Man on the Street

Brother Rap — X-Clan: Holy Rum Swig (1992)

Can I Get Some Help — Ice-T: Freedom of Speech (1989)

Can I Get Some Help — Kool G Rap: Play It Kool (1990)

Can I Get Some Help — Shyheim: Here Come the Hits (1994)

Can I Get Some Help — Tim Dog: Fuck Compton (1991)

Can Mind — Brand Nubian: All for One (1991)

Can Mind — Terminator X: Juvenile Delinquitz (remix) (1991)

Chase — Fun DMC: Back from Hell (remix) (1990)

Chase — Fun DMC: The Ave (1990)

The Chicken — 2 Live Crew: I Ain't Bullshittin' (1990)

The Chicken — Big Daddy Kane: Calling Mr. Welfare (1989)

Coldblooded — Lord Finesse: Baby, You Nastyn (1990)

Coldblooded — Schoolly D: Who's Schoolin' Who (1991)

Coldblooded — WC & the Maad Circle: A Crazy Break (1991)

Cold Sweat — Three Times Dope: Straight Up (1989)

Cold Sweat — Chubb Rock: What's the Word? (1991)

Cold Sweat — DJ Jazzy Jeff & the Fresh Prince: Taking It to the Top (1987)

Cold Sweat — Ice Cube: Jackin' 4 Beats (1991)

Cold Sweat — Public Enemy: Prophets of Rage (1988)

Cold Sweat — Public Enemy: Welcome to the Terrordome (1990)

Cold Sweat — Public Enemy: How To Kill a Radio Consultant (1991)

Cold Sweat — Sweet Tee: I Got Da Feelin'(1989)

Cold Sweat — Terminator X: Juvenile Delinquentz (1991)

Cold Sweat — UTFO: Wanna Rock (1989)

Don't Be a Dropout — Red Hot Lover Tone: Like a Virgin (1992)

Don't Tell a Lie about Me and I Won't Tell the Truth on You — Low Profile: Easy Money (1990)

Don't Tell It — Boogie Down Producitons: Poetry (1991)

Don't Tell It — Eric B. & Rakim: Move the Crowd (remix) (1987)

Don't Tell It — Kool G. Rap: Money in the Bank (1990)

Down and out in New York City — Rakim: New York (1997)

Escape-ism — Audio Two: What More Can I Say? (1988)

Escape-ism — Big Daddy Kane: Raw (1988)

Escape-ism — Craig Mack: Get Down (remix) (1994)

Escape-ism — Cypress Hill: How I Could Just Kill a Man (remix)(1992)

Escape-ism — Heavy D: Overweight Lovers in the House (1987)

Escape-ism — Ice-T: Home of the Bodybag (1991)

Escape-ism — Ice-T: Street Killer (1991)

Escape-ism — Kool Moe Dee: Here We Go Again (1991)

Escape-ism — Kool Moe Dee: Death Blow (1991)

Escape-ism — Kriss Kross: Warm It Up (1992)

Escape-ism — Lords of the Underground: Psycho (1993)

Escape-ism — Mellow Man Ace: River Cubano (1990)

Escape-ism — Onyx: Throw Ya Gunz (1993)

Escape-ism — Paris: Days of Old (1992)

Escape-ism — Public Enemy: Don't Believe the Hype (1988)

Escape-ism — Run DMC: Back from Hell (1990)

Escape-ism — TLC: Ain't 2 Proud 2 Beg (1992)

For Goodness Sakes, Look at Those Cakes — De La Soul: Afro Connections at Hi 5 (1991)

Funky Drummer — 2 Live Crew: Coolin' (1989)

Funky Drummer — Above the Law: Untouchable (1990)

Funky Drummer — Big Daddy Kane: Mortal Combat (1989)

Funky Drummer — Beastie Boys: Shadrach (1989)

Funky Drummer — Biz Markie: Spring Again (1989)

Funky Drummer — BWP: Different Category (1991)

Funky Drummer — Choice: Bad Ass Bitch(1990)

Funky Drummer — Chubb Rock: Bump the Floor (1989)

Funky Drummer — Compton's Most Wanted: Wanted (1991)

Funky Drummer — Compton's Most Wanted: Final Chapter (1990)

Funky Drummer — Coldcut: Say Kids, What Time Is It? (1987)

Funky Drummer — Criminal Nation: I'm Rollin'(1990)

Funky Drummer — Criminal Nation: Insane (1990)

Funky Drummer — Criminal Nation: Right Crowd (1990)

Funky Drummer — De La Soul: Oodles of O's (1991)

Funky Drummer — DJ Jazzy Jeff & the Fresh Prince: Pump up the Bass (1988)

Funky Drummer — DJ Jazzy Jeff & the Fresh Prince: Hip Hop Dancer's Theme (1988)

Funky Drummer — DJ Jazzy Jeff & the Fresh Prince: Magnificent Jazzy Jeff (1987)

Funky Drummer — DJ Jazzy Jeff & the Fresh Prince: Too Damn Hype (1989)

Funky Drummer — DJ Jazzy Jeff & the Fresh Prince: Jazzy's Groove (1989)

Funky Drummer — The DOC: Let the Bass Go (1989)

Funky Drummer — Digable Planets: Where I'm From (remix) (1993)

Funky Drummer — Dr. Dre: Let Me Ride (1993)

Funky Drummer — Eazy-E: We Want Eazy (remix) (1988)

Funky Drummer — Eric B. & Rakim: Relax with Pep (1992)

Funky Drummer — Eric B. & Rakim: Lyrics of Fury (1988)

Funky Drummer — Enigma: Carly's Song (1993)

Funky Drummer — Father MC: Ain't It Funky (1990)

Funky Drummer — Freddie Foxx: F.F. Is Here (1989)

Funky Drummer — Fine Young Cannibals: I'm Not the Man I Used To Be (1989)

Funky Drummer — Gang Starr: 2 Deep (1992)

Funky Drummer — Geto Boys: Read These Nikes (1990)

Funky Drummer — Geto Boys: Mind of a Lunatic (1990)

Funky Drummer — Guy: I Like (remix)(1988)

Funky Drummer — Heavy D: We Got Our Own Thang (remix) (1989)

Funky Drummer — Heavy D: Peaceful Journey (1991)

Funky Drummer — Ice Cube: Jackin' 4 Beats (1991)

Funky Drummer — Ice Cube: Endangered Species (1990)

Funky Drummer — Ice-T: O.G. Original Gangster (19910)

Funky Drummer — Ice-T: I Ain't New Ta This (1993)

Funky Drummer — Ice-T: Radio Suckers (1988)

Funky Drummer — Jaz: The Originators (1990)

Funky Drummer — Kid 'N Play: Foreplay (1991)

Funky Drummer — Kid 'N Play: Slippin'(1991)

Funky Drummer — Kool Moe Dee: Knowledge Is King (1989)

Funky Drummer — Kool Moe Dee: I'm Blowin' Up (1989)

Funky Drummer — Kool Moe Dee: Bad, Bad, Bad (1991)

Funky Drummer — Kool G. Rap: It's a Demo (1989)

Funky Drummer — Kool G. Rap: Butcher Shop (1989)

Funky Drummer — Korn & the Dust Brothers: Kick the PA (1997)

Funky Drummer — Kriss Kross: Jump (1992)

Funky Drummer — Kriss Kross: Lil' Boys in Da Hood (1992)

Funky Drummer — LL Cool J: Boomin' System (1990)

Funky Drummer — LL Cool J: Mama Said Knock You Out (1990)

Funky Drummer — LL Cool J: Nitro (1989)

Funky Drummer — LL Cool J: Fast Peg (1989)

Funky Drummer — Leaders of the New School: Teachers, Don't Teach Us Nonsense!! (1991)

Funky Drummer — Leaders of the New School: Sobb Story (1991)

Funky Drummer — Mantronix: Fresh Is the Word (remix) (1985)

Funky Drummer — Masters at Work: Justa Lil' Dope (1991)

Funky Drummer — MC Lyte: Brooklyn (1993)

Funky Drummer — George Michael: Waiting for That Day (1998)

Funky Drummer — Michie Mee: Jamaican Funk Canadian Style (1991)

Funky Drummer — Mechel'le: No More Lies (1990)

Funky Drummer — Mellow Man Ace: River Cubano (1990)

Funky Drummer — Mobb Deep: Flavor for the Non-Believers (1993)

Funky Drummer — Naughty by Nature: Ready for Dem (1993)

Funky Drummer — Naughty by Nature: Hot Potato (1993)

Funky Drummer — Nikki D: Freak Accident (1991)

Funky Drummer — Nikki D: Gotta Up the Anti for the Panties (1991)

Funky Drummer — NWA: Fuck tha Police (1988)

Funky Drummer — NWA: Quiet on tha Set (1988)

Funky Drummer — Sinead O'Connor: I Am Stretched on Your Grave (1990)

Funky Drummer — Paperboy: Nine Yards (1993)

Funky Drummer — Paris: I Call Him Mad (1990)

Funky Drummer — Paris: On the Prowl (1990)

Funky Drummer — The Pharcyde: Officer (1993)

Funky Drummer — Pete Rock & CL Smooth: Go with the Flow (1991)
Funky Drummer — Prince: Gett Off (1991)
Funky Drummer — Prince: My Name Is Prince (1992)
Funky Drummer — Public Enemy: Bring the Noise (1988)
Funky Drummer — Public Enemy: Terminator X to the Edge of Panic (1988)
Funky Drummer — Public Enemy: She Watch Channel Zero (1988)
Funky Drummer — Public Enemy: Rebel Without a Pause (1988)
Funky Drummer — Public Enemy: Fight the Power (1990)
Funky Drummer — Public Enemy: Hazy Shade of Criminal (1992)
Funky Drummer — Redman: Rated R (1992)
Funky Drummer — Run DMC: Back from Hell (1990)
Funky Drummer — Run DMC: Word Is Born (1990)
Funky Drummer — Run DMC: Beats to the Rhyme (1988)
Funky Drummer — Salt-N-Pepa: Let the Rhythm Run (1988)
Funky Drummer — Scarface: Born Killer (1991)
Funky Drummer — South Central Cartel: Neighborhood Jacka (1991)
Funky Drummer — Sir Mix-a-Lot: No Holds Barred (1992)
Funky Drummer — Slick Rick: Moment I Feared (1989)
Funky Drummer — Stetsasonic: Speaking of a Girl Named Susie (1991)
Funky Drummer — Stetsasonic: Hip Hop Band (1991)
Funky Drummer — Style: Victim to the Vinyl (1991)
Funky Drummer — Sublime: Scarlet Begonias (1992)
Funky Drummer — Sweet Tee: It's My Beat (1989)
Funky Drummer — Tim Dog: Goin' Wild in the Penile (1991)
Funky Drummer — Tim Dog: Low Down Nigga (1991)
Funky Drummer — TLC: Shock Dat Monkey (1992)
Funky Drummer — Tung Twista: No Peace Sign (1991)
Funky Drummer — 2Pac, featuring Richie Rich: Lie To Kick It (1997)
Funky Drummer — Ultramagnetic MC: Give the Drummer Some (1988)
Funky Drummer — WC & the Maad Circle: Ghetto Serenade (1991)
Funky Drummer — Alyson Williams: Sleep Talk (1989)
Funky Drummer — YZ: Return of the Holy One (1992)
Funky President — 2 Live Crew: So Funky (1990)
Funky President — A Tribe Called Quest: Show Business (1991)
Funky President — A Tribe Called Quest: Oh My God (remix) (1993)
Funky President — Big Daddy Kane: Word to the Mother (Land) (1988)
Funky President — Big Daddy Kane: Give It to Me (1993)
Funky President — Brand Nubian: To the Right (1991)
Funky President — Brand Nubian: All for One (1991)
Funky President — Dana Dane: Little Bit of Dane Tonight (1992)
Funky President — Das EFX: The Want EFX (remix) (1992)
Funky President — Das EFX: East Coast (1992)
Funky President — Das EFX: Looseys (19920
Funky President — DJ Jazzy Jeff & the Fresh Prince: Who Stole My Car? (1989)
Funky President — DJ Jazzy Jeff & the Fresh Prince: Jazzy's in the House (1988)
Funky President — Eric B. & Rakim: Eric B. Is President (1987)
Funky President — Eric B. & Rakim: Eric B. Made My Day (1990)
Funky President — Gang Starr: Knowledge (1989)

Funky President — Gang Starr: Gotta Get Over (1999)
Funky President — Geto Boys: Read These Nikes (1990)
Funky President — Guru: Take a Look (At Yourself) (1993)
Funky President — Guru: Trust Me (1993)
Funky President — Heavy D: We Got Our Own Thang (1989)
Funky President — Heavy D: Gyrlz, They Love Me (1989)
Funky President — Ice Cube: I Wanna Kill Sam (1991)
Funky President — Ice Cube: Horny Lil' Devil (1991)
Funky President — Ice Cube: Jackin' 4 Beats (1991)
Funky President — Kid 'N Play: Ain't Gonna Hurt Nobody (1991)
Funky President — Kid 'N Play: Last Night (1988)
Funky President — KRS One: Outta Here (1993)
Funky President — Large Professor: I Juswannachill (1996)
Funky President — LL Cool J: Fast Peg (1989)
Funky President — LL Cool J: Ain't No Stoppin' This (1993)
Funky President — LL Cool J: 6 Minutes of Pleasure (1990)
Funky President — Lord Finesse: Hey Look at Shorty (1991)
Funky President — Low Profile: Easy Money (1990)
Funky President — Marley Marl: Duck Alert (1988)
Funky President — Naughty by Nature: Guard Your Grill (1991)
Funky President — Naughty by Nature: Hip Hop Hooray (1993)
Funky President — NWA: Fuck Tha Police (1988)
Funky President — Mica Paris: More Love (1990)
Funky President — Pete Rock & CL Smooth: Anger in the Nation (1992)
Funky President — Pete Rock & CL Smooth: Tell Me (1994)
Funky President — Pete Rock & CL Smooth: Skinz (1992)
Funky President — Poor Righteous Teachers: Rock Dis Funky Joint (1990)
Funky President — Public Enemy: Fight the Power (1990)
Funky President — Run DMC: Not Just Another Groove (1990)
Funky President — Salt-N-Pepa: Shake Your Thang (1988)
Funky President — Silk Tymes Leather: The Woman in Me (1991)
Funky President — Slick Rick: Why, Why, Why (1999)
Funky President — Stetsasonic: Uda Man (1991)
Funky President — Terminator X: Homey Don't Play Dat (1991)
Funky President — Terminator X: Vendetta. . .The Big Getback (1991)
Funky President — Ultramagnetic MC: I Like Your Style (1996)
Get on the Good Foot — 2 Live Crew: Break It on Down (1989)
Get on the Good Foot — Three Times Dope: From Da Giddy Up (1989)
Get on the Good Foot — Big Daddy Kane: Mister Cee's Master Plan (1988)
Get on the Good Foot — Boogie Down Productions: Jack of Spades (1989)
Get on the Good Foot — Criminal Element: Hit Me with the Beat (1989)
Get on the Good Foot — EPMD: Jane 3 (1991)
Get on the Good Foot — Grand Master Flash & the Furious Five: Gold (1988)
Get on the Good Foot — MC Hammer: Pump It Up (Here's The News) (1988)
Get on the Good Foot — Kool Moe Dee: They Want Money (1989)
Get on the Good Foot — Kool Moe Dee: Death Blow (1991)
Get on the Good Foot — Kool Moe Dee: Gangster Boogie (1991)
Get on the Good Foot — Mister Lee: Pump That Body (remix) (1990)
Get on the Good Foot — South Central Cartel: Neighborhood Jacka (1991)
Get on the Good Goot — Stetsasonic: Hip Hop Band (1991)

Get Up, Get into It, Get Involved — 2 Live Crew: Do the Bart (1990)

Get Up, Get into It, Get Involved — 2 Live Crew: Drop the Bomb (1987)

Get Up, Get into It, Get Involved — Three Times Dope: No Words (remix) (1990)

Get Up, Get into It, Get Involved — Big Daddy Kane: Set It Off (1988)

Get Up, Get into It, Get Involved — Boogie Down Productions: South Bronx (1991)

Get Up, Get into it, Get Involved — Beastie Boys: Sounds of Science (1989)

Get Up, Get into It, Get Involved — Neneh Cherry & Guru: Sassy (1992)

Get Up, Get into it, Get Involved — Gang Starr: Gotch U (1989)

Get Up, Get into It, Get Involved — Heavy D: Flexin' (1989)

Get Up, Get into It, Get Involved — Ice-T: Home Invasion (1993)

Get Up, Get into It, Get Involved — Kid Capri: Apollo (1991)

Get Up, Get into It, Get Involved — Kool G. Rap: Poison (1989)

Get Up, Get into It, Get Involved — LL Cool J: Mr. Goodbar (1990)

Get Up, Get into It, Get Involved — Leaders of the New School: Connections (1993)

Get Up, Get into It, Get Involved — Organized Konfusion: Maintain (1994)

Get Up, Get into It, Get Involved — Professor Griff & the Last Asiatic Disciples: Pawns in the Game (1990)

Get Up, Get into It, Get Involved — Public Enemy: Terminator X to the Edge of Panic (1988)

Get Up, Get into It, Get Involved — Public Enemy: Night of the Living Baseheads (1988)

Get Up, Get into It, Get Involved — Public Enemy: Party for Your Right To Fight (1988)

Get Up, Get into It, Get Invovled — Public Enemy: Welcome to the Terrordome (1990)

Get Up, Get into It, Get Involved — Public Enemy: Nighttrain (remix) (1991)

Get Up, Get into It, Get Involved — Public Enemy: Brother's Gonna Work It Out (1990)

Get Up, Get into It, Get Involved — Public Enemy: Can't Truss It (1991)

Get Up, Get into It, Get Involved — Public Enemy: Shut 'Em Down (1991)

Get Up, Get into It, Get Involved — Rob Base & DJ E-Z Rock: Make It Hot (1988)

Get Up, Get into It, Get Involved — Salt-N-Pepa: Doper than Dope (1990)

Get Up, Get into It, Get Involved — Schoolly D: Get Off Your Ass and Get Involved (1991)

Get Up, Get into It, Get Involved — Schoolly D: Godfather of Funk (1991)

Get Up, Get into It, Get Involved — Special Ed: Come One, Let's Move It (reimix) (1990)

Get Up, Get into It, Get Involved — Terminator X: Vendetta . . . The Big Getback (1991)

Get Up, Get into It, Get Involved — Tim Dog: Fuck Compton (1991)

Get Up Offa That Thing — Boogie Down Productions: South Bronx (1991)

Get Up Offa That Thing — Beck: Diskobox (1999)

Get Up Offa That Thing — Criminal Element: Here We Go Again (1989)

Get Up Offa That Thing — Hen-Gee & Evil-E: Lil' Trig (1991)

Get Up Offa That Thing — Ice-T: Killing Fields (1997)

Get Up Offa That Thing — Schoolly D: How a Black Man Feels (1991)

Get Up Offa That Thing — Public Enemy: Rebel Without a Pause (1988)

Get Up Offa That Thing — WC & the Maad Circle: Get Up on That Funk (1991)

Get Up I Feel Like Being a Sex Macnine — Biz Markie: Nobody Beats the Biz (1988)

Get Up I Feel Like Being a Sex Machine — Lord Finesse: Isn't He Something (1991)

Give It Up or Turnit a Loose (remix) — Miles Davis: Blow (1992)

Give It Up or Turnit a Loose (remix) — Def Jef: Poet with a Soul (1989)

Give It Up or Turnit a Loose (remix) — Doug E Fresh: Guess? Who? (1988)

Give It Up or Turnit a Loose (remix) — Everlast: Syndicate Soldier (1990)

Give It Up or Turnit a Loose (remix) — Gang Starr: Gotch U (1989)

Give It Up or Turnit a Loose (remix) — NWA: 100 Miles and Runnin' (1990)

Give It Up or Turnit a Loose (remix) — Paris: Wretched (1990)

Give It Up or Turnit a Loose (remix) — Professor Griff & the Last Asiatic Disciples: Pass the Ammo (1990)

Give It Up or Turnit a Loose (remix) — Public Enemy: Burn Hollywood Burn (1990)

Give It Up or Turnit a Loose (remix) — Public Enemy: Welcome to the Terrordome (1990)

Give It Up or Turnit a Loose (remix) — Schoolly D: Who's Schoolin' Who? (1991)

Give It Up or Turnit a Loose (remix) — Seady B: Let the Hustlers Play (1988)

Give It Up or Turnit a Loose (remix) — Tone Loc: Freaky Behavior (1991)

Give It Up or Turnit a Loose (remix) — Twin Hype: Tales of the Twins (1989)

Give It Up or Turnit a Loose (remix) — Ultramagnetic MC: Give the Drummer Some (1988)

Give it Up or Turnit a Loose (remix) — Young Black Teenagers: Loud and Hard To Hit (1991)

Give Me Some Skin — South Central Cartel: Pops Was a Rolla (1991)

Honky Tonk Popcorn — Big Daddy Kane: Mortal Combat (1989)

Honky Tonk Popcorn — The Beatnuts: Are You Ready (1994)

Hot (I Need To Be Love Love Loved) — Above the Law: Livin' like Hustlers (1990)

Hot (I Need To Be Love Love Loved) — Downtown Science: Fat Shout (1991)

Hot (I Need To Be Love Love Loved) — Ice Cube: Alive on Arrival (1991)

Hot (I Need To Be Love Love Loved) — MC Lyte: When in Love (1992)

Hot (I Need To Be Love Love Loved) — Steady B: Attitude Problem (1989)

Hot Pants — Compton's Most Wanted: Final Chapter (1990)

Hot Pants — EPMD: Hit Squad Heist (1991)

Hot Pants — Eric B & Rakim: Paid in Full (1987)

Hot Pants — Insane Poetry: Angel of Death (1992)

Hot Pants — Kool Moe Dee: Funke Wisdom (1991)

Hot Pants — Marley Marl: The Rebel (1988)

Hot Pants — Original Flavor: Give 'Em Some Wrek (1992)

Hot Pants — Professor Griff & the Last Asiatic Disciples: Pawns in the Game (1990)

I Can't Stand It (76) — Everlast: Pass It On (1990)

I Can't Stand It (76) — Lord Finesse: Funky on the Fast Tip (1991)

I Don't Want Nobody To Give Me Nothin' — Guy: Gotta Be a Leader (1990)

I Don't Want Nobody To Give Me Nothin' — Ice-T: Power (1988)

I Got Ants in My Pants — Big Daddy Kane: Get Down (1994)

I Got Ants in My Pants — Cypress Hill: How I Could Just Kill a Man (remix) (1992)

I Got Ants in My Pants — Father MC: Dance 4 Me (1990)

I Got Ants in My Pants — Public Enemy: Don't Believe the Hype (1988)

I Got Ants in My Pants — Public Enemy: How To Kill a Radio Consultant (1991)

I Got To Move — Cypress Hill: How I Could Just Kill a Man (remix) (1992)

I Got To Move — Double XX Posse: Headcracker (1992)

I Got You (I Feel Good) — Gang Starr: Gotch U (1989)

I Got You (I Feel Good) — Public Enemy: Contract on the World (Love Jam) (1990)

I Need Help — Eric B & Rakim: No Omega (1990)

I Need Help — LL Cool J: Why Do You Think They Call It Dope (1989)

I'm Shook — C&C Music Factory: Things That Make You Go Hmmmm (1991)

In the Middle — Chubb Rock: The Organizer (1991)

It's a Man's, Man's, Man's World — Big Daddy Kane: Mortal Combat (1989)

It's a Man's, Man's, Man's World — Black Moon: Black Smif-N-Wessun (1993)

It's a Man's, Man's, Man's World — Heavy D: You Ain't Heard Nuttin' Yet (1989)

It's a Man's, Man's, Man's World — Ice Cube: It's a Man's World (1990)

It's a Man's, Man's, Man's World — Ice Cube: Jackin' for Beats (1991)

It's a Man's, Man's, Man's World — 2Pac, featuring Dramacydal, C- Bo & Storm: Tradin' War Stories (1996)

It's a New Day — EPMD: Gold Digger (1991)

It's a New Day — Young Black Teenagers: Loud and Hart To Hit (1991)

It's a New Day (live) — Artifacts: Dynamite Soul (1994)

It's a New Day (live) — Big Daddy Kane: The House That Cee Built (1989)

It's a New Day (live) — Big Daddy Kane: Calling Mr. Welfare (1989)

It's a New Day (live) — Black Moon: Enta Da Stage (1993)

It's a New Day (live) — The DOC: It's Funky Enough (1989)

It's a New Day (live) — Doug E Fresh: World's Greatest Entertainer (1988)

It's a New Day (live) — Lord Finesse: Isn't He Something? (1991)

It's a New Day (live) — Public Enemy: Who Stole the Soul? (1990)

It's a New Day (live) — Da Youngstas: Iz U Wit Me (1993)

Just Enough Room for Sotrage — A Tribe Called Quest: Lyrics To Go (1993)

Licking Stick-Licking Stick — GrandMaster Flash & the Furious Five: Cold in Effect (1988)

Licking Stick-Licking Stick — GrandMaster Flash & the Furious Five: This Is Where You Got It From (1988)

Licking Stick-Licking Stick — Queen Latifah: Fly Girl (1991)

The Little Groove Maker, Part 1 — De La Soul: Me, Myself & I (1989)

Lowdown Popcorn — Organized Konfusion: Audience Pleasers (1991)

Make It Funky — A Tribe Called Quest: What Really Goes On (1996)

Make It Funky — Coolio: Geto Hilights (1995)

Make It Funky — Kool Moe Dee: Funke Wisdom (1991)

Make It Funky — Public Enemy: Who Stole the Soul? (1990)

Make It Good to Yourself — Kool G. Rap: Play It Again, Polo (1990)

Make It Good to Yourself — Public Enemy: One Millian Bottlebags (1991)

Make It Good to Yourself — Redhead Kingpin & the FBI: Scam! (1989)

Maybe the Last Time — The Pharcyde: I'm That Type of Nigga (1993)

Mind Power — De La Soul: Stakes Is High (1996)

Mind Power — D-Nice: And You Don't Stop (1990)

Mind Power — Ice-T: Mind over Matter (1991)

Mind Power — Kool Moe Dee: To the Beat Y'All (1991)

Mind Power — The Lady of Rage: Breakdown (1997)

Mind Power — LL Cool J: Illegal Search (1990)

Mind Power — Pete Rock & CL Smooth: All the Places (1994)

Mind Power — Slick Rick: Get a Job (1994)

Mind Power — Terminator X: Back to the Scene of the Bass (1991)

Mind Power — WC & the Maad Circle: You Don't Work U Don't Eat (1991)

Mother Popcorn — Doug E Fresh: On the Strength (1988)

Mother Popcorn — Heavy D: Flexin' (1989)

My Thang — DJ Jazzy Jeff & the Fresh Prince: Brand New Funk (1988)

My Thang — Downtown Science: If I Was (1991)

My Thang — EPMD: Gold Digger (1991)

My Thang — Jeru the Damaja: Frustrated Nigga (1996)

My Thang — Kool Moe Dee: I'm a Player (1987)

My Thang — LL Cool J: Murdergram (Live at Rapmania) (1990)

My Thang — Lords of the Undergroud: Funky Child (1993)

Never Can Say Goodbye — Massive Attack: Better Things (1994)

Night Train — Kool Moe Dee: How Ya Like Me Now (1987)

Nose Job — Three Times Dope: No Words (1990)

Nose Job — Boogie Down Productions: The Racist (1990)

Nose Job — Gang Starr: What You Want This Time? (1991)

Papa Don't Take No Mess — Biz Markie: The Vapors (1988)

Papa Don't Take No Mess — Mary J. Blige: You Don't Have To Worry (1993)

Papa Don't Take No Mess — Choice: HIV Positive (1992)

Papa Don't Take No Mess — Downtown Science: If I Was (1991)

Papa Don't Take No Mess — Eric B & Rakim: Move the Crowd (remix) (1987)

Papa Don't Take No Mess — Janet Jackson: That's the Way Love Goes (1993)

Papa Don't Take No Mess — Kool Moe Dee: I'm a Player (1987)

Papa Don't Take No Mess — Kool Moe Dee: How Kool Can One Black Man Be? (1991)

Papa Don't Take No Mess — Snoop Doggy Dogg: Vapors (1996)

Papa's Got a Brand New Bag — Kool Moe Dee: How Ya Like Me Now (1987)

Papa's Got a Brand New Bag — Kool Moe Dee: I'm a Player (1987)

Papa's Got a Brand New Bag — No Face: Stole My Shit (1990)

Papa's Got a Brand New Bag — Pahrcyde: I'm That Type of Nigga (1990)

Papa's Got a Brand New Bag — Salt-N-Pepa: Swift (1990)

The Payback — The Alkaholiks: Last Call (1993)

The Payback — The Almighty R.S.O.: Badd Boyz (1993)

The Payback — Big Daddy Kane: Just Rhymin' with Da Biz (1988)

The Payback — Black Moon featuring Smif-N-Wessun: Headz Ain't Ready (1995)

The Payback — Boss: Born Gangstaz (1993)

The Payback — Chi-Ali: Shorty Said Nah (1992)

The Payback — Compton's Most Wanted: Final Chapter (1990)

The Payback — Coolio: Sticky Fingers (1994)

The Payback — Criminal Nation: Mission of Murder (1990)

The Payback — Da Lench Mob: Guerillas in the Mist (1992)

The Payback — Das EFX: Brooklyn to T-Neck (1992)

The Payback — Das EFX: Mic Checka (1992)

The Payback — Das EFX: They Want EFX (remix) (1992)

The Payback — Das EFX: Wontu (1993)

The Payback — Def Squad, featuring Biz Markie: Rhymin' Wit' Biz (1998)

The Payback — En Vogue: Hold On (1990)

The Payback — En Vogue: (My Lovin') You're Never Gonna Get It (1992)

The Payback — EPMD: The Big Payback (1989)

The Payback — EPMD: Mr. Bozack (1991)

The Payback — EPMD: I'm Mad (1991)

The Payback — EPMD: Boon Dox (1992)

The Payback — Heavy D: Black Coffee (1994)

The Payback — Ice Cube: Jackin' 4 Beats (1991)

The Payback — Ice Cube: Wrong Nigga To Fuck Wit (1991)

The Payback — Jodeci: In the Meanwhile (1994)

The Payback — Kool Moe Dee: Mo' Better (1991)

The Payback — LL Cool J: Boomin' System (1990)

The Payback — LL Cool J: Straight from Queens (1993)

The Payback — Low Profile: Comin' Straight (1990)

The Payback — Mary J. Blige: Everything (1998)

The Payback — Massive Attack: Protection (1994)

The Payback — MC Lyte: Ruffneck (1993)

The Payback — MC Ren: Mr. Fuck-Up (1993)

The Payback — Me Phi Me: Keep It Goin' (1992)

The Payback — NWA: SA Prize Pt. 2 (1990)

The Payback — Professor X: Definition of a Sissy (1991)

The Payback — Queen Latifah: If You Don't Know (1991)

The Payback — R Kelly: Hump Bounce (1995)

The Payback — Redheaded Kingpin & the FBI: A Shade of Red (1989)

The Payback — Redman: Day of Sooperman Lover (1992)

The Payback — Redman: Blow Your Mind (1992)

The Payback — Redman: Tonight's Da Night (remix) (1992)

The Payback — Erick Sermon: Safe Sex (1993)

The Payback — Shaq: I'm Outstanding (1993)

The Payback — Silk: Happy Days (1992)

The Payback — Slick Rick: Slick Rick-The Ruler (1991)

The Payback — Terminator X: Buck Whylin' (1991)

The Payback — 2Pac: Souljah's Revenge (1993)

The Payback — Total, featuring Norious BIG: Can't You See? (1996)

The Payback — Ultramagnetic MC: Yo! Black (1993)

The Payback — Karyn White: Hungah (1994)

The Payback — Wreckx-n-effect: Wreckxs Shop (1992)

Please Please Me — Ice Cube: Horny Lil' Devil (1991)

Popcorn with Feeling — Brand Nubian: Who Can Get Busy like This Man (1991)

Popcorn with Feeling — Heavy D: Blue Funk (1993)

Popcorn with Feeling — Run-DMC: Bob Your Head (1990)

Public Enemy No. 1 — Brand Nubian: Punks Jump up To Get Beat Down (1993)

Sayin' It and Doin' It — Schoolly D: Who's Schoolin' Who? (1991)

Say It Loud (I'm Black and I'm Proud) — Big Daddy Kane: Long Live the Kane (1988)

Say It Loud (I'm Black and I'm Proud) — BLACKstreet: Good Lovin' (1996)

Say It Loud (I'm Black and I'm Proud) — Brand Nubian: Dedication (1991)

Say It Loud (I'm Black and I'm Proud) — Cypress Hill: Insane in the Brain (1993)

Say It Loud (I'm Black and I'm Proud) — EPMD: Brothers on My Jock (1991)

Say It Loud (I'm Black and I'm Proud) — Eric B. & Rakin: Move the Crowd (Democratic 3 Beatmix) (1987)

Say It Loud (I'm Black and I'm Proud) — Intelligent Hoodlum: Black and Proud (1990)

Say It Loud (I'm Black and I'm Proud) — LL Cool J: Nitro (1989)

Say It Loud (I'm Black and I'm Proud) — The Real Roxanne: Her Bad Self (1988)

Say It Loud (I'm Black and I'm Proud) — Run DMC: Naughty (1990)

Say It Loud (I'm Black and I'm Proud) — Salt-N-Pepa: Do You Want Me? (1990)

Say It Loud (I'm Black and I'm Proud) — Vanilla Ice: Ice Cold (1990)

Sex Machine — Big Daddy Kane: Get Down (1991)

Sex Machine — Criminal Element: Hit Me with the Beat (1989)

Sex Machine — Everlast: Syndication (remix) (1990)

Sex Machine — MC Hammer: They Put Me in the Mix (1988)

Sex Machine — Heavy D: Big Tyme (1989)

Sex Machine — Mister Lee: Pump That Body (1990)

Sex Machine — Redman: Jam 4 U (1992)

Shoot Your Shot — Pete Rock & CJ Smooth: All Souled Out (1991)

Shoot Your Shot — Public Enemy: Nighttrain (1991)

Slaughter's Theme — Ice-T: This One's for Me (1989)

Slaughter's Theme — Lord Finesse: Isn't He Something? (1991)

Spinning Wheel — Color Me Badd: Slow Motion (1991)

The Sporting Life — Scarface: The Pimp (1991)

Soul Power Part1 — Boogie Down Productions: Poetry (1991)

Soul Power Part 1 — Das EFX: Mic Checka (1992)

Soul Power Part 1 — Das EFX: Undaground Rappa (1993)

Soul Power Part 1 — EPMD: Total Kaos (1989)

Soul Power Part 1 — Kool Moe Dee: Let's Get Serious (1991)

Soul Power Part 1 — Public Enemy: Night of the Living Baseheads (remix) (1988)

Soul Power Part 1 — Public Enemy: What Kind of Power We Got? (1994)

Soul Power Part 1 — Scarface: Body Snatchers (1991)

Soul Power Part 1 — Stetsasonic: Speaking of a Girl Named Suzy (1991)

Soul Pride — Digable Planets: 9th Wonder (Blackitolism) (1994)

The Spank — 2Pac: Trapped (1992)

Stoned to the Bone — 3rd Bass: Steppin' to the AM (1989)

Stoned to the Bone — Del Tha Funkee Homosapien: Mistadobalina (1991)

Stoned to the Bone — MC Ren: Same Old Shit (1993)

Stoned to the Bone — NWA: Alawyz into Something (1991)

Stoned to the Bone — Terminator X: Homey Don't Play That (1991)

Super Bad — Three Times Dope: I Got It (1990)

Super Bad — Color Me Badd: Color Me Badd (remix) (1991)

Super Bad — MC Hammer: Here Comes the Hammer (1990)

Super Bad — Kool Moe Dee: I Go to Work (1989)

Take Some and Leave Some — EPMD: Mr. Bozack (1991)

Take Some and Leave Some — Ice Cube: Bird in the Hand (1991)

Take Some and Leave Some — Lord Finesse: Here I Come (1990)

Take Some and Leave Some — Lord Finesse: Funky on the Fast Tip (1991)

Take Some and Leave Some — Pete Rocke & CL Smooth: All the Places (1994)

Take Some and Leave Some — Salt-N-Pepa: Solo Power (Syncopated Soul) (1988)

Take Some and Leave Some — Soul for Real: You Just Don't Know (1996)

Talkin Loud and Sayin Nothing — Big Daddy Kane: Keep'em on the Floor (1990)

Talkin Loud and Sayin Nothing — Brothers Like Outlaw: Trappec into Darkness (1992)

Talkin Loud and Sayin Nothing — De La Soul: Down Syndrome (1996)

Talkin Loud and Sayin Nothing — Everlast: Syndication (1990)

Talkin Loud and Sayin Nothing — Leaders of the New School: Sobb Story (1991)

Talkin Loud and Sayin Nothing — Run DMC: Beats to the Rhyme (1988)

There It Is — Criminal Element: Hit Me with the Beat (1989)

There It Is — Ice Cube: AmeriKKKa's Most Wanted (1990)

There It Is — Jungle Brothers: JB's Comin' Through (1993)

There It Is — Prince: Get Off (1991)

There It Is — Public Enemy: Anti-Nigger Machine (1990)

There It Is — Terminator X & Godfather of Threat: Sticka (1994)

There It Is — Zhigge: No Time To Fess (1992)

There Was a Time — Chubb Rock: Treat 'Em Right (1991)

There Was a Time — Downtown Science: Keep It On (1991)

Unity — Beastie Boys: Shake Your Rump (1989)

Untitled Instrumental — Scarface: Murder by Reason of Insanity (1991)

Untitled Instrumental — Schoolly D: Godfather of Funk (1991)

White Lightnin' (I Mean Moonshine) — Gang Starr: I'm the Man (1992)

White Lightnin' (I Mean Moonshine) — Leaders of the New School: Sobb Story (1991)

You Got To Have a Mother for Me — DJ Quik: Tear It Off (1991)

You Got To Have a Mother for Me — LL Cool J: Why Do You Think They Call It Dope (1989)

You Got To Have a Mother for Me — Schoolly D: Gangster Boogie (1988)

You Mother You — Main Source: Just a Friendly Game of Baseball (1991)

Your Love — Boogie Down Productions: The Kenny Parker Show (1990)

Your Love — Ed OG: Let Me Tickle Your Fancy (1990)

Your Love — Queen Pen: Man Behind the Music (1997)

## BOBBY BYRD

**BORN:** *8/15/34, Toccoa, GA*

The longest serving of all James Brown's myriad bandmates, Byrd first met the singer when the latter, an inmate at the Toccoa, GA, correctional facility, visited Byrd's high school with the prison basketball team. The two remained in touch; both had fierce local reputations as pianists (Brown's nickname at the time was Music Box) and, following Brown's parole in June 1952, he lodged with the Byrd family for several weeks.

Byrd was leading a vocal group, the Avons, at the time; Brown joined in 1953, following the death of Avon Troy Collins. Lining-up as Sylvester Keels, Doyle Oglesby, Fred Pulliam, Nash Knox and Roy Scott, plus Byrd, Brown and another new recruit, Johnny Terry, this group metamorphosed into the Flames (and later, the Famous Flames) in 1954.

The group broke up in 1957 in a dispute over billing— newly recruited manager Ben Bart wanted to rename them James Brown & the Famous Flames. Brown and Byrd remained in contact, however. Indeed, Brown helped Byrd get a job at King Records, where label boss Syd Nathan employed him to rewrite demo tapes received at the office, then cut the "new" songs with King artists. In his autobiography, Brown recalls one such submission, "The Sweetest Letter." It was received from unknowns Sam Moore and David Prater; they eventually became Stax records stars Sam and Dave. Revamped as "There's a Difference," it was recorded by Little Willie John for the B-side of his 1960 single "Sleep."

Byrd rejoined Brown for the singer's debut at the Harlem Apollo on April 24, 1959 (Byrd had just two days notice before the show), and remained on board as vocalist and organist for the next decade. He also began taking a solo spot at live shows and, in 1963, Byrd cut his solo debut, "I Found Out."

The follow-up, "I'm Just a Nobody," became a regional success in late 1963, while a duet with James Brown Revue star Anna King, "Baby Baby Baby," breached the R&B Top 60. Another 45, 1965's "We Are in Love," made the Top 20 and Byrd continued releasing sporadic singles (and one album, 1970's *I Need Help*) throughout the remainder of his time with Brown. Backing musicians on these recordings were drawn from Brown's own band, while the relationship was further cemented when Byrd married Vicki Anderson (b. Myra Barnes), lead female vocalist with Brown's Revue.

Anderson quit the Revue in 1967 to be replaced by Marva Whitney; she returned in 1970, when Whitney left, but quit again in December 1971. Byrd remained on board for a little over another year, releasing a clutch of further singles for the Brownstone label formed by Brown and former Dade label chief Henry Stone. Byrd and Anderson then settled in Houston, TX, with Anderson's daughter, Carleen (20 years later, a recording artist in her own right). There, Byrd set about consolidating his career, scoring his first truly solo hit, "Try It Again," in 1973.

When Brown's next tour brought him to Houston, the pair reunited for the handful of shows scheduled around Texas. Later, with Byrd now riding high with 1975's "Back from The Dead" single and gigging with the Bootsy Collins-era JBs as his backing musicians, Brown joined him onstage in Miami for versions of "Try Me" and "Sex Machine."

Byrd rejoined Brown for a European tour later that same year, but quit again once they returned home. He made occasional returns to Europe in his own right, however, where he found himself elected a figurehead of sorts within the acid jazz scene of the late '80s.

In 1987, Eric B. and Rakim furthered Byrd's renown with a sample of 1971's "I Know You Got Soul" in their smash single of the same name. In 1988, Byrd and Anderson toured again with James Brown and, by 1990, Byrd was celebrating such unexpected renewals with a compilation wryly titled *Finally Getting Paid*. His 1994 album *On the Move* featured contributions from both Vicki and Carleen Anderson, brother Tony Byrd, plus guests Emilio Castillo and Sultan Mohammed. Included were new versions of past hits "Sayin' It and Doin' It" and "Back from the Dead."

## BOBBY BYRD COMPLETE DISCOGRAPHY
### SINGLES/CHART LOG
1963 I Found Out/They Are Saying (Federal)
1963 I'm Just a Nobody (part one)/(part two) (Smash)
1964 I Love You So/Write Me a Letter (Smash)
1964 I've Got a Girl/I'm Lonely (Smash)
1965 We Are in Love/No-One Like My Baby (Smash—#14 R&B/#120 pop)
1965 The Way I Feel/Time Will Make a Change (Smash)
1965 Let Me Know/You're Gonna Need My love (Smash)
1966 Oh What a Night/Lost in the Mood of Changes (Smash)
1966 Let Me Know/Ain't No Use (Smash)
1967 I Found Out/I'll Keep Pressing On (King)
1967 Funky Soul (part one)/(part two) (King)
1968 My Concerto/You Gave My Heart a Brand New Song To Sing (King—withdrawn)
1970 Hang Ups We Don't Need/You Gave My Heart. . . (King)
1970 It's I Who Loves You/I'm Not To Blame (King)
1970 I Need Help (part one)/(part two) (King—#14 R&B/#69 pop)
1970 You've Got To Have a Job/You've Got To Change Your Mind (King)
1971 I Know You Got Soul/It's I Who Loves You (King—#30 R&B/#117 pop)
1971 Hot Pants—I'm Coming/Hang It Up (Brownstone—#34 R&B/#85 pop)

1971 Keep On Doin' What You're Doin'/Let Me Know (Brownstone—#40 R&B/#88 pop)
1972 If You Got a Love You Better/You've Got To Change your Mind (Brownstone)
1972 Never Get Enough/My Concerto (Brownstone)
1972 Sayin' It and Doin' It/Never Get Enough (Brownstone)
1973 I Need Help/Signed, Sealed and Delivered (Brownstone)
1973 Try It Again/I'm on the Move (Kwanza—#82 R&B)
1975 Back from the Dead/The Way To Get Down (International Bros—#57 R&B)
1975 Headquarters (Augusta GA)/(instrumental) (International brothers)
1977 Here for the Party/Byrd's in Flight (Strawberry)
1979 Gasoline/What Goes Around Comes Around (Audio Latino)
1980 Real Good Feeling/Here for the Party (Mia Sound)
1989 What Goes Around/Picture Perfect/Why Did This Happen to Me (Rhythm Attack)
1993 I'm on the Move/Don't Throw Your Love In A Garbage Can (Soulciety)

### BOBBY BYRD WITH ANNA KING
1964 Baby Baby Baby/(instrumental) (Smash—#52 R&B)

### BOBBY BYRD WITH JAMES BROWN
1968 You've Got To Change Your Mind/I'll Lose My Mind (King—#47 R&B/#102 pop)

### BOBBY BYRD WITH VICKI ANDERSON
1968 Here Is My Everything/Loving You (ABC)

### LPs
🎱 1970 I Need Help (King)
Apparently recorded live, Byrd's remarkable vocals hang high over a wild funk feast, including "Funky Soul," "My Concerto," "You Got To Have A Job," and the title track.
🎱 1994 On The Move (Instinct)
High on his acid-jazz revival, a powerful return highlighted by a handful of well-chosen revivals.

### SELECTED COMPILATIONS AND ARCHIVE RELEASES
🎱 1990 Finally Getting Paid (Rhythm Attack)
Byrd's post-Brown career neatly encapsulated.
🎱 1995 Bobby Byrd Got Soul (Polydor)
The King/People years.

### SELECTED SAMPLES
Hot Pants — 3rd Bass: Oval Office (1989)
Hot Pants — A Lighter Shade of Brown: Paquito Soul (1990)
Hot Pants — A Tribe Called Quest: Every Thing Is Fair (1991)
Hot Pants — Big Daddy Kane: Raw (1988)
Hot Pants — Big Daddy Kane: Raw 91 (1991)
Hot Pants — Big Daddy Kane: Nuff Respect (1993)
Hot Pants — James Brown: Static (1988)
Hot Pants — Chubb Rock: Bonus Beat (1989)

Hot Pants — Criminal Nation: Insane (1990)

Hot Pants — Das EFX: Straight out of Da Sewer (1991)

Hot Pants — Doctor Ice: The Mic Stalker (1989)

Hot Pants — Johnny Gill: Rub You the Right Way (1990)

Hot Pants — Heavy D: The Lover's Got What U Need (1991)

Hot Pants — Ice Cube: I Wanna Kill Sam (1991)

Hot Pants — Ice Cube: Jackin' 4 Beats (1990)

Hot Pants — King Sun: Pure Energy (1990)

Hot Pants — LL Cool J: It Gets No Rougher (1989)

Hot Pants — LL Cool J: How I'm Coming (1993)

Hot Pants — M.A.R.R.S.: Pump Up the Volume (1987)

Hot Pants — MC Brains: Everybody's Talking About MC Brains (1992)

Hot Pants — Alexander O'Neal: Every Time I Get Up (1991)

Hot Pants — Public Enemy: Can't Do Nuttin' for Ya Man (1990)

Hot Pants — Public Enemy: Caught, Can We Get a Witness? (1988)

Hot Pants — Public Enemy: 1 Million Bottlebags (1991)

Hot Pants — Run DMC—What's It All About? (1990)

Hot Pants — Salt-N-Pepa: Solo Power (Syncopated Soul) (1988)

Hot Pants — Sir Mix a Lot: One Time's Got No Case (1996)

Hot Pants — Stone Roses: Fool's Gold (1989)

Hot Pants — Too Nice: Cold Facts (1990)

Hot Pants — Vanilla Ice: Cool as Ice (1991)

Hot Pants — Alyson Williams: Sleep Talk (1989)

I Know You Got Soul — Eric B & Rakim: I Know You Got Soul (1987)

I Need Help — Compton's Most Wanted: Final Chapter (1990)

I Need Help — DJ Jazzy Jeff & the Fresh Prince: You Got It (1989)

I Need Help — Double XX Posse: Executive Class (1992)

I Need Help — Everlast: I Got the Knack (1990)

I Need Help — Ice Cube: Jackin' 4 Beats (1990)

I Need Help — Kool Moe Dee: Rise'n'Shine (1991)

I Need Help — Kool G. Rap: It's a Demo (1989)

I Need Help — Original Flavor: Give 'Em Some Wrek (1992)

I Need Help — Professor Griff: Pawns in the Game (1990)

I Need Help — Public Enemy: Party for Your Right To Fight (1988)

I Need Help — Public Enemy: Cold Lampin' with Flavor (1988)

I Need Help — Public Enemy: Fight the Power (1990)

I Need Help — Roxanne ft Chubb Rock: Gear (1992)

I Need Help — Salt-N-Pepa: A Salt with Deadly Pepa (1988)

I Need Help — Special Ed: Come On, Let's Move It (1990)

If You've Got a Love. . . — Eric B. & Rakim: Set 'Em Straight (1990)

Never Get Enough — Diamond D: Best Kept Secret (remix) (1992)

## DAPPS, see BEAU DOLLAR & THE DAPPS

## DR. JOHN, see FRONTIERS OF FUNK: GUMBO AND THE GROOVE

## DYKE & THE BLAZERS

FORMED: 1964, Phoenix, AZ

ORIGINAL: Arlester "Dyke" Christian (b. 1943, Brooklyn; d. 3/30/71—vcls), Alvester Jacobs (gtr), Alvin Battle (bs),

Bernard Williams (sax), Clarence Towns (sax), Willie Earl (drms)

If they are remembered for no other reason, Dyke & the Blazers sealed their place in history when they became the first act ever to take the word "funk" into the R&B chart, with February 1967's "Funky Broadway." In their wake, Wilson Pickett, Jerry-O, Clarence Carter, Bull & the Matadors, Arthur Conley and Calvin Arnold all made their own contributions to the repertoire. But not only were the Blazers the first, they were also the funkiest. Indeed, veteran Cincinnati funk-guitarist Danny Adler credits them alongside James Brown and Beau Dollar & the Dapps as "the only band playing 'real' funk at that time," an achievement that vocalist Arlester Christian's tragically early death may have obscured but will never be forgotten.

The Blazers themselves were better known as the O'Jays' backing musicians when Christian—the band's bassist—took them for his own; the break came when the group found themselves stranded in Phoenix, AZ, unable to afford the fare back to homebase Buffalo. Making the city their home, the group originally cut "Funky Broadway" in 1966, for release on the local Artco independent label; the Original Sound picked up nationwide distribution in early 1967 and "Funky Broadway" entered the R&B Top 20 that spring.

Distilled down from a lengthy jam—a procedure that shaped most of the Blazers' best records, and their live performances too—the single's incendiary blend of raw guitars, prominent horns and bellowed vocals was patently influenced by James Brown, another reason why their own fame never truly broke out of the R&B charts. But a follow-up single, "So Sharp," maintained the Blazers' visibility and, that same summer, Wilson Pickett took his own version of "Funky Broadway" to the top of the R&B chart.

"Funky Walk," a hit, and "Funky Bull," a miss, followed during 1968 before 1969 brought Dyke & the Blazers' biggest hits: R&B Top 10/pop Top 40 smashes "We Got More Soul" and the double A-sided success "Let a Woman Be a Woman, Let a Man Be a Man"/"Uhhh" (a gutbucket first album track, which truly out-Browned James Brown himself).

By now, Christian was basing himself in Los Angeles, recording with a coterie of musicians that included future Earth Wind & Fire-guitarist Al McKay and members of Charles Wright Watts 103rd Street Band. The Blazers themselves remained on call for the chaotic stage shows, which were their forte. The improvement in musicianship, however, scraped away much of the visceral appeal of those earlier records; Christian himself was not a great singer, but he worked in the confines of his original band. His attempt to wring a melody out of the standard "You Are My Sunshine" may have become a Top 30 hit, but it lacked punch, a fate also suffered by "Runaway People," during summer 1970.

That was Christian's final hit. He was killed in a street shooting in Phoenix on March 13, 1971.

## DYKE CHRISTIAN & THE BLAZERS COMPLETE DISCOGRAPHY
### SINGLES/CHART LOG
1966 Funky Broadway (part one)/(part two) (Artco)
1967 Funky Broadway (part one)/(part two) (Original Sound—#17 R&B/#65 pop)
1967 So Sharp/Don't Bug Me (Original Sound—#41 R&B/#130 pop)
1967 Funky Walk (part one)/(part two) (Original Sound—#22 R&B/#67 pop)
1968 Funky Bull (part one)/(part two) (Original Sound)
1969 We Got More Soul/Shotgun Slim (Original Sound—#7 R&B/#35 pop)
1969 Let a Woman Be a Woman (Original Sound—#4 R&B/#36 pop)/Uhh (#20 R&B/#118 pop)
1969 You Are My Sunshine/City Dump (Original Sound—#30 R&B/#121 pop)
1970 Uhh/My Sister's and My Brother's Day Is Coming (Original Sound)
1970 Runaway People/I'm So All Alone (Original Sound—#32 R&B/#119 pop)

### LPs
🎵 1967 The Funky Broadway (Original Sound—#186 pop)
The title track and the later hit "Uhhh" capture the Blazers' majestically dissolute lurch, a proto-funk pounding cut straight from the Godfather's book.

### SELECTED COMPILATIONS AND ARCHIVE RELEASES
🎵 1968 Dyke's Greatest Hits (Original Sound)

### SELECTED SAMPLES
Broadway Combination — Big Daddy Kane: Chocolate City (1993)
Broadway Combination — Deee-Lite: Vote Baby Vote (1993)
Let a Woman Be a Woman — 3XDope: From Da Giddy Up (1989)
Let a Woman Be a Woman — Above the Law: Menace to Society (1990)
Let a Woman Be a Woman — Beck: Jackass (1996)
Let a Woman Be a Woman — Digital Underground: No Nose Job (1991)
Let a Woman Be a Woman — Kid 'N Play: Damn That DJ (1988)
Let a Woman Be a Woman — King Tee: Diss You (1990)
Let a Woman Be a Woman — Leaders of the New School: Case of the PTA (1991)
Let a Woman Be a Woman — Run DMC: Faces (1990)
Let a Woman Be a Woman — Stetsasonic: Sally (1988)
Let a Woman Be a Woman — 2pac: If My Homie Calls (1992)
Let a Woman Be a Woman — X-Clan: Rhythm of God (1992)
Runaway People — Ice T: Mic's Contact (1991)
Runaway People — Professor Griff & the Last Asiatic Disciples: Mental Genocide (1991)

We Got More Soul — Public Enemy: Anti-Nigger Machine (1990)

## YVONNE FAIR, see JAMES BROWN

## FUNK BROTHERS, see FRONTIERS OF FUNK: MOTOWN GETS WITH IT

## JIMI HENDRIX, see FRONTIERS OF FUNK: THE PSYCHE-FUNKA-DELIA EXPERIENCE

## THE IMPRESSIONS, see CURTIS MAYFIELD (PART 2)

## ISLEY BROTHERS
**FORMED:** *1955, Lincoln Heights, OH*
**ORIGINAL:** *O'Kelly Isley (b. 12/25/37, Lincoln Hts; d. 3/31/86), Rudolph Isley (b. 4/1/39, Lincoln Hts), Ronald Isley (b. 5/21/41, Lincoln Hts), Vernon Isley (d. 1955)*

Originally a gospel quartet formed by brothers O'Kelly, Rudolph, Ronald and Vernon Isley, the Brothers performed regularly around Lincoln Heights, OH, during the early-mid-'50s, but came close to shattering after Vernon was killed in a bicycling accident. Only slowly regrouping and resuming work, the brothers relocated to T-Neck, NJ, and turned to doo wop for a string of tiny labels around their newly adopted hometown.

In 1959, a Top 50-berth for the raucous "Shout" was the launching pad for a career of countless twists as the Isleys moved from vital R&B to luscious Motown-style soul, and shot through with an instinctive understanding of what one day emerged as funk all draped in the brothers' trademark soaring vocals. In 1962, their take on the Top Notes' "Twist and Shout" in turn inspired a cover by the Beatles, suggesting a rock and soul fusion that the Isleys adopted as a virtual blueprint over the next four years. Two years later, "Testify" found them publicly allying themselves with the hard-hitting likes of James Brown, Little Richard, Ray Charles and the then prodigious talent of "Little" Stevie Wonder.

"Testify," of course, occupies another, even weightier, place in history as one of the first singles ever to feature a young Jimi (or, as he was known then, Jimmy) Hendrix. The guitarist was a member of the Isleys' backing group for four months, June through October 1964, arriving at a time when the Isleys themselves were going through a transitional phase, caught in the four year no-man's land that separated their last hit, "Twistin' with Linda," from their next, "This Old Heart of Mine."

They were also in the process of setting up their own record label, T-Neck (named for their New Jersey home-

**Ronald, Ernie, and Marvin Isley.**

base), and looking for a new guitarist when a friend, Tony Rice, saw Hendrix playing in the houseband at New York's Palm Cafe and recommended him to the Isleys

A churning rhythmic blues, "Testify" was haunted by at least an echo of all that Hendrix journeyed on to achieve; touring with the Isleys in the record's wake, he showed off even more of his repertoire, including playing his guitar with his teeth. It was a trick the Isleys were more than happy to encourage—unlike other acts with whom the young Hendrix worked, anything that added to their reputation was welcome, even a flashy backing musician with a taste for crowd-pleasing novelty. "They used to let me do my own thing because it made them more bucks," Hendrix said later, but he also knew that the Isleys' own trip was based around more than neat presentation and sweet vocal harmony. They wanted excitement, action, drama. It oozed from their records; it issued from their live shows; now it poured from their guitarist.

Interviewed for the *Experience Hendrix* magazine in 1999, younger brother Ernie Isley recalled watching from the side of the stage as Kelly called Hendrix to the front, to

"show them how it's done. And [Jimi'd] do something like play the guitar behind his back and everyone would go, 'my God, how did he do that?' They did a show with Eric Burdon and the Animals in 1964, and the Animals were going out of their minds." (Two years later, Animals bassist Chas Chandler, coincidentally or otherwise, became Hendrix's manager.)

Hendrix quit the Isleys in October 1964, following the "Last Girl" single. He reunited with them in August 1965, meeting them in New York to cut a new single, "Move Over and Let Me Dance." A year after that, as Ronnie Isley remarked in the liner notes to the Hendrix-era Isleys compilation *In the Beginning*, "he went to England, we went to Detroit."

The T-Neck label's distribution deal with Atlantic had proven no more successful than any of their other post-"Twist and Shout" releases, so when Motown came a-wooing in 1966, the brothers saw little sense in turning them down. Paired with songwriters Holland-Dozier-Holland, the Isleys scored immediately with "This Old Heart of Mine," one of the all-time classic Motown tearjerkers; they followed through with a brace of lesser smashes before "Take Me in Your Arms (Rock Me a Little While)" restored them to the R&B Top 30 in 1968.

Again, however, the Isleys remained just a few steps short of genuine stardom, a frustration that was not helped by the maddening frictions within Motown itself. Finally, in 1969, the brothers pulled away from the label and returned to New Jersey to relaunch T-Neck and reinvent themselves.

Eschewing the sessionmen and backing musicians who had sustained them through the '60s, they instead recruited brothers Ernie (b. 3/7/52, Lincoln Hts—guitar, drums) and Marvin (bass), plus Rudolph's brother-in-law, Chris Jasper (b. 12/30/51, Lincoln Hts—keyboards), to the setup as full-time accompanists. The three newcomers were already playing together as the Jassmen Trio, performing spot-on covers of Ramsey Lewis and Young-Holt Unlimited instrumentals, a repertoire that represented precisely the kind of perfectionism the elder Isleys wanted for themselves.

The brothers' old mohair suits were next to go, cast aside in favor of a theatrical wardrobe of furs, velvets, satins and silks. But the most crucial change was in their approach to their music. No more dance-craze novelties ("Twist and Shout") or production-line love songs; the Isleys' outspoken concerns were now the same as those that fired the other music that mattered: the social and personal politicization of former Motown labelmates Marvin Gaye, the Temptations and Stevie Wonder, the increasingly ambitious orientation of Sly Stone and Jimi Hendrix, and the knowledge that personal freedom is the most creative force on earth.

That was as true for their future as it was for their past. Journalist William C. Rhoden, writing in the liners for the Isleys' It's Your Thing box set confirms, "their separation from Motown was liberating because it exploded the myth that 'color' and racial affiliation, in and of themselves, were liberating." Motown, in its own way, was as blinkered and hidebound as society itself. The Isleys dreamed of a society where such restrictions simply didn't exist.

That was the cultural inspiration behind 1969's "It's Your Thing," the first release on the reborn T-Neck label—and the Isleys' first #1 hit. "It was such an important record," Bobby Womack mused. "It was like an abstract picture with a message. 'Dig it any way you wanna. Whatever turns you on.' People love the freedom to draw their own conclusions."

"It's Your Thing" scooped a Best R&B Vocal Grammy; it was also the musical impetus behind the string of giant grooves that followed between 1969–71: "I Turned You On," "Keep On Doin," the colossal jam "Get into Something'"

and, of course, "Freedom" itself. The Isleys' most significant release during this period, however, was the *Givin' It Back* album, a collection of covers of predominantly White rock songs, performed with a fervor that all but reinvented them.

"The choices were significant," Ernie Isley recalled. "We liked the songs, of course, and we figured we could push some boundaries. That someone might recognize a song with a familiar title. Slowly, people started checking us out."

Neil Young's "Ohio," written in the aftermath of the deaths of four Kent State University students at a peace rally in 1970; Stephen Stills' "Love the One You're With"; even James Taylor's hitherto mawkish "Fire and Rain" were funked up for the occasion; while Eric Burdon and War's "Spill the Wine" slammed the album back to its own basics with uncommon passion.

So much about the Isleys stood out, but if there was one side to the band that encapsulated their uniqueness, it was Ernie Isley. He had been playing guitar for little more than a year when he was recruited to the group; Marvin Isley recalled, "Ernie was playing drums . . . then 'Classical Gas' (a 1968 instrumental by folk guitarist Mason Williams) broke and Ernie exploded, 'I wanna play like that!' I told him to stick with his drums." Ernie was adamant, however, practicing in private until one day, "Kelly comes downstairs . . . 'who's that playing?' When he finds out it's Ernie, he calls over to Ronald who can't believe his ears."

Ernie's guitar drenched, but never dominated, his first recordings with the band. In concert, however, he grew ever more prominent and finally, in 1973, it was time to truly let the monster out of the cage, across the brothers' 3 + 3 album. Two cuts in particular were earmarked for the occasion, a cover of Seals and Crofts' "Summer Breeze" and a remake of the Isleys' own 1964 single "Who's That Lady," transformed from a mere lovely ballad into an acid-blues guitar jamboree.

"When I finished that solo," Ernie recalled, "Kelly looked at me for 15 minutes straight without blinking. I felt like I'd discovered how to ride a bike and eat ice cream at the same time." Equally incredible, Marvin continued, was the reaction from their fellow college students (the three younger members were still completing their studies when 3 + 3 was released), "and we'd hear 'Who's That Lady' blasting clear across the campus. People were coming to our room, asking for autographs, and we were just regular guys trying to get a college education."

When "Who's That Lady" first reached radio, a rumor circulated that the track was a previously unheard collaboration with Hendrix himself, particularly in the UK, where the song gave the Isleys their first Top 20 entry in four years. But then "Summer Breeze" came along and the guitar was even more incredible. For anybody caught up in '70s rock's most enduring obsession, to crown the new Jimi Hendrix, the quest was already over, but the search, of course, had barely begun. For the only thing Ernie Isley truly had in common with Hendrix was that he didn't sound like anybody else on earth. His style was utterly unique.

*Live It Up*, in 1974, confirmed its predecessor's qualities; the following year, the infectious, defiant "Fight the Power" launched *The Heat Is On* with equal grit. "One of my favorite albums," Jasper reflected. "Very funky. 'For the Love of You,' 'Fight the Power,' they stand the test. And those stadium shows! The brotherhood and competition with P-Funk, Rufus and Chaka [Khan], The Brothers Johnson, Teddy Pendergrass, Maze." As the Isley Brothers toured America in the company of the biggest acts of the era, Jasper insists, "We were *living* history."

Of all the secrets behind the Isleys' longevity, of course, their willingness to change with the times, *just ahead of the times*, is one of the most successful. In 1976, the *Harvest for the World* album announced such a change, a shift from the visceral funk of the past half decade to a brighter, effervescent dance sound that blasted the disco scene wide open to the Isleys—without ever demanding anything in return. Even 1979's worryingly titled "It's a Disco Night (Rock Don't Stop)" was cut entirely on the brothers' own musical terms and it was only as the '80s brought fresh musical schisms into play that the Isleys' earlier unity and single-mindedness crumbled.

In 1984, Ernie and Marvin Isley and Chris Jasper departed the group to form their own Isley Jasper Isley. Their elder brothers promptly returned to their earlier three piece format, but recorded just one album, 1985's *Masterpiece*, before Kelly suffered a fatal heart attack. Soon after, Rudolph quit to enter the church.

Ronald Isley continued alone and, in 1990, enjoyed hits with both his wife, Angela Wimbush, and with longtime admirer Rod Stewart, including a new version of "This Old Heart of Mine". That same year, Ernie and Marvin returned to form a new Isley Brothers lineup and, two years later, the group reunited with the spirit of Jimi Hendrix when they were both among the inductees to the Rock & Roll Hall of Fame.

Fronting an all-star guitar team-up—Carlos Santana, Jimmy Page and Keith Richards included—Ernie took the lead in a colossal jam through Hendrix's "Purple Haze." "I strapped on my guitar over my tuxedo and I went up there

and sang and played lead in front of all these guys. At one point, tuxedo on and all, I threw the guitar behind my back. When it was over, I'm coming off stage and Carlos Santana came over to me, shook my hand and said, 'hey man, nice playing.' I'm thinking, 'boy, if the guys in study hall could see me now'."

### ISLEY BROTHERS COMPLETE DISCOGRAPHY
#### SINGLES/CHART LOG

1957 Angels Cried/The Cow Jumped over the Moon (Teenage)
1957 The Drag/Rockin' MacDonald (Mark-X)
1958 Don't Be Jealous/This Is the End (Cindy)
1958 I Wanna Know/Everybody's Gonna Rock 'n' Roll (Gone)
1958 My Love/The Drag (Gone)
1959 I'm Gonna Knock on Your Door/Turn to Me (RCA)
1959 Shout (part one)/(part two) (RCA—#47 pop)
1959 Respectable/Without a Song (RCA)
1960 He's Got the Whole World in His Hands/How Deep Is the Ocean (RCA)
1960 Gypsy Love Song/Open Up Your Heart (RCA)
1960 Say You Love Me/Tell Me Who (RCA)
1961 Jeepers Creepers/Teach Me How To Shimmy (Atlantic)
1961 Shine On Harvest Moon/Standing on the Dancefloor (Atlantic)
1961 Your Old Lady/Write to Me (Atlantic)
1961 A Fool for You/Just One More Time (Atlantic)
1962 Right Now/The Snake (Wand)
1962 Shout (part one)/(part two) (RCA—reissue #94 pop)
1962 Twist and Shout/Spanish Twist (Wand—#2 R&B/#17 pop)
1962 Twistin' with Linda/You Better Come Home (Wand—#54 pop)
1963 Nobody but Me/I'm Laughing to Keep from Crying (Wand)
1963 I Say Love/Hold On Baby (Wand)
1963 She's Gone/Tango (UA)
1963 Surf and Shout/Whatcha Gonna Do (UA)
1963 Please Please Please/You'll Never Leave Him (UA)
1964 Who's That Lady/My Little Girl (UA)
1964 Testify (part one)/(part two) (T-Neck)
1964 Looking for a Love/The Last Girl (Atlantic)
1965 Simon Says/Wild as a Tiger (Atlantic)
1965 Move over and Let Me Dance/Have You Ever Been Disappointed (Atlantic)
1965 I Hear a Symphony/Who Could Ever Doubt My Love (VIP)
1966 Love Is a Wonderful Thing/Open Up Your Eyes (Veep)
1966 This Old Heart of Mine/There's No Love Left (Tamla—#6 R&B/#12 pop)
1966 Take Some Time Out for Love/Who Could Ever Doubt My Love (Tamla—#66 pop)
1966 I Guess I'll Always Love You/I Hear a Symphony (Tamla—#31 R&B/#61 pop)
1967 Got To Have You Back/Just Ain't Enough Love (Tamla—#47 R&B/#93 pop)
1967 One Too Many Heartaches/That's the Way Love Is (Tamla)
1968 Take Me in Your Arms/Why When Love Is Gone (Tamla—#22 R&B/#121 pop)

1968 Behind a Painted Smile/All Because I Love You (Tamla)

1969 Take Some Time Out for Love/Just Ain't Enough Love (Tamla)

1969 It's Your Thing/Don't Give It Away (T-Neck—#1 R&B/#2 pop)

1969 I Turned You On/I Know Who's Been Sockin' It to You (T-Neck—#6 R&B/#23 pop)

1969 Black Berries (part one)/(part two) (T-Neck—#43 R&B/#79 pop)

1969 Was It Good to You/Got To Get Myself Together (T-Neck—#33 R&B/#83 pop)

1969 Bless Your Heart/Give the Women What They Want (T-Neck—#29 R&B/#105 pop)

1970 Keep On Doin'/Save Me (T-Neck—#17 R&B/#75 pop)

1970 If He Can You Can/Holdin' On (T-Neck—#21 R&B/#113 pop)

1970 Girls Will Be Girls/Get Down off of the Train (T-Neck—#21 R&B/#75 pop)

1970 Get into Something (part one)/(part two) (T-Neck—#25 R&B/#89 pop)

1970 Freedom/I Need You So (T-Neck—#16 R&B/#72 pop)

1971 Warpath/Got To Find Me One (T-Neck—#17 R&B/#111 pop)

1971 Love the One You're With/He's Got Your Love (T-Neck—#3 R&B/#18 pop)

1971 Spill the Wine/Take Inventory (T-Neck—#14 R&B/#49 pop)

1971 Lay Lady Lay/Vacuum Cleaner (T-Neck—#29 R&B/#71 pop)

1972 Lay Away/Feel Like the World (T-Neck—#6 R&B/#54 pop)

1972 Pop That Thang/I Got To Find Me One (T-Neck—#3 R&B/#24 pop)

1972 Work To Do/Beautiful (T-Neck—#11 R&B/#51 pop)

1973 It's Too Late/Nothing To Do but Today (T-Neck—#39 R&B)

1973 That Lady (part one)/(part two) (T-Neck—#2 R&B/#6 pop)

1973 What It Comes Down To/Highways of My Life (T-Neck—#5 R&B/#55 pop)

1974 Summer Breeze (part one)/(part two) (T-Neck—#10 R&B/#60 pop)

1974 Live It Up (part one)/(part two) (T-Neck—#4 R&B/#52 pop)

1974 Midnight Sky (part one)/(part two) (T-Neck—#8 R&B/#73 pop)

1975 Fight the Power (part one)/(part two) (T-Neck—#1 R&B/#4 pop)

1975 For the Love of You/Walk Your Way (T-Neck—#10 R&B/#122 pop)

1976 Who Loves You Better (part one)/(part two) (T-Neck—#3 R&B/#47 pop)

1976 Harvest for the World (part one)/(part two) (T-Neck—#9 R&B/#63 pop)

1977 The Pride (part one)/(part two) (T-Neck—#1 R&B/#4 pop)

1977 Livin' the Life/Go for Your Guns (part one)/(part two) (T-Neck—#4 R&B/#40 pop)

1977 Voyage to Atlantis/Do You Wanna Stay Down (T-Neck—#50 R&B)

1978 Take Me to the Next Phase (part one)/(part two) (T-Neck—#1 R&B)

1978 Groove with You/Footsteps in the Dark (T-Neck—#16 R&B)

1978 Showdown (part one)/(part two) (T-Neck)

1979 I Wanna Be with You (part one)/(part two) (T-Neck—#1 R&B)

1979 Winner Takes All/Fun and Games (T-Neck—#38 R&B)

1979 It's a Disco Night/Ain't Givin' Up on Love (T-Neck—#27 R&B/#90 pop)

1980 Don't Say Goodnight (part one)/(part two) (T-Neck—#1 R&B/#39 pop)

1980 Here We Go Again (part one)/(part two) (T-Neck—#11 R&B)

1980 Say You Will (part one)/(part two) (T-Neck)

1981 Who Said/(Can't You See) What You've Done to Me (T-Neck—#20 R&B)

1981 Hurry Up and Wait/(instrumental) (T-Neck—#17 R&B/#58 pop)

1981 I Once Had Your Love/(instrumental) (T-Neck—#57 R&B)

1981 Inside You (part one)/(part two) (T-Neck—10 R&B)

1982 Welcome into My Heart/Party Night (T-Neck—#45 R&B)

1982 The Real Deal/(instrumental) (T-Neck—#14 R&B)

1982 It's Alright with Me/(instrumental) (T-Neck—#59 R&B)

1983 Between the Sheets/(instrumental) (T-Neck—#3 R&B/#101 pop)

1983 Choosey Lover/(instrumental) (T-Neck—#6 R&B)

1984 Let's Make Love/(instrumental) (T-Neck)

1985 Colder Are My Nights (instrumental) (WB—#12 R&B)

1986 May I?/(instrumental) (WB—#42 R&B)

1987 Smooth Sailin' Tonight/(instrumental) (WB—#3 R&B)

1987 Come My Way/(instrumental) (WB—#71 R&B)

1988 I Wish/(instrumental) (WB—#74 R&B)

1989 Spend the Night/(instrumental) (WB—#3 R&B)

1989 You'll Never Walk Alone (WB—#25 R&B)/One of a Kind (#38 R&B)

1992 Sensitive Lover /(instrumental) (WB—#24 R&B)

1992 Whatever Turns You On/(album version) (WB—#46 R&B)

1994 I'm So Proud/(album version) (WB—#66 R&B)

1996 Let's Lay Together/(instrumental) (Island—#24 R&B/#93 pop)

1996 Floatin' on Your Love/(remixes) (Island—#14 R&B/#47 pop)

1997 Tears/(album version) (Island—#12 R&B/#55 pop)

### ISLEY JASPER ISLEY

1984 Look the Other Way/(instrumental) (CBS—#14 R&B)

1985 Kiss and Tell/(instrumental) (CBS—#52 R&B/#63 pop)

1985 Caravan of Love/I Can't Get Over Losin' You (CBS—#1 R&B/#51 pop)

1986 Insatiable Woman/Break This Chain (CBS—#13 R&B)

1987 Eighth Wonder of the World/Broadway's Closer to Sunset Boulevard (CBS—#18 R&B)

1987 Givin' You Back My Love/I Can Hardly Wait (CBS—#15 R&B)

### RONALD ISLEY/ANGELA WINBUSH

1990 Lay Your Troubles Down/Hello Beloved (Mercury—#10 R&B)

### RONALD ISLEY/ROD STEWART

1990 This Old Heart of Mine/You're in My Heart (WB—#10 pop)

### RONALD ISLEY/BOBBY WOMACK

1994 Trying Not To Break Down/Wish (Continuum—#94 R&B)

### LPs

**6** 1960 Shout! (RCA)

**5** 1962 Twist and Shout (Wand)

**6** 1966 This Old Heart of Mine (Tamla—#15 R&B/#140 pop)

**6** 1967 Tamla Motown Presents. . . (Tamla)

**7** 1968 Soul on the Rocks (Tamla)

**9** 1969 It's Our Thing (T-Neck—#2 R&B/#22 pop)

It's hard to say what was more shocking, the affirmative energy of the album itself, or the bold swerve away from the Motown sound. Either way, the Isleys' first truly self-defining album remains a classic.

**8** 1970 The Brothers Isley (T-Neck—#20 R&B/#180 pop)

**7** 1971 Givin' It Back (T-Neck—#13 R&B/#71 pop)

Audacious all-covers album occasionally runs out of gas, but never loses its nerve.

**6** 1972 Brother, Brother, Brother (T-Neck—#5 R&B/#29 pop)

**6** 1973 The Isleys Live (T-Neck—#14 R&B/#139 pop)

Oddly unfulfilling snapshot of the Isleys' peak period, marred by too many lackluster covers, and nowhere near enough of Ernie's guitar.

**9** 1973 3 + 3 (T-Neck—#2 R&B/#8 pop)

The rock-funk-soul fusion peaks across "That Lady," "Summer Breeze" and "Listen to the Music"; the rest of the set doesn't quite match the same standards, but what could?

**8** 1974 Live It Up (T-Neck—#1 R&B/#14 pop)

With the entire album pursuing the Isleys' new-found fascination with texture and effects, the highlight title track rides a quintessentially funky keyboard rhythm, reminiscent of Stevie Wonder's "Superstition" and punctuated by outrageous, and outrageously brief, bursts of electric guitar.

**8** 1975 The Heat Is On (T-Neck—#1 R&B/#1 pop)

Dynamite. The slow jams "For the Love of You" and "Make Me Say It Again" are cool evening enders; while "Fight the Power" takes the aggressive stomp of "Live It Up" to the next level.

**7** 1976 Harvest for the World (T-Neck—#1 R&B/#9 pop)

The wind cries disco and the Isleys heed the call. The title track is a solemn suite of superlative soul; the remainder of the album tentatively toes the new dancefloor.

**7** 1977 Go for Your Guns (T-Neck—#1 R&B/#6 pop)

**6** 1978 Showdown (T-Neck—#1 R&B/#4 pop)

**6** 1979 Winner Takes All (T-Neck—#3 R&B/#14 pop)

**7** 1980 Go All the Way (T-Neck—#1 R&B/#8 pop)

The strongest of the Isleys' disco-era albums, although the finest track, "Don't Say Goodnight," is best heard via the *It's Your Thing*'s box set alternate take.

**6** 1981 Grand Slam (T-Neck—#3 R&B/#28 pop)

**5** 1981 Inside You (T-Neck—#8 R&B/#45 pop)

**5** 1982 The Real Deal (T-Neck—#9 R&B/#87 pop)

**6** 1983 Between the Sheets (T-Neck—#1 R&B/#19 pop)

Predicting the soft electrofunk of the imminent Isley Jasper Isley spin-off, but like all the Isleys' '80s albums, unable to discern a direction of its own.

**6** 1985 Masterpiece (WB—#19 R&B/#140 pop)

**5** 1987 Smooth Sailing (WB—#5 R&B/#64 pop)

**5** 1989 Spend the Night (WB—#4 R&B/#89 pop)

**5** 1990 Come Together (WB)

**6** 1992 Tracks of Life (WB—#19 R&B/#140 pop)

**6** 1993 Live (Elektra—#34 R&B)

**5** 1996 Mission To Please (WB - #2 R&B/#31 pop)

## SELECTED COMPILATIONS AND ARCHIVE RELEASES

**6** 1971 In the Beginning: With Jimi Hendrix (T-Neck)

Self-explanatory souvenir of Hendrix's short spell with the band, padded out with period extras

**7** 1973 Greatest Hits (T-Neck—#24 R&B/#195 pop)

**7** 1976 The Best (Buddah—#49 R&B)

**6** 1977 Forever Gold (T-Neck—#40 R&B/#58 pop)

**7** 1979 Timeless (T-Neck—#70 R&B/#204 pop)

**8** 1991 Isley Brothers Story, Vol. 1: Rock 'n' Soul Years 1959–68 (Rhino)

**8** 1991 Isley Brothers Story, Vol. 2: The T-Neck Years 1969–85 (Rhino)

Far-reaching collections, sensibly divided.

**9** 1999 It's Your Thing (Legacy)

Peerless three-CD collection unearths several rarities and unreleased cuts, alongside the expected treasures.

## SELECTED SAMPLES

Ain't I Been Good to You? — Boss: Recipe of a Hoe (1993)

Ain't I Been Good to You? — Public Enemy: Shut Em Down (remix) (1991)

Between the Sheets — Audio Two: The Questions (1988)

Between the Sheets — Rob Base: Break of Dawn (1994)

Between the Sheets — Common Sense: Breaker 1/9 (1994)

Between the Sheets — Da Brat: Funkdafied (1994)

Between the Sheets — Heavy D: Nuttin but Love (remix) (1994)

Between the Sheets — Keith Murray: The Most Beautifullest Thing (1994)

Between the Sheets — Notorious BIG: Big Poppa (1994)

Between the Sheets — Naughty by Nature: Written on Ya Kitten (1993)

Between the Sheets — Skee-lo: Superman (1995)

Between the Sheets — A Tribe Called Quest: Bonita Appelbum (1990)

Between the Sheets — Underground Kingz: Crampin' My Style (1992)

Coolin' Out — Coolio: Mama, I'm in Love with a Gangsta (1994)

Fight the Power — Cypress Hill: The Phuncky Feel One (1992)

Fight the Power — Insane Poetry: The House That Dripped Blood (1992)

Fight the Power — WC & the Madd Circle: Back on the Scene (1991)

Footsteps in the Dark — Compton's Most Wanted: Can I Kill It? (1991)

Footsteps in the Dark — Ice Cube: It Was a Good Day (1992)

For the Love of You — College Boyz: Hollywood Paradox 1992)

For the Love of You — Dr. Dre & Ed Lover: For the Love of You (1994)

For the Love of You — Masta Ace Inc.: INC Ride (1995)

For the Love of You — Poison Clan: Ho Stories (1993)

For the Love of You — Slick Rick: Sittin' in My Car (remix) (1994)

For the Love of You — Thug Life: Bury Me a G (1994)

Groove with You — Channel Live: Who U Represent? (1995)

Groove with You — Isaac 2 Isaac: Ol' Skool (1995)

Groove with You — MC Lyte: 2 Young for What? (1991)

I Turned You On — Big Daddy Kane: Prince of Darkness (1991)

I Turned You On — Eazy-E: Eazy Duz-It (1988)

I Turned You On — ESP: Oh Well (1991)
It's Your Thing — Kris Kross: Jump (1992)
It's Your Thing — Salt-N-Pepa: Shake Your Thing (1988)
Make Me Say it Again, Girl — Bone Thugs N Harmony: Crossroad (1995)
Make Me Say it Again, Girl — Naughty by Nature: Hip Hop Hooray (1993)
Summer Breeze — DJ Shadow: Midnight in a Perfect World (Gab Mix) (1996)
Take Me to the Next Phase — Stetsasonic: So Let the Fun Begin (1991)
Work to Do — Average White Band: Work To Do (remake) (1998)
Work To Do — Vanessa Williams: Work To Do (1991)

## FELA RANSOME KUTI

**BORN:** *1938, Abeokuta, Nigeria, died: 8/2/97*

He has been called the African James Brown, although not necessarily by James Brown himself. Reflecting upon a visit to Nigeria in 1970 with the JBs, Brown mused "some of the ideas my band was getting from [his] band had come from me in the first place." "But," he continued, "that was okay with me. It made the music that much stronger."

By the time of that visit, Kuti had been establishing himself as a force on the Nigerian music scene for some 15 years. In 1954, aged 16, he joined his first group, the Cool Cats, a long-running Menudo-like act playing the local jazz variant known as high life, and whose membership was in a permanent state of movement; players came and went, but the Cool Cats went on forever. These activities were interrupted in 1958, when his parents sent him to London to study medicine, a path already taken by his sister and two older brothers.

Kuti's parents were comfortably middle class. His father, Reverend Israel Ransome-Kuti, was principal of the Abeokuta Grammar School and the first man in the neighborhood to purchase a motor car; his mother, Funmilayo, was a known power in left wing politics, leader of the first demonstrations during the 1940s against Nigeria's colonial master, Britain, and the first Nigerian woman ever to visit the Soviet Union.

Their hopes for their third son were not to be borne out. Abandoning any thoughts of medicine as soon as he arrived in London, Kuti enrolled instead at the Trinity School of Music, where he formed a new high life act, Koola Lobitos, with other Nigerian musicians he met in the city.

The band became a fixture on London's burgeoning R&B scene, witnessed by any number of the future stars then moving around the same circuit—Georgie Fame, the Rolling Stones, Alexis Korner, Cyril Davies and so forth. The group also cut a single for Emile Shalit's Melodisc label, a London-based company specializing in what were then classified as ethnic interests; the label's ska and calypso catalog was the first to be established outside of Jamaica. Renamed Fela Kuti & his Highlife Rakers for the occasion, they cut four tracks for the label: "Aigana" and "Fela's Special" which were selected as the singles, "Highlife Rakers' Calypso #1" and "Wa Ba Mi Jo Bosue."

Kuti returned to Nigeria following graduation in 1962, accompanied by several of the Koola Lobitos regulars. The group signed with the Phillips label's Nigerian wing and, over the next two years, released a number of singles, including several under the name Highlife Jazz Band ("Onifere," "Yeshe Yeshe" and an early version of the later classic "Mr. Who Are You").

Then in 1964, Kuti met another former Cool Cat, drummer Tony Allen, now playing with the Western Toppers Band, and recruited him to Koola Lobitos. With a lineup of Kuti, Allen, Yinka Roberts (gtr), Fred Lawal (gtr), Ojo Okeji (bs), Isaac Olasugba (sax), Tex Becks (sax), Uwaifo (sax), Tunde Williams (trum), Eddie Aroyewu (trum), the band underwent a seismic change in direction, from straightforward high life jazz to a complicated, virtuosic hybrid, which even the musicians eventually realized was so convoluted that nobody was actually able to dance to it!

They scaled back their ambition, introducing straightforward arrangements and simple hooks, and issued a string of further singles, together with at least one self-titled album. This was the sound that, in 1968, Kuti christened Afrobeat, popularizing the phrase with his next release, *Afro-Beat Live*. It was the events of the following year, however, that truly defined the music he was making.

In 1969, Koola Lobitos relocated to Los Angeles to escape a homeland embroiled in civil war over the breakaway nation of Biafra. Koola Lobitos had initially come down firmly on the side of the government forces with a single, "Keep Nigeria One," issued shortly before their departure. The growing awareness that Biafra was rapidly turning into a major humanitarian tragedy, however, changed their perspective, all the more so after the band reached the US.

There, Kuti came face to face with the influences that dictated his future direction. First there came a political awakening aroused by Sandra Isidore, a Black American woman who introduced Kuti to the full spectrum of Black radicalism, from Malcolm X and Eldridge Cleaver to Angela Davis and the Last Poets. Then there was a musical rebirth, as he allied his own music with that coming out of Black America, the formative funk of James Brown and Sly Stone, the hard R&B of Archie Bell & the Drells and the Isley Brothers. In pure musical terms, it wasn't that vast a leap from the direction in which Koola Lobitos were already moving, but the hybrid itself was startling.

Kuti renamed the band Nigeria 70 and, with a lineup of Kuti (vcls, pno, trum), leader Allen (drms), Tutu Shoronmu (gtr), Segun Edo (gtr), Tommy James (bs), Igo Chico (sax), Lekan Animashaun (sax), Isaac Olaleye (maraccas), James Abayomi (sticks), Henry Kofi (perc) and Daniel Koronteg (perc), the group remained in Los Angeles for nine months, some time after their visas expired, playing the club circuit and developing their repertoire.

Nigeria 70's US sojourn finally ended after a promoter turned them into the Immigration and Naturalization Service; before they left, however, Nigeria 70 went into the studio to record material for release (in Nigeria only) as singles over the next year or so. Again deeply indebted to America's own funk pioneers, the songs were performed in English rather than Kuti's native Yoruba, to ensure his message reached the largest number of people possible. (These recordings were subsequently released as the *69 Los Angeles Sessions* album.)

The ploy worked. A hit with "Jeun Ko'Ku" ("eat and die") provided the financing Kuti required to open his own club, the Afro-Shrine, at the Empire Hotel, and the band—now renamed Africa 70—were instant superstars, Kuti's hard-hitting plea for a return to an African culture striking the same chord with young Nigerians as the similar stateside messages had among young Black Americans.

The watching authorities were edgy, but seemed powerless—not only did Kuti have the respect of the people, he was also attracting attention from elsewhere. James Brown was only one of several international stars to visit Kuti; Ginger Baker, former drummer with rock supergroup Cream, was also entranced by Africa 70, visiting Kuti in 1971 and recording a live album, *Fela Ransome Kuti & Ginger Baker Live*. Baker subsequently formed his own troupe of Nigerian musicians, Salt; he also returned to Nigeria to help Kuti establish the country's first 16-track recording studio. It opened in 1973. Africa 70's "He Miss Road," produced by Kuti and Baker, was one of the studio's first recordings; in the meantime, Kuti traveled to London to record what became the *London Scene* album.

Such connections ensured Kuti retained a profile in the west far greater than any other African artist; ensured, too, that his own music retained a cross-cultural flavor, which other, less well-traveled, African performers could only aspire to.

Years later, when the Anglo-American music industry formulated the "world music" genre to encompass any foreign musical form, which didn't slip comfortably into the tyrannical hegemony of rock, pop and soul, Kuti's inclusion remained a glaring miscalculation, so effortlessly had the disciplines of his Afro-beat been absorbed into those genres. (At the same time, however, Afro-beat remained very much its own master. The handful of groups who did launch western careers in Kuti's shadow, the London-based Ghanaian rock act Osibisa and the renowned Burundi drummers being the most prominent, were similarly, and equally gratuitously, marginalized.)

Africa 70 were at their peak through the first half of the 1970s. Between 1972, when the sexually charged "Na Poi" was banned by the Nigerian Broadcasting Company (and became a massive hit as a consequence) and 1977, the band were fabulously prolific, maintaining an output of two, sometimes three albums a year, each one dominated by jams that extended across one and sometimes both sides of the vinyl, almost as though they were singles. In fact, Kuti himself seems to have regarded them as such. In one interview, asked why he did not cut "conventional" length records like other (western) artists, Kuti responded, "I can't stand all that short music. We dance long distance here, so no three-minute music for me."

"Gentlemen" was the first release to feature Kuti himself playing tenor sax; Igo Chico quit shortly before sessions began, one of a handful of personnel changes that shaped the band as the decade progressed. By 1974, Afrika 70 lined up as: Ogene Kologbo (gtr), Leke Benson (gtr), Franco Aboddy (bs), Ukem Stephen (trum), Tunde Williams (trum), Christopher Uwaifa (sax), Nicholas Addo (perc) and James Bayomi (sticks), together with Kuti and remaining founders Lekan Animashaun, Tony Allen (drms), Henry Kofi (perc) and Isaac Olaleyo (maraccas).

1974 was the year in which Kuti's increasingly violent confrontations with the Nigerian military regime of Olusegun Obasanjo exploded into the open, as he declared his home to be the independent Kalakuta ("rascal") Republic. The response came in the form of increased police harassment and raids, culminating with Kuti's arrest for marijuana possession. He was found not guilty, only for the police to return the following day, November 23, intending to plant another joint on him.

They were foiled when Kuti snatched the joint and swallowed it. He was arrested anyway and imprisoned—the police intended waiting until the drugs passed through his system, then using his feces as evidence against him. With the aid of his fellow prisoners, Kuti was able to make an unsupervised trip to the bathroom, void the incriminating matter and then produce a "clean" sample the following day. He was freed and responded with the self-explanatory "Expensive Shit."

The Kalakuta Republic continued to grow both in size and in its capacity to annoy and frustrate the authorities. Kuti himself adopted the surname Anikulapo ("he who carries death in his pouch"), debuting this new identity on 1976's "Yellow Fever." The B-side, incidentally, was given over to a reworking of the controversial "Na Poi," retitled "Na Poi 75."

1976 saw the release of Kuti's bestselling record yet, an open assault on the Nigerian military, "Zombie." Of course it was banned, but its success spilled beyond the record stores that carried it and into the streets; soon, it's "no brains, no sense, march march march" refrain could be heard all over Nigeria, sung by children to mock the military. With Kuti having already snubbed the ruling party by boycotting the second World Black Festival of Arts and Culture, held in Lagos that year, "Zombie" simply added insult to injury. Still, nobody could have predicted the brutality that followed.

With tensions between the Kalakuta Republic and the government now at an all time high, a February 1977, confrontation between Kuti's bodyguards and two soldiers ended with the soldiers being savagely beaten and their motorcycles burned. Days later, on February 18, 1977, the military responded with a full-scale assault on the Kalakuta compound, some 1,000 soldiers attacking an admittedly hostile, but otherwise peaceful, civilian camp.

The compound was burned to the ground, its 60 inhabitants beaten, tortured and raped. Firefighters who arrived on the scene were forced back; press photographers were openly attacked. Kuti's 78-year-old mother was thrown from a window and later died from her injuries. Kuti himself received a fractured skull. Laughably, the government subsequently attributed the attack to "unknown soldiers"—a title and theme that later became one of Kuti's bestselling records.

For a time, Kuti and his entourage holed up in the Crossroads Hotel in Lagos, venturing out only to record what became the "Stalemate," "Fear Not for Man" and "Shuffering and Shmiling" hits. Kuti also spent some time in Ghana, organizing a tour for later in 1978. However that, too, ended in chaos when rioting broke out during a show in the capital, Accra (not surprisingly, during an impassioned performance of "Zombie"). The Ghanaian authorities promptly arrested the entire band, which now included some 70 musicians, including all 27 of Kuti's wives (married

in a joint ceremony on the first anniversary of the Kalakuta attack).

Deported back to Nigeria, Kuti and Africa 70 spent July through September 1978, squatting at the Lagos headquarters of his record company, Decca Afrodisia. It was not a development that Decca themselves approved of, particularly in the wake of Kuti's latest release, "Sorrows, Tears and Blood."

Recorded following the destruction of Kalakuta, the master tape of "Sorrows, Tears and Blood" was promptly confiscated by the government. Kuti was forced to go to court to retrieve the recordings, only for Decca to refuse to release them on the grounds that they were seditious. When further scheduled releases, too, were postponed, Kuti responded by forming his own label, Kalakuta; "Sorrows, Tears and Blood" became the label's first release.

Late in 1978, Kuti and Africa 70 were invited to Germany to perform at the Berlin Jazz Festival. One track from the show, the 20 minute "VIP," was released as Africa 70's next album in early 1979; it also proved their final release. Immediately following the concert, the band broke up in protest at Kuti's latest scheme—plowing the profits from the concert into a political campaign. (Tony Allen went on to form the Afro-Beat specialists Mighty Irokos; following their 1983 breakup he moved into session work, before 1999 united him with former P-Funk vocalist Gary "Mudbone" Cooper in a new outfit, Mudbone & the Medicine.)

With Nigeria preparing to go to the polls in 1979, Kuti announced his intention of running for President at the head of a new political party, Movement of the People. His candidacy was eventually disqualified, but still the elections saw the Nigerian military government finally overthrown by a new civilian administration, ushering in a new dawn for both the country and for Kuti. He toured constantly and commenced a new stream of releases, including a collaboration with Roy Ayers, *Music of Many Colours*. But he was also courting official disapproval once again.

The civilian government installed in 1979 transpired to be no less corrupt than its military predecessor, a point that Kuti was swift to make in his music. In 1981, "Authority Stealing," however, was a step too far; Kuti could not even find a pressing plant in Nigeria willing to touch the song. Finally, he had the record manufactured in Ghana and then smuggled back to Nigeria, for release on Kalakuta. Shortly after, a violent confrontation with Lagos police saw him hospitalized, close to death.

He recovered and bounced back with Egypt 80, a 30-piece outfit (including a ten-man horn section led by Africa

70 mainstay Lekan Animashaun), and the mighty "Original Suffer Head." It revealed Kuti to be as defiant as ever, despite his recent experiences, but his ability to elude his foes was running out. In 1983, his plans to run again for President were ended by another police assault on his home, while a military coup led by General Buhari ensured that there would be no more elections either. Soon after, Kuti was arrested on currency charges and sentenced to an unprecedented five years imprisonment.

The western media was outraged. Attention was drawn to Kuti's predicament in every available arena. Led by Amnesty International, so much pressure was placed upon the Nigerian authorities that finally, the country's new leader, General Babangida, was forced to reopen the investigation. It swiftly transpired that the sentencing judge had himself been under pressure from the then incumbent Buhari to rid Nigeria of her most troublesome son. The judge was dismissed and Kuti was freed, having served 20 months.

He immediately reformed Egypt 80, frequently employing up to 80 musicians at a time and, with his European and American profile now higher than at any time since the Ginger Baker days, Kuti spent much of the 1980s touring. New and archive releases, too, were making their appearance on foreign shores, opening further doors not only for Kuti's own music, but for a host of other African artists and sounds.

Of his late-'80s releases, two sets recorded with producer Wally Badarou, "Teacher . . ." and the politically universal "Beasts of No Nation," were especially well received by a western music media which had barely noticed Kuti's pre-imprisonment work, but was now hastening to re-evaluate it. They, in particular, were utterly baffled by Kuti's near impenetrable silence through the 1990s—a silence broken only by the news that he was seriously ill, suffering from AIDS-related complaints. Kuti died on August 2, 1997.

He was buried ten days later. Over 150,000 people attended his memorial, a massive concert in Lagos' Tafawa Balewa Square, where his body lay in state in a glass coffin. A band playing his music led the funeral cortege the 20 miles to the cemetry. The journey took seven hours; Kuti's manager, Rikki Stein, later estimated that a million people turned out to pay their final respects.

Much of Kuti's musical legacy has since been assumed by his son, Fema.

## FURTHER READING
*Fela Kuti* by Michael Veal (Temple University Press, 2000)

## FELA KUTI DISCOGRAPHY
Note: with close to 100 releases, many of which were available in Nigeria only, a full discography has not been attempted. In addition, Kuti's ambiguous relationship with conventional distinctions between LPs and singles is maintained. Regardless of length, all two-song releases are treated as "singles"; only releases with more songs are considered LPs. Titles marked with an asterisk were reissued on CD during 2000/2001 (MCA).

### SINGLES

### FELA RANSOME KUTI AND HIS HIGHLIFE RAKERS
1960 Aigana/Fela's Special (Melodisc—UK)

### FELA RANSOME KUTI/THE HIGHLIFE JAZZ BAND (1962–64)
196? Onifere/? (Phillips—Nigeria)
196? Yeshe Yeshe/? (Phillips—Nigeria)
196? Mr Who Are You?/? (Phillips/Nigeria)

### FELA RANSOME KUTI AND THE KOOLA LOBITOS (1965–68)
196? Die Die/Kusimilaya (Parlophone—Nigeria)
196? Fire/Oni Machine (Parlophone—Nigeria)
196? Orit She/Eke (Parlophone—Nigeria)
196? Wa Dele/Laise (Parlophone—Nigeria)
196? Yese/Egbin (Parlophone—Nigeria)
196? Omuti Te Se/? (unknown—Nigeria)
196? Bonfo/Fere (RK—Nigeria)
196? Abiara/Ajo (Phillips WA—Nigeria)
196? My Baby Don Love Me/Home Cooking (Phillips WA—Nigeria)
196? Onicodo/Alagbara (Phillips WA—Nigeria)
196? Waka Waka/Se E Tunde (Phillips WA—Nigeria)
1969 Keep Nigeria One/? (unknown—Nigeria)

### FELA RANSOME-KUTI AND THE NIGERIA 70
1970 Blackman's Cry /Beautiful Dancer (HMV—Nigeria)
1971 Jeun K'oku (part one)/(part two) (HMV—Ghana)
1972 Shenshema (part one)/(part two) (HMV—Nigeria)
1972 Monday Morning (part one)/(part two) (HMV—Nigeria)
1972 Fogo Fogo (part one)/(part two) (HMV—Nigeria)
1972 Going in and Going Out (part one)/(part two) (HMV—Nigeria)

### FELA RANSOME KUTI/GINGER BAKER
1972 Egbe Mi O/Chop & Quench (Regal Zonophone—UK)

### FELA RANSOME KUTI AND THE AFRICA 70
1971 Why Black Man Dey Suffer/Ikoyi Mentality vs. Mushin Mentality (African Songs—Nigeria)
1972 Alijon-Jon-Ki-Jon (part one)/(part two) (HMV—Ghana)
1972 Ariya (part one)/(part two) (HMV—Nigeria)
1972 Shakara Oloje/Lady (EMI—Nigeria)*
1972 Na Poi/You No Go Die Unless You Wan Die (HMV—Nigeria)
1973 Gentleman/Fefe Naa Efe/Igbe (EMI—Nigeria)*

1974 Alagbon Close/I No Get Eye For Black (Jofabro—Nigeria)

1975 He Miss Road/Monday Morning in Lagos/It's No Possible (EMI—Nigeria)*

1975 Expensive Shit/Water No Get Enemy (Editions Makossa)*

1975 Noise for Vendor Mouth/Mattress (Afrobeat—Nigeria)*

1975 Everything Scatter/Why No Know Go Know (Coconut—Nigeria)*

1975 Confusion (part one)/(part two) (EMI—Nigeria)*

1976 Kalakuta Show/Don't Meke Garnan Garnan (Editions Makossa)*

1976 Ikoyi Blindness/Gba Mi Leti Ki N'dolowo (Africa Music—Nigeria)*

1976 Yellow Fever/Na Poi 75 (Decca Afrodisia—Nigeria)*

1976 Upside Down/Go Slow (Decca Afrodisia—Nigeria)*

1976 No Bread/Unnecessary Begging (Editions Makossa)*

1976 Before I Jump like Monkey Give Me Banana [Monkey Banana]/Sense Wiseness (Coconut—Nigeria)*

1976 Again, Excuse O [Excuse O]/Mr. Grammatology-Lisationalism Is the Boss (Coconut—Nigeria)*

1976 Zombie/Mr. Follow Follow (Creole—UK)*

1977 Johnny Just Drop (JJD) (part one)/(part two) [recorded live] (Decca Afrodisia—Nigeria)*

1977 Opposite People/Equalisation of Trouser and Pant (Decca Afrodisia—Nigeria)*

1977 Mr. Big Mouth/The Beginning (Decca Afrodisia—Nigeria)

1977 Stalemate/African Message (Don't Worry About My Mouth O) (Decca Afrodisia—Nigeria)*

1977 Fear Not for Man/Palm Wine Sound (Decca Afrodisia—Nigeria)*

1977 Why Black Man Dey Suffer/Male (Decca Afrodisia—Nigeria: unreleased)

1977 Observation No Crime/Lady (Decca Afrodisia—Nigeria: unreleased)

1977 I Go Shout Plenty/Frustration (Decca Afrodisia—Nigeria: unreleased)

1977 No Agreement/Dog Eat Dog (Decca Afrodisia—Nigeria)*

1977 Sorrow, Tears and Blood/Colonial Mentality (Kalakuta—Nigeria)*

1977 Shuffering and Shmiling (part one)/(part two) (Coconut—Nigeria)*

1978 Shuffering and Shmiling/Perambulator (Barclay—France)

1979 Unknown Soldier (part one)/(part two) (Phonodisk Skylark—Nigeria)*

1979 Vagabonds in Power (VIP) (part one)/(part two) (Kalakuta—Nigeria)*

1979 International Thief Thief (part one)/(part two) (Kalakuta—Nigeria)*

1980 Authority Stealing (part one)/(part two) (Kalakuta—Nigeria)*

1981 Coffin for Head of State (part one)/(part two) (Kalakuta—Nigeria)*

## TONY ALLEN AND THE AFRICA 70 (WITH FELA RANSOME-KUTI )

1976 Jealousy/Hustler (Sound Workshop—Nigeria)

1977 Progress/Afro Disco Beat (Coconut—Nigeria)

1979 No Accommodation for Lagos/African Message (Phonogram—Nigeria)

## FELA ANIKULAPO-KUTI AND THE EGYPT 80

1981 Original Sufferhead/Power Show (Lagos Int'l—Nigeria)*

1983 Perambulator/Frustration (Lagos Int'l—Nigeria)

1985 Army Arrangement (part one)/(part two) (Celluloid)

1986 Teacher Don't Teach Me Nonsense (part one)/(part two) (Polygram—Nigeria)*

1989 Beasts of No Nation (part one)/(part two) (Kalakuta—Nigeria)*

1989 Overtake Don Overtake Overtake (part one)/(part two) (Kalakuta—Nigeria)*

1990 Confusion Break Bones (part one)/(part two) (Kalakuta—Nigeria)

1990 Just like That/Movement of the People Political Statement #1 (Kalakuta—Nigeria)

1992 Underground System/Pansa Pansa (Kalakuta—Nigeria)*

## LPs

### FELA RANSOME KUTI AND THE KOOLA LOBITOS (1965–68)

**6** 196? Fela Ransome Kuti and the Koola Lobitos (EMI—Nigeria)

**7** '64–68 (MCA 2001)

Strictly high life recordings, historically fascinating if nothing else.

**7** 1968 AFRO-BEAT LIVE (Phillips—Nigeria)

Still formative, but now recognizably rhythmcentric.

### FELA RANSOME-KUTI AND THE NIGERIA 70

**6** 1970 Fela's London Scene (Editions Makossa)

LP featuring five tracks, with the slinky "J'Ehin J'Ehin" an almost dub-inflected standout. Reissued on CD in 2000 (MCA).

### FELA RANSOME KUTI/GINGER BAKER

**5** 1971 Live! (Regal Zonophone—UK)

**5** 1971 Stratavarious (Atco)

Baker's sincerity cannot be doubted, but neither can the record label's sense of who the star of the show was. *Live* was reissued on CD in 2001 (MCA).

### FELA RANSOME KUTI AND THE AFRICA 70

**6** 1971 Open and Close (EMI—Nigeria)

Reissued on CD in 2001 (MCA).

**8** 1972 Music of Fela—Roforofo Fight LP (Jofabro—Nigeria)

**8** 1973 Afrodisiac LP (Regal Zonophone UK)

Four tracks and a genuinely uplifting sense of adventure. Reissued on CD in 2001 (MCA).

### FELA ANIKULAPO-KUTI AND THE EGYPT 80

**8** 1984 Live in Amsterdam—Music Is the Weapon (EMI—UK)

Though lacking the instinctive majesty of earlier combos, still Egypt 80 represented one of the most powerful live acts to visit Europe during the early '80s. A small club audience gets its money's worth and then some. Reissued on CD in 2001 (MCA).

**7** 1985 Army Arrangement/Cross Examination/Gov't. Chicken Boy (Celluloid)

Left unfinished when Kuti was jailed, the album was completed by producer Bill Laswell, recruited to the cause by Kuti's US label of the time. His contributions to the final project are typically idiosyncratic, but largely unobtrusive. Reissued on CD in 2001 (MCA).

**5** **1980 Music of Many Colors (Phonodisk—Nigeria)**

An odd, sometimes awkward collaboration that doesn't let either musician truly stretch out. Reissued on CD in 2001 (MCA).

## SELECTED COMPILATIONS AND ARCHIVE RELEASES

**7** **1975 Fela's Budget Special (EMI—Nigeria)**

Nigerian compilation album reprising "Monday Morning in Lagos," "Shenshema," "Don't Gag Me," "Beggar's Song," "Alu Jon Jon Ki Jon" and "Chop and Quench."

**7** **1992 Black Man's Cry (Shanachie)**

Six track compilation of '70s material, targeted toward listeners lured in by Kuti's funk reputation (the title track) and his political flammability ("Zombie").

**6** **1994 The '69 Los Angeles Sessions (Stern's—UK)**

Reissued on CD in 2001 (MCA).

**9** **2000 The Best Best Of (MCA)**

Two-CD, 13-track compilation heading up MCA's ambitious 22-CD Kuti reissue series.

## SELECTED SAMPLES

Sorrow, Tears and Blood — X-Clan: Grand Verbalizer, What Time Is It? (1992)

# THE LAST POETS

**FORMED:** *1969, Harlem, NY*

**ORIGINAL LINE-UP:** *Abiodun Oyewole (vcls), Jalal Mansur Nuriddin aka Alafia Pudim aka Lightnin' Rod (vcls), Umar Bin Hassan (vcls), Nilaja (perc)*

Quizzed about their musical inspirations, the Last Poets unhesitatingly concur with the music archaeologists who can reel off a litany of Black poets and writers who set their words to music during the '50s and '60s: Langston Hughes (who recorded with Charles Mingus), occasional Sun Ra conspirator Imamu Amiri Baraka, Archie Shepp and Max Roach.

But precious few acts, those same historians agree, so effectively bridge the gap between the Black nationalist funk and soul of the early '70s and the first stirrings of hip-hop culture close to a decade later. Nor have any so effectively maintained their position at the forefront of the revolution, which they predicted, without ever tampering with a vision *Rolling Stone* magazine, in 1970, summed up as "nothing more than [a] heighten[ing of] . . . a new Black urban street poetry." Journalist Jonathan Cott continued, "at a New York high school assembly commemorating Malcolm X's death. . . . the 'predominantly Black' students hooted the principal down and kids got up on stage and read their poems—charged statements like those

of the [Last] Poets, rhythmically asserting Black consciousness. . . ."

The Last Poets were formed by Jalal Nuriddim, Umar Hassan and Abiodun Olewoye; the trio met in prison (Nuriddim was jailed for refusing the draft) and, upon their release, reunited at the East Wind poetry workshop in Harlem, in 1968. Other performances took place on neighborhood street corners, but they didn't formally become a "group" until the following May 16, Malcolm X's birthday. Their name was taken from South African writer Little Willie Copaseely's insistence that the poets of the day would be the last, before the world was taken over by guns.

With the original trio swollen by the arrival of percussionist Nilaja and fellow street rappers David Nelson, Gylan Kain and Felipe Jeliciano, local television picked up on the Last Poets; one such profile brought them to the attention of Alan Douglas, owner of the tiny Douglas Communications label. While nominally a jazz concern (Douglas' own track record included recording Eric Dolphy and John McLaughlin), Douglas was also establishing itself as a home for more unconventional artists. Douglas had already signed Timothy Leary; the Last Poets only added to the label's reputation.

Douglas was also working with Jimi Hendrix at this time. When the Poets came to record their debut album that November, the guitarist dropped by the studio with his current drummer, Buddy Miles; the pair backed Nurridim on one track, "Doriella Du Fontaine," part of a longer "Jail Toasts" suite—oddly, the piece would not make the final album.

*Last Poets* was released in June 1970, around the same time as one track from the set, "Wake Up Niggers," was included in the soundtrack to Mick Jagger's controversial acting debut, *Performance*. It is unlikely whether such an honor impacted upon *Last Poets* own performance. While the soundtrack stiffed, the Poets soared into the pop Top 30, an astonishing achievement for an album of such violent racial intensity—albeit one that history, strangely, appears to have forgotten.

Author David Toop, having noted (in 1999's *Rap Attack 3*) that the Poets set the stage for "wall poems and street verse . . . [to] climb not only the R&B charts but also pop hit parades all over the world," then mourns, "there was little chance of the same success coming to the Last Poets." In fact, the album remained on the R&B chart for close to nine months, and stayed in the pop listings for over seven.

Plans for the Last Poets to tour in the album's wake were

placed on hold when Oyewole was sentenced to 14 years imprisonment on a robbery charge. Further disruption occurred when Nelson, Kain and Luciano broke away to form a rival group, the Original Last Poets, riding the Poets' own success back into the Top 50 in the new year with the album *Right On*.

The Last Poets themselves followed through with *This Is Madness* in April 1971, which brought the team to the attention of President Nixon's Counter-Intelligence Programming list. Less successful than its predecessor, it was also Hassan's farewell. He quit in 1972 to join a religious group.

Recruiting jazz drummer Suliaman El Hadi, Nuriddim and Nilaja recorded *Chastisement*, an album whose increased musical content was described by its makers as "jazzoetry." Two years later, *At Last* descended totally into the realm of free-form jazz. Nuriddim also cut a solo album, 1973's *Hustler's Convention*, under his Lightnin' Rod pseudonym. A concept album resembling a soundtrack album, *Hustler's Convention* included contributions from Eric Gale and Kool & the Gang and became a firm favorite on the early New York hip-hop scene.

The departure of Nilaja in 1974 left Nuriddim the sole remaining Last Poet. With El Hadi and drummer Bernard Purdy, he cut one final album under the band name, *Delights of the Garden* in 1977. The Last Poets effectively disbanded soon after, just as another generation was arising to take up their original mantel.

The Last Poets resurfaced in 1984 as both Nuriddin and Oyewole returned with new singles under the old name, Nuriddin's "Long Enough" and Oyewole's "Super Horror Show." Nuriddin then reunited with El Hadi and, mentored by former P-Funk keyboard player Bernie Worrell and producer Bill Laswell, he released the Last Poets album *Oh My People*, a powerful return to lyrical form that was followed, four years later, *Freedom Express*, recorded in London with Aswad guitarist Curtis Lugay.

Nuriddin then turned his attention to production, working with the British acid-jazz group Galliano; in the meantime, Laswell linked with another founding Poet, Hassan, to record 1993's *Be Bop or Be Dead* album. Oyewole's *25 Years* followed, again cut firmly in the mould of "classic" Last Poets.

By 1994, Hassan, Oyewole and drummer Don "Babatunde" Eaton had claimed the Last Poets name for themselves and cut the *Holy Terror* album with Laswell again at the controls, and contributions from George Clinton and Bootsy Collins. The same core grouping followed through with 1997's *Time Has Come*, aided this time by Pharaoh

Sanders (sax), Senegalese drummer Aiyb Dieng and rapper Chuck D.

Nuriddin and El Hadi retaliated with their own Last Poets release, the "Scatterbrain" single.

### THE LAST POETS COMPLETE DISCOGRAPHY
#### SINGLES
1972 Tribute to Orabi/Bird's Word (Blue Thumb)

#### LPs
**10** 1970 Last Poets (Douglas—#3 R&B/#29 pop)
The sole Poets album to feature all four founding members and the most powerful. Conventional instrumentation is restricted to the tribal percussion; voices provide the rhythms, whether incessantly chanting "next stop" through "On the Subway," "ooh- ah" through "Black Thighs," or simply "niggers . . ." during "Niggers Are Scared of Revolution." Initially disconcerting, *Last Poets* is nevertheless flawlessly arranged, deeply provocative and darkly thought provoking.

**8** 1971 This Is Madness (Douglas—#14 R&B/#104 pop)
**7** 1972 Chastisement (Blue Thumb)
**4** 1974 At Last (Blue Thumb)
Unrecognizable, as the last Last Poet in the house switches off the rapping and delves into the chaos of free form.

**4** 1977 Delights in the Garden (Casablanca)
**5** 1984 Oh My People (Celluloid)
**6** 1988 Freedom Express (Celluloid)
Picking up where its Laswell-produced predecessor left off, powerful jazz-funk instrumentation pushes the vocals along, occasionally detracting from the characteristically strong lyrics, but at least making for a comfortable listening experience.

**7** 1994 Holy Terror (Black Ark/Rykodisc)
**6** 1997 Time Has Come (Mouth Almighty)
Heavily atmospheric, the overall mood is more akin to an electro performance of the *Missa Luba* than any past Poets performance, although too often, things slip into conventional Axion/Laswell patterns and rhythms. Half a great album, half a so-so one.

### LIGHTNIN' ROD (NURIDDIM)
#### LP
**8** 1973 Hustler's Convention (Douglas)
With Kool & the Gang serving up the funk stew, Nuriddim tracks a rap concept album jammed with gamblers, pimps and general double dealers—the soundtrack to the greatest blaxploitation movie never made.

## ABIODUN OYEWOLE

**LP**

**8** **1994 25 Years (Axiom)**
The best of the spin-offs opens with the ghost of the first Poets' "tick tock" refrain, looped through a virtual amalgam of early-Poets/Gil Scott Heron revolutionary rhetoric. The closing "25 Years," meantime, sums up Oyewole's own reflections on the years that have passed since that time. It's as brutally truthful as anything he has ever said.

## UMAR BIN HASSAN

**LP**

**6** **1993 Be Bop or Be Dead (Axiom)**

## THE ORIGINAL LAST POETS

**7** **1971 Right On! (Juggernaut—#43 R&B/#106 pop)**
Despite its historically dubious origins, a worthy (if overly similar) successor to *Last Poets*.

### SELECTED SAMPLES

Black People What Y'all Gon' Do Chant — Professor Griff & the Last Asiatic Disciples: Real African People (1990)

Black Soldier — X-Clan: Tribal Jam (1990)

Mean Machine — M.A.A.R.S.: Pump Up the Volume (1987)

Niggers Are Afraid of Revolution — Brand Nubian: Concerto in X Minor (1991)

Related To What? — 2 Live Crew: Get the Fuck out of My House (1989)

Run Nigga — NWA: 100 Miles and Runnin' (1990)

Run Nigga — Yo-Yo: Girls Got a Gun (1993)

Time — A Tribe Called Quest: Excursions (1991)

Time — Brand Nubian: Concerto in X Minor (1991)

Time — Justice System: Due Our Time (1994)

Tribute to Obabi — A Tribe Called Quest: Excursions (1991)

Tribute to Obabi — X-Clan: Shaft's Big Score (1990)

True Blues — Terminator X & Andreas 13: The Blues (1991)

## THE MAR-KEYS

**FORMED:** *1958, Memphis, TN*
**ORIGINAL LINE-UP:** *Packy Axton (tnr sax), Steve Cropper (b. 10/21/41, Willow Spring, MO—kybds, gtr), Charlie Freeman (gtr), Donald Dunn (b. 11/24/41—Memphis TN—bs), Don Nix (b. 9/27/41, Memphis TN—sax), Jerry Lee "Smoochy" Smith (kybds), Terry Johnson (drms)*

A high school R&B instrumental outfit, the Royal Spades became houseband at the Satellite (soon to be Stax) label in 1960; label co-owner Estelle Axton's was tenor saxophonist Packy's mother.

Renamed the Mar-Keys, early personnel changes set the stage for their career, with the departure of Freeman (he later returned for live work) and the arrival of Joe Arnold (tenor sax) and Bob Snyder (baritone). In this form the Mar-Keys cut their first single, "Last Night," for release in June 1961.

Conceived more or less as a Hank Ballard tribute, which was simultaneously ideal for dancing the twist (the popular dance-craze of the day), the sound that rapidly came to epitomize the little Memphis label was born on "Last Night," a swinging Southern-flavored honk, powered by Johnson's thumping drums and a galloping organ courtesy of Cropper and Smith.

Satellite became Stax in 1961; the first release on the new label was the Mar-Keys' "The Morning After," both titularly and musically an obvious follow-up to "Last Night," possibly too obvious. Nowhere near as memorable, it struggled into the R&B Top 60.

Cropper quit the Mar-Keys following disagreements with Packy Axton during their first national tour; he joined fellow Stax studio mavens Booker T. & the MGs and, over the next two years, the two groups became increasingly intertwined. A string of subsequent Mar-Keys singles were written by and featured members of the MGs, with their final single, January 1963's "Bo Deal," a tremendous Cropper composed barrage of bass.

With Dunn having followed Cropper into the MGs, the Mar-Keys broke up during 1964. Nix went into sessions and production, later joining Delaney and Bonnie's group (he also wrote the R&B anthem "Goin' Down"); Freeman joined the Dixie Flyers; Axton, meanwhile, formed another Stax instrumental act, the Barracudas. (Their "Yank Me (Doodle)" single featured keyboards from Isaac Hayes.) From there, Axton broke with the label for a time, linking with Los Angeles DJ The Magnificent Montague's Pure Soul label for November 1965's "Hole in the Wall"—an R&B Top Five 45 that featured Booker T. & the MGs among the backing musicians. (Axton and Freeman both passed away during the 1970s.)

Meanwhile, Stax horn players Wayne Jackson and Andrew Love revived the Mar-Keys name during late summer 1964, cutting a pair of Stax 45s, "Bush Bash" and Isaac Hayes' "Banana Juice," with a band that again, at least partly, comprised MGs members. The spirit of the Mar-Keys was also invoked in early 1965 when "Boot-Leg," an outtake from the Axton-era's last days, was activated as a single under the MGs name, even though Booker T. was not even present during the session. Hayes, again, filled in.

Equally bizarre circumstances surrounded the revitalized Mar-Keys' own next single. "Philly Dog" was born out of a Rufus Thomas session that simply hadn't gelled.

Thomas left, so the musicians (Jackson, Love and tenor saxophonist Gene Parker fronted the lineup) continued playing with the song, eventually relaxing into a jam that had little to do with Thomas' own composition (they retained his name in the writing credits as a courtesy) but took on a life of its own regardless.

In June 1967, the Mar-Keys (alongside Booker T. & the MGs) accompanied Otis Redding at the Monterey Pop Festival; by 1969, however, Jackson and Love had allowed the Mar-Keys' name to slip away, preferring to work as the Memphis Horns. *Memphis Experience*, including a phenomenal version of the Temptations' "Cloud Nine," was their final release under the old name.

As the Horns, and with a constantly changing lineup, Jackson and Love established themselves among the most in-demand horn sections of the 1970s, at the same time recording several strong albums in their own right, with assistance from Booker T. and Charlie Freeman's Dixie Flyers. A deal with RCA launched the band on its most successful period, with four top-selling singles during 1976–78.

Though the Horns were less active during the '80s, Jackson and Love maintained their partnership, sessioning with rockers U2, Primal Scream, Billy Joel, Sting, etc. A more lasting relationship was launched with Robert Cray, with whom they first recorded in 1990 and were still touring in 1999. The duo also recorded their own *Flame Out* album in 1992. Shortly after, the original Mar-Keys' best-known number, "Last Night," was resurrected as the theme tune to the BBC TV comedy *Bottom*.

### THE MAR-KEYS DISCOGRAPHY
#### CHART LOG
1961 Last Night/Night Before (Satellite—#2 R&B/#3 pop)
1966 Philly Dog/Honey Pot (Stax—#19 R&B/#89 pop)

#### ALBUMS
**6** 1961 Last Night (Stax)
Neither of the Mar-Keys' albums live up to the visceral thrill of their debut hit, with *Last Night* itself suffering from a surfeit of soundalikes.
**5** 1962 Do the Popeye with the Mar-Kays (Stax)
**6** 1966 Great Memphis Sound (Stax)
The punchy reinvention of the band as a horn section plus accompanists resulted in an album packed with instrumentals that at least threatened the supremacy of "Last Night." None, however, surpass it.
**6** 1968 Mellow Jello (Stax)
**8** 1969 Damnifiknow (Stax—#34 R&B)

The Mar-Keys' only chart album, and their best. The horns have a unique character of their own, shading the fringes of the funk to come, but remembering Stax's own traditions too.
**6** 1971 Memphis Experience (Stax)

### SELECTED COMPILATIONS AND ARCHIVE RELEASES
**6** 1967 Back to Back (split LP w/Booker T. & the MGs) (Stax)

### SELECTED SAMPLES
Grab This Thing — Cypress Hill: Insane in the Brain (1993)
Grab This Thing — Grand Puba: 360 Degrees (What Goes Around) (1992)
Grab This Thing — Pete Rock & CL Smooth: The Creator (1991)

### MEMPHIS HORNS
#### CHART LOG
1976 Get Up and Dance/Don't Abuse It (RCA—#61 R&B/#108 pop)
1977 What the Funk/Love Is Happiness (RCA—#83 R&B)
1977 Just for Your Love/Keep On Smilin' (RCA—#17 R&B/#101 pop)
1978 Our Love Will Survive/(Let's Go) All the Way (RCA—#42 R&B)

#### LPs
**8** 1970 Memphis Horns (Cotillion)
As much a shop window for the Horns' wares as an album per se, nevertheless a powerpacked jamboree pushing deep into both rock and funk territory.
**7** 1972 Horns for Everything (Million)
**5** 1976 High on Music (RCA)
**5** 1977 Get Up and Dance (RCA—#32 R&B/#201 pop)
**6** 1978 Band II (RCA—#48 R&B/#163 pop)
Jim Gilstrap, David T. Walker and Michael McDonald weigh in on vocals, as the Horns (and arranger Sonny Burke) extract exquisite soul smoothies from "Our Love Will Survive," "Livin' for the Music" and "You."
**4** 1979 Welcome to Memphis (RCA)

### WAYNE JACKSON/ANDREW LOVE
**5** 1992 Flame Out (Lucky Seven)

### THE ROBERT CRAY BAND, FEATURING THE MEMPHIS HORNS
**6** 1990 Midnight Stroll (Mercury—#81 R&B/#51 pop)

### SELECTED SAMPLES
Just for Your Love—Leaders of the New School: What's Next? (1993)

## MEMPHIS HORNS, see MAR-KEYS

## THE PARLIAMENTS, see GEORGE CLINTON (PART 2)

## SANTANA, see FRONTIERS OF FUNK: THE PSYCHE-FUNKA-DELIA EXPERIENCE

## SLY AND THE FAMILY STONE, see SLY STONE

## STAX/VOLT RECORDS

With the possible exception of Motown, Stax is the most famous soul/R&B label in the world and home to some of the best-loved artists. Otis Redding, Sam & Dave, Rufus Thomas, the Mar-Keys, Isaac Hayes, Eddie Floyd and Johnnie Taylor did more than create great records, they laid the foundations for everything the genre went on to achieve, while the story of funk, in particular, looked to the Stax stable not only for guidance, but for its very parenthood.

Stax was launched by Jim Stewart, a Memphis State graduate and former Army Special Serviceman. A talented fiddler, he spent his evenings playing with various Western swing groups, with his interests also turning toward record production. In 1957, Stewart cut a single with DJ Fred Bylar, a country song called "Blue Roses," released on his own Satellite label—named for the recently launched Russian space probe *Sputnik*.

The following year, with financing from Stewart's sister Estelle Axton, Satellite purchased its own recording equipment and set up shop in a Brunswick, TN, warehouse, before returning to Memphis in 1960 and moving into a disused movie theater on East McLemore. The label's product was sold from a record store at the front of the building.

Having achieved early hits with the father-daughter team Rufus and Carla Thomas, in 1961, the label learned of an older, California-based company with a claim on the Satellite name. Moving to head off any possible problems, Stewart and Axton decided to rename their company, combining the first two letters of their surnames to create Stax.

The label had already recruited its own houseband, Axton's son Packy's high school combo, the Royal Spades. Renamed the Mar-Keys, this group provided backing on most early label 45s, until the emergence of Booker T. & the MGs at the sister label Volt. Joined by Mar-Key guitarist Steve Cropper, the MGs first complemented, but ultimately succeeded the Mar-Keys as the very sound of Stax Records. Nevertheless, the Mar-Keys' debut single, "Last Night," remained a crucial step in the label's development.

Though there are certainly similarities to be gleaned by playing "Last Night" side by side with James Brown's "Suds" (released just weeks earlier) and though, too, the company's early ear for country and pop had more or less been retired by this point, still records like Prince Conley's (admittedly spellbinding) blues "I'm Going Home" and ballads and slow movers by the Thomases and Barbara Stephens sounded positively old-fashioned alongside the Mar-Keys.

The instrumental prowess of Stax's housebands remained the label's most identifiable feature, but it was with vocal talent that the company made its name. In October 1962, the label released the first single by Otis Redding. William Bell, the Mad Lads, Sam & Dave, David Porter, Johnnie Taylor, Isaac Hayes, Eddie Floyd and bluesman Albert King joined the roster over the next five years, often performing songs written and/or produced by members of the MGs.

As Stax's best-known musicians, the MGs plus the Mar-Keys' horn section also accompanied Otis Redding to the Monterey Pop Festival in June 1967. Alongside Jimi Hendrix, Redding emerged one of the stars of the performance; however, fate would not allow him to truly follow up the triumph.

During fall 1967, Redding was kept out of action following an operation to remove polyps from his throat; he recovered and went straight into the studio with producer Cropper for three weeks. It was December 8 before he again faced his public, hooking up with Stax studio ingenues the Bar-Kays for shows in Nashville, Cleveland and Madison. The plane carrying Redding and the musicians crashed as it approached the latter city—the singer and all but two of the group were killed.

Written by Cropper and Redding himself while they were in California for Monterey, "(Sitting on The) Dock of the Bay" (the last song Redding ever recorded) was released a month later. His first ever pop Top 20 hit, it spent a month atop that chart and three weeks at #1 on the R&B lists. Cropper and the rest of the MGs subsequently completed the album Redding had been working on; it, too, was an R&B chart-topper.

Redding's death coincided with the end of another era, as Stax's long-standing relationship with Atlantic Records came to a close in May 1968. However, the label itself went from strength to strength as a new generation moved up to take Stax into the '70s.

The undisputed star of the newly formed Enterprise subsidiary, Isaac Hayes emerged from the shadows of songwriting and sessions to become a superstar; the Staple Singers, the Emotions and the Dramatics followed, while the Bar-Kays were reborn first as the new Stax houseband, then as hitmakers in their own right. 1972's *Wattstax*, a day long festival showcasing the best of current Stax talent, spun off one of the most successful music movies of the early decade.

By the mid-'70s, however, the label's importance and impact alike were fading. A handful of notable releases included the soundtracks to *Sweet Sweetback's Baadasss Re-*

*venge* and the *Wattstax* movie; for the most part, however, Stax had swung away from even a pretence of its earlier pre-eminence.

Attempts to move into rock, via oddball UK prog act Skin Alley and some early Black Oak Arkansas material were doomed to failure, while 1974 saw Stax sign teenaged British singer Lena Zavaroni, an unashamedly MOR performer discovered via a primetime TV talent contest called *Opportunity Knocks*. Stax could fall no further from grace, and beset, too, by mounting financial problems by 1976, the label had effectively ceased operations. The following year, company and catalog were purchased by Fantasy Records.

### STAX RECORDS DISCOGRAPHY 1959–72
### SINGLES

The entire Satellite/Stax/Volt etc. singles catalog has been presented within three CD box sets (A-sides only) as follows:
1991 The Complete Stax/Volt Singles 1959–1968
1993 The Complete Stax/Volt Soul Singles, Vol. 2: 1968–1971
1994 The Complete Stax/Volt Soul Singles, Vol. 3: 1972–1975

### LPs
701 Booker T. & the MGs: Green Onions
702 Gus Cannon (Banjo & Vocal with Will Shade): Walk Right In
703 various artists: The Treasure Chest of Goldies
704 Rufus Thomas: Walking the Dog
705 Booker T. & the MGs: Soul Dressing
706 Carla Thomas: Comfort Me
707 Mar-Keys: Great Memphis Sound
708 Sam & Dave: Hold On I'm Comin'
709 Carla Thomas: Carla
710 various artists: Memphis Gold
711 Booker T. & the MGs: And Now
712 Sam & Dave: Double Dynamite
713 Booker T. & the MGs: In the Christmas Spirit
714 Eddie Floyd: Knock on Wood
715 Johnnie Taylor: Wanted One Soul Singer
716 Otis Redding/Carla Thomas: King and Queen
717 Booker T. & the MGs: Hip Hug-Her
718 Carla Thomas: The Queen Alone
719 William Bell: Soul of a Bell
720 Mar-Keys/Booker T. & the MGs: Back to Back
721 various artists: Live in London, Vol. 1
722 various artists: Live in London, Vol. 2
723 Albert King: Born Under a Bad Sign
724 Carla Thomas: Live at the Bohemian Cavern (unissued)
724 Booker T. & the MGs: Doin' Our Thing
725 Sam & Dave: Soul Men
726 various artists: Memphis Gold, Vol. 2
2001 Booker T. & the MGs: Soul Limbo

2002 Eddie Floyd: I've Never Found a Girl
2003 Albert King: Live Wire/Blues Power
2004 Staple Singers: Soul Folk in Action
2005 Johnnie Taylor: Who's Making Love
2006 Booker T. & the MGs: Uptight (Soundtrack)
2007 various artists: Soul Explosion
2008 Johnnie Taylor: Raw Blues
2009 Booker T. & the MGs: The Booker T. Set
2010 Albert King: Years Gone By
2011 Eddie Floyd: Rare Stamps
2012 Johnnie Taylor: Rare Stamps
2013 John Lee Hooker: That's Where It's At
2014 William Bell: Bound to Happen
2015 Albert King: King Does the King's Thing
2016 Staple Singers: We'll Get Over
2017 Eddie Floyd: You've Got To Have Eddie
2018 Soul Children: Soul Children
2019 Carla Thomas: Memphis Queen
2020 Cropper/King/Pop Staples: Jammed Together
2021 Ollie & the Nightingales: Ollie & Nightingales
2022 Rufus Thomas: May I Have Your Ticket Please (unissued)
2023 Johnnie Taylor: The . . . Philosophy Continues
2024 various artists: Boy Meets Girl
2025 Mar-Keys: Damifiknow!
2026 Delaney & Bonnie: Home
2027 Booker T. & the MGs: McLemore Avenue
2028 Rufus Thomas: Do the Funky Chicken
2029 Eddie Floyd: California Girl
2030 Johnnie Taylor: One Step Beyond
2031 various artists: Gold Soul
2032 Johnnie Taylor: Greatest Hits
2033 Booker T. & the MGs: Greatest Hits
2034 Staple Singers: Staple Swingers
2035 Booker T. & the MGs: Melting Pot
2036 Mar-Keys: Memphis Experience
2037 William Bell: Wow . . .
2038 Israel Tolbert: Popper Stopper
2039 Rufus Thomas: Doing the Push and Pull at PJ's
2040 Albert King: Lovejoy
2041 Eddie Floyd: Down to Earth
2042 Ernie Hines: Electrified (unissued)
2043 Soul Children: Best of Two Worlds
2044 Carla Thomas: Love Means . . .
2045 Jean Knight: Mr. Big Stuff
2046 Calvin Scott: I'm Not Blind . . . I Just Can't See
2047 Jimmy McCracklin: Yesterday Is Gone

### VOLT LABEL LISTING
### LPs
411 Otis Redding: Sings Soul Ballads

412 Otis Redding: Otis Blue

413 Otis Redding: The Soul Album

414 Mad Lads: In Action

415 Otis Redding: Complete & Unbelievable: The Otis Redding Dictionary of Soul

416 Otis Redding: Live in Europe

417 Bar-Kays: Soul Finger

418 Otis Redding: History Of

419 Otis Redding: The Dock of the Bay

6001 Barnes/Mancha: Rare Stamps

6002 Darrell Banks: Here To Stay

6003 Jimmy Hughes: Something Special

6004 Bar-Kays: Gotta Groove

6005 Mad Lads: Mad, Mad, Mad, Mad Lads

6006 Steve Cropper: With a Little Help from My Friends

6007 Mavis Staples: Mavis Staples

6008 Emotions: So I Can Love You

6009 Maceo Woods: Hello, Sunshine

6010 Mavis Staples: Only for the Lonely

6011 Bar-Kays: Black Rock

6012 Margie Joseph: Makes a New Impression

6013 Maceo Woods: Step to Jesus

6014 Kim Weston: Kim Kim Kim

6015 Emotions: Untouched

6016 Margie Joseph: Phase 2

6017 Lou Johnson: With You in Mind

6018 Dramatics: Whatcha See Is Whatcha Get

6019 Dramatics: A Dramatic Experience

6020 Mad Lads: A New Beginning

6021 Emotions: Songs of Innocence, Songs of Experience (unissued)

6022 Inez Foxx: At Memphis

6023 Bar-Kays: Cold Blooded

## SLY STONE

**BORN:** *Sylvester Stewart, 3/15/43, Denton, TX*

As one of the single most influential figures in the entire history of Black music, Sly Stone presides over a legacy of almost unremitting musical brilliance; as one of the most wasteful figures in that same lexicon, his career simultaneously represents some of its greatest lost opportunities. Through the early '60s, Stone's genius was evident in his writing and production work; through the latter part of that decade, it was visible in everything he did. But the shattering success that he attained was to exact a price every bit as large as the legend he created, until even Stone's music was but a shadow of its former self and the man himself had withdrawn completely.

Nevertheless, during the five years when Stone and his Family Stone were at their peak, their revolutionary fusion of psychedelic soul and rock-shocked funk not only delivered a stream of bestselling albums, it rewrote itself into the very fabric of modern music. Acts as far apart as Jane's Addiction, Duran Duran, Fred Wesley and the Jazz Crusaders have covered Stone's music, while his acknowledged influence—as a musician, a visionary and simply as a cultural icon—ensures that of his contemporaries and peers, only James Brown and George Clinton could possibly claim to rival his impact.

Stone was just eight when he made his recording debut, alongside brother Freddie and sisters Rose, Vaetta (all vcls) and Loretta (pno) as the Stewart Four. The quintet cut a 78 for their Sunday School, comprising the hymns "On the Battlefield for My Lord" and "Walking in Jesus' Name." Already Stone was teaching himself guitar and piano; over the next few years, he also mastered bass, drums and horns and, after leaving school, he enrolled in a Music Theory course at Vallejo's Solano College.

With brother Freddie, Stone formed the Stewart Brothers and cut a pair of doo-wop singles for local labels Ensign and Keen; he also cut one single under the pseudonym of Danny Stewart and a second under his own name, before quitting Texas for the Bay Area. There he formed a new band, the Biscaynes, who swiftly became the Viscanes, recording doo-wop, but onstage performing an incendiary pop/R&B hybrid.

Stone's interests continued in that direction following the Viscanes' breakup. He landed a gig as DJ at KSOL in Oakland and put together a one-man road show, based equally upon his hard-hitting musical tastes and already outrageous personality. He was also forging a relationship with Top 40 DJs Bobby Mitchell and Tom Donahue as they set about forming their own record label, Autumn Records. Brought onboard as Autumn's in-house composer and producer, a position he kept for the next three years, Stone was responsible for hits by Bobby Freeman and the Beau Brummels, alongside garage punks the Chosen Few, the Mojo Men and the Spearmints.

Warner Brothers paired Stone with soul singer Gloria Scott; he also recorded some demos with the young Billy Preston, "Ain't That Lovin' You Baby" and "Little Latin Lupe Lu." In terms of actual releases, his own recording career might well have stalled through this period (there were just three Autumn releases by Stone alone, the dance-craze cash-in "I Just Learned How To Swim," "Buttermilk" and "Temptation Walk"), but his studio expertise was increasing all the time.

An album's worth of outtakes from the Autumn period

**Sly Stone at the Woodstock festival: there really was a riot going on.**

were subsequently released across sundry albums, indicating just how far reaching Stone's tastes were. "In the Still of the Night" is a moody Spector-esque mega-production; "Don't Say I Didn't Warn You" is quintessential girl group material; "The Seventh Son" was convincing Chicago R&B; "Every Dog Has His Day" was subsequently reworked as "Dog." Nothing was wasted.

Amid such activity, Stone kept a close eye on the local club scene, watching as a San Francisco sound began radiating out from Haight Ashbury and tailoring his radio show—now broadcast through Oakland's KDIA—toward all that was happening on the streets. He cut a single with the Great Society, led by the pre-Jefferson Airplane Grace Slick and, mindful of the direction in which the musical wind was blowing, Stone returned to regular live work with a new act, the punningly named Stoners, featuring sister Rose and trumpeter Cynthia Robinson. The Stoners in turn developed into the Family Stone, following the arrival of brother Freddie, horn player Jerry Martini, Larry Graham (bass) and Greg Errico (drms).

Early demos by the band include versions of Wink Mar-

tindale's "Deck of Cards," Otis Redding's "I Can't Turn You Loose" and Herbie Hancock's "Watermelon Man," alongside a clutch of increasingly distinctive Stone originals, including the disjointed Stax-esque instrumental "Rock Dirge," "Take My Advice" and "If You Were Blue."

Stone's involvement with Autumn had faded by now; in late 1966, the new team made their debut with a single for the independent Loadstone label, a reasonably faithful rendition of Otis Redding's "I Can't Turn You Loose" alongside Stone's own "I Ain't Got Nobody." It did little commercially, but so impressed Columbia's Epic subsidiary that they scooped up the Family Stone in early 1967, at a time when many other San Francisco concerns (the Grateful Dead and the Airplane, of course, notwithstanding) were still struggling to land a local label deal.

The Family Stone's appeal was obvious from the outset. While skin color persuaded the marketing department to target them toward a soul and R&B audience, their music flew off on another tangent altogether, nodding toward Frank Zappa's Mothers of Invention in one moment, toward the Fifth Dimension in another, and—though America had yet to experience him in his full glory—Jimi Hendrix in another.

The only constant was the dance rhythms that were pounded out by both drummer Errico and bassist Graham, made even James Brown's assault sound muted. It was a wild potpourri of sound and sensation, effortlessly slammed onto tape once Stone got his Family into the studio to record their debut album. The ensuing record's title, *A Whole New Thing*, only began to describe its contents.

It is said that Epic had very little understanding of their latest recruit; that the suits simply didn't know what to make of a man who answered to the name Sylvester one day and Sly the next, and frequently credited songs to both of them at once. In later years, the issue of ego versus alter-ego was blamed for many of Stone's subsequent problems; at the time, however, the apparent ease with which Stone could slip between the mild-mannered one and the wild child other was simply fascinating.

Epic decided not to pull a single from the album, whether through genuine uncertainty or through an awareness of the nature of the scene from which Stone had emerged. Although the LP record had been around for over a decade at that point, the industry instinct hitherto insisted that albums were of little overall importance, that the majority of acts need do nothing more than tape a batch of filler material to wrap around their most recent singles.

Now the mood was changing, at least in the rock world. There, the example of superstars like the Beatles, Bob Dylan and their ilk had given the LP a brand new importance. Still, Epic was taking a major chance in affording the Family Stone a similar luxury; no Black act had ever succeeded in winning a rock audience before, no rock audience had ever given itself over to a R&B group. Everybody had heard of crossover hits; Epic was hoping for a crossover *act*, and Stone was ready to deliver.

The Family Stone had already recorded "(I Want To Take You) Higher" before they began work on their next album; released as a single in late 1967 it did not chart, but it made radio playlists regardless and set the stage for their next release, "Dance to the Music." An instant smash in the new year, it was followed by an album of the same name, a piece de resistance that stripped away all the esotericism of its predecessor and went straight for the funk-rock jugular. The album was only a minor hit, but again, it blazed a trail, which the Family Stone wasn't slow to follow.

There would be one hiccup; reacting to the success of "Dance to the Music," the band quickly turned out a third album, *Life*, devoted almost in its entirety to flippant dance music. Illustrating the uncertainty with which both the Black and White markets viewed Stone, *Life* barely registered anywhere—five weeks climbing to and from #195 on the pop charts and not a mention on the R&B listings. A single of the title track fared equally poorly, but Stone already had salvation in his palm, a new 45, "Everyday People." This time, it went all the way to #1.

*Stand!* followed in April 1969, bringing with it a remarkable double A-sided single, the title track, backed by a dramatic remake of "(I Want To Take You) Higher," which climbed even further in stature following the Family Stone's appearance at the Woodstock festival. Both on the day and, later, in the movie of the event, "Higher" became a mammoth mantra, half a million festival-goers dancing and chanting along with Stone and establishing the song, in the process, as a part of the hippy landscape.

Stone was at his peak. *Stand!* was a massive hit—within a year, even James Brown had borrowed one of its song titles, "Sex Machine." A new single, "Hot Fun in the Summertime," soared to #2. When the band closed the year with another double A-side, coupling the hippy soul of "Everybody Is a Star" with the hard-hitting funk of "Thank You (Falettinme Be Mice Elf Agin)," nobody was surprised to see the two sides respectively top the pop and R&B charts.

1970 should have been a year of consolidation; instead, it became one of controversy. Stone's late arrival for a show in DC provoked a major riot, while he lost the support of many Black radio stations after commenting angrily on what he saw as their divisive (Blacks-only) playlisting policies. Epic's hopes for a new album were left to wither; in their stead came legends of debauchery, gunplay and violence, a nonstop party fuelled by drugs, sex and alcohol, and by a parade of visitors, musicians and hangers-on alike.

There was talk of threats made by Black militants who disliked Stone's conciliatory approach toward rock, and from White supremacists who disapproved of the same thing for opposite reasons. Everywhere one turned there was another Stone story, more outrageous than the last, and the band's only recordings came when Stone led them into the studio to back Joe Hicks (aka Abaci Dream) on his "I'm Going Home" and "Life and Death in G & A" singles. Finally Epic pulled out a greatest hits collection as a stopgap and hoped that the wayward star might deliver the following year.

He did, eventually. With the lineup enlivened by the presence of Bobby Womack, among others, fall 1971 finally brought the darkly political *There's a Riot Going On*. An instant hit, of course, it was accompanied by the chart-topping (and deeply self-analytical) "Family Affair" single, a powerful follow-up, "Runnin' Away," and a fresh bout of very bizarre publicity, after a US record buyer sued on the grounds that the album's title track was, in fact, silence.

*There's a Riot Going On* was the classic Family Stone's final album. Graham quit to form his own Graham Central Station; Errico, too, departed. Preparing to return to the studio, Stone replaced them with Rusty Allen and Andy Newmark, then added his brother-in-law Bubba Banks, saxophonist Pat Rizzo and the vocal trio Little Sister, led by the youngest Stone sibling, Vaetta. "Right now I've got myself a whole new lease on life," he told Britain's *New Musical Express*. "You've just gotta go so far one way and then you become more aware. There's so much vitality around me these days. Nowadays it's fun for me to go on stage and it's also fun for me to come offstage, knowing I've done a good show."

He claimed to have changed. "Some of the things that happened in the past were my fault, but I'm sure I've now corrected. All those things like why we didn't turn up for dates or why we were late or why we kept people waiting. Well, we're no longer associated with those reasons — or. . . those people."

Stone's professed rebirth survived just one album, 1973's *Fresh*, widely regarded as the last essential Family Stone release. The 1974 *Small Talk* album, recorded with drummer Bill Lordan replacing Newmark, was an unsatisfying record that Stone himself claimed was his celebration of love (he married girlfriend Kathy Silva onstage at Madison Square Garden later in the year) and laziness — summed up in what many critics felt was the ominously autobiographical "Can't Strain My Brain."

Stone broke up the Family Stone following their 1974 tour and, in 1975, released his first solo album, *High on You*; it fared poorly and Stone promptly convened a new Family Stone for 1976's *Heard Ya Missed Me, Well I'm Back*. Unfortunately, he'd apparently heard wrong and Stone sank back into legend, this time remaining there for much of the remainder of the decade.

Signing to Warner Brothers, he finally re-emerged in 1979 with *Back on the Right Track*, an optimistically titled debut that his old label, Epic, did their best to undermine with their own version of a "new" album, a collection of disco mixes of Stone's greatest hits, propitiously dubbed *Ten Years Too Soon*.

Neither release performed well (the latter mercifully so), and Stone was next sighted alongside George Clinton in what was, though few people realized it, the last gasp of the P-Funk empire. Funkadelic's *The Electric Spanking of War Babies*, the album that introduced Stone to the troupe, was their last; shortly after, Clinton's Uncle Jam label also collapsed, taking with it hopes for a new Stone album any time soon.

Stone stuck around for the formation of Clinton's next creation, the P-Funk All-Stars; a series of 1981 sessions not only produced material for the *Urban Dancefloor Guerillas* album, but also turned up the first fruits of what became Stone's own next album.

Clinton's *Family Series Volume One* collection features one wild Stone/Clinton demo from this period, "Who in the Funk Do You Think You Are?"; reworked, the song reappeared on Stone's *Ain't but the One Way* album in 1983. He and Womack then teamed up for the latter's *The Poet* album cycle, while a union with Jesse Johnson (ex-Time) brought a surprise success with "Crazay" in 1986.

Temporarily reinvigorated, Stone signed with A&M and cut a new single, "Eek-a-Bo-Static." It did nothing, however, and plans for an album fell through; instead, his only other recording that year was a duet, "Love and Affection," with the Motels' Martha Davis, recorded for the *Soul Man* movie soundtrack.

Having already been busted for coke possession in 1983, Stone reached his personal nadir in 1989 when he was sentenced to nine months in a federal drug clinic, following a cocaine bust. The decade since then continued turbulent and, in musical terms, silent, his only appearances being on 13 Cats' 1991 album *March of the 13 Cats* and at The Rock and Roll Hall of Fame induction ceremony in 1993. Of course, rumors of a return to action have circulated without a break, while George Clinton and Prince have both purportedly discussed working with him. (Larry Graham's association with Prince has added further fuel to that particular legend.) Further reports have linked Stone with Avenue Records, home of War's back catalog.

### SLY STONE COMPLETE DISCOGRAPHY
### SINGLES/CHART LOG
### THE STEWART FOUR
1952 On the Battlefield for My Lord/Walking in Jesus' Name (Church of God in Christ, Northern Sunday School Division)

### THE STEWART BROTHERS
1959 The Rat/Ra Ra Roo (Ensign)
1960 Sleep on the Porch/Yum Yum Yum (Keen)

### DANNY STEWART
1961 A Long Time Alone/I'm Just a Fool (Luke)

**SYLVESTER STEWART**

1961 Help Me with My Broken Heart/A Long Time Alone (G&P)

**THE BISCAYNES**

1961 Yellow Moon/Uncle Sam Needs You (VPM)

**THE VISCANES**

1961 Yellow Moon/Heavenly Angel (VPM)

1961 Stop What You're Doing/I Guess I'll Be (Tropo)

**SLY STEWART**

1964 I Just Learned How To Swim/Scat Swim (Autumn)

**SLY**

1965 Buttermilk (part one)/(part two) (Autumn)

1965 Temptation Walk (part one)/(part two) (Autumn)

**SLY & THE FAMILY STONE**

1966 I Ain't Got Nobody/I Can't Turn You Loose (Loadstone)

1967 I Want To Take You Higher/Underdog (Epic)

1968 Dance to the Music/Let Me Hear It from You (Epic #9 R&B/#8 pop)

1968 Life/M'Lady (Epic—#93 pop)

1968 Everyday People (Epic #1 R&B/#1 pop)/Sing a Simple Song (#28 R&B/#89 pop)

1969 Stand (Epic #14 R&B/#22 pop)/I Want To Take You Higher (#24 R&B/#60 pop)

1969 Hot Fun in the Summertime/Fun (Epic #3 R&B/#2 pop)

1970 Thank You (Falettinme Be Mice Elf Agin) (Epic #1 R&B/Everybody Is a Star (#1 pop)

1971 Family Affair/Luv'n'Haight (Epic #1 R&B/#1 pop)

1972 Runnin' Away/Brave and Strong (Epic #15 R&B/#23 pop)

1972 Smilin'/Luv'n'Haight (Epic #21 R&B/#42 pop)

1973 If You Want Me To Stay/Thankful 'n' Thoughtful (Epic #3 R&B/#12 pop)

1973 Frisky (Epic #28 R&B/#79 pop)/If It Were Left Up to Me (#57 R&B)

1974 Time for Livin'/Small Talk (Epic #10 R&B/#32 pop)

1974 Loose Booty/Can't Strain My Breath (Epic #22 R&B/#84 pop)

1977 Family Again/Nothing Less Than Happiness (Epic #85 F&B)

1979 Remember Who You Are/Sheer Energy (Warners #38 R&B/#104 pop)

1980 Same Thing/Who's To Say (Warners)

**SLY STONE**

1975 I Get High on You/That's Loving You (Epic #3 R&B/#52 pop)

1975 Le Lo Li/Who Do You Love (Epic #75 R&B)

1976 Crossword Puzzle/Greed (Epic)

**SLY STONE/JESSE JOHNSON**

1986 Crazay/Drive Yo Cadillac (A&M #2 R&B/#53 pop)

**LPs**

**SLY & THE FAMILY STONE**

**8** 1967 A Whole New Thing (Epic)

Purposefully obtuse, no genuinely standout tracks, but home, nevertheless, to some remarkable grooves best ex-

perienced in one breathless sitting. The 1995 reissue appends the previously unreleased gem "What Would I Do."

**9** 1968 Dance to the Music (Epic—#11 R&B/142 pop)

The first unqualified masterpiece. Concise on the hits, majestic on the medley, Stone's rocking R&B awareness takes on a classic pop edge too. Is there anyone who can't sing "Dance to the Music"?

**7** 1969 Life (Epic—#195 pop)

Rushed and insubstantial, but tight enough to include "M'Lady" (the entire album's UK title) and the bouncing "Fun."

**9** 1969 Stand! (Epic—#3 R&B/#13 pop)

Impossible to believe this album was released as early as 1969; impossible, too, to believe that it took the rest of the world so long to catch up with it. "Everyday People" can seem a little cloying (although it isn't), but "Stand," the revised "Higher" and the unequivocal chant "Don't Call Me Nigger, Whitey" don't even look at rock and R&B traditions. Slyly stoned to the $n$th degree, they reinvent them.

**10** 1971 There's a Riot Goin' On (Epic—#1 R&B/#1 pop)

The deep funk drive of "Thank You for Talkin' to Me Africa" (remaking the earlier ". . . Falettin Me") is a deceptively familiar closing cut. Elsewhere, however, the album alternately drifts and drives across the landscapes laid out by *Stand*, en route to the whispered, creeping paranoia of "Family Affair," the laconic sweetness of "(You Caught Me) Smilin'" and "Just like a Baby" and the cut 'n' thrust vamp of "Africa Talks to You." Loose-limbed but never uncoordinated, it's funk from under the floorboards. Way under.

**7** 1973 Fresh (EPIC—#1 R&B/#7 pop)

Adding little to the sound perfected on its two predecessors, but bolstered by the ineffable "If You Want Me To Stay" and a crooked-grin revamp of "Dance to the Music" ("Keep On Dancing"), *Fresh* also serves up Rose and Sly's genuinely haunting, and somehow regretful take on "Que Sera Sera."

**6** 1974 Small Talk (Epic—#15 pop)

**5** 1976 Heard Ya Missed Me, Well I'm Back (Epic—#33 R&B)

**5** 1979 Back on the Right Track (Epic—#31 R&B/#152 pop)

**SLY STONE**

**LPs**

**6** 1975 High on You (Epic—#11 R&B/#45 pop)

**7** 1983 Ain't but the One Way (WB)

A return to form, if not to brilliance, with "Who in the Funk Do You Think You Are" a lightly cliched, but nevertheless demanding drive through the heart of Stone's greatest idiosyncrasies. A freakily rearranged version of the Kinks' "You Really Got Me" is also a highlight.

## SELECTED COMPILATIONS AND ARCHIVE RELEASES

**7** 1971 **Greatest Hits (Epic—#1 R&B/#42 pop)**

Singles-heavy roundup of the best of the band so far.

**3** 1980 **Ten Years Too Soon (Epic)**

Dreadfully dated and misguided disco remix collection, masochistically enjoyable as a kitsch period piece.

**8** 1992 **Takin' You Higher: The Best Of (Epic)**

In the continuing and inexplicable absence of a full Stone box set, this set (the CD successor to 1982's *Anthology* collection) offers the broadest cross-section of classic Stone, although the selection itself leaves much to be desired.

**9** 1998 **The Masters (Eagle—UK)**

Although this material has been circulating since at least 1972, Eagle's 27 track roundup of earlysingles, Autumn sessions and sundry other odds is the best summary of Stone's pre-Family Stone material (even if the band does take full credit on the sleeve!). Pitfalls include an absolute lack of recording information, and the inclusion of several patently non-Stone performances, but the presence of material dating back to the 1961 Danny Stewart 45 makes this an unqualified must-have.

**8** 2001 **Who In The Funk Do You Think You Are? (Rhino Handmade)**

Limited edition (5000 copies) compilation features Stone's 1979 and 1983 albums, plus 5 bonus tracks.

## SELECTED SAMPLES

Brave & Strong — Beastie Boys: 3 Minute Rule (1989)
Crossword — De La Soul: Say No Go (1989)
Dance to the Music — Beastie Boys: Egg Man (1989)
Don't Call Me Nigga, Whitey — Ice Cube: Horny Lil' Devil (1991)
Don't Call Me Nigga, Whitey — KAM: Stereotype (1993)
Family Affair — Digital Underground: Family of the Underground (1991)
Hot Fun in the Summertime — Jungle Brothers: Sunshine (1989)
I Ain't Got Nobody (For Real) — Stereo MC: Ain't Got Nobody (1990)
I Want To Take You Higher — DOC: Mind Blowin' (remix) (1989)
I Want To Take You Higher — Grandmaster Flash & the Furious Five: Magic Carpet Ride (1988)
I Want To Take You Higher — Schoolly D: Dis Groove Is Bad (1987)
If You Want Me To Stay — Bell Biv Devoe: She's Dope (remix) (1991)
If You Want Me To Stay — Dana Dane: Tales from the Dane Side (1990)
If You Want Me To Stay — DOC: Comm 2 (1989)
If You Want Me To Stay — Warren G.: Reality (1997)
Life — Beck: Sissyneck (1992)
Life — Cypress Hill: Insanse in the Brain (1993)
Loose Booty — Bell Biv Devoe: Ghetto Booty (1993)
Loose Booty — Beastie Boys: Shadrach (1989)
Loose Booty — Fu-Schnickens: True Fu-Schnick (remix) (1992)
Poet — Beastie Boys: 3 Minute Rule (1989)
Poet — De La Soul: Description (1989)

Poet — Def Jef: A Poet's Predlue (1989)
Running Away — A Tribe Called Quest: Description of a Fool (1991)
Sing a Simple Song — Alkaholiks: Make Room (1993)
Sing a Simple Song — Arrested Development: Mr. Wendal (1992)
Sing a Simple Song — Mary J. Blige: Live Is All We Need (remix) (1997)
Sing a Simple Song — Boss: Drive by (remix)(1993)
Sing a Simple Song — Chubb Rock: Lost in the Storm (1992)
Sing a Simple Song — Cree Summer: Miss Moon (1999)
Sing a Simple Song — Compton's Most Wanted: I Don't Dance (1992)
Sing a Simple Song — College Boyz: Underground Blues (1992)
Sing a Simple Song — Da Lench Mob: Buck the Devil (1992)
Sing a Simple Song — Das EFX: Mic Checka (remix) (1992)
Sing a Simple Song — De La Soul: Eye Know (1989)
Sing a Simple Song — Diamond D: Check One, Two (1992)
Sing a Simple Song — Domino: Sweet Potato Pie (1993)
Sing a Simple Song — Domino: Long Beach Thang (1993)
Sing a Simple Song — Domino: Getto Jam (1993)
Sing a Simple Song — Dr. Dre: Deep Cover (1996)
Sing a Simple Song — Digital Underground: The Humpty Dance (1990)
Sing a Simple Song — Digital Underground: Return of the Crazy One (1993)
Sing a Simple Song — Ed OG: Skinny Dip (Got It Goin' On) (1994)
Sing a Simple Song — Erick Sermon: Stay Real (1993)
Sing a Simple Song — Fu-Schnickens: Props (1992)
Sing a Simple Song — Fu-Schnickens: Sneakin' Up on Ya (1994)
Sing a Simple Song — Grandmaster Flash & the Furious Five: Kid Named Flash (1987)
Sing a Simple Song — Gold Money: Nothin' (1992)
Sing a Simple Song — Group Home: Supa Star (1995)
Sing a Simple Song — Ice Cube: Who's the Mack? (1990)
Sing a Simple Song — Ice Cube: Jackin' for Beats (1992)
Sing a Simple Song — Ice Cube: Gangsta's Fairy Tale 2 (1992)
Sing a Simple Song — Ice Cube: Really Doe (1993)
Sing a Simple Song — Jungle Brothers: For the Headz at Company Z (1993)
Sing a Simple Song — Jungle Brothers: Simple as That (1993)
Sing a Simple Song — Jungle Brothers: JB's Comin' Through (1993)
Sing a Simple Song — Jodeci: You Got It (1994)
Sing a Simple Song — KAM: Ain't That a Bitch (1993)
Sing a Simple Song — KAM: Holiday Madness (1993)
Sing a Simple Song — KAM: Stereotype (1993)
Sing a Simple Song — KAM: Pull Ya Hoe Card (1995)
Sing a Simple Song — Kriss Kross: Can't Stop the Bumrush (1992)
Sing a Simple Song — KRS-One: Sound of Da Police (1993)
Sing a Simple Song — LL Cool J: How I'm Comin (1993)
Sing a Simple Song — LL Cool J: Mama Said Knock You Out (1990)
Sing a Simple Song — Marky Mark & the Funky Bunch: You Gotta Believe (1992)
Sing a Simple Song — Naughty by Nature: Ready for Dem (1993)
Sing a Simple Song — Ol' Dirty Bastard: Hippa to Da Hoppa (1995)
Sing a Simple Song — Papa Chuk: Trunk of Funk (1994)
Sing a Simple Song — Paris: Check It Out Ch'all (1992)

Sing a Simple Song — Pharcyde: I'm That Type of Nigga (1993)

Sing a Simple Song — Pete Rock & CL Smooth: Anger in the Nation (1992)

Sing a Simple Song — Pete Rock & CL Smooth: For Pete's Sake (1992)

Sing a Simple Song — Public Enemy: Party for Your Right To Fight (1988)

Sing a Simple Song — Public Enemy: Can't Truss it (1991)

Sing a Simple Song — Public Enemy: Brothers Gonna Work It Out (1990)

Sing a Simple Song — Public Enemy: Get the F out of Dodge (1991)

Sing a Simple Song — Public Enemy: Living in a Zoo (1994)

Sing a Simple Song — Redman: Time 4 Sum Aksion (1992)

Sing a Simple Song — Redman: Blow Your Mind (1992)

Sing a Simple Song — Redman: So Ruff (1992)

Sing a Simple Song — Run DMC: In the House (1993)

Sing a Simple Song — Salt-N-Pepa: Somma Time Man (1993)

Sing a Simple Song — Scarface: Your Ass Got Took (1991)

Sing a Simple Song — Schooly D: Dis Groove Is Bad (1987)

Sing a Simple Song — Sir Mix-A-Lot: Jack Back (1992)

Sing a Simple Song — Stereo MC: The Other Side (1992)

Sing a Simple Song — Terminator X: Back to the Scene of the Bass (1991)

Sing a Simple Song — TLC: Ain't 2 Proud 2 Beg (1992)

Sing a Simple Song — TLC: What About Your Friends? (1992)

Sing a Simple Song — TLC: Hat 2 Da Back (1992)

Sing a Simple Song — A Tribe Called Quest: Jazz (We've Got) (remix) (1992)

Sing a Simple Song — 2Pac: Peep Game (1993)

Sing a Simple Song — 2Pac: Souljah's Revenge (1993)

Sing a Simple Song — 2Pac: Temptations (1995)

Sing a Simple Song — 2Pac: Young Niggaz (1995)

Sing a Simple Song — UTFO: Rough and Rugged (1989)

Sing a Simple Song — X Clan: Funk Liberation (1992)

Sing a Simple Song — Yo-Yo: Mackstress (1993)

Stand — Three Times Dope: Believe Dat (1989)

Stand — 7A3: Coolin in Cali (1988)

Stand — Kool Moe Dee: Rise 'N' Shine (1991)

Stand — Professor Griff & the Last Asiatic Disciples: L.A.D. (1990)

Stand — Public Enemy: Who Stole the Soul? (1990)

Stand — Scarface: The Diary (1994)

Stand — A Tribe Called Quest: Rap Promoter

Thank You (Falletin Me Be Mice Elf Again) — 7A3: Coolin in Cali (1988)

Thank You (Falletin Me Be Mice Elf Again) — Janet Jackson: Rhythm Nation (1989)

Thank You for Takin' Me to Africa — Public Enemy: Air Hoodlum (1992)

Thank You for Takin' Me to Africa — WC & the Maad Circle: Out On A Furlough (1991)

Thankful & Thoughtful — PM Dawn: Comatose (1991)

Trip to Your Heart — LL Cool J: Mama Said Knock You Out (1990)

Turn Me Loose — Public Enemy: Power to the People (1990)

Underdog — Cypress Hill: Real Estate (1992)

Underdog — Public Enemy: Fear of a Black Planet (1990)

You Caught Me Smilin' — Funkdoobiest: It Ain't Going Down (1995)

You Caught Me Smilin' — Justin Warfield: Season of the Vic (1991)

## THE TEMPTATIONS, see FRONTIERS OF FUNK: MOTOWN GETS WITH IT

## ALLEN TOUSSAINT, see FRONTIERS OF FUNK: GUMBO AND THE GROOVE

## VOLT RECORDS, see STAX/VOLT RECORDS

## WATTS PROPHETS

FORMED: 1965, Los Angeles, CA

ORIGINAL LINE-UP: *Dee Dee McNeil (vcls, pno), Anthony Hamilton (vcls), Otis O'Solomon (vcls), Richard Dedeaux (vcls)*

Funk in the late '6os wasn't only a musical force. It was also a political power, one whose voice was raised through Black America, amplified through the revolutionary rhetoric of church and campus and disseminated through whichever medium it could find. Music, of course, was the most obvious avenue, but poetry, too, played its part.

From the East Coast the Last Poets grabbed a chart album and enjoyed the patronage of Jimi Hendrix and Mick Jagger. On the West Coast, however, it was the Watts Prophets who held sway.

The quartet first met in the aftermath of the 1965 Watts riots, at author Budd Schulberg's Watts Writers Forum. The Forum itself had become swiftly established as a meeting place for the city's Black radical community, but also as a voice of reason within the increasingly turbulent politics of the time. Robert Kennedy visited during his campaign for the 1968 Democratic Party nomination and pronounced himself impressed; the FBI, however, were less enamored and eventually arranged for the Workshop to be torched.

Despite regular performances at the Workshop, the Prophets themselves claimed that their work was never intended to be political — "we were just calling what we saw," Hamilton told author David Toop. Nevertheless, what they called voiced what much of their audience was thinking, including their wilful misappropriation of one of JFK's best-loved speeches, "ask not what you can do for your country, 'cos what in the fuck has it done for you?"

By 1970, the Prophets' reputation was beginning to reach music industry ears. Hamilton appeared on a poetry compilation, *Black Voices on the Streets of Watts*, alongside Ed Bereal and sundry other fellow spokesmen. A number of labels approached the Prophets, only to draw back upon encountering the full impact of their performance. Finally, the small ALA label moved in and 1971 saw the Watts Prophets' first (and, as it transpired, only) album released in a sleeve that spoke volumes—a photo montage drifted from a Bobby Seale election poster, through Watts and the ghetto to Malcolm X, and onto a camouflage clad child holding a gun.

In commercial terms, *Rappin' Black in a White World* didn't stand a chance; it was another 15 years before such sentiments (not to mention such a delivery) would be accepted in the marketplace, and the Prophets couldn't wait that long.

McNeil quit for a career in cabaret; the remainder of the Prophets continued on as a trio, regularly performing but rarely recording. They were not forgotten, however. A track on Quincy Jones' 1975 album *Mellow Madness* featured an O'Solomon lyric, while the Prophets were recruited to Stevie Wonder's *Songs in the Key of Life* album the following year. There was also talk of a second Watts Prophets album to be released on Bob Marley's Tuff Gong label—Hamilton met the reggae superstar following his 1979 ordainment into the Ethiopian Orthodox Christian Church. Unfortunately, Marley's death in 1981 saw the project dropped.

Still they persisted although, for many modern listeners (familiar with the Prophets only through the admiration of current artists) they were as much legend as legendary. That changed in 1997, when the Prophets—with Horace Tapscott replacing the long absent McNeil—signed with Brit-ain's Acid Jazz label and cut *When the '90s Came*, a set steeped deeply within their own legend, but effortlessly contemporary all the same. Reissues of Rapping and the *Black Voices on the Streets of Watts* poetry album followed.

## WATTS PROPHETS DISCOGRAPHY
### LPs
**8** **1971 Black Rapping in a White World (ALA)**
Taut, abrupt and outspoken, with arrangements snowballing across a belligerent babel, *Black Rapping* remains uneasy listening even after 15 years of modern rap.

**7** **1997 When the '90s Came (ffrr)**
Anybody searching for evidence of how much the world has changed since the late '60s needs look no further than reviews of the Prophets' second album. In 1971, their debut was widely regarded as a call for revolution. In 1997, one popular internet music encyclopedia suggested that fans might also want to check out the CD of Princess Diana's funeral service. Well, they are both spoken word . . .

### SELECTED SAMPLES
Dem Niggers Ain't Playin'— Coolio: Bring Something Back Fo Da Hood (1994)

## MARVA WHITNEY, see JAMES BROWN

## STEVIE WONDER, see FRONTIERS OF FUNK: MOTOWN GETS WITH IT

# FRONTIERS OF FUNK: GUMBO AND THE GROOVE

The story of New Orleans funk begins with jazz, which is the city's most famous musical export. But it also begins at the bottom, with the drums that Mac "Dr. John" Rebennack, the city's most favored son, once described as "chronic to our thing." Writing in his 1994 autobiography, *Under a Hoodoo Moon*, Dr. John insisted, "in New Orleans roots music, the drummer is crucial . . . because he lays down the foundation of what New Orleans music is all about: The Funk."

And though that funk comes in many shapes and many colors, from the wild piano of R&B veteran Professor Longhair to the rocking soul of Joe Tex, from the smooth rhythmic passages of the Neville Brothers to the swampy juju pounding of Dr. John himself, still the Big Easy remains untouchable, the number one funk town in America.

Throughout the '50s and '60s, the city led the way in steaming R&B—Little Richard recorded many of his greatest records there, with local musicians adding to the flavor. During the '70s, producer Allen Toussaint's Sea Saint studios entertained artists as disparate as Paul McCartney and Labelle, Robert Palmer and King Biscuit Boy, and all went away with what they came for. McCartney's "Listen to What the Man Said" (a pop #1 from 1975) is as true to its source as Little Richard's "Tutti Frutti," while Labelle were simply an under-achieving soul vocal group before they linked with Toussaint and the Meters for "Lady Marmalade," a crossover smash in late 1974.

The Meters were the first true modern funk act to be spawned by New Orleans (Chocolate Milk were the second); their sound the catalyst that pulled together the manifold pulses of local musical life into one single school of thought: Creole, cajun, Black and White. Objectively, one could argue that without the Meters, even the aforementioned Dr. John quote would not exist (or, at least, not mean so much); that the nonstop party that is Mardi Gras, Bourbon Street and the French Quarter would have simply continued to dance to the delta drumbeats, and never the twain would meet. Plenty of other musical forms are built from the percussive roots up, after all.

Funk, however, is in the eye of the beholder—that is its beauty and that is its strength. Different ears hear different things and New Orleans caters to them all. Rising up from the Caribbean, the rhythms of mento and calypso, even ska and rocksteady, percolate throughout the bayou. (Of the Meters' finest achievements, both "Ease Back" and "Zony Mash" pack bass lines that will delight the most purist reggae lover.)

The sounds of Africa, too, inform the New Orleans beat; the city's Congo Square (now Louis Armstrong Plaza) was the first and, for a long time, only neighborhood in all of 18th century America to allow Blacks to celebrate their own musical heritage, and that is the wild celebration upon which all of New Orleans' music was built. Small wonder then, that with such a heritage behind him, '50s-era sessionman Earl Palmer, born and bred in New Orleans, has been called the world's first funk drummer—and again, a string of primal Little Richard hits back up the claim.

But New Orleans is also a keyboard town, home to Huey Smith, James Booker, Fats Domino, Allen Toussaint, Dr. John, Art Neville, the spiritual sons of perhaps the wildest pianist of them all, the immortal Professor Longhair.

Henry Roeland Byrd, aka Professor Longhair (b. 12/19/18, d. 1/30/80), was 31 when he cut his first record, the perennial "Mardi Gras in New Orleans," but he was already a veteran of the French Quarter scene as both a bar musician and a street dancer. Over the next five years, Longhair (so named for obvious reasons) dominated the local scene without ever truly impacting outside of the city limits. His sole national hit, in 1950, was the unabashedly novelty flavored "Bald Head," cut for Mercury under the name of Roy Byrd and His Blues Jumpers.

Pounding R&B as wild as any on the scene at the time was Longhair's stock-in-trade. His records were a whirlwind of activity, the instruments racing one another to the beat, while above it all, Longhair's distinctive vocals tangled, then mangled his blistered blues with juke-joint intensity. Even on wax, the singer was a jumping live experience, comparable to James Brown and Little Richard long before anyone had heard either name.

Indeed, Longhair might even have eclipsed them both had a minor stroke not halted his activities during the mid-'50s; he returned to action later in the decade, but the first flush of the R&B/rock 'n' roll hybrid he pioneered had already run its course. By 1964, Longhair had virtually abandoned music (or, more accurately, music had abandoned him) and he was working at a local record store, sweeping floors.

Longhair's lack of mainstream commercial success was not indicative of New Orleans' own musical profile. More than 60 locally produced hits made the pop Top 100 during 1962–63 alone, while the likes of Smiley Lewis, Lloyd Price (1952's

"Lawdy Miss Clawdy" is frequently cited among the first ever rock 'n' roll records), Fats Domino, Frankie Ford (whose 1959 "Sea Cruise" was subsequently covered by pop sensations Herman's Hermits) and Huey "Piano" Smith (author of the staple "Rockin' Pneumonia and the Boogie Woogie Flu") kept the city's R&B roots steaming even after they stopped scoring hits.

If any one performer could rival Longhair's musical impact, however, it was Lee Dorsey (b. 12/24/24), best known to pop audiences for the crossover neo-novelty smashes "Ya Ya" (subsequently covered by John Lennon), "Holy Cow" and "Working in a Coalmine." But he was responsible, too, for a chain of ferocious proto-funk R&B pounders cut for the Fury and Amy labels during the '60s: "Ride Your Pony," "Get Out of My Life, Woman," "Go Go Girl," "Yes We Can" (later covered by the Pointer Sisters) and, of course, in 1969 the self-defining "Everything I Do Gohn Be Funky (From Now On),"—the dominant notion in Dorsey's music for the remainder of his life. (He died 12/1/86; his last hit, "Night People," fell in early 1978).

Allen Toussaint (b. New Orleans, 1/14/38) was Dorsey's collaborator throughout the bulk of his career. Himself a piano prodigy whose roots lay in Longhair and Fats Domino, but whose future established him as the premier producer in the city—one whose work positively dripped the molten essence of New Orleans.

Toussaint explained that essence to journalist Eric Olsen. "In New Orleans, the music isn't just in the clubs or on the dancefloor, it's in everything. You can feel it in the street, see it in the buildings, taste it in the food. The syncopation and the strut of the second line brass bands [those that follow the main musicians at carnivals. etc.], the frenzied intensity of the Mardi Gras Indian chants [captured in the Meters' Wild Tchoupitoulas project], and the driving rhythms of blues, jazz and R&B are as essential to this city as eating and sleeping." Toussaint's own accomplishments became living evidence of that fact.

Teenaged sessions with R&B star Smiley Lewis and gigs alongside Earl King at the Dew Drop Inn brought Toussaint to the attention of Fats Domino. In 1957, Toussaint actually stood in for Domino on "I Want You To Know," pulling off a note-perfect Fats piano solo when the artist was unable to attend the session. The following year, Toussaint cut his first album, *The Wild Sound of New Orleans* for RCA (under the name Al Tousan); the record sold well locally and, six years later, provided Dixieland trumpeter Al Hirt with his first hit, "Java."

In 1960, Toussaint became A&R man for Joe Banashak's newly formed Minit label; one of his first duties was to oversee an open audition night, which Banashak hoped would unearth new talent for the company. It succeeded beyond anybody's wildest dreams; in one evening, Toussaint discovered Aaron Neville, Irma Thomas, Benny Spellman and Jessie Hill (b. 12/9/32), with the latter promptly bringing Toussaint his first Minit smash, the oft-imitated "Ooh-Poo-Pah-Doo," in March 1960.

Further hits with Clarence "Frogman" Henry, Chris Kenner, Barbara George and Ernie K-Doe followed, the latter's "Mother-in-Law" becoming the first national chart-topper ever recorded in New Orleans. But it was the emergence of Lee Dorsey (Toussaint arranged "Ya Ya," and became his producer soon after) that gave him a consistent and prolific hitmaker.

Toussaint was drafted in 1963; but when he resumed his musical career two years later, it was as though the hiatus never happened. Aaron Neville's "Tell It like It Is" and Betty Harris' "Nearer to You" both charted and, by 1968, Toussaint had appointed the Meters as his houseband, confident that they would bring their own sensibilities—equally informed by James Brown and Jimmy Smith, Booker T. and Ernie K.—to bear on anything and everything Toussaint chose to throw at them.

The Meters were behind Dorsey's "Gohn Be Funky," of course, but they also contributed to Toussaint's work with Little Feat, the Louisiana-based, deep south flavored rock outfit who epitomized Americana for many White rock critics of the early '70s. But if Toussaint was to be regarded as the heart of the New Orleans music scene through the '70s, its soul was to be found elsewhere, dripping from the pure voodoo funk of Mac "Dr. John" Rebennack, author of what remains the definitive portrait of New Orleans music, "Walk on Gilded Splinters."

Drawn from his eminent *Gris Gris* debut album (1968), "Walk on Gilded Splinters" has earned covers from as far afield as soul songstress Marsha Hunt and English rockers Humble Pie, yet still it oozes the aura of the bayou—the dank, sinister darkness that a hundred movies and a thousand novelists have tried in vain to recapture as art, invoked instead as timeless ritual.

Born in 1940, Rebennack was still in his late teens when he established himself alongside the city's most remarkable sessioneers. He haunted Cosimo Matassa's legendary studios, getting to know local musicians and just hanging out, graduated to playing keyboards and guitar on records by Longhair, Frankie Ford, Joe Tex and others, and by 1958, was established as a songwriter, musician and producer at Johnny Vincent's Ace label, one of the so-called Funk Clique gathering of New Orleans' top sessionmen. Released in 2000, the *Return of the Mac* compilation gathered up 28 tracks from the period 1959–61 alone, including his own first single, 1959's ominous "Storm Warning."

In 1964, Rebennack almost lost a finger when he tried to prevent a friend from being pistol-whipped. The injury left him unable to play guitar; he switched to keyboards and, around 1965, relocated to Los Angeles, where he became a regular member of producer Phil Spector's houseband.

Rebennack toyed with a couple of groups during this period, the Zu Zu Band (formed with Jessie Hill) and Morgus & the Three Ghouls; but it was 1968 before he arrived at his future identity, Dr. John Creaux the Night Tripper, purveyor of dark Creole invocations, secret voodoo ritual and blistered, bayou imagery. Onstage outrageous robes and feathered head-dresses, scantily clad dancers and liquid lights heightened the impressions left by his lyrics; offstage, his records alone were enough to immolate the imagination.

In later years, earnest archaeologists would pinpoint *Gris Gris* as the third key offshoot of the same psychedelic miasma that spawned the Latin funk of Santana and Malo and the acid funk of George Clinton and Sly & the Family Stone. That much is true, but it's also misleading. Those acts drew their sources from within the realms of human experience. Dr. John's incorporated the "un-human" as well.

Not all of Dr. John's albums were as terrifying as *Gris Gris*, not all of his songs as powerful as "Splinters." Indeed, by the late '70s, he had dropped much of the early theatrics and confirmed himself instead as one of America's greatest blues jazzmen. But the same psilocybic gumbo nightmare still lay at the heart of the best of them.

It was Dr. John who hauled Professor Longhair back into contention in 1971, encouraging him to make a comeback at that year's New Orleans Jazz and Heritage Festival. Near simultaneously, the Meters used his "Hey Now Baby" as the model for their own "Cabbage Alley" and, when Paul McCartney was casting around for eye-opening talent to play his 1975 *Venus and Mars Are Alright Tonight* record release party, he had no hesitation in booking the Professor. (The Meters were also on the bill.)

The ultimate gathering of New Orleans' funk talent occurred when PBS brought Longhair, the Meters and Dr. John together as part of the *Soundstage* concert series. By that time, of course, funk itself had rocketed away on tangents that the protagonists themselves probably never imagined—and that the acclaimed program's viewers might never trace back to such idiosyncratic roots.

But the musicians knew, the music remembered and the thread, which has bound the New Orleans sound since the beginning, remains unbroken.

### RECOMMENDED LISTENING

#### Dr. John: *Gris Gris* (Atlantic 1968)
Joined by Jessie Hill—Dr Poo Pah Doo—and Dr. (Harold) Battiste of Scorpio, the Night Tripper lives up to his name with a dark, freaky ghost-train through bayou backwater, which the tourist guides never visit. "Gilded Splinters," "Danse Kalinda Ba Boom" and "Gris Gris Gumbo Ya Ya" dominate, but John's crooked Creole incantations are unforgettable throughout.

#### Professor Longhair: *Rock and Roll Gumbo* (Atlantic, 1977)
Riveting versions of "Junco Partner," "Stag-o-Lee" and "Rockin' Pneumonia," a seething remake of "Mardi Gras in New Orleans" and the self-affirming "They Call Me Dr. Professor Longhair" push the Fess into overdrive. Accompanying musicians include veteran Texan Clarence "Gatemouth" Brown and Dr. John sideman Julius Farmer.

#### Wild Magnolias: *Wild Magnolias* (Polydor, 1974)
The New Orleans Project, featuring Willie Tee, Earl Turbinton, Larry Panna and Julius Farmer serve up a to-die-for slice of classic bayou funk, including "Soul Soul Soul" and "Corey Died on the Battlefield." Tee's keyboards are exquisite.

#### Wild Tchoupitoulas: *The Wild Tchoupitoulas* (1976)
Aka the Meters and the reunited Neville family, but also an evocative portrait of the primal heart of Mardi Gras traditions.

**various:** *Eddie Bo's Funky Funky New Orleans — Rare & Unreleased New Orleans Funk 1968–1971* (Funky Delicacies/Tuff City)

Fiery collection focussing on Bo's little-known time as New Orleans producer. Classic grooves from the Vibrettes, Chuck Carbo, the Scram Band & Smokey Johnson, the Explosions and Bo himself.

**various:** *The New Orleans Hit Story: 20 Years of Big Easy Hits 1950–70* (Charley 1993)

Essential gathering of predominantly Top 100 hits, with heavy Toussaint involvement. It closes just as things start to get funky, but still serves up an invaluable introduction.

**various:** *Gumbo Ya Ya Yah!* (P-Vine 1995)

Subtitled "New Orleans Funky Classics," but in truth a random gathering of sides by some of the artists who made that funk possible—Professor Longhair, Ernie K, Huey Smith, Lil Millet, Big Boy Myles, Jerry Byrne and more. Annotated in Japanese only, but a vivid snapshot all the same.

# FRONTIERS OF FUNK: THE PSYCHE-FUNKA-DELIC EXPERIENCE

James Brown formulated funk, Sly Stone created it. But still it took the lightning bolt of consciousness and energy that permeated all of American life in the late '6os to give life to their Funkenstein, the collision of art, culture, politics and music . . . so much music, so many different types of music that history glibly records as "psychedelia."

To ears yet to be clogged by the pernicious ghettoization of modern musical marketing, "psychedelia" meant just what it promised, the coming together of a myriad disparate visions, arts and dreams into one multi-colored, multi-faceted whole. But it was no coincidence that the most revolutionary talents of the era emerged from worlds removed from the rock and pop metier—for which psychedelia is best remembered today—Stone, of course, but also voodoo bluesman Jimi Hendrix, Latin magician Carlos Santana and R&B genius Otis Redding.

For though psychedelic *rock* remained the province of the rock 'n' roller, psychedelic *music* was rooted in an artform that jazz and R&B artists had been perfecting for years and, if anybody demanded further proof of that, they needed only visit the Monterey International Pop Festival in June 1967.

The first major festival of the age, most eyes were on the heroes of the rock scene—the Dead, the Who, the Beach Boys, Janis Joplin. But their ears and feet were somewhere else entirely, with Hendrix, with Redding, with the driving dance of Booker T. and the MGs and the dramatic Afro punch of Hugh Masekela. Both Hendrix and Redding went into the festival all but unknown to White American audiences. They emerged superstars.

It took rock 'n' roll musicians a long time to come to terms with jamming. Of course, they'd always done it in the privacy of their own garage, just kicking back and letting rip, playing till someone thought of something more pressing . . . a new three-minute pop song, maybe, or an overdue trip to the barber. But in a genre born of the blessings of the short, sharp shockability of a marketplace drip-fed radio and TV, there was little room for such indulgences elsewhere, not on stage and certainly not in the studio.

So, it was a very big deal indeed when Bob Dylan released close to six minutes of "Like a Rolling Stone" on the top side of a 1965 single; and almost as big a one when the Rolling Stones followed through with "Going Home," a 12-minute opus, which devoured more than half a side of an album. But still the liberation was slow in pushing through, slow enough that when a new scene began percolating out of the San Francisco Bay area during 1965–66, fuelled by the more-or-less newly introduced drug LSD, but fired by the realization that there was more to life than verse-chorus-verse, the outside world was swift to give it a name. Several names . . . psychedelia, acid rock, freak out music.

The former stuck, but the others all fit. There were no limits; a song was as long as it wanted to be and traveled as far as it liked. In fact, songs themselves were an out-moded concept; freaking out meant shedding one's conditioning, releasing one's consciousness, opening brain and body to the music alone. Consciously unconscious, some people called it, but George Clinton, years later, perhaps put it best, "free your mind and your ass will follow."

The new climate, of course, demanded new talent: the hokey country-rockers who became the Grateful Dead; the faintly freaky folkies of the Jefferson Airplane; lumpen bluesmongers Big Brother & the Holding Company; in the two-bit bars where they earned a pre-psych crust, acts like these were barely holding their own. But time flies when you're tripping and even more so when the audience is as well. You wanna blow like Charlie Parker? You wanna get down like James Brown? Rock 'n' roll had always been open to outside influences; now it was to be blasted open by them. Jazz, soul, the classics, R&B, anything and everything was fair game, for themes, for concepts, for energies. Especially for energies.

The Santana Blues Band slipped into this scene without a word of warning. They didn't even have a name for their first few shows, but then they opened for Paul Butterfield at the Fillmore, one afternoon in January 1967, and so many people asked who they were that they took the first thing that came to mind.

There was nobody else that sounded remotely like them, even with the Bay Area bursting at the seams with new excitement. Maybe some of Sly & the Family Stone's more incendiary rhythms touched upon areas that Santana made their own. Maybe Big Brother had a similar grasp on the simple dynamics of wild improvisation in the key of blues; and maybe the Grateful Dead were capable of launching themselves toward the same expanding universes where Santana plied their most notable trades. But those similarities only drew people into earshot. It was the music that kept them there.

The son of a Tijuana mariachi musician, Santana himself was a genius guitarist, capable of finding notes and then holding them forever, before finally letting them slip gracefully away the moment he found one he seemed to like more. But the first thing the unsuspecting listener heard were the rhythms, piling atop and over one another until you could watch the backline drummer and percussionists all night and never guess where it all was coming from.

One of them, Michael Carabello, learned from his love of James Brown and Sly Stone; another, Michael Shrieve, was into Coltrane and Miles Davis; a third, Chepito, was into Eddie Palmieri and African music. The ensuing fusion was heart-stopping, especially when you topped up your senses with the obligatory tab, because that's when you noticed the guitar, scything through the beat, racing on overhead, forming its own intricate patterns in the gaps between the drums. "Everything about Santana was just jams," Santana himself acknowledged. "No beginning, no middle, no end. We just made a gumbo together."

The group worked constantly, building their repertoire as they gathered an audience, ricocheting between the city's most happening clubs and venues: the Fillmore, the Carousel, the Straight and all points in between. Long before the term had any meaning beyond a solid groove that made you wanna keep on dancing while all hell broke loose inside your skull, Santana were being called the funkiest unsigned thing in 'Frisco—the mystery was, how they managed to remain unsigned for so long.

As 1967 became 1968, Santana were headlining the Fillmore with rugged regularity, rocking the Sky River Rock Festival, conquering the Atlantic City Pop bash. Their demos, however, couldn't get arrested. Too Latin, said some people; too funky, said others; too rocky said more and, if you put yourself in their shoes, it wasn't hard to understand their uncertainty. In and of themselves, all three ingredients were eminently saleable, and you could even get a hit by mixing two of them. But putting all three together was utterly unheard of and that was before you added the rest of the Santana experience. "Can't play," condemned Atlantic Records founder Ahmet Ertegun when he caught the band at the Fillmore. "Furthermore, won't sell."

Only one man was genuinely interested in Santana, Columbia Records producer David Rubinson. He understood Latin music—he'd produced conguero Mongo Santamaria. He understood blues— he'd also worked with Taj Mahal. And he understood rock. It was this understanding that finally swayed Columbia Records; that, and the fact that the last two acts they'd signed from San Francisco, Janis Joplin and Sly & the Family Stone (on the Epic subsidiary), were both already threatening major dividends.

Sly Stone hung over the city scene as though he were already the legend he'd one day become. As house producer at Autumn Records, he once pushed local folk-rockers the Great Society, through 50 takes of a single song before he agreed their performance was ready for release. Now their singer, Grace Slick, was fronting the Jefferson Airplane, up there with the Grateful Dead among San Francisco's most sainted offspring.

But did Stone show any regret? Of course not. Rather, he watched how far out the White bands could go, then made sure that his group traveled even further with their debut album, the very deliberately titled *A Whole New Thing*, of such dazzling stylistic extremes that Stone himself felt obliged to pull back next time out. At a time, October 1967, when the rest of the city's music scene was still trying to absorb the lessons of the Beatles' *Sgt. Pepper's Lonely Hearts Club Band*, *A Whole New Thing* was just that, an album unquestionably rooted in familiar territory, but absolutely unwilling to spend any time there. The first sound you heard was a horn croaking "Frere Jacques," but *A Whole New Thing* would not come so close to home again.

Santana offered the same other-worldliness. Without ever aspiring toward the same peaks of sonic dislocation as Stone, the group shared his disdain for convention—that included the *un*-conventions of the age itself. Occasionally, you might catch a quaint snatch of Mexican folk or Afro-Cuban jazz percolating through the naive enthusiasm. But you can also hear the future as well: the streetwise Chicano ballet of War, the crafted deliberation of Tower of Power, and the looseness, of course, of a whole new generation of what the media was soon dubbing Latin Rockers. Soon after, as in the summer

**FUNK**

of 1969, Santana appeared at the Woodstock Festival and transformed the whole circus into an unscheduled Mardi Gras.

David Rubinson produced the first Santana album, but it took time. His first attempt to record the band, live at the Fillmore in December 1968, was abandoned on the night; his second, in Los Angeles in the new year, ended up being scrapped because not one member of the group actually liked what they heard on the tapes. Finally, they settled into a studio just outside San Francisco, slamming down an album, *Santana*, which defied every uncertainty ever voiced about their music.

Interviewed for the booklet accompanying the 1998 remastered edition of the album, Rubinson recalled, "when it came out, you could not turn on the radio for six weeks without hearing the damn record. In the middle of all that vapid bullshit that was going on with psychedelia and mandala that was happening in '69, here was the essence, boiled down to drums and percussion and pulse. It was just balls out music, and that's what people wanted to hear."

Santana were not alone in stealing the show at Woodstock. Sly Stone was there as well, performing an epic set climaxed by "I Want To Take You Higher," a song whose very title—let alone its stoned groove majesty—was in perfect tune with the mood of the day. When the *Woodstock* movie was released the following June, those were the moments that lodged in the soul. But there was another that lodged in the heart, the final sunrise of the entire event, as Jimi Hendrix shook the stage with his "Star Spangled Banner."

And if it wasn't telling enough that, just as occurred at Monterey, the most pervasive images of the entire event should again be Black men, what greater synchronicity could there have been than for Hendrix to follow up Woodstock by completing the equation that Stone and Santana had already begun, with the launch of his own Band of Gypsies—the ultimate expression of the rock in his heart, the funk in his soul and the soul in his spirit.

It was a dramatic combination, and Hendrix begged his audience not to judge it in advance. But even he admitted that, with a lineup like the Band of Gypsies'—drummer Buddy Miles and bassist Billy Cox joined Hendrix on stage—a few preconceptions were inevitable. And, with the slabs of solid jam that comprised their repertoire—"Machine Gun," "Message to Love," "We Gotta Live Together'—those preconceptions weren't going to be far wrong. But they were also rooted in a reality that wouldn't be truly appreciated until after Hendrix's death, when the critics stopped simply calling him one of the greatest musicians of all time, and set about trying to prove it.

What was the first funk record ever made? There are a lot of contenders, most of them involving James Brown. But there's also the Isley Brothers' "Testify," recorded in 1964, with an unknown Jimmy Hendrix on guitar and Ronald Isley letting rip with that full-throated roar that became such an integral part of the genre in the '70.

Now, stick with the Isleys, and fast forward to 1973, three years after Hendrix's death. A lot of people, clocking the directions in which the guitarist was moving during his last year on earth, have asked, what would he, could he, have done next? Ernie Isley's guitar solo howling out of that year's "That Lady" answers the question, and does so with such style that there were rumors at the time that it really WAS Hendrix, returning from beyond the grave . . . or at least, an opened archive to help out his old employers.

Of course it wasn't, but standing at the crossroads between "Testify" and "That Lady" (and countless other, similar, examples), Band of Gypsies represented an occasion of utterly pregnant magnitude—*not* for what was played (for the show itself was uniformly lackluster), nor for what it portended for Hendrix himself (the Band broke up onstage at its very next show). It was important because Band of Gypsies wasn't simply a crossover act. It was a fusion, of all the music Hendrix had ever heard, of all he had ever played and, during the handful of moments of unquestioned brilliance that the show threw up, all he had ever dreamed of playing.

It is neither a surprise nor contentious to describe Hendrix as a rock artist. Though he cut his musical teeth on the American R&B circuit (aside from the Isleys, he also worked with Lonnie Youngblood, Ike and Tina Turner, Little Richard, King Curtis and Curtis Knight between 1962–66), Seattle-born James Marshall Hendrix did not become Jimi until late 1966, when ex-Animals bassist Chas Chandler caught him playing in Greenwich Village, New York, and shipped him to the UK as an exotic star-in-the-making.

For six months, the three-man Jimi Hendrix Experience were Britain's secret weapon in the psychedelic wars between Swinging London and San Francisco's Haight-Ashbury scene. Three singles, "Hey Joe," "Purple Haze" and "The Wind

Cries Mary," became hits before Hendrix even began looking for an American record deal; his first album, *Are You Experienced* was released a month before he returned to his homeland. That incendiary appearance at Monterey in June 1967, changed all of that, though, and for much of the next two years, Hendrix toured the US almost ceaselessly.

His audience, however, was predominantly White, and while his music proudly acknowledged his roots, it did so from behind precisely the facade that a man labelled "the wild man of pop" was expected to possess. Wild studio effects and gimmickry swamped the production (Hendrix was one of the first artists to truly appreciate the possibilities inherent in stereo mixing), flash, outrageous guitar swamped the songs. A brilliant writer in his own right, he was not afraid to tackle the classics either; but from Chuck Berry's "Johnny B. Goode" to Dylan's "All Along the Watchtower," Hendrix covered other people's material in every sense of the word, burying the song beneath his own personality, then marking the grave with feedback and lighter fluid.

By spring 1969, however, Hendrix was visibly beginning to flag. The Experience broke up bad-temperedly, manager Chandler had moved on no less unhappily, and Hendrix's own attempts to record a new album, his fourth (*Are You Experienced* was followed by *Axis: Bold as Love* and the double *Electric Ladyland*), had stalled amidst a morass of studio outtakes and unwieldy jams. Woodstock, in many people's eyes, was the high point of his career. In Hendrix's own mind, it was one of the lowest. He began scheming Band of Gypsies soon after.

History today disregards the once-prevalent rumors that Hendrix was pressured into forming an all-Black group by sundry activist and nationalist groups. According to Cox, interviewed by Hendrix biographer Caesar Glebbeek, Experience drummer Mitch Mitchell was Hendrix's first choice, but backed out when he learned that the new act would be based in the US. Buddy Miles, on the other hand, was readily available and willing as well. That the rhythm section was naturally, infinitely, funkier than the Experience had ever been was partly down to chemistry, but also followed a thought process that was becoming increasingly apparent in Hendrix's studio work.

Band of Gypsies debuted at the Fillmore East on New Year's Eve 1969, with a second show the following day; highlights were subsequently released as a contractual obligation live album, titled simply *Band of Gypsies*. And immediately it was apparent that Hendrix's fusion was doomed to failure. The rock press was uniformly critical of both the show and album; the R&B media all but ignored it. *Band of Gypsies* peaked at #14 on the R&B chart (#5 pop), the lowest placing for any new Hendrix material since his breakthrough.

But again, if the music fell short of expectations, the message did not. In terms of portent and accomplishment, *Band of Gypsies* is today regarded as one of Hendrix's most influential and insightful albums and, though Hendrix swiftly abandoned the project itself, he never lost sight of its goals—even if his own future was to be so harshly limited. Hendrix died in London on September 18, 1970, just nine months after the final Band of Gypsies show.

But the last group he ever jammed with was War, fronted by his old friend (and Chas Chandler's Animals colleague) Eric Burdon, at Ronnie Scott's in London on September 16, and the last gig he attended was Sly & the Family Stone, earlier that same evening. And how ironic is that, the last live music Jimi Hendrix should experience, would be the first to acknowledge his influence as it came to grips with the decade just beginning?

While rock 'n' roll praised Hendrix as high as the sky and a slew of well-meaning guitar-garroting tributaries welled up from the waters that he had stirred, it was funk that kept his spirit alive and followed the musical courses he'd created. Anyone, it seemed, could ape his guitar style. But it was a select few indeed who would advance his vision.

The early Earth Wind & Fire surely rehearsed, figuratively if no way else, in Hendrix's "Roomful of Mirrors"; you can hear his "Machine Gun" through most of Funkadelic's first album. Indeed, George Clinton had known Hendrix since the guitarist's time with bluesman King Curtis; and Eddie Hazel knew his music like other men know their wives. It was only inevitable that some of Hendrix's magic would rub off on the mothership as it commenced its ascent to the stars. The only difference, of course, was that the music was no longer psychedelic. From hereon in, it was Funkadelic.

### RECOMMENDED LISTENING

#### Band of Gypsies: *Band of Gypsies* (Capitol, 1970)
Hopelessly over-indulgent, whether sampled on the original single disc release or swallowed whole as a remastered two-CD package. But still the anti-war "Machine Gun" has frightening power.

**FUNK**

**Eric Burdon and the Animals:** *Winds of Change* (MGM, 1967)

Utterly entranced by the possibilities of psychedelia, but already looking toward future fusion, Burdon twists between lightweight hippy philosophy ("Good Times," "San Francisco Nights") and vivid portents of his later collaboration with War—most notably, "Paint It Black" (to be reprised on *Black Man's Burdon*), "Black Plague" and an answer to Jimi Hendrix's first album, "Yes, I Am Experienced."

**Lenny Kravitz:** *Let Love Rule* (Virgin, 1990)

Los Angeles-flower adult Kravitz was barely three when psychedelia hit its stride, but it obviously made a major impression. 23 years on, he distilled its essence, added some of his own, and made a few of the short-circuit connections that other period bands neglected.

**Quicksilver Messenger Service:** *Happy Trails* (Capitol, 1969)

For sheer jam endurance (with a bit of soul as well, something conspicuously lacking from certain other bands of that bent), proof that rock 'n' roll may have started short, but learned fast. Mammoth recountings of "Who Do You Love" and "Mona" are based in the blues, but it's where they go from there that matters.

**Santana:** *Tropical Spirits* parts 1/2 (Purple Pyramid, 2000)

Though Santana's eponymous debut album is considered the classic, their earlier demos (available in myriad permutations over a string of budget-and-other albums—this is the best) capture the band at its most blisteringly raw, patently searching out their future on the cuts that were subsequently re-recorded for *Santana* ("Jingo," "Soul Sacrifice," "El Corazon Manda") and exercising their instincts on those that wouldn't.

# FRONTIERS OF FUNK: MOTOWN GETS WITH IT

Famously, Berry Gordy so disliked the term "funk" that, when his Motown label came to release an album by a band whose very name contained the offending word, he personally instructed the group to change its name.

Equally famously, when two of the greatest jewels in the Motown crown demanded they be permitted to record music in keeping with their personal feelings, Gordy came close to losing both of them, so vehemently did he oppose their wishes.

Yet, as the '60s ended and the '70s began, the Motown studios in Detroit not only continued living up to their historic nickname of Hitsville, they did so with one finger so firmly on the pulse of the changing marketplace that even the undisputed masters of the one musical form that Motown still failed to fully endorse—funk, of course—kept one eye firmly on the label's output, knowing that even the omnipotent Gordy could not and, ultimately, would not, stand in the way of his artists' progress.

Marvin Gaye's epochal *What's Going On* album (1971), conceived around his brother Frankie's experiences in and after Vietnam, but convened around a rat's nest of social wrongs, may have been couched in the singer's customary silken tones and arrangements, but still it packed a musical punch as profound as any of the outlaw's genre's heavy-hitters.

Stevie Wonder, too, reflected the change in Motown's musical temperament, spending the first half of the '70s progressing from the sophisticated soul bubblegum of "Uptight," "I Was Born To Love Her" and "My Cherie Amour" to the scintillating electricity of "Higher Ground," the urban sprawl of "Living in the City" and the sly, Sly-jive of "Boogie on Reggae Woman." In their own right, Wonder and Gaye had simply struck blows for their own musical individuality. Collectively, however, they confirmed a revolution that invigorated the new decade, even as it completely restructured Motown.

No longer would the company shy away from contemporary issues ("message songs," as the label somewhat patronizingly referred to anything that didn't deal with traditional subjects), passing them on to the less-established likes of Edwin Starr and the Undisputed Truth. No more would controversy and contentiousness be relegated to the more obscure Motown label subsidiaries. And no longer would there be such a thing as a single "Motown" sound.

From the exuberant bubblegum of the young Jackson Five to the gutbucket insistence of the Commodores' "Machine Gun," from the synthesizer assault that Wonder borrowed from the rock group Tonto's Expanding Headband to the sinewy seduction of Diana Ross' "Love Hangover," a whole new musical experience erupted into view. And though Motown purists and nostalgics bemoan the loss of that early, indefinable, Motown "magic," if the history of funk were rewritten without the repercussions of Motown's radical denouement, it would be a shorter and far sadder saga.

The popular image of Motown throughout the '60s was of a massive pop conveyor belt, churning out a steady stream of dynamically arranged, effortlessly performed, honking, bopping dance pop classics, and each one only as unique as the performers who were lined up to record them.

Occasionally something emerged to shatter the image. Marvin Gaye's moody "I Heard It Through the Grapevine," the Supremes' phase-drenched "Reflections" and socially volatile "Love Child" all shocked with their shaking of the Motown "formula." So (earlier in the decade) did the chain of hard-riding, sax-driven instrumentals by Junior Walker & the All-Stars, which nodded toward both James Brown and the Memphis-based Stax label (at that time Motown's greatest rival in the R&B market). Indeed, February 1965's "Shotgun" not only out-vamped the master Brown, it out-gunned him as well; "Papa's Got a Brand New Bag" was still six months away when "Shotgun" commenced its rocket ride to the top of the charts.

Yet "Shotgun" did not appear on any one of the labels best associated with Hitsville at that time, the Motown, Gordy and Tamla imprints that carried the unmistakable imprimatur of the Temptations, the Miracles, Martha Reeves or the Four Tops. Rather, it was farmed away to Soul, a barely tested subsidiary that Gordy purposely reserved for hardcore R&B releases unsuitable for the parent companies (as an interesting aside, Gordy actually copyrighted the word "Soul," some time before it became common parlance for secular Black music).

"Shotgun's" success, then, not only took the Motown hierarchy by surprise, it also flew in the face of everything they believed about their market. One year later, Stevie Wonder had a similarly disrupting effect when he took a version of

Bob Dylan's "Blowing in the Wind" to the top of the R&B chart, solidifying his belief—as author Nelson George put it—"that Black musical tastes weren't as narrow as most record companies, including Motown, often thought they were."

"Blowing in the Wind," of course, also damned another Motown convention. Since the beginning, hit songs had largely been kept within the family (the label's own Jobete music publishing house), a tradition that, in turn, ensured that a "good" Motown song might pass through half a dozen performers' hands before it was finally consigned to the past, and the only difference between any version might be the tempo at which the musicians played it. Or it might not, because even they were generally the same.

Convened over a period of months (and countless sessions), the houseband at Motown played an inestimable role in shaping the label's musical identity. Like the MGs at Stax, the group was drawn from the cream of locally available musicians; unlike the MGs, or any other studio group of the age, the Funk Brothers enjoyed a success that crossed every conceivable boundary and border. R&B chart-toppers were a regular occurrence; pop smashes rolled out with production line precision. Not only were the Funk Brothers unstoppable, they seemed infallible as well.

Unnamed at the time, the Funk Brothers were integral to label founder Berry Gordy's dream from the outset. The first ever release on his Tamla label 1959's "Come to Me," featured ex-Jackie Wilson bassist James Jamerson and drummer Benny Benjamin, alongside Thomas Bowles (sax), Eddie Willis (gtr) and Joe Messina (gtr).

Over the next five years, other musicians moved in and out of the orbit as individual producers, circumstances and availability demanded. By 1964, however, the group had settled down to a solid core of Jamerson, Benjamin and former Aretha Franklin/Lloyd Price-pianist Earl Van Dyke, with guitarist Robert White completing the core quartet.

Aside from a handful of European tours, the Funk Brothers rarely strayed far from Detroit.—Indeed, the very nature of the Motown operation insisted that they be on call at all hours (a separate road band accompanied Motown artists when they toured), to put in anything up to 12 hours a day in the Snakepit (as they called the tiny Motown Studio A). Neither were the musicians allowed any more creative freedom than individual producers (and the omnipresent Gordy) deemed appropriate to whichever song they were recording at the time.

The atmosphere was stifling. On the one occasion that the Funk Brothers were permitted to record their own album, Motown not only picked the tracks (instrumental versions of label hits) and the arrangements (there was to be no deviation from the songs' original melody lines); the label even selected a new name for the group, Earl Van Dyke & the Soul Brothers. Gordy believed that the word "funk" had no place around such an operation as his.

The Brothers' only opportunity to relax, then, came after-hours, when the quartet headed down to the Chit Chat Club to jam the riffs and ideas that would be brought back to the studio for infusion into the next Motown classic. Until the club was destroyed during the Detroit riots of June 1967, "many of the grooves that made it to vinyl over at Hitsville actually had their origins in the Chit Chat jam sessions," Van Dyke told journalist Allan Slutsky.

The end of the Chit Chat also marked the end of this particular incarnation of the Funk Brothers. After years of increasing substance abuse, Benjamin was now so unreliable that even his once instinctive time-keeping had fallen apart. Increasingly, Uriel Jones replaced him on sessions. Bob Babbitt now vied with Jamerson for the title of Motown's supreme bassist. And Dennis Coffey and Melvin "Wah Wah Watson" Ragin had moved into the front rank of guitarists. And with the new faces came, of course, new ideas, personified by staff producer Norman Whitfield.

Inspired by both the emergent rock funk fusion sounds of Sly & the Family Stone and the socially aware songs of Motown's latest writing team, the Clan (R. Dean Taylor, Pam Sawyer, Frank Wilson and Deke Richards, authors of the Supremes' "Love Child"), Whitfield and partner Barrett Strong commenced their assault on Motown's ingrained sensibilities with "Cloud Nine," a psychedelic soul synthesis that combined momentum and message to emerge utterly unique.

With the Temptations set to record the song, Babbitt, Jones, Coffey and Ragin were all present for the session, the first named to lay down the pulsing beat that drove the song inexorably on, the latter to layer the rock inflected guitars Whitfield required.

According to drummer Jones, interviewed by author Nelson George, Whitfield "came into the studio one day and said 'I wanna do something different. I wanna do something fresh.'" And he succeeded. "Cloud Nine" blasted into the R&B chart in November 1968, eventually spending three weeks at #2. It was held at bay, ironically, by another Whitfield/Strong composition, Marvin Gaye's "I Heard It Through the Grapevine."

Of the two, "Grapevine" was subsequently adjudged one of the greatest records ever made. "Cloud Nine" was simply one of the most important. As George remarked in his history of Motown, *Where Did Our Love Go*, "Isaac Hayes, Barry White, Curtis Mayfield . . . Gamble and Huff, men who became the cutting edge of Black music in the early '70s, all owed a debt to 'Cloud Nine' for opening up Black music and preparing the Black audience for more progressive directions."

Neither would the innovation end there. The accompanying album of the same name followed the title track first with a new, supremely funky rendition of "Grapevine"(its signature riff subverted to the ghost of a piano fighting to be heard through the drums), then with "Run Away Child, Running Wild," a sprawling nine-minute soundscape that added spacey organ and heartbroken "I want my momma" wailing to the mix, and still it emerged a mere shadow of what the same team would create the following year.

*Psychedelic Shack* (1970) caught the Temptations not only tracing the title track's convulsive funkadelia, but followed through with the eight-plus minute "Take a Stroll Thru Your Mind," possibly the most adventurous (and certainly the most experimental) cut ever to grace a Hitsville release. A crazy paving acid trip, "Take a Trip" was the culmination of a Whitfield vision that returning bassist Jamerson summed up, so succinctly, as "monstrous funk."

Familiar refrains and beats raced past like highway signs. Ghostly guitars scythed through the walking bass. The history of Motown itself was drenched in a lysergic dreamscape that alternately lulled and lured the listener, before the entire thing climaxed with one monstrous gong blast, as shattering to the senses as the firearm blast that opened "Shotgun" five years earlier.

Neither were the Temptations to be the sole beneficiaries of Whitfield's inventiveness. Throughout 1970–71, Rare Earth (the first White rock act to be signed to Motown, albeit for the short-lived Rare Earth subsidiary) and Edwin Starr were both propelled to glory on the back of Whitfield's funk-caked streams of socio-political consciousness, with Starr's "War"—reprised from *Psychedelic Shack* to become a pop #1 during fall 1970—swiftly ascending to the stature of social anthem.

Starr's Christmas-time follow-up, "Stop the War Now," was even more outspoken, while the New Year's "Funky Music Sho' Nuff Turns Me On" (backed by a dangerous new interpretation of "Cloud 9") evidenced just how strongly the winds of change had blown through Motown. Once, Berry Gordy would not even allow the word "funk" on the sleeve of an album that, in all fairness to the Brothers, was highly unlikely to bother the chart. Now it was emblazoned across a follow-up to one of Motown's biggest hits of the past 12 months.

If Whitfield and (suddenly, less significantly) the Clan were the spearhead that drove Motown into the new decade, they were not alone. Funk Brother Earl Van Dyke released a solo album, *The Earl of Funk* in September 1970, a set of lunging lounge piano recreations of the day's biggest hits, complete with stylized renditions of Sly Stone's bass blurge "Thank You Falettin Me Be Mice Elf Again" and the Meters' "Cissy Strut." Meanwhile, Jobete staff writer Al Cleveland and the Four Tops' Renaldo Benson took advantage of the new climate to present Marvin Gaye with "What's Going On?"—a reflective and apparently all-encompassing contemplation of the state of the nation.

It was a powerful song and, in its implications, a frightening one. Gaye himself resisted recording it for several weeks before throwing himself into first the song itself, and then an entire album in a similar vein.

Now it was Motown's turn to draw the line. With Gordy allegedly pronouncing "What's Going On" the worst record he'd ever heard, Gaye's album sat on the shelf for close to six months, even after "What's Going On" itself, reluctantly released as a single, topped the R&B chart. It was June 1971, before Motown saw fit to release the parent album. Their reluctance to commit either artist or label to this radical new direction was so strong that it even broke another of the company's most ironclad traditions: always have a fresh smash ready the moment the last one begins slipping down the chart.

Of course, once *What's Going On* proved its commercial worth, there was to be no holding back. Two further singles, "Mercy Mercy Me (The Ecology)" and "Inner City Blues (Make Me Wanna Holler)" topped the chart, making 1971 Gaye's most successful year in such terms since 1968 and "Grapevine." *What's Going On* itself topped the R&B chart for nine weeks while, across the spectrum, music critics flocked to heap fresh and further accolades upon it.

In 1985, Nelson George described *What's Going On* as "a recording on par" with Sly Stones' *Stand* and the Beatles' *Sgt. Pepper's Lonely Hearts Club Band*. Ten years later, *Mojo* magazine adjudged it #6 in a wide-ranging poll of the 100 Greatest Albums Ever Made. (*Stand* came in at #65, *Pepper* at #51.)

Even more important, however, was the opinion of Gaye's own peers. It is no coincidence whatsoever that *What's Going On* should be followed, almost immediately, by commentary as hard-hitting as Funkadelic's *America Eats Its Young*, Sly & the Family Stone's *There's a Riot Goin' On* and Isaac Hayes' *Shaft*. Indeed, Hayes himself acknowledged that his soundtrack was inescapably informed by "what happened in the '60s, the civil rights struggle, the Vietnam issues and so forth."

All three were cut in the shadow of *What's Going On*. All three brought to the mass marketplace a Black consciousness that hitherto had been buried away either in the polemic of one-off 45s ("War," the Temptations' "Ball of Confusion"), or else consigned to the obscurity of underground cult acts.

Certainly Stevie Wonder understood the implications of Gaye's new stance, instantly combining the despite-it-all success of *What's Going On* with his own plans for artistic independence. Wonder's 21st birthday on May 13, 1971, also marked the expiration of his existing contract with Motown. Of course he renewed it, but only after leaving the company on tenterhooks through weeks of renegotiation, and only after informing them that he now intended to explore his own creativity as thoroughly as he and his advisers had explored their options before signing the deal.

He proved true to his word. Absolutely inspired within the recently (September 1970) deceased Jimi Hendrix's Electric Lady Studios in New York, a year's worth of sessions saw Wonder complete the heart of four albums: *Music of My Mind*, *Talking Book* (both 1972), *Innervisions* (1973) and *Fulfillingness' First Finale* (1974). Each one kept pace with developments not only elsewhere within the worlds of soul, funk and R&B, but in the heart of rock territory too. During this same period, Wonder guested on recordings by Peter Frampton, Dave Mason and James Taylor; he toured with the Rolling Stones and he wrote songs for Jeff Beck. It was a ferocious burst of creativity that only let up when Wonder was involved, and almost killed, in a highway accident in 1973.

By the time he returned to action in 1976 with the *Songs in the Key of Life* double album, Wonder was one of the biggest stars in the world; his new album, one of the most eagerly anticipated in history. And his record label, home now to acts as far apart as the Commodores and the Undisputed Truth, Jerry Butler and the Dynamic Superiors, actor Albert Finney and diva Thelma Houston, was also home to some of the most esoteric and adventurous sounds around. It was, indeed, all a very long way from the Motown of old.

## FUNKY MOTOWN: RECOMMENDED LISTENING

### Mandre: *Mandre* (Motown, 1977)
The first of three seductive slow jam albums cut by superstar session player Andre Lewis following stints with Buddy Miles and Frank Zappa (his "Dirty Love" is given the P-Funk treatment within). Heavily electronic and at least partially conceptual, Lewis washes lavish synths over some dynamic bass, while sound effects predict disco's forthcoming fascination with *Star Wars*.

### Rare Earth: *Greatest Hits and Rare Classics* (Motown 1991)
It isn't difficult to see why Rare Earth never really caught on, but hand them a Motown classic ("Get Ready") or a Whitfield number ("Hum Along and Dance," "Big John Is My Name," "Midnight Lady," "I'm Losing You") and they draw a tangible line between hard rock and rootsy funk.

### Edwin Starr: *Involved* (Gordy, 1971)
A standard Motown star-sings-hits-by-other-stars album, dignified by the nature of the hits sung by the star: "Ball of Confusion," "Cloud Nine" and "Stand," alongside Starr's own three recent hits.

### The Temptations: *Psychedelic Shack* (Gordy, 1970)
The title track is irresistible and a take on "War," complete with marching military refrain, at least aims for the passion Edwin Starr later brought to it. But the key cuts are "Friendship Train," a seven-minute refrain that rattles by like an express, and the segued salvo that closes side one: "Hum Along and Dance" and "Take a Stroll Through Your Mind." Both leave you with no alternative but to obey. A staggering achievement.

### Earl Van Dyke: *The Earl of Funk* (Soul, 1970)
Excuse the arrangements and picture what lies beneath. For every "Wichita Linesman" there's a "Cissy Strut," for every "Cherie Amour" there's a "Stingray." And one wonders precisely how ironic his choice of "Thank You (Falettin Me Be

Mice Elf Again)" really was. Apparently recorded live, Van Dyke's funky organ drums up some haunting originals: "Fuschia Moods," "The Stingray," "The Whip a Rang," and "The Flick" are highlights.

### Jr. Walker & the All-Stars: *Shotgun* (Soul, 1965)

Nothing can recapture the first time you heard "Shotgun" itself, but the album of the same name tries hard, taut saxophone fission hitting hard with "Shake and Fingerpop," "Shoot Your Shot," "Do the Boomerang" and more.

### Stevie Wonder: *At the Close of a Century* (Motown, 1999)

Four CD box tracing Wonder from 1963's "Fingertips" through to a 1996 collaboration with Babyface. Not surprisingly, the real meat is in the earlier half of the set, with disc two, dedicated to the 1971–74 period, a shameless festival of funky exploration. Of the later recordings, 1980's "Master Blaster," a funk-reggae tribute to Bob Marley, makes you wish that all slow declines could sound so good.

# PART TWO: CLASSIC FUNK

## ACT ONE

**FORMED:** *1972, Los Angeles, CA*
**ORIGINAL LINE-UP:** *Raeford Gerald (producer)*

Producer of Millie Jackson's first three albums, and writer of some of her best known hits ("My Man, a Sweet Man," "I Miss You Baby," "Breakaway," "How Do You Feel the Morning After"), Raeford Gerald convened the slick jamming Act One around a group of sessionmen he frequently worked with on other projects.

Signing with Jackson's then-label Spring, Act One scraped two R&B chart hits during 1973, the pounding "Friends or Lovers" and "Takes Two of Us," both drawn from their eponymous album. They then scored an unexpected success in the UK when the infectious "Tom the Peeper" single crept into the Top 40 in 1974, primarily on the strength of its popularity on the Northern Soul dancefloors.

The song did little in America, however, and Gerald did not follow it up. By 1975, he was working with soulman Joe Simon on his hit *Get Down* album; Gerald later reunited with Jackson for 1999's *Between the Sheets*.

### ACT ONE DISCOGRAPHY
### CHART LOG

1973 Friends or Lovers/I Never Had a Love like Yours (Spring—#22 R&B/
    #101 pop)
1973 Takes Twoo of Us/A Whole Lot of Lovemaking (Spring—#90 R&B)

### LP
**6** 1974 Act One (Spring)
Well played, but generally workmanlike horn driven funk highlighted by "Tom the Peeper."

## ALL THE KING'S MEN, see MACEO PARKER

## AVERAGE WHITE BAND

**FORMED:** *1972, Dundee, Scotland*
**ORIGINAL LINE-UP:** *Hamish Stuart (b. 10/8/49, Glasgow—gtr, vcls), Onnie McIntyre (b. 9/25/45, Lennox, Scotland—gtr, vcls), Alan Gorrie (b. 7/19/46, Perth, Scotland—bs, vcls), Roger Ball (b. 6/4/44, Dundee, Scotland—kybds, sax), Malcolm Duncan (b. 8/24/45, Montrose, Scotland—tnr sax), Robbie McIntosh (b. 1950, Scotland; d. 9/23/74,—drms)*

The Average White Band (AWB) initially formed around the idea of a single unit functioning along the same lines as the great studio housebands of the '60s—Booker T. & the MGs, the Funk Brothers, etc. All six members had strong, if understated pedigrees: Onnie McIntyre and Alan Gorrie were ex-Hopscotch, a low-grade Scottish soul act of the late '60s; Robbie McIntosh was ex-Brian Auger's Oblivion Express, one of the hottest jazz fusion squads around; Roger Ball, Malcolm Duncan and Hamish Stuart were well-known sessionmen.

The unifying factor was the musicians' fondness for the one musical style none of them had been asked to play, a hard-hitting funk R&B sound. AWB's name, therefore, was a suitably self-deprecating commentary on their intentions; their sound, though at times clinical, was a vibrant contradiction of all that implied. Gorrie explained, "it's the only music that we've ever as a group gotten off on. It's . . . the only language that we ever understood and that's why we arrived at the policy of making our own R&B music."

In December 1972, AWB won an utterly unexpected (if anonymous) hit backing Chuck Berry on the UK #1 "My Ding-a-Ling." They followed up with a well-received opening slot at Eric Clapton's January 1973, London comeback show. But even after signing with MCA, AWB seemed destined for obscurity. Their debut album, *Show Your Hand*, and early singles "Put It Where You Want It" and "How Can You Go Home," did little and AWB were dropped. The same evening that they heard the news, however, they were introduced to Atlantic Records executive Jerry Wexler, producer of so many of their own favorite records. The following morning, Wexler signed AWB to the US wing of Atlantic—ironically, the UK label had already turned them down on several occasions.

Atlantic promptly dispatched them to New York's Atlantic Recording Studio with the legendary Arif Marden. "He allowed us to express what was really inside ourselves in terms of composition and the direction we took in the studio," Gorrie reflected; the result, an eponymous album and the Grammy winning "Pick Up the Pieces" single, slammed AWB to the top of both the US pop and R&B charts, an unheard-of achievement for a white group—average or otherwise.

"Pick Up the Pieces" itself started life as an unnamed jam recorded in tribute to one of AWB's biggest influences, James Brown (the JBs' "Gimme Some More" is an undeniable parent of the signature riff). Saxophonist Ball wrote the horn line in the studio; Gorrie then came up with the

**Scotland's Average White Band—a distinct cut above the norm.**

notion of adding a chant—apparently his original suggestion was "pick up the peas," after another JBs cut, "Pass the Peas."

"Pick Up the Pieces" was released in the UK in July 1974, and flopped; a follow-up, "Nothing You Can Do," went no further. But worse was to follow. Even as AWB were gearing up for the record's American release, they were shattered by the heroin overdose and death, at a Hollywood party, of drummer McIntosh on September 23, 1974.

Stunned, AWB returned home, before replacing McIntosh with another Brian Auger graduate, Steve Ferrone. Then it was back to the US to tour and marvel as both album and single stormed the chart. Heeding the lessons learned in the UK (where a reissued "Pick Up the Pieces" had finally charted), Atlantic opted not to pull a second single from the album, insisting instead that the band cut something else in the spirit of the hit.

They emerged with another James Brown-type jam, "Cut

the Cake," which effortlessly returned AWB to the Top Ten in April 1975. Utterly unflattered by such tributes, Brown himself responded by remixing and overdubbing a 1971 JBs' rhythm track, "Hot Pants Road," and releasing it (on the specially formed Identify label) as "Pick Up the Pieces One by One," under the name AABB (the Above Average Black Band).

AWB's second album, also titled *Cut the Cake* (and dedicated to McIntosh), followed in June. It emulated its predecessor in going gold, while the following year's *Soul Searching* ultimately went platinum as AWB continued touring the US; a souvenir of their endeavors, 1977's *Person To Person*, was recorded at shows in Philadelphia, Pittsburgh and Cleveland.

AWB's live activities slowed somewhat following this, as the individuals found themselves in constant demand for session work—finally fulfilling their own initial vision for the group. Gorrie, Stuart, McIntyre and Ferrone joined

Chaka Khan on her 1978 *Chaka* debut; the entire AWB backed Dick Morrissey and Jim Mullen on their jazz-fusion classic *Up* in 1977.

AWB were in Florida recording their next album when an Atlantic executive suggested they take a day out of their schedule to cut a single, "Get It Up for Love," with Ben E. King. Recorded in a day, the session was so successful that Gorrie immediately suggested the partnership continue on over the course of an entire album. Atlantic agreed and after one further single, "A Star in the Ghetto," the *Benny and Us* album was released during summer 1977. The team-up also toured Europe and played the Montreaux Jazz festival.

In 1978, the group's own next album, *Warner Communications*, went gold and kept AWB's head above the all-pervasive tides of disco—at the same time severing their last links with funk, in favor of a gentle (some said generic) soul sound. Interviewed for the R&B Network, Gorrie reflected, "What happened was, the style of music we played went away at the end of the '70s and disco took over. Disco was a nail in R&B's coffin at that time." The musicians, too, had drifted apart and, as the decade ended, so did AWB's pre-eminence.

*Feel No Fret* (1979) was a weak set met by poor sales and it was indeed ironic that, as the American market tired of the band, their homeland, which had hitherto ignored almost every release since "Pick Up the Pieces," was paying attention again. *Feel No Fret* became AWB's first British Top 20 entry since their debut, while the singles "Walk On By" and "When Will You Be Mine" both made the Top 50.

Departing Atlantic in 1979, AWB signed with Arista, with their UK profile still outweighing their American status. "Let's Go Round Again" climbed to #12 in April 1980; the album *Shine* made #14. But the writing was on the wall. The *Volume Eight* album made a brave attempt to lure old listeners into the group's new sound, combining a string of early hits with a clutch of new songs. But AWB recorded just one more album, 1982's *Cupid's in Fashion* (with ex-Plasmatics guitarist Ritchie Stotts as special guest), before splitting in early 1983.

The musicians scattered. Steve Ferrone joined Duran Duran as they prepared to record the Nile Rodgers' produced *Notorious* album; Hamish Stuart linked first with ex-Beatle Paul McCartney for his *Flowers in the Dirt* album and tour, then joined Eric Clapton's backing group. Gorrie signed with A&M and released a solo album, *Sleepless Nights*, before convening a 1989 AWB reunion with Ball and McIntyre, plus yet another ex-member of Brian Auger's

Oblivion Express (and former Santana vocalist), Alex Ligertwood. Elliot Lewis (kybds) and Tiger McNeil (drms) completed the lineup.

The *Aftershock* album followed, but did little and AWB vanished again, resurfacing once more in 1994, following the UK success of the *Let's Go Round Again* best-of album. (A remix of the title cut was also a hit.) With drummer Pete Abbott on board, the independently released *Soul Tattoo* appeared in Europe and Japan in late 1996. *Face to Face*, a live set recorded in San Francisco in October 1997, followed.

Abbot quit in 1998 to marry; he was replaced by former Bootsy Collins sideman Fred Angelo and AWB celebrated their 25th anniversary with fall tours of the UK and US. They continued gigging through 1999, not only celebrating their own music but also promoting keyboard player Lewis' solo album, *Get Back What You Give*.

## AVERAGE WHITE BAND COMPLETE DISCOGRAPHY
### SINGLES/CHART LOG
1973 Put It Where You Want It/Reach Out (MCA)

1973 This World Has Music/The Jugglers (MCA)

1974 How Can You Go Home/Twilight Zone (MCA)

1974 Nothing You Can Do/I Just Can't Give You Up (Atlantic)

1974 Pick Up the Pieces/Work To Do (Atlantic—#5 R&B/#1 pop)

1975 Cut the Cake/Person to Person (Atlantic—#7 R&B/#10 pop)

1975 If I Ever Lose This Heaven/High Flyin' (Atlantic—#25 R&B/#39 pop)

1975 School Boy Crush/Groovin' the Night Away (Atlantic—#22 R&B/#33 pop)

1976 Queen of My Soul/Would You Stay (Atlantic—#10 R&B/#40 pop)

1976 A Love of Your Own/Soul Searchin' (Atlantic—#35 R&B/#101 pop)

1977 Cloudy/Love Your Life (Atlantic—#55 R&B)

1978 Your Love Is a Miracle/One Look over My Shoulder (Atlantic—#33 R&B)

1978 Big City Lights/She's a Dream (Atlantic)

1979 Walk On By/Too Late To Cry (Atlantic—#32 R&B/#92 pop)

1979 Feel No Fret/Fire Burning (Atlantic)

1980 Let's Go Round Again/Shine (Arista—#40 R&B/#53 pop)

1980 For You, for Love/Whatcha Gonna Do for Me (Arista—#60 R&B/#106 pop)

1980 Into the Night/? (Arista)

1982 Easier Said than Done/? (Arista)

1982 Cupid's in Fashion/? (Arista)

1988 The Spirit of Love/remixes (Track—#47 R&B)

### AVERAGE WHITE BAND WITH BEN E. KING
1977 Get It Up/Keepin' It to Myself (Atlantic—#21 R&B)

1977 A Star in the Ghetto/What Is Soul (Atlantic—#25 R&B)

1977 Fool for You Anyway/The Message (Atlantic)

### LPs
**4** 1973 Show Your Hand (MCA)

Enthusiastic but generally dull collection, reissued in 1976 as *Put It Where You Want It* (#39 R&B/#39 pop)

**7** **1974 Average White Band (Atlantic—#1 R&B/#1 pop)**
"Pick Up the Pieces" dominates, just as Atlantic insisted it did, when they refused to endanger AWB's success by releasing a second single from the album. It dominates, but it is by no means representative; AWB's forte at this point was funked-up rock, tastefully embellished with horns and wah-wah, but built around tightly constructed songs all the same. Only "Pick Up the Pieces" indicates their jam capabilities; it alone fulfills them.

**5** **1975 Cut the Cake (Atlantic—#1 R&B/#4 pop)**
Brutally formulaic repeat of the last album, even down to the "Pick Up More Pieces" vibe of the title track.

**4** **1976 Soul Searching (Atlantic—#9—#2 R&B/#9 pop)**
The rut gets deeper. The band's playing remains breathtakingly precise, but the songs are almost totally devoid of soul and content.

**6** **1977 Person to Person (live) (Atlantic—#9 R&B/#28 pop)**
**5** **1978 Warmer Communications (Atlantic—#12 R&B/#28 pop)**
The slow jam "Your Love Is a Miracle" lures the listener in with more aplomb than anyone had a right to expect. Unfortunately, the rest of the album does not live up to its promise, sucking everything into a funk-lite swamp that even a reprise of the "Pieces" horn pattern (during the dangerously titled "Same Feeling, Different Song") cannot avoid.

**4** **1979 Feel No Fret (Atlantic—#30 R&B/#32 pop)**
**4** **1980 Shine (Arista—#38 R&B/#116 pop)**
**3** **1982 Cupid's in Fashion (Arista—#49 R&B/#202 pop)**
**4** **1989 Aftershock (Track—#69 R&B)**
**5** **1996 Soul Tattoo (AWB)**
**7** **1997 Face to Face—Live (AWB)**
An energetic, even enthusiastic reminder of past glories, looser than their last live album and benefiting accordingly.

## AVERAGE WHITE BAND WITH BEN E. KING

**6** **1977 Benny and Us (Atlantic—#14 R&B/#33—pop)**
King is the star of the show, AWB a better-than-competent backing band.

## SELECTED COMPILATIONS AND ARCHIVE RELEASES
1980 Volume VIII (Atlantic—#182 pop)
Part new material ("Kiss Me," "Love Gives, Love Takes Away," "Love Won't Get in the Way"), part greatest hits. The decline from first to last is breathtaking.

## SELECTED SAMPLES
A Love of Your Own — Brownstone: Love Me like You Do (1997)

A Star in the Ghetto — NWA: If It Ain't Ruff (1988)
If I Ever Lose This Heaven — Gumbo: Jungle (1993)
I'm the One — Brand Nubian: Word Is Bond (1994)
The Jugglers — Ice Cube: What They Hittin' Foe? (1990)
Love Your Life — A Tribe Called Quest: Check the Rhime (1991)
Love Your Life — Kool Keith: Get Off My Elevator (1999)
Pick Up the Pieces — Awesome Dre & Hardcore Committee: You Can't Hold Me Back (1989)
Pick Up the Pieces — Changing Faces: I Got Somebody Else (1997)
Pick Up the Pieces — Chris Rock featuring Old Dirty Bastard: Me & ODB (1999)
Pick Up the Pieces — Cash Money & Marvelous: Who's in the Place? (1988)
Pick Up the Pieces — Doug E Fresh: On the Strength (1988)
Pick Up the Pieces — Public Enemy: Night of the Living Baseheads (remix) (1988)
Pick Up the Pieces — Style: Set the Mood (1991)
Pick Up the Pieces — Tim Dog: You Ain't Shit (1991)
Person to Person — Big Daddy Kane: Mr. Pitiful (1990)
Person to Person — Brand Nubian: Word Is Bond (1994)
Person to Person — Boss: Recipe of a Hoe (1993)
Person to Person — Brothers like Outlaws: Trapped into Darkness (1992)
Person to Person — Changing Faces: I Got Somebody Else (1997)
Person to Person — EPMD: Richter Scale (1997)
Person to Person — Insane Poetry: Angel of Death (1992)
Person to Person — Low Profile: That's Why They Do It (1990)
Person to Person — Luke: Cowardz in Compton (1993)
Person to Person — Mellow Man Ace: Gettin' Stupid (1990)
Person to Person — Public Enemy: Air Hoodlum (1992)
Person to Person — Puff Daddy, featuring Foxy Brown: Friend (1997)
Person to Person — Steady B: Stone Cold Hustler (1989)
Person to Person — Tim Dog: Goin Wild in the Penile (1991)
Reach Out — Boogie Down Productions: House Niggas (1990)
Reach Out — Ice Cube: Steady Mobbin' (1991)
Reach Out — Lifers Group: Jack U. Back (So You Wanna Be a Gangsta) (1993)
Reach Out — Lifers Group: Rise or Fall (1993)
Schoolboy Crush — Artifacts: What Goes On? (1994)
Schoolboy Crush — Color Me Badd: Thinkin' Back (remix) (1991)
Schoolboy Crush — De La Soul: Do as De La Does (1989)
Schoolboy Crush — Double XX Posse: School of Hard Knocks (1992)
Schoolboy Crush — Eric B & Rakim: Microphone Friend (1988)
Schoolboy Crush — EPMD: Can't Hear Nothin' but the Music (1992)
Schoolboy Crush — EPMD: Give the People (remix) (1991)
Schoolboy Crush — Father MC: One Night Stand (1992)
Schoolboy Crush — Janet Jackson: New Agenda (1993)
Schoolboy Crush — Diana King: Shy Guy (1995)
Schoolboy Crush — Da Lench Mob: You and Your Heroes (1992)
Schoolboy Crush — Nas: Halftime (1994)
Schoolboy Crush — Public Enemy: Pollywanacracka (1990)
Schoolboy Crush — Ras Kass: Soul on Ice (1996)
Schoolboy Crush — Special Ed: Think About It (1989)

Schoolboy Crush — TLC: Ain't 2 Proud 2 Beg (1992)
Schoolboy Crush — Too Short: Life Is Too Short (1989)
Schoolboy Crush — X-Clan: Grand Verbalizer, What Time Is It? (1990)
Soul Searching — Private Investigators: U Fi Listen (1993)
Stop The Rain — Gang Starr: Gotta Get Over (1999)
Sweet & Sour — Justin Warfield: Cool like the Blues (1993)
T.L.C. — Boogie Down Productions: Ya Know the Rules (1990)
T.L.C. — The Lox: The Heist (1998)
Your Love Is a Miracle — DelTha Funkee Homosapien: Hoodz Come in Dozens (1991)
Your Love Is a Miracle — WC & the Maad Circle: Get Up on That Funk (1991)

## BABY HUEY AND THE BABYSITTERS

**BORN:** *James Thomas Ramsey, 1954, Richmond IN; died: 10/28/70*

Contrary to his stagename, Baby Huey was a behemoth of a man, who blended psychedelia and R&B harder and hotter than almost anybody else at the time. He emerged on the Chicago scene in 1967, forming the ten-piece Babysitters and signing to the tiny local USA label.

The band's first single, "Messin' with the Kid," became an immediate local smash and was promptly picked up for wider distribution by St. Lawrence; a second single, "Monkey Man," followed and, in 1969, Curtis Mayfield signed the Babysitters to his own Curtom label.

Mayfield's own "Mighty Mighty," the Babysitters' first single, was a riotous slab of funk, apparently recorded live and edited down from a massive rap jam to a little more than two and a half minutes. It didn't chart, but with the group's live appeal as vast as Huey himself, a breakthrough appeared imminent.

In early 1970, Huey and the Babysitters traveled to Los Angeles with producer Mayfield and arranger Donnie Hathaway to cut their debut album, *The Baby Huey Story: Living Legend*—they also played the Whisky A Go-Go, and at least one witness, Eric Bloom of future heavy metal superstars Blue Oyster Cult, summed up Huey's uncompromising lifestyle when he recalled, "I was hangin' with them a lot and it was a very bizarre trip. I remember goin' to this Whisky and doin' all . . . kinds of stuff." Just weeks after the album was completed Huey died following a drug overdose.

The album's title now doubly ironic, *Living Legend* was released in early 1971 and became a minor hit; the Babysitters, meanwhile, changed their name to Goliath, regrouping around a new vocalist, 18-year-old Chaka Khan. In this form, the group landed a weekly residence at Chicago club Nero's Pit, largely performing Top 40 material, but also issuing a single on Curtom, before breaking up when Khan quit to join Rufus in 1972.

**BABY HUEY AND THE BABYSITTERS DISCOGRAPHY**

*LPs*

**10** 1971 The Baby Huey Story: The Living Legend (Curtom—#38 R&B/#214 pop)

Blistering brilliance, all the promise of the party-time "Mighty Mighty" fulfilled without a false step. A second Mayfield composition, "Hard Times," blisters with all the fire of great Chicago soul, but every track's a thunderous mass of dancing, shouting, thumping funk, with Huey's trademark bellow inciting a riot every time he opens his mouth.

### SELECTED SAMPLES
Hard Times — Tha Alkaholiks: Soda Pop (1993)
Hard Times — Biz Markie: The Dragon (1989)
Hard Times — Black Moon: Powaful Impak! (1993)
Hard Times — Chemical Brothers: Playgound for a Wedgeless Firm (1995)
Hard Times — Chill Rob G: Ride the Rhythm (1990)
Hard Times — Ice Cube: The Birth (1991)
Hard Times — Saafir: Joint Custody (1994)
Hard Times — Supercat: Ghetto Red Hot (1992)
Hard Times — A Tribe Called Quest: Can I Kick It? (remix) (1990)
Hard Times — Yaggfu Front: Slappin' Suckas Silly (1993)
Listen To Me — Eric B. & Rakim: Follow the Leader (1988)
Listen To Me — Public Enemy: Revolutionary Generation (1990)

## THE BAR-KAYS

**FORMED:** *1966*

**RE-FORMED:** *1968, Memphis TN*

**ORIGINAL (1968) LINEUP:** *James Alexander (bs), Ben Cauley (trum), Harvey Henderson (sax), Ronnie Gordon (kybds), Michael Toles (gtr) Roy Cunningham (drms) Willie Hall (drms)*

Originally known as the River Arrows, and then the Imperials, this Memphis soul group was discovered by Otis Redding while they were working at a barberstore next door to the Stax/Volt Studios. He recruited them as counterparts to the already revered Booker T. & the MGs houseband and Mar-Keys horn section.

Comprising Jimmy King (gtr), Ronnie Caldwell (orgn), James Alexander (bs) Carl Cunningham (drms), Phalon Jones (sax) and Ben Cauley (trum), the Bar-Kays backed many of the great Stax artists of the mid-late-'60s and scored their own major hit during the summer of 1967 with the instrumental "Soul Finger" (its B-side, the Steve Cropper/Booker T. Jones composition "Knucklehead," also charted.)

"Give Everybody Some" followed, before Redding took the Bar-Kays out on tour that winter as his backing group. Of course they would not return; on December 10, Redding's private plane crashed into a lake near Madison, WI. Aside from the singer, Bar-Kays King, Caldwell, Cunningham and Jones also perished.

Two members of the Bar-Kays remained—Alexander, who missed the flight, and Cauley, who survived it— and, by late 1968, the pair were rebuilding around producer Allen Jones and local musicians Harvey Henderson, Ronnie Gordon, Michael Toles, Roy Cunningham and Willie Hall.

One final single by the original Bar-Kays, a distinctive cover of the Beatles' "A Hard Day's Night," appeared on Stax in early 1968; the new lineup, meanwhile, slipped quietly into circulation at the label, accompanying Isaac Hayes on his *Hot Buttered Soul* LP and appearing on albums by Rufus Thomas, the Staple Singers and Albert King. They also released their own "Copy Cat" single, an entertaining guessing game beneath whose girlish chanted title and driving horns there lurked a riff distinctly similar to Jimi Hendrix's "Foxy Lady." Who, however, was the copy cat meant to be?

The group underwent several early lineup changes; Cunningham and Gordon quit in 1970; keyboard player Winston Stewart came in, together with vocalist Larry Dodson (of Stax balladeers' the Temprees). Toles and original member Cauley were next to depart, joining Isaac Hayes' group; they were replaced by Vernon Burch and Charles Allen just as the Bar-Kays enjoyed a hit with 1971's (inevitably) wah-wah soaked "Son of Shaft."

Further singles "Dance, Dance, Dance," "You're Still My Brother," "It Ain't Easy" and "Coldblooded," released between 1971 and 1975, failed to chart; however, 1971's *Black Rock* album at least offered a fitting description for the group's music, which had hitherto evaded the most inquisitive critics.

Drawing equally, indeed, from both Black R&B and White rock influences, the Bar-Kays' pounding rhythms and jams were one of the highlights of the Stax label festival Wattstax, in 1972; however, awareness of the group's fiery innovation was largely restricted to the cult circuit. Although their live shows were becoming increasingly popular, their records, for the most part, sold poorly. The darkly political *Do You See What I See* (1972) and *Cold Blooded* (1974) were both solid albums, but did nothing saleswise. Meanwhile, the Bar-Kays were blowing away all challengers on the road, upstaging almost anybody they toured with.

Early comparisons with Sly & the Family Stone (whose vocal style Dodson shared) were soon outweighed by references to P-Funk, whose outlandish dress sense the Bar-Kays parallelled, and even rocker Alice Cooper—one of

Dodson's most treasured stage props was a live boa constrictor.

The Stax/Volt label folded in 1975; the following year the Bar-Kays signed with Mercury. Lining up as Dodson (vcls), Alexander (bs), guitarist Larry Smith (who replaced Burch prior to *Cold Blooded*), Charles Allen (trum), Henderson (sax), Stewart (kybds) and Beard (drms), the Bar-Kays' first release for their new label, the kicking "Shake Your Rump to the Funk," powered into the R&B Top Five. At last all the work of the past five years was paying off.

Further exposure was gained when the Bar-Kays toured with P-Funk through late 1976. "Too Hot To Stop" and "Spellbound" were hits and the band's Mercury debut album, *Too Hot To Stop* emerged one of the crucial funk albums of 1976.

The Bar-Kays grasped success with all hands. Through the end of the '70s, they achieved five major R&B hits, "Let's Have Some Fun," "Attitudes," "I'll Dance," "Shine" and "Move Your Boogie Body." The albums *Flying High on Your Love* (1978), *Light of Life* and *Injoy* were all similarly successful; there was even room in the chart for the Bar-Kays' back catalog as Fantasy—owners, now, of the Stax back catalog—unearthed an album's worth of material recorded following *Cold Blooded* and released it as the (possibly spitefully titled) *Money Talks* album. An accompanying single, "Holy Ghost," made the R&B Top 20 effortlessly.

As the decade progressed, of course, the Bar-Kays' early funk intensity was necessarily colored by the demands of the new disco audience. The musicians retained their sense of fun, however, loading every release with both musical and visual puns. Both 1978's *Light of Life* (rush-released to compete with *Money Talks*) and 1980's *As One* arrived in sleeves parodying Earth Wind & Fire's Egyptology fixation.

In addition, the members' photographs on the inner sleeve of *Light* noted each musician's astrological sign in honor of another disco fad, fired by the Floaters' grotesque "Float On" smash hit. The Bar-Kays were also now sporting silver spacesuits, acknowledging the scene's sudden fixation with *Star Wars*.

The band's lineup expanded with their ambitions. *Light of Life* debuted a new ten-piece Bar-Kays, as Frank Thompson (trom), Mark Bynum (kyds) and Sherman Guy (perc) joined the group; they gathered menacingly beneath a lamp post on the sleeve of 1981's *Nightcruising* album, their determined appearance a visual match to the album's own statement of intent, "when you're daring and think you've gone too far," counselled a message on the inner sleeve, "you're only halfway there."

*Nightrider* was almost pure disco—and disco at its purest, a long way from the Bar-Kays of old, but irresistible once it caught you on the dancefloor. Thus, the band marched on into the '80s, seemingly unaffected by anything beyond the need to continue having as much fun as possible, as loudly as they could.

Gleefully embracing the growing importance of electronics and technology in dance music, the Bar-Kays continued scoring hits into the mid-'80s, with a well-received role on the soundtrack to the 1984 movie *Breakdance*, further evidencing their ability to move with the times.

*Breakdance* brought the Bar-Kays their biggest 45 yet, the platinum "Freakshow on the Dancefloor." Another example of their wicked ability to parody their peers, "Freakshow" borrowed just enough from Midnight Star's "No Parking on the Dancefloor" to prove that the two songs' similarities were pointedly deliberate; the follow-up, "Dirty Dancer," made a similar gesture toward Michael Jackson's "Billie Jean."

Successive departures had by now seen the lineup whittled down to a mere trio of Dodson, Stewart and Henderson; even Alexander had gone to pursue a career in A&R. But it took the death of longtime producer Allen Jones from a heart attack on May 5, 1987, to finally slow the Bar-Kays—that year's *Contagious* comprised their last ever recordings with Jones. The following year, the Bar-Kays recorded their final album, *Animal*, bringing the wheel full circle with a guest appearance from Sly Stone.

Touring rigorously, Henderson, Dodson and Stewart kept the Bar-Kays' name alive through the early '90s. But a new deal with the Jaguar label fell through and, by 1993, Stewart had had enough. He quit upon the combo's return from a Japanese tour that year, soon to be followed by Henderson. Dodson, however, promptly reunited with founder member Alexander, for a 1994 concert in Memphis.

The pair convened a veritable Bar-Kays all-star lineup comprising fellow founder Cauley, plus Henderson, Stewart, *Animal*-era sidemen Mark Bynam and Frank Thompson, Hubert Crawford, Ben Jones, Sherman Guy, Larry Johnson and Roy Cunningham. They then signed with BMG subsidiary Zoo, and cut the single "Put a Little Nasty on It"; soon after, the label closed, and the Bar-Kays shifted to Memphis indie Basix for the *48 Hours* album.

With the act sliding readily into the burgeoning funk revival/nostalgia circuit of the '90s, a new lineup crystallized around Dodson, Anderson, Bryan Smith, Michael Anderson (gtr), Tim Horton, Curt Clayton (kybds) and Derek Dabbs, plus a vocal trio. Following another single, "The

Slide," the Bar-Kays signed to the Curb label; 1996's "Everybody Wants That Love" became a local success, while a new album, originally called *Boys in the Band*, but ultimately (and somewhat misleadingly) released as *The Best of Bar-Kays*, arrived that October.

### BAR-KAYS DISCOGRAPHY
### CHART LOG

1967 Soul Finger/Knucklehead (Volt—#3 R&B/#17 POP)

1967 Give Everybody Some/Don't Do That (Volt—#36 R&B/#91 pop)

1968 Hard Day's Night/I Want Someone (Volt)

1968 Copy Cat/In the Hole (Volt)

1969 Don't Stop Dancing to the Music (part one)/(part two) (Volt)

1969 Midnight Cowboy/A. J. the Housefly (Volt)

1970 Sang and Dance/I Thank You (Volt)

1970 Montego Bay/Humpin' (Volt)

1971 Son of Shaft (Volt—#10 R&B/#53 pop)

1972 Dance, Dance, Dance/Memphis Sunrise (Volt)

1973 You're Still My Brother/You're the Best Thing (Volt)

1973 It Ain't Easy/God Is Watching (Volt)

1974 Coldblooded/? (Volt)

1976 Shake Your Rump to the Funk/Summer of Our Love (Mercury—#5 R&B/#23 pop)

1977 Too Hot To Stop (part one)/Bang Bang (Mercury—#8 R&B/#74 pop)

1977 Spellbound/You're So Sexy (Mercury—#29 R&B)

1978 Let's Have Some Fun/Cozy (Mercury—#11 R&B/#102 pop)

1978 Attitudes/Can't Keep My Hands off You (Mercury—#22 R&B)

1978 Holy Ghost/Monster (Stax—#9 R&B)

1978 I'll Dance/Angel Eyes (Mercury #28 R&B)

1979 Shine/Are You Being Real (Mercury—#14 R&B/#102 pop)

1979 Move Your Boogie Body/Love's What It's All About (Mercury—#3 R&B/#57 pop)

1980 Today's the Day/Loving You Is My Occupation (Mercury—#25 R&B/#60 pop)

1980 Boogie Body Land/Running in and out of My Life (Mercury—#7 R&B)

1981 Body Fever/Deliver us (Mercury—#42 R&B)

1981 Hit And Run/Say It Through Love (Mercury—#5 R&B/#101 pop)

1982 Freaky Behavior/Backseat Driver (Mercury—#27 R&B)

1982 Do It (Let Me See You Shake)/Feels like I'm Falling in Love (Mercury—#9 R&B)

1983 She Talks to Me with Her Body/Anticipation (Mercury—#13 R&B)

1984 Freakshow on the Dance Floor/Lovers Should Never Fall in Love (Mercury—#2 R&B/#73 pop)

1984 Dirty Dancer/? (Mercury—#17 R&B)

1984 Sexomatic/? (Mercury—#12 R&B)

1985 Your Place or Mine/(instrumental) (Mercury—#12 R&B)

1985 Banging the Walls/Gina (Mercury—#67 R&B)

1987 Certified True/It Be That Way Sometimes (Mercury—#9 R&B)

1987 Don't Hang Up/Contagious (Mercury—#56 R&B)

1989 Struck by You/Your Place or Mine (Mercury—#11 R&B)

1989 Animal/Time Out (Mercury—#66 R&B)

1993 Put a Little Nasty on It/Funkahawlix mix (Zoo)
1994 Old School Mega Mix/Out of My Mind (Basix)
1995 The Slide/? (Basix—#82 R&B)
1996 Everybody Wants That Love/Soul Finger '96 (Curb)

## LPs

**6** **1967 Soul Finger (Stax)**
Pumping soul-inflections cut firmly in the mold of Booker T.

**5** **1969 Gotta Groove (Stax—#40 R&B)**
Tentative and generally lightweight set, although a handful of cuts shine.

**7** **1971 Black Rock (Volt—#12 R&B/#90 pop)**
Sly's "Dance to the Music" sets the stage for a fast-paced dance party marred only by a redundant stab at "Montego Bay."

**7** **1972 Do You See What I See (Volt—#45 R&B/#212 pop)**
**8** **1974 Cold Blooded (Volt)**
The culmination of the Bar-Kays' early development, a deep funk piledriver that never lets up.

**9** **1976 Too Hot To Stop (Mercury—#8 R&B/#69 pop)**
How great is this album? As good as "Shake Your Rump" and the title track, exhilaratingly punching out the next person to say that disco killed funk.

**7** **1977 Flying High on Your Love (Mercury—#7 R&B/#47 pop)**
**7** **1978 Light of Life (Mercury—#15 R&B/#86 pop)**
If gimmicks be the food of life, goof on. *Light of Life* magpie-magical disco-funk throws in everything from "Let's All Chant" bird calls to TSOP strings, and onto a Jimmy Castor rhythm ("Give It Up") that defies all resistance.

**5** **1979 Injoy (Mercury—#2 R&B/#35 pop)**
**4** **1980 As One (Mercury—#6 R&B/#57 pop)**
The blurting bass of "Boogie Body Land" is as compulsive as anything in the Bar-Kays' catalog, but a surfeit of so-so ballads send it all downhill from there.

**4** **1981 Night Cruisin' (Mercury—#6 R&B/#55 pop)**
It's hard to deny the electrobubble lunacy of "Freaky Behavior," although the novelty synths are beginning to grow tiresome.

**5** **1982 Propositions (Mercury—#9 R&B/#51 pop)**
**6** **1984 Dangerous (Mercury—#7 R&B/#52 pop)**
A wide-screen amalgam of everything that mainstream dance music became in the early-mid-'80s, hung around the monster "Freakshow on the Dancefloor."

**5** **1985 Bangin' the Wall (Mercury—#11 R&B/#115 pop)**
**4** **1987 Contagious (Mercury—#25 R&B/#110 pop)**
**4** **1988 Animal (Mercury—#36 R&B)**
**5** **1994 48 Hours (Basix)**
**5** **1996 The Best of Bar-Kays (Curb)**

## SELECTED COMPILATIONS AND ARCHIVE RELEASES

**7** **1978 Money Talks (Fantasy—#21 R&B/#72 pop)**
Chronologically and schematically the follow-up to *Cold-Blooded*, packed with langorous, lurching stomps and all eight minutes of the hypnotic "Holy Ghost."

**8** **1992 The Best of the Bar-Kays (Stax)**
13 tracks round up a random selection of Stax-era A-sides and B-sides.

One or two seem darkly dated today, but the best of the batch (the laconic near-instrumental "Humpin'," the incendiary "Sang and Dance," a surprisingly effective "Midnight Cowboy") joyously fuse the essentials of funk with a vibe that couldn't have come from anywhere but Stax.

**6** **1993 The Best of the Bar-Kays (Mercury)**
**6** **1996 The Best of the Bar-Kays, Vol. 2 (Mercury)**

## SELECTED SAMPLES

Copy Cat — Cypress Hill: Real Estate (1992)
Cozy — MC Lyte: All That (1991)
Do You See What I See? — Black Sheep: U Mean I'm Not (1991)
Hit & Run — Coolio: County Line (1994)
Holy Ghost — Beastie Boys: Hey Ladies (1989)
Holy Ghost — Kid 'N Play: Gittin' Funky (1988)
Holy Ghost — M.A.R.R.S.: Pump Up the Volume (1987)
Holy Ghost — Public Enemy: Fear of a Black Planet (1990)
Holy Ghost — Steady B: Keeper of the Funk (1991)
Holy Ghost — 2Pac: Trapped (1992)
Holy Ghost — 2Pac: Last Wordz (1993)
Humpin' — Black Sheep: Choice Is Yours (1991)
Humpin' — Cypress Hill: Funky Cypress Hill Shit (1992)
Humpin' — Cypress Hill: Real Estate (1992)
Humpin' — Ice Cube: Amerikkka's Most Wanted (1990)
In the Hole — Compton's Most Wanted: Dead Men Tell No Lies (1992)
In the Hole — Fu-Schnickens: Ring the Alarm (1992)
In the Hole — Genius/GZA: Living in the World Today (1995)
In the Hole — Kool G Rap: Crime Pays (1992)
In the Hole — Yo-Yo: Hoes (1992)
Jiving 'Round — Del Tha Funkee Homosapien: Ya Lil' Crumbsnatchers (1991)
Jiving 'Round — Kool G Rap: Crime Pays (1992)
Jiving 'Round — Run DMC: The Ave (1990)
Let's Have Some Fun — Above the Law: Harda U R Tha Doppa U Faal (1993)
Let's Have Some Fun — Blackstreet: Fix (remix) (1996)
Let's Have Some Fun — Eazy E: No More ?'s (1988)
Move Your Boogie Body — Gospel Gangstaz: Mobbin' (Gang Affiliated) (1995)
Move Your Boogie Body — Lighter Shade of Brown: If You Wanna Groove (1994)
Sang and Dance — De La Soul: Breakadawn (1993)
Sang and Dance — Will Smith: Gettin' Jiggy Wit It (1997)

Shake Your Rump to the Funk — Eazy E: No More ?'s (1988)
Son of Shaft — Bomb The Bass: Beat Dis (1988)
Son of Shaft — De La Soul: Plug Tunin' (Are You Ready for This) (1989)
Son of Shaft — Public Enemy: Caught, Can We Get a Witness (1988)
Son of Shaft — Public Enemy: Night of the Living Baseheads (1988)

## BLACK NAZTY

**FORMED:** *1971, Detroit, MI*
**ORIGINAL LINE-UP:** *Audrey Matthews (vcls), Curtin Hobson
(gtr), Mark Patterson (bs), Mike Judkins (kybds), Sam
Burns (trom), Artwell Matthews (drms), James Maddox
(perc, vcls)*

Musically outspoken, if heavily influenced by the then
emergent P-Funk sound, the unequivocally named Black
Nazty were formed in 1971 by Artwell and Audrey Matthews
(children of Detroit entrepreneur Johnnie Mae Matthews)
and bassist Patterson. Other members followed and in 1973,
Black Nazty signed to the Stax subsidiary Enterprise. They
released their debut single, "Gettin' Funky 'Round Here"
later that same year.

An album, 1974's *Talking to the People*, and a second
single, "Talkin' to the People" itself, followed, but the collapse of Stax in 1975 left the group floundering.

Now lining up as the Matthews siblings, Patterson, Alice
Myers (perc, vcls), Larry Thomas (kybds), Jackie Casper
(gtr) and Mike Judkins (kybds), by early 1976 the group had
abbreviated their name to Nazty alone. They were then
picked up by the little-known gospel label Mankind in early
1976, and scratched a minor R&B hit that summer, with
the excellent "It's Summertime."

Unfortunately, the follow-up "I Got To Move," and album *Nazty's Got the Move*, were no more successful than
any previous releases and, by 1978, the Matthews and Patterson had formed a new group, General Assistance & the
ADC Band. Retaining Judkins alone from Nazty, the group
also featured Pervis Johnson (gtr) and Kublah Khan (perc).

An album, *Looking for My Roots* was released on Matthews Senior's Northern label, before they again shortened
their name, to the ADC Band, and signed with Cotillion.
Still hotly pursuing George Clinton's form of funk, the
ADC Band achieved instant glory with "Long Stroke" (the
title track from their latest album); subsequent releases,
however, would struggle to make the lower limits of the
R&B chart and the group finally folded in 1982.

### BLACK NAZTY DISCOGRAPHY
### CHART LOG
### THE NAZTY
1976 It's Summertime/Look What You've Done (Mankind—#100 R&B)

### ADC BAND
1978 Long Stroke/That's Life (Cotillion—#6 R&B/#101 pop)
1979 Fire Up/More and More Disco (Cotillion—#72 R&B)
1979 Talk That Stuff/ADC Is Back (Cotillion—#69 R&B)
1980 In the Moonlight/Everyday (Cotillion—#75 R&B)
1980 Hangin' Out/Tripwire (Cotillion—#67 R&B)
1982 Roll with the Punches/Funk on Fire (Cotillion—#46 R&B)

### LPs
### BLACK NAZTY
**8** 1974 **Talking to the People (Enterprise)**
The essential album in the Matthews' canon, deep, dark
funk with a solid psyche-funk-adelic bent.

### THE NAZTY
**7** 1976 **Nazty's Got The Move (Mankind)**
Brighter, lighter, friendlier . . . think "Flashlight" amplified
through the national grid. Great mothership-friendly cover
as well.

### GENERAL ASSISTANCE AND THE ADC BAND
**6** 1978 **Looking for My Roots (Northern)**
Uncertain set, casting lingering looks toward funk, but
knowing that the future lies somewhere else entirely.

### ADC BAND
**6** 1978 **Long Stroke (Cotillion—#16 R&B/#139 pop)**
With the exception of the remarkably P-funky title track,
this set continues backing off the funk and includes the so-
abysmal-it's-amusing "Reggae Disco."
**5** 1979 **Talk That Stuff (Cotillion—#62 R&B)**
**6** 1980 **Renaissance (Cotillion—#69 R&B)**
**5** 1981 **Brother Luck (Cotillion)**
**6** 1982 **Roll with the Punches (Cotillion)**

## HAMILTON BOHANNON

**BORN:** *3/7/42, Newnan, GA*

Graduating Clark College with a Bachelors degree in musical education, Bohannon originally began a career in
teaching before joining his first band; unnamed by history,
the group apparently also included guitarist Jimmy (later
Jimi) Hendrix, himself then an unknown struggling to
make a living on the chitlin circuit.

Bohannon did not remain in obscurity for long. In 1965,
he was recruited to Stevie Wonder's road band, charged
with recreating in concert the awesome percussives of studio drummer Benny Benjamin. He succeeded; Bohannon
remained alongside Wonder for much of the next two years,
an extraordinarily powerful drummer whose instinctive un-

derstanding of rhythm saw him promoted to leader and arranger for the Motown road band until well into the '70s.

The values brought to that gig were the same as those applied to his own music; the buoyant rhythmic foundation over which Bohannon layered irresistible chants and mantras, and the almost ethereal vocal and self-aggrandizing lyrical stance (most of his greatest songs dropped his own name into the hookline somewhere) ensured that his records remained instantly recognizable.

Bohannon's solo career commenced in 1973 when he signed with soul singer Carl Davis' Dakar label and released the *Stop and Go* album, entirely self-written, produced and arranged. The following year brought *Keep on Dancin'* and, more importantly, "South African Man," an insistent percussion-led 45 that cracked the R&B chart that November.

Bohannon followed through with the similarly constructed "Footstompin' Music" and "Disco Stomp" (from *Insides Out*) and, while he registered only lightly on American ears, British audiences were absolutely entranced.

"South African Man" reached #22 in early 1975, while "Disco Stomp" climbed to #6 a full three months before it charted in the US. Belated releases for "Footstompin' Music" and "Happy Feeling" made it four British winners during 1975 alone. The signature riff of "Disco Stomp," meanwhile, reappeared in the UK chart that fall as "New York Groove" by London glam heroes Hello (later covered by KISS guitarist Ace Frehley); Bohannon responded with his own reworking of the same theme, "East Coast Groove."

Recorded with his now regular team of Rick Rouse (bs), Nimrod Lumpkin (gtr), Ted Waterhouse (kybds) and Lorenzo Brown (drms) plus Counts guitarist LeRoy Emmanuel and keyboard player Mose Davis, Bohannon's second 1975 album, *Bohannon*, saw him beginning to embrace disco textures, again in deference to his European following. His future was clear, even before he titled his next album *Phase II*.

Bohannon quit Dakar in 1976, moving to major label Mercury. There, following a lowly placing for the sweeping "Bohannon's Disco Symphony," he won his biggest ever US smash in summer 1978, with "Let's Start the Dance," a duet with Carolyn Crawford (backing vocalist on several earlier recordings).

He never returned to such heights. Four further chart entries, including a cover of Marvin Gaye's "Baby I'm for Real," missed the Top 40 and, in 1980, Hamilton Bohannon reinvented himself as Bohannon alone, launching his own Phase II label with fall's "Throw Down That Groove."

He spent the next three years on much the same level as he had spent the '70s, a regular minor hitmaker with a sharp eye for changes in the musical temperature. "Let's Start II Dance Again" (1981), credited to Bohannon featuring Dr. Perri Johnson, offered a rap inflected remake of "Let's Start the Dance." "I've Got the Dance Fever" in 1982 featured a rap intro by Rick Alston; "Make Your Body Move" paired Bohannon with Ray Parker, Jr.

Despite gathering at least some interest from a whole new audience after the New York's Tom Tom Club (a spin-off from Talking Heads) namechecked him during their "Wordy Rappinghood," Bohannon enjoyed just one further hit, late 1983's "Wake Up." Since that time, he has become little more than a cult nostalgia act, although he has been the subject of several "best of" compilations in the US and Europe.

## CHART LOG
### HAMILTON BOHANNON
1974 South African Man (part one)/Have a Good Day (Dakar—#78 R&B)

1975 Foot Stomping Music/Dance with Your Parno (Dakar—#39 R&B/#98 pop)

1975 Disco Stomp (part one)/(part two) (Dakar—#62 R&B)

1976 Bohannon's Beat (part one)/East Coast Groove (Dakar—#65 R&B)

1977 Bohannon's Disco Symphony/Moving Fast (Mercury—#67 R&B)

1978 Let's Start the Dance/I Wonder Why (Mercury—#9 R&B/#101 pop)

1979 Me and the Gang/Summertime Groove (Mercury—#82 R&B)

1979 Cut Loose/Listen to the Children Play (Mercury—#43 R&B)

1979 The Groove Machine/Love Floats (Mercury—#60 R&B)

1980 Baby I'm for Real/Hurry Mr. Sunshine (Mercury—#54 R&B)

### BOHANNON
1980 Throw Down the Groove (part one)/(part two) (Phase II—#59 R&B)

1980 Dance Dance Dance All Night/April My Love (part one) (Phase II—#76 R&B)

1981 Don't Be Ashamed To Call My Name/? (Phase II—#54 R&B)

1981 Goin' for One Another/The Happy Dance (Phase II—#91 R&B)

1981 I've Got the Dance Fever(rap) (Phase II—#72 R&B)

1982 The Party Train (part one)/(part two) (Phase II—#69 R&B)

1983 Make Your Body Move/Come Back My Love (Phase II—#63 R&B)

1983 Wake Up/Enjoy Your Day (Phase II—#87 R&B)

### LPs
### HAMILTON BOHANNON
**8** 1973 Stop & Go (Dakar)

Tentatively, Bohannon's masterpiece, relentless rhythms and gutbucket textures and above it all, the mighty stomp.

**7** 1974 Keep on Dancin' (Dakar—#49 R&B)

**7** 1975 Insides Out (Dakar—#28 R&B)

Essentially one long reprise of the quintessential "Disco Stomp," extended not only in its own right but across the rest of the album as well.

**6** 1975 Bohannon (Dakar—#21 R&B)

Seven solid dance grooves flavored with a firm eye for the on-coming disco movement, Bohannon's patent funk rhythms sidestepped (on side one) into a new dance direction with strings pumped higher in the mix, and eschewed altogether on the other, as Bohannon turned the tempo even lower than the lights.

**6** 1976 Dance Your Ass Off (Dakar—#47 R&B)

The title says it all!

**5** 1977 Phase II (Mercury—#46 R&B/#203 pop)

**5** 1978 Summertime Groove (Mercury—#14 R&B/#58 pop)

Tightening his grip on the last dance disco floor, a weak set but worth hearing for the title track.

**5** 1979 Cut Loose (Mercury—#34 R&B)

**4** 1980 Music in the Air (Mercury—#72 R&B)

### BOHANNON

**4** 1980 One Step Ahead (Phase II)

**3** 1981 Goin' for Another One (Phase II)

**4** 1981 Alive (Phase II)

**3** 1983 Make Your Body Move (Phase II/Compleat)

**5** 1983 Bohannon Drive (Phase II/Compleat)

**4** 1984 Motions (MCA)

**4** 1989 Here Comes Bohannon (MCA)

**5** 1990 It's Time To Jam (Southbound)

**4** 1996 Stomp (Dance Street)

### SELECTED COMPILATIONS AND ARCHIVE RELEASES

**8** 1978 Bohannon's Best (Brunswick)

His best, indeed. "Disco Stomp" and "South African Man" top the playlist, but there's nary a dull (or even less than scintillating) groove in sight.

**6** 1995 Very Best Of (Rhino)

Handpicked by Bohannon himself, a career spanning collection that sadly loses interest around the 1977–78 mark. Rather like everyone else did.

### SELECTED SAMPLES

Save Their Souls — Bell Biv Devoe: Hootie Mack (1993)

Save Their Souls — Chubb Rock: Stop That Train (1989)

Save Their Souls — Jay-Z: Cashmere Thoughts (1996)

Save Their Souls — Jungle Brothers: All I Think About Is You (1993)

Save Their Souls — Kool G. Rap: Fuck U Man (1992)

Save Their Souls — Total: Someone like You (1996)

Singing a Song for My Mother — Ed OG: I Got To Have It (1990)

Singing a Song for My Mother — Heavy D: Love Sexy (1993)

Singing a Song for My Mother — Intro: Let Me Be the One (1993)

## BOOTSY'S RUBBER BAND, see BOOTSY COLLINS

## DAVID BOWIE, see THE BRITISH ROCK FUNK CONNECTION

## BROTHER TO BROTHER

**FORMED:** 1973, St Louis, MO

**ORIGINAL LINE-UP:** Michael Burton (vcls), Billy Jones (gtr, kybds), Frankie Prescott (bs), Yogi Horton (d. 6/8/87—drms)

Brother to Brother were one of the myriad politically themed funk acts emerging onto the US club scene through the early '70s, signing with a minor label and then fading away as disco took over.

Recruited to the Turbo label, the group started well, battering the R&B Top Ten with a delicious cover of Gil Scott Heron's "In the Bottle." A minor classic album of the same name followed, but the original Brother to Brother broke up soon after, with both Prescott and Horton moving into sessions.

Michael Burton and Billy Jones alone then pieced together a new, expanded lineup around Bernadette Randle (kybds), John Williams (bs) and Clarence Oliver (drms) and, in 1976, Brother to Brother returned with *Let Your Mind Be Free*. While the title track was a surprisingly under-performing choice of 45, "Chance with You" made the R&B Top 30. Unfortunately, Brother to Brother broke up again shortly after.

Of the four original members, drummer Horton traveled the furthest, launching a career in session work that saw him become a part of Aretha Franklin's regular backing group, as well as serve with Ashford & Simpson, Cheryl Lynn, Diana Ross, George Benson, Luther Vandross and Hall & Oates. He also infiltrated that select company of funk musicians adopted by the New York new wave community. Talking Heads David Byrne and Jerry Harrison both employed him on solo recordings; so did Blondie's Debbie Harry, Yoko Ono and the B52s. He died in New York on June 8, 1987.

### CHART LOG

1974 In the Bottle/The Affair (Turbo—#9 R&B/#46 pop)

1976 Let Your Mind Be Free/(instrumental) (Turbo—#71 R&B)

1976 Chance with You/Joni (Turbo—#30 R&B)

### LPs

**8** 1974 In the Bottle (Turbo—#45 R&B)

Pointedly political, a mood reflected in the pent-up power of the hit title track, but spread elsewhere, too, through great vocals, monster rhythms and a thunderous bass to boot.

**7 1976 Let Your Mind Be Free (Turbo—#33 R&B)**
Less acerbic than its predecessor, but still packing a beefy aural punch.

### SELECTED SAMPLES
In The Bottle — Rottin Rascalz: Ohh Yeah (1995)

## DONALD BYRD AND THE BLACKBYRDS
**FORMED:** *1974, Washington, DC*
**ORIGINAL LINE-UP:** *Joe Hall (b. 1954, Washington DC—vcls, bs), Kevin Toney (b. 1953, Detroit, MI—vcls, kybds), Barney Perry (b. 1953, Buffalo, NY—gtr), Donald Byrd (b. 12/9/32, Detroit MI—trum), Allan Barnes (b. 1949, Detroit—reeds), Keith Kilgo (b. 1954, Baltimore, MD—vcls, drms), Pericles Jacobs (b. 1951, Washington, DC—perc)*

In a career that dated back to the late '50s, Blackbyrds founder Donald Byrd had long since established himself within the leading ranks of jazzmen willing to embrace commercial soul and R&B textures in his music. A graduate of Wayne State University, where he received a Bachelors degree in music in 1954, and the Manhattan School of Music, where he earned his Masters, Byrd worked alongside Max Roach, Art Blakey, Sonny Rollins and Pepper Adams, before decamping to Europe during 1962 to study composition.

Byrd returned to the US the following year to teach at Rutgers, Howard University and the Hampton Institute. He continued performing, however, and during the '60s released a string of well-received jazz albums on Blue Note. Then, in 1969, he found himself with an unexpected success when "Slow Drag" breached the R&B Top 30. Recorded with the hard bop quartet of Billy Higgins (drms, vcls), Sonny Red (alto sax), Cedar Walton (pno) and Walter Booker (bs), the album's success was such that Byrd immediately abandoned his proposed next album (it was finally released in 1981 as *The Creeper* and set to work instead on 1970's *Fancy Free*, a set that moved unrepentantly toward funky dance rhythms.

With Jimmy Ponder on guitar and Duke Pearson supplying some revolutionary electric piano, *Fancy Free* served unequivocal notice of Byrd's immediate intentions; Pearson reappeared on *Electric Byrd* later that same year, and while neither this album nor 1971's Afro-jam flavored *Ethiopian*

*Knights* returned Byrd to the chart, still his music continued pushing toward funk.

Byrd's breakthrough came in spring 1973, when the *Black Byrd* album entered the R&B chart, to be followed swiftly by a single of the same name. The latter peaked at #19, breached the pop Top 100 and suddenly this 40-year-old university professor was being feted as a rising star.

With musicians drawn from the *Blackbyrd* sessions crew, Hall, Toney and Killgo, Byrd launched into a remarkable prolific phase, releasing albums both under his own name and as a member of the Blackbyrds. In terms of material, there was little to choose between them—both were, naturally, horn heavy, both were so fascinated by both the musical and the commercial possibilities of Byrd's flight into funk that the jazz community's cries of "sell out" did not halt their journey.

The two acts were phenomenally successful. Signing to Fantasy, the Blackbyrds' first single, "Do It, Fluid," broke out of college radio (primarily Howard University's WHUR) and reached #23 in fall 1974, to be followed in the new year by the massive "Walking in Rhythm," a TopTen smash in both the R&B and pop charts. A second R&B Top Five, "Happy Music," arrived precisely a year later, while a total of four all-new Blackbyrds albums (including the soundtrack *Cornbread, Earl and Me*) during 1974–75 were equally successful.

Byrd, meanwhile, established the Mizell brothers, Fonce (horns, vcls) and Larry (kybds), as the core musicians behind his own string of best-selling singles and albums during that same period—a remarkable run highlighted by the funk fusion concept set *Street Lady*. He also passed his law degree, making one wonder just how he found the time to actually get everything done.

The cries of Byrd's old jazz admirers continued to be drowned out. Adding Patrice Rushen (kybds) to the studio crew, and increasingly laying down his trumpet in favor of lead vocals, Byrd scored another distinctive hit with 1977's cover of "Dancing in the Street" (he had already covered the Temptations' "Just My Imagination") from his *Caricatures* album.

The following year, Byrd left the venerable Blue Note label for a new career at Elektra. Blue Note, he insisted, had never enjoyed his new music. He recalled taking a James Brown record into the office; it was promptly thrown out of the window. His first album for the new label, possibly appropriately, was titled *Thank You for F.U.M.L.*—for Funking Up My Life.

The Blackbyrds, too, were going from strength to strength. With the lineup expanding to include Orville Saunders (gtr) and Jay Jones (sax), the group landed another pair of effortless Top Ten albums; *Unfinished Business* in 1976, and *Action* in 1977, made it three gold albums on the trot, while the band was also charting high on the pop listings.

Unfortunately, their music was also becoming increasingly formulaic, losing much of its early funky drive in favor of an all-encompassing dancefloor friendliness that, as is so often the case, promptly lost the attention of everybody it was targeted toward. The *Night Grooves* compilation was an unexpected failure in 1978 and it would be three years more before another Blackbyrds album appeared, the less than stellar *Better Days*.

It was to be their final release. In 1979, Byrd's own second album for Elektra had debuted a new group, 125th Street, NYC; now that group was to become his principle outlet and in 1981, they went into the studio with Isaac Hayes. They emerged with three successive hits, with "Love Has Come Around" a smooth Top 20 hit. However, when "I Need Your Love" and "Sexy Dancer" failed to repeat that performance, Byrd broke up the band and, by 1982, his attention had returned to academia. He received his doctorate from Columbia Teachers College that same year.

He returned, too, to his jazz roots, recording with Joe Henderson, Bobby Hutcherson, Kenny Garrett and Mulgrew Miller among others. In 1994, however, demand from the burgeoning funk revival circuit, together with a massive upsurge of interest brought on by the regular appearance of Byrd samples, saw him lured back into the R&B marketplace by ex-Gang Starr rapper Guru. A Blackbyrds reunion followed.

### DONALD BYRD/BLACKBYRDS DISCOGRAPHY
### CHART LOG
### DONALD BYRD
1973 Black Byrd/Skip Jar Blues (Blue Note—#19 R&B/#88 pop)
1975 Change (Makes You Want To Hustle) (part one)/(part two) (Blue Note—#43 R&B)
1976 (Fallin' like Dominoes)/Just My Imagination (Blue Note—#61 R&B)
1977 Dancing in the Street/Onward Til Morning (Blue Note—#95 R&B)
1979 Loving You/Cristo Redentor (Elektra—#74 R&B)

### BLACKBYRDS
1974 Do It Fluid (Fantasy #23 R&B/#69 pop)/Summer Love (#101 pop)
1975 Walking in Rhythm/The Baby (Fantasy—#4 R&B/#6 pop)
1975 Flyin' High/All I Ask (Fantasy—#22 R&B/#70 pop)
1976 Happy Music/Love So Fine (Fantasy—#3 R&B/#19 pop)

1976 Rock Creek Park/Thankful 'Bout Yourself (Fantasy—#37 R&B/#93 pop)
1977 Time Is Movin'/Lady (Fantasy—#15 R&B/#95 pop)
1977 Party Land/In Life (Fantasy—#30 R&B)
1977 Soft and Easy/Something Special (Fantasy—#20 R&B/#102 pop)
1978 Supernatural Feeling/Lookin' Ahead (Fantasy—#19 R&B/#102 pop)
1980 What We Have Is Right/What's on Your Mind (Fantasy—#38 R&B)
1981 Love Don't Strike Twice/Don't Know What To Say (Fantasy—#52 R&B)

### DONALD BYRD AND 12TH STREET, NYC
1981 Love Has Come Around/Love for Sale (Elektra—#15 R&B)
1982 I Love Your Love/Falling (Elektra—#77 R&B)
1982 Sexy Dancer/Midnight (Elektra—#38 R&B)

### SELECTED ALBUMS
### DONALD BYRD
**7** 1970 Fancy Free (Blue Note—#50 R&B)
Introducing the electric keyboard, which flavored much of Byrd's R&B work, this final fling with the old jazz disciplines barely hints at the future, but has an exhilarating sheen regardless.

**6** 1970 Electric Byrd (Blue Note)
Four tracks blend a distinctly samba-esque funk with occasional passages of Miles Davis-like experimentation. Not an easy listen, but the ideas take hold.

**8** 1971 Ethiopian Knights (Blue Note)
Heavy Afro rhythms chase three lengthy jams, and when they catch them it's wonderful.

**6** 1973 Black Byrd (Blue Note—#2 R&B/#36 pop)
Larry Mizell's production can be a little heavy-handed and certainly Byrd's experience deserved stronger songs. But the performances are tight and imaginative, and few records shout "early-'70s jazz-funk cross-over artist" louder than this.

**6** 1974 Street Lady (Blue Note—#6 R&B/#33 pop)
**5** 1975 Stepping into Tomorrow (Blue Note—#7 R&B/#42 pop)
**8** 1975 Places and Spaces (Blue Note—#6 R&B/#49 pop)
The best of Byrd's funk albums, but also the most derivative with producer Mizell apparently staying up very late with the Sly Stone/Earth Wind & Fire albums, then figuring out how to make everything sound like Stevie Wonder.

**5** 1977 Caricatures (Blue Note—#12 R&B/#60 pop)
Upon release, "Science Funktion" was certainly one of the finest thus-themed songs on the dancefloor; time and repetition have dulled its effect somewhat, but alongside a masterful cover of "Dancing in the Street," it does make *Caricatures* seem bearable.

**3** 1978 Thank You . . . For F.U.M.L. (Elektra)
But no thanks for disco-ing up ours.

## SELECTED COMPILATIONS AND ARCHIVE RELEASES

**7** 1977 Donald Byrd's Best (Blue Note—#46 R&B/#167 pop)

Byrd's label apparently hated his new music, but they certainly loved the hits. "Blackbyrd," "Change" and the remarkable "Lansana's Priestess" are well-chosen highlights.

## BLACKBYRDS

**8** 1974 The Blackbyrds (Fantasy—#14 R&B/#96 pop)

"Do It Fluid," "Reggins" and "The Runaway" ensure this remains the Blackbyrds' finest hour, rhythmic and soulful, with Byrd himself in astonishing form.

**7** 1974 Flying Start (Fantasy—#5 R&B/#30 pop)

**5** 1975 Cornbread, Earl and Me (Fantasy—#19 R&B/#150 pop)

Loose fitting soundtrack to the movie of the same name; the titles ("Candy Store Dilemma," "One Eye Two Step") are generally more intriguing than the music.

**5** 1975 City Life (Fantasy—#3 R&B/#16 pop)

"Happy Music," "Flyin' High" and "Rock Street Park" all made the pop 100. Little else recommends a dull, workmanlike performance.

**5** 1976 Unfinished Business (Fantasy—#6 R&B/#34 pop)

**6** 1977 Action (Fantasy—#8 R&B/#43 pop)

**4** 1981 Better Days (Fantasy—#40 R&B/#133 pop)

## SELECTED COMPILATIONS AND ARCHIVE RELEASES

**6** 1978 Night Grooves (Fantasy—#43 R&B/#159 pop)

A good grounding in the Blackbyrds' hits, although if you have the first two albums, you won't be needing much more.

**6** 1989 Greatest Hits (Fantasy)

## DONALD BYRD AND 125TH STREET, NYC

1979 Donald Byrd and 125th Street, NYC (Elektra—#71 R&B/#204 pop)
1981 Love Byrd (Elektra—#15 R&B/#93 pop)

## SELECTED SAMPLES

All I Ask — 2pac: Lord Knows (1995)
Blackbyrds' Theme — Queen Latifah: Bad as a Mutha (1991)
Blackbyrds' Theme — Lord Finesse: Back to Back Rhyming (remix) (1990)
Blackbyrds' Theme — Jungle Brothers: Tribe Vibes (1989)
Do It Fluid — Stetsasonic: So Let the Fun Begin (1991)
Do It Fluid — Style: In Tone We Trust (1991)
Dreaming About You — Da Lench Mob: Lord Have Mercy (1992)
Life Styles — Salt-N-Pepa: Solo Power (Let's Get Paid) (1988)
Mysterious Vibes — Almighty RSO: One in the Chamba (1994)
Reggins — Hard 2 Obtain: LI Groove (remix) (1994)
Riot — Ghostface Killah: Black Jesus (1996)
Rock Creek Park — Eric B. & Rakim: The R (1988)
Rock Creek Park — De La Soul: Ghetto Thang (1989)
Rock Creek Park — Big Daddy Kane: Raw '91 (1991)
Rock Creek Park — NWA: Quiet on Tha Set (1989)
Rock Creek Park — Massive Attack: Blue Lines (1991)
Rock Creek Park — Ice Cube: I Wanna Kill Sam (1991)
Rock Creek Park — Heavy D: Swinging with Da Hevsta (1991)
Rock Creek Park — Grandmaster Flash & the Furious Five: We Will Rock You (1987)
Spaced Out — MC Lyte: Cappucino (1989)
The Runaway — Kid 'N Play: Gittin Funky (1988)
Wilford's Gone — Hard 2 Obtain: LI Groove (remix) (1994)
Wilford's Gone — Gang Starr: Say Your Prayers (1991)
Wilford's Gone — Compton's Most Wanted: Def Wish (1991)

# JIMMY CASTOR

**BORN:** 6/2/43, *New York City, NY*

As a teenage doo-wop singer, Jimmy Castor was 13 when he wrote and recorded his first single, "I Promise To Remember," with the Juniors in 1956. A second single, "This Girl of Mine," followed in 1957, by which time Frankie Lymon & the Teenagers had recorded their own version of "I Promise To Remember," a #10 R&B hit in fall 1956.

Castor occasionally appeared live with the Teenagers, sometimes standing in for Lymon himself, before moving into session work as a saxophonist around 1960. He cut a solo single, "Poor Loser," in 1963, but he also took time to complete his schooling and it was 1966 before Castor returned full time to music, signing to the Decca label for the impulsively good time "In a Boogaloo Bag." It flopped and he moved on to Smash, scoring with "Hey Leroy, Your Mama's Callin' You" and finally laying bare the foundations for what eventually proved a career's worth of novelty funk recordings.

"Hey Leroy" was followed by three further singles, including the Vietnam-topical "Leroy's in the Army," none of which made any impression. A short stay with Capitol Records saw Castor cut three further 45s, "Hey Shorty," "Psycho Man" and "Helpless," again to no commercial avail.

"Leroy" was revived once again in 1972. Now helming a new act, the Jimmy Castor Bunch, Castor debuted on RCA with "My Brightest Day," then followed through with "Say Leroy (The Creature from the Black Lagoon Is Your Father)," a funking great record that genuinely deserved some attention. It got none, but success was nevertheless just around the corner.

Lining up as Castor, Harry Jensen (gtr), Doug Gibson (bs), ex-Fatback Band keyboard player Gerry Thomas, Bobby Manigault (drms) and Lennie Fridie (perc), the Bunch grabbed their first hit with what initially seemed a simple (if belated) successor to British trio Hotlegs' "Neanderthal Man" smash of two years earlier, "Troglodyte

(Cave Man)." Whatever its inspiration, the percussion and grunt-led single was massive and, while a similarly themed follow-up, "Luther the Anthropod," bombed, a change-of-pace follow-up, "Soul Serenade," at least registered some chart action.

Signing next to Atlantic, Castor returned to a familiar format with 1974's "Maggie," before scoring another self-defining hit with "The Bertha Butt Boogie" in 1975. Then, over the next five years, the Jimmy Castor Bunch were unstoppable, a pounding, hammering assault on the disco sensibilities.

Gerry Thomas, who had continued supplying his erstwhile Fatback Bandmates with material throughout the Bunch's reign, finally returned to that group in 1977; the Bunch, however, continued riotously on. They invoked "King Kong" with one breath, the "Space Age" with another and, while the novelties were interspersed with more conventional material, still the E (for Everything) Man, as Castor now termed himself, was to remain a force both to be reckoned with and, for disco fainthearts, to be feared. Leroy returned once again on, of course, "The Return of Leroy" (1977), Bertha Butt resurfaced on the *Star Wars* influenced "Bertha Butt Encounters Vadar" 45 (1978); the Bunch themselves encountered "Dracula" (1976) and even launched a ferocious attack on AOR slow dancer "You Light Up My Life."

Castor broke up the Bunch in 1980, commencing a solo career with a painfully sincere rendition of Elvis Presley's "Can't Help Falling in Love," in spring 1980. He returned to type in 1982, signing with the Salsoul label for an updated version of 1974's "E-Man," "E-Man Boogie 82" (followed, in 1983, by "E-Man Boogie 83"), and delivered another characteristic hit with 1984's "Amazon."

The successes finally dried up after that, but Castor appeared once again in the R&B Top 30 in 1988, when he joined soul singer Joyce Simms on "Love Makes a Woman." By the end of the '80s, Castor had left the music industry once again, but returned in 1999 with a reconvened Bunch, releasing the single, "I Got Something for Ya," and album JCB.

## CHART LOG
### JIMMY CASTOR
1966 Hey Leroy, Your Mama's Callin' You/Ham Hocks Espanol (Smash—#16 R&B/#31 pop)
1980 Can't Help Falling in Love/Stay with Me (Long Distance—#93 R&B)
1984 Amazon/She's an Amazon (Dream—#84 R&B)
1985 It Gets to Me/(instrumental) (Dream—#81 R&B)

### JIMMY CASTOR BUNCH
1972 Troglodyte/I Promise To Remember (RCA—#4 R&B/#6 pop)
1973 Soul Serenade/Tribute to Jimi (RCA—#72 R&B)
1975 The Bertha Butt Boogie (part one)/(part two) (Atlantic—#22 R&B/#16 pop)
1975 Potential/Daniel (Atlantic—#25 R&B)
1975 King Kong (part one)/(part two) (Atlantic—#23 R&B/#69 pop)
1976 Supersound/Drifting (Atlantic—#42 R&B)
1976 Bom Bom/What's Best (Atlantic—#97 R&B)
1976 Everything Is Beautiful to Me/Magic in the Music (Atlantic—#67 R&B)
1977 Space Age/Dracula (part two) (Atlantic—#28 R&B/101 pop)
1978 Maximum Stimulation/It Was You (Atlantic—#82 R&B)
1979 Don't Do That (part one)/(part two) (Cotillion—#50 R&B)

### JIMMY CASTOR/JOYCE SIMMS
1988 Love Makes a Woman/All and All (Sleeping Bag—#29 R&B)

### LPs
### JIMMY CASTOR
6 1967 Hey Leroy (Smash)
If there were ever a missing link between the Coasters and rap, Castor wrote a song about it. Leroy sets the ball rolling; the rest of the album is cut in a similar, if less compulsive vein.
4 1980 C (Long Distance)

### JIMMY CASTOR BUNCH
7 1972 It's Just Begun (RCA—#11 R&B/#27 pop)
Indeed it has. "Troglodyte" is untenably compulsive and, with maximum exposure, quite hateful. But the rhythms knew their business and even fake funk sounds convincing if it's loud enough.
6 1972 Phase Two (RCA)
Leroy's family tree and apeboy Luther are the standouts, but Castor also makes a pretty mess of "First Time Ever I Saw Your Face."
5 1973 Dimension III (RCA—#49 R&B)
6 1974 The Everything Man (RCA)
6 1975 Butt of Course (Atlantic—#34 R&B/#74 pop)
The Butt, of course, is the boogie-ing Bertha. So it's the same old lunacy as before, pumped through Elton John's "Daniel" and the Stylistics' "You Make Me Feel Brand New."
5 1975 Super Sound (Atlantic—#30 R&B)
6 1976 E Man Groovin' (Atlantic—#29 R&B/#132 pop)
4 1977 Maximum Stimulation (Atlantic)
4 1978 Let It Out (Drive)
5 1979 The Jimmy Castor Bunch (Cotillion)
6 2000 J3C (Orchard)

Nothing new, but plenty of old, borrowed and slightly blue to reawaken past guilty pleasures.

## SELECTED COMPILATIONS AND ARCHIVE RELEASES
**7** 1976 **Best of the Jimmy Castor Bunch (RCA)**
There's a gynormous hole where Bertha's butt should boogie, but you can't get too much of the rest. Can you?
**7** 1995 **Everything Man: The Best Of (Rhino)**

## SELECTED SAMPLES
E-Man Boogie — Young Black Teenagers: Nobody Knows Kelli (1991)
I Promise To Remember — Big Daddy Kane: Mister Cee's Master Plan (1988)
It's Just Begun — 2 Live Crew: Get Loose Now (1989)
It's Just Begun — Eric B & Rakim: Musical Massacre (1988)
It's Just Begun — Everlast: Syndicate Soldier (1990)
It's Just Begun — Grandmaster Flash & the Furious Five: She's Fresh (1982)
It's Just Begun — Jungle Brothers: On the Run (1988)
It's Just Begun — Marky Mark & the Funky Bunch: Last Song on Side B (1991)
It's Just Begun — M.A.R.R.S.: Pump Up the Volume (1987)
King Kong — Coldcut: Stop This Crazy Thing (1988)
King Kong — Jungle Brothers: Sounds of the Safari (1988)
The Return of Leroy — Beastie Boys: Hold It Now, Hit It (1986)
The Return of Leroy — Jungle Brothers: JB's Comin' Through (1993)
Troglodyte — En Vogue: Time Goes On (1990)
Troglodyte — NWA: Gangsta Gangsta (1989)
Troglodyte — NWA: Dayz of Wayback (1991)
Troglodyte — Professor Griff & the Last Asiatic Disciples: Pawns in the Game (1990)
Troglodyte — X-Clan: Fire and Earth (100% Natural) (1992)

# GEORGE CLINTON
**BORN:** 7/22/40, *Kannapolis, NC*

North Carolina born, Newark-raised George Clinton is the single most influential figure in the history of funk, the first musician to actively sense the possibilities raised by a blending of, primarily, R&B, psychedelia and even the garage roar of rock iconoclasts the MC5 and the Stooges. The result was a sound that utterly reinvented dance music during the '70s, bringing funk alive for an audience who had scarcely even glanced in its direction in the past.

Adding Clinton's intuitive sense of natural outrage and theatrics to the brew only heightened the impact. Throughout the early '70s, the UK music press had little difficulty in allying Parliament to the similarly colorful Glam Rock movement then sweeping that country; later in the decade, American critics acknowledged that Clinton alone was capable of giving heavy metal superstars KISS a run for their extravagantly costumed money—a comparison that was only exacerbated after Clinton signed with the same record label, Casablanca.

## THE PARLIAMENTS: 1956–69
Clinton's first group, the barbershop/doo-wop Parliaments, was formed while he was still attending junior high in Newark, New Jersey. Lining up as Clinton, Charles "Butch" Davis, Gene Boykins, Herbie Jenkins and Glenn Carlos, the Parliaments made their first recordings in 1956, "Sunday Kind of Love" and "The Wind." It was another two years, however, before the group released their first single, "Poor Willie," in May 1958.

The lineup shifted gradually. Calvin Simon replaced Boykin; Johnny Murray replaced Robert Lambert who, in turn, replaced Herbie Jenkins. Grady Thomas took over from Mitchell. Three further singles followed, "Lonely Island," "I'll Get You Yet" and "My Only Love," while the Parliaments continued playing around town. Their most regular gig was a barbershop in Plainfield, NJ, the Silk Palace. There the Parliaments joined fellow regulars the Sensation Six, the Gospel Clefs, the Monotones and the Fiestas—all used the Palace both for rehearsing and performing.

By 1961, however, Clinton was—in his own words— "wiped out by the '50s," all the more so after he heard Smokey Robinson's "Shop Around," the R&B chart-topper that launched the Motown label into the soul stratosphere. At the same time, one of his friends, Sidney Barnes, was joining that label as a producer and writer, based out of the newly opened Jobete Music office in New York City. Barnes told Clinton to bring the Parliaments in for an audition— and was blown away by their performance. Even then, and even within the strictures of the Parliaments, Clinton was experimenting with harmonies, melody and rhythm.

As a publishing company, Jobete's prime purpose was to record demos of the songs that their contracted writers were delivering, and to encourage other artists to record them. It was a powerful operation, but Clinton's work immediately set him apart—not only from his fellow writers and performers, but from the musical mainstream in general. His songs were so individual, so unique, that nobody else dared touch them.

Finally, the Jobete team decided to launch their own label within the Motown family, Soul Records, and release Clinton and the Parliaments' work themselves. (Junior Walker & the All-Stars were among the other non-traditional Motown acts placed on the label.) Motown's own internal politics ensured that little came of the union,

**An uncharacteristically pensive-looking George Clinton.**

however, and in 1964 Clinton relocated to Detroit (the others remained in New Jersey), to sign the Parliaments directly with Motown.

Again, little happened. Clinton recalled, "I could tell we weren't gonna go nowhere, because all the [other] groups they had [were] from Detroit. And you could just forget it after the Temptations, 'cause they were the best of their thing." Clinton contented himself behind the scenes at Motown, writing and demoing his own songs, and plowing his wages into making his own records. In partnership with Joe Martin, one of Motown's east coast distributors, Clinton launched Marton Records, a tiny operation that ultimately released just four singles including one, "Accidental Love," by Vivian Lewis, mother of Clinton's son, Tracey (the future Treylewd).

An even more important venture launched when Clinton was approached by Ed Wingate, head of the Detroit based Golden World and Ric-Tic labels. A well-known nightclub owner, Wingate opened both the labels and the Golden World studios specifically to compete with Motown—and he succeeded. Well aware that Motown's rates of pay were notoriously low, Wingate blithely invited the cream of the label's sessionmen, the legendary Funk Brothers among them, to earn some extra money at Golden

World. With such an arsenal, 1965–66 saw Golden World not only rivalling Motown's commercial success, but emulating the Motown sound as well. Edwin Starr's "Agent Double-O-Soul" and (especially) "Stop Her on Sight" rank among the greatest non-Motown Motown records ever made.

For Clinton himself, Golden World was invaluable, not only offering him the studio freedom he relished but encouraging him to explore that freedom to its limit. Clinton's writing partner at the time, Sidney Barnes, later recalled, "George was [Wingate's] boy. He loved George." And he gave him free run of the studio.

Clinton repaid Wingate's faith handsomely. He co-produced Barbara Lewis' "Hello Stranger" and Darrell Banks' "Open the Door to Your Heart." He masterminded the Debonaires' recording career. Clinton even found time to cut a new Parliaments' single for the label, "Heart Trouble," with a lineup wholly unrecognizable from the vocal group's original incarnation: Clinton, and the New Jersey-based Clarence "Fuzzy" Haskins, Grady Thomas, Calvin Simon and Raymond Davis (ex-Del Larks).

The Golden World operation closed in 1968, sold to Motown for a million dollars. The studio became Motown Studio B, Edwin Starr became a Motown artist and Clinton became full-time Motown staff writer. With Barnes, he co-wrote "Can't Shake It Loose," originally recorded by Pat Lewis, but subsequently covered by the Supremes on their *Love Child* album. Another Clinton/Barnes co-composition, "I Bet You," earned covers by Theresa Lindsay, Billy (brother of Jerry) Butler and the Jackson Five (for the *ABC* album and also as a giveaway on the back of a cornflakes box). Two other Clinton compositions, "Touch the One You Love" and "Little Christmas Tree," were later recorded solo by the young Michael Jackson.

Such activities did not stop his moonlighting, however. LeBaron Taylor, president of Golden World's Ric-Tic subsidiary, had formed a new label, Revilot, and Clinton and Barnes promptly joined him there.

The first order of business was to record a new Parliaments single—albeit without the Parliaments. Simon had been drafted and was already in Vietnam; the rest of the band were still living in New Jersey and couldn't afford to fly out to Detroit. Clinton alone made the record, then, calling in a local pickup group, the Holidays, to accompany him. "(I Wanna) Testify" was released in May 1967, and rocketed straight into the upper echelons of the soul chart, coming to rest at #3. Pop radio went crazy for it too. The single breached the Top 20 and, in June 1967, the reunited Parliaments played the biggest show of their lives, at the Apollo in Harlem. It was a disaster.

With the Parliaments augmented by bass guitarist William "Billy Bass" Nelson and the Apollo houseband, everything that could go wrong did. Painstakingly rehearsed dance steps collapsed into chaos; lyrics were forgotten, tempos were misplaced. The Parliaments played just one show as headliners; the remainder of their engagement saw them second-billed to the original opening act, the O'Jays.

The Parliaments continued gigging through the summer, but outside events were moving in on them. After one show, playing alongside the Four Tops at Newark's Bradford Theater, the band left the venue to discover the streets aflame as rioting exploded all around. They returned to Detroit, just as that city, too, went up in flames. Slowly, Clinton began to formulate a new vision, of a music that spoke as loudly, and as violently, as the riots themselves.

It was Billy Bass who first suggested the Parliaments recruit a rhythm section. Tired of being forever reliant on housebands, he saw the Parliaments becoming a self-contained unit and, when Clinton agreed, he made another suggestion: that they also seek out another Plainfield, NJ, native, guitarist Eddie Hazel.

The duo next approached the Boyce Brothers, Richard (bs) and Frankie (gtr). Also from Plainfield, their group, Jo-Jo & the Admirations, had often opened for the Parliaments. However, Frankie Boyce had just been drafted out to Vietnam (he would die there); in his stead, they recruited United Soul guitarist Gary Shider. A drummer Clinton knew in Washington DC, named Stacy, and organist Mickey Atkins (born in Harrisburg, PA) followed, and the newly constituted team began rehearsing.

Stacy lasted just a handful of shows before being replaced by Tiki Fulwood, the extravagant house drummer at the Uptown Theater in Philadelphia. And it was with the arrival of his powerhouse style that Clinton now set his own dreams in motion.

Unlike many soul and R&B musicians at that time, Clinton had never thought of "Black" music as being specifically Black—or of rock 'n' roll as having become exclusively White. Through most of the '60s, of course (and particularly in the aftermath of the British Invasion's wholesale absorption of America's early blues heritage), his had been a minority opinion, but the times were changing—all the more so after 1967 brought the emergence of Jimi Hendrix, a Black man playing White rock, and a guitarist whom Clinton remembered from years before, when Hendrix was simply Jimmy James, sideman to the likes of King Curtis, the Isley Brothers and Little Richard. "To me, that's the ultimate," Clinton recalled. "If he done changed to get that deep, 'oh, okay, here's another style.'"

The Parliaments began changing overnight. Taking their cue from the psychedelic fashions of the hippy movement, out went the Parliaments' old straight tuxes and smart grooming, in came bright pink jackets and crazy bell-bottoms. "We took it to exaggeration," Clinton said. "We wore sheets, we wore the suit bags that our suits came in." Billy Bass went even further; tiring one day of his bandmates constantly referring to him as the baby of the group, he walked out onstage wearing nothing more than a diaper and combat boots.

It was a show at Sacred Heart College in Connecticut that fit the final piece into the Parliaments' deranged jigsaw. The band's equipment was late in arriving, so they borrowed from the support act, Vanilla Fudge, a double stack of Marshall amps, a triple stack of SVTs and a set of oversized fiber-glass drums. Three weeks later, the Parliaments took delivery of precisely the same setup for themselves.

Word of the Parliaments' new-found craziness spread, all the more so after it became apparent that their music was just as liberated. Tight songs became sprawling jams around the funkiest of rhythms—but in an age before either popularity or familiarity had acquainted listeners with that expression, audiences (particularly White audiences) swiftly conferred another label on the music—one long psychedelic freak out.

Not everybody who encountered the Parliaments was as immediately enamored as the hippies. More than one club owner, having booked the band on the strength of "Testify" and the clean-cut image in the promo photos, was horrified to be confronted by a vision of color, hair and flesh (Clinton had developed a habit of stripping onstage) that they now presented. A new single, "All Your Goodies Are Gone," in October, went some way toward clearing up the confusion, but still the Parliaments continued weaving their baffling spell over North American clubs and owners until well into 1969.

In the meantime, four further singles had failed even to brush the soul charts: "Little Man," "Look at What I Almost Missed," "A New Day Begins" and "Good Old Music." And while a reissued "A New Day Begins" did make the R&B Top 50 in May 1969, by that time a new day truly had begun.

Contractual snarls were engulfing the Parliaments, snarls within which Clinton had no wish, right now, to entangle himself. So, when Armen Boladian, Revilot's distributor, announced he was forming his own label, Westbound, Clinton glimpsed a unique solution to the band's problems. It was only their name, after all, that was under contract elsewhere; the members themselves were free agents. All they had to do, then, was change their name. In May 1969, Westbound released "Music for My Mother," the first single by the by now self-explanatorily named Funkadelic.

### FUNKADELIC 1969–71

Clinton recalled, "We said, 'We're gonna be the blackest, we gonna be the funkiest, we gonna be dirty.' We were playing stuff in the studio that the engineer didn't even want his name on. You turned on a Funkadelic record with earphones on, drums running across your head, panning the foot, we panned everything. Matter of fact, you didn't even have to be high to get off into that. We went to colleges where they weren't taking anything, but they were tripping on the records."

What set Funkadelic apart, aside from the nature of their records, was their intention. Even the slowly politicizing, gradually hardening Motown sound was still conceived with the magic word "crossover" in mind, while Sly Stone, the only other headline maverick on the R&B scene at that point, was about to explode despite himself, courtesy of a barnstorming appearance at the Woodstock festival.

Funkadelic would not cross over, did not play Woodstock; they remained ferociously underground, even after the hits started mounting up. They remained loyal, of course, to homebase Detroit, and through 1969–70, Funkadelic were as likely to be found playing a biker bar with the garage rock bands MC5, the Amboy Dukes or the Stooges, as turning out in a theater, co-billed with the Temptations or the Four Tops.

Guitarist Tawl Ross (born Lucius Ross, Plainfield, NJ) was drawn from the seemingly bottomless trove of brilliant, unknown north Jersey musicians. Calvin Simon was drawn back into the fold, and with two further singles, "I'll Be You" and "I Got a Thing, You Got a Thing, Everybody's Got a Thing," under their belt, Funkadelic worked toward their eponymous debut album.

The lineup began expanding. Guitarists Dennis Coffey and Ray Monette, bassist Bob Babette, keyboard players Ivy Hunter and Earl Van Dyke and drummer Brad Innis, all Motown sessionmen, were in evidence on Funkadelic.

More crucial, however, was the arrival, shortly after the album was completed, of the classically trained Bernie Worrell, replacing Atkins. He made his debut with Funkadelic when they backed Hot Buttered Soul singer Rose Williams on her "Whatever Makes My Baby Feel Good" single in fall 1969; his first Funkadelic record was their own next single "I Wanna Know If It's Good to You," and their second album, the mighty Free Your Mind and Your Ass Will Follow.

Famously, the album was recorded in one day, with the entire studio tripping on acid—certainly it had a lysergic edge to it that traveled far beyond the outermost realms of even the most liberal interpretation of the band's name. Indeed, as one tried to settle into the mammoth freak-form title track, it was difficult to comprehend precisely what Funkadelic even hoped to achieve. The album stalled at #92 on the US chart; its successor, August 1971's apocalyptic Maggot Brain, did not even climb that far. But already Clinton was moving on.

### PARLIAMENT 1970–71

Within Funkadelic's hierarchy, the original Parliament members had always remained separate from their bandmates, financially and creatively—a situation that naturally caused a number of disagreements. The arrival on the scene of Jeffrey Bowen, one of Clinton's old Motown friends and now a producer at the Invictus label, only complicated things further. Even with the old contractual wrangles still in place, he wanted to reform the Parliaments and Clinton agreed.

The "Testify"-era Parliaments lineup was on board: Clinton, Davis, Haskins, Simon and Thomas. Of course they were backed by the Funkadelic mainstays of Bass, Hazel, Fulwood, Ross and Worrell, plus guitarist Garry Shider and drummer Tyrone Lampkin, whom Clinton first noticed when the drummer's then-current group, the hard rocking Gutbucket, opened for Parliament in Connecticut.

But that is all they were, backing musicians. *Osmium*, the slightly-renamed Parliament's debut album, had absolutely nothing to do with the Funkadelic sound—nothing, in fact, to do with anything even the Invictus staff had been expecting. Linking with English folk singer Ruth Copeland (Bowen's wife), the group flirted with every musical genre Clinton took a fancy to, including an utterly skewed take on country and western. Then they did it all again, backing Copeland on her debut album, *Self Portrait*.

*Osmium* flopped as, indeed, did all five of Parliament's Invictus singles, but the Funkadelic crew had had enough. Unanimously, Bass, Hazel, Fulwood and Worrell quit, to join Copeland's own band. The ensuing record, 1971's *I Am What I Am*, included three songs co-written by Copeland and Clinton, plus a pair of very well-executed Rolling Stones covers. But it was to be a short-lived defection, ending after Copeland—touring with Sly & the Family Stone—introduced her fellows as Funkadelic and allowed them to perform one of her encores. The crowd's reaction was so intense that Sly promptly told Copeland to find another band, or another gig. She found another band.

### FUNKADELIC 1971–74

The errant Funkadelics went on to work with Chairmen of the Board and sundry other Invictus acts but, by late summer 1971, Worrell, Hazel and Billy Bass, at least, were back alongside Clinton. Lampkin was recalled to replace Fulwood and a new guitarist, Harold Beane of Isaac Hayes' group, was brought in.

Further Parliament projects had been placed on hold for the foreseeable future, but still the new members were not to enjoy an easy baptism. Less than a week after they were recruited and, without any rehearsal whatsoever, Lampkin and Beane found themselves simultaneously preparing to make their stage debut and record Funkadelic's first live album, at Rochester, MI's Meadowbrook. In fact, none of the musicians knew what labelhead Boladian was planning until they arrived at the venue to discover an engineer setting up the recording equipment.

The show did not go well and the album was shelved for another 20-plus years. (It finally appeared as *Funkadelic*

*Live* in 1996). Despite Clinton announcing, "bear with us, we have a new drummer," the rhythms were completely out of sequence—so much so that Billy Bass finally walked offstage in frustration. Neither would he return for long. Incensed at what he saw as Worrell's promotion to his, Bass', own established role as Funkadelic's musical director, the bassist quit in early 1972. He was replaced by ex-JBs bassist Bootsy Collins.

Mallia Franklin, Clinton's girlfriend's sister, alerted Funkadelic to Collins after catching him accompanying singer Gloria Taylor (then riding the success of "You Got To Pay the Price" and "Grounded") at a show in Toledo. Clad in lace body stocking and hotpants, with a tambourine taped to one foot, Collins immediately—and inevitably—captured Franklin's attention. On her advice, Clinton then caught Collins' own act, the Pacemakers, at Detroit's Soul Expression.

The group's vocalist, Philippe Wynne, had recently joined the Spinners; Clinton then recruited the remainder of the Pacemakers en masse: Bootsy and his brother, Catfish (born Phelps Collins), percussionist Frankie Kash (born Frank Waddy), tenor sax player Robert McCullough and trumpeter Clayton "Chicken" Gunnels, just as work began on Funkadelic's next album, 1972's double *America Eats Its Young*.

They played little part in the sessions. Visualizing a personal empire as vast as any previous musical conglomerate (Motown and James Brown were fixed role models), Clinton drew in musicians from across the funk and soul spectrum. A total of four drummers and percussionists, four guitarists and three bassists appeared on the finished album, together with a seven-piece horn section, eight string players, steel guitarist Ollie Strong and comedian James Wesley Jackson, contributing "juice harp."

Amid this vast conspiracy of musicians, Clinton engineered a state of absolute flux, drawing musicians in for single sessions, occasional shows, even full tours; bassist Prakash John (born in Toronto, Canada) joined for one American jaunt. Still, the Collins brothers contributed one track, "Philmore," all but single-handedly, and it was clear that they were to prove an integral part of Clinton's future plans. Another vital component was United Soul bassist Cordell "Boogie" Mosson, while Gary Shider found himself in the unenviable position of having to replace Eddie Hazel, currently serving time in jail after assaulting an air hostess during a flight. Hazel appeared on just one track on the album.

Stageshows, too, became ever more adventurous; one of Shider's first gigs, during a tour of colleges, was highlighted by a naked Clinton rising from a casket, to reveal stars, moons and penises shaved into his scalp. Even without mainstream radio play (American broadcasters still frowned on the word "funk") and with the R&B chart only cautiously accepting this freakish phenomenon, Funkadelic was a cult monster, arriving in every town to be greeted by screaming auditoriums full of fans.

*Cosmic Slop*, in July 1973, was the album that Clinton credits as merging Funkadelic's live reputation with their studio capabilities. A ferociously slimmed down band comprising Worrell, Mosson, Lampkin, Shider and Polish guitarist Ron Bykowski (plus returning "Guest Funkadelic Maggot" Fulwood for one cut) slammed out the band's cleanest-sounding record yet and were rewarded when DC radio went mad for it. A breakthrough was clearly imminent although, typically, Clinton was not about to make it easy.

### P-FUNK 1974–81

Through 1974, as another sprawling mass of musicians worked on the next Funkadelic album, *Standing on the Verge of Getting It On*, Clinton was also overseeing the return of Parliament. Funkadelic called on Thomas, Davis, Simon, Haskins, Worrell, Mosson, Hazel (who co-wrote much of the album under his own mother's name, Grace Cook), Shider, Fulwood and Bykowski, plus drummers Lampkin and Gary Bronson, bassist Jimmy Calhoun and pianist Leon Patillo. With the addition of the returning Bootsy Collins, essentially the same team of musicians would almost simultaneously be recording Parliament's *Up for the Down Stroke*.

Reaching the stores just one month after *Standing on the Verge*, *Up for the Down Stroke* was released on Casablanca, the label formed by former Buddah Records chief Neil Bogart. In fact, Parliament were the first group Bogart signed to the label, to be followed by Donna Summer and KISS.

It was a smart move on both sides. Bogart had an almost sixth sense for scenting hits (which is why he signed KISS after every other label in the land had run away laughing), while Clinton admitted that this latest incarnation of Parliament was intended to showcase the commercial side of his art. Indeed, remakes of three '60s-era Parliaments' singles, the B-side "The Goose," "All Your Goodies Are Gone" and, of course, "Testify" could not have been intended any other way, while the opening title track was an even more radio friendly piece de resistance. Suddenly, Parliament found themselves soaring where Funkadelic had never been able to tread, into the middle regions of the pop Top 100.

With two bands now operating at contrasting ends of the success spectrum—Parliament as genuine chartbusters, Funkadelic as a roaring cult institution—Clinton knew the time had come to begin closing ranks. Funk was breaking out everywhere, not only in the R&B charts, but across the white mainstream as well. In 1974, English rocker David Bowie enjoyed his first significant US success with the James Brown-esque "Fame." Now the Rolling Stones were preparing their funk album, the pounding *Black and Blue*. After five years of being the only funk band in the rock 'n roll circus, suddenly Funkadelic had some strong competition.

Convening Worrell, Mosson, Fulwood and Shider and guitarist Michael Hampton alongside the full Parliament vocal line of Simon, Davis, Thomas and Haskins, plus guest appearances from Bootsy, Billy Bass, Hazel and Bykowski (the album's "Alumni Funkadelic"), Clinton set about cutting the most commercial Funkadelic album yet, *Let's Take It to the Stage*, hand in hand with the contrastingly funkiest Parliament album so far, *Chocolate City*—his own tribute, of course, to the loyal DC. And though *Stage* steadfastly refused to break Funkadelic's non-charting streak, *City* made the Top 100.

The lineup on that album was stellar. Inaugurating what became a fixture within the P-Funk set-up were the Horny Horns, featuring further ex-JBs Fred Wesley and Maceo Parker. The renowned Brecker Brothers, Michael and Randy, too, were recruited to the cause, while another Plainfield-born star-in-the-making joined the party, vocalist Glen Goins. Wesley later described Goins as the best vocalist he'd ever heard. Worrell reflected that, had Goins lived (he died of Hodgkins disease in 1978), he would have become the number one top male vocalist in America.

The same gathering was back in the studio within months of *Chocolate City*'s release, hammering down the next Parliament album, *Mothership Connection*, for release in February 1976. A dynamic statement of intent, it was the culmination of everything Clinton had been working toward for over a decade, and it could scarcely have been more successful. The album stormed to #13; a single, "Give Up the Funk (Tear the Roof off the Sucker)," tore to #15; and, as if to cement the empire's dominance, Goins, Shider, Collins, Worrell and Fulwood returned to the chart behind soul man Johnnie Taylor (died May 2000) on what emerged one of the defining singles of the age, "Disco Lady." An R&B chart-topper for six weeks, #1 on the pop charts for four, "Disco Lady" would become the first single ever to be certified platinum by the RIAA.

Avant-garde rocker Frank Zappa, too, was keen to work with the same musicians, offering them $500 a week each to join him in the studio for sessions. They turned him down; there was simply too much going on back aboard the Mothership. (Goins and Wesley briefly moved outside of the Funk Mob the following year, for Albert King's *King Albert* album.)

As "Tear the Roof off the Sucker" (sensibly, "Give Up the Funk" was retitled for still-cautious radio) continued climbing the chart, Parliament enjoyed their first sold-out headlining tour, and set about repaying the audience with a show they'd never forget. Certainly Clinton's old co-writer Sidney Barnes still remembers the day he received a phone call from Clinton announcing, "Guess what? I got a spaceship."

The stage set was designed by Jules Fisher and organized by Bob DeDeckere. The eternal example of labelmates KISS notwithstanding, only the Commodores and, more famously, Earth Wind & Fire were truly exploring theatrics onstage at that time, but Clinton didn't even regard their efforts as competition. Armed with seven truckloads of equipment and scenery—the spaceship was joined by a Rolls Royce, a pyramid and a mass of pyrotechnic devices—Parliament ran the entire show through its paces at KISS' own rehearsal studio, an aircraft hanger in Newburgh, NY.

Music and theater combined dramatically; the arrival of the spaceship would be foretold every night by Goins, standing alone onstage and announcing, "I think I hear the Mothership coming. I think I see the Mothership coming." It landed, a door opened and Clinton, a behemoth in silver, stood in the open hatch. Except it wasn't Clinton any more. It was Dr. Funkenstein. And the night was his to do with as he wanted. (Excerpts from a 1976 show at the Houston Summit appeared on 1986's *The Mothership Connection* album.)

Off the road, things were just as hectic. With guitarist Hampton now firmly assimilated as Eddie Hazel's full-time replacement and drummer Jerome Brailey pounding like a veteran, Funkadelic's final album for the Westbound label, *Tales of Kidd Funkadelic*, kept up the heat. Simultaneously, the band recorded almost enough material for an entire second album, for release in late 1976 as *Hardcore Jollies*, their first for new label Warner Brothers. (The set includes a guest appearance from Buddy Miles and was further bolstered with a raw, live version of "Cosmic Slop.")

The long-promised first album by Bootsy's Rubber Band—in reality, another gathering of the Parliament/Funkadelic P-Funk clan—appeared that same year, together with a solo set by Fuzzy Haskins. Accompanied by Fulwood, Mosson, Bykowski, Collins and Worrell, he turned in a workmanlike set that at least brought a vinyl birth to one of Parliament's most popular live tracks, "Cookie Jar." It sold poorly, however, and attention turned back to what the audience, at least, now regarded as the main attraction, a new Parliament album.

*The Clones of Dr. Funkenstein* arrived in October 1976, just eight months after its predecessor. Conceptually as well as chronologically a follow-up to *Mothership*, it climbed immediately into the Top 20, a seamless slab of contagiously commercial funk. It suddenly appeared that the studio had little room for any of the old "-adelia" anymore.

Live, however, Parliament remained as uncompromisingly jam-heavy as ever, an attribute hammered harder home by their next release, the double album *Live/P-Funk Earth Tour*. Recorded two nights apart in Los Angeles and Oakland in January 1977, and bolstered by the inclusion of two new studio tracks ("This Is the Way We Funk with You" and an old song, "Fantasy Is Reality"), the album highlighted material by both Parliament and Funkadelic. The totality of P-Funk was unfurled.

It was a breathlessly fertile period. Individual musicians were frequently involved in up to four albums at a time, with work continuing even as they toured. It was a common occurrence for the P-Funk musicians to finish a show, then head straight into the nearest studio to record ("Bop Gun" was taped in Atlanta, immediately after a gig at the Omni). The band's United Studios homebase outside Detroit, too, was constantly in action, even while Clinton and company were out of town. Any musicians left behind simply joined producer Ron Dunbar to continue recording.

With so much activity, 1977 saw the P-Funk empire spread its wings even further. Albums appeared from Fred Wesley & the Horny Horns (*A Blow for Me, a Toot for You*) and Eddie Hazel (*Game, Dames and Guitar Thangs*; Clinton was already scheming the Brides of Funkenstein duo of Dawn Silva and Lynn Mabry; and Parlet, built around longtime backing vocalists Jeanette Washington, Debbie Wright and Mallia Franklin. And a second Bootsy Collins set (*Ahh . . . The Name Is Bootsy, Baby!*) confirmed Collins' independence at the same time as re-emphasizing the true nature of the co-operative. Shider, Hampton, Brailey, Worrell, Wesley and Parker were all involved in the sessions.

However, all was not well within the community. Increasingly, Parliament vocalists Haskins, Davis, Thomas and Simon saw Clinton taking over roles that they had once at least had a share in, creatively and economically—saw, too, the public at large and the business in general feting Clinton as the band's leader and motivating force. It was plain, too, that they would never regain their lost footing and, immediately following the last show of P-Funk's spring 1977, tour, at the Los Angeles Coliseum on June 4, all four quit the group.

Davis soon returned, admitting that the money from P-Funk's recently signed Warner Brothers deal played a major part in his decision, but the others could not be swayed. Goins and Brailey, too, departed, chafing over Clinton's creative and financial stranglehold on the band. Goins formed his own group, Praxis, with Brailey producing.

Clinton did not replace them, instead getting down to work on the next Parliament album—and their most successful yet. *Funkentelechy vs. the Placebo Syndrome* was released in December 1977, its contents drawn from a sprawl of sessions over the past two years. "Flash Light" was an outtake from the last Bootsy album; "Funkentelechy" itself dated back to 1975 and Jerome Brailey's first ever session with Clinton. Nevertheless, both musically and politically ambitious, *Funkentelechy* continues to stand as a still photograph of American pop culture in the late '70s—lyrics borrow as unashamedly from television commercials as from current drug slang (the cocaine-laced "Sir Nose").

The album spent three weeks at #2 on the R&B chart, a single of "Flash Light" stayed at #1 for just as long. Powered by Worrell's incredible bass keyboard line, while Catfish Collins pinned everything down with a brittle guitar line. "Flash Light" also became such a live favorite that Clinton arranged to have P-Funk brand flashlights manufactured for sale at live shows. Between two and three thousand were sold every night and, when the band performed "Flash Light" itself, the entire auditorium would be illuminated by the audience's answering beams.

P-Funk toured through much of 1978, solo and spin-off albums ricocheting out as they traveled, and warming up the audience for a tremendous Christmas doubleheader, Parliament's *Motor Booty Affair* and Funkadelic's definitive *One Nation Under a Groove*, their first with Clinton's latest noteworthy recruit, former Ohio Players keyboardist Walter "Junie" Morrison, co-writer of almost all the album's most crucial cuts.

In 1976, *Hardcore Jollies* had already debuted Funkadelic in the Top 100. *One Nation* broke Parliament into the Top 20, even as its title track broached the US pop Top 30, a political anthem far beyond its own parochial borders, a lyrical reaffirmation of funk's power and glory that served as a triumphant rallying point for the myriad new fans suddenly flocking to the P-Funk banner.

In their moment of greatest strength, however, the P-Funk crew were at their weakest. Money lay at the heart of many of the disagreements, power at the soul of others. With so many musicians around, all jostling for their day in the sun, it didn't matter how many projects Clinton was juggling, he still couldn't keep everybody happy. But he would not tolerate discontent either.

Rick Gardner and Frank Waddy, saxophonist and drummer for Bootsy's Rubber Band, decided the time had come to procure a manager for themselves and do things "by the book" as Waddy put it, requesting traveling expenses and decent hotel accommodations. Collins responded by dropping them from the session, Clinton by dropping them from the pay roll.

Parlet were brindling at their own lack of success, coming to the conclusion that they had been put together as little more than a tax write-off, and that despite Clinton debuting the newly organized P-Funk Horns (Greg Boyer, Greg Thomas and Bennie Cowan) on their sophomore album, *Invasion of the Body Snatchers*.

Old resentments, too, bubbled back to the surface. Jerome Brailey launched his own band, Mutiny with an undisguised assault on what he saw as Clinton's dictatorship, the *Mutiny on the Mamaship* album. (Clinton is renamed for the album's purposes as "Lump," and is pictured walking the plank, pirate style, on the album's inner sleeve.)

Meanwhile, Haskins, Thomas and Simon had regrouped under the aegis of the LAX label and, figuring they had as much right to the Funkadelic name as their former bandmates, began work on an album of their own, *Connections and Disconnections*, complete with the caveat "none of the concepts on this album are related to George Clinton." In any event, it would be another two years before the album appeared (and 12 before the true ownership of the name was finally established). But still, the mood in the P-Funk camp was worsening under so many sustained attacks.

"One Nation Under a Groove" had broken Funkadelic onto the pop chart, but to some of the members, that was all it was, pop. Shider called the song "bubblegum" and complained, "Funkadelic was supposed to be rock." Hampton was convinced that for the first time in the band's history, "People were kicking our ass—the Aerosmiths and

Deep Purples and Ozzy Osbourne. [We] got more or less softer and softer."

Neither was there any reversal in sight. *Uncle Jam Wants You*, the next Funkadelic album, was musically lightweight and lyrically gimmicky, while a new Parliament album, *Gloryhallastoopid*, wasn't simply weak and repetitive, it also embraced the very "blahs" that its Funkadelic twin was supposed to protect people from, with the hand-clap powered "Party People" and the unabashedly disco-id "The Freeze."

Clinton's attention, however, was elsewhere: attending the launch, through a distribution deal with CBS, of his own Uncle Jam record label, and locked into a dispute with Funkadelic's label, Warner, over the band's own next record. Clinton had his heart set on a double; Warners insisted it could only be a single set. The arrival of Sly Stone as a full-time P-Funker introduced yet another element of chaos into the group; Clinton's own battle with an addiction to freebase cocaine unleashed further demons. And suddenly, the whole edifice came tumbling down.

January 1981's *Trombipulation* proved the final Parliament album; April's *The Electric Spanking of War Babies*, recorded with an all-but unrecognizable cast of musicians, became Funkadelic's farewell. Uncle Jam collapsed soon after, as war broke out between CBS and Warner Brothers over the rights to release a Roger Troutman/Zapp album, which Clinton produced and Uncle Jam financed. Wrapping up the defiantly titled Greatest Funk on Earth tour, P-Funk played their final show in Detroit shortly after the release of *War Babies*. The musicians were then handed $20 each and sent home.

### GEORGE CLINTON/P-FUNK ALL-STARS 1982–DATE

Shrugging off industry-wide predictions of his imminent demise, Clinton was back on his feet within a year. Surrounding himself with much of the classic P-Funk crew, he launched his own Hump label with a pair of singles ("Hydraulic Pump" and "One of Those Summers") by the ad-hoc P-Funk All Stars, a new group pieced together by Clinton and Sly Stone.

With a lineup that included Shider, Hazel, Wesley, Parker, Hampton, Silva and Bootsy, latter-day P-Funkers DeWayne "Blackbyrd" McKnight, Philippe Wynne and Junie Morrison, plus new recruits Bobby Womack, David Lee Chong and Gary Cooper (among many others), the All-Stars followed through with "Generator Pop" and the *Urban Dancefloor Guerrillas* album. Only a still shaky financial situation seemed to cloud the horizon. The version

of *Urban Dancefloor* that finally saw daylight was substantially shorter than Clinton originally envisioned (it would be 1995 before the unabridged album was released, as *Hydraulic Funk*). Finally bowing to economic reality, Clinton disbanded the All Stars and signed with Capitol as a solo artist.

Of course Bootsy, Worrell, Shider, Wesley, Parker, Junie Morrison, Hazel, Davis, the Brides and Parlet all joined him for 1982's *Computer Games*, a heavily synthesized, clearly new wave-influenced album that nevertheless packed a pair of stunning funkers, "Loopzilla" and "Atomic Dog."

It was followed, in 1983, by *You Shouldn't Nuf Bit Fish*, a set that took its lead from "Loopzilla"'s namechecking of Afrika Bambaataa's "Planet Rock" and acknowledged the growing power of rap (the opening "Nubian Nut")—one of several musical styles that sustained Clinton (and, via a steady stream of borrowed loops, vice versa) through the '80s.

However, Clinton's uncertainty over precisely which direction he intended pursuing was laid bare by his next two albums. Recorded around the same time as he produced the Red Hot Chili Peppers' sophomore album, 1985's *Some of My Best Jokes Are Friends*, paired Clinton with such techno wonderkids as Thomas Dolby, Tackhead/Living Colour producer Doug Wimbish and Slave's Steve Washington, but never really rose above the synthesizer overkill of the production. Dolby's *Aliens Ate My Buick* album, incidentally, featured an unreleased track from the *Jokes* sessions, "Hot Sauce."

*R&B Skeletons in the Closet*, in 1986, meanwhile, found Clinton shining the spotlight upon the current state of Black American music, highlighting the often under-stated presence of soul, funk and indeed R&B skeletons in the closet of every major contemporary artist. Again it was a good idea, let down by the execution and Clinton lapsed into silence immediately after.

He resurfaced in 1989, first with the lackluster *George Clinton Presents Our Gang Funky* album, then as the latest—and most surprising—recruit to Prince's Paisley Park label. The company's other signings, after all, had been unknowns whom Prince, with a barely disguised nod in Clinton's own direction, could mold to his own specifications. Clinton, however, not only arrived fully-formed, he was also one of the role models after whom Prince's entire musical career was modeled.

A new Clinton solo album, *The Cinderella Theory*, included songwriting contributions from as far afield as Public Enemy's Chuck D. and Flavor Flav and Clinton's son Treylewd, while the supporting musicians included Bootsy, Andre Foxxe Williams, Steve Washington and Blackbyrd McKnight. Clinton also recorded at least one song, "Soul Psychedelicide," with Prince. But plans for a new Funkadelic album to appear alongside *Cinderella, By Way of the Drum*, proved overly optimistic (the title track did make it out as a single) and it was four years more before Clinton released another new album.

Much of what became 1993's *Hey Man . . . Smell My Finger* was already present (at least in rudimentary form) in Clinton's 1989–90 live show, while the album itself was recorded a full year before it was finally released.

Produced by new jack stars William Bryant III and Kerry Gordon, *Hey Man . . .* followed *Cinderella* in recruiting a host of Clinton's acolytes both as rappers and guest musicians. Bootsy and Catfish, Shider, Parker, Wesley, Worrell, and Blackbyrd again brought continuity from the past. Red Hot Chili Peppers' Anthony Kiedis and Flea repaid Clinton's decade-old production favors; Dr. Dre, Ice Cube, J Cool and MC Breed weighed in on vocals, while Bill Laswell and Herbie Hancock also contributed.

In 1993, Clinton also relaunched his own dream of a record label, debuting One Nation with "Dope Dog", an album length collection of remixes of another 1989 tour favorite. The following year further enhanced his mainstream rehabilitation when he was recruited to provide the soundtrack to the movie *PCU*, a post-*Animal House* effort that was absolutely dwarfed by its predecessor, and utterly swamped by its soundtrack. Romping through both his own back catalog ("Tear the Roof off the Sucker" received a tumultuous workout) and his mentor's (Prince's "Erotic City"), Clinton turned in a set that really deserved a better commercial fate than it ultimately received.

Clinton's adoption by the rap community had already been confirmed; 1994 acknowledged his importance to the alternative rock crowd as well, as he joined the traveling festival Lollapalooza, on a bill also featuring Smashing Pumpkins, the Beastie Boys, the Breeders, A Tribe Called Quest, Nick Cave and Green Day. Nightly—and even without the vast extravaganzas of old—Clinton stole the show.

Victory in the long-running dispute over the Parliament and Funkadelic names saw Clinton return to his best known brand names in 1995, for the Parliament, Funkadelic and P-Funk All Stars single "Follow the Leader." Departing Paisley Park, 1995 then saw Clinton sign with Sony 550, and celebrate further with the unequivocally titled *The Awesome Power of a Fully Operational Mothership* (TA-

POAFOM) album, a vital return to funk form fired by the archetypes reinstalled by co-producers Bootsy, Worrell and Junie Morrison.

Two years later, his long-gestating "Dope Dogs" concept was expanded into an entire album, credited to Clinton and the All-Stars, while Clinton and company simultaneously maintained a barrage of live work, including a well-received appearance at Woodstock '99. Other Clinton projects during 1999–2000 included joining with Bobby Womack and Ronny Isley (among others) on a projected doo-wop covers album; guesting on new recordings by Bernie Worrell and Snoop Dogg; and accompanying Forche on the minor R&B chart single "Dog Food."

## GEORGE CLINTON COMPLETE DISCOGRAPHY
### THE PARLIAMENTS
1958 Poor Willie/Party Boys (APT)
1959 Lonely Island(You Made Me Wanna) Cry (Flipp)
1965 Heart Trouble(That Was) My Girl (Golden World)
1967 (I Wanna) Testify/I Can Feel the Ice Melting (Revilot—#3 R&B/#20 pop)
1967 All Your Goodies Are Gone (Let Hurt Put You in the Loser's Seat)/Don't Be Sore at Me (Revilot—#21 R&B)
1967 Little Man/The Goose (That Laid the Golden Egg) (Revilot)
1967 Look at What I Almost Missed/What You Been Growing (Revilot)
1968 A New Day Begins/I'll Wait (Revilot)
1968 Good Old Music/Time (Revilot)
1969 A New Day Begins/I'll Wait (Atco—#44 R&B)

### A PARLIAMENT THANG
1970 I Call My Baby Pussycat/Little Ole Country Boy (Invictus)

### PARLIAMENT
1970 The Silent Boatman/Livin' the Life (Invictus)
1971 Red Hot Mama/Little Ole Country Boy (Invictus)
1971 The Breakdown/Little Ole Country Boy (Invictus—#30 R&B/#107 pop)
1972 Come in out of the Rain/Little Ole Country Boy (Invictus)
1974 I Call My Baby Pussycat/Little Ole Country Boy (HDH)
1974 Testify/I Can Move You (If You Let Me) (Casablanca—#77 R&B)
1974 The Goose (part one)/(part two) (Casablanca)
1974 Up for the Down Stroke/Presence of a Brain (Casablanca—#10 R&B/#63 pop)
1975 Chocolate City (long version) (Casablanca—#24 R&B/#94 pop)
1975 Ride On/Big Footin' (Casablanca—#64 R&B)
1976 P-Funk (Wants To Get Funked Up)/Night of the Thumpasorus Peoples (Casablanca—#33 R&B)
1976 Tear the Roof off the Sucker/P-Funk (Casablanca—#5 R&B/#15 pop)
1976 Star Child (Mothership Connection)/ Supergroovalisticprosifunkstication (The Thumps Bump) (Casablanca—#26 R&B)
1976 Do That Stuff/Handcuffs (Casablanca)
1977 Dr. Funkenstein/Children of Production (Casablanca—#43 R&B/#102 pop)

1977 Fantasy Is Reality/The Landing of the Holy Mothership (Casablanca—#54 R&B)

1977 Bop Gun (Endangered Species)/I've Been Watching You (Move Your Sexy Body) (Casablanca—#14 R&B/#102 pop)

1978 Flash Light/Swing Down, Sweet Chariot (Casablanca—#1 R&B/#16 pop)

1978 Funkentelechy (part one)/(part 2) (Casablanca—#27 R&B)

1978 Aqua Boogie (A Psychoalphadiscobetabioaquadoloop)/(You're a Fish and I'm a) Water Sign (Casablanca—1 R&B/#89 pop)

1979 Rumpofsteelskin/Liquid Sunshine (Casablanca—#63 R&B)

1979 Party People/Party People (Reprise) (Casablanca—#39 R&B)

1979 Theme from the Black Hole/(You're a Fish and I'm a) Water Sign (Casablanca—#8 R&B)

1980 Agony of Defeet/The Freeze (Sizzaleenmean) (Casablanca—#7 R&B)

1980 The Big Bang Theory (part one)/(part two) (Casablanca—#50 R&B)

1981 Crush It/Body Language (Casablanca)

## FUNKADELIC

1969 Music for My Mother/instrumental (Westbound—#50 R&B)

1969 I'll Bet You/Qualify & Satisfy (Westbound—#22 R&B/#63 pop)

1969 I'll Bet You (alt version)/Open Your Eyes (Westbound)

1970 Focus on Funkadelic (part one)/(part two) (Westbound)

1970 Can't Shake It Loose/As Good As I Can Feel (Westbound—release cancelled)

1970 I Got a Thing, You Got a Thing/Fish'n'Chips And Sweat (Westbound—#30 R&B/#80 pop)

1970 I Wanna Know If It's Good to You? (instrumental) (Westbound—#27 R&B/#81 pop)

1971 You and Your Folks, Me and My Folks/Funky Dollar Bill (Westbound—#42 R&B/#91 pop)

1971 Can You Get to That/Back in Our Minds (Westbound—#44 R&B/#93 pop)

1972 Hit It and Quit It/A Whole Lot of B.S. (Westbound)

1972 A Joyful Process (#49 R&B/#118 pop)/Loose Booty (Westbound—#38 R&B/#118 pop)

1973 Cosmic Slop/If You Don't Like the Effects, Don't Produce the Cause (Westbound)

1974 Standing on the Verge of Getting It On/Jimmy's Got a Little Bit of Bitch in Him (Westbound—#27 R&B)

1975 Red Hot Momma/Vital Juices (Westbound—#73 R&B)

1975 Better by the Pound/Stuff & Things (Westbound)

1976 Let's Take It to the Stage/Biological Speculation (Westbound—#89 R&B)

1976 Undisco Kidd/How Do Yeaw View You (Westbound—#30 R&B/#102 pop)

1977 Comin' Round the Mountain/If You Got Funk, You Got Style (WB—#54 R&B)

1977 Smokey/Soul Mate (WB)

1978 Maggot Brain/Chant (WB)

1978 (Think! It Ain't Illegal Yet)/Lunchmeataphobia/P.E. Squad + Doo Doo Chasers (Special EP, included with One Nation . . . LP) (WB)

1978 One Nation Under a Groove (part one)/(part two) (WB—#1 R&B/#28 pop)

1979 Cholly Funk Getting Ready To Roll/Into You (WB—#43 R&B)

1979 (Not Just) Knee Deep (part one)/(part two) (WB—#1 R&B/#77 pop)

1979 Uncle Jam (part one)/(part two) (WB—#53 R&B)

1981 The Electric Spanking of War Babies/instrumental (WB—#60 R&B)

1981 Shockwaves/Brettino's Bounce (WB)

## FUNKADELIC (no Clinton involvement)

1981 Connections and Disconnections/? (LAX—#68 R&B)

## P-FUNK ALL-STARS

1982 Hydraulic Pump (part one)/(part two) (Hump—#66 R&B)

1982 One of Those Summers/It's Too Funky in Here (Hump—#77 R&B)

1983 Generator Pop/Hydraulic Pump (Uncle Jam—#62 R&B)

## GEORGE CLINTON

1982 Loopzilla (Edit)/Pot Sharing Tots (Capitol)

1982 Atomic Dog/Atomic Dog (instrumental) (Capitol)

1982 Atomic Dog/Loopzilla (Capitol)

1982 Atomic Dog/Man's Best Friend (Capitol)

1983 Get Dressed (part one)/(part two) (Capitol)

1983 Nubian Nut/Free Alterations (Capitol)

1984 Quickie/Last Dance (Capitol)

1984 Last Dance/Last Dance (Capitol)

1985 Double Oh-Oh/Bangladesh (Capitol)

1985 Bullet Proof/Silly Millameter (Capitol)

1985 Do Fries Go with That Shake/Pleasures of Exhaustion (Capitol)

1986 Hey Good Lookin'/Hey Good Lookin' (Capitol)

1986 R&B Skeletons in the Closet/Nubian Nut (Capitol)

1989 Why Should I Dog U Out? (Edit)/(part two) (Paisley Park)

1990 Tweakin'/French Kiss (Paisley Park)

1993 Paint the White House Black/instrumental (Paisley Park)

1994 Erotic City/Stomp (Fox)

1996 If Anybody Get's Funked Up (It's Gonna Be You) (remix)/LP version (Sony 550)

### LPs
## FUNKADELIC

**10** 1970 Funkadelic (Westbound)

"Mommy? What's a Funkadelic?" Opening with a statement of intent that mystified more than it explained, *Funkadelic* is a shattering blend of R&B sensibilities and acid soaked rock effects. Eddie Hazel's guitar chimes, assaults and ultimately explodes; the production treats the studio like one giant toybox and the feedback is a living creature. Play it loud.

**8** 1971 Free Your Mind . . . and Your Ass Will Follow (Westbound)

Under 25 minutes long, with almost half that devoted to the feedback choked title track. The slight "Funky Dollar Bill" is easily skipped, but the riffing "I Wanna Know . . ." and the spacey, backward backing track of "Eulogy and Light" prove that *Funkadelic* wasn't a freakish fluke.

**8** **1971 Maggot Brain (Westbound)**

Worrell's organ-led "Hit It and Quit It" takes the prog rock excursion to its limit, coming over like an obscure 45 by a British band you've never heard of; the lazy "You and Your Folks," in contrast, is almost mundane R&B call and response . . . so, the first Funkadelic clinker? Maybe . . . but bracketing the filler, Hazel's squealing guitar solo title track and the roughshod "Wars of Armageddon" turn all the equations on their head.

**7** **1972 America Eats Its Young (Westbound)**

Sprawlingly diverse double highlighted by the rap "Loose Booty" and a few moments recalling Isaac Hayes' weirder moments, all orchestral muttering and wah-wah guitar.

**7** **1973 Cosmic Slop (Westbound)**

**8** **1974 Standing on the Verge of Getting It On (Westbound)**

Rocked up renditions of old Parliaments numbers, "Red Hot Mama" and "I'll Wait" (retitled "I'll Stay") drag the mood down a little, but bad taste comes to the rescue with the bizarre "Jimmy's Got a Little Bit of Bitch in Him" and "Good Thoughts, Bad Thoughts." The title track, meanwhile, blends rock, soul and even a snatch of music hall over an all-pervading funk.

**9** **1975 Let's Take It to the Stage (Westbound)**

Laconic, deranged and tight as a duck's ass. . . the first Funkadelic album to eschew the jam mentality (only three songs break the four-minute barrier) and a party favor of the first order. X-rated lyrics and concepts and some excruciating funk puns are bound up in concise dance stompers epitomized—musically and thematically—by the positively lethal "Get Off Your Ass and Jam." The title rhymes with "shit, goddamn."

**6** **1976 Tales Oo Kidd Funkadelic (Westbound)**

A transitional album, the first non-essential Funkadelic set yet. But still the sinewy "Undisco Kid" recalls the unrepentant weirdness of pure funkadelia, while there's also an early version of "I'm Never Gonna Tell It," later reworked for Philippe Wynne's solo album.

**7** **1976 Hardcore Jollies (WB)**

**7** **1978 One Nation Under a Groove (WB)**

The title track notwithstanding, a functional album at best. By 1978, the independence and vitality of funk was very old news indeed, while an otherwise dynamic Michael Hampton's showcase, "Who Says a Funk Band Can't Play Rock?" addressed a question that Clinton answered years before. (In any case, a live version of "Maggot Brain" tacked on the end of the album more than cleared up that equation for any late-comers.)

**6** **1979 Uncle Jam Wants You (WB)**

Though still joyously defiant in the face of disco (the sleeve insists "Funkadelic is rescuing dance music from the blahs"), *Uncle Jam* labors beneath a self-conscious air only halfway redeemed by "Freak of the Week," "(Not Just) Knee Deep" and the gargantuan 10 minute title track.

**6** **1981 The Electric Spanking of War Babies (WB)**

**SELECTED COMPILATIONS AND ARCHIVE RELEASES**

**6** **1975 Funkadelic's Greatest Hits (Westbound)**

**7** **1992 Music for Your Mother (The Singles) (WB)**

**9** **1996 Live (WB)**

Exceptional 1971 recording, suffers from a few performance jitters but otherwise functions precisely as the band's reputation says it should.

**6** **1997 Finest (Westbound)**

Eventful but unimaginative compilation rounds up 13 prime album cuts, two odd singles and a short live "Maggot Brain."

**PARLIAMENT LPs**

**LPs**

**8** **1971 Osmium (Invictus)**

Scattershot collection of styles, moods and occasionally brilliant moments places Parliament into an oddly Rolling Stones-ish urban rock/blues mold (*Let It Bleed* sounds great alongside it). Country, folk and gospel all get a look in, together with some startling efforts that don't fit any bag.

**7** **1974 Up for the Down Stroke (Casablanca)**

Melodic commercial funk is the order of the day, vocal chants and catchphrases (the title track is nothing but) lending the affair a superficial breezy air, which it really doesn't deserve, as the whacked out "The Goose" remake, and the sleazy "All Your Goodies Are Gone" quickly prove.

**6** **1975 Chocolate City (Casablanca)**

Slight collection seemingly more concerned with a hip-shaking party than pushing any of Clinton's usual frontiers. "Big Foot" has a mischievous Motown vibe, though, and the title track is a fine rap experiment.

**9** **1976 Mothership Connection (Casablanca)**

The moment where the realities of P-Funk as two functioning bands begins to blur, highlighted by the formal caution of "P-Funk (Wants To Get Funked Up)," the relentless stomp of "Tear the Roof Off" and, finally, "Night of the Thumpasorus People," which sounds precisely like its title demands.

**6** **1977 The Clones of Dr. Funkenstein (Casablanca)**

Riding the Horny Horns across seas of unrelenting light-heartedness, *Clones* opens with the portentously biblical scene-setter "Prelude," then rushes downhill from there. By the time you hit the closing "Funkin' for Fun". . . it really isn't even amusing.

**9 1977 Live/P-Funk Earth Tour (Casablanca)**

Phenomenal recounting of the live show, the album closes with a studio stunner: "Fantasy Is Reality," a gospel swing funker driven equally by the Brides and a guitar oddly borrowed wholesale from English rocker Marc Bolan.

**10 1977 Funkentelechy vs. the Placebo System (Casablanca)**

Back to P-Funk basics, six solid grooves packed to the rafters with chants, rhythms, effects and excitement. The marathon "Funkentelechy," ten more minutes of "Sir Nose" and the pointed "Bop Gun" are stamping, synthing highlights, and "Flash Light," of course, is "Flash Light."

**8 1978 Motor-Booty Affair (Casablanca)**

The alternately exhilarating and infuriating "Aqua Boogie" takes the fascination with freaky effects to new heights, but little about this album remains in one place for too long, lending it a dishevelled, even un-danceable, air. But "Mr. Wiggles" warns you of that; it's definitely not your average 50 yard dash of funk.

**6 1979 Gloryhallastoopid—Or Pin the Tail on the Funky (Casablanca)**

**5 1981 Trombipulation (Casablanca)**

### SELECTED COMPILATIONS AND ARCHIVE RELEASES

**9 1993 Tear the Roof Off: 1974–80 (Casablanca—#79 R&B)**

Generally flawless two-CD beginners' guide.

**9 1999 The 12" Collection and More (Casablanca)**

Absolutely essential collection hauls out the startling nine to ten-minute versions of "Aqua Boogie," "Flash Light," "Agony of DeFeet," "Ridin' High" and "Black Hole/Big Bang," plus (slightly) shorter alternate/original versions of Parlet's "Ridin' High," "Testify," "Oh I" and "Up for the Down Stroke."

### GEORGE CLINTON/P-FUNK ALL STARS LPs

**8 1982 Computer Games (Capitol)**

Heavily electronic but undeniably Funkadelic. "Atomic Dog" and "Loopzilla" should be familiar to all.

**6 1984 You Shouldn't Nuf Bit Fish (Capitol)**

**6 1985 Some of My Best Jokes Are Friends (Capitol)**

**6 1986 R&B Skeletons in the Closet (Capitol)**

Stepping back from the electro-overkill of the last two albums, a hip-hop-influenced mish-mash of dance styles that is only partially successful.

**5 1988 The Cinderella Theory (Paisley Park)**

Less a comeback, more a reminder of how deeply embedded in the R&B psyche Clinton had become. Disciples queue up to appear (but only occasionally truly perform)

alongside him and the lasting effect is of watching a party from the other side of the street.

**8 1990 Live at the Beverly Theatre in Hollywood (Westbound)**

Live two-CD set from 1983 featuring epic renditions of its best cuts ("Cosmic Slop," "Maggot Brain," "One Nation," "Atomic Dog"), clean sound and a coherent performance.

**6 1993 Hey Man, Smell My Finger (Paisley Park)**

### SELECTED COMPILATIONS AND ARCHIVE RELEASES

**7 1987 The Mothership Connection Live from Houston (Capitol)**

One side highlights a 1976 Houston show, the other serves up a three track "best of" Clinton's recent solo work.

**6 1993 Dope Dog (One Nation)**

Basically, 11 different remixes of the title track, ranging from the superb to the mundane.

**9 1994 Parliament & Funkadelic Live 1976–93 (Essential—UK)**

Superlative four-CD collection tracing the P-Funk family's live career from shows in Denver (1976), San Diego, Oakland (1977), DC, Monroe, Hampton, (1978), Dayton (1981), Los Angeles (1983), Tokyo, Chicago and Memphis (1993), plus three 1972 recordings. Sound quality is variable and annotation is minimal, but the sheer wealth of material (and excitement) is unimpeachable.

**5 1996 Greatest Funkin' Hits (Capitol)**

Remix collection packing a few interesting twiddly bits, but nothing to get too excited over.

**7 2000 Greatest Hits (Capitol)**

Generally worthwhile 12 track rendering of the Capitol years, features the non-CD "broadcast version" of "Loopzilla," together with the expected cuts.

### P-FUNK ALL STARS LPs

**8 1983 Urban Dancefloor Guerrillas (Uncle Jam)**

One of the great P-Funk albums, strong funky drumming and bass forming the kind of bedrock every Clinton song should have had, but which they sometimes lost sight of in search of the gimmicks. Don't let the late date put you off—"Pumpin' It Up" would have fit on any past triumph.

**8 1996 T.A.P.O.A.F.O.M. (MJJ-EPIC)**

### SELECTED COMPILATION AND ARCHIVE RELEASES

**8 1995 Hydraulic Funk (Westbound—UK)**

The original *Urban Dancefloor* was cut back from Clinton's original vision; restored, the missing elements prove that the scissors rarely lied.

### P-FUNK GUITAR ARMY

**4 1994 Tribute to Jimi Hendrix, Vol. I (P-Vine)**

**2 1995 Tribute to Jimi Hendrix: Return of the Gypsy (P-Vine)**

Largely disappointing/disposable tribute albums produced by Clinton and featuring several P-Funk alumni.

## THE GEORGE CLINTON FAMILY SERIES (ESSENTIAL—UK)

An on-going anthology of rare and unreleased cuts from the George Clinton archives. The following indexes volumes one through five chronologically by artist.

Jerome & Jimmy Ali: She's Crazy (1980) (v2)
Sidney Barnes: Secrets (1980) (v4)
Brides . . . w/Dr. Funkenstein: Rat Kissed the Cat (1977) (v5)
Brides of Funkenstein: Love Is Something (1977) (v2)
Brides of Funkenstein: Ice Melting in Your Heart (1977) (v5)
Brides of Funkenstein: Take My Love (1977) (v4)
Brides of Funkenstein: Up Up and Away (1979) (v5)
Brides of Funkenstein: Love Don't Come Easy (1980) (v3)
Brides of Funkenstein: 20 Bucks (1980) (v4)
Brides of Funkenstein: Just for Play (1980) (v4)
Jessica Cleaves: Off Tthe Wall (1978) (v4)
Jessica Cleaves: Send a Gram (1980) (v1)
Jessica Cleaves: I Really Envy the Sunshine (1980) (v3)
Jessica Cleaves: Eyes of a Dreamer (1981) (v5)
Jessica Cleaves: My Love (1981) (v2)
George Clinton/Bootsy Collins: [commercials] (v2)
Bootsy Collins: The Chong Show (1979) (v1)
Ron Dunbar: These Feets Are Made for Dancing (1982) (v1)
Gary Fabulous/Black Slack: Funkin' For (1980) (v3)
Flo: Common Law Wife (1972) (v3)
Ron Ford: Monster Dance (1980) (v3)
Ron Ford: Rock Jam (1980) (v2)
Ron Ford: Thumparella (1981) (v5)
Ron Ford: Bubblegum Gangster (1981) (v2)
Four Tops: To Care (1978) (v4)
Andre Foxxe: Better Days (1984) (v1)
Funkadelic w/Diane Brooks: Every Little Bit Hurts (1972) (v5)
Funkadelic: In the Cabin of My Uncle Jam (1976) (v2)
Funkadelic: Clone Commando (1976) (v2)
Funkadelic: Too Tight for Light (1979) (v5)
Funkadelic: I Angle (1980) (v4)
Funkadelic: May Day (1981) (v3)
Funkadelic: Sunshine of Our Love (1984) (v1)
Jimmy G: Shove On (1981) (v2)
Jimmy G: Get It On (1981) (v4)
Lonnie Greene: I Didn't Know That the Funk Was Loaded (1980) (v5)
Michael Hampton: We're Just Funkers (1980) (v3)
Horny Horns: Lickety Split (1979) (v3)
Treylewd: She Never Do's Things (1978) (v4)
Treylewd: Personal Problems (1981) (v2)
Treylewd/Flastic Brain Flam: Michelle (1978) (v1)
Treylewd/Flastic Brain Flam: Clone Ranger (1978) (v5)
Tracey Lewis/Andre Foxxe: I Can't Stand It (1981) (v3)

Junie Morrison: Superspirit (1978) (v3)
Junie Morrison: Triune (1978) (v4)
Junie Morrison: Can't Get Over Losing you (1978) (v5)
Muruga: Superstar Madness (1980) (v4)
Parlet & the Brides: Think Right (1980) (v2)
Parliament: Does Disco Go with DAT? (1979) (v2)
Parliament: Live Up (1975) (v4)
Parliament: Flatman and Bobin (1978) (v5)
Parliament: Every Booty (1979) (v2)
Parliament: Go Fer Yer Funk (1980 w/James Brown) (v1)
Nick Savannah and Dwarf: Comin' Down from Your Love (1981) (v4)
Sterling Silver Starship: Booty Body (1980) (v3)
Sterling Silver Starship: Funk It Up (1981) (v1)
Sly Stone: Who In the Funk (1981) (v1)
Bernie Worrell: Who Do You Love (1978) (v5)
Philippe Wynne: I Found You (1981) (v5)

## THE FUNK MOB

A comprehensive index of all musicians featured on the core P-Funk family albums 1969–81.

### KEY:

AE = America Eats Its Young
B1 = Bootsy LP Stretchin' Out in Bootsy's Rubber Band
B2 = Bootsy LP Aah . . . The Name Is . . .
B3 = Bootsy LP This Boot Is Made . . .
B4 = Bootsy LP Ultra Wave
BF1 = Brides of Funkenstein LP Funk or walk
BF2 = Brides of Funkenstein LP Never Buy Texas
CC = Chocolate City
CD = Clones of Dr. Funkenstein
CS = Cosmic Slop
ES = Electric Spanking
F1 = Funkadelic
FH1 = Fuzzy LP A Whole Nother Thang
FH2 = Fuzzy LP Radio Active
FP = Funkentelechy vs. the Placebo Syndrome
FYM = Free Your Mind
G = Gloryhallastoopid
GD = Eddie Hazel LP Games, Dames and Guitar Thangs
HH1 = Horny Horns LP A Blow for Me
HH2 = Horny Horns LP Say Blow by Blow Backwards
HH3 = Horny Horns LP The Final Blow
HJ = Hardcore Jollies
KF = Tales of Kidd Funkadelic
LP = Let's Take It . . .
MB = Maggot Brain
MoB = Motor Booty Affair
MC = Mothership Connection
O = Osmium
ON = One Nation Under a Groove

PP1 = Parlet LP *Pleasure Principle*
PP2 = Parlet LP *Invasion of the Booty Snatchers*
PP3 = Parlet LP *Play Me or Trade Me*
PW = Philippe Wynne LP *Wynne Jammin*
RC = Ruth Copeland LP *Self Portrait*
RC2 = Ruth Copeland LP *I Am What I Am*
SB = Sweat Band LP *Sweat Band*
SV = *Standing on the Verge*
T = *Trombipulation*
UD = *Up for the Down Stroke*
UJ = *Uncle Jam Wants You*
WOO = Bernie Worrell LP *All the Woo in the World*

Jerome Ali (gtr) PP2/3,ES
Jimmy Ali (bs) PP2/3,T,ES
Frederick Allen (kybds) B1
Mickey Atkins (kybds) F1
Donald Austin (gtr) FH1
Bob Babbitt (bs) RC,F1
Walter Babiuk (vls) AE
Leslyn Bailey (vcls) B1
Ron Banks (vcls) BF1
Sidney Barnes (vcls)
Harold Beane (gtr, vcls) AE
Marcus Belgrave (hrns) PW
Kenny Birch (gtr) PW
Fred Boldt (hrns) PW
Boom (hrns) MC
Raputin Boutte (vcls) MC
Greg Boyer (hrns) MoB,PP2/3,UJ,G
Jerome Brailey (drms) MC,HJ,KF,CD,GD,B2,HH1,FH2,FP,ON,HH3
Michael Brecker (sax) CC,MC,B1/2,CD,HH1/3,T,ES
Randy Brecker (trum) CC,MC,B1/2,CD,HH1/3,T
Lloyd Bridges (vcls) SB
Gary Bronson (drms) SV,UD
Diane Brooks (vcls) AE
Linda Brown (vcls) MoB,UJ
Raymond Lee Brown (hrns) PP3
Frank Bryant (bs) PW
Jeff Bunn (bs) PP2,UJ,BF2
Ron Bykowski (gtr, vcls) RC2,CS,SV,UD,LT,FH1
Danny Cahn (hrns) T
Jimmy Calhoun (bs) SV
Angelo Carlisi (hrns) PW
Gordon Carlton (gtr, vcls) PP2/3,G,T,ES,PW
Janice Carlton (vcls, perc) PP2/3
Dave Case (kybds) RC2
Casper (vcls) B2/4,WOO
Bruce Cassidy (trum) AE
Dennis Chambers (drms) UJ,G,BF2
Peter Chase (whistle) UD

Bryna Chimenti (vcls) MC
David Lee Chong (kybds) G,T,ES,PW
Arnie Chykowski (trum) AE
Jessica Cleaves (vcls) KF,UJ,G,BF2,HH2,T,PW
Dennis Coffey (gtr) RC,F1,PW,FH2
Bootsy Collins (bs, gtr, drms, vcls) AE,UD,CC,MC,LT,KF,B1–4,FH1,CD,GD,HH1–3,FP,BF1/2,ON,PP1–3,MoB,WOO,UJ,G,T,SB,ES
Phelps Collins (gtr, vcls) AE,B1–4,HH1–3,FP,BF1,MoB,WOO,PP2/3,G
Kenny Colton (drms) PP2/3,G,BF2,T,ES
Gary Cooper (drms, vcls) CC,MC,KF,B1–3,CD,GD,BF1,PP1/2,MoB,WOO, HH2/3
Ruth Copeland (vcls) RC/2
Danny Cortez (hrns) FP
Benny Cowan (hrns) MoB,PP2/3,G,T
Randy Crawford (vcls) HH1
Rodney Crutcher (gtr) BF2,HH2/3
Lige Curry (vcls,bs) UJ,T,PP3,ES
Rodney Curtis (bs) BF1/2,ON,PP1,WOO,UJ,G,HH2/3,ES,PW
Cynthia Davis (vcls) KF
Donna Davis (vcls) KF
Maurice Davis (hrns) PW
Ray Davis (vcls) F1,FYM,O,MB,AE,CS,SV,UD,CC,MC,LT,HJ,KF,CD,FP,ON MoB,PP2,UJ,G,BF2,T,SB,PW
Tony Davis (vcls) G,T,PP3
Larry Demps (vcls) BF1
Darryl Dixon (hrns) FP,T
Gwen Dozier (vcls) T,PP3
Valerie Drayton (hrns) FP
Dawn Driver (vcls) T
Doug Duffey (kybds) GD
Ron Dunbar (vcls) G,T,PP3
Debbie Edwards (vcls) MC,KF,CD
Janice Evans (vcls) PP2/3,G,T,SB
Rick Evans (gtr) B4
Joe Farrell (hrns) MC
Ronni Faust (vcls) T,SB
Ernie Fields Jr. (hrns) PP3
Eli Fontaine (sax) WOO,
Ron Ford (vcls) ON,PP1–3,MoB,UJ,G,T,PW
Mallia Franklin (bvoc) CC,ON,PP1/2,MoB,WOO,UJ,BF2,T
Larry Fratangelo (perc) BF1/2,ON,MoB,PP2/3,UJ,G,HH3,B3,T,ES,PW
Zachary Frazier (drms) AE
Tiki Fulwood (drms) RC/2,F1,FYM,O,MB,AE,CS,SV,UD,CC,MC,LT,FH1,GD,UJ
Dr. Funk (vcls) PP2/3,BF2,HH2,T,PW
Rick Gardner (trum, vcls) B1/2/3,CD,HH1/2,FP,PP1,MoB,WOO
Rick Gilmore (gtr) PP1
Cynthia Girty (vcls) B4
Glen Goins (vcls, gtr) MC,HJ,KF,CD,GD,HH1/3,FP,B2,PP1/2,FH2,WOO,UJ
John Glover (kybds) PW
Ronnie Greenaway (trum, vcls) AE
Lonnie Greene (drms,vcls) T

Richard Griffith (trum, vcls) B2–4,HH1–3,FP,PP1/3,MoB,WOO,T,SB

Clayton Gunnels (trum, vcls) AE

Larry Hackett (vcls) G,

Michael Hampton (gtr) MC,LT,HJ,KF,B1/2/3,CD,GD,HH1/2/3,FP,BF1/2,ON,PP1–3,FH2,MoB,WOO,UJ,G,T,SB,PW,ES

Willie Hampton (gtr) PW

Lee Harrison (hrns) PW

Fuzzy Haskins (vcls, drms) F1,FYM,O,MB,AE,SV,UD,CC,MC,LT,HJ,KF,FH1/2,CD

Dawn Hatcher (bs) RC2

Larry Hatcher (hrns, vcls) G,B4,T,SB,PP3

Shirley Hayden (vcls) MoB,PP2/3,G,T,SB,PW

Eddie Hazel (gtr, vcls) RC/2,F1,FYM,O,MB,AE,SV,UD,CC,LT,GD,WOO,UJ,BF2,ES

Larry Heckstall (vcls) MoB,UJ,G,T

Nina Hoover (vcls) T

Telma Hopkins (vcls) PP1,B4,FH2,PW

Sheila Horne (vcls) UJ,G,BF2,HH2,T,SB,PW

Gary Hudgins (kybds) UJ,BF2,PW

Ivy Hunter (kybds) F1

Arnold Ingram (kybds) PW

Brad Innis (drms) F1

Archie Ivy (vcls) MC

James W. Jackson (harp) MB,AE

McKinley Jackson (trom) MB

Ted Jackson (hrns) PW

Cheryl James (vcls) MoB,PP2/3,T,PW

John Jaszez (vcls) PP3

Prakash John (bs, vcls) AE,CC

Joel Johnson (kybds) B2–4,BF1,PP2,HH2/3,SB

Mark Johnson (kybds) B4

Robert Johnson (vcls) B1–4,MoB,PP2,G,HH2,T,SB,PW

Jerry Jones (drms) BF2,B4,SB,PW

Taka Kahn (vcls) MC,KF,CD,HH1

Steve Kennedy (vcls) AE

Ty Lampkin (drms) O,AE,CS,SV,CC,BF1,ON,MoB,WOO,UJ,G,HH3,T,PP3,ES,PW

Ronald Laurie (clo) AE

Clay Lawrey (hrns) FP

Bobby Lewis (banjo) ON

Diane Lewis (vcls) MB

Pat Lewis (vcls) MB

Tracey Lewis (vcls) G,BF2,T

Overton Loyd (vcls) MoB

Robert McCullough (tenor) AE

Jeanette McGruder (vcls) UJ,G,BF2,HH2,T,SB,PW

Dewayne McKnight (gtr, bs, drms) UJ,G,BF2,ES

David McMurray (lyricon) B4

Lynn Mabry (vcls) GD,HH1,FP,BF1,ON,MoB,WOO,B4

Man in the Box (drms) UD,CC

David Majal (hrns) T,PP3

John Mical (hrns) T

Buddy Miles (perc) HJ

Carolyn Miles (vcls) B4

George Minger (hrns) BF1

God Momms (vcls) T

Ray Monette (gtr) RC/2,F1

Tim Moore (gtr) PP2,

Walter Morrison (kybds, gtr, vcls) ON,MoB,UJ,G,T,ES

Cordell Mosson (bs, drms, gtr) AE,CS,SV,UD,CC,MC,LT,HJ,KF,B1,FH1/2,CD,GD,FP,ON,UJ,G,HH2/3,PP3

Bruce Nazarian (gtr, bs) FH2,BF2,PW

Bill Nelson (bs, gtr, vcls) RC/2,F1,FYM,O,MB,UD,LT,GD,PP1,WOO,UJ, HH2/3

Kevin Oliver (gtr) PP2

Stevie Pannell (vcls, bs) T,PP3,PW

Maceo Parker (tnr./alt sax, kybds, vcls) MC,B1–4,CD,HH1–3,FP,PP1/3,MoB,WOO,G,T,SB

Leon Patillo (kybds) SV

Chanta Payne (vcls) PW

Mike Payne (vcls) MoB,UJ,G,T,SB,PW

Sam Peakes (hrns) G

Jerry Paul Podgajski (perc) FH2

Victoria Polley (vln) AE

Albert Pratz (vln) AE

Wayman Reed (hrns) BF1

Greg Reilly (vcls) PP3

Bill Richards (vln) AE

Pat Rizzo (sax) ES

Cynthia Robinson (trum) ES

Rudy Robinson (kybds) BF2,PW

Ernie Rodgers (hrns) PW

Barry Rogers (hrns) T

Jerome Rogers (kybds, vcls) UJ,G,BF2,HH2/3,T,PW

Lucius Ross (gtr, vcls) RC,F1,FYM,O,MB

Timmy Ryan (vcls) FH2

Manon Saulsby (kybds,vcls) PP2/3,T,ES

Peter Schenkman (clo) AE

Joe Sera (vln) AE

Garry Shider (vcls, gtr) O,MB,AE,CS,SV,UD,CC,MC,LT,HJ,KF,B1/2,CD,GD,HH1–3,FP,BF1/2,FH2,ON,PP1–3,MoB,WOO,UJ,G,T,SB,PW,ES

Kevin Shider (vcls) T

Linda Shider (vcls) G,T,SB

Dawn Silva (vcls, vcls) GD,HH1/2,FP,BF1/2,ON,MoB,WOO,UJ,G,B4,T,SB

Calvin Simon (vcls, perc) F1,FYM,O,MB,AE,CS,SV,UD,CC,MC,LT,HJ,KF,CD

Carl Small (perc, vcls) PP2/3,G,BF2,HH3,B3/4,T,SB,PW

Nolan A. Smith (hrns) PP3

Stanley Solomon (vla) AE

Herb Sparkman (vcls) F1

David Spradley (kybds) B4,PP3

Raymond Spruell (vcls) MB

Al Stanwyck (trum) AE

Donald Sterling (bs, vcls) PP2/3,G,BF2,HH2/3,T,ES,PW

Sly Stone (vcls, gtr, kybds, drms) ES
Ollie Strong (stl gtr) AE
Gordon Stump (hrns) PW
Mike Sutter (hrns) PW
Sonny Talbert (kybds) B1
Barry Taylor (hrns) T
David Taylor (hrns) T
J.S. Theracon (kybds, gtr, vcls) MoB,WOO,UJ
Grady Thomas (vcls) F1,FYM,O,MB,AE,SV,UD,CC,MC,LT,HJ,KF,CD
Greg Thomas (vcls, hrns) ON,MoB,PP2/3,UJ,G,B3,T
Tony Thomas (gtr, vcls) T
David Tofani (hrns) T
Roger Troutman (gtr, bs, kybds) ES
John Trudell (hrns) PW
Danny Turner (hrns) BF1
Earl Van Dyke (kybds) F1
Joyce Vincent (vcls) PP,B4,FH2,PW
Pam Vincent (vcls) MC,KF
Frank Waddy (drms, vcls) AE,B1/2/3,HH1/3,BF1,PP1/2
Patty Walker (vcls) T,SB
Tony Walker (vcls) B4
Randy Wallace (alto, vcls) AE
Jeanette Washington (vcls) FP,ON,PP1—3,MoB,WOO,G,T,SB
Fred Wesley (tromb, kybds, vcls) CC,MC,B1—4,CD,HH1—3,FP,PP1/3,MoB, WOO,T,SB, ·
James Wesley (vcls) UJ
Andre Williams (vcls) G,T,PP3,PW
Christopher Williams (vcls) B3
Jesse Williams (drms) HH3
Rose Williams (vcls) MB
Aaron Willis (harmon) T
Ernestro Wilson (kybds, vcls) PP2/3,BF2,T
Bernie Worrell (kybds, mel, vcls) RC/2,FYM,O,MB,AE,CS,SV,UD,CC,MC,LT,HJ, KF,B1/2/3,FH1/2,CD,GD,HH1/2/3,FP,BF1/2,ON,PP1/2,MoB,WOO,UJ,G,T, SB,PW
Debra Wright (vcls) MC,KF,FP,ON,PP1,MoB,WOO
Jim Wright (drms) PP1,WOO,
Philippe Wynne (vcls) UJ,G,T,SB,PW
Joey Zalabok (vcls) MoB

## SELECTED SAMPLES
### THE PARLIAMENTS
I'll Wait — De La Soul: Millie Pulled a Pistol on Santa (1991)

### P-FUNK/GEORGE CLINTON
A Joyful Process — Eazy: Eazy-Duz-It (1988)
A Joyful Process — Smokin' Suckas Wit Logic Uncle Tom Artist (1993)
Adolescent Funk — Dr. Dre: Bitches Ain't Shit (1993)
All Night — Arrested Development: Ease My Mind (1994)
All Night — Gang Starr: Blowin' Up the Spot (1994)
All Your Goodies Are Gone — Boss: Born Gangstaz (1993)

All Your Goodies Are Gone — Poison Clan: Afraid of the Flavor (1993)
All Your Goodies Are Gone — Salt-N-Pepa: Tramp (1987)
All Your Goodies Are Gone — Salt-N-Pepa: Everybody Get Up (1988)
Aquaboogie — Above the Law: Call It What You Want (1993)
Aquaboogie — Cypress Hill: Psychobetabuckdown (1992)
Aquaboogie — Da Lench Mob: Lost in Tha System (1992)
Aquaboogie — Digital Underground: Flowin' on the D-Line (1991)
Aquaboogie — Digital Underground: Underwater Rimes (1990)
Aquaboogie — Digital Underground: Return of the Crazy One (1994)
Aquaboogie — Digital Underground: No Nose Job (1991)
Aquaboogie — Dr. Dre: Dre Day (Extended) (1993)
Aquaboogie — En Vogue: This Is Your Life (1992)
Aquaboogie — Ice T: The Syndicate (1988)
Aquaboogie — Ice Cube: Dirty Mack (1992)
Aquaboogie — Schoolly D: Super Nigger (1991)
Aquaboogie — Too Short: Dead or Alive (1990)
Aquaboogie — Young Black Teenagers: Traci (1991)
Atomic Dog — 2Pac: Holler if Ya Hear Me (1993)
Atomic Dog — Above the Law: Why Must I Feel like Dat (1993)
Atomic Dog — Above the Law: Process of Elimination (1993)
Atomic Dog — Big Daddy Kane: Get Down (1991)
Atomic Dog — Biz Markie: The Dragon (1989)
Atomic Dog — BLACKstreet: Booti Call (1994)
Atomic Dog — College Boyz: Underground Blues (1992)
Atomic Dog — Compton's Most Wanted: I Gots Ta Get Over (1993)
Atomic Dog — Compton's Most Wanted: I Don't Dance (1991)
Atomic Dog — Consolidated: You Suck (1992)
Atomic Dog — Digital Underground: Doowhatchalike (1990)
Atomic Dog — Digital Underground: Bran New Swetta (1993)
Atomic Dog — Fu-Schnickens: Back Off (1992)
Atomic Dog — Geto Boys: Homie Don't Play That (1991)
Atomic Dog — Guy: D-O-G Me Out (1990)
Atomic Dog — Ice Cube: Ghetto Bird (1993)
Atomic Dog — Ice Cube: 2 N the Morning (1994)
Atomic Dog — Ice Cube: Better Off Dead (1990)
Atomic Dog — Ice Cube: Nigga Ya Love To Hate (1990)
Atomic Dog — Ice Cube: Man's Best Friend (1991)
Atomic Dog — Ice Cube: No Vaseline (1991)
Atomic Dog — Ice-T: Funky Gripsta (1993)
Atomic Dog — Insane Poetry: How Ya Gonna Reason with a Psycho (1992)
Atomic Dog — K-Solo: I Can't Hold It Back (1992)
Atomic Dog — KAM: Peace Treaty (1993)
Atomic Dog — Kool Moe Dee: Here We Go Again (1996)
Atomic Dog — Kriss Kross: Party (1992)
Atomic Dog — MC Hammer: Pumps and a Bump (1995)
Atomic Dog — MC Ren: Hound Dogz (1992)
Atomic Dog — Paris: Bush Killa (1992)
Atomic Dog — Paris: Coffee, Donuts & Death (1992)
Atomic Dog — Pete Rock & CL Smooth: The Basement (1992)
Atomic Dog — PM Dawn: Comatose (1991)

Atomic Dog — Public Enemy: Pollywannacraka (1990)

Atomic Dog — Redman: Watch Yo Nuggets (1992)

Atomic Dog — Redman: Bobyahed2dis (1994)

Atomic Dog — Redman: Winicumuhround (1994)

Atomic Dog — Redman: Slide and Rock On (1994)

Atomic Dog — Scarface: Diary of a Madman (1991)

Atomic Dog — Snoop Doggy Dogg: Who Am I. . .See What's My Name (1993)

Atomic Dog — South Central Cartel: South Central Madness (1991)

Atomic Dog — Stetsasonic: Speaking of a Girl Named Suzy (1991)

Atomic Dog — Terminator X: DJ Is the Selector (1991)

Atomic Dog — X-Clan: Earth Bound (1990)

Big Bang Theory — Above the Law: V.S.O.P. (1993)

Big Bang Theory — College Boyz: How Ta Act (1992)

Big Bang Theory — Compton's Most Wanted: I Don't Dance (1991)

Big Bang Theory — DJ Quik: Amerika'z Most Complete Artist (1992)

Big Bang Theory — Dr. Dre: Dre Day (Extended) (1993)

Big Bang Theory — Geto Boys: Life in the Fast Lane (1990)

Big Bang Theory — Ice Cube: Alive on Arrival (1991)

Big Bang Theory — K-Solo: I Can't Hold It Back (1992)

Big Bang Theory — Paris: It's Real (1994)

Big Bang Theory — Redman: Blow Your Mind (1992)

Big Bang Theory — Yo-Yo: Westside Story

Body Language — Terminator X: Wanna Be Dancin' (1991)

Bop Gun — Ice Cube: Endangered Species (Tales from the Darkside) (1990)

Bop Gun — Redman: So Ruff (1992)

Bop Gun — Digital Underground: The Humpty Dance (1990)

Bop Gun — Redman: Da Funk (1992)

Chocolate City — Ice Cube: I Wanna Kill Sam (1991)

Chocolate City — Kool G Rap: Live and Let Die (1992)

Chocolate City — Nemesis: Temple of Boom (1993)

Chocolate City — Totally Insane: Here We Go Again (1996)

Colour Me Funky — Above the Law: The Harder U R Tha Doppa U Faal (1993)

Colour Me Funky — Above the Law: Who Ryde (1994)

Colour Me Funky — Del Tha Funkee Homosapien: Pissin' on Your Steps (1991)

Colour Me Funky — Digital Underground: Dope-a-Delic (Do-U-B-Leeve-in-D-Flo?) (1993)

Colour Me Funky — Dr. Dre: The Roach (1993)

Come in out Of . . . — Jungle Bros: I'm in Love with Indica (1993)

Cosmic Slop — Smokin' Suckas Wit Logic: Jah Sent (1993)

Cosmic Slop — DOC: Beautiful but Deadly (1989)

Cosmic Slop — Ice Cube: Doing Dumb Shit (1991)

Deep — Kool Moe Dee Pump Your Fist (1989)

Deep — Public Enemy: Revolutionary Generation (1990)

Do That Stuff — Nice & Smooth: Funky for You (1989)

Do That Stuff — Yo-Yo: Mackstress (1993)

Dr. Funkenstein — Scarface: Lettin' Em Know (1993)

Dr. Funkenstein — Too Short: It's Your Life (1990)

Dr. Funkenstein — Ice-T: Bitches 2 (1991)

Dr. Funkenstein — No Face: We Wants To Fuck (1990)

Eulogy and Light — Above the Law: Black Triangle (1993)

Flash Light — 3 Times Dope: Make Dat Move (1990)

Flash Light — Above the Law: Never Missin a Beat (1993)

Flash Light — Above the Law: Wicked (1991)

Flash Light — Ahmad: Can I Party? (1994)

Flash Light — Boss: Born Gangstaz (1993)

Flash Light — Criminal Nation: I'm Rollin' (1990)

Flash Light — Da Lench Mob:Guerillas in the Mist (1992)

Flash Light — De La Soul: Shwingalokate (1991)

Flash Light — Del Tha Funkee Homosapien: Sunny Meadowz (1991)

Flash Light — Digital Underground: Sons of the P (1991)

Flash Light — Digital Underground: Arguin' On the Funk (1991)

Flash Light — Digital Underground: Body Hats (1992)

Flash Light — Digital Underground: Rhymin on the Funk (1990)

Flash Light — Digital Underground: DooWatchaLike (1990)

Flash Light — Digital Underground: The Danger Zone (1990)

Flash Light — Genius: True Fresh MC (1990)

Flash Light — Ice Cube: Wrong Nigga To Fuck Wit (1991)

Flash Light — Ice T: Home Invasion (1993)

Flash Light — Ice Cube: Man's Best Friend (1991)

Flash Light — Jungle Bros: Sunshine (1989)

Flash Light — Kool G Rap: Operation CB (1992)

Flash Light — Lords of the Underground: Keepers of the Funk (1994)

Flash Light — Masta Ace Incorporated: Jeep Ass Niguh (1993)

Flash Light — MC Ren: Final Frontier (1992)

Flash Light — MC Ren: Mr. Fuck Up (1993)

Flash Light — MC Ren: One False Move (1993)

Flash Light — Public Enemy: Nighttrain (1991)

Flash Light — Public Enemy: Anti-Nigger Machine (1990)

Flash Light — Redman: Rockafella (1992)

Flash Light — Redman: So Ruff (1992)

Flash Light — Run DMC: Back from Hell (1990)

Flash Light — X-Clan: Xodus (1992)

Flash Light — X-Clan: Heed the Words of a Brother (1990)

Freak of the Week — Above the Law: Call It What You Want (1993)

Freak of the Week — Compton's Most Wanted: Straight Checkn 'Em (remix) (1991)

Freak of the Week — Digital Underground: Heartbeat Props (1991)

Freak of the Week — Too Short: The Dangerous Crew (1993)

Free Your Mind . . . — Kriss Kross Freak Da Funk (1992)

Free Your Mind . . . — X-Clan Shaft's Big Score (1990)

Funk Gets Stronger (part one) — Digital Underground: Fool Get a Clue (1996)

Funkentelechy — Dr. Dre: Dre Day (Extended) (1993)

Funkentelechy — Digital Underground: Shake and Bake (1993)

Funkentelechy — Ice Cube: Doing Dumb Shit (1991)

Funkentelechy — Stetsasonic: So Let the Fun Begin (1991)

Gamin On Ya — Bloods & Crips: Shuda Beena B-Dog (1993)

Gamin On Ya — Ice Cube: Us (1991)

Gamin On Ya — WC & the Madd Circle: Ghetto Serenade (1991)

Get Off Your Ass And . . . — 2Pac Holler if Ya Hear Me (1993)

Get Off Your Ass And . . . — Eazy E: Eazy-Duz-It (1988)

Get Off Your Ass And . . . — Ice-T: 99 Problems (1993)

Get Off Your Ass And . . . — Public Enemy: Bring the Noise (1988)

Get Off Your Ass And . . . — Yo-Yo: They Shit Don't Stink (1993)

Give Up the Funk — Gerardo: We Want the Funk (1991)

Give Up the Funk — Grandmaster Flash & the Furious Five: Tear the Roof Off (1987)

Give Up the Funk — Heavy D.: More Bounce (1989)

Give Up the Funk — MC Hammer: Turn This Mutha Out (1988)

Give Up the Funk — No Face: We Wants To Fuck (1990)

Give Up the Funk — Schoolly D: Godfather of Funk (1991)

Give Up the Funk — Snoop Doggy Dogg: What's My Name (1993)

Give Up the Funk — Steady B: Keeper of the Funk (1991)

Give Up the Funk — Too Short: No Love from Oakland (1992)

Gloryhallastoopid — DelTha Funkee Homosapien: Mistadobalina (1991)

Gloryhallastoopid — DelTha Funkee Homosapien: Sunny Meadowz (1991)

Good Ole Music — 2Pac: Young Black Male (1992)

Good Ole Music — Above the Law: Pimp Clinic (1993)

Good Ole Music — Above the Law: Another Execution (1990)

Good Ole Music — Biz Markie: She's Not Just Another Woman (Monique) (1989)

Good Ole Music — College Boyz: Politics of a Gangster (1992)

Good Ole Music — Common Sense: Tricks Up My Sleeve (1992)

Good Ole Music — Compton's Most Wanted: They Still Gafflin' (1991)

Good Ole Music — DOC: DOC & the Doctor (1989)

Good Ole Music — Greg Osby: Thelonious (1993)

Good Ole Music — Ice Cube: The Wrong Nigga To Fuck Wit (1991)

Good Ole Music — Jungle Brothers: Jimbrowsky (1998)

Good Ole Music — Scarface: Good Girl Gone Bad (1991)

Good Ole Music — Stetsasonic: Free South Africa (1991)

Good Ole Music — Tone Loc: On Fire (1989)

Hardcore Jollies — DJ Quik: Born and Raised in Compton (1991)

Hit It nd Quit It — Ant Banks: Hit It (1993)

Holly Wants To Go . . . — Digital Underground: Hollywantstaho (1993)

How Do Yeaw View You — Luke: Freestyle Joint (1994)

I Can Move You — Above the Law: Process of Elimination (1993)

I Can Move You — Above the Law: Why Must I Feel like Dat (1993)

I Got a Thing . . . — Bell Biv Devoe: Ghetto Booty (1993)

I Got a Thing . . . — Ice Cube: Who Got the Camera (1992)

I Bet You — Beastie Boys: Car Thief (1989)

I Bet You — Del Tha Funkee Homosapien: Dark Skin Girls (1991)

I Bet You — Ice-T: Mind Over Matter (1991)

I'll Stay — De La Soul: Millie Pulled a Pistol on Santa (1991)

I'll Stay — CrucialConflict: Hay (1996)

I've Been Watching You — NWA: Don't Drink That Wine (1991)

Knee Deep — Above the Law Never Missin a Beat (1993)

Knee Deep — Above the Law: G in Me (1994)

Knee Deep — Above the Law: Call It What You Want (1993)

Knee Deep — Bobby Brown: Get Away (1992)

Knee Deep — College Boyz: How Ta Act (1992)

Knee Deep — De La Soul: Me Myself and I (1989)

Knee Deep — Digital Underground: Kiss You Back (1991)

Knee Deep — Dr. Dre: Dre Day (1993)

Knee Deep — EPMD: Golddigger (1991)

Knee Deep — Everlast: Never Missin' a Beat (1990)

Knee Deep — Geto Boys: Homie Don't Play That (1991)

Knee Deep — Keith Murray: Dip Dip Di (1994)

Knee Deep — LL Cool J: Nitro (1989)

Knee Deep — Paris: It's Real (1994)

Knee Deep — Snoop Doggy Dogg: What's My Name? (1993)

Knee Deep — Snoop Doggy Dogg: G-Funk Intro (1993)

Knee Deep — Tone Loc: Funky Cold Medina (1989)

Knee Deep — X-Clan: Funkin Lesson (1990)

Knee Deep — Yo-Yo: Ain't Nobody Better (1991)

Last Dance — Erick Sermon: Hittin' Switches (1993)

Let's Take It (live) — Ahmad: Can I Party? (1994)

Let's Play House — Ant Banks: Sittin' on Somethin' Phat (1993)

Let's Play House — Digital Underground: The Humpty Dance (1990)

Let's Take It to The . . . — EPMD: I'm Mad (1991)

Little Ole . . . — De La Soul: Potholes in My Lawn (1989)

Loose Booty — EPMD: Who's Booty (1989)

Maggot Brain — Smokin' Suckas Wit Logic: Gangsta Story (1993)

Mommy, What's a Funkadelic — De La Soul: Millie Pulled a Pistol on Santa (1991)

Mommy, What's a Funkadelic — Kool G. Rap: Two to the Head (1992)

Mothership Connection — Run DMC: Groove to the Sound (1990)

Mothership Connection — Tone Loc: The Homies (1989)

Mothership Connection — Yo-Yo: Make Way for the Motherlode (1991)

Mothership Connection — Above the Law: Pimp Clinic (1993)

Mothership Connection — Dr. Dre: Let Me Ride (1993)

Mothership Connection — Digital Underground: Tales of the Funky (1991)

Mothership Connection — Eazy-E: We Want Eazy (1988)

Mothership Connection — Infinite Mass: Mah Boyz (1997)

Mr. Wiggles — Ice Cube: Givin Up the Nappy Dug Out (1991)

Mr. Wiggles — Schoolly D: It's Krack (1987)

Mr. Wiggles — Yo-Yo: Westside Story (1993)

Nappy Dugout — Ant Banks: Hit It (1993)

Nappy Dugout — Ice Cube: U Ain't Gonna Take My Life (1994)

Nappy Dugout — Poison Clan: Listen (1993)

Nappy Dugout — Tim Dog: Goin' Wild in the Penile (1991)

No Head No Backstage Pass — Eric B & Rakim: Lyrics of Fury (1988)

One of Those Funky — Ice Cube: I Wanna Kill Sam (1991)

One Nation Under a Groove — Above the Law: Uncle Sam's Curse (1994)

One Nation Under a Groove — Above the Law: 4 the Funk of It (1991)

One Nation Under a Groove — Digital Underground: Tales of the Funky (1991)

One Nation Under a Groove — EPMD: So Whatcha Sayin (1999)

One Nation Under a Groove — Ice Cube: Bop Gun (One Nation) (1993)

One Nation Under a Groove — LL Cool J: All We Got Left Is the Beat (1993)

One Nation Under a Groove — MC Hammer: They Put Me in the Mix (12" also)(1988)

One Nation Under a Groove — Spice 1: Peace to My Nine (1992)

One Nation Under a Groove — Steady B: Mac Daddy (1989)

One Nation Under a Groove — X-Clan: Earth Bound (1990)

One Nation Under a Groove — X-Clan: Funkin' Lesson (1990)

P.E. Squad — Scarface: Strictly for the Funk Lovers (1993)

P-Funk — DelTha Funkee Homosapien: Sunny Meadowz (1991)

P-Funk — Dr. Dre: The Roach (1993)

P-Funk — Ice Cube: Say Hi to the Bad Guy (1992)

P-Funk — K-Solo: Premonition of a Black Prisoner (1992)

P-Funk — NWA: 1–900–2-Compton (1991)

P-Funk — Paris: Outta My Life (1994)

P-Funk — Redman: Da Funk (1992)

P-Funk — Terminator X: High Priest of Turbulence (1991)

P-Funk — Tone Loc: Don't Get Close (1989)

P-Funk — Yo-Yo: Make Way for the Motherlode (1991)

Placebo Syndrome — De La Soul: Shwingalokate (1991)

Prelude — Eazy E: Prelude (1988)

Prelude — X Clan: Xodus (1992)

Pumping It Up — Del Tha Funkee Homosapien: What Is a Booty (1991)

Pumping It Up — Digital Underground: Rhymin' on the Funk (1990)

Pumping It Up — DJ Quik: Loked Out Hood (1991)

Pumping It Up — Geto Boys: Homie Dont Play That (1991)

Pumping It Up — X-Clan: Funkin Lesson (1990)

Rumpofsteelskin — Del Tha Funkee Homosapien: Dr. Bombay (1991)

Rumpofsteelskin — Del Tha Funkee Homosapien: Sleepin on My Couch (1991)

Rumpofsteelskin — Ice Cube: You Can't Fade Me (1990)

Sexy Ways — Fu-Schnickens: Props (1992)

Sir Nose D'Voidoffunk — Black Sheep: Have U.N.E. Pull (1991)

Sir Nose D'Voidoffunk — E Forty: Nuttin Ass Nigga (1994)

Sir Nose D'Voidoffunk — Ice Cube: Gangsta's Fairytale 2 (1992)

Sir Nose D'Voidoffunk — Ice Cube: It Was a Good Day (remix) (1992)

Sir Nose D'Voidoffunk — Ice Cube: Steady Mobbin (1991)

Sir Nose D'Voidoffunk — NWA: Niggaz 4 Life (1991)

Sir Nose D'Voidoffunk — Schoolly D: Godfather of Funk (1991)

Sir Nose D'Voidoffunk — Yo-Yo: Givin' It Up (1993)

Sir Nose D'Voidoffunk — Yo-Yo: Westside Story (1993)

Standing On the Verge . . . — Ice Cube: Endangered Species (Tales from the Darkside) (1990)

Swing Down (live) — Dr. Dre: Let Me Ride (1993)

Take Your Dead Ass Home — Too Short: Hoes (1992)

The Song Is Familiar — MC Lyte: All That (1991)

The Motor Booty Affair — Digital Underground: Sex Packets (1990)

The Motor Booty Affair — Digital Underground: Packet Reprise (1990)

The Motor Booty Affair — Willie D: I'm Going out Lika Soldier (1992)

The Freeze — Digital Underground: Wheee! (1993)

The Freeze — Ice Cube: Look Who's Burnin' (1991)

The Freeze — Kris Kross: 2 Da Beat Ch'Yall (1993)

Theme from the Black Hole — Above The Law: V.S.O.P. (1993)

Theme from the Black Hole — Compton's Most Wanted: I Don't Dance (1991)

Theme from the Black Hole — Digital Underground: Same Song (1990)

Theme from the Black Hole — Ice Cube: Steady Mobbin' (1991)

Theme from the Black Hole — Kausion: What You Wanna Do (1995)

Theme from the Black Hole — Redman: Blow Your Mind (1992)

Trombipulation — Digital Underground: Dope-a-Delic (Do-U-B-Leev-in-D-Flo?) (1993)

Unfunky UFO — Ice Cube: Dirty Mack (1992)

Up for the Down Stroke — Nemesis: Temple of Boom (1993)

Up for the Down Stroke — Salt-N-Pepa: Everybody Get Up (1988)

Water Sign — Geto Boys: Straight Gangstaism (1993)

You and Your Folks . . . — Insane Poetry: Manic Depressive (1992)

You and Your Folks . . . — Chris Rock: Your Mother's Got a Big Head (1991)

## BOOTSY COLLINS

**BORN:** *William Collins, 10/26/51, Cincinatti, OH*

Phelps "Catfish" Collins was already regarded among the finest guitarists in Cincinnati when his younger brother William, aka Bootsy, first picked up a bass, initially wanting simply to play alongside his fast moving sibling.

Early years rehearsing with other aspiring young musicians, including future Roogalator frontman Danny Adler, gave way to a regular band called the Pacesetters, featuring the Collins brothers, Frank Waddy (drms), Clayton Gunnels (trum) and Robert McCullough (tnr sax).

Like so many other aspiring musicians, the five regularly hung out at King Records' complex of studio, pressing plant, distribution house and management company; unlike so many others, they were eventually invited in and allowed to play. By 1968, the Pacesetters were King's house-band, recording and jamming with Bobby Byrd, Marva Whitney, Kay Robinson, Vicki Anderson, Bill Doggett, even jazzman Arthur Byrd. Inevitably, they also came to James Brown's attention.

Brown and Byrd frequently sat in with the Pacesetters while they rehearsed, getting the feel of the band members. From there, they were sent out on the road—again at Brown's instigation—backing Whitney and Hank Ballard on club tours. Frequently dubbed the New Dapps, in honor of another (recently disbanded) group Cincinnati with whom Brown was working, Beau Dollar & the Dapps, the Pacesetters also cut one unreleased single with Brown, "More Mess on My Thing." But still they could never have dreamed what Brown had in store for them.

Brown recruited the Pacesetters to his own side in typically apocalyptic fashion. Culminating a long running dispute over money, Brown's own then-current band were

**The name is Bootsy, baby. Even his bass was a star.**

threatening to refuse to play a March 1970, show at the National Guard Armory in Columbus, GA. Brown called back to Cincinnati and told Byrd to round up the Pacesetters, put them on a plane and get them to the venue. They were then put on the biggest stage they'd ever seen, in front of the largest crowd they'd ever heard. Brown fired his regular band that same evening.

Renamed the JBs, the Pacesetters remained behind Brown for a little over a year, "the nucleus," Brown reflected in his autobiography, "of a very good band. They were studio musicians," Brown continued, "so when I hummed out solos and things, they knew how to give me what I wanted." Trumpeter Daryl Jamison, longtime Brown associate Bobby Byrd and returning drummer John Starks completed the core of the JBs.

Ultimately, this incarnation of the JBs cut a mere handful of studio tracks with Brown, but each was to prove a crucial recording, beginning with their epochal debut "Sex Machine" and, later, "Superbad." Albums of the same titles

followed (*Sex Machine* was recorded live); Brown also produced three singles by the JBs themselves: "The Grunt," "These Are the JBs" and "Across The Track" (released as "The Believers").

For their own part, the Pacesetters never viewed their months with Brown as any kind of permanent gig. Brown was already a veteran, set in his ways and adamant that the musicians he worked with followed suit. The Pacesetters, however, were just starting out—young, wild and uncontrollable. Furthermore, they had discovered LSD; it contributed even further to the mayhem they habitually wrought on stage.

Tours of Nigeria, where the party met Fela Ransome Kuti, and Europe were followed by a two week engagement at the Copacabana in New York, broken after a week by Brown's awareness that his idea of music, and that of the Copa's audience, would never have anything in common.

January 1971, also brought the Collins' lineup's final session with Brown, cutting "Soul Power." Less than two months later, history repeated itself when the Pacesetters confronted Brown over wages, then quit when nothing more than half-pay was forthcoming. They had played with him for precisely 381 days.

Returning to Cincinnati, the Pacesetters hooked up with soul vocalist Philippe Wynne and returned to the clubs and theaters through the remainder of 1971, opening local shows for the likes of Gladys Knight, the Dells and Erma Franklin. They worked for a time as the Pacemakers, before becoming the House Guests and developing the outrageous dress sense that—even before the band members themselves had ever seen the group—was earning them comparisons with Funkadelic. By the time the House Guests did understand what people were talking about, they were already too set in their ways to change.

The band self-released a pair of singles, "What So Never the Dance" and "My Mind Sets Me Free," but the Cincinnati scene was boring them. They played some shows behind Bobby Byrd, following his departure from James Brown's organization and, in early 1972, the House Guests relocated to Detroit, where they were approached to become the Spinners vocal group's latest backup group. The band members declined, but told Wynne to pursue the similarly vacant lead vocalist role. As Bootsy later put it, the rest of the musicians now had eyes only for "the group of maniacs with George Clinton."

They were finally introduced by Mallia Franklin, Clinton's girlfriend's sister. She saw the House Guests when they gigged with singer Gloria Taylor (then riding the hits "You Got To Pay the Price" and "Grounded") at an Afro Artists International show in Toledo. In a lace body stocking and hotpants, with a tambourine taped to one foot, Collins inevitably caught Franklin's attention.

Taking the band under her wing, Franklin invited the House Guests to become her own house guests, and encouraged them to continue bending their sound toward a Funkadelic shape. That achieved, she then booked the group into Detroit's Soul Expression nightclub and invited Clinton down to see them. He hired the band en masse.

It was, as Funkadelic manager Ron Scribner recalled, "the time when [people] started to become . . . movable parts." Augmented by keyboard player Bernie Worrell and guitarist Harold Beane, the House Guests completed one tour with Clinton under the banner of Funkadelic, and contributed to the sessions that eventually produced the *America Eats Its Young* album. They appeared on three tracks: "Loose Booty," driven along by Bootsy's already unmistakable bass, "Balance" and his own "Philmore."

It was, initially, a short-lived dalliance. By the end of 1972, the House Guests had returned to Cincinnati and changed their name again, to the Complete Strangers. With Baltimore vocalist Gary "Mudbone" Cooper fronting the band, they began gigging again, and cut a single, the two part "Fun in Your Thang," for the General American label. Further demos were recorded but they remained in contact with Clinton and Bootsy, at least, was back on the scene in 1974, for the sessions that produced Parliament's *Up for the Down Stroke* album.

Thereafter, few P-Funk related albums passed by without some contribution from Collins, whether he was in the studio at the time, or by virtue of Clinton's penchant for retrieving one project's outtakes for the next album's heart. However, unlike so many other of the musicians who moved into the P-Funk orbit, Bootsy was adamant that he remained a free agent.

In mid-1975, with Clinton's promises of beginning work on Bootsy's own album still nothing more substantial than promises, Bootsy began looking elsewhere for backing. He found it with producer Jeffrey Bowen at the Invictus label (home of Parliament's first album and singles in 1970).

It was a move deliberately calculated to stir Clinton into action; in fact, when Clinton called him back to Detroit, Collins was already in Los Angeles with Bowen discussing what Invictus could do for, what was currently being called, Bootsy's Early Sunn. He returned to Detroit immediately and, gathering together musicians from Complete Strangers (Cooper, Catfish and Waddy), P-Funk (Gary Shider, Michael Hampton and Bernie Worrell) and the JBs (Fred Wesley and Maceo Parker), began work on *Stretchin' Out in Bootsy's Rubber Band*. The group, of course, took their name from the album.

Setting the pace for future Bootsy albums, *Stretchin'* inaugurated several Bootsy traditions, including that of placing each album in the care of a seemingly improvised alterego. *Stretchin'* was to see the birth of Caspar the Ghost, clearly a by-product of Collins' childhood TV viewing, but an endearing character all the same. Material was drawn from throughout Collins' writing career—"I'd Rather Be with You" and "Vanish in Our Sleep" dated back to his days with the JBs, "Psychoticbumpschool" grew out of a House Guests song called "Be Right Back," "Stretchin' Out" itself was based around the rhythms Bootsy heard in Nigeria with James Brown.

Signed to Warner Brothers and added to the bill for the next P-Funk tour, Bootsy's Rubber Band spent much of 1976 on the road with a lineup drawn from the album sessions. The Complete Strangers lay at the heart of the hurricane, Leslyn Bailey was added on vocals, Wesley and Parker added horns, while Mudbone introduced two musicians from one of his old Baltimore groups, Frederick Allen (kybds) and Robert Johnson (vcls).

A stage show to rival P-Funk grew up, the bizarrely bespectacled Bootsy at the front of an extravagantly costumed band, pumping his custom built Space Bass (pictured on the back of *Stretchin' Out*. And while solid gigging dragged "Stretchin' Out" into the R&B Top 20, a tight 45-minute live set left more than enough room for the Rubber Band to develop the jams and riffs that would be refined for the group's second album, January 1977's *Ahh . . . The Name Is Bootsy, Baby*. Then, with that completed, another year of touring loomed, both as part of the P-Funk circus and in their own right.

That spring, the Rubber Band played their first headline shows, scoring a massive hit with "The Pinocchio Theory" and not faltering even after vocalist Bailey quit, apparently unable to take the madness any longer.

It was madness, too. Faced with an act exploding across the country, Warner Brothers demanded a third album little more than a year after the first. Bootsy responded with *Bootsy? Player of the Year*. Introducing a new manic persona, "Bootzilla," the first single from the album topped the R&B chart in spring 1978, just as the never-ending tour finally graduated to the arena circuit. But behind the scenes, Bootsy himself was utterly lost and bewildered by the entire experience. Suddenly, making music was only a small part of his job. Reminiscing in the liner notes to the *Back in the Day* compilation, Bootsy recalled how he was also responsible for a host of other things as well, "management decisions, trucks, buses . . . how many of this, how much of that. How much is this person gonna get paid. Who gets a raise. Who gets laid off. I had never dreamed of that kind of pressure." Presumably, it never occurred to him to hire a tour manager!

Such troubles did not impact upon the live performance; one show from the 1978 tour, in Washington, DC, was released as a live album in Japan in 1995, and evidenced the Rubber Band at full stretch. Appearances, however, were deceptive.

Finally coming off the road in spring 1978, with rumors of drug abuse and discontent swirling around him, Bootsy announced he wanted to take a year off to try and rediscover himself. The defining moment came, he said, when he went home one day to visit his mother, still clad in full Bootsy regalia. She told him, "You're in the house now; you can take those glasses off."

With *Billboard* magazine reporting that Bootsy had been hospitalized (again drugs were implicated), the star began turning down shows. High-earning festivals through the summer of 1978 were routinely dismissed as he took another piece of advice from his mother: if you ever get to the point where you don't know what to do, don't do anything.

Under pressure from Warner Brothers, Bootsy did reconvene the Rubber Band for a new album, 1979's *This Boot Is Made for Fonk-N*, and an edit of the nine-minute epic "Jam Fan (Hot)" kept him in the R&B Top 20. But the Rubber Band had effectively broken up, its disparate elements scattered through a wealth of other P-Funk projects: the Horny Horns, the Brides of Funkenstein and P-Funk itself.

In 1980, a rejuvenated Bootsy returned to the fray, first convening the ad-hoc Sweat Band for one eponymous album (the first ever release on Clinton's Uncle Jam label), then cutting his first solo album, *Ultra Wave*. A scaled back lineup saw Catfish and Johnson alone retained from the Rubber Band, alongside the Horny Horns, David Spradley, Joel Johnson and David Lee Chong (kybds), Carl Small (perc) and vocals from the Brides, Parlet, the Brandy duo of Telma Hopkins and Joyce Vincent, and another vocal trio Godmoma (Cynthia Girty, Tony Walker, Carolyn Myles) whom Bootsy himself was currently nurturing.

He returned to the stage in 1981 as part of Clinton's Greatest Funk on Earth tour; from there, he went back to the studio with Godmoma. Their album *Here*, was released in 1982, a far funkier effort than either Parlet or the Brides (with whom, inevitably, Godmoma would be compared). Indeed, many critics even preferred it to Bootsy's own next release, that same year's *The One Giveth, the Count Taketh Away* (originally to be titled *The Secret Life of Fruit*).

Bootsy's final Warner Brothers album, *The One Giveth* was dominated by the liquid "Body Slam," a total remix revision of another of the album's cuts, "Countracula." It made #12, Bootsy's biggest single since "Jam Fan" three years earlier and, while the album sank, Bootsy himself was approaching a rebirth of sorts. He kicked the cocaine habit that, it now transpired, had been haunting him since the last days of the Rubber Band and threw himself back into his work.

At least, that was the intention. A few weeks on the road with Clinton's Atomic Dog show, however, persuaded him that everything that had driven him away in the past was still lurking out there. "I had thought some of it would have changed, but everything there was the same. I didn't even know how to react to the same old crap. I immediately said to myself, 'Uh uh, I don't think so.'"

Returning to Cincinnati, Bootsy moved into session work; 1984 brought a fascinating collaboration with Talking Heads' Jerry Harrison, Bonzo Goes to Washington's "5 Minutes." Bootsy also guested on recordings by Herbie Hancock, Rolling Stones guitarist Keith Richards, Japanese maestro Ryuichi Sakamoto, Afrika Bambaataa and others. A new album in 1988, *What's Bootsy Doin'*, nudged him back toward the limelight, and saw him reunite with Catfish and the Horny Horns, plus guitarists Ron Jennings and Stevie Salas and keyboard players Trey Stone, Mico Wave and Wes Boatman.

It was an uncertain comeback, however, laden with the fashionable synth and techno stylings that his new label, Columbia, deemed necessary to compete. Yet, alongside Clinton's near-simultaneous *The Cinderella Theory*, *What's Bootsy Doin'* became one of the building blocks upon which the funk revival of the '90s was built, the old school's acknowledgement of the impact of the new, but also a chance for the new to reacquaint itself with what made the old so special in the first place.

Bootsy grasped the new movement, and its accompanying technology, with the 1990 mini-album *Jungle Bass*. Produced by Bill Laswell during the sessions for Maceo Parker's *All The King's Men* album, four distinctly individual versions of the title track ranged in length between three and 13 minutes as all concerned came to grips with a cyberfunk vibe that could easily have been pursued onto a full length album. Instead, while the partnership with Laswell spilled out into further albums by Praxis, Zillatron and Axiom Funk, for his own next album, Bootsy returned to basics with a vengeance.

The catalyst for Bootsy's rebirth was his collaboration with former Sex Pistols manager Malcolm McLaren, on 1989's *Waltz Darling* album. Credited to McLaren & the Bootzilla Orchestra, the album followed past McLaren solo projects in blending classical, rock and R&B disciplines, often with seamless guile. Bootsy contributed to just four cuts, most notably the opening "House of the Blue Danube" (a virtual duet for Bootsy's bass and Jeff Beck's guitar), but the activity reawakened his hunger. Within months, Bootsy was working with New York club trio Deee-Lite, joining the sessions for their 1990 debut album *World Clique*, then heading out on tour with them—his first since the Atomic Dog outing seven years earlier. Back home, he convened the New Rubber Band, naturally (and inevitably)

drawing from the coterie of past sidemen, then launched a tour in his right.

Several visits to Japan prompted a deal with the P-Vine label and the release of the *Blasters of the Universe* album, a double set recorded at his own home studio and titled for a jam Bootsy recorded with Eddie Hazel in the mid-'70s. The album finally made it out in the US in 1994, even as the New Rubber Band undertook another successful tour of Japan. In 1995, the *Keepin' Dah Funk Alive 4–1995* live album was recorded during this latest outing, at Tokyo's Jungle Bass funk mecca on June 24–25. He produced the debut album by Freekbass and grabbed a hit alongside rapper Dru, while a new Bootsy album, *Fresh Outa P University* arrived in 1997, a single disc in the US, a mighty double album in Europe.

In 2000, Bootsy launched a songwriting collaboration with former Eurythmic Dave Stewart, having appeared in Stewart's debut as a movie director, *Honest* and jammed (with Stewart and U2's The Edge) at the film's Cannes festival premier. He also rejoined James Brown for live shows, including the much-hyped opening of the Experience Music Project in Seattle.

### BOOTSY COLLINS COMPLETE DISCOGRAPHY
### SINGLES/CHART LOG

1976 Stretchin' Out (In a Rubber Band)/Physical Love (WB—#18 R&B)
1976 I'd Rather Be with You/Vanish in Our Sleep (WB—#25 R&B)
1976 Psychoticbumpschool/Vanish in Our Sleep (WB—#69 R&B/#104 pop)
1977 The Pinocchio Theory/Rubber Duckie (WB—#6 R&B)
1977 Can't Stay Away/Another Point of View (WB—#19 R&B/#104 pop)
1978 Bootzilla/Vanish in Our Sleep (WB—#1 R&B)
1978 Hollywood Squares/What's a Telephone Bill (WB—#17 R&B)
1979 Jam Fan (Hot)/She Jam (Almost Bootsy Show) (WB—#13 R&B)
1979 Bootsy Get Live (part one)/(part two) (WB—#38 R&B)
1979 Under the Influence of a Groove (part one)/(part two) (WB)
1980 Mug Push/Scenery (WB—#25 R&B)
1980 F-Encounter/(instrumental) (WB—#51 R&B)
1981 Is That My Song?/It's a Musical (WB)
1982 Take a Lickin' and Keep On Kickin'/Shine-O-Myte (No Rap Version) (WB—#29 R&B/#103 pop)
1982 Shine-O-Myte (Rap Popping)/So Nice You Name Him Twice (WB—#78 R&B)
1982 Body Slam/I'd Rather Be with You (WB—#12 R&B)
1988 Party On Plastic/remixes (Columbia)
1988 First One to the Egg Wins/First One to the Egg Wins (Columbia)
1988 Party On Plastic/Save What's Mine for Me (Columbia—#27 R&B)
1990 Jungle Bass/remixes (4th & Broadway—#91)

### DRU DOWN FEATURING BOOTSY COLLINS
1997 Baby Bubba (version) (Relativity—#84 R&B)

## BOOTSY'S RUBBER BAND

### LPs

**9** **1976 Stretchin' Out in Bootsy's Rubber Band (WB—#10 R&B/#59 pop)**

Rambunctious set divided almost equally between extraordinarily up-tempo funk rockers (he is a bassist, after all!) and the quieter ballads, which Clinton himself eschewed placing on P-Funk albums.

**10** **1977 Ahh . . . The Name Is Bootsy, Baby! (WB—#1 R&B/#16 pop)**

How do you follow a masterpiece? With an even greater one. Casper returns with another fonkin' great slab, elastic bass pinging against songs that clash silly lyrics with serious intent and deceptively light-weight titles. But "Rubber Duckie" is a triumph, "What's a Telephone Bill?" packs some dreadful dialtone puns and "Munchies for Your Love" would be a fuzzy, frantic highlight of any P-Funk phase you could name.

**9** **1978 Bootsy? Player of the Year (WB—#1 R&B/#16 pop)**

Four deep funk jams live up to past precedents, three ballads sag a little. But "Bootzilla" was a worthy successor to "Flash Light" atop the R&B chart, while "Roto Rooter" quickly flushes disappointment away. Catches Catfish at his craziest, as well.

**7** **1979 This Boot Is Made for Fonk-N (WB—#9 R&B/#52 pop)**

Rushed, but juicy jam heavy and home to "Under the Influence of a Groove," a key ingredient in Clinton's later "Kickback."

## [WILLIAM] BOOTSY COLLINS

**7** **1980 Ultra Wave (WB—#30 R&B/#70 pop)**

Issued under Bootsy's name alone, a partial departure from the Rubber Band daze, including a straightforward bluesy dance number ("Is That My Song") and a convincing new wave piece ("Sound Crack").

**6** **1982 The One Giveth, the Count Taketh Away (WB—#18 R&B/#120 pop)**

The bitterness behind "Countracula" (say it fast) and the smooth production make for a light-weight dance set, likeable but disappointing.

**5** **1988 What's Bootsy Doin'? (Columbia—#58 R&B)**

Hanging out with the electrofunk crowd, from the sound of things.

## BOOTSY COLLINS & BOOTSY'S NEW RUBBER BAND

### LPs

**6** **1994 Blaster of the Universe (Rykodisc)**

Two CDs is one too many, but with the electronics back on the shelf, any return to basics is welcome. Reconvening many past P-Funkers, and packed with earthy downhome jams, *Blaster* is definitely worth investigating. Just don't expect miracles.

**7** **1995 Keepin' Dah Funk Alive 4–1995 (Rykodisc)**

Another double, but live this time, and no matter what goes down in the studio, the stage is Bootsy's. Highlighting both his own catalog and P-Funk's, the main drawback is that Bootsy himself isn't present throughout the show.

**6** **1997 Fresh Outa P-University (WEA)**

## SELECTED COMPILATIONS AND ARCHIVE RELEASES

**9** **1994 Back in the Day: The Best of Bootsy (WB—#59 R&B)**

More or less definitive WB years collection, includes a vivid live "Psychoticbumpschool," plus a genuinely thoughtful round-up of the classics.

## SWEAT BAND

### SINGLES

1980 Body Shop/Love Munch (Uncle Jam)

1980 Freak To Freak (Uncle Jam)

### LP

**9** **1980 Sweat Band (Uncle Jam)**

Bootsy himself isn't necessarily the star, only the ringleader, on an album that rounds up a lot of stray P-Funkers, but even more stray P-Funk genius. In terms of showcases (Parker, the Brides, Gary Shider all shine), it outweighs most of the rest of the period's releases, a diverse set that never takes its eyes off the one.

## SELECTED SAMPLES

Ahh . . . The Name Is . . . — Eazy E: We Want Eazy (1988)

Body Slam! — Above the Law: VSOP (1993)

Bootsy Get Live — Keith Murray: The Most Beautifulest Thing (1995)

Bootzilla — Eazy E: Eazy Duz It (1988)

Bootzilla — Digital Underground: Rhymin' on the Funk (1990)

Bootzilla — Digital Underground: Danger Zone (1990)

Bootzilla — Doctor Ice: Word to the Wise (1989)

Can't Stay Away — NWA: To Kill a Hooker (1991)

Can't Stay Away — NWA: Don't Drink That Wine (PSA) (1991)

Fat Cat — Above the Law: Pimp Clinic (1993)

Hollywood Squares — Too Short: I'm a Player (1993)

Hollywood Squares — LL Cool J: All We Got Left Is the Beat (1993)

Hollywood Squares — Da Lench Mob: Mellow Madness (1994)

I'd Rather Be with You — Adina Howard: A Freak like Me (1995)

I'd Rather Be with You — NWA: I'd Rather Fuck You (1991)

Munchies for Your Love — Kokane: No Pain, No Gain (1994)

Pinocchio Theory — Sir Mix-A-Lot: Sleepin' Wit My Fonk (1994)

Under the Influence. . . — TreyLewd: The Next Thing You Know (1992)

Under the Influence. . . — Keith Murray: How's That (1995)

Vanish in our Sleep — Scarface: I Need a Favor (1993)

## LYN COLLINS

**BORN:** *6/12/48, Abilene, TX*

The sixth and, to many listeners, greatest of all James Brown's so-called Funky Divas, Collins was the leading lady in Brown's Revue throughout the early-mid-'70s, replacing Vicki Anderson at the end of her second stay in 1971.

Her predecessors set a high standard—Yvonne Fair, Sugar Pie DeSanto, Anna King, Anderson and Marva Whitney all fronted the Revue during the '60s—but from the moment Brown heard Collins' voice, on a demo she sent him after catching the Revue around 1968, he had her earmarked for future attention.

Her opportunity came on February 15, 1971, when Brown took Collins into Bobby Smith's Studio in Macon, GA, to cut five songs. Two of these, "Just Won't Do Right" and "Wheels of Life," were scheduled for a single, first on the King label, then on Brown's own People; in any event, they finally appeared on Polydor in December 1971, just as Anderson quit the Revue.

Collins immediately replaced her and, beginning with March 1972's "Oh, Uncle Sammy," backed by a tremendous reading of "Ain't No Sunshine," Collins joined the JBs as the most prolific and successful act in the People label stable. (Of course, the JBs backed her throughout this period.) Her second single for the label, May 1972's feminist war-cry "Think (About It)," was R&B Top Ten, to be followed chartward by the "What My Baby Needs Now" duet with Brown.

Although Collins later insisted that she would have preferred to "sing more and scream less," her dramatic performances and astonishing power soon saw her dubbed the Female Preacher—a tag amply justified by her in-concert showstopper, Isaac Hayes' "Do Your Thing" (a version recorded at the Apollo in September 1972 was subsequently included on the *Funky People Volume 2* compilation).

In similar form, she was featured in both of Brown's 1973 soundtrack recordings, scoring further hits with the self-defining "Mama Feelgood" (from *Black Caesar*) and "How Long Can I Keep It Up" (from *Slaughter's Big Rip Off*), and also recorded two albums in her own right, making the R&B Top 40 with *Think (About It)*. Although she never again returned to the heights of "Think," Collins remained a chart regular until 1975, when her soulful version of Harold Melvin's "If You Don't Know Me by Now" made #82. She recorded one final single with Brown in 1976, "Mr. Big Stuff," then moved into session work.

A new Collins single, "Shout," was released in Belgium in the late '80s; she again resurfaced in 1993 alongside Ja-maican dancehall singer Patra (b. Dorothy Smith, 11/22/72) on a new version of "Think (About It)." It made #89 in the US. Collins also appeared on several "Funky People" tours during the '80s and –'90s, alongside fellow Brown alumni Anderson and Bobby Byrd, Whitney and the JB Horns.

### LYN COLLINS DISCOGRAPHY

#### SINGLES/CHART LOG

1971 Just Won't Do Right/Wheels of Life (Polydor)
1972 Oh, Uncle Sammy/Ain't No Sunshine (People)
1972 Think (About It)/Ain't No Sunshine (People—#9 R&B/#66 pop)
1972 Me And My Baby Got Our Own Thing Going/I'll Never Let You Break My Heart Again (People)
1973 Mama Feelgood/Fly Me to the Moon (People—#37 R&B)
1973 How Long Can I Keep It Up (part one)/(part two) (People—#45 R&B)
1973 Take Me Just as I Am/People Make the World a Better Place (People—#35 R&B)
1973 We Want To Parrty Parrty Parrty/You Can't Beat Two People in Love (People—#64 R&B)
1974 Don't Make Me Over/Take Me Just as I Am (People)
1974 Give It Up or Turnit a Loose/What the World Needs Now Is Love (People—#77 R&B)
1974 Rock Me Again and Again . . . (Six Times)/Wide Awake in a Dream (People—#53 R&B)
1975 You Can't Love Me If You Don't Respect Me/Rock Me Again and Again . . . (Six Times) (People)
1975 How Long Can I Keep It Up?/Baby Don't Do It (People)
1975 If You Don't Know Me by Now/Baby Don't Do It (People—#82 R&B)
1976 Mr. Big Stuff/Rock Me Again and Again and Again (People)
1988 Shout/? (ARS—Belgium)

#### LYN COLLINS AND JAMES BROWN

1972 What My Baby Needs Now/This Girl's in Love with You (People—#17 R&B/#56 pop)

#### PATRA FEATURING LYN COLLINS

1993 Think (About It) (remix) (Epic—#89 R&B)

#### ALBUMS

**9** 1972 Think (About It) (People—#34 R&B)
With a presence as powerful as her voice, Collins' debut is hard funking attitude at its best. The hot JBs' arrangements and playing are as great as on any of Brown's own albums, and Collins herself never backs down from the comparison.

**7** 1975 Check Me Out If You Don't Know Me by Now (People)

#### SELECTED SAMPLES

Ain't No Sunshine — Ol Dirty Bastard: Don't U Know (1995)
Do Your Thing — Above the Law: Another Execution (1990)
Do Your Thing — Compton's Most Wanted: N 2 Deep (1992)
Mama Feelgood — Big Daddy Kane: Raw (1988)
Mama Feelgood — Big Daddy Kane: Get Down (1991)

Mama Feelgood — Freestyle Fellowship: 5 O'Clock Follies (1999)

Mama Feelgood — MC Lyte: Throwin' Words at U (1989)

Mama Feelgood — Steady B: Use Me Again (1989)

Put It on the Line — Allure: When You Need Someone (1997)

Put It on the Line — Above the Law: Freedom of Speech (1990)

Put It on the Line — LL Cool J: I Shot Ya (1995)

Rock Me Again and Again and . . . — Low Profile: Pay Ya Dues (1990)

Think (About It) — 2 Live Crew: Get Loose Now (1989)

Think (About It) — Three Times Dope: From Da Giddy Up (1989)

Think (About It) — Rob Base & D.J. E-Z Rock: It Takes Two (1988)

Think (About It) — Rob Base & D.J. E-Z Rock: Don't Sleep on It (1988)

Think (About It) — Biz Markie: Road Block (1991)

Think (About It) — Boyz II Men: Motownphilly (1991)

Think (About It) — Criminal Element: Hit Me with the Beat (1989)

Think (About It) — Chubb Rock: Ya Bad Chubbs (1989)

Think (About It) — Chubb Rock: Bump the Floor (1989)

Think (About It) — Das EFX: Mic Checka (1992)

Think (About It) — De La Soul: Jenifa (Taught Me) (1989)

Think (About It) — DJ Jazzy Jeff & the Fresh Prince: Girlie Had a Mustache (1989)

Think (About It) — Dream Warriors: Face in the Basin (1991)

Think (About It) — Eric B. & Rakim: Rest Assured (1992)

Think (About It) — Eric B. & Rakim: What's on Your Mind? (1992)

Think (About It) — Eric B. & Rakim: No Omega (1990)

Think (About It) — EPMD: The Joint (1997)

Think (About It) — EPMD: Golddigger (1991)

Think (About It) — Geto Boys: Seek and Destroy (1990)

Think (About It) — Heavy D: You Ain't Heard Nuttin Yet (1989)

Think (About It) — Heavy D: Somebody for Me (1989)

Think (About It) — Heavy D: Flexin' (1989)

Think (About It) — Intelligent Hoodlum: Party Pack (1990)

Think (About It) — Janet Jackson: Alright (1989)

Think (About It) — Janet Jackson: FreeXone (1997)

Think (About It) — K-9 Posse: Ain't Nothin' To It (remix) (1989)

Think (About It) — Kid 'N Play: Gittin' Funky (1988)

Think (About It) — Kid 'N Play: Do This My Way (1988)

Think (About It) — Kool Moe Dee: Let's Get Serious (1991)

Think (About It) — Kool Moe Dee: Time's Up (1991)

Think (About It) — Kool Moe Dee: Let's Get Serious (1991)

Think (About It) — Kool Moe Dee: I Go to Work (1989)

Think (About It) — Kool G Rap: Trilogy of Terror (1989)

Think (About It) — Lil' Kim: Dreams (1996)

Think (About It) — Marky Mark & the Funky Bunch: On the House Tip (1991)

Think (About It) — MC Brains: Everybody's Talking About MC Brains (1992)

Think (About It) — Michie Mee: On This Mic (1991)

Think (About It) — Mister Lee: Break Out (1990)

Think (About It) — New Edition: Hit Me Off (remix) (19??)

Think (About It) — Nice & Smooth: Gold (1989)

Think (About It) — NWA: Appetite For Destruction (1991)

Think (About It) — Organized Konfusion: Organized Konfusion (1991)

Think (About It) — Paris: Wretched (1990)

Think (About It) — Paris: Break the Grip of Shame (1990)

Think (About It) — Prince Johnny C: Sunshine (1992)

Think (About It) — Public Enemy: Who Stole The Soul? (1990)

Think (About It) — Public Enemy: Pollywannacraka (1990)

Think (About It) — Public Enemy: 911 Is a Joke (1990)

Think (About It) — Public Enemy: Anti-Nigger Machine (1990)

Think (About It) — The Real Roxanne: Roxanne's on a Roll (1988)

Think (About It) — Red Hot Lover Tone: Gigolows Got It Goin' On (1992)

Think (About It) — Redhead Kingpin & the FBI: Superbad, Superslick (1989)

Think (About It) — Roxanne Shante: Bad Sister (1989)

Think (About It) — Roxanne Shante: My Groove Gets Better (1989)

Think (About It) — Roxanne Shante: Go On Girl (1989)

Think (About It) — Salt-N-Pepa: Negro Wit An Ego (1990)

Think (About It) — South Central Cartel: Ya Getz Clowned (1991)

Think (About It) — Schoolly D: Mama Feel Good (1991)

Think (About It) — Silk Tymes Leather: The Woman in Me (1991)

Think (About It) — Slick Rick: Children's Story (1989)

Think (About It) — Slick Rick: Mistakes of a Woman in Love with Other Men (1991)

Think (About It) — Slick Rick: Slick Rick — The Ruler (1991)

Think (About It) — Slick Rick: I Shouldn't Have Done It (1991)

Think (About It) — Snoop Doggy Dogg: Ain't No Fun (If The Homies Can't Have None) (1993)

Think (About It) — Special Ed: I'm The Magnificent (1989)

Think (About It) — Steady B: Nasty Girls (1989)

Think (About It) — TLC: Das Da Way We Like 'Em (1992)

Think (About It) — UMCs: Never Never Land (1991)

Think (About It) — Young Black Teenagers: Nobody Knows Kelli (1991)

Think (About It) — Yo-Yo: The Bonnie & Clyde Theme (1993)

Think (About It) — YZ: The Ghetto's Been Good To Me (1993)

We Want To Parrty, Parrty, Parrty — Eric B. & Rakim: Pain in Full (1987)

We Want To Parrty, Parrty, Parrty — Illegal: On Da M.I.C. (1993)

We Want To Parrty, Parrty, Parrty — Legion: Legion Groove (1995)

You Can't Love Me If You Don't Respect Me — Tha Alkaholiks: Who Dem Niggas (1993)

You Can't Love Me If You Don't Respect Me — EPMD: For My People (1991)

## THE COMMODORES

**FORMED:** *1967, Tuskegee, AL*

**ORIGINAL LINE-UP:** *Thomas McClary (gtr), Michael Gilbert (bs), Lionel Richie (sax), Milan Williams (keyboards), William King (trum), Jimmy Johnson (sax), Andre Callaghan (drms)*

Few bands have been so misguidedly served by their own career as the Commodores. For the first five years of their recording career—and for several years before that—there were few finer funk acts in America. "Rise Up," the flip of their 1969 single "Keep n Dancing," is a pulsing bass boogie

**Thomas McClary and Lionel Ritchie, flying high with the Commodores.**

with James Brown horns and Booker T. keyboards; "Machine Gun," the Commodores' pop chart debut in 1974, stands among the greatest instrumental jams of its era; and "Young Girls Are My Weakness," from their debut album, is a leering chant that stands alongside the nastiest records of the age.

Yet the Commodores today are best remembered for two of the dominant hits of the mid-late-'70s, the laid back "Easy" and the eternal "Three Times a Lady," and for vocalist Lionel Richie's subsequent career as poster child of the '80s ballad crowd. Of course, the ease with which they adapted to and, ultimately, helped shape the direction of soul music in the late '70s can only be regarded as testament to the group's talents and perceptions. But it also ensured an entire generation grew up without any reference to the Commodores' early-mid-'70s funk heyday. It's an injustice that history might never correct.

The Commodores formed at Tuskegee Institute in Ala-bama in 1967, from the wreckage of two other groups. Richie, McClary and King were members of the (self-confessedly horrible) Mystics, Williams was with the Jays. Joined by Johnson, Gilbert and Callaghan, the band changed their name to the Commodores in 1968; according to legend, King picked the name at random from a dictionary.

Early shows in Tuskegee, Montgomery and Birmingham, AL, saw the group's high octane, high volume, horn-heavy funk swiftly become a firm local favorite and, in 1969, the Tuskegee Institute dispatched the Commodores to New York to appear at a benefit concert/talent show. There they were spotted by Benjamin Ashburn, a Harlem PR man currently working as a rep for a local liquor wholesaler. He kept in touch with the Commodores and, when they returned to New York the following year, he became their manager.

The band's early days in New York were difficult. On one

occasion, they were turned down for a show at Smalls Paradise club in Harlem by a club owner who insisted that funk was on the wane. However, he called them back a few days later, to fill in for a last-minute cancellation and was stunned to see them play to a full house. He had no way of knowing that almost every person in the room was either friends with, or family of, the band, and promptly rebooked the Commodores for a two week residency.

Late in 1969, Ashburn arranged for the Commodores to audition with Atlantic Records. They cut an album's worth of mostly instrumental material with producer Jerry Williams, including dramatically idiosyncratic versions of the Intruders' "Cowboys to Girls," Johnny Taylor's "Who's Making Love," Sly Stone's "Sing a Simple Song" and an up-tempo reinvention of the Temptations "(I Know) I'm Losing You." Atlantic, however, issued just one single, a cover of Alvin Cash's "Keep On Dancing."

The single went nowhere and, to compound the band's misfortune, the year also saw their lineup all but halved as Callaghan quit, and Johnson and Gilbert were drafted to Vietnam. They were replaced in the new year by Ronald LaPread, bassist with another Tuskegee group, the bluesy Corvettes, and lead vocalist/drummer Walter Orange, of the J-Notes.

Meanwhile, Ashburn was still pushing the band's name forward at every opportunity he could, pulling off a masterstroke when he arranged for Commodores to perform at a music business attorney's conference he himself had organized. There, Motown executive Suzanne DePasse was sufficiently impressed; she arranged for them to audition for the opening spot on the Jackson Five's forthcoming world tour.

Ashburn contacted the Commodores in Tuskegee and told them to return to New York that evening— he didn't tell them why. Neither would anybody at the audition explain what it was all about. It was another two weeks before the Commodores discovered what they'd let themselves in for—an outing that kept them on the road for much of the next two years.

In early 1972, a deal with the Motown subsidiary Mowest saw the Commodores—in time honored Motown fashion—placed with staff songwriters/producers Pam Sawyer and Gloria Jones to cut their next single, the freakishly funky "The Zoo (The Human Zoo)." Released in March, it sold poorly, a fate that also awaited their follow-up, "Don't You Be Worried." Still, by 1973, the Commodores had been transferred to Motown itself, debuting with "Are You Happy"—significantly, the first Commodores recording to

feature lead vocals by Richie. Again the record went nowhere.

The Commodores finally charted with May 1974's "Machine Gun," a scorching Milan Williams instrumental that utterly captivated American dancefloors. Produced by James Anthony Carmichael, the synth-ridden groove made the R&B Top Ten, the pop Top 30 and broke out across Europe as well.

August 1974, saw the release of the band's debut album, also titled *Machine Gun*. "I Feel Sanctified," featuring the joint vocals of Richie and Orange, gave the Commodores a second hit, but it was their increasingly extravagant live shows that earned the group the most attention, as they launched into what amounted to a two year tour of the US, opening for Stevie Wonder, the Rolling Stones (themselves riding their own take on funk, the *Black and Blue* album) and the O'Jays, before inching into their own headline spots.

That leap became even easier following the release of the Commodores' next single, the R&B chart topper "Slippery When Wet" (a title later borrowed by rockers Bon Jovi), and their second album, *Caught in the Act*. The album breached the Top 30 and, through 1975, the Commodores were actively pursuing the title of America's hottest funk act. Unfortunately, it was not a title they necessarily coveted.

Sensing a gradual shift in the demands of the dancefloor audience—toward disco, certainly, but also toward the overwrought twist of soft soul that modern music critics term "quiet storm" (in honor of the Smokey Robinson song)—the Commodores returned to the studio to cut the album that assured their domination of the remainder of the decade, *Movin' On*.

The first single from the album spelled out the band's intentions, Richie's gentle "Sweet Love." "Just To Be Close to You," from 1976's *Hot on the Tracks*, made a similar gesture of doe-eyed soulfulness; and though the Commodores' first single of 1977, "Fancy Dancer" (written by Richie and LaPread) proved that they could still provide a punch when they wanted to, the evidence was that they didn't want to very often.

Their next album, *The Commodores* (retitled *Zoom* in Europe), arrived in spring 1977. It was an impressive piece of work, all the more so once the stylus struck Orange's "Brick House." The last song recorded for the album, but ironically set to become the Commodores' personal anthem, "Brick House" was a pounding percussion driven funk feast that clearly remembered where the band had come from.

But it was to be utterly overshadowed, commercially and historically, by the song that had "crossover" written all over it even before it commenced its chartbound assault. Richie's melancholy "Easy" was a showcase for guitarist McClary, who turned in a breathtaking solo over much of the record. It was also the hammer that banged the final nail into the coffin of the Commodores' past.

"Too Hot Ta Trot," a disco groove first recorded as a (studio) bonus on fall 1977's double *Live* album (recorded during the Commodores' 72-city US tour earlier that same year) opened the disco doors even wider after it was included in the movie *Thank God It's Friday*. The *Natural High* album (1978) became the Commodores' first platinum disc, simultaneously ingratiating them to a middle-class audience who simply couldn't get enough of Richie's sensuous croon; and that same year's "Three Times a Lady" inexplicably became Motown's biggest-selling single of all time. The band had found their sound. And, it wasn't simply miles removed from even their most generous roots, it might as well have been from another planet.

The 1980's *Heroes* album caught the Commodores themselves trying to break the mold a little, with an experimental, rock-inclined sound. Compared to recent releases, however, it fared poorly, a disappointment rendered all the more noticeable when Richie alone upped his own profile further by teaming with Diana Ross for "Endless Love."

Richie quit the Commodores in 1981, following the *In the Pocket* album; his successor was the unknown Kevin Smith. Thomas McClary was the next to depart, to be replaced by English-born vocalist J.D. Nicholas (ex-Heatwave). His arrival injected some old-fashioned virtues into the Commodores; unfortunately, Motown offered their own vote of confidence with the release of two consecutive greatest hits collections and, though the Commodores remained with the label for another two years, it was clear where the company's sympathies lay.

In 1985, Souther's "Nightshift," a tribute to Marvin Gaye and Jackie Wilson, won the Commodores their first ever Grammy. But the group quit Motown following a dispute over whose next album was going to be released first, the Commodores' or Lionel Richie's *Dancing on the Ceiling*. They moved to Polydor, gathering immediate hits with "Goin' to the Bank" and the *United* album, but the success was impossible to sustain. The Commodores' next album, *Rock Solid*, missed the chart altogether and the band's slide was unstoppable. Orange, King and Nicholas alone fly the original Commodores banner today, from a comfortable perch on the nostalgia circuit.

## THE COMMODORES COMPLETE DISCOGRAPHY
### SINGLES/CHART LOG

1969 Keep on Dancing/Rise Up (Atlantic)

1972 I'm Looking for Love/At the Zoo (Mowest)

1973 Determination/Don't You be Worried (Mowest)

1973 Are You Happy/There's a Song in My Heart (Motown)

1974 Machine Gun/There's a Song in My Heart (Motown—#7 R&B/#22 pop)

1974 I Feel Sanctified/It Is as Good as You Make It (Motown—#12 R&B/#75 pop)

1975 Slippery When Wet/The Bump (Motown—#1 R&B/#19 pop)

1975 This Is Your Life/Look What You've Done to Me (Motown—#13 R&B)

1975 Wide Open (Motown — unreleased)

1976 Sweet Love/Better Never than Forever (Motown—#2 R&B/#5 pop)

1976 Come Inside/Time (Motown—unreleased)

1976 High on Sunshine/Thumpin' Music (Motown—unreleased)

1976 Just To Be Close to You/Thumpin' Music (Motown—#1 R&B/#7 pop)

1977 Fancy Dancer/Cebu (Motown—#8 R&B/#39 pop)

1977 Easy/Can't Let You Tease Me (Motown—#1 R&B/#4 pop)

1977 Brick House/Captain Quickdraw (Motown—#4 R&B/#5 pop)

1977 Too Hot Ta Trot/Funky Situation (Motown—#1 R&B/#24 pop)

1978 Three Times a Lady/Look What You've Done to Me (Motown—#1 R&B/#1 pop)

1978 Flying High/X-Rated Music (Motown—#21 R&B/#38 pop)

1978 Say Yeah (Motown—unreleased)

1979 Sail On/Thumpin' Music (Motown—#8 R&B/#4 pop)

1979 Still/Such a Woman (Motown—#1 R&B/#1 pop)

1979 Wonderland/Lovin' You (Motown—#21 R&B/#25 pop)

1980 Old Fashion Love/Sexy Lady (Motown—#8 R&B/#20 pop)

1980 Heroes/Funky Situation (Motown—#27 R&B/#54 pop)

1980 Jesus Is Love/Mighty Spirit (Motown—#34 R&B)

1981 Lady (You Bring Me Up)/Gettin' It (Motown—#5 R&B/#38 pop)

1981 Oh No/Lovin' You (Motown—#5 R&B/#4 pop)

1982 Why You Wanna Try Me/X-Rated Movie (Motown—#42 R&B/#66 pop)

1982 Painted Pictures/Reach High (Motown—#19 R&B/#70 pop)

1983 Sexy Lady/Reach High (Motown)

1983 Only You/Cebu (Motown—#20 R&B/#54 pop)

1984 Been Lovin' You/Turn Off the Lights (Motown)

1985 Nightshift/I Keep Runnin' (Motown—#1 R&B/#3 pop)

1985 Animal Instinct/Lightin' Up the Sky (Motown—#22 R&B/#43 pop)

1985 Janet/I'm in Love (Motown—#65 R&B/#87 pop)

1986 Goin' To The Bank/Serious Love (Polydor—#2 R&B/#65 pop)

1987 Take It from Me/I Wanna Rock You (Polydor—#38 R&B)

1987 United In Love/Talk To Me (Polydor)

1988 Solitaire/Stretchhh (Polydor—#51 R&B)

1989 Ain't Givin' Up/Grrip (Polydor)

### LPs

⑧ 1974 Machine Gun (Motown—#22 R&B/#138 pop)

Relentless horns and rhythms cut in the JBs' mold pump through the quirky consciousness of "Zoo," the lazy loping "I Feel Sanctified" and "Young Girls . . . ," and on to the mammoth, Stevie Wonder flavored title track.

**7** 1975 Caught in the Act (Motown—#7 R&B/#26 pop)

**7** 1975 Movin' On (Motown—#7 R&B/#29 pop)

Just six tracks, but they're mostly good 'uns. "(Can I) Get a Witness" and "Cebu" are the heaviest highlights, but "Sweet Love" suggests a future away from the funk, sounding suspiciously like Creedence's "Have You Ever Seen the Rain."

**6** 1976 Hot on the Tracks (Motown—#1 R&B/#12 pop)

**4** 1977 Commodores (Motown—#1 R&B/#3 pop)

"Brick House" and "Squeeze the Fruit" offer a deceptive return to roots; the guitar drenched "Easy" a blatant shortcut to MOR riches.

**5** 1977 Live! (Motown—#2 R&B/#3 pop)

Disappointingly restrained set reaches such a nadir with the nearly guitar-free "Easy," that even 12 relatively raunchy minutes of "Brick House" cannot salvage the show.

**4** 1978 Natural High (Motown—#1 R&B/#3 pop)

**3** 1979 Midnight Magic (Motown—#1 R&B/#3 pop)

A lackluster gathering of cliched love songs and wholesome affectations.

**4** 1980 Heroes (Motown—#3 R&B/#7 pop)

Insubstantial nod back toward earlier triumphs, marred by the fact they've forgotten how to funk.

**3** 1981 In the Pocket (Motown—#4 R&B/#13 pop)

Richie's final album with the band is dignified by the inclusion of "Lady" (a song he'd already gifted to Kenny Rodgers), but crippled by the high gloss mediocrity of all the band now represented.

**3** 1983 13 (Motown—#26 R&B/#103 pop)

**6** 1985 Nightshift (Motown—#1 R&B/#12 pop)

Orange's title track is a gentle gem; the remainder of the album founders in its slipstream, although newcomer Nicholas sounds strong.

**5** 1986 United (Polydor—#17 R&B/#101 pop)

**6** 1988 Rock Solid (Polydor)

**4** 1993 No Tricks (Navarre)

*SELECTED COMPILATIONS AND ARCHIVE RELEASES*

**6** 1978 Greatest Hits (Motown—#24 R&B/#23 pop)

**5** 1982 All The Great Hits (Motown—#12 R&B/#137 pop)

**7** 1983 Anthology (Motown—#50 R&B/ #141 pop)

This key collection packs the first four album highlights into 11 tracks, then takes the story up to '79 across ten more.

**8** 2000 Early Gold and New Spins (Golden Lane)

The 1969 Atlantic sessions find the band plowing the James Brown/Bar-Kays influenced groove that had sustained them back in Tuskegee. Four "bonus exclusive millennium remixes" add some extra sparkle.

**7** 2001 Anthology (Universal)

*SELECTED SAMPLES*

Assembly Line — Guy: Her (1990)

Assembly Line — Boogie Down Production: House Niggas (1990)

Assembly Line — 3rd Bass: Wordz of Wizdom (remix) (1989)

Assembly Line — Eric B. & Rakim: Let the Rhythm Hit 'Em (remix) (1990)

Assembly Line — Chemical Brothers: Chemical Beats (1995)

Assembly Line — Jungle Brothers: Black Woman (1989)

Assembly Line — Kool G Rap: It's a Demo (1989)

Assembly Line — U.N.K.L.E.: Unreal (1998)

Brickhouse — Dream Warriors: Follow Me Not (remix) (1991)

Brickhouse — Lost Boyz: Music Makes Me High (1996)

Easy — Geto Boys: Six Feet Deep (1993)

Fancy Dancer — Original Flavor: I Like It (Freestyle) (1992)

Girl, I Think the World About You — De La Soul: Buddy (1989)

Machine Gun — Beastie Boys: Hey Ladies (1989)

Say Yeah — Tamia: So into You (1998)

Zoom — Tricky: Tricky Kid (1995)

## RUTH COPELAND

**BORN:** *Durham, England*

A massively influential figure in the formative days of George Clinton's P-Funk empire, English folk-blues singer Copeland arrived in Detroit with her husband, Motown staff producer Jeffrey Bowen. He moved to Holland Dozier Holland's Invictus label in 1970, and Copeland became the company's first White signing as a member of the band New Play.

Written by Copeland, future P-Funk producer Ron Dunbar and Edith Wayne, New Play's debut single, "Music Box," was the second ever release on the label (following Chairman of the Board's "Finder's Keepers"). New Play broke up, however, and Copeland launched a solo career. But first she was to play a major role in the creation of Parliament's debut album, *Osmium*.

Copeland co-produced the sessions with George Clinton and wrote the country spoof "Little Old Country Boy" and the folky bagpipe-led "The Silent Boatman"; the two songs, more than any other, shaped *Osmium*'s reputation as something more than a "regular" funk album. (She also contributed the prayer segment of the plaintive gospel "Oh Lord, Why Lord.") Two further Copeland efforts, "Come in out of the Rain" (co-written with Clyde Wilson) and "Breakdown" (with Wilson and Clinton) appeared as Parliament singles in 1971/72.

The *Osmium* sessions over, attention then turned to Copeland's own debut album, *Self Portrait*. The full Funkadelic band of Clinton, Eddie Hazel, Lucius Ross, Bernie Worrell, Billy Nelson and Tiki Fulwood appeared on the album, which included a remake of "The Silent Boatman," plus two tracks co-written with the musicians, "Your Love Been So Good to Me" (Copeland/Ross/Clinton) and "I Got a Thing for You Daddy" (Copeland/Hazel/Clinton). *Self Portrait* is not, by a long chalk, a funk record, but alongside the more esoteric elements of *Osmium*, it slides effortlessly into the P-Funk canon.

The same can be said of Copeland's sophomore effort, 1971's *I Am What I Am*, the principle difference being, this time the band was her own. Bass, Hazel, Fulwood and Worrell had all quit Funkadelic, first joining Copeland in the studio, then accompanying her in concert. There, Copeland turned in some blistering shows, all the more so after she took to introducing her bandmates as Funkadelic. That, however, was a step too far for Sly Stone, when they toured together in 1971. Already discomforted by her introductions, he was further enraged when Copeland began allowing her colleagues to take one of her encores. According to legend, Copeland was issued an ultimatum, to find another band or get off the tour. She opted for the former.

Following these adventures, Copeland faded from view. A third album, *Take Me to Baltimore* (featuring P-Funk sessioners the Brecker Brothers among its supporting cast), appeared in 1976, since when she is rumored to have found a new career making violins.

### RUTH COPELAND
#### LPs
**8** 1971 Self Portrait (Invictus)
Folky blues infected soul, a disappointment for anyone seeking P-Funk power, but richly enjoyable regardless.
**9** 1971 I Am What I Am (Invictus)
Across an album comprising three more songs written with Clinton and two Rolling Stones covers (lengthy workouts of "Play with Fire" and "Gimme Shelter"), the team produced an electrifying blues-funk hybrid pinned by some of Hazel's best ever guitar work.
**5** 1976 Take Me To Baltimore (RCA)
Competent, but generally characterless funky soul set.

#### SELECTED COMPILATIONS AND ARCHIVE RELEASES
**9** 1997 Self Portrait/I Am What I Am (Deepbeats—UK)
Taking the edge of a high priced collectors market, a CD round-up of her first two albums, credited to Ruth Copeland & The Parliaments.

## THE COUNTS
**FORMED:** *1971, Detroit, MI*
**ORIGINAL LINE-UP:** *Mose Davis (kybds, vcls), Leroy Emmanuel (gtr, vcls), Raoul Keith Mangrum (bs), Demetrious "Demo" Cates (wind, vcls), Andrew Gibson (drms, vcls)*

The Counts were one of a number of Detroit-based funk bands who grew up in the wake of, and in competition with, the early Funkadelic, albeit one that leaned in a considerably jazzier direction.

After close to a year spent working the local club circuit, the sextet came to the attention of veteran producer Ollie McLaughlin (best known for his work with Barbara Lewis in the early-mid-'60s); he, in turn, took them to the Westbound label and the Counts' debut single, "Thinking Single," was issued in late spring 1972. An album, *What's Up Front That Counts* followed, a six-track instrumental jam that pushed the Counts into the pop Top 200 for a couple of weeks, and kept them on the road for much of the year.

Slimming down to a quartet of Davis, Emmanuel, Cates and Gibson, the Counts relocated to Atlanta in 1973. There they signed with Aware Records and released the *Love Signs* album that fall, followed by the singles "Funk" and "Sacrifice." Emmanuel and Davis also appeared on Hamilton Bohannon's *Bohannon* album. The Counts, however, continued to struggle and, when 1975's *Funk Pump* album barely scratched the R&B Top 60, the band faded.

### THE COUNTS DISCOGRAPHY
#### LPs
**8** 1972 What's Up Front That Counts (Westbound—#35 R&B/#193 pop)
With three songwriters in the band (Davis, Emmanuel and Cates), the Counts were always going to sound uneven; first time out, however, six dirty instrumental jams keep all their other instincts in check.
**5** 1973 Love Signs (Aware—#45 R&B)
At their best, they plowed a dramatic funky groove. At the other end of the scale, however, they were capable of some quite unnecessary balladeering, even toying with jazz muzak with a cover of Carole King's mawkish "Jazzman."
**4** 1975 Funk Pump (Aware—#58 R&B)

#### SELECTED COMPILATIONS AND ARCHIVE RELEASES
1996 It's What's in the Groove (Southbound)

#### SELECTED SAMPLES
Motor City —Raw Stylus: Pushing Against the Flow (1995)
Pack of Lies — Snoop Doggy Dogg: Who Am I. . . . See What's My Name? (1993)

Since We Said Goodbye — Gravediggaz: Mommy, What's a Gravedigga? (remix) (1994)

## CURTOM RECORDS

Although it was 1968 when Curtis Mayfield and partner Eddie Thomas launched the Curtom label, they had been operating under that name for some five years beforehand, with their own music publishing house. Among the company's better known properties was "I've Been Loving You Too Long," composed by former Impressions vocalist Jerry Butler and a million-seller for Otis Redding.

Mayfield and Thomas also launched several labels of their own: the Mayfield, Thomas and Windy C imprints. The first and last of these had both closed by early 1968, Thomas continued on into the new era ushered in by Curtom.

Operating out of the former RCA recording studios in Chicago (now renamed Curtom Studios), with distribution through the local Chi Sound Inc., the new label was inaugurated that spring with singles by local songstress Junie Conquest ("What's This I See?"), Philadelphia's Symphonics ("When I Grow Old") and DC natives the Winstons ("Need a Replacement"). These were followed in early summer with a single by longtime Mayfield associates the 5 Stairsteps, formed by the multi-talented Burke Family.

Their first ever release, "Don't Waste Your Time," had debuted the Windy C label; this latest one, "Don't Change Your Love," fittingly, debuted the latest addition to the Burke family, the co-credited two-year-old Cubie. It reached #15 on the R&B chart, and while "Stay Close to Me," a cunning rewrite of "This Old Heart of Mine," bombed, three further Curtom releases kept the group's visibility high.

Mayfield was still performing and recording with the Impressions at this time, and that band's career proved Curtom's most successful, particularly through the label's infancy. However, Donny Hathaway also enjoyed some chart action with "I Thank You Baby," a duet with Junie Conquest, while Baby Huey & the Babysitters seemed destined for stardom before Huey's untimely death.

It was Huey's manager, Marv Stuart, who first suggested that Mayfield break away from the Impressions for a solo career; Stuart also took over from Eddie Thomas as co-owner of Curtom when Thomas moved into artist management. The Thomas label also folded, but was swiftly replaced by Gemigo, an imprint launched for Mayfield's own replacement in the Impressions, Leroy Hutson.

Few of the acts signed to Curtom proved successful. Goliath, formed from the wreckage of the Babysitters, remained small fry despite the presence of a young Chaka Khan, while blues shouter Ruby Jones and the Jackson 5-esque Love's Children went nowhere equally fast. Veterans Major Lance, Gene Chandler and the vocal group Natural Four also found hits hard to come by and Curtom's biggest-selling release beyond the Mayfield/Impressions axis proved to be the soundtrack to the 1975 Bill Cosby/Sidney Poitier comedy *Let's Do It Again*. Performed by the Staple Singers, the title track reached #1 on both the pop and R&B lists, Curtom's first ever chart-topper. (Mayfield also produced the Singers' next album, for Warner Bros).

Hutson protege Linda Clifford also turned out a string of minor singles during the late '70s, but further recruits like Rasputin's Stash and the Jones Girls (no relation to Ruby) did little.

In 1978, Curtom inked a new distribution deal with the RSO label, a move that saw Mayfield make some genuinely inspired signings, only to see them crushed by a lack of promotion or worse. Mystique, formed by another ex-Impression, Ralph Butler, deserved to make an impact with their tight soul; so did Philly mastermind Bunny Sigler, Florida hopefuls TTF (Today Tomorrow Forever) and one-time David Bowie associate Ava Cherry. All, however, released records unnoticed by the outside world, but the worst was still to come.

In 1980, Curtom enjoyed its biggest success in several years when Fred Wesley's "House Party" breached the R&B Top 40. A full album was recorded, but RSO's own financial difficulties ensured that the record was left on the shelf. By the end of the year, RSO had crumbled and Curtom collapsed alongside it.

Mayfield continued to use the Curtom identity for his production work during the early '80s, before reviving the label itself in 1988. A handful of new signings followed, but Curtom became better known for a number of classic '70s reissues (including, of course, Mayfield's own). More recently, the European Charly label has maintained a steady steam of welcome archive releases, including a two-CD label retrospective.

*CURTOM LABEL*
*COMPLETE LP DISCOGRAPHY*
*RELEASES 1968–78*
8001 Impressions: This Is My Country
8002 5 Stairsteps & Cubie: Love's Happening
8003 Impressions: The Young Mod's Forgotten Story
8004 Impressions: The Best Impressions: Curtis, Sam and Fred
8005 Curtis Mayfield: Curtis

8006 Impressions: Check Out Your Mind!

8007 Baby Huey & the Babysitters: The Baby Huey Story/The Living Legend

8008 Curtis Mayfield: Curtis/Live!

8009 Curtis Mayfield: Roots

8010 unissued

8011 Ruby Jones: Ruby Jones

8012 Impressions: Times Have Changed

8013 unissued

8014 Curtis Mayfield: Superfly (Soundtrack)

8015 Curtis Mayfield: Back to the World

8016 Impressions: Preacher Man

8017 unissued

8018 Curtis Mayfield: In Chicago

8019 Impressions: Finally Got Myself Together

8020 Leroy Hutson: The Man

8600 Natural Four: Natural Four

8601 Curtis Mayfield: Sweet Exorcist

8602 Impressions: Three the Hard Way

8603 unissued

8604 Curtis Mayfield: Got To Find a Way

### RELEASES 1979–80

5001 Curtis Mayfield—There's No Place Like America Today

5002 Leroy Hutson—Hutson

5003 Impressions—First Impressions

5004 Natural Four—Heaven Right Here On Earth

5005 Staple Singers—Let's Do It Again (Soundtrack)

5006 Ed Townsend—Now

5007 Curtis Mayfield—Give, Get, Take And Have

5008 Natural Four—Nightchaser

5009 Impressions—Loving Power

5010 Leroy Hutson—Feel The Spirit

5011 Leroy Hutson—Hutson II

5012 Mystique—Mystique

5013 Curtis Mayfield—Never Say You Can't Survive

5014 Barbara Mason & Bunny Sigler—Locked In This Position

5015 unissued

5016 Linda Clifford—Linda

5017 Curtis Mayfield—Short Eyes

5018 Leroy Hutson—Closer To The Source

5019 Mavis Staples—A Piece Of The Action

5020 Leroy Hutson—Love Oh Love

5021 Linda Clifford—If My Friends Could See Me Now

5022 Curtis Mayfield—Do It All Night

### SELECTED COMPILATIONS AND ARCHIVE RELEASES

**8** **1996 various artists—The Curtom Story (Charly)**

51 track label retrospective scoops up the best of both the original and the revived (1968) Curtom catalogs, with the emphasis on quality as opposed to mere rarity— the much sought after Goliath single is absent, and rightfully so according to the liner notes. Excellent contributions from Baby Huey, Bobby Franklin's Insanity, Moses Dillard & The Tex Town Display, Ground Hog (aka Hutson) and, of course, Fred Wesley document the label's strengths.

## CARL DOUGLAS

**BORN:** *1942, Kingston, Jamaica*

Jamaican-born, California-bred, Carl Douglas originally relocated to London in his mid-teens to pursue a Bachelors degree in mechanical engineering. By the early '60s, he was also fronting a semi-professional R&B covers act, the Charmers, breaking away in 1965 at the urging of booking agent John Gunnell. He formed a new group, the Big Stampede and, through the mid-'60s, they become a major attraction on the swinging London soul circuit. Ben E. King, Georgie Fame and Zoot Money all sat in with the band— so did Jimi Hendrix, shortly after he arrived in the city in September 1966.

In terms of recapturing the manic excitement of a Stax roadshow, the Big Stampede's live show was second to none; their records, however, did little. "Crazy Feeling" and "Let the Birds Sing" both flopped; so did a pair of Douglas solo efforts, "Nobody Cries" and "Sell My Soul to the Devil" and, by 1967, Big Stampede had broken up.

A solo appearance at the Cannes Film Festival in 1967 saw Douglas introduced to French superstar Johnny Halliday's backing musicians—a tight aggregation that Douglas promptly lured to his own side, combining them with a Spanish soul group called The Lynx and renaming the ensuing melange The Explosion.

This aptly named lineup spent the next two years touring mainland Europe, before Douglas alone returned to London in 1970 to join a hard rocking funk group called the Gas; their original vocalist, Bobby Tench, had just been recruited to the Jeff Beck Group.

Renaming themselves Gonzalez, the band became a regular fixture on the UK club circuit, expounding a contagious funk rock sound interspersed by highlights from Douglas' own parallel solo career. Through the early '70s, the singer maintained a barrage of singles, including "Do You Need My Love," "Somebody Stop This Madness," "Marble and Iron" and a cover of Bill Withers' "Lean on Me." He also linked with India-born producer Biddu Appian to record the main theme to the 1972 Chuck Connors movie *Embassy*.

Gonzalez signed with EMI in 1973, shortly before embarking upon a UK tour with the visiting Curtis Mayfield; it was he who suggested Douglas quit Gonzalez for a solo career, after catching Douglas alone jamming onstage with the Average White Band. Douglas took his advice shortly before work began on Gonzalez's debut album in early 1974, launching his latest career twist with the soft soul ballad "I Want To Give You My Everything," written by Larry ("Rhinestone Cowboy") Weiss. The B-side was a song he had offered Gonzalez the previous year, but they had rejected as a frivolous novelty, "Kung Fu Fighting."

Producer Biddu agreed with them and gave Douglas just 15 minutes to record the song. But Pye Records A&R man Robyn Blanchflower, visiting the studio that day, was convinced "Kung Fu Fighting" was a sure-fire monster. The sides were flipped and "Kung Fu Fighting" was released as Douglas' debut in August 1974. A month later, it was topping charts all over the world, with sales of over 10 million. "Dance the Kung Fu," won another month on the British chart; an album, *Kung Fu Fighting and Other Great Love Songs* (*Kung Fu Fighter* in the UK), was released in time for Christmas.

Unfortunately, the album wound up stuffing more remainder bins than Xmas stockings; "Kung Fu Fighting" was already being written off as a one-off joke and few among even its most rabid fans imagined that Douglas had anything more impressive up his sleeve. (Gonzalez, fearful that "Kung Fu Fighting"'s infamy might now begin rubbing off on them, promptly titled their own sophomore album *Music Is Our Only Weapon*.)

Subsequent Douglas singles, too, failed. "Blue Eyed Soul," "I Want To Give You My Everything," "Love Peace and Happiness" and "Shanghai'd" were all passed over, as were two further albums, 1975's *Love Peace and Happiness* and 1977's *Keep Pleasing Me*. Douglas did manage one more hit single, when December 1977's "Run Back" made #25 in Britain; two decades later, he celebrated another after Bus Stop revived "Kung Fu Fighting" for a single of their own, and invited Douglas to guest on it.

### CHART LOG
1974 Kung Fu Fighting/Gamblin' Man (20th Century—#1 R&B/#1 pop)
1975 Dance The Kung Fu/Changing Times (20th Century—#8 R&B/#48 pop)

### LPs
**8** 1974 **Kung Fu Fighting and Other Great Love Songs (20th Century—#1 R&B/#37 pop)**
An excellent album, albeit in a very mid-'70s soft-soul kind of way. Biddu's string arrangements, simultaneously lush and explosive, were magnificent; while Douglas' treatment of the (largely self-composed) material drew upon all the experience his decade in clubs and bars had granted him.

**8** 1975 **Love, Peace and Happiness (20th Century)**
Another triumph, with one track, "M.O.R.F.," ranking among the finest slabs of Britfunk ever made—and that despite its self-deprecating insistence that it was nothing more than "Middle of the Road Funky."
**6** 1977 **Keep Pleasing Me (Pye—UK)**

### SELECTED COMPILATIONS AND ARCHIVE RELEASES
**8** 1998 **The Soul of the Kung Fu Fighter (Sequel—UK)**
Sensible collection gets the hits out of the way early on, then digs deep into all three 1970s' solo albums. The Bus Stop reprise winds things up.

### SELECTED SAMPLES
Kung Fu Fighting — Fat Boy Slim: (in concert break)

## EARTH WIND & FIRE
**FORMED:** *1969, Chicago, IL*
**ORIGINAL LINE-UP:** *Wade Flemmons (vcls), Sherry Scott (vcls), Michael Beale (gtr), Verdine White (b. 7/25/51, IL—bs), Don Whitehead (kybds), Leslie Drayton (trum), Alex Thomas (trom), Chet Washington (tnr sax), Maurice White (b. 12/19/41, Memphis TN—drms), Phillard Williams (perc)*

The son of a medical student, Maurice White began his musical career at age six, singing and touring the south-east with a gospel quartet, the Rosehill Jubilettes. He began learning drums at age 13 and, with classmate Booker T. Jones, was soon playing in various Porter Junior High jazz combos.

In 1961, White moved to Chicago to study at Chicago Music Conservatory. He was still a student in 1963, when he made his recorded debut on Betty Everett's "You're No Good." Soon established as house drummer at the Chess Studios, he became one of the local R&B scene's most in-demand sessionmen, working (among others) with Etta James, Billy Stewart, Chuck Berry, the Impressions, Jackie Wilson, Muddy Waters and Fontella Bass. He also spent a week touring with John Coltrane, deputizing for the indisposed Elvin Jones.

In 1965, White was invited to join the Ramsey Lewis Trio, at a time when Lewis was still in the first flush of crossover success with "The In-Crowd," "Hang on Sloopy" and a cover of the Beatles' "A Hard Day's Night," all Top 30 pop hits through 1965–66.

White replaced Isaac "Red" Holt in the Trio; also making his debut on Lewis' next hit, "Wade in The Water," was former Ike Cole bassist Cleveland Eaton. However, despite this promising start the new lineup was never to enjoy the

**Verdine White, Maurice White, and Roland Bautista heading for that boogie wonderland.**

success of its predecessor. A second hit, "Up Tight," in late 1966, was not followed up until 1969 brought another Beatles' cover, "Julia"—by which time White was preparing to move on, to launch his own project, the Salty Peppers.

He had already formed his own production company, Hummit Productions, with keyboard player Don Whitehead and vocalist Wade Flemmons (b. 9/25/40, Coffeyville, KS; d. 10/13/93), a former teen sensation who notched a run of R&B hits during 1958–61, but was now fresh back from two years in Vietnam. Hummit comprised a modest demo studio, a photography studio and an office, but it was there that White's next venture took shape.

As a quartet completed by White's brother Verdine, the Salty Peppers cut a single, "La La Time," for release on their own Hummit label in early 1969. It immediately caught the attention of Capitol Records, who signed the group and lured them to Los Angeles to make an album. In the event, they cut just one further single, "Uh Huh Yeah," before they were dropped.

Undeterred, the Peppers decided to expand their lineup and, by June 1970, the original group had been swollen by the arrival of Sherry Scott, Michael Beale, Leslie Drayton, Alex Thomas, Phillard Williams and Chet Washington. Renamed in honor of White's astrological profile, Earth Wind & Fire signed with Warner Brothers in late 1970 and cut their eponymous debut album with producer Joe Wissert, for release the following spring.

All concerned were confident that Earth Wind & Fire—a pop group, said White, made up of jazz musicians—were going places. Indeed, *Earth Wind & Fire* reached the R&B Top 30, while the single "Love Is Life" (reprised from a Salty Peppers' B-side) proved a minor hit, alerting director Melvin Van Peebles to the band, just as he was preparing to score the movie *Sweet Sweetback's Baadasssss Song*.

Despite the ensuing soundtrack's immediate success, Earth Wind & Fire's second WB album, *The Need of Love*, fared poorly and, by early 1972, the original lineup had all but disbanded. The Whites were working to rebuild, however, recruiting the four octave vocals of Philip Bailey (b. 5/8/51, Denver, CO—in Los Angeles as musical director for the Stovell Sisters gospel act). He in turn introduced Larry Dunn (b. Lawrence Dunhill—6/19/53, kybds), while auditions eventually turned up Jessica Cleaves (.b 1948—vcls, ex-Friends of Distinction), Roland Bautista (gtr), Ronnie Laws (b. 10/3/50, Houston, TX—sax, gtr), Al McKay (gtr, perc—ex-Watts 103rd Street Rhythm Band), Bobby Bryant and Oscar Brashear (trum) and Ralph Johnson (drms).

New management in the form of Bob Cavallo and Joe Ruffalo brought Earth Wind & Fire a succession of shows opening for former Loving Spoonful vocalist John Sebastian, an odd pairing but one which ensured that whatever happened in the future, the group's appeal would not be confined to a strictly R&B crowd. Certainly Columbia Records chief Clive Davis was impressed when he caught them at Rockefeller Center, buying out their WB contract and signing them immediately to his label.

In November 1973, *Last Days and Time* commenced its slow rise into the R&B Top 20. Despite featuring a couple of contentious covers (Pete Seeger's "Where Have All the Flowers Gone?" and Bread's "Make It with You"), it was a genuinely cohesive and at times, innovative album, while Earth Wind & Fire were also becoming an increasingly impressive, not to mention ambitious live draw.

While underground college radio sang their praises, Earth Wind & Fire toured with Funkadelic, the Stylistics, Mandrill, War, Eddie Kendricks and B.B. King, growing more outrageous every time. Conscious from the start of the value of theatrics, White encouraged his bandmates to dress as extravagantly as they could, in tights, platform boots, anything that came to mind.

The following summer, "Evil" brought Earth Wind & Fire the chart breakthrough they had been threatening. Recorded with guitarist Johnny Graham (ex-New Birth) replacing the solo-bound Laws, and another of Bailey's Denver friends, Andrew Woolfolk (soprano sax) now the sole brass player, it breached both the R&B Top 30 and the pop Top 50, hauling the *Head to the Sky* album in its wake. It eventually became the Earth Wind & Fire's first gold record.

Bautista quit, while Cleaves, too, departed, simply disappearing following a show in Boston. She married, then moved to Detroit, bound for George Clinton's P-Funk empire. White opted not to replace either of them, and Earth Wind & Fire completed their next album, *Open Our Eyes*, as an octet, with one of White's old Chess comrades, Charles Stepney, moving in as arranger and occasional co-

writer. "Mighty Mighty" and "The Kalimba Story" (titled for the handheld African thumb piano, which was White's sonic trademark) stormed into the R&B Top Five in the new year, while *Open Our Eyes* topped the chart, on its way toward an eventual platinum disc.

The group's earnings were poured straight back into the live show. In an age when P-Funk alone had persuaded American audiences that concerts could offer far, far more than a simple musical recital, Earth Wind & Fire began expanding their stage set even as White's imagination broadened its own horizons. At Madison Square Garden, opening for Sly Stone, Verdine White astonished audiences by being whisked into the air on an all-but invisible hoist; at the California Jam, where Earth Wind & Fire were the only Black act to appear on a stage creaking beneath the biggest names in rock (Deep Purple and Emerson Lake & Palmer were among the headline attractions), few witnesses to their performance ever forgot it.

Late 1974 saw White return to his roots when he led Earth Wind & Fire into a collaboration with Ramsey Lewis. Recording an album, *Sun Goddess*, the pairing also ran up two hit singles, "Hot Dawgit" and "Sun Goddess" itself. The group's presence (and commercial omnipresence) was also responsible for their casting in the 1974 movie *That's the Way of the World*. There, they appeared alongside Harvey Keitel in the latest effort from director Sig (*Superfly*) Shore.

The movie told the story of a conscientious record company exec (Keitel) whose is forced to choose between his personal dream, a Black rock group called The Group (Earth Wind & Fire), and what Keitel's character describes as a "bullshit whitebread bubblegum" singing family—in other words, an everyday tale of the music industry.

It was an absolute flop, but—despite doubling as its soundtrack—Earth Wind & Fire's own latest release, *That's the Way of the World*, in early 1975, broke them into the mainstream. With domestic sales eventually topping five million, it remained on the pop chart for over a year, topping the lists for three weeks and unleashing two of Earth Wind & Fire's most memorable hits, the title track and the chart-topping/Grammy-winning "Shining Star."

Augmented by the Whites' younger brother Jeff (ex-Donny Hathaway—gtr), the group responded with a lavish tour, which included their own sell-out Madison Square gig and incorporated pyrotechnics, Egyptology and conjuring acts. The stageset itself was designed by Doug Henning and his then little known assistant, David Copperfield, and offered viewers a maze of levitating musicians, secret passages and magical disappearances, a revolving drum riser and the astonishingly powerful musical show captured in part on Earth Wind & Fire's next album, November 1975's *Gratitude*.

Three of the four sides were recorded live, during stops in Chicago, Los Angeles, St. Louis, Atlanta, Boston, New York City, DC and Philadelphia. The fourth comprised five songs recorded in June 1975, during a break in the tour, spotlighting Earth Wind & Fire's horn section of Don Myrick, Louis Satterfield and Michael Harris and promptly spinning off two further singles, "Sing a Song" and "Can't Hide Love."

A European tour with Santana saw Earth Wind & Fire's profile go into overdrive there (by 1977, they were UK Top 20 regulars), while the band's success suddenly thrust White into yet another new spotlight; during 1976 alone, he produced albums by Deniece Williams, Chicago vocal trio The Emotions (with whom he had played during the early '60s, while they were known as the Heavenly Sunbeams) and, again, Ramsey Lewis, at the same time as completing Earth Wind & Fire's own latest offering. He would remain an in-demand producer.

Earth Wind & Fire's eighth album, *Spirit*, was released in September 1976. It was, compared to its predecessors, a downbeat set—the death of the group's longtime arranger, Charles Stepney, earlier in the year, struck the musicians hard and the new album's title track was a very personal tribute to him. Yet it was also a triumphant album, as the band's ability to combine pounding rhythms with sultry-but-so-commercial ballads had become all but second nature.

The album rose to #2 on the strength of the hits "Getaway," "On Your Face" and "Saturday Nite," and also introduced another group trademark, the Egyptian-flavored album covers, which both echoed their stage show and helped shape perceptions of the music itself. No less than P-Funk's crazy cartoons, Earth Wind & Fire created a brand identity that remained with them until the end. The following year's *All 'n' All* pursued the mystic imagery even further, serving up the sinewy chart-topper "Serpentine Fire," alongside that most superlative of disco floorshakers, "Fantasy."

A rivetting version of the Beatles' "Got To Get You into My Life," taken from the otherwise misconceived *Sgt. Pepper's Lonely Hearts Club Band* movie soundtrack, and "September," excised from the band's first best of collection, kept Earth Wind & Fire at #1 through 1976–77. At the 1978 Grammys, they were nominated for six awards and took home three of them, for best R&B group performance (*All*

'n' All*), best R&B instrumental ("Running") and best arrangement ("Got To Get You into My Life"). Two successive #2s followed, with the Grammy-winning ballad "After the Love Has Gone" and "Boogie Wonderland," the latter a fine collaboration with the Emotions. (The instrumental B-side earned the group a second Grammy that year). White opened a new studio in Los Angeles, the Complex, and launched his own Columbia distributed record label. American Recording Company (ARC) debuted with Earth Wind & Fire's own *Best Of* set, then continued strongly with releases by the Emotions, Deniece Williams, DJ Rogers, and the Pockets, an R&B combo discovered and produced by Verdine White.

Earth Wind & Fire's 1979 album, *I Am*, continued both their massive success and their willingness to push at boundaries—Verdine White later called it their own *Abbey Road*. However, critics were increasingly pointing out that mainstream success was seriously diluting their original forcefulness, a failing that audiences were not slow in acknowledging either. Although it made the Top Ten and was eventually to go gold, 1980's *Faces* became Earth Wind & Fire's least successful album in five years.

Al McKay quit for a career in record production. Roland Bautista returned for 1981's *Raise* and a return to form of sorts, with "Let's Groove" and the Grammy-winning "Wanna Be with You." But though two further albums, *Powerlight* and *Electric Universe*, saw the band—now comprising the White trio, Bailey, Dunn, Bautista, Woolfolk and Johnson—moving successfully into techno funk-lite territory, both sold poorly and, in March, 1984, Earth Wind & Fire broke up. Bailey later admitted that they should have done so four years earlier.

Bailey had already launched a smooth-soul solo career the previous year, and in 1985 he landed a transatlantic chart-topper when he teamed up with MOR pop singer Phil Collins for the single "Easy Lover" (Collins had previously used the Earth Wind & Fire horn section on several of his own recordings.) White, too, was to cut a solo album, 1985's *Maurice White*, and made the Top Ten with a sumptuous cover of Ben E. King's "Stand by me." In early 1987, however, Bailey, Johnson, Maurice and Verdine White, Woodfolk, guitarist Sheldon Reynolds (from the Commodores' backing group) and Sonny Emory (drms—ex-Crusaders) reconvened as Earth Wind & Fire, and grabbed a comeback hit in October with "System of Survival."

The following month, the album *Touch the World* suggested that Earth Wind & Fire's popularity had not been dented by their absence—it made the R&B Top Three and spent over six months on the chart. Earth Wind & Fire themselves remained on the road for nine months, including an appearance alongside Kool & the Gang at the Star Spangled Celebration, a July 4, 1988, event hosted by Patrick Duffy and screened by ABC.

Further hits followed through 1988, including another soundtrack classic, "Turn On (The Beat Box)," from Jackie Mason's *Caddyshack II*, while 1990 saw Earth Wind & Fire team with teenaged singing group The Boys, to cut the title track to their next album, *Heritage*. Two collaborations with rapper MC Hammer followed: "For the Love of You," which he co-wrote with Stephanie Mills, and "Wanna Be the Man," which featured the Hammer on co-vocals.

1993 brought the next Earth Wind & Fire album, as they signed to Reprise for the Top 40 *Millennium Yesterday Today*; the single, "Sunday Morning," also gave the band their first pop success since 1988 (and their first Grammy nomination in a decade). However, after 30 years on the road, Maurice White, at least, felt it was time for a change. In 1996, he announced his retirement from live work (he continued on in the studio); his final shows with Earth Wind & Fire, in Japan, were subsequently released as a live album.

Offstage at last, White returned to production work with Jonathan Butler, Gerald Albright and the Urban Knights duo of Ramsey Lewis and Grover Washington. He also launched a new label, Kalimba. Earth Wind & Fire themselves cut the *In the Name of Love* album, simultaneously cementing their position among the godfathers of funk by linking with rappers Sunz of Man for a version of "Shining Star." Fugees vocalist Wyclef Jean, who also appeared on the record, subsequently signed Earth Wind & Fire to his own Refugee Camp label, and penned the group's contribution to the *PJs* movie soundtrack. Earth Wind & Fire were inducted into the Rock & Roll Hall of Fame in March 2000.

### EARTH WIND & FIRE COMPLETE DISCOGRAPHY
### SINGLES/CHART LOG
### THE SALTY PEPPERS

1969 Uh Huh Yeah/Your Love Is Life (Capitol)
1969 La, La, La (part 1) 2. La, La, La (part 2) (Capitol)

### EARTH WIND & FIRE

1971 This World Today/Fan the Fire (WB)
1971 Love Is Life/This World Today (WB—#43 R&B/#93 pop)
1971 I Think About Lovin' You/C'mon Children (WB—#44 R&B)
1973 Evil/Clover (Columbia—#25 R&B/#50 pop)

1973 Keep Your Head to the Sky/Build Your Nest (Columbia—#23 R&B/#52 pop)
1974 Mighty Mighty/Drum Song (Columbia—#4 R&B/#29 pop)
1974 Kalimba Story/Tee Nine Chee Bit (Columbia—#6 R&B/#55 pop)
1974 Devotion/Fair But So Uncool (Columbia—#23 R&B/#33 pop)
1975 Shining Star/Yearnin' Learnin' (Columbia—#1 R&B/#1 pop)
1975 That's the Way of the World/Africano (Columbia—#5 R&B/#12 pop)
1975 Sing a Song/(instrumental) (Columbia—#1 R&B/#5 pop)
1975 Can't Hide Love/Gratitude (Columbia—#11 R&B/#39 pop)
1976 Getaway/(instrumental) (Columbia—#1 R&B/#12 pop)
1976 Saturday Nite/Departure (Columbia—#4 R&B/#21 pop)
1977 On Yer Face/Departure (Columbia—#26 R&B)
1977 Serpentine Fire/(instrumental) (Columbia—#1 R&B/#13 pop)
1977 Fantasy/Runnin' (Columbia—#12 R&B/#32 pop)
1977 Got To Get You into My Life/I'll Write a Song for You (Columbia—1 R&B/#9 pop)
1978 September/Love's Holiday (ARC—#1 R&B/#8 pop)
1979 After the Love Has Gone/Rock That! (ARC—#2 R&B/#2 pop)
1979 In the Stone/You and I (ARC—#23 R&B/#58 pop)
1979 Star/You and I (ARC—#47 R&B/#64 pop)
1980 Let Me Talk/(instrumental) (ARC—#8 R&B/#44 pop)
1980 You/Share Your Love (ARC—#10 R&B/#48 pop)
1980 And Love Goes On/Win or Lose (ARC—#15 R&B/#59 pop)
1981 Let's Groove/(instrumental) (ARC—#1 R&B/#3 pop)
1981 Wanna Be with You/Kalimba Tree (ARC—#15 R&B/#51 pop)
1981 Fall in Love with Me/Lady Sun (Columbia—#4 R&B/#17 pop)
1983 Side by Side/Something Special (Columbia—#15 R&B/#76 pop)
1983 Spread Your Love/Hearts to Heart (Columbia—#57 R&B)
1983 Magnetic/Speed of Love (Columbia—#10 R&B/#57 pop)
1983 Touch/September (Columbia—#23 R&B/#103 pop)
1983 Moonwalk/We're Living in Our Own Time (Columbia—#67 R&B)
1987 System of Survival/ Writing on the Wall (Columbia—#1 R&B/#60 pop)
1987 Thinking of You/Money Tight (Columbia—#3 R&B/#67 pop)
1987 Evil Roy (part one)/(part two) (Columbia—#22 R&B)
1987 You and I/Musical Interlude: New Horizons (Columbia—#29 R&B)
1988 Turn On (The Beat Box) (part one)/(part two) (Columbia—#26 R&B)
1989 Megamix (September — Let's Groove—Rock That—Boogie Wonderland)/Rock That! (Columbia)
1990 For the Love of You/Motor (Columbia—#19 R&B)
1993 Sunday Morning/The L Word (Reprise—#20 R&B/#53 pop)
1993. Spend the Night/Even If You Wonder (Reprise—#42 R&B)
1993 Two Hearts/Honor the Magic (Reprise—#88 R&B)
1999 Megamix 2000/September '99 (Columbia)

### EARTH WIND & FIRE/RAMSEY LEWIS

1975 Hot Dawgit/Tambura (Columbia—#61 R&B/#50 pop)
1975 Sun Goddess/Jungle Strut (Columbia—#20 R&B/#44 pop)

### EARTH WIND & FIRE/THE EMOTIONS

1979 Boogie Wonderland/(instrumental) (ARC—#2 R&B/#6 pop)

**EARTH WIND & FIRE/THE BOYS**

1990 Heritage/Gotta Find Out (Columbia—#5 R&B)

**EARTH WIND & FIRE/MC HAMMER**

1990 Wanna Be the Man/Welcome (Columbia—#46 R&B)

**EARTH WIND & FIRE**

**LPs**

**8** 1971 Earth Wind & Fire (WB—#24 R&B/#172 pop)

Taking their lead from the recent success of Santana, EW&F rise from the psychedelic stew with a riveting blend of Latin, jazz and R&B sensibilities. It's a little sloppy in places, but never less than adventurous.

**6** 1971 Sweet Sweetback's Baadasssss Song (Stax—#13 R&B/#139 pop)

**7** 1972 The Need of Love (WB—#35 R&B/#89 pop)

**7** 1972 Last Days and Time (Columbia—#15 R&B/#87 pop)

Gently hinting at the band's later embrace of lighter funk textures, *Last Days* is very much a showcase for individual talents—Bailey shines on "Where Have All the Flowers Gone." The horns power the electrifying "Time Is on Your Side" (the album's most up-tempo number); the instrumental "Power" brings everyone together for a hypnotic jam.

**8** 1973 Head to the Sky (Columbia—#2 R&B/#27 pop)

The frenetic "Build Your Nest" and the lushly textured "Evil" evidence the band's development, with the closing 13-minute "Zanzibar" returning to the latter's Latin jazz premise for an exhilarating virtuoso workout.

**6** 1974 Open Our Eyes (Columbia—#1 R&B/#15 pop)

With a formula now creeping into view, ballads, jazz and funk alternate more or less equally, and the album's strongest points are its most unusual: the muscular "Kalimba Story," the (obviously) percussive "Drum Song" and the neo-jam "Tee Nine Chee Bit."

**6** 1975 That's the Way of the World (Columbia—#1 R&B/#1 pop)

**9** 1975 Gratitude (live) (Columbia—#1 R&B/#1 pop)

The best evidence there is of the band's early magnificence, four cuts from *That's the Way* ("Shining Star" among them) dwarf their studio counterparts, while the opening "Africano"/"Power" medley disgraces EW&F's later reputation for lightweight funk.

**5** 1976 Spirit (Columbia—#2 R&B/#2 pop)

High energy all the way, but a little samey as well. Hear the three Top 30 smashes ("Getaway," "Saturday Night" and "On Your Face") and you've heard the rest of the album.

**6** 1977 All 'n' All (Columbia—#1 R&B/#3 pop)

"Fantasy" was a pop masterpiece any way you looked at it, "Serpentine Fire" and "Jupiter" worthy companions.

But they alone distinguish another predictably workaday album.

**5** 1979 I Am (ARC—#1 R&B/#3 pop)

**6** 1980 Faces (ARC—#2 R&B/#10 pop)

**5** 1981 Raise! (ARC—#1 R&B/#5 pop)

**6** 1983 Powerlight (Columbia—#4 R&B/#12 pop)

**8** 1983 Electric Universe (Columbia—#8 R&B/#40 pop)

The naysayers deny it but (alongside Herbie Hancock's *Future Shock*), if there was a better electrofunk album released that year, it remains well hidden. The wide-open production is plugged with brittle pop and effects, the guitars are dangerous, the bass a burbling, subterranean brute. The ballads let things sag in places, but up the tempo and the album cooks.

**6** 1987 Touch the World (Columbia—#3 R&B/#33 pop)

**7** 1990 Heritage (Columbia—#19 R&B/#70 pop)

**6** 1993 Millennium, Yesterday, Today (Reprise—#8 R&B/#39 pop)

**7** 1996 Plugged in and Live/Greatest Hits Live in Tokyo (Pyramid—#75 R&B)

No competition for *Gratitude*, of course, but still an enjoyable souvenir.

**6** 1996 Avatar (Pyramid)

**6** 1997 In the Name of Love (Pyramid—#50 R&B)

**SELECTED COMPILATIONS AND ARCHIVE RELEASES**

**7** 1974 Another Time (WB—#29 R&B/#97 pop)

Reissue of first two albums.

**7** 1978 The Best Of, Vol. 1 (ARC—#3 R&B/#6 pop)

Smoothly packaged hits collection lacking, of course, EW&F's more experimental excursions (including anything from even the first two Columbia albums), but adding non-LP material to the brew.

**6** 1991 The Best Of, Vol. 2 (Columbia—#74 R&B/#190 pop)

More of the same, except the best was not so easy to find any longer.

**8** 1992 The Eternal Dance (Columbia)

Three-CD box set, sensibly divided 1971–75 (disc one: three unreleased tracks), 1975–77 (disc two: three unreleased tracks) and 1978–89 (disc three: four unreleased tracks). Essential roundup that naturally loses its punch around the halfway mark, but still retains one's interest.

**7** 1998 Greatest Hits (Remastered) (Columbia)

**MAURICE WHITE SOLO LP**

**6** 1985 Maurice White (Columbia)

**SELECTED SAMPLES**

Bad Tune — Brand Nubian: Dance to My Ministry (1991)

Bad Tune — Diamond D: Feel the Vibe (1992)

Bad Tune — DJ Shadow: In/Flux (1998)

Brazilian Rhyme — Professor X: The Sleeper Has Awakened! (1991)

Brazilian Rhyme (Interlude) — A Tribe Called Quest: Mr. Muhammad (1990)

Brazilian Rhyme (Interlude) — Fugees: Refugees on the Mic (remix) (1994)

Devotion — Mack 10, featuring K-Dee: Mozie Wozie (1995)

Devotion — Yo-Yo: You Can't Play with My Yo-Yo (1991)

Devotion (live) — Naughty by Nature: Rhyme'll Shine On (1991)

Devotion — Scarface: Now I Feel Ya (1995)

I Can Feel It in My Bones — EPMD: Boon Dox (1992)

I Think About Loving You — Fugees: Nappy Heads (1994)

I'll Write a Song for You — 2pac: Hold on Be Strong (1996)

Moment of Truth — Third Eye: Ease Up (1993)

Moment of Truth — Kid 'N Play: Energy (1990)

Moment of Truth — LL Cool J: Murdergram (Live at Rapmania) (1990)

Power — Organized Konfusion: Prisoners of War (1991)

Runnin' — Organized Konfusion: Walk into the Sun (1991)

Saxophone Interlude — Digable Planets: Swoon Units (1993)

Shining Star — Sunz of Man: Shining Star (1998)

Shining Star — Roots, featuring D'Angelo: The 'Notic (1999)

Shining Star — Public Enemy: Prophets of Rage (1988)

Shining Star — MC Lyte: Paper Thin (1988)

Shining Star — De La Soul: Roller Skating Jam Named Saturdays (1991)

Sunshine — Wyclef Jean: To All the Girls (1998)

Sunshine — Big Punisher, featuringNext: Sex, Money & Drugs

Sunshine — Arrested Development: Natural (1992)

Tee Nine Chee Bit — Medina Green: Crosstown Beef (1998)

You Can't Hide Love — Audio Two: I Don't Care (1988)

## ENTERPRISE RECORDS

A Stax Records subsidiary launched in 1968 with the first Isaac Hayes album, Enterprise was originally intended to be a jazz label. In the event, the five years during which Enterprise remained in operation saw it offering up an eclectic mix of material that ranged from primal funk and R&B (Hayes, co-writer David Porter, Detroit's Black Nazty, etc.) through gospel and, increasingly predominantly, country. Highly regarded by collectors, the label was not a commercial success—Hayes alone proved a reliable hit-maker.

### ENTERPRISE LP LISTING

13–100 Isaac Hayes: Presenting
13–101 Maynard Ferguson: Ridin' High
13–102 Father Herrera & Trio: Jazz Goes to Church
1001 Isaac Hayes: Hot Buttered Soul
1002 Moloch: Moloch
1003 Sid Selvidge: Portrait
1004 January Tyme: First Time from Memphis
1005 Little Sonny: New King of the Blues Harmonica
1006 Barbara Lewis: Many Grooves

1007 Jerry Miller: Rated X: Suggested for Mature Souls
1008 Terry Manning: Home Sweet Home
1009 David Porter: Gritty, Groovy & Gettin' It
1010 Isaac Hayes: The . . . Movement
1011 Dallas County: Dallas County
1012 David Porter: Into a Real Thing
1013 Billy Eckstine: Stormy
1014 Isaac Hayes: . . . To Be Continued
1015 Caboose: Caboose
1016 Stillrock Featuring Don Preston: Stillrock
1017 Billy Eckstein: Feel the Warm
1018 Little Sonny: Black and Blue
1019 David Porter: Victim of a Joke?
1020 Eric Mercury: Funky Sounds
1021 Ben Atkins: Patchouli
1022 Hevy Gunz: Dope on Dope & Dope Doops
1023 O. B. McClinton: . . . Country
1024 River City Street Band: River City Street Band
1025 Freddie Robinson: At the Drive In
1026 David Porter: Sweat and Love
1027 River City: Anna Divina
1028 Joe Hicks: Mighty Joe Hicks
1029 OB McClinton: Obie from Senatobie
1030 24 Carat Black: Ghetto—Misfortune's Wealth
1031 Black Nazty: Talking to the People
1032 Don Nix: Hobos, Hero's & Street Corner
1033 Eric Mercury: Love Is Taking Over
1034 Louis Paul: Louis Paul
1035 Freddie Robinson: Off the Cuff
1036 Little Sonny: Hard Goin' Up
1037 O.B. McClinton: Live At Randy's Rodeo
1038 Eddie Bond: Legend of Buford Pusser
5001 Frank Wess: Wess to Memphis
5002 Isaac Hayes: Shaft (Soundtrack)

## FUNKADELIC, see GEORGE CLINTON

## FUNK INC.
**FORMED:** *1969, Indianapolis, IN*
**ORIGINAL LINE-UP:** *Steve Weakley (gtr), Bobby Watley (orgn), Eugene Barr (sax), Jimmy Munford (drms), Cecil Hunt (cngs)*

After close to two years plowing a tight, all-instrumental jazz-funk groove around their Indianapolis hometown, Funk Inc were discovered in 1971 by producer Bob Porter (b. 6/20/40, Wellesley, MA), later renowned for his pains-taking research work on the Atlantic records jazz catalog, but at the time working for the local Prestige label.

Home to such hard bop heroes as Rusty Bryant, Charles

Kynard, Johnny Hammond Smith, Boogaloo Joe Jones and the young George Benson, Prestige signed the band in mid-1971. Riding the acclaim for Funk Inc.'s electrifying live shows, their self-titled, improvisation heavy, debut album, made the R&B Top 50 that fall.

The following year, Funk Inc. served up more of the same with the less successful *Chicken Lickin'* and *Hangin' Out* sets; it took a dramatic swerve away from the overt jazz material, into the aptly named *Superfunk* album, to return Funk Inc. to the chart in December 1973. The set rose to the edge of the Top 30, encouraging the musicians to delve even deeper into commercial territory. Their hitherto unsullied instrumentals were now accompanied by backing vocals, spontaneous improvisation gave way to crafted arrangements—and Funk Inc. began to fall apart. *Priced to Sell*, Top 30 in early 1975, was their final album.

The members parted and, over the next twenty years, little was heard of any of them. Barr and Munford both passed away in relative obscurity, Watley alone appears to have continued in music. By the early '90s, however, Funk Inc.'s reputation was on the rise, as the British acid-jazz scene came to ever greater prominence and brought with it a wealth of resurgent interest. In 1994, Watley, Weakley and Hunt reconvened under the old band name.

The new lineup's first release, that same year, was a jazz-lite Christmas album, *Piano-el*, the trio performing seven soul and pop standards accompanied by a variety of singers and other musicians. In 1995, joined by Teddy Patterson (sax), Doug Swanigan (gtr) and Phil Brines (drms), Watley and Hunt returned to the studio (and to Funk Inc. basics) to cut the well-received *Urban Renewal*.

## FUNK INC. DISCOGRAPHY
### LPs
**9** **1971 Funk Inc. (Prestige—#45 R&B/#211 pop)**
Bands like Earth Wind & Fire would soon make a killing from territory first explored by Funk Inc., swirling jazz grooves tied to a deep funking rhythm. Individual songs are irrelevant (even covers are radically reworked); *Funk Inc.* is simply a non-stop party.

**8** **1972 Chicken Lickin' (Prestige)**
"Let's Make Peace and Stop the War" is the killer cut, a slamdunk honking monster that conveys its message without a word. Other cuts can appear less focussed, but the overall album is very impressive.

**6** **1972 Hangin' Out (Prestige)**
**8** **1973 Superfunk (Prestige—#31 R&B)**
"Message from the Meters" is a deceptive opener: maybe a

soupcon of gumbo creeps into view, but *Superfunk* itself is as straightforward as you could wish, a groove heavy party animal that doesn't even try to be memorable. It is, however, often irresistible.

**4** **1974 Priced To Sell (Prestige—#30 R&B)**
**3** **1994 Piano-el: An Artist Collection, Vol. 2 (Pure & Simple)**
Jazz-lite, an irrelevance to past (and future) Funk Inc. releases.

**5** **1995 Urban Renewal (Milestone)**
The '90s funk revivals rarely recapture the raison d'etre of the past, but this one tries, upping the rhythms while never losing sight of the band's new acid-jazz audience.

## SELECTED COMPILATIONS AND ARCHIVE RELEASES
**7** **1988 Acid Inc.: The Best of Funk Inc. (BGP)**
A fair career summary, but a better Best Of would have simply drawn from the first two albums.

## SELECTED SAMPLES
Bowlegs — Boogie Down Productions: Ya Strugglin' (1990)

Chicken Lickin' — 3rd Bass' No Static at All (1991)

Goodbye, So Long — Brand Nubian: Hold On (remix) (1994)

Goodbye, So Long — Lench Mob: All on My Nut Sac (1992)

Kool Is Back — Black Sheep: North South East West (1994)

Kool Is Back — Brand Nubian: Pass the Gat (1993)

Kool Is Back — Compton's Most Wanted: I Give Up Nuthin (1990)

Kool Is Back — Compton's Most Wanted: Growin' Up in the Hood (1991)

Kool Is Back — Erick Sermon: Ill Shit (1993)

Kool Is Back — Everlast: Tired (1999)

Kool Is Back — Full Force: Alice, I Want You Just for Me (1986)

Kool Is Back — Geto Boys' The Other Level (1991)

Kool Is Back — Grand Puba: Check Tha Resume (1992)

Kool Is Back — Ice-T: 409 (1987)

Kool Is Back — Jeru The Damaja: Come Clean (1994)

Kool Is Back — Keith Murray: Sychosymatic (1994)

Kool Is Back — Milli Vanilli: Girl You Know It's True (1989)

Kool Is Back — Nice & Smooth: Hit Me (1989)

Kool Is Back — Pete Rock & CL Smooth: I Got a Love (1994)

Kool Is Back — Queen Latifah: Nature of a Sista (1991)

Kool Is Back — Rasco: Suckas Don't Respect It (1998)

Kool Is Back — Schoolly D: B-Boy Rhyme and Riddle (1987)

Kool Is Back — West Coast Rap All Stars' We're All in the Same Gang (1990)

Message from the Meters — Eric B. & Rakim: Keep 'Em Eager To Listen (1990)

The Better Half — Leaders of the New School: Daily Reminder (1993)

The Better Half — Blood of Abraham: Stabbed by the Steeple (1993)

Thrill Is Gone — Alkaholics: 21 and Under (1995)

## GONZALEZ

**FORMED:** *1974, London, England*

**ORIGINAL LINE-UP:** *Carl Douglas (vcls), Gordon Hunte (gtr), Phil Chen (bs), Roy Davies (kybds), Steve Gregory (sax), Chris Mercer (sax), Mick Eve (sax), Richard Bailey (drms), Allan Sharpe (perc)*

Gonzalez existed more as a concept than a full-time concern, made up of as many as 30 (and seldom less than 15) musicians, drawn from a pool of Britain's finest session men, all of whom shared a desire to play the dirtiest funk the country had ever produced.

Purposefully modeled on the then-newly emergent Earth Wind & Fire, Gonzalez grew out of an earlier soul-funk act, the Gas, led by vocalist Bobby Tench. He quit in 1970 to join the Jeff Beck Group and was replaced by Jamaican-born Carl Douglas, then regarded among Britain's best R&B vocalists. Of the other founding members, Roy Davies was ex-the Butts Band with former Doors members John Densmore and Robbie Krieger; Chris Mercer was ex-bluesmen John Mayall and Keef Hartley and, along with Lisle Harpe, had played with Anglo-American rockers Juicy Lucy; Gordon Hunte once worked with reggae star Johnny Nash. Other recruits recorded with Georgie Fame's Blue Flames, one of the tightest and most authentic British R&B acts of the '60s.

Signed by EMI in 1973, Gonzalez toured the UK with Curtis Mayfield; it was he who recommended that Douglas go solo, advice the singer took shortly before Gonzalez started work on their debut album. He was replaced by George Chandler; then, while Douglas stormed to #1 with the novelty "Kung Fu Fighting," his former bandmates released the well received *Gonzalez*, following up in 1975 with *Our Only Weapon Is Our Music* — titled to distance Gonzalez from their ex-singer's greatest hit.

Gonzalez then took a year-long break before resurfacing in 1977 with *Haven't Stopped Dancing*, its title song contributed by former Motown songwriter Gloria Jones, then resident in London as consort of rocker Marc Bolan. Jones and her brother Richard also co-produced the album and, despite the recent birth of her son, Rolan, she made a couple of live appearances with Gonzalez, opening for Bob Marley at Cardiff City soccer ground and at the Wigan Casino, capital of Britain's Northern Soul community (one of Jones' own '60s singles, "Tainted Love," was a firm favorite on that circuit.) Gonzalez reciprocated by joining Jones on her own gestating solo album, *Vixen*.

*Haven't Stopped Dancing* was released in the US in 1978; it did little, but reissued toward the end of the year as *Ship-*

*wrecked*, it finally became a minor hit in early 1979, with the title track also climbing into the pop Top 30.

But a new album that same year, *Move It to the Music*, flopped, despite a powerful production effort by Donna Summer/Giorgio Moroder co-conspirator Pete Bellotte and, when 1980's *Watch You Step* suffered a similar fate, EMI dropped the band. Still Gonzalez continued working until 1986, several members becoming involved with the briefly successful Funkmasters. Gonzalez finally broke up following the death of founder Davies.

### GONZALEZ DISCOGRAPHY
#### CHART LOG
1978 Shipwrecked (Capitol—#52 R&B/#67 pop)
1979 Haven't Stopped Dancing Yet/Just Let It Lay (Capitol—#46 R&B/#26 pop)

#### LPs
**7** 1974 Gonzalez (EMI—UK)
A gritty, if occasionally well-mannered album, defiantly funky and higher on substance than the contemporary Average White Band.
**7** 1975 Our Only Weapon Is Our Music (Capitol)
Still too polite to really hit home, Gonzalez nevertheless turn in an effervescent floor filler.
**9** 1979 Haven't Stopped Dancing (Capitol)
Their most adventurous album, gleefully mixing funk, disco and pop elements, but with little regard for commerce. "Rockmaninoff" is a good-natured instrumental packed with clever, twiddly bits, while the brainless disco "Dancing" itself is the Koolest gangbang of the year.
**6** 1979 Move It to the Music (Capitol)
**5** 1980 Watch You Step (Capitol)

## LARRY GRAHAM

**BORN:** *8/14/46, Beaumont, TX*

One of the most distinctive bassists of his generation, and one of the most influential ever, Graham developed that distinction while playing in a trio led by his mother, former Lowell Fulson pianist Dell Graham, and trying to compensate for the fact that the group had no drummer.

The Dell Graham Trio was a fixture on the Bay Area lounge circuit through the early-mid-'60s; Larry was initially the Trio's guitarist, doubling as bassist by operating the relevant pedals of an organ with his foot. It was a haphazard style and, when the organ finally gave out, he switched to bass guitar, which was when drummer Ruben Kerr departed. Interviewed by *Black Stars* magazine a decade later, in 1974, Graham determined his style was "a result of trying to play the bass and keep the rhythm at the same time. It's like overplaying, you try to compensate for what is missing."

In fact, what he did was create a percussive thumping sound that bewitched everybody who came in earshot of it—none so much as Sly Stone, a local DJ/record producer then in the throes of putting together his own group, Sly & the Family Stone. On the recommendation of a persistent fan, Stone caught Graham at a Trio gig at Relax with Yvonne's, a club on Haight/Ashbury, and immediately offered him a place in the new band.

Graham became one of the foundation stones of that group, his unique bass and baritone vocals as much a signature as Stone's own tenor rasp. Indeed, over the next six years, through the crucial *Dance to the Music, Life, Stand* and *There's a Riot Goin' On* albums, Graham arguably rewrote the book on acid-funk bass, at the same time as providing the bedrock upon which the greatest of Stone's grim visions was effortlessly built. He also wrote a number of the Family Stone's best-loved songs, beginning with "Let Me Hear It from You," a heartbreaking ballad included on the Stone's *A Whole New Thing* debut album. It was, with hindsight, inevitable that Graham's departure should also mark the beginning of the end for the Family Stone.

Graham first began looking outside of the band in early 1972, when he took another Bay Area group, Hot Choclet, under his wing. At that point he intended simply to produce them; however, by the end of the year he and Stone had broken up and Graham found himself joining Hot Choclet. He renamed them Graham Central Station partly to trade upon his own name and reputation and partly to avoid confusion with a British combo of a similar name—and just in time. Within a year, the British Hot Chocolate were enjoying a de facto US success after New York-rockers The Stories snatched a US pop #1 with their "Brother Louie" single, a cover of the UK band's latest homeland hit.

Graham Central Station, was launched in early 1973, with a lineup of Graham, fellow ex-patriate Texan Patrice "Chocolate" Banks (vcls), David Vega (gtr), Hershall Kennedy (trum, kybds), Robert Sam (kybds) and Willie Sparks (drms). They quickly earned a powerful live reputation and, by the end of the year, had signed to Warner Brothers, stablemates and frequent live companions of Tower of Power, whose Lenny Williams received a special thank you on the Station's debut album.

The growling monster that was *Graham Central Station* was released in January 1974, an immediate R&B Top 20 entry and source of the Top Ten single "Can You Handle It." By the end of the year, *Release Yourself* had proven a similarly successful follow-up, but it was with their third album. summer 1975's *Ain't No Bout-a-Doubt It*, that Graham Central Station truly crashed into the mainstream.

On the back of almost constant live work, the album went gold—the first such honor ever scored by a Black Warner Brothers artist, while the "Your Love" single (based around the 1969 Family Stone classic "Hot Fun in the Summertime") topped the R&B chart, displacing KC & the Sunshine Band in the process.

Graham Central Station would not return to that particular pinnacle again; the onset of disco and a decline in the R&B market's enthusiasm for the road warriors of past years was matched by the musicians' own apparent uncertainty about their future direction. "Your Love" had introduced a magical falsetto to Graham's already legendary three-and-one-half octave range and the singer was anxious to explore a more tender musical style, one that also reflected his newly embraced faith as a Jehovah's Witness.

The departures of Banks and Sparks during 1976 only weakened things further; they were replaced by Gaylord Birch and Gail Muldrow and Graham Central Station enjoyed one further notable hit in 1977, "Now Do-U-Wanta Dance," a hefty funk workout further characterized by the then-still novel use of a vocoder, feeding Graham's vocals into his bass.

The accompanying album, titled for the hit, became Graham Central Station's final chart entry. In 1978, with Graham's wife Tina replacing Muldrow (and Graham's own name now topping the credits), the Station released two final, somewhat desultory, albums before Graham broke away to launch a solo career—one that moved as far away from the pounding funk of old as it could.

Composed by Sam Dees, the smooth romantic ballad "One in a Million" became Graham's first solo single, and an immediate R&B chart topper in mid-1980. "When We Get Married," a cover of an Intruders' oldie, followed it into the Top Ten, while his debut album, *One in a Million You*, gave him his second gold disc. The self-composed title track to his second album, *Just Be My Lady*, continued Graham's rebirth into 1981; but once again, Graham appeared to be left behind as a new wave of solo soul/R&B balladeers emerged to overtake him.

By 1985, without a hit in two years, Graham had parted company with Warner Brothers and was now concentrating on studio work, recording with artists as far apart as Johnny Mathis and Jeffrey Osborn, the Crusaders, the Fortran Five and Carlos Santana. Teaming up with Aretha Franklin, he also scraped a minor 1987 hit with "If You Need My Love

Tonight," while Japanese audiences were treated to a genuine spectacle when, touring on a 1985 bill with the Crusaders, Graham and Stanley Clarke agreed to stage a Battle of the Basses.

Another partnership saw Graham join forces with former Brothers Johnson guitarist George Johnson to produce a Japanese vocalist named Noriko "Mimi" Miyamoto. In 1992, the pair convened a Graham Central Station reunion to accompany one of Miyamoto's homeland tours; the lineup was completed by former members Kennedy, Sam and Birch.

Three years later, with several other one-off revivals behind them, the Station regrouped once again, for tours of the US, Europe and Japan. This time lining up as Graham, Kennedy and original vocalist Banks, plus Dean Gant (kybds), Wilton Rabb (gtr) and Noel Closson (drms), gigs with Earth Wind & Fire, Teena Marie and Sinbad followed, while Graham Central Station were also one of the hits of the 1995 Soul Music festival in Aruba.

The group continued touring through 1996–97 and, following yet another personnel shuffle, Graham led the reunion through a new studio album; wife Tina, Sam, Rabb, Closson and saxophonist Jerry Martini recorded *By Popular Demand* for release in Japan in 1997.

It was while the Station were playing a show in Memphis that Graham was contacted by Prince, who was also in town that night. They met up later that evening to jam; Prince promptly invited Graham aboard his own upcoming Jam of the Year World Tour before taking the full Graham Central Station lineup into the studio to record a new album, February 1999's GCS2000, for release on Prince's own NPG label. Produced by Prince and featuring contributions from the New Power Generation and labelmate Chaka Khan, the album also spawned a remarkable New Power Generation/Graham Central Station hybrid, the NPGCS, featuring Graham, Mike Scott (gtr), Morris Hayes (kybds), Kirk Johnson (drms) and backing vocalists Tina Graham and Marva King.

Graham was inducted into the Rock & Roll Walk Of Fame in Los Angeles in 1999, alongside Bootsy Collins, Vanilla Fudge bassist Tim Bogert, Stanley Clarke and (posthumously), Funk Brothers founder James Jamerson.

### LARRY GRAHAM/GRAHAM CENTRAL STATION DISCOGRAPHY
### CHART LOG
### GRAHAM CENTRAL STATION
1974 Can You Handle It?/Ghetto (WB—#9 R&B/#49 pop)
1974 Release Yourself/Tis Your Kind of Music (WB—#56 R&B)
1974 Feel The Need/We Bes Gettin' Down (WB—#18 R&B)
1975 Your Love/I Believe in You (WB—#1 R&B/#38 pop)
1975 It's Alright/Luckiest People (WB—#19 R&B/#92 pop)
1976 The Jam (long version) (WB—#15 R&B/#63 pop)
1976 Love/Why? (WB—#14 R&B)
1976 Entrow (part one)/(part two) (WB—#21 R&B)
1977 Now Do-U-Wanta Dance/Got To Go Through It (WB—#10 R&B)
1977 Stomped Beat Up and Whooped/Ole Smokey (WB—#25 R&B)

### LARRY GRAHAM AND GRAHAM CENTRAL STATION
1978 My Radio Sure Sounds Good to Me/Turn It Out (WB—#18 R&B)
1978 Is It Love?/Are You Happy? (WB—#65 R&B)
1979 (You're a) Foxy Lady/Tonight (WB—#37 R&B)
1979 Star Walk/Boogie Baby (WB—#85 R&B)

### LARRY GRAHAM
1980 One in a Million You/The Entertainer (WB—#1 R&B/#9 pop)
1980 When We Get Married/Tonight (WB—#9 R&B/#76 pop)
1981 Just Be My Lady/Feels like Love (WB—#4 R&B/#67 pop)
1981 Guess Who/Sweetheart (WB—#69 R&B)
1982 Don't Stop When You're Hot/I Love Loving You (WB—#16 R&B/#102 pop)
1982 Sooner or Later/I Feel Good (WB—#27 R&B/#110 pop)
1983 I Never Forgot Your Eyes/Movin' Inside Your Love (WB—#34 R&B)

### LARRY GRAHAM/ARETHA FRANKLIN
1987 If You Need My Love Tonight/He'll Come Along (Arista—#88 R&B)

### GRAHAM CENTRAL STATION LPs
**10** 1974 Graham Central Station (WB—#20 R&B/#48 pop)
A warm a cappella opener welcomes you to the show—and then all hell breaks loose. Hints of the Family Stone naturally abound, but GCS is its own beast entirely, popping, yowling, slurring and so heavy that even the ballads punch you out.

**9** 1974 Release Yourself (WB—#22 R&B/#51 pop)
—More of the manic-packed same, even down to a jokey-weird intro that is just long enough to fool you into thinking the next track won't make you jump. But of course it does—"Release Yourself" is mach 10 mayhem, and again the ballads are deceptive. But nothing can prepare you for the garage funk take on the Detroit Emeralds' "Feel The Need"!

**8** 1975 Ain't No Bout-a-Doubt It (WB—#4 R&B/#22 pop)
**8** 1976 Mirror (WB—#7 R&B/#46 pop)
The military marching "Entrow" introduces "GCS, the baddest group from east to west"—and if you excise the drab "Love" and the pointless "I Got a Reason," it could be correct. "Forever," a synth-led tour de force and the lurching "Do Yah" are peaks, and only familiarity with the sound weakens the album.

**6** 1977 **Now Do U Wanta Dance** (WB—#12 R&B/#67 pop)

**8** 1993 **Live in Japan 92** (Edoya—Japan)

Fine comeback album hits all the right highpoints in front of an audience that clearly can't believe its luck.

**7** 1996 **Live in London** (Funk—UK)

**8** 1997 **By Popular Demand** (P-Vine—Japan)

**6** 1999 **GCS 2000** (NPG)

Reinvents the sound, if not necessarily the freshness of classic GCS. Workmanlike but worthy.

### LARRY GRAHAM & GRAHAM CENTRAL STATION LPs

**2** 1978 **My Radio Sure Sounds Good to Me** (WB—#18 R&B/#105 pop)

A horrible record, emotionless ballads, cracked vocals ("Is It Love" tries the Sly slur, but just sounds sickly) and cheesy synths for the sake of 'em.

**4** 1979 **Star Walk** (WB—#44 R&B/#136 pop)

A shock improvement, with "Foxy Lady" even recalling why the band was so great in the first place. But the synths are still overpowering and the opportunist title track needs a time machine to salvage it.

### LARRY GRAHAM LPs

**4** 1980 **One in a Million You** (WB—#2 R&B/#26 pop)

**3** 1981 **Just Be My Lady** (WB—#8 R&B/#46 pop)

**3** 1982 **Sooner or Later** (WB—#15 R&B/#142 pop)

**3** 1983 **Victory** (WB—#52 R&B/#173 pop)

**4** 1985 **Fired Up** (WB—UK)

### SELECTED SAMPLES

It Ain't No Thang to Me — Da Lench Mob: Lost in Tha System (1992)

The Jam — Biz Markie: Pickin' Boogers (1988)

The Jam — Chill Rob G: Court Is Now in Session (1990)

The Jam — DJ Jazzy Jeff & the Fresh Prince: Numero Uno (1989)

The Jam — Eric B. & Rakim: Move the Crowd (remix) (1987)

The Jam — Geto Boys: Mind Playing Tricks on Me (1991)

The Jam — Insane Poetry: Six in the Chamber (1992)

The Jam — Jungle Brothers: Sounds of the Safari (1988)

The Jam — LL Cool J: Fast Peg (1989)

The Jam — M.A.R.R.S.: Pump Up the Volume (1987)

The Jam — Method Man: Release Yo' Delf (remix) (1994)

The Jam — Notorious BIG: Friend of Mine (1994)

The Jam — Paris: Days of Old (1992)

The Jam — Schoolly D: Livin' in the Jungle (1991)

The Jam — Soul II Soul: Keep on Movin' (1989)

The Jam — Soul II Soul: Back to Life (However Do You Want Me) (1989)

People — Das EFX: Baknaffek (1993)

People — KAM: Drama (1993)

## GRAHAM CENTRAL STATION, see LARRY GRAHAM

## HERBIE HANCOCK

**BORN:** *4/12/40, Chicago, IL*

Since his emergence in 1961, the classically trained Hancock had recorded a string of stylishly intriguing solo albums for Blue Note, at the same time as establishing himself among the most in-demand sessionmen on the east coast. His imprimatur can be found on classic recordings by Donald Byrd, Wayne Shorter, Wes Montgomery, Freddie Hubbard, Tony Williams, George Benson, Roy Ayers and many more, while he was also responsible for the cult classic soundtrack to Michelangelo Antonioni's swinging '60s movie *Blow Up*.

In 1968, Hancock quit Davis to launch a journey into the then revolutionary pastures of electronic jazz, delving into effects as much as emotions across a sequence of almost avant-garde albums cut during the early '70s. His ambition, unfortunately, was never to be rewarded with commercial success and in 1973, finances caused Hancock to abandon the experiment. He remained intrigued with technology, however. Indeed, even as Hancock pieced together a new vision, he determined that nothing in his past could prepare the listener for the visceral impact of what emerged as the Head Hunters.

Hancock had already touched on funk with 1971's *Fat Albert's Rotunda* album; and employed the then startling sounds of an ARP synthesizer on his last album, 1973's *Sextant*. But in both instances, he did so sparingly. Now the music and the instrument alike became the heart and soul of his sound.

His bandmates, too, were chosen for their willingness to adapt with the music. Other musicians with an eye for fusion chose jazzmen who could turn their hands to funk. Hancock took the opposite approach, recording *Head Hunters* with fellow Davis sideman Bennie Maupin (sax, clar, flte), Paul Jackson (bs), Harvey Mason (drms) and Bill Summers (perc). The results saw Hancock completely reinventing his own reputation, beginning with a steaming revision of his own "Watermelon Man," a cut from his 1962 debut album, *Takin' Off*. Another cut, "Sly," was Hancock's tribute to Sly Stone, the man whose example set him off on this route in the first place; the album's attendant single, "Chameleon," reiterated that same debt.

Interviewed in 1977, Hancock explained his decision to depart jazz. "Funk . . . that music has such strong roots in the Earth. With all the earthiness there's always room for flight. The biggest reason I enjoy this new kind of funk is the contrast between the wide open improvisations and the funky foundation at the bottom. It gives the music a character that is broad, vast, yet in touch with the people."

Indeed it was. *Head Hunters* soared to the top of the jazz chart, even as jazz purists threw their hands up in horror. More impressive, however, was the album's performance in the R&B charts, where it spent two weeks at #2, and the pop lists, where it made #13.

The success of *Head Hunter* paid some unexpected dividends. Hancock's last label, Warner, promptly produced a compilation album drawn from the *Mwandishi* trilogy of the early '70s (so named for the African name Hancock adopted during that period), earning attention for a series of courageous albums that had hitherto been ignored. Hancock & the Head Hunters, meanwhile, were commissioned to produce a soundtrack to the new Charles Bronson movie, *Death Wish*, even as they got to grips with their own next release, *Thrust*.

With Mike Clark, a former associate of Jackson's, replacing Mason, the Head Hunters' second album was followed by *Flood*, a live set recorded during 1974's Japanese tour. The band then returned to the studio for the crucial *Man Child* album, recorded with renowned jazz-funk producer David Rubinson (Malo, Santana, the Meters, Elvin Bishop etc).

"Hang Onto Your Hang-Ups," a monster groove first aired (as a 20-minute, side-long behemoth) on *Flood*, opened the album, but equally impressive was the litany of guest stars suddenly turning out on Hancock's side. Motown sideman Melvin "Wah Wah Watson" Ragin (who recently worked alongside several other Head Hunters on Bobby Womack's *Safety Zone* album), Stevie Wonder, future Pflunk/Red Hot Chili Pepper-guitarist Blackbyrd McKnight and the Brothers Johnson's Louis Johnson all contributed to *Man-Child*. Johnson also co-wrote one track, "The Traitor."

The Head Hunters, meanwhile, had spun off as their own entity, cutting a full frontal funk album, *Survival of the Fittest* in 1975; this lineup, Maupin, Summers, Clark, Jackson, McKnight and Mason, then reconvened with Wah Wah Watson and another newcomer, Ray Parker, Jr., for Hancock's own next album, *Secrets*.

Like Hancock, Watson's musical abilities were matched only by his fascination with electronic technology and many contemporary commentators noted that this new album essentially doubled as a demonstration disc for all that the modern age could pack into a studio. It was a path, of course, that ultimately led Hancock to the electrofunk apotheosis of his '80s output. In 1976, however, *Secrets*' opener,

"Doin' It," was at least as mindblowing as anything he would go on to achieve.

In 1976, Hancock abandoned the Head Hunters in favor of several new directions. The most critically lauded, of course, followed a one-off reunion with the 1965 Miles Davis Quintet of Ron Carter, Tony Williams and Wayne Shorter, with Freddie Hubbard sitting in for Davis at the 1976 Newport Jazz Festival. Overwhelmed by the response, the quintet, now named VSOP (Very Special One-time Performance), undertook a full world tour during 1977 (further reunions followed throughout the '80s).

Commercially, Hancock continued scoring hits, although the creative tenor of his music had unquestionably reached an impasse. The albums *Sunlight* (1977), *Feets, Don't Fail Me Now* (1979), *Mr. Hands* and *Monster* (1980) all caught Hancock treading disco water to little advantage for listener and performer alike. However, 1978's direct-to-disc *Direct Step* was a reassuring return to form, recutting both Head Hunters and *Sunlight*-era material with a core cast of Jackson, Summers and Maupin joined by Ray Obiedo (gtr) and Alphonse Mouzon (drms).

In 1981 Hancock reunited with Louis Johnson for *Magic Windows*, a solid return to firm funk ground, but his reemergence as both a creative and a commercial force occurred with 1982's *Lite Me Up!*, recorded with former Heatwave maestro Rod Temperton. Hancock linked next with producer Bill Laswell, chasing *Lite Me Up!*'s example into *Future Shock*, an album of electronic funk mayhem that not only caused a mass re-evaluation of Hancock's own ouvre, it reinvented MTV as well. Brilliantly realized by English directors Lol Creme and Kevin Godley, the album's first video, "Rockit," was purposefully conceived as a way of circumventing the video station's unspoken aversion toward Black artists. Hancock himself appears as a mere image on a flickering TV screen, in a roomful of robotic limbs and automations.

"Rockit" (and its follow-up, "Autodrive") ranked among the crossover hits of the year, and were followed by a second album in a similar vein, *Sound System*. Hancock, however, was already mapping out another change of direction, combining with Gambian kora virtuoso Foday Musa Suso for much of the album, matching the sci-fi electronics with an invigorating Afro-beat vibe that culminated, two years later, with the live album *Jazz Africa*.

Hancock would nod once more toward the freaked funk of *Future Shock*; 1988's *Perfect Machine* saw Bootsy Collins, Ohio Players maestro Leroy Bonner and a returning Laswell embark upon what proved Hancock's last album in that style—his last, indeed, for another seven years.

Hancock guested on new albums by Bernie Worrell, Bill Laswell, George Clinton and more, but a union with Quincy Jones' Qwest label produced nothing more than the *Tribute to Miles* album in 1992. Hancock returned to full time recording in 1994, returning, too, to his first love, jazz, with pop a delightful but scarcely dependable sideline.

Hancock launched his own Hancock Records label, in 1989, with a Head Hunters reunion. Michael Clark, Paul Jackson, Bennie Maupin and Bill Summers led an enjoyable (if less than innovative) updating of the old group sound. Hancock's contributions, however, were confined to just four tracks.

## HERBIE HANCOCK DISCOGRAPHY
### CHART LOG
1974 Chameleon/Vein Melter (Columbia—#18 R&B/#42 pop)
1974 Palm Grease/Butterfly (Columbia—#45 R&B)
1976 Doin' It/People Music (Columbia—#83 R&B, #104 pop)
1978 I Thought It Was You/No Means Yes (Columbia—#85 R&B)
1979 Ready or Not/Trust Me (Columbia—#25 R&B)
1980 Stars in Your Eyes/Go for It (Columbia—#33 R&B)
1980 Making Love/It All Comes Around (Columbia—#73 R&B)
1981 Everybody's Broke/Help Yourself (Columbia—#46 R&B)
1981 Magic Number/Help Yourself (Columbia—#59 R&B)
1982 Lite me Up/Satisfied with Love (Columbia—#52 R&B)
1982 Gettin' to the Good Part/The Fun Tracks (Columbia—#47 R&B)
1983 Rockit (LP version) (Columbia—#6 R&B/#71 pop)
1983 Autodrive/Chameleon (Columbia—#26 R&B)
1984 Megamix/TFS (Columbia—#36 R&B/#105 pop)
1984 Hardrock (edit) (Columbia—#41 R&B)
1988 Vibe Alive/Maiden Voyage/P Bop (Columbia—#25 R&B)

### LPs
### HERBIE HANCOCK AND THE HEAD HUNTERS
**8** 1974 Head Hunters (Columbia—#2 R&B/#13 pop)
**8** 1974 Thrust (Columbia—#2 R&B/#13 pop)

Three-quarters jazz-funk, one quarter ("Butterfly") ballad, an incredibly sophisticated album that was a million miles from the dancefloor, but spellbinding regardless.

**6** 1974 Death Wish (original soundtrack) (Columbia—#38 R&B)
**9** 1975 Flood—Herbie Hancock Live in Japan (Columbia)

An essential performance reduces the best of its predecessors to one solid jam.

**9** 1975 Man-Child (Columbia—#6 R&B/#21 pop)

"Hang Onto Your Hang-Ups," condensed from a sidelong freak-out on *Flood*, introduces the Head Hunters' at their peak; difficult to dance to, but contagious enough that you want to regardless.

**6** 1976 Secrets (Columbia—#8 R&B/#49 pop)

### THE HEADHUNTERS
**6** 1975 Survival of The Fittest (Arista)

Comparatively mundane, although few could fault the musicianship.

**7** 1998 Return of the Headhunters (Hancock)

Capably blending a classic feel with modern-day technology, the band over-ride the general absence of Hancock with a series of well-designed jams.

### HERBIE HANCOCK: FUNK YEARS LP DISCOGRAPHY
**7** 1970 Fat Albert Rotunda (WB)
**7** 1971 Mwandishi (WB)
**7** 1972 Crossings (WB)

The so-called Mwandishi triology lies closer to avant jazz than funk, but the occasional nudge gives each album an unexpected edge. Indeed, distilled for the *Treasure Chest* compilation, one can almost hear the Head Hunters coming.

**7** 1973 Sextant (Columbia)

"Rain Dance" would become one of Hancock's best-loved cuts, a lengthy excursion through that precise musical moment where jazz forgets its own hang-ups and plays with other peoples' instead.

**4** 1978 Sunlight (Columbia—#31 R&B/#58 pop)

Whether Hancock was really lost, or just sounded like it, is an unanswerable question. Still, little of *Sunlight* sparkles.

**8** 1979 Direct Step (Sony—Japan)

Live in the studio, direct to disc recording that draws from several past years worth of music for a remarkably loose and funky collection.

**3** 1979 Feets Don't Fail Me Now (Columbia—#16 R&B/#38 pop)
**3** 1979 The Piano (Columbia)
**4** 1980 Mr. Hands (Columbia—#46 R&B/#117 pop)
**5** 1980 Monster (Columbia—#19 R&B/#38 pop)

Hancock stirs some rock into the disco miasma, but to little effect.

**6** 1981 Magic Windows (Columbia—#40 R&B/#140 pop)

Future Hancock producer Bill Laswell acknowledges this album's importance, the first of Hancock's attempts to "reach out" toward the newly gestating New York underground. He continued, "it was based on . . . listening to Talking Heads or something." And it shows.

**7** 1982 Lite Me Up (Columbia—#31 R&B/#151 pop)

The future starts here. Again, like *Magic Windows*, it pales in comparison to Hancock's next three albums, but the roots are strong and well worth investigating.

**10** 1983 Future Shock (Columbia—#10 R&B/#43 pop)

The essential electrofunk album. Its effects, of course, seem utterly dated by modern standards, but its execution remains stark and staggering, a looselimbed blend of industrial textures, hip-hop breaks and deep throat bass lines. Try it loud on headphones.

**8  1984 Sound System (Columbia—#34 R&B/#71 pop)**
No simple son of its father, an Afro-beat pounding counteracts the electro to devastating effect.

**8  1988 Perfect Machine (Columbia—#65 R&B)**
Utterly over the top, an audacious electrofunk jamboree, essentially encapsulating everything its predecessors had suggested was possible, then taking them beyond the realms of imagination.

### HERBIE HANCOCK: OTHER RECORDINGS

(The following discography is included for reference only. Individual albums have not been graded or reviewed.)

1962 Takin' Off (Blue Note)
1963 My Point of View (Blue Note)
1963 Inventions and Dimensions (Blue Note)
1964 Empyrean Isles (Blue Note)
1965 Maiden Voyage (Blue Note)
1966 Blow Up (original soundtrack) (MGM)
1968 Speak like a Child (Blue Note)
1969 The Prisoner (Blue Note)
1974 Dedication (Sony—Japan)
1977 The Herbie Hancock Trio (Columbia)
1978 Ron Carter/ Herbie Hancock/ Tony Williams: Third Plane (Milestone)
1992 A Tribute to Miles (Qwest)
1994 Dis Is Da Drum (Mercury)

### VSOP

1977 V.S.O.P. (Columbia—#24 R&B/#79 pop)
1977 The Quintet (Columbia)
1977 Tempest in the Colosseum (Columbia)
1978 Live Under the Sky (Sony—Japan)
1979 Five Stars (Sony—Japan)

### KIMIKO KASAI WITH HERBIE HANCOCK

1979 Butterfly (Sony—Japan)

### HERBIE HANCOCK/FODAY MUSO SOSA

1985 Village Life (CBS)
1987 Jazz Africa (CBS)

### HERBIE HANCOCK/DAVE HOLLAND/JACK DEJOHNETTE/PAT METHENY

1990 Parallel Realities Live (Jazz Door)

### SELECTED COMPILATIONS AND ARCHIVE RELEASES

**7  1974 Treasure Chest (WB—#31 R&B/#158 pop)**
Well-conceived if thematically disruptive collection drawn from the Mwandishi albums.

1989 Quartet (recorded 1982) (CBS—France)
1992 Herbie Hancock Trio with Ron Carter + Tony Williams 1981 (Sony—Japan)
1994 Herbie Hancock Quartet Live, 1988, 1992 (Jazz Door)
1994 Herbie Hancock Trio Live in New York 1993 (Jazz Door)

### SELECTED SAMPLES

Bring Down the Birds — Deee-Lite: Groove Is in the Heart (1990)
Cantaloupe Island — US Three: Cantaloop (1993)
Chameleon — 2Pac: If My Homie Calls (1992)
Chameleon — Coolio Etc: Get Up Get Down (1995)
Chameleon — Digital Underground: Underwater Rimes (remix) (1989)
Chameleon — Kool G. Rap: Money on My Brain (1995)
Chameleon — Nas: Dr. Knockboot (1999)
Chameleon — Organized Konfusion: Open Yyour Eyes (1991)
Fat Mama — 2Pac: If My Homie Calls (1992)
Fat Mama — Mad Flava: Bump Ya Head (1994)
God Made Me Funky — Biz Markie: Albee Square Mall (1988)
God Made Me Funky — Common Sense: Pitchin' Pennies (1992)
God Made Me Funky — De La Soul: Take It Off (1989)
God Made Me Funky — Digital Underground: Underwater Rimes (1989)
God Made Me Funky — Downtown Science: Down to a Science (1991)
God Made Me Funky — Eric B. & Rakim: Beats for the Listeners (1988)
God Made Me Funky — Eric B. & Rakim: To the Listeners (1988)
God Made Me Funky — Fugees: Ready or Not (1996)
God Made Me Funky — Jungle Brothers: Braggin & Boastin (1988)
God Made Me Funky — Marky Mark: Wildside (1991)
God Made Me Funky — NWA: Approach to Danger (1991)
God Made Me Funky — Quiet Boys: Never Change (1996)
God Made Me Funky — Tony D: Check the Elevation (1991)
God Made Me Funky — X-Ecutioners: The Countdown (1997)
Hang Onto Your Hang Ups — Lords of the U: Sleep for Dinner (1993)
I Remember I Made You Cry — Mobb Deep: Drink Away the Pain (Situations) (1995)
If You've Got It . . . — Boogie Down Prod: Ruff Ruff (1992)
If You've Got It . . . — Professor Griff: Jail Sale (1991)
Oh! Here He Comes — Del Tha Funkee Homos: No More Worries (1994)
Oliloquy Valley — Eric B. & Rakim: Untouchables (1990)
Oliloquy Valley — Simple E: Play My Funk (1994)
Quasar — The Mighty Bop, featuring EJM: Freestyle Linguistique (1995)
Rain Dance — Digable Planets: It's Good to Be Here (1993)
Rain Dance — Organized Konfusion: The Extinction Agenda (1994)
Toys — Beatnuts: Yeah You Get Props (1994)
Watermelon Man — Born Jamerican: State of Shock IV (1997)
Watermelon Man — Diamond Shell: Captain Speakin' (1991)
Watermelon Man — Digable Planets: Escapism (Gettin' Free) (1992)
Watermelon Man — LL Cool J: 1–900-LL-Cool-J (1989)
Watermelon Man — Organized Konfusion: Open Your Eyes (1991)
Watermelon Man — Original Flavor: Gumdrops (1992)
Watermelon Man — Schoolly D: Smoke Some Kill (1988)

Watermelon Man — Style: Pray for Death (1991)
Watermelon Man — Supercat: Dolly My Baby (remix) (1992)
Watermelon Man — US Three: Eleven Long Years (1993)
Watermelon Man — Young Black Teenagers' Looney Toonz (1993)

# FUZZY HASKINS

**BORN:** *Clarence Haskins, 6/8/41, Elkhorn, WV*

Through the late '50s, Fuzzy Haskins was a member of the Plainfield, NJ-based Bel-Airs, one of a number of doo-wop acts operating in the Newark area. George Clinton''s Parliaments were also from Plainfield, and extrovert Haskins joined them in 1965, as they were preparing to record the "Heart Trouble" single. Two years later, the Parliaments landed on the chart with "Testify"—recorded by Clinton and the Detroit combo, the Holidays, because his bandmates could not afford to travel that city.

It was while the Parliaments toured the US in the wake of "Testify" that they commenced the transformation into Funkadelic, a musical shift that, at least in part, echoed Haskins' own sartorial style—and then eclipsed it, as Funkadelic established themselves as the freakiest funkers around.

An accomplished songwriter, Haskins contributed "I Got a Thing, You Got a Thing, Everybody's Got a Thing" to Funkadelic's eponymous debut album (he also handled the lead vocal). Other early Haskins compositions included "My Automobile," for the first Parliament revival in 1970 and "Back in Our Minds" (*Maggot Brain*, while he co-wrote "All Your Goodies Are Gone," "I Misjudged You" (*Chocolate City*) and "Good to Your Earhole" (*Let's Take It to the Stage*).

At the same time, his distinctive vocals, frequently to the fore of the P-Funk sound, ensured that by the time he became the first member of the aggregation to launch a solo career, in 1976, he was already guaranteed an enthusiastic audience.

Despite its title, *A Whole Nother Thang* did not deviate too far from the mothership norm; self-produced, the album featured regular P-Funkers Tiki Fulwood, Bootsy Collins, Ron Bykowski, Cordell Mosson and Bernie Worrell among its supporting cast, while nine self-composed songs (the instrumental "Fuz And Da Boog" was co-written with Mosson) were firmly rooted in funk and dance.

One track, "Cookie Jar," was already a live favorite—a second version of the track subsequently appeared on the Brides of Funkenstein's debut album. Another cut, however, seemingly pointed toward a grimmer future; "Which Way Do I Disco" was apparently directed at the increasing

commercialization of the P-Funk package and has since been cited as an early warning of Haskins' future intentions. Following a P-Funk show in Los Angeles on June 4, 1977, Haskins quit, together with fellow Parliament founders Ray Davis, Calvin Simon and Grady Thomas. (Davis returned shortly after.)

Haskins immediately began work on a second album, *Radio Active*. Again, many of the P-Funk regulars joined him at the sessions, including Jerome Brailey, Bruce Nazarian, Michael Hampton, Glen Goins, Gary Shider, Mosson and Worrell, and again the result was a powerful, varied collection.

Haskins' next move, however, was not so well-judged, as he linked with Simon and Thomas to reclaim the Funkadelic name from Clinton. Working with an entirely new crew, comprising Michael Williams (gtr, kybds, vcls), Billy Mims (vcls, clav, gtr), Ben Powers, Jr. (drms, bs, vcls), Ken Blackmon (kybds), Stan Thorn (kybds) and Johnny Riley (kybds, vcls), the trio created a set that echoed many of Clinton's Funkadelic tricks, but adamantly informed its audience, "none of the concepts on this album are related to George Clinton." Released in March, 1981, *Connections and Disconnections* limped into the chart on the strength of the band name, but dropped out again after just one month.

Haskins left the music industry soon after. Between 1981 and 1991 he devoted his life to God. It was during a live recording at the church, which he was attending, that he was reunited with Westbound Records chief Armen Boladian; Funkadelic had spent six years at his label in the early 1970s. Haskins' own solo records also appeared through the imprint.

Reflecting on the meeting, Haskins drew the unavoidable conclusion that such a coincidence was no coincidence at all, that "it was the will of God that our paths crossed that night and . . . I am back doing what I love to do . . . making music funky."

Haskins' long-delayed third solo album, *TriXXX of the Trade*, followed just as the classic Parliament lineup of Clinton, Haskins, Simon, Thomas and Davis was reunited for the first time in 20 years, for their induction into the Rock & Roll Hall of Fame. All but Clinton then reconvened as Original P, performing early P-Funk material together with new material. An album, 1998's *What Dat Shakin'*, followed.

*LPs*

**8** 1976 **A Whole Nother Thang** (Westbound)

Pure P-Funk madness, with the band screaming blue murder behind him, and Haskins pulling every trick out of his vocal book. "Mr. Junkman," an unsubtle addendum to Curtis Mayfield"s "Pusherman," is a low point, but elsewhere, A *Whole Nother Thang* is exactly the sort of thang you'd hope it to be.

### 6 1978 Radio Active (Westbound)

Inconsistent set that bounds from the sublime nastiness of "Not Yet," to the ridiculously drab "I Think I Got My Thang Together." At its best it echoes early P-Funk ("Sinderella," "Silent Day"), but those peaks are all too scarce.

### 6 1997 TriXXX of the Trade (Westbound)

Well-made, if none too memorable return that spends too much time trying to re-establish Haskins' Phunklord credentials, without enough songs to justify the stance.

#### SELECTED COMPILATIONS AND ARCHIVE RELEASES

### 7 1994 A Whole Nuther Radioactive Thang (Westbound)

Reissue of the first two albums, plus outtake "Right Back Where I Started From."

#### FUZZY HASKINS/FUNKADELIC

### 3 1981 Connections and Disconnections (LAX)

The pledge is that George Clinton had nothing to do with this album—and it shows. Uninspired funk, which barely even tries to get excited.

#### FUZZY HASKINS/ORIGINAL P

#### LP

### 7 1998 What Dat Shakin' (Westbound)

The inclusion of three versions of the infectious title track notwithstanding, a varied and confident set, although it sorely misses the madcap genius once associated with these guys.

#### SELECTED SAMPLES

Love Is Now Forever—Black Sheep: To Whom It May Concern (1991)

## ISAAC HAYES

**BORN:** *8/20/42 (some sources state 1938), Covington TX*

Orphaned as a child and raised by his grandparents, Hayes moved to Memphis in his late teens, where he led a string of short-lived combos around the club circuit. A self taught sax, piano and organ player, Hayes appeared with the Teen Tones, Sir Calvin and his Swinging Cats and Memphis singer Jeb Stuart's backing band, the Doo-Dads. He also cut one single with producer Chips Moman, "Laura we're on Our Last Go-Round" in 1962, before he was recruited to Mar-Keys saxophonist Floyd Newman's live group.

From there, Hayes became a regular at Stax studio sessions, often standing in for the MGs' keyboard player, Booker T. after he began attending college in Indiana. Floyd Newman's December 1963, "Frog Stomp" single was co-written with an uncredited Hayes, the first of many compositions for the label.

In 1964, Hayes was responsible (with future Bar-Kays drummer Carl Cunningham and Rufus Thomas' son Marvell) for the Mad Lads' "Sidewalk Surf" single. Hayes was credited as Ed Lee, forced into a pseudonym by a publishing contract signed earlier in his career. Again as Lee, he also began writing with another Stax sideman, David Porter. Porter's own recording of "Can't You See When I Want To," in January 1965, debuted the partnership (five years later, Porter succeeded with a remake of this same song).

By summer 1965, Hayes was again able to put his own name to his writing credits and the Hayes/Porter team was officially launched on August 13, with the release of Sam and Dave's sophomore Stax 45, "I Take What I Want," and Rufus Thomas and Carla Thomas' "When You Move You Lose." Thereafter, the Hayes/Porter team was responsible for hits across the Stax spectrum, including Carla Thomas' "B-A-B-Y," Sam & Dave's "Hold On, I'm Coming" and "Soul Man," Ruby Johnson's "I'll Run Your Hurt Away" and the Astors' "In the Twilight Zone"—a song that was subsequently, memorably, borrowed by Blondie as the basis for "Rifle Range."

Another project reunited Hayes with two former schoolfriends, Eddie Harrison and Billy Moore, with whom he had played in the high school-era Missiles. Now they were members of the Premiers; Hayes and Porter's "Make It Me" would be their Stax debut. Hayes' own debut as a Stax recording artist, contrarily, was with a cover, the lazy sax-led instrumental "Blue Goose," cut with his old colleagues from the Doo-Dads, renamed Sir Isaac & the Doo-Dads for the occasion.

By 1967, Hayes was involved in virtually every aspect of the recording process at Stax, as a writer, a musician and an arranger; Otis Redding's "Try a Little Tenderness" is frequently cited among his greatest triumphs in the latter category. He also cut a Christmas single with Booker T. & the MGs, a version of his own "Winter Snow," but still Hayes continued to hanker for his own recording career.

Impetus for what he would achieve was coming at him from every direction: Otis Redding's success at the rock-oriented Monterey Pop festival in summer 1967; David Porter's admiration for the newly emergent Sly & the Family Stone, elements that he incorporated into the first Sam and

Isaac Hayes: the self-styled Black Moses.

Dave single of 1968, "I Thank You." Hayes plays a clavinet on the song, forcing guitarist Steve Cropper to adopt the dirtiest guitar sound of his career and creating an intricate sonic soup whose importance, of course, only became apparent in later years. Few musicians venturing into what became funk over the next few years, however, truly escaped the shadow of "I Thank You."

In January 1968, Hayes finally recorded what became his debut album. Taking over the studio following a company party, Hayes and the MGs rhythm section of Al Jackson and Duck Dunn relaxed into a late night, laidback jazz jam, released later in the year as *Presenting Isaac Hayes,* and accompanied by a single of the improvised vamp, "Precious, Precious."

Inaugurating a new Stax subsidiary, what was intended to be the jazz specialist Enterprise, the album did little, but with Stax giving him the go-ahead to continue, Hayes changed direction entirely for the massive *Hot Buttered*

*Soul.* With Hayes accompanied by the Bar-Kays, *Hot Buttered Soul* featured just four cuts, the shortest, Charles Chalmer's "One Woman," coming in at five minutes; the longest, Jimmy Webb's "By The Time I Get to Phoenix," close to a marathon 19 minutes.

Somehow, "Phoenix" and the 12-minute "Walk on By" were edited down for a double A-sided single. It became Hayes' first hit, but just as potently, it introduced Hayes' startling image to the world, shaven headed and bedecked in medallions, slow-rapping super cool sensuality over a landscape that slid from lush orchestrations to snapping guitar with barely a pause. It was, with the obvious physical modifications, a role model Barry White would soon be taking to extraordinary commercial heights, although Hayes ran him a close second.

*Hot Buttered Soul* was the first of five consecutive R&B chart-toppers from Hayes. Indeed, over the next two years, he spent 49 weeks at #1; by comparison, the entire Motown family (the Temptations, Diana Ross and the Jacksons were all at the peak of their powers) mustered just three weeks longer between them.

Hayes' next album, *The Isaac Hayes Movement*, debuted Hayes' own band of that same name: Lester Snell (kybds), Charles Pitts (gtr), Ronald Hudson (bs), Willie Hall (drms) and Gary Jones (perc); and even without any substantial smash singles, both it and 1970's *To Be Continued* were massive hits. But it was Hayes' next release, the soundtrack to the Richard Roundtree movie *Shaft*, that established the benchmark by which his career (and every other movie soundtrack of the '70s) would henceforth be judged.

*Shaft* was Hayes' first attempt ever at writing a movie score; he worked, initially, from a 16mm copy of three scenes, basing what became the opening theme on a short piece of wah-wah guitar inflected funk he'd written, but never previously found a use for. Touring at the same time as he worked on the score ensured, Hayes and his band (now featuring James Alexander in place of bassist Hudson) remained fresh; so did the external influences that Hayes brought to bear on the project, "a lot of what happened in the '60s, the civil rights struggle, the Vietnam issues and so forth." Quoted in the Blaxploitation movie history *What It Is, What It Was*, Hayes continued, "Society was more liberal and having more fun at that time. I tried to make the tracks like that."

He succeeded beyond anybody's wildest dreams. In 1972, Hayes became the first African-American ever to receive an Oscar for Best Musical Score. He also picked up two Grammys and a Golden Globe, but he insisted that "one of the greatest compliments I ever got [was when] Dominic Frontiere, whom I respected so much and looked up to for what he had done in films, walked in and fell on his knees and kissed the back of my hand. He said, Thank you. Thank you for taking us out of the dark ages.'"

*Shaft* was unique, not in terms of its actual mechanics (a good movie soundtrack *should* reflect what's going on on-screen), but in its dynamics. "There was a lot of freedom," Hayes explained. "You were disciplined because you had to match a lot of dramatic cues on the film. But you had creative freedom to interpret how you felt they should be played against the scene. Since I did not have formal training, I was not restricted [in] what I could hear, what I could imagine. That's why the sound is so unique." But even he never dreamed that "almost everything that followed for almost a decade had that same kind of sound, like *Shaft*. It revolutionized music in film and . . . television."

It also sent Hayes' own career skyward. *Black Moses*, his next album, went straight to #1 despite its proportions—a double set, it included heavily stylized versions of "Never can Say Goodbye," Gamble and Huff's "Never Gonna Give You Up" and Curtis Mayfield's "Need To Belong to Someone," alongside a Bacharach-David song, "(They Long To Be) Close to You," which had already become massive once that year, for the Carpenters. (Hayes was a special guest on Bacharach's 1972 UK TV special, performing "Windows of the World.")

Hayes toured through 1971–72, including the headline spot at the Stax label's Wattstax festival at the Los Angeles Coliseum. Unfortunately his role in the movie/LP documentary of the event was limited after MGM, distributors of *Shaft*, sued over the inclusion of great swathes of that soundtrack. However, Hayes was nevertheless represented by a gargantuan version of "Ain't No Sunshine," an all-but unrecognizable piano-led rap suddenly crashing into the signature theme.

Hayes also established his own Isaac Hayes Foundation, set up to create low income housing for the poor and elderly. In the interim, a reissue of his debut album kept the charts warm while America awaited his own next release, another double album set, *Live at the Sahara Tahoe*.

Accompanied again by Pitts, Snell, Hall and Jones, plus William Murphy (bs), Sidney Kirk (pno), an eight-piece horn section led by Floyd Newman, the Hot Buttered Soul Ltd. vocal group and the Al Trouti Orchestra, Hayes' show was superslick, deliciously paced and arranged, incontinent with virtuosity and showmanship. As a physical experience, it was amazing; as a musical experience, on the other hand, it was maybe a little too much of a good thing. The album spent just two weeks at the top of the R&B chart, then slipped fast. Before the end of the year, Hayes responded with a new studio set, *Joy*; it peaked at #2, but still picked up a gold disc.

In 1974 Hayes moved into acting, appearing alongside Lino Ventura and Fred Williamson in *Three Tough Guys*; he followed up with a role in Jonathan Kaplan's *Truck Turner*, turning in competent soundtracks to both. Acting soon became at least as important to Hayes as his music. Indeed, by the mid'90s, he was adamant that younger fans knew him more for his thespian abilities than his records. Nevertheless, he maintained a relatively high profile through the '70s, breaking with Stax in 1975 following a dispute over royalties and launching his own label, Hot Buttered Soul. But *Chocolate Chip*, his first release for that label, was also to be his final #1.

Hot Buttered Soul folded in 1977 and Hayes moved to Polydor, at the same time quitting Memphis for a new base in Atlanta. He was regularly appearing on television now, guesting in *The Rockford Files* and *Starsky and Hutch*; he also starred in John Carpenter's *Escape from New York* movie. His records were dipping into the disco movement with some success, but he was also fighting a losing battle against mounting financial problems—at one point he was said to be six million dollars in debt. In 1979, Hayes filed for bankruptcy, ironically, around the same time as he enjoyed his biggest hit in six years.

"When disco hit, I heard myself everywhere, in so many songs and styles, until I decided to chill. Finally, I took the unlikeliest disco song, an old Roy Hamilton tune, and gave it a new dance spin. It worked," recalled Hayes. Recorded with Millie Jackson, "Do You Wanna Make Love" returned Hayes to the R&B Top 20, while an accompanying album of duets made #9. Two albums later, however, Hayes retired from music to concentrate on acting.

Hayes made his first comebacks in 1986, leading off with the latest in a long succession of recordings titled "Ike's Raps"—semi-lectures on the evils of the day, in this instance crack cocaine. The accompanying *U-Turn* and *Love Attack* albums were not a success, however, and Hayes returned to acting, resurfacing only to cut a 1991 duet with Barry White, the lascivious "Dark and Lovely."

The mid-'90s brought another outbreak of Hayes-mania, at the hands of a rap and hip-hop community, which never tired of sampling his work. Hayes released two new albums in 1995, a smooth vocal set, *Branded*, and a driving instrumental album suitably titled *Raw and Refined*, drawn from a stockpile of grooves and rhythms dating back to the late '60s. The opening "Birth of Shaft" was itself drawn from the original sessions for that soundtrack.

Most remarkable of all, however, Hayes finally celebrated another #1 single. As one of the vocal stars of the cult cartoon *South Park*, where he gave voice to the school cook, Chef, Hayes topped the UK chart, in December 1998, with the risque "Chocolate Salty Balls." Further attention, of course, came his way following the 2000 release of a new *Shaft* movie, complete with Hayes' own spectacular remake of the original theme.

### ISAAC HAYES COMPLETE DISCOGRAPHY
### SINGLES/CHART LOG
1964 Sweet Temptation/Laura (Brunswick)
1965 Blue Goose/? (Volt)
1969 Precious Precious/Going to Chicago Blues (Enterprise)

1969 By The Time I Get to Phoenix (Enterprise—#37 R&B/#37 pop)/Walk on By (#13 R&B/#30 pop)
1970 I Stand Accused/I Just Don't Know What To Do with Myself (Enterprise—#23 R&B/#42 pop)
1970 The Look of Love/Ike's Mood (Enterprise)
1971 Never Can Say Goodbye/I Can't Help It If I'm Still in Love with You (Enterprise—#5 R&B/#22 pop)
1971 Theme from Shaft/Cafe Regio's (Enterprise—#2 R&B/#1 pop)
1972 Do Your Thing/Ellie's Love Thing (Enterprise—#3 R&B/#30 pop)
1972 Let's Stay Together/Soulville (Enterprise—#25 R&B/#48 pop)
1972 Theme from the Men/Type Thang (Enterprise—#19 R&B/#38 pop)
1973 (If Loving You Is Wrong)/Rolling Down a Mountainside (Enterprise)
1973 Joy (part one)/(part two) (Enterprise—#7 R&B/#30 pop)
1974 Wonderful/Someone Made You for Me (Enterprise—#18 R&B/#71 pop)
1974 Title Theme/Hung Up on My Baby (Enterprise—#72 R&B)
1975 Chocolate Chip/(instrumental) (HBS/ABC—#13 R&B/#92 pop)
1975 Come Live with Me/Body Language (HBS/ABC—#20 R&B)
1976 Rock Me Easy Baby (part one)/(part two) (HBS/ABC)
1976 Juicy Fruit (Disco Freak) (part one)/(part two) (HBS/ABC)
1977 Out of the Ghetto/It's Heaven to Me (Polydor—#42 R&B/#107 pop)
1978 Moonlight Lovin'/It's Heaven to Me (Polydor—#96 R&B)
1978 Zeke the Freak/If We Ever Needed Peace (Polydor—#19 R&B)
1978 Feel Like Makin' Love (part one)/(part two) (Stax)
1979 Just the Way You Are (part one)/(part two) (Polydor)
1979 Don't Let Go/You Can't Hold Your Woman (Polydor—#11 R&B/#18 pop)
1980 A Few More Kisses To Go/What Does It Take (Polydor—#89 R&B)
1980 I Ain't Never/Love Has Been Good to Us (Polydor—#49 R&B)
1980 It's All in the Game/Wherever You Are (Polydor—#86 R&B/#107 pop)
1981 I'm So Proud/I'm Gonna Make You Love Me (Polydor)
1981 Fugitive/Lifetime Thing (Polydor)
1986 Ike's Rap/Hey Girl (Columbia—#9 R&B)
1987 Thing For You/Thank God for Love (Columbia—#43 R&B)
1987 If You Want My Lovin'/(instrumental) (Columbia)
1988 Showdown/(instrumental) (Columbia—#40 R&B)
1988 Let Me Be Your Everything/Curious (Columbia)
1995 Walk on By/(Al Green cut) (Capitol)

### ISAAC HAYES AND DAVID PORTER
1972 Ain't That Loving You/Baby I'm a Want You (Enterprise—#37 R&B/#86 pop)

### ISAAC HAYES MOVEMENT
1976 Disco Connection/St. Thomas Square (HBS/ABC—#60 R&B)

### ISAAC HAYES AND DIONNE WARWICK
1977 By the Time I Get to Phoenix—I Say a Little Prayer/That's the Way I Like It—Get Down Tonight (HBS/ABC—#65 R&B)

### ISAAC HAYES AND MILLIE JACKSON
1979 Do You Wanna Make Love/I Changed My Mind (Polydor—#30 R&B)
1980 You Never Cross My Mind/Feels like the First Time (Polydor—#78 R&B)

## ISAAC HAYES AND KIM WATERS
1990 Just Be My Lady/? (Warlock—#71 R&B)

## ISAAC HAYES AND BARRY WHITE
1992 Dark and Lovely/Love Is in Your Eyes (A&M—#29 R&B)

## LPs
**6** 1968 Presenting Isaac Hayes (Enterprise) (Atlantic—#25 R&B/ #102 pop)

Reissued as *In The Beginning*.

**10** 1969 Hot Buttered Soul (Enterprise—#1 R&B/#8 pop)

The Hayes formula would grow stale fast, but first time around, it was revelatory. Two pop classics ("Walk on By," "Phoenix"), two originals, drawn tantalizingly out into hyperspace length, half-cinerama, half-sensurround and with orchestration to die for.

**8** 1970 The Isaac Hayes Movement (Enterprise—#1 R&B/#8 pop)

"I Just Don't Know What To Do with Myself" and the Beatles' "Something" are this album's gargantuan feasts, "I Stand Accused" the timeless hit.

**6** 1970 To Be Continued (Enterprise—#1 R&B/#11 pop)

Okay, enough's enough. Just a look at the track listing lets you know what you're getting, elongated versions of "Our Day Will Come," "The Look of Love," "You've Lost That Loving Feeling," and the sensation that once, Hayes reinvented schmaltz, then redeployed it for the boudoir brigade. Now he redefines it and even bedtime seems tiresome.

**9** 1971 Shaft (Enterprise—#1 R&B/#1 pop)

**6** 1972 Black Moses (Enterprise—#1 R&B/#10 pop)

Great title, great cover, and some great raps. But a couple of Curtis Mayfield cuts notwithstanding, no surprises.

**5** 1973 Live at the Sahara Tahoe (Enterprise—#1 R&B/#14 pop)

**5** 1973 Joy (Enterprise—#2 R&B/#16 pop)

**4** 1974 Tough Guys (soundtrack) (Enterprise)

**4** 1974 Truck Turner (soundtrack) (Enterprise—#17 R&B/#156 pop)

**8** 1975 Chocolate Chip (HBS—#1 R&B/#18 pop)

Hayes' finest album since *Shaft*, and five self-composed tracks at least lurk around the same pastures. "Body Language" has a sultry, dangerous quality, while "Chocolate Chip" packs a lifetime of energy into a ten-minute groove cruelly split between vocal and instrumental versions.

**7** 1975 Disco Connection (HBS—#19 R&B/#85 pop)

**8** 1976 Groove-a-Thon (HBS—#11 R&B/#45 pop)

You don't realize how much disco stole from "Shaft" until you hear Hayes stealing it back. Lyrically limited and musically minimal, *Groove-a-Thon* is a triumph of tongue-in-cheek restraint, and great to get down to as well.

**7** 1976 Juicy Fruit (Disco Freak) (HBS—#18 R&B/#124 pop)

**7** 1977 New Horizon (Polydor—#26 R&B/#78 pop)

**6** 1978 For the Sake of Love (Polydor—#15 R&B/#75 pop)

**6** 1979 Don't Let Go (Polydor—#9 R&B/#39 pop)

**5** 1980 And Once Again (Polydor—#26 R&B/#59 pop)

**6** 1981 Lifetime Thing (Polydor)

**4** 1986 U-Turn (Columbia—#32 R&B)

Misjudged cross between wise elder statesman and wearisome elder brother, although the band is hot.

**5** 1988 Love Attack (Columbia—#70 R&B)

**6** 1995 Branded (Pointblank—#75 R&B)

An interesting, if restrained, album, but it does include a delicious reworking of "Hyperbolicsyllabic . . ."

**8** 1995 Raw and Refined (Pointblank)

An incredible album—arguably the bulk of Hayes' career has been funk by default, but here (raw and *un*-refined would have been a better target), the specter that overhangs every album is unleashed, with the murderous "Birth of Shaft" good enough to win inclusion on Hayes' own next "best of" style collection.

## ISAAC HAYES AND DIONNE WARWICK
**5** 1977 A Man and a Woman (HBS—#20 R&B/#49 pop)

## ISAAC HAYES AND MILLIE JACKSON
**6** 1979 Royal Rappin's (Polydor—#17 R&B/#80 pop)

Two voices, one word, sex.

## SELECTED COMPILATIONS AND ARCHIVE RELEASES
**8** 1975 The Best of Isaac Hayes (Enterprise—#57 R&B/#165 pop)

**6** 1975 Use Me (Enterprise)

**6** 1977 Memphis Movement (Enterprise)

**8** 1978 Hot Bed (Enterprise)

**8** 1978 The Isaac Hayes Chronicles (Enterprise)

The latter pair, taken together, offer the best overall examination of Hayes' Stax years, *Chronicles* rounding up the hits, *Hot Bed* picking up some rarities and album cuts.

**2** 2000 Ultimate Collection (Hip-O)

Disappointing overall, 16 tracks attempt to chronicle Hayes' entire career, but omit too many classics ("I Stand Accused" paramount) in favor of lesser, later material.

## SELECTED SAMPLES
A Few More Kisses To Go — Redman: Tonight's Da Night (1992)

A Friends Place — Red Hot Lover Tone: Give It Up (remix) (1992)

Blue's Crib — Compton's Most Wanted: Another Victim (1993)

Breakthrough — Gang Starr: Tonz 'O' Gunz (1994)

Bumpy's Lament — Blaque: Leny (1999)

Bumpy's Lament — Mobb Deep: Right Back at You (1995)

Buns O Plenty — Compton's Most Wanted: Straight Checkn' Em (1991)

Buns O Plenty — KRS-One: Wannabemceez (1995)

Do Your Thing — Big Daddy Kane: Smooth Operator (1989)

Do Your Thing — Bushwick Bill: Already Dead (1995)

Do Your Thing — Compton's Most Wanted: N 2 Deep (1992)

Do Your Thing — Lifers Group: Out of Sight, out of Mind (1993)

Hyperbolicsyllabicsesquedalymistic — Above the Law; Just Kickin' Lyrics (1990)

Hyperbolicsyllabicsesquedalymistic — DJ Quik: Born nd Raised in Compton (1991)

Hyperbolicsyllabicsesquedalymistic — Ice Cube: I Gotta Say What Up!! (1991)

Hyperbolicsyllabicsesquedalymistic — NWA: Prelude (1991)

Hyperbolicsyllabicsesquedalymistic — Nemesis: Temple of Boom (1993)

Hyperbolicsyllabicsesquesalymistic — Public Enemy: Black Steel in the Hour of Chaos (1988)

Hyperbolicsyllabicsesquesalymistic — Soul Assassins featuring Dr. Dre: Puppet Master (1997)

House of Beauty — Ice Cube: Turn Off the Radio (1990)

Ike's Mood 1/You've Lost That Lovin' Feelin' — The Alkaholiks: Mary Jane (1993)

Ike's Mood 1/You've Lost That Lovin' Feelin' — Biz Markie: Make the Music with Your Mouth Biz (1988)

Ike's Mood 1/You've Lost That Lovin' Feelin' — Biz Markie: Cool V's Tribute to Scratching (1988)

Ike's Mood 1/You've Lost That Lovin' Feelin' — Das EFX: East Coast (1992)

Ike's Mood 1/You've Lost That Lovin' Feelin' — Jeru The Damaja: Jungle Music (1994)

Ike's Mood 1 You've Lost That Lovin' Feelin' — JVC Force: Styl n' Lyrics (1988)

Ike's Mood 1/You've Lost That Lovin' Feelin' — LL Cool J: Six Minutes of Pleasure (remix) (1990)

Ike's Mood 1/You've Lost That Lovin' Feelin' — The Lox: Bitches from Eastwick (1998)

Ike's Mood 1/You've Lost That Lovin' Feelin' — Mary J. Blige: I Love You (1994)

Ike's Mood 1/You've Lost That Lovin' Feelin' — Massive Attack: One Love (1991)

Ike's Mood 1/You've Lost That Lovin' Feelin' — Naughty By Nature: Knock 'Em out Da Box (1993)

Ike's Mood 1/You've Lost That Lovin' Feelin' — Ron C: On and On (1992)

Ike's Rap III — Portishead: Glory Box (1995)

Ike's Rap III — Tricky: Hell Is Round the Corner (1995)

Joy — Big Daddy Kane: Float (1991)

Joy — Biz Markie: Young Girl Bluez (1993)

Joy — Boogie Down Productions: Poisonous Products (1992)

Joy — Compton's Most Wanted: I'm Wit Dat (1990)

Joy — Destiny's Child featuring Wyclef Jean & Pras: Illusion

Joy — Geto Boys: Mind Playing Tricks on Me (1991)

Joy — Geto Girlz: My Many's Playin' Tricks on Me

Joy — Ice Cube: You Know How We Do It (1993)

Joy — Eric B. & Rakim: Keep the Beat (1992)

Joy — Jungle Brothers: Behind the Bush (1988)

Joy — Kool G Rap: She Loves Me, She Loves Me Not (1989)

Joy — Lifers Group: Jack U Back (So You Wanna Be a Gangsta) (1993)

Joy — Mase: Puff's Intro (1997)

Joy — Massive Attack: Lately (1991)

Joy — Scarface: Mind Playin' Tricks (1994)

Joy — TLC: Creep (remix) (1994)

Joy — Yo-Yo: Home Girl Don't Play Dat (1992)

No Name Bar — DJ Magic Mike: Feel the Bass 2 (1997)

No Name Bar — The DOC: Let the Bass Go (1989)

No Name Bar — E Forty: Rat Heads (1994)

No Name Bar — 2Pac: Souljah's Story (1993)

Our Day Will Come — Massive Attack: Exchange (1998)

The Look of Love — Compton's Most Wanted: Niggaz Strugglin' (1992)

The Look of Love — Jay Z: Can I Live (1996)

The Look of Love — Lost Boyz: Is This Da Part? (1996)

The Look of Love — LL Cool J: Hollis to Hollywood (1995)

The Look of Love — Snoop Doggy Dogg: Gz Up, Hoes Down (1993)

The Look of Love — Special Ed: Neva Go Back (1995)

The Look of Love — Smif-N-Wessun: Stand Strong (1995)

Theme from Shaft — Jay-Z: Resevoir Dogs (1998)

Theme from Shaft — LL Cool J: Get Down (1987)

Theme from Shaft — Public Enemy: Caught, Can We Get a Witness? (1988)

Theme from Shaft — Young MC: Know How (1989)

Walk from Regio — Beastie Boys: Sounds of Science (1989)

Walk from Regio — Camp Lo: Nicky Barnes AKA It's Alright (1997)

Walk from Regio — Grooverider: On the Double (1998)

Walk on Ey — Bushwick Bill: Only God Knows (1995)

Walk on Ey — Compton's Most Wanted: Hood Took Me Under (1992)

Walk on Ey — Cypress Hill: Whatta You Know (1996)

Walk on By — Faith Evans: No Other Love (1995)

Walk on By — MF Doom: Dead Bent (1999)

Walk on By — Notorious BIG: Warning (1994)

Walk on By — One Twelve: Call My Name (1996)

Walk on By — Sounds of Blackness: Everything Is Gonna Be Alright (1994)

Walk on By — 2Pac: Me Against the World (1995)

Walk on By — Westside Connection: Do You Like Criminals? (1996)

## EDDIE HAZEL

**BORN:** *4/10/50 Brooklyn, NY; died: 12/23/92*

Having moved to Plainfield, NJ, as a child, the young Hazel was one of a number of juvenile musicians who gathered in one another's backyards to jam the hits of the day. He immediately attracted attention—another of the young aspirants, bassist Billy Nelson, recalled seeing the then-12-year-old Hazel play the Surfaris' "Wipe Out." "All the guitar players up there took a lead solo. When it came time for Eddie to take [one], that motherfucker played some totally other shit. I knew then that he was good."

With friend Harvey McGee, Hazel and Nelson formed the Wonders, their repertoire concentrating on Motown covers. During the mid-'60s, the Wonders played regularly around Plainfield; the highlight of their career was the holiday weekends when promotor Sammy Campbell (of local stars The Del-Larks) organized a show highlighting the best of local musical talent. The Del-Larks and George Clinton's Parliaments headlined, the Wonders appeared further down the bill.

By 1967, Hazel's local reputation had taken him to Newark, where he began working with producer George Blackwell. Nelson, meanwhile, joined the Parliaments as they toured to promote their debut smash "Testify"; he brought Hazel into the band that summer, as the group commenced its drift into the unique psychedelic funk that would, by 1969, see the group rename itself (and its music) Funkadelic.

Hazel's scything performance on "I'll Bet You," the second single, and the restrained wah-wah backwash to its follow-up, "I've Got a Thing," set the stage for the remainder of his stay with Funkadelic, a span encompassing the stream of self-defining albums bracketed by *Funkadelic* (1970) and *Maggot Brain* (1971).

There, across the epic ten-minute "Free Your Mind and Your Ass Will Follow" and "Maggot Brain" (from the albums of the same name) and more, the fearless Hazel not only redefined the role of the guitar in funk. He impacted upon rock 'n' roll with a quiet passion that only Jimi Hendrix (who died in London in September 1970, the same month Funkadelic's debut album was released in Britain) and the Isley Brothers' similarly mercurial Ernie Isley came close to emulating. Before Hazel came along, Bootsy Collins mused, "Black rock guitar players on the radio had a sound that was really cheesy compared to the rock heavyweights." Thereafter, even giants like Jimmy Page, Jeff Beck and Ritchie Blackmore knew they'd met their match.

Famously, Hazel's signature tune, "Maggot Brain," came about after Clinton asked him to think of the saddest thing he could (Hazel imagined the death of his mother), then express it through his guitar. In one take, Hazel laid down a ten-minute minor key anthem; remains synonymous not only with his name, but with the guitar itself.

Hazel's time with Funkadelic was tumultuous. Together with bandmates Nelson, Tiki Fulwood and Bernie Worrell, he quit Funkadelic in spring 1971, to work with Ruth Copeland and Chairman of the Board. Hazel returned for Clinton's fall US tour (source of the *Funkadelic Live . . . 1971* album) and also played some of the sessions that produced 1972's transitional *America Eats Its Young* album.

It was clear, however, that his blisteringly abrasive playing style was not part of the group's future direction; and that his equally uncompromising lifestyle was going to lead him even further astray. Never afraid to experiment with drugs ("maggot brain" was, in fact, one of Hazel's nicknames among his bandmates). Hazel's unpredictability reached its nadir when he was convicted of assault after biting an air hostess while high on the drug angel dust.

Hazel was sentenced to a spell in Lampoc Prison; 1973's *Cosmic Slop* album thus became Funkadelic's first to be recorded without him—and their most conventional sounding release yet. He reappeared for *Standing on the Verge of Getting It On*, adopting the pseudonym Grace Cook (his mother's name) and co-writing much of the album. But he remained excruciatingly unpredictable. Again quitting P-Funk later in 1974, he auditioned for the Chambers Brothers, at Boston's Sugar Shack—and was turned down. Apparently, he was so locked inside his own world that he was still playing long after the other musicians finished the song.

Nevertheless, he was on fine form when he and Nelson joined the Temptations for their *A Song for You* (1975) and *Wings of Love* (1976) albums, while 1975 also saw Hazel move back into the mothership's orbit when he contributed an electrifying solo to "Whatever Makes My Baby Feel Good" (from Parliament's *Up for the Down Stroke* album). He also had a hand in writing several tracks on the *Hardcore Jollies* and *Tales of Kidd Funkadelic* albums.

Work began on a Hazel solo album in 1976. Clinton and Hazel produced, while the accompanying musicians were drawn, of course, from throughout the P-Funk universe. Material ranged even further afield, from Bootsy to the Beatles, all stacking up to create one of the defining P-Funk albums.

Over the next two years, Hazel appeared on several further P-Funk albums, including Worrell's debut, the Brides of Funkenstein's sophomore set and Funkadelic's own *Uncle Jam* and *Electric Spanking* sets. Harking back, as it did, to the abandon of early Funkadelic, his collaboration with Sly Stone on the latter album's "Funk Gets Stronger II" was a fitting swansong. In 1978–79 Hazel worked with Bonnie Pointer, contributing to her first two Motown solo albums (*Bonnie Pointer* and *Bonnie Pointer II*).

Hazel remained alongside Clinton during the first half of the '80s, working both on his albums and on sundry spin-offs. In 1983, Hazel co-produced several tracks with former Parlet vocalist Mallia Franklin for eventual inclusion on her *Funken Tersepter* album. The guitarist' health, however, was failing; he was racked by stomach problems and, as the decade progressed, Hazel was working less and less. Indeed, at one point he was both penniless and homeless but, when warned by his doctors to give up both drink and drugs, he could only go halfway and stop drinking.

By 1992, Hazel appeared to have turned the corner. Living back at his mother's house in Plainfield, he was actively excited about making music again. Encouraged by this apparent turnaround, Worrell and Nelson introduced him to producer Bill Laswell, who immediately began recording a new Hazel solo album with Worrell, Nelson and another former P-Funk-er, drummer Jerome Brailey.

Hazel was also discussing a Band of Gypsies-type power trio with that trio's own co-founders, Buddy Miles and Billy Cox, while there was talk, too, of a reunion with Clinton. Both projects were set for launch in early 1993. Unfortunately, Hazel could not wait that long. He died from liver failure and internal bleeding on December 23, 1992. Fittingly, his mother had "Maggot Brain" played at the funeral.

Highlights of the Laswell sessions saw the light of day on the *Axiom Funk* album in 1994; two further posthumous releases, the *Jams from the Heart* EP and *Rest in P* album, culled unreleased material from the 1976 solo sessions.

## EDDIE HAZEL COMPLETE DISCOGRAPHY
### SINGLES
1977 California Dreamin'/instrumental (WB)

### EP
1994 Jams from the Heart (P-Vine—Jap)

### LP
**9** **1977 Games, Dames and Guitar Thangs (WB)**
Thoroughbred genius and one of THE greatest P-Funk spin-offs of all. A cover of the Beatles' "I Want You (She's So Heavy)" allows Hazel to show off his effortless command of the rock idiom, without really straying from Funk Central. A spacey reinvention of the Mamas & the Papas' "California Dreaming" turns winsome hippy into soaring lover, while "Physical Love," is remixed from Bootsy Collins' first album, to spotlight Hazel's breathtaking guitar.

### SELECTED COMPILATIONS AND ARCHIVE RELEASES
**6** **1994 Rest in P (P-Vine—Jap)**
Neither a study in funk nor overtly guitar-fired, essentially a jazz-inflected set highlighted by the epic blues (and sole vocal track) "We Three," co-written with Clinton. Overall, it's okay, but if you're searching for why Eddie Hazel was so great, this is not the place to start. (The album incorporates cuts from the *Jams from the Heart* EP)

Frantic Moment—Gang Starr: Take Two & Pass (1992)

## HOT CHOCOLATE
**FORMED:** *1969, London, England*
**ORIGINAL LINE-UP:** *Errol Brown (b. Jamaica—vcls), Harvey Hinsley (b. Mitcham, England—gtr), Patrick Olive (bs), Larry Ferguson (b. Nassau, Bahamas—kybds), Tony Connor (b. Romford, England—drms)*

Hot Chocolate was the vision of vocalist Brown and his songwriting partner Tony Wilson, two London teenagers whose big break came in 1969, when they formulated a version of John Lennon's "Give Peace a Chance" and approached the Beatles' Apple organization for permission to record the altered lyrics. Their request came to the attention of Lennon himself, who met with the duo and offered the pair a one-off deal with Apple itself. An Apple secretary, Mavis Smith, came up with a name for the duo, the Hot Chocolate Band, and "Give Peace a Chance" was released in the UK in October 1969.

It did little, but, armed with the Lennon seal of approval, Brown and Wilson contacted Mickie Most, one of the country's leading independent producers, then in the process of putting his own RAK label together. They had a new song, "Bet Yer Life I Do," that they thought was perfect for one of his acts, '60s bubble-boppers Herman's Hermits. Most agreed; indeed, all three of the songs they played him at their first meeting would swiftly be recorded, by the Hermits, another former Beatles protege Mary Hopkin ("Think About Your Children") and by (the newly abbreviated) Hot Chocolate themselves. "Love Is Life" became their first single for RAK and reached #6 in the UK in August, 1970.

From the outset, Hot Chocolate's musical palate was never to be confined to one style, ranging from straight pop to punchy disco, from moody ballads to a captivating funk-lite, fronted by Brown's incredible voice. Throughout, the unifying factor was Brown and Wilson's readiness to broach subjects they felt passionately about. In 1973, successive British 45s dealt with politics ("Rumours") and racism ("Brother Louie"—covered in the US by the Stories). The title track to their debut album, 1975's *Cicero Park*, took an outspoken stance against pollution; while 1974's UK #3 "Emma" merged funeral drums with psychedelic guitars for one of the all-time great death songs. A decade later, gothic rockers The Sisters of Mercy included the song in their live set without raising a single eyebrow.

It was Hot Chocolate's adaptability that saw them survive not only the departure of songwriter Wilson (he wasn't replaced; Brown was more than capable of stepping into the breach), but also a number of career troughs that might have left lesser temperaments foundering. When "Emma" was followed by the flops "Cheri Babe" and "Blue Night," Hot Chocolate simply bounced back with 1975's horn-driven floor shaker "Disco Queen." They followed that through with the orchestrated Curtis Mayfield-influenced "Say a Little Prayer," then slammed to #2 in Britain with the pop-funk classic "You Sexy Thing," a song they'd previously buried away on the B-side of "Blue Night."

"Disco Queen" became Hot Chocolate's first US hit, during summer 1975; "You Sexy Thing" followed, soaring into the pop Top Three. Two further singles, the grinding, bass-heavy "Don't Stop It Now" and "So You Win Again" (their first UK #1), were less successful, but again the band proved their resilience by storming the Top Ten with 1978's "Every1's a Winner"—an utterly irresistible wall of funk with a guitar sound straight out of vintage Sly Stone.

That track marked the peak of Hot Chocolate's success, both in the US and the UK. Nevertheless, the act remained reliable hitmakers in their homeland until as late as 1984, while remixes of "You Sexy Thing," "Every1's A Winner" and 1982's "It Started with a Kiss" maintained their chart profile into the early '90s. Hot Chocolate themselves broke up in 1985, after which Brown launched a short-lived solo career.

### HOT CHOCOLATE COMPLETE DISCOGRAPHY
### SINGLES/CHART LOG

1969 Give Peace a Chance/Living Without Tomorrow (Apple)
1972 You Could Have Been a Lady/Everybody's Laughing (RAK)
1972 I Believe in Love/Caveman Billy (RAK)
1972 Mary Anne/Ruth (RAK)
1973 Brother Louie/I Want To Be Free (RAK)
1973 Rumors/? (Bell)
1974 Emma/A Love like Yours (Bell)
1975 Emma/A Love like Yours (Big Tree)
1975 Disco Queen/Makin' Music (Big Tree—#40 R&B/#28 pop)
1975 You Sexy Thing/Amazing Skin Song (Big Tree—#6 R&B/#3 pop)
1976 Don't Stop It Now/Beautiful Lady (Big Tree—#43 R&B/#42 pop)
1976 Heaven Is in the Back Seat of My Cadillac/? (Big Tree)
1977 So You Win Again/Part of being with You (Big Tree—#82 R&B/#31 pop)
1977 Man To Man/? (Big Tree)
1978 Every1's a Winner/Power of Love (Infinity—#7 R&B/#6 pop)
1979 Going Through the Motions/Don't Turn It Off (Infinity—#43 R&B/#53 pop)
1979 I Just Love What You're Doing/Congas Man (Infinity)
1979 Mindless Boogie/Dance (Infinity)

1982 Are You Getting Enough Happiness/One Night's Not Enough (EMI America—#50 R&B/#65 pop)
1983 It Started with a Kiss/Bed Games (EMI America)

*LPs*
**7** 1975 Cicero Park (Big Tree—#55 pop)
The effervescent "Disco Queen" notwithstanding, most notable for the sultry "Emma" and the sinister "Brother Louie," the band's most individual hits and those that prove (contrary to much of the rest of the record) that Hot Chocolate are something more than a gently funky pop group.
**5** 1975 Hot Chocolate (Big Tree—#34 R&B/#41 pop)
**3** 1976 Man to Man (Big Tree—#172 pop)
**4** 1978 Every1's a Winner (Infinity—#18 R&B/#31 pop)
The title track and "So You Win Again" vie with the "Emma"-like "Confetti Day" for the most satisfying tracks; elsewhere, the album wallows just a little too much in discoid balladry.
**8** 1979 Going Through the Motions (Infinity—#112 pop)
Hard hitting cynicism permeates the grooves, peaking with the less-than-frivolous "Mindless Boogie," an eight-minute summation of all that the last few years had wrought, set to a bubbling bass beat and a taste of the band's later interest in synths. The live "Congas Man" packs a punch, too.
**5** 1980 Class (RAK—UK)
**6** 1982 Mystery (EMI America)
**4** 1983 Love Shot (RAK—UK)

### SELECTED COMPILATIONS AND ARCHIVE RELEASES
**6** 1977 10 Greatest Hits (Big Tree)
**8** 1979 20 Hottest Hits (EMI—UK)
Classy collection that rounded up all the band's hits so far, adding the deliciously conspiratorial "Rumours" to the litany of genuine stand-outs.
**7** 1993 Every 1's a Winner (EMI)
A sensible summation of the band's US career, omitting only one crucial single ("Rumours"), but avoiding many of the less well-advised later moves.

### SELECTED SAMPLES
You Sexy Thing — A Tribe Called Quest: Can I Kick It (1990)

## HORNY HORNS, see MACEO PARKER, FRED WESLEY

## HOT CITY BUMP BAND
**FORMED:** *1973, Melbourne, Australia*
**ORIGINAL LINE-UP:** *Chuck McKinney (b. Chicago, IL—vcls), Margaret McKinney (vcls), John Adolphus (gtr), David Green (bs), David McMaster (org), Mick Holden (drms), Robert Ellis (b. West Indies—cngas)*

Australia's first ever funk group was formed by American Chuck McKinney and his Australian-born wife Margaret, members of the rock-dominated Melbourne production of *Hair*. Assailing the Melbourne club circuit in late 1973, the band was originally greeted with shock and incomprehension; however, a heavily stylized version of the Beatles' "Come Together" proved an immense live favorite and, having signed to the Wizard label, it became their debut single in mid-1974.

Steadily building local support via their live shows, the Hot City Bump Band scored Melbourne city hits with further singles "Time Is on Your Side" and "Do What You Wanna Do," before early summer 1975, brought their debut album, *Come Together*.

That fall, he group overcame the departure of founding guitarist John Adolphus; he was replaced by Noel Davies for Australian tours with Osibisa, the Temptations and Gladys Knight & the Pips. A new single, "Ain't No Use," appeared in January 1976; just days later, however, the Hot City Bump Band announced they were breaking up.

The McKinneys and bassist David Green promptly formed a new group, City Strut, but it faded unrecorded. Chuck McKinney then launched a solo career with a smooth version of Harold Melvin's "If You Don't Know Me By Now," forming his own eponymous band before joining Margaret as a session vocalist.

*LP*

**8** **1975 Come Together (Wizard—Aus)**
Fiery debut reflects the band's birth and baptism on the hardnosed Melbourne club circuit.

## INVICTUS RECORDS

Although the Invictus and Hot Wax labels formed by renegade Motown songwriters Brian and Eddie Holland and Lamont Dozier (H-D-H) are best regarded today as the repository of some of the finest soul of the early '70s, the label was also home to some dynamite funk—the first album and attendant singles by Parliament, two great sets by Ruth Copeland and the Chairmen of the Board's *Skin I'm In*.

It also became a training ground for one of the great unsung heroes of the then-embryonic P-Funk empire, writer/producer Ron Dunbar—untried when he and partner Edith Wayne first saw their name on a record label; unstoppable thereafter. "Give Me Just a Little More Time," the first smash by Chairmen of the Board, and Freda Payne's impossibly magnificent "Band of Gold," established the team, while Wright herself also launched a singing career in her own right under the alias of the Honey Comb. (Wright was sister to singer Darlene Love.)

Other recruits were equally inspired. English folk singer Copeland, wife of another former Motown staffer, Jeffrey Bowen, was a member of New Play. Freda Payne's sister, Scherrie, arrived with the Glass House. Steve Mancha brought two groups to the party, 8th Day and the wonderfully named 100 Proof Aged in Soul, while the label houseband, McKinley Jackson and the Politicians, built up a following in their own right after their one-and-only album arrived packing heat in the shape of "The World We Live In."

Two years and just 45 singles old, by 1971 Invictus/Hot Wax had clocked up a staggering 34 Top 100 hits, and H-D-H were on their way to launching a third label, Music Machine. Considerably less successful at the time, that concern's Just Brothers can today claim to be one of the best known acts in the entire roster, courtesy of Fat Boy Slim's "Rockefeller Skank," which sampled their "Sliced Tomatoes."

The Invictus bubble burst slowly and, ironically, under circumstances not dissimilar to those that had precipitated H-D-H's departure from Motown in the first place. A dispute over artistic control saw Freda Payne go on strike for much of 1971–72. Chairman of the Board launched litigation against the company in 1972; the following year, the Holland brothers initiated legal proceedings against Dozier after he quit the team to become a staff producer at ABC—taking Payne and McKinley Jackson with him. Four years earlier, Motown chief Berry Gordy had done likewise when H-D-H jumped ship.

Although the label continued to produce some remarkable records, most notably (again) Chairmen of the Board's hard funking and almost gratuitously aggressive *Skin I'm In*, by late 1973 both Hot Wax and Music Machine had folded. Invictus, too, was soon in limbo (it briefly flickered back to life during 1976–77, but to no avail), and the Hollands returned to Motown.

### INVICTUS LABEL LISTING: THE CLASSIC YEARS 1969–72
### SINGLES
9071 The Glass House- Crumbs off the Table/Bad Bill of Goods
9072 The New Play: The Music Box/Gift of Me
9073 Freda Payne: Unhooked Generation/Easiest Way To Fall
9074 Chairmen of the Board: Give Me Just a Little More Time/Since the Days of Pigtales
9075 Freda Payne: Band of Gold/Easiest Way To Fall
9076 Glass House: I Can't Be You (You Can't Be Me)/He's in My Life

9077 A Parliament Thang: I Call My Baby Pussycat/Little Old Country Boy

9078 Chairmen of the Board: (You've Got Me)Dangling on a String/I'll Come Crawling

9079 Chairmen of the Board: Everything's Tuesday/Patches

9080 Freda Payne: Deeper and Deeper/The Unhooked Generation

9081 Chairmen of the Board: Pay to the Piper/Bless You

9082 Glass House: Stealing Moments/If It Ain't Love

9083 Barrino Brothers: Trapped in a Love/When Love Was a Child

9084 Barrino Brothers: I Shall Not Be Moved/When Love Was a Child

9085 Freda Payne: Cherish What Is Dear to You (While It Is Near to You)/They Don't Owe Me a Thing

9086 Chairmen of the Board: Chairman of the Board/When Will She Tell Me She Needs Me

9087 The 8th Day: She's Not Just Another Woman/I Can't Fool Myself

9088 Ruth Copeland: Hare Krishna/No Commitment

9089 Chairmen of the Board: Hanging On (to) a Memory/Tracked and Trapped

9090 Glass House: Touch Me Jesus/If It Ain't Love It Don't Matter

9091 Parliament: Red Hot Mama/Little Ole Country Boy

9092 Freda Payne: Bring the Boys Home/I Shall Not Be Moved

9093 General Johnson: I'm in Love Darling/Savannah Lady

9094 Lucifer: Old Mother Nature/What I Am

9095 Parliament: Breakdown/Little Ole Country Boy

9096 Ruth Copeland: Gimme Shelter/No Commitment

9097 Glass House: Look What We've Done to Love/Heaven's There To Guide Us

9098 8th Day: You've Got To Crawl/It's Instrumental To Be Free

9099 Chairmen of the Board: Try on My Love For Size/Working on a Building of Love

9100 Freda Payne: You Brought the Joy/Suddenly It's Yesterday

9101 John Billy West: Nothing but a Devil/Yeah I'm the Devil

9102 Billie Sands: Solo/I Don't Want To Lose a Good Thing

9103 Chairmen of the Board: Men Are Getting Scarce/Bravo! Hurray!

9104 Barrino Brothers: I Had It All/I Shall Not Be Moved

9105 Chairmen of the Board: Elmo James/Bittersweet

9106 General Johnson: All We Need Is Understanding/Savannah Lady

9107 8th Day: If I Could See the Light/(instrumental)

9108 Lucifer: We Gotta Go/Don't You

9109 Freda Payne: I'm Not Getting Any Better/The Road We Didn't Take

9110 Holland-Dozier: Don't Leave Me/(instrumental)

9111 The Glass House: Let It Flow/Playing Games

9112 Harrison Kennedy: Sunday Morning People/Up—The Organization

9113 Lucifer: Old Mother Nature/Bloodshot Eyes

9114 Scherrie Payne: VIP/It Ain't the World

9115 Melvin Davis: I'm Worried/Just as Long

9116 Danny Woods: Let Me Ride/It Didn't Take Long

9117 8th Day: Eeny-Meeny-Miny-Moe/Rocks in My Head

9118 Glass House: Giving Up the Ring/Let It Flow

9119 Harrison Kennedy: Come Together/Sunday Morning People

9120 Ty Hunter: Hey There Lonely Girl/I Don't See Me in Your Arms

9121 Barrino Brothers: I Had It All/Try It, You'll Like It

9122 Chairmen of the Board: Everybody's Got a Song To Sing/Working on a Building of Love

9123 Parliament: Come in out \of the Rain/Little Ole Country Boy

9124 8th Day: I Gotta Get Home/Good Book

9125 Holland-Dozier: Why Can't We Be Lovers/Don't Leave Me

9126 Chairmen of the Board: Let Me Down Easy/I Can't Find Myself

9127 unissued

9128 Freda Payne: He's in My Life/Through the Memory of My Mind

9129 Glass House: Thanks I Needed That/I Don't See Me in Your Eyes Anymore

9130 Barrino Brothers: Livin' High off the Goodness of Your Love/(instrumental)

9131 unissued

9132 Danny Woods: Everybody's Tippin'/Roller Coaster

9133 Holland-Dozier: Don't Leave Me Starvin' for Your Love (part one)/(part two)

## LPs

7300 Chairmen of the Board: Give Me Just a Little More Time

7301 Freda Payne: Band of Gold

7302 Parliament: Osmium

7303 Ruth Copeland: Self Portrait

7304 Chairmen of the Board: In Session

7305 Glass House: Inside the Glass House

7306 The 8th Day: 8th Day

7307 Freda Payne: Contact

7308 Barrino Brothers: I Shall Not Be Moved

7309 Lucifer: Lucifer

7310 unissued

7311 Lucifer: Black Mass

9801 Chairmen of the Board: Bittersweet

9802 Ruth Copeland: I Am What I Am

9803 General Johnson: Generally Speaking

9804 Freda Payne: Best of Freda Payne

9805 unissued (Glass House)

9806 Harrison Kennedy: Hypnotic Music

9807 various artists: Invictus' Greatest Hits

9808 Danny Wood: Aries

9809 8th Day: I Gotta Get Home

9810 Glass House: Thanks, I Needed That

9811 Barrino Brothers: Livin' High off the Goodness

## SELECTED COMPILATIONS AND ARCHIVE RELEASES

**8** 1998 Invictus Chartbusters (Sequel—UK)

This 24-track collection ranges across the catalog, including "Band of Gold" (Freda Payne), "Women's Love Rights" (Laura Lee), "Why Can't We Be Lovers" (Lamont Dozier), "Crumbs off the Table" (Glass House), "Pay to the Piper" (Chairmen of the Board) and "She's Not Just Another Woman" (8th Day).

**7** 1998 Invictus Unconquered: The Best Of, Vol. 1 (Deep Beats—UK)

**7** 1998 Invictus Unconquered: Cherish What Is Dear To You (Sequel—UK)

**8** 1999 Invictus Club Classics (Sequel—UK)

Powered as much by the songs' latter-day resonance as by their original impact, *Club Classics* revolves around cuts that have, via sample or otherwise, resurfaced in the late '80s and '90s. 23 cuts include "Bar B Q Ribs" (Raynel Wynglas), "Music Box" (Ruth Copeland), "Sittin on a Time Bomb" (Lee Charles), "Taster of the Honey" (Jones Girls) and "Crumbs off the Table" (Laura Lee). The Just Brothers' "Sliced Tomatoes," hardly surprisingly, opens the set. Check it out now.

## THE JBs

**FORMED:** *1970, Cincinatti, OH/Columbus, GA*

**ORIGINAL LINE-UP:** *Phelps Collins (gtr), Bootsy Collins (bs), Clayton Gunnels (trum), Robert McCullough (tnr sax), Frank Waddy (drms)*

James Brown's backing band through much of the '70s, the JBs also enjoyed a long and, at times, highly successful career in their own right, chiefly performing instrumentals both written and produced by Brown himself. In that time, the group's lineup changed on numerous occasions. Their name, too, varied as Brown's insatiable appetite for studio work found an outlet in the JBs' own prolificness.

In the process, they established themselves as perhaps the most influential, and surely the most imitated, funk act of the age, a process that peaked when Brown himself, reacting to the Average White Band's apparent wholesale co-opting of the group's sound, rechristened the JBs as the Above Average Black Band and released a parody of AWB's own greatest effort, "Pick up the Pieces."

Their work under Brown's own name notwithstanding, over 40 JBs singles would appear under close to 20 different names (or variations on a name), the vast majority appearing during the 1971–75 period during which the JBs were helmed by Fred Wesley and Maceo Parker. Later in the decade, following that pair's departure to the equally incestuous P-Funk dynasty, releases slowed somewhat, but still the JBs maintained a presence on the schedules.

The original JBs lineup came together in March, 1970, around Cincinnati hopefuls, the Pacesetters, with whom Brown had been involved for around a year. A long-running dispute over wages had seen Brown's existing band arrive at their latest show, in Columbus, GA, refusing to take the stage unless Brown improved their pay. Brown promptly had the Pacesetters flown in from Cincinatti and played the show with them, then sacked the old group.

Brown originally intended calling the crew the New Breed; with further consideration, he plumped for the JBs shortly before his next studio date.

Augmented by trumpeter Daryl Jamison, organist Bobby Byrd and drummer John Starks (St. Clair Pinckney and Fred Wesley returned before year's end), the JBs' first session with Brown, in late April 1970, began as a jam through "Give It Up," which slowly turned into "Get Up, I Feel like Being a Sex Machine." Over the next six months, that particular masterpiece was followed by "Super Bad" and "Get Up, Get into It, Get Involved." The JBs also accompanied Revue singer Vicki Anderson on her singles "Message from the Soul Sisters" and "Super Good," and backed Kay Robinson on "The Lord Will Make a Way Somehow."

A chance to compare the new band and the old came in September 1970, when Brown released the *Sex Machine* album, partly recorded live the previous October in Augusta, GA, and completed with the results of a King Studios session with the JBs. It was not always a pleasing comparison; writing in the liner notes to Brown's *Funk Power* compilation, Brown employee Alan Leeds, recalled, "two weeks into their new jobs, the [band] struck me as everything the classic Brown bands were not—loose, unpolished, occasionally out of tune. . . ."

But then they clicked. With Bootsy Collins deliberately modeling himself partly on Sly & the Family Stone bassist Larry Graham, partly on his own predecessor, Charles Sherrell (according to Brown, it was Sherrell who originated the notion of thumping the strings for extra rhythmic impact), the JBs "forged James Brown's funk into the sound of the '70s." Brown himself noted in his autobiography, "They were studio musicians, so when I hummed out solos and things, they knew how to give me what I wanted."

Less than a month after the "Sex Machine" session, Brown took the group back into the studio to record the first JBs single, "The Grunt"; it was followed by "These Are the JBs" and the first of many pseudonymous releases, "Across the Track," released under the name of the Believers. However, this particular incarnation of the JBs was not to last. Following sessions in January 1971, cutting Brown's "Soul Power" and Lyn Collins' "Wheel of Life," another dispute over money arose and this time, the musicians did not simply threaten to quit. They actually did so.

Brown promptly set about rebuilding the group around those players who remained: Wesley, Byrd, Starks, guitarist Hearlon Martin and saxophonist Pinckney, adding Robert Coleman (gtr), Jimmy Parker (sax), Russell Crimes and Jerome Sanford (trum), Fred Thomas (bs), John Morgan (drms) and Johnny Griffin (kybds) to cut Brown's own "Escape-ism" in early April 1972.

By June, sessions had begun for the next crop of JBs singles, with the wailing sax-led "Pass the Peas." Over the next three months, "My Brother" and the JBs' first R&B Top 20 entry, "Gimme Some More," would be taped. The group also recut a Brown song recorded two years earlier by Hank Ballard, "From the Love Side"—the new version, credited to the Sons of Funk, was titled "From the Back Side."

The JBs' contagious "Givin' Up Food for Funk" surprisingly missed the chart in July 1972; It was the last single released under the JBs' name alone. Moving bandleader Fred Wesley to the fore, Brown rechristened the group Fred Wesley & the JBs and relaunched them with a cover of the O'Jays' recent "Back Stabbers." Other rearrangements followed: Herbie Hancock's "Watermelon Man" was subjected to a powerful funk revision some months before Hancock himself released his own rearranged version on his *Head Hunters* album; the performance was backed by a strong horn-powered interpretation of Gilbert O'Sullivan's "Alone Again, Naturally"—a song that, in years to come, assumed fresh significance in R&B circles, when it became the center of a test case involving sampling.

The return of Maceo Parker to the fold in early 1973 precipitated the JBs' period of greatest chart success, as the title track from that year's *Doing It to Death* album became a summertime R&B chart-topper and a pop Top 30 smash. The group followed through with "If You Don't Get It the First Time, Back Up and Try It Again, Party," from the forthcoming *Damn Right I Am Somebody* album; that album also provided the JBs' next two hits, "Same Beat" and the title track.

Meanwhile, the JBs were also busy operating under a slew of aliases, backing Parker in the guise of Maceo & the Macks; providing the backing on further singles by Anderson and Lyn Collins; and looking in on sundry media crazes of the age. As the Last Word, they celebrated the new bump dance fad with "Keep On Bumping." When that was ousted by the hustle, they became the Hustlers; and when the success of the movie *The Exorcist* seemed set to create an epidemic of Satanic frenzy across the US, they became the Devils and unleashed "The X-Sorcist."

The Watergate political scandal provoked musical comment in the form of "You Can Have Watergate, Just Give Me Some Bucks and I'll Be Straight" and "Rockin' Funky Watergate." (Ironically, Brown and the JBs played President Nixon's inauguration ball in 1968, thus placing themselves at both the beginning and the end of the ill-fated admin-

istration.) The aforementioned Above Average Black Band then raised a wry smile with "Pick Up the Pieces One by One."

For no apparent reason, 1974 saw the group's name change again, to Fred & the New JBs. The core of the band remained much the same as it had been for the past year or so—Wesley, Maceo and Jimmy Parker, Pinckney, Thomas, Morgan and Starks, plus percussionist Johnny Griggs and guitarist Charles Sherrell. However, a truly new JBs lineup was not far away.

In 1975, Parker and Wesley quit to join George Clinton's P-Funk, uniting with fellow former JBs Bootsy and Phelps Collins and company. Brown, whose own career was now slipping, regrouped, but the JBs' period of true success was over. It was 1977 before the group returned to the chart, when Brown himself took leadership credit for the first time, on "Give Me Some Skin."

With the lineup now including Brown veteran Jimmy Nolen (gtr), David Weston (bs), Charles Sherrell (pno), Tony Cook (drms), Johnny Griggs (cngas) and a horn section of Russell Crimes, Joe Poff and Peyton Johnson, further attempts to relaunch the JBs in their own right, as JBs Wedge and JBs International, failed. By 1980, the JBs own identity had once again been absorbed back into Brown's own. It re-emerged in 1990 under the aegis of Parker and Wesley's JB Horns combo.

## JBs COMPLETE DISCOGRAPHY

For releases credited to Maceo [Parker]/the Macks, Vicki Anderson, James Brown, Lyn Collins, see individual artist entries.

### SINGLES/CHART LOG

#### JBs MARK 1 (BOOTSY COLLINS ETC)

1970 The Grunt (part one)/(part two) (King)
1970 These Are the JBs (part one)/(part two) (King)

#### AS THE BELIEVERS

1971 Across the Track (part one)/(part two) (Brownstone)

#### JBs MARK 2 (FRED WESLEY ETC.)

1971 My Brother (part one)/(part two) (People)
1971 Gimme Some More/The Rabbit Got the Gun (People—#11 R&B/#67 pop)
1972 Pass the Peas/Hot Pants Road (People—#29 R&B/#95 pop)
1972 Givin' Up Food for Funk (part one)/(part two) (People)

#### AS THE SONS OF FUNK

1971 From the Back Side (part one)/(part two) (King)

#### FRED WESLEY AND THE JBs

1972 Back Stabbers/JB Shout (People)

1972 Everybody Plays the Fool/Use Me (People—unissued)
1973 Watermelon Man/Alone Again, Naturally (People)
1973 Sportin' Life/Dirty Harri (People)
1973 Doing It to Death/Everybody Got Soul (People—#1 R&B/#22 pop)
1973 If You Don't Get It the First Time/You Can Have Watergate (People—
#24 R&B/#104 pop)
1973 Same Beat (part one)/(part two) (People—#26 R&B)
1974 Damn Right I Am Somebody (part one)/(part two) (People—#32 R&B)
1974 Rockin' Funky Watergate (part one)/(part two) (People)
1974 Little Boy Black/Rockin' Funky Watergate (part two) (People—unissued)

## AS THE LAST WORD
1974 Keep On Bumping Before You Give out of Gas/Funky and Some (Polydor)

## AS THE DEVILS
1974 The X-Sorcist/Hip Hugger (People)

## AS THE FIRST FAMILY
1974 Control (part one)/(part two) (Polydor)

## FRED AND THE NEW JBs
1974 Breakin' Bread/Funky Music Is My Style (People—#80 R&B)
1975 Makin' Love/Rice'n'Ribs (People—#64 R&B)
1975 Thank You for Letting Me Be Myself and Be Yours (part one)/(part two)
(People—unissued)
1975 It's the JBs Monaurail (part one)/(part two) (People—#63 R&B)

## AS AABB
1975 Pick Up the Pieces One by One/COLD (Identify)

## AS THE HUSTLERS
1975 Hustling/Soft Hustle (People)

## THE JBs
1975 Thank You for Letting Me Be Myself (part one)/(part two)
1976 All Aboard the Soul Funky Train/Thank You . . . (People)

## JBs WEDGE
1976 Bessie (part one)/(part two) (Brownstone)

## THE JBs WITH JAMES BROWN
1976 Everybody Wanna Get Funky One More Time (part one)/(part two)
(People)
1977 Give Me Some Skin/People Wake Up and Live (Polydor—#20 R&B)

## JAMES BROWN AND THE NEW JBs
1977 If You Don't Give a Dogone About It/People Who Criticize (Polydor—
#45 R&B)

## JBs INTERNATIONAL
1977 Music for the People/Crossover (Polydor)
1977 Nature (part one)/(part two)
1978 Disco Fever (part one)/(part two) (Polydor)

## THE JBs
1979 Rock Groove Machine (part one)/(part two) (Drive)

## LPs

## THE JBs
**9** 1971 Food for Thought (People—#34 R&B)
Dramatic instrumental set bears comparison with any of Brown's own. The best cuts are the looser jams: "The Grunt," "Pass the Peas," etc., but nothing disappoints.

## FRED WESLEY AND THE JBs
**7** 1973 Doing It to Death (People—#7 R&B/#77 pop)
The title track would later be reinvented for the next album's "If You Don't Get It," but here it's in its funky prime.
**8** 1974 Damn Right I Am Somebody (People—#20 R&B/#197 pop)

## FRED AND THE NEW JBs
**8** 1974 Breakin' Bread (People—#36 R&B)
Dynamic set that justifies Wesley's pre-eminence with some hot compositions and hotter playing— the title track is classic Fred.

## THE JBs
**6** 1975 Hustle with Speed (People)
Slowing down despite the promise of "It's the JB's Monaurail," the album relies too heavily on repetition and reputation.

## JBs INTERNATIONAL
**8** 1978 Disco Fever (Polydor)
The title is as much a misnomer as a symptom of the times, although the album itself does little more than nod in the direction of past glories. Jimmy Nolen and St. Clair Pinckney still hold the fort; Martha & the Lazers add some fine vocals. And most of the titles include the word "disco."

## THE JBs
**6** 1979 Groove Machine (Drive)
The infectious full-length title track still defies the passing years; elsewhere, the album offers few surprises.

## SELECTED COMPILATIONS AND ARCHIVE RELEASES
**9** 1995 Funky Good Time: The Anthology
A two-CD/30-track collection drawing together the very cream of the JB's repetoire, including each of the hits (and mostly the misses), extended versions and a handful of key rarities.
**7** 1997 Funky Men (Disky—Germany)
Not a JBs compilation per se, but close enough; 14 highlights from the post-Wesley-era include "The Way To Get Down" (the JBs featuring Maxxi), "Rock Groove Machine" (the JBs), "Bessie" (JBs Wedge) and "Nature" (JBs Internationals), together with cuts by Brown and Byrd.

**6** **2000 Pass the Peas (Polydor)**

Oddly unadventurous roundup of Polydor singles and LP cuts.

## SELECTED SAMPLES

Blow Your Head — Alkaholiks: Make Room (1993)

Blow Your Head — Compton's Most Wanted: Rhymes Too Funky (part one) (1990)

Blow Your Head — Compton's Most Wanted: Straight Checkin' 'Em (1991)

Blow Your Head — DOC: Portrait of a Master Piece (1989)

Blow Your Head — Everlast: Fuck Everyone (1990)

Blow Your Head — Public Enemy: Public Enemy No. 1 (1988)

Blow Your Head — Special Ed: The Mission (1990)

Blow Your Head — Terminator X: High Priest of Turbulence (1991)

Damn Right I Am . . . — Ice T: Lifestyles of the Rich and Infamous (1991)

Damn Right I Am . . . — Professor Griff: Crucified (1991)

Damn Right I Am . . . — Salt-N-Pepa: Let the Rhythm Run (1988)

Damn Right I Am . . . — 3RD Bass: Pop Goes the Weasel (1991)

Gimme Some More — Compton's Most Wanted: Final Chapter (1990)

Gimme Some More — Kool Moe Dee: The Don (1989)

Gimme Some More — LL Cool J: It Gets No Rougher (1989)

Gimme Some More — Public Enemy: Power to the People (1990)

Gimme Some More — Public Enemy: Cold Lampin' with Flavor (1988)

Givin Up Food for Funk — Geto Boys: Mind of a Lunatic (1990)

Givin Up Food for Funk — Big Daddy Kane: Wrath of Kane (1989)

Givin Up Food for Funk — Big Daddy Kane: Raw '91 (1991)

Givin Up Food for Funk — Insane Poetry: The House That Dripped Blood (1992)

Givin Up Food for Funk — Pharcyde: I'm That Type of Nigger (1993)

Hot Pants Road — Grandmaster Flash & the Furious Five: On the Strength (1988)

Hot Pants Road — Public Enemy: Fight the Power (1990)

Hot Pants Road — Roxanne Shante: Have a Nice Day (1989)

I Wanna Get Down — Ice Cube: Who's the Mack? (1990)

I'm Payin' Taxes — Doctor Ice: The Mic Stalking (1989)

JB's Monaurail — III All Skratch: Classic Shit (III's Sold) (1994)

JB's Monaurail — College Boys: Victim of the Ghetto (remix) (1992)

JB's Monaurail — Compton's Most Wanted: Final Chapter (1990)

More Peas — Tim Dog: Bronx Nigga (Blue Note Mix) (1991)

More Peas — WC & the Maad Circle: Behind Closed Doors (1991)

More Peas — Steady B: Ego Trippin' (1989)

More Peas — Slick Rick: I Shouldn't Have Done It (1991)

More Peas — Showbiz & AG: Soul Clap (1992)

More Peas — Organized Konfusion: Fudge Pudge (1991)

More Peas — MC Lyte: Search 4 Tha Lyte (1991)

More Peas — MARRS: Pump Up the Volume (1987)

More Peas — Lords of the Underground: Here Come the Lords (1993)

More Peas — Kris Kross: Way of Rhyme (1992)

More Peas — Cypress Hill: Phuncky Feel One (1992)

More Peas — Frankie Cutlass: Puerto Rico (1994)

Pass the Peas — Eric B & Rakim: I Ain't No Joke (1987)

Pass the Peas — Heavy D. & the Boyz: Moneyearnin' Mount Vernon (1987)

Pass the Peas — Grandmaster Flash & the Furious Five: On the Strength (1988)

Pass the Peas — Roxanne Shante: Have a Nice Day (1989)

Pass the Peas — Heavy D. & the Boyz: Overweight Lover's in the House (1987)

Pass the Peas — Eric B. & Rakim: Move the Crowd (1987)

Pass the Peas — De La Soul: Ring Ring Ring (Ha Ha Hey) (1991)

Pass The Peas — Pharcyde: I'm That Type tf Nigger (1993)

Pass The Peas — De La Soul: Pass the Plugs (1991)

Rockin' Funky Watergate — Pharcyde: 4 Better or 4 Worse (1993)

Same Beat (part one) — Run DMC: The Ave (1990)

Same Beat (part one) — Ice T: The Iceberg (1989)

Same Beat (part one) — EPMD: Who's Booty (1989)

Same Beat (part one) — Jungle Brothers: J. Beez Comin' Through (1989)

The Grunt — Joe Public: Live & Learn (1999)

The Grunt — Compton's Most Wanted: Final Chapter (1990)

The Grunt — Chubb Rock: The One (1991)

The Grunt — Terminator X: Vendetta . . . The Big Getback (1991)

The Grunt — Steady B: Hustler Mac (1991)

The Grunt — Erick Sermon: Payback II (1993)

The Grunt — Salt-N-Pepa: Break of Dawn (1993)

The Grunt — Roxanne Shante: Have a Nice Day (1989)

The Grunt — Pharcyde: Officer (1993)

The Grunt — Public Enemy: Terminator X to the Edge of Panic (1988)

The Grunt — Public Enemy: Rebel Without A Pause (1988)

The Grunt — Public Enemy: Night of the Living Baseheads (1988)

You Can Have Watergate — Compton's Most Wanted: One Time Gaffled Them Up (1990)

You Can Have Watergate — Zhigge: Toss It Up (1992)

You Can Have Watergate — Yo-Yo: Girl Don't Be No Fool (1991)

You Can Have Watergate — Special Ed: The Mission (1990)

You Can Have Watergate — Run DMC: The Ave (1990)

You Can Have Watergate — Geto Boys: Read These Nikes (1990)

You Can Have Watergate — Everlast: Syndication (remix) (1990)

You Can Have Watergate — Downtown Science: If I Was (1991)

# KOKOMO

**FORMED:** 1973, London, England

**ORIGINAL LINE-UP:** Frank Collins (vcls), Paddy McHugh (vcls), Dyan Birch (vcls), Jim Mullen (gtr), Alan Spenner (vcls, bs), Neil Hubbard (gtr, vcls), Mel Collins (sax), Tony O'Malley (kybds), Terry Stannard (drms), Jody Linscott (cngas)

Ranked alongside Gonzalez and the Average White Band as prime exponents of Britain's white funk movement, Kokomo formed in May 1973, from the remains of a variety of projects from across the UK spectrum. Mel Collins was exprog rockers King Crimson; Neil Hubbard and Alan Spenner worked with Joe Cocker's Grease Band; Frank Collins led '60s pop sensations Arrival.

A ten-piece aggregation with four lead vocalists—a rare sight among even the funkiest White bands—Kokomo launched onto the UK pub scene later than year, swiftly engendering an entire new wave of young British groups. By the time the band played their first full UK tour, co-headlining the Naughty Rhythms pub rock showcase (with rockers Dr. Feelgood and Chili Willi & the Red Hot Peppers), both Supercharge and the newly inaugurated partnership of Ian Dury and Chaz Jankel were both embarking in a similar direction to Kokomo.

Independently booked and organized, Naughty Rhythms brought Kokomo to the attention of CBS and that summer, their self-titled debut album was released to wild reviews. CBS labelmate Bob Dylan, too, was impressed; when the band visited New York in July, to promote Kokomo, they were invited down to Columbia Studios for two days to record tracks for Dylan's forthcoming Desire album. Only one song from the sessions (the Latin-flavored "Romance in Durango") made the finished album; among the cuts left on the shelf was a dynamic disco-funk flavored version of "Hurricane."

With Kokomo making a strong showing in the US R&B chart, Kokomo returned to the UK to tour through the fall. Drummer Stannard quit to be replaced by American born John Sussewell; Mullen and Linscott, too, departed shortly before the group set to work on their sophomore album, Rise And Shine—previewed with the mini hit "Use Your Imagination."

It was a competent set but, despite again breaching the US pop Top 200, it could not compete either with its predecessor or with Kokomo's reputation. In January 1977, following a handful of Christmas period shows with Hubbard and Spenner's former employer, Joe Cocker, Kokomo broke up.

Several one-off reunions followed over the next five years; finally, at the height of the early-'80s Britfunk boom led by Light of the World, Linx and Spandau Ballet, the Rise and Shine-era lineup reconvened for a third album, again titled Kokomo. It sold poorly and the band split once again.

### KOKOMO DISCOGRAPHY
### CHART LOG
1976 Use Your Imagination/That's Enough (Columbia—#81 R&B)

### LPs
**8** 1975 Kokomo (Columbia—#34 R&B/#159 pop)

Considerably less studious than other Britfunk albums, Kokomo is one melting jam after another, its main drawback being a certain sameyness.

**6** 1976 Rise And Shine (CBS—#194 pop)
**7** 1932 Kokomo (CBS)

Distinctly low-pressure, good time funk, a timely reminder of just how influential Kokomo had been.

## KOOL & THE GANG

**FORMED:** 1961, Jersey City, NJ

**ORIGINAL LINE-UP:** Charles "Claydes" Smith (b. 9/6/48, Jersey City, NJ—gtr), Robert "Kool" Bell (b. 10/8/50, Youngstown, OH—bs), Ronald Bell (b. 11/1/51, Youngstown OH—sax, kybds), Clifford Adams (trom), Woody Sparrow (gtr), Robert "Spike" Mickens (b Jersey City, NJ—trum), Dennis Thomas (b. 2/9/51, Jersey City, NJ—sax), "Funky" George Brown (b. 1/5/49, Jersey City, NJ—drms)

Kool & the Gang formed as the Jazziacs in Jersey City in 1961. The Bell brothers' father was a professional boxer and keen jazz enthusiast (Thelonious Monk was a family friend) and his love of music was effortlessly passed on to his children and their friends. All of the original Jazziacs (the Bells, Adams, Sparrow, Mickens, Thomas) attended Lincoln High in Jersey City, and all learned their musical basics playing together on sticks and cans, pursuing a naive, but nevertheless effective, line in the African percussion that would develop into one of the essential funk rudiments.

Robert Bell mastered the bass and, by 1966, the group's sound had taken on a distinctly jazzy air. Charles Smith and George Brown joined and, as their reputation developed, the Jazziacs' shows at Jersey City's St. John's nightclub became a veritable magnet for visiting jazzmen; Pharaoh Sanders, McCoy Tyner and Leon Thomas all sat in with the band.

In 1968, the Jazziacs were invited to join the Soultown Revue, a live ensemble that toured the north-east performing the day's biggest hits behind a clutch of regular vocalists. A name change, to the New Dimensions, followed. One night, however, they arrived at the venue to find themselves mysteriously billed as Kool & the Flames—which became Kool & the Gang after Robert Bell adopted "Kool" as his onstage nickname. A crowd pleasing instrumental of the same name slipped into their live set and, in 1969, producer Gene Redd (former King Records A&R man) signed the group to his Redd Coach label.

Effortlessly reproducing the sound of the wild club evenings where they were at their best, complete with back-

**Kool & the Gang: celebrating the science of sound.**

ground noise and talking, "Kool & the Gang" was released as the group's debut single that summer. By fall, its local success had prompted the De-Lite label to move in for the band, reissuing "Kool & the Gang" and enjoying an immediate R&B Top 20 hit. A second single, "The Gang's Back Again" (backed with the doppelganger "Kool's Back Again") followed, as the group unveiled their eponymous debut album.

In June 1970, "Let the Music Take Your Mind" became Kool & the Gang's third hit and first vocal cut, loose banter slipping into the jazz grooves and indicating the direction that the band would increasingly be taking in the future. (In the wake of its success, the track was added to later pressings of the *Kool & the Gang* album).

Joined now by Ricky Westfield (keyboards), the group's live performance continued to slam from strength to strength, encouraging the release of two live albums in the course of a year; *Live at the Sex Machine* in February 1971, and *Live at PJs* in December, a faithful document of a typically frenzied May night in Hollywood, featuring dy-

namic reworkings not only of original material, but also of pop staples "Walk On By" and "Wichita Linesman." Both albums charted and, in between times, the singles so far were repackaged beneath the only vaguely presumptuous title of *The Best of Kool & the Gang.*

Kool & the Gang continued refining their sound over the next two years, even as they developed their approach—musically and spiritually. With the entire band becoming adherents of the Nation of Islam, the Bell brothers were given new Muslim names—Khalis Bayyan (Ronald) and Amir Bayyan (Robert)—by Wallace Muhammad, son of the movement's founder Elijah Muhammad, in 1972. This new philosophy, coupled with the musicians' increasingly heavy funk approach, emerged full-blooded on the *Wild and Peaceful* watershed album, and 1973's "Funky Stuff" finally gave them their R&B Top Five breakthrough.

Long accustomed to crafting their songs out of rehearsal jams, Kool & the Gang created "Funky Stuff" at Media Sound Studio on New York City's West 57th Street—so tiny a studio, Robert Bell still recalls how odd it was to find themselves sharing the building with Santana, and how exciting the fusion as their sounds bled through the walls and floors. Modified and mutated, this fusion was recaptured in *Wild and Peaceful*'s nine-minute title track, a subtle weaving of Afro-Latin jazz forging a powerful alliance with nasty funk of the hits. Breaching the pop Top 30, "Funky Stuff" effortlessly hauled "Jungle Boogie" and "Hollywood Swinging" into contention too. (It also popularized the dancefloor ubiquity of ear-piercing whistle blasts.)

Talking with writer Cleveland Brown, James Brown said of Kool & the Gang, "They're the second-baddest out there. They make such bad records that you got to be careful when you play a new tape on the way home from the record store. Their groove is so strong you could wreck." He knew what he was talking about. Kool & the Gang were unique, wildly experimenting on the edge of the funk jazz crossover and scoring pop hits as well. Suddenly, James Brown's words, "the second baddest," sounded less of an endorsement and more like fighting talk. "We are scientists of sound," the Gang announced in "Heaven at Once," "we are mathematically puttin' it down," and few bands have so accurately pinpointed their style in song.

Yet there was no cold calculation to Kool. Ronald Bell acknowledged that much of what the group was doing was wholly improvised, the musicians simply pursuing the groove and rhythms to see where they led. "Some," he said, "succeeded; some didn't." But they never tired of the chase.

By April 1974, "Hollywood Swinging" was topping the R&B chart; "Higher Plane," the first single from Kool & the Gang's next album, *Light of Worlds* followed it, while "Light of Worlds" itself was nominated for a Best R&B Instrumental Performance Grammy at the 1974 awards ceremony. (It was beaten out by MFSB's "TSOP.") "Rhyme Tyme Boogie" peaked at #3. The Don "Boogie Man" Boyce-led title track from their next album, the superlative *Spirit of the Boogie*, gave the band their third #1 in April 1975.

Kool & the Gang visited Europe that summer, recording a tumultuous show at London's Rainbow Theatre for inclusion on their next album, *Love and Understanding*, and igniting a frenzy of funk awareness within the local press. Yet as fast as it rose, Kool & the Gang's profile began slipping as they struggled to come to terms with the disco explosion. Even their inclusion in the Grammy winning *Saturday Night Fever* soundtrack could not prevent them from being forgotten (their contribution to that collection, the thunderous "Open Sesame," was already over a year old)

and, as subsequent singles missed the pop 100 altogether, it seemed an era was over.

Westfield's departure exacerbated this sense but, behind the scenes, Kool & the Gang were preparing for absolute reinvention. Late in 1978, the band recruited two vocalists, the short-lived Earl Toon, Jr. and a former New Jersey nightclub singer, James Warren Taylor (b. 8/16/53, Laurens, SC).

They also struck up a partnership with the legendary Brazilian jazz fusion arranger/producer Eumir Deodato. Robert Bell told *Rolling Stone* "We just started talking. We all came from a jazz background, so the chemistry was there. We talked about not being over-creative and Deo has the same problem, so he kept saying, 'let's not go way out to left field. Let's keep it simple and basic and clean.'"

Toning down the tumultuous funk of their earlier work, Kool & the Gang finally re-emerged with "Ladies Night," their most successful single yet. (The album of the same name became their first platinum disc.) An untrammelled explosion of party-pounding frenzy, "Ladies' Night" topped the R&B chart for three weeks, and made #8 on the pop charts, the year's ultimate ultra funky, feel-good club anthem. According to Robert Bell, the song is "about hanging out at the time and going to the clubs on Friday night. Friday was always ladies night. And I thought we should just take that."

A lot of others agreed with him. "Ladies Night" inspired covers by both KC & the Sunshine Band and Joyce Kennedy, yet Kool & the Gang had only begun their comeback. From 1980's *Celebrate* album, "Celebration" spent six weeks atop the R&B chart, two weeks at number one on the pop chart, clocking up American sales of two million plus even as Ronald Bell enthused, "This is going to be an international anthem. To be played at weddings, bar mitzvahs, and all joyous occasions beyond our time on Earth! This is going to change us!"

When Iran released the American hostages, which the revolution had been holding at the embassy in Teheran, on January 26, 1981, "Celebration" was the record played to welcome them home. Walter Mondale took the song to celebrate his nomination as the Democratic Party's presidential candidate in 1984. More recently, "Celebration" has been adopted as the theme for the Oakland A's baseball team. And once again, a slew of cover versions followed: '50s-era heroes The Platters turned in a characteristically rearranged version; the Kingston Players, the Mini Pops and the Merenbooty Girls also enjoyed some success with the song.

Still working with Deodato, Kool & the Gang released their third successive platinum album in 1982. Once again, *Something Special* bristled with gems: the pulsing "No Show," and another Top Ten hit, "Get Down on It," included. Their renewed fame had again reached across the ocean to Europe. "Get Down on It" became Kool & the Gang's first ever UK Top Five hit, an event celebrated with a solidly sold out tour that fall, an outing that included four nights in London alone. There, the group's slickly choreographed stageshow won the undying admiration even of the city's normally cynical music press, not only powering the team to ever greater heights of acclaim in Britain, but also prompting their UK record label to release the first in what became a flood of *Greatest Hits* collections, the non-stop dance party *Twice as Kool*.

*As One*, in fall 1982, marked the end of Kool & the Gang's relationship with Deodato, and the dawn of a new era. It was a suitable farewell to one of the most explosive combinations in dance history, one that could have demanded no stronger a curtain call than "Let's Go Dancing (Ooh La La La)" the partnership's eighth successive Top 40 smash.

Suspicions that Kool & the Gang's revival owed much to Deodato's influence were immediately disproved as the band launched a string of further monster hits during 1984–85: "Joanna," "Tonight," "Misled," "Fresh" and the Adult Contemporary #1 "Cherish." *In the Heart*, their first post-Deodato album, went gold; 1984's beat- and guitar-led *Emergency* soared to platinum, 1985's *Forever*, too, went gold. If there was a downside to this success, however, it was the loss of their original audience. By the mid-'80s, Taylor himself estimated that Kool & the Gang had crossed over so successfully that their audiences were now 90 percent White.

The departure of Taylor for a solo career halted even this momentum. Replacing him with Gary Brown, Odeen Mays and former Dazz Band frontman Skip Martin, Kool & the Gang scratched three further minor R&B hits, "Rags to Riches," "Raindrops" and "Never Give Up." But their solitary new album, 1989's *Sweat*, was wholly unsuccessful and Brown departed the following year. The similarly disappointing *Unite* followed in 1993 but, with Taylor's solo career having proven a non-starter in its own right, few were surprised when he rejoined Kool & the Gang in 1995, for the following year's *State of Affairs* set.

The reunion also recorded a clutch of greatest hits for a second album in 1996. Neither were a success, but Kool & the Gang's legacy continued to grow, a favorite among sample-hungry performers and a staple on the funk revival circuit.

## KOOL AND THE GANG COMPLETE DISCOGRAPHY
### SINGLES/CHART LOG

1969 Kool & the Gang/Raw Hamburgers (De-Lite—#19 R&B/#59 pop)

1970 The Gang's Back Again/Kool's Back Again (De-Lite—#37 R&B/#85 pop)

1970 Let the Music Take Your Mind/Chocolate Buttermilk (De-Lite—#19 R&B/#78 pop)

1970 Funky Man/1–2–3–4–5–6–7–8 (De-Lite—#16 R&B/#87 pop)

1971 Who's Gonna Take the Weight (part one)/(part two) (De-Lite—#28 R&B/#113 pop)

1971 I Want To Take You Higher/Pneumonia (De-Lite—#35 R&B/#105 pop)

1972 Love the Life You Live (part one)/(part two) (De-Lite—#31 R&B/#107 pop)

1973 Funky Stuff/More Funky Stuff (De-Lite—#5 R&B/#29 pop)

1973 Jungle Boogie/North East South West (De-Lite—#2 R&B/#4 pop)

1974 Hollywood Swinging/Dujii (De-Lite—#1 R&B/#6 pop)

1974 Higher Plane/Wild Is Love (De-Lite—#1 R&B/#37 pop)

1974 Rhyme Tyme People/Father Father (De-Lite—#3 R&B/#63 pop)

1975 Spirit on the Boogie (De-Lite—#1 R&B/#35 pop)/Summer Madness (#38 R&B)

1975 Caribbean Festival (disco version) (De-Lite—#6 R&B/#55 pop)

1976 Love & Understanding/Sunshine And Love (De-Lite—#8 R&B/#77 pop)

1976 Universal Sound/Ancestral Ceremony (De-Lite—#71 R&B/#101 pop)

1976 Open Sesame (part one)/(part two) (De-Lite—#6 R&B/#55 pop)

1977 Super Band/Sunshine (De-Lite—#17 R&B/#101 pop)

1978 Slick Superchick/Life's a Song (De-Lite—#19 R&B/#102 pop)

1978 Everybody's Dancin'/Stay Awhile (De-Lite—#65 R&B)

1979 Ladies' Night/If You Feel Like Dancing (De-Lite—#1 R&B/#8 pop)

1980 Too Hot/Tonight's the Night (De-Lite—#3 R&B/#5 pop)

1980 Celebration/Mornin' Star (De-Lite—#1 R&B/#1 pop)

1981 Take It To the Top/Love Affair (De-Lite—#11 R&B)

1981 Jones vs. Jones/Night People (De-Lite—#33 R&B/#39 pop)

1981 Take My Heart/Just Friends (De-Lite—#1 R&B/#17 pop)

1982 Steppin' Out/Love Festival (De-Lite—#12 R&B/#89 pop)

1982 Get Down on It/Steppin' Out (De-Lite—#4 R&B/#10 pop)

1982 Big Fun/No Show (De-Lite—#6 R&B/#21 pop)

1982 Let's go Dancin'/Be My Lady (De-Lite—#7 R&B/#30 pop)

1983 Street Kids/As One (De-Lite—#78 R&B)

1983 Joanna/Place for Us (De-Lite—#1 R&B/#2 pop)

1984 Tonight/Home Is Where the Heart Is (De-Lite—#7 R&B/#13 pop)

1984 Straight Ahead/September Love (De-Lite—#49 R&B/#103 pop)

1984 Misled/Rollin' (De-Lite—#3 R&B/#10 pop)

1985 Fresh/In the Heart (De-Lite—31 R&B/#9 pop)

1985 Cherish/(instrumental) (De-Lite—#1 R&B/#2 pop)

1985 Emergency/You Are the One (De-Lite—#7 R&B/#18 pop)

1986 Victory/Bad Woman (De-Lite—#2 R&B/#10 pop)

1987 Stone Love/Dance Champion (De-Lite—#4 R&B/#10 pop)

1987 Holiday/(jam mix) (De-Lite—#9 R&B/#66 pop)

1988 Rags to Riches/(remix) (De-Lite—#38 R&B)
1989 Raindrops/Amor Amore (De-Lite—#27 R&B)
1989 Never Give Up/Amor Amore (De-Lite—#74 R&B)

## LPs

**5** **1969 Kool & the Gang (De-Lite—#43 R&B)**
Sparse vocals and lots of jazzy grooves set the standard for the early years.

**6** **1971 Live at the Sex Machine (De-Lite—#6 R&B/#122 pop)**
Considerably less dynamic than its reputation insists, further marred on CD by a stodgy sound, a jazzy jam through "Walk On By" approaches virtuoso muzak territory; "Wichita Linesman" never leaves it and the highlight, predictably, is Sly Stone's "I Want To Take You Higher," lurching into a badass "Funky Man."

**4** **1971 Live at P.J.'S (De-Lite—#24 R&B/#171 pop)**
Despite a ten-minute plus slab of "Ike's Theme"/"You've Lost That Loving Feeling" in the middle of the set, the disc is better left to the serious collector.

**6** **1972 Music Is the Message (De-Lite—#25 R&B)**
From the title track to "Funky Granny," to "Blowin' in the Wind," the first Kool set to genuinely recapture their imagination.

**5** **1973 Good Times (De-Lite—#34 R&B/#142 pop)**
**7** **1973 Wild and Peaceful (De-Lite—#6 R&B/#33 pop)**
The fresh funk of "Jungle Boogie" and the down and dirty grooves of "Hollywood Swinging" set a tone full of controlled jams that come across as spontaneously fluid. The sounds of K&TG finding their stride.

**6** **1974 Light of Worlds (De-Lite—#16 R&B/#63 pop)**
**10** **1975 Spirit of the Boogie (De-Lite—#5 R&B/#48 pop)**
The utterly staggering climax of this stage of the band's development. From the foldout African artwork sleeve, to the spiritual and musical purity of "Ancestral Ceremony," "Jungle Jazz" and "Mother Earth," the album lashes a reverence for their roots to street smart hard funk and a keen awareness of their own role in the latter's development. "Ancestral Ceremony" quotes from past Kool songs, while the pounding "Jungle Jazz" tracks back to the original jam that created "Jungle Boogie." Dominated by and delving into rhythm and chant, *Spirit of the Boogie* is quintessential Kool.

**8** **1976 Love & Understanding (De-Lite—#9 R&B/#68 pop)**
Even with three of its eight cuts recorded live at London's Rainbow (a punchy "Hollywood Swinging," "Summer Madness" and "Universal Sound"), *Love and Understanding* is dominated by the opening title cut and its closing

near-instrumental shadow, "Come Together," horn heavy, insistent and dramatic. Yet there are also signs of the band's eventual musical course, in the lackluster "Sugar" and "Do It Right Now," while "Cosmic Energy" rides the basics of a great groove, but cuts off long before it gets going.

**7** **1975 Open Sesame (De-Lite—#9 R&B/#110 pop)**
Shazaam! "I Am the Genie of Funk" is still one of the best lyrics ever penned, even though the set in total doesn't fully deliver.

**6** **1977 The Force (De-Lite—#33 R&B/#142 pop)**
A little fusion, a little funk and lots of disappointment. From the *Star Wars*-ian title to the songs themselves, it's easy to see where the force was not.

**5** **1978 Everybody's Dancin' (De-Lite—#71 R&B/#207 pop)**
**6** **1979 Ladies' Night (De-Lite—#1 R&B/#13 pop)**
The band's first real shift from dirty funk to mainstream pop is apparent in the masterful title track, which retained a groove and became a club standard as well. "Too Hot" and "Tonight's the Night" repeat the feat.

**7** **1980 Celebrate! (De-Lite—#2 R&B/#10—pop)**
The album rode in on a major dancefloor hit and the acknowledgement that, though disco was dead, there was still life left on the Excess Express. Thumping bass and drums drive the "Love Festival," while the sinewy "Night People" joined the title cut as dancehall fixtures throughout the early '8cs.

**8** **1981 Something Special (De-Lite—#1 R&B/#12 pop)**
From the smooth groove of "Get Down on It" to the ballad "No Show," it's obvious that K&TG can do it all and do it well. An excellent set that changes pace, but keeps the sound intact.

**7** **1982 As One (De-Lite—#5 R&B/#29 pop)**
A surprisingly successful blend of jazzed funk with a reggae beat, "Let's Go Dancing" brought the warm sands of Jamaica to the Jersey clubs. It's a mix of style that couldn't have been created by any other band. Following the death of Bob Marley, this song, perhaps, was a tribute to the great reggae master, by the masters of funk.

**6** **1983 In the Heart (De-Lite—#5 R&B/#29 pop)**
With "Joanna" setting the pace, the set swerves fully out of the funk fast lane and onto the R&B expressway.

**5** **1984 Emergency (De-Lite—#3 R&B/#13 pop)**
**5** **1986 Forever (Mercury—#9 R&B/#25 pop)**
JT Taylor's last hurrah with the band is competent, but doesn't have anywhere near the driving grooves of Kool's early material. Total MOR smoothies.

**2** **1989 Sweat (Mercury—#52 R&B)**

Not even recommended for the completist. This is the sound of a band who lost the only lead singer they'd ever had. Beware!

**4** **1993 Unite (RCA)**
**5** **1996 State of Affairs (Curb)**

Comeback set with JT Taylor. Not too bad.

**2** **1998 All Time Greatest Hits (Curb)**

Deceptively packaged hit re-recordings, not nearly as good as the originals!

**5** **1998 Greatest Hits Live (Rhino)**

### SELECTED COMPILATIONS AND ARCHIVE RELEASES

**6** **1971 The Best Of (De-Lite—#32 R&B/#157 pop)**
**7** **1974 Kool Jazz (De-Lite—#26 R&B/#187 pop)**
**5** **1975 Greatest Hits! (De-Lite—#21 R&B/#81 pop)**
**8** **1978 Spin Their Top Hits (De-Lite)**

The essential primer to Kool's funk period, tracking the best of the pre-Deodato hits, at the same time as amplifying their diversity.

**7** **1988 Everything's Kool & the Gang (Mercury—#58 R&B/#109 pop)**

Strong collection of the band's '80s-era hits.

**8** **1993 The Best of Kool & the Gang (Mercury)**

Fabulous collection of the band's best funk era and pop material.

**7** **1994 Celebration (Mercury)**

Everything you need, if you need it, from 1979 to 1987.

**7** **1999 12" Collection And More (Polygram)**

A great collection of old and new from this stellar series. Includes the Spanish language "Celebramos!" A must have for the clubber.

**8** **2000 20th Century Masters—The Millennium Collection: The Best of Kool & the Gang**

### SELECTED SAMPLES

Chocolate Buttermilk — Chubb Rock: the Night Scene (1991)
Chocolate Buttermilk — Heavy D: Let It Flow (1989)
Chocolate Buttermilk — Eric B & Rakim: Keep 'Em Eager To Listen (1990)
Chocolate Buttermilk — Eric B & Rakim: No Omega (1990)
Chocolate Buttermilk — Marley Marl: SImon Says (1988)
Chocolate Buttermilk — Pete Rock & CL Smooth: Straighten It Out (1992)
Chocolate Buttermilk — Special Ed: Ready 2 Attack (1990)
Chocolate Buttermilk — Stetsasonic: The Hip Hop Band (1991)
Chocolate Buttermilk — Style: Set the Mood (1991)
Chocolate Buttermilk — Young Black Teenagers: Proud To Be Black (1991)
Cosmic Energy — Big Daddy Kane: Nuff' Respect (1993)
Duji — Chi-Ali: Funky Lemondade (1992)
Duji — Gang Starr: Jazz Thing (1999)
Duji — Pete Rock & CL Smooth: It's on You (1994)

Electric Frog (part one) — A Tribe Called Quest: Mr. Muhammed (1990)
Funky Granny — Das EFX: Baknaffek (1993)
Funky Man — Fat Joe: Watch Out (1995)
Funky Man — Public Enemy: Night of the Living Baseheads (1988)
Funky Man — Zhigge: Harlem (1992)
Funky Stuff — Beastie Boys: Hold It Now, Hit It (1986)
Funky Stuff — NWA: Appetite for Destruction (1991)
Funky Stuff — Terminator X: Ain't Gut Nuttin' (1991)
Get Down on It — Jermain Dupri featuring Snoop Doggy Dogg: We Just wanna Party with You (1997)
Give It Up — A Tribe Called Quest: Scenario (1991)
Give It Up — Beastie Boys: Professor Booty (1992)
Give It Up — Compton's Most Wanted: Compton 4 Life (1992)
Give It Up — Cypress Hitll: Phunky Feel One (1992)
Give It Up — Deee-Lite: Deee-Lite Theme (1990)
Give It Up — Eric B & Rakim: Don't Sweat the Technique (1992)
Give It Up — Gang Starr: Take A Rest (1991)
Give It Up — Lionrock: Morning Will Come When I'm Not Ready (1995)
Give It Up — Greg Osby: 3-D Lifestyles (1993)
GIve It Up — MC Brains: Everydoby's Talking About MC Brains (1992)
Give It Up — NWA: Real Niggaz (1990)
Give It Up — Organized Konfusion: Intro (1991)
Give It Up — X-Clan: Shaft's Big Score (1990)
Good Times — Cypress Hill: Light Another (1992)
Good Times — Ice Cube: The Product (1991)
Good Times — Queen Latifah: Ladies First (1989)
Heaven at Once — Fugees: Nappy Heads (1994)
Hollywood Swinging — 7A3: Coolin' In Cali (1988)
Hollywood Swinging — DJ Kool: Let Me Clear My Throat (1996)
Hollywood Swinging — Mase: Feel So Good (1997)
Hollywood Swinging — Mack 10: Inglewood Swangin' (1997)
Hollywood Swinging — Professor Griff & the Last Asiatic Dicsiples: 1–900 Stereotype (1990)
Hollywood Swinging — Terminator X: The Blues (1991)
Hollywood Swinging — Too Short: Money in the Ghetto (1993)
Jungle Boogie — Big Daddy Kane: Get Down (1991)
Jungle Boogie — Beastie Boys: Hey Ladies (1989)
Jungle Boogie — BWP: Wanted (1991)
Jungle Boogie — Compton's Most Wanted: Compton Cyco (1994)
Jungle Boogie — Coldcut: Say Kids, What Time Is It? (1987)
Jungle Boogie — Das EFX: Straight Out of the Sewer (1992)
Jungle Boogie — EPMD: Can't Hear Nothing But the Music (1992)
Jungle Boogie — EPMD: You're a Customer (1988)
Jungle Boogie — EPMD: You Gots To Chill (1988)
Jungle Boogie — EPMD: Richter Scale (1997)
Jungle Boogie — Ice Cube: The Product (1991)
Jungle Boogie — Insane Poetry: How Ya Gonna Reason with a Psycho (1992)
Jungle Boogie — Insane Poetry: Grim Reality (1992)
Jungle Boogie — Janet Jackson: You Want This (1993)
Jungle Boogie — Jeru the Damaja: Frustrated Nigga (1996)

Jungle Boogie — KAM: Neva Again (1993)

Jungle Boogie — Madonna: Erotica (1992)

Jungle Boogie — MC Lyte: I Am the Lyte (1989)

Jungle Boogie — Public Enemy: Welcome to the Terrordome (1990)

Jungle Boogie — Redman: So Ruff (1992)

Jungle Boogie — Redman: Jam 4 U (1992)

Jungle Boogie — Threat; Let the Dogs Loose (1993)

Jungle Jazz — 3rd Bass: Brooklyn-Queens (remix) (1991)

Jungle Jazz — Biz Markie: I'm the Biz Markie (1993)

Jungle Jazz — Brand Nubian: Drop the Bomb (1991)

Jungle Jazz — Hi-C: Leave My Curl Alone (remix) (1992)

Jungle Jazz — Jade: Don't Walk Away (1993)

Jungle Jazz — Gus Gus: Believe (1997)

Jungle Jazz — M.A.R.R.S.: Pump Up the Volume (1987)

Jungle Jazz — Public Enemy: Anti Nigger Machine (1990)

Jungle Jazz — Stetsasonic: So Let the Fun Begin (1991)

Kool It (Here Come the Fuzz) — Brand Nubian: Slow Down (1991)

Kool It (Here Come the Fuzz) — Janet Jackson: New Agenda (1993)

Kool It (Here Come the Fuzz) — Kool G. Rap: Bad to the Bone (1990)

Ladies Night (remix) — Lil' Kim featuring Da Brat, Left Eye, Missie Elliot & Angie Martinez: Not Tonight (remix) (1996)

Let the Music Take Your Mind — Boss: Process of Elimination (1993)

Let the Music Take Your Mind — Ice Cube: Amerikkka's Most Wanted (1990)

Let the Music Take Your Mind — Ice-T: Freedom of Speech (1989)

Life Is What You Make It — Cypress Hill: Phunky Feel One (1992)

Life Is What You Make It — Style: What A Brother Know (1991)

Little Children — AZ: Ho Happy Jackie (1995)

Love Is the Life You Live — Freestyle Fellowship: Way Cool (1993)

Love Is the Life You Live — Geto Boyz: Trigga Happy Nigga (1990)

Love Is the Life You Live — Yo-Yo: Make Way for the Motherlode (1991)

Mother Earth — 3rd Bass: Steppin' to the AM (1989)

Music Is the Message — Queen Latifah: King & Queen Creation (1989)

N.T. — 3rd Bass: Gladiator (remix) (1989)

N.T. — A Tribe Called Quest: Mind Power (1996)

N.T. — Big Daddy Kane: On the Move (1989)

N.T. — Brand Nubian: Slow Down (1991)

N.T. — BWP: Cotex (1991)

N.T. — Chill Rob G: Let Me Show You (1990)

N.T. — Chubb Rock: Which Way Is Up? (1992)

N.T. — Compton's Most Wanted: Compton 4 Life (1992)

N.T. — Da Lench Mob: Ankle Blues (1992)

N.T. — De La Soul: Keepin' the Faith (remix) (1991)

N.T. — Diamond D: Best Kept Secret (1992)

N.T. — DJ Quik: Amerika'z Most Complete Artist (1992)

N.T. — Double XX Posse: Headcracker (1992)

N.T. — Eric B & Rakim: Move the Crowd (remix) (1987)

N.T. — Geto Boys: Cereal Killer (1993)

N.T. — Geto Boys: Damn It Feels Good To Be a Gansta (1992)

N.T. — Kool G Rap: Truly Yours (1989)

N.T. — Kriss Kross: Jump (1991)

N.T. — Lord Finesse: Praise the Lord (1991)

N.T. — Lords of the Underground: What's Goin On? (1993)

N.T. — Mellow Man Ace: Talkapella (1990)

N.T. — Main Source: Scratch & Kut (1991)

N.T. — MC Serch: Don't Have To Be (1992)

N.T. — Mark Morrison: Return of the Mack (remix) (1997)

N.T. — Nas: It Ain't Hard To Tell (1994)

N.T. — NWA: Gangsta Gangsta (1989)

N.T. — NWA: Niggaz 4 Life (1991)

N.T. — Professor Griff & the Last Asiatic Disciples: Pawns in the Game (1990)

N.T. — Public Enemy: B Side Wins Again (1990)

N.T. — Run DMC: Back from Hell (remix) (1990)

N.T. — Shabba Ranks: The Jam (1991)

N.T. — Steady B: Going Steady (1989)

N.T. — Stetsasonic: Blood, Sweat and No Tears (1991)

N.T. — Stetsasonic: So Let the Fun Begin (1991)

N.T. — Terminator X: Can't Take My Style (1991)

N.T. — UMC: Siwng It To the Area (1991)

N.T. — Warren G: Runnin Wit No Breaks (1994)

N.T. — Yo-Yo: Woman To Woman (1992)

N.T. — YZ: Return of THe Holy One (1992)

Rated X — Ice Cube: Turn Off the Radio (1990)

Rated X — Ice Cube: The Product (1991)

Rated X — Kool Moe Dee: Rise 'N' Shine (1991)

Rated X — Queen Latifah: Queen of Royal Badness (1989)

Soul Vibrations — A Tribe Called Quest: Scenario (remix) (1991)

Soul Vibrations — Biz Markie: Things Get a Little Easier (1989)

Soul Vibrations — Donald D: Notorious (1989)

Soul Vibrations — LL Cool J: Cheesy Rat Blues (1990)

Spirit of the Boogie — KAM: Peace Treaty (1993)

Spirit of the Boogie — Notorious BIG: Friend of Mine (1994)

Summer Madness — Coolio: Mama I'm in Love Wit a Gangsta (1994)

Summer Madness — Miles Davis: Doo Bop Song (1992)

Summer Madness — DJ Jazzy Jeff & the Fresh Prince: Summertime (1991)

Summer Madness — Ice Cube: You Know How We Do It (1993)

Summer Madness — Mad Skillz: Get Your Groove On (1996)

Summer Madness — Montell Jordan: Somethin' 4 Da Honeyz (1995)

Summer Madness — Lost Boyz: Intro (1995)

Summer Madness (live) — Domino: Do You Qualify? (1993)

Who's Gonna Take the Weight? — A Tribe Called Quest: Oh My God (1993)

Who's Gonna Take the Weight? — Criminal Element: Hit Me with the Beat (1989)

Won's Gonna Take the Weight? — Cypress Hill: When the Ship Goes Down (remix) (1993)

Who's Gonna Take the Weight? — Diamond D: Best Kept Secret (1992)

Who's Gonna Take the Weight? — Diamond D: What You Seek (1992)

Who's Gonna Take the Weight? — Heavy D: Letter To the Future (1991)

Who's Gonna Take the Weight? — Public Enemy: Louder than a Bomb (1988)

Who's Gonna Take the Weight? — Stetsasonic: In Full Gear (1988)

## LAFAYETTE AFRO ROCK BAND

**FORMED:** *1970, Long Island, NY*
**ORIGINAL LINE-UP:** *Larry Jones (gtr), Lafayette Hudson (bs), Frank Abel (kybds), Ronnie James Buttacavoli (horns), Arthur Young (horns), Ernest "Donny" Donable (drms), Keno Speller (perc), Arthur Young (perc)*

Formed as the Bobby Boy Congress, after original vocalist Bobby Boy, the musicians moved to France in 1971, having failed to attract any attention in their homeland. Bobby Boy returned home very soon after; his bandmates renamed themselves Ice and were soon regularly appearing in Paris' predominantly African Barbesse district. There they were discovered by producer Pierre Jaubert and recruited as houseband at his Parisound studio.

It was Jaubert who initiated the group's name change to the Lafayette Afro Rock Band in 1973, following the release of the album *Each Man Makes His Own Destiny*. Encouraged by their Barbesse audience, the group's musical direction had altered dramatically, blending powerful Afro-beat tendencies with their original solid (if workmanlike) funk.

Having replaced guitarist Jones with Michael McEwan, the band's next album, 1974's *Soul Makossa*, became their most successful, at the time and subsequently—the record was released in the US as *Movin' and Groovin'*. Though it did not chart, it apparently made sufficient impact that, 20 years on, its highlights were being regularly sampled. *Malik*, the following year, has been similarly treated; Public Enemy's "Show 'Em Whatcha Got" (from the *It Takes a Nation of Millions* album) makes excellent use of the sax intro from "Darkest Night."

In 1975, producer Jaubert made his bid for Eurodisco production mastermind status by disguising the musicians as Crispy and Company and cutting the novelty dance track "Brazil." It was a smash across Europe, reaching #26 in the UK, with a follow-up effort, "Get It Together," climbing five places higher. Evidencing their versatility, however, that same year also saw the group work with jazzman Mal Waldron and blues guitarist Sunnyland Slim.

In 1976, tiring of the nomenclatural connotations of the Lafayette Afro Rock Band, the group reverted to the Ice name and cut *Frisco Disco*, another disco set. It was not successful; however, yet another alias, Captain Dax, landed a bestseller in Japan with the novelty "Dr. Beezar, Soul Frankenstein."

A third Ice album, *Afro Agban*, in 1978, and a return to the Crispy and Co. identity for *Funky Flavored* followed, but their failure proved the last straw. By the end of the year, the musicians had returned to the US, disbanding the group upon arrival.

## LAFAYETTE AFRO BAND DISCOGRAPHY
### ICE LPs

**5** 1972 **Each Man Makes His Own Destiny (Makossa—Fr)**
Unspectacular rent-a-funk set, studiously overproduced, but intriguing in its precision.

**4** 1976 **Frisco Disco (Makossa—Fr)**
**5** 1977 **Afro Agban (Makossa—Fr)**

### LAFAYETTE AFRO BAND LPs

**8** 1974 **Soul Makossa (Makossa—Fr)**
Released in the US as *Movin' and Groovin'* (Musicdisc), the album upon which the band's entire reputation is built, a dramatic Afro-funk fusion that eschews songs for grooves, lyrics for chants and rhythms for sheer liquidity.

**7** 1975 **Malik (Makossa—Fr)**
Megaton percussion, super-fuzz guitar and a "magic bag" vocoder effect that brought an other worldly feel to the magic Third World sound.

### SELECTED COMPILATIONS AND ARCHIVE RELEASES

**6** 1978 **Afon: 10 Unreleased Afro Funk Recordings (Superclasse—FR)**
Occasional cuts reach the peaks of *Movin' and Groovin'*, but a general lack of focus leaves the album feeling dangerously unfinished.

**7** 1999 **Darkest Light: The Best of (Strut—UK)**
The ultimate point of entry, collecting Ice, Mal Waldron, Crispy & Co. and Dr. Beezar alongside the Lafayette centerpiece. "Soul Frankenstein," "The Gap (instrumental)," "Conga," "Malik," "Soul Makossa," "Scorpion Flower," "Nicky" and "Darkest Light" are the most obvious high points.

### SELECTED SAMPLES

Darkest Light — Freestylers: Freestyle Noize (1998)
Darkest Light — Heavy D: You Can't See What I See (1996)
Darkest Light — Masters at Work: Justa lil' Dope (1991)
Darkest Light — Public Enemy: Show 'Em What'cha Got (1988)
Darkest Light — Tuff Crew: Soul Food (1989)
Darkest Light — Wreckx-N- Effect: Rump Shaker (1992)
Hihache — Biz Markie: Nobody Beats the Biz (1988)
Hihache — Channel Live: Build and Destroy (1995)
Hihache — De La Soul: Oodles of O's (1991)
Hihache — Digital Underground: No Nose Job (remix) (1991)
Hihache — GRavediggaz: 2 Cups of Blood (1994)
Hihache — Montell Jordan: This Is How We Do It (1995)
Hihache — Kriss Kross: Alright (1993)
Hihache — LL Cool J: Jingling Baby (1989)
Hihache — Naughty By Nature: Ghetto Bastard (1991)
Hihache — Nice & Smooth: No Delayin' (1989)

Hihache — Original Flavor: I Like It (Freestyle) (1992)
Hihache — Public Enemy: Can't Truss It (1991)
Hihache — Souls of Mischief: Dirty D's Theme (Hoe or Die) (1995)
Hihache — Wu-Tang Clan: Wu-Tang Ain't Nuthing Ta F' Wit (1993)

## MACEO AND MACKS, see MACEO PARKER

## MALO

**FORMED:** *1970, San Francisco, CA*
**ORIGINAL LINE-UP:** *Arcelio Garcia (perc, vcls), Jorge Santana (gtr, vcls), Abel Zarate (gtr), Pablo Tellez (bs), Richard Kermode (kybds), Luis Gasca (trum), Richard Spremich (drms), Richard Bean (perc, vcls)*

The sudden insurgence of Latin funk acts that burst over the US in the early 1970s was, naturally, a consequence of the emergence of Santana. Few of these groups survived more than an album or two before the inevitable comparisons ground them down. Malo, on the other hand, flourished under such categorization and not only for their music. With frontman Jorge Santana bearing both a visual and a vocal resemblance to his superstar brother Carlos, the die would have been cast whatever music Malo played.

Originally called the Malibus, they were spotted by David Rubinson, the man who signed Santana to Columbia (and later produced the Meters' final album). Despite the family connection, the Malibus were as concerned with hard-nosed funk as they were with extolling their Latin influences, an independence that thoroughly impressed Rubinson.

He signed the newly renamed Malo (Spanish for "bad") to Warner Brothers in 1971, at a time when the local *Night Times* newspaper was trumpeting Malo as "the hottest rock property in the Bay Area right now." The band had their press unveiling on January 10, 1972, just as copies of their Rubinson-produced debut album reached radio. KSAN slammed *Malo* into rotation, and the group launched a tour with Quicksilver. Within a week of release, local sales of *Malo* topped 7,000 as it drove into the Top 20. A single, "Suavecito," readily followed.

The group ranked among the main attractions at the final Fillmore shows (their fluid fusion is captured on the *Last Days at the Fillmore* live album). However, constant lineup changes led to diminishing returns for Malo's next two albums, *Dos* and *Evolution*, released in fall 1972 and spring 1973. Garcia quit and, while Santana held a lineup together for one final album, *Ascension*, the funk had gone east with the vocalist. Malo split in mid-1974.

Jorge Santana resurfaced briefly with salsa superstars Fania All-Stars, guesting alongside drummer Billy Cobham on the *Latin Soul Rock* album. He also cut a solo album, *Jorge Santana*, for Tomato in 1978. He became better known, however, for his early-'90s partnership with brother Carlos and nephew Carlos Hernandez, as the Santana Brothers.

Garcia, meanwhile, was working as a mechanic at a Brooklyn cosmetics factory when he decided to form an 11-piece East Coast Malo in 1981. The group flourished locally for the next three years, but by 1985, Garcia was back in San Francisco and piecing together a new lineup, debuting at a benefit show opening for Tower of Power. Pete Escovido, ex-Azteca, was also on the bill.

Buoyed by a well-received 1992 "best of" collection, Malo cut a moderately successful comeback album, 1995's *Senorita*, following through with a 25th anniversary tour. However, it was not until 1999 that Malo truly re-emerged from the shadows, when alternative rockers Sugar Ray sampled "Suavecito" for their "Every Morning" hit. In its wake, Santana returned to the fold and Malo was relaunched in early 2000 with the two founder members joined by Pablo Benavidez (vcls), Gabriel Manzo (gtr), Ramiro Amador (bs), Zach Bonilla (kybds) Steve Rocha (trom), Tom Bertetta (trum), David George (drms), Gibby Ross (perc) and Tony Menjivar (perc).

### MALO DISCOGRAPHY
### CHART LOG
1972 Suavecito/Nena (WB—#18 pop)

### LPs
**8** 1972 Malo (WB—#14 pop)
An inventive offering established Malo as something more than funky Santana wannabes. The epic "Just Say Goodbye" proves Santana's guitar sound to be just as individual as his brother's, the much-sampled "Suavecito" adds warm vocals to a charming lite-funk soundscape, and the screaming "Peace" simply rocks.
**6** 1972 Dos (WB—#62 pop)
**5** 1973 Evolution (WB—#101 pop)
**4** 1974 Ascension (WB—#188—pop)
Without the funk rock sensibilities of Garcia, a distinctly underwhelming set of Latin rhythms and sparse ideas.
**4** 1995 Senorita (GNP)
Competent comeback offers no musical surprises and suffers from a paucity of fresh ideas.
**7** 1996 Rockin' the Rockies (GNP)

Oldies heavy live album, a little more tempered than the "classic" lineup sounded, but still an exciting affair.

### SELECTED COMPILATIONS AND ARCHIVE RELEASES

**7** 1992 The Best of Malo (GNP)

Sensible, if unadventurous sampling of the band's WB years.

**6** 2001 Celebracion (Rhino Handmade)

Limited edition, four-CD box set comprising 41 tracks (one unreleased). The group's entire WB catalog.

### SELECTED SAMPLES

Suavecito — Sugar Ray: Every Morning (1999)

## CURTIS MAYFIELD

**BORN:** *6/3/42, Chicago; died: 12/26/99*

When Curtis Mayfield passed away the day after Christmas 1999, the majority of the obituaries dispensed by the world's music press were swift to remember him—and rightly so— as one of the sweetest soul singers of the past 40 years. As the voice behind "We're a Winner," "Keep On Pushing," "People Get Ready," "Move On Up," "Sweet Exorcist," "Between You Baby and Me," and the prime instigator behind a staggering 69 US R&B chart hits between 1958 and 1997, Mayfield's active impact upon the Black music scene of the '60s and '70s is incalculable; his effect on that of the '80s and '90s just as prodigious.

A gospel singer as a child, Mayfield was 12 when he joined the Northern Jubilee Gospel Singers, a group linked to his grandmother's Traveling Soul Spiritualist Church. Within two years, Mayfield and another of the Singers, 17-year-old Jerry Butler, joined the Roosters, a secular group formed by singers Sam Gooden and the brothers Richard and Arthur Brooks, replacing the recently departed Emanuel Thomas and Fred Cash.

The Roosters became Jerry Butler & the Impressions and, in 1958, their first single, "For Your Precious Love," was released by Vee-Jay. It flopped, as did a reissue on Falcon. Finally, a third release on the Abner label cracked the pop Top 20. A follow-up, "Come Back My Love," was less successful and Butler quit for a solo career; the remaining Impressions replaced him with the returning Fred Cash. Mayfield then wrote Butler's chart-topping "He Will Break Your Heart" in 1960. He plowed his earnings from the 45 into taking the Impressions to New York to record a set of demos that ultimately landed them a deal with ABC-Paramount.

The band was relaunched onto the commercial stage in 1961, when "Gypsy Woman" powered to #2 on the R&B chart; two years later, despite the departure of the Brook brothers, the Impressions unveiled "It's Alright," an R&B chart-topper and pop #4.

However, they were also evincing a pronounced social consciousness. "Keep On Pushing," the Impressions' fourth R&B Top Ten 45 in 1964, was immediately taken up by the infant civil rights movement, just as author Mayfield intended it to be. But its message was cleverly coded, cloaked in seemingly innocuous religious imagery that only translated to listeners who already knew which side of the struggle they were on.

That same year's "I'm So Proud"—again a Black power anthem before the expression had even entered the popular vocabulary—and 1965's emotion-soaked "People Get Ready," made similar leaps into the consciousness of what society, at least, regarded as a radical minority. (Years later, director Spike Lee included "People Get Ready" among four Impressions songs featured in his *Get on the Bus* movie, documenting the Million Man march.)

Not until 1968, the year in which the struggle exploded into the frontline of American life, would the Impressions' joyful subversion finally be revealed. Led by Chicago's WLS, a string of US radio stations banned the group's MLK-inspired "We're a Winner."

Now recording for Mayfield's own Curtom label, the Impressions responded by ditching the smart suits and ties that had been their stagewear through the early-mid-'60s, and began turning out in the street clothes, which were themselves a badge of recognition in the movement, turtlenecks, leather jackets, wide pants, sailor's caps.

Equally dramatically, however, they preached moderation. The 1969 R&B #1 "Choice of Colors" pointedly asked, "how long have you hated your White teacher," an outright rejection of the race war rhetoric that was both the White establishment's greatest fear and the Black radical's fondest threat. The single's B-side, "Mighty Mighty (Spade And Whitey)" put a similar question in even stronger terms. Mayfield later took to opening his live show with the song.

Mayfield launched a solo career in 1970, initially to fulfill his (White) business manager Marv Stuart's insistence that the commercial tide was turning in the favor of singer-songwriters and that Mayfield really ought to give it a go. He responded with *Curtis*, a devastating statement of intent that may have continued walking the same lyrical path as the Impressions, but could not have ventured further afield musically.

The opening "(Don't Worry) If There's a Hell Below, We're Going To Go," an R&B Top Three that November, set the tone for the album, although Mayfield's gospel back-

**The late, great Curtis Mayfield.**

ground could not be completely subjugated. "Move On Up," a massive UK hit (and absolute flop in the US), was the match of anything the Impressions ever recorded, but it unquestionably benefitted from its surroundings, emerging as defiant as it was triumphant. A little over a decade later, British punks The Jam covered the song as a symbol of their solidarity with their country's leftist working class. Utterly unsurprisingly, the group grafted a light funk rhythm to their arrangement.

Mayfield's willingness to explore funk, he told *Goldmine* magazine, was a natural extension of his Chicago upbringing. "For me, it was just the way. I had my guitar and, along with the gospel, I heard plenty of rhythm and blues and blues per se." He also nursed a deep love of Jimi Hendrix, whose own fusion of those musical forms had itself pointed him in the direction Mayfield was now taking. And, like Hendrix, he had no fear of taking a wrong turning while he traveled.

"I'd never taken any music lessons so I didn't really know the forms—eight bars, 16 bars, this, that. So I played and wrote as I felt it." Every so often, he recalled, his backing band "would make comments like, 'gosh, this is a terribly

strange key to play in.' [But] they just had to follow as I wrote it." Besides, to an audience already schooled in the wild waters of psychedelic rock and regarding funk as the logical inheritor of that genre's freedom, Mayfield's approach was valued precisely for its idiosyncrasies.

Riding the success of *Curtis*, Mayfield toured with a combo drawn from among his oldest musical friends: Phil Upchurch, a session guitarist whose work encompassed great swathes of the Vee Jay, Okeh and Chess catalogs of the '60s; bassist Lucky Scott, nephew of the Impressions' Sam Gooden; and percussionist Henry Gibson. A dynamic live show was captured for the *Curtis/Live* album, released as Mayfield returned to the Impressions for what became the *Check Out Your Mind* album.

That was his last record with the band. Commercially, Mayfield's solo career had risen higher than the Impressions' had climbed in years, while his commitments to Curtom were also consuming vast tracts of time. Mayfield quit the Impressions in mid-1971, as their latest single, "Love Me," climbed to #25 and his own *Curtis/Live!* album, recorded at New York's Bitter End club, stormed to #3. (The Impressions regrouped with vocalist Leroy Hutson.)

By late 1971, Mayfield's third solo album, *Roots*, was spinning off the hits "Get Down," "We Got To Have Peace" and another of Mayfield's dramatic funk/gospel fusions, "Beautiful Brother of Mine." But it was with the following year's *Superfly* movie soundtrack that Mayfield finally made the socio-political and musical transition that both his group and solo work had been aiming for, a suite of songs that, no less than the Issac Hayes' *Shaft* the previous year, so effortlessly complimented the action on screen that it is impossible to even think of one without recalling the other.

Director Sig Shore and screenwriter Philip Fenty delivered the movie script to Mayfield while he was performing at the Lincoln Center in New York; Mayfield was so excited at the prospect that he wrote the first song for the soundtrack on the plane home from New York.

In keeping with his long established program of subterfuge, however, little about Mayfield's soundtrack actually echoed the theme of the finished movie. While the film apparently glorified cocaine, the soundtrack slammed it and, while contemporary audiences commented upon the dichotomy, Mayfield's unrepentant explanation has since become regarded among the album's greatest strengths. In that same *Goldmine* interview, he acknowledged, "when I saw [the movie], I thought 'this is a cocaine infomercial.' That's all it was. I didn't want to be part of that infomercial, so it was important to me that I left the glitter. I tried to tell the stories of the people in depth."

Mayfield's commentary did not escape completely unscathed. The bitterest of his compositions, "Freddie's Dead," appeared only as an instrumental in the movie; the lyrics, however, were no secret as the full version was released as a single and sauntered to #2.

Encouraged by the massive success of *Superfly*, Mayfield wasted little time in completing his own next release, *Future Shock*, a concept album germinated on a tour of US bases in Europe, but based around the experiences of a GI returning home from Vietnam. It was a theme that Marvin Gaye had already explored with the bitter *What's Going On*, but Mayfield's superior lyrical talents raised the temperature from polemic to politics and further still, into the soul of its protagonist.

*Sweet Exorcist*, the last of Mayfield's Top Ten albums, was also to prove the last to evidence his observations on (and, where necessary, condemnation of) modern society. Later, he admitted that the decline in both his musical and commercial fortunes was simply the outcome of trying to do too much.

The success of *Superfly* saw his name top the shortlist for almost every blaxploitation movie of the era. He wound up scoring six more films between 1972–77: *Claudine* (1974), *Pipedreams* (1976, with soundtracks performed by Gladys Knight & the Pips), *Let's Do It Again* (1975, with the Staples Singers), *Sparkle* (1976, with Aretha Franklin), *A Piece of The Action* (1977, with Mavis Staples) and, under his own name, *Short Eyes* (1977). Small wonder that, when it came to his own career, he was rapidly running out of ideas.

Through the mid-late-'70s, Mayfield moved increasingly toward a disco-fuelled soft option. Curtom was on the verge of collapse and, in one final desperate bid for mainstream success, Mayfield paired himself with Bunny Sigler, Norman Harris and Ronald Tyson, a team of producers/arrangers/musicians first convened at Gamble and Huff's Philly label.

Mayfield himself was a firm admirer of Gamble and Huff. Interviewed for the booklet accompanying the duo's 1997 *The Philly Sound* box set, he confessed, "they overwhelmed us. . . . They walked a thin line in many directions, but you always knew they were steering the ship." In the hands of their crew members, however, Mayfield was sucked into a vortex he would only recognize after the fact, the knowledge that "the music I made only sold when I was just being Curtis. When I tried to be other than what I was, you could forget it."

Two albums, *Do It All Night* in 1978 and *Heartbeat* in 1979, were indeed forgettable, and in 1979, Mayfield signed Curtom's distribution over to RSO, a label best known for its success with the Bee Gees and the *Saturday Night Fever* soundtrack. Curtom's identity was promptly swallowed into the parent label, which itself folded a year later.

Mayfield continued recording with varying degrees of success through the early '80s, reawakening his political conscience as he did so. He signed with Boardwalk, the label launched by former Casablanca chief Neil Bogart; but *Honesty*, in 1982, was his last new release for three years. He then relaunched Curtom in 1985; *We Come in Peace with a Message of Love*, in 1985, was followed by the self-explanatory *Live in Europe* in 1988, while Mayfield also recorded a single with British soul hopefuls The Blow Monkeys, the biting "Celebrate (The Day After You)," a single dedicated to Prime Minister Margaret Thatcher.

In 1989, a new Mayfield soundtrack, *I'm Gonna Git You Sucker* announced Mayfield's return to full action. The acclaimed *Take It To the Streets*, was released in 1990 and, in early July, Mayfield recorded a single with rapper Ice-T,

"Superfly 90." (T had previously sampled "Pusherman" in his own "I'm Your Pusher.") But it all came tumbling down a month later, at an outdoor show at Brooklyn's Wingate high School on August 13, 1990, when high winds blew a lighting tower down upon him. Several of Mayfield's vertebrae were crushed and he was left quadraplegic, paralyzed from the neck down.

Mayfield's career came to a halt, of course. Now, however, it was time to finally receive the recognition of his peers. In 1991, Mayfield was inducted into the Rock & Roll Hall of Fame, alongside the Impressions; three years later, the NAACP Hall of Fame opened its doors to him. In 1995, he received the Grammy Lifetime Achievement Award, 22 years after *Superfly* earned him his first and only nomination. He was also honored with three separate tribute albums and, in 1997, he returned to the studio under the aegis of hip-hop pioneer Darryl Simmons.

With Narada Michael Walden, Roger Troutman and Organized Noise also on board, *New World Order* saw Mayfield turn full circle, to the gospel of the early Impressions, and the political doublespeak of his peak. Hopes, however, that his body would mend alongside his spirit were tragically misplaced. He developed diabetes, a disease that ultimately forced doctors to amputate Mayfield's right leg in 1998 and, over the next year, his health spiraled downward. He died on December 26, 1999, at North Fulton Regional Hospital, in Roswell, GA.

### CURTIS MAYFIELD COMPLETE DISCOGRAPHY
### SINGLES/CHART LOG
### JERRY BUTLER AND THE IMPRESSIONS

1958 For Your Precious Love/Sweet Was the Wine (Abner—#3 R&B/#11 pop)
1958 Come Back My Love/Love Me (Abner—#29 R&B)
1959 The Gift of Love/At the Country Fair (Abner)

### THE IMPRESSIONS

1959 Senorita I Love You/Lonely One (Abner)
1960 Say That You Love Me/A New Love (Abner)
1960 Listen/Shorty's Got To Go (Bandera)
1961 Gypsy Woman/As Long as You Love Me (ABC-Paramount—#2 R&B/#20 pop)
1962 Grow Closer Together/Can't You See? (ABC-Paramount)
1962 Little Young Lover/Never Let Me Go (ABC-Paramount)
1962 You've Come Home/Minstrel and Queen (ABC-Paramount)
1963 I'm the One Who Loves You/I Need Your Love (ABC-Paramount)
1963 Sad Sad Girl and Boy/Twist and Limbo (ABC-Paramount)
1963 It's All Right/You'll Want Me Back (ABC-Paramount—#1 R&B/#4 pop)
1964 Talking About My Baby/Never Too Much Love (ABC-Paramount—#12 R&B)

1964 Girl You Don't Know Me/A Woman Who Loves Me (ABC-Paramount)
1964 I'm So Proud/I Made a Mistake (ABC-Paramount—#14 R&B)
1964 Keep On Pushing/I Love You (Yeah) (ABC-Paramount—#14 R&B)
1964 You Must Believe Me/See the Real Me (ABC-Paramount—#15 R&B)
1965 Amen (ABC-Paramount—#17 R&B/#7 pop)/Long Long Winter (#35 R&B)
1965 People Get Ready (ABC-Paramount—#3 R&B/#14 pop)/I've Been Trying (#35 R&B)
1965 Woman's Got Soul/Get Up and Move (ABC-Paramount—#9 R&B/#29 pop)
1965 Meeting Over Yonder/I've Found That I've Lost (ABC-Paramount—#12 R&B/#48 pop)
1965 I Need You (ABC-Paramount—#26 R&B/#64 pop)/Never Could Be You (#35 R&B)
1965 Just One Kiss from You/Twilight Time (ABC-Paramount)
1965 You've Been Cheating/Man Oh Man (ABC-Paramount—#12 R&B/#33 pop)
1966 Since I Lost the One I Love/Falling in Love with You (ABC-Paramount)
1966 Too Slow/No-one Else (ABC-Paramount)
1966 Can't Satisfy/This Must End (ABC—#12 R&B/#65 pop)
1966 Love's a Coming/Wade in the Water (ABC)
1967 You Always Hurt Me/Little Girl (ABC—#20 R&B/#96 pop)
1967 You've Got Me Running/It's Hard To Believe (ABC—#50 R&B)
1967 I Can't Stay Away from You/You Ought To Be in Heaven (ABC—#34 R&B/#30 pop)
1968 We're a Winner/It's All Over (ABC—1 R&B/#14 pop)
1968 We're Rolling On (part one)/(part two) (ABC—#17 R&B/#59 pop)
1968 I Loved and Lost/Up Up and Away (ABC—#9 R&B/#61 pop)
1968 Fool for You/I'm Loving Nothing (Curtom—#3 R&B/#22 pop)
1968 This Is My Country/My Woman's Love (Curtom—#8 R&B/#25 pop)
1968 Don't Cry My Love/Sometimes I Wonder (ABC—#44 R&B/#71 pop)
1969 East of Java/Just Before Sunrise (ABC)
1969 My Deceiving Heart/You Want Somebody Else (Curtom—#23 R&B/104 pop)
1969 Seven Years/The Girl I Find (Curtom—#15 R&B/#84 pop)
1969 Choice of Colors/Mighty Mighty Spade and Whitey (Curtom—#1 R&B/#21 pop)
1969 Say You Love Me/You'll Always Be Mine (Curtom—#10 R&B/#58 pop)
1970 Wherever She Leadeth Me (Curtom #31 R&B/#128 pop)/Amen (1970) (#44 R&B/#110 pop)
1970 Check Out Your Mind/Can't You See (Curtom—#3 R&B/#28 pop)
1970 (Baby) Turn Onto me/Soulful Love (Curtom—#6 R&B/#56 pop)
1971 Ain't Got Time/I'm So Proud (Curtom—#12 R&B/#53 pop)
1971 Love Me/Do You Wanna Win (Curtom—#25 R&B/#94 pop)

### CURTIS MAYFIELD

1970 (Don't Worry) If There's a Hell Below/The Makings of You (Curtom—#3 R&B/#29 pop)
1970 Beautiful Brother of Mine/Give It Up (Curtom)
1971 Mighty Mighty (Spade and Whitey) (live)/? (Curtom)

1971 Get Down/We're a Winner (live) (Curtom—#13 R&B/#69 pop)

1972 We Got To Have Peace/Love to Keep You in My Mind (Curtom—#32 R&B/#115 pop)

1972 Beautiful Brother of Mine/Love to Keep You in My Mind (Curtom—#45 R&B)

1972 Move On Up/Underground (Curtom)

1972 Freddie's Dead/Underground (Curtom—#2 R&B/#4 pop)

1972 Superfly/Underground (Curtom—#5 R&B/#8 pop)

1973 Future Shock/The Other Side of Town (Curtom—#11 R&B/#39 pop)

1973 If I Were Only a Child Again/Think (Curtom—#22 R&B/#71 pop)

1973 Can't Say Nothin'/Future Song (Curtom—#16 R&B/#88 pop)

1974 Kung Fu/Right On for the Darkness (Curtom—#3 R&B/#40 pop)

1974 Sweet Exorcist/Suffer (Curtom—#32 R&B)

1975 Mother's Son/Love Me (Curtom—#15 R&B)

1975 So in Love/Hard Times (Curtom—#9 R&B/#67 pop)

1976 Only You Babe/Love To the People (Curtom—#8 R&B)

1976 Party Night/PS I Love You (Curtom—#39 R&B)

1977 Show Me Love/Just Want To Be with You (Curtom—#41 R&B)

1977 Do Do Wap Is Strong in Here/Need Someone To Love (Curtom—#29 R&B)

1978 You Are You Are/Get a Little Bit (Curtom—#34 R&B)

1978 Do It All Night/Party Party (Curtom—#96 R&B)

1978 In Love in Love in Love/Keeps Me Loving You (Curtom)

1979 This Year/(instrumental) (RSO/Curtom—#40 R&B)

1980 Love Me Love Me Now/It's Alright (RSO/Curtom—#48 R&B)

1980 Tripping Out/Never Stop Loving Me (RSO/Curtom—#46 R&B)

1981 She Don't Let Nobody (But Me)/You Get All My Love (Boardwalk—#15 R&B/#103 pop)

1981 Toot & Toot & Toot/Come Free Your People (Boardwalk—#22 R&B)

1982 Hey Baby/Summer Hot (Boardwalk—#68 R&B)

1982 Dirty Laundry/Nobody But You (Boardwalk)

1985 Baby It's You/Breakin' in the Streets (CRC—#68 R&B)

1988 Move On Up/Little Child Runnin' Wild (Curtom)

1989 I Mo' Git You Sucka/He's a Fly Guy (Curtom)

1990 Homeless/People Never Give Up (Curtom)

1990 Do Be Down/Got To Be Real (Curtom)

1990 Dirty Laundry/We Gotta Have Peace (Curtom)

1996 New World Order/(instrumental) (WB—#49 R&B)

1997 No-one Knows About a Good Thing/We People Who Are Darker than Blue (WB—#61 R&B)

1997 Back To Living Again (LP version) (WB—#88 R&B)

## CURTIS MAYFIELD/LINDA CLIFFORD

1979 Between You Baby and Me (RSO/Curtom—#14 R&B)/You're So Good to Me (#46 R&B)

1980 Love's Sweet Sensation/(instrumental) (RSO/Curtom—#34 R&B)

## CURTIS MAYFIELD/BLOW MONKEYS

1987 Celebrate (The Day After You)/? (RCA—UK only)

## CURTIS MAYFIELD/ICE T

1990 Superfly 1990/remix (Capital)

## LPs
### THE IMPRESSIONS

(The following is included for reference only. Individual albums have not been graded or reviewed.)

### ALBUMS

1963 The Impressions (ABC—#43 pop)

1964 The Never Ending Impressions (ABC—#52 pop)

1964 Keep On Pushing (ABC—#4 R&B/#8 pop)

1965 People Get Ready (ABC—#1 R&B/#23 pop)

1965 One By One (ABC—#4 R&B/#104 pop)

1966 Ridin' High (ABC—#4 R&B/#79 pop)

1967 The Fabulous Impressions (ABC—#16 R&B/#184 pop)

1968 We're a Winner (ABC—#4 R&B/#35 pop)

1968 This Is My Country (Curtom—#5 R&B/#107 pop)

1969 The Young Mod's Forgotten Story (Curtom—#21 R&B/#104 pop)

1970 Check Out Your Mind (Curtom—#22 R&B)

### SELECTED COMPILATIONS AND ARCHIVE RELEASES

1965 Greatest Hits (ABC—#2 R&B/#83 pop)

1968 The Best Of (ABC—#23 R&B/#172 pop)

1973 Curtis Mayfield/His Early Years with the Impressions (ABC—#180 pop)

1977 The Vintage Years (Sire—#199 pop)

Excellent overview featuring 13 tracks apiece by the Impressions and the solo Jerry Butler, plus the two hit singles from *Superfly*

1997 The Very Best Of the Impressions (Rhino)

### CURTIS MAYFIELD

**10** 1971 Curtis (Curtom—#1 R&B/#19 pop)

The opening "Hell" sets the stage, the gospel tinged "Move On Up" confirms it, lacing through paranoid distortion and proto-dub echo that bleeds almost unwillingly into churning, string-driven funk, underpinned throughout by a bass line poised just on the audible side of sub-sonic assault.

**7** 1971 Curtis/Live (Curtom—#3 R&B/#21 pop)

Surprisingly mellow in-concert set, Mayfield luxuriating in front of a too-laid-back audience. A handful of tracks ("Stone Junkie," "People Get Ready," "Hell") stand out, but a sycophantic crowd reduces much of the performance to a stand-up routine.

**7** 1972 Roots (Curtom—#6 R&B/#40 pop)

**9** 1972 Superfly (soundtrack) (Curtom—#1 R&B/#1 pop)

The powerhouse musical performances are clearly influenced by *Shaft*, but grinding lyrical realism makes *Superfly* a discomforting potent commentary. A deluxe edition released in 2000 appends bonus material, but adds little to the original album's grandeur.

**7** 1972 Back To the World (Curtom—#1 R&B/#16 pop)

Led by the heavy horns of "Future Shock" and the turbulent "Can't Say Nothin'," the album echoes *Superfly*'s grit, albeit through a gauze of gentleness.

**6** 1974 Sweet Exorcist (Curtom—#2 R&B/#39 pop)

The super-slinky "Kung Fu" belies the increasingly romantic sounds now pleasing Mayfield.

**6** 1974 Curtis in Chicago (Curtom)

A second live album, tighter than its predecessor, but slicker, too.

**6** 1975 Got To Find a Way (Curtom—#17 R&B/#76 pop)

**5** 1975 There's No Place like America Today (Curtom—#13 R&B/ #120 pop)

**4** 1976 Give, Get, Take and Have (Curtom—#16 R&E/#171 pop)

The sensuous "Only You Babe" drapes its sheen over the entire album, a late-night, low-lights affair that never gets past second base.

**5** 1977 Never Say You Can't Survive (Curtom—#32 R&B/#173 pop)

**5** 1978 Short Eyes (soundtrack) (Curtom—#59 R&B)

Without saying he kept all his best songs for soundtracks, there's no denying "Do Do Wap Is Strong in Here" rates among Mayfield's best late '70s compositions. The remainder of the album, though, struggles to keep up.

**4** 1978 Do It All Night (Curtom—#52 R&B)

**4** 1979 Heartbeat (RSO—#19 R&B/#42 pop)

**3** 1980 Something To Believe In (RSO—#33 R&B/#128 pop)

**3** 1981 Love Is the Place (Boardwalk—#39 R&B)

A change of label, but no change in direction—typically shiney early-'80s production married to largely indistinguishable balladeering.

**3** 1983 Honesty (Boardwalk—#49 R&B)

**5** 1985 We Come in Peace with a Message of Love (Curtom)

**7** 1988 Live in Europe (Curtom—UK only)

An anonymous sounding band cannot disguise the adulation of the audience, or Mayfield's gratitude. His best live album, marred only by a few weak choices of material.

**6** 1989 I'm Gonna Git You Sucka (soundtrack) (Arista)

**6** 1990 Live at Ronnie Scotts (Essential—UK only)

**6** 1990 Take It To the Street (Curtom—#59 R&B)

Imbibing the lessons of recent years—personal and musical—a strong album with some genuine return-to-form moments ("Do Be Down," "Dirty Laundry")

**6** 1990 Return of Superfly (soundtrack) (Capitol)

**6** 1997 New World Order (WEA—#24 R&B/#137 pop)

### CURTIS MAYFIELD/LINDA CLIFFORD
### LP

**3** 1980 The Right Combination (RSO)

### SELECTED COMPILATIONS AND ARCHIVE RELEASES

**8** 1974 Move On Up: The Best of Curtis Mayfield (Curtom)

Well-planned digest of the best of the early solo years.

**9** 1996 People Get Ready: The Curtis Mayfield Story (Rhino)

A genuine labor of love, celebrating Impressions and solo material in deservedly equal quantities.

**8** 1997 The Very Best of Curtis Mayfield (Rhino)

A companion to the Impressions best of (above), 18 tracks trace Mayfield's '70s career.

### SELECTED SAMPLES
### THE IMPRESSIONS

We're a Winner—Biz Markie: I Hear Music (1989)
We're a Winner—Souls of Mischief: Limitations (1993)

### CURTIS MAYFIELD

Back to the World — De La Soul: Ghetto Thang (1989)
Cannot Find a Way — Too Short: I Ain't Nothin' But a Dog (1992)
Can't Say Nothin' — Dream Warriors: U Could Get Arrested (1991)
(Don't Worry) If There's a Hell Below — Artifacts: Notty Headed Niggaz (1994)
(Don't Worry) If There's a Hell Below — Big Daddy Kane: Niggaz Never Learn (1993)
(Don't Worry) If There's a Hell Below — Bushwick Bill: Letter from the KKK (1992)
(Don't Worry) If There's a Hell Below — Del Tha Funkee Homosapien: Don't Forget (1994)
(Don't Worry) If There's a Hell Below — EPMD: Hardcore (1991)
(Don't Worry) If There's a Hell Below — EPMD: Crossover (remix) (1992)
(Don't Worry) If There's a Hell Below — NWA: Niggaz 4 Life (1991)
(Don't Worry) If There's a Hell Below — Stetsasonic: Heaven Help the M.F.'s (1991)
(Don't Worry) If There's a Hell Below — Eddie, You Should Know Better— Snoop Doggy Dogg: Gz Up, Hoes Down (1993)
Freddie's Dead — Brand Nubian: Gangbang (1994)
Freddie's Dead — Gang Starr: Gusto (1989)
Freddie's Dead — MC Hammer: That's What I Said (1988)
Freddie's Dead — Master P: Kenny's Dead (1998)
Future Shock — Cypress Hill: Something for the Blunted (1992)
Future Shock — Ice Cream Tea: New Revolution (1989)
Give Me Your Love — Big Daddy Kane: Get Bizzy (1991)
Give Me Your Love — Mary J. Blige: I'm The Only Woman (1994)
Give Me Your Love — Digable Planets: Nickel Bags (1993)
Give Me Your Love — EPMD: Can't Hear Nothing but the Music (1992)
Give Me Your Love — Snoop Doggy Dogg: Bathtub (1993)
Gyspy Woman — Craig Mack: Project Funk Da World (1994)
Hard Times — Causal: Follow the Funk (1994)
Hard Times — Geto Boys: Murder After Midnight (1993)
Kung Fu — Above the Law: Process of Elimination (1993)
King Fu — Compton's Most Wanted: Growin' Up in the Hood (1991)
Make Me Believe in You — Ice-T: Depths of Hell (1993)
Mother's Son — LL Cool J: Soul Survivor (1993)

Pusherman — Eminem: I'm Shady (1999)

Pusherman — Ice-T: I'm Your Pusher (1988)

Pusherman — Zhigge: Zhigge Man (1992)

Right On for the Darkness — Eric B. & Rakim: Don't Sweat the Technique (remix) (1992)

Right On for the Darkness — Gang Starr: Take a Rest (1991)

Right On for the Darkness — Mase featuring Total: What You Want (1997)

Right On for the Darkness — R Kelly: Did You Ever Think (1998)

Stone Junkie — Apache: Wayz of A Murderahh (1993)

Stone Junkie — EPMD: Who Killed Jane? (1992)

Stone Junkie — Jeru the Damaja: Invasion (1996)

Superfly — Beastie Boys: Egg Man (1989)

Superfly — Geto Boys: Do It like a G.O. (1990)

Tripping Out — Camp Lo: Black Nostaljack AKA Come On (1997)

You're So Good to Me — Mary J Blige: Be Happy (1994)

You're So Good to Me — Ill Al Skratch: I'll Take Her (1994)

## THE METERS

**FORMED:** *(as Neville Sounds): 1962, New Orleans, LA*

**ORIGINAL LINE-UP:** *Leo Nocentelli (gtr), George Porter, Jr. (bs), Art Neville (b. Arthur Lanon Neville, 12/17/37 — keyboards), Zigaboo Modeliste (b. Joseph Modeliste — drms)*

They have been described, and rightfully so, as the ultimate New Orleans funk combo. Rightfully, because as with so much other music emanating from that city, the Meters' funk was as distinct and distinctive as New Orleans itself.

Whether in their own right, across eight albums released between 1969 and 1977, or as the musicians behind a slew of early-mid-'70s albums by Robert Palmer, Little Feat, Frankie Miller (and, of course, Dr. John — who *is* New Orleans to many rock 'n' roll fans), the Meters' metier was an extravagant sonic hybrid that was as comfortable hitting the Creole rhythms of the city's ancient past, as it was pursuing the Rolling Stones into deepest urban blues territory. Indeed, when the Stones toured in 1975–76, at the height of their own flirtation with the disciplines of funk, the Meters were their first choice for opening act.

Neither would the Meters' demise in 1977 see any slackening in their influence or involvement, as the continuing saga of the Neville Brothers has proven. From Ice Cube to NWA, Salt-N-Pepa to Public Enemy, the Meters have permeated modern American music, while the Red Hot Chili Peppers created a fascinating fusion of their own when they recruited George Clinton to produce a cover of the Meters' "Africa." The Meters may not have created New Orleans funk, but they certainly showed everyone what it was.

"I think we brought it to the rest of the country and the rest of the world," George Porter, Jr. says in the liner notes to the Meters' anthology *Funkify Your Life*. "There would always be some guys that got together on the weekend and jam, and there'd be some serious funk going on. We just happened to be in the right place and the right time, because we were the only organized group that played it all the time."

The Meters' story began when Art Neville, the eldest of four brothers, formed his own first group, the Hawketts, at high school in the early '50s. A seven-piece R&B outfit, the Hawketts scored locally in 1954 with "Mardi Gras Mambo," released on the legendary blues label Chess and, naturally, reissued annually in time for Mardi Gras, long after the Hawketts broke up in the early '60s.

In 1957, still a Hawkett, Neville launched a parallel solo career with Specialty Records, scoring further local hits with the energetic "Cha Dooky Doo" and "Zing Zing." He put his career on hold the following year when he joined the US Navy. He was replaced in the Hawkettes by brother Aaron (b. 1/24/41, New Orleans), but returned to the band in 1962.

The Hawkettes split soon after, and Neville united with both Art and younger brother Cyril (b. 1/10/48 — vcls, perc) in a new project, the Neville Sounds.

A tight R&B combo, Neville Sounds linked with New Orleans producer Allen Toussaint (who also produced several solo Art and Aaron Neville singles), and became one of the dominant live acts on the city scene for much of the next six years. They had a long standing residency at the Nite Cap nightclub and it was there that Art Neville first began laying the groundwork for his own musical future, after he persuaded the club owner to install a Hammond B-3 organ.

With that instrument to the fore, the Nevilles' sound began to edge toward Art's own ideal of a cajun-twisted Booker T. & the MGs. A shifting lineup settled around the George Porter/Zigaboo Modeliste bass and drums team (the pair were also cousins) and former Lee Dorsey guitarist Nocentelli. By 1968, Neville Sounds' electrifying R&B funk groove was drawing attention from all over town. So much so that when the owner of Bourbon Street's prestigious Ivanhoe Bar contacted Art Neville with the offer of a regular gig, he had one major condition — that the band leave the vocalists behind.

Aaron and Cyril departed to form their own group, the Soul Machine; Art, Modeliste, Porter and Nocentelli took over the Ivanhoe. There, they developed a set that stretched

**The funky soul of sophistication, Big Easy style—the mighty Meters.**

the audience as much as it did the musicians, the rhythm section opening their set with a three songs burst of ballads and Miles Davis jazz, before Art Neville joined them and kicked them into a solid jam mode.

Porter recalled, "we would stretch out and once Leo started soloing, the chord structure would disappear, so I had to play chord structures and fills. Being a frustrated guitar player, when he started playing those funky lines and licks, I started playing those things as a bass player."

Soon, Allen Toussaint and partner Marshall Sehorn were regulars in the Ivanhoe audience, adopting the Neville Sounds as house-band at their studio and putting them to work backing Lee Dorsey, Betty Harris and Toussaint himself (across what became his 1970 album *Toussaint*). In late 1968, meanwhile, the group changed their name to the Meters and, signing to the New York based Josie label, cut their first single, "Sophisticated Cissy." Of course, Toussaint produced.

R&B Top 40 in February 1969, "Sophisticated Cissy" was followed up the chart by the loping "Cissy Strut" and, that summer, the Meters' eponymous debut album, one of the first recordings made at Toussaint and Sehorn's newly equipped eight track studio. Subsequently voted *Billboard*'s top R&B instrumental album of the year, *The Meters* launched the band on tour through the southern states, an outing that tightened their live performance even as it allowed their improvisational instincts to stretch ever further afield.

Much of the Meters' sophomore album, 1970's *Look-Ka Py Py*, was composed on the road; the title chant actually came together in the car on the way to a show. Other material was jammed into shape in the studio, spontaneous riffs and rhythms that built up seemingly effortlessly. Then, they'd simply pluck a title out of thin air. "Because we were an instrumental band," said Nocentelli, "and it didn't matter too much."

From the outset, the Meters were never locked into any particular musical style. A distinctly bayou-flavored funk remained the dominant mood, but they were as likely to spin off a Scottish reel ("Dry Spell," from *Look Ka Py Py*) as a solid progressive rock number ("Stay Away," from 1972's *Cabbage Alley* album). Neither were they confined solely to instrumentals. While the vocal refrains on their second album were restricted to the chant of the title song, 1971's *Struttin'* album caught Art Neville's voice breaking out over a dramatic reworking of Lee Dorsey's "Ride Your Pony," and Modeliste's rooster impressions echoing across the memorable "Chicken Strut."

*Struttin'* was the Meters' final album for Josie, although the label would continue releasing singles through 1971, "A Message from the Meters," "Stretch Your Rubber Band," "Doodle Oop" and "Hey Pocky A-Way" served up a string of Top 50 hits, even as the Meters worked to refine and redirect their sound even further. Having now broken through the vocal barrier, Modeliste and Nocentelli, the band's primary songwriters, were becoming increasingly interested in the craft of actually composing, as opposed to improvising, songs.

They toyed with a reggae hybrid on the remarkable "Zony Mash" B-side, while fuzz guitars and wah-wah effects

became another striking element of the group's arsenal. "Good Old Funky Music," their final Josie single (and first non-charting 45) even gave Funkadelic a run for their money in the psychedelic groove stakes.

With critical acclaim rising around them, the Meters signed with Reprise late in 1971, following through with *Cabbage Alley* and a tour with Sly & the Family Stone the following year. It was with 1974's *Rejuvenation*, however, that the Meters truly peaked, a solid funk album built around "Africa" and the minor hit "People Say," a powerful example of the musicians' taste in social commentary. Nocentelli's personal favorite Meters album, however, was to be the least successful; it missed the R&B chart altogether, their first album to do so, ironically at a time when their peers could not speak highly enough of them.

Summer 1974, brought English R&B singer Robert Palmer to Toussaint's Sea Saint studios, to cut his superlative solo debut, *Sneaking Sally Through the Alley*, with members of both the Meters and Little Feat. Further Englishmen Frankie Miller and Jess Roden followed Palmer to New Orleans. The Meters dominate Roden's eponymous 1974 debut album, pushing an already strident vocalist to even greater heights.

Other groups, too, called upon the group's services, all entering the studio in search of some of the magic that permeated the Meters' own music. All came away with at least a piece of it: King Biscuit Boy, Labelle (whose seminal "Lady Marmalade" drew one of their finest ever performances out of the musicians), Dr. John, Toussaint, of course, and ex-Beatle Paul McCartney, who booked into Sea Saint studio in February 1975, as he pieced together the *Venus and Mars* album.

At McCartney's request, the Meters (together with New Orleans legend Professor Longhair) performed live at that album's release party, on board the *Queen Mary* ocean liner in Long Beach, CA. Their performance has since been released as *Uptown Rulers! Live on the Queen Mary*.

The Rolling Stones were next to pay court to the Meters, catching their set on board the *Queen Mary* and inviting them along on their 1975 North American and 1976 European tours. Unfortunately, as the Meters' reputation continued to grow, their commercial success continued to dip. Despite the addition of Cyril Neville to further bolster the vocal department, 1975's *Fire on the Bayou* album barely improved on the performance of its predecessor. The Meters' projected next album was actually rejected by their label while they were on the road with the Stones.

Before leaving for Europe, the Meters went into Sea Saint and cut some 25 tracks live in the studio, aiming to recapture their in concert energy on vinyl. Sehorn mixed the material while the band were away, only for Reprise to nix around half of it. Attempting to salvage the project, the Meters cut further material once they returned home, but their sound had changed again and, in any case, the mood was broken.

The collection that appeared in late 1976 as *Trick Bag* was patchy at best, and precipitated the Meters' break with Toussaint and Sehorn. The producers turned immediately to Chocolate Milk, fellow New Orleans funksters who they were already grooming as a new Meters-of-sorts. The Meters chose to record their next album in San Francisco with David Rubinson (Malo, Herbie Hancock, Taj Mahal, etc.).

Art and Cyril Neville, however, were tiring of the group's continued half-life. Earlier in the year, the pair had reunited with brother Aaron and fourth sibling, Charles, to cut an album under the guise of Wild Tchoupitoulas, a moving tribute to their own Mardi Gras Indian heritage. Although the remainder of the Meters accompanied the brothers on this album, it was clear that the Nevilles were looking for more from their reunion than just the one album. When "Be My Lady," the Meters' latest single, collapsed at #78 in late 1977; the die was cast. Art Neville quit shortly before they were due to make their first headlining appearance on television's *Saturday Night Live* (an earlier visit, on March 19, 1977, saw them appearing alongside Dr. John).

Cyril Neville followed him and, by early 1978, the newly named Neville Brothers quartet were signed to Capitol and preparing to release their eponymous debut album. Porter, Nocentelli and Modeliste, after a short period attempting to continue on as the Meters, finally broke up around the same time.

Porter formed a new outfit, Joy Ride, but their solitary album remains unreleased; he and Modeliste then formed the Metrics for some live work during 1982–83, performing with David Torkanowsky, Scott Goudreaux and Tony DeGrady. He subsequently released several solo albums— *George Porter, Jr.* (1980), *George Porter and the Runnin' Pardners* 1990, *Count On You* (1994), *Things Ain't What They Used To Be* (1994)—and enjoyed a successful career as a session musician; he recorded three successive albums with singer Tori Amos.

It was left, however, to occasional Meters reunions to truly rekindle the original group's magic. They played one-off shows in 1980 and 1984, before 1989 saw Art Neville, Porter and Nocentelli (now gigging together as Geo-Leo)

and Modeliste reunite again following a potent on-stage jam at a nightclub during the New Orleans Jazz festival.

Immediately Neville, Porter and Nocentelli announced they wanted to make the reunion permanent; Modeliste declined and was replaced by David Russell Batiste, a local session drummer whose past credits included albums with Toussaint, Robbie Robertson and Harry Connick, Jr.

Of course the Meters' schedule was built around the Neville Brothers' own. In late 1991, a "Legendary" Meters lineup comprising Porter, Nocentelli, Batiste and Torkanowsky toured Europe with the JB Horns of Maceo Parker, Fred Wesley and Pee Wee Ellis; shows in Aarburg, Switzerland, were subsequently released as the two-CD set *Live at the Moonwalker.*

In January 1994, following the departure of Nocentelli, former Neville Brothers guitarist Brian Stoltz was brought in to usher in the new Funky Meters, tenacious road warriors, but as yet unrecorded.

Nocentelli moved into songwriting and session work, launching his own project, Nocentelli. Former Neville Brothers bassist Darryl Johnson is an occasional member. Modeliste also returned from retirement for a stint with the group. Nocentelli's debut album was the self-explanatory, *Live in San Francisco.*

The original Meters reconvened on November 11, 2000, for a show at the Warfield in San Francisco.

## THE METERS COMPLETE DISCOGRAPHY
### SINGLES/CHART LOG
1969 Sophisticated Strut/Sehorns Farms (Josie—#7 R&B/#34 pop)
1969 Cissy Strut/Here Comes the Meter Man (Josie—#4 R&B/#23 pop)
1969 Ease Back/Ann (Josie—#20 R&B/#61 pop)
1969 Dry Spell/Little Old Money Maker (Josie—#39 R&B)
1969 Look-Ka Py Py/This Is My Last Affair (Josie—#11 R&B/#56 pop)
1970 Chicken Strut/Hey! Last Minute (Josie—#11 R&B/#50 pop)
1970 Hand Clapping Song/Joog (Josie—#26 R&B/#89 pop)
1970 A Message from the Meters/Zony Mash (Josie—#21 R&B)
1971 Stretch Your Rubber Band/Groovy Lady (Josie—#42 R&B)
1971 Doodle Oop/I Need More Time (Josie—#47 R&B)
1971 Good Old Funky Music/Sassy Lady (Josie)
1972 Do the Diert/Smiling (Reprise)
1972 Cabbage Alley/The Flower Song (Reprizse)
1972 Chug Chug Chug a Lug (part one)/(part two) (Reprise)
1974 Hey Pocky A-Way/Africa (Reprise—#31 R&B)
1974 People Say/Loving You Is on My Mind (Reprise—#52 R&B)
1975 Running Away/They All Ask'd for You (Reprise)
1976 Disco Is the Thing Today/Mr. Moon (Reprise—#87 R&B)
1976 Trick Bag/Find Yourself (Reprise)
1977 Be My Lady/No More Okey Doke (WB—#78 R&B/#78 pop)

## ALBUMS

**9** **1969 The Meters (Josie—#23 R&B/#108 pop)**

Steamy, organ led melodies floating deceptively over the maniac bass, drums and syncopated riffery—a formula that would sustain the band over three successive albums and never grow boring.

**9** **1980 Look-Ka Py Py (Josie—#23 R&B/#198 pop)**

**7** **1970 Struttin' (Josie—#32 R&B/#200 pop)**

When producer Toussaint heard one of the group's new tunes, he remarked, "Oh, the same old stuff." The band promptly titled that cut "Same Old Thing," although *Struttin'* would also stutter a little, most noticeably on the vocal numbers—great playing, weak singing.

**8** **1972 Cabbage Alley (Reprise—#48 R&B)**

Rewrapping their trademark sound in some of the modern studio's favorite toys (phasing, echo, delay), the Meters ensure they don't move too far off base with a ferocious take on Professor Longhair's "Hey Now Baby."

**10** **1974 Rejuvenation (Reprise)**

The funkiest, fieriest of all Meters albums, undented by either time or familiarity. The anthemic "Africa," "People Say" and "Hey Pocky A-way" are untrammelled delights, coiled and flexing around the rhythms, while the band's grip on funk and rock has never been tighter.

**9** **1975 Fire on the Bayou (Reprise—#41 R&B/#179 pop)**

At its best, scarcely less powerful than its predecessor, although a couple of duff tracks do undermine things somewhat.

**6** **1977 New Directions (Reprise)**

A patchy attempt to try, indeed, some new directions, a few of which work but, overall, leave one wishing they'd just stuck with the same old stuff again. A stab at emulating the MGs' take on the *Hang 'Em High* western theme is an irrefutable highlight, however.

## SELECTED COMPILATIONS AND ARCHIVE RELEASES

**6** **1992 Meters Jam (Rounder)**

**6** **1992 Good Old Funky Music (Rounder)**

Two albums bring together the unused *Trick Bag* sessions in their entirety, unmixed live in the studio material that captures the spontaneity of the moment, but does not noticeably salvage the concept.

**8** **1992 Uptown Rulers! Live on the Queen Mary (Rhino)**

From 1975, a short but so sharp recounting of the band at their *Rejuvenation/Bayou* peak.

**7** **1994 The Legendary Meters Featuring the JB Horns: Live at the Moonwalker, Vols. 1 & 2 (Lakeside Music—Swtz)**

**9** **1995 Funkify Your Life (Rhino)**

Two-CD box set recounting the full Meters story via choice album cuts and scarce singles.

## SELECTED SAMPLES

9 Till 5 — Jungle Brothers: Black Is Black (1988)
Britches — Main Source: Peace Is Not the Word To Play (1991)
Britches — Apache: Hey Girl (1993)
Cardova — MC Lyte: Shut the Eff Up! (Hoe) (1989)
Cardova — Boss: Livin Loc'ed (1993)
Cardova — NWA: She Swallowed It (1991)
Cardove — King Tee: Can This Be Real? (remix) (1990)
Chicken Strut — Queen Latifah: Wrath of My Madness (1989)
Cissy Strut — Del Tha Funkee Homosapien: Same Ol' Thing (1991)
Cissy Strut — Salt-N-Pepa: I Don't Know (1990)
Cissy Strut — Runaway Slaves: Booty Mission (1992)
Cissy Strut — Run DMC: Bob Your Head (1990)
Cissy Strut — Master P: 211 (1994)
Cissy Strut — NWA: Niggaz 4 Life (1991)
Dry Spell — Compton's Most Wanted: 8 Iz Enough (1992)
Ease Back — MC Lyte: Please Understand (1989)
Ease Back — Queen Latifah: That's the Way We Flow (1991)
Find Yourself — Naughty By Nature: Feel Me Flow (1995)
Funky Miracle — Digital Underground: DFLO Shuttle (1991)
Funky Miracle — Gang Starr: Take a Rest (1991)
Go for Yourself — Boogiemonsters: Honeydips in Gotham (1994)
Groovy Lady — Jingle Brothers: I'm Gonna Do You (1988)
Groovy Lady — LL Cool J: Droppin 'Em (1989)
Handclapping Song — Das EFX: Klap Ys Handz (1992)
Handclapping Song — Channel Live: What! (Cause and Effect) (1995)
Handclapping Song — Salt-N-Pepa: Beauty and the Beat (1987)
Handclapping Song — Marley Marl: The Symphony (part two) (1991)
Handclapping Song — Illegal: Crumbsnatchers (1993)
Handclapping Song — Gang Starr: DJ Premier in Deep Concentration (1989)
Handclapping Song — Chi-Ali: Let the Horns Blow (1992)
Handclapping Song — Black Eyed Peas: Clap Your Hands (1998)
Handclapping Song — A Tribe Called Quest: Clap Your Hands (1993)
Handclapping Song — Redman: Da Funk (1992)
Handclapping Song — Eric B & Rakim: Put Your Hands Together (1988)
Handclapping Song — Del Tha Funkee Homosapien: Same Ol' Thing (1991)
Here Comes the Metermen — Run DMC: How'd Ya Do It Dee? (1988)
Here Comes the Metermen — Big Daddy K: Long Live the Kane (1988)
Here Comes the Metermen — Digable Planets: Black Ego (1994)
Here Comes the Metermen — DJ Shadow: Changeling (1996)
Hey, Last Minute — Tone Loc: The Homies (1989)
Hey, Last Minute — Pharcyde: On the DL (1993)
Hey, Last Minute — Gang Starr: Mostly Tha Voice (1994)
Hey, Last Minute — Big Daddy Kane: Long Live the Kane (1988)
Hey Pocky A-way — Boogie Down Productions: The Homeless (1990)
Hey, Last Minute — Salt-N-Pepa: Let the Rhythm Run (1988)
Jungle Man — Mad Flava: What's A Dog 2 Do? (1994)

Just Kissed My Baby — Positive K: How the Fuck! Would You Know (1992)
Just Kissed My Baby — EPMD: Never Seen Before (1997)
Just Kissed My Baby — Public Enemy: Timebomb (1988)
Just Kissed My Baby — Special Ed: Fly MC (1989)
Just Kissed My Baby — Public Enemy: Terminator X Speaks with His Hands (1988)
Just Kissed My Baby — Lord Finesse: Party Over Here (remix) (1991)
Just Kissed My Baby — Dream Warriors: Answer for the Owl (1991)
Little Old Money Maker — Kool Moe Dee: Rise 'N' Shine (1991)
Live Wire — Gang Starr: Cause And Effect (1989)
Live Wire — Big Daddy Kane: Troubled Man (1991)
Liver Splash — Double XX Posse: We Got It Goin On (1992)
Liver Splash — Big Daddy Kane: Death Sentence (1991)
Liver Splash — Big Daddy Kane: Raw '91 (1991)
Look Ka Py Py — Cypress Hill: Phunky Feel One (1992)
Message from the Meters — Tone Loc: Loc'in on the Shaw (1989)
Message from the Meters — 3rd Bass: Merchant of Grooves (1991)
Never Seen Before — De a Soul: Declaration (2000)
People Say — Ice-T: Fried Chicken (1991)
Pungee — Ice Cube: Color Blind (1991)
Rigor Mortis — Jungle Brothers: I'm Gonna Do You (1988)
Rigor Mortis — Del Tha Funkee Homosapien: Same Ol' Thing (1991)
Same Old Thing — Pete Rock & CL Smooth: Good Life (remix) (1991)
Same Old Thing — Private Investigaters: But She's Not My G (1993)
Same Old Thing — D-Nice: And There U Have It (1991)
Thinking — Scarface; I'm Dead (1991)
Thinking — Heavy D & the Boyz: Gyrlz, They Love Me (1989)
Tippi Toes — Illegal: Ban Da Iggidy (1993)
Yeah, You're Right — Compton's Most Wanted: 8 Iz Enough (1992)

## ZIGABOO MODELISTE

**BORN:** *Joseph Modeliste, New Orleans, LA*

Following the breakup of the Meters in 1978, self-styled "King of the Funk Drums" Zigaboo Modeliste was promptly recruited by Rolling Stones guitarist Keith Richards, as a member of his New Barbarians side project. The band toured the US during spring 1979, also playing one-off shows in Canada and England, but broke up following Richards' return to the Stones. The New Barbarians played one show without him, in Milwaukee, WI, in January 1980. It ended when the disappointed audience rioted.

Modeliste returned to New Orleans, playing around the club circuit and taking part in the one-off Meters reunions in 1980 and 1984. By the mid-'80s, however, he had all but retired from the music industry, and while he attended another Meters reunion show in 1989, he absented himself from the ensuing tour.

Modeliste finally re-emerged in the early '90s under the aegis of producer Bill Laswell, appearing on two Axiom

albums, Nicky Skopelitis' *Ekstasis* and Third Rail's *South Delta Space Age*. From his base in Berkeley, CA, he then formed his own Zigaboo Modeliste & the Aahkestra project, returning to New Orleans in 1997 for the first in what has since become an unbroken sequence of appearances at the Jazz Festival. A second annual event, launched in 1999, is the Krewe of Zigaboo party.

Another occasional Modeliste project, The Funk Revue, played a handful of shows around New Orleans that same spring, including Jazzfest's opening party at the Howling Wolf bar. Modeliste was joined onstage by Renard Poche (gtr – Dr. John Band), Nick Daniels (bs — the Neville Brothers) and David Torkanowsky (kybds — Astral Project). At a separate Funk Revue performance, Art Neville came onstage for a version of the Meters' own "Cabbage Alley"

Modeliste's solo debut album, *Zigaboo.Com* was released via the internet in early 2000. Featuring the already established live favorites "Funky Nasty Cigarettes" and "Shake What You Got," the album was also highlighted by "ZIG Me," cowritten by Modeliste and Porter, Jr.

### ZIGABOO MODELISTE AND THE AAHKESTRA DISCOGRAPHY
**6** 2000 Zigaboo.Com (JZM)
Heavily jazz-funk flavored set, redolent of early Meters in places, but prone, too, to makeweight noodling.

## JUNIE MORRISON, see THE OHIO PLAYERS

## NEW BIRTH
**FORMED:** 1970, *Detroit, MI*
**ORIGINAL LINEUP INC:** *Ann Bogan (vcls), Melvin Wilson (vcls), Leslie Wilson (vcls), Bobby Downs (vcls), Londee Loren (vcls), Alan Frye (vcls), Tony Churchill (sax, vcls), Austin Lander, James Baker (kybds), Robert Jackson (sax)*

In 1970, following seven years in A&R at Motown, industry veteran Harvey Fuqua launched his own production company through the RCA label and began seeking new talent. Among the acts he came into contact with at Motown was a Louisville, KY, funk instrumental combo called the Nite-Liters, who frequently accompanied Motown acts at local shows, but who also gigged in their own right with the addition of vocalists Bobby Downs, Londee Loren and Alan Frye, themselves collectively known as the New Birth.

Fuqua was simultaneously keeping tabs on a Detroit vocal group, Love, Peace and Happiness, formed by ex-Marvelettes vocalist Ann Bogan (she also accompanied Fuqua himself in the short-lived duo Harvey & Ann), and featuring the remarkable Wilson brothers, Melvin and Leslie.

Visualizing the potential of a collective formed around these acts, Fuqua recruited all three, delivering the entire package to RCA in 1970. Taken from their self-titled debut album, the Nite-Liters debuted the arrangement with "Con-Funk-Shun" (from whence the late-'70s' funk giants Con Funk Shun took their name) and, within a year, both their densely packed follow-up, "K-Jee," and the New Birth's sweet cover of Perry Como's "It's Impossible" had become hits.

The three groups toured together during 1971, with the Nite-Liters providing backing throughout, and initially it seemed that the instrumentalists were going to prove the most successful. Without exception, the band's albums prove remarkable documents of a tight, energetic unit capable of shifting moods and grooves in a moment, without ever losing sight of their manic funkiness. The group also followed "K-Jee" with the double-sided "Afro Strut"/"We Got To Pull Together," Top 30 at a time when the New Birth and Love, Peace and Happiness were barely scratching the Top 50.

Two subsequent Nite-Liters singles, "Cherish Every Precious Moment" and "Funky-Doo" missed the chart, however, and by early 1973, Fuqua had blended all three groups into one, under the umbrella name of the New Birth. The new aggregation immediately enjoyed a #4 R&B with a cover of Bobby Womack's punchy "I Can Understand It"; the parent album, Birth Day, topped the R&B chart.

The band was briefly joined by Johnny Graham, who departed for Earth Wind & Fire in 1974, while lightweight covers of Elvis Presley's recent "Until It's Time for You To Go" and Skylark's "Wildflower" sandwiched another Top Ten 45, 1974's "It's Been a Long Time." All three releases pushed the aggregation further away from the Nite-Liters' original funk sound (zero reaction to a final Nite-Liters single, "Pe-Foul," confirmed their demise). This drift continued into the latter part of the decade, following the New Birth's break with Fuqua, RCA and manager Jerry Weintraub.

With the lineup expanding to include new recruits Ben Boxtel, Roger Voice and James Hall, signing with Buddah (and dropping "the" from their name), New Birth won a summer 1975, smash with "Dream Merchant." It was, however, their last significant hit. Moving to Warner Brothers, the follow-up, a syrupy version of the Beatles' "The Long and Winding Road" halted at #91 and, in 1977, the Wilson brothers quit. Two years later, New Birth broke up altogether. Ironically, their last single, "I Love You," was proving their most successful in four years.

New Birth reunited in 1994 around the returning Wilsons, and fellow vocalists Barbara Wilson and Danette Williams. A new album, *God's Children*, was released in Europe in 1998.

## CHART LOG
### NITE-LITERS
1971 K-Jee/Tanga Boo Gonk (RCA—#17 R&B/#39 pop)
1972 Afro-Strut (RCA—#24 R&B/#49 pop)/Pull Together (#27 R&B)

### LOVE, PEACE AND HAPPINESS
1972 I Don't Want To Do Wrong/Lonely Room (RCA—#41 R&B)

### THE NEW BIRTH
1971 It's Impossible/Honeybee (RCA—#12 R&B/#52 pop)
1972 Unh Song/Two Kinds of People (RCA—#45 R&B)
1973 I Can Understand It/Oh Baby, I Love the way (RCA—#4 R&B/#35 pop)
1973 Until It's Time for You To Go/You Are What I'm All About (RCA—#21 R&B/#97 pop)
1974 It's Been a Long Time/Keep On Doin' It (RCA—#9 R&B/#66 pop)
1974 Wildflower/Got To Get a Knutt (RCA—#17 R&B/#45 pop)
1974 I Wash My Hands of the Whole Damn Deal (part one)/(part two) (RCA—#46 R&B/#88 pop)
1974 Comin' from All Ends/Patiently (RCA—#76 R&B)

### NEW BIRTH
1975 Grandaddy (part one)/(part two) (Buddah—#28 R&B/#95 pop)
1975 Dream Merchant/Why Did I (Buddah—#1 R&B/#36 pop)
1976 Long And Winding Road/Hurry Hurry (WB—#91 R&B)
1976 Fallin' in Love (part one)/(part two) (WB—#51 R&B)
1977 Deeper/(instrumental) (WB—#65 R&B)
1978 The Mighty Army/Hurry Hurry (WB—#49 R&B)
1979 I Love You/Fastest Gun (Ariola America—#28 R&B)

## LPs
### THE NITE-LITERS
9 **1970 The Nite-Liters (RCA)**
Short songs but a high groove quotient, echoing the Meters' MGs fixation, but slamming into focus across downhome grinds like "Snap Your Twig," "Itchy Brother" and the virtual statement of intent, "Down and Dirty."

8 **1971 Morning, Noon and the Nite-Liters (RCA—#31 R&B/#167 pop)**
Ranging across the musical spectrum, but seldom losing sight of a pronounced Isaac Hayes-meets-the-JBs influence, *Morning* . . . includes a glacial cover of the Carpenters' "We've Only Just Begun" among other party-funk instrumental treats.

8 **1972 Instrumental Directions (RCA—#41 R&B/#198 pop)**
More of the same, highlights this time including a funkier-than-funky cover of the *Shaft* theme, and a masterful visit

to "MacArthur Park." The sax-screaming "Afro-Strut" is a drop-dead beauty.

**9 1972 Different Strokes (RCA)**

Howling hot stuff packs "Do the Granny," "Theme from Buck and the Preacher," Quincy Jones' "Money Runner" and the manic "Funky Vamp" into a flawless barrage of sound.

**7 1973 Anal-Y-Sis (RCA—#34 R&B)**

A (comparatively) weaker set as the band's ambition is toned down to meet the lighter-weight sensibilities of the impending New Birth. But still "Serenade for a Jive Turkey," "Damn" and "Pee-Foul" restore past glories.

### THE NEW BIRTH

**6 1970 New Birth (RCA)**

Lucid but lightweight set cut firmly in the then-prevalent soul vocal group mold. Flashes of the accompanying Nite-Liters' own brilliance are kept to a minimum.

**5 1971 Ain't No Big Thing, But It's Growing (RCA—#50 R&B/#189 pop)**

Covers of pop standards "Fire and Rain," "I Want To Make It with You" and "Let It Be Me" lead the band into a lukewarm approximation of the Isleys' near-simultaneous *Givin' It Back*.

**5 1972 Comin' Together (RCA—#40)**

**4 1973 Birth Day (RCA—#1 R&B/#31 pop)**

The iron hand of Fuqua's quality control keeps New Birth locked on a straight course down the middle of the road. "Until It's Time for You To Go" epitomizes the sweet-but-so-sickly sounds.

**4 1974 It's Been a Long Time (RCA—#7 R&B/#50 pop)**

**3 1974 Comin' from All Ends (RCA—#20 R&B/#56 pop)**

A nadir of sorts, but revolution is coming: "I Wash My Hands of the Whole Damn Deal" speaks of more than a broken love affair.

### NEW BIRTH

**7 1975 Blind Baby (Buddah—#17 R&B/#57 pop)**

With the Nite-Liters contingent now ascendent again, New Birth break with past traditions for an album that spreads more energy over six tracks than its predecessors did over 30.

**4 1976 Love Potion (WB—#22 R&B/#168 pop)**

The band found its feet—and then found something to do with them, executing a neat Ohio Players-flavored disco-funk boogie. Unfortunately, it's really only interesting for the first couple of songs.

**3 1977 Behold the Mighty Army (WB—#28 R&B/#164 pop)**

### SELECTED COMPILATIONS AND ARCHIVE RELEASES

**4 1975 Best of New Birth (RCA)**

**4 1977 Reincarnation (RCA)**

**4 1998 Wildflowers (BMG)**

Three collections concentrating on the Fuqua years, without much to distinguish any of them.

### SELECTED SAMPLES
#### NITE-LITERS

Bakers Instant — Brothers like Outlaw: Kickin' Jazz (1992)

Buck & the Preacher — Steady B: Get On Down (1991)

Buck & the Preacher — Scarface: Born Killer (1991)

Funky-Vamp — Chi-Ali: Chi-Ali vs. Vanilla Shake (1992)

Tanga Boo Gonk — Brand Nubian: Wake Up (remix) (1991)

Valdez in the Country — Dr. Dre: Lyrical Gangbang (1993)

#### NEW BIRTH

Got To Get a Knutt — Public Enemy: Lost at Birth (1991)

Got To Get a Knutt — De La Soul: This Is a Recording 4 Living In A Full Time Era (L.I.F.E.) (1989)

Go To Get A Knutt — De La Soul: Can U Keep a Secret? (1989)

Honeybee — X-Clan: Verbal Milk (1990)

Honeybee — Wu-Tang Clan: Clan in Da Front (1993)

Honeybee — Prime Minister Pete Nice & Daddy Rich: Sleeper (1993)

It's Been a Long Time — Somethin' for the People: My Love Is the SHHH! (1997)

It's Been a Long Time — Master P: Ice Cream Man (1996)

Keep On Doin It — Black Sheep: The Choice Is Yours (Revisited) (1990)

Keep On Doin It — Big Daddy Kane: Stop Shammin' (1993)

You Are What I'm All About — Junior MAFIA: Player's Anthem (1995)

You Are What I'm All About — Jeru the Damaja: Ya Playin' Yaself (1996)

## THE NITE-LITERS, see NEW BIRTH

## THE OHIO PLAYERS

**FORMED:** *1967, Dayton, OH*

**ORIGINAL LINE UP:** *Joe Harris (vcls), Bobby Lee Fears (vcls), Dutch Robinson (vcls), Dale Allen (vcls), Leroy "Sugarfoot" Bonner (gtr), Marshall Jones (bs), Ralph Middlebrooks (d. 1997—sax, trum), Clarence Satchell (d. 1995—sax), Greg Webster (drms)*

The Ohio Players started life as Robert Ward & the Untouchables in Dayton, OH, in 1959, with Ralph Middlebrooks, Clarence Satchell, Marshall Jones and drummer Cornelius Johnson. Changing their name to the Ohio Untouchables, they joined the tiny LuPine label in 1961 (the company was launched by one of Ward's relatives). The group was recruited primarily to accompany other Lupine acts, including the Falcons vocal group, featuring the young and unknown Eddie Floyd and Wilson Pickett.

**The classic Players line-up: (l-r) Sugarfoot, PeeWee, Billy (above), Satch (below), Diamond, Merv, Jones.**

The Falcons' first single for the label (earlier releases appeared on Chess and UA), "I Found a Love," made the R&B Top Ten in spring 1962. Its success prompted the Untouchables to relocate to LuPine's Detroit base and, later in the year, the band cut their own first single, "She's My Heart's Desire." "Love Is Amazing" and "Uptown" followed.

Ward quit the group in 1964 to pursue a solo career (Johnson also departed); the Untouchables recruited the blues oriented Bonner as Ward's replacement, adding drummer Greg Webster, plus vocalists Dutch Robinson, Dale Allen, Bobby Lee Fears and Joe Harris. They returned to Dayton and, over the next three years, continued gigging around the local circuit. The group changed their name to the Ohio Players in 1967, celebrating with a one-off single on the Tangerine label, "Neighbors."

The next year, the group was recruited as studio house-band at New York's Compass label, recording a mass of material both alongside other label acts (Helena Ferguson

and Gloria/Towanda Barnes among them), and in their own right. In 1972, these tapes were gathered together as the *First Impressions* album; they have since appeared under a variety of titles and guises.

The Ohio Players' only bona fide Compass releases, however, were a pair of singles in early 1968, "Trespassin'," which clearly indicates their debt to the Stax sound of the time, and "It's a Cryin' Shame," a worthy effort lost as the Compass label slipped into financial difficulties.

The group moved to Capitol Records and, in late 1968, released the *Observations in Time* album, alongside two further 45s, "Bad Bargain" and "Find Someone to Love"—the latter backed by an impassioned R&B interpretation of "Somewhere Over the Rainbow" that, legend insists, was the version played at Judy Garland's funeral in June 1969.

By then, the band had left the confines of Ohio and were touring the country, jamming long and loud on stage, and defining the combination of funk grooves and soul inflected ballads that would make them famous. Right now, however, they were getting nowhere and in early 1970, the group returned to Dayton and broke up.

Robinson, Fears and Harris all launched solo careers (the latter subsequently joined Undisputed Truth); the remaining members simply jammed around town, gradually reforming around the arrival of vocalist/keyboardist Walter "Junie" Morrison, Bruce Napier (trum) and Marvin Pierce (trom). They announced their return with a new single, "Pain," originally released independently but soon picked up by the Detroit label Westbound. An album of the same title followed in 1971 and finally, twelve years of gigging paid off as *Pain* edged into the R&B Top 30.

The massive *Pleasure* appeared in late 1972; their breakthrough single, the novelty-inclined "Funky Worm," followed in winter 1973, the first of five R&B chart-toppers, which the Ohio Players amassed over the next three years.

The *Ecstasy* album was less successful, however. The group's sound was changing fast, abandoning ballads in favor of a heavier funk sound, helped along by plenty of horns and Bonner's fat blues guitars. *Ecstasy* echoed the indecision that accompanied the change. As 1974 dawned, however, the group again found themselves surrounded by internal conflicts. Webster was replaced with drummer James "Diamond" Williams, William Beck was added on keyboards and Bonner took over lead vocals, as Junie Morrison announced he, too, was quitting for a solo career. (He released two albums on Westbound, later surfacing within George Clinton's P-Funk empire.)

The group's Westbound contract, too, was at an end; signing to the major Mercury, they kicked off a stellar string of three consecutive platinum albums with the R&B chart-topper *Skin Tight* in spring 1974. The transformation was complete now. *Skin Tight* introduced a savage stew of raw funk, superlative soul and heavy blues, swirling behind Bonner's breathtaking tenor—a distinctive sound that was echoed later in the decade by the likes of Con Funk Shun's Michael Cooper and Cameo's Larry Blackmon.

Only six tracks long and full of loose jams and serious grooves, *Skin Tight* spawned two hugely successful singles, "Jive Turkey" in the late spring and the title track later that summer. DJs, however, were spinning the entire LP; the band's sexy LP sleeves were as famous as their music. And, buoyed by the enthusiasm, the Ohio Players raced back to the studio to cut their next album, *Fire*.

The album topped both the R&B and pop charts that autumn, the cue for Ohio Players to throw themselves onto the road as one of the most spectacular touring acts of the age. Always a strong touring act, they were now able to mount huge shows, while their public profile was vast enough for the *Midnight Special* TV show to devote an entire program to the band.

Culminating with *Honey*, 1975 would be the Ohio Players' finest year yet. Not only did the album again take the #1 spot on the R&B charts, it slammed into the pop charts as well, reaching #2. The band was seemingly unstoppable. Three singles, too, made strong statements: the innuendo laden "Fopp," the mellow jazz "Sweet Sticky Thing" and, rounding out the year in unforgettable fashion, "Love Rollercoaster."

There are few songs that ink themselves indelibly into the cultural milieu, but "Love Rollercoaster" did it, not only topping the chart, but remaining a favorite in every arena that can accommodate it, from oldies radio to modern samplers, and onto TV commercials—the high tech company Intel used the song to promote its pentium processors in the late '90s.

But all good rides have to stop sometime, though no one would have predicted that the Ohio Players' time at the top would slow down so quickly. While the disco infused "Who'd She Coo" reached #1 on the R&B charts and gave the band their first and only UK hit, when it peaked at #43, their next album, *Contradiction*, was regarded a total let down, critically and commercially. Though it shot to #1 as a matter of course, the sheer impossibility of following *Fire* and *Honey* left the album floundering for friends, amid a sea of negative reviews.

Mercury moved to repair the damage with the compilation, *Ohio Players Gold*, gathering up the best of the band's recent material, alongside a pair of unreleased tracks, "Feel the Beat (Everybody Disco)" (a surprisingly minor hit in early 1977) and "Only a Child Can Love."

The *Angel* album followed in 1977, bearing with it a long-demanded studio version of the call and response live favorite "O-H-I-O." Just one year after "Who'd She Coo" ruled the roost, the Ohio Players had racked up their final R&B Top 20 hit. Their soundtrack for the Fred Williamson movie *Mr. Mean*, faltered at #11 and didn't even make the pop Top 60.

Times were changing. Disco was now fueling the record buying public and the Ohio Players were suddenly irrelevant. They were still hot sellers but they weren't hitting the platinum or even the gold highs anymore.

In a bid to turn their fortunes around, the Ohio Players wrote, produced and played the Kitty & the Haywoods album, *Love Shock*, in 1977, but it registered nothing more than a chart flicker with the title track. Satchell also led the group in writing and producing the debut album for Faze-O in 1977 (the saxophonist alone also remained on hand for the remainder of that band's career). The Ohio Players themselves returned to action with 1978's double album *Jass-Ay-Lay-Dee*, their last for Mercury.

The album reached #15 on the R&B charts and spawned the effects laden "Funk-O-Nots" single, but overall, *Jazz-Ay-Lay-Dee* simply echoed the state of the band. Having churned out hit after hit for almost a decade without a break, they were tired and sounded it. Moving to Arista and adding percussionists Reubens Bassini and Azzedin Weston, the Ohio Players recorded another less than stellar album, *Everybody Up*, then broke up.

Williams, Willis and Beck promptly formed their own new group, Shadow, in 1979. Signing to Elektra, they released their debut, *Love Life*, in 1979, together with two minor singles, "I Need Love" and "No Better Love." Shadow released two further albums in 1980–81, *Shadow* and *Shadows in the Street*, both produced by Leon Ware, best known for his work with Marvin Gaye. The group broke up in late 1981.

Bonner, Middlebrooks, Jones and Pierce, meanwhile, rebuilt the Ohio Players with David Johnson (pno), Michael Jennings (trom), Dean Sims (trum), Shawn Dedrick (vcls), Wes Boatman (kybds) and Floyd Bailey (drms). This lineup cut *Ouch*, the first of two albums for Casablanca label mastermind Neil Bogart's Boardwalk label. Within the year, all the newcomers bar Johnson had departed, to be replaced by Jimmy Sampson (drms) and Vincent Thomas (perc) for *Tenderness*. Now based permanently back in Dayton, the Ohio Players finally called it quits in 1984, following the little-noticed, but contrarily best-in-years album *Graduation*.

Bonner began collaborating with fellow Ohioan and longtime friend Roger Troutman, whose own group, Zapp, had enjoyed immense success during the early '80s. Bonner now joined him at his Troutman Sound Systems studio to work on a solo album, 1985's *Sugar Kiss*. Troutman produced the set and Bonner returned the favor, guesting on Troutman's own next LP.

The pull of the Ohio Players remained strong, however, and in 1988, Bonner, Beck, Williams, Willis and Jones reformed the group with Darwin Dortch (bs) and Ronald Nooks (kybds). Still a ferociously tight live band, they now updated the Ohio Players sound with a trace of hip-hop. The resultant *Back* album was strong enough to scratch the R&B Top 60 that fall, but the reunion's future was clearly

on the road—a 1996 live album, *Ol' School*, captured a typically smoking show.

Two former members of the Ohio Players passed away during the 1990s; Satchell died in 1995, Middlebrook in 1997.

### THE OHIO PLAYERS COMPLETE DISCOGRAPHY
### SINGLES/CHART LOG
### OHIO UNTOUCHABLES

1962 She's My Heart's Desire/What To Do (LuPine)
1962 Love Is Amazing/Forgive Me Darling (LuPine)
1962 I'm Tired/Uptown (LuPine)

### THE OHIO PLAYERS

1967 Neighbors/A Thing Called Love (Tangerine)
1968 Trespassin'/You Don't Mean It (Compass—#50 R&B)
1968 It's a Cryin' Shame/I've Got To Hold On (Compass)
1969 Bad Bargain/Here Today And Gone Tomorrow (Capitol)
1969 Find Someone To Love/Over the rainbow (Capitol)
1971 Pain (part one)/(part two) (Westbound—#35 R&B/#64 pop)
1972 Pleasure/I Wanna Hear from You (Westbound—#45 R&B)
1972 Walt's First Trip/Varce Is Love (Westbound)
1973 Funky Worm/Paint Me (Westbound—#1 R&B/#15 pop)
1973 Ecstasy/Not So Sad and Lonely (Westbound—#12 R&B/#13 pop)
1974 Sleep Talk/Food Stamps Y'All (Westbound)
1974 Jive Turkey (part one)/(part two) (Mercury—#6 R&B/#47 pop)
1974 Skin Tight/Heaven Must Be like This (Mercury—#2 R&B/#13 pop)
1974 Fire/Together (Mercury—#1 R&B/#1 pop)
1975 I Want To Be Free/Smoke (Mercury—#6 R&B/#44 pop)
1975 Sweet Sticky Thing/Alone (Mercury—#1 R&B/#33 pop)
1975 Love Rollercoaster/It's All Over (Mercury—#1 R&B/#1 pop)
1975 Happy Holidays (part one)/(part two) (Mercury)
1976 Rattlesnake/Good Forever (Westbound #69 R&B/#90 pop)
1976 Fopp/Let's Love (Mercury—#9 R&B/#30 pop)
1976 Who'd She Coo?/Bi-Centennial (Mercury—#1 R&B/#18 pop)
1976 Far East Mississippi/Only a Child Can Love (Mercury—#18 R&B)
1977 Feel the Beat (Everybody Disco)/Contradiction (Mercury—#31 R&B/#61 pop)
1977 Body Vibes/Don't Fight My Love (Mercury—#19 R&B)
1977 O-H-I-O/Can You Still Love Me (Mercury—#9 R&B/#45 pop)
1977 Merry Go Round/Angel (Mercury—#77 R&B)
1977 Good Luck Charm (part one)/(part two) (Mercury—#51 R&B/#101 pop)
1978 Magic Trick/Mr. Mean (Mercury—#93 R&B)
1978 Funk-O-Nots/Sleepwalkin' (Mercury—#27/#105 pop)
1978 Time Slips Away/Nott Enuff (Mercury—#53 R&B)
1979 Everybody Up/Take De Funk Off, Fly (Arista—#33 R&B)
1979 Don't Say Goodbye/Say It (Arista)
1981 Try A Little Tenderness/Try To Be a Man (Boardwalk—#40 R&B)
1981 Skinny/Call Me (Boardwalk—#46 R&B)
1981 Star of the Party/Better Take a Coffee Break (Boardwalk)

1984 Sight for Sore Eyes/(instrumental) (AIR City—#83 R&B)
1988 Sweat/(LP version) (Track—#50 R&B)
1988 Let's Play (From Now On)/Show Off (Track—#33 R&B)

## LPs

**7** **1968 Observations in Time (Capitol)**

Pre-funking soul that contains their frightening version of "Somewhere over the Rainbow," but also packs the powerful punch of a heavily Stax/Isleys influenced soul-funk band, layering hot horns around sweaty vocals. Reissued as *The Ohio Players* in 1974 (Capitol—#32 R&B) and under a myriad of guises since then.

**6** **1972 Pain (Westbound—#21 R&B/#177 pop)**

Full of jazz breaks layered in the grooves highlighted by "Pain" and "Players Balling." Tight arrangements and intense energy keep it real.

**7** **1973 Pleasure (Westbound—#4 R&B/#63 pop)**

**8** **1973 Ecstasy (Westbound—#19 R&B/#70 pop)**

With "Food Stamps Y'All" and the title track especially, the album reflects the band's increasing proficiency for creating a perfect blend of funk.

**8** **1974 Skin Tight (Mercury—#1 R&B/#11 pop)**

The set that kicked off their rise to stardom with "Jive Turkey" and "Skin Tight" leading the pack of dirty, sweaty funk.

**9** **1975 Fire (Mercury—#1 R&B/#1 pop)**

Smooth music dominates in an unending circular flow that wraps around the vocals and often lets the words take center stage. It all sounds best on "Fire" and "I Want To Be Free."

**9** **1975 Honey (Mercury—#1 R&B/#2 pop)**

Excellent from beginning to end—full of vocal harmonies and grooves. The dirty guitars on "Fopp" are barely tempered by the over the top antics on the anthemic "Love Rollercoaster" and the lascivious "Sweet Sticky Thing."

**7** **1976 Contradiction (Mercury—#1 R&B/#12 pop)**

Great mid period funk. Horn heavy with lots of fresh guitar riffing, "Who'd She Coo" is sweet, while "Far East Mississippi" is hot and sticky, and reaches back to blues roots.

**6** **1977 Angel (Mercury—#9 R&B/#41 pop)**

The Players ride the disco train swapping fierce funk for mediocre chart grabbers, but we still love "O-H-I-O" and "Body Vibes," which added structure to the jams.

**3** **1977 Mr. Mean (Mercury—#11 R&B/#68 pop)**

A soundtrack showcasing the softer (read un-funky) side of the band. Understated and subtle to the point of horizontal, this is not your everyday OP set.

**4** **1978 Jass-Ay-Lay-Dee (Mercury—#15 R&B/#69 pop)**

Dated in the face of the new funk wave, the OP seemed to have reached the bottom of their bag of tricks.

**3** **1979 Everybody Up (Arista—#19 R&B/#80 pop)**

**5** **1981 Tenderness (Boardwalk—#49 R&B/#165 pop)**

This comeback album after a two year hiatus from the public this isn't bad, but doesn't have the energy of earlier LPs. Includes a warm cover of Otis Redding's "Dock of the Bay."

**3** **1982 Ouch (Boardwalk)**

Exactly.

**4** **1984 Graduation (AIR City)**

Utterly overlooked, *Graduation* features the ultra-nasty "Fast Track," for which it can almost be forgiven its other big-ballad sins.

**4** **1988 Back (Track Record—#55 R&B)**

Hip-hop hooks and ultra slick production slide in over the trademark horns and dirty jams. Disappointing.

**6** **1996 Ol' School (Castle—UK)**

Released in the US in 1998 as *Sweet Sticky Thing* (Capitol/EMI), a gee-it's-wunnerful-to-be-here-tonite . . . live set, built around a strong set of classic oldies.

### SELECTED COMPILATIONS AND ARCHIVE RELEASES

**8** **1968 First Impressions (Trip)**

Pre *Observations in Time* set hooking a tight rock sensibility around their stock-in-trade R&B shouters.

**7** **1974 Climax (Westbound—#24 R&B/#102 pop)**

An in-between labels set of vintage Westbound sessions.

**8** **1975 Greatest Hits (Westbound—#22 R&B/#92 pop)**

**7** **1975 Rattlesnake (Westbound—#8 R&B/#61 pop)**

Fascinating exhumation of unreleased 1972–73-era material, capturing the band somewhere between pain and ecstasy.

**8** **1976 Ohio Players Gold (Mercury—#10 R&B/#31 pop)**

Great hits compilation with "Love Rollercoaster."

**7** **1977 Best of the Early Years (Westbound—#58 R&B)**

**6** **1989 O-H-I-O (Polygram)**

Not a bad hits collection with "Funk-O-Nots," "Who'd She Coo" and "Far East Mississippi."

**9** **1995 Funk on Fire: The Mercury Anthology (Mercury)**

Two disc best of the best with unreleased tracks and all the faves is a must for the fan. With "Love Rollercoaster" and "Skin Tight," well, "Heaven Must Be like This"!

**6** **1996 Jam (Polygram)**

Live set of the hits. Not great but some of the versions are interesting. Best for the collector.

**7** **1998 Orgasm: The Very Best of the Ohio Players (Southbound—UK)**

Great comp of the best of the Westbound years.

**8** **2000 Gold Soul (Golden Lane)**

Two for the price of one—remastered gold disc collects *Observations in Time* and *First Impressions*.

## SELECTED SAMPLES

Climax — Too Short: It Don't Stop (1992)

Dirty Worm — Brotha Lynch Hung: Deep Down (1995)

Dirty Worm — Sicx: Once upon a Time (1998)

Dirty Worm — Too Short: Sample the Funk (1995)

Ecstasy — Jay-Z featuring Notorius BIG: Brooklyn's Finest (1996)

Ecstasy — A Tribe Called Quest: Scenario (remix) (1991)

Far East Mississippi — Style: Just a Little Something (1991)

Far East Mississippi — Chop Shop: Hurt Me (1996)

Fopp — Jay-Z: Rap Game/Crack Game (1997)

Funky Worm — X Clan: Xodus (1992)

Funky Worm — Too $hort: Sample the Funk (1995)

Funky Worm — De La Soul: Me Myself & I (1989)

Funky Worm — Yo-Yo: Letter To the Pen (1993)

Funky Worm — Rumpletilskinz: Attitudes (1993)

Funky Worm — Redman: Cosmic Slop (1994)

Funky Worm — Snoop Doggy Dogg: Serial Killa (1993)

Funky Worm — Tim Dog: Skip to My Loot (1993)

Funky Worm — Kris Kross: 2 Da Beat Ch'yall (1993)

Funky Worm — Keith Murray: Most Beautifullest Thing . . . (1994)

Funky Worm — Naughty By Nature: Klickow-Klickow (1995)

Funky Worm — NWA: Gangsta, Gangsta (1989)

Funky Worm — Above the Law: Black Superman (1994)

Funky Worm — South Central Cartel: Ya Want Sum a Dis (1991)

Funky Wrom — Domino: That's Real (1993)

Funky Worm — Three TimesDope: Mr. Sandman (1990)

Funky Worm — NWA: Dopeman (1989)

Funky Worm — AMG: Vertical Joyride (1992)

Funky Worm — Above the Law: B.M.L. (Commercial) (1991)

Funky Worm — Dr. Dre: The Chronic (1993)

Funky Worm — Beastie Boys: Funky Boss (1992)

Funky Worm — Ice Cube: Wicked (1992)

Funky Worm — Erick Sermon: Ill Shit (1993)

Funky Worm — Insane Poetry: If Rhymes Could Kill (1992)

Funky Worm — Bushwick Bill: Dollars and Sense (1992)

Funky Worm — Terminator X: Back To the Scene of the Bass (1991)

Funky Worm — PMD: I Saw It Cummin' (1994)

Funky Worm — DJ Jazzy Jeff & the Fresh Prince: Boom, Shake the Room (1993)

Funky Worm — Lifers Group: Jack U. Back (So You Wanna . . .) (1993)

Funky Worm — Kris Kross: Jump (1992)

I Wanna Know . . . — Compton's Most Wanted: 8 Iz Enough (1992)

I Wanna Know . . . — Black Sheep: City Lights (1994)

Introducing the Players — King Tee: Drunk Tekneek (1993)

Introducing the Players — Above the Law: Pimpology 101 (1993)

Laid It — EPMD: I'm Mad (1991)

Little Lady Maria — Puff Daddy: Senorita (1997)

Love Rollercoaster — Digable Planets: 9th Wonder (1994)

Love Rollercoaster — George Clinton: Dis Beat Disrupts (1993)

Never Had a Dream — Lord Finesse: Track the Movement (1990)

Never Had a Dream — Ice Cube: Down for Whatever (1993)

Never Had a Dream — Gang Starr: Lovesick (1991)

Never Had a Dream — BUMS: Suck My Dick (1995)

Our Love Has Died — Naughty By Nature: Shout Out (1995)

Our Love Has Died — Capital Tax: In Memory Of (1993)

Pain — Queen Mother Rage: To Be Real (1991)

Pain — Father MC: I've Been Watching You (1990)

Pain — Pete Rock & CL Smooth: Soul Brother # 1 (1992)

Pain — Organized Kon: Who Stole My Last Piece of Chicken? (1991)

Pain — Sounds of Blackness: I Believe (1994)

Pain — Gang Starr: Lovesick (1991)

Pain — Da King & I: Krak Da Weazel (1993)

Pain — Shyheim: Here I Am (1994)

Pain — A Tribe Called Quest: What Really Goes On (1996)

Players Balling — NWA: Dayz of Wayback (1991)

Players Balling — Keith Murray: Escapism (1994)

Players Balling — Pete Rock & CL Smooth: Lot's of Lovin' (1992)

Pride and Vanity — Naughty by Nature: Everyday All Day (1991)

Pride and Vanity — Leaders of the New School: Noisy Meditation (1993)

Pride and Vanity — Leaders of the New School: Classic Material (1993)

Pride and Vanity — Mary J Blige: What's the 411? (1992)

Pride and Vanity — Ice-T: Bitchess 2 (1991)

Pride and Vanity — Fat Joe Da Fat Gangsta: Da Fat Gangsta (1993)

Pride and Vanity — EPMD: Hardcore (1991)

Pride and Vanity — Digital Underground: Tie the Knot (1991)

Pride and Vanity — Diamond D: Pass Dat Shit (1992)

Skin Tight — Young MC: I Let 'Em Know (1989)

Skin Tight — Young MC: Know How (1989)

Skin Tight — Geto Boys: Talkin' Loud Ain't Saying Nothin' (1990)

Sweet Sticky Thing — Tony! Toni! Tone!: Gangsta Groove (1993)

What's Goin' On — Pete Rock & CL Smooth: Lot's of Lovin' (1992)

Who'd She Coo? — Penthouse Players Clique: Pimp Lane (1992)

Dirty Worm — Street Military: Another Hit (1993)

## ROBERT PALMER, see THE BRITISH ROCK FUNK CONNECTION

## MACEO PARKER

**BORN:** *2/14/43, Kinston, NC*

The son of musical parents (both sang in church, while his father also played piano and drums) Maceo Parker began playing baritone saxophone after seeing the instrument at a parade through town (he later switched to tenor). His brothers, too, were aspiring musicians: Melvin played drums and Kellis trombone and, by the time they were in fifth grade, they had already formed their first combo, the Blue Note Juniors, so-named in honor of their uncle's group, Bobby Butler & the Mighty Blue Notes. Indeed, their uncle frequently took them to his band's shows, where they performed a song or two during the intermission.

After graduating high school, all three brothers went on to college at North Carolina A&T, majoring in music. There they joined different bands and, one night around 1962, Melvin's group were booked into the El Morocco Club in Greenville, NC. In the audience that night was James Brown, who immediately offered Melvin a job the moment the boy had finished his studies. Two years later, Melvin and Maceo turned up together, backstage at one of Brown's shows, to ask if the offer still held. It did.

The pair arrived in time for one of the most crucial recording sessions in Brown's entire career, the smash "Out of Sight;" within a year, it was utterly reworked to become "Papa's Got a Brand New Bag."

Melvin Parker remained alongside Brown into 1966, until the arrival of John Starks and Clyde Stubblefield; Maceo, on the other hand, "has quit and been fired more times than either one of us can count," as Brown put it in his autobiography. However, he was generally on board for the most significant recordings of the next five years, his tight, punching sax leads all but duetting with Brown himself. "That's right, you keep playing, Maceo," Brown shouts during "Get It Together." "'Cause the groove is there."

Parker's first major break with Brown came on March 9, 1970, at the height of a dispute over payments. Hours before the group was due to take the stage in Columbus, GA, they announced *en masse* that they were quitting unless they were paid. Brown called their bluff, sacking them and taking the stage that night with a young Cincinnati act he had been grooming for just such an eventuality, the Facesetters, aka the first generation of the JBs

With brother Melvin, plus fellow defectors Jimmy Nolen and Alphonso Kellum (gtr), Bernard Odum (bs), Joseph Davis and Richard Griffith (trum) and Eldee Williams (sax), Parker immediately formed his own All the King's Men, signing with the Southbound label and cutting the album *Doing Their Own Thing*. Sales were poor; however, it is said that Brown himself was instrumental in discouraging radio play. And, after a second record, *Funky Music Machine* was cut for Excello but never released, the band broke up.

Parker and Nolen returned to Brown in early 1973, alongside Fred Wesley, Starks, guitarist Hearlon Martin and sax player St. Clair Pinckney; Brown also prompted Parker to launch a new sideline, Maceo & the Macks, for a string of singles released through the singer's own People label.

Between 1973–74, Maceo & the Macks released four sin-gles, "Party," "Soul Power 74," "I Can Play for (Just You and Me)" and "Cross the Track." Of course, the Macks simply disguised Brown and the rest of the JBs, but with Parker's sax way out front, his billing was richly deserved. Indeed, there would also be a pair of singles and one album, *Us*, credited to Maceo alone, further emphasizing his individuality, while the JBs themselves continued to spit out a stream of singles.

However, such activity could not disguise the fact that after two decades on top, Brown's magic was slipping. By 1975, the singer was in virtual semi-retirement; money was again an issue, but this time, there were not even that many gigs. Finally, Parker and Wesley quit, following erstwhile JBs Phelps Collins and Bootsy Collins into George Clinton's P-Funk organization.

There they formed the bedrock of the Horny Horns, a stellar horn section completed by jazzmen Michael and Randy Brecker and a regular fixture within the sprawling P-Funk empire for much of the remainder of the decade. Debuting on 1976's breakthrough *Mothership Connection* album, Parker and company received their first true taste of Clinton's vision on the accompanying tour, a lavish extravaganza built around the arrival onstage of a massive space ship.

Aided by the rest of the mothership crew, and fronted by Wesley, the Horny Horns released two albums during their lifetime, *A Blow for Me* and *Say Blow by Blow Backwards*. (A third, *The Final Blow*, was created from outtakes and remixes in 1994.) Both were largely comprised of existing P-Funk recordings, reworked for horns; much of *A Blow for me* was built around outtakes from Bootsy's Rubber Band's first albums.

Parker returned to James Brown in 1986 (he maintained his connection with Clinton by appearing on the *Hey Man . . .* album, among other projects), touring through the next two years of an increasingly successful comeback. Brown's incarceration in 1988, however, sent Parker off in yet another direction.

In 1990, awaiting Brown's release, Parker relaunched his solo career with the album *Roots Revisited*. Hooking up with German producer Stephen Meyer, Parker found himself luxuriating in the freedom to explore wherever he wanted, through jazz and soul as well as funk. The album topped the *Billboard* Jazz Chart for two months, while *Rolling Stone* named Parker Best Jazz Artist of the Year.

Also in 1990, Parker reunited with Wesley and Pee Wee Ellis as the JB Horns, named, of course, in a bid to keep Brown's name in the public eye during his imprisonment. Their debut album, *Pee Wee, Fred and Maceo*, was a wild

632 Fred Wesley & the JBs: Same Beat (part one)/(part two)

633 Lyn Collins: Take Me Just as I Am/Don't Make Me Over

634 Maceo & the Macks: I Can Play For (Just You And Me)/Doing It to Death

635 Lee Austin: I'm in Love/Moonlight

636 Lyn Collins: Give It Up or Turnit a Loose/What the World Needs Now

637 The Devils: Th X-Sorcist/Hip Hug Her

638 Fred Wesley & JBs: Damn Right I Am Somebody (part one)/(part two)

639 Sweet Charles: Soul Man/Why Can't I Be Treated like A Man

640 Maceo: Drowning in the Sea of Love/Show and Tell

641 Lyn Collins: Rock Me Again and Again . . ./Wide Awake in a Dream

642 The Progressors: The Brother's Under Pressure/I'm So Lonely

643 Fred Wesley & the JBs: Rockin' Funky Watergate (part one)/(part two)

644 The Insiders: In the Midnight Hour/Lonely Teardrops

645 Sweet Charles: Dedicated To the One I Love/Give the Woman a Chance

646 Fred Wesley & the JBs: Little Boy Black/Rockin' Funky Watergate (part two)

647 Maceo & the Macks: Cross the Track/The Soul of A Black Man

648 Fred Wesley & the New JBs: Breakin' Bread/Funky Music Is My Style

649 Johnny Scotton: You Don't Wanna Do Nothin', Do Ya/With Your Love for Me

650 Lyn Collins: Rock Me Again and Again/You Can't Love Me

651 Fred Wesley & the New JBs: Makin' Love/Rice & Ribs

652 unissued

653 Sweet Charles: I Won't Last a Day Without You/I'll Never Let You Break My Heart Again

654 Fred & the New JBs: Thank You for Lettin' Me Be Myself and Be Yours (part one)/(part two)

655 Fred & the New JBs: It's the JBs Monaurail (part one)/(part two)

656 Sweet Charles: Hang Out and Hustle/Together

657 Lyn Collins: How Long Can I Keep It Up/Baby Don't Do It

658 The Hustlers: Hustling/Soft Hustle

659 Lyn Collins: If You Don't Know Me By Now/Baby Don't Do It

660 The JBs: Thank You for Lettin' Me Be Myself and Be Yours (part one)/(part two)

661 Maceo: Future Shock (part one)/(part two)

662 Lyn Collins: Mr. Big Stuff/Rock Me Again and Again . . .

663 The JBs: All Aboard the Soul Funky Train/Thank You (part one)

664 The JBs with James Brown: Everybody Wanna Get Funky One More Time (part one)/(part two)

*LPs*

5601 The JBs: Food for Thought

5602 Lyn Collins: Think (About It)

5603 Fred Wesley & the JBs: Doing It to Death

6601 Maceo: Us

6602 Fred Wesley & the JBs: Damn Right I Am Somebody

6603 Sweet Charles: For Sweet People

6604 Fred & the New JBs: Breakin' Bread

6605 Lyn Collins: Check Me Out If You Don't Know Me By Now

6606 The JBs: Hustle with Speed

*SELECTED COMPILATIONS AND ARCHIVE RELEASES*

**8** 1986 Funky People, Vol. 1 (Polydor)
**7** 1988 Funky People, Vol. 2 (Polydor)
**8** 2000 Funky People, Vol. 3 (Polydor)

Three volume series anthologizing both the artists and the output of Brown's early-mid-'70s People label. The inclusion of rare and unreleased material ensures they are of especial interest to serious Brown collectors; however, general fans and curious initiates are encouraged to check them out as well. The following indexes volumes 1–3 alphabetically by artist.

AABB — Pick Up the Pieces One by One (v3)

Vicki Anderson — If You Don't Give Me What I want (v3)

Hank Ballard — From the Love Side (v2)

Hank Ballard/The Dapps — How You Gonna Get Respect (v3)

Myra Barnes (Vicki Anderson) — Super Good

Myra Barnes (Vicki Anderson) — Message from the Soul Sisters (v2)

Believers — Mr. Hot Pants (v3)

James Brown — Talkin' Loud and Sayin' Nothin' (v3)

Bobby Byrd — I Know You Got Soul (v2)

Bobby Byrd — Hot Pants (v2)

Lyn Collins — Rock Me Again and Again. . . (v1)

Lyn Collins — Think (About It) (v1)

Lyn Collins — Do Your Thing (v2)

Lyn Collins — Mama Feelgood (v1)

Lyn Collins — Put It on the Line (v2)

Lyn Collins — Take Me as I Am (v1)

Lyn Collins — Give It Up or Turnit a Loose (v3)

Beau Dollar — Who Knows (v3)

Dee Felice Trio — There Was a Time (v3)

JBs — Hot Pants Road (v1)

JBs — Givin' Up Food for Funk (v1)

JBs — Gimme Some More (v1)

JBs — Pass the Peas (v1)

Maceo & the Macks — Parrty (part one) (v1)

Maceo & the Macks — Cross the Track (v2)

Maceo & the Macks — Soul Power 74 (v2)

Sweet Charles — Hang Out and Hustle (v3)

Fred Wesley & the JBs — Blow Your Head (undubbed) (v3)

Fred Wesley & the JBs — I'm Paying Taxes, What Am I Buying (v2)

Fred Wesley & the JBs — If You Don't Get It the First Time (v1)

Fred Wesley & the JBs — Same Beat (part one) (v1)

Fred Wesley & the JBs — You Can Have Watergate (v2)

Fred Wesley & the JBs — Damn right I Am Somebody (v1)

Fred [Wesley] & the New JBs — It's the JBs Monaurail (part one) (v1)

Fred Wesley & the JBs — Blow Your Head (v2)

Marva Whitney — It's My Thing (live) (v3)

Marva Whitney — What Do I Have To Do (v2)

## P-FUNK, see GEORGE CLINTON

**THE ROLLING STONES, see THE BRITISH ROCK FUNK CONNECTION**

## RUFUS

**FORMED:** *1970, Chicago, IL*
**ORIGINAL LINE-UP:** *Al Ciner (gtr), Kevin Murphy (kybods), Ron Stockers (kybds, vcls) Dennis Belfield (bs), Andre Fischer (drms)*

In the early 1970s, Rufus created the quintessential marriage between rock 'n' roll and funk. Where many of their funky peers only hinted at the guitar riffs, which they imbedded in the groove, Rufus gave their songs the full-on garage treatment, tinged with leftover psychedelia to create a fusion of many styles including, but certainly not limited to, jazz, gospel, country and, of course, funk.

Rufus grew in part out of an earlier Chicago bar group, the American Breed, formed in 1966 around Al Ciner and Kevin Murphy. Quickly picking up on the then-prevalent psychedelic pop sound, American Breed made a brief if indelible splash on the pop charts with "Bend Me, Shape Me" in late 1967.

Murphy was drafted soon after, his departure was the first of several lineup changes that saw the band forever in a state of flux. Finally, the American Breed splintered, and Ciner, the returning Murphy and vocalist Paulette McWilliams regrouped as Ask Rufus in 1969. Adding Ron Stockert, Andre Fischer and Dennis Belfield, they shortened their name to Rufus in 1970 and signed with Epic. They recorded two singles, "Read All About It" and "Follow the Lamb," before McWilliams left for a solo career in 1971.

Rufus continued to play the Chicago club circuit however, and it wasn't long before another powerful singer caught their attention. Chaka Khan was lead vocalist for Goliath, a group that evolved from local heroes Baby Huey & the Babysitters. The two bands often sat in on one anothers' shows; Khan's recruitment was an easy and obvious fit.

With Khan's vocals fronting the fusion, Rufus began traveling around the Midwest where constant gigging helped to develop their sound. Signing to ABC Records, the band relocated to California, and cut their debut album, *Rufus*. Combining original material with a clutch of well-chosen covers (Allen Toussaint's "Whoever's Thrilling You (Is Killing Me)" became the album's first single), the summer 1973 release broke into the R&B Top 50. It also won Rufus the admiration of Ashford & Simpson and Stevie Wonder, whose songs were covered on the set; both immediately gifted further material for inclusion on their sophomore set, 1974's *Rags to Rufus*.

*Rags* broke Rufus in the US, hitting #4 on both the R&B and pop charts that spring and spawning two smash singles: Wonder's "Tell Me Something Good," which featured the composer himself on keyboards, and "You Got the Love," which gave Rufus their first R&B chart-topper that fall. Rounding out a superb set were Ashford/Simpson's "Ain't Nothin' but a Maybe" and "You Got the Love," a Chaka Khan/Ray Parker, Jr. collaboration.

Rufus seemed to be beginning the ultimate ride, but all was not well within the ranks. Khan was already a hot commodity, but ABC were intent on turning up the heat even further, singling her out for a "featuring" credit on the sleeve of *Rags to Rufus* and treating her, indeed, as a solo star in the making. Even more damaging, the democratic spread of vocals that characterized *Rufus* was now subverted behind Khan. Ron Stockert was openly rebellious, his frustrations echoed by both Ciner and Dennis Belfield, who felt the group was becoming simply a vehicle for Khan's diva persona. Khan, too, was unhappy but, as she told *Goldmine* in 1997, there was nothing she could do to circumvent ABC's agenda.

Rufus exploded. Ciner, Stockton and Belfield quit *en masse* immediately before recording commenced on the next LP—Stockton and Belfield returning to their rock roots in Three Dog Night. Rufus, now a trio of Khan, Murphy and Fischer, replaced them with Tony Maiden (gtr) and Bobby Watson (bs).

*Rufusized* appeared at the end of 1974 and, while the crisis certainly affected the members themselves, it didn't even dent the band's public appeal. The album shot to #2 on the R&B charts and was quickly joined by the singles "Once You Get Started" and "Please Pardon Me (You Remind Me of A Friend)." Indeed, 1975 would be a huge year for Rufus. They supported the Rolling Stones on their 1975 US tour (alongside the Meters), then unleashed *Rufus, Featuring Chaka Khan*, fattening the sound with horns courtesy of Tower of Power. Released in the late fall, it shot straight to the top of the R&B chart.

The album's three singles fared equally well; "Sweet Thing" hit #1, "Dance Wit' Me" peaked at #5 and, mere months after the Bee Gees stormed the charts with "Jive Talkin'," Rufus took the song back to the charts in summer 1976.

*Ask Rufus* (1977) was another phenomenal success, spending some 27 weeks on the charts. Rufus' sound was fattened further as percussionist Milt Holland and keyboardist Gary Wolinski added to the groove, while Rolling Stones guitarist Ron Wood guested on the album's "A-Flat Fry."

Fischer quit, to be replaced by John Ronison; 1978's *Street Player*, in turn, proved to be Khan's final album with Rufus; after five years, she was eager to launch her solo career. The band's internal relationships had reached their breaking point by the time Khan left, although of course she could not simply walk away from Rufus. Her contract demanded two more albums.

Rufus brought in two backing vocalists, Maxayn Lewis and Lalomie Washburn, to fill some of the holes for their next album, 1979's *Numbers*. But it was quickly apparent that Rufus without Khan would never stand a chance. The album peaked at a disappointing #15 on the R&B charts in early 1979, while the single, "Blue" reached #16. Khan's return later in the year, on the other hand, produced Rufus' fourth #1 album, the Quincy Jones produced *Masterjam*.

Khan departed again immediately after, and Rufus followed through with *Party 'Til You're Broke*, a respectable seller but scarcely a massive hit. Neither, surprisingly, did the second Khan reunion set, *Camouflage*, restore Rufus to favor, although a string of live shows in early 1982 were massively successful. Another Chaka-less album, March 1983's *Seal in Red*, barely cracked the R&B Top 50 before fading away, and fall 1983, brought the release of Rufus' final album, *Live-Stompin' at the Savoy*.

A massive double, three sides were recorded live with Khan at New York's Savoy Theatre over three nights, February 12–14, 1982. The fourth, again recorded with Khan, comprised all new studio material, including "Ain't Nobody," which promptly became one of the best-loved songs in Rufus' entire canon. The single slammed straight into the R&B charts at #1 and became one of THE summer sensations of 1983. Rufus disbanded soon after.

Maiden, Watson, Murphy and Khan reunited in February 2000 to film a set for the Experience Hendrix Music project.

### RUFUS DISCOGRAPHY
#### CHART LOG
1973 Whoever's Thrilling You (Is Killing Me)/I Finally Found You (ABC—#40 R&B)
1973 Feel Good/Keep It Coming (ABC—#45 R&B)
1974 Tell Me Something Good/Smokin' Room (ABC—#3 R&B/#3 pop)
1974 You Got the Love/Rags to Rufus (ABC—#1 R&B/#11 pop)
1975 Once You Get Started/Rufusized (ABC—#4 R&B/#10 pop)
1975 Please Pardon Me (You Remind Me of A Friend)/Watching You (ABC—#6 R&B/#48 pop)
1975 Sweet Thing/Circles (ABC—#1 R&B/#5 pop)
1976 Dance Wit' Me/Everybody's Got an Aura (ABC—#5 R&B/#39 pop)
1976 Jive Talkin'/On Time (ABC—#35 R&B)
1977 At Midnight (My Love Will Lift You Up)/Better Days (ABC—#1 R&B/#30 pop)
1977 Hollywood/Earth Song (ABC—#3 R&B/#32 R&B)
1977 Everlasting Love/Close the Door (ABC—#17 R&B)
1978 Stay/Change Your Ways (ABC—#3 R&B/#105 pop)
1978 Blue Love/Turn (ABC—#34 R&B/#105 pop)
1979 Do You Love What You Feel/Dancin' Mood (MCA—#1 R&B/#30 pop)
1980 Any Love/What Am I Missing? (MCA—#24 R&B/#102 pop)
1980 I'm Dancin for Your Love/Walk the Rockaway (MCA—#43 R&B)
1981 Sharing the Love/We Got the Way (MCA—#8 R&B/#91 pop)
1982 Better Together/True Love (MCA—#66 R&B)
1983 Ain't Nobody/Sweet Love (Warners—#1 R&B/#22 pop)
1984 One Million Kisses/Stay (Warners—#37 R&B/#102 pop)
1979 Keep It Together (Declaration of Love)/Red Hot Poker (ABC—#16 R&B/#109 pop)
1981 Tonight We Love/Afterwords (MCA—#18 R&B)
1981 Hold on To A Friend/Party 'Til You're Broke (MCA—#56 R&B)
1982 Better Together/True Love (MCA—#66 R&B)
1983 Take It To the Top/Distant Lover (Warners—#47 R&B)
1983 Ain't Nobody/Sweet Thing (live) (Warners—#1 R&B/#22 pop)
1984 One Million Kisses/Stay (Warners—#37 R&B/#102 pop)

#### LPs
**4** 1973 Rufus (MCA—#44 R&B/#175 pop)
**9** 1974 Rags to Rufus (MCA—#2 R&B/#7 pop)
A stunning LP that reflects their fully gelled sound. "You Got the Love" lays down the funk tone while Stevie Wonder's "Tell Me Something Good" became a classic. Elsewhere the Ashford/Simpson stunner "Ain't Nothin' but a Maybe" allows Khan to use her voice to its fullest potential.
**7** 1974 Rufusized (MCA—#4 R&B/#4 pop)
Often more rock than funk, a fact that betrays the band's roots, there are nonetheless some pure grooves in "I'm a Woman," "Right Is Right" and "Once You Get Started."
**7** 1975 Rufus Featuring Chaka Khan (MCA—#1 R&B/#7 pop)
Khan's voice again takes to the skies with a soulful edge on "Sweet Thing" and "Dance Wit Me." Less funky than expected, the set also includes a gallant cover of the Bee Gee's "Jive Talkin'."
**5** 1977 Ask Rufus (MCA—#1 R&B/#12 pop)
"At Midnight (My Love Will Lift You Up)" kicks off this set, putting the funk back in the mix, while adding a jazzy edge that suits Khan's voice perfectly. The rest of the LP, while excellent soft soul, doesn't pack a real punch.
**8** 1978 Street Player (ABC—#1 R&B/#14 pop)
A stellar set on par with the *Rags*-era material. The grooves are ferocious and match Khan's vocals in intensity through-

out, especially on "Destiny," while "Stranger To Love" and "Blue Note" are close seconds. "Turn," meanwhile, remains some of the band's best funk.

**4** **1979 Numbers (ABC—#15 R&B/#81 pop)**
No Chaka, few ideas.

**6** **1979 Masterjam (MCA—#1 R&B/#14 pop)**
It's obvious that disco impacted the band heavily. Songs stand out on one hand as pop/soul masterpieces and Khan is magnificent, but the funk suffers as a result.

**3** **1981 Party 'Til You're Broke (MCA—#24 R&B/#73 pop)**
Another post-Chaka LP. The set is competent with all the usual riffery that set Rufus apart from many. Khan's absence, however, is a gaping hole.

**4** **1981 Camouflage (MCA—#15 R&B/#98 pop)**
A suprisingly underwhelming reunion with Khan.

**5** **1983 Seal in Red (WB—#49 R&B)**

**7** **1983 Live-Stompin' at the Savoy (WB—#4 R&B/#30 pop)**
Three superb sides of live performance include passionate reworkings of "Tell Me Something Good" and "What Cha' Gonna Do for Me." Side four is filled with throwaway new material, bar the stunning "Ain't Nobody."

### SELECTED COMPILATIONS AND ARCHIVE RELEASES
**8** **1996 Very Best of Rufus & Chaka Khan (MCA)**
All the hits and no misses. A great comp.

### SELECTED SAMPLES
Magic in Your Eyes — Nicole Renee: Wickedness (1998)
Ooh I Like Your Lovin' — Boogie Down Productions: The Blueprint (1989)
You Got the Love — Tone Loc: On Fire (1989)

## SNAFU, see THE BRITISH ROCK FUNK CONNECTION

## SUPERCHARGE, see THE BRITISH ROCK FUNK CONNECTION

## TOWER OF POWER
**FORMED:** *1968, San Francisco, CA*
**ORIGINAL LINE-UP:** *Rufus Miller (vcls), Emilio Castillo (b. Detroit, MI, 1950—sax), Joe DeLopez (gtr), Rocca Prestia (b. Francis Prestia III—bs), Mic Gillette (trum), Steve Kupka (sax), Skip Mesquite (sax), Jack Castillo (drms)*

Half Mexican, half Greek, Detroit born Emilio Castillo arrived in Fremont, CA, with his family in 1962. Together with brother Jack and guitarist Joe DeLopez, he formed his first band, Black Orpheus, in 1966, shortly after sneaking (under-age) into a Hayward, CA, club and catching a performance by the then unknown Sly Stone.

Immediately captivated by Stone's heady R&B brew, the Castillos then saw a local soul act, the Spiders, and promptly decided to steer Black Orpheus in a similar direction. With the addition of Rufus Miller, Skip Mesquite and Rocca Prestia, Black Orpheus changed their name to the Motowns at the suggestion of their manager, the Castillos' mother. The group gigged only occasionally—their youth ensured few clubs would, or even could, book them—although on the occasions they did play, clad in matching outfits and with their dance steps expertly synchronized, they never failed to make an impression.

Certainly Stephen Kupka, the baritone sax playing roadie for another local outfit, the Loading Zone, was already aware of them when he met Emilio Castillo at the Alameda County Fair in summer 1967; he joined the Motowns the following June. Trumpeter Mic Gillette (the son of Harry James & the Dorseys trombonist Ray Gillette) followed.

The Motowns continued inching ahead through 1968 and 1969, but gigs remained at a premium as the Bay Area was consumed by the psychedelic scene whose epicenter, at the corner of Haight and Ashbury, continued to attract would-be musicians from all across the country. Neither were the new music's shockwaves confined to the world of rock 'n' roll. Sly Stone's appearance at the Woodstock Festival in August 1969, opened soul and R&B to exactly the same musical forces—a point driven further home by the emergence that same year of George Clinton's Funkadelic.

Of course the Motowns' own music was adapting to the changing scenery; their name and the uniformed image, however, remained locked in an earlier age. That summer, then, Castillo announced that both had to go. Henceforth, the band would be called Tower of Power—and their music would be pumped up to match.

It was very much a last ditch effort. The group was barely making enough money to cover expenses and Castillo later admitted that if things hadn't started improving, the Motowns would certainly have split. As it was, they were on the verge of breaking up when they applied for an audition at the fabled Fillmore theater.

They were accepted and that fall 1969, Tower of Power appeared at one of the venue's regular Audition Nights, well aware that this one performance would either catapult them to the stars, or slam them back into oblivion. After the show, Castillo was sure it was the latter; they played one song, their own "Social Lubrication," but one look at Fillmore promotor Bill Graham's face convinced him that the great man hated every minute of it. Immediately afterward, Castillo headed up to Detroit, where his parents were now living, only to turn around again almost as immediately, after an excited Kupka called him up. Graham's expression had

**Oakland's finest—Tower of Power.**

nothing to do with what he'd seen. In fact, he was now offering them a regular show.

Soon, Tower of Power were appearing regularly at what was, at that time, the West Coast's most prestigious venue, their skillful blending of R&B and Latino influences combining to forge a funk sound as unique as any on the scene. Bill Graham himself was absolutely besotted with the band and, even before he signed them to his own San Francisco record label, he made sure they received the best exposure he could muster. When Aretha Franklin announced she intended recording her next album live at the Fillmore, Graham arranged for Tower of Power to appear as opening act.

Behind the scenes, however, life was not so smooth. David Rubinson, Graham's partner in San Francisco Records (and subsequently, producer of both Malo and the Meters), felt that Tower of Power's rhythm section was too weak, prompting the removal of Jack Castillo and DeLopez. They were replaced by Willie James Fulton (gtr) and David Garibaldi (drms); the latter joined just two weeks before the

group were scheduled to record their first single, "Sparkling in the Sand."

The changes were a taste of things to come. In short succession, Mic Gillette quit to join another San Francisco combo, Cold Blood, as they set out on tour—apparently he would avoid the draft by doing so. Recently recruited second trumpeter Ken Balzell departed, to be replaced by Greg Adams; another trumpeter, David Padron, was also involved as the sessions for that solitary single expanded toward an entire album. And still the lineup was not settled. Vocalist Miller quit during the recording itself; Rick Stevens, nephew of Ivory Joe Hunter, was recruited in his stead. It would be Stevens who sang lead on "Sparkling in the Sand."

Powered by phenomenal Bay Area sales, "Sparkling in the Sand" and the album, the Rubinson-produced *East Bay Grease*, both edged into the lower reaches of the pop chart, landing fine reviews in *Downbeat* and *Rolling Stone* ("knockout dance music") and setting up tours of the Southwest, Mexico City and the East Coast. Their local renown, meanwhile, saw the Tower of Power horn section alone recruited to play on Janis Joplin's former colleagues, Big Brother & the Holding Company's latest album, *Be a Brother.*

Tower of Power themselves contributed four tracks to the Bay Area compilation album, *Lights Out . . . Voco Presents the Soul of the Bay Area*, while the news that San Francisco Records had folded was more than offset by the knowledge that several major labels were now waiting in the wings.

They signed with Warner Brothers and began work immediately on their second album. As concise as its predecessor was sprawling, *Bump City* took the first giant steps toward defining what became the Tower of Power sound, hard funking, but utterly radio friendly, every song falling just a few inches short of a genuine jam, but loose enough that you never really noticed. "You're Still a Young Man," Tower of Power's first Warner single, broke the pop Top 30; the album faltered at #85, but with their live show gathering converts everywhere, a breakthrough was imminent.

Certainly the band's peers were impressed. In the studio, Booker T. & the MGs guitarist Steve Cropper joined producer Ron Capone at the mixing stage, while Tower of Power themselves became all but synonymous with studio perfectionism, and not only on their own records. During 1971–72, the ever-active Tower of Power horns guested on the debut album by Little Feat (lending that outfit a funkiness that remains an integral part of their own musical legend) and the third album by Santana.

Mesquite and Stevens quit in mid-1972. (Stevens later joined Brass Horizon; in 1974, however, he was convicted of kidnapping and three murders.) The pair were promptly replaced by 18-year-old Lenny Pickett (who turned down an offer from Cold Blood to take the Tower gig) and vocalist Lenny Williams (born in Pine Bluff, AR). He made his debut just six days after joining and got through the show (opening for Curtis Mayfield) reading lyrics from a piece of paper. Pickett, meanwhile, was already perfecting the dervish mambo dance that became his onstage trademark; a whirl of gold lame, platform shoes and Afro hair highlighted each show as he threw himself into the audience.

Pickett's sense of theater brought an entire new dimension to Tower of Power, lending their shows a visual dimension to match the already powerful musical impact. The lineup was still evolving, however; Bruce Conte, another refugee from Loading Zone, replaced Fulton, a former research chemist, Brent Byars, came in on congas and organist Chester Thompson, hot from a well-received solo

album, *Powerhouse*, arrived to bring yet another ingredient to the stew.

In July 1973, Tower of Power's new single "So Very Hard To Go," breached the pop Top 30; it was followed by the group's third album, *Tower of Power*, a #15 that brought the band their first (and thus far, only) gold disc. They also made their debut on television's *Soul Train*, disavowing great swathes of their radio audience from the belief that, after three successive balladic hits, Tower of Power were a Bay Area version of the sweet soul Stylistics — a common misconception at the time, and one that the musicians would be gleefully demolishing with their next album.

Like its predecessor, *Tower of Power* had kept things short, with just two tracks edging over the five minute mark. But *Back to Oakland*, luxuriously recorded with an unchanged lineup, was dominated by the marathon "Squib Cakes," an eight-minute jam that proved Tower of Power could let rip with the best of them. So, at the other end of the scale, did "Oakland Stroke," a frantic two-minute boogie that opened the album at a manic 132 bpm.

The departure of Garibaldi saw Tower of Power return to the studio almost immediately, to break in his successor, David Batlett. The result, fall 1974's *Urban Renewal* furthered the group's musical development, while the Tower of Power horns, too, continued expanding horizons, working with Roy Buchanan, Graham Central Station, Rufus and British pop soul singer Linda Lewis. At the same time they brought a taste of unaccustomed funkiness to albums by Elton John, Rod Stewart, Rolling Stones bassist Bill Wyman and rocker Sammy Hagar.

Lennie Williams was next to go, departing for a successful solo career around the same time as Garibaldi returned to the fold; new vocalist Hubert Tubbs, however, was to see his reign dawn with Tower of Power's first flop album, 1975's adventurously soulful *In the Slot*. Instantly falling back on their strengths — the funk — Tower of Power responded with their most powerful album yet, the in concert *Live and in Living Color*, a dramatic, jam-packed set. Its only failing was, in an age when double live albums were all but the industry norm, it emerged as a mere single disc.

*Live* was Tower of Power's final Warner Brothers album; early in 1976, they joined Columbia, a decision Castillo later confessed was to irrevocably damage the group's standing, commercially and creatively. Through the late '70s, Tower of Power became an increasingly marginal sideline to the more lucrative disco boom and, while the likes of War and P-Funk proved that it was possible to maintain a high funk profile in the face of all else, for others, it was a definite case of sink or swim. Tower of Power sank.

Personnel problems continued to cloud the horizon. Hubert Tubbs left; in his stead came Edward McGee, a vocalist who impressed everybody at his audition but, according to Camillo, went downhill from there. McGee cut just one album with the group, 1976's *Ain't Nothin' Stoppin' Us Now*, before being replaced by ex-Spectrum vocalist Michael Jefferies.

Garibaldi left again; So did Prestia. Both subsequently returned, but in the meantime, Ronnie Beck and Victor Conte (brother of Bruce) were recruited as Tower of Power cut 1978's *We Came To Play*, with Steve Cropper returning to oversee the sessions. It was a lackluster performance from all concerned, however, and after one further album, 1979's distinctly disco-fied *Back on the Streets*, produced nothing more than the R&B chart mini-hit "Rock Baby," Tower of Power and Columbia parted company.

Beck and the Conte brothers left in late 1979. Garibaldi returned, joined by Danny Hoefer (gtr) and Vito San Filippo (bs), and in 1981, Tower of Power were invited to cut a direct-to-disc audiophile recording for Sheffield Labs. Reprising three old songs and introducing two new ones, *Direct* was recorded with Willie James Fulton back on guitar, plus a sixth horn player, Rick Waychesko. The band also recorded a new single, "It's as Simple as That," for European release and, toward the end of 1981, signed again with Warner Brothers. However, the group's own internal state was so chaotic that there was never any chance of new music being released. It was 1999 before their 1981 sessions finally saw release, as the *Dinosaur Tracks* album.

Pickett, Gillette and Thompson quit; the latter joined Santana, Pickett became an integral part of the *Saturday Night Live* musical troupe. New members came and went. Marc Russo (sax), Mike Cichowicz (trum) and Mark Sanders (drms) passed through. And though Tower of Power regained some lost visibility through a link up with rock singer Huey Lewis and the News (who recorded "Simple as That," a track from the ill-fated WB album), still a new deal proved elusive—even as the Tower of Power horns continued in constant demand, recording with Dionne Warwick, LaToya Jackson, country star Rodney Crowell and rockers Heart and Molly Hatchet.

By the time Tower of Power were finally able to record their next album, 1986's *TOP*, the lineup was led by former Kenny G vocalist/keyboard player Ellis Hall, while drummer Mick Mestek, returning bassist Rocca Prestia, Richard Elliot (sax) and Lee Thornberg (trum) joined an aggrega-

tion that gave new meaning to the word "unsettled." Castillo, Fulton and Kupka alone remained a link with the band's glory days.

*TOP* was unlikely to change that; it was initially released in Scandinavia only, by the Glenyd Grammafon APS label, finally appearing (in abridged form, and retitled *Power*) in the US the following year. One track, the instrumental "Boys Night Out," gained some attention after it was included in the soundtrack to the movie *Arthur 2*. Otherwise, it would be another four years (and further lineup changes) before Tower of Power re-emerged with new management, a major label deal (Epic) and another album, *Monster on a Leash*.

Who would have recognized this group from the Tower of Power of old, however? Fronted by the first White vocalist in their history, Tom Bowes, the core trio was joined now by former Maria Muldaur keyboard player Nick Milo, ex-Jefferson Starship guitarist Carmen Grillo and one-time Gap Band sideman Russ McKinnon (drms), to turn in a seamless pop-soul collection. It was a direction they pursued again on 1993's *TOP* (their second use of that title, of course), but was quickly reversed for 1995's *Souled Out*, new vocalist Brent Carter's debut with a band that really had been traveling too far to change direction for long.

Now lining up as Castillo (sax), Grillo (gtr), Milo (kybds), Kupka (sax), Prestia (bs), Carter (vcls), Bill Churchville (trum, trom), Barry Danielian (trum and flglhrn), David Mann (sax) and Herman Matthews (drms), Tower of Power turned back the clock with a passion and, while the return to form may have pleased die-hard fans alone, it was both impressive and heartfelt, as the group proved with the title track from their next album, *Rhythms and Business*—a caustic discussion of musicians who sell out their soul, just to sell records.

In 1998, Tower of Power launched their 30th anniversary celebrations with the *What Is Hip* anthology and a triumphant tour—subsequently commemorated with the *Soul Vaccination* live album. Mic Gillette and David Garibaldi both returned to the ranks for a time, while a host of extra-curricular activities ensured that the musicians remained constantly active: regular gigs by Kupka's Strokeland Super Band, and albums by Prestia (*Everybody on the Bus*), Adams' (the jazzy *Hidden Agenda*) and latter-day guitarist Jeff Tamelier (*Strat Got Yo Tongue*).

Into 2000, Tower of Power themselves continued touring, gigging with the Average White Band during April and James Brown through May.

## TOWER OF POWER COMPLETE DISCOGRAPHY
### SINGLES/CHART LOG

1970 Sparkling in the Sand/? (San Francisco—#107 pop)

1972 You're Still a Young Man/Skating on Thin Ice (WB—#24 R&B/#29 pop)

1972 Down to the Nightclub/What Happened to the World That Day? (WB—#66 pop)

1973 So Very Hard To Go/Clean Slate (WB—#11 R&B/#17 pop)

1973 This Time It's Real/Soul Vaccination (WB—#27 R&B/#65 pop)

1973 What Is Hip?/Clever Girl (WB—#39 R&B/#91 pop)

1974 Time Will Tell/Oakland Stroke (WB 27 R&B/#69 pop)

1974 Don't Change Horses (In the Middle of a Stream)/I Got the Chop (WB—#22 R&B/#26 pop)

1975 Only So Much Oil in the Ground/Give Me the Proof (WB—#85 R&B/#102 pop)

1975 Willing To Learn/Walking Up Hip Street (WB—#77 R&B)

1975 You're So Wonderful, So Marvelous/Stroke '75 (WB—#57 R&B)

1975 Soul of a Child/Treat Me like Your Man (WB)

1976 You Ought To Be Havin' Fun/While We Went to the Moon (Columbia—#62 R&B/#68 pop)

1977 Ain't Nothin' Stoppin' Us Now/Because I Think the World of You (Columbia—#95 R&B)

1978 Lovin' You Is Gonna See Me Through/I Am a Fool (Columbia—#98 R&B/#106 pop)

1978 Love Bug/We Came To Play (Columbia)

1979 Rock Baby/Heaven Must Have Made You (Columbia—#61 R&B)

1979 In Due Time/And You Know It (Columbia)

1981 It's as Simple as That/You Taught Me How To Love (Fusion)

1987 Credit/? (Cypress)

1987 Baby's Got the Power/? (Cypress)

## TOWER OF POWER
### LPs

**7** 1970 East Bay Grease (San Francisco—#106 pop)

Muscular rhythms, gravel-raw vocals and horns that just don't let up are the hallmarks of an album that doesn't know the meaning of either finesse or restraint. Even though it sometimes lurches into sloppiness, it's explosive from start to finish.

**7** 1972 Bump City (WB—#16 R&B/#85 pop)

A considerably more commercial effort than its predecessor—only one of the ten tracks broke the five minute barrier, compared with all six on *East Bay Grease*. The brevity doesn't always work in its favor, and the ballads are slick but cloying. Still there are few finer statements of intent than the opening "You Got To Funkifize."

**6** 1973 Tower of Power (WB—#11 R&B/#15 pop)

**8** 1974 Back to Oakland (WB—#13 R&B/#26 pop)

Chester Thompson's "Squib Cakes" is TOP at their most majestically primal. The band lock into place in the open-

ing moments, solos fly from every direction, and nobody watches the clock. The rest of the album pales by comparison, but the virtuoso "Oakland Stroke" and "I Got the Chop" ensure that the landscape continues expanding.

**5** 1974 Urban Renewal (WB—#19 R&B/#22 pop)

The hard-nosed funk takes a total backseat, as TOP echo their early hit singles with a disco-ey ballad style across the bulk of the album. Elsewhere, "Maybe It'll Rub Off," a JBs-esque chant, is shattered by an out-of-place organ break, while a tendency toward autopilot scars other would-be highlights ("You're the Most," "Only So Much Oil in the Ground").

**5** 1975 In the Slot (WB—#29 R&B/#67 pop)

**9** 1976 Live and in Living Color (WB—#29 R&B/#99 pop)

Packs every last ounce of the band's energies into the grooves, including a 23-minute jam through "Knock Yourself Out," from *East Bay Grease*, "Sparkling in the Sand," two cuts from *Bump City* and, courageously, just one track from the band's most successful era, "What Is Hip," from *Tower of Power*.

**5** 1976 Ain't Nothin' Stoppin Us Now (Columbia—#25 R&B/#42 pop)

**5** 1978 We Came To Play! (Columbia—#33 R&B/#89 pop)

**5** 1979 Back on the Streets (Columbia—#28 R&B/#106 pop)

After two albums of desultory soul balladeering, a tentative dip into disco waters . . . but no sign of an improvement.

**8** 1981 Direct (Sheffield Labs)

A snarling dynamo, five years of underachievement and commercial pressure shrugged off in an instant, as TOP blast back to their peak . . . almost as though much of the last decade never happened.

**3** 1987 Power (Cypress)

Aka the Scandinavian *TOP*, shorn of two tracks, but not that it matters—weak songs fanned into half-life by a band that really doesn't seem to care that much.

**4** 1991 Monster on a Leash (Epic)

**3** 1993 TOP (Epic—#92 R&B)

**5** 1995 Souled Out (Epic)

Recovering from their recent facelessness, a boisterous, buoyant collection suffers only from a shortage of genuinely memorable songs.

**4** 1997 Rhythm and Business (Epic)

**6** 1999 Soul Vaccination: Tower of Power Live (Epic)

## SELECTED COMPILATIONS AND ARCHIVE RELEASES

**5** 1999 Dinosaur Tracks (Rhino Handmade)

Limited edition album reprieves the album's worth of material canned in 1982, and maybe reminds us that not every "lost" album needs to be found. "Simple as That" deftly destroys Huey Lewis' version, but it's a peak the rest of the album seldom revisits.

### 8 1999 What Is Hip? (Rhino)

Tremendous two-CD collection spanning the band's heyday, mercifully eschewing the album weeds in favor of the hits and the heavyweights only.

### SELECTED SAMPLES

Drop It in the Slot — Beastie Boys: Egg Man (1989)
Ebony Jam — De La Soul: A Rollerskating Jam Named Saturdays (1991)
Sparkling in the Sand — Diamond D: Sally Got a One Track Mind (1992)
Squib Cakes — MC900 Ft Jesus: Killer Inside Me (1991)

## UNDISPUTED TRUTH

**FORMED:** *1970, Detroit, MI*
**ORIGINAL LINE-UP:** *Joe Harris (vcls), Billie Calvin (vcls), Brenda Evans (vcls)*

Billie Calvin and Brenda Evans were originally members of the Delicates, an act discovered by singer Bobby Taylor (he also alerted Motown to the Jackson Five) in 1969. The Delicates themselves did little, although Calvin and Evans were ranked among the label's frontline backing vocalists, appearing on releases by Diana Ross, the Four Tops and Edwin Starr among others.

The Delicates split in 1970, at which point Motown staff producer Norman Whitfield introduced a third vocalist, former Ohio Untouchables member Joe Harris, and began grooming the trio for stardom as the Undisputed Truth.

Clad in white facepaint, blonde afros and tight silver spacesuits, the spectacularly theatrical Undisputed Truth led Motown into the new age of supercharged funk, a la Earth Wind & Fire and George Clinton's P-Funk axis. For his own part, Whitfield—writing the liners to the band's sophomore album—described them as "a perfect cross between Sly and the Fifth Dimension" and created a debut album that drew similar boundaries without ever stepping outside of the established Motown format.

The group's first single was a cover of the Temptations' "Save My Love for a Rainy Day," while their debut album included remakes of the same outfit's "Ball of Confusion" and Marvin Gaye's "I Heard It Through the Grapevine," all Whitfield co-compositions. But Whitfield also gifted them with "Smiling Faces Sometimes," a richly paranoid political observation that took the Undisputed Truth to #3 on the pop chart in June 1971. (A simultaneous Temptations version appeared only on their *Sky's the Limit* LP).

The revolutionary political stance that the Undisputed Truth intended to represent was furthered across a dramatic second album, *Face to Face With*. . . . But the Motown hierarchy was strangely unimpressed, affording the band only minimal promotion. Even worse, the group's third album, *Law of the Land*, passed by all but unnoticed, only for its best track, summer 1972's "Papa Was a Rolling Stone," to then be handed to the Temptations, for a pop chart-topper just weeks after the Undisputed Truth's version peaked 62 places lower.

Calvin and Evans departed the group after this; they were replaced by Tyrone "Lil Ty" Berkeley, Tyrone Douglas, cosmic witch doctor Calvin "Dhaak" Stevens and Virginia McDonald and, with another Whitfield discovery, Total Concept Unlimited, installed as their backing band, the Undisputed Truth's next albums, *Down to Earth*, *Cosmic Truth* and *Higher than High*, continued their adventurous course and, in chart terms, their downward spiral.

Whitfield's departure from Motown brought about at least a partial revival in the Undisputed Truth's fortunes, all the more so after Douglas and McDonald quit in 1976, to be replaced by Taka Boom, sister of Rufus vocalist Chaka Khan. Another contender for the vacant microphone was Gwen Dickey, who Whitfield promptly drafted into Total Concept Unlimited, as those musicians launched a parallel career as Rose Royce.

Boom debuted with the Undisputed Truth on 1976's *Method to the Madness* album, a discofied lurch away from the weightier issues of past recordings. "You + Me = Love" went Top 50 in both the US and the UK (their only British success) and remained a dancefloor staple for much of the next year; "Let's Go Down to the Disco" followed, and the album became the Undisputed Truth's first R&B Top 20 entry since their debut.

Unfortunately, the success could not obscure internal tensions within the band as Boom, in particular, bridled against Whitfield's control over every aspect of the Undisputed Truth's creativity. He selected the songs, the arrangements, the musicians. Within a year, Boom had departed for the Glass Family. (She later reunited with Whitfield and Harrison for '80's Dream Machine project.) For the Truth themselves, there would be one final minor single, "Show Time," in spring 1979, and the utterly unsuccessful *Smokin'* album. The band broke up before year's end.

### UNDISPUTED TRUTH COMPLETE DISCOGRAPHY
### SINGLES/CHART LOG

1971 Save My Love for a Rainy Day/Since I've Lost You (Gordy—#43 R&B)
1971 Smiling Faces Sometimes/You Got the Love I Need (Gordy—#2 R&B/#3 pop)
1971 You Make Your Own Heaven and Hell/Ball of Confusion (Gordy—#24 R&B/#72 pop)

1972 What It Is/California Soul (Gordy—#35 R&B/#71 pop)

1972 Papa Was a Rolling Stone/Friendship Train (Gordy—#24 R&B/#63 pop)

1972 Girl You're Alright/With a Little Help (Gordy—#43 R&B/#63 pop)

1973 Mama I Got a Brand New Thing/Gonna Keep On Tryin' (Gordy—#46 R&B/#109 pop)

1973 Law of the Land/Just My Imagination (Gordy—#40 R&B)

1974 Help Yourself/What's Going On (Gordy—#19 R&B/#63 pop)

1974 I'm a Fool for You/The Girl's Alright with Me (Gordy—#39 R&B)

1974 Big John Is My Name/L'il Red Riding Hood (Gordy)

1975 Earthquake Shake/Spaced Out (Gordy)

1975 UFOs/Got To Get My Hands on Some Lovin' (Gordy—#62 R&B)

1975 Higher than High/Spaced Out (Gordy—#77 R&B)

1975 Boogie Bump Boogie/I Saw Her When You Met Her (Gordy)

1976 You + Me = Love/(instrumental) (Whitfield—#37 R&B/#48 pop)

1976 Let's Go Down to the Disco/Loose (Whitfield—#68 R&B)

1977 Hole in the Wall/Sunshine (Whitfield)

1979 Show Time (part one)/(part two) (Whitfield—#55 R&B)

1979 I Can't Get Enough of Your Love/Misunderstood (Whitfield)

## LPs

**8 1971 The Undisputed Truth (Gordy—#7 R&B/#43 pop)**

Earthy harmonies and funk mutant arrangements are the logical successors to Whitfield's last Temptations albums, understated funk grooves lapping against the psychedelic rock shore, and restating the political intentions of great swathes of the producer's own past.

**10 1972 Face To Face With (Gordy—#16 R&B/#114 pop)**

The Temptations' "You Make Your Own Heaven and Hell Right Here on Earth" and a freakish nine-plus minute revision of Marvin Gaye's "What's Going On" maintain the first album's subversive punch, while a band drawn from the best musicians Motown had to offer simply cooks deep in the mix.

**8 1973 Law of the Land (Gordy—#52 R&B/#191 pop)**

Superb versions of "Just My Imagination" and "Killing Me Softly" see the band's focus shifting from politics to relationships, but with no loss of punch. Anybody familiar only with the Temptations' version of "Papa Was a Rolling Stone" is in for a major shock.

**7 1974 Down To Earth (Gordy—#35 R&B/#208 pop)**

**5 1975 Cosmic Truth (Gordy—#42 R&B/#186 pop)**

In the '60s, Motown made much capital from having one band pay tribute to the hits of another. An Undisputed-Truth-sing-the-Temptations album might not have had the same commercial punch, but the raw material's there. "(I Know I'm) Losing You" makes a triumphant appearance here, although elsewhere, the Truth's magic is wearing thin . . . rather like the revamped lineup's vocals.

**4 1975 Higher than High (Gordy—#52 R&B/#173 pop)**

**3 1977 Method to the Madness (Whitfield—#16 R&B/#66 pop)**

After the last album's "Boogie Bump Boogie" nadir, "Let's Go Down to the Disco" cuts the final ties with the band's original integrities. Bland dancefodder, although "You + Me = Love" remains a guaranteed floor filler.

**3 1979 Smokin' (Whitfield)**

### SELECTED SAMPLES

Smiling Faces Sometimes — George Clinton: Paint the White House Black (1993)

Smiling Faces Sometimes — Willie D: F . . . the KKK (1989)

Spaced Out — Redman: Journey Throo Da Darkside (1994)

# WAR

**FORMED:** *1969, Compton/Long Beach, CA*

**ORIGINAL LINE-UP:** *Howard Scott (b. 3/15/46, San Pedro, CA—gtr), Morris "BB" Dickerson (b. 8/3/49, Torrence, CA—bass), Lonnie Jordan (b. 11/21/48, San Diego, CA—kybds), Charles Miller (b. 6/2/39, Olathe, KS; d. 1980—sax), Harold Brown (b. 3/17/46, Long Beach, CA—perc)*

The core of what became War was one of the constants of the California soul club circuit during the '60s, operating and recording under a variety of names. Brown and Scott set the ball rolling in 1962, when they formed the Creators. By 1965, with Jordan, Dickerson and Miller on board, they were recording for the Dore label and scrabbled at least an iconographical hit when their "Burn Baby Burn" single was adopted by the Watts ghetto rioters. (It was also the theme song of Los Angeles DJ Magnificent Montague.)

Emboldened, the Creators began to broaden their sound to incorporate jazz, salsa and even ska, with earthier elements coming into play after the legendary Bobby Womack joined the group in 1966, as a temporary replacement for the recently drafted Scott. Dickerson also departed, to be replaced by Pete Rosen.

As the Romeos, this lineup linked with Magnificent Montague's Mark II label and recorded a handful of singles. Scott's return in 1969, however, set the band off on another track, slipping into a funk-flavored instrumental groove under a new name, the Nightshift.

Now lining up as Jordan, Brown, Miller, Rosen, Scott and percussionist Thomas "Papa Dee" Allen (b. 7/18/31, Wilmington DE; d. 8/30/88—percussion), the Nightriders were hired to back football star/aspiring vocalist Deacon Jones at North Hollywood's Rag Doll Club.

It was an inauspicious situation, but the enterprising Rosen nevertheless invited everybody he could to see them play. Among the people who came were, English R&B vo-

War: Lonnie Jordan, Harold Brown, Howard Scott, Papa Allen, BB Dickerson, Lee Oskar, Charles Miller (l-r).

calist Eric Burdon, Danish harmonica player "Lee" Oskar (b. Oskar Hansen, 3/24/48, Copenhagen, Denmark) and '60s pop producer Jerry Goldstein. It probably wasn't the response that Deacon Jones was expecting, but all three were blown away by his backing musicians.

Within days, Oskar had been recruited into the Nightriders. Goldstein was installed as their manager and producer; and Burdon picked up the entire package to work as his own backing band, renaming them War and immediately going on the road. They spent the next year touring, an exciting phase tragically broken by the drug overdose death of Rosen. Dickerson returned to fill the gap and, in early 1970, the combination began work on their debut album, *Eric Burdon Declares War*.

The team scored an immediate smash with the classic "Spill the Wine," a cut based around a true-life incident, after Jordan indeed spilled a bottle of wine over one of the studio's consoles. The group continued touring and, late in the year, a second single, "They Can't Take Away Our Music" (featuring guest vocalist Sharon Scott) previewed the

band's second album, the punningly named *Black Man's Burdon*.

War and Burdon parted in early 1971, following a poorly received European tour and, by April, War alone were bubbling under the pop 100 with "Lonely Feelin'," their own debut single. An eponymous album that same month merely nudged the Top 200, but when August 1971, brought the hit "All Day Music," their immediate future was assured.

Constant gigging saw War effortlessly establish themselves. Their second album, also titled *All Day Music*, made the Top 20; but it was with 1972's *The World Is a Ghetto* that the band's hard-hitting funk rock sound truly impacted. The album topped the chart; three successive singles made the pop Top Ten (the Grammy nominated "The Cisco Kid" went gold); and, by 1973, War were as popular in stoner rock circles as with the R&B audience. Eric Burdon's original vision was fulfilled.

Tightening up a cut first recorded (as a live performance) on *All Day Music*, "Me and Baby Brother," from 1973's

*Deliver the Word*, epitomized War's sound, a compulsive funk-rock hybrid growling along on an hypnotic wave of bass. *War Live*, a stop-gap set recorded in November 1972, and designed to maintain the group's profile amid their constant gigging, then established itself among the crucial live albums of the era.

War were one of the undisputed stars of the First Annual Benefit for the Congressional Black Caucus in September 1974, appearing alongside Curtis Mayfield, Kool & the Gang, Jimmy Witherspoon and Gladys Knight, and contributing a wild 16-minute version of "Gypsy Man" to the ensuing souvenir album. However, an ambitious plan to launch what they described as a *Sesame Street*-type television program aimed at aspiring young musicians slowed War's momentum somewhat.

In the event, 1975's *Why Can't We Be Friends* proved well worth the wait, featuring as it did War's signature song, the Chicano cruising jam "Low Rider," together with the effervescent title track. Its success also prompted a reissue of the two albums recorded with Eric Burdon, and launched Oskar on a parallel solo career with a successful album, *Lee Oskar*, and the memorable "BLT" single.

However, War saw their commercial stock plummet, with the onset of what was, to them, the anathemic disco boom, which coincided with the band's own drive back toward an exotic funk-jazz brew. A *Greatest Hits* package, featuring one new song, "Summer," proved their final major album smash. "LA Sunshine," from 1977's *Platinum Jazz* album (released on the once-prestigious Blue Note jazz label), and the compulsively delirious title cut from the following year's *Galaxy* both did well. But they appealed to an audience that had little sense of who War were—and even less interest. Indeed, though "Galaxy" earned the band only their second international smash (following "Low Rider"), the album climbed no higher than #15 in the US.

What hindsight insists was an ill-advised switch to the MCA label, and the arrival, in 1978, of a full time female vocalist, Alice Tweed Smyth, lessened the group's fire even further, while the departure of bassist Dickerson, to be replaced by ex-Ballin' Jack member Luther Rabb, saw one of the key components of the original War sound disappear. Miller, too, quit, but 1979's recruitment of Pat Rizzo (horns) and another ex-Ballin' Jack member, percussionist Ron Hammond, added little more than weight of numbers to the ensemble.

Jordan released a solo album, *Different Moods of Me* in 1978; the following year saw Oskar relaunch his own solo career, although the ensuing *Before the Rain* fared little better than War's own recent releases. But worse was to come. First, an ambitious sequence of separate but related albums, *The Music Band*, *The Music Band 2* and *The Music Band—Live*, was critically hammered and commercially disastrous. Then, with War still reeling, former saxophonist Miller was murdered during a robbery.

A shocked War came to an abrupt halt. It was 1982 before the band reappeared, signed now to RCA and returning, somewhat, to basics—Smyth had departed and the *Outlaw* album saw the team looking back toward their musical heyday with increasing passion. The commercial failure of *Life (Is So Strange)* in 1983, however, brought an end to their relationship with both their new label and with long-time producer Jerry Goldstein.

Brown quit in 1984, and the group drifted through the remainder of the '80s, watching from the sidelines as their past again rose before them in the hands of the new rap movement. War's sinewy old rhythms were tailor-made, it seemed, for the new music, while their reputation as precursors of so much of the '80s underground scene was furthered when renowned dance producer Arthur Baker took a remix of "Low Rider" into the R&B Top 60—War's first such success since 1983.

Again, however, tragedy awaited. On August 30, 1988, Papa Dee suffered a brain hemorrhage and died while on stage with the band. Once more, War retreated from view and it was 1992 before they resurfaced with a lineup of founders Jordan, Scott and the newly returned Brown, percussionist Hammond, and newcomers saxophonists Charley Green and Kerry Campbell, percussionist Sal Rodriguez, harmonica player Tetsuya Nakamura and programmer Rae Valentine.

In 1992, War made their own much anticipated contribution to the rap scene with the release of *Rap Declares War*, an album that matched their instrumental talents with an all-star hip-hop cast. Two years later, in 1994, War produced a new album; though an unnamed set, its peace symbol logo became widely regarded as its title. War's own Avenue label also arranged the reissue of much of War's back catalog through Rhino, reclaiming a little more of both their heritage and their legend.

### WAR COMPLETE DISCOGRAPHY
### SINGLES/CHART LOG
### WITH ERIC BURDON
1970 Spill the Wine/Magic Mountain (MGM—#3 pop)
1970 They Can't Take Away Our Music/Home Cookin' (MGM—#50 pop)
1977 Magic Mountain/Home Dream (ABC)

## WAR

1971 Lonely Feeling/Sun Oh Sun (UA—#38 R&B/#107 pop)
1971 All Day Music/Get Down (UA—#18 R&B/#35 pop)
1972 Slippin' into Darkness/Happy Head (UA—#12 R&B/#16 pop)
1972 The World Is a Ghetto/Four Cornered Room (UA—#3 R&B/#7 pop)
1973 The Cisco Kid/Beetles in the Bog (UA—#5 R&B/#2 pop)
1973 Gypsy Man/Deliver the Word (UA—#6 R&B/#8 pop)
1973 Me And Baby Brother/In Your Eyes (UA—#18 R&B/#15 pop)
1974 Ballero/Slippin' into Darkness (UA—#17 R&B/#33 pop)
1975 Why Can't We Be Friends/In Mazatlin (UA—#9 R&B/#6 pop)
1975 Low Rider/So (UA—#1 R&B/#7 pop)
1976 Summer/All Day Music (UA—#4 R&B/#7 pop)
1977 LA Sunshine/Slowly We Walk Together (Blue Note—#2 R&B/#45 pop)
1977 Galaxy (part one)/(part two) (MCA—#5 R&B/#39 pop)
1978 Hey Senorita/Sweet Fighting Lady (MCA—#70 R&B)
1978 Youngblood/(instrumental) (UA—#21 R&B)
1978 Sing a Happy Song/This Funky Music Makes You Feel Good (UA—#87 R&B)
1979 I'm the One Who Understands/Corns And Cal-louses (MCA)
1979 Good Good Feelin'/Baby Face (MCA—#12 R&B/#101 pop)
1979 Don't Take It Away/Music Band 2 (MCA—#32 R&B)
1980 I'll Be Around /The Music Band 2 (MCA—#96 R&B)
1981 Cinco De Mayo/Don't Let No-One Get You Down (LAX—#90 R&B)
1982 You Got the Power/Cinco De Mayo (RCA—#18 R&B/#66 pop)
1982 Outlaw/I'm About Somebody (RCA—#13 R&B/#94 pop)
1983 Life (Is So Strange)/WWIII (RCA—#50 R&B)
1985 Groovin'/(instrumental) (Coco Plum—#79 R&B)
1987 Livin' in the Red (instrumental) (Priority—#59 R&B)
1987 Low Rider - Arthur Baker remix (remixes) (Priority—#59 US)
1994 Peace Sign/(remixes) (Avenue—#64 R&B)

### LPs

### WITH ERIC BURDON

**8** **1970 Eric Burdon Declares War (MGM—#47 R&B/#18 pop)**

Patchy, but across eleven tracks (divided into four suites), there's no doubting the purity of either Burdon's ambition or War's ability. Fifteen minutes alternately dedicated to and built around John D. Loudermilk's "Tobacco Road" encapsulate the essence of the union, a driving gutbucket vamp with Lee Oskar's harmonica to the fore, and the bass-drums interplay maintaining a tempo that pursues Burdon even through the seemingly ad-libbed "I Have a Dream" center section.

**7** **1970 The Black Man's Burdon (MGM—#39 R&B/#82 pop)**

### WAR

**9** **1971 War (UA—#42 R&B/#190 pop)**

Culled from a succession of white-hot studio jams, War's loosest album compensates for its lack of focus with some

of the most substantial sonics of the age. This record is heavy!

**10** **1971 All Day Music (UA—#6 R&B/#16 pop)**

The dynamic "Nappy Head" plays on War's Latin influences, while a non-stop party atmosphere ensures that even a couple of dull grooves sound exciting. The prototype "Baby Brother" is the highlight, a bluesy jam that captures the full frenzy of the live War experience.

**7** **1973 The World Is a Ghetto (UA—#1 R&B/#1 pop)**

"Cisco Kid" is, quite simply, scintillating; elsewhere, "Where Was You At" blends bluesy harmonica with James Brown passion, and "City Country City" utterly invokes a lost JBs jam. But then you flip the vinyl over and side two—dominated by the ten-minute title ballad—really doesn't cut it.

**7** **1973 Deliver the Word (UA—#1 R&B/#6 pop)**

Strong set brings the band's softer side into focus once again, then clashes it with a prog jazz element that pays memorable dividends—most of them within the mammoth mantric "Gypsy Man." The long-awaited studio take of "Baby Brother" returns to cutting, concise funk stomp form and "Southern Part of Texas" bleeds uncontrollably out of "Cisco Kid" territory.

**8** **1974 War Live! (UA—#1 R&B/#13 pop)**

There's no place to hide. "Sun Oh Sun" may make an unconvincing opener, but it hits its stride quickly and *War Live!* becomes irresistible. Don't miss the sidelong, rap-heavy "Get Down," a hyper-funky drum solo during "Darkness" and a truly wicked "Ballero."

**8** **1975 Why Can't We Be Friends (UA—#1 R&B/#8 pop)**

Cut from the same cloth as *Deliver the World*, so the stomping funk is the exception, not the rule—particularly once Oskar's utterly apposite "Latin Lament" medley gets going. But "Heartbeat" and "Low Rider" give the album invincible character, and the skank-worthy title track is just knock-down, balls-out grin-a-minute fun.

**6** **1977 Platinum Jazz (Blue Note—#6 R&B/#23 pop)**

Double album opens with the amazing "War Is Coming," a funky Latin shuffle that encapsulates everything that was great about the band. Redundant revisions of sundry older cuts lessen the impact, however, while the full 12-minute "LA Sunshine" gets awfully dull, awfully fast.

**5** **1978 Galaxy (MCA—#6 R&B/#15 pop)**

A rhythm slipped from Chakachas' "Jungle Fever," a lyric drawn from *Star Wars* culture, a compulsive hook, a powerhouse beat and an FX-wired weird bit in the middle . . . how could the title track go wrong? Well, grafting it to an album devoid of anything else even half as interesting might be the place to start.

**4 1978 Youngblood (MCA—#40 R&B/#69 pop)**
Generally bland soundtrack.

**3 1979 The Music Band (MCA—#11 R&B/#41 pop)**
**3 1979 The Music Band 2 (MCA—#34 R&B/#111 pop)**
**2 1980 The Music Band Live (MCA)**
Spread across three albums, sad disco jazz with a hint of old-time rhythm finally scrapes the bottom with an elevator-lite instrumental version of "The World Is a Ghetto" (vol 2).

**4 1982 Outlaw (RCA—#15 R&B/#48 pop)**
**7 1983 Life (Is So Strange) (RCA—#36 R&B/#164 pop)**
A remarkable album, all the more so since it was so utterly unexpected. Opens with a wild, scratchy chant-jam, digs into cool, deep reggae, throws some disco wah-wah over a sleepy seductive wash, and then wipes out New York City with the extraordinary "World War Three" concept medley. A veritable colossus.

**4 1984 Where There's Smoke (Coco Plum)**
. . . there's ashes.

**6 1992 Rap Declares War (Avenue)**
An acquired taste, but a rewarding one.

**6 1994 Untitled (Peace Sign) (Avenue—#52 R&B/#200 pop)**

### SELECTED COMPILATIONS AND ARCHIVE RELEASES
**6 1976 Greatest Hits (UA—#12 R&B/#6 pop)**
**5 1976 Love Is All Around (ABC—#140 pop)**
**7 1987 The Best of War & More (Rhino—#156)**
Concise (13 track) round-up of the expected high points, including the Arthur Baker "Low Rider" remix.

**7 1999 Grooves and Messages (BMG)**
Two-CD set echoes much of the above, but totally remastered and bolstered with a fabulous "2000" version of "Galaxy" and a bass sound to die for. The hits hog disc one, a string of self-conscious name remixes take up disc two and, though less compulsive, aren't completely devoid of merit.

### SELECTED SAMPLES
Cisco Kid — 7A3: Drums of Steel (1988)
Cisco Kid — Janet Jackson: You (1997)
Deliver the Word — Gang Starr featuring Scarface: Betrayal (1939)
Four Corner Room — Scarface: Your Ass Got Took (1991)
Galaxy — Boogie Down Productions: Nervous (1988)
Galaxy — Mellow Man Ace: Mentirosa (1990)
Galaxy — De La Soul: IC Y'all (2000)
Heatbeat — Nice & Smooth: Funky for You (1989)
Low Rider — Beastie Boys: Slow Ride (1986)
Low Rider — OffSpring: Pretty Fly (For a White Guy) (remix) (1998)

Low Rider — Stereo MC: Ain't Got Nobody (1990)
Magic Mountain — De La Soul: Potholes in My Lawn (1989)
Magic Mountain — Portishead: Wandering Star (1995)
Sing a Happy Song — Brand Nubian: Feels So Good (1991)
Sing a Happy Song — Dream Warriors: U Never Know a Good Thing Till U Lose It (1991)
Slippin' Into Darkness — Eazy E: Sippin On a 40 (1996)
Slippin' Into Darkness — Mantronix: Join Me Please (Home Boys Make Some Noise) (1988)
Slippin' Into Darkness — Poor Righteous Teachers: Rock This Funky Joint (1990)
Slippin' Into Darkness — Poor Righteous Teachers: Self Styled Wisdom (1991)

## LEE OSKAR
### CHART LOG
1976 BLT (UA—#23 R&B/#59 pop)
1976 Sunshine Keri (UA—#85 R&B)
1978 Before the Rain (Elektra—#91 R&B)
1979 Feelin' Happy (Elektra—#89)

### LPs
**6 1976 Lee Oskar (UA—#29 R&B)**
Pleasant late-night stuff, softly jazzy, lightly funked—think Al Jarreau with a mouth organ.

**4 1979 Before the Rain (Elektra—#86 R&B)**
**4 1981 My Road Our Road (Elektra—#162 R&B)**
Virtuoso harmonica playing, of course, backed with portentous orchestrations and some very early-'80s style electric keyboards.

### SELECTED COMPILATIONS AND ARCHIVE RELEASES
**5 1995 The Best of Lee Oskar (Elektra)**
Probably a lot more Lee than you need.

## FRED WESLEY
**BORN:** 7/4/43, Mobile, AL

The son of band leader and high school teacher Fred Wesley, Sr., Wesley was three when his grandmother encouraged him to learn his first musical instrument, the piano. Inspired by one of his father's students, trombonist Harry Freeman, he turned to horns several years later, beginning with first trumpet, before picking up trombone at junior high. Soon he was playing in music teacher EB Coleman's combo.

Throughout his teens, Wesley's principle interest was jazz and be bop; he frequently joined his father onstage, playing drums as well as trombone. The education served him well. In 1961, when Wesley was 17, he was recruited to Ike and Tina Turner's band, at that point one of the tightest R&B outfits in the country.

His stay was curtailed first by a bout of pneumonia, then by the draft. Stationed at Redstone Arsenal in Huntsville, AL, Wesley joined the 55th Army Band as a featured soloist and, by the time his service was completed, in 1967, he had graduated from the Armed Forces School of Music.

Newly married and a father, Wesley was on the verge of quitting music and becoming the first Black milkman in Mobile when he received a call from Waymon Reed, an old friend who was now playing reeds with James Brown. The group was looking for a trombone player and Reed had recommended Wesley for the gig.

Wesley made his recorded debut with Brown on 1968's seminal "Say It Loud, I'm Black and I'm Proud" and, over the next 18 months, he became an integral part of the group, a vital foil for the mighty Maceo Parker. Indeed, as they steered Brown's music toward ever funkier heights across the remainder of the decade; the two also ignited a partnership that has persisted on and off ever since.

Wesley's time with Brown ended in March 1970, when the entire group quit in a row over money. Brown paid the musicians a salary, rather than a share of the actual gig and recording receipts, at a time when his own earnings seemed stratospheric. Brown promptly replaced the defectors with a new lineup, the Phelps and Bootsy Collins-led Pacesetters, renaming them the JBs and continuing on much as before.

Slowly, however, members of Brown's original outfit began trickling back; Wesley himself rejoined around Christmas 1970, cutting the epochal "Super Bad" in January 1971. That session proved to be the Pacesetters' last with Brown and over the next few weeks, Brown set about rebuilding the group around Wesley and the omnipresent Bobby Byrd. Drummer John Starks, guitarist Hearlon Martin and saxophonist St Clair Pinkney were retained from the old JBs. Adding Robert Coleman (gtr), Jimmy Parker (sax), Russell Crimes and Jerome Sanford (trums), Fred Thomas (bs), John Morgan (drms) and Johnny Griffin (kybds), Brown now relaunched the JBs, fronted both onstage and on their own records by Wesley.

Brown's own People label was up and running and, at the end of June 1971, this latest incarnation of JBs cut their first single for the label (the Bootsy-era lineup had already recorded several 45s). "Pass the Peas" became the first of a chain of remarkable JBs instrumental hits over the next three years, released either as the JBs, Fred Wesley & the JBs or, as the group lineup evolved, Fred & the New JBs. The band also cut five albums during that same span, dynamic collections that not only ranked alongside, but sometimes eclipsed, Brown's own output.

Along with Parker, Wesley quit the JBs in 1975, to rejoin Bootsy Collins and company aboard George Clinton's P-Funk mothership. There the pair remained for some five years, a vital component not only in the expanding lunacy of the Parliament and Funkadelic universe, but also fronting a side project of their own, Fred Wesley & the Horny Horns. Between 1977–79, the Horny Horns released two albums, A Blow for Me and Say Blow by Blow Backwards. (A third, The Final Blow, was created from outtakes and remixes in 1994).

In 1980, Wesley cut his first solo album, House Party, for Curtis Mayfield's Curtom label. Unfortunately, both the label and its parent company, RSO, were on their last legs. Although a 12-inch single of the title track became a club hit, the album itself was canned on the eve of release, with only a handful of promotional copies making it out. (It finally received a full release in 1993.)

In 1981, Wesley was contacted again by Waymon Reed. He was now working with the Count Basie Orchestra and, once again, was searching for a trombonist. Wesley leaped at the opportunity, remaining with the Orchestra for the next three years before leaving to concentrate on production and session work. Recording with Whitney Houston, Curtis Mayfield and Dr. John, he also produced the debut album by the SOS Band and Cameo's 1989 hit, "The Skin I'm In." By the end of the decade, however, Wesley was again contemplating a solo career, signing with German producer Stephen Meyer, as part of a package that also included Maceo Parker and Pee Wee Ellis. The three promptly grouped together as the JB Horns, cutting Pee Wee, Fred and Maceo in 1990. Wesley (like Parker) also began work on a solo album, New Friends.

Since that time, Wesley has continued on with both the Horns and his own albums, blending a scintillating jazz funk brew that has won as many new, young, fans as it has thrilled older devotees. He has also maintained contact with past employers. His 1999 album, Full Circle: From Be Bop To Hip Hop, featured contributions from P-Funkers Bootsy Collins and Bernie Worrell, and Brown associates Bobby Byrd and Vicki Anderson among others; the following year, Wesley was alongside James Brown when he played the opening of the Experience Music Project in Seattle.

### FRED WESLEY DISCOGRAPHY
(For releases credited to the JBs (and pseudonyms), Fred/ Fred Wesley & the [New] JBs, Vicki Anderson, James

Brown, Lyn Collins, Maceo Parker, see under individual artists.)

SINGLES/CHART LOG
**FRED WESLEY**
1980 House Party/I Make Music (Curtom—#40 R&B)

**HORNY HORNS**
1977 Up for the Down Stroke/Four Play (Atlantic)
1977 Up for the Down Stroke/When in Doubt: Vamp (Atlantic—#93 R&B)

**FRED WESLEY**
LPs
**8** 1980 House Party (Curtom)

A thumping, club friendly groove, Wesley's pumped-up horns feeding the dancefloor with some genuinely memorable melodies.

**7** 1990 New Friends (Antilles)

Strong jazz textures dominate a tasteful album, although excursions into calypso, soul and funk ("D-Cup And Up") rise up above the brew. Maceo Parker and pianist Geri Allen co-star.

**6** 1991 Comme Ci Comme Ca (Antilles)

Gentle hard bop seasoned by Theresa Carroll's captivating vocals. Closes with the unutterably lovely "Prayer," possibly Wesley's finest hour.

**6** 1992 Swing and Be Funky (Minor Music)
**8** 1994 Amalgamation (Minor Music)

A dramatic album, funky spontaneity with more twists than a mountain road, winding up with a delicious rendering of George Michael's "Careless Whisper."

**5** 1995 To Someone (Good Hope)
**6** 1995 La Bossa—Funk Meets Jazz (P-Vine)
**8** 1999 Full Circle: From Be Bop to Hip-Hop (Cleopatra)

The supporting cast of unrepentant old funkers doesn't divert Wesley from his jazzier ambitions, although "Rehab" ("Wesley's signature thang," according to the liners) and the Gary Cooper-led "Mo'Money" are gems. A Vicki Anderson vocal on "Beautiful Temptress" and the rap "Hey You in the Neighborhood" add to the variety.

**HORNY HORNS**
**6** 1977 A Blow for Me, a Toot for You (Atco)

Essentially reworking the P-Funk archive, blasting into view with an earthmoving "Up for the Down Stroke," a honking, stomping good time.

**6** 1979 Say Blow by Blow Backwards (Atlantic)

SELECTED COMPILATIONS AND ARCHIVE RELEASES
**5** 1994 The Final Blow (AEM)

A handful of cuts deserved a better fate than the cutting room floor, but for the most part, outtakes are outtakes.

**JB HORNS**
LPs
**6** 1990 Pee Wee, Fred & Maceo: The JB Horns (Gramavision)

If you go in expecting more of the old JBs magic, you'll come out disappointed. Brasher than either Wesley or Parker's solo work, all three members go for the jazz jugular.

**7** 1993 Funky Good Time/Live (Gramavision)
**6** 1994 I Like It like That (SoulCiety)
**6** 1999 JBs Reunion (P-Vine—Japan)

SELECTED COMPILATIONS AND ARCHIVE RELEASES
**6** 1994 The Legendary Meters Featuring the JB Horns: Live at the Moonwalker, Vols. 1 & 2 (Lakeside Music—Swtz)

SELECTED SAMPLES
A Blow for Me . . . — Def Jef: Black to the Future (1990)
A Blow for Me . . . — Raw Fusion: Hoochified Funk (1994)
A Blow for Me . . . — Sade: Feel No Pain (1993)
Between Two Sheets — DJ Quik: Deep (1991)
Four Play — Aaron Hall: Curiosity (1995)
Four Play — Beastie Boys: Get It Together (1994)
Four Play — Black Sheep: Butt in the Meantime (1990)
Four Play — DJ Quik: Deep (1991)
Four Play — Digital Underground: Packet Man (1989)
Four Play — Digital Underground: Rhymin' on the Funk (1989)
Four Play — Gang Starr: Step in the Arena (1991)
Four Play — Nice & Smooth: Sky's the Limit (1994)
Four Play — Penthouse Players Clique: P.L.F. (1992)
Peace Fugue — Raw Fusion: Freaky Note (1994)

# WESTBOUND RECORDS

Armen Boladian was a distributor for Detroit label Revilot when he announced he was launching his own label, Westbound, in 1969. Early signings the Detroit Emeralds, Funkadelic and the fast-rising Ohio Players established the nature of the company; over the next five years, Westbound was responsible for one of the strongest funk and R&B catalogs in America, one that would remain years ahead of any other label's own attempts to move into a similar field.

In 1972, Boladian expanded his horizons even further with the funk jazz label Eastbound, primarily drawing artists from the wealth of sidemen passing through the studio in the early 1970s. Stuff's Gordon Edwards and Cornell Dupree both recorded for Eastbound, alongside Bill Mason and Gary Chandler respectively. Eastbound folded in 1975 following the demise of distributors Chess—several acts, including the Fantastic Four, were transplanted to Westbound, as that label found new distribution through 20th Century. Unfortunately, the loss of many of the label's bigger acts, including the Ohio Players and the P-Funk axis, saw Westbound's significance decline considerably.

By the late 1970s, only the Detroit Emeralds remained consistent hitmakers, although disco funkers CJ & Co provided some light relief during 1978. Finally, following a period under Atlantic Records' aegis, Westbound folded in 1979.

### LPs

2000 Funkadelic: Funkadelic
2001 Funkadelic: Free Your Mind . . . and Your Ass Will Follow
2002 Catfish Hodge: For Free
2003 Teegarden & Van Winkle: Teegarden & Van Winkle
2004 Assemblage: The Assemblage Album
2005 Frut: Keep On Truckin'
2006 Detroit Emeralds: Do Me Right
2007 Funkadelic: Maggot Brain
2008 Frut: Spoiled Rotten
2009 Jonathon Round: Jonathon Round
2010 Teegarden & Van Winkle with Bruce: On Our Way
2011 Counts: What's Up Front That Counts
2012 Denise Lasalle: Trapped by a Thing Called Love
2013 Detroit Emeralds: You Want It, You Got It
2014 unissued
2015 Ohio Players: Pain
2016 Denise Lasalle: On the Loose
2017 Ohio Players: Pleasure
2018 Detroit Emeralds: I'm in Love with You
2019 Skip Van Winkle Knape & David Teegarden: Experimental Groundwork
2020 Funkadelic: America Eats Its Young
2021 Ohio Players: Ecstasy
2022 Funkadelic: Cosmic Slop
1000 Byron MacGregor: The Americans
1001 Funkadelic: Standing on the Verge of Getting It On
1002 unissued
1003 Ohio Players: Climax
1004 Funkadelic: Greatest Hits
1005 Ohio Players: Greatest Hits
200 Junie: What We Do
201 Fantastic Four: Alvin Stone (The Birth and Death of a Gangster)
202 Catfish Hodge: Soap Operas
203 Etta James: Etta James
204 Melvin Sparks: Melvin Sparks
205 unissued
206 unissued
207 Spanky Wilson: Specialty of the House
208 Funkadelic: Standing on the Verge of Getting It On

209 Denise Lasalle: Here I Am Again
210 unissued
211 Ohio Players: Rattlesnake
212 Dennis Coffey: Finger Lickin' Good
213 Houston Person: Get Out of My Way
214 unissued
215 Funkadelic: Let's Take It To the Stage
216 Funkadelic: Funkadelic
217 Funkadelic: Free Your Mind . . . and Your Ass Will Follow
218 Funkadelic: Maggot Brain
219 Ohio Players: Pain
220 Ohio Players: Pleasure
221 Funkadelic: America Eats Its Young
222 Ohio Players: Ecstasy
223 Funkadelic: Cosmic Slop
224 King Errisson: The Magic Man
225 unissued
226 Fantastic Four: Night People
227 Funkadelic: Tales of Kidd Funkadelic
228 Junie: Suzie Super Groupie
229 Fuzzy Haskins: A Whole Nother Thang
300 Dennis Coffey: Down Home
301 unissued
302 Detroit Emeralds: Feel the Need
303 Funkadelic: The Best of the Early Years
304 Ohio Players: The Best of the Early Years
305 Mike Theodore Orchestra: Cosmic Wind
306 Fantastic Four: Got To Have Your Love
307 King Errisson: L.A. Bound
800 St. James Choir: The Gospel According to the . . .
6100 CJ & Co.: Devil's Gun
6101 Detroit Emeralds: Let's Get Together
6102 Fuzzy Haskins: Radio Active
6103 Caesar Frazer: Another Life
6104 CJ & Co.: Deadeye Dick
6105 Dennis Coffey Band: A Sweet Taste of Sin
6106 Carlis Munro: I Was Made for Love
6107 various artists: Westbound Disco Sizzlers
6108 Fantastic Four: B.Y.O.F. (Bring Your Own Funk)
6109 Mike Theodore Orchestra: High on Mad Mountain
6110 Crowd Pleasers: Crowd Pleasers

## BARRY WHITE

**BORN:** *Barry Eugene Carter, 9/12/44, Galveston, TX*

Layering deep, sensuous and sexually charged lyrics over a growling, sweeping, slow funk base, session veteran White ranked among the unlikeliest "pop" stars of the early-mid-'70s, a behemoth of a man whose critics dubbed him "the walrus of love," but whose audience—one that reached far beyond the sex-starved White housewives of popular legend—regarded him as the pinnacle of passionate masculinity. That his husky vocals and risque subject matter utterly eclipsed the vitality of his music was, under those conditions, unavoidable; it is only in recent years that he has fully regained the admiration that his talents as an arranger and producer deserved.

White was born in Texas, but raised in Los Angeles, where his family relocated when he was six months old. He joined a Baptist choir when he was 8; at 10, he was the church's regular organist and, in 1956, aged 11, White made his recorded debut as pianist on doo-wopper Jesse Belvin's R&B Top Ten 45 "Goodnight My Love (Pleasant Dreams)." White's mother was herself an accomplished pianist, but her attempts to teach him the instrument in conventional style were fruitless. White preferred to learn in his own way and later acknowledged, "one of the greatest gifts she gave me was when she said okay."

Already he had isolated what became his two most consuming (and, eventually, inextricably intertwined) passions, music and love. According to his own autobiography, at 14, he was advising neighborhood teens (and older) about their love lives. But it took a brush with the law to truly launch White on his future path, after he was arrested for stealing tires and sentenced to four months in juvenile hall.

Upon his release, he joined a local vocal group, the Upfronts and, between 1960–62, sang bass on four of that group's singles, released through future Motown artist Henry Lumpkin's Lummtone label. White also performed (and recorded) with a couple of other local acts, the Atlantics and the Majestics; all three band went nowhere and White concentrated instead on carving out a career as a songwriter, arranger and session musician for a number of tiny southern California labels.

In 1962, his studio debut saw him supplying syncopated handclaps to Guggee Renee's "Tossin' Ice Cubes." It sounded easy, but three union musicians had already failed to nail the beat before studio chief Leon Renee noticed White watching the proceedings from a corner of the studio. He was paid $100 for his efforts, but more importantly, word went around that he had a great sense of rhythm. Further sessions quickly followed.

At the Marc label in 1963, White played on Bob (Relf) and Earl (Nelson)'s immortal "Harlem Shuffle." At Mirwood, two years later, he arranged the massive "The Duck" for Jackie Lee—a pseudonym for Earl alone. (White also co-wrote the B-side with Lee, "Ooh Honey Baby"). With White on drums, the pair toured in the new year, including an eight-day engagement at the Harlem Apollo (opening for the Marvellettes and the Exciters).

1965 also saw White record his own first single, "A Man Ain't Nothin'," under the name Lee Barry. It flopped, but White was still moving forward. Shortly after returning from tour, he was offered the post of head of A&R at Bronco-Mustang, a new label formed by former Sam Cooke/Ritchie Valens manager Bob Keane as Los Angeles' answer to Motown.

It was a period of intense activity. For his first Bronco session, White co-wrote and played virtually every instrument on Viola Wills' "Lost Without the Love of My Guy," while he co-produced (with Keane) two singles for another of Keane's most legendary recruits, Bobby Fuller. Fuller returned the favor by describing White as "the most outrageous arranger around . . . a brother who knows how to make Top 40 hits for White kids."

White also wrote and produced veteran Texan Johnny Wyatt's "This Thing Called Love;" but his greatest Bronco success came after he reunited with "Harlem Shuffle" arranger Gene Page to record 18-year-old singer Felice Taylor. Casting her firmly in the sonic mould of the Supremes, the team earned hits in both the US and UK with "It May Be Winter Outside (But in My Heart It's Spring)." (White subsequently re-recorded the song with his own Love Unlimited Orchestra) and "I Feel Love Comin' On."

White's second solo single, "All in the Run of a Day," was the final release within the Bronco-Mustang stable. The label closed down during 1967 and White returned to session work. With Keane and Page, he co-produced Danny Wagner's *The Kindred Soul of Danny Wagner* album; he guested on Sarah James & the Soul Babies' "Takin' Care of Business" single, and wrote and produced "Doin' the Banana Split," a 1969 single released in the name of the TV characters of the same name. That year, too, White released his third single, a cover of Elvis Presley's "In the Ghetto," under the name Gene West.

Following the demise of Bronco, White was offered a staff job at Motown, turning it down in favor of a similar post with the publishers Aaron and Abby Schroeder. His reasoning was simple; at Motown, he would simply be one small fish in a very large pond. At the Schroeders' newly opened Los Angeles office, he would be the pond; and with a wife and four children to fend for, that was an important consideration. Plus, his new post also gave him his own publishing wing, Savette.

Still able to work freelance as well, in 1969 White recorded a brace of demos with vocalist Andrea "Trixie" Roberton for the Sidewalk label (owned by Larry Nunes, Bob Keane's partner at Mustang-Bronco). Robertson in turn introduced him to the Croonettes, a San Pedro vocal group comprising Diane Parson and sisters Glodean and Linda James. Renaming them Love Unlimited, White groomed them for close to a year before he was ready to begin recording; now a partner in Larry Nunes' new Mo'Soul production company, the hiatus was a luxury he considered essential to the trio's launch. (Nunes was subsequently installed as White's manager, a role he kept until his retirement in 1976.)

White had already made a dry run of the girls' extravagantly orchestrated and arranged sound with "Oh Love (Well, We Finally Made It)," by Bob Relf's new outfit, Smoke. Love Unlimited's debut single, "Walking in the Rain with the One I Love," however, took those experiments to an entirely new level.

More than two decades later, White acknowledged that the crucial moment in this process came with his first exposure to the Philly songwriting duo of Kenny Gamble and Leon Huff White; interviewed for that duo's 1997 box set, White explained, "when I was coming up in the business, the Motown sound was like a revolution. It changed my whole approach and philosophy about strings and rhythms. Gamble and Huff took those concepts even further . . . they showed me how many different ways you can write and arrange for an orchestra; that artistically and commercially, everything was possible."

And so it was. Indeed, with its chattering girls-talk intro bleeding into Glodean's murmured opening verse, through to White's own guest appearance on the other end of the telephone, "Walking In the Rain with the One I Love" had as much in common with Philles, the label formed a decade previous by producer Phil Spector, as with Philly. It was a combination that would prove devastatingly potent.

Even though he was simply a single voice on "Walking in the Rain," and a brief one at that, still the single slammed White into the spotlight. And when his efforts to find a second band to compliment Love Unlimited's releases failed to turn up any suitable contenders, he decided to remain there. At Glodean James' prompting, White recorded "I'm Gonna Love You Just a Little Bit More, Baby," for release under his own name and, in April 1973, won his own first hit.

Love Unlimited's "Oh Love, Well We Finally Made It," followed in July and, at the end of the year, the 40-piece Love Unlimited Orchestra waded into the fray with the chart topping "Love's Theme" and a gold album, *Rhapsody in White* (A teenaged Kenny G was one of the horn players in the Orchestra). White himself followed up with "Never Gonna Give You Up" that fall, launching a period of absolute chart supremacy. At one point during 1974, White had four albums—his own *Can't Get Enough*, Love Unlimited's *Under the Influence Of* and the Orchestra's *Rhapsody in White* and *Together Brothers*—and six singles in the chart simultaneously. By early 1977, the three acts had amassed an incredible 28 R&B chart hits between them.

White knew what people wanted and exactly how to give it to them. Commenting on his recipe for love, White insisted, "A lot of people make love in one way. . . . I am not that human being." Self-ordained or otherwise, the High Priest of Romance played heartstrings like he conducted orchestral ones.

Of the three acts under his banner, White was by far the most prolific. While Love Unlimited and the Orchestra tended to release just two singles apiece every year; White himself unveiled three or even four. "Can't Get Enough of Your Love, Baby" became his first #1 in summer 1974, entering the charts just three weeks after White and Glodean James married, on July 4. "You're My First, My Last, My Everything" made #2, while White, Love Unlimited and the Orchestra embarked on a massive, and utterly self-contained, world tour.

"What Am I Gonna Do with You" continued White's Top Ten run into 1975, but though he was to remain a high profile fixture on the R&B chart, the pop hits began to slow thereafter. Once past the initial flush of success, White's label, 20th Century, had never concerned themselves too much with promotion, apparently believing that White's name alone was sufficient to sell records. As the frenetic upstart disco took root, however, that was clearly no longer the case.

White himself did his utmost to persuade 20th Century to put more muscle behind his releases. At one meeting, the singer lay his gun on the table in full view of the label executives, while suggesting they might like to contribute to his records' promotion—and apparently, they agreed. The densely seductive "It's Ecstasy When You Lie Down Next to Me," from 1977's *Barry White Sings for Someone You Love* album, climbed to #4 on the pop charts and topped the R&B listings for five weeks that October. A year later, however, the truly inspired "Your Sweetness Is My Weakness," one of White's most electrifying records ever, barely scraped to #60 on the pop chart, despite a three week berth at #2 on the R&B charts.

White left 20th Century in late 1978, launching his own Unlimited Gold label through CBS in early 1979 (the label had existed sporadically since 1975, largely for Love Unlimited releases). However, the singer's remarkable run was about to close, coincidentally around the same time as White's longtime friend and manager, Larry Nunes, suffered a fatal heart attack. White was first to admit that he missed Nunes' advice and experience as Unlimited Gold records struggled to get off the ground.

The label's first CBS release, White's own "Any Fool Could See," barely made the Top 40. Subsequent singles by White fared just as poorly, while Love Unlimited's final burst of releases, "High Steppin', Hip Dressin' Fella," "I'm So Glad That I'm a Woman" and "If You Want me, Say It," were similarly underwhelming. White tried interesting CBS in other acts on the label to no avail. A pair of singles recorded with wife Glodean couldn't even break the R&B Top 70 and, in early 1983, Unlimited Gold quietly notched up its final mini-hit, White's "Passion." A year later, White folded the label and prepared to try and rebuild his life.

His finances were in a perilous state; his marriage to Glodean—though they remained close friends—was similarly parlous. His brother Darryl, having spent most of his life in prison, had been murdered in December 1983. (Early Los Angeles radio reports of the tragedy claimed it was Barry who was dead.) His mother was in the early stages of Alzheimer's disease. For three years, White struggled. Then, in 1986, he was offered a new deal by A&M.

Immediately, the old confidence returned. Even as he himself acknowledged that "I wasn't quite as hot as I'd been in the past; rap and hip-hop were coming on strong," a new album, The Right Night and Barry White, at least made the pop Top 200, while a world tour—his first live shows in four years—and a UK hit with a modern remix of 1973's "Never Never Gonna Give Ya Up" confirmed the wisdom of his comeback.

Tragedy marred his dream of reforming Love Unlimited, when Diane Parson died of cancer, aged just 30. (Linda James, too, was unavailable, having married and moved to Switzerland.) But Glodean and two of White's daughters, Bridget and Shaherah, united as Love U II and, when White returned to the studio for his second A&M album, he could not have chosen a more appropriate title, The Man Is Back.

He returned to the pop Top 40 after a 12 year absence, teaming with Quincey Jones, James Ingram, El DeBarge and Al B. Sure! for 1990's "The Secret Garden (Sweet Seduction Suite)." And, the following year, the Put Me in Your Mix album broke the pop Top 100, again for the first time in over a decade. A duet with Isaac Hayes, "Dark and Lovely," restored that fallen idol, too, to the chart.

Elsewhere, too, White's influence over an entire new generation was bearing fruit. In 1991, rapper Big Daddy Kane charted with White's "All of Me"; two years later, Taylor Dane revived "Can't Get Enough of Your Love, Babe." It was 1994's The Icon of Love, however, that truly returned White to the top. The album went double platinum, stormed the Top 20 and span off the hits "Practice What You Preach" and "Come On."

The following year, White charted again with another all-star collaboration with Quincy Jones, "Slow Jams" (also featuring Babyface and Tamia with Portrait). White's own next album, 1999's Staying Power, was similarly littered with star names, including guest appearances from Chaka Khan, Bones Thugs N Harmony and Lisa Stansfield.

### FURTHER READING

Love Unlimited: Insights on Life and Love by Barry White with Marc Eliot (Broadway Books, 1999)

### BARRY WHITE COMPLETE DISCOGRAPHY
### SINGLES/CHART LOG
### THE UPFRONTS

1960 Too Far To Turn Around/Married Jive (Lummtone)
1961 Send Me Someone To Love Who Will Love Me/Baby for Your Love (Lummtone)
1962 I Stopped the Duke of Earl/Baby for Your Love (Lummtone)
1962 It Took Time/Baby for Your Love

### THE MAJESTICS

1963 Strange World/Everything Is Gonna Be Alright (Linda)
1963 Tracy (All I Have Is Yours)/Flame of Love (Faro)

### THE ATLANTICS

1963 Let Me Call You Sweetheart/Home on the Range (Rampart)

### LEE BARRY

1965 A Man Ain't Nothin'/I Don't Need It (Downey)

### GENE WEST

1969 In the Ghetto/Little Girl (Original Sound)

### BARRY WHITE

1967 All in the Run of a Day/Don't Take Your Love from Me (Bronco)
1973 I'm Gonna Love You Just a Little Bit More Baby/Just a Little Bit More Baby (20th Century—#1 R&B/#3 pop)
1973 I've Got So Much To Give/(instrumental) (20th Century—#5 R&B/#32 pop)
1973 Never Never Gonna Give You Up/(extended) (20th Century—#2 R&B/#7 pop)

1974 Honey Please Can't You See/(instrumental) (20th Century—#6 R&B/#44 pop)

1974 Can't Get Enough of Your Love, Babe/Just Not Enough (20th Century—#1 R&B/#1 pop)

1974 You're My First, My Last, My Everything/More than Anything, You're My Everything (20th Century—#1 R&B/#2 pop)

1975 What Am I Gonna Do with You/What Am I Gonna Do with You, Baby (20th Century—#1 R&B/#8 pop)

1975 I'll Do Anything You Want Me To Do/Anything You Want Me To (20th Century—#4 R&B/#40 pop)

1975 Let the Music Play/(instrumental) (20th Century—#4 R&B/#32 pop)

1976 You See the Trouble with Me/I'm So Blue When You Are Too (20th Century—#14 R&B)

1976 Baby We Better Try To Get It Together/If You Know, Won't You Tell Me (20th Century—#29 R&B/#92 pop)

1976 Don't Make Me Wait Too Long/Can't You See It's Only You I Want (20th Century—#20 R&B/#105 pop)

1977 I'm Qualified To Satisfy You/(instrumental) (20th Century—#25 R&B)

1977 It's Ecstasy When You Lay Down Next To Me/I Never Thought I'd Fall in Love with You (20th Century—#1 R&B/#4 pop)

1977 Playing Your Game, Baby/Of All the Guys in the World (20th Century—#8 R&B/#101 pop)

1978 Oh What a Night for Dancing/You're So Good When You're Bad (20th Century—#13 R&B/#24 pop)

1978 Your Sweetness Is My Weakness/It's Only Love Doing Its Thing (20th Century—#2 R&B/#60 pop)

1979 Just the Way You Are/Now I'm Gonna Make Love To You (20th Century—#45 R&B/#102 pop)

1979 I Love To Sing the Songs/Oh Me Oh My (20th Century—#53 R&B)

1979 How Did You Know It Was Me?/Oh Me Oh My (20th Century—#64 R&B)

1979 Any Fool Could See/You're the One I Need (Unlimited Gold—#37 R&B)

1979 It Ain't Love, Babe/Hung Up in Your Love (Unlimited Gold—#58 R&B)

1980 Love Ain't Easy/I Found Love (Unlimited Gold—#75 R&B)

1980 Sheet Music/(instrumental) (Unlimited Gold—#43 R&B)

1980 Love Makin' Music/Ella Es Todo Mi (Unlimited Gold—#25 R&B)

1980 I Believe in Love/You're the One I Need (Unlimited Gold—#71 R&B)

1981 Louie Louie/Ghetto Letto (Unlimited Gold)

1981 Beware/Tell Me Who Do You Love (Unlimited Gold—#49 R&B)

1982 Change/I Like You, You Like Me (Unlimited Gold—#12 R&B)

1982 Passion/It's All About Love (Unlimited Gold—#65 R&B)

1983 America/Life (Unlimited Gold)

1983 Don't Let 'Em Blow Your Mind/Dreams (Unlimited Gold)

1987 Sho' You Right/You're What's on My Mind (A&M—#17 R&B)

1987 For Your Love/I'm Ready for Love (A&M—#27 R&B)

1988 Right Night/There's a Place (A&M)

1989 I Wanna Do It Good To Ya (A&M #26 R&B)/Super Lover (#34 R&B)

1990 When Will I See You Again/Goodnight My Love (A&M—#14 R&B)

1991 Put Me in Your Mix/? (A&M—#2 R&B)

1994 Practice What You Preach/Come On (A&M—#1 R&B/#18 pop)

1995 Come On/My Kinda Place (A&M—#12 R&B/#87 pop)

1995 There It Is/? (A&M—#54 R&B)

### BARRY WHITE/GLODEAN

1981 Didn't We Make It Happen/Our Theme (part two) (Unlimited Gold—#78 R&B)

1981 I Want You/Our Theme (part one) (Unlimited Gold—#79 R&B)

1981 You're the Only One for Me/This Love (Unlimited Gold)

### BARRY WHITE WITH QUINCEY JONES ETC

1990 Secret Garden /(instrumental) (Qwest—#1 R&B/#31 pop)

1996 Slow Jams/(remix) (Qwest—#19 R&B/#68 pop)

### BARRY WHITE WITH BIG DADDY KANE

1991 All of Me/? (Cold Chillin'—#14 R&B)

### BARRY WHITE/ISAAC HAYES

1992 Dark and Lovely/? (A&M—#29 R&B)

### LPs

**8** **1973 I've Got So Much To Give (20th Century—1 R&B/#16 pop)**
Setting the stage for all that was to come, five lushly orchestrated slow groove orgasms, always excellent, often ecstatic. The hit title track and the molten "I'm Gonna Love You Just a Little Bit More," drawn out far beyond their knee-trembler 45 equivalents, are acts of love in their own right.

**10** **1973 Stone Gon' (20th Century—#1 R&B/#20 pop)**
The enervating funk washes "Honey, Please Can't Ya See" and "Never Never Gonna Give You Up" are the national anthems of passion, but that's simply because they're so familiar. Up-tempo elegance, peek-a-boo wah-wah and always, those climactic strings take the entire album as high as White will ever go.

**7** **1974 Can't Get Enough (20th Century—#1 R&B/#1 pop)**
The title track was a massive hit, but also the first crack in White's seamless armor, a song as opposed to a symphony, and the first one to actively encourage the Isaac Hayes comparisons, which so amused White's detractors. Never mind, the headboard hammering "You're My First . . ." more than makes up for it.

**7** **1975 Just Another Way To Say I Love You (20th Century—#1 R&B/#17 pop)**
Actually, it's exactly the same way, and though White's style hasn't slipped an inch, he is running out of ways to thrill.

**7** **1976 Let the Music Play (20th Century—#8 R&B/#42 pop)**

**6** **1976 Is This Whatcha Want? (20th Century—#25 R&B/#125 pop)**

**7** **1977 Barry White Sings for Someone You Love (20th Century—#1 R&B/#8 pop)**
Still recognizably White, still impossibly romantic, but the sheets are a little dirtier and the lights aren't quite so low. "It's Ecstasy When You Lay Down" is a mudbath of rudely

percolating rhythm, while "Oh What a Night for Dancing" is, oddly, about dancing.

**5 1978 The Man (20th Century—#1 R&B/#36 pop)**

A lovely cover of "Just the Way You Are" is the highlight, but its mawkish sentimentality is a long way from the lust of yore.

**4 1979 The Message Is Love (Unlimited Gold—#14 R&B/#67 pop)**

**5 1979 I Love To Sing the Songs I Sing (20th Century—#40 R&B/ #132 pop)**

**6 1980 Barry White's Sheet Music (Unlimited Gold—#19 R&B/#85 pop)**

The best of a bad bunch; White's problem, first noted on *The Man*, is the sudden conviction that he's simply singing songs, which he does very well, rather than orchestrating some vast sexual olympiad. Three minutes may be long enough for the real thing, but on record it should last a little bit more.

**5 1981 Beware (Unlimited Gold—#40 R&B/#207 pop)**

**4 1982 Change (Unlimited Gold—#19 R&B/#148 pop)**

**5 1983 Dedicated (Unlimited Gold)**

**6 1987 The Right Night and Barry White (A&M—#28 R&B/#159 pop)**

**6 1989 The Man Is Back! (A&M—#22 R&B/#143 pop)**

Not yet he isn't . . . but he's getting closer.

**7 1991 Put Me in Your Mix (A&M—#8 R&B/#96 pop)**

Sensational comeback. White is older and shorter of breath of course, and he still hasn't recovered the staying power of old. But across ten short songs (including a preposterous "Volare"), the old sensual flair flickers with brightening passion.

**7 1994 The Icon Is Love (A&M—#1 R&B/#20 pop)**

**8 1999 Staying Power (A&M—#13 R&B/#43 pop)**

Solid smooth grooves from beginning to almost-end; duets with Chaka Khan and Lisa Stansfield prove that White's old wickedness is again firing on all cylinders. Thumping covers of War's "Low Rider" and Sly Stone's "Thank You" wrap things up in dirty style.

## BARRY WHITE/GLODEAN

**5 1981 Barry & Glodean (Unlimited Gold—#44 R&B/#201 pop)**

## SELECTED COMPILATIONS AND ARCHIVE RELEASES

**9 1975 Greatest Hits, Vol. 1 (20th Century—#15 R&B/#23 pop)**

**6 1980 Greatest Hits, Vol. 2 (20th Century)**

**6 1994 All Time Greatest Hits (Mercury—#70 R&B)**

**8 1998 Boss Soul: The Genius of Barry White (Del Fi)**

Utterly rivetting study of White's early years, drawing together 16 singles from his time at Bronco, including productions/compositions for Viola Wills, Johnny Wyatt and Felice Taylor, plus both sides of White's own Downey and Bronco 45s. The style, of course, is strictly mid-'60s sub-Motown, but White's sultry growl is already firmly in place.

**8 2000 The Ultimate Collection (UTV)**

Two-CD set serves up 30 tracks, concentrating on the shorter single-length versions of the hits and highlights through 1999, plus a handful of Love Unlimited cuts.

## SELECTED SAMPLES

I'm Gonna Love You Just a Little More, Babe — Big Daddy Kane: Brother, Brother (1991)

I'm Gonna Love You Just a Little More, Babe — Beavis & Butthead: Come to Butt-Head (1993)

I'm Gonna Love You Just a Little More, Babe — Compton's Most Wanted: Wanted (1991)

I'm Gonna Love You Just a Little More, Babe — Daft Punk: Da Funk (1997)

I'm Gonna Love You Just a Little More, Babe — De La Soul: De La Orgy (1989)

I'm Gonna Love You Just a little More, Babe — Eirc B. & Rakim: Move the Crowd (remix) (1987)

I'm Gonna Love You Just a Little More, Babe — Everlast: Goodbye (1990)

I'm Gonna Love You Just a Little More, Babe — Kool G. Rap: Edge of Sanity (1992)

I'm Gonna Love You Just a Little More, Babe — LL Cool J: Farmers Blvd (Our Anthem) (1990)

I'm Gonna Love You Just a Little More, Babe — NWA: She Swallowed It (1991)

I'm Gonna Love You Just a Little More, Babe — NWA: One Less Bitch (1991)

I'm Gonna Love You Just a Little More, Babe — Queen Latifah: Latifah's Law (1989)

I'm Gonna Love You Just a Little More, Babe — South Central Cartel: County Bluz (1991)

I'm Gonna Love You Just a Little More, Babe — Tone Loc: Cutting Rhythms (1989)

It's Ecstasy When You Lay Down Next To Me — Mary J. Blige: You Bring Me Joy (1994)

It's Ecstasy When You Lay Down Next To Me — Mad Lion: Own Destiny (1995)

It's Ecstasy When You Lay Down Next To Me — Nice & Smooth: Gold (1989)

Love Serenade — Fat Joe: Part Deux (1995)

Love Serenade — Gravediggaz: Never Gonna Come Back (1997)

Love Serenade — Scarface: Money and the Power (1991)

Never, Never Gonna Give You Up — Ant Bank: Livin the Life (1993)

Never, Never Gonna Give You Up — Ill Al Skratch: Where My Homiez? (Come Around My Way) (1994)

Playing Your Game Baby — Big Daddy Kane: Brother Man, Brother Man (1993)

Playing Your Game Baby — Black Moon: I Got Cha Opin (remix) (1993)

Playing Your Game Baby — C&C Music Factory, featuring Patra: Take a Toke (1994)

Playing Your Game Baby — Lost Boyz: Da Game (1996)

Playing Your Game Baby — Ron C: SMooth Attack (1992)

Playing Your Game Baby — X-Clan: Verbal Papp (1992)

Standing in the Shadows of Love — Black Eyed Peas: Fallin Up (remix) (1998)

You're the One I Need — Big Daddy Kane: Lyrical Gymnastics (1994)

You're the One I Need — Lost Boyz: Keep It Real (1996)

You're the One I Need — 2Pac: Streetz R Deathrow (1993)

## NORMAN WHITFIELD

BORN: *1943, Harlem, NY*

Norman Whitfield had been a mid-level staff producer at Motown since the early '60s, when he was plucked from the ranks of local kids who saw the studios as just another hang out. Impressed by the youngster's enthusiasm and curiosity, label head Berry Gordy recruited him to what he, Gordy, called Motown's quality control department, where Whitfield was paid $15 a week to give an honest opinion on the label's latest records.

Whitfield produced his first Motown record, the Velvelettes' "Needle in a Haystack," in 1964. Later that same year he cut "Girl (Why You Wanna Make Me So Blue)" with the Temptations, taking over from Smokey Robinson as that band's regular producer in 1966. Over the next two years, he co-wrote (with Barrett Strong) and produced many of their best-remembered hits, including "(I Know) I'm Losing You," "Ain't Too Proud To Beg" and "I Wish It Would Rain," while maintaining a stream of hits elsewhere at Motown with Gladys Knight & the Pips and Jimmy Ruffin.

In 1967, Knight's version of a new Whitfield/Strong composition, "I Heard It Through the Grapevine," topped the R&B chart for six weeks and remained at #2 on the pop listings for three. Some months later, however, Whitfield decided to try out a new arrangement of the song, slower, moodier, less jazzy, and pocked with sensibilities that owed as much to recent rock productions as to the brassy blare of Motown. With one of Marvin Gaye's greatest ever vocals pushed to the forefront, and exactly one year after Knights' version topped the charts, "Grapevine" returned to #1 for a further seven weeks, then racked up the same span on the pop listings.

It was the biggest 45 in Motown's history, but Whitfield had only just launched his sonic revolution. A pair of incredible albums with the Temptations—*Cloud Nine* (1969) and *Psychedelic Shack* (1970)—proved that Whitfield and, by logical extension, Motown, could compete with the ideological stars of Sly Stone, Isaac Hayes and Curtis Mayfield. Now he set his sights upon another movement percolating beneath the fast-growing banner of funky R&B and one that, somewhat ironically, was being fostered by one of Motown's own former junior staffers, the theatrical smorgasbord that was George Clinton and Funkadelic.

A degree of rivalry surely influenced Whitfield's planned attack. Not only did Funkadelic hail from the Motown heartland of Detroit, but the band's Parliament alter-ego were currently recording for Invictus, the label fronted by another ex-Motown team, Holland-Dozier-Holland. If any group deserved to be shown who was boss, it was Funkadelic.

Whitfield's primary weapon of choice was the Undisputed Truth, a heavily costumed vocal trio whose mission, Whitfield insisted, was to perpetuate "the cosmic thing." Even before the trio's first single was recorded, he was predicting a hit within their first three releases. In fact, he did it within two, as "Smiling Faces Sometimes," a darkly conspiratorial assault on the Nixon government, rose to #3 on the pop chart and only just missed out on the R&B top spot.

Undisputed Truth remained Whitfield's favorites through the remainder of his years with Motown. He departed in 1975, as the label entered a fallow period dominated either by fading stars or self-sufficient supermen, and launched his own Whitfield label around former Motown acts, Undisputed Truth, Willie Hutch and Junior Walker, plus one new group, Rose Royce, formed from Edwin Starr's back-up band, Total Concept Unlimited.

Introduced to the world via the movie *Car Wash*, Rose Royce proved Whitfield's strongest property. Yet, having done so much to predict and even incite the disco boom of decade's end, Whitfield was now being overtaken by it. With painful irony, Whitfield's last major smash of the era was with a record whose embrace of "new technology" would, in fact, hasten his demise even further. In late 1978, Rose Royce's "Love Don't Live Here Anymore" topped charts all over Europe, made #2 in Britain (and a surprisingly paltry #32 in the US), and ushered in the era of the electronic linn drum. Soon, such machines dominated the dancefloor and the organic rhythms and purity of Whitfield's heyday were a thing of the distant past.

He struck back in 1980 with a new group, Mammatapee, featuring Ella Faulk (vcls), Isy Martin (gtr), Mark Kenoly (bs), Walter Downing (kybds) and Jimi Veldez (drms), and backed by an all-star session aggregation led by Junior Walker and Motown guitarist Melvin Ragin. However, the group's sub-Rose Royce disco funk made no impression whatsoever, and by the early '8os, Whitfield had closed the label and withdrawn from the landscape.

Since that time, he has resurfaced only occasionally, producing the soundtrack to 1988's *I'm Gonna Git You Sucka* movie, and working with the Gap Band among others.

### SELECTED PRODUCTIONS

1965 Temptations: The Temptin' Temptations (Gordy)
1966 Temptations: Gettin' Ready (Gordy)
1967 Temptations: With a Lot o'Soul (Gordy)
1967 Gladys Knight & the Pips: Everybody Needs Love (Soul)
1967 Jimmy Ruffin: Ruff'n'Ready (Motown)
1968 Marvin Gaye: I Heard It Through the Grapevine (Motown)
1968 Temptations: Wish It Would Rain (Gordy)
1968 Marvin Gaye: In the Groove (Tamla)
1968 Gladys Knight & the Pips: Feelin' Bluesy (Soul)
1969 Temptations: Cloud Nine (Gordy)
1969 Temptations: Puzzle People (Gordy)
1969 Marvin Gaye: That's the Way Love Is (Tamla)
1969 Gladys Knight & the Pips: Nitty Gritty (Soul)
1969 Marvin Gaye: MPG (Tamla)
1970 Temptations: Psychedelic Shack (Gordy)
1970 Rare Earth: Ecology (Rare Earth)
1970 Edwin Starr: War and Peace (Gordy)
1971 Undisputed Truth: Face to Face with the Truth (Gordy)
1971 Undisputed Truth: Undisputed Truth (Gordy)
1971 Temptations: The Sky's the Limit (Gordy)
1971 Temptations: Solid Rock (Gordy)
1971 Edwin Starr: Involved (Gordy)
1972 Temptations: All Directions (Gordy)
1973 Temptations: 1990 (Gordy)
1973 Undisputed Truth: Law of the Land (Gordy)
1974 Undisputed Truth: Down to Earth (Gordy)
1975 Yvonne Fair: The Bitch Is Black (Motown)
1975 Undisputed Truth: Cosmic Truth (Gordy)
1976 soundtrack: Car Wash (MCA)
1977 Rose Royce: In Full Bloom (Ol' Skool)
1977 Undisputed Truth: Method to the Madness (Whitfield)
1978 Spyder Turner: Music Web (WB)
1978 Rose Royce: Strikes Again (Whitfield)
1979 Rose Royce: Rainbow Connection (Whitfield)
1979 Willie Hutch: In Tune (Whitfield)
1979 Undisputed Truth: Smokin' (Whitfield)
1980 Mammatapee!: Mammatapee! (Whitfield)
1980 Dream Machine: Dream Machine (Whitfield)
1988 soundtrack: I'm Gonna Git You Sucka (Arista)

## CHARLES WRIGHT AND THE WATTS 103RD STREET RHYTHM BAND

**FORMED (AS THE WRIGHT SOUNDS):** *1962, Los Angeles, CA*
**ORIGINAL LINE-UP:** *Charles Wright (b. 1940, Clarksville, Mississippi—gtr), Al McKay (gtr), Melvin Dunlap (bs), Big John Raynford (sax), Bill Cannon (sax), Ray Jackson (trom), Gabriel Fleming (trum), Joe Banks (trum), James Gadson (drms)*

Any discussion of the groups who were present as funk approached its late-'6os Year Zero has to include Charles Wright & the Watts 103rd Street Rhythm Band. The first R&B group to sign to the Warner Brothers label—paving the way, therefore, for fellow pioneers Tower of Power and the Meters—Wright and company were among that select few who spotted a musical opening somewhere between the groove of James Brown, the soul of Otis Redding and the liquid excitement of Jimi Hendrix, and stepped right into it.

Alongside Sly & the Family Stone, they had the West Coast funk scene sewn up two years before many people were even aware such a thing existed; and by the time they broke up in 1975, they had laid the groundwork for much of the music that followed.

Born in Mississippi, but raised in Los Angeles, where his family moved in 1952, Wright was originally more interested in sports than music. When he was 14, however, the family moved into a house whose furnishings included an old upright piano. Wright took to it immediately and, the following year, he heard, and fell in love with, Jesse Belvin's "One Little Blessing."

With the audacity of starstruck youth, Wright promptly looked up the singer's number in the phone book and called him; Belvin, for his part, was sufficiently impressed to check the boy out.

Initially, Belvin placed Wright in one of the teenage doo-wop outfits he was nurturing at the time, the Turks. The following year, as a member of the Twilighters, Wright scored his first hit with "Eternally." He also became an increasingly integral part of Belvin's own set-up, recording with him until Belvin was killed in a car crash on February 6, 1960.

Wright's own next project was the Shields, who debuted with "You Cheated," a 1958 R&B/pop Top 20 hit. The Shields released two further singles, "I'm Sorry Now" and "Fare Thee Well My Love" before breaking up, and Wright spent some time with the Gallahads, cutting "I'm Without a Girlfriend" and "Lonely Guy" for entrepreneur Bob Keene's Del Fi label.

He obviously made an impression; when Wright left the Gallahads, Keane promptly offered him an A&R position at the company. There he worked with Caesar & the Romans, playing almost all the instruments on their "I Never Will Forget." He was joined in the studio by a young drummer who Keane had also taken under his wing, Barry White.

Wright made several attempts to form a vocal group of his own, but was never able to find the right combination of singers. In 1962, then, he changed tack and put together a straightforward soul group, Charles Wright & the Wright Sounds.

With the core lineup of Wright, Dunlap, Raynford and Gadson in place through much of this period, the Wright Sounds established themselves among the leading lights on the south-central Los Angeles/Hollywood club circui. They were unique in that the entire rhythm section, Wright, Melvin Dunlap, James Gadson and a second guitarist, were left handed. "We came about the music from our own original perspective," Wright remarked in the autobiographical notes published on his website. "I was the only guy in town who struck a guitar hitting the high pitched strings first."

It was a unique sound, so much so that Wright found so much demand for his services as a sessionman that he had to drop out of school; he was studying music at the Los Angeles City College. The group also had a weekend residency at Hollywood's Haunted House, which packed the venue for some two and a half years.

In 1967, the Wright Sounds were "discovered" by Fred Smith, one of the key African-American producers on the Los Angeles scene at that time. He began hiring Wright for regular session work, backing Jackie Lee, Bob and Earl and more, and recording their own material during studio downtime.

It was during one of these sessions that the Wright Sounds (augmented by a visiting Bobby Womack) cut "Spreading Honey," a funking instrumental jam that they handed to DJ Magnificent Montague to use as the theme for his KGFJ show. By summer, demand for the song was so strong that Smith finally released it as a single on his own Keymen label. Renamed the Watts 103rd Street Rhythm Band for the occasion, Wright and company were promptly rewarded with a Top 100 pop hit. (This was the group's first release. Contrary to other published sources, they were never known as the Soul Runners; nor did they have a hit under that name.)

Another of the acts Smith was producing at this time was comedian Bill Cosby; he requested the Wright Sounds as his backing group after overhearing them rehearsing in an adjoining studio. Together, this unlikely-sounding team landed a top-selling version of Stevie Wonder's "Uptight," reworked as "Little Ole Man," and cut a pair of albums together. Equally important, however, Cosby introduced Watts 103rd to his own label, Warner Brothers, just as Wright decided to sack half the band and launch an entirely new lineup, retaining Gadson and Dunlap, and recruiting Al McKay, John Raynford, Bill Cannon, Ray Jackson, Gabriel Fleming and Joe Banks.

Watts 103rd toured with Cosby, then went into the studio with Wright himself producing. Recorded live in the studio, an album, *Hot Heat and Sweat Groove*, and two early singles attracted little attention, before late 1968 brought a hit with the impulsive "Do Your Thing." Based around Wright's on stage exhortations to an audience, while the band jammed behind him, "Do Your Thing" spent four months on the R&B chart, climbing to #12—and going one better on the pop chart.

Adhering to the same format, Watts 103rd next unleashed the Top 40 album *Together*, followed in July 1969 by "Till You Get Enough," allegedly the inspiration behind the Rolling Stones' "Gimme Shelter." It gave the group a #12 and, alongside the rush-released *In the Jungle, Babe* album, was the last to be issued under the name of the Watts 103rd Street Rhythm Band alone. For future releases, Wright's own name was appended to the group's.

Taken from *In the Jungle, Babe*, "Must Be Your Thing" and "Love Land," a soulful revision of an old doo-wop number, kept the profile high. It was with July 1970's *Express Yourself*, however, that Wright and the Watts truly struck paydirt. The title track itself was originally a chant that developed out of a protracted version of "Do Your Thing" on stage one night; Wright wrote the finished song in his hotel immediately after the show. It climbed to #3 on the R&B chart and swiftly became the group's best known, and best remembered, hit.

"Solution to Pollution" was a disappointing follow-up later that year, but spring 1971, saw the band return to the R&B Top Ten with "Your Love (Means Everything to Me)," from the album *You're So Beautiful*. The group's name had altered slightly again, losing the "Rhythm." The cosmetic change was short-lived, however. The band broke up at the end of the year, and when Wright resurfaced in 1972, he was working solo.

While McKay joined the newly configured Earth Wind & Fire, *Rhythm and Poetry*, Wright's solo debut (and final album for WB), marked his own move away from funk, toward the yearning soul sound that he followed across three albums for ABC through the mid-'70s.

Wright faded from view after that, re-emerging in the mid-'90s after growing interest in Watts 103rd through the early '90s saw a "best of" package inaugurate WB's Warner Archives series of remastered classics. A second collection, combining *In the Jungle Babe* and *Express Yourself* albums followed in 1997, prompting Wright to relaunch the band itself for a short tour. Solo again, he then recorded 1999's *Going to the Party* album. He also became heavily involved in the student initiative program JAM.

### CHARLES WRIGHT AND THE WATTS 103RD RHYTHM BAND COMPLETE DISCOGRAPHY
### SINGLES/CHART LOG
### THE WATTS 103RD STREET RHYTHM BAND

1967 Spreadin' Honey/Charley (Keymen—#44 R&B/#73 pop)
1968 Brown Sugar/Caesar's Palace (WB)
1968 Bottomless/65 Bars and a Taste of Soul (WB)
1969 Do Your Thing/A Dance, a Kiss and a Song (WB—#12 R&B/#11 pop)
1969 Till You Get Enough/Light My Fire (WB—#12 R&B/#67 pop)

### CHARLES WRIGHT AND THE WATTS 103RD RHYTHM BAND

1969 Must Be Your Thing/Comment (WB—#35 R&B/#103 pop)
1970 Love Land/Sorry Charlie (WB—#23 R&B/#16 pop)
1970 Express Yourself/Living on Borrowed Time (WB—#3 R&B/#12 pop)
1970 Solution for Pollution/High as Apple Pie (WB—#96 pop)

### CHARLES WRIGHT AND THE WATTS 103RD BAND

1971 Your Love (Means Everything to Me)/What Can You Bring Me (WB—#9 R&B/#73 pop)
1971 Nobody/Wine (WB)
1972 I've Got Love/Let's Make Love—Not War (WB)
1972 Soul Train/Run Judy Run (WB)
1972 Here Comes the Sun/You Gotta Know Whatcha Doin' (WB)

### CHARLES WRIGHT

1973 Liberated Lady/You Threw It All Away (Dunhill/ABC)
1973 What Cums Naturally (part one)/(part two) (Dunhill/ABC—#27 R&B)
1974 The Weight of Hate/You Threw It All Away (ABC/Dunhill)
1974 Don't Rush Tomorrow/Is It Real (ABC/Dunhill)
1975 Is It Real/One Lie (ABC)

### ALBUMS
### THE WATTS 103RD STREET RHYTHM BAND

**8** 1968 The Watts 103rd St Rhythm Band (aka Hot Heat and Sweat Groove) (WB)

The group's loosest album, live in the studio with constant high temperature jams redolent of Sly's Family Stone.

**7** 1969 Together (WB—#40 R&B/#140 pop)

**10** 1969 In the Jungle, Babe (WB—#42 R&B/#145 pop)

The Sly Stone influence still permeates, with a steaming instrumental cover of "Everyday People" physically outfunking the original. Less satisfying (but seriously soulful) is a slinky version of "Light My Fire," while Bobby Womack's 'I'm a Midnight Mover' sends the band spiraling back to their '60s club days with stunning aplomb.

### CHARLES WRIGHT AND THE WATTS 103RD RHYTHM BAND

**9** 1970 Express Yourself (WB—#27 R&B/#182 pop)

The bland opener, "Road Without an End," disguises a tiger of an album, the momentum building toward two separate slices of "High as Apple Pie," the first a foreboding piano-led shouter. The second, an impassioned gospel chant slipping into darkness. And then, of course, there's "Express Yourself," which has a Jackson 5 rhythm, and more than a hint of go-go round the edges. If any song demanded an eternal extended version, it's this one.

### CHARLES WRIGHT AND THE WATTS 103RD BAND

**8** 1971 You're So Beautiful (WB—#39 R&B/#147 pop)

### CHARLES WRIGHT

**5** 1972 Rhythm and Poetry (WB)
**5** 1973 Doing What Comes Naturally (Dunhill/ABC—#45 R&B)
**4** 1974 Ninety Day Cycle People (Dunhill/ABC)
**4** 1975 Lil' Encouragement (ABC)
**6** 1998 Going to the Party (A Million Dollars)

### SELECTED COMPILATIONS AND ARCHIVE RELEASES

**9** 1993 Express Yourself: The Best of . . . (WB)

It's hard to go wrong!

### SELECTED SAMPLES

A Dance, a Kiss and a Song — Jungle Brothers: Good Lookin Out (1993)
Fried Okra — A Tribe Called Quest: Can I Kick It (remix) (1990)
Giggin' Down 103rd — Funkdoobiest: The Funkiest (1993)
High as Apple Pie—Slice II — Gang Starr: No Shame in My Game (1992)
Soul Con-Certo — A Tribe Called Quest: Can I Kick It (remix) (1990)
That's All That Matters Baby — Naughty by Nature: Craziest (1995)
What Can You Bring Me? — Brand Nubian: Punks Jump Up To Get Beat Down (1993)

# BLAXPLOITATION: FUNK GOES TO THE MOVIES

**Y**ou can't keep a good man down. In June 2000, almost thirty years after Gordon Parks, Sr.'s Black detective adventure *Shaft* first slammed onto the screen, the smooth-talking, gun-toting, lady-killing John Shaft was back at the top of the box office.

The times had changed, of course. Now it was Samuel L. Jackson who walked the walk and talked the talk, while Richard Roundtree, the "original" Shaft, was content to do the talk show round, and watch while late-night TV reprised his own work. Musically, too, the landscape had lurched away from the street fighting funk of Isaac Hayes' original score, and into the sprawl of 21st century urban dance: R. Kelly, Big Gipp, OutKast and Too $hort.

But the themes remained unchanged, and the beast untamed. The only question left unanswered was—what next? The original *Shaft*, after all, was more than just a movie. It was also the trigger that ignited a craze that engrossed Hollywood for the next half-decade.

In the early '70s, the media delighted in creating ever- narrowing stereotypical genres to describe any artform that did not fall directly into its own narrow mainstream. Some were based upon unimpeachable criteria: disco music, disaster movies, that sort of thing. Some were insulting (few German musicians truly appreciated having their records corralled together as Krautrock) and some were utterly irrelevant beyond a convenient hook for lazy journalists to swing from. And though history is still uncertain precisely which category the catchall term for Afro-American-made adventure movies falls into, there is no doubt that "Blaxploitation" became more than a simple marketing term. It became a way of life.

It was not, though hindsight mutters otherwise, intended as a pejorative term. Neither was it an especially accurate one. The "blax-" bit was self-explanatory. But "-ploitation," as in *exploitation* . . . well, who exactly was exploiting who? Not the movie makers, many of whom had been struggling to introduce strong Black leads into their films for years. Nor the studios, who were as surprised as anybody by the public demand for such movies. And certainly not the viewing public, who proved no more gullible in this genre as they were in any other.

However, there were certain parameters the term did embrace, including a keen appreciation of B-moviedom—those less than glossy, lowly budgeted and poorly scripted would-be epics that had been around since the days when killer tomatoes stalked the earth, and giant spiders devoured entire cities. Since that time, of course, the genre had grown, to encompass gory horror, schlocky romance—anything, in fact, that fell beyond the remit of the major Hollywood studios. Which, as the '70s dawned, is precisely where the majority of Black American actors and directors were living. That the first and best movies created under the Blaxploitation tag did, in fact, succeed in utterly blurring the commercial and production values that defined B movies in the first place, is simply further fuel to the fires burning around the name.

Historically, it was Sidney Poitier who created a space for Black actors in Hollywood. Through groundbreaking films like 1955's rock 'n' roll tinderbox *Blackboard Jungle* and 1961's *A Raisin in the Sun*, through to 1967's *To Sir, with Love* and the highly charged *Guess Who's Coming to Dinner*, Poitier unflinchingly brought the Black character out of the shadows of supporting roles and caricatures, and onto the front of the big screen.

Richard Pryor's film career got its true start with his first starring role in the hippie drenched skit-fest *Dynamite Chicken* in 1970; comedian Bill Cosby turned to drama in the civil war-era *Man and Boy*, the following year. How effective such characters were in addressing a Black audience, however, is questionable.

In the highly charged racial atmosphere of late-'60s America, was it enough for Black characters to simply be accepted into the confines of white society? Did Black society itself not have a place on-screen as well? Mirrored against what was happening across the country at the time, the images were completely disparate. There had to be an alternative, something that could tap into the truth of urban living, culturally, visually and musically.

The founding father of what became the Blaxploitation picture was the young Afro-American director Melvin Van Peebles. He had spent much of his celluloid apprenticeship in France, before moving to Hollywood in 1970 to shoot *The Watermelon Man*—the story of a White bigot who awakens one morning to discover he is now Black. A year later, riding the relative success of that film, Van Peebles decided to follow through with a movie, which not only reflected facets of his own experience as an African American, but was also directly targeted at a Black audience—something *The Watermelon Man*, for all its powers of observation, had not been. It was called *Sweet Sweetback's Baadasssss Song*.

Immediately, he ran into problems. No major (or even minor) studio was interested in his proposal; finally, Van Peebles financed the project himself. Distributors balked; the movie opened with only two theaters in the US willing to screen it, one in Detroit and one Atlanta. The media ignored it, reviewers avoided it, and Van Peebles admits that he'd spent so much money getting the movie made, that he didn't have anything left for advertising. What he did have, however, was a dynamite soundtrack, and one that was to revolutionize the relationship between films and music, as profoundly as *Sweet Sweetback's Baadasssss Song* was to change film's relations with its audience.

"Music was not used as a selling tool in movies at the time," he recalled. "Even musicals, it would take three months after the release of the movie before they would bring out an album." Van Peebles' idea was to reverse that situation completely, to preview the movie with its soundtrack, building an awareness of the product without recourse to any of Hollywood's traditional avenues.

Stax Records agreed to release the soundtrack, written by Van Peebles himself, and performed by the then-unknown Earth Wind & Fire. The label, too, was stepping into the unknown, but of course, once *Sweet Sweetback's Baadasssss Song* hit (and it hit big, becoming the most successful independent American film yet released), Stax would be richly rewarded for their foresightedness. MGM, having already been prompted to recast the in-production *Shaft* to feature a Black lead character, now redesigned their soundtrack requirements too. Stax Records were asked to take over.

*Shaft* was a mainstream moneymaker for MGM and really jumpstarted the genre. With a superb and now classic score by Isaac Hayes, the film also heralded the rapid rise of the blaxploitation soundtrack. Curtis Mayfield answered the call with *Superfly* in 1972, while James Brown and Fred Wesley followed suit with *Black Caesar* in 1973.

The flood continued, even after the true age of blaxploitation movies passed into history. *What It Is . . . What It Was!*, Gerald Martinez, Diana Martinez and Andres Chavez's lavishly illustrated study of the blaxploitation phenomenon, unearths over 130 movies that can be categorized under the label, all but a handful of them dating from the peak span of 1971–78, from *Shaft* to *Youngblood*, by which time the genre had undergone such a colossal change in both intent and execution as to deserve an even more disparaging name than (in some viewers' eyes) it already had.

The accompanying soundtracks follow suit. Funk, of course, was the music of choice, partly in imitation of Isaac Hayes' masterful *Shaft* score, of course (White cop TV shows would still be perpetuating that pattern into the '80s), but also because funk was, at that time, the music of the streets, the city and the society in the lens.

From the Blackbyrds (*Cornbred, Earl and Me*) to the Ohio Players (*Mr. Mean*), then, and from Rose Royce (*Car Wash*) to War (*Youngblood*), the blaxploitation boom spun off some classic music, and suffered some absolute tripe as well. Some of the best albums accompanied the worst films, some of the greatest movies were saddled with the most unbearable soundtracks. But all played some part in affecting the remarkable, even unimaginable, change that so indelibly swept the American movie industry as the '70s progressed, paving the way, of course, for the later likes of Spike Lee, but also opening the doors for the summer sensation of 2000 as well. Shaft was back, and now, nobody noticed that he was Black as well.

## BLAXPLOITATION'S GREATEST HITS

**FILM:** SWEET SWEETBACK'S BAADASSSSS SONG
**DIRECTOR:** Melvin Van Peebles
**YEAR:** 1971
**CAST:** Melvin Van Peebles, Simon Chuckster, Hubert Scales
**SOUNDTRACK:** Stax Records
**ARTIST:** Earth, Wind & Fire

This was the film that kickstarted the whole movement, a gritty slab of inner city realism designed to reflect the ongoing racial tensions then sweeping the country.

*Sweet Sweetback's Baadasssss Song* was fabricated reality—harsh and wholly urban, a Black film from a Black perspective. It was something never before seen in the cinema. But more importantly, it was a fitting statement for the times, the story of the quintessential pimp (Sweetback) who stumbles upon a young Black man being beaten by the cops for his revolutionary politics, steps in to help the youth and becomes awakened himself to the need for radical militant action against the "establishment."

**FUNK**

In his transformation, he becomes a hero, an idol, and ultimately an icon for an uneasy local community. The Black Panthers subsequently adopted *Sweet Sweetback's Baadasssss Song* as a virtual training film, requiring all new recruits to see it.

Of course, the film captured only a very small slice of Black urban experience. But still its overall impact was huge, both visually and musically; the marriage of horny funk and political manifesto was perfect, while the movie's rapid-fire success promptly opened eyes in Hollywood itself. In the end, as Van Peebles himself has observed, that success "took away the revolutionary context, in such a way to be counter-revolutionary." But regardless of how far future films would stray from what Peebles achieved with *Sweet Sweetback's Baadasssss Song*, still they passed through the door he had opened, one through which the movie-going public could glimpse a world as similar—or as different—as an image in a mirror.

**FILM:** SHAFT
**DIRECTOR:** Gordon Parks, Sr.
**YEAR:** 1971
**CAST:** Richard Roundtree, Moses Gunn, Charles Cioffi
**SOUNDTRACK:** Enterprise Records
**ARTIST:** Isaac Hayes

Certainly the best known and most easily identified of all blaxploitation movies made throughout the '70s—in part due to Isaac Hayes' Oscar-winning theme song—*Shaft* may not have packed the political punch of its predecessor, but it did impact the genre in a way that no other film ever would. Backed with MGM dollars for marketing and advertising, the film stormed the US, made a superstar of Richard Roundtree, and ensured that African-American filmmakers would rarely hear the word "no" again. But would that have been the case if the film had appeared as it was intended?

Shaft, John Shaft. . . . There can be no denying it, the hero's very name had an extraordinarily Bond-esque ring to it, a ring that often dictated the form of the subsequent genre. But that was what was intended in the first place; as White private eye, Shaft stepped out of novelist Ernest Tidyman's imagination, a lot more groomed than he ever was gritty. It was only after the shock success of *Sweet Sweetback's Baadasssss Song* that the studio heads looked again at their model, and realized it could become even more powerful.

As Melvin Van Peebles explained in *What It Is . . . What It Was!*, "*Sweet Sweetback's Baadasssss Song* was so successful that everybody jumped on the bandwagon. The original Shaft was a White guy. They [MGM] threw in a couple of 'mother fucks,' found a Black guy [Richard Roundtree] and made themselves a Black detective."

Slick and very well directed, *Shaft* spawned two silver screen sequels and a short-lived television show. All were stuffed to the gills with non-stop action, crash bang cinematography and sex, sex, sex. What those follow-ups didn't have, however, was Isaac Hayes' score, with its resonating vibrancy of a rich funk tapestry. Few soundtracks have ever done their job more brilliantly.

Shaft returned the following year with *Shaft's Big Score!*, this time finding himself smack in the middle of some *West Side Story*-esque warfare involving Harlem hoods and Mafia mobsters.

Like its predecessor, *Shaft's Big Score!* was action-packed from beginning to end, battling the bad guys with boats, helicopters, cars, the lot. Of course it fell short of expectations; most sequels do and besides, one James Bond is enough.

Isaac Hayes obviously agreed, eschewing the chance to revisit his greatest triumph and leaving the bulk of the soundtrack (MGM, 1972) to director Parks himself. Hayes served up just one track, "Type Thang." A third movie, *Shaft in Africa* (director John Guillerman, 1973), was generally regarded as even more tired than its predecessor ("the Brother Man in the Motherland. . . ." said the posters), a modern re-run classic that even today's viewer will inevitably find a parody of the original vision. A Four Tops fired soundtrack (ABC) is nevertheless prized on the collector market.

**FILM:** SUPERFLY
**DIRECTOR:** Gordon Parks. Jr.
**YEAR:** 1972

**CAST:** Ron O'Neal, Carl Lee, Sheila Frazier, Julius Harris, Charles MacGregor
**SOUNDTRACK:** Curtom
**ARTIST:** Curtis Mayfield

Like father, like son? Hardly. If Gordon Parks Senior's John Shaft was the new Black hero, then Gordon Parks Junior's Youngblood Priest was the anti-hero, an inner city coke dealer out to make his retirement fund with one last sweet deal, while "sticking it to the man" one last, glorious time.

True, the film edged toward very dark comedy, its perceived amorality actually intended as folly. But that didn't change its overall appearance. Blacks Against Narcotic Genocide (BANG) went so far as to picket outside cinemas showing the film. Community leaders spoke out against it; even Curtis Mayfield, composing the movie's soundtrack, described it as an infomercial for cocaine, and penned a score purposefully designed to oppose the action taking place around it.

Yet the ensuing conflict between sound and scene only added to the movie's impact; it certainly aided its success. While the *Superfly* soundtrack spun off two Top Ten singles and topped the chart in its own right, box office takings ran *Shaft* a close second, ultimately taking in almost $19 million (*Shaft* topped $23 million).

**FILM:** CLEOPATRA JONES
**DIRECTOR:** Jack Starrett
**YEAR:** 1973
**CAST:** Tamara Dobson, Bernie Casey, Brenda Sykes, Antonio Fargas, Bill McKinney, Dan Frazer, Shelley Winters
**SOUNDTRACK:** WB
**ARTIST:** JJ Johnson

"She's '10 miles of bad road for every hood' in town!" announced the posters; "6 feet 2" and all of it Dynamite." In a droll comedy thriller, the amazonian Dobson portrays a federal drug agent with a penchant for heroics, battling drug dealers puppeted by, of all people, Shelley Winters.

Following the traditional patterns of action and romance, *Cleopatra Jones* kicks some serious ass, has some serious sex and cleans up some serious bad guys, and all in under two hours. JJ Johnson's jazzy soundtrack fills the bits in-between.

**FILM:** BLACK CAESAR
**DIRECTOR:** Larry Cohen
**YEAR:** 1973
**CAST:** Fred Williamson, Julius Harris, Val Avery, Art Lund, Gloria Hendry
**SOUNDTRACK:** Polydor
**ARTIST:** James Brown, Fred Wesley

More James Cagney than James Bond, *Black Caesar* does indeed reinvent the mob movie boom of the '30s, chronicling the rise of a small time gangster as he moves up the Harlem crime ladders to reach the top.

Focussing on the themes of poor boy makes good, while giving back to the community that sheltered him, the film nevertheless packed its share of terse content. Opening with the young Tommy Gibbs (Williamson) being cruelly beaten by the cops, *Black Caesar* personified the duality of being a genuinely "good" person, placed on the wrong side of the law by society's own blindness to its own inate evils. Gibbs' greatest crime is to rebel against the corruption that is masked by the badge of the law.

*Caesar* also stands apart through its apparent aversion to the staples of violence and murder—the most harrowing scene, in which Gibbs is kicked to death—was cut before the movie was ever screened, allowing him to live on for an immediate sequel.

Shorn of the heaps of broken corpses, the movie ironically emerges even more brutal. If you can't see what happened, you can only imagine it, a private nightmare that James Brown's kick-ass soundtrack only exaggerates. Featuring dynamic contributions from Fred Wesley, the JBs and Lyn Collins (the astonishing "Mama Feelgood"), plus Brown himself, the album is nothing short of a full frontal funk assault.

**FILM:** HELL UP IN HARLEM
**DIRECTOR:** Larry Cohen
**YEAR:** 1973
**CAST:** Fred Williamson, Julius Harris, Margaret Avery, Gerald Gordon, Gloria Hendry
**SOUNDTRACK:** Motown
**ARTIST:** Edwin Starr

Cohen and Williamson reunite for a straightforward sequel to *Black Caesar*, as Williamson's gangster-with-a-heart-of-gold finds himself persecuted by his own son, himself manipulated by the local D.A.'s office. It's a neat idea, but the drama and suspense that made the first movie so memorable seem to have gone out of the door.

With an increasingly incensed Gibbs searching for his kidnapped children and seeking revenge for the murder of his wife, the film more than compensates for its predecessor's bloodless restraint with a veritable orgy of gratuitous violence. Indeed, even as Gibbs emerges triumphant at the end, the expectant viewer is more likely to feel an aching void where *Black Caesar* left breathless excitement.

No such problems with the soundtrack. Although much of Freddie Perren and Fonze Mizell's score screams "Shaft," some excellent textures and themes are further enhanced by the addition of Edwin Starr.

**FILM:** SLAUGHTER'S BIG RIP OFF
**DIRECTOR:** Gordon Douglas
**YEAR:** 1973
**CAST:** Jim Brown, Ed MacMahon, Brock Peters, Don Stroud, Gloria Hendry
**SOUNDTRACK:** Polydor
**ARTIST:** James Brown

Another in the line of gangster mystery shoot 'em ups, a sequel to Jack Starrett's 1972 *Slaughter*, *Slaughter's Big Rip Off* follows Beret Slaughter's vendetta against a Mafia gang who murdered one of his friends.

Armed only with a copy of the gang's payroll, his trusty machine gun and—*Rambo* fans will enjoy this—his Green Beret training, Slaughter of course lives up to his name, before relocating abroad for some well deserved R&R. And though many voiced dismay at the predictability of it all, really; isn't the predictability comforting?

James Brown and Fred Wesley again scored a funk packed soundtrack, much of it improving on *Black Caesar*'s occasionally tentative score as Brown settled comfortably into the moviemaker's demands.

**FILM:** COFFY
**DIRECTOR:** Jack Hill
**YEAR:** 1973
**CAST:** Pam Grier, Booker Bradshaw, Robert DoQui, Allan Arbus
**SOUNDTRACK:** Polydor
**ARTIST:** Roy Ayers

Pam Grier's meteoric ascent to cult superstardom ensures that any one of her early-mid-'70s movies can be accorded classic status, simply because of her presence. From *The Big Bird Cage* and *Foxy Brown*, to *Blacula* and *Drum* (and on, of course, to Tarantino's *Jackie Brown*), Grier's characters were undeniably sexy, strong, and strongwilled, establishing her as an icon for an entire generation, a no holds barred heroine of sorts for a nation of women who were finally finding their voice. Grier found hers in *Coffy*.

Violent, discomforting and edgy, *Coffy* was a reflection on the horrors of drug abuse, delving deep into the gritty realism of pushers and addicts as Grier seeks to avenge the death of her eleven–year-old sister. She emerges triumphant, but more importantly, heroic. And if some of her methods are a little less than saintly, so were the people she was dealing with.

Against so relentless a backdrop, the still jazzbound Roy Ayers' score was a masterpiece of calm and understatement, punctuating the action not with the street smart abrasion of a James Brown or Curtis Mayfield, but with a cool, unruffled sophistication that is chilling for its absolute detachment. Watch the movie with a friend, but never listen to the soundtrack in the dark.

**FILM:** THREE THE HARD WAY
**DIRECTOR:** Gordon Parks, Jr.
**YEAR:** 1974
**CAST:** Jim Brown, Fredd Williamson, Jim Kelly, Sheila Frazier, Jay Robinson, Charles MacGregor, Howard Platt, Alex Rocco
**SOUNDTRACK:** Curtom
**ARTIST:** The Impressions

Another absolutely outrageous film from Gordon Parks, Jr., *Three the Hard Way* took blaxploitation to a new level of farce and satire, embodying the best tricks of the low-budget disaster epic, tying them to a particularly genocidal White supremacist plot, then floating everything from Parks' own unique vision of society.

Parallels with late-'50s cold war monster movies are doubtless deliberate. Paranoia and camp make especially active bedfellows, while adding an appositely serious sounding Impressions soundtrack to the brew sparked some interesting subliminal comparisons with *Superfly*.

**FILM:** THREE TOUGH GUYS
**DIRECTOR:** Duccio Tessari
**YEAR:** 1974
**CAST:** Lino Ventura, Fred Williamson, Isaac Hayes, Paula Kelly
**SOUNDTRACK:** Enterprise
**ARTIST:** Isaac Hayes

Isaac Hayes had already scored big with *Shaft*, but now combined soundtrack duties with an onscreen role as well, stepping impressively out amid the carnage that only an ex-cop and an ex-priest can wreak while trying to hunt down the man who lost the lawman his badge. It's vendetta time!

A slick Italian-American joint production, *Three Tough Guys* flipped tables on an astounded audience as Williamson appeared as the villain to Hayes' good guy. Indeed, as highly regarded a musician as Hayes already was, he found acting equally to his taste, offering up a performance that almost outshone his score.

**FILM:** TRUCK TURNER
**DIRECTOR:** Jonathan Kaplan
**YEAR:** 1974
**CAST:** Isaac Hayes, Yaphet Kotto, Nichell Nichols, Alan Weeks, Dick Miller
**SOUNDTRACK:** Enterprise
**ARTIST:** Isaac Hayes

Fresh from the set of *Three Tough Guys*, Hayes reprises both his acting and musical roles, this time starring as a bounty hunter, Turner, in a topsy-turvy action packed world tailor-made for Hayes' larger than life persona.

Indeed, while other directors were busy taking their calling oh-so-seriously, Kaplan and company simply set out to have fun, an untrammelled joy that came across in the finished print, as Hayes himself later explained. "I don't think we took ourselves too seriously, maybe some people did. It was fun to see, at last, the brother on the screen being a hero, being a sex symbol, having the upper hand, and winning for a change."

**FILM:** YOUNGBLOOD
**DIRECTOR:** Noel Nossack
**YEAR:** 1978
**CAST:** Laurence-Hilton Jacobs, Ren Woods, Brian O'Dell, Tony Allen, Vince Cannon
**SOUNDTRACK:** MCA

**ARTIST:** War
**LABEL:** MCA

This film arrived very late in the day and foundered in the wake of the disco revolution—itself already well catered for by the Norman Whitfield assembled *Car Wash* boom. Steadfastly true to old themes, however, *Youngblood* tells the tale of ghetto culture as a young boy tries to leave the harsh life behind, whilst simultaneously refusing to sever ties with his former gang.

As would be expected, full on urban warfare ensues, but times had changed. Movie-goers were no longer the politicized beasts they once were; now the theaters were full of *Saturday Night Fever* and *Youngblood* inevitably foundered.

The soundtrack, too, suffered from the sea-change; even two years earlier, War's funk-lite score would have been kindly received, and it certainly worked well with the action on-screen. But in 1978, it seemed dated, and completely out of fashion. But it wasn't simply the movie that passed into oblivion. A genre, too, had outlived its usefulness.

### FURTHER READING

*What It Is . . . What It Was!* by Gerald Martinez, Diana Martinez and Andres Chavez (Hyperion Books, 1998)

### RECOMMENDED LISTENING

### THE BEST OF BLAXPLOITATION (Global)
TRACKS: Shaft: Isaac Hayes/The Ghetto: Donny Hathaway/Inner City Blues: Grover Washington Jr/Superfly: Curtis Mayfield/The Bottle: Gil Scott-Heron/Papa Was a Rollin' Stone: Temptations/Woman of the Ghetto: Marlena Shaw/Am I Black Enough for You?: Billy Paul/Death Wish: Herbie Hancock/The Boss: James Brown/Trouble Man: Marvin Gaye/Home Is Where the Hatred Is: Esther Phillips/Ain't No Love in the Heart of the City: Bobby Bland/I'm Gonna Tear Your Playhouse Down: Ann Peebles/Celestial Blues: Gary Bartz Nu Troop/If You Want Me To Stay: Sly Stone/All the Way Lover: Millie Jackson/I'd Rather Be with You: Bootsy Collins/September 13th: Deodato/Little Child Running Wild: Curtis Mayfield/Be Thankful for What You Got: William DeVaughan/Expansions: Lonnie Liston Smith/Gun: Gil Scott-Heron

Accusations that the quality of blaxploitation soundtracks began high (*Shaft*) then declined with the standards of the movies are blown out of the water by this phenomenal collection tracing the history of the genre through some of its finest moments.

### BEST OF BLAXPLOITATION: HARLEM HUSTLE (Global)
TRACKS: Law of the Land: the Temptations/Am I Black Enough for You: Billy Paul/Death Wish: Herbie Hancock/If There's a Hell Below: Curtis Mayfield/September 13th: Deodato/Grandma's Hands: Gil Scott-Heron/Who Is He & What Is He To You: Bill Withers/Truck Turner: Isaac Hayes/Son of Shaft: Bar-Kays/Mister Magic: Grover Washington, Jr./Theme from Cleopatra Jones: Joe Simon/Flying Machine: War/Sweet Sweetback's Theme: Earth Wind & Fire/I Want You: Marvin Gaye/Theme from Savage: Don Julian/For the Love of Money: O'Jays/Strawberry Letter 23: Brothers Johnson/Natural High: Bloodstone/Inside My Love: Minnie Riperton/One Gun Salute: Donald Byrd/Always There: Ronnie Laws/God Made Me Funky: Headhunters/Get Up, I Feel like a Sex Machine: James Brown

And if one volume was not enough. . . .

# THE BRITISH ROCK FUNK CONNECTION

B ritish rock groups have never been afraid of R&B. It might not, as ornery American critics point out every time an MOR superstar attempts a weak assault on another Motown gem, be in their blood, but it is certainly in their genes, and has been since the '40s and '50s, when merchant seamen returned home from trips to America, their suitcases stuffed with blues-wailin' vinyl.

In the years before their 1962–63 breakthroughs, the Beatles cut their teeth on R&B and Motown. The Rolling Stones delved even deeper, to the blues of Muddy Waters and Howling Wolf. And though they took the experience little further, the British club landscape of the mid-late-'60s was littered with bands who not only performed the Black American hits of the day, they performed in the style of the hitmakers, too.

The young Rod Stewart was a member of an all-White band based almost shamelessly upon the James Brown revues, while vocalist Steve Marriott broke up his first hitmakers, pop darlings the Small Faces, specifically to form a new group, Humble Pie, as a mirror on current (late-'60s) developments on the American R&B scene. By 1971, Humble Pie were one of the most popular British acts in America but, more importantly, Marriott was widely acclaimed among the most convincing white R&B vocalists ever. In terms of sheer groove intensity, Pie's side-long version of Dr. John's bayou-funk masterpiece "Walk on Gilded Splinters," captured on the *Rockin' the Fillmore* live album, has seldom been bettered.

Marriott was not alone in mastering the nuances of the genre. Noddy Holder, vocalist with a little-known midlands club combo called the N Betweens, recalls a late-'60s trip to the Bahamas, where they landed a residency playing a backwoods hotel resort. During the evening, they entertained the tourists. Into the night, they played for the locals and Holder recalled, "[they] couldn't believe their ears. Bahamians had never seen anyone actually perform James Brown's music before. Watching a bunch of White guys doing it was astonishing to them. James Brown was a god on this island." (With a somewhat different approach, but with no less effervescence, the N Betweens would later re-emerge as pop hitmakers Slade.)

Amid so much activity, the first English musician to consciously approach funk head-on was Eric Burdon, the 28-year-old vocalist with Newcastle-based blues outfit the Animals. In 1969, following the demise of both that group and their acid-stoked successors, the New Animals, Burdon's search for a new backing band ended at Hollywood's Rag Doll Club, when he was introduced to the Nightriders.

Burdon had been growing increasingly anxious to explore what he saw as the next logical step in the development of psychedelic rock, following his friend Jimi Hendrix into the realm of funk, but imbibing Hendrix's earthy explorations with a more danceable element. He saw the all-instrumental Nightriders as the ideal vehicle for his new passion.

Changing their name to War (allowing for a punningly titled debut album, *Eric Burdon Declares "War"*), Burdon employed the band for the next two years, pursuing an idiosyncratic post-psychedelic sound that blended War's own chicano jazz-funk instincts with the singer's astonishing vocals and ear for extemporization. The team eventually broke up following a disastrous European tour, but the possibilities that their union had raised remained a vivid temptation.

Watching Burdon's developments, and simultaneously plotting his own move in a similar direction, was guitarist Jeff Beck. Like Burdon, Beck was a graduate of one of Britain's finest blues academies, in this instance the Yardbirds. Since that time, he had flirted with mainstream pop success and also, with a band fronted by vocalist Rod Stewart, and published the blueprint for the blues-rock explosives of Led Zeppelin. But with an increasingly jazz-inflected feel coming into his playing, Beck was looking beyond the horizons of his past for inspiration. He found it when he hooked up with Bobby Tench, vocalist with the soul-funk club act the Gas (soon to reach a wider audience themselves as Gonzalez) and jazz pianist Max Middleton.

Like Burdon with War, Beck retained this lineup for just two albums, 1971's *Rough and Ready* and 1972's *Jeff Beck Group*. Unlike Burdon, it would be the second album, not the first, that truly encapsulated his intentions. Working with producer Steve Cropper, the Memphis-born guitarist with Booker T. & the MGs, Beck conceived an album that slammed soulful instrumentals into passionate vocal numbers, highlighted by Mar-Kays bassist Don Nix's "Going Down" (a song simultaneously in the repertoire of hard rock blues devotees Stone the Crows) and a distinctly Dr. John-inflected Cropper-Beck composition, "Sugar Cane."

**FUNK**

Beck also served notice of one of his own personal friendships, with Stevie Wonder. This album featured a devastating instrumental version of "I Can't Give Back the Love I Feel for You," a cut from Mrs. Wonder, Syreeta Wright's recently released *Syreeta* debut album. Beck's next, recorded with Americans Tim Bogert and Carmine Appice, would include a near-definitive take on Wonder's own "Superstition."

Wonder had personally promised that song to Beck, and Motown's decision to release the original version as a single shortly before Beck's rendition, caused something of a breach between the two. They finally reunited around two new songs offered up for Beck's 1975 album *Blow by Blow*, "Cause We've Ended as Lovers" and "Thelonius." "He's such a ball of energy," Beck told the British music paper *Sounds*. "He could give you 50 hours of unrecorded material!"

*Blow by Blow* was the album that saw Beck's funkiest instincts come to the fore, teaming up with Beatles producer George Martin for a record that, while taking Beck further than ever from his roots as one of Britain's prime guitar gods, only spurred him on toward his future—and a career crossroads that was going to pay dividends whichever way he went. How does any musician choose between the offer of a job with the Rolling Stones, and the chance of partnerships with jazzmen Jan Hammer and Stanley Clarke?

Beck chose the latter, working with Clarke over the course of the four albums—*Journey to Love* (1975), *Schooldays* (1976), *Modern Man* (1978) and *I Wanna Play with You* (1979)—that prefaced Clarke's plunge into full-blooded funk with the Clarke-Duke Project. His work with Hammer, meantime, included the studio album *Wired* (1976) and the frenetic in concert fusion *Live* (1977).

His sojourn with the Rolling Stones, brief and unofficial though it was, did not, however, go unrecorded. Like Beck, the Stones were perennial scholars of the American R&B scene, and vice versa, as the overall mood of Parliament's *Osmium*, and Ruth Copeland's Funkadelic fired take on "Gimme Shelter" prove.

Without ever reverting to the slavish devotion of their earliest blues-inspired recordings, the Stones had long since mastered the art of the funk vibe (the slide from "Ventilator Blues" into "Just Want To See His Face" to 1972's *Exile on Main Street* would not have been out of place on a Sly & the Family Stone session), while their last album, 1974's *It's Only Rock 'n' Roll* physically climaxed with the bona fide funk of the sinister slithering "Fingerprint File."

The Beck sessions would continue this vibe. Versions of "Freeway Jam" (a fast-paced groove from *Blow by Blow*) and a raucous take on Martha & the Vandellas' "Heatwave" were both taped during Beck's two-week sojourn at the Stones' Rotterdam rehearsal space in early 1975. Both set a mood that would only be enhanced by further recordings with Americans Harvey Mandel and Muscle Shoals sessioneer Wayne Perkins (the tightly-coiled "Black and Blue Jam" (abbreviated and overdubbed to become the *Tattoo You* album's centerpiece "Slave") and a churning instrumental jam through Shirley & Co.'s contemporaneous "Shame Shame Shame."

Compared with what purists call "the real thing," a lot of these efforts were clumsy to say the least. Unreleased rehearsal tapes from the Stones' *Black and Blue* sessions often reveal the musicians to be uncertain whether they are attempting to play reggae or funk, and end up simply jamming aimlessly around Bill Wyman bass lines whose greatest virtue is their insistence.

But other times, the band banged the nail on the head and the beat on the one, and suddenly everything makes sense. They relax into "Hot Stuff" as though it were the most natural rhythm in the world, while 17 minutes of "Hey Negrita," taped during eventual full-time guitarist Ronnie Wood's first audition with the group, are positively relentless.

Wood and Keith Richard's crooked guitar lines instinctively take on the inspired jauntiness, which propelled the Stones through another two decades-plus of music, while Mick Jagger offered up one of his most impassioned vocal performances . . . and that despite the song's lyrics being little more than a meaningless succession of mantric exhortations. Selected to open side two of the finished album, "Hey Negrita" would remain one of the Stones' best performances of the decade.

Despite (or possibly, because of) such successes, the *Black and Blue* album emerged one of the most divisive records in the Rolling Stones' history; the band's embrace of the funk ethic misread in the White rock media as an attempt to leap aboard the then-rolling disco bandwagon and condemned accordingly. Unfortunately, it was also a very easy accusation to throw, not only at the Stones, but also at the handful of other British rock acts who, as the decade approached its cleavage, made similar moves away from their top pop heartland.

First off the mark was Robert Palmer, best known as vocalist with the Humble Pie-ish rock/R&B act Vinegar Joe. That band split in late 1973 and Palmer promptly decamped to New Orleans and hooked up with Allen Toussaint, Little Feat's Lowell George and the Meters to record *Sneaking Sally Through the Alley*, the quintessential "blue eyed soul" album and certainly the finest British funk excursion of the '70s.

Much of the material was recorded first take, according to Palmer, "A half hour after we sat down in the studio, [George's] 'Sailing Shoes' was cut." For the title track, "we played the demo twice, broke for lunch, ran through it again and that one was down." The spontaneity shows.

Within a year, Philadelphia-based duo Daryl Hall and John Oates would be taking Palmer's blueprint to heights of their own. Other ears, however, moved a little faster. Even as Palmer and company were wrapping up *Sally* at the Sea Saint Studios in New Orleans, David Bowie was passing through the south with his own latest American tour, his first since he retired his fame-making Ziggy Stardust persona in 1973, but one that, with its Broadway style sets and choreography, was no less ambitious than any he had played in the recent past.

Bowie, however, was tiring of the theatrics. His latest band had been handpicked, as Bowie himself put it, for its "funky" sound; at its core were Earl Slick, Michael Kamen and David Sanborn, members of the jazz fusion outfit the New York Rock Ensemble. Later, former Main Ingredient guitarist Carlos Alomar and backing vocalist Luther Vandross were added to the entourage. All had an incredible impact upon Bowie, joining him in rearranging songs (the glam rock anthem "All the Young Dudes," transformed into a gospel ballad; the riff-sodden "Jean Genie" slowed to quaalude camp vamp) and, as the tour progressed, so the musicians relaxed, bringing their own visions further to bear.

A former member of Dr. John's Brethren, pianist Mike Garson opened the show, leading the ensemble through a brief jazz set building up to Bowie's arrival on stage. The old Stax stomper "Knock on Wood" was introduced to the main set. But it was Alomar who made what would, in hindsight, be the greatest contribution, jamming such a great version of James Brown's "Footstompin'" music during rehearsals one day that Bowie promptly inserted the song into his live set.

Bowie was no stranger to funk; a version of the 1969 Marva Whitney-James Brown duet "You've Gotta Have a Job" regularly featured in his repertoire during 1970–71. Still it was a surprise when Bowie appeared on television's Dick Cavett's *Wide World of Entertainment* show in early December 1974, to lead the group through a genuinely foot-stomping version of the Brown number; and an even greater one when he and Alomar joined forces with Beatle John Lennon to record a new song around the same signature riff, "Fame."

Appended at the last minute to Bowie's forthcoming new album, the otherwise Philly ballad-inflected *Young Americans*, "Fame" pushed Bowie to #21 on the R&B chart and topped the pop listing during fall 1975, his first American success of any significance, and it was difficult for observers to say in which direction the crossover really flowed.

Even with its superstar nosejob, "Footstompin' Music" remained readily identifiable within "Fame"'s gritty framework, and it was apparent from the fate of subsequent Bowie releases that it was not a newly converted pop audience that pushed the record so high up the chart. It would be another eight years before Bowie again returned to such heights (with 1983's "Let's Dance," significantly his only other R&B chart entry), while a second Top Ten single in 1975, the ominous funk rumble of "Golden Years," climbed so high only after Bowie made an appearance on TV's *Soul Train*.

Neither was the funk of "Fame" a passing fancy. Rather, as "Golden Years" proved, it proved the musical launching pad for Bowie's own next album, the lushly miasmic electro-stomp of *Station To Station* (1976), an album worth checking out if only for the mutant groove of the title track and the epic, Alomar-powered "Stay."

Interestingly, Lennon would also be present for another, equally unexpected funk reinvention, hanging (if not actively working) with Elton John while the bespectacled glam pianist responded to Bowie's breakthrough first with the Gamble and Huff-inflected "Philadelphia Freedom" (1975), then, appropriately in the light of the well-publicized rivalry between Elton and Bowie, "Grow Some Funk of Your Own" (1976).

Neither was especially convincing, as their chart fates proved: "Philadelphia Freedom" reached #32 on the R&B charts, "Grow Some Funk" missed them altogether, and it is ironic that the closest Elton ever came to a truly instinctive funk workout was apparently as unintentional as this latest crop of songs was deliberate. The languorously lethal slow handclap vamp of 1973's "Bennie and the Jets" was a major R&B hit, and one whose success led Elton, in turn, to become the first White guest ever to play *Soul Train*. Compared with "Bennie," his new material simply wasn't in the same ballpark.

In any case, it was already too late for Elton, or anybody else for that matter, to pledge their troth to the funkwagon. The onset of disco created more than a new set of possibilities for the enterprising crossover artist, it created a new set of pitfalls as well and now, when rock artists were accused of "going disco," it was usually because they had.

The absurd spectacle of Wild Cherry notwithstanding, it would be another five years before funk resurfaced as a viable, thriving musical form in White rock circles, through the efforts of Britons Light of the World, the Gang of Four and the early Spandau Ballet. It would be even longer before their better established peers could return to the same battlegrounds themselves.

## RECOMMENDED LISTENING

**Jeff Beck: *Blow by Blow* (Epic, 1975)**
It all seems (and sounds) a little dated now, particularly when the vocoder comes in, but Beck's playing is electrifying and the band, which includes Stevie Wonder and Phil Chen, is magnificent, driving Beck through the jazz-funk masterpiece "Freeway Jam," a red-hot cover of the Beatles' "She's a Woman" and Wonder's vital "Cause We've Ended as Lovers."

**David Bowie: *Young Americans* (RCA 1975)**
Bowie's most emotional album, built around the breakdown of both his marriage and his management, but fired by a fascination for contemporary R&B. The singer himself called it "plastic soul," and it's true to a point. Some of the ballads are a little overblown, and Bowie occasionally lets ambition get in the way of his vocal capabilities. But the jerking "Fame," the slowed down "Right" and the ingenious title track are invested with considerably more dynamism than posterity lets on.

**Eric Burdon/War: *Eric Burdon Declares "War"* (MGM, 1970)**
It certainly has its faults (the unfulfilled meandering of "The Vision of Rassan"), but still funk's first full-blooded collaboration with English rock signposts an edgy fusion that was never truly tamed. The impulsive "Spill the Wine" serves up a capsule introduction to the album's full intentions; while the epics "Tobacco Road" and "Blues for Memphis Slim" slam stream-of-consciousness blues poetry into the already bubbling melting pot of War's own musical influences.

**Fancy: *Something To Remember* (RCA, 1975)**
Best remembered for a deeply sensual cover of "Wild Thing," Fancy regrouped around new vocalist Annie Kavanagh and built their sophomore album around an extended funk rock cover of Stevie Wonder's "I Was Born To Love Her." Other cuts struggle to match the same standard, but that one performance ensured that *Remember* remained unforgettable.

**Humble Pie: *Performance—Rockin' the Fillmore* (A&M, 1971)**
Pie's hard rock approximation of R&B never sounded better. The later (1973) *Eat It* was an earthier album, but *Performance* packs truly revelatory versions of "Rolling Stone" and "Gilded Splinters," each extended over a full side of vinyl, together with a crop of shorter, but no less shattered originals.

**Robert Palmer: *Sneaking Sally Through the Alley* (Island 1974)**
Side one is all but seamless, as "Sailing Shoes," "Hey Julia" and "Sally" itself segue together into one long, sinewy whole. Side two, meanwhile, is dominated by the smokey "Through It All There's You," close to 13 minutes of sighing bass and spectral piano flourishes, which only slowly, almost lackadaisically, pick up the tempo as the song builds toward its extended—and so archetypically Meters-esque-breakneck coda.

**The Rolling Stones: *Black and Blue* (Rolling Stones Records, 1976)**
That's Black, as in the music that the Stones always loved the most, and blues as in the music they made at the start. Put the two together and *Black and Blue* emerged an affirmation of everything they had done since they first stumbled out of suburbia, and the promise of a lot of what they would accomplish subsequently. Without "Hey Negrita" there might never have been a "Miss You"; without "Hand of Fate" they might never have created "Emotional Rescue." The notion that they had merely "gone disco" was too simpleminded for words.

**Snafu: *All Funked Up* (Capitol, 1975)**
Formed by former Procol Harum/Freedom drummer Bobby Harrison, Snafu cut three albums in an increasingly funk-flavored mode, with the third, *All Funked Up*, an occasionally heavy-handed, but always enthusiastic reaction to the

band's recent European tour with War—primal rhythms, driving grooves, and a spectacular cover of Stevie Wonder's "Keep On Running."

**Supercharge:** *Local Lads Make Good* (Virgin, 1976)

The problem with Supercharge was, nobody knew whether or not they were serious. Live, they alternated exhilarating, but defiantly cliched funk with unapologetically slapstick comedy routines, and their debut album followed suit. So, while "Get Down Boogie" has all the ingredients for a lost funk classic, and much of the album follows delirious suit, everything is rendered completely untrustworthy by "She Moved the Dishes First," a hilarious Drifters pastiche discussing the etiquette of urinating in the kitchen sink.

# PART THREE: DISCO FUNK

## AURRA

**FORMED:** 1979, *East Orange, NJ*

**ORIGINAL LINEUP:** *Starleana Young (b. 1961, White Sulphur Springs, WV—vcls, perc), Curt Jones (b. 1957, Linden, NJ—vcls, gtr, perc)*

Aurra first emerged as an offshoot of the ever-growing Slave family, formed around Curt Jones and Starleana Young, both then members of the Symphonic Express vocal group. The pair were initially recruited to Slave itself. Young performed backing vocals on 1978's *The Concept* album; Jones debuted on the following year's *A Touch of Love.*

At the same time, Young also launched a solo career, cutting the "Heartbreaker" single with her brothers William and Mike. They, too, were drawn into the burgeoning Aurra concept, albeit only briefly. By the time Slave overseer Steve Washington was ready to send his baby into the studio, the brothers had quit to form their own group, Young & Company.

*Aurra* was released through Salsoul's short-lived Dream subsidiary in 1980. A single, "In the Mood To Groove," made minor inroads into the R&B chart, but their label's low profile rubbed off on Aurra; for their next album, the group was transferred to the Salsoul parent, with immediate results.

The shifting nature of Aurra ensured that *Send Your Love* was recorded with a very different lineup than its predecessor; indeed, Young and Jones were the only constants in the group's story. Bassist Buddy Hankerson quit to join Young & Company. Other musicians involved on *Aurra* returned to Slave, only to be "replaced" by other members of that band. Washington himself contributed guitar, bass, trumpet, drums and percussion; Slave co-founder and saxophonist Thomas Lockett also contributed. There was an appearance, too, from Jennifer Ivory, Slave's business coordinator and also a strong songwriter. She co-wrote six of *Send Your Love*'s eight tracks, including the Top 20 hit "Are You Single."

Aurra's third album was previewed with another hit, the band's biggest, December 1981's "Make Up Your Mind"; in the new year, *A Little Love* breached the pop Top 40. However, Aurra never returned to such peaks. Their next set, *Live and Let Live* was a major disappointment, spawning nothing more than a pair of low-charting singles, while financial disagreements between Washington and the Young/Jones axis began flaring. A breakup was inevitable.

In 1983, Washington launched a new Aurra with his ex-wife, former Brides of Funkenstein vocalist Sheila Horne, Mark Stevens (brother of Chaka Khan and Taka Boom), and regular Aurra live guitarist AC Drummer. *Satisfaction* was scheduled for release through Quincy Jones' Qwest label; it was cancelled following legal intervention from Young and Jones, themselves still working as Aurra.

Signing with Virgin, the duo enjoyed hits in the UK with "Like I Like It," and in the US with "You and Me Tonight." Legal action from Washington then prompted them to change their name to Deja for the remainder of their career. Following the *Serious* album (produced by The Time's Monty Moir) in 1987, Young quit for a solo career. (She also worked with Kool & the Gang vocalist James Taylor, soon to become her husband.) Jones replaced her with Mysti Day for one final album, 1989's *Going Crazy*. He subsequently launched his own solo career as Trilogy.

### AURRA DISCOGRAPHY
### CHARTLOG
### AURRA

1980 In the Mood (To Groove)/You're the Only One (Dream—#86 R&B)
1981 Are You Single/Living Too Fast (Salsoul—#16 R&B)
1981 Make Up Your Mind/(instrumental) (Salsoul—#6 R&B/#71 pop)
1982 A Little Love/In My Arms (Salsoul—#36 R&B)
1982 Checking You Out/It's You (Salsoul—#64 R&B)
1982 Such a Feeling/One More Time (Salsoul—#40 R&B)
1983 Baby Love/Positive (Salsoul—#78 R&B)

### DEJA

1987 You and Me Tonight/Premonition (Virgin—#2 R&B/#54 pop)
1988 That's Where You'll Find Me/Life (Virgin—#17 R&B)
1989 Made To Be Together/Sexy Dancer (Virgin—#23 R&B)
1989 Going Crazy/Waiting Downtown (Virgin—#57 R&B)

### LPS
### AURRA

**7** 1981 Send Your Love (Salsoul—#22 R&B/#103 pop)

A lighter version of Slave, hard on the electro-disco rhythms but with sufficient funk punch to satisfy fans of the mother ship.

**7** 1982 A Little Love (Salsoul—#12 R&B/#38 pop)

**8** 1983 Live and Let Live (Salsoul—#36 R&B/#208 pop)

Aurra's finest hour, blending savvy electro-funk know-how with some tight balladeering.

**6** 1985 Like I Like It (Virgin)

*DEJA*
**5** 1987 Serious (Virgin—#27 R&B)
**3** 1989 Made To Be Together (Virgin—#96 R&B)

*STARLEANA YOUNG SOLO*
**5** 1991 Starleana Young (Virgin)

## ROY AYERS

**BORN:** *9/10/40, Los Angeles, CA*

A jazz vibraphonist who decided, very early on, that no single musical genre could hold him for long, Roy Ayers' current status as the Godfather of Acid Jazz owes little to any conscious effort on his part, and much to his unending restlessness. To paraphrase a lyric from his own "What You Won't Do for Love," from 1979's funk classic *No Stranger To Love* album, he's tried everything, but he won't give up.

Ayers' first instrument was piano. Encouraged by his mother, herself a music teacher, he wrote his first songs at age five, hammering out rudimentary boogie woogie. The following year, his parents took him to see Lionel Hampton, master of the vibraphone. Hampton gave the boy his first pair of mallets and, though it was another decade before Ayers turned his attention to that instrument, around 1957, that meeting remained a crucial moment in his musical development.

In 1961, aged 21, Ayers moved onto the Los Angeles jazz scene, gigging with Teddy Edwards, Chico Hamilton and pianist Jack Wilson. It was the latter who gave Ayers his first taste of studio work, recruiting him to play vibes on the *Brazilian Mancini* album in 1962. A year later, Wilson repaid the favor, appearing on Ayers' own first album, *West Coast Vibes*, alongside Curtis Amy (sax), Bill Plummer (bs) and Tony Bazley (drms). Ayers also recorded with the Gerald Wilson Orchestra during this period, establishing himself as one of the most in-demand vibes players on the West Coast.

In 1966, bassist Reggie Workman introduced Ayers to Herbie Mann at a show at the Lighthouse in Hermosa Beach. Ayers joined Mann's band, remaining on board for the next four years and appearing on Mann's two greatest albums, *Memphis Underground* and *Live at the Whisky A Go-Go*. The exposure also landed him a solo deal with Mann's label, Atlantic, and during 1967–68, Mann produced three Ayers solo albums, *Virgo Vibes*, *Daddy Bug and Friends* and *Stoned Soul Picnic*.

Ayers left Mann's band in 1969 and cut the *Daddy's Back* album, with guests Herbie Hancock, Ron Carter and Freddy Waites. The following year, he signed with Polydor

for *He's Coming* before launching his own group, Ubiquity, from his new base in Manhattan.

Ubiquity became the vehicle that launched Ayers as an international star in his own right, a wildly eclectic combo whose musical tastes ranged both the jazz and pop spectrums, but imbibed everything with a funk base clearly influenced by Donald Byrd's recent crossover recordings. Ayers' soundtrack for the 1973 Pam Grier movie, *Coffy*, was as masterful as the movie itself, but Ubiquity's upward trajectory reached its climax in 1975 with the release of *Mystic Voyage*. With vocals by Edwin Birdsong and Chicos, the album spawned a minor hit title-track single, but also crashed the R&B Top 20 in its own right.

Led off by its pop smash title track in 1976, *Everybody Loves the Sunshine* introduced pianist Phillip Woo to the ever-changing Ubiquity roster and climbed to #10. (A fresh version of the title track appeared on the Ayers-produced *Come into My Knowledge* album by Ramp.)

With the outrage of his old jazz purist supporters ringing in his ears, Ayers swiftly followed through with the defiantly pop-funk flavored *Vibrations* (January 1977) and *Lifeline* (June 1977). "Running Away," from the latter, became Ayers' first Top 20 hit that fall, after which he abandoned the Ubiquity identity for a full solo career. The infectious "Freaky Deaky" debuted him in this new guise and, while it was undeniable that Ayers' move into funk territory was a stunning loss to the jazz community, it was unquestionably a gain for R&B. (This fact was exacerbated by the launch of Ayers' own Uno Melodic label, for which he produced classic soul sides by Ethel Beatty, Sylvia Striplin, '80s Ladies and more.)

Recorded with an ever-changing array of sidemen, including Woo, drummers Bernard Purdie and Gene Dunlap, bassists Kerry Turman and William Allen and guitarist Chuck Anthony, both *You Send Me* (1978) and *No Stranger to Love* (1979) were masterful sets. The latter boiling the entire dance scene down to six separate, but intriguingly inter-connected tracks, effortlessly absorbing disco gloss into the dirty funk grooves, then breaking for vibraphone solos, which became one of the signature sounds of 1979.

Accusations that Ayers had sold out continued to fly out of the jazz world, although a union with former Crusaders trombonist Wayne Henderson paid both critical and commercial dividends. Similarly, Ayers' next project, linking with Nigerian Afro-beat pioneer Fela Ransome Kuti, did much to still the dissent; 1980's *Music of Many Colors* was a revelatory collision, forging a mood that Ayers alone continued on 1981's *Africa Is the Center of the World*.

**The master of the vibraphone, Roy Ayers.**

As Ayers' direction changed during the early '80s, so the hits began to slow down. He remained a major live attraction in Europe and Japan, however, a figurehead of the slowly burgeoning acid jazz movement and, gradually, the American underground, too. Further rebirth was ignited by A Tribe Called Quest's use of a sample from Ayers' "Daylight" and, in 1993, Ayers linked with ex-Gang Starr rapper Guru for the *Jazzmatazz Volume One* album. Subsequent projects have maintained a low profile, although Ayers did guest on Eric Benet's 2000 hit "When You Think of Me."

### ROY AYERS DISCOGRAPHY
### CHARTLOG
### ROY AYERS UBIQUITY

1976 Mystic Voyage/Evolution (Polydor—#70 R&B)
1976 The Golden Rod/Tongue Power (Polydor—#70 R&B)
1977 Running Away/Cincinatti Growl (Polydor—#19 R&B)

### ROY AYERS

1978 Freaky Deaky/You Came into My Life (Polydor—#29 R&B)
1978 Get On Up, Get On Down/And Don't You Say No (Polydor—#56 R&B)
1979 Love Will Bring Us Back Together/Leo (Polydor—#41 R&B)

1979 Don't Stop the Feeling/Don't Hide Your Love (Polydor—#32 R&B)
1980 What You Won't Do for Love/Shack Up Pack Up (Polydor—#73 R&B)
1984 In the Dark/Love Is in the Feel (Polydor—#35 R&B)
1985 Poo Poo La La/Sexy Sexy Sexy (Columbia—#89 R&B)
1985 Slip 'n' Slide/Can I See You (Columbia—#49 R&B)
1986 Hot/Virgo (Columbia—#20 R&B)
1986 Programmed for Love/For You (Columbia—#62 R&B)

### ROY AYERS/WAYNE HENDERSON

1978 Heat of the Beat/No Deposit No Return (Polydor—#59 R&B)

### SELECTED LPS
### ROY AYERS UBIQUITY

6 1971 Ubiquity (Polydor)
6 1973 Virgo Red (Polydor)

Widely regarded as Ayers' most transitional release, straight jazz looking toward righteous R&B, without making a commitment to either.

7 1974 Change Up the Groove (Polydor)
9 1975 A Tear to a Smile (Polydor)

One of the albums upon which Ayers' funk fusion reputation is based, a masterpiece through "2000 Black," "Magic Lady," "Ebony Blaze" and a genius on the title cut.

**7** **1975 Mystic Voyage (Polydor—#13 R&B/#90 pop)**
The funk's at a premium ("Brother Green," "Spirit of Doo Doo," "Funky Motion" of course), but the mellowness has its moments.

**7** **1976 Everybody Loves the Sunshine (Polydor—#10 R&B/#51 pop)**
The monster title track lures you in, but the real meat lays in sun-drenched jazzy grooves like "The Golden Rod," "Third Eye" and the marvelous "Keep On Walking."

**6** **1976 Vibrations (Polydor—#11 R&B/#74 pop)**

**7** **1977 Lifeline (Polydor—#9 R&B/#72 pop)**
The stellar space groove title track throws killer electronics at you, although there's maybe one too many soft soul fillers.

### ROY AYERS: THE FUNK YEARS

**7** **1971 He's Coming (Polydor)**
With Billy Cobham and Sonny Fortune among the abetters, a righteous swamp of jazz, soul and funk, aggressively dissimilar to Ayers' later, lighter material, but no disappointment.

**8** **1973 Coffy [soundtrack] (Polydor)**
Jazzy vibes and cool funk collide on a smooth slab of dramatic understatement. Predominantly instrumental, but cuts like "Making Love," "Brawling Broads" and "King George" don't need words.

**7** **1977 Crystal Reflections (Muse)**

**6** **1978 Let's Do It (Polydor—#15 R&B/#33 pop)**

**7** **1978 You Send Me (Polydor—#16 R&B/#48 pop)**
Dripping summertime vibes in every sense of the word; Carla Vaughn sings like a nightingale on the title cut. "Can't You See Me?" and "Get On Up, Get On Down" up the tempo further, and the bass-popping "Rhythm" rides a beat you won't believe. The wacky "It Ain't Your Sign" is an absolute standout.

**7** **1979 Fever (Polydor—#25 R&B/#67 pop)**

**8** **1980 No Stranger to Love (Polydor—#22 R&B/#82 pop)**
Ayers' finest disco-funk album. Six tracks drawn out to gargantuan proportions, all solid righteous rhythm, handclaps and synthesizer flourishes. Mondee Oliver's irresistible scat on the mighty "Don't Stop the Feeling" leaves you begging for more.

**6** **1980 Love Fantasy (Polydor—#47 R&B/#157 pop)**

**7** **1981 Africa, Center of the World (Polydor—#43 R&B/#197 pop)**

**5** **1981 Feelin' Good (Polydor—#45 R&B/#160 pop)**

### ROY AYERS/FELA ANIKULAPO-KUTI AND THE AFRICA 70

**5** **1980 Music of Many Colours (Phonodisk—Nigeria)**

### ROY AYERS: OTHER RECORDINGS

(The following discography is included for reference only. Individual albums have not been graded or reviewed.)
1963 West Coast Vibes (United Artists)
1967 Virgo Vibes (Atlantic)
1967 Daddy Bug & Friends (Atlantic)
1968 Stoned Soul Picnic (Atlantic)
1969 Daddy's Back (Atco)
1972 Live at the Montreux Jazz Festival (Verve)
1983 Drivin' On Up (Uno Melodic)
1983 Silver Vibrations (Uno Melodic)
1984 In the Dark (Columbia—#50 R&B/#201 pop)
1985 You Might Be Surprised (Columbia—#31 R&B)
1987 I'm the One (For Your Love Tonight) (Columbia)
1988 Drive (Ichiban—#60 R&B)
1989 Wake Up (Ichiban—#60 R&B)
1991 Searchin' (Ronnie Scott's)
1992 Double Trouble (Uno Melodic)
1995 Good Vibrations (Ronnie Scott's)
1995 Naste (RCA—#71 R&B)
1996 Essential Groove Live (Ronnie Scott's)

### ROY AYERS/WAYNE HENDERSON

1978 Step into Our Life (Polydor—#45 R&B)
1980 Prime Time (Polydor—#62 R&B/#205 pop)

### SELECTED COMPILATIONS AND ARCHIVE RELEASES

1995 Evolution: The Polydor Anthology (Polydor Chronicles)
1995 Vibesman Live at Ronnie Scott's (Music Club)
2000 The Uno Melodic Story (Charly)

### SELECTED SAMPLES

Come into My Knowledge — Mad Skillz: Doin' Time in the Cypha (1996)
Daylight — A Tribe Called Quest: Bonita Applebaum (1990)
Everybody Loves the Sunshine — PM Dawn: So On and So On (1993)

## TAKA BOOM

**BORN:** *Yvonne Stevens, 10/8/54, Chicago, IL*

Sister of Chaka Khan and Aurra guitarist Mark Stevens, Boom formed her first band, the Crystalettes, with Chaka while both were still in high school. Covering the top soul hits of the day, the girls' first shows were for their mother's friends before they graduated to local talent shows.

As the Crystalettes dissolved, the pair joined the harder edged, politically focussed Shades of Black in the late '60s; both adopted their better-known names at that time. Shades of Black disbanded in 1971 and Boom briefly hooked up with another Top 40 band, Sweet Fire. By 1972, however, she had relocated to Los Angeles where she married tenor saxophonist John "Boom" Brumbach, a session musician whose career includes stints with Rufus, Dennis Coffey, Sly Stone, The Gap Band and the P-Funk axis.

It was through Brumbach that Boom, too, moved into session work. She recorded with Carl Carlton in 1974, and in 1976 contributed to Parliament's *The Mothership Connection* and *Clones of Dr. Funkenstein* albums. That same year also saw her drafted into Norman Whitfield's The Undisputed Truth, winning out over future Rose Royce star Gwen Dickey at the auditions. However, her stay was limited to just one album, 1977's *Method to the Madness*, before she quit, complaining about producer Whitfield's control over the band. She reunited with Whitfield and Undisputed Truth vocalist Joe Harris in 1980 for the producer's Dream Machine project.

Boom's next stop was producer Jim Callon's disco project, the Glass Family, cutting an independent EP and a charting single, "Mr. DJ You Know How To Make Me Dance," in 1978 before the band folded and Boom moved on. In late 1978, she signed a solo deal with Ariola, retreating to the studio with Brumbach to record her eponymous debut. Released in the spring 1979, the album cracked the Top 50 in the R&B charts and spawned two singles, "Night Dancin'" and "Red Hot."

Moving to New York in the early '80s, Boom next linked with the Prelude label for a string of singles, including 1982's "Love Party" and the Bob Esty produced "To Hell with Him" the following year. Both were subsequently included on the *Boomerang* album in 1984, before Boom and Prelude parted company later that year.

Linking with Billy Rush (ex-Bruce Springsteen), Boom's next album, 1985's *Middle of the Night*, spawned the hit single title track, but still she remained very much a minor player on the R&B scene, forever overshadowed by sister Chaka. Back in Los Angeles, she guested on Bootsy Collins' *What's Bootsy Doin'?* album in 1988; but by 1991, based now in Phoenix, she had all but turned her back on R&B and was concentrating instead on blues. She next moved to London, where she joined the blues group The Blues of Cain—Boom also appeared on the UK dance charts in 1997 with the solo "Surrender" single. She also worked with UK hipsters Sha-Boom and Joey Negro and DJ Disciple.

## TAKA BOOM DISCOGRAPHY
### CHARTLOG
### GLASS FAMILY
1978 Mr. DJ, You Know How To Make Me Dance/No One Can Find Love (JDC—#88 R&B)

### TAKA BOOM
1979 Night Dancin'/Cloud Dancer (Ariola—#20 R&B/#74 pop)
1979 Red Hot/Troubled Water (Ariola—#70 R&B)
1985 Middle of the Night/LP version (Mirage—#63 R&B)

### LPS
**8** 1979 Taka Boom (Ariola—#48 R&B/#171 pop)
Boom demonstrates her range, moving from the ultra funk of "Dance like You Do at Home," to the pure disco driven "Red Hot."
**6** 1984 Boomerang (Ariola)
A less than stellar set includes the pre-*Boomerang* indie singles "To Hell with Him" and "Love Party."

### WITH BILLY RUSH
**6** 1985 Middle of the Night (Mirage)
Pure pop exemplified by the title track.

## BRASS CONSTRUCTION
FORMED: *1968, Brooklyn, NY*
ORIGINAL LINEUP: *Randy Muller (b. Guyana—vcls, kybds, perc, flute), Joseph Arthur Wong (b. Trinidad—gtr), Wade Williamston (bs), Morris Price (trum, perc, vcls), Wayne Parris (b. Jamaica—trum, vcls), Jesse Ward (sax, vcls), Michael Grudge (b. Jamaica—sax, vcls), Sandy Billups (cngs, vcls), Larry Payton (drms)*

Randy Muller was born and raised in British Guyana, playing in a string of juvenile steel bands before the family relocated to New York in 1963. He formed his first serious outfit, Dynamic Soul, with a group of fellow George Gershwin Junior High students, seemingly picked as much for their own cosmopolitan backgrounds as for their musical abilities. The presence of Jamaicans Wayne Parris and Michael Grudge, and Trinidad-born Joseph Arthur Wong ensured that Dynamic Soul absorbed Muller's own formative influences as avidly as the R&B of the day.

Dynamic Soul became Brass Construction in 1973, by which time their effortless blending of African, American and Caribbean sounds had developed into a truly potent hybrid, a throbbing big band sound that was to help define the dancefloors of the last half of the American '70s. Recruited as houseband at producer Jeff Lane's management and production company, Dock, the Brass Construction became an ever-present factor on Dock releases, with Muller scoring his first successes as producer and arranger of the B.T. Express. Muller became a virtual member of that band, while he also played with a third outfit, the Panharmonics, alongside singer Rafael Cameron.

**Brass Construction: Randy Muller, Joe Wong, Wayne Parris, Morris Price, Jesse Ward, Mickey Grudge, Sandy Billups, Wade Williamston, Larry Payton.**

Brass Construction landed their own record deal in 1975, signed by UA as cohorts—and, ultimately, as successors to the label's other major funk signing, War. They swiftly proved that the label's faith in Muller's abilities was not misplaced.

Adding the vocal punch of the sisters Bonnie, Delores and Denise Dunning, FDR High students who Muller discovered performing at a Miss Black America pageant, Brass Construction's debut single, the monstrous, synth-powered instrumental "Movin'," topped the R&B chart and made the pop Top 20 in early 1976, having already proven a smash hit in Europe.

The *Brass Construction* album, too, was a massive success. However, a follow-up single cut in suspiciously similar style to the hit, "Changin'," was a comparative miss and, while Brass Construction returned to the R&B Top Ten with "Ha Cha Cha (Funktion)" in spring 1977, neither it nor its parent album, *Brass Construction II*, ever seemed

likely to eclipse the majesty of the band's debut, commercially or musically.

Indeed, it swiftly transpired that the savage funk assault of *Brass Construction I*, like that of the early B.T. Express, was simply the storm before the increasing calm of Muller's interest in disco. Brass Construction lumbered toward decade's end with a succession of increasingly sickly sweet dance songs, dignified only by the band's still pumping brass section and their continued fascination with rhythm.

*Brass Construction III* in 1977 spun off the mildly memorable "LOVE-U" and "Celebrate," but Muller's own greatest success came when he teamed with jazzman Charles Earland for "Let the Music Play," a trans-Atlantic hit in 1978.

By the early '80s, when the group switched from UA's Liberty successor to Capitol Records, Brass Construction were all but unrecognizable. In the liner notes to Brass Construction's *Movin' and Changin'* compilation, Muller himself admitted, "We were pretty tired. Brass started out with some songs and a concept and some fresh ideas. And we spent our whole lives getting them together. Next thing you know, we were a success. We had fancy arrangers flown into our sessions, we used the fanciest studios and hired the fanciest musicians. Eventually the music got watered down. And a little stale."

Heading up his own Alligator Bit Him production company, Muller himself was now heavily involved in the disco-funk sounds of Rafael Cameron, Tamiko Jones and Skyy. The latter's "Call Me" proved as memorable a hit as any recent Brass Construction release, and the band seemed destined for further success after Muller transplanted the Dunning sisters into its ranks.

*Conversations*, Brass Construction's first album for Capitol, proved to be the band's final US chart hit. Two further sets, *Renegades* and *Conquest*, passed by unnoticed (despite the return, for the latter, of the Dunning sisters, plus fellow Skyy alumni Solomon Roberts and Anibal Sierra) and, by the mid-'80s, Brass Construction had slipped out of view in their homeland.

Europe, however, remained loyal. "Give and Take" came close to the British Top 60 in 1985 and, as the acid house movement kicked in toward the end of the decade, Brass Construction found themselves touching a whole new audience via a string of sometimes superlative remixes. A powerful "Acieed Mix" of "Ha Cha Cha" nudged the UK chart in 1987, followed by a Top 30 berth for "Movin' '88."

### BRASS CONSTRUCTION CHARTLOG

1976 Movin'/Talkin' (UA—#1 R&B/#14 pop)
1976 Changin'/Love (UA—#24 R&B)
1977 Ha Cha Cha (Funktion)/Sambo (Conditions) (UA—#8 R&B/#51 pop)
1977 The Message (Inspiration)/What's on Your Mind (UA—#42 R&B)
1977 What's on Your Mind/The Message (Inspiration) (UA—#69 R&B)
1978 LOVE-U/Get It Together (UA—#18 R&B/#104 pop)
1978 Celebrate/Top of the World (UA—#77 R&B)
1978 Help Yourself/Pick Yourself Up (UA—#58 R&B)
1978 Get Up/Perceptions (What's the Right Direction) (UA—#56 R&B)
1980 Right Place/It's Alright (UA—#41 R&B)
1980 How Do You Do (What You Do to Me)/Don't Try To Change Me (Liberty—#71 R&B)
1982 Can You See the Light/E.T.C. (Liberty—#23 R&B)
1982 Attitude/Hotdog (Liberty—#59 R&B)
1983 Walkin' the Line/Forever Love (Capitol—#28 R&B)
1984 Never Had a Girl/Breakdown (Capitol—#38 R&B)
1984 Partyline/We Can Bring It Back (Capitol—#53 R&B)
1985 Give and Take/My Place (Capitol—#76 R&B)

### LPS

**9** 1976 Brass Construction (UA—#1 R&B/#10 pop)
Make no bones about it, this is all the Brass anyone needs, the gargantuan eight-plus minutes "Movin'" is a funk juggernaut plowing down everything in its path, "Changin'" doesn't change a thing, and if the laid-back "Love" suggests the band had other grooves on their mind, those things weren't so bad either.

**6** 1976 Brass Construction 2 (UA—#3 R&B/#26 pop)
"Ha Cha Cha" is a delirious funk chant, straight out of the "Movin'" manual of soundalike stompers, but elsewhere, *II* sags like the morning after a really great party, which, in a way, it was.

**5** 1977 Brass Construction 3 (UA—#16 R&B/#66 pop)
Some snarling guitar and percussion on "LOVE-U" raises hopes high, but the song . . . indeed, the entire album, doesn't really go anywhere from there.

**3** 1978 Brass Construction 4 (UA—#24 R&B/#174 pop)
**4** 1979 Brass Construction 5 (UA—#18 R&B/#89 pop)
"Get Up To Get Down" reflects on early BC triumphs and conjures up a bass to boil your head with. There's also some adventurous electronics flickering across the stage, but once again, one killer song doesn't make a worthwhile album.

**3** 1980 Brass Construction 6 (UA—#32 R&B/#121 pop)
**3** 1982 Attitudes (Liberty—#21 R&B/#114 pop)
**4** 1983 Conversations (Capitol—#29 R&B/#176 pop)
**3** 1984 Renegades (Capitol—#31 R&B)
**3** 1985 Conquest (Capitol)

### SELECTED COMPILATIONS AND ARCHIVE RELEASES

**7** 1993 The Best of Brass Construction: Movin' & Changin' (EMI)
**7** 1997 Get Up To Get Down: Brass Construction's Funky Feeling (Capitol)
Two collections trace the band's development, although unless you really need those latter-day hits, a copy of their debut album has all the essential bits and more.

**7** 1998 Live (Collectibles)
Powerful 1977 recording offers little deviation from the studio versions, but how much more punch do you really need?

### SELECTED SAMPLES

Changin'— MC Lyte: When in Love (1991)
Changin' — Schoolly D: Black Jesus (1991)
Get Up To Get Down — Ahmad: Touch the Ceiling (1994)
Get Up To Get Down — Rufus Blaq, featuring Spinderella: Don't Worry (My Shorty) (1998)
Movin' — DJ Quik: Niggaz Still Trippin' (1992)
Movin' — DJ Quik: Quik Is the Name (1991)

Movin' — Bucketheads: Got Myself Together (1995)

The Message (Inspiration) — NWA: I Ain't Tha 1 (1988)

What's on Your Mind (Expression) — Biz Markie: Cool V's Tribute to Scratching (1988)

What's on Your Mind (Expression) — Lord Finesse: Baby, You Nasty (single mix) (1990)

## BRICK

**FORMED:** *1972, Atlanta, GA*

**ORIGINAL LINEUP:** *Jimmy Brown (vcls, sax), Reggie Hargis (gtr), Ray Ransom (pno), Donald Nevins (sax), Eddie Irons (drms)*

Brick's infectious jazz-funk grooves spent close to four years on the Atlanta club circuit before the band cut their first single, "Music Matic," for the tiny Main Street label in late 1975. Though only a minor R&B hit, it nevertheless brought the band to the attention of the Bang label, who signed Brick the following year and unleashed what became one of the biggest funk successes of the year, the maddeningly memorable "Dazz."

Topping the chart for a solid month, within two years the song's title, a contraction of the band's chosen hybrid of "danceable disco-jazz," had been borrowed by another band, the Dazz Band, and lent itself to another hit. Brick's second monster, "Dusic," applied a similar trick to "disco music," as the band itself abandoned their original form in favor of an increasingly disco-fied approach—first as they consolidated their success and then, through the early '80s, as they tried to recapture it.

1980's *Waiting on You* was a powerful release regardless, while a union with Raydio vocalist/producer Ray Parker, Jr. for 1981's *Summer Heat* album, brought Brick both a return to early form and a final hit, the frantic "Sweat (Til You Get Wet)." The band faded away soon after.

### BRICK

### CHARTLOG

1975 Music Matic/Good High (Main Street—#82 R&B)

1976 Dazz/Southern Sunset (Bang—#1 R&B/#3 pop)

1977 What It's All About/Can't Wait (Bang—#8 R&B)

1977 Dusic/Happy (Bang—#2 R&B/#18 pop)

1977 Ain't Gonna' Hurt Nobody/Honey Chile (Bang—#7 R&B/#92 pop)

1979 Raise Your Hands/Life Is What You Make It (Bang—#34 R&B)

1979 Dancin' Man/We'll Love (Bang—#47 R&B)

1980 All The Way/Spread Love (Bang—#38 R&B/#106 pop)

1980 Push Push/All the Way (Bang—#21 R&B)

1981 Sweat (Til You Get Wet)/Seaside Vibes (Bang—#10 R&B)

1981 Wide Open/Seaside Vibes (Bang—#58 R&B)

1982 Free Dancer/Stick by You (Bang—#62 R&B)

### LPS

**8** 1976 Good High (Bang—#1 R&B/#19 pop)

Heavy on the jazz stylings, the album as a whole is most memorable for "Dazz," although the lengthy "Sister Twister" stands as an epic achievement.

**8** 1977 Brick (Bang—#1 R&B/#15 pop)

A chunky guitar keeps the opening "Ain't Gonna Hurt Nobody" funky fresh, an impression that the first half of the album readily maintains. The mood shifts with "Dusic"—the "fonky fonky fonky" refrain offering a cute counterpoint to the somewhat worrying flute solo, before Brick drift into a defiant ballad mode that, by the time you reach "Fun," owes as much to Jamaican lovers rock as anything else.

**5** 1979 Stoneheart (Bang—#25 R&B/#100 pop)

**3** 1980 Waiting on You (Bang—#31 R&B/#179 pop)

The slow burning "Push Push" had already proven Brick's most successful (and enjoyable) single in three years; unfortunately, nothing else even pretends to rise above the Chic-shaped hole Brick have fallen into . . . and that's Chic if they weren't very good.

**3** 1981 Summer Heat (Bang—#13 R&B/#89 pop)

### SELECTED COMPILATIONS AND ARCHIVE RELEASES

**7** 1995 The Best of Brick (Sony Legacy)

Straightforward summary of the hits, with the attendant highs and lows.

### SELECTED SAMPLES

Dazz — Compton's Most Wanted: Compton 4 Life (1992)

Dazz — Dana Dane: Cinderfella Dana Dane (1987)

Dazz — Das EFX: Rap Scholar (1998)

Dazz — DJ Quik: Dollaz + Sense (1995)

Dazz — Ice Cube: No Vaseline (1991)

Dazz — MC Lyte: Search 4 the Lyte (1991)

Dazz — The Real Roxanne: Howie's Teed Off (1988)

Dazz — Snoop Doggy Dogg: Snoopafella (1999)

Dusic — M.C. Hammer: It's All Good (1994)

Dusic — Hi-C: Leave My Curl Alone (1992)

Fun — Akinyele: Put It in Your Mouth (1996)

Living from the Mind — Tung Twista: Ratatattat (1991)

Living from the Mind — Yaggfu Front: Lookin' for a Contract (1993)

## THE BRIDES OF FUNKENSTEIN

**FORMED:** *Detroit, 1977*

**ORIGINAL LINEUP:** *Lynn Mabry (vcls), Dawn Silva (b. Sacramento, CA—vcls)*

Dawn Silva and Lynn Mabry had been a part of the P-Funk setup for over a year when George Clinton first paired them as the Brides, although their own partnership dated back even further. Mabry was Sly Stone's cousin; Silva was "discovered" by Family Stone mainstay Cynthia Robinson, while rehearsing in her parents' garage with a high school band called Windsong. The group, led by Silva and her sister, concentrated on Top 40 material and Robinson's intitial approach fell on deaf ears. It was another year before Silva finally accepted Robinson's offer. She made her debut on Stone's *High on You* album in 1975.

They encountered Clinton when the Family Stone appeared as special guests during P-Funk's November 1976 US tour. Stone eventually dropped out of the tour, but Clinton asked Mabry and Silva to join the sessions for The Horny Horns' "Get Up on the Down Strolls" single, followed by guitarist Eddie Hazel's then in-progress solo album, *Games, Dames and Guitar Thangs*. From there, they moved onto Funkadelic's own *Funkentelechy vs. the Placebo Syndrome*. Thereafter, the electrifying tones of Silva and Mabry remained an integral part of the P-Funk family.

According to Silva, Clinton told them that he was forming them into their own band, the Brides of Funkenstein, precisely seven days before he signed the group to Atlantic Records. His precise words, she recalled, were, "you're gonna have your own group whether you like it or not." Indeed, work on the Brides' debut album had already commenced, Clinton culling material from both P-Funk and Bootsy Collins' stockpile of unreleased tapes, then having Silva and Mabry sing over the backing tracks.

Such origins were no reflection, of course, on the quality of either the album or the project itself. The Brides proved a sensation when they toured as one of the opening acts on P-Funk's 1978 US outing. (Their November 1st and 2nd shows at the Howard Theater in DC were recorded for a deeply posthumous live album.) Silva and Mabry were joined onstage by the Bridesmaids, Jeanette McGruder, Sheila Horne (wife of Slave frontman Steve Washington) and Babs Stewart. Their backing musicians included DeWayne "Blackbyrd" McKnight (gtr), Jeff Bunn (bs), Joel Johnson (kybds), Frank Waddy (drms) and a brass section comprising Horny Horns mainstays Maceo Parker, Richard Griffith and Fred Wesley.

Further tours of the US, Europe and Japan followed before Mabry quit; she went on to join fellow P-Funk-er Bernie Worrell on the Talking Heads' *Stop Making Sense* album. Mabry has since toured with George Michael and recorded with After 7, Bobby Lyle and Elton John. Horne and McGruder were promptly promoted to full Bride status in her stead, and work began on the band's second album, *Never Buy Texas from a Cowboy*.

With Clinton delegating at least some of the leg work to recent P-Funk recruit Ron Dunbar (co-writer of both the 15 minute title track and the closing "Didn't Mean To Fall in Love"), *Texas* was less reliant on existing material than its predecessor, but emerged just as rivetting. (Outtakes from both Brides albums appeared within the *George Clinton Family Series* albums.)

However, as the P-Funk empire crumbled, so did the Brides. With Ron Ford, Ron Dunbar and Clinton all at the controls, sessions for a third album (to be titled *The Shadow on the Wall Shaped like the Hat Wore*) were launched but aborted during 1980. Material scheduled for this set subsequently appeared both within the *Family Series* of compilations and, heavily reworked, on Clinton's own *Cinderella Theory* album.

The group did live on long enough to tour Japan in 1981, their funk instincts now almost wholly subverted by a new wave faddishness. Silva had recently discovered the music of Lene Lovich, incorporating her "Lucky Number" into the live set and adding other elements of Lovich's sound to the package. (Plans for the two acts to tour together sadly failed to materialize.) Well-received gigs with the Talking Heads, Grace Jones and Was Not Was greeted this transformation, but still the band broke up later that same year.

Horne subsequently joined her now ex-husband Washington's Aurra side project; Silva joined the Gap Band's live revue, and appeared on 1983's *Jammin'* album. She has since worked with Roy Ayers, Cristal Waters, the Eurythmics, Ice Cube and Coolio.

Silva also recorded a solo album for Polygram during the late 1980s; it was cancelled shortly before release, but she resurfaced in 2000 with a new set, *All My Funky Friends*.

### THE BRIDES OF FUNKENSTEIN COMPLETE DISCOGRAPHY
#### SINGLES/CHARTLOG
1978 Amorous/War Ship Touchante (Atlantic—#76 R&B)

1978 Disco To Go/When You're Gone (Atlantic—#7 R&B/#101 pop)

1979 Mother May I/Didn't Mean To Fall in Love (Atlantic)

1979 Never Buy Texas from a Cowboy (part one)/(part two) (Atlantic—#67 R&B)

#### LPS
**8** 1978 Funk or Walk (Atlantic)

From the opening "Disco To Go" (at one point, the projected title track for Bootsy Collins' second album) on in, *Funk or Walk* was to prove one of the most enjoyable of all period P-Funk spin-offs, powered by the Brides' genuinely powerful vocals and bastioned by some generally inspired playing.

**9** 1979 Never Buy Texas from a Cowboy (Atlantic)

It's very easy to pick on any individual P-Funk project as the greatest of them all, but you'd need to go a long way to beat this album's title track, a 15-minute distillation of everyone's favorite bits of the post-1975 empire. It's fired by vocals that range from raunchy to righteous in the space of a breath, and loop around at least three separate, ultra-memorable melodies. The rest of the album struggles to match the momentum, but as good as *Funk or Walk* was, this one's better.

### SELECTED COMPILATIONS AND ARCHIVE RELEASES

**5** 1993–95: tracks on George Clinton Family Series ols.

Virtually another album's worth of unreleased Brides material appears on these compilations, the earliest a collaboration with Dr. Funkenstein himself, 1977's "Rat Kissed the Cat" (vol. 5). Three other tracks from 1977, "Love Is Something" (vol. 2), "Take My Love" (vol. 4) and "Ice Melting in Your Heart" (vol. 5) also appear, alongside a second album out-take, "Up up and Away" (vol. 5). The Brides' other contributions to the series were culled from the abandoned third album: "Love Don't Come Easy" (vol. 3), "20 Bucks" and "Just for Play" (both vol. 4).

**8** 1994 Live at Howard Theatre, Washington (P-Vine)

### DAWN SILVA

**9** 2000 All My Funky Friends (JDC)

Quite simply, one of the finest true funk albums of the 1990s, from the opening assurances of "As Long As It's on the One," to the ferocious remake of "Disco to Go." Silva is in devastating voice, while co-consipirator D'La Vance guides the musicians to the frontlines of funk. An astonishing re-awakening!

### SELECTED SAMPLES

Disco To Go — Too Short: Giving Up the Funk (1995)

## THE BROTHERS JOHNSON

**FORMED:** *1975, Los Angeles, CA*

**ORIGINAL LINEUP:** *George Johnson (b. 5/17/53), Louis Johnson (b. 4/13/55)*

George Johnson was three when he was given his first guitar, an empty milk carton with elastic bands for strings, designed by his father after the boy saw Elvis Presley on the *Ed Sullivan Show*.

Five years later, his father and uncle together built him an electric guitar, modeled on a Fender Stratocaster; Johnson learned to play listening to BB King records. When younger brother Louis began showing a similar interest, dad bought him a bass and an amp. Older brother Tommy was then fitted out with a drum kit, and with cousin Alex Weir on rhythm guitar, the Johnson Three-Plus-One began playing parties, dances and weddings around their Los Angeles home, armed with a repertoire that topped 300 songs.

By 1968, the group had graduated to clubs, playing the soul and pop hits of the day. Hoping to expand their sound, they were auditioning keyboard players when they were introduced to Billy Preston, himself looking for a guitarist to join his next European tour. He offered the gig to George; brother Louis then came on board when Preston's bassist quit on the eve of a follow-on US tour. The pair subsequently appeared on Preston's *Music Is My Life* album, becoming an integral part of his regular touring band for the next three years.

In 1973, the Johnsons auditioned for Stevie Wonder's band at the Record Plant in Los Angeles; there they were spotted by Quincy Jones, who promptly recruited them for his own session in a neighboring studio. Moving into Jones' guest house, the brothers spent much of the next year on the road and in the studio with their mentor, recording his August 1975's Top 20 album *Mellow Madness*.

George and his girlfriend (soon to be wife) Valerie also co-wrote the single "Is That Love We're Missin'," released in October 1975, and credited to Jones and the Brothers Johnson. An immediate Top 20 R&B hit, the song established the Brothers as a genuine power and the duo promptly signed to A&M.

With Jones at the helm and a strong coterie of sessionmen (cousin Alex Weir among them), the Brothers Johnson's debut album appeared in spring 1976, heralded by the massive hit "I'll Be Good to You." "Get the Funk out Ma Face" followed, while a third single from the album, "Free and Single," bridged the gap while the Brothers and producer Jones worked on their sophomore set, *Right on Time*. Released in May 1977, it again produced an R&B chart topper, "Strawberry Letter 23," bolstered by a great guitar solo by Lee Ritenour, although two follow-up singles did less well.

The brothers continued session work throughout this period; George recorded with George Duke (*I Love the Blues* in 1975, *Liberated Fantasies* in 1976), while 1976 also brought a return engagement with Preston appearing on his *Billy Preston* album. The following year, Louis joined an all-star cast on Harvey Mason's *Funk in a Mason Jar* and, in 1979, the brothers were recruited to play percussion on Rufus's *Masterjam* album.

Their own career, meanwhile, continued strongly. The *Blam!* album returned the Brothers Johnson to the top of the R&B chart, with Ashford-Simpson's "Ride O Rocket," and the dynamite "Ain't We Funkin' Now," maintaining their 45s profile. Two years later, *Light Up the Night* saw former Heatwave maestro Rod Temperton join the team, writing or co-writing all but two of the album's nine tracks. Another guest, Michael Jackson, had a hand in one of the exceptions, "This Had To Be."

That was the Brothers' final album with Jones; his acrimonious split from A&M saw the label place an injunction on the Brothers to stop them from even communicating with him. They ended up self-producing their next album, *Winners*, and scoring another hit, "Real Thing," but though they continued recording during 1984, their own interest was wandering.

The A&M dispute solved, Louis rejoined Quincy Jones for albums by Patti Austin (*Every Home Should Have One*, 1980), the Crusaders (*Standing Tall*, 1981), Michael McDonald (*If That's What It Takes*, 1982), as well as Michael Jackson's epochal *Thriller* (1982). George, meanwhile, concentrated on his involvement with a Christian organization, while spending time with his growing family. When the duo came to record 1983's *Blast* album, they had just one side's worth of new material to offer, prompting A&M to transform the set instead into a "latest and greatest" collection.

Uniting with producer Leon Silva, the Brothers Johnson recorded the *Control* album in 1984, then effectively parted for the next four years. A reunion in 1988 brought the *Kickin'* album, but it sold poorly and the comeback single "Kick It to the Curb," didn't even make the R&B Top 50. The pair broke up again soon after.

In 1992, George joined Larry Graham's reformed Graham Central Station for a tour of the Far East, accompanying Japanese vocalist/guitarist Noriko "Mimi" Miyamoto. Returning to the US, George then reformed the Brothers Johnson—without his brother!—but following a US tour in the mid-'90s, he announced his retirement. Louis, meanwhile, now runs a bass academy in north Hollywood.

### THE BROTHERS JOHNSON DISCOGRAPHY CHARTLOG

1975 Is It Love That We're Missin'/Cry Baby (A&M—#18 R&B/#70 pop)
1976 I'll Be Good to You/The Devil (A&M—#1 R&B/#3 pop)
1976 Get the Funk out Ma Face/Tomorrow (A&M—#4 R&B/#30 pop)
1976 Free and Single/Thunder Thumbs and Lightnin' Licks (A&M—#26 R&B/#103 pop)
1977 Strawberry Letter 23/Dancin' and Prancin' (A&M—#1 R&B/#5 pop)

1977 Runnin' for Your Lovin'/Q (A&M—#20 R&B/#107 pop)
1978 Love Is/Right on Time (A&M—#50 R&B)
1978 Ride-O-Rocket/Dancin' and Prancin' (A&M—#45 R&B/#104 pop)
1978 Ain't We Funkin' Now/Dancin' and Prancin' (A&M—#45 R&B/#102 pop)
1980 Light Up the Night/Streetwave (A&M—#16 R&B)
1980 Treasure/Smilin' on Ya (A&M—#36 R&B/#73 pop)
1981 The Real Thing/I Want You (A&M—#11 R&B/#67 pop)
1981 Dancin' Free/Do It for Love (A&M—#51 R&B)
1982 Welcome to the Club/Echoes of an Era (A&M—#13 R&B)
1983 I'm Giving You All of My Love/The Real Thing (A&M—#75 R&B)
1984 You Keep Me Coming Back/Deceiver (A&M—#53 R&B/#102 pop)
1988 Kick It to the Curb/P.O. Box 2000 (A&M—#52 R&B)

### LPS

**8** **1976 Look Out for Number One (A&M—#1 R&B/#9 pop)**
"I'll Be Good To You" is a monster based around Sly Stone's "Time For Living" and driven by Louis' bass (following lines that George first sketched on guitar). The manic jam "Get the Funk out Ma Face" is just as diverting, but don't be alarmed by the so-abrupt ending. It's just George randomly cutting the master tape with a razorblade. The studio techs were mortified at such a breach of recording etiquette, but it works.

**7** **1977 Right on Time (A&M—#2 R&B/#13 pop)**
**6** **1978 Blam! (A&M—#1 R&B/#7 pop)**
**8** **1980 Light Up the Night (A&M—#1 R&B/#5 pop)**
Bubbly and commercial, an unchallenging dancefloor disc that nevertheless packs more worthy numbers than the chart statistics let on—with the hottest guitar sound around and a great Alex Weir vocal, why wasn't "You Make Me Wanna Wiggle" a single? Meanwhile, sharp ears will discern the roots of "Thriller" lurking within the Michael Jackson co-composition, "This Had To Be." Oddly, Rod Temperton, the composer of "Thriller," appears almost everywhere else on the album.

**6** **1981 Winners (A&M)**
**5** **1984 Out of Control (A&M—#20 R&B/#91 pop)**
**7** **1988 Kickin' (A&M)**
Nowhere near as turgid as it reputation insists, although the hot electro production would probably have worked better four years earlier. Still, "I Fresh" is a lovely Sly Stone style mover, while Stone himself helps arrange some classic horns on the Prince-like "Balls of Fire."

### SELECTED COMPILATIONS AND ARCHIVE RELEASES

**6** **1983 Blast! (The Latest and the Greatest) (A&M—#23 R&B/#138 pop)**
The hit side is spectacular, the new material adequate. The band still awaits a definitive roundup.

Ain't We Funkin' Now — Doug E. Fresh: I'm Gettin Ready (1988)

Ain't We Funkin' Now — Kid 'N Play: Last Night (1988)

Ain't We Funkin' Now — Public Enemy: Revolutionary Generation (1990)

Ain't We Funkin' Now — Queen Latifah: Nature of a Sista' (1991)

Land of Ladies — Brand Nubian: Love Me or Leave Me Alone (remix) (1993)

Strawberry Letter 23 — Chubb Rock: She's with Someone (1989)

Strawberry Letter 23 — DJ Quik: Safe + Sound (1995)

Strawberry Letter 23 — Positive K, featuring M.O.P.: How Yah Livin' (1997)

Strawberry Letter 23 — Yo-Yo: Woman to Woman (1992)

Tomorrow — Grand Puba: Amazing (1995)

Tomorrow — Mase featuring Monifah: I Need To Be (1997)

Tomorrow — OC: Far from Yours (1997)

## B.T. EXPRESS

**FORMED:** *1972, Brooklyn, NY*

**ORIGINAL LINEUP:** *Barbara Joyce Lomas (vcls), Richard Thompson (gtr, vcls), Louis Risbrook (bs, orgn, vcls), Bill Risbrook (sax), Carlos Ward (sax), Dennis Rowe (perc), Leslie Ming (drms)*

Randy Muller was already leading two bands of his own, the Panharmonics and Brass Construction, when he helped manager Jeff Lane put together a new New York dance band, the King Davis House Rockers in 1972, installing himself as songwriter, producer and arranger as the band launched into the city nightlife.

Changing their name first to the Madison Street Express, then to the Brooklyn Trucking Express, the band became the abbreviated B.T. Express in 1974, just as they signed with the Roadshow label.

With Muller firmly at the helm, the band's debut single, saxophonist Nicholls' "Do It ('Til You're Satisfied)," rocketed up both the R&B and pop charts, finally coming to rest at #1 and #2 respectively. "Express" followed it to similar peaks as the band's debut album (named for the first hit) soared into the Top Five and work was already underway on B.T. Express' sophomore album, 1975's *Non-Stop*, when Muller was diverted by Brass Construction landing a deal with United Artists.

The new album was a hit and "Give It What You Got," B.T. Express' next single, went Top 40 (the flip, "Peace Pipe," was rediscovered during the early days of house in Chicago). But a bizarre cover of the Carpenters' "Close to You," could only make #31 and, with Muller's attention firmly directed elsewhere, the third B.T. Express album would show a distinct slackening off, musically and commercially. Teenage keyboard player Michael Jones (b. Brooklyn, 1959), drafted in to assume at least some of Mul-

ler's former duties, brought some new ideas into focus, but B.T. Express' headlong rush toward generic disco territory only gathered momentum as 1976/77 progressed.

A switch to Columbia in mid-1976 saw B.T. Express celebrate another major hit, with the infectious "Can't Stop Groovin' Now, Wanna Do It Some More." Their popularity was now at an all-time high. Touring the Far East, they were invited to perform for King Aduldet of Thailand and his family; back in Brooklyn, Borough President Howard Golden honored the band's achievements with a parade to City Hall, declaring the day B.T. Express Day. The group would also perform for President Jimmy Carter.

But the 1978 departure of Barbara Lomas' so-distinctive vocal powers damaged B.T. Express beyond repair, and it was a pale ghost indeed that finally reached the end of the decade with one final stab at the R&B Top 30, the blandly treasonable "Give Up the Funk (Let's Dance)."

Jones, too, quit, ultimately to reinvent himself as techno funk star Kashif; B.T. Express would roll on for just a few months more without him, then split.

### B.T. EXPRESS DISCOGRAPHY
### CHARTLOG

1974 Do It ('Til You're Satisfied) (remix) (Roadshow—#1 R&B/#2 pop)

1975 Express (remix) (Roadshow—#1 R&B/#4 pop)

1975 Give It What You Got (Roadshow—#5 R&B/#40 pop)/Peace Pipe (#31 pop)

1976 Close to You/Whatcha Think About That? (Roadshow—#31 R&B/#82 pop)

1976 Can't Stop Groovin' Now, Wanna Do It Some More/Herbs (Columbia—#6 R&B/#52 pop)

1976 Energy To Burn/Make Your Body Move (Columbia—#37 R&B)

1977 Shout It Out/Ride on B.T. (Columbia—#12 R&B)

1980 Give Up the Funk (Let's Dance)/Better Late than Never (Columbia—#24 R&B)

1980 Does It Feel Good/Have Some Fun (Columbia—#76 R&B)

1980 Stretch/Just Want To Hold You (Columbia—#51 R&B)

### LPS

**8** **1974 Do It ('Til You're Satisfied) (Roadshow—#1 R&B/#5 pop)**
Arguably, B.T. Express were never built for the long haul, but their debut is defiant enough to at least make a second album worth investigating. The title hit influences much of the rest of the set, but that's not a bad thing.

**7** **1975 Non-Stop (Roadshow—#1 R&B/#19 pop)**
Still strong, if not quite as memorable. Again, the hits are the best bits.

**5** **1976 Energy To Burn (Columbia—#11 R&B/#43 pop)**

**4** **1977 Function at the Junction (Columbia—#39 R&B/#111 pop)**

**6** 1978 Shout (Columbia—#16 R&B/#67 pop)

Faceless, but competently disco-funky, horns punching the ceiling, Thompson's always exemplary guitar slicing some nice shapes round the rhythm, and lyrics as dauntlessly dumb as the era demanded. "Put It In" ranks among their best post-Muller creations.

**5** 1980 B.T. Express 1980 (Columbia—#29 R&B/#164 pop)

Moving back toward their homefunk base, 1980 echoes the tighter grooves that salvaged *Shout*, although again, the going's tough.

**3** 1982 Keep It Up (Coast to Coast—#49 R&B)

### SELECTED COMPILATIONS AND ARCHIVE RELEASES

**5** 1980 Greatest Hits (CBS)
**6** 1997 The Best of B.T. Express (Rhino)

### SELECTED SAMPLES

Do You Like It — Above the Law: Menace to Society (1990)
Do You Like It — DJ Quik: Loked Out Hood (1991)
Do You Like It — DJ Quik: Tear It Off (1991)
Do You Like It — Zhigge: Harlem (1992)
Everything Good to You . . . — DMX: Get at Me Dog (1998)
Everything Good to You . . . — EPMD: Get the Bozack (1989)
Everything Good to You . . . — Mase: Will They Die 4 You (1997)
Express — Gang Starr: Gusto (1989)
Express — Leaders of the New School: Sound of the Zeekers (1991)
Express — Rell featuring Jay-Z: Love for Free (1998)
Happiness — 3rd Bass: Problem Child (1991)
If It Don't Turn You On . . . — Big Daddy Kane: Smooth Operator (1989)
If It Don't Turn You On . . . — Dr. Dre: Stranded on Death Row (1993)
If It Don't Turn You On . . . — En Vogue: Lies (remix) (1990)
If It Don't Turn You On . . . — EPMD: So Whatcha Sayin'? (1989)
If It Don't Turn You On . . . — Gang Starr: Premier & the Gure (1989)
If It Don't Turn You On . . . — Ice Cube: Jackin' for Beats (1991)
If It Don't Turn You On . . . — Lootpack: WhenIMondamic (1999)
If It Don't Turn You On . . . — Nemesis: Str8 Jackin' (1993)
If It Don't Turn You On . . . — SWV: Use Your Heart (1996)
Once You Get It — Above the Law: Menace to Society (1990)
Once You Get It — DJ Quik: Loked Out Hood (1991)
Once You Get It — DJ Quik: Tear It Off (1991)
This House Is Smokin' — 3rd Bass: Triple Stage Darkness (1989)
This House Is Smokin' — Above The Law: Menace to Society (1990)
What You Do In The Dark — Del Tha Funkee Homosapian: Wrongplace (1993)
You Got It I Want It — Coolio: Smokin' Stix (1994)

## CAMEO

**FORMED:** *1974, New York, NY*
**ORIGINAL LINEUP:** *Wayne Cooper (vcls), Eric Duram (gtr), Gary Dow (bs), Gregory Johnson (kybds), Tomi Jenkins (vcls, perc), Nathan Leftenent (trum), Arnett Leftenent (sax), Larry Blackmon (vcls, drms, bs)*

A resilient funk band unafraid to move with the times, Cameo revolved around a small nucleus of musicians headed by Larry Blackmon, who formed the band with Gregory Johnson as the New York City Players during the early-'70s. That group became Cameo in 1974, apparently after objections from the Ohio Players, but also as their jazz roots began to shift toward a funkier root.

Signed to the Casablanca Records imprint Hot Chocolate, Cameo's first single, "Find My Way," was released to immediate local club success in 1976. With Blackmon producing, the band maintained the momentum with their debut album, *Cardiac Arrest*, released in the summer of 1977. But it was their next single, "Rigor Mortis," that set the stage for the band's future success, breaking them in the R&B Top 40.

Blackmon was working at a gent's outfitter near Wall Street at the time, and was in the middle of a fitting when he heard "Rigor Mortis" had become a WBLS radio World Premier—meaning it would be played once every two hours for the next week. "I just left the customer standing there waiting for me to chalk his pants," Blackmon recalled. "I knew right then it was all over."

A hectic live schedule saw the increasingly theatrical Cameo supporting P-Funk, the O'Jays and the Bar-Kays, as they spent much of 1977–78 on the road. In the midst of that, "Funk Funk" brought a Top 20 berth, while two albums in 1978, *We All Know Who We Are* and *Ugly Ego*, furthered Cameo's popularity.

In 1979, *Secret Omen* and the single "I Just Want To Be" became Cameo's biggest hits yet, at the same time signposting the direction that sustained the band into the new decade. Relocating to Atlanta, GA, and grasping the new electronics, which were just coming into fashion, incorporating them seamlessly into the Cameo sound, the group all but reinvented themselves—and did so in record time. In 1980 they released another two albums, the chart-topping *Cameosis* and *Feel Me*, the former spawning the irreverent club classic "Shake Your Pants."

A massive, US tour that summer utilized three semi trucks worth of stage sets and costumes, the props for a spectacle worthy of the Mothership-era Parliament. Cameo had by now grown to incorporate over a dozen musicians: the full-time nucleus of Blackmon, Wayne Cooper, Gregory Johnson, Tomi Jenkins and the Leftenent brothers, augmented by Anthony Lockett (bs), Aaron Mills (gtr), Thomas

**The ubiquitous red codpieces thrust Cameo into the limelight.**

Campbell (kybds), Charlie Singleton (vcls, gtr), Vince Wilburn and Damon Mendes (both drms) and Jeryl Bright (trom).

This lineup came off tour and cut 1981's *Knights of the Sound Table*, then immediately returned to the road for one final round of flamboyance. Although their shows remained massively successful, the staging costs, coupled with so many musicians' salaries, were prohibitive. Blackmon shaved the lineup down to a tight core comprising Jenkins, Singleton, Nathan Leftenent and himself, a unit that has remained intact ever since.

The group continued developing. Reacting to the now complete electronic takeover of the dancefloor, but refusing to follow so many other bands and allow the technology to swallow them whole, Cameo's next album, *Alligator Woman*, was an almighty synthesis of old funk and new noises, a peerless hybrid that presented them with their fifth

Top Ten album, and three hit singles, "Just Be Yourself," "Alligator Woman" and "Flirt."

*Alligator Woman* was Cameo's final album for Hot Chocolate; Blackmon had now launched his own imprint, Atlanta Artists, debuting it with the *Style* album in spring 1983, then following through with the monster *She's Strange* in 1984. Both the album and the hip-hop inflected title track 45 topped the R&B charts, paving the way for four years of absolute R&B chart domination by the band. Their next album, 1985's *Single Life*, spent three weeks at #2 and housed the Top Three singles "Attack Me with Your Love" and "Single Life" itself; 1986 brought *Word Up*, #1 for five weeks that fall, with both the title track and "Candy" racking up another five between them.

The band's videos, too, took a stranglehold on the imagination, a blur of Gaultier leather and the now infamous red codpiece. "Word Up" itself was nominated for a

Grammy (losing out to Prince's "Kiss"; "Back and Forth," the album's third single, reached #3, and the band's acclaim now crossed the Atlantic, serving up a string of hits across Europe.

Cameo launched another major tour in support of *Word Up*, remaining on the road during much of 1987. It was fall 1988 then, before their next album arrived, and it was immediately apparent that, at least in commercial terms, the band had peaked. *Machismo* barely scraped the Top Ten, and that despite a guest appearance from Miles Davis, and a sterling Fred Wesley production job on the single "Skin I'm In." Worse was to follow: 1990's *Real Men . . . Wear Black* faltered at #18; 1994's *In the Face of Funk* barely made the Top 100. By 1996, Cameo were confined to the funk nostalgia circuit, cutting a "greatest hits—live" type album to little response whatsoever.

Constant attention from samplers, however, together with several well-received retrospective CDs ensured that Cameo never completely fell by the wayside, and they returned in 2000 with a genuine return-to-form, *Sweet Sexy Thing*.

## CAMEO DISCOGRAPHY
### CHARTLOG

1977 Rigor Mortis/Stay by My Side (Chocolate City—#33 R&B/#103 pop)
1977 Post Mortem/Smile (Chocolate City—#70 R&B)
1977 Funk Funk/Good Times (Chocolate City—#20 R&B/104 pop)
1978 It's Serious/Inflation (Chocolate City—#21R&B)
1978 It's Over/Inflation (Chocolate City—#60 R&B)
1978 Insane/I Want You (Chocolate City—#17 R&B)
1979 Give Love a Chance/Two of Us (Chocolate City—#76 R&B)
1979 I Just Want To Be/The Rock (Chocolate City—#3 R&B)
1979 Sparkle/Macho (Chocolate City—#10 R&B)
1980 We're Goin' out Tonight/On the One (Chocolate City—#11 R&B)
1980 Shake Your Pants/I Care for You (Chocolate City—#8 R&E)
1980 Keep It Hot/I Care for You (Chocolate City—#4 R&B)
1981 Feel Me/Is This the Way (Chocolate City—#24 R&B)
1981 Freaky Dancin'/Better Days (Chocolate City—#3 R&B/#102 pop)
1981 I Like It/The Sound Table (Chocolate City—#25 R&B)
1982 Just Be Yourself/Use It or Lose It (Chocolate City—#12 R&B/#101 pop)
1982 Flirt/I Owe It All to You (Chocolate City—#10 R&B)
1982 Aligator Woman/Soul Army (Chocolate City—#54 R&B)
1983 Style/Enjoy Your Life (Atlanta Artists—#14 R&B)
1983 Slow Movin'/For You (Atlanta Artists—#47 R&B)
1984 She's Strange/Tribute to Bob Marley (Atlanta Artists—#1 R&B/#47 pop)
1984 Talkin' out the Side of Your Neck/Leve-Toi (Atlanta Artists—#21 R&B)
1984 Hangin' Downtown/Cameo's Dance (Atlanta Artists—#45 R&B)
1985 Attack Me with Your Love/Love You Anyway (Atlanta Artists—#3 R&B)
1985 Single Life/I've Got Your Image (Atlanta Artists—#2 R&B)

1985 A Good-Bye/Little Boys—Dangerous Toys (Atlanta Artists—#76 R&B)
1986 Word Up/Urban Warrior (Atlanta Artists—#1 R&B/#6 pop)
1986 Candy/She's Strange (Atlanta Artists—#1 R&B/#21 pop)
1987 Back and Forth/You Can Have the World (Atlanta Artists—#3 R&B/#50 pop)
1988 You Make Me Work/DKWIG (Atlanta Artists—#4 R&B/#85 pop)
1988 Skin I'm In/Honey (Atlanta Artists—#5 R&B)
1989 Pretty Girls/Pretty Girls (dub) (Atlanta Artists—#52 R&B)
1990 I Want It Now/DKWIG (Polygram—#5 R&B)
1990 Close Quarters/Honey (Polygram—#38 R&B)
1992 Emotional Violence (Reprise—#47 R&B)
1992 That Kind of Guy (Reprise—#53 R&B)
1994 Slyde (W2F—#57 R&B)
1995 You Are My Love/You Are My Love (extended) (W2F—#99 R&B)

### LPS

**7** 1977 Cardiac Arrest (Chocolate City—#16 R&B/#110 pop)
In 1977 disco was the moneymaker, but Cameo debuted instead with hard funk cut in the image of their forefathers, mixing up the styles of the Ohio Players and Parliament (and others!) into a glorious, if occasionally tentative, new brew.

**7** 1978 Ugly Ego (Chocolate City—#16 R&B/#83 pop)
Chunky slab of classically inclined funk, laden with lots of horns and thumping breaks.

**5** 1978 We All Know Who We Are (Chocolate City—#15 R&B/#58 pop)
Not as good as its predecessors, the band's sound is scattered from the funk of "C on the Funk" to the more dubious premise of the discofied "It's Serious."

**6** 1979 Secret Omen (Chocolate City—#4 R&B/#46 pop)

**7** 1980 Feel Me (Chocolate City—#6 R&B/#44 pop)
"Is This the Way" gets the funky groove going while the title track proves the band is not only masters of funk but of delicious ballads as well.

**7** 1980 Cameosis (Chocolate City—#1 R&B/#25 pop)
The band is finally beginning to hit its stride. The inspired "Shake Your Pants" emerges a luscious progenitor of what was to come, the hi-energy only barely tempered by the honesty of the smooth R&B ballad "I Care for You."

**7** 1981 Knights of the Sound Table (Chocolate City—#2 R&B/#44 pop)
A strong set that keeps the band's foot firmly in the '70s, but clearly hints at the radical electronic groove to come.

**6** 1982 Alligator Woman (Chocolate City—#6 R&B/#23 pop)
**6** 1983 Style (Atlanta Artists—#14 R&B/#53 pop)
**7** 1984 She's Strange (Atlanta Artists—#1 R&B/#27 pop)
**7** 1985 Single Life (Atlanta Artists—#2 R&B/#58 pop)

**9** **1986 Word Up (Atlanta Artists—#1 R&B/#8 pop)**

A genre defining—and defying—album tears up the dancefloors with "Word Up," "Candy" and "Back and Forth," as the band became stylistic groundbreakers. A tight, standout masterpiece.

**7** **1988 Machismo (Atlanta Artists—#10 R&B/#56 pop)**

Two years on the road were too long. Cut off from the contemporary mainstream, the sounds seem dated and the ideas less than fresh. Not bad, just uneven.

**5** **1990 Real Men . . . Wear Black (Atlanta Artists—#18 R&B/#84 pop)**

**6** **1994 In the Face of Funk (Way 2 Funky—#83 R&B)**

**8** **1996 Nasty (Intersound)**

Energetic live set reprising all the hits.

**8** **2000 Sexy Sweet Thing (Crash)**

Despite the rap of "Antidote" and the balladic "She Wants Some More," *Sweet Sexy Thing* finds an unselfconscious middle ground between the primal funk of the early albums, and the electro-wizardry of the biggest hits, and relishes the freedom of both. Arguably, the best thing they've recorded since 1986.

### SELECTED COMPILATIONS AND ARCHIVE RELEASES

**6** **1993 The Best of Cameo (Mercury—#44 R&B)**

**7** **1996 The Best of Cameo Vol. 2 (Mercury)**

**6** **1998 Ballads Collection (Polygram)**

**7** **1998 Greatest Hits (Polygram)**

**9** **1999 12" Collection & More (Polygram)**

With the band exhibiting a firm (and so rare) grasp on the true purpose of the 12-inch extended mix, Cameo's greatest hits as they were meant to be heard.

### SELECTED SAMPLES

Back and Forth — Fu-Schnickens: Movie Scene (1992)

Candy — 2Pac featuring Snoop Dogg, Nate Dogg & Dru Down: All About U (1996)

Funk Funk — Too Short: In the Trunk (1992)

Hangin' Downtown — Group Home: Supa Star (1995)

I Just Want To Be — DJ Quik: Quik Is the Name (1991)

Rigor Mortis — Brand Nubian: Brand Nubian (1991)

Rigor Mortis — DJ Quik: Get at Me (1995)

Rigor Mortis — Jungle Brothers: Feelin' Alright (1989)

Rigor Mortis — Heavy D: Big Tyme (1989)

Shake Your Pants — Beastie Boys: Hey Ladies (1989)

Shake Your Pants — Boyz II Men: Can't Let Her Go (1997)

Strange — 2Pac: Young Niggaz (1995)

The Two of Us — 2Pac: I Wonder I Heaven Got a Ghetto (remix) (1997)

Why Have I Lost You? — Above the Law: Ballin' (1990)

Why Have I Lost You? — Bone Thugs-N-Harmony: Blaze It (1997)

## RAFAEL CAMERON

**BORN:** *1951, Georgetown, Guyana*

Raphael Cameron already had several years singing on the Georgetown hotel circuit beneath his belt when he moved to Brooklyn, New York, in 1973, to seek a career in journalism. Like so many other bands in his homeland, Cameron's groups—the Night People and the In Crowd—concentrated on Top 40 material, albeit with a marked R&B bias. This was the experience that he brought to bear in Brooklyn, when he joined the Panharmonics.

Fronted by keyboard player Randy Muller, the leader also of Brass Construction, the Panharmonics used funk as a middle ground between a host of other musical styles. Reggae, calypso, salsa, R&B, soul and pop all had a place in the band's musical arsenal. The Panharmonics were never more than a part-time diversion for Muller, however, and when Brass Construction landed a record deal in 1975, he quit. The Panharmonics folded soon after.

Cameron's path again crossed with Muller's in late 1976. Cameron had spent the intervening year songwriting, producing a portfolio that Muller was keen to nurture. In 1979, having already arranged for Cameron to cut a solo album for the Salsoul label, Muller then introduced the singer to Skyy, the Brooklyn funk band that he was then producing. Funk Deluxe, Skyy's instrumental disco-funkmeister alias, accompanied Cameron on his debut album. Muller produced it.

Under the abbreviated name of Cameron, his debut single, "Magic of You," and the album, *Cameron*, were released in spring 1980, to immediate acclaim. The LP wound up selling over 300,000 copies in the US, breaking the UK Top 20 and topping the charts in Cameron's native Guyana. A year later, with the singer restoring his Christian name to the credits, "Funtown USA" and "Boogie's Gonna Get Ya" helped push his sophomore album, *Cameron's in Love*, to similar heights, earning him *Record World* magazine's Best New Male Vocalist award in the process. In 1982 he received further accolades, with the R&B Music Awards naming Cameron Single Male Artist of the Year, while two self-penned singles, the balladic "Desires" and the punchy "Shake It Down," continued his unbroken run of hits.

The demise of the Salsoul label, however, thrust Cameron into a hole, which nobody expected. The artist of the year could not find another record deal, and eventually he just stopped looking. When journalist Maria Granditsky caught up with Cameron in New York in 1998, he was working in a bank and had only just returned to music, cutting a gospel album, *I'm New in Christ Jesus* the previous year.

## RAFAEL CAMERON DISCOGRAPHY
### CHARTLOG
### CAMERON
1980 Magic of You/Feelin' (Salsoul—#16 R&B)
1980 Funkdown/Can't Live Without Ya (Salsoul—#33 R&B)
1981 Feelin'/Together (Salsoul—#67 R&B)

### RAFAEL CAMERON
1981 Funtown USA/In Love (Salsoul—#21 R&B)
1981 Boogie's Gonna Get Ya/Daisy (Salsoul—#53 R&B)
1982 Desires/Angel Eyes (Salsoul—#59 R&B)
1982 Shake It Down/I Love You (Salsoul—#81 R&B)

### LPS
**7** 1980 Cameron (Salsoul—#18 R&B/#67 pop)
"Let's Get It Off," Cameron's biggest dance hit, typifies this disco-esque set.
**8** 1981 Cameron's in Love (Salsoul—#29 R&B/#101 pop)
Cameron's great vocals treat the light pop/funk of "Boogie's Gonna Get Ya'," "All That's Good To Me" and "Funtown USA" to a smooth ride.
**6** 1982 Cameron All the Way (Salsoul—#43 R&B)

## CHOCOLATE MILK
**FORMED:** *1974, New Orleans, LA*
**ORIGINAL LINEUP:** *Frank Richard (vcls), Mario Tio (gtr), Robert Dabon (kybds), Amandee Castanell (sax), Joe Foxx (trum), Dwight Richards (vcls, drms)*

Launched by drummer Dwight Richards, Chocolate Milk formed as a low-key New Orleans jazz quartet, shifting their focus to R&B and funk after noting the commercial success now attending other jazz influenced R&B bands. The lineup was duly expanded and the revamped Chocolate Milk launched themselves onto the local scene at a time when the scene itself was at its most combustible.

The Meters, the houseband at local producer Allen Toussaint and Marshall Sehorn's Seasaint Studios, had recently broken out as one of the most in-demand acts in the country, and early witnesses to Chocolate Milk's show were convinced this new band was set to follow them. Inevitably, Toussaint himself was quick to check them out, although the group's first sessions with him were essentially unproductive.

Further sessions, however, unveiled "Action Speaks Louder than Words," a sinewy funk slab underpinned by a massive squelchy bass sound; the performance earned Chocolate Milk a deal with RCA and a summer 1975, R&B Top 20 hit.

While tours with the Bar-Kays, Kool & the Gang and Parliament established Chocolate Milk on the live circuit, further hit singles "How About Love" and "Comin'" followed over the next two years, with 1978's "Girl Callin'" (composed by Toussaint) becoming the band's biggest hit yet. However, RCA's belief that Chocolate Milk could go even further if they were parted from Toussaint saw the band's next album, the George Tobin-produced *Hipnotism*, stall mid-chart.

The label promptly assigned the group another producer, Bar-Kays guru Allan Jones, and this time it worked. Joining Jones in Memphis, where the producer effortlessly relit the funk fires that *Hipnotism* had allowed to burn out, Chocolate Milk hit immediate paydirt with the title track from their next album, 1981's *Blue Jeans*. The single remained on the R&B chart for almost five months, even after the follow-up, "Let's Go All the Way," commenced its climb to the edge of the Top 40.

The new mood of optimism did not last, however. Over the next 18 months, just two Chocolate Milk singles made the R&B chart, while the late-1982 *Friction* album likewise failed to take off. The band called it quits the following year.

### CHOCOLATE MILK DISCOGRAPHY
### CHARTLOG
1975 Action Speaks Louder than Words/Ain't Nothin' But a Thing (RCA—#15 R&B/#69 pop)
1976 How About Love/Party Happy (RCA—#79 R&B)
1976 Comin'/Starbright (RCA—#56 R&B)
1978 Girl Callin'/Thinking of You (RCA—#14 R&B/#103 pop)
1979 Say Won'tcha/DOC (RCA—#39 R&B)
1979 Groove City/Save the Last Dance (RCA—#59 R&B)
1980 Hey Lover/Would It Be Alright (RCA—#40 R&B)
1981 Blue Jeans/Dawn (RCA—#15 R&B)
1982 Let's Go All the Way/Honey Bun (RCA—#41 R&B)
1982 Take It Off/Honey Bun (RCA—#39 R&B)
1983 Who's Getting It Now/Sweet Heat (RCA—#65 R&B)

### LPS
**9** 1975 Action Speaks Louder than Words (RCA—#34 R&B/#191 pop)
Super tight rhythms and heavy bass drive this New Orleans-tinged funk right over the edge. Full of lush sounds from the slow grooving title track to the now classic "Time Machine," a stunning debut in modern Meters style.
**8** 1976 Chocolate Milk (RCA—#18 R&B)
**7** 1978 We're All in This Together (RCA—#34 R&B/#171 pop)
Easing off the funk, CM still managed to turn in a notable performance, especially on "Grand Theft."

**6** 1979 Milky Way (RCA—#52 R&B/#161 pop)
**5** 1980 Hipnotism (RCA—#69 R&B)
**7** 1981 Blue Jeans (RCA—#22 R&B/#162 pop)

Cameo-tinged title track proves the band can still get a groove going, while producer Jones' naturally grafts in a strong Bar-Kays element.

**5** 1982 Friction (RCA—#50 R&B)

### SELECTED COMPILATIONS AND ARCHIVE RELEASES

**8** 1998 Ice Cold Funk: The Greatest Grooves Of (Razor & Tie)

Super collection of all their best, from "Action Speaks Louder than Words" to "Girl Callin'" and "Take It Off."

### SELECTED SAMPLES

Action Speaks Louder than Words — Eric B. & Rakim: Move the Crowd (remix) (1987)

Action Speaks Louder than Words — Stetsasonic: Don't Let Your Mouth Write a Check like That (1991)

Girl Callin' — Immature: We Got It (1995)

Runnin' Away — Miles Davis: Blow (1992)

## STANLEY CLARKE, see THE CLARKE-DUKE PROJECT

## THE CLARKE-DUKE PROJECT

**FORMED:** 1980, Los Angeles, CA

**ORIGINAL LINEUP:** Stanley Clarke (b. 6/30/51, Philadelphia, PA—bs), George Duke (b. 1/12/46, San Rafael, CA—kybds)

The mass exodus of jazzmen into funk and R&B during the '70s was the starting point for any amount of fascinating fusions, both musically and, in terms of crossover success, commercially. Few, however, brought together such titans of the genre as the Clarke-Duke Project, and fewer still paid such dividends without ever compromising the reputations of the players themselves.

Of the pair, Clarke was the better known. Starting out playing accordion and, later, cello, by his teens Clarke had moved onto bass, swiftly mastering both the acoustic and electric instruments. His first bands, through his teens, were R&B and rock oriented, but Clarke first came to attention in the early '70s as the brilliant bassist behind such jazz stars as Pharoah Sanders, Gil Evans, Mel Lewis, Horace Silver, Stan Getz, Dexter Gordon and Art Blakey. He truly came into his own, however, when he joined Return to Forever in 1972.

Charismatically fronted by Chick Corea (kybds), plus Flora Purim (vcls) and Lenny White (drms), Return to Forever's audacious repertoire of jazz values and rock stylings all but singlehandedly determined the direction the ensu-ing fusion would take. Indeed, by the time of 1977's mammoth Live: The Complete Concert box set, Return to Forever's influence could be seen across the progressive rock scene.

As the band's second songwriter (behind Corea), Clarke was responsible for some of Return to Forever's most distinctive performances, including "After the Cosmic Rain," from 1973's seminal Hymn of the Seventh Galaxy album, "Vulcan Worlds," from 1974's Where Have I Known You Before and "Magician," from 1976's Top 30 hit Romantic Warrior.

Clarke also pursued a parallel recording career during this period, albeit to little attention. In 1975, however, he scored an R&B Top Ten hit with Journey to Love, an album featuring contributions from bandmates Corea and White, plus English guitar legends John McLaughlin and Jeff Beck and, for the first time, George Duke.

A disciple of jazzman Les McCann, Duke's eponymous Quartet (completed by David Simmons—trum, John Heard—bs, George Walker—drms) worked the San Francisco club circuit during the mid-'60s, cutting one album of jazz standards in 1966, Presented by the Jazz Workshop 1966 of San Francisco (Saba).

The pianist linked with jazz violinist Jean-Luc Ponty in 1968, appearing on that year's Electric Connection album. Experience and the Frank Zappa tribute King Kong followed; Duke also worked for some eight months with Don Ellis' Orchestra, before 1970 saw him recruited by Zappa himself, for the Chunga's Revenge album.

Following a brief sojourn with Cannonball Adderley, during which time he also cut a second solo album, Live in LA, Duke returned to Zappa for much of the early-mid'70s, contributing to the albums Just Another Band from LA, The Grand Wazoo, Waka Jawaka, Overnight Sensation, Apostrophe and One Size Fits All. He is one of the stars of the Roxy and Elsewhere live album. He also appears in the 1971 movie 200 Motels.

Zappa, meantime, was one of the guests (alongside Return to Forever vocalist Purim) on Duke's 1974 Feel solo album. Indeed, several of Zappa's band members would appear on Duke's albums during this period, while Duke also recorded his own distinctive versions of several Zappa compositions, including "Echidna's Arf" and "Uncle Remus."

Duke quit Zappa's band in 1975, and, reuniting with George Duke Quartet bassist Heard, plus new drummer Leon Chancler, he cut the esoteric Faces in Reflection album. The set proved that, despite his outside interests,

Duke was still first and foremost a jazzman. However, his next couple of releases would see him drifting closer to a funk vibe, all the more so after he linked with Clarke.

Like Duke, many of the guest stars on Clarke's *Journey to Love* reappeared on the bassist's next album, 1976's *School Days*. Perhaps shockingly in view of its subsequent stellar reputation, the album was not an immediate commercial hit. But with Beck and Duke still on hand, Clarke followed through with the similarly styled *Modern Man* and the half-live *I Wanna Play for You*. Clarke was now as integral to Duke's recordings as he was to the bassist's, starring on Duke's smash hit 1978 album *Reach for It*, and, over the next two years, the pair's activities continued intertwined.

Other promising unions passed by unfulfilled. Duke and drummer Billy Cobham shone briefly across 1979's *BC* album; Clarke, George Benson, Wynton Marsalis and others hit some fascinating heights with their joint project Fuse One. But the true chemistry was between Duke and Clarke and, in 1981, they formally announced the formation of their own funk band, the prosaically titled Clarke/Duke Project.

*Clarke Duke Project Volume One* was launched with the single "Sweet Baby" that spring. The album followed it up the chart, becoming Clarke's biggest seller since *Journey to Love,* and establishing the duo as *the* supergroup pairing for the new decade.

It was not to be an exclusive arrangement. Both Clarke and Duke continued their solo activities into the early '80s, Duke scoring with *Dream On* and *Guardian of the Light,* Clarke with *Let Me Know You,* before the duo reconvened in 1983. However, adding to the sense of anticipation surrounding *The Clarke/Duke Project II,* the pair were absent from one another's intervening records. The ploy worked; both album and the "Heroes" single were hits, while the presence of Billy Cobham among the album's guest drummers lent even greater weight to the proceedings.

Six years (and a number of other, often worthier, projects) elapsed before the Duke/Clarke Project again came together, convincing many observers that at least some of the partnership's own magic had dissipated. Indeed, 3, in 1989, was released at a time when neither musician's profile truly required it. Clarke had just returned vividly to his jazz roots with the acclaimed *If This Bass Could Only Talk* album; Duke was firmly established as the visionary producer behind hits by Philip Bailey, Melissa Manchester and Jeffrey Osborne.

Against all odds, then, 3 emerged their mightiest album yet; but it was also the Project's final recording. Into the '90s, both Clarke and Duke returned to their own careers, Clarke concentrating on soundtrack work, Duke continuing in production and session work.

## THE CLARKE-DUKE PROJECT DISCOGRAPHY
### CHARTLOG
1981 Sweet Baby/Never Judge a Cover by Its Book (Epic—#6 R&B/#19 pop)
1981 I Just Want To Love You/Finding My Way (Epic—#49 R&B)
1983 Heroes/Atlanta (Epic—#37 R&B)
1990 Lady/Find Out Who You Are (Epic—#67 R&B)

## STANLEY CLARKE
### CHARTLOG
1976 Silly Putty/Hello Jeff (Nemperor—#94 R&B)
1978 Slow Dance/Rock 'n' Roll Jelly (Nemperor—#76 R&B)
1980 We Supply/Underestimation (Epic—#43 R&B)
1982 Straight to the Top/The Force of Love (Epic—#81 R&B)
1984 Heaven Sent You/Speedball (Epic—#21 R&B)
1985 Born in the USA/Campo Americano (Epic—#52 R&B)

## GEORGE DUKE
### CHARTLOG
1977 Reach for It/Just for You (Epic—#2 R&B/#54 pop)
1978 Dukey Stick (part one)(part two) (Epic—#4 R&B)
1978 Movin' On/The Way I Feel (Epic—#68 R&B)
1979 Say That You Will/I Am for Real (Epic—#25 R&B)
1979 I Want You for Myself/Party Down (Epic—#23 R&B)
1982 Shine On/Positive Energy (Epic—#15 R&B)
1982 Ride on Love/Let Your Love Shine (Epic—#83 R&B)
1983 Reach Out (part one)/(part two) (Epic—#59 R&B)
1985 Thief in the Night/La La (Elektra—#37 R&B)
1986 Broken Glass/Island Girl (Elektra—#57 R&B)
1986 Good Friend/African Violet (Elektra—#60 R&B)
1992 No Rhyme No Reason/The Morning After (WB—#24 R&B)
1995 Love Can Be So Cold/Buffalo Soldiers (WB—#78 R&B)

## THE CLARKE/DUKE PROJECT
### LPS
**9** 1981 The Clarke-Duke Project (Epic—#7 R&B/#33 pop)
Adeptly combining original compositions with a stunning reappraisal of the ubiquitous "Louie Louie," a titanic partnership begins strongly and never lets up. Funk-jazz at its finest.

**4** 1983 II (Epic—#44 R&B/#146 pop)
A savage disappointment. The guiding principles of the first album, to pursue a funk groove which their regular releases generally skimmed over, was lacking here as well, together with anything to distinguish it from a myriad other R&B-lite offerings.

**8** 1990 3 (Epic—#52 R&B)

A techno-funk beast that nodded most overtly toward vintage P-Funk with a cover of "Mothership Connection," and became positively nasty on "Pit Bulls (An Endangered Species)." A handful of the wide-screen ballads, which were Duke's current stock in trade, lower the tone a little, but still 3 was a triumph.

## STANLEY CLARKE
### SELECTED ALBUMS
**5** 1972 Children of Forever (Polydor)
**6** 1974 Stanley Clarke (Nemperor)
**6** 1975 Journey to Love (Nemperor—#8 R&B/#34 pop)
**8** 1976 School Days (Nemperor)
Masterful set dominated by its eight-minute title track and the manic pulse of Clarke's thumb slap bass playing.
**7** 1978 Modern Man (Nemperor—#25 R&B/#57 pop)
**8** 1979 I Wanna Play for You (Nemperor—#36 R&B/#62 pop)
Half live recordings, half dexterous drama—and not only in terms of the musicians' virtuosity. "Jamaican Boy" toys expertly with reggae; "Just a Feeling," a true Duke showcase, comes firmly to grips with a disco funk vibe.
**5** 1980 Rocks, Pebbles and Sand (Epic—#40 R&B/#95 pop)
Not an altogether successful funk rock experiment, with the rock on one side, the funk on the other. Both tend to be very overdone, though the rock songs are an exhilarating barrage of screaming guitars and thundering drums, and the funk numbers heap molten pace onto precise rhythms, it quickly becomes apparent that that's all they are. No form, and way too much content.
**5** 1982 Let Me Know You (Epic—#25 R&B/#114 pop)
**7** 1984 Time Exposure (Epic—#52 R&B/#149 pop)
Beck returns, and so do Clarke's better songwriting skills. Though there's a distinct "Rockit" era Herbie Hancock influence at large, the title track is a fabulous mound of colossal funk, while the sci-fi theme of many of the lyrics is amply explored by the instrumentation.
**7** 1985 Find Out! (Epic)
Another thrilling techno-funk excursion, raised to unexpected heights by a mean version of Springsteen's "Born in the USA." And this time, nobody could mistake the song's sentiments.
**5** 1986 Hideaway (Epic)
More or less a last hurrah for Clarke's solo funk rock visions, but also a dry run for his later work with rock drummer Stewart Copeland in Animal Logic. Copeland is one of several big-name guests, and does beef up the sound some. But the album's real selling point is a reunion with the School Days-era band for "Old Friends."

**5** 1988 If This Bass Could Only Talk (Portrait)
**6** 1992 Passenger 157 (Epic)
**4** 1993 East River Drive (Epic—#54 R&B)
**7** 1993 Live at the Greek (Epic)
**6** 1994 Live in Montreaux (Jazz Door)
**7** 1995 At the Movies (Epic Soundtrax)

## GEORGE DUKE
### SELECTED ALBUMS
**8** 1969 Save the Country (Liberty)
Standout combination of soul and jazz that blend for a truly tripped out groove. Don't miss "Soul Watcher," "Alcatraz" and "Since You Asked."
**8** 1969 George Duke Aka Pacific Jazz (UA)
**5** 1971 Live in L.A. (Sunset)
**7** 1974 Feel (MPS)
Classic crossover jazz, smack in the heart of Zappa territory.
**9** 1974 Faces in Reflection (MPS)
Primarily instrumental, this excellent set is '70s fusion at its best. Whether it's funk, jazz or full-on rock doesn't matter, Duke makes sure it's all three at once. "Psychosomatic Dung" and "North Beach" are shatteringly fabulous.
**7** 1975 I Love the Blues: She Heard My Cry (MPS/BASF—#36 R&B/#169 pop)
**7** 1975 The Aura Will Prevail (BASF)
**7** 1976 Liberated Fantasies (BASF—Ger)
**6** 1976 Live: On Tour in Europe (Atlantic)
Culled from 1976 shows in England and Switzerland, Duke powers through a high profile set highlighted by "Space Lady" and "Juicy."
**6** 1977 From Me to You (Epic)
A sonically heady mix where the songs start off in one vein, before spinning out into another entirely. Some seriously heavy guitar riffing scars "What Do They Fear?"
**8** 1977 Reach for It (Epic—#4 R&B/#25 pop)
Leaving jazz almost totally behind, Duke swings into full funk mode, ripping through a tight set highlighted by the title track but also standing out on "Lemme at It," "Hot Fire" and "Searchin' My Mind."
**7** 1978 Don't Let Go (Epic—#5 R&B/#39 pop)
Another strong R&B set heavy on the soul, but with some solid funk mixed in.
**5** 1979 Follow the Rainbow (Epic—#17 R&B/#56 pop)
This collection of up-tempo dance tunes leans heavily toward disco, although "I Am for Real" leads off some noteworthy borrowings from the Parliament/Funkadelic songbook.
**7** 1979 Master of the Game (Epic—#18 R&B/#125 pop)

**9** 1979 A Brazilian Love Affair (Epic—#40 R&B/#119 pop)

Duke takes a break from funk but doesn't go back to jazz. Instead he lands somewhere in the Latin American middle, with an outstanding set recorded in Brazil. Hot shots include "Cravo E Canela" and "Ao Que Vai Nascer" and, of course, the excellent title track.

**7** 1982 Dream On (Epic—#17 R&B/#48 pop)

**5** 1983 Guardian of the Light (Epic—#46 R&B/#147 pop)

**5** 1985 Thief in the Night (Elektra—#52 R&B/#183 pop)

**5** 1986 George Duke (Elektra—#56 R&B)

**8** 1989 Night After Night (Elektra—#87 R&B)

What a great way to end the decade! After a string of mediocre albums, Duke is back to his best with a funk driven pop set that includes a cover of L.T.D.'s "Love Ballad."

**6** 1992 Snapshot (WB—#36 R&B)

**7** 1993 Muir Woods Suite (WB)

Odd live performance of music for orchestra and jazz ensemble from the Montreaux Jazz Festival—a contemplative, moody suite.

**8** 1995 Illusions (WB—#33 R&B)

With lots of texture, masterful sonic layering and heavy on the Moog, this set has a decidedly delicious retro feel. Viva la '70s!

**7** 1997 Is Love Enough? (WB—#65 R&B)

A typical Duke tapestry of style, from funk to stirring ballads, but still fresh enough.

**7** 1998 After Hours (WB)

Duke's first all-instrumental set in almost two decades is a stunning cycle of grooving mood, focused enough to keep the progression forward, yet mellow enough to ensure there's no rush to get to the end.

## CON FUNK SHUN

**FORMED:** *1972, Memphis, TN*

**ORIGINAL LINEUP:** *Michael Cooper (b. 11/15/52—Vallejo, CA; vcls, gtr), Cedric Martin (bs, vcls), Danny Thomas (clav, kybds, vcls), Felton Pilate (trom, bs, trum, kybds, gtr, vcls), Paul Harrell, aka Zebulon Paulle Harrell (sax, flte, vcls), Karl Fuller (trum, flugel, vcls), Louis McCall (drms)*

High school students Cooper and McCall first came together in 1968 in their hometown of Vallejo, CA, as Projekt Soul. Joined first by fellow classmates Cedric Martin, Danny Thomas, Paul Harrell and Karl Fuller, then by the multi-instrumentalist Felton Pilate, the Projekt Soul sextet became staunch favorites on the Bay Area Top 40 circuit.

In 1971, the band's manager, Joe Connors, arranged for Projekt Soul to accompany Stax Records hitmakers The Soul Children when they played the Bay Area that summer. Like many other vocal groups of the time, the Children traveled alone, relying upon promoters and booking agents to provide a new group of suitable musicians in every town.

The show was a success, but Projekt Soul's hope that the gig might lead to further, similar, opportunities went unfulfilled. Indeed, when the Soul Children returned to Oakland's Showcase club on August 4, 1972, they arrived with a backing band already in tow.

Projekt Soul attended the show anyway and, when the Soul Children's Norman West asked what they were doing these days, Cooper replied, "Waiting for you to ask us to be your backing band." Incredibly, West did just that, dismissing the other musicians on the spot, and recruiting Projekt Soul in their place.

Relocating to the Soul Children's native Memphis, Projekt Soul were employed in the pre-production room at Stax, working with various songwriters and musicians as they dropped in to run through new ideas. The group appeared in the hit movie *Wattstax*, stylishly backing the Soul Children, but their interest was now moving toward writing and recording their own material.

Projekt Soul broke with Stax in 1973, and linked with Ted Sturges, owner of the Audio Dimensions studio. Changing their name to Con Funk Shun, in honor of the Nite-Liters instrumental which was a highlight of their live set, the band signed with the Fretone label and cut a couple of singles. However, they also recorded a wealth of other material, unreleased at the time, but later gathered together as the pounding jazz funk hybrid *Organized Con Funk Shun*. A second album of material from this period, *The Memphis Sessions*, appeared some years later.

Con Funk Shun remained with Sturges for three years, until 1976. At that point, they signed with Mercury and recorded their official debut album, *Con Funk Shun*, for release in late 1976. A schizophrenic set, as likely to drift into soft soul as hard funk, it did little, a fate that also awaited their next single, the album's closing track, "Sho Feels Good To Me" (re-recorded from the 1973 sessions) in January 1977.

Its follow-up, however, topped the R&B chart for two weeks, introducing the world to what became one of Con Funk Shun's most endearing trademarks. "Ffun" was Cooper's tribute to the group Brick, effortlessly recapturing the spirit of that band's sound, even as they pursued a unique vibe that was all their own. "Foley Park," from their debut album, had made a similar gesture toward Van McCoy's "The Hustle"; "Shake and Dance with Me," from their

Con Funk Shun: Mike Cooper, Louis McCall, Karl Fuller, Paul Harrell, Cedric Martin, Felton Pilate, Danny Thomas.

third, would mischievously plunder the Archies' "Sugar Sugar."

Taken from the Ron Capone-produced *Secrets* album, "Ffun" remained on the R&B chart for five months, dropping out just as the band's next single, "Confunkshunizeya," climbed in. "Shake and Dance with Me" followed, its ascent into the R&B Top Five finally powering the third Con Funk Shun album, *Loveshine*, into the Top 40. (This album also debuted longtime guest percussionist Sheila Escovedo, later to find fame as Prince protege Sheila E.)

Aiming to consolidate their breakthrough, Con Funk Shun's subsequent album was to prove their funkiest yet. In 1979, *Candy* featured an opening cut recorded live, where the band's undeniable strengths were, naturally, at their best. Elsewhere, Pilate's "Chase Me"—originally written, he claimed, with the Isley Brothers in mind—was a dramatic stomp, with growled vocals and an irresistible bass rhythm.

Con Funk Shun maintained this same momentum for *Spirit of Love*, an album whose somewhat slick artwork disguised some genuinely earthy funk, and some surprising

uses of modern technology. Pilate had made no secret of his hatred of the machinery now creeping into the dance music scene, sensibly arguing that if you want a career as a musician, you should learn to play an instrument. But the opening cut, "Got To Be Enough" was written on a $150 drum machine he had recently picked up, before being punched up by McCall's unquestionably live drumming and the Earth Wind & Fire horn section. "Got To Be Enough" gave the band their fourth R&B Top Ten hit in four years, while Con Funk Shun's continued pre-eminence was confirmed when "Too Tight," later in the year, returned them to the pop Top 40 for the first time since "Ffun."

Never afraid of traditional soul balladry, Con Funk Shun's early-mid-'80s releases delved deep into that territory, as their output—and success—grew increasingly haphazard. The albums *Touch*, *7* (titled both for the number of band members and to show their disdain for the 1973 album) and *To the Max* returned ever diminishing sales. However, Pilate insists that, had Mercury only followed the band's intuition when it came to selecting the first single from the latter, the group's story may well have taken an altogether different turn.

Two tracks presented themselves as potential singles, "Love's Train" and "Ms. Got-the-Body," with the label favoring the latter. It reached a respectable #15 on the R&B chart, but to this day, the band's own choice, "Love's Train," remains a radio favorite and has been called Con Funk Shun's best-loved song.

Still, "Ms. Got-the-Body" did revitalize the group's fortunes somewhat. While 1983's *Fever* album, well produced by Brazilian Eumir Deodato (fresh from a run of hits with Kool & the Gang) fared no better than its predecessors, bassist Martin's "Baby I'm Hooked" went Top Five.

Sessions for their next album, *Electric Lady*, saw the band working with a string of different producers—Jerome Gaspar, Maurice Starr, Billy Osborne and Larry Smith, at a variety of studios. The results were predictably patchy, but with the rap-flavored title track rising to #4 and the album itself hitting #62—Con Funk Shun's biggest hit in five years—it seemed that a whole new lease of life was there for the taking.

It was not to be. In early 1986, Pilate quit the band, to be replaced by Melvin Carter—Con Funk Shun's first-ever lineup change. The group promptly earned another Top Ten hit with the title track from 1986's *Burning Love*, but the band's entire dynamic had been lost. Cooper quit soon after to launch his own successful solo career, and Con Funk Shun effectively came to a halt.

Back in Vallejo, Pilate opened his own recording studio and signed a production deal with Fantasy Records. There, he linked with Christian rapper Holy Ghost Boy (b. Stanley Kirk Burrell, 3/30/63, Oakland, CA) and, had Fantasy not dropped them both before their efforts could come to fruition, the future of hip-hop may have turned out quite different. Holy Ghost Boy promptly changed his name to MC Hammer and, with a loan from Oakland Athletics outfielders Dwayne Murphy and Mike Davis, launched his own Bustin' Records label, linking with Pilate to produce a single, "Ring 'Em," and the album, *Feel My Power*. For Pilate, who had long before decried rap as a passing fad, the irony of suddenly finding himself ranked among the genre's top-selling producers remains a favorite anecdote.

After several years in dispute with other claimants, Cooper and Felton regained control of the Con Funk Shun band name in the mid-'90s, relaunching the band for a New Year's Eve show in Oakland. With a constantly shifting lineup, they have continued working since then; a live album, sensibly titled *New Live Album*, was released in 1996.

Con Funk Shun also contributed to the *United We Funk* collection of revitalized '80s-era funk acts—Rick James, the Gap Band and the SOS Band were similarly involved.

## CON FUNK SHUN DISCOGRAPHY
### CHARTLOG
1977 Sho Feels Good to Me/Foley Park (Mercury—#66 R&B)
1977 Ffun/Indian Summer Love (Mercury—#1 R&B/#23 pop)
1978 Confunkshunizeya/Who Has the Time (Mercury—#31 R&B/#103 pop)
1978 Shake and Dance with Me/I'll Set You out O.K. (Mercury—#5 R&B/#60 pop)
1978 So Easy/Tears in My Eyes (Mercury—#28 R&B)
1979 Chase Me/I Think I Found the Answer (Mercury—#4 R&B)
1979 (Let Me Put) Love on Your Mind/Fire When Ready (Mercury—#24 R&B)
1980 Da Lady/Images (Mercury—#60 R&B)
1980 Got To Be Enough/Early Morning Sunshine (Mercury—#8 R&B/#101 pop)
1980 By Your Side/Spirit of Love (Mercury—#27 R&B)
1980 Happy Face/Honey Wild (Mercury—#87 R&B)
1980 Too Tight/Play Widit (Mercury 38 R&B/#40 pop)
1981 Ladies Wild/Pride and Glory (Mercury—#42 R&B)
1981 Bad Lady/California 1 (Mercury—#19 R&B)
1982 Straight from the Heart/California 1 (Mercury—#79 R&B)
1982 Ain't Nobody, Baby/Ever Love (Mercury—#31 R&B)
1983 Ms. Got-the-Body/Hide and Freak (Mercury—#15 R&B)
1983 You Are the One/Let's Ride and Slide (Mercury—#47 R&B)
1983 Baby, I'm Hooked (Right into Your Love)/Thinking About You, Baby (Mercury—#5 R&B/#76 pop)
1984 Don't Let Your Love Grow Cold/Lovin' Fever (Mercury—#33 R&B/#103 pop)
1985 Electric Lady/Pretty Lady (Mercury—#4 R&B/#102 pop)
1985 I'm Leaving Baby/Love's Train (Mercury—#12 R&B)
1985 Tell Me What (I'm Gonna Do) (remix) (Mercury—#47 R&B)
1986 Burnin' Love/Candy (Mercury—#8 R&B)
1986 She's a Star/Rock It All Night (Mercury—#80 R&B)
1996 Throw It Up, Throw It Up/remix (Intersound—#84 R&B)

## CON FUNK SHUN
### LPS
**7** 1976 Con-Funk-Shun (Mercury)
A confident set splits evenly between horn heavy funk jams ("Music Is the Way" and "Sho Feels Good to Me") and contemplative ballads ("Another World" and "Tell Me That You Like It"), with a few inbetweeners for variety.

**9** 1977 Secrets (Mercury—#6 R&B/#51 pop)
The band takes the solid beginning of their debut and hones it into solid gold. Super tight horns and grooves are captured best on the smash hit "Ffun," but really, the entire set powers through with glints of jazz, soul and synthesized electronics coming to the surface.

**7** 1978 Loveshine (Mercury—#10 R&B/#32 pop)

Con Funk Shun pull back to lay down a mellow groove, punctuated by the catchy "Shake and Dance with Me."

**6** 1979 Candy (Mercury—#7 R&B/#46 pop)

Put your hands together for this live set from the Automatt in San Francisco. But after the loud, audience-heavy "Fire When Ready," the band settles down to more relaxed soul grooves.

**6** 1980 Touch (Mercury—#7 R&B/#51 pop)

**6** 1980 Spirit of Love (Mercury—#7 R&B/#30 pop)

A commercial hit driven primarily by "Got To Be Enough," the group seem to be stuck in a rut—a competent, tight, well-received rut, but a rut just the same.

**7** 1981 Con Funk Shun 7 (Mercury—#17 R&B/#82 pop)

**7** 1983 To the Max (Mercury—#9 R&B/#115 pop)

Best on "Got the Body," "Love's Train" and "Let It Ride nd Slide" Con Funk Shun once again deliver a super tight crop of mellow funk and delicious R&B ballads.

**7** 1984 Fever (Mercury—#12 R&B/#105 pop)

Brings back the funk on the opening "Can You Feel the Groove Tonight," then keeps the mood flowing with "Indiscreet Sweet" on side one, and "Lovin' Fever" and "Hard Lovin'" on the flip.

**5** 1985 Electric Lady (Mercury—#9 R&B/#62 pop)

A total departure from any past effort, the band utilizes all the popular technology of the '80s to create a synthesized groove. Not bad, but certainly derivative.

**6** 1986 Burnin' Love (Mercury—#25 R&B/#121 pop)

Retaining some of the electronic ethics, but infusing them with more traditional grooves, the group keep their sound contemporary, but grounded—heard best on "She's Sweet," "Do Ya" and "She's a Star."

**6** 1996 New Live Album (Intersound)

**7** 1997 Live for Ya Ass (Castle—#74 R&B)

Great new live set from San Francisco proves Con can still funk with the best of 'em, through an outrageously energetic hits concert.

### SELECTED COMPILATIONS AND ARCHIVE RELEASES

**9** 1976 Organized Con Funk Shun (Pickwick)

Despite the band's own disdain for the release, *Organized Con Funk Shun* captures them in drop-dead early '70s funking temper, crashing through "Funky Things on My Mind" and a righteous prototype of "Sho' Feels Good to Me." One ballad, "Do You Really Know What Love Is," disrupts the damage in the nicest possible way, and had this album actually appeared at the time, the mid-'70s might have been a very different place.

**7** 1977 The Memphis Sessions (51 West/CBS)

Marvin Gaye's "You Sure Love To Ball" highlights further material from the 1973–76 period, mostly mellower than the *Organized* crop, but strong R&B all the same.

**8** 1993 The Best of Con Funk Shun (Mercury—#43 R&B)

Fat, fine collection with all the hits, plus the sleepers, which never charted but impacted nonetheless.

**7** 1994 Ffun (Special Music)

**7** 1996 The Best of Con Funk Shun, Vol. 2 (Polygram)

Hits collection includes the extended "Too Tight."

**7** 1998 Ballads Collection (Polygram)

### MICHAEL COOPER
### CHARTLOG
### LPS

**7** 1987 Love Is Such a Funny Game (King Jay—#21 R&B/#98 pop)

A nice set lets Cooper showcase his gorgeous voice in a variety of musical grooves. Best on "Dinner for Two" and "To Prove My Love." Includes a cover of the Carole King classic "You've Got a Friend."

**6** 1989 Just What I Like (King Jay—#27 R&B)

**5** 1992 Get Closer (Reprise—#56 R&B)

### SELECTED SAMPLES
Ffun — DJ Quik: Niggaz Still Trippin' (1992)

Ffun — Pete Rock & C.L. Smooth: Skinz (1992)

## CROWN HEIGHTS AFFAIR

**FORMED:** *1973, New York, NY*

**ORIGINAL LINEUP:** *Phil Thomas (vcls), William Anderson (gtr), Muki Wilson (bs), Howard Young (kybds), Bert Reid (sax), Raymond Reid (trom), James Baynard (sax), Raymond Rock (drms, vcls)*

Named for their native New York neighborhood, Crown Heights Affair emerged onto the city scene in early 1973 from the same ferment that produced Brass Construction, B.T. Express and Fuel/Skyy (the latter's drummer, Tommy McConnell, was a member for a time).

A vitality-packed and extraordinarily punchy funk octet, Crown Heights Affair's future seemed assured when they were signed to RCA and had an immediate local hit with the 1974 single "Super Rod." "Leave the Kids Alone," the following year, broke the band into the R&B Top 100, but after just one eponymous album, Crown Heights Affair parted company with RCA and switched to De-Lite, a label then in the very vanguard of the disco-funk movement. There, the group was paired with producers/writers Britt Britton and Freda Nerangis and, in 1975, they emerged reinvented as one of the key bands of the forthcoming firestorm.

Tellingly backed by a self-confessed "disco version," "Dreaming a Dream," Crown Heights Affair's first single under the new regime, slammed the band into the R&B Top Five. Though they never attained those heights again, they remained consistent hitmakers for the next five years. A succession of albums, too, made the R&B Top 100 and, while the band's US crossover appeal was more limited, they also unleashed a number of major UK/European hits, beginning with "Galaxy of Love" and "I'm Gonna Love You Forever."

The band broke with Britton/Nerangis following 1978's *Dream World* album; Crown Heights' affair with the R&B Top 100 ran out soon after and, while "Somebody Tell Me What To Do" brought a brief renewal of past glories in 1982, the group returned to the club circuit for much of the '80s.

Both Anderson and the Reid brothers quit the band in 1986, for careers in production; they returned eight years later, to oversee Crown Height's 1994 album *I Got Something for Ya* and the "You Gave Me Love" single. Further singles "It's Time To Get Up" and a remake of 1978's "Say a Prayer for Two" followed, while 1998 brought the *Dream on Danceland* album, built around re-recorded oldies and more recent material.

## DISCOGRAPHY
### CHARTLOG
1974 Leave the Kids Alone/Rip Off (RCA—#96 R&B)

1975 Dreaming a Dream (disco version) (De-Lite—#5 R&B/#43 pop)

1975 Every Beat of My Heart (new disco version) (De-Lite—#20 R&B/#83 pop)

1976 Foxy Lady/'Picture Show (De-Lite—#17 R&B/#49 pop)

1977 Dancin'/Love Me (De-Lite—#16 R&B/#42 pop)

1977 Do It the French Way/Sexy Ways (De-Lite—#60 R&B)

1978 Say a Prayer for Two/Galaxy of Love (De-Lite—#41 R&B)

1979 Dance Lady Dance/Come Fly with Me (De-Lite—#20 R&B)

1980 You Gave Me Love/Tell Me You Love Me (De-Lite—#74 R&B/#102 pop)

1980 Sure Shot/I See the Light (De-Lite—#72 R&B)

1982 Somebody Tell Me What To Do/You Gave Me Love (De-Lite—#31 R&B)

### LPS
**8** 1974 Crown Heights Affair (RCA)

In terms of the band's original aims and vision, this is the only album that matters. "Super Rod" and "Leave the Kids Alone" are especially monumental.

**6** 1975 Dreaming a Dream (De-Lite—#28 R&B/#121 pop)

Disco colossus "Na Na Hey Hey" joins the title track and "Every Beat of My Heart" in hot-wiring CHA for the new age; "Foxy" gives fresh hope to all the evening's wallflowers.

**6** 1976 Foxy Lady (De-Lite—#59 R&B)

**5** 1976 Do It Your Way (De-Lite—#41 R&B/#207 pop)

**6** 1978 Dream World (De-Lite—#56 R&B/#205 pop)

**4** 1979 Dance Lady Dance (De-Lite—#40 R&B/#207 pop)

**6** 1980 Sure Shot (De-Lite—#50 R&B/#148 pop)

If you have to own a second CHA album (after the first), this one's worth it for the hopping "Use Your Body and Soul." Otherwise, grab the greatest hits collection.

**5** 1982 Think Positive (De-Lite)

**4** 1983 Struck Gold (De-Lite)

Stranded without too many hot ideas, the band at least looks back on their beginnings with fondness, and toys with recreating them. Unsuccessfully, one might add.

**6** 1994 I Got Something for Ya (Unidisc)

**6** 1998 Dream on Danceland (Snapper)

### SELECTED COMPILATIONS AND ARCHIVE RELEASES
**6** 1996 Dreams of De-Lite (Castle)

Lacks the RCA-era monsters, but a fine education in the days of disco.

### SELECTED SAMPLES
Far Out — Pete Rock & C.L. Smooth: Tell Me (1994)

## DAZZ BAND
**FORMED:** *1977, Cleveland, OH*

**ORIGINAL LINEUP:** *Bobby Harris (vcls, sax), Eric Fearman (gtr). Michael Wiley (bs), Kevin Frederick (kybds), Pierre DeMudd (horns), Skip Martin III (b. Sennie Martin III—horns), Isaac Wiley (drms), Kenny Pettus (perc)*

Saxophonist Bobby Harris launched what became the Dazz Band in 1977, after uniting his own group, Bell Telefunken, with the houseband from the Kinsman Grill in Cleveland. Emerging a classic funk octet in the style of Earth Wind & Fire, he christened the new unit Kinsman Dazz, a tribute to the recent hit single by Atlanta funk combo Brick. Dazz was also a contraction of the phrase "danceable jazz," a description that ideally fit this new band's attack.

Signing with the 20th Century label during 1978, Kinsman Dazz debuted with the minor hit "I Might as Well Forget About Loving You" toward the end of the year. They followed through with winter 1979's "Catchin' Up on You," but other releases were less successful and the band switched to Motown during 1980, abbreviating their name to the Dazz Band at the same time.

"Shake It Up" became the group's first hit—again twelve months after their last. Over the next six years, however, the Dazz Band achieved a virtual residency in the R&B

chart, beginning with the ballad "Invitation To Love" (the title track from their debut album) in March 1981.

They followed up with another slow dance, "Knock Knock" (and a second album, *Let the Music Play*), but anybody who had pegged the Dazz Band as some kind of post-Commodores ballad machine was to be seriously disavowed by their next release, "Let It Whip." Fearlessly embracing a pronounced new wave production, married to a driving, infectious funk rhythm, the Grammy winning "Let It Whip" topped the R&B chart for five weeks in May 1982, and remained on the chart for the next six months.

"Keep It Alive (On the K.I.L.)," the synthesizer and sound-effects laden title track to the band's newly released third album, followed. It climbed no higher than #20, but nevertheless confirmed the Dazz Band's aggressive dance (some say proto hip hop) tendencies—a mood enhanced in early 1983 by the album *On the One* and a Top Ten hit for its title track, "On the One for Fun."

Hastening to employ new recording technology as soon as it became available (they were one of the first R&B acts to actively embrace found sound samples), the Dazz Band next unleashed the techno-funk masterpiece "Joystick" (once more, the new album's title track), in November 1983. Twelve months later, they grabbed another major hit on both sides of the Atlantic with "Let It All Blow," taken from the *Jukebox* album.

Eric Fearman and Kevin Frederick quit in early 1985. They were replaced by Marlon McClain (gtr) and Keith Harrison (kybds) in time for the *Hot Spot* album; Steve Cox (kybds) and Jerry Bell (vcls) were also added to the lineup. However, a shift from Motown to the Geffen label in 1986 saw the Dazz Band's profile take a serious denting. After two years of reliable Top 30 action, the band snatched just two further hits with the new label, "L.O.V.E. M.I.A." and "Wild and Free," in 1986.

The parent *Wild and Free* album, meanwhile, saw the group's hitherto fearless development suddenly halt at a spot that sounded both distinctly dated and increasingly indebted to recent Prince releases. The unspecified involvement of Earth Wind & Fire's Maurice White apparently made no difference whatsoever.

The 1988 departures of Skip Martin (for Kool & the Gang) and Kenny Pettus coincided with the band's next move, from Geffen to RCA, where "Single Girls" finally returned them to the Top 20. It was a false dawn, however; the Eumir Deodato produced *Rock the Room* album failed to sell, while their new lineup of Harris, Harrison, De-Mudd, McClain, Cox, Dave O (kybds), Juan Lively (vcls) and Alan Palanker (kybds) was already sounding tired.

RCA dropped the band and they effectively broke up. It would be 1995 before the Dazz Band resurfaced, when Harris and McClain alone convened a new lineup featuring Nate Phillips (bs), Nikes McKinney (kybds), Greg Adams (trum) and the brothers Tommy (gtr) and Derek Organ (drms), for the *Streetlights* album and "Nasty Boogie" single. Two years later, linking with Intersound, the live *Double Exposure* captured a powerfully funk-heavy set high on nostalgia but higher still on fresh energy. Again, McClain and Harris were the sole original members.

However, the Dazz Band's new lease on life drew both Martin and Pettus back into the fold. They were augmented by a strong new lineup: Teri Stanton (vcls), Kevin Kendricks and Michael Norfleet (kybds) and Raymond Calhoun (drms). And, with George Clinton joining another original member, Pierre DeMudd, among the guest vocalists, the group cut an album that, defiantly, earned them some of the best reviews of their entire career. *Here We Go Again* was further highlighted by covers of Bootsy Collins "I Rather Be with You" and P-Funk's "Summer Swim," while the single "Girl Got Body" returned the band to the R&B charts.

## DAZZ BAND DISCOGRAPHY
### CHARTLOG

1980 Shake It Up/Only Love (Motown #65 R&B)
1981 Invitation To Love/Magnetized (Motown—#51 R&B/#109 pop)
1981 Knock! Knock!/Sooner or Later (Motown—#44 R&B)
1982 Let It Whip/Everyday Love (Motown—#1 R&B/#5 pop)
1982 Keep It Live (On the K.I.L.)/ This Time It's Forever (Motown—#20 R&B)
1983 On the One for Fun (Motown—#9 R&B)
1983 Cheek to Cheek/Can We Dance (Motown—#76 R&B)
1983 Party Right Here/Gamble with My Love (Motown—#63 R&B)
1983 Joystick/Don't Get Caught in the Middle (Motown—#9 R&B/#61 pop)
1984 Swoop (I'm Yours)/Bad Girl (Motown—#12 R&B)
1984 Let It All Blow/Now That I Have You (Motown—#9 R&B/#84 pop)
1985 Heartbeat/Rock with Me (Motown—#12 R&B/#110 pop)
1985 Hot Spot/I've Been Waiting (Motown—#21 R&B)
1986 L.O.V.E. M.I.A./A Place in My Heart (Geffen—#48 R&B)
1986 Wild and Free/Last Chance for Love (Geffen—#44 R&B)
1988 Anticipation/If It's Love (RCA—#38 R&B)
1988 Single Girls/All the Way (RCA—#19 R&B)
1988 Open Sesame/(instrumental) (RCA—#83 R&B)
1997 Ain't Nuthin' but a Jam Y'all/(instrumental) (Intersound—#58 R&B)
1998 Girl Got Body/Here We Go Again (Intersound—#81 R&B)

### LPS
**7** 1980 Invitation To Love (Motown)

**7** 1981 Let the Music Play (Motown—#36 R&B/#154 pop)
Nice, smooth pop set with little of the funk that would soon dominate their sound.

**8** 1982 Keep It Live (Motown—#1 R&B/#14 pop)
When they're good they're great, although the overall album is uneven. However, the absolutely outstanding "Let It Whip" makes up for any wobbles.

**7** 1983 On the One (Motown—#12 R&B/#59 pop)
**8** 1983 Joystick (Motown—#12 R&B/#73 pop)
**7** 1984 Jukebox (Motown—#18 R&B/#83 pop)
Joyous techno-funk, with a sound that hindsight insists pre-empted much of what English producer Trevor Horn soon achieved with the Art of Noise and Frankie Goes to Hollywood.

**5** 1986 Wild and Free (Geffen—#37 R&B/#100 pop)
The unmistakable sound of mid-'80s smarmy electro and tinky-tinky dance is all-pervading, as the band ditch some of their older school styling for the sake of current musical trend.

**5** 1988 Rock the Room (RCA—#91 R&B)
**7** 1995 Under The Streetlights (Lucky—#42 R&B)
Comeback from the band proves that older can sometimes be wiser, as the band dumps the weakness of their later '80s sound for an edgier, older, funk groove—although the mix of ballads detracts from the energy of the album. Includes the "Dazz Mega Mix" of older classics.

**7** 1997 Double Exposure (Intersound)
Live and loving it! From "Double ZZ" to "Knock Knock" and, of course, "Let It Whip," Dazz come through with high energy.

**7** 1998 Here We Go Again (Intersound—#99 R&B)
Great set that runs the gamut from the smooth R&B of "Oh What a Night" to the old school funk of "Ride" and the more contemporary "Bop Gun."

### SELECTED COMPILATIONS AND ARCHIVE RELEASES
**7** 1987 Greatest Hits (Motown)
**8** 1994 Funkology: The Definitive Dazz Band (Motown)
Chunky and complete—all the hits.

## THE FATBACK BAND

FORMED: 1970, New York, NY

ORIGINAL LINEUP: Bill Curtis (vcls, drms), Johnny King (gtr), Johnny Flippin (bs), Gerry Thomas (kybds), George Williams (trum), Earl Shelton (sax), George Adam (flute)

More than almost any other group of the era, the Fatback Band told the story of R&B as it traveled through the changing moods of the '70s and into the mid-'80s. In a career that ultimately saw them amass 31 R&B chart hits, the band unveiled a chain of crucial milestones in funk's journey from its psychedelic R&B roots, through disco and pop and on into the realms of hip-hop.

"Street Dance," from 1973, the double whammy of "Do the Bus Stop" and "Spanish Hustle" in 1975–76, "Freak the Freak the Funk (Rock)" and "King Tim III" in 1979, and, as aptly titled as any song could be, 1983's "Is This the Future?" serve up a virtual beginners' guide to the development of modern R&B. And all without once crossing into the pop Top 100.

The Fatback Band came together in the late '60s as the houseband at Bill Curtis' own Fatback label, a tiny New York operation whose acts included the Diplomats, the Puzzles and Mary Davis. Little of Fatback's output sold and, by 1972, Curtis had abandoned the label and was concentrating on the Fatback Band itself.

Signing to Perception, the group's first album, *Let's Do It Again*, and single, the frantic instrumental "Soul March," flopped in early 1973. However, the "Street Dance" 45 made the R&B Top 30 later that same year, while both "Nija (Nija) Walk (Street Walk)" and a reactivated "Soul March" reached the lower reaches of the chart soon after.

Accompanied by the *Keep On Steppin'* and *Yum Yum* albums, other lesser hits followed during 1974–75. The group was attaining some fame on the British northern soul circuit, however. "Keep On Brother, Keep On" became a firm dancefloor favorite and, in 1975, the Fatback Band achieved a surprise UK breakthrough when the absurdly hypnotic good times "Yum Yum (Gimme Some)" breached the Top 40, and "Do the Bus Stop" stomped to #18.

The group's lineup was still fluctuating throughout this period. Saxophonist Earl Shelton quit in 1974, following the sophomore *Keep On Steppin'* album, but returned in 1977. Guitarist King departed in 1975, but rejoined in 1979, with Kenny Ballard replacing him in the interim; keyboard player and arranger Gerry Thomas left to join novelty-funk wonders the Jimmy Castor Bunch.

He was replaced first by Saunders McCrae, then by Calvin Duke, but Thomas remained in contact with his former bandmates. In early 1976, he handed them a new song he'd written called "(Do the) Spanish Hustle," patently unsuitable for the Bunch, but ideal for the Fatback Band. It rocketed them to #10 in Britain, #12 on the US R&B chart (and #101 on the pop lists), and helped propel their latest (sixth) album, *Raisin' Hell*, into the Top 200.

**The full weight of the Fatback Band.**

Even more importantly, however, "Spanish Hustle" allowed the band to break out of the thoroughbred funk ranks at precisely the right time. Disco was coming, and the Fatback Band's fast-paced grooves were ideal for the Studio 54 crowd, even as they kept the funk audience happy as well.

Like Shelton, Thomas returned to the Fatback Band in 1977, as the group shortened their name to Fatback alone and delivered the *NYCNY USA* album. Meanwhile, the singles "The Booty," "Master Booty," "The Double Dutch" and "(Do the) Boogie Woogie" continued their fascination with new dance crazes. Elsewhere, "Freak the Freak the Funk (Rock)" took Chic's earlier interest in (of course) the Freak, and applied it to standards that even old school fans understood.

Fatback's pointedly tongue-in-cheek relationship with disco was a frequent source of unease, even within the band itself; but somehow they pulled it off—all the more so after they delivered the *Fired Up and Kickin' and Ready To Go*

album. The record was divided into two halves, the "freak party" side for the disco crowd, the "foot-stompin'" side for the funkers. They were rewarded when the funk driven "I Like Girls," became their first ever R&B Top Ten hit in spring 1978.

Fatback's eagle eye for new fashions and movements peaked when they encountered the B-Boy party scene in the Bronx. By mid-1979, DJ rappers the Cold Crush Brothers, the Funky 4+1 and Afrika Bambaataa were regularly releasing live tapes of their performances. Eazy AD of the Cold Crush Brothers claims sales of 500,000 plus tapes long before any rap *records* were ever released.

When Fatback recruited a rapper/MC of their own, Tim Washington, aka King Tim III, the original intention was simply to bring a new dimension to their live shows. It was the response of audiences that prompted them to combine one of King Tim's raps over a track called "Catch the Beat," retitle it "King Tim III" and—much against the better instincts of their record label—place it on the B-side of their next single, "You're My Candy Sweet."

But nobody could have predicted what happened next. New York DJs completely ignored "Candy Sweet," and instead slammed all six minutes of "King Tim III" into constant rotation. Rap had hit the record racks.

The release, just one week later, of the Sugarhill Gang's "Rapper's Delight," a similarly themed union with "We Got the Funk" hitmakers Positive Force, stole some of Fatback's thunder. But while history recalls "Rapper's Delight" as the first rap record to make the pop Top 40, by a matter of seven days "King Tim III" was the first to make the R&B chart.

Johnny King returned to Fatback following "King Tim III" and the accompanying XII album. Now, with a lineup of Curtis, Flippin, Williams, Thomas, King, Billy King (perc) and George Victory (gtr), the band recorded their most successful album yet, 1980's Hot Box. A pop Top 50 hit (going gold in the process), it spawned the synthesizer bass-driven hits "Backstrokin'" and another remarkable King Tim led rap, "Gotta Get My Hands on Some Money." By the end of the year, another album, 14 Karat had unleashed one more heavy funk hit, "Let's Do It Again," notable (amongst so much else) for a veritable bass battle between Flippin and synth wizard Thomas.

Further lineup changes, meanwhile, had seen Fatback redesigned once again. As the group prepared to follow-up 1982's On the Floor with Fatback album, Curtis, Flippin and Thomas alone remained from the original lineup, joined by keyboard player Michael Walker, guitarist Herb Smith and saxophonist Ed Jackson.

Still Fatback continued developing. Thomas' "Angel," while not the band's first soft, slow smoocher, was certainly an effective contribution to the so-called "quiet storm" balladeering now moving toward center stage, while "Take It Any Way" (1981) and "On the Floor" (1982) ensured they maintained contact with their roots. And in 1983, the cynically ominous "Is This the Future" returned them to streetwise urbanity with the recruitment of New York rapper Gerry Bledsoe to deliver a despairing recitation on modern city life.

Another guest, Evelyn Thomas, powered "Spread Love" into 1985, but Fatback's departure from Spring Records, their label for the past nine years, marked the end of the line. Signed now to Cotillion, two final singles made the lower reaches of the R&B chart during 1985, while their next two albums failed to make any impact whatsoever. Finally, Fatback broke up in 1987, bowing out with a live

album that proved, no matter how much else had changed over the years, their understanding of funk remained as strong as it ever was.

### FATBACK COMPLETE DISCOGRAPHY
### SINGLES
### THE FATBACK BAND

1973 Soul March/To Be with You (Perception—#69 R&B)
1973 Street Dance/Going To See My Baby (Perception—#26 R&B)
1973 Nija (Nija) Walk (Street walk)/Soul Man (Perception—#56 R&B)
1974 Keep On Steppin'/Breaking Up (Event—#50 R&B)
1974 Wicki Wacky/Can't Fight the Flame (Event—#94 R&B)
1975 (Hey I) Feel Real Good (part one)/(part two) (Event)
1975 Yum Yum (Gimme Some)/Let the Drums Speak (Event—#80 R&B)
1975 Do the Bus Stop/Gotta Learn To Dance (Event—#37 R&B)
1976 Spanish Hustle/Put Your Love (Event—#12 R&B/#101 pop)
1976 Party Time/Groovy Kind of Day (Spring—#84 R&B)
1976 The Booty/That's the Way You Want It (Spring—#32 R&B)
1977 Double Dutch/Spank the Baby (Spring—#52 R&B)

### FATBACK

1977 NYCNY USA/Soulfinger (Spring)
1977 Master Booty/Zodiac Man (Spring—#88 R&B)
1978 Mile High/Midnight Freak (Spring)
1978 I Like Girls/Get Out on the Dance Floor (Spring—#9 R&B/#101 pop)
1978 Boogie Freak/I'm Fired Up (Spring)
1979 Freak the Freak the Funk (Rock)/Wild Dreams (Spring—#36 R&B)
1979 (Do the) Boogie Woogie/Hesitation (Spring)
1979 You're My Candy Sweet (#67 R&B)/King Tim III (Spring—#26 R&B)
1979 Love in Perfect Harmony/Disco Bass (Spring—#59 R&B)
1980 Gotta Get My Hands on Some (Money)/Street Band (Spring—#6 R&B)
1980 Backstrokin'/Love Spell (Spring—#3 R&B)
1980 Let's Do It Again/Come and Get the Love (Spring—#55 R&B)
1981 Angel/Concrete Jungle (Spring—#67 R&B)
1981 Take It Any Way You Want It/Lady Groove (Spring—#19 R&B)
1981 Kool Whip/Keep Your Fingers Out of the Jam (Spring—#64 R&B)
1981 Rockin' to the Beat/Wanna Dance (Spring—#50 R&B)
1982 Na Na Hey Hey Kiss Her Goodbye/So I'm in Love/Chillin' Out (Spring)
1982 She's My Shining Star/UFO (Unidentified Funk Object) (Spring—#76 R&B)
1983 The Girl Is Fine (dance version) (Spring—#28 R&B)
1983 Is This the Future/Double Love Affair (Spring—#43 R&B)
1983 Up Against the Wall/With Love (Spring)
1984 I Wanna Be Your Lover/? (Spring)
1984 You've Got That Magic/? (Cotillion)
1984 Call Out My Name/I Love You So (Cotillion—#70 R&B)
1985 Lover Undercover/? (Cotillion)
1985 Girls on My Mind/Osiris (Cotillion—#79 R&B)

### FATBACK/EVELYN THOMAS

1985 Spread Love/(Instrumental) (Spring—#88 R&B)

LPS

THE FATBACK BAND

1972 Let's Do It Again (Perception)

Storming bursts of rhythm layered with dramatic guitars and vocal hooks.

1974 Keep On Steppin' (Event)

1975 Yum Yum (Event)

1976 Raising Hell (Event—#37 R&B/#158 pop)

1976 Night Fever (Spring—#31 R&B/#182 pop)

## FATBACK

### LPS

### THE FATBACK BAND

**8** 1972 Let's Do It Again (Perception)

Shows the band in fine funk style, before they added that disco groove. From "Goin' To See My Baby" to "Take a Ride (On the Soul Train)" this LP's a funk must have!

**8** 1973 Feel My Soul (Perception)

Johnny King's soulful vocals take center stage on a mighty, mellow album that nevertheless has a potent groove working under the surface.

**10** 1973 People Music (Perception)

"Nija Walk," "Soul March" and Isaac Hayes' "Soul Man" highlight a solid classic; the band's statement of intent, "Fatbackin'," has seldom been equaled. When people rank the Fatbacks among the funkiest bands of all time, this is what they mean.

**8** 1974 Keep On Steppin (Event)

Great hard funk with lots of groove, and includes the now classic "Wicky Wacky"

**7** 1975 Yum Yum (Event)

**7** 1976 Raising Hell (Event—#37 R&B/#158 pop)

A solid album, although the great funk of songs like "(Are You Ready) To Do the Bus Stop" and "Put Your Love (In My Tender Care)" is undermined somewhat by the speculative "Spanish Hustle."

**5** 1976 Night Fever (Spring—#31 R&B/#182 pop)

Very scary disco ranges from "Night Fever" (and it's not the Bee Gees song), to a cover of the Four Seasons' "December 1963 (Oh What a Night)." However, the band does pull some funk out with "A Little Funky Dance" and "No More Room on the Dance Floor."

## FATBACK

**8** 1977 NYCNYUSA (Spring—#54 R&B)

From the infectious funk of "Soul Finger (Gonna Put on You)" to the wonderfully euphemistic "Spank the Baby," Fatback meld funk with the day's popular club sounds for an overall easy groove.

**8** 1978 Fired Up and Kickin' 'N' Ready To Go (Polydor—#17 R&B/#73 pop)

Great LP with something for everyone. The set is divided into sections with Freak Party side's "I'm Fired Up" kicking things off, with the mellow thumper "I Like Girls" on the foot stomping flip.

**7** 1979 Bright Lites, Big City (Spring—#57 R&B)

**6** 1979 Fatback XII (Spring—#16 R&B/#89 pop)

The album itself is fair, but Fatback had their ear to the ground and their eyes on music's future. The vision is brought to life on the outstanding "King Tim III (Personality Jock)" recorded with rapper King Tim III. His rhymes over their funk were not only groundbreaking, but also predated, if only briefly, "Rapper's Delight."

**6** 1980 Hot Box (Spring—#7 R&B/#44 pop)

**7** 1981 Tasty Jam (Spring—#17 R&B/#102 pop)

Leaving recent gimmicky trappings behind, this set resonates with more traditional funk grooves. It's a smooth ride from "Take It Any Way You Want It" and "Keep Your Fingers out the Jam" to "Kool Whip."

**7** 1981 Gigolo (Spring—#68 R&B/#148 pop)

Fatback's full on funk on "Rockin' to the Beat" and "Rubdown," tempering the tempo with the R&B-sy ballad, "I'm So in Love."

**6** 1982 On the Floor with Fatback (Spring—#28 R&B/#204 pop)

**6** 1983 Is This the Future? (Spring—#27 R&B)

Ironic title for a set that has a (by 1983) very retro feel. Danceable light funk dominates here, but please skip "Funky Aerobics (Body Movement)," which is just plain silly.

**5** 1984 With Love (Spring—#64 R&B)

**6** 1984 Phoenix (Cotillion—#67 R&B)

**5** 1985 So Delicious (Cotillion)

**6** 1987 Live (Start)

### SELECTED COMPILATIONS AND ARCHIVE RELEASES

**6** 1976 Best of the Fatback Band (Spring)

**7** 1980 14 Karat (Spring—#16 R&B/#91 pop)

Includes tracks from the early "Let's Do It Again" to 1980's "Backstrokin'" and "Got To Get My Hands (On Some Money)."

**7** 1995 24 Karat: The Best (Southbound)

**8** 1997 Fattest of Fatback (Rhino)

Great collection of hits features full-length album tracks and single versions.

### SELECTED SAMPLES

Backstrokin' — Above the Law: V.S.O.P. (1993)

Backstrokin' — KAM: Givin' It Up (1995)

Gigolo — Above the Law: Me vs. My Ego (1993)

Gigolo — Eazy E: Any Last Werdz (1993)

Gotta Learn How To Dance — Everlast: Death Comes Callin (1998)

Gotta Learn How To Dance — Kool G. Rap: The Streets of New York (1990)

Kiba — Lord Finesse: Back to Back Rhyming (1990)

Let the Drums Speak — Jungle Brothers: Acknowledge Your Own History (1989)

Love Spell — Too Short: Gotta Get Some Lovin' (1993)

Put Your Love (In My Tender Care) — Beastie Boys: High Plains Drifter (1989)

Put Your Love (In My Tender Care) — Bjork: One Day (1993)

Put Your Love (In My Tender Care) — Gang Starr: Suckas Need Bodyguards (1994)

Put Your Love (In My Tender Care) — Kool G. Rap: Money in the Bank (1990)

Put Your Love (In My Tender Care) — Mad Kap: Beddie-Bye (1993)

Put Your Love (In My Tender Care) — Naughty by Nature: Written on Ya Kitten (remix) (1993)

Put Your Love (In My Tender Care) — The Pharcyde: Soul Flower (remix) (1993)

Put Your Love (In My Tender Care) — Poetess: For Rhyme's Sake (1992)

Put Your Love (In My Tender Care) — Poor Righteous Teachers: Pure Poverty (1991)

Put Your Love (In My Tender Care) — Yvette Michelle: DJ Keep Playin' (Get Your Music On) (1997)

Wicky-Wacky — A Tribe Called Quest: Show Business (1991)

What's Up Front That Counts — Eric B. & Rakim: Relax with Pep (1992)

What's Up Front That Counts — Queen Latifah: Mama Gave Birth to the Soul Children (1989)

## FAT LARRY'S BAND

**FORMED:** 1976, *Philadelphia, PA*

**ORIGINAL LINEUP:** *Ted Cohen (gtr), Larry LaBes (bs), Erskine Williams (kybds), Art Capehart (trum), Jimmy Lee (sax, trom), Doug Jones (sax), Larry James (b. 8/2/49 Philadelphia, d. 12/5/87 — drms), Darryl Grant (perc)*

Few groups better illustrated funk's ability to laugh at itself than Fat Larry's Band. Larry was fat; this was his band. Their name was a no-brainer, although the group's propensity for wild on-stage partying could not disguise the sheer depth of musicianship wrapped up within the hijinx.

Fat Larry himself was a Philly sessionman during the late '60s and early '70s, best known for his work with the Delfonics and Blue Magic. He formed his own band in 1976 at the dawn of the disco era, signing to the legendary Stax label (just as it was bought into the Fantasy stable) and immediately making it apparent that he didn't care what genre his particular brand of high-spirited jazz-funk was placed into, so long as people could dance to it.

It was an attitude that served the band much better in the UK than at home. Summer 1977 saw "Center City" rise to the edge of the UK Top 30, some nine months before

"Peaceful Journey" brought the band their first (very minor) R&B hit at home. A brief flirtation with the abbreviated name FLB saw "Boogie Town," a British Top 50 hit in March 1979, make #43 at home before the band reverted to their full nomenclatural glory for "Lookin' for Love" that fall. It kept them in the R&B Top 50, but little else.

With the group still confined to the ranks of period also-rans, Fat Larry's Band's third album, *Stand Up*, was attended by a pair of further mini-hits, including an unconventional version of the Beatles' "Here Comes the Sun" and "Act Like You Know"—a song better remembered for the Whatnauts' 1982 remake, "Help Is on the Way."

When the band chose to cover the Commodores' "Zoom" in 1982, few American listeners paid any attention then. In the UK, however, where Fat Larry's good time stomp fed effortlessly into the country's appetite for light-hearted dance music, the single soared to #2, its ascent characterized by some huge jumps—from #40 to #17 to #3 to #2 in just one month. It was ultimately held off the top by reggae tots Musical Youth's "Pass the Dutchie," but Fat Larry still wrapped up the year with the country's bestselling single by an American band. (The accompanying album, *Breakin' Out*, made #58 in Britain.)

It would be another four years before "Zoom" even sniffed the US R&B chart, when it struggled to #89, then fell out again. By that time, Fat Larry's Band themselves were on the way out. A new album, *Nice*, did no better than any past release and the group had all but broken up when news came of Fat Larry's death from a heart attack on December 5, 1987.

### *FAT LARRY'S BAND DISCOGRAPHY*
#### *CHARTLOG*

1978 Peaceful Journey/FLB (Stax—#94 R&B)

1979 Boogie Town/Passing Time (Fantasy—#43 R&B)

1979 Lookin' for Love/Countryside (Fantasy—#47 R&B)

1980 Here Comes the Sun/Everything Is Disco (Fantasy—#44 R&B)

1980 How Good Is Love/Like To Get To Know You Better (Fantasy—#78 R&B)

1982 Act Like You Know/Get Down Get Funky (WMOT—#67 R&B)

1986 Zoom/Which One Should I Choose (Omni—#89 R&B)

### *LPS*

**8** 1977 Feel It (Atlantic)

Heavy on the disco beat, the band nonetheless captures some great funk moments, from the throaty vocals of "Feel It" to the horn heavy "Music Maker."

**7** 1978 Off the Wall (Stax)

**7** 1980 Stand Up (Fantasy—#72 R&B)

**6** **1982 Breakin' Out (Virgin)**

Good, if somewhat formulaic set of danceable lite funk. Both the title track and "Act Like You Know" stand out in this vein, while the band swings round to smooth soul on "Zoom."

**5** **1983 Straight from the Heart (Virgin)**

**5** **1986 Nice (Omni)**

### SELECTED COMPILATIONS AND ARCHIVE RELEASES
**7** **1979 Best of the Fat Larry Band (Fantasy)**

Nice collection of early hits that includes the energetic "Close Encounters of a Funky Kind."

**6** **1995 Greatest Hits (Fantasy)**

### SELECTED COMPILATIONS AND ARCHIVE RELEASES
1979 Best of the Fat Larry Band (Fantasy)
1995 Greatest Hits (Fantasy)

### SELECTED SAMPLES

Down on the Avenue — Ice-T: Freedom of Speech (1989)
Down on the Avenue — Jungle Brothers: All I Think About Is You (1993)
Down on the Avenue — NWA: Something Like That (1988)
Down on the Avenue — Run DMC: The Ave (1990)
Down on the Avenue — Scarface: Your Ass Got Took (1991)
Down on the Avenue — Scarface: I'm Dead (1991)

## FAZE-O

**FORMED:** *1976, Chicago, IL*

**ORIGINAL LINEUP:** *Keith "Chop Chop" Harrison (kybds, vcls, perc), Ralph "Love" Aitkens (gtr), Tyrone 'Flye' Crum (bs), Roger "Dodger" Parker (drms, Robert "Bip" Neal, Jr., (perc, vcls)*

Chicago area funk band Faze-O began essentially as a side project for the Ohio Players, and specifically for Players sax man Clarence Satchell. Signing to She Records, the group released their first album, *Riding High* in 1977. All of the songs were co-written with the Ohio Players, who produced and arranged (under the moniker Tight Corporation) as well. The album crept into the R&B charts early in 1978, alongside a single of the same name.

Increasingly self-confident, Faze-O put more of themselves into their second set, *Good Thang*, handling most of the composing in-house. Satchell co-wrote one track, "Who Loves You," but was retained as producer, and once again, both the album and the title track made the R&B Top 50. However, just one further Faze-O album would appear, 1979's *Breakin' the Funk* (again produced by Satchell) before the band called it quits.

### FAZE-O COMPLETE DISCOGRAPHY
### SINGLES
1978 Riding High/True Love (She—#19 R&B)
1978 Good Thang/Who Loves You (She—#43 R&B)
1979 Breakin' the Funk/See You Through the Night (She—#63 R&B)

### LPS
**8** **1977 Riding High (She—#19 R&B/#98 pop)**

The outstanding "Funky Reputation" is sadly sandwiched between the ballads on side one, but the flip picks up the pace with "Toe Jam," "Get Some Booty" and "Test-This-Is-Faze-O."

**6** **1978 Good Thang (She—#40 R&B/#154 pop)**

**7** **1979 Breakin' the Funk (She—#48 R&B)**

Bowing to the overwhelming influence of disco, the band nevertheless are tighter, more polished and self-assured than ever. Their weakness, however, remains the ballad, and thankfully "See You Through the Night" is the last track on the LP.

### SELECTED SAMPLES

Ridin' High — Brothers like Outlaws: The Real McKoy (1992)
Ridin' High — Dream Warriors: Twelve Sided Dice (1991)
Ridin' High — EPMD: Please Listen to My Demo (1989)
Ridin' High — EPMD: Funky Piano (1991)
Ridin' High — Fat Joe: Shit Is Real (remix) (1995)
Ridin' High — Fresh 4: Wishing on a Star (1989)
Ridin' High — KAM: Hang 'Um High (1993)
Ridin' High — Kriss Kross: Tonite's Tha Night (1996)
Ridin' High — Low Profile: Keep 'Em Flowin (1990)

## THE GAP BAND

**FORMED:** *1969, Tulsa, OK*

**ORIGINAL LINEUP:** *Charles Wilson (vcls, kybds, perc), Ronnie Wilson (trum, kybds), Robert Wilson (bs, vcls)*

The children of a Pentecostal preacher, Ronnie, Charlie, Robert and sister Loretta Wilson originally sang together as a self-contained choir at their father's church. At junior high, Ronnie joined another vocal band, singing at local country clubs, before forming his own group in 1969.

Brother Charlie joined after being lured away from a rival band with the promise of more money. Fourteen-year-old Robert then came on board as bassist, despite never having played the instrument before. According to group legend, he nevertheless performed his first show without any rehearsal.

For a time, the trio gigged as the Wilson Brothers, before renaming themselves after the three main streets running through hometown Tulsa's Black business district, the Greenwood Archer and Pine Band. It was a short-lived con-

**Robert, Charlie, and Ronnie Wilson—the Gap Band.**

ceit. Realizing that their name was too long to comfortably fit on a bill poster, the group abbreviated to the G.A.P. Band. By the time fellow Oklahoman Leon Russell recruited the Wilsons as his backing group, they were the Gap Band; this final change was brought upon them by a concert promoter, who simply got it wrong on a poster.

The group's lineup was notoriously fluid. Guitarist Tuck Andress, one half of the Tuck and Patti jazz duo, was a member for a time; when Russell discovered the group, however, they were again the trio of Ronnie, Robert and Charlie. In this form, they made their recorded debut on Russell's own *Stop All That Jazz* album in 1974 and, the following year, cut their own debut, *Magician's Holiday* for his Shelter label.

They promoted it on the road with Russell, touring almost solidly for two years, and performing in front of massive crowds as opening act for the Rolling Stones, Queen and Kansas. The brothers also became a familiar force on the session circuit. Charlie recorded with Billy Preston, DJ Rogers, and Russell's wife, Mary McCreary; Robert worked with Ike Turner and also appeared on Russell's own next record, *Wedding Album*; Ronnie recorded with reggae icon Jimmy Cliff.

In 1977, Shelter dropped the Gap Band and, following one final single on parent label A&M, the Wilsons relocated to Los Angeles. There they signed with Tattoo, and two heavily Sly Stone-influenced singles—"Out of the Blue" and "Little Bit of Love"—made minor inroads into the R&B chart. But an accompanying eponymous album did nothing, despite guest appearances from Leon Russell and Chaka Khan, and by early 1978, the Gap Band was concentrating exclusively on live work.

With anything up to 14 musicians on stage at one time, the band were a hot concert attraction, earning warm comparisons with any of the better-known theatrical mavens of the day—a compliment their music only exaggerated. In a period when Sly Stone was fast moving out of the public eye, and P-Funk were moving into the arena circuit, the Gap Band's West Coast club dates provided an irresistible middle ground—all the more so since their good-natured sound (and unforgettable cowboy chic outfits) clearly showed no interest whatsoever in the forces of the demon disco. The downside of that, of course, was that very few record companies were showing any interest in them.

In 1978, DJ Rogers introduced the trio to Lonnie Simmons, a businessman who had just launched a partnership with a Los Angeles clothing store and a couple of local nightclubs, in order to open a new recording studio, Total Experience. This was part of an ambitious plan aimed at launching his own management and record company as well.

Simmons signed the Gap Band and, having first trimmed the sprawling lineup down to the core Wilson trio, he landed them a deal with Mercury. With Simmons producing (a role he would retain until the band themselves took over for their fifth album), March 1979 saw the Gap Band's first single for the label, "Shake," slam to #4 on the R&B chart.

"Open Up Your Mind" followed, while 1979–80 brought "Steppin' Out"—inspired by the then burgeoning skateboarding culture—and "Get Up and Dance (Oops Up Side Your Head)," a monstrous jam developed on stage one night after an ecstatic audience called the band back for an encore with that very chant.

Released in late 1979, the Gap Band's second Mercury album, II went gold, while the Wilsons themselves were attracting so much attention that, when Stevie Wonder was casting around for musicians to guest on his Hotter Than July album, the Gap Band were among his first choices. He subsequently returned the favor, appearing alongside Brides of Funkenstein vocalist Dawn Silva on the group's fifth album, in 1983. Cavin Yarbrough (of Yarbrough & Peoples) and future Tower of Power drummer Russ McKinnon ranked among the Gap Band's other high profile guests over the years.

Gap Band III and IV were the peak of the group's commercial prowess. Both went platinum, and between 1980–87, the Gap Band were scarcely out of the R&B chart, running up 24 hits, including three #1s. "Burn Rubber" topped the chart in 1980, while 1982's "Early in the Morning" debuted manager/producer Simmons' newly inaugurated Total Experience label in similar style. "You Dropped a Bomb on Me," that same summer, climbed to #2. "Outstanding" returned them to the top in early 1983.

The Gap Band's pop chart performances were less impressive ("Early in the Morning" was their sole Top 30 entry), but still the group represented one of the funk success stories of the '80s, clashing eminently danceable music with an often wicked sense of humor. "Burn Rubber," for ex-

ample, was based around their road manager's sad tale about how he arrived home to find his girlfriend had left so fast she "burned rubber through the back door." Other bands might have turned the experience into broken-hearted blues. The Gap Band transformed it into a riot.

Neither did the Gap Band's popularity ever really decline. Even when they released a very uncharacteristic ballad as a single, a cover of the Friends of Distinction hit "Goin' in Circles," in early 1986, they soared to #2. "Automatic Brain," "Big Fun" and "Zibble Zibble" followed. But by the end of that year, the brothers agreed it was time to take a break, both from manager Simmons and from one another.

Ronnie had recently been Born Again, and was more interested in pursuing a return to the church than making music. (He later joined Melba Moore and others in the traveling play Momma I'm Sorry.) Charlie was working as a session musician, alongside Ray Charles, Quincy Jones and the Eurythmics, and the Gap Band took a hiatus, broken only by a cut recorded for the soundtrack to the movie Penitentiary III.

They reunited in 1988 to work with veteran producer Norman Whitfield, recording the title theme to a second movie, I'm Gonna Git You Sucka. The brothers then signed with Capitol and recorded a new album, Round Trip, home to the Gap Band's fourth R&B chart-topper, "All of My Love."

The group disappeared again soon after, while Charlie Wilson worked on a solo album, 1992's You Turn My Life Around. The following year, the Gap Band again regrouped and released Testimony, an album that saw them try their hands at rap (contributed by Almighty Gee) and inspirational ballads, albeit with less than satisfactory results. The similarly underwhelming Ain't Nothin' Like a Party followed but, as the '90s funk revival found its feet, so the Gap Band rediscovered theirs.

A live album in 1996 proved the Wilsons had lost none of their ability to excite, while the Gap Band also contributed to the United We Funk collection of revitalized '80s-era funk acts, alongside Rick James, the SOS Band and Con Funk Shun. A new full-length album, 1999's Y2K: Funkin' Till the Millennium Comz, positively exploded with confidence, as guests Snoop Dogg, Casey Wilson and DJ Quik filed through to add their own stamp of approval on the old school.

### GAP BAND COMPLETE DISCOGRAPHY
### SINGLES
1974 Backbone/Loving You Is Everything (Shelter)

1974 I Like It/Tommy's Groove (Shelter)

1976 Hard Time Charlie/This Place Called Heaven (A&M)

1977 Out of the Blue (Can You Feel It)/Silly Grin (Tattoo—#42 R&B)

1977 Little Bit of Love/Knucklehead Suckin' (Tattoo—#95 R&B)

1979 Shake/Got To Get Away (Mercury—#4 R&B/#101 pop)

1979 Open Up Your Mind (Wide)/I Can Sing (Mercury—#13 R&B)

1979 Steppin' (Out)/You Are My High (Mercury—#10 R&B/#103 pop)

1980 I Don't Believe You Want To Get Up and Dance (Oops, Up Side Your Head)/Who Do You Call (Mercury—#4 R&B/#102 pop)

1980 Party Lights/Boys Are Back in Town (Mercury—#36 R&B)

1980 Burn Rubber (Why You Wanna Hurt Me)/Nothin' Comes to Sleepers (Mercury—#1 R&B/#84 pop)

1981 Yearning for Your Love/When I Look in Your Eyes (Mercury—#5 R&B/#60 pop)

1981 Humpin'/No Hiding Place (Mercury—#60 R&B)

1982 Early in the Morning/I'm in Love (Total Experience—#1 R&B/#24 pop)

1982 You Dropped a Bomb on Me/Lonely Like Me (Total Experience—#2 R&B/#31 pop)

1982 Outstanding/Boys Are Back in Town (Total Experience—#1 R&B/#51 pop)

1983 Party Train (dance mix) (Total Experience—#3 R&B/#101 pop)

1983 Jam the Motha'/Munchkin People (Total Experience—#16 R&B)

1984 Not Guilty/? (Mega—#77 R&B)

1984 I'm Ready (If You're Ready)/Shake a Leg (Total Experience—#74 R&B)

1984 Beep a Freak (dub version) (Total Experience—#2 R&B/#103 pop)

1985 I Found My Baby/(instrumental) (Total Experience—#8 R&B)

1985 Disrespect/(instrumental) (Total Experience—#18 R&B)

1985 Desire (LP version) (Total Experience—#46 R&B)

1985 The Christmas Song/Joy to the World (Total Experience)

1986 Going in Circles/I Believe (Total Experience—#2 R&B)

1986 Automatic Brain (rap version) (Total Experience—#78 R&B)

1986 Big Fun (serious dub mix) (Total Experience—#8 R&B)

1987 Zibble, Zibble (Get the Money)/(instrumental) (Total Experience—#15 R&B)

1987 Sweeter Than Candy/Penitentiary III/(instrumental) (RCA—#40 R&B)

1988 Straight from the Heart (dub mix) (Total Experience—#36 R&B)

1988 I'm Gonna Git You Sucka/Clean Up Your Act (Arista—#14 R&B)

1989 All of My Love (7" mix) (Capitol—#1 R&B)

1990 Addicted to Your Love (remixes) (Capitol—#8 R&B)

1990 We Can Make It Alright/? (Capitol—#18 R&B)

1995 First Lover (radio mix) (Raging Bull—#59 R&B)

1995 Got It Goin' On (radio edit) (Raging Bull—#75 R&B)

## LPS

**7** 1974 Magician's Holiday (Shelter)

A strange set, as influenced by label head Redbone as by the band's own inate style. "Backbone," which has plenty of it, and "Tommy's Groove" are the highlights.

**8** 1977 The Gap Band (Tattoo)

Not to be confused with their similarly titled Mercury de-but, but a tough set featuring those two wonderful, but so overlooked, Tattoo singles, plus a clutch of other heads-down boogie monsters.

**7** 1979 The Gap Band (Mercury—#10 R&B/#10 pop)

Uneven, but it does shine at times. Although the band is still some way away from their strongest material, they rip through some heavy funk. Includes "Open Your Mind (Wide)" and the sweet ballad "You Can Count on Me."

**8** 1979 The Gap Band II (Mercury—#3 R&B/#42 pop)

Dominated by the outstanding Parliament-esqe "I Don't Believe You Want To Get Up and Dance (Oops!)," the funkfest continues with "Party Lights" and "Steppin' (Out)." All this is only tempered mildly by the ubiquitous ballads "No Hiding Place" and "You Are My High."

**7** 1980 The Gap Band III (Mercury—#1 R&B/#16 pop)

Outrageous funk on "Humpin'" and "Burn Rubber on Me (Why You Wanna Hurt Me)" set the pace for this set, which only drops a notch from its predecessor.

**9** 1982 The Gap Band IV (Mercury—#1 R&B/#14 pop)

The group reaches their apex with one hit after another, including "You Dropped a Bomb on Me" and "Outstanding." Smooth and tight all the way, all howling horns, bad-ass bass and great vocals.

**8** 1983 The Gap Band V: Jammin' (Mercury—#2 R&B/#28 pop)

It must have been tough to follow up *IV*, but the band does so with exuberance and energy to spare. Slick R&B groovers like "Shake Leg" are the order of the day, while Stevie Wonder guests on "Someday."

**7** 1985 The Gap Band VI (Total Experience—#1 R&B/#58 pop)

**3** 1986 The Gap Band VII (Total Experience—#6 R&B/#159 pop)

Sadly, strangely, stagnant.

**4** 1987 The Gap Band VIII (Total Experience—#29 R&B)

**5** 1988 Straight from the Heart (Total Experience—#74 R&B)

**6** 1990 Round Trip (Capitol—#20 R&B/#189)

A better set than they'd turned out in five years, the brothers rebound mightily on "It's Our Duty" and Addicted to Your Love."

**6** 1994 Testimony (Rhino)

**5** 1995 Ain't Nothing but a Party (Raging Bull)

Over slick and more soul-oriented than the fierce funk that made them stars. Self-deprecating song titles like "Over the Funkin' Hill" don't help matters much.

**6** 1996 Live And Well (Intersound—#54 pop)

Competent live set from the mid-'90s covers all the hits and a few key misses.

**6** 1999 Y2K: Funkin' Till 2000 Comz (Crash)

While updating their sounds with rappers Snoop Doggy Dogg and DJ Quik among others, the band still mixes it up with old style funk and soul grooves.

## SELECTED COMPILATIONS AND ARCHIVE RELEASES

**7** 1985 Gap Gold: The Best of the Gap Band (Mercury—#46 R&B/ #103 pop)

All the hits through 1985, from "Shake" to "Burn Rubber (Why You Wanna Hurt Me)."

**8** 1995 The Best of the Gap Band (Mercury)

The best of the "best of" packed with chart hits and album goodies too.

**6** 1997 Greatest Hits (PSM)

**7** 1998 Ballads Collection (Polygram)

**6** 1998 The Best of the Gap Band 2 (Simitar)

Nice compilation targets lesser-known oldies but goodies.

**8** 1999 12" Collection & More (Polygram)

Great for the true fan, with the hits remixed to their extended best.

**7** 2000 20th Century Masters—Millennium: The Best of the Gap Band (Polygram)

## SELECTED SAMPLES

Burn Rubber — No Face: Fake Hair Wearin' Bitch (1990)

Humpin' — Paperboy: Bumpin' (Adaptation of Humpin') (1993)

Oops Up Side Your Head — DJ Quik: Mo' Pussy (1992)

Oops Up Side Your Head — Snoop Doggy Dogg: Snoop's Upside Ya Head (1996)

Outstanding — BLACKstreet: U Blow My Mind (1994)

Outstanding — Ice Cube: True to the Game (1991)

Outstanding — Kurious: I'm Kurious (1994)

Outstanding — Paris: Assata's Song (1992)

Outstanding — Paris: Thinka 'Bout It (1992)

Outstanding — R. Kelly: Summer Bunnies (1993)

Outstanding — Redman: Blow Your Mind (1992)

Outstanding — Soul for Real: Every Little Thing I Do (1995)

Shake — DJ Quik: Mo' Pussy (1992)

Tommy's Groove — Brand Nubian: Ragtime (1991)

Yearning for Your Love — A Tribe Called Quest: Like It Like That (1998)

Yearning for Your Love — Nas: Life's a Bitch (1994)

Yearning for Your Love — Paris: Outta My Life (1994)

Yearning for Your Love — The Pharcyde: Runnin' (remix) (1995)

## HEATWAVE

**FORMED:** *1976, Germany*

**ORIGINAL LINEUP:** *Johnnie Wilder (b. Dayton, OH—vcls, perc), Keith Wilder (b. Dayton, OH—vcls), Eric Johns (b. USA—gtr), Jesse Whittens (gtr), Rod Temperton (b. Hull, England—kybds), Mario Mantese (b. Spain— bs), Ernest Berger (b. Czechoslovakia—drms)*

The Wilder brothers, Johnny and Keither, formed Heatwave in 1976, following their discharge from the US Army. Initially based in Germany, where the pair were stationed (and had performed with various club bands), the pair relocated to the UK after a music press ad introduced them to songwriter Rod Temperton. Quite accidentally, the arrival of fellow Americans Jesse Whitten and Eric Johns, Czech-born Ernest Berger and Spaniard Mario Mantese conspired to bring Heatwave a cosmopolitan sound, which Temperton swiftly turned to his musical advantage.

At a time when the first wave of disco was beginning to crash onto European shores, Temperton melded the band members' "exotic" origins to a truly international funk rhythm and, having swiftly made a name for themselves on the live circuit, Heatwave came to the attention of London's GTO Records.

They were placed in the care of Barry Blue, a veteran session guitarist and producer, whose career also included a run of surprisingly enduring glitter/dance UK hits during 1973–75 ("Dancing on a Saturday Night," "Do You Wanna Dance," "Hot Shot"). Blue's crystalline ear for sound found a seamless soulmate in Temperton's writing, and Heatwave began work on their debut album in fall 1976.

Tragedy struck the group when rhythm guitarist Whitten was murdered before they even entered the studio. He was replaced by Roy Carter and, in January 1977, Heatwave's first single, "Boogie Nights," was released in Britain.

A pounding mini moog-led mantra, "Boogie Nights" climbed to #2 in the UK. Six months later, its US counterpart climbed just as high, even as "Too Hot To Handle" romped to #15 in Britain and the band's debut album, also titled *Too Hot To Handle*, made #46 in the UK.

Sensing that, despite its British success, the "Too Hot" ballad may, contrarily, have not been hot enough for American tastes, Heatwave followed up with the hard-hitting "The Groove Line." It slammed to #12 in the UK, and reached #7 in the US. Again produced by Blue and composed by Temperton, their second album, *Central Heating* followed, breaching the UK Top 30 and spawning two of the era's most memorable hit ballads, "Mind Blowing Decisions" and "Always and Forever."

Guitarist Johns quit the band during 1978; so did Temperton, embarking upon a songwriting career that saw him pen material for Quincy Jones and his proteges: the Brothers Johnson, Rufus, George Benson, Herbie Hancock and Karen Carpenter. Temperton also launched a partnership with Michael Jackson and contributed "Rock with Me" and "Off the Wall" to the singer's 1979 album, *Off the Wall,* before 1982 brought him mega-success as author of three songs, including the title track for *Thriller*.

Despite his departure, Temperton continued supplying Heatwave with new material, contributing all but one of the ten tracks scheduled for the band's next album, 1979's *Hot Property*. Unfortunately, before work could begin on it, disaster struck the band again; bassist Mantese was so seriously injured in a car accident, that he had no option but to leave the group. He was replaced by Derek Bramble and, with Calvin "Just Duke" Duke (kybds) and William Jones (gtr) on board, Heatwave recorded the album with producer Phil Ramone.

But the fates had not finished with the band. As the remarkably ambitious *Hot Property* stuttered to a halt just inside the Top 40, rhythm guitarist Carter left for a career in production (he would swiftly hit paydirt with electro-funkers Linx); synth player Keith Harrison replaced him. Then Johnnie Wilder, too, was involved in a terrible motor crash, and was left paralyzed from the neck down. Courageously, Wilder rejoined Heatwave in the studio for 1980's *Candles*, but his injuries necessitated recruiting a new vocalist for live work, James Dean "JD" Nicholas. Wilder concentrated on work on the other side of the mixing desk.

With Temperton maintaining his involvement as composer and arranger, November 1980 saw Heatwave unleash the dense "Gangsters of the Groove" for their final US pop hit. Early in the new year, riding constant club action, it made the UK Top 20 and pulled the album into the Top 30 in its wake. But Heatwave's day was fast coming to a close. "Jitterbugging," the second single from the album, made #34 in Britain; "Where Did I Go Wrong," in the US, barely scratched the R&B Top 75.

For their fifth album, *Current*, Heatwave returned to producer Barry Blue and scraped a minor hit with Temperton's "Lettin' It Loose" in mid-1982. By the end of the year, however, Bramble had quit; he, too, moved into production, working with David Bowie on 1984's *Tonight* album and, later, with British hopeful Jaki Graham. Nicholas also left, for the demanding role of replacing Lionel Ritchie in the Commodores. Heatwave effectively broke up.

The Wilder brothers remained silent through the remainder of the '80s, although 1989 brought a low-key comeback with *The Sound of Soul*, followed in 1991 by a minor UK hit with a remix of "Mind Blowing Decisions." Johnnie Wilder also cut a spiritual album, *My Goals* (and an a cappella single "In the Garden") for the Light label in 1990. This flurry of activity preceded a second comeback in the mid-'90s, highlighted by a successful US tour for a new Heatwave lineup fronted by Keith Wilder alone, with Kevin Sutherland (kybds), Dave Williamson (bs), Byron Byrd (kybds) and Bill Jones (gtr). A surprisingly entertaining live album, *At the Greek Theater, Hollywood*, followed in 1997.

## HEATWAVE
### HEATWAVE DISCOGRAPHY
### CHARTLOG
1977 Boogie Nights/All You Do Is Dial (Epic—#5 R&B/#2 pop)
1977 Always and Forever/Super Soul Sister (Epic—#2 R&B/#18 pop)
1978 The Groove Line/Happiness Togetherness (Epic—#3 R&B/#7 pop)
1978 Mind Blowing Decisions/Beat Your Booty (Epic—#49 R&B)
1979 Eyeballin'/Birthday (Epic—#30 R&B)
1980 Gangsters of the Groove/Find Someone like You (Epic—#21 R&B/#110 pop)
1981 Where Did I Go Wrong/Dreamin' You (Epic—#74 R&B)
1982 Lettin' It Loose/Mind What You Find (Epic—#54 R&B)

### LPS
**9** **1976 Too Hot to Handle (Epic—#5 R&B/#11 pop)**
The set has a strong dance ethic, but is imbued with plenty of funk from "Ain't No Half Steppin'" to the unimpeachable classic "Boogie Nights." The other standout is, of course, 1976's prom theme "Always and Forever."

**8** **1977 Central Heating (Epic—#2 R&B/#10 pop)**
Smooth grooves dominate this set, especially on "Send Out for Sunshine," while "Central Heating" is a mover *par excellence* Plus, where would we be now without "The Groove Line"?

**7** **1978 Hot Property (Epic—#16 R&B/#38 pop)**
The set doesn't pack the same punch as its predecessors. But, split between quiet soul ballads, funk grooves and hard disco—heard best on "One Night Tan," the LP is still worth a dance or two.

**6** **1981 Candles (Epic—#24 R&B#71 pop)**
**6** **1982 Current (Epic—#21 R&B/#156 pop)**
**5** **1989 Sound of Soul (Blatant)**
**7** **1997 Live at the Greek Theater (Century Vista)**
Unlike most of their peers' latter live performances, Heatwave are scorching! Energetic and effusive, they lay down long grooves that just get everyone in the mood for more. Includes "Boogie Nights" and "You Can't Get It." Of course.

### SELECTED COMPILATIONS AND ARCHIVE RELEASES
**7** **1984 Greatest Hits (Epic)**
**8** **1996 The Best of Heatwave: Always & Forever (Epic/Legacy)**
All you'll need from this great band. Includes all the hits, plus disco versions of several songs including "Groove Line."

Ain't No Half Steppin' — Doug E. Fresh: Keep Risin to the Top (1988)
Mind Blowin' Decisions — A Tribe Called Quest, featuring Faith Evans & Raphail Saddig: Stressed Out (remix) (1996)
Groove Line — Public Enemy: Sophisticated Bitch (1987)
Mind Blowin' Decisions — Doug E. Fresh: Keep Risin' to the Top (1988)
Mind Blowin' Decisions — Pete Rock: Soul Survivor (1998)
Star of the Story — A Tribe Called Quest: Verses from the Abstract (1991)

## HI TENSION

**FORMED:** *1972, London, England*
**ORIGINAL LINEUP:** *David Joseph (vcls, kybds), Paul Phillips (gtr), Ken Joseph (bs), Paul McLean (sax), Bob Sydor (sax), Ray Alan Eko (sax), Peter Thomas (trom), Guy Barker (trum), David Reid (drms), Paapa Mensah (drms), Jeff Guishard (perc)*

Formed as a vehicle for vocalist Joseph's wild funk songwriting, Hi Tension started life as Hot Waxx, one of the crucial attractions on the early-'70s British club scene. Regulars on the northern soul circuit, where their high energy performances were as indefatigable as the all-night dancers, Hi Tension finally landed a record deal in 1977.

They signed to Island partly on the strength of their live reputation and partly via the utterly irresistible qualities of their best number, a funked up answer to the "Hustle"/ "Spanish Hustle" hits of recent years, "The British Hustle."

Produced by Kofi Ayivor and Alex Sadkin, Hi Tension's first single, "Hi Tension," made #13 in the UK in spring 1978, paving the way for "British Hustle" that summer. It reached #8; oddly, however, as swiftly as Hi Tension broke through, they faded away. A third single, "There's a Reason," bombed, while the band's debut album, released at the end of the year, climbed no higher than #74. The group was dropped soon after.

Hi Tension resurfaced in the mid-'80s with a new core lineup of Ken Joseph and Jeff Guishard, plus conductor Leroy Williams. A pair of lightweight independent singles made no impression, however, and Hi Tension faded again.

### *HI TENSION DISCOGRAPHY*
*LP*

**7** 1978 Hi Tension (Island)

Pulsing energy, thunderous bass, and some so-sweetly dated disco-era flourishes, slam the band through the hits "British Hustle" and "Hi-Tension."

## INSTANT FUNK

**FORMED:** *1968, Trenton, NJ*
**ORIGINAL LINEUP:** *James Carmichael (vcls), Kim Miller (gtr), George Bell (gtr), Raymond Earl (bs), Dennis Richardson (kybds), Larry Davis (trum), Johnny Onderlinde (sax), Eric Huff (trom), Scotty Miller (drms)*

Trenton Junior High students Raymond Earl and Scotty Miller formed their first band, the Music Machine, in the mid-'60s. An enthusiastic R&B combo, the group gigged extensively around New Jersey, but remained unknown and unsung until they encountered the TNJs (Trenton New Jerseys), a newly formed vocal trio comprising James Gist, Elijah Jones and Greg Jamerson. They were in search of a reliable, hardworking backing band, while Music Machine were in search of direction. The two groups dovetailed perfectly.

With Miller's brother Kim coming in on guitar, Music Machine became the TNJs' regular backing band in mid-1967. At this point, the TNJs' manager introduced the package to Walter "Bunny" Sigler, a Philadelphia based singer and producer then riding high with the hit medley "Let the Good Times Roll and Feels So Good." According to band legend, the first time Sigler saw them, the TNJs were performing his own "You Got Your Hooks in Me."

In 1968, Sigler took the TNJs to local label Newark, cutting their debut single, "She's Not Ready." Switched to the Cameo-Parkway label, the group followed through with "I Think I'm Falling in Love." However, it swiftly transpired that Sigler was more interested in the Music Machine than the TNJs. By 1969, he had recruited Earl & the Millers to back him on his own recordings, changing their name to Instant Funk—apparently because it only took them an instant to get down to it.

In 1971, Sigler linked with the production team of Kenny Gamble, Leon Huff and Thom Bell at the forefront of the Philly International Records (PIR) label. Gamble and Huff, of course, would become the label's focus; they had already established themselves as a formidable team, co-writing hits for the Intruders, Archie Bell & the Drells, Jerry Butler, the O'Jays and more.

At PIR, however, Gamble and Huff's reputation—and their success—went into overdrive. Within nine months of the label's launch, PIR had sold over ten million singles, scoring #1s with Billy Paul, the O'Jays and Harold Melvin & the Bluenotes, and establishing a brandname, Philly, which was as instantly identifiable as Motown or Stax had ever been.

The musicians who accompanied PIR's artists were drawn from a vast pool, including members of Trammps, the Salsoul Orchestra and, at Sigler's prompting, Instant Funk. Their first session for the label produced Sigler's own version of the O'Jays' "Love Train" and the *Keep Smilin'* album, and the band remained by Sigler's side throughout the remainder of the decade.

The trio were also to be found backing many of PIR's other stars—the O'Jays, South Shore Commission ("Free Man," as a promo, the first 12-inch disco mix single in US music history), the resurgent Archie Bell & the Drells, jazz guitarist Gabor Szabo (on a re-recording of "Keep Smilin'"), Carl Carlton and Lou Rawls. Sessions with keyboard player Dexter Wansel (his 1976 *Life on Mars*) and guitarist Theodore Life (1978's *That's Life*) then saw these musicians drawn into Instant Funk itself.

Under Sigler's tutelage, Instant Funk's first single, the instrumental "Float like a Butterfly," appeared in 1976. It was followed by an album, *Get Down with the Philly Jump*, a fine slab of what Sigler's liner notes called "sweet sophisticated funk with a driving beat, the kind that got the whole world on its feet." The album sold poorly, but Sigler was not to be deterred. He encouraged the band to expand its lineup even further, recruiting pianist Dennis Richardson and percussionist Charles Miller.

In early 1978, Sigler broke from Philly and launched his own production company, Bundino Productions Unlimited, which was distributed by Norman Harris' Gold Mind label. (Harris was guitarist with the Salsoul Orchestra.)

Even more so than at PIR, Instant Funk became one of Salsoul's premier in-house bands, while continuing to work outside the label's own stable. They accompanied Evelyn "Champagne" King on her hits "Shame," "I Don't Know If It's Right" and "Music Box," and recorded with the Pips (the *Callin'* LP) and the O'Jays. Of course, they were also present on Sigler's own next album, *I've Always Wanted To Sing, Not Just Write Songs*; band members contributed two tracks to the album, "I'm Funkin' You Tonight" and "Let's Get Freaky Now."

Sigler debuted on Gold Mind with the Top Ten hit single "Let Me Party with You (Party Party Party)," edited down from the 12-minute title track of his latest album. Instant Funk, of course, backed him throughout the album, while the guest vocalists included another Sigler discovery, James Carmichael (ex-Tapestry, Bittersweet). Convinced that a powerful vocalist was all that was standing between Instant Funk and a successful career of their own, Sigler promptly drafted Carmichael into the band, adding guitarist George Bell and a horn section around the same time.

The Gold Mind label folded in early 1979. But with Salsoul picking up the roster, Instant Funk's instantly successful eponymous debut album was released in spring, 1979, just as the new lineup's first single, "I Got My Mind Made Up (You Can Get It Girl)" soared to the top of the R&B chart. Hooking listeners with a scandalized sounding refrain of "say what?" provided by Pinky, a North Carolina girl who happened to be around the studio at the time; "I Got My Mind Made Up" became a million seller. Its success in New York City (some 400,000 copies were sold in the city alone) prompted Manhattan Borough President Andrew Stein to proclaim May 22, 1979, "Instant Funk Day."

Instant Funk followed up with the Latin flavored "Crying," a song that Sigler later suggested may not have been the right choice. "Instant Funk [have] been accepted as a disco band, but they were really a funk band," he reflected in the liner notes to Instant Funk's 1996 *Greatest Hits* anthology. "They were Instant Funk, not Disco Funk." But "Crying" blurred such distinctions, while Sigler also acknowledged that success, too, had altered the makeup of the band. "When you have more chiefs than indians, you're gonna have problems. On the first album, I was chief. On the second, everybody was a chief."

That second album was *Witch Doctor*, cut with what became the band's permanent lineup of Earl, the Miller brothers, Carmichael, Bell, Richardson, Williams, Eric Huff (trom), Johnny Onderline (sax) and Larry Davis (trum). "Bodyshine," the band's first 1980 hit, featured the added punch of the Brecker Brothers. In the meantime, a dynamic remix of *Witch Doctor*'s none too subtle ode to oral sex, "Slap Slap Lickedy Lap" brought the group to the attention of Isley Brothers guitarist Ronnie Isley, who recruited Instant Funk as support for his own band's next tour.

*Witch Doctor* itself, meanwhile, became the object of considerable controversy; the sleeve design depicted the band members in full ritualistic drag (complete with bubbling cauldron), while the title track slunk in on sinewy rhythms, primitive chants and lyrics full of bones and ju ju men. Accusations of religious impropriety swiftly followed. According to an incredulous Sigler, "One guy told me he couldn't listen to the record because it was against his religion."

Riding the controversy, Instant Funk shared a *Midnight Special* TV bill with rock shocker Alice Cooper, using the opportunity to further emphasize the hard-edged funk rock sound that would characterize their third album, *The Funk Is On*.

The album was launched with a new single; the densely packed Randy Muller (Brass Construction) composed title track in November 1980. But Instant Funk's hardest-hitting album yet was an inexplicable flop and, over the next two years, the band concentrated on live work and sessions alone.

Recorded with a slimmed down lineup of Earl, the Miller brothers, Carmichael, Bell, Richardson, Williams, and Davis, Instant Funk's fourth album, 1982's *Looks So Fine*, was a tour de force Sigler's vocals highlighted the title track, and the mini hit "Why Don't You Think About Me," one of two tracks produced by the band themselves. The album's masterpiece, however, was "Punk Rockin' (Slam Dunk the Funk)," a teasing parody of Rick James' self-professed funk punk, a classic groove unfortunately overlooked in the wake of Sun's near-simultaneous "Slam Dunk the Ffunk."

Members continued departing. Both Davis and Bell quit during 1982, even as Sigler and the surviving Instant Funkers, Earl, the Millers, Richardson and Carmichael got to grips with V, the band's fifth album. The loss of the horns, however, was more than remedied by the band's eager embrace of electronics and techno.

The vocoder-led "No Stoppin' That Rockin'," its composite elements indebted equally to classic Philly soul and modern Afrika Bambaataa, made #32 in early 1983 — Instant Funk's first R&B Top 40 hit since "Witch Doctor." The triumphant "Who Took Away the Funk" followed. Penned by ex-Heatwave guitarist Roy Carter, this monster lament for the death of the old school effortlessly (and, of course, purposefully) recaptured the golden age of P-Funk in its insistent chant and solid jam.

Despite the obvious vitality, which remained Instant Funk's most potent calling card, Carmichael quit in mid-1983, to be replaced by former TNJ Elijah Jones. Other new recruits included Michael Gist (perc) and pianist Donald Lamons (rapper on "Don't Call Me Brother"), while Manchild/West Street Mob frontman Reggie Griffin weighed in on sax and linn drum. Again it was a powerful lineup, but in October, "(Just Because) You'll Be Mine" became Instant Funk's last R&B chart entry.

The demise of the Salsoul label spelled the beginning of the end for Instant Funk. Breaking with Sigler, they released the "Tail Spin" single through the Philadelphia independent label Pop Art (better known as home to Salt-N-Pepa's embryonic Super Nature incarnation), but it sold poorly. A period of increasingly desultory live work followed, and by 1986, Instant Funk were no more.

Earl moved into production (his first studio was in the basement of the Millers' mother's home). There he began working with Terrence Reed, the son of one of the TNJs' own, pre-Music Machine backing band, scoring a 1987 hit with "Love Rap Ballad" under the name True Love. Earl and Sigler, too, have continued working together on recordings by Patti Labelle (1994's "If I Don't Have You"), the Wootens and an off-Broadway production, *20th Century R&B*.

### INSTANT FUNK DISCOGRAPHY
#### CHARTLOG
1979 I Got My Mind Made Up (You Can Get It)/Wide World of Sports (Salsoul—#1 R&B/#20 pop)
1979 Crying/Never Let It Go Away (Salsoul—#41 R&B)
1979 Witch Doctor/I Want To Love You (Salsoul—#35 R&B)
1980 Bodyshine/Scream and Shout (Salsoul—#41 R&B/#103 pop)
1980 The Funk Is On/You're Not Getting Older (Salsoul—#87 R&B)
1982 Why Don't You Think About Me/Punk Rockin' (Salsoul—#59 R&B)
1983 No Stoppin' That Rockin'/(instrumental) (Salsoul—#32 R&B)
1983 Who Took Away the Funk/I'll Be Good to You (Salsoul—#70 R&B)
1983 (Just Because) You'll Be Mine/Funkiest Party in the World (Salsoul—#71 R&B)

#### LPS
**6** **1976 Get Down with the Philly Jump (PIR)**
A brain-blistering collision of two musical forms that really didn't spend that much time together, hard earthy funk and sweet Philly soul.

**8** **1979 Instant Funk (Salsoul—#1 R&B/#12 pop)**
Airtight funk grooves make liberal use of fierce guitar and furious bass riffing, making it easy to see why the band were in such demand as session musicians. Who wouldn't want their own record to sound this good? Includes the smash hit "I Got My Mind Made Up (You Can Get It Girl)."

**8** **1979 Witch Doctor (Salsoul—#23 R&B/#129 pop)**
You can throw them onto the disco floor, but they'll never stay there for long. Innovative latter-day funk adds a rock sound to the mix on "Bodyshine," while the title track seethes as wickedly as you like.

**7** **1980 The Funk Is On (Salsoul—#62 R&B/#130 pop)**
Another solid set keeps the funk fires burning on the title track, while allowing the band to experiment on "Can You See Where I'm Coming From." The result is a fresh twist on an old sound.

**6** **1982 Looks So Fine (Salsoul—#43 R&B/#147 pop)**

**6** **1983 V (Salsoul—#38 R&B)**

**5** **1984 Kinky (Salsoul)**

**8** 1996 Greatest Hits (Capitol)

Great collection that's got all the hits in a package as tight as the band's own sound. The 12-inch dance mix of "I Got My Mind Made Up" is unbeatable.

### SELECTED SAMPLES

I Got My Mind Made Up . . . — De La Soul: Roller Skating Jam Named "Saturdays" (1991)

I Got My Mind Made Up . . . — Public Enemy: Welcome to the Terrordome (1990)

I Got My Mind Made Up . . . — Terminator X featuring Whodini: It All Comes Down to Money (1994)

## RICK JAMES

BORN: *James Johnson, Jr., 2/1/48, Buffalo, NY*

Rick James has spent much of his career shrugging off the traditional trappings of funk—the sounds of James Brown and Parliament—and replacing them with his self-defined brand of "punk funk." And while success certainly followed the formula, James' own career wound a path that was both rocky and rich.

Growing up in the 1950s, James' musical background was eclectically diverse, spanning the rock 'n' roll of Elvis Presley, and the R&B roots of the Drifters, the cool jazz of Thelonious Monk and his mother's favorite, Nancy Wilson. An uncle, Temptations' vocalist Melvin Franklin, also was a strong influence.

James picked up instruments naturally, without lessons or guidance and, by the time he was nine years old, he was singing both at school and on the street with his friends, as well as playing drums. In his early teens, James joined an African style group, but put his ambitions on hold when he dropped out of school and, lying about his age, joined the military reserves.

He was still underage when he was placed on active duty. However, rather than admitting he was too young to be shipped out to Vietnam, James went AWOL, eventually relocating to Toronto, Canada, where he returned to his R&B roots and began singing.

Linking with local musicians, "Rick James Matthews," formed the Mynah Birds in 1965. According to *Great Rock Discography* author Martin Strong, the band cut one single, "Myhah Bird Hop," for the Canadian arm of Columbia Records before James' uncle Melvin helped the band land a deal with Motown. After some lineup shuffles, the Myhah Birds also featured bassist Bruce Palmer and guitarist Neil Young. Goldie McJohn (who called James "the black Mick

Jagger"), later to join Steppenwolf, was also a member at one point, though he was gone by the time Young came into the Mynah Birds.

Despite the risk of James' arrest, the band, by this time including Young and Palmer, recorded in Detroit; British author Johnny Rogan, in his 1982 *Neil Young* biography, alleges the Mynah Birds released "a couple of singles . . . which were almost immediately deleted." In fact, the band recorded about an album's worth of material, all of which remains unreleased. (Following guitarist Young's rise to fame, Motown finally scheduled a release in late 1969, assigning the LP catalog number Motown MS 697. However, pressure from Young apparently stymied the project.)

Inevitably, the military caught up with James, bursting into the studio one day and arresting him. Only after he finally admitted his age was he released, by which time the Mynah Birds had already broken up. Young and Palmer later relocated to Los Angeles and helped form Buffalo Springfield; James, meanwhile, remained in Detroit, as a Motown staff writer.

Spending the next year dividing his time between the US and London (where he briefly fronted a blues band, the Main Line), James returned to the US and joined White Cane, alongside J. Sonny Nicholas (gtr), Denny Gerard (bs), Ed Roth (orgn), Ian Kojima (sax), Bob Boughty (trum), Norman Wellbanks (drms) and Cleveland Hughes (perc). The group recorded one album, *Great White Cane* for MGM's Lion subsidiary, but remained unknown.

By 1977, James was working with a new group, the Stone City Band, exploring a funk-rock fusion quite unlike any other, one which prided itself upon maintaining a tight structure that was never allowed to wander into the jam.

The Stone City Band backed James across an album's worth of recordings and in late 1977 he returned to the Motown family, signing to the Gordy subsidiary. The album, credited to Rick James and the Stone City Band, appeared in spring, 1978; *Come and Get It* immediately rocketed up both the R&B and pop charts. A single, "You and I," topped the R&B chart. A barely disguised paean to marijuana, "Mary Jane," made the Top 3.

It was a phenomenal rebirth, and one which James' second album, early 1979's *Bustin' Out of L Seven* only enlarged upon. Three singles, "Bustin' Out," "High on Your Love Suite" and "Fool on the Street" peeled straight into the charts and, that summer, James launched his first major US tour, supported by a young and unknown Prince. Released in late fall, 1979, the *Fire It Up* album capped off a sensational year, while James also scored as the writer and

**A superfreak in the garden of love—Rick James.**

producer behind teenage singer Teena Marie's "I'm a Sucker for Your Love" hit.

In 1980, the excitement begin to flag. *Garden of Love*, James' fourth album, failed to match the accomplishments of its predecessors and, amid swarming rumors of drug abuse, James dropped out of sight. He soon resurfaced, however, crashing to the top of the R&B charts with a new album, *Street Songs*, and another rapid-fire burst of hit singles, "Give It to Me Baby," "Ghetto Life" and the utterly irresistible "Super Freak."

A massive hit, its unmistakable riff and great groove dominating that summer of 1981, "Super Freak" was the ultimate fruition of the mix of sounds that James had been honing for so many years. The song was nominated for a Grammy for Best Rock Vocal Performance and, although it eventually lost out to Rick Springfield's "Jessie's Girl," the song and that riff would become a vital part of an enduring musical tapestry—even before it was lifted almost wholesale for MC Hammer's 1990 smash "U Can't Touch This." (According to James, he was initially strongly opposed to sampling, and infuriated when he heard "his" song on the radio. He became even angrier when he learned that his own lawyers had approved Hammer's use of the loop. But then, he says, they revealed how big his checks were going to be, and suddenly sampling didn't seem such a terrible thing after all.)

"Super Freak" was also remarkable in that it brought together four of the Temptations on backing vocals, a successful collaboration that pushed James to reunite all seven members of the band for a new single. "Standing at the Top," credited to the Temptations, featuring Rick James, reached #6 on the R&B charts and was included on James own 1982 LP, *Throwin' Down*. The following year, James duetted with another Motown great, Smokey Robinson, for his *Cold Blooded* album's "Ebony Eyes."

Next, James launched the Mary Jane Girls, a quartet (Joanne McDuffie, Kim Wuletich, Candice Ghant and Yvette Marina) conceived as a tribute to the great girl groups of his youth. With James writing and producing, the band released two albums, in 1983 and 1985, both R&B Top Ten hits. Another successful collaboration with Eddie Murphy saw James produce the comedian's 1985 hit "Party All the Time." (James' own "Can't Stop" was included in the soundtrack to Murphy's *Beverly Hills Cop* movie that same year.)

James seemed unstoppable, a human hit machine. But there were cracks in the armor that were becoming harder to ignore. James had long been famed for his prodigious use of drugs and, despite having cleaned up in 1980, the rumors were again flying. Several times he was hospitalized, and even as 1985's *Glow* swept chartward, his life appeared in total disarray, as he battled an addiction to cocaine. Problems with Motown, too, were looming. Indeed, the label dropped him in 1986 after one final release, the Top 20 hit *The Flag*.

James again disappeared from view, but returned in 1988 on Reprise Records to release *Wonderful*, and close out a tumultuous decade with two excellent singles—a collaboration with rapper Roxane Shante, "Loosey's Rap," which brought James his first R&B #1 since 1983, and a remarkable

ode to his old icons the Drifters with "This Magic Moment/Dance with Me."

James spent the next several years living hard, a cycle that finally came crashing to a halt in 1991, when he and his girlfriend, Tanya Hijazi, were arrested on a variety of charges, including false imprisonment and aggravated mayhem. His mother died in the midst of that controversy, devastating James and pushing him even closer to the brink. The following year he was arrested again, this time on a drugs charge. Finally, in 1994, he was sentenced to five years and four months, in Folsom State prison, on charges of assaulting two women and cocaine use.

Released within two years, James was clean and ready to pick up the music where he had left off. But his still-flourishing bad boy reputation ensured he would find it very difficult to land a new record deal. He was finally picked up by the tiny Private Eye label and, drawing from a stockpile of songs written during his prison time, he recorded the *Urban Rhapsody* album in 1997. Working with guests Bobby Womack, Snoop Doggy Dogg and the Mary Jane Girls' McDuffie, James recorded sufficient material to fill a double album, but ultimately whittled it down to a concise single disc.

James also contributed to the *United We Funk* collection of revitalized '80s-era funk acts; the SOS Band, the Gap Band and Con Funk Shun were similarly involved.

### RICK JAMES DISCOGRAPHY
#### CHARTLOG
1978 You and I/Hollywood (Gordy—#1 R&B/#13 pop)
1978 Mary Jane/Dream Maker (Gordy—#3 R&B/#41 pop)
1979 High on Your Love Suite/Stone City Band, Hi! (Gordy—#12 R&B/#72 pop)
1979 Bustin' Out/Sexy Lady (Gordy—#8 R&B/#71 pop)
1979 Fool on the Street/Jefferson Ball (Gordy—#35 R&B)
1979 Love Gun/Stormy Love (Gordy—#35 R&B)
1980 Come into My Life (Part 1)/CIML (Part 2) (Gordy—#26 R&B)
1980 Big Time/Island Lady (Gordy—#17 R&B)
1981 Give It to Me Baby/Don't Give Up on Love (Gordy—#1 R&B/#40 pop)
1981 Super Freak (Part 1)/(Part II) (Gordy—#3 R&B/#16 pop)
1981 Ghetto Life/Below the Funk (Pass the J) (Gordy—#38 R&B/#102 pop)
1982 Standing on the Top (Part 1)/(Part 2) (Gordy—#6 R&B/#66 pop)
1982 Dance Wit' Me –(Part 1)/(Part 2) (Gordy—#3 R&B/#64 pop)
1982 Hard To Get/My Love (Gordy—#15 R&B)
1982 She Blew My Mind (69 Times)/(instrumental) (Gordy—#62 R&B)
1983 Cold Blooded/(instrumental) (Gordy—#1 R&B/#40 pop)
1983 U Bring the Freak Out/Money Talks (Gordy—#16 R&B/#101 pop)
1983 Ebony Eyes/1,2,3 (You Her and Me) (Gordy—#22 R&B/#42 pop)
1984 17/(instrumental) (Gordy—#6 R&B/#36 pop)

1984 You Turn Me On/Fire and Desire (Gordy—#31 R&B)
1985 Can't Stop/Oh What a Night (4 Luv) (Gordy—#10 R&B/#50 pop)
1985 Glow/(instrumental ) (Gordy—#5 R&B/#106 pop)
1985 Spend the Night with Me/(instrumental) (Gordy—#41 R&B)
1986 Sweet and Sexy Thing/(instrumental) (Motown—#6 R&B)
1988 Loosey's Rap/(instrumental) (Reprise—#1 R&B)
1988 Wonderful/(instrumental) (Reprise—#50 R&B)
1989 This Magic Moment/Dance with Me/(instrumental) (WB—#74 R&B)
1997 Players Way/? (Private Eye)

## LPS

**7** 1978 Come and Get It! (Gordy—#3 R&B/#13 pop)

A nice debut nodding toward Motown standards and disco, but the funk bubbles underneath the surface break out occasionally with some great grooves.

**8** 1979 Bustin' Out of L Seven (Gordy—#2 R&B/#16 pop)

From top to bottom, shout out loud funk a la Funkadelic and Sly. Thoroughly danceable from "Bustin' Out" to "Cop N Blow," with "Fool on the Street" presaging James' later material.

**6** 1979 Fire It Up (Gordy—#5 R&B/#34 pop)

Losing some punch in comparison, this set feels more like transitional material—spread equally between disco/pop, funk and the rock edge that would soon come to the fore, although the title track and "Come into My Life" is fun.

**5** 1980 Garden Of Love (Gordy—#17 R&B/#83 pop)

James takes a break from funk with a quality collection of smooth soul groovers.

**10** 1981 Street Songs (Gordy—#1 R&B/#3 pop)

James' greatest. A delicious blend of classic funk, merging maniacally into his own aggressive punk/funk sound, and even that's not enough to keep "Super Freak" in check. An expanded "deluxe edition" was released in 2001 (Universal).

**8** 1982 Throwin' Down (Gordy—#2 R&B/#13 pop)

There's a little something for everyone here, from ballads to punk/funk, including "Standing on the Top," James' duet with the Temptations.

**6** 1983 Cold Blooded (Gordy—#1 R&B/#16 pop)

Despite the inclusion of esteemed guests Billy Dee Williams, Grand Master Flash and Smokey Robinson (on the smash hit "Ebony Eyes"), and the now expected crop of top-notch punk-funkers, much of James' own performance feels just a little lost and weary.

**7** 1985 Glow (Gordy—#7 R&B/#50 pop)

Good comeback album that adds more rock to the R&B.

**4** 1986 The Flag (Gordy—#16 R&B/#95 pop)

Formulaic funk. Give it a miss.

**5** 1988 Wonderful (Reprise—#12 R&B/#148 pop)

The album gave us "Loosey's Rap," but not much else.

**6** 1997 Urban Rhapsody (Private I—#31 R&B/#170 pop)

Fine, friendly comeback album that recycles the aggro sounds of '80s-era James and updates the whole package with additions from Snoop Doggy Dogg and Rappin' 4-Tay.

### SELECTED COMPILATIONS AND ARCHIVE RELEASES

**6** 1984 Reflections: Greatest Hits (Motown)

**6** 1986 Greatest Hits (Motown)

**8** 1992 Rick and Friends (Priority)

Nice collection of James' collaborations with other musicians, plus some of the Mary Jane Girls stuff.

**9** 1994 Bustin' Out: The Very Best of Rick James (Motown)

Fat 27 track career spanning collection.

**6** 1995 Motown Legends: Give It to Me Baby (Motown)

Collection of earlier Motown material.

**7** 2000 20th Century Masters: The Millennium Collection—The Best of Rick James

Worthy, if cruelly but short, hits collection.

### WHITE CANE

**6** 1972 Great White Cane (Lion)

Unremarkable funk-rock album, its modern collectibility owes everything to James and little to its contents.

### SELECTED SAMPLES

Bustin' Out — Keith Murray: Get Lifted (1994)
Give It to Me Baby — MC Hammer: Let's Get It Started (1988)
Mary Jane — BWP: No Means No (1991)
Mary Jane — Compton's Most Wanted: Late Night Hype (1990)
Mayy Jane — Coolio: I Remember (remix) (1994)
Mary Jane — Da Brat: Sittin' on Top of the World (1996)
Mary Jane — Dana Dane: Rollin' Wit Dane (1995)
Mary Jane — Diamond Shell: Grand Imperial Diamond Shell (1991)
Mary Jane — Dr. Dre & Ed Lover: For the Love of You (1994)
Mary Jane — EPMD: Jane (1988)
Mary Jane — EPMD: Jane II (1989)
Mary Jane — EPMD: Who Killed Jane (1992)
Mary Jame — EPMD: Jane 5 (1997)
Mary Jane — Kriss Kross: I'm Real (1993)
Mary Jane — Redman: Smoke Buddah (1996)
Moonchild — Mary J. Blige: Love Is All We Need (1997)
Moonchild — Diamond D: Cream N Sunshine (1997)
Moonchild — Jay-Z: You're Only a Customer (1997)
Super Freak — MC Hammer: U Can't Touch This (1990)

## KC & THE SUNSHINE BAND

**FORMED:** *1973, FL*
**ORIGINAL LINEUP:** *Harry Wayne "KC" Casey (b. 1/31/51—vcls, kybds), Jerome Smith (b. 6/8/53—gtr), Richard*

*Finch (b. 1/25/54—bs), Charlie Williams (b. 11/18/54—trom), Robert Johnson (b. 3/21/53—drms), Fermin Goytisolo (b. 13/31/51—perc)*

Full of smooth funk grooves and an insatiable bubblegum sensibility, KC & the Sunshine Band carved an indelible niche for themselves in the annals of 20th century music by crossing every genre available, from funk and soul to Calypso and pop. Their sound was always lighthearted and a call to hit the dancefloors—no matter the country or audience.

Harry Casey was working in a Hialeah, FL, record store in the early '70s, picking up the store's stock from area distributors. At one of his regular calls, Tone Distributors, he was invited in to meet singer Clarence Reid; immediately impressed by the studio setup, Casey began spending time there, helping out around the warehouse and, eventually, being hired as an occasional session pianist.

It was there, too, that he met Richard Finch, a young engineer. The duo began jamming together, graduated to writing songs and, in early 1973, launched themselves as KC & the Sunshine Junkanoo Band. "Junkanoo" was a rowdy Caribbean dance music the duo first heard played at Clarence Reid's wedding.

Released through Tone's own TK label, that fall brought their debut single, "Blow Your Whistle," a compulsive dancefloor number that cracked the R&B Top 30, but just as importantly, launched the pair as the studio's new golden boys. "Rock Your Baby," written and produced for George McCrae, topped charts around the world in spring 1974. They also recorded with Betty Wright among others, before TK suggested they relaunch the Sunshine Junkanoo Band.

Adding Jerome Smith, Robert Johnson and Fermin Goytisolo, the newly abbreviated KC & the Sunshine Band cut their first album, *Do It Good*, in late 1974. It did little, but two singles enjoyed a very different fate. "Sound Your Funky Horn" was an immediate US hit; "Queen of Clubs" made the Top Ten in the UK (it finally charted in America following a 1976 reissue).

KC & the Sunshine Band opened 1975 with their first American tour, and while another single, "I'm a Push-over," barely made the R&B Top 60, their next release, April's "Get Down Tonight," topped both the pop and R&B charts. The *KC & the Sunshine Band* album followed later in the summer and again reached the top of the charts, while the group's signature hit, "That's the Way (I Like It)," proved similarly successful that fall.

Attempts to establish the Sunshine Band themselves as a hit-making concern were less well-starred. Although an album, *The Sound of Sunshine*, fared well. Two singles, "Shotgun Shuffle" and a reprise of "Rock Your Baby," were only minor hits. The fans, it seemed, had spoken. KC & the Sunshine Band were a package deal; without KC, there was no sunshine.

The group toured heavily, their success alone brushing away the disdain of so-called "serious" funk and R&B fans. For middle America, they were indeed the epitome of funk, as was proven at the end of the year, as KC & the Sunshine Band won two Grammy nominations for Best Artist and Best R&B Vocal Performance for "Get Down Tonight." Casey and Finch also received two nominations—in the same category! "Where Is the Love," co-written with (and for) Betty Everett, pipped "That's the Way (I Like It)" for Best Rhythm & Blues Song.

In 1976, KC & the Sunshine Band firmly hitched their wagon to the disco train, with their third LP, *Part 3*, and a stream of effervescent—not to mention inescapable—singles. "(Shake, Shake, Shake) Shake Your Booty" became one of 1976's summer anthems, knocking the Ohio Players off the top of the chart; while "I Like To Do It," "I'm Your Boogie Man," "Wrap Your Arms Around Me" and "Keep It Comin' Love", kept up the pressure well into 1977.

Whether by accident or design, KC & the Sunshine Band released no new product during 1977—the year, of course, in which *Saturday Night Fever* so thoroughly redesigned the disco/R&B landscape. They returned in 1978, however, having imbibed every lesson that monster taught. "Boogie Shoes," the flip from "Shake Your Booty," was included on the film's soundtrack, and KC re-released the song in its own right in early 1978. It was an effortless Top 30 hit, and became their biggest-selling release ever.

It would be hard for KC & the Sunshine Band to compete with such a heady peak, so they didn't even try. Instead, 1978's *Who Do Ya (Love)* album scaled back the sound a little, returning to the funk grooves that dominated their earlier sound. The following year's *Do You Wanna Go Party* continued in a similar vein, while the group proved that they were capable of even greater musical extremes, when the ballad "Please Don't Go" topped the pop chart without even figuring in the R&B listings.

Casey, meanwhile, was also nurturing a new talent, singer Teri DeSario, recording two singles with her in 1980. "Yes, I'm Ready" and "Dancin' in the Streets," furthered the Band's recent achievements, with the former topping the Adult Contemporary chart, and reaching #2 on the pop. However time was running out. The Band's *Space Cadet* album failed to chart, and in 1981, the TK label folded, a victim of the disco boom's own abrupt dissipation. KC & the Sunshine Band disbanded soon after.

Casey retained the group's name briefly, signing with Epic and releasing the album *The Painter*. Again it missed the chart, and Casey was still considering his next move when he was involved in a horrific automobile accident in early 1982. Suffering extensive nerve damage, he was confined to a wheelchair for much of the year, undergoing months of grueling physical therapy and rehabilitation.

He recovered and, in early 1983, recorded the album *All in a Night's Work*, again credited to KC & the Sunshine Band. It did nothing in the US, but one single from the set, "Give It Up," took the UK by storm, topping the chart for three weeks in August. But a follow-up, "(You Said) You'd Gimme Some More," could only scrape to #41, and with the album also failing to live up to the single's success, Casey briefly retired the Sunshine Band name. One final album credited to KC alone, *KC Ten*, was released in 1984, on Casey's own Meca label.

With a new generation of Sunshine Bandsmen, KC continued touring the United States, performing a nostalgia-choked greatest hits set, and filling venues from coast to coast. The band also enjoyed a massive resurgence in the mid-late-'90s, showering their audience with a host of compilation best-ofs and remix collections, while rockers White Zombie covered "I'm Your Boogie Man" for the soundtrack to *The Crow: City of Angels*. Finally, in 1998, that old familiar sound returned to the chart once more, when Casey teamed with rappers 2 Live Crew to record "2 Live Party."

### KC & THE SUNSHINE BAND DISCOGRAPHY
### CHARTLOG
#### KC & THE SUNSHINE JUNKANOO BAND
1973 Blow Your Whistle/I'm Going To Do Something Good (TK—#27 R&B)

#### KC & THE SUNSHINE BAND
1974 Sound Your Funky Horn/Why Don't We Get Together (TK—#21 R&B)
1974 Queen of Clubs/Do It Good (#25 R&B/#66 pop—in 1976)
1975 I'm a Pushover/You Don't Know (TK—#57 R&B)
1975 Get Down Tonight/You Don't Know (TK—#1 R&B/#1 pop)
1975 That's the Way (I Like It) (TK—#1 R&B/#1 pop)
1976 (Shake, Shake, Shake) Shake Your Booty/Boogie Shoes (TK—#1 R&B/#1 pop)
1976 I Like To Do It/Come On In (TK—#4 R&B/#37 pop)
1977 I'm Your Boogie Man (TK—#3 R&B/#1 pop)
1977 Wrap Your Arms Around Me (TK—#24 R&B)
1977 Keep It Comin' Love/Baby I Love You (TK—#1 R&B/#2 pop)
1978 Boogie Shoes/I Get Lifted (TK—#29 R&B/#35 pop)
1978 It's the Same Old Song/Let's Go Party (TK—#30 R&B/#35 pop)

1978 Do You Feel All Right/I Will Love You Tomorrow (TK—#62 R&B/#63 pop)
1979 Who Do Ya Love/Sho-Nuff (TK—#88 R&B/#68 pop)
1979 Do You Wanna Go Party/Come to My Island (TK—#8 R&B/#50 pop)
1979 Please Don't Go/I Betcha Didn't Know That (TK—#25 R&B/#1 pop)
1983 Give It Up/Uptight (Meca—#18 pop)

#### THE SUNSHINE BAND
1975 Shotgun Shuffle/Hey J (#25 R&B/#88 pop)
1976 Rock Your Baby/S.O.S. (TK—#70 R&B)
1978 Black Water Gold/Part 2 (TK—#75 R&B)

#### KC WITH TERI DESARIO
1980 Yes, I'm Ready/With Your Love (Casablanca—#20 R&B/#2 pop)
1980 Dancin' in the Streets/Moonlight Madness (Casablanca—#66 pop)

#### KC & SUNSHINE WITH 2 LIVE CREW
1998 2 Live Party/(mixes]) (Lil' Joe—#52 R&B/#102 pop)

### LPS
**5** 1974 Do It Good (TK)
**8** The band's funkiest effort was also their least successful. Go figure.
**8** 1975 KC & the Sunshine Band (TK—#1 R&B/#4 pop)
Practically a hits collection in its own right. "Boogie Shoes," "Get Down Tonight", and "That's The Way (I Like It)" changed the way people danced, with an infectious hint of funk masquerading as disco gold.
**7** 1976 Part 3 (TK—#5 R&B/#13 pop)
KC toned down the disco and brought up the grooves, while "Shake Your Booty" and "Wrap Your Arms Around Me" stomped the competition on the dancefloor.
**5** 1978 Who Do Ya (Love) (TK—#25 R&B/#36 pop)
A harder edge returns, but an uneven set with no real hits, and a dire warning that perhaps the band had run out of material.
**6** 1979 Do You Wanna Go Party (TK—#19 R&B/#50 pop)
**6** 1981 Space Cadet (TK)
**5** 1981 The Painter (Epic)
**5** 1982 All in a Night's Work (Epic)

#### THE SUNSHINE BAND
**7** 1975 The Sound of Sunshine (TK—#24 R&B/#131 pop)

#### KC
**4** 1984 KC Ten (Meca—#93 pop)
The sounds of something that should have stopped—long ago.

### SELECTED COMPILATIONS AND ARCHIVE RELEASES
**7** 1980 Greatest Hits (TK—#62 R&B/#132 pop)
**6** 1983 Their Greatest Hits (Epic)

**7** 1990 Greatest Hits Vol. 2 (Hollywood)

**8** 1990 Best of KC & the Sunshine Band (Rhino)

A nice, fat, 16-track boogiefest.

**7** 1994 KC & the Sunshine Band and More (Rhino)

Reissue of the second album includes remixes, plus "Do It Good" and "I'm a Pushover" from the first.

**5** 1995 Part 3 And More (Rhino)

Like its predecessor a straightforward album reissue, appended with bonus material including solo KC material from the '80s.

**5** 1995 Get Down (Live) (Intersound)

Live set includes "James Brown Medley." Uh huh uh huh.

**6** 1996 The Gold Collection (EMI)

**6** 1997 I'm Your Boogie Man and Other Hits (Rhino)

**5** 1997 Shake Shake Shake and Other Hits (Rhino)

**6** 1998 Let's Party (EMI)

**5** 1998 Dance Remixes (Rhino)

A dangerously compulsive collection utterly dismisses the mindless purity of the original recordings, and instead tries to reinvent the hits as something meatier. Unfortunately, it was the mindless purity that made them matter in the first place.

**7** 1999 25th Anniversary Edition (Rhino)

Nice two-CD set collects all the '70s hits, plus goodies from the '80s and rarities.

## SELECTED SAMPLES

Ain't Nothin' Wrong — Digable Planets: Where I'm From (1993)

Ain't Nothin' Wrong — Soul II Soul: Feeling Free (1989)

Boogie Shoes — Grand Puba: That's How We Move It (remix) (1992)

Do You Wanna Go Party — Ice-T: What You Wanna Do? (1989)

Get Down Tonight — Bamboo: Bamboogie (1998)

Get Down Tonight — Busta Rhymes: Get High Tonight (1997)

Get Down Tonight — Kid 'N Play: Funhouse (1990)

That's The Way — 2 Live Crew: Face Down, Ass Up (1990)

That's THe Way — DJ Jazzy Jeff & the Fresh Prince: Scream (1993)

What Makes You Happy — Young Black Teenagers: Mack Daddy Don of the Underworld (1991)

## CHAKA KHAN

**BORN:** *Yvette Marie Stevens, 3/23/53, Chicago, IL*

Although Chaka Khan's initial claim to fame was as vocalist for the funk rock band Rufus, it was her solo career that placed her on a pedestal. She remains one of the very few funk superstars who were able to break away from the bands that defined them, and emerge not as an appendage or splinter, but as a fully fledged performer whose canon utterly eclipsed their past.

Alongside her sister Yvonne (aka Taka Boom), Khan launched her career as a teenager in a school group, the Crystalettes. She moved onto the politically aware Shades of Black in the late '60s, where both sisters adopted their better-known monikers.

Leaving home to get married in 1969, Khan joined local heroes the Baby Sitters in 1972, following the death of the group's original vocalist, Baby Huey. The group changed its name to Goliath and cut a 45 for Curtis Mayfield's Curtom label; it went nowhere, but Khan was already attracting attention from elsewhere. Another band on the Chicago circuit, Rufus, had recently parted company with their vocalist, Paulette McWilliams. They asked Khan to replace her.

Things moved quickly. By mid-1973, Rufus signed to ABC. By mid-1974, they were stars, with Khan singled out for especial attention almost from the beginning. By the end of 1974, the original Rufus had broken up in the face of ABC's constant demands for her to be given even more of the spotlight. The new lineup convened for the band's third album apparently had less objections to the set being titled *Rufus Featuring Chaka Khan*.

Khan went on to record nine records with the band over the course of the next decade, and in 1977, began work on what became her solo debut, *Chaka*, backed by members of the Average White Band. (Rufus' Tony Maiden added guitar to "I Was Made To Love Him"—a cover, of course, of Stevie Wonder's "I Was Made To Love Her.")

Produced by Arif Mardin and leaning more toward disco than the funkified sonics of Rufus, Khan nevertheless turned in a stunning debut, scoring an instant hit with Ashford & Simpson's "I'm Every Woman," a song the duo wrote specifically for her. It was also nominated for a Grammy for Best Female R&B Vocal Performance. *Chaka*, too, was a weighty hit, and while a second single, "Life Is a Dance" didn't fare quite as well, still it was an impressive start.

Khan quit Rufus to launch her solo career, although her contract demanded she return for two subsequent albums: 1979's *Masterjam* and 1981's *Camouflage*. She also returned to the stage with the band in February 1982, for the New York shows recorded for 1983's *Stompin' at the Savoy* live album.

Maintaining her solo career throughout this period, Khan's 1980 album *Naughty* repeated much the same format as its predecessor, including an Ashford & Simpson composed opening cut, "Clouds." (They also wrote the closing "Our Love's in Danger.") Late 1982 then saw the release of Khan's own fourth album, the Grammy-winning *Chaka Khan*. She also aligned herself with jazz keyboardist

**Chaka Khan—the woman she is.**

Chick Corea on his *Echoes of an Era* album, eschewing the R&B/pop vocal style of her own career to demonstrate a breathtaking command of jazz.

Khan's masterpiece, however, was still to come; 1984's *I Feel for You* granted her a recognition that spanned not only genres, but generations as well. The title track, a Prince composition first recorded on his *Prince* album, featured contributions from Stevie Wonder and Melle Mel. This not only updated Khan's sound, it also sent her off in a new, updated direction. Almost as a matter of course, the single captured another Grammy, while the album, too, was nominated.

*I Feel for You* marked the peak of Khan's pop ambitions, as she now entered a period of fruitful collaborations that not only continued to push her profile, but also helped satisfy her creative yearnings as well.

In 1986, Khan joined English rock singer Steve Winwood on the sessions for his single "Higher Love"; she also appeared alongside David Bowie on the Arif Mardin produced *Labyrinth* soundtrack. Three years later, Quincy Jones recruited Khan to perform two tracks on his *Back on the Block* album, a set designed to recreate four decades of musical change, from bebop to rap. She also duetted with Siedah Garrett on "The Places You'll Find Love" and with Ray Charles on "I'll Be Good to You"—an old Brothers Johnson song.

Khan herself released just two solo albums during this time, later admitting that she had become increasingly dissatisfied with the direction her own music was taking. Both *Destiny* in 1986 and *CK* in 1988 were very dance-oriented sets, focussing ever less on her own vocal strengths. The 1992 album *The Woman I Am*, too, proved a less than satisfying showcase, and that despite winning yet another Grammy. It was also her last contracted album for WB, and she did not seem in much of a hurry to resign with the label.

Moving to London, Khan intentionally dropped from sight for a time. She worked in theater for a while, and collaborated with Mary J. Blige on "Not Gon' Cry," for the *Waiting to Exhale* soundtrack. Other partnerships included hit couplings with Guru, Brandy and Me'Shell Ndege-Ocello, and a reunion with Quincy Jones, Khan contributing one song, "Stomp," to his 1996 *Q's Jook Joint* album.

Of course the layoff was not permanent; following a tentative return to the limelight in 1996, with the handpicked compilation, *Epiphany: The Very Best of Chaka Khan*, Khan then signed to Prince's NPG label. Her ninth solo album, *Come 2 My House*, was released in 1998.

## CHAKA KHAN DISCOGRAPHY

### CHARTLOG

1978 I'm Every Woman/A Woman in a Man's World (WB—#1 R&B/#21 pop)

1979 Life Is a Dance/Some Love (WB—#40 R&B)

1980 Clouds/What You Did (WB—#10 R&B/#103 pop)

1980 Papillon (aka Hot Butterfly)/Too Much Love (WB—#22 R&B)

1980 Get Ready, Get Set/So Naughty (WB—#48 R&B)

1981 What 'Cha Gonna Do for Me/Lover's Touch (WB—#1 R&B/#53 pop)

1981 We Can Work It Out/Only Once (WB—#34 R&B)

1981 Any Old Sunday/Heed the Warning (WB—#68 R&B)

1982 I Know You, I Live You/And the Melody Still Lingers On (Night in Tunisia) (WB)

1982 Got To Be There/Pass It On, a Sure Thing (WB—#5 R&B/#67 pop)

1983 Tearin' It Up/So Not To Worry (WB—#48 R&B)

1984 I Feel for You/Chinatown (WB—#1 R&B/#3 pop)

1985 This Is My Night/Caught in the Act (WB—#11 R&B/#60 pop)

1985 Through the Fire/La Flamme (WB—#15 R&B/#60 pop)

1985 (Krush Groove) Can't Stop the Street/(instrumental) (WB—#18 R&B)

1985 Own the Night/(instrumental) (MCA—#66 R&B/#57 pop)

1986 The Other Side of the World/(instrumental) (WB—#81 R&B)

1986 Love of a Lifetime/Coltrane Dreams (WB—#21 R&B/#53 pop)

1986 Tight Fit/Who's It Gonna Be? (WB—#28 R&B)

1987 Earth to Mickey/My Destiny (WB—#93 R&B)

1988 It's My Party/Where Are You Tonite (WB—#5 R&B)

1989 Baby Me/Everybody Needs Some Love (WB—#12 R&B)

1989 Soul Talkin'/I'm Every Woman (WB)

1992 Love You All My Lifetime/Keep Givin' Me Lovin' (WB—#2 R&B/#68 pop)

1992 You Can Make the Story Right/Love with No Strings (WB—#8 R&B)

1992 I Want (LP version) (WB—#62 R&B)

### CHAKA KHAN/QUINCY JONES/RAY CHARLES

1989 I'll Be Good to You/(instrumental) (Qwest—#1 R&B/#18 pop)

### CHAKA KHAN/QUINCY JONES/SIEDAH GARRETT

1990 The Places You Find Love/(long version) (Qwest—#39 R&B)

### CHAKA KHAN/GURU

1995 Watch What You Say/Respect the Architect (EMI—#93 R&B)

### CHAKA KHAN/BRANDY/TAMIA/GLADYS KNIGHT

1996 Missing You/So Right for Life (EastWest—#10 R&B/#25 pop)

### CHAKA KHAN/ME'SHELL NDEGEOCELLO

1996 Never Miss the Water/Papillon (WB—#36 R&B/#102 pop)

### LPS

**8** 1978 Chaka (WB)

If anyone imagined Khan would stumble as a solo artist, such notions were swiftly disavowed. Instead, she ripped up the formbook in every way. Highlights are the powerful "I'm Every Woman" and "Life Is a Dance."

**7** 1980 Naughty (WB)

While not quite as even as her debut, the LP is notable for "Clouds" and the audacious jazz-funk "Papillon."

**6** 1981 What Cha' Gonna Do for Me (WB)

Khan's powerful vocals still pack a punch. Includes a cover of the Beatles' "We Can Work It Out," given a work out indeed.

**8** 1982 Chaka Khan (WB)

Khan hit her stride with a tight set of songs that cradled her gorgeous vocals in upbeat rhythm.

**9** 1984 I Feel for You (WB)

Dominated by the outstanding title track, the rest of the album rises to the occasion with good funk grooves and Khan's trademark scaling vocals. Don't miss "Through the Fire," "This Is My Night" and "Caught in the Act."

**6** 1986 Destiny (WB)

**7** 1988 C.K. (WB)

Khan recovered from *Destiny*'s faceless dance-pop stumble with another full LP's worth of good material. Despite her own misgivings, perhaps her most underrated album.

**6** 1992 The Woman I Am (WB)

A graceful transition into the '90s highlighted by the stellar "Love You All My Lifetime" and the title track. But the musical tide had turned, and much of the album sounded dated.

**8** 1998 Come 2 My House (NPG)

Great later-day material—mostly from Prince—that Khan takes out of the stratosphere. The singles "Spoon," "Don't Talk to Strangers" and "This Crazy Life of Mine" deserve all the attention you can give them.

### CHAKA KHAN/CHICK COREA, FREDDIE HUBBARD, JOE HENDERSON, LENNY WHITE, STANLEY CLARKE

**8** 1982 Echoes of an Era (Elektra)

An amazing full-on jazz album, and Khan's love of the genre is evident.

**4** 1989 Life Is a Dance: The Remix Project (WB)

Some people make a living from remixing others' hits. In the art world, that would be called wanton vandalism.

**8** 1996 Epiphany: The Very Best of Chaka Khan (WB)

Outstanding compilation that covers the full range of Khan's material from ballads and funkers to jazzy grooves. A must have.

### SELECTED SAMPLES

Ain't Nobody — Eric B. & Rakim: I Know You Got Soul (remix) (1987)

Fate — Stardust: Music Sounds Better with You (1998)

## LAKESIDE

**FORMED (AS OHIO LAKESIDE EXPRESS):** *1968, Dayton, OH*
**ORIGINAL LINEUP:** *Tiemeyer McCain (vcls), Otis Stokes (vcls), Mark Wood (vcls), Thomas Oliver Shelby (vcls), Steve Shockley (gtr), Marvin Craig (bs), Norman Beavers (kybds), Fred Alexander (drms), Fred Lewis (perc)*

Although Lakeside did not emerge nationally until the late '70s, the Dayton band's roots reached back a decade, to the mid-'60s. Steve Shockley and Mark Wood led the Young Underground, a band who came close to signing with Curtis Mayfield's original Windy C. label in 1966, after winning a label-sponsored talent contest. The label folded and, instead, the Young Underground joined Mayfield's partner, Eddie Thomas, at a new company, Lakeside.

The label offices were directly across the river from the *Lakeside Express* newspaper offices; Thomas had already made it plain that he did not like the band's current name and suggested they change it to the Ohio Lakeside Express. The group agreed and over the next two years, cut a handful of singles for the label, adding former Bad Bunch vocalists Thomas Shelby and Otis Stokes as they did so.

Around 1970, the Lakeside Express decided that the local scene, while buoyant, was also stifling; there were only so many clubs in Dayton, and so many recording studios. They needed to broaden their horizons, and chose to do so in Oklahoma City.

Things were little better there, however, so Lakeside (as they were now calling themselves) continued heading west, finally relocating to Los Angeles in 1972. There they ran into a band they'd encountered several times before on the road, the Dallas based Liquid Funk—like Lakeside, heavily influenced by the Meters, Isaac Hayes and Booker T. That band was faltering, however; they had come to Los Angeles in search of work, but the members were homesick. Only drummer Fred Alexander wanted to stay. He joined Lake-

side, just as the group landed a month long residency at the Club Citadel. From there they moved on to the Crenshaw Palace, where they were spotted by Motown producer Frank Wilson, then working with the Supremes.

Wilson took the group into the studio and cut a number of tracks. However, the partnership never got off the ground and the band returned to the clubs, before finally signing to ABC in 1976.

Again, Lakeside had found but a temporary resting place, as ABC was bought out (by MCA) shortly after the release of the group's debut album, and the band found their services were no longer required.

Norman Whitfield expressed an interest in picking them up for his own Whitfield label, but Lakeside balked at the producer's demand of total control over their output. Their debut proved them to be competent songwriters and musicians; the last thing they saw themselves doing was recycling "I Heard It Through the Grapevine" and "Ball of Confusion" one more time.

The smaller Solar label also made a move for Lakeside, this time on their own terms, and in late 1977, the group signed. Like the Whitfield label, Solar, too, was based around a singular musical vision, created by founder Dick Griffey and producer Leon Sylvers. The offer to Lakeside, however, gave them the freedom to write, produce (and choreograph!) their own albums, together with the opportunity to become Solar's in-house band. The group was soon accompanying fellow Solar stars Carrie Lucas, Shalamar and the Whispers (Shockley co-wrote their "And the Beat Goes On" hit with producer Sylvers.)

Lakeside's Solar debut, *Shot of Love*, followed in late summer, 1978, presenting the band in hilarious "Robin Hood and his Merry Men" type costumes, and packing the irresistible Latin funk 45 "It's All the Way Live." After so many years of disappointment, Lakeside were stunned when the single slammed into the R&B Top 5.

Adopting a new image, cowboys, Lakeside next unveiled *Rough Riders*. The album was less successful, but Lakeside unequivocally bounced back with 1980's deep bass *Fantastic Voyage*, which married an electronics-tinged pirates theme with a wild party groove and another extraordinarily garish stage presentation. The set punched out two monster hits, "Your Love Is on the One" and the chart-topping title track.

Again, Lakeside found it difficult to follow-up the smash, as *Keep On Moving Straight Ahead* faltered on the fringe of the Top 30. They restored their position, however, with

*Your Wish Is My Command*, generally a softer album than past offerings, but one that was characterized by a fine, soulful rendition of the Beatles' "I Want To Hold Your Hand" and a title track that knowingly conjured up delirious memories of Kool & the Gang's "Open Sesame."

Lakeside continued moving in a similarly softer direction when the folky-guitar and synth based "Real Love" brought them a Top 20 hit in 1983—although they could still let rip when they wanted to, as the insistently slinky "Raid" proved that same year. However, the band's latest image of Chicago gangsters caused something of an uproar among the more hysterical media elements, and Lakeside found themselves defending their look against accusations that they were glorifying violence.

Chastened, the group's next album, *Outrageous*, was based around an "Indiana Jones in outer space" theme, with the music nodding toward the new wave- funk sound currently being popularized by labelmates Midnight Star. It proved Lakeside's final Top Ten hit, and marked the beginning of the end for the classic Lakeside lineup.

Stokes, McCain and Shelby all quit, leaving vocals to Wood and new recruit Barrington Scott (ex-Eighth Day). And, while Lakeside returned to the R&B charts during 1987 and again in 1990, it was 1994 before they truly made another splash, when Coolio sampled "Fantastic Voyage" for a monster hit of the same title. It reached #3 on the pop charts, earning Coolio a platinum disc and thrusting Lakeside—who had been quietly touring the oldies circuit for the past five years—back into the headlines. A "greatest hits live" type album was released in 1997.

## LAKESIDE DISCOGRAPHY
### CHARTLOG
1978 It's All the Way Live (part one)/(part two) (Solar—#4 R&B/#102 pop)
1979 Given In to Love/One Minute After Midnight (Solar—#73 R&B)
1979 Pull My Strings/Visions of My Mind (Solar—#31 R&B)
1980 Form 9:00 Until/All in My Mind (Solar—#44 R&B)
1980 Fantastic Voyage/I Can't Get You out of My Head (Solar—#1 R&B/#55 pop)
1981 Your Love Is on the One/I Love Everything You Do (Solar—#14 R&B)
1981 We Want You (On the Floor)/All for You (Solar—#44 R&B)
1982 I Want To Hold Your Hand/Magic Moments (Solar—#5 R&B/#102 pop)
1982 Something About That Woman/The Songwriter (Solar—#25 R&B)
1983 Raid/The Urban Man (Solar—#8 R&B)
1983 Turn the Music Up/Alibi (Solar—#38 R&B)
1983 Real Love/Tinsel Town Theory (Solar—#17 R&B)
1984 Outrageous/So Let's Love (Solar—#7 R&B/#101 pop)
1984 Make My Day/I'll Be Standing By (Solar—#37 R&B)
1987 Relationship/Homewrecker (Solar—#24 R&B)

1987 Bullseye/Sensations (Solar—#33 R&B)
1990 Money/? (Solar—#62 R&B)

## LAKESIDE DISCOGRAPHY
### LPS
**6** 1977 Lakeside Express (ABC)
**8** 1978 Shot of Love (Solar—#10 R&B/#74 pop)
Settling down after their uneven debut, the band pulled it all together with great grooves, sliding from the Ohio style funk of the title track and "It's All the Way Live" to the ballad "Visions of My Mind."
**7** 1979 Rough Riders (Solar—#21 R&B/#141 pop)
It's still an all night funk party, although *Riders* misses some of the energy from last time around. Still, there's a clutch of excellent songs, including "From 9:00 Until."
**7** 1980 Fantastic Voyage (Solar—#2 R&B/#16 pop)
From the smash hit title track, to "Your Love Is on the One," the set again lays down pure funk next to heavy soul, although the songs still feel like they'd benefit from the energy of the live Lakeside treatment.
**6** 1981 Keep On Moving Straight Ahead (Solar—#32 R&B/#109 pop)
**5** 1982 Your Wish Is My Command (Solar—#9 R&B/#58 pop)
Reasonable, if by now predictable. Includes a cover of the Beatles "I Want To Hold Your Hand."
**6** 1983 Untouchables (Solar—#10 R&B/#42 pop)
**7** 1984 Outrageous (Solar—#11 R&B/#68 pop)
"Outrageous" was the high point in an otherwise mediocre album. The band was still cranking out smooth, tight, rhythm, but other people were doing it a lot better.
**6** 1987 Power (Solar—#35 R&B)
**5** 1990 Party Patrol (Solar)
**7** 1997 Invasion (Greatest Hits Live '97) (Intersound)
Late in the day live performance features all the hits including "Fantastic Voyage."

### SELECTED COMPILATIONS AND ARCHIVE RELEASES
**7** 1989 The Best of Lakeside (Solar)
Expected collection of hit singles.
**8** 1998 Galactic Grooves: The Best of Lakeside (Capitol)
Nice set featuring the great funk singles the band is remembered for, plus a few of their more outstanding ballads.
**8** 1999 Fantastic Voyage (Sequel—UK)
More Lakeside than you could shake a stick at, two stuffed CDs serving up full-length versions of the singles and key album cuts, although nothing from the Motown/ABC years.

### SELECTED SAMPLES
Eveready Man — 2Pac: Nothin' but Love (1997)

Fantastic Voyage — Coolio: Fantastic Voyage (1994)

Fantastic Voyage — Gospel Gangstaz: Gospel Gangsta Voyage (1995)

## LTD

**FORMED:** *1968, Greensboro, NC*

**ORIGINAL LINEUP:** *John McGee (gtr), Henry Miller (bs), Jimmie Davis (kybds), Carle Vickers (trum), Arthur Carnegie (sax), Toby Wynn (sax), Abraham Miller (sax), Jake Riley (trom), Jeffrey Osborne (drms, vcls)*

Having met as backing vocalists in Sam and Dave's live band, Jimmie Davis and Henry Miller relocated to New York City in 1968 to form their own band, Love, Tenderness and Devotion—swiftly abbreviated to LTD. There they recruited guitarist John McGee and singing drummer Jeffrey Osborne, plus a fierce five-piece horn section, but several years of local gigging took the band nowhere and, by 1973, LTD had shifted operations to Los Angeles. There they recruited Osborne's brother Billy (kybds) and, in 1974, they signed to A&M.

LTD's eponymous debut was released in spring 1974, a minor hit followed by the R&B Top 50 charting *Gittin Down* in 1975. Slowly picking up momentum, the band finally broke through in 1976 with *Love to the World*, and the accompanying singles "Love Ballad" (a summertime #1) and "Love to the World."

LTD charged back into the studio to record the chart-topping *Something To Love*, which was released in summer 1977. The album was the perfect blend of soul and funk and produced another mid-summer monster, "(Every Time I Turn Around) Back in Love Again."

The band's stellar run continued until the end of 1980. *Togetherness* in 1978, *Devotion* in 1979 and *Shine On* in the fall of 1980 were all massive sellers, but the departure of Osborne for a solo career dealt LTD a savage blow. They replaced him with Leslie Wilson and Andre Ray, but neither *Love Magic* (1981) nor *For You* (1983) could recapture past glories, and LTD disbanded in 1984.

The group were gone, but not forgotten. As classic funk began to enjoy a resurgence in the early to mid-'90s, McGee decided to reform LTD, inviting jazz singer Greg Henneghan to front the crew. With a full band in place, a newly energized LTD was relaunched with a major tour in 1996, and a new album, *Marry You*, in 1999.

### LTD DISCOGRAPHY
#### CHARTLOG

1976 Love Ballad/Let the Music Keep Playing (A&M—#1 R&B/#20 pop)

1977 Love to the World/Get Your It Together (A&M—#27 R&B/#91 pop)

1977 (Every Time I Turn Around) Back in Love Again/Material Things (A&M—#1 R&B/#4 pop)

1978 Never Get Enough of Your Love/Make Someone Smile, Today (A&M—#8 R&B/#56 pop)

1978 Holding On (When Love Is Gone)/Together Forever (A&M—#1 R&B/#49 pop)

1978 We Both Deserve Each Other's Love/It's Time To Be Real (A&M—#19 R&B/#107 pop)

1979 Dance 'N' Sing 'N'/Give It All (A&M—#15 R&B)

1979 Share My Love /Sometimes (A&M—#69 R&B)

1979 Stranger/Sometimes (A&M—#14 R&B)

1980 Where Did We Go Wrong/Stand Up L.T.D. (A&M—#7 R&B)

1980 Shine On/Love Is What You Need (A&M—#19 R&B/#40 pop)

1981 Kickin' Back/Now (A&M—#10 R&B/#102 pop)

1982 April Love/Stay On The One (A&M—#28 R&B)

1983 For You/Party with You (All Night) (Montage—#50 R&B)

### LTD
#### LPS

**6** 1974 Love, Togetherness & Devotion (A&M—#54 R&B)

**6** 1975 Gittin' Down (A&M—#40 R&B)

**9** 1976 Love to the World (A&M—#7 R&B/#52 pop)

Fast paced and horn heavy, intricate bass lines dominated the title track, "Time for Pleasure" and "Get It Together," while "The Word" took the pace down a little, making way for the smooth "Love Ballad."

**8** 1977 Something To Love (A&M—#1 R&B/#21 pop)

Not the heavyweight match of its predecessor, the set nevertheless rips through some serious funk on "Every Time I Turn Around," while "Never Get Enough of Your Love" heads straight to the disco.

**8** 1978 Togetherness (A&M—#3 R&B/#18 pop)

Osborne delivers vocals to die for, from the kickoff of "Holding On When Love Is Gone," through the edgy funk of "Jam," and into snappy ballad "Don't Stop Loving Me Now." Great set, but the funkiness is fading.

**6** 1979 Devotion (A&M—#5 R&B/#29 pop)

Lots of bass in between the ballads. Not a bad album—but it lacks the intensity of earlier releases. Even the mighty "Dance 'N' Sing 'N'" sounds soft.

**7** 1980 Shine On (A&M—#6 R&B/#28 pop)

Osborne's last LP with the band claws back some energy, with "Getaway" and "Love Is What You Need" almost sounding like old times again.

**6** 1981 Love Magic (A&M—#21 R&B/83 pop)

**6** 1994 For You (Hot Production—#66 R&B)

**4** 1999 Marry You (Clout)

Sometimes comebacks are a good idea—and sometimes they're not.

**8** **1996 Greatest Hits (A&M)**

Compact collection that gives nods to both the pre- and post-Osborne eras.

## MAZE

**FORMED (AS RAW SOUL):** *1972, Philadelphia, PA*

**ORIGINAL LINEUP:** *Frankie Beverly (vcls), Wayne Thomas (gtr), Sam Porter (kybds), Robin Duke (bs), Roame Lowry (perc), McKinley Williams (drms), Joe Provost (perc)*

Vocalist Frankie Beverly had been recording since the mid-'60s, issuing a handful of singles ("Because of My Heart" among them) on small Philadelphia labels with the vocal group Frankie Beverly and the Butlers. He formed the deeply funky Raw Soul in the early '70s, gigging around Pennsylvania before relocating the band to San Francisco.

Plying a frenetic blend of Santana/Sly Stone flavored funk around the Bay Area, Raw Soul released at least one 45 on a local label, "Open Up Your Heart," and landed a residency at the Scene nightclub. However, a meeting with one of Marvin Gaye's girlfriends led to the group being recruited to open several shows for Gaye himself during 1976. It was he who suggested they change their name to something more appropriate to their increasingly sophisticated sound. They chose Maze.

Basking in the exposure, which Gaye's patronage conferred, Maze signed with Capitol in late 1976. Their first R&B chart entry, "While I'm Alone," followed in March 1977, igniting a sequence of close to 30 hits over the next 17 years. Indeed, Maze rapidly established themselves among the most consistent R&B/funk bands of that period, with their sense of adventure epitomized by a collaboration with rapper Kurtis Blow on 1980's "Joy and Pain."

Maze's prime environment, however, was the stage. Although each of their first four albums made the R&B Top Ten and went gold, nobody was surprised when 1981's *Live in New Orleans* became their first Top Three hit. Recorded with new keyboard player Phillip Woo (one of several lineup changes the band underwent), *Live* also spawned three hit singles, "Running Away," "Before I Let Go" and "We Need Love To Live."

Further touring kept Maze out of the studio through much of 1982. They bounced back the following year with *We Are One*, but it was 1985 before their recorded career finally attained the same extraordinary heights as their live reputation. That April, the *Can't Stop the Love* album hit the R&B #1 spot, to be joined at the top by the single, "Back

in Stride." The group's success percolated over to the UK as well. Despite climbing no higher than #36 with "Too Many Games," Maze staged a phenomenal run of six sold-out nights at London's Hammersmith Odeon.

Maze followed up with the *Live in Los Angeles* set, three sides recorded in concert the previous year, a fourth comprising all new studio material. It was three years before the group's next album appeared, during which time they broke with Capitol. 1989, however, brought Maze a second brace of R&B chart-toppers, the "Can't Get Over You" single and *Silky Soul* album. Another long lay-off preceded the release of *Back to Basics* in 1993; the band's time since then has been spent touring (of course!) and overseeing 1999's massive overhaul of their back catalog.

### MAZE DISCOGRAPHY

#### CHARTLOG

1977 While I'm Alone/Colour Blind (Capitol—#21 R&B/#89 pop)
1977 Lady of Magic/Time Is on My Side (Capitol—#13 R&B/#108 pop)
1978 Workin' Together/You're Not the Same (Capitol—#9 R&B)
1978 Golden Time of Day/Travelin' Man (Capitol—#39 R&B)
1978 I Wish You Well/Song for My Mother (Capitol—#61 R&B)
1979 Feel That You're Feelin'/Welcome Home (Capitol—#7 R&B/#67 pop)
1979 Timin'/Call On Me (Capitol—#55 R&B)
1980 Southern Girl/I Want To Thank You (Capitol—#9 R&B)
1980 The Look in Your Eyes/Roots (Capitol—#29 R&B)
1981 Running Away/Family (Capitol—#7 R&B)
1981 Before I Let Go/Joy and Pain (Capitol—#13 R&B)
1982 We Need Love To Live/You (Capitol—#29 R&B)
1983 Love Is the Key/Lady of Magic (Capitol—#5 R&B/#80 pop)
1983 Never Let You Down/Lovely Inspiration (Capitol—#26 R&B)
1983 We Are One/Reason (Capitol—#47 R&B)
1984 I Wanna Thank You/I Love You Too Much (Capitol—#59 R&B)
1985 Back in Stride/Joy and Pain (Capitol—#1 R&B/#88 pop)
1985 Too Many Games/Twilight (Capitol—#5 R&B/#103 pop)
1985 I Want To Feel I'm Wanted/Twilight (Capitol—#28 R&B)
1986 I Wanna Be with You/(instrumental) (Capitol—#12 R&B)
1986 When You Love Someone/Happy Feelin's (Capitol—#38 R&B)
1989 Can't Get Over You/Africa (WB—#1 R&B)
1989 Silky Soul/Midnight (WB—#4 R&B)
1990 Love's on the Run/(instrumental) (WB—#13 R&B)
1990 Songs of Love/(instrumental) (WB—#37 R&B)
1993 Laid Back Girl/Twilight (WB—15 R&B)
1993 The Morning After/Laid Back Girl (WB—#19 R&B/#115 pop)
1994 What Goes Up (remix) (WB—#32 R&B)

#### LPS

**9** **1977 Maze Featuring Frankie Beverly (Capitol—#6 R&B/#52 pop)**

No disco for this band, as they swung the musical tide in the opposite direction with Beverly's excellent voice laying down the funky soul over smooth, tight arrangements. Totally fresh.

**8 1978 Golden Time of Day (Capitol—#9 R&B/#27 pop)**

A strong follow-up is again infused with a perfect groove. Includes the mildly politicized "Workin' Together," while "Travelin' Man" and "Song for My Mother" are equally outstanding.

**7 1979 Inspiration (Capitol—#5 R&B/#33 pop)**

**7 1980 Joy and Pain (Capitol—#5 R&B/#31 pop)**

A solid set features the title track, "Look in Your Eyes" and the major R&B hit "Southern Girl."

**8 1981 Live in New Orleans (Capitol—#3 R&B/#34 pop)**

Excellent double three-sides, live album that crackles with energy, while the group's smooth grooves keep the crowd from burning. This is how this band should be heard.

**7 1983 We Are One (Capitol—#5 R&B/#25 pop)**

**6 1985 Can't Stop the Love (Capitol—#1 R&B/#45 pop)**

Still wildly popular, the band put synthesized spin on "Back in Stride" for some updated funk.

**6 1986 Live in Los Angeles (Capitol—#12 R&B/#92 pop)**

**8 Another peak performance and crowning achievement, at least across the three live sides.**

**5 1989 Silky Soul (WB—#1 R&B/#37 pop)**

An even, tight set with political overtones on "Mandela" and "Africa."

**6 1993 Back to Basics (WB—#3 R&B/#37 pop)**

Full on soul that could as easily have been recorded in the mid-'70s, as the mid-'90s.

*SELECTED COMPILATIONS AND ARCHIVE RELEASES*

**7 1989 Lifelines Volume One (Capitol—#57 R&B)**

All the hits, both up-tempo and down, from the Capitol era.

**8 1996 Anthology (Right Stuff—#57 R&B)**

**7 1998 Greatest Slow Jams (Right Stuff)**

*SELECTED SAMPLES*

Before I Let Go — Criminal Element: Hit Me with the Beat (1989)

Before I Let Go — Keith Murray: The Rhyme (1996)

Before I Let Go — Steady B: Use Me (1987)

We Are One — WC & the Maad Circle: Better Days (1998)

While I'm Alone — Nate Dogg: G-Funk (1998)

## MIDNIGHT STAR

**FORMED:** *1976, Louisville, KY*

**ORIGINAL LINEUP:** *Belinda Lipscomb (vcls), Jeffrey Cooper (gtr), Kenneth Gant (bs), Boaz Watson (kybds), Reginald Calloway (hrns), Vincent Calloway (hrns), William Simmons (sax), Melvin Gentry (drms)*

Midnight Star was formed at Kentucky State University in 1976, as a heavy funk antidote to the increasingly insipid disco music then filtering into the eight members' lives. The band initially played for fun only, jamming around campus and sundry Louisville hangouts, and rehearsing at the Calloway brothers' parents' home.

In 1977, the members decided to drop out of college and dedicate themselves full-time to Midnight Star, decamping to New York in search of a record deal. They didn't find one, but word of their electrifying stage performances did reach Solar Records chief Dick Griffey in Los Angeles and, in early 1979, he signed the band.

Midnight Star's debut album, *The Beginning*, was recorded with producer Harvey Mason and spawned one minor hit, "Make It Last." Next time around, then, Griffey paired the band with Leon Sylvers, the man responsible for most of Solar's greatest successes, and immediately the group hit paydirt.

Working with Midnight Star's already developed theatrical sense, Sylvers reinvented their stage show as a space-age cosmic party. At the same time he brightened the still funk-deep vistas of the band's music to create a furious pop funk fusion overflowing with hook-laden melodies, catchy choruses and some astonishing vocal harmonies. *Standing Together* unleashed the compulsively driven "Tuff" and "I've Been Watching You" singles; then, with Reggie Calloway moving into the producer's chair, *Victory* recruited Bootsy Collins to add bass and guest vocals to the mighty "Hot Spot."

Recruiting ex-Mantra drummer Bobby Lovelace, Melvin Gentry was freed to spend more time accompanying Lipscomb at the microphone, and Midnight Star cut 1983's *No Parking on the Dance Floor*, the crossover breakthrough they'd been threatening. The title track and the Shalamar-esque sing-along "Wet My Whistle" were both hits. But it was the frenzied, effects-crazed "Freak-a-Zoid" that slammed Midnight Star up the chart, haunting the #2 spot for a month (it was held back by Mtume), while the album remained in the same position for ten weeks, behind Rick James' omnipresent *Cold Blooded*.

*No Parking* took four months to go gold (it eventually went double platinum). Its follow-up, the riotous *Planetary Invasion*, did it within a week, as Midnight Star's finest moment yet, "Operator," cruised to #1 and stayed there for five weeks. "Operator" also became the band's first pop Top 20 hit and introduced Midnight Star to the UK as well. The following year, "Headlines" (the latest album's title track) and "Midas Touch" followed it across the Atlantic, while

**Belinda Lipscomb and Melvin Gentry of Midnight Star.**

Midnight Star's compulsive sound had not gone unnoticed elsewhere.

"Midas Touch" is frequently cited as the inspiration behind Babyface's latter-day work with the Whispers. Reggie Calloway himself was now in high demand as a producer for other acts. Natalie Cole, Gladys Knight and Levert all enjoyed success with his so distinctive approach and it was little surprise, in 1987, when he and brother Vincent quit Midnight Star to form their own production company, Calloco Productions. The pair also launched a recording career under the name Calloway, scoring their biggest hit with a song co-written by Lipscomb and Gentry, "I Wanna Be Rich."

Opting not to replace the errant duo, Midnight Star linked with producer Larkin Arnold, best known for his early-'80s work with Marvin Gaye, and cut 1988's *Midnight Star* album. East Coast rapper Ecstasy (of Whodini) guested on the remarkable "Don't Rock My Boat" single, a dazzling hybrid of hard rap and smooth R&B. However, the departure of the Calloways had taken its toll on Midnight Star; they cut one further album, 1990's *Work It Out*, before breaking up.

## MIDNIGHT STAR DISCOGRAPHY
### CHARTLOG

1980 Make It Last/Follow the Path (Solar—#85 R&B)
1981 I've Been Watching You/Open Up to Love (Solar—#36 R&B)
1981 Tuff/I Got What You Need (Solar—#60 R&B)
1982 Hot Spot/I Won't Let You Be Lonely (Solar—#35 R&B/#108 pop)
1982 Victory/Love Is Alive (Solar—#83 R&B)
1983 Freak-a-Zoid/Move Me (Solar—#2 R&B/#66 pop)
1983 Wet My Whistle/You Can't Stop Me (Solar—#8 R&B/#61 pop)
1984 No Parking (On the Dance Floor)/Feels So Good (Solar—#43 R&B/#81 pop)
1984 Operator/Playmates (Solar—#1 R&B/#18 pop)
1985 Scientific Love/Make Time (Solar—#16 R&B/#80 pop)
1985 Body Snatchers/Curious (Solar—#31 R&B)
1986 Headlines/(instrumental) (Solar—#3 R&B/#69 pop)
1986 Midas Touch/Searching for Love (Solar—#7 R&B/#42 pop)
1986 Engine #9/Searching for Love (Solar—#11 R&B)
1988 Don't Rock the Boat/(instrumental) (Solar—#3 R&B)
1988 Snake in the Grass/(remix) (Solar—#10 R&B)
1989 Love Song/(instrumental) (Solar—#55 R&B)
1990 Do It (One More Time)/(remix) (Solar—#12 R&B)
1990 Luv-U-Up/? (Solar—#58 R&B)

## LPS

6 **1979 The Beginning (Solar)**
5 **1981 Standing Together (Solar—#54 R&B)**
7 **1982 Victory (Solar—#58 R&B/#205 pop)**

Firmly on the upswing, the band's synth sounds haven't quite gelled, but both the title track and "Hot Spot" know what's coming.

9 **1983 No Parking on the Dance Floor (Solar—#2 R&B/#27 pop)**

Practice makes perfect, and this set of stellar synthi-funk was some of the greatest. Taking elements of Euro-disco, funk ethics and hard synth breaks, the band dominated the dancefloor with the title track, "Freak-a-Zoid" and "Wet My Whistle." Nothing could be more '80s.

8 **1984 Planetary Invasion (Solar—#7 R&B/#32 pop)**

Midnight Star take a sci-fi holiday as they blister through a set utilizing the ever popular vocoder and much electronic knob twiddling. "Scientific Love" and "Bodysnatchers" are standouts.

7 **1986 Headlines (Solar—#7 R&B/#56 pop)**
6 **1988 Midnight Star (Solar—#14 R&B/#96 pop)**

Not a bad album, but the departure of the Calloways crippled the band's overall sound.

5 **1990 Work It Out (Solar—#41 R&B)**

### SELECTED COMPILATIONS AND ARCHIVE RELEASES

8 **1999 Wet My Whistle (Sequel—UK)**

The best "best of," this double includes all the hits plus Calloway solo material.

### SELECTED SAMPLES

Curious — Eric B. & Rakim: What's on Your Mind (1994)
Curious — Kurious: I'm Kurious (1994)
Curious — Mic Geronimo: Wherever You Are (remix) (1995)

## MUTINY

**FORMED:** *1979, Detroit, MI*

**ORIGINAL LINEUP:** *Jerome Brailey (vcls, drms), Lenny Holmes (gtr), Skitch Lovett (vcls, gtr), Raymond Carter (vcls, bs), Nat Lee (kybds), Darryl Dixon (hrns), Marvin Daniels (hrns), Melvin El (hrns)*

Once (and not unreasonably) described as the funkiest drummer in the world, Jerome Brailey's acrimonious departure from P-Funk was followed initially by his involvement with fellow defector Glen Goins of Praxis. That project petered out with Goins' death; Brailey then formed Mutiny, intended as a commentary on his experiences with George Clinton.

Despite only luring one other P-Funker into the group, saxophonist Darryl Dixon, the band's *Mutiny on the Ma-maship* debut album painted a masterful, if uncomplimentary, portrait of P-Funk politics, with an excellent, heavy funk sound, cut expertly from classic cloth. Clinton himself later admitted he would have loved to release the record on his own Uncle Jam label—and that despite its uncomplimentary nature (he is invoked throughout the album as "Lump").

Although the Mutiny concept seemed very much a one-off, Brailey followed up with a remarkably powerful successor in 1980, *Funk Plus the One*. However, it was 1983 before Mutiny resurfaced on Brailey's own J. Romeo label, with *A Night out with the Boys*. Unfortunately, J. Romeo's distribution was weak and the album was barely made available.

Brailey worked as a session musician throughout much of the '80s, resurfacing in 1993, when Clinton invited him to join the P-Funk All Stars. That sojourn came to an end when Brailey took a week away to record with former Eurythmic Dave Stewart, and was promptly replaced in the All Stars lineup, a blow that prompted him to immediately piece together New Mutiny, cutting a hard hitting rap single, "Sneaking Up Behind You."

Alongside fellow P-Funkers Bernie Worrell and Eddie Hazel, Brailey also linked with producer Bill Laswell's Axiom Funk/OG Funk conglomerate and, in 1995, Brailey and Laswell hatched Mutiny's belated fourth album, *Aftershock 2005*. Outtakes from this and earlier Mutiny projects subsequently appeared through Brailey's own Rome Dog label.

### MUTINY COMPLETE DISCOGRAPHY

#### SINGLES

1979 Funk 'N' Bop/? (Columbia)
1980 Semi-First Class Seat/? (Columbia)
1983 Peanut Butter and Jam/(same) (J. Romeo)
1994 Sneaking Up Behind You/? (Rad)

#### LPS

9 **1979 Mutiny on the Mamaship (Columbia)**

Superb concept album that trashes George Clinton and Parliament all the way through. From "Lump" to "Funk 'N' Bop" and "Go Away from Here," it's a winner.

8 **1980 Funk Plus the One (Columbia)**

Full of fresh funk ranging from the super horn heavy "Don't Bust the Groove," to the bass barrage "Will It Be Tomorrow?," and all combinations in between.

7 **1983 A Night out with the Boys (J. Romeo)**

Lifting lyrics from a variety of other musical sources, then pursuing them in some startlingly fresh directions, a fulfilling slice of updated funk classicism, if occasionally a little obscure.

**6** 1995 **Aftershock 2005 (P-Vine – Ja)**

As with so many Laswell productions, you know what you're getting long before you get in—extraordinarily intelligent rhythms and textures, deep meaning and miasmic production. Then he drops the songs on top. Released in the US in 1996 (Black Arc)

### SELECTED COMPILATIONS AND ARCHIVE RELEASES

**6** 1999 **Black Hat Daddy and the Silver Comb Gang (Rome Dog)**
**7** 1999 **P-Funk in Latin Groove (Rome Dog)**
**7** 1999 **Funky Mad Men (Rome Dog)**

## PARLET

**FORMED:** *1978, Detroit, MI*
**ORIGINAL LINEUP:** *Jeanette Washington (vcls), Debbie Wright (vcls), Mallia Franklin (vcls)*

Having debut on Parliament's *Chocolate City* album in 1975, Mallia Franklin was one of the longest serving female vocalists aboard the Mothership when George Clinton formulated a P-Funk-ified answer to the classic girl groups of the '60s, Parlet. Debbie Wright came aboard during the *Mothership Connection* sessions; former James Brown vocalist Jeanette Washington arrived for 1977's *Funkentelechy vs. the Placebo Syndrome.*

Clinton already had the Brides of Funkenstein up and running, but clearly envisioned Parlet as a very separate proposition, harking back to an earlier, purer era of soulfunk. Indeed, his original plan was to title them the Parlettes, confirming the trio as a female version of the original Parliaments. They became Parlet during the sessions for their first album.

Like the Brides' debut album, 1978's *Pleasure Principle* (a title later borrowed by English electro artist Gary Numan) was largely comprised of already existing material, with only the trio's vocals added. It was an entertaining set, but sold poorly. Dismayed at this lack of success, Franklin and Wright both left Parlet soon after. Washington later reflected, "[the record company and Clinton] didn't do anything promotion-wise with Parlet. And from my understanding, there was never any intention to really put Parlet out there. After the first year or so, it really became a job. [The] newness wore off and it was like, 'Okay, here we go. Next hotel.'"

Washington herself persevered, and with the errant pair replaced by Janice Evans and Shirley Hayden (previously heard among the backing vocalists on Parliament's *Motor-*

*Booty Affair* album), Clinton assigned a regular band to Parlet, including Jerome Ali (gtr), Jimmy Ali (bs), Donny Sterling (bs), Ernestro Wilson (kybds, sax), Mannon Saulsby (kybds, sax), Kenny Colton (drms) and Janice Carlton (perc). This pool of musicians accompanied Parlet on their rare live appearances and also joined them in the studio for 1979's *Invasion of the Booty Snatchers.* (Of course, other P-Funkers were also present.)

Like its predecessor, *Invasion . . .* performed poorly, spawning just one minor R&B chart hit—and that despite emerging as a riveting fusion of funk and disco, Clinton's least facetious assault yet on the bodies and souls of the dancefloor.

*Play Me or Trade Me*, the third Parlet album, followed in 1980. A return to the funkier pastures of *Pleasure Principle*, it was also notable for the inclusion of "Funk Until the Edge of Time," the only Parlet song to feature a member of the band among its co-writers (Washington penned it with Ron Dunbar and bassist Steve Pannell). However, again sales were low and, as the P-Funk empire itself wound down, Parlet folded.

Franklin released her first solo album in 1995; *Funken Tersepter* was compiled from sessions dating back to 1981, when she worked with producer Gary Shider, and included subsequent dates with Walter "Junie" Morrison (1982 and 1986) and Eddie Hazel (1983), usually with great swathes of the P-Funk crew on board.

### PARLET COMPLETE DISCOGRAPHY
#### SINGLES/CHARTLOG

1978 Cookie Jar/Are You Dreaming? (Casablanca)
1978 Pleasure Principle (part one)/(part two) (Casablanca—#66 R&B)
1979 Don't Ever Stop/Huff-N-Puff (Casablanca)
1979 Ridin' High (part one)/(part two) (Casablanca—#49 R&B)
1980 Help from My Friends/Watch Me Do My Thang (Casablanca—#73 R&B)
1980 Wolf Tickets (part one)/(part two) (Casablanca—#67 R&B)

#### LPS

**8** 1978 **Pleasure Principle (Casablanca)**
Reprising the epic "Cookie Jar" from Fuzzy Haskins' solo debut, *Pleasure Principle* is also notable for some dynamic performances from the individual musicians (bassist Rodney Curtis and the Horny Horns both shine), while Parlet also execute the best ballads P-Funk ever performed.

**6** 1979 **Invasion of the Booty Snatchers (Casablanca)**
"No Rump To Bump" and "Huff—Puff" are disco floor giants, and if there's any serious flaw, it's that even the short songs take five or six minutes to finish.

**7** 1980 **Play Me or Trade Me (Casablanca)**

Touching the peaks of the first album, combined with some remarkably fresh-sounding new material. "Funk Until the Edge of Time" is phenomenal.

### SELECTED COMPILATIONS AND ARCHIVE RELEASES
**7** 1994 The Best of Parlet (Casablanca)

Intelligent collection, although not a patch on the full albums.

### SELECTED SAMPLES
Love Amnesia — Ice Cube: Steady Mobbin'
Wolf Tickets — Del: Dr. Bombay

### MALLIA "QUEEN OF FUNK" FRANKLIN
**LP**
**6** 1995 Funken Tersepter (P-Vine—Japan)

Vintage '80s-era funk mob sessions sadly, "updated" with '90s remixes and technology, all rendering it even more dated than it might have been to begin with.

## PRAXIS
**FORMED:** *1978, Detroit, MI*
**ORIGINAL LINEUP:** *Glen Goins (vcls, gtr), Kevin Goins (vcls, gtr) Harvey Banks (gtr), Eugene Jackson (bs), Richard banks (kybds), Darryl Dixon (sax, clar, flte), Monica Peters (trum), Greg Fitz (kybds), Jeff Adams (drms), Darryl Deliberto (cngs)*

Having quit P-Funk in a dispute over wages following the release of 1977's *Funkentelechy vs. the Placebo Syndrome* album, vocalist Glen Goins linked with brother Kevin in a new band, Praxis.

Largely co-written and produced with fellow P-Funk renegade Jerome Brailey, Praxis' eponymous debut was intended as a showcase for the remarkable talents Goins had; but sparingly employed as a member of P-Funk, Fred Wesley once described him as the greatest vocalist he'd ever heard.

However, Goins was already suffering from Hodgkins Disease, which restricted his involvement in the sessions. His death in late 1978, again some months before the album's completion, initially (and understandably) left a question mark over the entire proceedings. Finally Kevin and Brailey opted to continue.

The album was released by Arista in late 1978. However, with no band to promote it, and neither Kevin Goins nor Brailey wishing to create one, *Quazar* passed by all but unnoticed. Promotion was restricted to one now collectable promo single, the self-explanatory "Funk 'N' Roll."

The Praxis name was revived by producer Bill Laswell in 1992, albeit without the participation of any of the founding members.

### DISCOGRAPHY
**9** 1978 Quazar (Arista)

Alongside co-producer Brailey's Mutiny, the most enjoyable album by any dissatisfied ex-P-Funker, honest enough to admit the mothership's importance, but strong enough to thrust its own personality to the fore. "Funk with a Big Foot" is everything its title says it should be, a yeti of a stomp; while "Funk with a Capital G" . . . , well, work it out for yourself.

**6** 1992 Transmutation (Axiom)

A typical Laswell/Axiom album, the usual mess of noise. . . sorry, experimental musical forms . . . but garnished with sufficient funk (and funkateers Bernie Worrell and Bootsy Collins both contribute) to maintain interest. Guitarist Buckethead adds to the fun, and it would be truly instructive to hear the same trio with a less self-conscious producer.

**2** 1994 Sacrifist (Axiom)

Out with the funk, in with the New York and Japanese avant-garde thrash merchants. "Interesting" becomes a very over-used description after a while.

## ROSE ROYCE
**FORMED:** *1976, Los Angeles, CA*
**ORIGINAL LINEUP:** *Gwen Dickey (vcls), Kenji Chiba Brown (gtr, vcls), Lequient "Duke" Jobe (bs, vcls), Victor Nix (kybds), Kenny "Captain Cold" Copeland (trum), Freddie Dunn (trum), Michael Moore (sax), Henry "Hammer" Garner (drms, vcls), Terral "Powerpack" Santiel (cngs)*

The instrumental core of what became Rose Royce originally formed in 1970, when a group of musicians, schooled in a myriad local backing groups, decided to put themselves forward as a self-contained outfit that could gig and record in their own right, as well as offer visiting performers a ready-made band. Naming themselves Total Concept Unlimited, the octet's first major engagement came in 1973, when Motown performer Edwin Starr hired them to accompany him on tours of Europe and the Far East. Starr then introduced them to his producer, Norman Whitfield, who promptly engaged Total Concept Unlimited as the studio band for the Temptations' "Let Your Hair Down" single—his last recording with that group.

From thereon in, Total Concept Unlimited became Whitfield's preferred studio act, joining him on albums by the Undisputed Truth and former James Brown diva Yvonne Fair (1975's sadly underrated *The Bitch Is Black*), before the producer quit Motown to launch his own Whitfield Records label.

In 1976, Undisputed Truth lost vocalists Tyrone Douglas and Virginia McDonald; auditions for the vacancies ultimately saw the recruitment of Taka Boom. However, another aspirant, Gwen Dickey (b. Miami, FL), also impressed, and was installed as Total Concept Unlimited's lead vocalist. She renamed herself Rose Norwalt, and the band was rechristened Rose Royce.

Rose Royce debuted on the Whitfield-designed soundtrack to the 1976 movie *Car Wash*, performing the chart-topping title track alongside two other future hits, "I Wanna Get Next to You" (with lead vocals from trumpeter Kenny Copeland) and "I'm Going Down." *Car Wash* subsequently won a Grammy for Best Original Score.

Replacing keyboard player Victor Nix with Michael Nash, Rose Royce returned to the studio in spring 1977 to record their next album, the R&B #1 hit *II/In Full Bloom*. A joyous fusion of classic funk and contemporary disco, interspersed with a handful of characteristic Whitman ballads. The album opened with the wistful "Wish Upon a Star," but was dominated by "Do Your Dance," a nine-minute funk workout, which was edited down for the band's fourth hit single. Further hits came as the band continued backing the Undisputed Truth and fellow Whitfield artist Willie Hutch; they also performed on Stargard's 1977 R&B chart-topper "Theme Song from *Which Way Is Up*," a Whitfield composition.

In 1978, Rose Royce's third album, *III/Strikes Again*, made R&B #4, again driven by a brace of stirring hits, "I'm in Love (And I Love the Feeling)" and, more significantly, "Love Don't Live Here Anymore," a spartan ballad that effectively introduced the electronic linn drum to mass consumption. The instrument had been used sparingly on "Do Your Dance" the previous year; now, it virtually duetted with Dickey, creating one of the most distinctive records of the year—and one of the most imitated of the age.

Certainly neither Rose Royce nor producer Whitman ever recovered from the storm that record unleashed. *Rose Royce IV/Rainbow Connection* failed to even scratch the Top 20 in 1979 and, in 1980, Dickey and guitarist Kenji Brown quit the band amid a string of undeachieving subsequent singles. They were replaced by Ricci Benson (vcls) and Walter McKinney (gtr), in which form Rose Royce cut their final R&B Top 30 album, *Golden Touch*.

Breaking with Whitfield, subsequent Rose Royce albums did little and, while the group maintained a sporadic presence in the R&B singles chart (most notably with 1986's Top 30 "Doesn't Have To Be This Way" and the following year's "Lonely Road," a collaboration with sax legend Grover Washington), they finally disbanded in 1987.

Rose Royce reformed in the '90s, with a lineup comprising founders Copeland, Freddie Dunn, Michael Moore and Henry Garner, plus Benson and McKinney. A live album, the predictably titled *Greatest Hits Live*, announced their return in 1995.

### ROSE ROYCE DISCOGRAPHY
#### CHARTLOG
1976 Car Wash/Water (MCA—#1 R&B/#1 pop)

1977 I Wanna Get Next to You/Sunrise (MCA—#3 R&B/#10 pop)

1977 I'm Going Down/Yo Yo (MCA—#10 R&B/#70 pop)

1977 Do Your Dance (part one)/(part two) (Whitfield—#4 R&B/#39 pop)

1977 Ooh Boy/You Can't Please Everybody (Whitfield—#3 R&B/#72 pop)

1978 Wishing on a Star/Love, More Love (Whitfield—#52 R&B/#101 pop)

1978 I'm in Love/Get Up off Your Fat (Whitfield—R&B #5)

1978 Love Don't Live Here Anymore/That's What's Wrong with Me (Whitfield—#5 R&B/#32 pop)

1979 First Come First Serve/Let Me Be the First To Know (Whitfield—#65 R&B)

1979 Is It Love You're After/You Can't Run From Yourself (Whitfield—#31 R&B/#105 pop)

1980 Pop Your Fingers/I Wonder Where You Are Tonight (Whitfield—#60 R&B)

1981 Golden Touch/Love Is in the Air (Whitfield—#56 pop)

1982 Best Touch/Dance with Me (Epic—#64 R&B)

1984 Magic Touch/You're So Fine (C&R—#77 R&B)

1986 Doesn't Have To Be This Way/You're My Peace of Mind (Omni—#22 R&B)

1987 Lonely Foad/I Found Someone (Omni—#45 R&B)

1987 If Walls Could Talk/? (Omni—#69 R&B)

### LPS
**8** 1976 Car Wash (MCA—#2 R&B/#14 pop)

Although shared with the rest of the soundtrack crew, a great debut highlights the band's tight, punchy energetic grooves, from the smashing title track to "Put Your Money Where Your Mouth Is" and "Daddy Rich."

**7** 1977 II/In Full Bloom (Whitfield—#1 R&B/#36 pop)

Rose Royce continue to cruise in style with their strong disco funk. The over eight-minute long "It Makes You Feel Like Dancing" is a winner, while "You Can't Please Everybody" and "Love, More Love" also get a groove going, and the sublime ballad "Wishing on a Star" is unbeatable.

**7** 1978 III/Strikes Again! (Whitfield—#4 R&B/#28 pop)

Another solid set of ballads and pop shakers includes the much imitated "Love Don't Live Here Anymore." Plus, how can you hate the carnival shill on "Get Up off Your Fat"?

**6** 1979 IV/Rainbow Connection (Whitfield—#22 R&B/#74 pop)

**7** 1981 Golden Touch (Whitfield—#30 R&B/#160 pop)

Solid throughout, the band persevere with their winning combination of funkified pop grooves. The title track was, and remains, an underrated gem.

**6** 1982 Stronger Than Ever (Epic—#50 R&B/#210 pop)

**6** 1984 Music Magic (Streetwave)

**6** 1987 Fresh Cut (Omni—#50 R&B)

Against all the odds, Rose Royce still turn a respectable groove, long after the genre's bloom has faded. Not a bad mix across "Holding On to Love," "You're So Fine" and "Long Distance Love Affair."

**7** 1995 Greatest Hits Live (Prime Cuts)

Live set covers all the classics with style.

### SELECTED COMPILATIONS AND ARCHIVE RELEASES

**8** 1980 Greatest Hits (Whitfield)

Respectable 14 track compilation takes care of the hits and throws in some other favorites to boot.

**8** 2000 Greatest Hits (Cleopatra)

Hits collection includes remixes of "Wishing on a Star" and "Car Wash."

### SELECTED SAMPLES

Born To Love You — Beastie Boys: Shake Your Rump (1989)
Daddy Rich — 3rd Bass: Merchant of Grooves (1991)
Daddy Rich — MC Serch: Return of the Product (1992)
Do Your Dance — Beastie Boys: Shadrach (1989)
Do Your Dance — Poor Righteous Teachers: Just Servin' Justice (1991)
Do Your Dance — Public Enemy: Aintnuttin Buttersong (1994)
I'm Going Down — Insane Poetry: Till Death Do Us Part (1992)
Love Don't Live Here Anymore — Dr. Dre: Big Ego (1999)
Love Don't Live Here Anymore — Geto Boys: Geto Fantasy (1996)
Ooh Boy — DJ Quik: Sweet Black Pussy (1991)
Ooh Boy — Mase featuring Billy Lawrence: Love U So (1997)
Ooh Boy — Snoop Doggy Dogg: Lodi Dodi (1993)
6 O'Clock DJ — Beastie Boys: Shake Your Rump (1989)
Yo-Yo — Beastie Boys: Shake Your Rump (1989)
Zig Zag — Downtown Science: Topic Drift (1991)
Zig Zag — Ice Cream Tee: Come On (1989)
Zig Zag — Tony D: Buggin' on the Line (1991)

## SKYY

**FORMED (AS FUEL):** *1976, Brooklyn, NY*
**ORIGINAL LINEUP:** *Bonnie Dunning (vcls), Delores Dunning (vcls), Denise Dunning (vcls), Anibal Anthony Sierra (gtr), Solomon Roberts, Jr. (gtr), Gerald LeBon (bs), Larry Greenberg (kybds), Tommy McConnell (drms)*

Solomon Roberts, Jr. was the teenage proprietor of Hole in the Ground Studios (actually a four track recorder in his parents' basement), the first port of call for any number of aspiring funk bands and musicians in late-'60s Brooklyn. Randy Muller's Dynamic Soul were regular visitors as they made the slow transformation into Brass Construction, so were Crown Heights Affair and Madison Street Express, the original incarnation of B.T. Express.

It was from within this resultant mutual appreciation society that Roberts formed his first serious band, Fuel, in 1976, joined in the venture by Gerald LeBon (ex-Moments and Sylvia Robinson), Tommy McConnell (ex-Crown Heights Affair), Anibal Sierra (ex- Ritchie Havens, Odyssey) and Larry Greenberg.

Both B.T. Express and Brass Construction had broken into the charts at that point; Roberts admitted that he learned much from watching both bands' progress. Indeed, Fuel's first taste of success came when Roberts and Sierra joined Randy Muller and Brass Construction vocalists Delores, Bonnie and Denise Dunning at the sessions for jazz saxophonist Charles Earland's 1978 hit album *Perceptions*. A single, "Let the Music Play," reached #46 in the UK that summer, lending fresh urgency to that country's already burgeoning domestic funk scene. The following year, the Dunning sisters joined Fuel full time, just as Roberts changed the band's name to Skyy.

In 1979, Roberts and Muller formed their own production company, Alligator Bit Him Productions, and signed Skyy to the Salsoul label. Muller also introduced another of his proteges, Guyana- born Rafael Cameron to the setup and, with the instrumental portion of Skyy established as Salsoul's in-house backing band, Funk Deluxe, work began on debut albums by both band and soloist.

With Muller as co-producer and songwriter, Skyy's debut album, the sci-fi themed *Skyy*, was an immediate hit. Like Brass Construction, Skyy had no qualms about adding disco to their funk. Unlike Brass Construction, they did not have a heritage that bad-tempered fans could claim they were betraying.

"First Time Around," Skyy's debut single, made the R&B Top 20 in May 1979; by the time Cameron's first hit, "Magic of You," struck a year later, Skyy had already notched up four more chart entries, although their greatest success was still to come. "Call Me," in November 1981, topped the R&B chart for two weeks and became the band's first pop smash as well.

That same month's *Skyy Line* album, the group's fourth, ultimately went gold. Live work took them as far afield as Nigeria, Europe and the UK, where "Let's Celebrate" gave the band a #67 hit under the alias New York Skyy—a name change necessitated by the existence of the similarly named, classical rock virtuosos Sky.

With Wayne Wilentz replacing Greenberg, Skyy spent much of 1982 on the road in the US, touring with Kool & the Gang. The ensuing non-stop party experiences inspired the band's most exciting album yet, 1982's *Skyjammer*. However, it was also their most divisive, a heroically rock and new wave inflected set that producer Randy Muller later claimed was one of the worst records he had ever made. A comparative commercial flop, it paved the way for Skyy's unabashed return to their funk roots for *Skylight*—their final Salsoul release before the company ceased operations.

In 1985, Skyy signed to Capitol, labelmates of Brass Construction (Roberts, Sierra and the Dunnings all appeared on the Construction's *Conquest* album). In early summer 1986, Skyy scored their first R&B Top Ten hit in five years, with "Givin' It (To You)." It marked a false dawn, however. No further singles charted and, when the *From the Left Side* album failed to meet expectations, Skyy and Capitol parted company.

Over the next three years, Skyy remained silent. But they resurfaced in 1989 on Atlantic, reliant now almost totally on ballads and armed with their biggest hits ever the chart-toppers "Start of a Romance" and "Real Love," and a hit album, also titled *Start of a Romance*. A similar pattern followed in 1992, when another long silence was shattered with a Top 20 single. However, the band had reached the end of the line; they broke up soon after, although a reunion was mooted around 1996, following the release of a *Best Of* compilation.

### SKYY DISCOGRAPHY
### CHARTLOG
1979 First Time Around/Disco Dancin' (Salsoul—#20 R&B)
1979 Let's Turn It Out/Let's Get Up (Salsoul—#65 R&B)
1980 High/Who's Gonna Love me (Salsoul—#13 R&B/#102 pop)
1980 Skyyzoo/Don't Stop (Salsoul—#32 R&B)
1980 Here's to You/Arrival (Salsoul—#23 R&B)
1981 Superlove/No Music (Salsoul—#31 R&B)
1981 Call Me/When You Touch Me (Salsoul—#1 R&B/#26 pop)
1982 Let's Celebrate/Gonna Get It On (Salsoul—#16 R&B)
1982 When You Touch Me/Girl in Blue (Salsoul—#43 R&B)
1982 Movin' Violation/Get into the Beat (Salsoul—#26 R&B)
1983 Let Love Shine/Together (Salsoul—#39 R&B)
1983 Bad Boy/Swing It (Salsoul—#39 R&B)

1983 Show Me the Way/Now That We've Found Love (Salsoul—#35 R&B)
1984 Dancin' To Be Dancin'/It's My Life (Salsoul—#49 R&B)
1986 Givin' It (To You)/Jealousitus (Capitol—#8 R&B)
1989 Start of a Romance/Sunshine (Atlantic—#1 R&B)
1989 Love All the Way/Groove Me (Atlantic—#47 R&B)
1989 Real Love/Feelin' It Now (Atlantic—#1 R&B/#47 pop)
1992 Up and Over/Medley (Atlantic—#16 R&B)
1992 Nearer To You/? (Atlantic—#73 R&B)

### LPS
**8** 1979 Skyy (Salsoul—#40 R&B/#117 pop)
Full on disco funk is the name of the game. Several six minute-plus songs, including "First Time Around," get a good groove going. A perfect band for the clubs.
**7** 1980 Skyyway (Salsoul—#17 R&B/#61 pop)
With a dancefloor slant, this album chugs along quite nicely adding a little rock 'n' roll guitar to shake things up.
**7** 1980 Skyyport (Salsoul—16 R&B/#85 pop)
**7** 1981 Skyy Line (Salsoul—#1 R&B/#18 pop)
From "Get into the Beat" to "Let's Celebrate" and "Jam the Box," a solid album from beginning to end.
**6** 1982 Skyyjammer (Salsoul—#22 R&B/#81 pop)
Much of the set was written during a raucous tour with Kool & the Gang and it shows. A love it or hate it album with more rock overtones, especially on "Movin' Violation;" it's still full of tracks to get people partying.
**6** 1983 Skyylight (Salsoul—#44 R&B/#183 pop)
The reception of the previous set sent the band back into the disco/funk grooves they knew so well. Includes the very funked up "Hey Girl."
**5** 1986 From the Left Side (Capitol—#33 R&B)
**7** 1989 Start of a Romance (Atlantic—#16 R&B/#155 pop)
**6** 1992 Nearer to You (Atlantic—#52 R&B)

### SELECTED SAMPLES
High — Too Short: Short But Funky (1990)
Let's Celebrate — Nice & Smooth: Step by Step (1991)

## SLAVE
**FORMED:** 1976, East Orange, NJ
**ORIGINAL LINEUP:** *Floyd Miller (vcls, trum), Danny Webster (gtr), Mark Adams (bs), Mark Hicks (kybds), Steve Washington (b. Newark, NJ—trum, gtr, bs), Tom Lockett (sax), Orion Wilhoite (sax), Tim Dozier (drms)*

One of the most ambitious R&B acts of the late '70s, blending funk basics with rock guitars, science fiction hooks and as much technology as they could lay their hands on; Slave was the brainchild of Steve Washington, nephew of Ohio Players trumpeter Ralph Middlebrooks.

**The extended family that was Slave.**

Washington frequently spent school holidays on the road with that band; back in hometown East Orange, he formed his first band, Black Satin Soul, with fellow high schoolers Mark Hicks and Tim Dozier. In 1976, that band joined forces with another local combo, the Young Mystics, formed by Floyd Miller, Tom Lockett and Mark Adams. Adding Danny Webster and Orion Wilhoite, Slave emerged early the following year with an eponymous album and an R&B chart-topper, "Slide."

Borrowing a leaf from George Clinton's book, Washington—or "Fearless Leader," as he was now being termed—swiftly began building a veritable empire around Slave. With the live show expanding into one of the most flamboyant of the age, new members arrived regularly to augment the troupe. At one point in 1979 (by which time Slave had amassed three hit albums and another Top 20 single, "Stellar Fungk"), the group boasted up to 18 members, including vocalists Steve Arrington and Starleana Young, and guitarist Curt Jones. The latter pair were eventually spun off as Aurra; other bands to emerge from the Slave Organization were Arrington's Hall of Fame and Mtume.

In 1980, the *Stone Love* album supplied Slave's biggest hit since their debut, when the "Watching You" single climbed to R&B #6. The following year, "Snap Shot" reached a similar peak. However, the departure of Arrington before 1983's *Vision of the Lite* album seriously reduced Slave's effectiveness, all the more so since Washington was simultaneously preoccupied with recording his own first solo album, *Like a Shot*, and piecing together a new Aurra lineup, following his break with Young and Jones. Washington and Horne also formed another new band, Civil Attack, in 1984. Very much a return to the dramatic funk of Slave's early years, the band's one album lucklessly appeared just as the Salsoul label folded.

1984's lackluster *New Plateau* marked the end of Slave's career-long relationship with the Cotillion label. They signed next with Ichiban, releasing two reasonably successful, but otherwise unfulfilling albums during 1986–87. Meanwhile, Washington continued his extracurricular activities. In 1985, he linked with George Clinton on the *Some of My Best Jokes Are Friends* and *R&B Skeletons in the Closet* albums, furthering his P-Funk connections by co-writing and producing five tracks for Jimmy G. & the Tackheads' *Federation of Tackheads* album.

Slave folded in 1987, following an EP cut for Westbound Records chief Armen Boladien. Washington and his second wife, Tracy, subsequently launched their own production company/studio, the Dept. of Funk Research, in East Orange. This in turn became TFL (The Funk Label), a multimedia organization whose releases include a solo album by one-time Aurra/Mtume bassist Ray Jack, the hip-hop themed *New Jeru Compilation* and Washington's own Rabbis project.

Under the aegis first of Webster, then of Hicks, two revived Slave incarnations, meanwhile, released two albums of new material during the early '90s, but peaked only when they turned their attention back to the oldies, re-recording a clutch of past hits for 1996's *Masters of the Funk*.

## FURTHER READING

*The Truth About Funk* by Steve Washington (TFL)

## SLAVE DISCOGRAPHY

### CHARTLOG

1977 Slide/Son of Slide (Cotillion—#1 R&B/#32 pop)
1978 The Party Song/We Can Make Love (Cotillion—#22 R&B/#110 pop)
1978 Baby Sinister/Can't Get Enough of You (Cotillion—#74 R&B)
1978 Stellar Fungk/Drac Is Back (Cotillion—#14 R&B)
1978 Just Freak/The Way You Love Is Heaven (Cotillion—#64 R&B/#110 pop)
1979 Just a Touch of Love/Shine (Cotillion—#9 R&B)
1980 Foxy Lady (Funky Lady)/Are You Ready for Love? (Cotillion—#55 R&B)
1980 Sizzlin' Hot/Never Get Away (Cotillion—#57 R&B)
1980 Watching You/Dreamin' (Cotillion—#6 R&B/#78 pop)
1981 Feel My Love/Stone Jam (Cotillion—#62 R&B)
1981 Snap Shot/Funken Town (Cotillion—#6 R&B/#91 pop)
1981 Wait for Me/Steal Your Heart (Cotillion—#20 R&B/#103 pop)
1982 Come To Blow Ya Mind/Stay in My Life (Cotillion—#81 R&B)
1983 Do You Like It. . .(Girl)/Friday Night (Cotillion—#73 R&B)
1983 Shake It Up/Rendezvous (Cotillion—#22 R&B)
1983 Steppin' Out/Show Down (Cotillion—#73 R&B)
1984 Ooohh/That's the Way I Like It (Cotillion—#41 R&B)
1986 Thrill Me/It's My Heart That's Breaking (Ichiban—#84 R&B)
1986 All We Need Is Time/Don't Waste My Time (Ichiban—#85 R&B)
1987 Juicy-O/? (Ichiban—#83 R&B)

### LPS

**8** 1977 Slave (Cotillion—#6 R&B/#22 pop)
This band was hot right from the start. A breathtaking slab of heavy, edgy funk, *Slave* includes "Slide," "Screw Your Wig on Tight," and the horn-drenched ballad "The Happiest Days."

**7** 1977 The Hardness of the World (Cotillion—#31 R&B/#67 pop)

**8** 1978 The Concept (Cotillion—#11 R&B/#78 pop)
Mellow vibes, which almost border on noodly, and lots of synthesizer drive this set, from the vocoder-whipped "Stellar Fungk" to the bright horns of "We've Got Your Party" and some truly serious guitar on "Let's Freak."

**7** 1979 Just a Touch of Love (Cotillion—#11 R&B/#92 pop)
**6** 1980 Stone Jam (Cotillion—#5 R&B/#53 pop)
Leaving behind the hard funk trappings of their early material, Slave take the groove 180 degrees into super smooth, superbly arranged songs. Includes "Let's Spend Some Time," "Feel My Love" and "Watching You."

**7** 1981 Show Time (Cotillion—#7 R&B/#46 pop)
**4** 1982 Visions of the Lite (Cotillion—#46 R&B/#177 pop)
**5** 1983 Bad Enuff (Cotillion—#30 R&B/#168 pop)
**6** 1986 Unchained at Last (Ichiban—#56 R&B)
**4** 1987 Make Believe (Ichiban—#44 R&B)
**4** 1991 Rebirth (Ichiban)
Samples, loops and the like try to bring the Slave's sound into the '90s. Unfortunately, it doesn't want to go there.

**4** 1994 Funk Strikes Back (Ichiban)
**4** 1996 Masters of the Funk (Ichiban)
Re-recordings . . . who needs them?

### SELECTED COMPILATIONS AND ARCHIVE RELEASES

**8** 1984 The Best of Slave (Cotillion)
Tight, snappy collection of the band's '70s-era hits.

**7** 1994 Stellar Fungk (Rhino—#44 R&B)
**7** 1998 From the Archives (Echo)

### STEVE WASHINGTON

**7** 1983 Like a Shot (Salsoul)

### STEVE WASHINGTON/CIVIL ATTACK

**6** 1984 Civil Attack (Salsoul)

### STEVE WASHINGTON

1983 Like a Shot (Salsoul)

### STEVE WASHINGTON/CIVIL ATTACK

1984 Civil Attack (Salsoul)

### SELECTED SAMPLES

Just a Touch of Love — De La Soul: Keepin' the Faith (1991)
Just a Touch of Love — Isis: Power of Myself Is Moving (1990)
Just a Touch of Love — Kriss Kross: Alright (1993)
Slide — A Tribe Called Quest: Go Ahead in the Rain (1990)
Slide — Professor Griff & the Last Asiatic Disciples: Pawns in the Game (1990)
Slide — Public Enemy: Can't Truss It (1991)
Son of Slide — Tone Loc: Next Episode (1989)
Watchin' You — EPMD: Never Seen You Before (remix) (1997)
Watchin' You — Snoop Doggy Dogg: Gin and Juice (1993)

## S.O.S. BAND

**FORMED:** *1977, Atlanta, GA*

**ORIGINAL LINEUP:** *Mary Davis (vcls, kybds), Bruno Speight (gtr), John Simpson III (bs), Jason TC Bryant (kybds), Billy R. Ellis (sax), Willie Killebrew (sax), James Earl Jonnes III (drms)*

Originally known as the Sounds of Santa Monica, the SOS Band were a regular sight at Lamar's Regal Room in Atlanta, a nightclub owned by would-be entrepreneur Milton Lamar. He became the band's manager, and in 1979, they signed to Clarence Avant's Tabu label. It was Avant who brought about the band's name change, although contrary to popular belief SOS was not simply an abbreviation of their old name; rather, Avant insisted, it was now short for the Sounds of Success.

The group was paired with producer Sigidi Abdallah, best known at that point for his work with Donald Byrd and the Black Byrds and LTD. (He also contributed backing vocals during Parliament's *Chocolate City* sessions; the liner notes misname him as Sigiti). With him at the helm, the SOS Band scored an immediate smash with "Take Your Time," a fine electro-funk anthem that topped the R&B chart and hit the pop Top Three. The infuriatingly contagious "SOS (Dit Dit Dit Dash Dash Dash Dit Dit Dit)" followed, while the SOS Band's eponymous debut went gold late in 1980.

Adding Abdul Raoof (trombone) and background vocalist Fredi Grace, the SOS Band promptly set about recording their second album. *Too*, however, struggled, while even newly recruited star producers Gene Dozier and Ricky Sylvers could not push *SOS III* beyond #27. But 1983 brought a massive resurgence in the band's fortunes as the band linked with producers Jimmy Jam and Terry Lewis for their fourth album.

*On the Rise*, unleashed two Top Five singles, "Just Be Good to Me" and "Tell Me If You Still Care." On the strength of a similarly successful title track, 1984's *Just the Way You Like It* made #6, while 1986's *Sands of Time* became the SOS Band's most successful offering since their debut, climbing to #4. The group also reached #2 with single "The Finest," featuring recently enlisted vocalist Mark Smith (b. 4/27/65; d. 10/4/92, ex-Force, X-Caliber) and guest star Alexander O'Neal.

Tours with Jermaine Jackson, Patti Labelle and Luther Vandross kept the SOS Band in the public eye. However, the band all but imploded during 1987, as charismatic vocalist Davis departed, followed by Smith, Jonnes, Simpson

and Killebrew. Davis launched a moderately successful solo career, scoring a minor hit in 1990 with "Separate Ways." Smith, newly ordained a minister, then began working on a contemporary gospel album; sadly, he commited suicide before it was completed.

The SOS Band's fortunes plummeted in the wake of the exodus. They linked with vocalist Penny Forde for "It's Time To Move," a contribution to 1988's *Police Academy 4* soundtrack, but the pairing did not gel and Forde departed for Chaka Khan's band.

SOS Band returned with new vocalist Chandra Currelly joining Fredi Grace up front, plus the rhythm section of Marcus Williams (drms) and Kurt Mitchell (bs). With producer Curtis F. Williams (ex-Kool & the Gang), they then set to work on their next album, 1989's *Diamonds in the Raw*.

The death of Ellis shortly before the album's completion saw the finished album dedicated to his memory. It was a worthy tribute. Although US sales were poor, *Diamonds in the Raw* was a hit across Europe, while the tour, which followed, spawned SOS Band's first live album, *Escape*, recorded in Amsterdam.

Recruiting Sultan Mohammed (sax), Lloyd L. Oby (trom), Roderick Smith (sax) and Gregory Mayfield (trum) to a powerful new horn section, SOS Band returned in 1991, buoyed by the massive international success enjoyed by a revitalized "Just Be Good to Me," within Beats International's "Dub Be Good to Me." (Beats mastermind Norman Cook is now better-known as Fat Boy Slim)

Grace departed, but founder bassist Alexander rejoined and, with the Tabu label's recently acquired new distribution through the major A&M, hopes were high for their next release. Unfortunately, *One of Many Nights* failed to chart altogether—despite boasting cover art by A&M label head Herb Alpert.

The SOS Band were one of the attractions at the 1993 North Sea Jazz festival, but the birth of Currelly's first child ensured the group were off the road for some time. In fact, it was two years before the SOS Band resurfaced, rejoined now by original vocalist Davis.

With a core lineup now of Davis, Bryant and Raoof, the SOS Band toured through the remainder of the decade, including a phenomenal set at Funkfest in 1999. They also contributed two tracks, "Girl's Night Out" and "Who Do You Tell," to the *United We Funk* collection of revitalized '80s-era funk acts; Rick James, Gap Band and Con Funk Shun were similarly involved.

## S.O.S. BAND DISCOGRAPHY
### CHARTLOG

1980 Take Your Time (Do It Right)(part one)/(part two) (Tabu—#1 R&B/#3 pop)

1980 S.O.S. (Dit Dit Dit Dash Dash Dash Dit Dit Dit)/Open Letter (Tabu—#20 R&B)

1980 Take Love Where You Find It/? (Tabu)

1981 What's Wrong with Our Love Affair?/Open Letter (Tabu—#87 R&B)

1981 Do It Now (part one)/(part two) (Tabu—#15 R&B)

1981 You/There Is No Limit (Tabu—#64 R&B)

1982 High Hopes/Good and Plenty (Tabu—#25 R&B)

1982 Groovin'/Your Love (Tabu)

1982 Can't Get Enough/High Hopes (Tabu)

1983 Have It Your Way/Your Love (Tabu—#57 R&B)

1983 Just Be Good to Me/(instrumental) (Tabu—#2 R&B/#55 pop)

1983 Tell Me If You Still Care/If You Want My Love (Tabu—#5 R&B/#65 pop)

1983 Open Letter/If You Want My Love (Tabu)

1984 For Your Love/On the Rise (Tabu—#34 R&B)

1984 Just the Way You Like It/Body Break (Tabu—#6 R&B/#64 pop)

1984 No One's Gonna Love You/I Don't Want Nobody Else (Tabu—#15 R&B/#102 pop)

1985 Weekend Girl/Feeling (Tabu—#40 R&B)

1986 The Finest/I Don't Want Nobody Else (Tabu—#2 R&B/#44 pop)

1986 Borrowed Love/Weekend Girl (Tabu—#14 R&B)

1986 Even When You Sleep/No One's Gonna Love You (Tabu—#34 R&B)

1987 No Lies/Even When You Sleep (Tabu—#43 R&B)

1989 I'm Still Missing Your Love (dub) (Tabu—#7 R&B)

1989 Just the Way You Like It/Borrowed Love (Tabu)

1990 Secret Wish/Crossfire (Tabu—#38 R&B)

1991 Sometimes I Wonder/(instrumental) (Tabu/A&M—#65 R&B)

### LPS

**7** 1980 SOS Band (Tabu—#2 R&B/#12 pop)

Of course "Take Your Time" and "SOS" dominate, but a glossy, horn-packed set bristles with energy throughout.

**5** 1981 Too (SOS 2) (Tabu—#30 R&B/#117 pop)

Typical second album—same sound, lesser songs, and a little heavy-handed as well. We all need a social conscience, but does it always have to be so mawkish?

**6** 1982 SOS Band III (Tabu—#27 R&B/#172 pop)

**6** 1983 On the Rise (Tabu—#7 R&B/#47 pop)

A truthful title, as the band rebuilds from the roots up, maintaining the funk, but acknowledging the '80s as well.

**8** 1984 Just the Way You Like It (Tabu—#6 R&B/#60 pop)

Exuberant, energetic set glosses over a few weak songs (and the rumors of Davis' imminent departure) to kick booty across the floor.

**7** 1985 Sands of Time (Tabu—#4 R&B/#44 pop)

**7** 1989 Diamonds in the Raw (Tabu—#43 R&B/#194 pop)

Nobody expected anything, but the band had something to prove. Curtis Williams' production brings the hint of a party-down Kool edge to the show, and if the songs don't exactly leap out, everything else does.

**7** 1991 One of Many Nights (Tabu/A&M)

"Get Hyped on This" invites the album's hottest cut, and overall it's not difficult to do. Currelly's heart-shattered "Broken Promises" is especially effective.

### SELECTED COMPILATIONS AND ARCHIVE RELEASES

**6** 1987 The Hit Mixes (Tabu)

**8** 1995 The Best of the SOS Band (Tabu—#27 R&B/#185 pop)

### SELECTED SAMPLES

Just Be Good to Me — Beats International: Dub Be Good to Me (1990)

Just Be Good to Me — 2Pac featuring Richie Rich: Heavy in the Game (1995)

No One's Gonna Love You — Maxwell: Ascension (Don't Ever Wonder) (remix) (1996)

No One's Gonna Love You — Spice 1: Welcome to the Ghetto (1992)

Take Your Time Do It Right — Black Sheep: Strobelite Honey (1990)

Tell Me If You Still Care — Mariah Carey: Always Be My Baby (remix) (1995)

Tell Me If You Still Care — DJ Jazzy Jeff & the Fresh Prince: I'm Looking for the One (To Be With Me) (1993)

Tell Me If You Still Care — L.L. Cool J.: Hip Hop (1995)

## STUFF

**FORMED:** 1975, New York, NY

**ORIGINAL LINEUP:** Cornell Dupree (gtr), Eric Gale (d. 5/25/94—gtr), Gordon Edwards (bs), Richard Tee (d. 7/12/93—kybds), Steve Gadd (drms), Christopher Parker (perc)

Originally conceived as a freelance answer to the Stax/Motown etc. housebands of the late '60s, Stuff formed in 1967 as Encyclopedia of Soul, with bassist Gordon Edwards the founding and longest serving member. Drummers Billy Cobham and Jimmy Johnson and alto saxophonist David Sanborn numbered among other members of the group, before Edwards pieced together a full-time, all-instrumental lineup in 1975.

Genuinely powerful, Stuff's eponymous debut album became a Top 60 R&B hit in early 1977. It was followed in summer by More Stuff, which offered more of the same, and left the group poised on the edge of a creative, if not necessarily commercial, breakthrough. Stuff, however, were clearly hoping for greater rewards. In 1979, Stuff It was encouragingly produced by legendary Booker T. & the MGs guitarist Steve Cropper, but served up little of either interest or substance, a failing amplified by 1980's Live in New York.

That was Stuff's final release before the individual musicians returned to session work. Richard Tee and Eric Gale died of cancer less than a year apart in 1993–94.

## LPS
**9 1976 Stuff (WB—#53 R&B/#163 pop)**
Lazily condemned for frequently sounding like a collection of funky backing tracks crying out for a vocalist ("Happy Farms" needs Mick Jagger), one wonders just how great it could have been if they'd found one. And that's before you get to the genuinely bizarre medley of "Dixie" and "Up on the Roof."
**6 1977 More Stuff (WB—#43 R&B/#61 pop)**
**5 1979 Stuff It (WB)**
Choral vocals straight out of a disco backing track aren't necessarily the best idea Stuff ever had, and many of the arrangements might be better suited to TV incidental music. But ghastly muzak renditions of lite-pop hits "Dance with Me" and Stevie Wonder's "Love Having You Around" are at least well executed, and played loud and loose, there is a certain guilty fission to it all.
**3 1980 Live in New York (WB)**
Imagine you're in an elevator and, every time the music stops, your fellow passengers applaud. Welcome to hell.

## SELECTED COMPILATIONS AND ARCHIVE RELEASES
**5 1996 Right Stuff (WB)**

# STYLUS
**FORMED:** *1975, Melbourne, Australia*
**ORIGINAL LINEUP:** *Peter Cupples (vcls, gtr, kybds), Ronnie Peers (gtr), Sam McNally (kybds), Ashley Henderson (bs), Peter Lee (drms)*

Stylus were the most successful of all the early-mid-'70s Australian funk rock bands (Skylight, Johnny Rocco, the Hot City Bump Band), not only threatening to break out beyond their homeland's shores, but also proving a powerful palliative to the weak American and European disco funk then infesting the national charts.

The group's roots lay in Mason's Jar, a rock band formed by keyboard player Ian Mason, and featuring future Stylus members Peter Cupples, Ronnie Peers, Ashley Henderson and Peter Lee. Jar folded when Mason quit after just one single (1975's "Let Me Love You"). Replacing him with Sam McNally and fleshing out the sound with Ronnie Peers, the group relaunched as Stylus, embarking on an intensive series of nationwide tours with local heroes Sherbert, and the visiting Focus and Ike & Tina Turner.

Stylus signed with Atlantic in early 1975, and debuted that summer with a cover of "Summer Breeze," the Seals and Croft song best known from the Isley Brothers R&B hit version. "World of Make Believe" followed, joining its predecessor in the Melbourne city charts, before the debut album *Where in the World* arrived shortly before Christmas.

Departing Atlantic following one more 45, "I'm Going Home," Stylus next released a single on the independent Crystal Clear label ("So Much Love"), then joined the EMI subsidiary Oz for *For the Love of Music* in 1976.

Lee quit, and was briefly replaced by Trevor Courtney, before Joe Tattersalls, of jazz-rock band Ayres Rock, moved in during 1977. This lineup cut *The Best Kept Secret*, which became Stylus' first American release, through the Motown subsidiary Prodigal (it was retitled *Stylus* for the occasion). The album did reasonably well, but Stylus themselves were suffering indecision over their future direction.

A second vocalist, Peter Roberts, was recruited, but Tattersalls then left, to be replaced by Mark Meyer, ex-European art-pop band Sailor. However, despite touring Australia with George Benson, *Part of It All*, Stylus' fourth album in summer 1979, bombed and the band broke up in late 1979.

## COMPLETE STYLUS DISCOGRAPHY
### SINGLES
1975 Summer Breeze/Feelin' Blue (WEA—Aus)
1975 World of Make Believe/Just Began (WEA—Aus)
1976 I'm Goin' Home/Where in the World (WEA—Aus)
1976 So Much Love/We All Need One Another (Crystal Clear—Aus)
1976 I Just Don't Want To Fall in Love Right Now/Funky Fig (Oz—Aus)
1977 Kissin'/For the Love of Music (Oz—Aus)
1978 Work Out Fine/Natural Feelin' (Oz—Aus)
1978 Look at Me/You Can't Get It out of Your Head (Oz—Aus)
1978 Got To Say Goodbye/Discover Your Life (Oz—Aus)
1979 If You Believe Me/Byron Bay (Oz—Aus)

### LPS
**4 1975 Where in the World? (WEA—Aus)**
Divorced from even a halfway authentic funk root, Stylus' early sound is formulaic, even clinical . . . the Average White Band with slide rules. But so precise!
**8 1976 For The Love Of Music (Oz—Aus)**
More feeling, more emotion . . . and more good songs as well. "Funky Fig" is suitably nutty.
**7 1978 Stylus (Prodigal)**
The Australian *Best Kept Secret* album, lavishly funk-lite, but smoothly enjoyable.
**5 1979 Part of It All (Oz—Aus)**

Disappointing and disjointed. A few good tracks are overwhelmed by too many mediocre ones.

## SUN

FORMED: *1975, Dayton, OH*

ORIGINAL LINEUP: *Byron Byrd (vcls, sax), Shawn Sandridge (gtr), Bruce Hastell (gtr), Hollis Melson (bs), Dean Hummons (kybds), John Wagner (trum), Christopher Jones (trum), Gary King (trom), Kym Yancey (drms), Ernie Knisley (perc)*

Emerging from the fetid funk hotbed of Dayton, Sun was the brainchild of Byron Byrd, the group's vocalist, principle writer, arranger and producer. The lineup was rarely stable; of Sun's founding lineup, Byrd, Gary King, Kym Yancey and Ernie Knisley alone enjoyed any longevity within the ranks. Other band members included guitarists Keith Cheatham, Sheldon Reynolds and Anthony Thompson, bassists Don Taylor and Curtis Hooks, keyboardists Dean Francis and Sonnie Talbert and horn players Larry Hatchet, Nigel Boulton and Robert Arnold.

Sun were very much a child of their times, tracing a similar musical trajectory to Earth Wind & Fire as they moved blithely between solid funk, slow jams and soulful ballads—tracing, too, the prevalent fashions of the era.

Astrology and *Star Wars* both flavored various Sun recordings, with 1979's *Destination: Sun* depicting its makers as heroic extraterrestrials, complete with solar names, "star tones" and an opening cut (the minor hit "Radiation Level"), which rhymed "rock with me" with "interplanetarily." Only the inventiveness of their music saved the group from absolute cliche, although that alone wasn't enough to bring them anything more than a stream of minor hits.

Sun burned out in 1984, following an ill-starred dalliance with early-'80s techno-funk. Byrd moved into production; among his better-known works were blues-rocker Roger Chapman's *Walking the Cat* in 1989 and former Black Uhuru vocalist Michael Rose's 1990 album *Proud*.

### SUN DISCOGRAPHY

#### CHARTLOG

1976 Wanna Make Love/Love Is Never Sure (Capitol—#31 R&B/#76 pop)

1977 Boogie Bopper/The Show Is Over (Capitol—#50 R&B)

1978 Dance (Do What You Wanna Do)/I Had a Choice (Capitol—#92 R&B)

1978 Sun Is Here/Long Drawn Out Thang (Capitol—#18 R&B)

1979 Radiation Level/(instrumental) (Capitol—#25 R&B)

1979 Pure Fire/Deep Rooted Feeling (Capitol—#67 R&B)

1980 Space Ranger (Majic's in the Air)/(instrumental) (Capitol—#56 R&B)

1981 Reaction Satisfaction (Jam Y'All: Funk Up)/It Seems So Hard (Capitol—#57 R&B)

1982 Slamm Dunk the Ffunk/I Wanna Be with You (Capitol—#81 R&B)

1984 Legs (Bring the Wolf out of Me)/True Love (Air City—#89 R&B)

#### LPS

**7** 1976 Live On Dream On (Capitol—#54 R&B)

Chunky rhythms and fractured horns make no attempt to hide earth, wind or fire, but inventive arrangements keep things interesting.

**8** 1977 Sun Power (Capitol—#39 R&B)

If you only hear one Sun album . . . the opening "Light Me Up" is a bubbling chameleon, on the floor funk with a chorus straight out of classic Motown. More slow grooves than in yer face funkers, the set climaxes with the hyper-suggestive "Organ Grinder."

**6** 1978 Sunburn (Capitol—#21 R&B/#69 pop)

**7** 1979 Destination: Sun (Capitol—#17 R&B/#85 pop)

It's completely predictable, of course, and has "1979" written all over it. But funky smooth grooves and a friendly popping bass are awfully hard to resist sometimes, and "Everybody Disco Down" is daft as a brush. Don't miss the electro effects in the run-off groove, either.

**6** 1980 Sun over the Universe (Capitol)

**6** 1981 Sun: Force of Nature (Capitol—#52 R&B/#205 pop)

#### SELECTED COMPILATIONS AND ARCHIVE RELEASES

**7** 1998 Greatest Hits (Capitol)

No surprises, but no disappointments either.

## WILD CHERRY

FORMED: *1974, Steubenville, OH*

ORIGINAL LINEUP: *Robert Parissi (vcls, gtr), Bryan Bassett (gtr), Allen Wentz (bs), Mark Avsec (kybds), Ron Beitle (drms)*

Few people would classify Wild Cherry's involvement with funk as anything more than a joke; fewer still, however, would consider a reference book complete if Wild Cherry weren't included. Alongside the equally ubiquitous KC & the Sunshine Band, after all, Wild Cherry came to epitomize "funk" for great swathes of the record-buying American public, an unlikely role that a host of modern TV-advertised compilation albums have been only too pleased to reinforce. What makes the whole thing even more inexplicable, of course, is that the band themselves were never convinced that the crown fit correctly. They just wanted to rock.

It was vocalist Robert Parissi who named the group, inspired by a box of cough drops lying by his bed during a stay in hospital in 1974. A hard rocking attraction on the local club scene, Wild Cherry released a couple of singles through the Brown Bag label, owned by Terry Knight of Grand Funk Railroad. Neither "Get Down" nor "Voodoo Doll" did anything, however, and by 1975, Wild Cherry had broken up. Parissi moved into steakhouse management, his bandmates dispersed.

But the following year, Parissi revived the old name with a new group of musicians, intending to continue in the same musical vein. Clubs that had previously welcomed the band with open arms, however, had either closed down or changed direction entirely. The only place Wild Cherry could get gigs were at discotheques, of course with an audience to match. It was at one such venue that a member of the audience finally lost patience with the band's interminable riffing, and demanded that the white boys play some funky music. Backstage that same night, Parissi wrote a song about just that.

Over the next few months, Wild Cherry worked hard to ensure "Play Some Funky Music" was not the sole offering of that ilk in their repertoire. A cover of the Commodores' "I Feel Sanctified" was added, together with a number of other self-composed cuts described by Parissi, in a *Billboard* interview, as an attempt "to do a white thing to R&B, adding some heaviness to it."

Wild Cherry signed with Sweet City Records and prepared their first single, "I Feel Sanctified." Both Sweet City and distributors Epic, however, felt that "Play That Funky Music" was a stronger choice, and events proved them correct. The single went to #1 on the pop chart, becoming only the second ever 45 to be certified platinum (following Johnnie Taylor's "Disco Lady"). An album, *Wild Cherry* followed, topping the R&B chart and making the pop Top Five.

But such success was strictly a one-off. Wild Cherry's second single, "Baby Don't You Know," faltered on the wrong side of the Top 40 and that despite packing an equally memorable hookline: "baby don't you know that the honky's got soul." Their second and third albums, too, sold a fraction of their platinum precursor and, when a fourth LP bombed completely, Wild Cherry broke up in February 1979. Parissi subsequently became a DJ, Marc Avsec joined the bands Breathless and Cellarful of Noise.

## CHARTLOG
1976 Play That Funky Music/The Lady Wants Your Money (Epic—#1 R&B/#1 pop)
1977 Baby Don't You Know/Get It Up (Epic—#41 R&B/#43 pop)
1977 Hot To Trot/Put Yourself in My Shoes (Epic—#62 R&B/#95 pop)
1977 Hold On/Are You Boogieing Around on Your Daddy (Epic—#61 pop)
1978 I Love My Music/Don't Stop Get Off (Epic—#49 R&B/#69 pop)

## LPS
**8** 1976 Wild Cherry (Sweet City—#1 R&B/#5 pop)
"Play That Funky Music" And they did, rather well, too, and certainly with a lot more aplomb than the more scholarly white funkers of the age. Indeed, so long as you don't take things too seriously, it's a very easy album to enjoy.

**7** 1977 Electrified Funk (Sweet City—#33 R&B/#51 pop)
"Baby Don't You Know" is "Funky Music" part two, apparently an autobiographical attempt to explain what happened after they wrote the song. The rest of the album dips a little toward loose-funk-by-numbers, but again the emphasis is on the looseness. At last, a white funk band that doesn't have a tropical plant up their ass.

**3** 1978 I Love My Music (Sweet City—#54 R&B/#84 pop)
Alright, you can ungrit your teeth. Even fans didn't like this one very much.

**3** 1979 Only the Wild Survive (Sweet Music)

# DISCO AND THE DEATH OF FUNK

James Brown reckons he saw it coming years before it finally hit, back when he toured Germany in 1971. Nightclubs dedicated purely to dancing to records were nothing new, of course. But this, as he wrote in his *Godfather of Soul* autobiography, was "a whole new scene," a culture that had no time for sweating musicians and heaving crowds, one that was devoted to dress, to dance and, to Brown's ears anyway, to extracting every last ounce of soul and humanity from the music and replacing it with superficiality.

Brown conceded that "disco is a very small part of funk." But, ". . . in funk, you dig into a groove, you don't stay on the surface. Disco stayed on the surface. It didn't worry me, though," he continued. "I didn't think it would make it across the water to America. Disco just didn't make any sense."

Neither, however, does the public's taste for new thrills. Fast forward five years, to 1975–76, and even Brown had to admit "disco had broken big." He still didn't understand its attraction, and didn't want to, either. "See, I taught them everything they know," he shrugged with becoming archness. "But not everything *I* know."

Brown was correct in almost all of his assumptions. Disco was soul-less; it was superficial and it was senseless. But it also brought funk, soul and R&B into the mainstream slipstream like nothing else before it. It made stars of nobodies (and nobodies of stars); and it served as the springboard for dance music in the '80s and '90s. And while disco is now synonymous with mirror balls, polyester suits and Tony Manero, it really accomplished much, much more.

Disco was 90 percent attitude, 10 percent lifestyle. It could only hurt you if you let it. That's what George Clinton meant when he sang of one nation under a groove, "getting down for the funk of it." Forget the labels, forget the critics, forget the narrow-minded fools who looked down their noses because they didn't like your musical taste, and just enjoy yourself because you can.

True, Clinton also hit out with "The Undisco Kidd" and "Freak of the Week," but the best of P-Funk ruthlessly satirized stereotypes. And what was more stereotypical, during 1977–78, than the funk or rock or jazz purist sneering "sell out" at the brethren who dared to use the "d" word in public? The Ohio Players were no more selling out when they cut "Everybody Disco" than electro-disco divas Lipps Inc. when they recorded "Funky Town." That the demise of a great many early-mid-'70s funk bands can be attributed almost exclusively to the onset of disco is true. But it was as much their failure and/or refusal to adapt that killed them, as any triumph of disposable synthetics over hardworking sincerity. In other words, on the dancefloor, no one can hear you sweat.

Funk is, of course, placed in an awkward position by disco because, as Brown pointed out, there are so many similarities. In terms of craftsmanship, disco was in many ways the crowning achievement of the previous two decades of American dance music, a form ruthlessly pillaged from others, then smoothed into one homogenous mass.

Many of the musicians involved at the studios best known for pumping out disco hits were sessionmen and studio players with years of funk, soul and R&B experience behind them, recruited precisely because of that fact. They knew what made a good dance record because they had recorded so many in the past. Similarly, the most skilled producers involved—Germans Giorgio Moroder and Pete Bellote (Donna Summer) and Michael Kunze (Silver Convention), American Steven Greenberg (Lipps Inc.), Asian Indian Biddu (Tina Charles, Carl Douglas), Brazilian Eumir Deodato (Kool & the Gang, Con Funk Shun)—were no strangers to the genre either. So they borrowed what they wanted from the past, their own and other people's, and if the ensuing synthesis maybe squeezed out some of the soul, they swiftly found other things to replace it with.

Disco's roots lay in a general backlash to the musical (and, to an equal extent, cultural) freedoms of the '60s and, particularly, the late '60s. It was primarily a white movement, the spawn of an uptight generation for whom the tight rhythms and tighter strings of the dancefloor offered a refreshing corollary to everything that the dippy, trippy music of the love 'n' acid generation represented. Regimented and calculated, there was no room for jamming and even less for improvisation. Everything was orchestrated, from the first string and horn note to the last squelch of guitar. Again employing George Clinton as an example, if anybody ever asks why it took until 1978 for P-Funk to translate their live superstardom into dancefloor superiority, there is only one thing that needs to be said to them: "Maggot Brain."

The first truly telling signs of what became a monstrous tidal wave were seen in 1973. The twin behemoths of funk and soul, in their increasingly ingenious attempts to fully crossover into the pop mainstream, had been executing some increasingly convoluted dance steps since the dawn of the decade. Individually and collectively, Isaac Hayes' "Shaft," the near rock thrust of Sly Stone, and Rufus' smokey soundtracks for undulating belly buttons, imperceptibly set the mirror ball revolving. All that was needed, then, was a sudden shock of electricity to coax gentle revolution into total social upheaval.

Across a broad spectrum of musical explorations, George McCrae's "Rock Your Baby," Jim Gilstrap's "Swing Your Daddy," Carl Douglas' "Kung Fu Fighting," and a host of early KC & the Sunshine Band hits, the term "disco" was in wide, and none too discriminating use long before the genre itself was formularized. By the time Labelle threw "Lady Marmalade" into the brew, in 1974, the die was already cast.

Chugging along in a long-term career, which had seldom got out of second gear, Labelle was actually one of the unlikeliest catalysts imaginable. Yet Patti Labelle herself knew something special was afoot the moment the "Lady Marmalade" sessions were over. "I loved the result. The minute we heard the Kenny Noland-Bob Crewe penned ode to Creole ladies of the night, we knew we had a hit on our hands. We just didn't know how big it would become." Appropriately produced by Allen Toussaint, with the Meters in full swing behind him, "Lady Marmalade' became the disco anthem of the '70s.

The song's immediate success is easy to pin down. It was indeed anthemic, catchy and hooky, the Meters themselves were smoking at that time, and the schoolboy French of the chorus won knowing smirks from ninth graders everywhere ("voulez vous couchez avec moi ce soir" does not, as one New Jersey area DJ once insisted, translate as "did you leave my cabbage in the bathroom?"). Under those conditions, how could it fail? And more importantly, how could it remain isolated? By 1976, "Lady Marmalade"'s basic recipe of rhythm, beat, strings and sex was being liberally spread across American radio, by some of radio's best-loved stalwarts.

One such was Van McCoy. Best known as a songwriter, he composed "Baby I'm Yours" for Barbara Lewis, "I Get the Sweetest Feeling" for Jackie Wilson, and many more, before finally emerging into the production limelight as the mastermind behind the Philly-sound vocal group, the Stylistics. Swimming with what was fast becoming a prevalent tide amongst sundry studio masterminds, McCoy issued his own *Disco Baby* instrumental album in 1975. He also fronted the Soul City Symphony and brought to the world a new dance sensation, The Hustle, reinvigorating a mania for "the dance of the moment" unparalleled since the early '60s.

Over the next couple of years, on either side of its incorporation into the genre-defining *Saturday Night Fever* soundtrack, "The Hustle" spawned a passel of imitations and parodies, everything from "The Latin Hustle" to the "San Francisco Hustle," to James Brown's "Soft Hustle." There was even a "British Hustle" and reformed glam rocker Barry Blue, who produced the song for Heatwave, admits, "Of course we were simply adapting Van's original, but why not? 'The Hustle' was universal!"

Diana Ross's epic "Love Hangover," in early 1976, marked the apogee of what could be described as disco's infancy, and a critical moment in the music's crossover path. Upwards of seven-minutes long, with Ross' super soft, super sexy vocals and a sensuous love-funky bass line sprinkled liberally with passionate strings, "Love Hangover" became THE cool down/heat up classic of the era, a pop and R&B chart-topper that comes from somewhere down below, perfect for checking out the tight pants on the other side of the dance floor. It also slipped effortlessly into place alongside the only other American chart-topper of the decade to present simulated orgasm as a spectator sport, Donna Summer's "Love To Love You Baby," which appropriately was just slipping out of the chart as "Love Hangover" slid in.

Producers Pete Bellote and partner Giorgio Moroder first ran into Summer when the transplanted American songstress started recording demos at their Musicland Studios in Munich in 1973. Two early singles, "Hostages" and "Ladies of the Night" proved hits on continental European dancefloors, but it was with "Love To Love You Baby," their third collaboration, that they struck the international motherlode—just months after countryman Michael Kunze first pinpointed it.

Late in 1974, Kunze unleashed an Anglo-American vocal trio, Silver Convention, upon Europe's defenseless dancers. The music termed as "disco" at that time was still very much in the tradition of Black American archetypes; European entries into the field tended to follow that model. But Silver Convention's "Fly Robin Fly" simply ripped the formbook to shreds. Quaalude paced, bolstered by a bass that literally pounded dancers into submission, but breaking periodically for the sweetest string section imaginable, "Fly Robin Fly" was a revelation, all the more so since little that Silver Convention managed thereafter came even close to repeating its impact. It was left to other minds to complete the revolution that "Fly Robin Fly" pronounced. Bellote and Moroder were right there, waiting.

"Love To Love You Baby" was first recorded as a scant three-minute quickie, then retooled into a 17-minute orgy at the suggestion of Casablanca Records chief Neil Bogart.

It was a dynamic concept, if not necessarily an original one. Three years earlier, Belgian funk band Chakachas achieved their sole US hit with the heaving, groaning "Jungle Fever." But in removing even the vaguest possibility that the vocalist on that song really was in the throes of some violent tropical malaise, "Love To Love You Baby" stepped fully fledged (if not fully dressed) into the realms of aural pornography.

In Britain, the BBC took one listen to Summer's unrelenting groans and promptly banned the record from the airwaves. It hit the Top 20 regardless. In America, the song went even further, topping the R&B chart, hitting #2 pop and establishing Summer, at least, as a star. But her producers were not far behind her, confirming their own credentials two years later as the creators of Summer's second masterpiece, "I Feel Love."

Powered by a battery of pulsing electronics, the throbbing sonics, which Moroder and Bellote were quick to christen "Motorik," "I Feel Love" was an absolute epiphany. In terms of the future evolution of dance music, disco and otherwise, it was James Brown, Sly Stone and George Clinton rolled into one and, while fellow Germans Kraftwerk (whose epochal *Trans-Europe Express* album was released almost simultaneously) have since been granted much of the historical credit for all that was subsequently wrought, in terms of sheer exposure, "I Feel Love" not only crossed the rubicon, it melted it.

Unquestionably the record established Germany at the forefront of what would now, both disparagingly and approvingly, be termed Euro-disco production. Moroder and Bellote themselves would go on to work with any number of European and American artists, with one of Moroder's most notable tasks being the reinvention of Gamble and Huff songstresses the Three Degrees, in 1978. If anybody demanded proof that the soul of the scene had finally shifted away from the American hit factories, that was it.

In swift succession, German disco factories sprang up like wildfires. Future Milli Vanilli mastermind Frank Farian launched Boney M.; Jurgen Korduletsch unleashed Lipstique. And elsewhere across continental Europe, too, things were cooking: France's La Belle Epoque and Space, Spain's Baccara, Holland's Pussycat, Sweden's resurgent ABBA and so forth. (Britain, having provided future archaeologists with a handful of mid-decade classics by Tina Charles and 5000 Volts, was now too deeply embroiled in the punk rock explosion to turn out more than a handful of contenders. The best of these, remarkably, all had names beginning with the letter "H": Heatwave, Hi-Tension and the reinvented Hot Chocolate.)

Abba notwithstanding, few of these ever followed up their moments of greatest glory; personal obscurity was the natural state of affairs. Indeed, it was through an absolute (if not necessarily welcome) sublimation of the artist that disco completely re-evaluated the nature of the pop music industry. In becoming the ultimate level playing field, disco utterly eschewed the cult of the ego, and the need for those egos to make lofty statements in their "art."

Vicki Sue Robinson, Anita Ward, Alicia Bridges, Santa Esmeralda, Cheryl Lynn, Rozlyn Woods, Amii Grant, Claudja Barry. . .without writing any of them off as simple one-hit wonders, one would be excused remembering them all as one-song wonders, so immortal were their greatest hits. Long after the names have been forgotten, the hits remain inviolate.

When disco superstars did emerge, therefore, it was not from the dancefloors, but from outside of the genre entirely, with the cinema its most seductive partner in crime. Donna Summer's status was consolidated by a handful more hits, but cemented into place by *Thank God It's Friday*. Norman Whitfield proteges Rose Royce were raised to glory by *Car Wash*. The Village People were thrust to immortality by *Can't Stop the Music*; and, of course, '60s pop superstars the BeeGees were catapulted to renewed fame by *Saturday Night Fever*, the highest grossing musical of all time, with the best-selling movie soundtrack of the next 20 years.

With a passion for overkill which is woefully familiar today, but really did seem a phenomenon in 1976–77, the market was saturated. Over-saturated. Disco themes turned up everywhere, from notebooks to lunch boxes, from prime time TV to, indeed, the latest offerings by artists who really should have been trusted to behave a little better. Books professed how to teach you to disco dance. Instructional records (home videos were still a few years away from mass consumption) demonstrated the difference between the New York Hustle and the Latin Hustle Plus, the Bus Stop and the Chicago Loop. And informative magazine articles kept apace with the life outside of the dancehalls.

*Life* magazine reported that within a year of the release of *Saturday Night Fever*, there were over 10,000 discotheques in the United States alone, with new ones opening at a rate of twenty a week. The Hilton Hotel chain was converting its unfashionable bars into trendy new discos, while the seediest bars converted themselves likewise, through the simple expedient of installing a mirror ball and a couple of turntables.

Entire communities found themselves caught up in regional dance competitions as a veritable army of little Tony Maneros, ably assisted, of course, by as many little Stephanies, vied for the lofty honor of local Disco Dancing Champion. There was even a proposal that airports attach discos to their passenger terminals, for the benefit of travelers with a few hours to kill between flights.

The record companies couldn't believe their luck. Visit any 25¢ record bin today, and it still overflows with thematic compilations spawned by such companies as K-Tel and Ronco. And it mattered not where the music came from, if it was a hardcore funk classic or a haddock-brained Eurotrash throwaway, just the inclusion of the magic word *Disco* in the LP's title was like a rumor of gold in a '49ers mining camp.

The flipside of this catalog of mass-marketing indignities, of course, was the sheer wealth of genuinely great songs that emerged from the post-*Saturday Night Fever* holocaust. Parliament's stroboscopic "Flashlight" was followed to glory by "One Nation Under a Groove," "Aqua Boogie" and "Not Just Knee Deep," presenting George Clinton with four R&B #1s (neatly divided between Parliament and Funkadelic) in one 20 month spell, after almost 20 years in the music business.

War's "Galaxy," Barry White's "It's Ecstacy When You Lay Down Next to Me," Marvin Gaye's "Got To Give It Up," the Ohio Players' "Use Ta Be My Girl" and the Isley Brothers' "Take Me to the Next Phase" were all great records crucially informed by the events of the past two years. Slave's "Slide," Maze's "Workin' Together," Brick's "Dazz," Con Funk Shun's "Ffun," Kool & the Gang's "Ladies Night," Earth Wind & Fire and the Emotions' "Boogie Wonderland," even such late-in-the-day hits as the Dazz Band's "Let It Whip," Midnight Star's "Operator" and Instant Funk's "Who Took Away the Funk" (a stupid question!) were each physically wrought by the light of the mirror ball. Had disco lived on, who knows what might have happened?

By the end of the '70s, however, it was fast becoming clear that most people had been there, done that and bought the souvenir polyester shirt. Because disco had started as a fringe cult, then driven so heartily into the mainstream, later contributions to the genre became nothing more than parodied ghostly echoes of their predecessors, well aware of what made money, and not caring a bit whether it made sense as well. But unlike other musical forms that rise and die, disco also spawned an angry music-squashing backlash, pioneered with a ferocity that actually rivaled the emotion behind the origins of the genre.

Instituted by many of the very same people who, just a year earlier, couldn't get enough of the stuff, the anti-disco bumperstickers, boycotts and record burnings spelled out a Dante-esque funeral, which just went on and on. Destroyed from without, self-destructing from within, finally the redneck rock-jock cliche was true. Of course disco sucked. All its teeth had been knocked out.

### RECOMMENDED LISTENING

No LPs to speak of, but ten singles that cannot be beat. Catch the 12-inch versions if you can.
Cerrone — "Supernature" (Cotillion, 1978)
Chic — "Le Freak" (Atlantic, 1978)
Gloria Gaynor — "I Will Survive" (Polydor, 1978)
Lipps Inc. — "Funky Town" (Casablanca, 1980)
Magazine 60 — "Don Quichotte" (Baja, 1986)
Musique — "In the Bush" (Prelude, 1978)
Diana Ross — "Love Hangover" (Motown, 1976)
Silver Convention — "Fly Robin Fly" (Midland International, 1975)
Donna Summer — "I Feel Love" (Casablanca, 1977)
Anita Ward — "Ring My Bell" (Juana, 1979)

# HOT GROOVES: COLD STORAGE

**Directory of Forgotten Funk Albums of the '70s, Ten-Star Collectibles One and All.**

**Azteca: *Azteca* (Columbia, 1972)**

There was Santana, there was Malo and there was Azteca, and West Coast Latin funk really didn't need anything more. Pete and the late (d. 1986) Coke Escovedo were the star attractions of an album that actually rustled the R&B Top 40. Key cuts include "Peace Everybody," "Can't Take the Funk out of Me" and the mighty "Azteca."

**Beginning of the End: *Funky Nassau* (Alston, 1971)**

Up from the Bahamas to funk your pants off. The title track was a major 1971 hit, and the choppy guitars and brittle horns that characterized it are in evidence across the entire LP. "Monkey Tamarind," "Surrey Ride," "In the Deep" and both halves of "Funky Nassau" head a non-stop party.

**Charles Hilton Brown: *Owed to Myself* (Schema, 1974—Italy)**

British Afro-funkers Assagai accompany Brown on a conga-fired trip to funk heaven. Comparisons between Brown and Otis Redding are borne out by his versions of "Try a Little Tenderness" and "Love Train" ("Ain't No Sunshine" is simply too dramatic for words), while the band's own alchemy is revealed on "GWF," an instrumental that just doesn't quit.

**Chairmen of the Board: *Skin I'm In* (Invictus, 1974)**

Magnificent Jeffrey Bowen production, with a band not hitherto associated with monster funk riffing, shattering horn climaxes and wah-wah-a-go-go. Every cut is a winner, particularly across side one, where Sly's wicked "Life and Death" brackets the soaring instrumental "White Rose" with a bass that sounds like a bear. Side two reverts to more familiar Chairmen territory, but does close with the titanic "Finders Keepers."

**Cymande: *Cymande* (Janus, 1972)**

Debut album by that most audacious of hybrids, a British funk dub band. Cymande always suffered in comparison with Osibisa and Assagai. In fact, they were way further out than either, never happier than when imagining what might happen if Lee Perry produced James Brown, in a room full of chanting ganga fiends. "Rastafarian Folk Song" states their case most sweetly; "Bra," "Rickshaw" and "Message" follow close behind. Eight years later, a lot of post-punk British bands would follow Cymande's lead, and take it to new heights entirely. But this is where it started.

**Eleventh Hour: *Hollywood Hot* (20th Century, 1976)**

Very chic edge-of-disco funk, vindicated by the quality of songwriting, Bob Crewe has a heavy hand in things, roping in a crop of the Los Angeles scene's most respected session musicians (Cindy Bullens had recently worked with Elton John) to help. Initially most notable for the minor hit title track, *Hollywood Hot*, then got hotter once people discovered their version of Crewe's own "Lady Marmalade"—a hit for Labelle, but here packing a vibrant funk rhythm lacking from the ladies' gumbo monster. A pumped up cover of the Isley Brothers' "It's Your Thing" is also worth investigating.

**Everyday People: *Everyday People* (Redd Coach, 1972)**

Gene Redd, Kool & the Gang's first producer and a former A&R man at King Records, had a hand in this, not only echoing his best-known clients' sound, but also throwing a few of their songs in as well. "Funky Granny" and "Who's Gonna Take the Weight" both compare well with the originals; but the funk drunk "Gold Smoke," "Mama Said-Papa Said" and "Funky Gene-Ra-Tion" prove there was more to Everyday People than a xerox machine.

**Fat: *Funky & Tough* (Bold, 1977)**

Released on TK's short-lived Bold subsidiary, Fat took their name from vocalist Eric "Fat" Gallon, a soulful baritone who carried the band's cool jazz-funk across the classics "Satan's Dream," "How Can I Explain," "Free My Mind," "Magician Man" and "Life Is a Beautiful Thing."

**Force of Nature: *Unemployment Blues* (Philadelphia International, 1976)**

Unequivocal proof that Instant Funk weren't the Philly Sound's only concession to sweat and groove, even if much of the album does prefer to hang around with a smoother kind of sound. The title track is a brassy construction with lyrics as loud as the horns, while "Toy Ball" echoes some of War's classier soul moods.

**Bill "Ravi" Harris & the Prophets: *Funky Sitar Man* (BBE, 1973—UK)**

When this album first appeared in the UK, there was a fear—and a very understandable one—that it was simply another in a long line of weird budget-label knock-offs, along the lines of *The Happy Hammond Goes Pop* or *400 Bagpipes Play a Tribute to the Beatles*. And it may well have been, but once inside, Harris co-conjured up surprisingly effective sitar-led renditions of the Meters' "Look Ka Py Py" and the JBs' "Pass the Peas," plus the matchless original "Path of the Blazing Sarong."

### High Voltage: *High Voltage* (Columbia, 1972)

Unquestionably cut in the Rufus mode, with vocalist Lalomie Washburn clearly aiming for the same range and volume as Chaka Khan. But strong songwriting saves the day, with a definite feel for funk rock with a capital "F."

### Little Beaver: *Black Rhapsody* (Cat, 1974)

Miami guitar legend Little Beaver never shook off the Shuggie Otis comparisons, even when driving his instrument through a solid all-funk instrumental album, dripping wah-wah and solos in equal doses, then drawing back just a little for a heroic take on the classic "Summertime."

### Mandrill: *Mandrill* (Polydor, 1970)

Never the most reliable band when it came to the actual contents of their records (the sleeves, contrarily, were uniformly excellent, in a very ape-centric way), this is one of the two Mandrill albums that everyone needs to hear; the other is 1973's *Composite Truth*. Stoned funk grooving across the immense "Peace & Love" suite, but with none of the wastrel Latin noodling that disfigured the rest of their canon.

### Osibisa: *Heads* (MCA, 1972)

Afro-beat with a prog rock frill, as the British scene begins succumbing to the march of the moog. (Plus, they shared their LP jacket designer with Yes.) But the band's own soul will not be subverted, such a moody, raw pounding that even the mellowness has teeth.

### Rasputin Stash: *Devil Made Me Do It* (Gemigo, 1974)

Alongside Baby Huey, this is *the* essential non-Mayfield Curtom family release, classic Chicago soul shot through with some ferocious funk. Occasional glimpses of the JBs are the initial high points, while "The Devil Made Me Do It" and "I Can Feel Your Jones" push things in a captivatingly funk rocky direction.

### Sins of Satan: *Future Star* (UA, 1977)

Five-piece band caught on the funk-disco cusp and, sadly, not taking full advantage of that wonderful band name. (Even better, their backing vocalists were called the Sexy Sins Destination Love. What were these people taking?) Mad synths solo over the bubbling drums in "Future Star," and "Love Brings Love" has a cool laid back feel to it, plus some great Bootsy-ish bass. The other must-hear highlights are "Realize the Jack" and the snakey-sinewy "Be Right Back."

### Skull Snaps: *Skull Snaps* (GSF, 1974)

"It's a New Day" will sound familiar, even if you've never heard it, so perfectly does it presage late-'90s hip-hop. But Skull Snaps themselves are utter unknowns; one album and they vanished. But what an album, a child of its times with smooth soul rubbing necks with organic funk, highlighted by "I'm Your Pimp" and "Trespasser."

# PART FOUR: THE NEW SCHOOL

## ACID JAZZ RECORDS

Dedicated to the lost grooves of the past and their obscure offspring of the present, London's Acid Jazz label was established in 1987 by Polydor Records executive Eddie Piller and London DJ Gilles Peterson, whose mid-'80s pirate radio programs had fuelled interest in the first place.

Broadcasting from a makeshift transmitter in his garden shed, Peterson filled the airwaves with little-known or, just as pertinently, critically reviled material from such jazz icons as Miles Davis (his electric period), Donald Byrd (the Black Byrds) and Herbie Hancock (the Head Hunters), albums that may have made a commercial splash, but which infuriated the purists who had hitherto followed their careers. Peterson's efforts became cult listening across London, leading him to a regular show on the legendary KISS-FM pirate radio station, and a diary full of solidly successful club dates.

Piller, meanwhile, was a northern soul devotee whose Re-elect the President label had discovered and nurtured jazz organist James Taylor. He also had a proven track record in A&R, as Acid Jazz's own first signings demonstrated. The Brand New Heavies, Galliano, Jamiroquai and D-Influence all numbered among Acid Jazz's prize captures.

It was the *Totally Wired* series of compilation albums that truly launched the label, working within Acid Jazz's rigid—and, at the time, desperately unfashionable—policy of "no house music." The label dug into the past (and Peterson's vast record collection) in search of obscure and underrated jazz-funk from the '70s, mixing that with material drawn from the fertile, but still absolutely unrecognized live scene springing up around the UK.

Peterson left Acid Jazz in 1989 to launch his own Talkin' Loud label (named after James Brown's "Talkin' Loud and Sayin' Nothin'"), and made an immediate impact with the first single by the Young Disciples, "Get Yourself Together." Releases by Galliano, Urban Sound and United Future Organisation followed, while the DJ was also instrumental in reforming early-'80s funkers Incognito.

Acid Jazz, meanwhile, continued pushing forward, launching its own London nightclub in December, 1994, the Blue Note (named, of course, for the classic jazz label) and maintaining its tradition of unearthing the past by resurrecting the debut LP by the Watts Prophets, together with the *Black Voices on the Streets of Watts* compilation and a

third, all new album. The Last Poets' *Freedom Express* was also an Acid Jazz label classic.

*Totally Wired*, too, continued on, reaching 20 volumes before the series ended; a second series was then launched in 2000.

### ACID JAZZ LABEL LISTING 1988–1999

AJCD 01 various artists: Totally Wired 1&2
JAZID 1 Galliano: Frederick Lies Still
JAZID 2 Bryon Morris: Kitty Bey
JAZID 3 Extasis: Psychedelic Jack
JAZID 4 A Man Called Adam: A.P.B.
JAZID 5 Johnny Daglo: Free Your Mind
JAZID 6 The Jazz Renegades: Playing for Real
JAZID 7 Bukky Leo: Rejoice in Righteousness
JAZID 8 The Last Poets: Freedom Express
JAZID 9 King Truman: Like a Gun
JAZID 10 The Quiet Boys featuring Galliano: Let the Good Times Roll
JAZID 11 Lazee Muthas: Cut & Run
JAZID 12 various artists: Hippy House & Happy Hop
JAZID 13 various artists: Totally Wired
JAZID 14 Ed Jones: The Homecoming
JAZID 15 A Man Called Adam: Earthly Powers
JAZID 16 various artists: Totally Wired Two
JAZID 17 Brand New Heavies: People Get Ready
JAZID 18 The Night Trains: Loaded
JAZID 19 Snowboy & the Latin Section: Ritmo Snowboy
JAZID 20 Steve White & Gary Wallace: Never Stop
JAZID 21 What's What: Open Channel D
JAZID 22 various artists: Totally Wired Three
JAZID 23 Brand New Heavies: The Brand New Heavies
JAZID 24 The Beaujolais Band: Mind How You Go
JAZID 25 The Brand New Heavies: Dream Come True
JAZID 26 Piece of Mind: Accept It like This
JAZID 27 Terry Callier: I Don't Want To See Myself Without You
JAZID 28 various artists: Totally Wired Four
JAZID 29 various artists: Best of Acid Jazz
JAZID 30 D-Influence: I'm the One
JAZID 31 various artists: Totally Wired Five
JAZID 32 The Apostles: The Apostles
JAZID 33 The New Jersey Kings: Party to the Bus Stop
JAZID 34 The Quiet Boys: Modal
JAZID 35 Dharma B., featuring Ace of Clubs: Everything Going to the Beat
JAZID 36 various artists: Totally Wired Six
JAZID 37 Rose Windross: Living Life Your Own Way
JAZID 38 various artists: Acid Jazz: Jazz
JAZID 39 The Brand New Heavies: Never Stop

JAZID 40 Snowboy & the Latin Section: Descarga Mambito
JAZID 41 Humble Souls: Beads, Things & Flowers
JAZID 42 Snowboy Featuring Noel McKoy: Lucky Fellow
JAZID 43 various artists: Totally Wired Seven
JAZID 44 The Quiet Boys: Make Me Say It Again
JAZID 45 The Quiet Boys: Can't Hold the Vibe
JAZID 46 Jamiroquai: When You Gonna Learn
JAZID 47 Sandals: A Profound Gas
JAZID 48 Mother Earth: Stoned Woman
JAZID 49 Pure Wilderness: Ain't No Use
JAZID 50 various artists: Totally Wired Eight
JAZID 51 various artists: Acid Jazz Mo'Jazz
JAZID 52 Hazardous Dub Company: Dangerous Dub Vol.1
JAZID 53 Humble Souls: Watch My Garden Grow
JAZID 54 various artists: Happy House & Hippy Hop II
JAZID 55 Mother Earth: Hope You're Feeling Better
JAZID 56 Diana Brown & Barrie K. Sharpe: Masterplan
JAZID 57 various artists: Totally Wired Nine
JAZID 58 Snowboy: The 3 Faces of Snowboy
JAZID 59 Humble Souls: How Now?
JAZID 60 Corduroy: *Dadmancat*
JAZID 61 Robbie Gordon: Still Growing
JAZID 62 Mother Earth: Freedom EP
JAZID 63 Vibraphonic: Vibraphonic
JAZID 64 A-Zel: Jazz Jupiter
JAZID 65 Vibraphonic Featuring Alison Limerick: Trust Me
JAZID 66 various artists: Best of Acid Jazz 2
JAZID 67 Humble Souls: Thoughts & Sound Paintings
JAZID 68 Corduroy: Something in My Eye
JAZID 69 Raw Stylus: Use Me
JAZID 70 unreleased
JAZID 71 The Subterraneans: Taurus Woman
JAZID 72 various artists: Totally Wired Ten
JAZID 73 Hazardous Dub Company: Dangerous Dub Vol. 2
JAZID 74 Ulf Sandberg Quartet: Ulf Sandberg Quartet
JAZID 75 Mother Earth: Grow Your Own EP
JAZID 76 Emperors New Clothes: Unsettled Life
JAZID 77 India: Liego-LA-India
JAZID 78 Cloud Nine: Millenium
JAZID 79 various artists: Totally Wired Italia
JAZID 80 Corduroy: The Frightners
JAZID 81 The James Taylor Quartet: The Money Spyder
JAZID 82 The James Taylor Quartet: Mission Impossible
JAZID 83 Mother Earth: The People Tree
JAZID 84 Night Trains: Lovesick
JAZID 85 Corduroy: High Havoc
JAZID 86 various artists: Further Adventures of Acid Jazz
JAZID 87 Cloud Nine: Promo
JAZID 88 The Whole Thing: The Whole Thing
JAZID 89 Cloud Nine: I Feel It

JAZID 90 various artists: The Best of Totally Wired
JAZID 91 The Beaujolais Band: Talk, Talk & More Talk
JAZID 92 Snowboy & the Latin Section: Something's Coming
JAZID 93 The Harvey Avenue Barrio Band: The Harvey Avenue Barrio Band
JAZID 94 Mother Earth: Find It
JAZID 95 Corduroy: Moterhead
JAZID 96 Night Trains: Hold Out EP
JAZID 97 Emperors New Clothes: Unsettled Life (Underdog Mix)
JAZID 98 Night Trains: Sleazeball
JAZID 99 Double Vision: Conscience
JAZID 100 Mother Earth: Jesse
JAZID 100L Mother Earth: Jesse Live
JAZID 101 various artists: Totally Wired Eleven
JAZID 102 Snowboy & the Latin Section: The Best of Snowboy
JAZID 103 various artists: Totally Wired Sweden
JAZID 104 Double Vision: Double Vision
JAZID 105 Corduroy: Mini
JAZID 106 Manasseh Meets the Equaliser: Dub the Millenium
JAZID 107 Corduroy: Out of Here
JAZID 108 Mother Earth: Institution Man
JAZID 109 Dread Flimstone: Bionic Dread
JAZID 110 The James Taylor Quartet: The James Taylor Quartet EP
JAZID 111 unissued
JAZID 112 The J.T.Q. & Alison Limerick: Love Will Keep Us Together
JAZID 113 Skunkhour: Skunkhour
JAZID 114 The Brand New Heavies: Original Flava
JAZID 115 The J.T.: In the Hand of the Inevitable
JAZID 116 Mother Earth: Free Thinker EP
JAZID 117 unissued
JAZID 118 Vibraphonic: Vibraphonic II
JAZID 119 Corduroy: Summer in My Eye
JAZID 120 various artists: Totally Wired Twelve
JAZID 121 The Quiet Boys: Bosh
JAZID 122 Emperors New Clothes: Wisdom & Lies
JAZID 123 New Jersey Kings: Stratosphere Breakdown
JAZID 124 The James Taylor Quartet: Whole Lotta Live
JAZID 125 Goldbug: Whole Lotta Love
JAZID 126 Snowboy & the Latin Section: Pit-Bull Latin Jazz
JAZID 127 unissued
JAZID 128 Emperors New Clothes: Darklight
JAZID 129 African Headcharge: Akwaaba
JAZID 130 unissued
JAZID 131 various artists: Athletico
JAZID 132 City Lix Featuring Carol Riley: Find Our Love
JAZID 133 Derek Dah Large: The Bloodsuckers
JAZID 134 various artists: Totally Wired Fourteen
JAZID 135 Skunkhour: Up to Our Necks
JAZID 136 Skunkhour: Feed
JAZID 137 Mister eXe: X Marks the Spot
JAZID 138 unissued

JAZID 139 unissued

JAZID 140 The James Taylor Quartet: Living Underground

JAZID 141 various artists: Best of Acid Jazz 3

JAZID 142 various artists: Jazz Jungle

JAZID 143 unissued

JAZID 144 various artists: Totally Wired 15

JAZID 145 various artists: Totally Wired Promo

JAZID 146 Snowboy: M.F.O.S.

JAZID 147 Snowboy: New Avengers

JAZID 148 unissued

JAZID 149 Corduroy: Double Pack

JAZID 150 Brand New Heavies: Shibuya 357

JAZID 151 various artists: Totally Wired 16

JAZID 159 Night Trains: Obstruct Doors, Cause Delay & Be Dangerous

JAZID 161 Night Trains: The Wave

JAZID 164 The Watts Prophets: Rappin' Black in a White World

JAZID 165 various artists: Black Voices on the Streets of Watts. . . .

JAZID 166 The Watts Prophets: When the '90s Came

JAZID 171 various artists: Swaraj

JAZID 172 various artists: TV & Movie Themes

JAZID 180 Cloud 9: Millenium

## ADU

**FORMED:** *1982, London, England*
**ORIGINAL LINEUP:** *Rauf Adu (vcls) and others*

Ghana-born, but London bred, Rauf Adu was house engineer at Essex Music during the late '70s, before moving onto the city poetry circuit in the early '80s. He published two volumes of poetry, *The Rise and Rise of General Gun* (1981) and *Word I View* (1985), while simultaneously working as a theater critic for the *West Indian World* newspaper. He was also composing strongly political, Afro-funk influenced songs, provocatively set within the increasingly depressing landscape of Thatcher's Britain.

In 1982, he formed Adu. Never boasting a stable lineup, they gigged around London for much of the next three years, issuing a one-off single, "Escape from Teletania," in September 1983. A year later, preparing for a second independent release, the group cut a strong set of demos at producer Nigel Gray's studio.

Leading off with the tribal jazz groove "Human to Human," the demo provoked immense interest around the UK music industry and, in late 1984, Adu signed with Modtone, a new label launched by *James Bond* moviemaker Chubby Broccoli's family.

"Human to Human" was released in early 1985 to enthusiastic local radio response. Nine months later, the seductive reggae-styled "Working for the Government" gave Adu a bestseller in Germany, provoking another flurry of interest

from the British press. A typical story headline, from a September, 1985, *Melody Maker*, was "Much Adu About Everything."

Certainly pre-empting later fascinations with "world music," Adu's live show was a tempestuous blur of sound and visuals, while songs like the solid stomp of "IOU" and "What Do You Want My Love For" displayed an awareness of organic funk basics, which was otherwise sadly lacking on the mid-'80s scene. Such attributes, however, came to naught. An Adu album was recorded, but failed to materialize and, by early 1986, the band had faded from view.

### ADU DISCOGRAPHY

1983 Escape From Teletania/? (Arro—UK)

1985 Human to Human/? (Modtone—UK)

1985 Working for the Government/? (Modtone—UK)

## BEGGAR AND CO.

**FORMED:** *1981, London, England*
**ORIGINAL LINEUP:** *Neville McKreith (gtr), Canute Wellington (trum), David Baptiste (trum)*

Formed from the three way split which sundered Britfunk pioneers Light of the World in 1980, Beggar and Co. debuted the following February with the powerful "(Somebody) Help Me Out." Released at the tail end of the earlier group's deal with the Ensign label, it slammed into the UK Top 20, prompting RCA to sign the new band.

*Monument*, which was indeed a monumental release, coalescing many of the disparate streams of funk then milling through the British funk underground, followed that summer. But it was their union with Spandau Ballet that cemented Beggar and Co.'s fame, as Canute Wellington and David Baptiste (plus Nathaniel Augustin, a latter-day Light of the World member) were recruited to add the brass hook to the Top 3 smash "Chant #1 (I Don't Need This Pressure On)." The record confirmed Spandau's funk credentials at the same time opening the door for their eventual surrender to pop stardom.

Beggar and Co. followed "Chant #1" with their own "Chant #2"—the somewhat opportunistic subtitle to "Mule"—and notched a second Top 40 hit. It was to be their final act, however; the band broke up in 1982. (Wellington subsequently became involved with George Michael's Wham!, contributing the signature horns to their "Wake Me Up Before You Go-Go" chart-topper.)

### DISCOGRAPHY

#### LP

**8** 1981 Monument (RCA—UK)

Not the first, but certainly one of the greatest manifestations of the Brit-funk groove, as it finally shed the shackles of the America prototype. Horns and voices to the fore, but guitar and keyboards are integral to the rhythm too.

## BRAND NEW HEAVIES

**FORMED:** *1985, London, England*
**ORIGINAL LINEUP:** *Simon Bartholomew (gtr), Andrew Levy (bs), Jan Kincaid (drms)*

Initially uniting as an instrumental trio, the Brand New Heavies emerged from London's burgeoning acid jazz revolution in the late-'80s. School friends Simon Bartholomew, Andrew Levy and Jan Kincaid grew up with a rabid fascination for old school funk and soul, adding these vital influences to the ferment already taking place on the London club scene via a string of self-released cassette tapes.

Soon the Brand New Heavies were one of the staples of the capital's active pirate radio stations, while DJs at the scene-setting Cat in the Hat club regularly cut from James Brown records to cassettes of the band's jams. Encouraged, the group began gigging in 1987, adding first a brass section, then vocalist Jay Ella Ruth. (Linda Muriel, later of Incognito, also performed with the team.)

Several record companies vied for the outfit's attention before the Acid Jazz label picked them up in 1990. The Brand New Heavies' eponymous debut album appeared the following year, a fat, tight, funk set that saw them eschew the genre's established practice of looping, sampling and sequencing in favor of actually playing all the old funk riffs themselves. The album reached #25 on the UK charts, but its biggest feat lay in breaking Brand New Heavies into the US R&B charts, where they came to rest at #17.

The Brand New Heavies toured both countries in its wake, afterwards Ruth departed, and was replaced by N'dea Davenport, a solo artist contracted to Acid Jazz's distributors, Delicious Vinyl. Re-recording several of the album's key tracks for singles, the group unleashed a stream of UK hits during 1992: "Never Stop" (#43), "Dream Come True" (#24) the *Ultimate Trunk Funk* EP (#19), "Don't Let It Go to Your Head" (#24) and a remixed "Stay This Way" (#40). The opening cut on the EP, the re-recorded "Never Stop," followed the album into the upper echelons of the US R&B listings.

The Brand New Heavies' refusal to embrace on-stage tapes and sequencers won them countless admirers; certainly their purity caught the eye of veteran Ray Charles, who invited them to perform at a concert celebrating his 50th year in the music business. Their second album, 1992's

*Heavy Rhyme Experience Vol. 1* featured contributions from such hip-hop stars as Pharcyde, Black Sheep and Grand Puba Maxwell.

Recorded in the US, and firmly absorbing the hip-hop culture, which had embraced the band, *Heavy Rhyme Experience Vol. 1* was taped live in the studio, an anomaly in the rap world. However, it could not repeat the success of its predecessor, reaching only #38 in the UK, while floundering at #49 on the US R&B chart.

Somewhat chastened by the experience, back in London the group began work on their third album, returning to basics for what they proclaimed the "natural" follow up to *Heavies*. It was a lofty pronouncement and anticipation for *Brother Sister* was correspondingly high; fortunately, nobody was disappointed. The spring 1994 release was certified platinum, and a fat clutch of singles brought their biggest UK 45s yet: "Dream On Dreamer" (#15), "Back to Love" (#23), a cover of Maria Muldaur's mid-'70s perennial "Midnight at the Oasis" (#13) and "Spend Some Time" (#26).

Launching a massive UK tour, the Brand New Heavies embarked on the major festival circuit during summer 1994. Those dates, however, marked the end of an era. Davenport left shortly after the tour finished, returning to the United States to relaunch her shelved solo career.

She was replaced by American singer Siedah Garrett, best known for her work on Michael Jackson's "I Just Can't Stop Loving You," but also a veteran of sessions with the Commodores, Quincy Jones and Aretha Franklin. A Brand New Heavies remix collection, *Excursions: Remixes & Rare Grooves* appeared in 1996, while the group worked on their fourth album. *Shelter* followed in spring 1997, accompanied by the band's first live dates in two years, and the now inevitable flood of UK singles: "Sometimes" (#11), "You Are the Universe" (#21) and Carole King's "You've Got a Friend" (#9). That year the group was nominated for a BRIT award, and also contributed "I Like It" to the *Love Jones* original soundtrack.

But all was not quite right. A scheduled European tour was cancelled and, in the summer of 1998, Garrett departed, citing internal conflicts. Carleen Anderson (ex-Young Disciples) was drafted for tours of the UK and Europe, leading up to the release of *Trunk Funk. . . .Best of the Brand New Heavies* in fall 1999. This "best of" set was wrapped around a handful of new tracks, including "Try My Love," "Saturday Night" and an old Young Disciples song, "Apparently Nothin'."

## US CHARTLOG

1991 Dream Come True/(same) (Delicious Vinyl—#63 R&B)
1991 Never Stop/(remix) (Delicious Vinyl—#3 R&B/#54 pop)
1991 Stay This Way/(remix) (Delicious Vinyl—#19 R&B)
1992 Dream Come True 92/(same) (Delicious Vinyl—#42 R&B)
1994 Dream On Dreamer/(remix) (Delicious Vinyl—#19 R&B/#51 pop)
1997 Sometimes/(remix) (Delicious Vinyl—#20 R&B/#88 pop)

## LPS
**8** **1991 The Brand New Heavies (Delicious Vinyl—#17 R&B)**
Takes acid jazz to a new level by incorporating the essential heartbeat rhythms of funk into fresh electronic territories, to create an organic hybrid of old and new. Don't miss "People Get Ready" and "Put the Funk Back in It"—a throwback to the golden old grooves of the '70s.
**6** **1992 Heavy Rhyme Experience Vol. 1 (Delicious Vinyl—#49 R&B/ #139 pop)**
A none-too-welcome step away from the roots, as some of rap's finest added a heavy slab of hip-hop to the annals of the new funk.
**7** **1994 Brother Sister (Delicious Vinyl—#26 R&B/#95 pop)**
Booty shaking, horn-heavy grooves dominate this set, and easily restored the BNH to their throne. "Snake Hips" in particular is outstanding!
**6** **1997 Shelter (Delicious Vinyl—#29 R&B)**
More R&B infused than past efforts, the set showcases a grown up BNH—albeit one that can still funk it up.

## SELECTED COMPILATIONS AND ARCHIVE RELEASES
**5** **1994 Original Flava (Acid Jazz)**
**8** Original flava, original grooves—the Heavies' early years.
**6** **1996 Excursions: Remixes & Rare Grooves (Delicious Vinyl—#70 R&B)**
**7** **1999 Trunk Funk . . . Best of the Brand New Heavies (London)**
The older material is self-explanatory, the new cuts highlight the continuing drift toward more mellow grooves.
**6** **1999 In Tha Beginning . . . (Music Club)**
Budget collection pairs highlights of the debut LP with gritty live tracks recorded in Tokyo.

## BROOKLYN FUNK ESSENTIALS
**FORMED:** *1993, New York, NY*
**ORIGINAL LINEUP:** *Lati Kronlund (bs) and guests*

Brooklyn Funk Essentials emerged as one of those rare outfits who not only demonstrated the convoluted path funk had taken in the '90s, but also typified the components that made early funk such an integral part of the world music experience. Indeed, the group's roots lay in a series of early-'80s sessions that paired veteran New York dance producer/remixer Arthur Baker with former James Brown horn player Maceo Parker.

Those session tapes lay in Parker's basement for another decade, before he played them for Lati Kronlund. The bassist immediately began work on them, adding local hip-hop and jazz artists to the mix to create a club sound that combined electronic beats, spoken word, reggae, hip-hop, jazz and soul, and packed explosive energy. Reggae master Papa Dee, vocalist Joi Caldwell, DJ Jazzy Nice, and Yuko Handa (later of Cibo Matto) all guested.

*Cool and Steady and Easy* was released in 1994, an underground smash that reverberated around the globe. In 1996, the Brooklyn Funk Essentials were invited to headline the World Music Festival in Istanbul, Turkey, turning in a blistering funk set topped by their take on the traditional "UskUdar." After inking a deal with Positiv Productions, they soon returned to Istanbul to record their next album.

In 1998, *In the Buzz Bag* recruited eleven Turkish musicians alongside the expected array of US performers and guests (including Papa Dee, Sha-Key, poet Everton Sylvester), resulting in a heady funk richly interpreted through the traditional Middle Eastern quarter scale.

Back in the US, Brooklyn Funk Essentials' third album, *Make 'Em Like It*, appeared in 2000.

## LPS
**8** **1995 Cool and Steady and Easy (Groovetown)**
A cover of Pharoah Sanders' "The Creator Has a Master Plan" is nothing short of smooth groove perfection, while "A Headnaddas Journey to the Planet Adidi-Skizm" nods to the old school stylings of Funkadelic. Inspired acid jazz grounded in some shockingly serious funk. Delicious!
**7** **1998 In the Buzz Bag (Shanachie)**
This horizon expanding set incorporates Middle Eastern flair into the funk, and then adds dub on "Istanbul Twilight." Great for the old school and interesting enough for the most dilettante of today's world music listeners. Oooh, and there's so many of them around.
**7** **2000 Make 'Em Like It (Shanachie)**
The band return to their "old" style, dropping the Turkish flair, but otherwise throwing in everything, including the kitchen sink.

## CHUCK BROWN AND THE SOUL SEARCHERS
**FORMED:** *1968, Washington, DC*
**ORIGINAL LINEUP:** *Chuck Brown (vcls, gtr), Le Ron Young (gtr), Jerry Wilder (bs), Curtis Johnson (kybds), Skip*

**The veteran Chuck Brown, going to a go-go.**

Fennell (kybds), LeRoy Fleming (sax), John Buchanan (trom), Donald Tillery (trum), Ricardo Wellman (drms), Gregory Gerran (perc)

Having sung and played piano in church as a child, Chuck Brown picked up guitar in his late teens, while serving an 11 year jail sentence at Lorton Penitentiary following a shooting incident. However, upon his release in 1951, Brown took up boxing, working as a sparring partner for Floyd Patterson, Zora Folley and others.

By the early '60s, Brown had returned to music, joining ex-Impressions singer Jerry Butler's band as guitarist, before enlisting with the Latin-soul group Los Latinos. He launched his own unit, the Soul Searchers, in 1968, initially playing Top 40 covers around the DC club circuit, but slowly graduating toward a harder, original output.

By the time the Soul Searchers emerged onto a wider stage in 1972, they had developed into a sophisticated, politically inspired act whose debut single, "We the People," hit the R&B Top 40 that summer. They followed up with

a growling version of James Brown's "Think" and an equally dramatic debut album, *We the People*.

Gradually cutting back the rhetoric, a fresh burst of activity in 1974 saw the Soul Searchers succeed with "Blow Your Whistle" (a riposte to the increasing amount of whistle blowing taking place elsewhere in the R&B scene) and the defiant "If It Ain't Funky." However, the group remained a minor league attraction, even after they departed Sussex Records for the Polydor major in 1975.

The two part "Boogie Up the Nation" launched this new relationship, but when the single stalled just inside the R&B Top 100, the Soul Searchers again fell off the radar. However, when they resurfaced in 1978, signed now to Source, it was with a record nobody could ignore.

Produced by James Purdie at Sigma Sound, Philadelphia, the James Brown-influenced "Bustin' Loose" was the first sizeable manifestation of "go-go," a new musical form taking root around their Washington, DC home base. This funk variation, with a close proximity to the underground hip-hop scene, was at least for a short time, the hottest new sound around.

"Bustin' Loose" topped the R&B chart for a month in early 1979, and sent the Soul Searchers' long-delayed second album, also titled *Bustin' Loose*, racing into the pop Top 40. As suddenly as they arrived, however, they apparently faded away. "Game Seven," their follow-up single, limped to an unimpressive #81; "Sticks and Stones," a full year later in 1980, barely improved upon that.

Though they continued gigging heavily, most frequently around Washington, DC, four years elapsed before the Soul Searchers again visited the R&B chart, when 1984's 12-inch "We Need Some Money (Bout Money)," broke the Top 30. By this time, fellow go-go heroes Trouble Funk, Experience Unlimited and Rare Essence were also threatening a breakthrough, but in fact, not one of them actually truly made it. The Soul Searchers themselves remained silent during much of go-go's brief day in the sun, but did join their disciples on the *Good To Go* soundtrack, while "We Need Some Money" reappeared on 1985's seminal *Go Go Crankin'* go-go compilation album.

Still, the Soul Searchers remained a strong live attraction and, while new record releases continued at a premium, they were usually worth waiting for. The group appeared on the movie soundtrack *Blue Iguana* and released several acclaimed EPs; further albums, however, were confined to concert recordings. Following the band's breakup, Brown alone moved into jazz-blues territory.

## CHUCK BROWN AND THE SOUL SEARCHERS DISCOGRAPHY
### US CHARTLOG

1972 We the People (part one)/(part two) (Sussex—#40 R&B)
1973 Think/1993 (Sussex—#43 R&B)
1974 Blow Your Whistle/Funk to the Folks (Sussex—#31 R&B)
1974 If It Ain't Funky/Wind Song (Sussex—#74 R&B)
1975 Boogie Up the Nation (part one)/(part two) (Polydor—#93 R&B)
1978 Bustin' Loose (part one)/(part two) (Source—#1 R&B/#34 pop)
1979 Game Seven (part two)/(part one) (Source—#81 R&B)
1980 Sticks and Stones (part one)/(part two) (Source—#55 R&B)
1984 We Need Some Money (Bout Money)/(two versions) (TTED—#26 R&B)

### LPs

**9** 1973 We the People (Sussex)

You get the definitive version of James Brown's "Think," plus a package that reads a riot act unheard since the first burst of Sly Stone.

**7** 1974 Salt of the Earth (Sussex)

**8** 1979 Bustin' Loose (Source—#5 R&B/#31 pop)

Although modern ears may detect an unexpected soulful mellowness—primal go-go scythes through seven solid grooves, defiant in the face of disco, delirious in the knowledge of the floodgates straining behind it. Brown recalls his days with Jerry Butler via the oddly gentle "Never Gonna Give You Up" (co-written by Butler and Gamble/Huff), while the #1 title cut isn't even the strongest track (a reprise of "If It Ain't Funky" is).

**8** 1980 Funk Express (Source)

**7** 1984 We Need Some Money (TTED)

Go-go central, cut at the right time, for the right label and with precisely the right swagger. All call and response monster grooves, even the confines of the studio can't kill the concert vibe.

**9** 1987 Any Other Way To Go (Mercury)

As go-go died, the man who created it takes over. The wrenchingly powerful "Run Joe" calypso, Sly Stone's "Family Affair," "Be Bumpin' Free" and "Go Go Drug Free" are as strong as anything the scene ever threw up.

**6** 1993 This Is a Journey Into Time (Future Sound)

**5** 1993 Live Pa Tape (three volumes) (Raw Ventures)

**8** 1993 Go Go Swing Live (Future Sound)

The best of all Brown's concert recordings, a riotous live album highlighting two decades of material, including "Stormy Monday" and "Family Affair" (both originally aired on *Any Other Way To Go*) and a tremendous version of Stevie Wonder's "Boogie On . . . Go Go Woman"

### SELECTED SAMPLES

Bustin' Loose — Coldcut: Hey Kids, What Time Is It? (1987)
Bustin' Loose — Eric B. & Rakim: Eric B. Made My Day (1990)

## DEFUNKT

**FORMED:** 1978, New York, NY

**ORIGINAL LINEUP:** *Janos Get (vcls), Clarice Taylor (vcls), Martin Aubert (gtr), Kelvyn Bell (gtr), Melvin Gibbs (bs), Martin Fisher (synth), Joseph Bowie (b. St Louis, MO—trom), Byron Bowie (flute, sax), Teddy Daniel (trum), Ronnie Burrage (drms), Charles "Bobo" Shaw (perc, vcls)*

Following in the footsteps of his elder brother, trumpet maestro Lester, Joseph Bowie's musical interests originally lay in jazz. Starting trombone lessons at age 11, by 15 he was a member of hometown St. Louis' Black Artist Group and was studying under Hamiett Bluiett, Julius Hemphill and Oliver Lake.

Relocating (via a Parisian sojourn) to New York where he managed the legendary off-Broadway La Mama Theater, in 1973 Bowie co-founded the experimental Human Arts

Ensemble. After returning to Missouri, he launched the similarly themed St. Louis Creative Ensemble with alto saxophonist Luther Thomas. As the decade progressed, however, Bowie found his attention leaning toward less rigid musical expression, crystallizing around his recruitment to Milwaukee sax maverick James Chance's jazz-punk combo The Contortions (he appears most impressively on the *Live in New York* album). There, Bowie further formulated an avant- garde funk vibe that he termed, with pinpoint phonetic accuracy, Defunkt . . . de-funked.

In his own words, the group combined "conscious[ness]-raising lyrics, a funky rhythmic approach, sinewy bass lines, metallic guitar [and] assaultive horns topped with maniacal vocals." It was a distinctive, if sometimes difficult brew, but launched onto the New York underground just as it lurched toward what critics termed the "No Wave" movement, Defunkt found themselves lauded in the same circles that followed Chance, John Zorn, Lydia Lunch and Bill Laswell's Material.

With its core based on the Contortions' horn section, Defunkt signed with legendary producer Joe Boyd's Hannibal label. Their eponymous 1980 debut album featured a stellar lineup built around Bowie, brother Byron and fellow Human Arts Ensemble founder Charles "Bobo" Shaw, guitarist Kelvyn Bell and vocalist Clarice Taylor. That latter pair alone remained on board for Defunkt's second Boyd-produced album, 1982's *Thermonuclear Sweat*, released following a killer 45, "Razor's Edge." Equally sharp on a cover of the O'Jays' "For the Love of Money," a young Vernon Reid was among the band's new recruits, a year before he formed the first incarnation of Living Colour.

Bowie disbanded Defunkt in 1983, and retired to St. Croix. He returned to New York three years later, however, and reassembled the group for live work. In 1988, they recorded the critically acclaimed *In America*, with a lineup featuring another former Contortion, Tomas Doncker (guitar) alongside the *Thermonuclear Sweat*-era rhythm section of Kenny Martin and Kim Clarke, and trumpeter John Mulkerin. This same unit formed the nucleus of subsequent Defunkt albums, as the band signed with the Enemy label and continued pursuing their singular sound.

In 1990, *Heroes* introduced covers of Jimi Hendrix's "Manic Depression" and "Foxy Lady" to Defunkt's repertoire, a prelude to the songs' reappearance on 1995's brilliantly conceived *Blues Tribute to Muddy Waters and Jimi Hendrix*, a 12-track set divided equally between the two masters' songs. The mid-'90s also saw Defunkt make serious inroads into the European market, signing with the Dutch

BlueFunk label and launching a summer festival tour on which they performed alongside Graham Central Station, Isaac Hayes, Maceo Parker and Groove Collective.

## DEFUNKT DISCOGRAPHY
### *LPS*
**8** 1980 Defunkt (Hannibal)
"Thermonuclear Sweat" really sums up the Defunkt sound. Each track is a blistering rip through jazz, fusion, funk and rock, peaking with "In the Good Times" and "Make Them Dance."

**7** 1982 Thermonuclear Sweat (Hannibal)
Confusingly (but accurately) titled after its predecessor's meltdown heart.

**7** 1988 In America (Antilles)
Outrageous comeback set, wild and disarming, if somewhat uneven. But with this much passion, perfection doesn't always pay.

**6** 1990 Heroes (DIW)

**8** 1992 Crisis (Enemy)
The band shake things up a little by bringing fresh elements to the mix. "Refuse To Love" is rock heavy while "Everyday They Come" slows down the tempo and sports vocals so atonal they border on dissonance; but it works, and it's nice to see that Bowie is still a fearless composer.

**6** 1993 Live at the Knitting Factory (Knitting Factory)

**6** 1994 Live & Reunified (Enemy)
Hot live set comprises a virtual best of, including "Hit Me," "Steppin' Off" and "Defunkt."

**4** 1994 Cum Funky (Enemy)
What sounds like it should be funky is just plain disappointing, from the lackluster music to lyrics that border at times on insipid. Give this one a miss.

**5** 1995 A Blues Tribute: Jimi Hendrix & Muddy Waters (Enemy)
Reworking past Defunkt Hendrix covers, then throwing in some new ones ("If 6 Was 9" is spectacular); the brutal Waters' covers include "Howlin' Wolf" and "Mannish Boy."

**5** 1995 One World (BlueFunk—Netherlands)

### *SELECTED COMPILATIONS AND ARCHIVE RELEASES*
**7** 1991 A Defunkt Anthology (Rykodisc)

## DIGITAL UNDERGROUND
**FORMED:** *1988, San Francisco, CA*
**ORIGINAL LINEUP:** *Eddie Humphrey (vcls), Ron "Money-B" Brooks (vcls), Gregory "Shock G." Jacobs (b. 8/25/63 kybds), Chopmaster J. (perc).*

A wild and funky corollary to the commercially burgeoning gangsta rap scene, Digital Underground's tripped-out psych riffs and serious funk fury brought a dazzling array of musicians together to create an infectious rap nodding—via samples and live sounds—to the golden age of P-Funk.

With a riotous stage show accentuated by Shock G.'s plaid-panted alter ego, the big nosed Humpty Hump, Digital Underground were already massive San Francisco club favorites by the time the rest of the US caught up with them. The band released their first single, "Your Life's a Cartoon," on the indie TNT, which sold briskly throughout California, (and utterly unexpectedly topped the chart in the Netherlands) and earned them a deal with Tommy Boy.

Summer 1989's "Doowutchayalike" gave Digital Underground their first minor hit; the *Sex Packets* quasi-concept album followed, but it was Shock G.'s anthemic "The Humpty Dance" that catapulted the group into the mainstream consciousness. It pranced into the R&B Top Ten and the pop Top 20, and also introduced Digital Underground's manic persona to the MTV audience. The song was nominated for Best Rap Performance at the Grammys; both single and album were certified platinum.

A remixed "Doowutchayalike" and the self-explanatory *This Is an EP Release* followed during 1991. Digital Underground made their movie debut in the comedy *Nothing but Trouble*, and "Same Song," from the accompanying soundtrack, introduced the then unknown 2Pac Shakur to the world. As D-Flow Production Squad, Digital Underground oversaw much of Shakur's subsequent solo career, including his debut, *2Pacalypse Now*. (The rapper died 9/13/96 of gunshot wounds sustained six days earlier.)

Money B., meanwhile, was also busy with his Raw Fusion collaboration with DJ Fuze, and the duo's 1991 *Live from the Styleetron* album spawned the hit "Rockin' to the PM."

That fall Digital Underground unleashed their second album, *Sons of the P*, which featured some three dozen guests rappers and musicians, including Fuze, Shakur and Live Quad's Big Stretch. *Sons* paid overt tribute to formative influence George Clinton, who co-wrote the title track and appeared as guest vocalist (three other tracks featured noticeable P-Funk samples). Digital Underground returned the favor in 1994, taking part in Clinton's "Paint the White House Black" video.

Following a quiet 1992, Digital Underground resurfaced the following year with a new album *The Body-Hat Syndrome* and an X-rated video for the first single "The Return of the Crazy One," reworked for broadcast, but the stuff of cult classics for fans and collectors. Unfortunately, the album swiftly faded from public view, while the second single, "Whassup Wit the Luv," barely scraped the R&B top 100.

*The Body-Hat Syndrome* also marked the end of Digital Underground's relationship with Tommy Boy. The face of rap was quickly changing, and Digital Underground were losing their way—ironically at the same time as Humpty Hump began carving out a sensational career of his own. The character's on-stage appeal was already so vast that Shock G. frequently recruited a friend to don the glasses and nose on stage, while he got on with the music. Now the character landed a cameo in the 1993 film *Who's the Man* (starring Dr. Dre and Ed Lover), followed by a popular Nike commercial alongside American basketball's Michael Jordan and Charles Barkley.

A second Raw Fusion album, *Hoochiefied Funk*, appeared in 1994; while that same year, G. produced the Oakland duo Luniz. Digital Underground themselves resurfaced in 1996 with *Future Rhythm*, their lowest charting album yet (R&B #26), and the members returned to their extra curricular activities. Money B. launched his own Bobby Beats label with the compilation *Money B. Presents . . . Folk Music Vol. 1 (Music by My Folks Fo' My Folks)*.

Digital Underground reconvened briefly to record with Prince, producing a song for his *Crystal Ball* album. They regrouped in 1998 for *Who Got the Gravy*, an album bolstered by appearances from Biz Markie, Big Pun and KRS-1, plus a radical new "character," pimped out attorney Peanut Hakim, a usual highlight of their subsequent 11-month tour. Money G.'s solo debut, *Talkin' Dirty* was released following the band's return home.

### DIGITAL UNDERGROUND
#### US CHARTLOG

1988 Your Life's a Cartoon/Underwater Rimes (TNT)

1989 Doowutchayalike/5 versions (Tommy Boy—#82 R&B)

1990 The Humpty Dance/Humpstramental mix (Tommy Boy—#7 R&B/#11 pop)

1990 Doowutchayalike (remix) (Tommy Boy—#29 R&B)

1991 Same Song/remix (Tommy Boy—#7 R&B/#61 pop)

1991 Kiss You Back/3 mixes (Tommy Boy—#13 R&B/#40 pop)

1992 No Nose Job/3 mixes (Tommy Boy—#28 R&B)

1993 The Return of the Crazy One/Carry the Way (Tommy Boy—#77 R&B)

1994 Wussup Wit the Luv/Doo Woo You—Part 1 (Tommy Boy—#99 R&B)

1996 Oregano Flow/(instrumental) (Critique—#75 R&B)

1996 Walk Real Kool (Critique—#95 R&B)

#### LPS

**10** 1990 Sex Packets (Tommy Boy—#8 R&B/#24 pop)

The brightest and best set of funk-fueled rap there is, Digital Underground pay homage to their icons within a complex texture of samples and original sound. Although the "Sex

Packets" cycle is the unquestioned highlight, fresh, intelligent lyrics make points with a sense of humor. And where would the world be without Humpty?

**9** **1991 Sons of the P (Tommy Boy—#23 R&B/#44 pop)**

And that's exactly what they are, a chain reaction of absurdly funkalicious songs, including the almost revoltingly compulsive "Kiss You Back." The sing-along nursery quality of Sly's "Everyday People" clashed with Funkadelic's "Knee Deep" to devastating (and devastatingly soppy) effect. The title track is equally outstanding, while "No Nose Job" catches up with our old friend Humpty, while imparting some socio-political commentary to boot.

**7** **1993 The Body-Hat Syndrome (Tommy Boy—#16 R&B/#79 pop)**
**6** **1996 Future Rhythm (Critique—#26 R&B/#113 pop)**

Loose, furious and typically great grooves again abound around a concept album dedicated to bringing funk into a new millennium.

**7** **1998 Who Got the Gravy? (Interscope—#90 R&B)**

Great set reaching back to Digital Underground's early days, with guest appearances from KRS-One and Biz Markie to further enliven things. Although many criticize the band for replaying the same tricks, they still have enough innovation and chops to make it work—every time.

### SELECTED COMPILATIONS AND ARCHIVE RELEASES
**7** **1999 The Lost Files of the Digital Underground (Lil Butta)**

A nifty collection of songs that were never included on earlier DU LPs.

## FISHBONE

FORMED: *1979, Los Angeles, CA*

ORIGINAL LINEUP: *Norwood Fishbone (b. John Norwood Fisher—vcls, bs), Kendall Jones (gtr), Chris Dowd (trum), Walter Kibby II (trum), Angelo Moore (vcls, sax), Phillip "Fish" Fisher (drms)*

A funk band in thought if not in deed, or so the alternative rock institution insists (motto: a category for everything, and everything in its category), Fishbone were still in junior high when they began playing an explosive mix of music that crossed virtually every generic barrier. Funk played a part in it, but so did ska, rock and reggae. Gigging constantly around the Los Angeles club circuit, Fishbone grabbed a virtual residency at Madame Wong's, where their frenetic live shows brought them to the attention of the major labels.

Signed by Columbia, Fishbone released their debut single in 1985; "Party at Ground Zero" instantly defined the band's hybrid sound, with the follow-ups "? (Modern In-

dustry)" and "Ugly" completing an immortal triptych. After so much excitement, however, their 1986 debut album *In Your Face* emerged a slickly produced shock and, while 1987's *It's a Wonderful Life (Gonna Have a Good Time)* EP at least tried to return to basics, it was onstage that Fishbone made the most sense.

By the time of 1988's "Freddie's Dead" (from the *Nightmare on Elm Street* sequel of the same name), and the *Truth and Soul* album, Fishbone were concentrating on a commercial soul-funk style. However, the two EPs *Ma and Pa* (1989) and *Set the Booty Upright Bonin' in the Boneyard* (1990), which broke the three year gap before the band's next album, found them battling some serious creative confusion.

Co-founder Chris Dowd quit, to be replaced by John Bigham shortly before work began on May 1991's belated third album, the double *The Reality of My Surroundings* and two accompanying EPs *Sunless Sunday* and *Fight the Youth*. Kendall Jones, too, departed, with Spacey T. enlisted just as Fishbone joined the 1993 Lollapalooza package, itself the prelude to the band's most eclectic album yet, *Give a Monkey a Brain and He'll Swear He's the Center of the Universe*.

Presumably designed with the rock mainstream in mind, a string of accompanying singles impacted US radio: "Swim," "Black Flowers," "Servitude" and "Unyielding Conditioning." All missed the chart, however, while the album itself missed the first stirrings of the ska third wave that Fishbone themselves had done so much to inspire.

Nevertheless, the affection Fishbone inspire among their alternative rock peers could be seen from the all-star lineup for Norwood Fishbone's benefit concert at the Hollywood Palladium in January 1994. The singer had been charged with kidnapping after an alleged attempt to abduct a friend who was reportedly suffering from mental problems. Porno for Pyros, Primus, Tool and Alice in Chains all turned out to raise money for his defense. (He was eventually acquitted.)

Previewed by the single "Alcoholic," 1996's *Chim Chim's Bad Ass Revenge* landed some supportive reviews, but the decade-long retrospective *Fishbone 101: Nuttasaurusmeg Fossil Fuelin'* proved Fishbone's last for Sony. Over the next five years, Fishbone themselves changed immensely. Though there was scarcely any letup in the band's traditionally hectic live schedule, drummer Fish Fisher departed, and was replaced first by Cameron Clinton, then Deion. Former Untouchables keyboardist Anthony Brewster also came on board briefly, before John McKnight was recruited.

**The manic exuberance of Fishbone.**

Founder members Angelo Moore, Fishbone and Walter Kibby, however, remained and, now signed with Hollywood, the band unveiled their next release, *Fishbone and the Familyhood Nextperience Presents the Psychotic Friends Nuttwerx*, in March 2000. Band side projects Trulio Disgracios, which dated back to the late '80s, and Dirty Walt & the Columbus Sanitations also released new albums.

### FISHBONE DISCOGRAPHY
### LPS
**4** 1986 In Your Face (Columbia)
**8** 1988 Truth and Soul (Columbia)
**8** 1991 The Reality of My Surroundings (Columbia)
Truly maniacal as "Everyday Sunshine" rewrites the book on subversive funk rock, while "These Days Are Gone' blazes with psychedelic savagery.
**6** 1993 Give a Monkey a Brain and He'll Swear He's the Center of the Universe (Columbia)
Eclectic meltdown stylistically reminiscent of the MC5's attempt to blend hard-nosed political hard rock with freeform Sun Ra cacophony. And sometimes it almost works.
**7** 1996 Chim Chim's Bad Ass Revenge (Arista)

**6** 2000 Fishbone and the Familyhood Nextperience Presents the Psychotic Friends Nuttwerx (Hollywood)

### SELECTED COMPILATIONS
**8** 1996 Fishbone 101: Nuttasaurusmeg Fossil Fuelin (Sony)
The whole story, rises and falls just like their career, but does round up the crucial earliest goodies.

### FREEEZ
**FORMED:** *1978, London, England*
**ORIGINAL LINEUP:** *John Rocca (b 9/23/60, London — vcls, gtr), Peter Maas (bs), Andy Stennet (kybds), Paul Morgan (drms)*

Founder John Rocca was working as a van driver for the specialist dance music store Disc Empire, when he formed Freeez in 1978. Taking their cue from the Do It Yourself ethic prevalent in late-'70s Britain, the group released their first single, "Keep in Touch," on their own (deliberately misspelled) Pink Rythm label in 1979.

"Keep in Touch" caused such a stir that it was picked up by the Calibre label and reissued in early 1980. It was one of the few homegrown dance records to percolate into the dance-crazed consciousness of the London nightclub scene in the months before the media christened its denizens "the New Romantics,"

The song climbed to #49, paving the way for a deal with Beggars Banquet. Their first single for their new label, "Southern Freeze," introduced vocalist Ingrid Mansfield-Allen to the proceedings, and peaked at #8 in February 1981. Freeez's debut album, also titled *Southern Freeze* made the Top 20 soon after, while the follow-up, "Flying High," reached the Top 40.

"Anti-Freeez" in late 1981 and the following year's "One to One" did little, however, and having added new vocalist Alison Gordon, Freeez traveled to New York to record with *producer du jour* Arthur Baker and arranger Jellybean.

The result was Freeez's biggest-seller, the UK #2 smash "IOU"; it also breached the American R&B Top 20 and came close to the pop 100. But their next single,"Pop Goes My Love," was less successful and, by the time "Love's Gonna Get You" flopped in the fall, the attendant album, *Gonna Get You*, had proven a shock under-performer as well.

Following 1984's *Anti-Freeez* album, Rocca launched a solo career, scoring an almost immediate US hit with "I Want It To Be Real," again recorded with Baker. The singer also linked with Andy Stennet in a new band, Pink Rhythm, debuting with the "Can't Get Enough of Your Love" single in mid-1985. The duo split in 1986.

Freeez, now lining up with Billy Crichton and Louis Smith alongside founders Peter Maas and Paul Morgan, also soldiered on, but achieved little. Two new singles during 1985, "That Beats My Patience" and "Train of Thought," bracketed the *Idle Vice* album, but by the end of the year, Beggars Banquet had dropped the band from its roster. They then broke up.

Although 1987 brought a UK hit remix of "IOU," it wasn't until the early '90s that Rocca returned to the public eye, fronting a new band, MIDI Rain. An album, *One*, received some interest upon release in 1994.

## US CHARTLOG
1983 IOU/I Dub U (Streetwise—#13 R&B/#104 pop)
1983 Pop Goes My Love/(edit) (Streetwise—#47 R&B/#104 pop)

## LPs
⑧ 1981 Southern Freeze (Beggars Banquet)
Sad but true, the only Freeez album that really matters, solid and gritty Brit-funk stomping, with keys and guitar filling in where the horns should go.

⑥ 1983 Gonna Get You (Beggars Banquet)
The isometric "IOU" flatters to deceive; Arthur Baker's great when it comes to electro-pop dance tunes, but Freeez are frozen out by the icyness.
⑤ 1984 Anti Freeez (Beggars Banquet)
⑤ 1985 Idle Vice (Beggars Banquet)

### SELECTED COMPILATIONS AND ARCHIVE RELEASES
⑦ 1996 The Best of John Rocca: IOU (Hot production)
This 12 track collection combines the best Freeez material with later, clubby solo recordings.

## GALACTIC
FORMED: *1994, New Orleans, LA*
LINEUP: *Theryl DeClouet (vcls), Jeff Raines (gtr), Robert Mercurio (bs), Rich Vogel (kybds), Ben Ellman (sax, hrmnca), Stanton Moore (drums)*

Galactic spearheaded the third generation of New Orleans based funk bands (successors, of course, to the Meters and Chocolate Milk), the brainchild of native New Yorkers Jeff Raines and Robert Mercurio, who attended college in the Big Easy.

Originally a loose group of musicians called Galactic Prophylactic, the slowly coalescing outfit were regulars at college parties, before eventually making their way onto the live circuit. Graduating to such frontline venues as Tipatinas, Raines and Mercurio, they were introduced to Theryl DeClouet in 1994, then a member of the highly rated Michael Ward and Reward funk band. He quit to join Galactic Prophylactic around the time they decided to abbreviate their name.

Masters of a style reminiscent of James Brown, the Meters and Sly Stone, but also extraordinarily independent, Galactic began recording their debut album in late 1994, after signing with the San Francisco indie Fog City Records, one of the key players in the Bay Area acid jazz explosion. Produced by label head Dan Prothero, the record was released in the summer of 1996 to local acclaim.

Galactic then embarked on a massive US tour, highlighted by a performance at the 1996 New Orleans Jazz & Heritage Festival. Other shows paired them with Maceo Parker, the Funky Meters, Johnny "Guitar" Watson, Run DMC and Widespread Panic; their links with the latter were instrumental in landing the group a berth on the 1998 HORDE festival tour.

In 1998, Galactic, now signed to Capricorn Records, released *Crazyhorse Mongoose*; two years later, *Late for the Future* appeared amid another grueling burst of live work.

## GALACTIC

### LPs

**7** 1996 **Coolin' Off (Fog City Records)**

With great funk grooves swanning around the acid jazz beats, it's hard to believe that Galactic aren't old funkers in disguise. From "Stax Anthem" to "Go-Go" and "Funky Bird," they have the formulae down pat, and the imagination to take them so much further.

**9** 1998 **Crazyhorse Mongoose (Capricorn Records)**

Tight down-and-dirty hot funk proves Galactic to be one of the very few modern funk bands who actually understand what they're doing.

**7** 2000 **Late for the Future (Polygram)**

Or not. An enjoyable album nevertheless evidences a worrying drift toward mainstream R&B/pop.

## IMAGINATION

**FORMED:** *1981, London, England*

**ORIGINAL LINEUP:** *Leee John (b. John McGregor, 6/23/57, London, England—vcls), Ashley Ingram (b. 11/27/60, Northampton, England—gtr), Errol Kennedy (b. Montego Bay, Jamaica—drms)*

At just 16, Leee John landed a development deal with EMI, recording demos with session superstars Phil Chung, Del Newman and the Thunderthighs vocal group. The project came to naught, and John turned toward the theater. Over the next five years he worked as a singing waiter at London's Encore revue bar, starred as the half-man, half-spider character, Brer Nancy, in a production in south London, and attended Anna Shear's drama school. During the late '70s, he also worked as a journalist at London's *West Indian Digest* newspaper, interviewing such stars as the Jacksons, Stevie Wonder and the Brothers Johnson.

Around 1979, John opted to return to music, linking with guitarist Ashley Ingram in the band Fuzz. They landed a regular gig at the George Canning pub in Brixton, where their live set blithely merged funk, dub and steel band sounds with a Top 40 repertoire. John told *The Face* magazine, "We did a wicked version of [Minnie Ripperton's] 'Loving You' and [Barry Briggs'] 'Sideshow,' and our 'Don't Leave Me This Way' [Thelma Houston] would wipe you out."

All of this was a long way from the imaginative account of their beginnings published following the duo's eventual breakthrough. Those reports claimed the pair had met in New York as members of the backing band shared by soul legends the Delfonics and the Chairmen of the Board. In fact, neither John nor Ingrams had left the country, rather,

they were among the pool of musicians hired to supply backing vocals for both those bands and for the Velvelettes, on their low-key British tours during 1980–81.

In early 1981, Fuzz met drummer Errol Kennedy, a former member of the London soul band Midnight Express; the trio formed Imagination soon after, naming their group in tribute to the recently murdered John Lennon. They soon came to the attention of Steve Jolley and Tony Swain, the production/writing team behind pop divas Bananarama, as well as the early funk rhythms of Spandau Ballet. John's outrageous persona—a self-proclaimed cross between Michael Jackson and Fred Astaire—immediately appealed to the pair, and the group were launched on the Red Bus label in May 1981, with "Body Talk."

Imagination courted controversy immediately. *Top of the Pops*, the flagship of British pop television, came close to banning them after deeming their stage act too sexy for early evening viewing; *The Sun* tabloid newspaper christened John "the Lover Boy of Pop." The band themselves became instant icons on the gay nightclub circuit. And amid all the excitement, "Body Talk" began a laborious haul to #4; its 18 week chart run was the longest enjoyed by any British 45 that year.

Imagination followed it with the mellow "In and out of Love," making it readily apparent that there was no defined Imagination sound. John told *The Face*, "I reject the idea that Black music has to be either heavily ethnic or disco drivel, and I'd like to think that we were sharpening up the entertainment end of the spectrum. I hope that we're encouraging new talent by being daring and a bit outrageous."

"Flashback" gave Imagination their third Top 20 entry in a year, while "Just an Illusion," a song that John himself claimed to hate, stormed to #2 in the New Year. Meanwhile, their debut album, *Body Talk*, made the UK Top 20, "Music and Lights" was a summertime Top Five smash, and their second album, *In the Heat of the Night*, went Top Ten. With Imagination's fame now spread across Europe, attention turned toward the US, with the release of the hard-nosed "Burnin' Up." Stateside releases of "Just an Illusion" and "Music and Lights" followed it into the R&B chart, while both Imagination albums cracked the Top 50 in 1982.

Not even the increasingly formulaic nature of the band's records could initially dent their success. Smoothing out the rougher funk edges, which characterized *Body Talk*, 1984's *New Dimension* found Imagination essentially pumping out romantic ballad after romantic ballad, a long way from their fiery beginnings, and no longer striking such a resonant chord in the hearts of the record buying public, either. That year's "Thank You My Love" became Imagination's final British hit for four years, with the harder "This Means War (Shoobedoodah Dabba Doobee)" closing the band's US account.

Down but not out, Imagination broke with Swain and Jolley and spent much of the next two years touring. They headlined a Prince's Trust Gala concert in London in 1984, appeared before a sold-out stadium audience of 100,000 in Algeria, and traveled across Europe and the Far East, before returning to London in 1986, for a fifth anniversary show at the Royal Albert Hall. A new record deal, with RCA, followed and, in early 1987, Imagination decamped to New York to record *Closer* with producer Arthur Baker. Two minor hits followed, "The Last Time" in the US and "Instinctual" in the UK (the latter also topped the US dance chart).

Kennedy quit the band during 1987; he was replaced by Peter Royer and Imagination's next album, *Imagination*, appeared in 1989, and reached #7 in Britain. A pulsing medley of re-recorded oldies, "Megamix," spent four months in the French Top Ten, while the band's fall 1989 world tour proved so successful that it was extended beyond its original six months, to include visits to Russia, India and the Pacific.

The *Fascination of the Physical* album in 1990 was Ingram's last with the group. He quit for a songwriting career (originally in partnership with Errol Kennedy), with the multi-instrumentalist Segun replacing him. The band finally broke up around 1995, and John embarked on a solo career.

### IMAGINATION DISCOGRAPHY
#### US CHARTLOG
1982 Burnin' Up/Flashback (MCA—#68 R&B)
1982 Just an Illusion/(instrumental) (MCA—#27 R&B/#102 pop)
1982 Music and Lights/(instrumental) (MCA—#52 R&B)
1983 Changes/So Good So Right (MCA—#46 R&B)
1983 Lookin' at Midnight/(instrumental) (Elektra—#64 R&B)
1984 This Means War/Wrong in Love (Elektra—#29 R&B)
1987 The Last Time/Touch (part one) (RCA—#88 R&B)

#### LPs
**8** 1981 Body Talk (MCA—#46 R&B)
Stellar set of disco/funk that's as perfect on the turntable as on the dancefloor. Great grooves all around, from the sweet and sexy "Body Funk" to the still fresh "Burnin' Up."
**7** 1982 In the Heat of the Night (MCA—#45 R&B)
Solid album of thoroughly danceable mid-tempo music with that unmistakeable early-'80s sound. From the club favorite "Just an Illusion" to the sweetly soulful "All Night Long," it's an easy, pleasing combination.

**7** 1984 New Dimension (Elektra—#44 R&B/#205 pop)
Released in Europe the previous year as *Scandalous*.
**6** 1986 Trilogy (Red Bus—UK)
**7** 1987 Closer (RCA)
Nice latter-day set that shuffles between funk, pop and dance grooves easily.
**5** 1989 Imagination (Stylus—UK)
**6** 1990 Fascination of the Physical (Stylus—UK)

### SELECTED COMPILATIONS AND ARCHIVE RELEASES
**6** 1983 Night Dubbing (MCA)
Eight-track collection of dub mixes of early hits, highlighted by a version of "Burnin' Up" that seems to predict much of the house movement of five years hence.
**6** 1984 Imagination Gold (Red Bus—UK)
**7** 1988 The Best Of (Arcade)
**6** 1989 Like It Is (RCA)
Hits collection features remixes by Frankie Knuckles, Graeme Park and Mike Pickering, while Imagination themselves add a brand new single, Love's Taking Over".
**7** 2000 Just an Illusion (BDU—Germany)
Sixteen-track "best of" includes all the hits, plus an edited live version of the band's "Megamix."

## INCOGNITO
FORMED: *1980, London, England*
ORIGINAL LINEUP: *Jean Paul Maunick (gtr), Paul Williams (bs), Peter Hinds (kybds)*

Created, like Beggar and Co., from the wreckage of the pioneering Light of the World in 1980, Incognito debuted that same summer with the "Parisienne Girl" single. Initially released as a private demo to London clubs, the song swiftly picked up sufficient local airplay to prompt Ensign, Light of the World's former label, to grant it a full release.

The single scratched the Top 75, and Incognito subsequently released an album, *Jazz Funk*, and a second single, "North London Boy," in 1981, before breaking up for the remainder of the decade. Paul Williams and ex-Light of the World member Ganiyu Bello formed a new band, the Team; Williams and Jean Paul Maunick also collaborated as the Warriors, releasing the *Behind the Mask* album before the former relocated to Finland for a time. Returning to the UK, the bassist was then involved with the jazz-soul band Working Week.

In 1990, Williams and Maunick were contacted by Talkin' Loud label supremo Gilles Peterson and asked to reform Incognito. Their name and reputation had soared in recent years as a new generation of acid jazz/jazz funk fans rediscovered their debut album and, in 1991, the duo linked with fellow Light of the World alumni Peter Hinds, and vocalist Linda Muriel (a veteran of several early Brand New Heavies recordings) for a new single, "Can You Feel Me."

Next up was a cover of Ronnie Laws' "Always There", with the duo opting, as was the prevalent fashion on the UK club scene, to work with a variety of guest vocalists and musicians, cutting the single with Jocelyn Brown. It made the UK Top Ten and was followed by "Crazy For You," featuring singer Chyna.

Subsequent Incognito recordings continued this practice: as of 1999's No Time Like the Future album, the brand name had employed the services of no less than ten vocalists (and 14 backing singers). Indeed, a constantly fluctuating lineup saw four bassists, five keyboard players, four drummers, seven percussionists and 37 horn players file through the ranks. Maunick alone has remained constant throughout the band's history.

Inside Life confirmed Incognito's resurgence, as a well-stylized cover of Stevie Wonder's "Don't You Worry 'Bout a Thing," and turned up another Top 20 winner in 1992. The following year saw Incognito's US breakthrough with the album Tribes, Vibes and Scribes, a set which in turn brought Maunick recognition as a producer (George Benson and Chaka Khan rank among his best-known clients).

Incognito's third album, Positivity, spawned their first US airplay favorite, "Deep Waters," featuring former Stock-Aitken-Waterman production house vocalist Maysa Leak. The album itself sold over 350,000 copies in the US, a stunning success that Incognito celebrated by confirming Leak as their first full-time vocalist. It was a short-lived concession; the attention focussed upon Leak in the wake of the breakthrough swiftly became uncomfortable, and she quit in late 1994 for a solo career (her debut album, Maysa, followed in 1995).

Returning to the earlier revolving door system of vocalists, 1995's 100 Degrees and Rising took Incognito into the pop Top 200, while the singles "Everyday" and "I Hear Your Name" highlighted their gentle shift away from overt jazz funk and into traditional soul/Philly territory. To judge from subsequent chart positions, it was not necessarily a move welcomed by the band's British fan base, but Incognito remained consistent hitmakers through the late '90s regardless.

Leaks returned to the band in 1996 for the Beneath the Surface album; Incognito also re-recorded the break-through "Always There," before undertaking a world tour captured on the Japanese Live in Tokyo album. US dates, however, were cancelled due to management problems, their sole American date was an unplugged show in Atlanta in June 1997, featuring Leaks and Maunick alone. In 1999, the No Time like the Future album broke the ensuing silence, and was followed in 2000 by a remix collection based on the same LP.

### INCOGNITO DISCOGRAPHY
#### LPs
**5** **1981 Jazz Funk (Ensign—UK)**

Subsequently an acid jazz classic, but one suspects that honor was due as much to elitist reaction to its obscurity as to its contents. Compared with other activity on the Brit-funk scene, Jazz Funk was a pedestrian effort, so intent on creating a fusion that it sometimes forgot precisely what it was fusing. "North London Boy" (allegedly written about Spandau Ballet) has a period charm, though.

**8** **1991 Inside Life (Talkin' Loud—UK)**

A decade later, Incognito know precisely who their audience is and what they want. The result is a revelatory soup of red-hot funk, hammering horns, and a mass of loops, samples and killer breaks.

**7** **1992 Tribes, Vibes and Scribes (Talkin' Loud—#74 R&B)**

Less funk and more jazz is the order of the day, as this (mid-period) Earth Wind & Fire-y set finds a mellow, predominantly instrumental groove . . . and stays there.

**6** **1993 Positivity (Talkin' Loud—#54 R&B)**

More jams and solos meander their way through the songs, but otherwise, no great departure.

**7** **1995 100 Degrees and Rising (Talkin' Loud—#29 R&B/#149 pop)**

**6** **1996 Beneath the Surface (Talkin' Loud)**

None-too-heady brew of smooth jazz and deep soul. The overall sound benefits from the return of singer Maysa Leak.

**6** **1997 Blue Moods (Talkin' Loud)**

**6** **1997 Live in Tokyo (Import—Jap)**

**5** **1999 No Time Like The Future (Talkin' Loud)**

It's nothing to run screaming from, but Incognito are sounding increasingly anonymous. As a whole, the album sounds better when put through the remix machine (see below).

### SELECTED COMPILATIONS AND ARCHIVE RELEASES
**6** **1996 Remixed (Talkin' Loud)**

**7** **1998 Greatest Hits (Jap)**

**7** **2000 Future Remixed (Talkin' Loud)**

Masters at Work, MJ Cole and others take Incognito's least exciting album, and turn it into a near-triumph of beats and textures.

## INCORPORATED THANG BAND

**FORMED:** *1987, Detroit, MI*

**ORIGINAL LINEUP:** *Claudia White (vcls), Angel Keener (vcls), Andre Foxxe (gtr), Lige Curry (vcls, bs), Christopher Bruce (gtr), Robert Garrett (kybds), Patrick Drummond (vcls, kybds) and Dean Ragland (drms)*

As a teen, Andre Foxxe Williams was little more than a dedicated P-Funk fan, one of the horde who followed the band around on tour and practiced his guitar in the hope of one day. . . . Unlike most of those others, that one day arrived. In 1981, Williams was recruited to Treylewd and Flastic Brain Flam, a group formed by George Clinton's son Tracey Lewis, alongside Tony Davis (drms), Stevie Pannall (bs) and David Spradley (kybds).

An album was recorded, but in the chaos surrounding the collapse of the P-Funk empire, it was shelved (a number of tracks eventually appeared piecemeal across the George Clinton *Family Series*) and the band folded.

Foxxe remained part of the P-Funk setup, however, and in 1984, sessions with Clinton and Garry Shider produced one cut, "Better Days," which also subsequently appeared within the Clinton *Family Series* (volume one). The following year, Foxxe made his debut on one of Clinton's own albums, as one of the nine guitarists featured on the *Some of My Best Jokes Are Friends* album.

In 1986, Foxxe recorded his first single, the Bootsy Collins composition "Pizzaz," backed by a new P-Funk powered band, Jam. Work began on an album around the same time, co-produced by Clinton and Foxxe, but again it was abandoned.

However, during 1988, the guitarist was one of the leading lights on yet another Clinton one-off, the Incorporated Thang Band, debuting with "Body Jackin'," one of the classic funk singles of the age and home to one of the best similes as well, "like chiropractors cracking backs, everybody's doing the jack."

The group recorded just one gloriously packaged album, 1988's *Lifestyles of the Roach and Famous*, featuring appearances by Bootsy Collins, Gary Shider, Robert Johnson, Joseph Fiddler and Blackbyrd. However, the sound was largely dominated by the synthesizers and drum machines, which were the preserve of former Slave electro wizard Steve Washington, and fans who decried Clinton's own embrace of electronics at that time were unlikely to enjoy ICT

any more. They disbanded soon after the album's release (keyboard player Garrett subsequently formed the Chicago-based Groovepushers).

In 1989, Foxxe was among the "playground screamers" featured on Clinton's misbegotten *Presents Our Gang Funky* album. He appeared on that same year's *The Cinderella Theory* set, and became an active member of the reborn P-Funk All Stars, resplendent in outfits ranging from a nun's habit to a wedding dress. In this role, he became a regular contributor to a slew of subsequent P-Funk related albums, including Trey Lewd's 1992 *Drop the Line* and, finally, his own long delayed solo debut, *I'm Funk and I'm Proud*.

With material drawn from as far back as 1985 and 1986, together with a handful of cuts featuring the Incredible Thang Band ("Squirrel Looking for a Nut," "Mature Freak," "Fox Hunt"), the album also included a collaboration with the Red Hot Chili Peppers. It was recorded around the time of the sessions for their Clinton-produced *Freaky Styley* album. The brief (93 second) "Reputation" featured Peppers vocalist Anthony Kiedis, bassist Flea, guitarist Hillel Slovak and drummer Cliff Martinez, alongside Foxxe and Mike Payne.

### INCORPORATED THANG BAND COMPLETE DISCOGRAPHY

**SINGLES**

1988 Body Jackin' (part one)/(part two) (WB)

1988 Still Tight (Tight Remix Edit)/Androgynous View (WB)

**LP**

**7** 1988 **Lifestyles of the Roach and Famous** (WB)

The Motown bass-led "I'd Do Anything for You" is the undisputed highlight of this heavily electro-textured album.

### JAM

**SINGLE**

1986 Pizazz/Black Beach (ITM)

### ANDRE FOXXE

**LP**

**7** 1993 **I'm Funk and I'm Proud** (P-Vine—Jap)

"Toyota Corolla," "Mature Freak," and "Fox Hunt" slide out of an above average modern-day P-Funk groove, although little about *I'm Funk* is especially distinguishable from so many other later Clinton productions.

## JAMIROQUAI

**FORMED:** *1991, London, England*

**ORIGINAL LINEUP:** *Jason Kay (vcls), Glenn Nightengale (gtr), Simon Bartholomew (gtr), Stuart Zender (bs), Toby*

**A man with a great taste in hats, Jason Kay of Jamiroquai prepares to blow your mind.**

*Smith (kybds), Gary Barnacle (sax, flte), John Thirkell (trum, flglhrn), Richard Edwards (trom), Nick Van Gelder (drms), Kofi Karikari (perc), Maurizio Ravalio (perc), D-Zire (DJ)*

The first acid jazz superstars, Jamiroquai's genre-defying fusion of ultra techno beats, funk, jazz and distinctly Stevie Wonder-esque soul emerged out of Jason Kay's early experiments with a drum machine. He pieced together the band to flesh out his earliest demos, taking the name Jamiroquai from the Native American tribe.

Discovered by the Acid Jazz label, the group's first single, fall 1992's "When You Gonna Learn," peaked just outside the Top 50, and prompted a major label bidding war for the band. Jamiroquai—or rather, Kay—were finally snapped up by Sony UK's S2 imprint for a reputed $1 million.

Brash, outspoken and instantly identifiable in his trademark buffalo hat, Kay had no problem whatsoever imprint-

ing himself upon the British landscape. Chasing the "Too Young To Die" 45, Jamiroquai's first album, *Emergency on Planet Earth* entered the UK charts at #1 in spring, 1993, becoming the biggest selling UK debut album of the year. Three further singles culled from the disc also charted: "Blow Your Mind" (#10), "Emergency on Planet Earth" (#32) and "When You Gonna Learn (Didgeridoo)" (#28).

A US release for *Emergency on Planet Earth*, however, passed by unnoticed, and 1995's sophomore *The Return of the Space Cowboy* did little to remedy the situation. Back in the UK, the album romped to #2, and spun off another clutch of British smashes: "Space Cowboy" (#17), "Half the Man" (#15) and "Stillness in Time" (#9).

The enthusiastic support of other musicians, including Earth Wind & Fire's Maurice White, increased the group's popularity in the US, while Europe and Japan, too, were becoming increasingly enthusiastic. A collaboration with

M-Beat raised the temperature even higher; "Do U Know Where You're Coming From" reached #12 in Britain and was a major smash across the continent. Finally, fall 1996's *Travelling Without Moving* album emerged the global monster that Jamiroquai had long threatened.

UK singles "Cosmic Girl" (#6), "Alright" (#6) and "High Times" (#20) showcased a whipsmart blend of jams, while MTV helped the band's stateside reputation by throwing "Virtual Insanity" (#3 UK) into rotation. *Traveling Without Moving* eventually captured a Grammy and four MTV awards, while Jamiroquai's contribution to 1998's *Godzilla* movie, "Deeper Underground," topped the UK chart and made major inroads in the US.

Jamiroquai's fourth album, *Synkronized* was released in summer 1999, prelude to an extensive tour of Britain, the US and Europe. The group also played a high profile role in England's annual Music Industry Soccer Six Tournament in May, and contributed to the *No Boundaries* Kosovo refugee charity compilation.

### JAMIROQUAI DISCOGRAPHY
#### LPS
**8** 1993 Emergency on Planet Earth (Epic)
A delicious blend of rock, funk and drugged out psychedelia, a little naive in its refusal to tone down the Stevie Wonder-isms, but hey, a little bit of familiarity never hurt anyone.

**8** 1994 The Return of the Space Cowboy (Epic)
**7** 1996 Travelling Without Moving (Epic—#24 pop)
Stuffed full of great loops, topped off with nuclear production, a soul-sexy, slap-happy brew of funk and electro gyrations, with a tinge of reggae on "Drifting Along" thrown in for good measure.

**7** 1998 Synkronized (Sony—#28 US)
Another horn-heavy, string-laden dance fest, it's disco-funk on speed. "Planet Home," meanwhile, leads a charge back to '70s roots, while remaining refreshingly contemporary.

## CHAZ JANKEL
**BORN:** *Charles Jeremy Jankel, 4/16/52, England*

One of the unsung heroes of British jazz-funk—at least until Quincy Jones landed a massive hit with his "Ai No Corrida"—pianist Jankel's first band of note was Call of the Wild, a high school-and-after outfit that specialized in Jimi Hendrix and Otis Redding style R&B. From there he drifted into session work, while recording a handful of singles, both under his own name and as one half of the soul duo Pure Gold.

In 1971, Jankel joined Byzantium, a jazz fusion group whose record label, A&M, proudly pronounced them as "one of the most exciting forces in the recording industry." The band released two albums, *Byzantium* and *Seasons Changing*, but split, otherwise unsung, during summer 1973. Jankel moved onto singer/songwriter Jonathan Kelly's Outside for 1974's *Waiting on You* album, then slipped back into session work. He played on Jamaican singer Susan Cadogan's Larry Lawrence production of *Hurts So Good*, covering one of Millie Jackson's contributions to the *Cleopatra Jones* soundtrack.

Then in March 1976, Jankel joined the London pub rock band Kilburn & the High Roads, which was fronted by 33-year-old former art teacher Ian Dury. The Kilburns spent much of their five year career attempting, as Dury put it, to blend American funk with English music hall—a peculiar hybrid which had already baffled two record companies (their first album, recorded for Raft, was never released; their second, through Dawn, sank without trace). Now the band itself was sinking, heavily in debt and utterly demoralized. Jankel's arrival was a blessing for Dury, but marked the end of the Kilburns.

In a 1999 BBC interview, the singer recalled, "I was playing the drums and behind me I heard a bit of funky music . . . and it was Chaz. As soon as I heard him play this very clarinetty type of piano, I knew that we had a shared thing." By the end of the week, Dury had folded the group, and began planning a solo career with Jankel as his writing partner.

In September 1976, the duo started work on an album that Dury—a cripple since a childhood polio attack—insisted would be called *Live at Lourdes*, accompanied by drummer Pete Van Hook and former Ginger Baker bassist Kuma Harada. It was an unashamedly funk-based album, built upon a slinking bass, and heavily ornamented by Jankel's jazzy keyboard flourishes. However, Dury was soon having second thoughts, especially after a DJ friend called him up after hearing one track, "Wake Up, Make Love To Me," and asked "what's with the Barry White impersonation?"

Stripping away almost every vestige of their former funkiness. dismissing, too, the two sidemen whose exquisite playing had given the album so much of its sheen, Dury and Jankel concentrated instead upon the vaudeville half of the singer's dream equation. They formed a new band, the Blockheads and, the following summer, a single, "Sex and Drugs and Rock and Roll," introduced Dury to the now-gathering hordes of British punk rock.

The album, meanwhile, was retitled *New Boots and Panties*, and re-recorded around Dury's pronounced cockney accent and a clutch of roughshod songs and arrangements that could, indeed, have stepped out of an old time English music hall. The merest ghost of the its former self remained detectable—a piano flourish borrowed from jazzman Bill Edmunds, a few bass notes lifted from a Charlie Haden riff, but what goes around comes around. The title track from Parliament spin-off Original P's 1998 *What Dat Shakin'* album utilizes much the same rhythm as "Sex and Drugs and Rock and Roll."

Over the next year, Dury and the Blockheads became one of the leading attractions on Britain's new wave scene, impacting hard when "What a Waste" (later sampled by A Tribe Called Quest) made the Top Ten; they peaked over Christmas, 1978, with the rambunctious UK chart-topper "Hit Me with Your Rhythm Stick." "Reasons To Be Cheerful (Part Three)" followed, a #3 smash that hindsight later marked out as the first-ever British rap record. Only then did Dury and Jankel feel comfortable returning to the album they'd wanted to make all along, the solid funk gem *Do It Yourself*. The critics slaughtered it.

Jankel quit the Blockheads in spring 1980, determined to follow the direction laid out by *Do It Yourself*. The remainder of the Blockheads (and their record company, of course), insisted on returning to the madcap mannerisms of its predecessor. Reuniting with Harada and Van Hooke, Jankel signed a solo deal with A&M and recorded his self-titled solo debut, an adventurous jazz-funk set highlighted, but by no means dominated, by "Ai No Corrida."

Nevertheless, "Ai No Corrida" became the benchmark by which Jankel's future work would be judged. Co-written with former Fox/Yellow Dog guitarist Kenny Young, the song reappeared the following year on Quincy Jones' *The Dude* album, soaring into the US pop Top 30 as a simultaneous single. In comparison, Jankel himself enjoyed just one minor US hit, when "Glad To Know You," from his third album, *Questionaire*, scratched the R&B Top 60.

Following one further album, 1983's *Chazabianca*, Jankel reunited with Dury to record the singer's *Lord Upminster* album in Nassau, with reggae superstars Sly and Robbie. The pair then parted ways again, Dury for a new career in acting, Jankel for one final solo album, 1985's *Looking at You*. From there the pianist returned to session work and production, before joining with Dury once again in 1990, when the Blockheads reconvened at a memorial concert for recently deceased drummer Charley Charles.

The band remained active over the next decade, although they released just one new album, 1998's *Mr. Love Pants*; shortly after, Dury announced he had been diagnosed with colon cancer. The singer died March 27, 2000. Jankel alone would lead the Blockheads at the June 16 tribute concert.

### DISCOGRAPHY
### US CHARTLOG
1982 Glad To Know You/3 Million Synths (A&M—#57 R&B/#102 pop)

### LPs
**7** **1980 Chaz Jankel (A&M)**
A shock after the shambolic majesty of his Blockhead years, Jankel keys into the jazzier side of the emergent Britfunk scene with ruthless syncopation, but standing just a little close to the lounge bar for comfort. "Ai No Corrida" stands head and shoulders over the rest of the set, and wipes the floor with Quincy Jones' version too.

**5** **1981 Chazanova (A&M)**
Little has changed; indeed, instead of one "Ai No Corrida," there are now several of the things, all suspiciously similar sounding. Not a triumph.

**8** **1981 Questionaire (A&M—#42 R&B/#126 pop)**
Much better. "Johnny Funk" recaptures much of Jankel's earlier flair for ruthless fun, while "3 Million Synths" and "Now You're Dancing" have a twinkle in the eye as well. Upbeat happy jazz-funk, lite but lurid too.

**6** **1983 Chazablanca (A&M)**
**6** **1985 Looking At You (A&M)**

## KASHIF

**BORN:** *Michael Jones, 1959, Brooklyn, NY*
Keyboardist Michael Jones was just 16 when he joined Brooklyn dance-funk aggregation B.T. Express in 1976. He remained there for three years, quitting shortly before the band itself sundered. Afterwards, he worked as a session musician for a time, touring with Stephanie Mills and the Four Tops, before forming the production house Mighty M. Productions with Paul Lawrence Jones and Morrie Brown. Recordings with Evelyn "Champagne" King ("I'm in Love," "Love Come Down"), Howard Johnson ("So Fine," "Keeping Love New") and Melba Moore ("Underlove") followed.

In early 1983, as Kashif, he signed with Arista at a time when the American music scene appeared ripe for a new wave of electronic-based funk. After just one album in this mold, however, the keyboardist began moving in a very different direction, establishing himself as a figurehead of what was later termed "Urban Contemporary" music. Throughout the decade Kashif maintained a chart profile, beginning in late 1982 with the R&B Top Five "Just Gotta Have You."

"Baby Don't Break Your Baby's Heart" brought another signature hit in 1984, while a collaboration with former Barry White/Love Unlimited Orchestra horn player Kenny G., "Love on the Rise," made the R&B Top 30 the following year. Increasingly AOR-oriented, Kashif's greatest successes, however, came via partnerships with Melba Moore, Dionne Warwick and Meli'sa Morgan ("Love Changes") between 1986–88, while he also worked with Whitney Houston, George Benson, Johnny Kemp, Giorge Pettus and Stacy Lattisaw.

In 1990, Kashif retired from recording and began hosting seminars for aspiring musicians. He finally returned to action in 1998 with the album *Who Loves You*, whose featured guests included Gerald Albright, Sheila E., Gary Taylor, Liz Hogue, Johnny Britt (from Impromp 2), Dwayne Wiggins (from Tony Toni Tone) and Michael White (Maze).

## KASHIF DISCOGRAPHY
### SINGLES/US CHARTLOG
1983 Just Gotta Have You/(instrumental) (Arista—#5 R&B/#103 pop)
1983 Stone Love/(instrumental) (Arista—#22 R&B)
1983 Help Yourself to My Love/The Mood (Arista—#28 R&B)
1984 Baby Don't Break Your Baby's Heart/(instrumental) (Arista—#6 R&B/#108 pop)
1984 Are You the Woman/Love Has No End (Arista—#25 R&B)
1985 Ooh Love/(instrumental) (Arista—#75 R&B)
1985 Condition of the Heart/Help Yourself to My Love (Arista—#34 R&B)
1986 Dancing in the Dark/Say You Love Me (Arista—#36 R&B)
1988 Love Me All Over/Kathryn (Arista—#14 R&B)
1988 Loving You Only/Vacant Heart (Arista—#60 R&B)
1989 Personality/Lovers and Friends (Arista—#6 R&B)
1990 Ain't No Woman/My Door (Arista—#33 R&B)

### KASHIF/KENNY G.
1985 Love on the Rise/Virgin Island (Arista—#24 R&B)

### KASHIF/MELBA MOORE
1986 Love the One I'm With/Don't Go Away (Capitol—#5 R&B)
1988 I'm in Love/Stay (Capitol—#13 R&B)

### KASHIF/DIONNE WARWICK
1987 Reservations for two/For Everything You Are (Arista—#20 R&B/#62 pop)

### KASHIF/MELI'SA MORGAN
1987 Love Changes/Midnight Mood (Arista—#2 R&B)

### LPs
**8** 1983 Kashif (Arista—#10 R&B/#54 pop)
Strong debut replaces horns and strings with synthesized sound, and includes some seriously funky bass riffing on "Stone Love."
**6** 1984 Send Me Your Love (Arista—#4 R&B/#51 pop)
They're still audible, but the funk rhythms are buried underneath archetypal '80s electro fiddling. Solid throughout, but not as bright as we expected.
**6** 1985 Condition of the Heart (Arista—#32 R&B/#144 pop)
Bypassing danceable pop for full on ballads and love songs, this super slick set is eminently hummable, but only if you're in the mood. Or in love.
**5** 1987 Love Changes (Arista—#17 R&B/#118 pop)
**5** 1989 Kashif (Arista—#29 R&B)
**7** 1998 Who Loves You (Expansion)
A heady mix of old school and fresh grooves; the Marvin Gaye-esque "Can We Just Get Along" highlights the moody vocal end of things, while "Brooklyn Breezes" offers some cool instrumental jazz, and "Good Ol' Days" rattles along like the old express.

### SELECTED COMPILATIONS AND ARCHIVE RELEASES
**6** 1998 The Definitive Collection (Arista)
14 track summary of the Arista years, heavy on the hits.

### SELECTED SAMPLES
Love Changes — Immature: Feel the Funk (1995)

## KIDDO
**FORMED:** *1983, Detroit*
**ORIGINAL LINEUP:** *Donny Sterling (vcls, gtr), Michael Hampton (gtr), Juice Johnson (bs), Arthur Brown (kybds), Leroy Davis (sax), Rock Goodin (drms), Willie Jenkins (perc)*

Following the breakdown of the P-Funk empire during 1980–81, *Electric Spanking of War Babies*-era vocalist Donny Sterling formed a new band, Sterling Silver Starship, with Rodney Crutcher (gtr), Tony Thomas (gtr) and Jerome Rogers (kybds). Producer Ron Dunbar oversaw the project.

The group today is familiar only from their pride of place in the George Clinton *And Family* series; indeed, Clinton reflected in the *Family Volume Three* liner notes, "they did a lot of tracks together, funky stuff." Sadly, little of it has seen daylight.

In common with much of the studio work taking place at this time, SSS was never seen as a long-term outfit and that is how it transpired. They released the superlative "Sunshine" single through Columbia, the Uncle Jam label's distributor, plus two great jams within the aforementioned *And Family* collections, before Sterling's attention turned to another project, Kiddo.

The group was initially conceived as a collaboration with fellow George Clinton alumni Michael Hampton. However, he departed shortly after the release of the band's debut album, 1983's *Kiddo*, and Sterling himself took over lead guitar for the band's sophomore set, 1984's *Action*. This album also featured contributions from Bernie Worrell and Gary Taylor.

## DISCOGRAPHY
### STERLING SILVER STARSHIP DISCOGRAPHY
#### SINGLE
1981 Sunshine (When I Got You)/? (Columbia)

#### KIDDO
#### LPs
⑤ **1983 Kiddo (A&M)**
Disappointing set that veers from fizzled funk to synth dance, although "Tired of Looking" is decent.
⑤ **1984 Action (A&M)**
Mid-decade crossover captures funk in the vein of Rick James, but without the same punch. It includes a cover of the Who's "I Can't Explain"—a full decade before Fat Boy Slim raised its signature riff to dancefloor prominence.

## BILL LASWELL
(producer)

A funk session bassist during the '70s, before forming his own studio supergroup Material in 1981, Laswell is a tireless explorer of the rhythms and textures that were subsequently incorporated into "world music." His pioneering attitude toward dance music has certainly attracted a number of significant admirers—George Clinton, Zigaboo Modeliste and Afrika Bambaataa included.

Laswell oversaw both Herbie Hancock's early-'80s electro-funk renaissance, and the Last Poets' *Oh My People* comeback. He was also deeply involved in Fela Kuti's *Army Arrangement* album, single-handedly completing the set after Kuti himself was jailed. Equally significantly, Laswell contributed a positively apocalyptic sheen to the Bambaataa/John Lydon Timezone project, "World Destruction," while a second Bambaataa collaboration, Shango, also paid musical dividends.

Joined by Material bandmates Bernard Fowler and Michael Beinhorn, Shango's solitary album, *Shango Funk*

*Theology* included a ferocious update of Sly Stone's "Thank You Falletin Me Bernice Elf Again," subverting the original's cataclysmic bass for a bubbling synth, plus three Material/Bambaataa collaborations.

Laswell's services were increasingly in demand among the rock cognoscenti throughout the late '80s; the new decade, however, brought a new focus, as Laswell launched his own Axiom label through Island Records. Devoted to further exploring the roots of funk, dub and electro, often with a defiantly experimental edge, Laswell recorded hours of material with a core of musicians largely drawn from the P-Funk crew.

A revival of the late Glen Goins' 1978 Praxis project, featuring original producer Jerome Brailey, Bernie Worrell and Bootsy Collins spawned two LPs, although a projected Eddie Hazel solo set was halted by the guitarist's death in December 1992. Laswell also worked with Collins on 1994's *Lord of the Harvest*, credited to Zillatron and featuring Worrell, Buckethead, the Last Poets' Umar Bin Hassan and Grandmaster Melle Mel.

Another well-received project was OG Funk, a 1993 vehicle built around original Funkadelic bassist Billy Nelson, but again featuring a crop of P-Funk alumni. The ensuing *Out of the Dark* album was dedicated to Hazel.

The culmination of this activity was 1994's *Funkcronomicon* double album, credited to Axiom Funk. A clever combination of both newly recorded material and outtakes and overflow from past sessions (a Maceo Parker/Sly Stone collaboration dated back to Parker's *All The Kings Men* album), the record also featured contributions from Worrell, Collins, Clinton and Hancock, plus Fred Wesley, Bobby Byrd, reggae rhythm masters Sly and Robbie and alternative rock stylist Anton Fier (ex-Feelies, Golden Palominos).

## BILL LASWELL SELECTED PRODUCTIONS
1983 Golden Palominos: The Golden Palominos (OAO/Celluloid)
1984 Gil Scott-Heron: Re-Ron (Arista)
1984 The Last Poets: Oh My People (Celluloid)
1984 Herbie Hancock: Sound System (Columbia)
1985 Herbie Hancock & Foday Muso Suso: Village Life (Columbia)
1985 Mick Jagger: She's the Boss (Atlantic)
1985 Manu Dibango: Electric Africa (Celluloid)
1985 Yoko Ono: Starpeace (Polydor)
1985 Fela Ransome Kuti: Army Arrangement (Celluloid)
1986 Motorhead: Organiasmatron (GWR)
1986 Public Image Limited: Album (Elektra)
1986 Laurie Anderson: Home of the Brave (WB)
1986 Ginger Baker: Horses and Trees (Celluloid)

1987 Riyuchi Sakamoto: Neo Geo (Epic)
1987 Sly and Robbie: Rhythm Killers (Island)
1987 Manu Dibango: Afrijazzy (Urban)
1987 Sonny Sharrock: Seize the Rainbow (Enemy)
1988 Stevie Salas: Colorcode (Island)
1988 Samulnori: Record of Changes (CMP)
1988 Iggy Pop: Instinct (A&M)
1988 Last Exit: Iron Path (Venture)
1988 Bootsy Collins: What's Bootsy Doin'? (Columbia)
1988 Herbie Hancock: Perfect Machine (Columbia)
1988 Last Poets: Freedom Express (Celluloid)
1989 Swans: The Burning World (Universal)
1989 Material: Seven Souls (Virgin)
1989 Ramones: Brain Drain (Sire)
1990 Jonas Hellborg: The Word (Mango)
1990 Ginger Baker: Middle Passage (Axiom)
1990 Nicky Skopelitis: Next to Nothing (Caroline)
1990 Maceo Parker: All the King's Men (4th & Broadway)
1991 Material: The Third Power (Axiom)
1991 Bernie Worrell: Funk of Ages (Rhino)
1992 Deadline: Dissident (Day Eight)
1992 Bomb: Hate Feel Love (Sire)
1993 Blind Idiot God: Cyclotron (Avant)
1993 Bernie Worrell: Blacktronic Science (Rhino)
1993 Nicky Skopelitis: Ekstasis (Axiom)
1993 Umar Bin Hassan: Be Bop or Be Dead (Axiom)
1994 Mephiskapheles: God Bless Satan (Pass the Virgin)
1994 Zillatron: Lord of the Harvest (Axiom)
1994 Abiodun Oyewole: 25 Years (Axiom)
1994 Hakim Bey: TAZ (Axiom)
1994 Last Poets: Holy Terror (Black Ark)
1994 Automaton: Dub Terror Exhaust (Strata)
1994 OG Funk: Out of the Dark (Rykodisc)
1995 Jah Wobble: Heaven and Earth (Island)
1995 Henry Threadgill: Makin' a Move (Sony)
1995 Axion Funk: Funkcronomixx (Axiom)
1996 Buckethead: Day of the Robot (Subharmonic)
1996 Aisha Kandisha's Jarring Effect: Shabeesation (Rykodisc)
1996 Pharoah Sanders: Message from Home (Verve)
1997 Bob Marley: Dreams of Freedom: Ambient Translations (Axiom)
1997 Death Cube K: Disembodied (Ion)
1997 Last Poets: Time Has Come (Mouth Almighty)
1998 Dubadelic: Bass Invaders (Wordsound)
1998 Buckethead: Colma (Cyber Ocatve)
1999 Buckethead: Monsters and Robots (EMI)

## LIGHT OF THE WORLD
**FORMED:** *1978, London, England*
**ORIGINAL LINEUP:** *Jean Paul Maunick (gtr), Neville McKreith (gtr), Paul Williams (bs), Peter Hinds (kybds), Canute Wellington (trum), David Baptiste (trum), Everton McCalla (drms), Chris Etienne (perc)*

Naming themselves after Kool & the Gang's 1974 *Light of Worlds* album, Light of the World were one of the spearheads of the late '70s Brit-funk movement. They easily stepped into the void left by Roogalator's decline, and were already a powerful live draw on the London scene when they signed to the Ensign label in mid-1978.

The band's first two singles, "Swingin'" and "Midnight Groovin'," were minor UK hits that same year, but the death of percussionist Chris Etienne understandably soured the launch of their self-titled debut album, and Light of the World spent much of the remainder of 1979 out of sight. They re-emerged in mid-1980 with new members Ganiyu Bello (perc) and Nat Augustin (trom) and, under the aegis of producer Augie Johnson of "Always There" hitmakers Side Effect, cut their sophomore *Round Trip* album.

Again Light of the World enjoyed some minor chart entries. Over the next six months, "London Town," an intriguing cover of Bob Marley's "I Shot the Sheriff" and "I'm So Happy" pushed the band's infectious brand of jazzy funk into the UK Top 40. Already, however, the scene had moved on; the new romantic pop-unk stylings of Spandau Ballet, the extravagant costume dramas of Imagination and the tight techno groove of Linx all broke through during 1981 and, by mid-year, Light of the World had sundered.

Two new bands grew out of the wreckage; Maunick, Williams and Hinds formed Incognito, while McKreith, Wellington and Baptiste became Beggar and Co. However, Bello, Tubbs and Augustin continued on as Light of the World, scoring one further mini hit in late 1981 with "Ride the Love Train," one of three singles from the hopefully titled *Check Us Out* album. Unfortunately, few people did, and the band called it a day. Bello later reappeared alongside Williams in the Team; he also worked with a '90s incarnation of Shakatak.

### LIGHT OF THE WORLD
#### LPs
**7** **1979 Light of the World (Ensign—UK)**
Jazzy Brit-funk cast in the style of Kool & the Gang, sounding best across the hits "Midnight Groovin'" and "Swingin'."

**6** **1980 Round Trip (Ensign—UK)**
**5** **1982 Check Us Out (EMI—UK)**
Faceless, soul-less jazz-funk lite in a similar vein to the elevator stylings of Level 42.

**8 1981 The Best Remixed (Mercury UK)**

Effective way of gathering together the 12-inch mixes that were, in fact, Light of the World's funky forte.

**8 1995 The Best of Light of the World (Music Club—UK)**

Probably a better bet than actually owning any of the albums, containing all the hits you'll need.

# LINX

**FORMED:** *1979, London, UK*

**ORIGINAL LINEUP:** *David Grant (b. 8/8/56, Kingston, Jamaica—vcls), Peter "Sketch" Martin (b. 1954, Antigua—kybds), Roy Carter (kybds), Andy Duncan (drms)*

Caribbean-born but London raised, David Grant and Peter Martin met while working in a hi-fi shop in the late-'70s, and formed Linx in 1979 initially as a vocal and keyboards electro-funk duo. Record company interest was minimal, and didn't improve after the pair were joined by drummer Andy Duncan and former Heatwave bassist Roy Carter, recruited both as a musician and producer.

Undeterred, in 1980 Grant and Martin formed their own production and publishing companies, Solid Foundation and Solid Music, self-releasing Linx's debut single, "You're Lying." A limited edition of 1,000 copies were pressed for sale through the one specialist funk record store in London, City Sounds. Days later, BBC radio's Saturday night DJ Robbie Vincent broadcast a copy and, within 72 hours, the entire batch was sold out.

Immediately the Chrysalis major—riding high on the success of the then-similarly themed Spandau Ballet—moved in to pick up Linx and reissue the single. They were rewarded with a #15 hit, a success effortlessly echoed by the band's next release, the Top Ten "Intuition." A debut album of the same name then spun off "Throw Away the Key" (#21), as the group expanded its live lineup, and took their highly stylized, very visual show on the road.

Both "You're Lying" and another album cut, "Together We Can Shine," charted in the US. In early summer 1981, Linx began recording their second album, *Go Ahead*, along with the attendant 45s "So This Is Romance" (#15), "Can't Help Myself" (#55) and "Plaything" (#48). Their future seemed guaranteed.

However, Linx had a shorter fuse than anybody imagined. In the studio one day in early 1982, the realization that they had already taken their music as far as it could go struck Grant and Martin with equal force. On the spot the pair agreed to break up the band.

Grant launched a solo career; he also linked with vocalist Jaki Graham for 1985's "Could It Be I'm Falling in Love," written and produced, coincidentally, by Linx bassist Carter's old Heatwave partner Derek Bramble.

## LINX DISCOGRAPHY
### US CHARTLOG
1981 You're Lying/(instrumental) (Chrysalis—#27 R&B)
1981 Together We Can Shine/Rise and Shine (Chrysalis—#45 R&B)

### LINX
### LPS
**8 1981 Intuition (Chrysalis—#39 R&B/#175 pop)**

This snappy set is thoroughly danceable, with a sound best appreciated on the title track and "Throw Away the Key."

**7 1981 Go Ahead (Chrysalis)**

### SELECTED COMPILATIONS AND ARCHIVE RELEASES
**7 1983 Last Linx (Chrysalis—UK)**

Collection of hits and singles, including the early "You're Lying."

**5 1993 The Best of David Grant and Linx (Chrysalis—UK)**

Half Linx hits and half David Grant solo. The Linx material is the better and deserved its own disc.

# POWER STATION

**FORMED:** *1984, New York, NY*

**ORIGINAL LINEUP:** *Robert Palmer (vcls), Andy Taylor (gtr), John Taylor (bs), Tony Thompson (drms)*

A spin-off from the massively successful British band Duran Duran, Power Station was intended to further pursue John Taylor's personal dream of combining the energy of the Sex Pistols with the style of Chic, underpinned by a strong funk root.

His and (the unrelated) Andy Taylor's initial aim was to record what John called "a really funky version of [the T. Rex classic] "Get It On" with the bassist's then-girlfriend Bebe Buelle, on vocals. Chic drummer Tony Thompson completed the projected lineup, but before recording could commence, Taylor and Buelle's relationship ended.

Still intrigued by the concept, however, the trio completed a demo of the song, together with a handful of new compositions. Vocalist Robert Palmer was then added as the project, now dubbed the Power Station, and the quartet began recording a full-fledged album.

With Thompson's Chic colleague bassist Bernard Edwards producing, and capturing a sound that neatly fell between the Taylors' funk instincts, Chic's disco savvy and Palmer's recently successful '80s dance quintessence, the

Power Station's eponymous debut album was released in spring 1985, on the heels of the Top Ten "Some Like It Hot." A second single, the promised "Get It On," followed, but before Power Station could launch their summer 1985 US tour, Palmer quit, returning to his solo career.

Palmer was replaced at ten days notice by Michael Des Barres, a long-standing fixture on both the UK and US hard rock scenes (past bands included Silverhead and Chequered Past). His performance was ideally suited to the vast live arenas into which Power Station's profile immediately placed them. However, his vocals utterly bulldozed many of the subtler nuances of the music, ensuring that what had started life as a genuinely sincere funk-rock hybrid was now more likely to be remembered as the Wild Cherry of the mid-'80s. A third single ("Communication") made the Top 40 in the fall, but once the tour was complete, Power Station broke up.

John Taylor returned to Duran Duran (Andy Taylor quit for a solo career) and, after the recruitment of former Average White Band drummer Steve Ferrone to fill another vacancy in the group, he led them into 1986's similarly funk-influenced *Notorious* album.

The original Power Station lineup reconvened in late 1993, but John Taylor departed for personal reasons before the new album's completion. It took 18 months for Andy Taylor and Thompson to bring the project back on course, at which point producer Edwards stepped in to add not just the remaining bass parts, but to re-record the Duran Duran star's contribution as well. Tragically, the album *Living in Fear* was still nearing completion when Edwards passed away from a virulent flu, 4/18/96.

A single of the album's "She Can Rock It" was a minor UK chart entry in October 1996; although the album followed in the UK a month later, it did not appear in the US until November 1997, on the heels of the latest Duran Duran LP. It was not a success.

### POWER STATION DISCOGRAPHY
#### US CHARTLOG
1985 Some Like It Hot/The Heat Is On (Capitol—#6 pop)
1985 Get It On/Go to Zero (Capitol—#9 pop)
1985 Communication/Murderess (Capitol—#34 pop)

#### LPs
**7** 1985 The Power Station (Capitol—#6 US)
Bernard Edwards is the soul of the band, and John Taylor emerges a considerably funkier bassist than any of Duran Duran's detractors ever dreamed. Sharp ideas resonate

through edgy pop and, though the material is sometimes flimsy, the overall vibe is at least respectable.

**3** 1996 Living in Fear (Chrysalis)
The allegedly long-awaited (but by whom?) follow-up, and could it be any blander? Not to mention painful. The band gamely try updating their sound and broadening their horizons with the headbanger "Dope." But it would have been better if they'd simply not bothered.

## PRINCE
**BORN:** *Prince Rogers Nelson, 6/7/58, Minneapolis, MN*

Prince has been one of the most scrutinized musicians ever to have graced a stage, alternately a pawn of the media and a master manipulator of ceremony who utterly dominated pop and R&B during the '80s, while remaining fearlessly independent of the demands of commerce.

Encouraged by his father, Minneapolis jazz musician John Nelson, Prince was both precocious and fiercely talented. Self-taught, he could play the piano by the age of seven and the guitar at thirteen; he later claimed music became an escape for an increasingly troubled home life.

Leaving home in his early teens to stay with a friend Andre Anderson (Andre Cymone) and his family, Prince's first band (with Anderson and his sister Linda) was Grand Central, who metamorphosed into Champagne around the time Prince reached high school. Existing on a diet of original compositions and current funk favorites (the band's repertoire included several Ohio Players covers), Champagne's constantly shifting membership included Terry Lewis and Morris Day (later of The Time), musicians with whom Prince formed close and lasting friendships.

Out of this flux came Flyte Tyme, the principle force on a teenaged Minneapolis scene, which Prince himself christened "uptown," and which was largely comprised of his own friends' bands—Lewis and Jellybean Johnson formed the nucleus of Flyte Tyme. Still a member of Champagne, Prince himself remained behind the scenes, writing songs, directing the action and, though it was several years before his machinations bore fruit, sowing the seeds of a familial empire at least as cohesive as those engineered by James Brown and George Clinton—both formative influences.

Leaving school at 16, Prince formed a bond with his cousin Shauntel's boyfriend, New York musician Pepe Willie. The couple had relocated to Minneapolis, and Willie often gave advice to his young nephew. Prince joined his mentor in the studio in early 1976, alongside Wendell Thomas (bs), Pierre Lewis (kybds) and future Madhouse drummer Dale Alexander.

**Prince—nothing compares 2 him.**

As 94 East, the team recorded five songs, "Games," "I'll Always Love You," "Better than You Think," "If We Don't" and "If You See Me"; posterity has since dubbed the tape the Cookhouse Five, in deference to the Cookhouse Studio where it was cut. Willie then returned to New York, where he landed 94 East a one-off single deal with Polydor.

Working with veteran Motown producer Hank Cosby, who added vocalist Colonel Abrams to the band. the group cut two new songs, Cosby's "Fortune Teller" and Willie's "10.15," but before the single was released. Polydor had second thoughts and dropped the band. 94 East recorded at least two further sets of demos (compiled on the *Symbolic Beginnings* collection), but fell apart soon after.

Prince's next collaborator/tutor was Chris Moon, the engineer on the 94 East sessions. Teaching Prince his way around a recording studio, Moon recorded a string of demos with the youngster, lengthy funk jams packed with increasingly steamy sexual imagery. These tapes, in turn, drew Minneapolis businessman Owen Husney into Prince's orbit; Husney formed a management company, American Artists, specifically to represent Prince, and in

late 1976, work began on a new set of demos. Then, with Husney filling the role of mentor, philanthropist and negotiator, Prince signed to Warner Brothers in March 1977, his opening demand being that he produce his own records.

It was an unprecedented demand, at least in a musician so young and apparently untried. Warners agreed to it, but behind the scenes, began negotiating with members of Earth Wind & Fire to take over the moment Prince realized he was out of his depth—as, the suits insisted, he inevitably would. Prince, in the meantime, started work, allegedly unaware that the constant stream of visitors, well-wishers and janitors passing through the studio were actually label and industry bigwigs, despatched to report back on his progress, or lack of it. He passed the audition regardless.

Warners' initial vision was to market Prince as a rival to the latest heavy-hitters to emerge from the Motown studios: the Commodores, with their increasingly silky, seductive soul; Rick James with his self-styled punk-funk and so forth. Prince's vision, contrarily, was simply to do what he wanted. Completely overlooking both time and budgetary constraints, he labored for five months writing, performing and producing his debut album, *For You*.

Released in fall 1978, on the heels of the "Soft and Wet" single, the album's lasciviously sweaty slab of sex funk completely blew all expectations out of the water, and eventually reached #21 on the R&B chart. Prince made his first live performance since the album's completion, headlining at his hometown's Capri Theater with a band comprising Cymone (bs), Bobby Rivkin (drms), Gayle Chapman and Matt Fink (both kybds) and rock guitarist Dez Dickerson. The latter was destined to become a mainstay of Prince's band and an integral part of his sound, his fluid style the bridge upon which Prince's funk and rock fusion would most successfully meet.

The show was a success, but Warners refused to finance a tour. Prince's live show was a free for all jam with little cohesion, and even less commercial appeal. Rather, the label wanted him to return to the studio to cut his second album, *Prince*.

Pausing only to dismiss manager Husney in favor of Earth Wind & Fire/Ray Parker, Jr.'s management team Cavallo & Ruffalo, Prince banged the new record out in six weeks, for release that fall. Even without live support, his reputation had spread sufficiently for *Prince* to crack the pop Top 30. More significantly, it climbed to #3 on the R&B listing, while "I Wanna Be Your Lover," the second single from the set (after "Why You Wanna Treat Me So Bad?") went all the way to the top. (Another track, "I Feel for You" passed unnoticed at the time, but gave Chaka Khan a global smash in 1984.)

Prince was finally given the go-ahead to take his show on the road, supporting Rick James on his American tour, in early 1980. It was not a successful pairing. While the onstage action was little short of sensational, with Prince and James both pushing the boundaries of funk and rock (and Prince's overtly sexual act pushing those of taste), offstage their rivalry was somewhat less than friendly.

Prince closed the tour in February with a headlining performance of his own in Minneapolis, introducing Lisa Coleman as replacement for the recently departed Chapman. Work then began on his third album, *Dirty Mind*.

A dramatic expansion of the sexual provocations Prince had always been toying with, the album was not, this time, greeted with the same indulgence as its predecessors. The title track single didn't crack the top 50 R&B, while the album itself only yielded one other single, "Uptown." Prince's first UK visit, following his spring 1981 US jaunt, was a disaster, the entire outing cancelled after a poorly received first night in London. The band's return to Minneapolis was marked by Cymone's departure from the group.

However, 1981 also saw the launch of the Time, the outfit that developed out of Prince's earlier plaything Flyte Tyme. Using the pseudonym Jamie Starr, Prince wrote and produced the group's debut album, then invited them to tour with him that fall, following the release of his own next album.

Further disappointment came with two poorly received shows opening for the Rolling Stones in Los Angeles in October; shaken, Prince walked off the stage the first night just a few songs into his set, and promptly boarded a plane back to Minneapolis. Dickerson somehow persuaded him to return for the second show, only for that to prove an even worse move.

Prince was boosted, however, by the release of *Controversy* the next month. An odd combination of political manifesto and sexual grind, the album pulled away from the slump of *Dirty Mind*, peaking at #3 on the R&B charts and just missing the Pop Top 20.

But it was the following year's double LP, *1999* that catapulted Prince straight into the mainstream. A monstrous electronic funk feast, *1999* was credited, for the first time, to Prince & The Revolution, and spun off three inescapable singles, "Let's Pretend We're Married," "Little Red Corvette" and, of course, the title track. It also prompted Prince to undertake his longest tour yet, a six month outing whose success was such that what was initially a slow-moving album finally peaked at #9, seven months after its release; *1999* would go on to spend a full two years on the pop chart.

The tour did not always run smoothly. Disagreements with members of Time saw Prince fire two of that group's lineup after they arrived late for a show (they were simultaneously producing the SOS Band while the tour was underway). Further disarray occurred when Dickerson quit on the eve of a proposed second visit to Britain; the sold out shows at London's Dominion Theatre were cancelled, while Prince sought a replacement.

He selected Wendy Melvoin, one half (with Revolution keyboardist Lisa Coleman) of the Wendy & Lisa duo, and in August, the new Revolution lineup debuted at the First Avenue club in Minneapolis, previewing material intended for Prince's next project, the semi-autobiographical *Purple Rain* movie.

Working with William Blinn and Albert Magnoli, Prince commenced filming in late fall, for a July 1984, opening. The film was presaged by the pop/R&B chart-topper "When

Doves Cry," while both the soundtrack and the subsequent tour that followed, joined the movie in the ranks of the year's most immense sellers.

Over half the songs off the soundtrack album became successful singles with "Let's Go Crazy" giving Prince his third #1, while "Take Me with U," "I Would Die 4 U," and the title track, became radio and club staples that year. Prince himself stepped out of the limelight briefly, relaunching an earlier side-project, Vanity 6, as Apollonia 6 (following the eponymous Vanity's replacement by his latest protege, Apollonia); then to mentor percussionist Sheila E. (born Sheila Escovedo) during the recording of her debut album, *The Glamorous Life*. Daughter of Latin funk hero Pete Escovedo, E. had been introduced to Prince by Carlos Santana, and would join the Revolution later in the year.

In 1985, Prince received a hail of accolades for the film and soundtrack; Prince and *Purple Rain* all but swept the American Music Awards in January, before picking up three Grammys and, across the ocean, two BRIT Awards. He was also invited to join both the USA for Africa and Live Aid famine relief events; he declined, but did contribute one song, "4 the Tears in Your Eyes," to the *USA for Africa* album.

Prince consumed much of early 1985 building his own studio outside Minneapolis, Paisley Park; he also established his own record label of the same name He then recorded his next album, *Around the World in a Day*, an informal set that developed from the *Purple Rain* tour rehearsals (and a songwriting reunion with his father). The album was released in the spring 1985, and showcased Prince's shift away from his trademark funk jams, and toward a poppier, and more spiritual mood.

Appearing with quiet promotion and nowhere near the fanfare of *Purple Rain*, the album nevertheless made #1 on the pop charts, and cruised into the R&B charts at #4, accompanied by the 45s "Raspberry Beret," "America" and "Pop Life."

Prince, meanwhile, waded through the remains of the Time to create a new group The Family. With Melvoin's sister Susannah, on vocals and the Time's Johnson and Benton rounding out the mix, plus Miko Weaver (gtr) and Eric Leeds (sax), this short-lived band recorded just one album before disintegrating. (Leeds subsequently reappeared in the Revolution.) The LP's most notable song, "Nothing Compares 2 U," of course, was reinvented by Sinead O'Connor in 1990.

Prince had also committed to making another feature film. Shot in the south of France by Mary Lambert, *Under the Cherry Moon* was a 180 degree turnaround from the extravagances of its predecessor. Shot in color, but ultimately released in black and white, it was almost universally (but very unjustly) panned, while Prince's refusal to release a conventional soundtrack album, hindered it further. Rather, elements of the movie were replayed on 1986's *Parade* (subtitled "music from *Under the Cherry Moon*"), issued two months before the movie's July premiere.

By that time, the album's first single, "Kiss," had already presented Prince with the unusual achievement of wrestling with himself for the US #1 position. "Kiss" topped the chart, "Manic Monday," written for the Bangles under the alias Christopher Tracy, was #2 behind it. A US tour followed, before Prince finally returned to the UK, at last, for three triumphant shows at Wembley Arena.

However, the gigs marked the end of an era. Tensions were again heating up among the various musicians in Prince's employ and, by the end of the year, he had disbanded The Revolution. Prince essentially closed the door on collaboration and returned to his earliest formula of one-man dynamo to record spring 1987's *Sign 'O' the Times* album.

It was released to much critical acclaim, although there were many who harshly criticized the LP, accusing Prince of losing the funky vibes he had been carrying for the better part of a decade. The album was a hit regardless, while hopes were high for the planned tour, as Prince convened a new band, retaining Leeds, Fink, Wally Safford and Greg Brooks from the Revolution, plus Sheila E., Mico Weaver (gtr), Seacer (bs) and Boni Boyer (kybds). However, both the US and UK dates were cancelled following a short string of European shows—the source of the *Sign 'O' the Times* live video released as a consolation prize later in the year.

*Sign 'O' the Times* was one of two albums Prince was recording near simultaneously; and one, therefore, of the two faces that Prince intended turning to his audience. *Sign 'O' the Times* was the calmer side of things; the wild funk, meanwhile, was channeled into what he called *The Black Album*. Warners, however, balked at releasing the album, presaging what soon erupted into a major confrontation between artist and label, *The Black Album* was canned (it was finally released in 1994), and Prince instead recorded 1988's *Lovesexy*.

Both the Paisley Park label and studios were running smoothly by this time and, at the end of 1988, Prince made his first major signings, former Staple Singers star Mavis Staples and funk godfather George Clinton. He also composed songs for Chaka Khan, Sheila Easton and Madonna, and provided the soundtrack for 1989's *Batman* movie. The "Batdance" single topped the chart during summer 1989; the album followed.

Prince spent the beginning of 1990 working on his *Graffiti Bridge* feature film and soundtrack. The album appeared late that summer (the movie premiered in November), again spawning a #1 single, "Thieves in the Temple." The movie, however, received atrocious reviews and disappeared quickly from theatres.

Prince, however, appeared too busy to notice. He worked with a revitalized Time on their 1990 album, *Pandemonium*, before launching the four month *Nude* world tour. In 1991, the revitalized Prince was riding high again, with a new band, The New Power Generation (NPG), and a new album, the rap-inflected *Diamonds and Pearls*. With an eclectic mix of updated funk and soul grooves, the album spawned four hot singles, including "Money Don't Matter 2 Night," while the accompanying tour was equally impressive, a homage/rival to Clinton's Mothership-era spectacles, complete with a lighted male/female symbol that drifted to stage spaceship style.

But all was not well. Prince was in the opening throes of what turned into a bitter, public battle with Warner Brothers over the renegotiation of his recording contract, a conflict that grew to incorporate everything from an artist's freedom to work (and release as many albums a year as he wanted!), to his right to own that work. The fight would dominate the press over some four years, often overshadowing the release of Prince's music.

The singer himself took to appearing in public with the word "slave" written on his face, protesting his alleged treatment by the company. His attempts to further distance himself from that servitude saw him celebrate his 35th birthday, in 1993, by officially changing his name to the unpronounceable symbol debuted on his latest album, 1992's *squiggle* (later adapted to TAFKAP, or The Artist Formerly Known as Prince). It was so ironic, then, that the LP itself opened with the ultra-funky and unequivocally affirmative "My Name Is Prince." The career retrospective *Hits/B-Sides* seemed to further bring down the curtain.

In 1994, Warners decided to close the Paisley Park label; Prince responded with the launch of a new, independent label, NPG, christening the imprint with "The Most Beautiful Girl in the World" single the following month. *The Beautiful Experience* EP followed later that spring, while Prince and the NPG also recorded the fat funk *Gold Nigga* for release through the (then infant) Internet.

Warners themselves retaliated with *Come*, a fall 1994 collection of outtakes and archive material, described by Prince as the type of material he would give to the label in order to fulfill his contract. In the event, the next two years saw Prince race to break his links with the label, finally engineering a release for *The Black Album*, and delivering three new albums (*The Gold Experience*, the soundtrack to Spike Lee's movie *Girl 6* and *Chaos and Disorder*).

The thrill of victory was soured in October 1996. Married to dancer Mayte Garcia the previous February 14, Prince's first son, Gregory, was born on October 16, but immediately rumors began to fly that the child had died within a week of his birth. Breaking his long-standing policy of refusing to comment on his private life (indeed, apparently taking a perverse delight in the welter of rumor that surrounded it), Prince agreed to an interview with *USA Today*, and firmly denied the stories. In June 1997, however, the Minneapolis county medical examiner's office confirmed that the child had died, having been born with a severe skeletal abnormality.

Despite the tragedy, which was then so fresh, November 1996, saw Prince go ahead with plans to release the three CD set *Emancipation*, before launching the *Love 4 One Anothers Charity Tour* in the new year. The album was distributed through EMI, but Prince also continued investigating the possibilities of the Internet, setting up a massive online site for NPG records, and unveiling another multi-disc package, the five CD *Crystal Ball*, in March 1998. (Retail outlets stocking the set offered only a four CD set, omitting the symphonic *Kamasutra*.)

Now working without either management or a major record label, Prince launched into a period of what, in the late '90s, struck observers as a period of unparalleled creativity. Indeed, even James Brown, at the height of his own prolificness, would have been hard pushed to match Prince's output. Just four months after *Crystal Ball*, a new album, *Newpower Soul* appeared in July 1998, while Prince also oversaw new releases by Chaka Khan and the reformed *Graham Central Station*, in whose honor, of course, he had named his own first band, Grand Central. Larry Graham himself appeared on both *Newpower Soul* and on Khan's album, also joining the New Power Generation on tour for dates in 1998, alongside Khan and fellow former Sly & the Family Stone mainstays Jerry Martini and Cynthia Robinson.

Prince's own output continued apace with the release of *NYC Live*, taken from a 1997 jam session at Paisley Park, and *The War*, a 1998 jam, while 1999 finally brought what many people called Prince's "comeback" album, *Rave Un2 the Joy Fantastic*, a one-off release through Arista. He then closed the century with a stellar pay per view New Year's extravaganza, a gig that also marked the last major appearance of his TAFKAP alias. He resumed work as Prince in early 2000.

## FURTHER READING

*Purple Reign* by Liz Jones (Citadel, 1998)

## PRINCE
### US CHARTLOG

1978 Soft and Wet/So Blue (WB—#12 R&B/#92 pop)

1978 Just as Long as We're Together/In Love (WB—#91 R&B)

1979 I Wanna Be Your Lover/My Love Is Forever (WB—#1 R&B/#11 pop)

1980 Why You Wanna Treat Me So Bad?/Baby (WB—#13 R&B)

1980 Still Waiting/Bambi (WB—#65 R&B)

1980 Uptown/Crazy You (WB—#5 R&B/#101 pop)

1981 Dirty Mind/When We're Dancing Close and Slow (WB—#65 R&B)

1981 Controversy/When You Were Mine (WB—#3 R&B/#70 pop)

1982 Let's Work/Ronnie, Talk to Russia (WB—#9 R&B/#104 pop)

1982 1999/How Come U Don't Call Me Anymore? (WB—#4 R&B/#12 pop)

1983 Little Red Corvette/All the Critics Love U in New York (WB—#15 R&B/#6 pop)

1983 Delirious/Horny Toad (WB—#18 R&B/#8 pop)

1984 Let's Pretend We're Married/Irresistible Bitch (WB—#55 R&B/#52 pop)

1984 When Doves Cry/Days (WB—#1 R&B/#1 pop)

1984 Let's Go Crazy/Erotic City (WB—#1 R&B/#1 pop)

1984 Purple Rain/God (WB—#4 R&B/#2 pop)

1984 I Would Die 4 U/Another Lonely Christmas (WB—#11 R&B/#8 pop)

1985 Take Me with U/Baby I'm a Star (WB—#40 R&B/#25 pop)

1985 Raspberry Beret/She's Always in My Hair (Paisley Park—#3 R&B/#2 pop)

1985 Pop Life/Hello (Paisley Park—#8 R&B/#7 pop)

1985 America/Girl (Paisley Park—#35 R&B/#46 pop)

1986 Kiss/Love or $ (Paisley Park—#1 R&B/#1 pop)

1986 Mountains/Alexa De Paris (Paisley Park—#15 R&B/#23 pop)

1986 Anotherloverholenyohead/Girls & Boys (Paisley Park—#18 R&B/#63 pop)

1987 Sign 'O' the Times/La, La, La, He, He, Hee (Paisley Park—#1 R&B/#3 pop)

1987 If I Was Your Girlfriend (Paisley Park—#12 R&B/#67 pop)

1987 U Got the Look/Housequake (Paisley Park—#11 R&B/#2 pop)

1987 Hot Thing/I Could Never Take the Place of Your Man (Paisley Park—#14 R&B/#63 pop)

1988 Alphabet Street/Alphabet Street (long version) (Paisley Park—#3 R&B/#8 pop)

1988 Glam Slam/Escape (Paisley Park—#44 R&B)

1988 I Wish U Heaven/Scarlet Pussy (Paisley Park—#18 R&B)

1989 Batdance/200 Balloons (WB—#1 R&B/#1 pop)

1989 Partyman/Feel U Up (WB—#5 R&B/#18 pop)

1989 Scandalous!/When 2 R in Love (WB—#5 R&B)

1990 Thieves in the Temple/Part II (Paisley Park—#1 R&B/#6 pop)

1990 New Power Generation/Part II (Paisley Park—#27 R&B/#64 pop)

1991 Gett Off/Horny Pony (Paisley Park—#6 R&B/#21 pop)

1991 Insatiable/I Love U in Me (Paisley Park—#3 R&B/#77 pop)

1992 Diamonds and Pearls (Paisley Park—#1 R&B/#3 pop)

1992 Money Don't Matter 2 Night/Call the Law (Paisley Park—#14 R&B/#23 pop)

1992 Sexy M.F./Strollin' (Paisley Park—#76 R&B/#66 pop)

1992 My Name Is Prince/Sexy Mutha (Paisley Park—#25 R&B/#36 pop)

1992 Damn U/Whom It May Concern (Paisley Park—#32 R&B/#108 pop)

1992 7/7 (acoustic version) (Paisley Park—#61 R&B/#7 pop)

1993 The Morning Papers/Live 4 Love (Paisley Park—#68 R&B/#44 pop)

1993 Pink Cashmere/Soft and Wet (remix version) (Paisley Park—#14 R&B/#50 pop)

1993 Nothing Compares 2 U/Peach (NPG—#62 R&B)

1994 The Most Beautiful Girl in the World/Beautiful (NPG—#2 R&B/#3 pop)

1994 Letitgo/Solo (WB—#10 R&B/#31 pop)

1994 Space/Space (album version) (WB—#71 R&B)

1995 Purple Medley/Purple Medley (remix) (WB—#74 R&B/#84 pop)

1995 I Hate U/I Hate U (remix)(NPG—#3 R&B/#12 pop)

1996 Gold/Rock 'N' Roll Is Alive! (And It Lives in Minneapolis)(NPG—#92 R&B)

1996 Girl 6/Nasty Girl (WB—#78 R&B)

1999 1999/Little Red Corvette (WB—#45 R&B)

### LPs

**6** 1978 For You (WB—#21 R&B/#163 pop)

**7** 1980 Prince (WB—#3 R&B/#22 pop)

An excellent slow-jam funk set, less muddled than *For You* and just beginning to develop the future trademark vocal and guitar sounds.

**8** 1980 Dirty Mind (WB—#7 R&B/#45 pop)

"When You Were Mine," "Uptown" and the funkfest of "Party Up" countered the libidinous raunch of "Head" and "Sister," lending some much needed balance to this concept album of sorts. Again, some amazing guitar riffs break through the still occasionally miasmic funk fog.

**7** 1981 Controversy (WB—#3 R&B/#21 pop)

Either loved or hated by the critics, this album divides neatly between sex on one side and politics on the other. Despite some wryly crass lyrics, the title track is a righteous new funk masterpiece, although other moments—notably "Ronnie, Talk to Russia"—verge on the mindless. Good, but uneven, effort.

**9** 1983 1999 (WB—#4 R&B/#9 pop)

Inescapable double album opens with the twin sucker punch of "1999" and "Little Red Corvette." Almost 20 years on, the rest of the record seems less memorable than it once was, but still a defining moment in pop history, as Prince finally breaks out the full "Prince" sound. From now on, half the world would be copying him.

**10  1984 Purple Rain (WB—#1 R&B/#1 pop)**
Slick pop, guitar riffs that won't stop, and more songs to become synonymous with the '80s. It's a joyous crash of sound from the hyperactive "Let's Go Crazy" and "When Doves Cry," to the more contemplative "I Would Die for You" and the title track; but what really impresses is the sheer cohesion of an album that skips so blithely between moods.

**7  1985 Around the World in a Day (Paisley Park—#4 R&B/#1 pop)**
No album could truly have followed *Purple Rain*, and this psych-tinged pop monster was as ill-equipped as any. Besides, the ever-so-annoying "Raspberry Beret" still over-rides every other track on the album.

**8  1986 Parade (Paisley Park—#2 R&B/#3 pop)**
Oh, how swift people were to condemn this album, and how foolish they look if you play it today. "Kiss" and "Girls and Boys" are unimpeachable, quirky funk pop that never forgets that clever production is only half of the job; you still need a good song to match it. Elsewhere . . . okay, some of *Parade* is self-indulgent twaddle, but when it's good, it's up there with the best.

**8  1987 Sign 'O' the Times (Paisley Park—#4 R&B/#6 pop)**
**7  1988 Lovesexy (Paisley Park—#5 R&B/#11 pop)**
**7  1989 Batman (WB—#5 R&B/#1 pop)**
**5  1990 Music from Graffiti Bridge (Paisley Park—#6 R&B/#6 pop)**
**7  1991 Diamonds and Pearls (Paisley Park—#1 R&B/#3 pop)**
From the rapturous "Thunder" to "Cream" and "Gett Off," the set is a return to a delicious mix of style. The band is tight, the songs are tighter and the slick sounds put Prince back on the fast track.

**8  1992 (SYMBOL) (Paisley Park—#8 R&B/#5 pop)**
**7  1995 The Gold Experience (WB—#2 R&B/#6 pop)**
**6  1996 Chaos and Disorder (WB/NPG)**
Full-on pop album with lots of rock riffing summed up, of course, on the effervescent "I Rock, Therefore I Am"

**6  1996 Girl 6 (WB—#15 R&B/#75 pop)**
**8  1996 Emancipation (NPG—#6 R&B/#11 pop)**
Ambitious and amazing three disc whopper to celebrate Prince's "rebirth." Each disc is a complete entity, running the gambit from pop to grooving funk and dance. An outrageous masterpiece.

**5  1998 Newpower Soul (NPG—#9 R&B/#22 pop)**
The set is full of funk, with a few ballads to cool down the grooving.

**5  1999 Rave Un2 the Joy Fantastic (NPG—#8 R&B/#18 pop)**

*SELECTED COMPILATIONS AND ARCHIVE RELEASES*
**6  1986 The Minneapolis Genius: 94 East (Hot Pink)**
Don't expect anything beyond a mostly anonymous session guitarist playing behind his cousin's boyfriend, co-writing one song ("Just Another Sucker") and contributing the occasional flash of intelligent guitar to a reasonable soulful stew. The future, however, was nowhere in sight.

**9  1993 The Hits B-Sides (Paisley Park—#6 R&B/#19 pop)**
This 56-track collection includes 18 rare B-sides and six unreleased cuts. Even if you know what to expect, the sheer range of material is staggering.

**7  1993 The Hits 1 (Paisley Park—#14 R&B/#46 pop)**
**7  1993 The Hits 2 (Paisley Park—#23 R&B/#54 pop)**
Condensed single disc versions of the above.

**4  1994 Come (WB—#2 R&B/#15 pop)**
Disappointing set of uneven material. Collectors need a copy . . . everyone else should buy something else.

**6  1994 The Black Album (WB—#18 R&B/#6 pop)**
The official release of the down and dirty funk set that had been circulating for five years as a bootleg. The wait was generally worthwhile, although legend did play its rootsiness up a little more than was deserved.

**6  1998 Crystal Ball (NPG—#59 R&B/#62 pop)**
A massive collection of outtakes—best for the diehard fan.

**7  1997 94 East Featuring Prince: Symbolic Beginnings (Charley—UK)**
Two CD set compiling the Cookhouse Five tapes, plus two subsequent sessions, outtakes, instrumental versions and jams. Prince is the little guitar sound in one speaker.

**6  1998 NYC Live (NPG)**
**6  1998 The War (NPG)**
**7  1999 The Vault: Old Friends 4 Sale (NPG—#27 R&B/#85 pop)**
Ten-track compilation of never before released material.

*SELECTED SAMPLES*
Alphabet Street — Arrested Development: Tennessee (1992)
The Ballad of Dorothy Parker — Digital Underground: Whassup Wit The Luv (1993)
The Ballad of Dorothy Parker — Lords of the Underground: Flow On (New Symphony) (1993)
Batdance — Sir Mix-a-Lot: Beepers (1989)
Controversy — Jungle Brothers: Black Is Black (1988)
Crazy You — Color Me Badd: How Deep (1993)
Darling Nikki — 2Pac: Heartz of Men (1996)
Electric Chair — Candyman: Nightgown (1990)
Gett Off — Da Lench Mob: Freedoms' Got an AK (1992)
Gett Off — House of pain: Jump Around (1992)
Gett Off — X-Clan: Funk Liberation (1992)

Hot Thing — Consolidated: America Number One (1985)

Housequake — Above the Law: G-Rupes Best Friend (1993)

Housequake — Bomb the Bass: Beat Dis (1988)

Housequake — Chubb Rock: Talkin' Loud, Ain't Sayin' Jack (1989)

Housequake — Digital Underground: Flowin' on the D-Line (1991)

Housequake — MC Hammer: They Put Me in the Mix (1988)

Housequake — Naughty by Nature: Let the Ho's Go (1991)

Housequake — Robert Plant: Hurting Kind (I've Got My Eyes on You) (1990)

Housequake — Sir Mix-a-Lot: Lockjaw (1992)

If I Was Your Girlfriend — Nemesis: Str8 jackin' (1993)

If I Was Your Girlfriend — Yo-Yo: Ain't Nobody Better (1991)

I Wanna Be Your Lover — DJ Quik: Safe + Sound (1995)

I Wanna Be Your Lover — Nice & Smooth: Sky's the Limit (1994)

Joy & Pain — A Tribe Called Quest: Go Ahead in the Rain (1990)

Joy & Pain — MC Solaar: Galaktika (1998)

Kiss — Criminal Element: Put the Needle to the Record (1989)

Let's Go Crazy — Eazy-E: Eazy-Duz-It (1988)

Let's Go Crazy — Public Enemy: Brothers Gonna Work It Out (1990)

Let's Work — MC Hammer: Work This (1990)

New Position — Arrested Development: Eve of Reality (1992)

Pop Life — Big Daddy Kane: Lover in You (1991)

Starfish & Coffee: Nice & Smooth: No Delayin' (1989)

When Doves Cry — Afrika Bambaataa & Jungle Brothers: Return to Planet Rock (remix) (1986)

When Doves Cry — Gold Money; Daddy Never Left Ya (1992)

When Doves Cry — MC Hammer: Pray (1990)

## THE RED HOT CHILI PEPPERS

**FORMED:** *1983, Los Angeles, CA*

**ORIGINAL LINEUP:** *Anthony Kiedis (b. 11/1/62, Grand Rapids, MI—vcls), Hillel Slovak (b. 4/13/62, Haifa, Israel—gtr), Flea (b. Michael Balzary, 10/16/62, Melbourne, Australia—bs), Jack Irons (b. 7/18/62, Los Angeles, CA—drms)*

In April 1983, bassist Flea, of ex-Los Angeles punk band Fear, linked with high school friends Anthony Kiedis, and Jack Irons and Hillel Slovak (both of Los Angeles art rockers What Is This?), as Tony Flow and His Miraculous Majestic Masters of Mayhem. Their debut performance at Los Angeles's Kit Kat Club, regarded as a strict one-off, culminated with the band members appearing onstage naked, bar strategically placed socks. The show was such a success that the quartet continued on as the Red Hot Chili Peppers, landing a residency at the local Cathay de Grand nightclub and swiftly becoming at least as big a local draw as What Is This?

A deal with EMI America followed within six months of their live debut; What Is This?, too, were offered a contract, and Slovak and Irons opted to remain with that band. Kiedis and Flea recruited Jack Sherman (guitar) and Cliff Martinez (ex-Weirdos, drums), and in late 1983 recorded their funk hip-hop hybrid debut album with ex-Gang of 4 member Andy Gill producing.

Slovak quit What Is This? following the release of *Red Hot Chili Peppers* in April, 1984, replacing Sherman for the recording of *Freaky Styley* with producer and guru George Clinton. It was, for the Peppers, a dream come true. "George Clinton is amazing," Kiedis enthused. "He's the ultimate hardcore funk creator in the world, ever. James Brown is the king of his field, but he was more pure funk. If anybody ever wanted to ask you what was the greatest funk-metal ever, it would be Parliament-Funkadelic. Their music is so great that I don't think people are even capable of understanding how great it is."

Flea agreed. "They just did the music they wanted to and it didn't fit into any category. I think what we're doing is very similar, except that they came out of the acid/hippy thing and we came out of the punk rock thing. Rock, funk, whatever you want to call it, they were one of the greatest bands."

Clinton lived up to their every expectation. Secluding the Peppers at his own United Sound studio, a farm on the outskirts of Detroit, he encouraged them to pour all their excesses into the music. "One thing Clinton told me about playing funk I'll never forget," Flea recalled, "is, 'you have to take it all the way home'." Kiedis concluded, "He's just a bottomless pit of funky creativity who I have a great deal of respect for. I'm so fortunate to have had the experience of making a record with him, it's something I'll never forget."

Clinton harnessed the Peppers' energy, focussed it and drove it home. He brought Maceo Parker and Fred Wesley into the sessions to contribute the horns that brought new shape and meaning to the Peppers' sound. He also introduced them to Andre Foxxe, with whom the band recorded the manic knockabout hardcore-funk fusion "Reputation" (released in 1992's on Foxxe's *I'm Funk and I'm Proud* album).

Two covers, Sly Stone's "If You Want Me To Stay" and the Meters' "Africa" (retitled "Hollywood"), allowed the group to delve deeper still into their own funk influences, even as they explored the direction they themselves wanted to take. Neither performance had much in common with the original versions, and that, too, was how it should be. Just as Clinton himself had regularly delighted in utterly reworking his own (and other people's) past on new albums, bringing new life to both the song and its makers, so now he encouraged the Peppers to do the same thing.

**Chili Peppers Anthony Kiedis and Flea.**

Such lessons remained with the Peppers through the tempestuous years that followed, all the more so since their early development was scarred by Slovak and Kiedis' escalating drug habits and a reputation for hell-raising, which seemed destined to ensure the group remained a second division act. Nevertheless, Irons returned to replace Martinez in 1986, confirming the vitality of the original lineup.

The Peppers' third album, *The Uplift Mofo Party*, again stalled, despite the gratuitous publicity generated by the track "Party on Your Pussy." But their first full European tour—celebrated by the Beatlesque sleeve to their *Abbey Road* EP—in early 1988 did better, and the band returned to Los Angeles to begin work on their next album.

However, the death of Slovak from a heroin overdose on June 25, 1988, left the Peppers directionless for close to a year. Irons quit, winding up in hospital before being pulled back on the road by Joe Strummer and, later, former What Is This? frontman Alan Johannes, with whom he formed

Eleven (Irons joined Pearl Jam in 1994). Kiedis, too, went to ground, holing up on a beach in Mexico before returning to Los Angeles to reform the Peppers.

With Dead Kennedys drummer DH Peligro and latter-day P-Funk guitarist "Blackbyrd" McKnight on board, the band made a tentative return to live work. Auditions then produced Chad Smith (b. 10/25/62, St. Paul, MN—ex-Toby Redd, drums), before Kiedis lured John Frusciante (b. 3/5/70, New York) from a Thelonious Monster audition.

Reuniting with *Mofo* producer Michael Beinhorn, the reconstituted Peppers released *Mother's Milk* in September 1989, followed by the airplay favorites "Knock Me Down," "Taste the Pain" and a frantic cover of Stevie Wonder's "Higher Ground." By late March, *Mother's Milk* had gone gold in the US, and early 1991 brought similar success for the *Psychedelic Sex Funk Live from Heaven* concert video.

The group signed to Warner Brothers that summer and recorded their new album, *Blood Sugar Sex Magik* with hip-hop producer Rick Rubin—the perfect combination in every sense of the word. A string of consecutive smash videos followed; "Give It Away" (their first bona fide hit single), the anti-drug ballad "Under the Bridge" and "Breaking the Girl" all impacted before *Blood Sugar* completed its rise up the US chart. The set eventually topped triple platinum, although the band's leap to superstardom was not without its casualties.

Frusciante quit midway through their Japanese tour; he was replaced by another Thelonious Monster graduate, Zander Schloss, who in turn gave way to Arik Marshall (b. 2/13/67—ex-Marshall Law).

Amid this chaos, the Peppers headlined Lollapalooza '92 and won Best Art Direction, Breakthrough Video and Viewers Choice categories at the MTV awards (for "Give It Away" and "Under the Bridge"). In 1992, the band wrapped up with Top 30 placings for material they once struggled to give away, as former label EMI released the career-spanning *What Hits?* package. A second compilation of B-sides and rarities, *Out in LA*, made further use of similar material.

Marshall quit in early 1993, having recorded the band's "Soul to Squeeze" single for the *Coneheads* soundtrack. He was replaced by Jesse Tobias (ex-Mother Tongue) for a handful of summer dates, including Britain's Glastonbury Festival, but the new man lasted little more than a month before Dave Navarro (b. 6/7/67, Santa Monica—ex-Jane's Addiction) was drafted in.

The Peppers then settled down to a period of comparative quiet, broken only by regular sessionwork for Flea, a competent trumpeter as well as bassist. Reissues of "Give It Away" and "Under the Bridge" prefaced the band's return to action at Woodstock 94. The quartet also opened two shows for the Rolling Stones in Pasadena that October, before completing their long-anticipated next album, *One Hot Minute*.

"My Friends" topped both the Modern Rock and Album Rock charts, while the album cuts "Warped" and "Aeroplane" were similarly successful. The band's schedule was severely disrupted, however, when Smith broke his wrist playing baseball. Even as they enjoyed another airplay hit with "Love Rollercoaster" (spun off the *Beavis and Butthead Do America* soundtrack), their fall US tour was cancelled, to be rescheduled for the new year, when it would kick off a well-received world tour.

Flea and Smith's Thermidor side project released their *Monkey on Rico* album that same spring, 1996; the following year, Flea joined Navarro in the oft-rumored Jane's Ad-

diction "relapse" reunion. Navarro, however, came off the road convinced that he never wanted to tour again; he quit the Peppers on April 3, 1998, although Spread, a side project he launched with Smith, would continue.

Navarro was replaced by the returning Frusciante, with the new lineup making its comeback at the Tibetan Freedom Concert on June 13, 1998. Work then began on the new album, 1999's *Californication*, followed by a prolonged bout of touring that included Woodstock 99, Britain's Reading Festival and Baltimore's HFStival. While they gigged, the single "Scar Tissue" established a new record stay at the top of *Billboard*'s Modern Rock Tracks chart. The band was also nominated for three Grammys.

### THE RED HOT CHILI PEPPERS COMPLETE DISCOGRAPHY
### SINGLES/US CHARTLOG
1984 Get Up and Dance/Baby Appeal (EMI America)
1985 Hollywood/Nevermind (EMI America)
1987 Fight Like a Brave/Fire (EMI Manhattan)
1988 Abbey Road EP (EMI Manhattan)
1990 Higher Ground/Millionaires Against Hunger (EMI Manhattan)
1991 Give It Away/Search and Destroy (WB—#73 pop)
1992 Under the Bridge/The Righteous and the Wicked (WB—#2 pop)
1992 Behind the Sun/Fire (EMI)
1993 Higher Ground/If You Want Me To Stay (EMI)
1993 Soul To Squeeze/Nobody Weird like Me (WB—#22 pop)
1999 Scar Tissue/? (WB—#9 pop)

### LPS
**8** **1984 Red Hot Chili Peppers (EMI America)**
They just wanna rap, blitz, yell and have fun. Nothing of tremendous consequence happens, but it's raucous, loud and completely uncontrollable. The funk-core revolution starts here.

**8** **1985 Freaky Styley (EMI America)**
More of the same, only less riotous. Producer George Clinton doesn't let things get too chaotic, and the band respond by matching the music to their attitude. Juvenile smut still rocks their boat, but at least they can laugh while they're leering.

**8** **1987 The Uplift Mofo Party Plan (EMI America—#148 pop)**
"Fight Like a Brave," "Party On Your Pussy" and then suddenly . . . a great song! Indeed, "Behind the Sun" so outclasses the rest of the album that the rest of the tracks probably beat it up later.

**9** **1989 Mother's Milk (EMI America—#52 pop)**
A faithful (albeit mach ten) rendition of "Higher Ground" is the undisputed classic, but "Taste the Pain" and the aptly named "Punk Rock Classic" help fire the Peppers' most

cohesive album yet . . . that's cohesive and genuinely listenable, by the way.

### 8 1991 Blood Sugar Sex Magik (WB—#3 pop)
Escape the interminable chainstore rap of "Give It Away" and the bleeding heart emotions of "Under the Bridge," and the Peppers strike surprising gold again. Producer Rubin reins in their last few stray weaknesses; it's PG party time from hereon in.

### 7 1995 One Hot Minute (WB—#4 pop)
After the chaos of the last few years, "Aeroplane" at least flies off in a reasonably hopeful direction. Sadly, the rest of the album struggles to catch up.

### 6 1999 Californication (WB—#3 pop)
The Peppers' continued slide into gameshow host sincerity is halted by the monster hit "Scar Tissue," but their peak days of danger seem a long way away now.

### SELECTED COMPILATIONS AND ARCHIVE RELEASES

### 7 1992 What Hits!? (EMI America—#22 pop)
Covering the band's pre-big time daze with all the expected chest-beaters, and little in the way of surprises. A helpful primer, but little else.

### 8 1994 Out in LA (EMI America—#82 pop)
A random collection of 12-inch remixes, occasional B-sides and the band's first ever demo, kinda Clash meet Clinton, and his name isn't Bill. Flea and Kiedis liner notes explain why.

### 7 1998 Under the Covers: Essential (Capitol)
Slick package wrapping up favorite covers—"Subterranean Homesick Blues," "Search Aand Destroy," "Fire"—caught live and otherwise. Two previously unreleased songs, "Dr. Funkenstein" and "Tiny Dancer," add to the weirdness.

### FURTHER READING
Red Hot Chili Peppers by Dave Thompson (St. Martin's Press, 1993)

## ROOGALATOR

**FORMED:** *1975, London, England*
**ORIGINAL LINEUP:** *Danny Adler (b. Cincinnati, OH—vcls, gtr), Paul Riley (bs), Nick Plytas (kybds), Dave Solomon (drms)*

A fixture on the Cincinnati club scene, guitarist Danny Adler cut his teeth working the same circuit as Dyke & the Blazers and Bootsy Collins' Pacesetters, frequently jamming with members of both bands. By 1971, however, he was based in the UK, a member of Smooth Loser, a group formed with fellow ex-pat Jeff Pasternak (bs) and Chris

Gibbons (gtr). After their breakup in 1972, Adler formed the first, very short-lived, incarnation of Roogalator.

Little came of it, and Adler moved into session work, highlighted by some monster jam sessions with drummer Ginger Baker's Nigerian group, Salt. He also spent time in Paris, studying jazz theory, then returned to London and suddenly things started moving. Linking with drummer Bobby Irwin, pianist Steve Beresford and keyboard player Nick Plytas, Adler recast Roogalator as an extraordinarily edgy funk-rock band, cut a demo and immediately began to attract interest. Neither Beresford nor Irwin wanted to take things any further, however, and with their first live shows now coming up fast, Adler and Plytas rebuilt.

Drummer Dave Solomon, a bandmate of both Plytas and Beresford in a Motown covers band, replaced Irwin; Irwin himself introduced Paul Riley, a member of pub scene heroes Chilli Willi & the Red Hot Peppers. He joined shortly before Roogalator's September 1975 debut and, within weeks, the UK music press was feting the group as the next big thing. One paper even described them as "the future of rock 'n' roll."

Neither was such applause simple hyperbole. At a time when British funk was still confined to the precise equations of Average White Band, Gonzalez *et al*, Roogalator played a jerky, minimalist funk that would, indeed, be absorbed by an entire future generation of local musicians. Like George Clinton five years before, and Prince five years hence, Roogalator isolated a funk that was utterly without precedent; unlike Clinton and Prince, however, they would not be around to reap the rewards of their foresight.

Roogalator's precipitous ride ended as suddenly as it began, with a disastrous showcase gig in London, opening for R&B mavens Dr. Feelgood. Drummer Solomon quit, to be replaced with the returning Irwin; Riley, too, departed, while his successor, Jeff Watts, lasted a matter of weeks. Irwin followed. Roogalator finally made their recorded debut in April with manager Robin Scott's brother Julian (bs) and Justin Hildreth (drms), cutting Adler's "Cincinnati Fatback" for the independent Stiff label.

A tumescent slab of triumphant fractured funk, namechecking the sights and sounds Adler grew up with "on the banks of the O-Hi-O," sales of "Cincinnati Fatback" were sufficient to prompt interest from Virgin Records. Roogalator, however, balked at the label's demands that they sign a publishing contract as well as a record deal, and after just one 1977 single, Plytas' "Love and the Single Girl," the band backed away.

But time was passing them by. Britain was in the throes of the punk rock explosion now; it would be another two years before dexterous funk returned to even the grassroots club scene. By the time manager Scott launched his own Do It label, and Roogalator cut their debut album in mid-1977, Adler simply wanted to get the old songs down on tape before moving on to something else.

When Nick Plytas quit, an era had clearly ended. As a trio, Roogalator toured on through 1978, cutting one more single ("Zero Hero") and demoing a second album. But further lineup changes rocked the group and, in July 1978, Roogalator came to the end of the line. Within twelve months, their praises were being played, if not overtly sung, by groups as far afield as Light of the World, the Gang of 4 and Spandau Ballet, spearheads of a Brit-funk movement, which Roogalator did not even know they were pioneering.

Striking out alone, Adler revived much of the projected second Roogalator album for his own solo debut, *The Danny Adler Story*. He subsequently worked with Rolling Stones drummer Charlie Watts' jazz band Rocket 88, reggae legend Niney the Observer, and James Brown drummer Tony Cook (1979's *Funky Afternoons*). He has also recorded a stream of extraordinarily eclectic albums over the past two decades.

### ROOGALATOR DISCOGRAPHY
#### LP
**6** **1977 Play It by Ear (Do It)**
Road-weariness and too many lineup changes squeezed much of the soul out of Roogalator long before they cut their first album. More pop than stylish, a mere ghost of their early audacity flaps through.

**8** **1998 Cincinnati Fatback (Proper—UK)**
Think Chuck Berry's "Promised Land" tied to Hendrix's "Star Spangled Banner," or Otis' "Dock of the Bay" if it was located on "Route 66." Think every thought you've ever dreamed when you're far away and homesick, then imagine what they'd sound like flooding out of a radio set halfway round the world. Congratulations: you've just heard "Cincinnati Fatback," a generous selection of the band's funkiest material, including demos and radio sessions.

## SHAKATAK
**FORMED:** *1980, London, England*
**ORIGINAL LINEUP:** *Keith Winter (gtr), George Anderson (bs), Bill Sharpe (kybds), Nigel Wright (kybds), Roger Odell (drms)*

A jazz-funk band launched from the same British underground scene as produced Level 42, Incognito and others,

Shakatak were widely perceived as simply a vehicle for keyboardist Bill Sharpe, all the more so after he united with new wave star Gary Numan in 1985. Yet Shakatak were also to rank among the most successful bands on that entire circuit, bursting into contention in summer 1980, with the club favorite "Steppin'," following with the UK Top 50 entry "Feels like the Right Time." Over the next two years, they constantly threatened a major breakthrough, and "Living in the UK," "Brazilian Dawn" and "Easier Said than Done" were all minor hits.

With Jill Saward taking lead vocals, Shakatak finally unleashed the expected monster in April 1982, with the cool "Nightbirds." It soared to #9 in Britain and gave the group their sole US success. A year later, "Dark Is the Night" returned them to the British Top 20, while "Down on the Street" brought them back again to #9 during summer 1984. A dynamic live album, recorded in London and Tokyo followed, before 1985 saw a collaboration with jazzman Al Jarreau, "Day by Day" (from the album of the same name).

The comparative over-excitability of Shakatak's early sound gave way, as the decade progressed, to a more sophisticated and increasingly straight jazz style. A clutch of instrumental albums released only in Japan indicated how little interest this change of direction received at home, although the success of 1987's "Mr. Manic and Sister Cool" single, from the *Manic and Cool* album, proved that Shakatak still had a UK audience.

Guitarist Winter quit shortly before work began on 1989's *Turn the Music Up* album; on the European tour, which followed, Shakatak played the first ever East Meets West concert in Berlin. They further proved their international appeal with consecutive Top 20 successes on the US Contemporary Jazz chart, with 1992's "Open Your Eyes" single topping the listing.

Gigging and recording regularly, Shakatak were now firmly ensconced within jazz territory, although they were still able to remember their roots, as they demonstrated with 1994's "Brazilian Love Affair" single, a cover of the George Duke classic. The band's lineup today remains Sharpe, Underwood, Odell and Saward.

### SHAKATAK DISCOGRAPHY
#### US CHARTLOG
1982 Night Birds/? (Polydor—#55 R&B/#202 pop)

#### LPS
**7** **1981 Drivin' Hard (Polydor)**
**8** **1982 Night Birds (Polydor)**

Great grooves to dance to, and some of Shakatak's finest material, including the now classic "Nightbirds" and "Easier Said than Done."

**7** 1982 Invitations (Polydor)

**5** 1983 Out of This World (Polydor)

Still pursuing the same wide-eyed "we're so happy" jazz-funk jamboree, with which they started, the razzle dazzle begins to wear a little thin.

**6** 1984 Down on the Street (Polydor)

**7** 1985 Shakatak Live (Polydor)

Live set covers all the hits, but also indicates that even if the records are impossibly slick, the show remains a non-stop party.

**7** 1986 Into the Blue (Polydor—Jap)

**6** 1987 Golden Wings (Polydor—Jap)

**6** 1988 Da Makani (Polydor—Jap)

A series of jazzy instrumental LPs released only in Japan. The sequence earned the band three consecutive Best Instrumental Album awards at the Japanese Phonograph Record Association awards.

**7** 1988 Manic & Cool (Polydor)

With a better sound than recent efforts, as though they've finally decided they want to play seriously, the band rips through a hefty jazz set with renewed energy.

**7** 1989 Nightflite (Polydor—Jap)

**8** 1989 Turn the Music Up (Polydor)

Introducing a heavier, edgier Shakatak . . . but retaining/reinvigorating all those endearing hooky bits that once consistently hit the charts.

**7** 1990 Perfect Smile (Polydor)

**7** 1991 Bitter Sweet (Polydor

Jazzy instrumentals and Latin-flavored breaks dominate, but be prepared for some updated hip-hop stylings as well.

**6** 1991 Open Your Eyes (Polydor)

**6** 1993 Street Level (Inside Out)

Fully absorbed within the acid jazz scene, more groovy funk and funky bass. How do they keep it up?

**6** 1993 Under the Sun (Inside Out)

**7** 1993 The Christmas Album (Inside Out)

**7** 1994 Full Circle (Inside Out)

**6** 1997 Let the Piano Play (Inside Out)

**7** 1998 Live at Ronnie Scotts (Indigo)

Excellent, smokey performance, but heaven help the '80s fan who wandered in off the street.

**6** 1998 Shinin' On (Instinct Jazz)

**7** 1999 View from the City (Inside Out)

**7** 1999 Magic (Instinct Jazz)

**6** 1999 Jazz in the Night (Inside Out)

### SELECTED COMPILATIONS AND ARCHIVE RELEASES

**8** 1988 Coolest Cuts (K-Tel)

Hits collection concentrates on the band's funkier material, but also includes some new material, together with some of those Japan-only cuts.

**7** 1988 The Very Best Of . . . (Polydor)

**6** 1991 The Remix Best Album (Polydor)

**6** 1996 Jazz Connections Series (Inside Out)

A collection of six compilations drawn from the Japanese albums.

## SKUNKHOUR

**FORMED (AS SKUNK):** *1991, Sydney, Australia*

**ORIGINAL LINEUP:** *Aya Larkin (vcls), Alan Blue (rap), Warwick Scott (gtr), Dean Sutherland (bs), Michael Sutherland (drms)*

Forming from the remains of a Sydney-based ska band led by the brothers Warwick and Dean Sutherland, Skunk launched onto Sydney's inner city nightclub circuit with a raw funk-rap hybrid that had few local precedents, but proved an immediate success regardless.

From the start, Skunk described their music as "controlled chaos," guitarist Warwick Scott insisting, "We have an audience that enjoys being challenged and that thrives on the excitement of stretching ourselves." However, he did admit to Australia's *Beat* magazine, "We did feel a bit out on a limb in terms of the mainstream sort of thing that was happening at the time."

Changing their name in tribute to poet Robert Lowell's *The Skunkhour*, the band replaced original rapper Alan Blue with vocalist Aya Larkin's brother Del (Blue relocated to Boston, MA, with Sound Unlimited), before embarking on a national tour with visiting UK acid jazz heroes Galliano in early 1993. The outting was followed by the release of the group's self-titled first album and the fall EP *Booty Full*.

Joined by keyboard player Paul Searles, Skunkhour signed with Mercury's Id offshoot and released two further EPs during 1994, *State* and *McSkunk*. After they switched to Epic for their sophomore album *Feed*, in April 1995, the UK Acid Jazz label then picked up the group's debut album for international distribution. The company also gave a European release to two further Australian EPs *Up to Our Necks* and *Sunstone*.

With strong European support, Skunkhour departed for their first overseas tours during 1996. Rapper Del Larkin quit following their return, but Skunkhour opted not to replace him, bringing the band back up to numerical strength with the addition of percussionist Chris Simmons. This powerful double percussive assault came to fruition during sessions at the Acid Jazz studios in London ("Foam," a highlight of their next album, *Chin Chin*, was recorded there).

Recorded with guest appearances from original Skunk rapper Blue and New Yorker Bubba, *Chin Chin* broke into the Australian Top 40, establishing Skunkhour among the leading attractions at the 1997 Equinox Festival. This activity preceded a two-year silence, during which time the band quit Epic for the newly formed Velvet label and linked with UK producer Steve James. The first fruits of this union, the "Home" single, appeared in October 1999. The group also contributed to the *Two Heads* movie soundtrack.

### SKUNKHOUR DISCOGRAPHY

#### LPs

**8** 1993 Skunkhour (Beast—Aus)
This stellar debut is a heady, intelligent urban funk brew, incorporating elements of rap, classic funk horns and bass with smooth soul. Released in the UK 1995 (Acid Jazz).

**7** 1995 Feed (Epic—Aus)

**7** 1997 Chin Chin (Epic—Aus)
Following much in the same vein as its predecessors, but without Del Larkin's raps, which actually opens things up far wider. Includes "Breathing Through My Eyes" and "Morning Rolls," plus the stunningly dirty "Weightlessness," which developed from a soundcheck jam in Germany.

## THE TIME

**FORMED:** *1981, Minneapolis, MN*
**ORIGINAL LINEUP:** *Morris Day (vcls), Jesse Johnson (gtr), Monte Moir (kybds), James "Jimmy Jam" Harris III (kybds), Terry Lewis (bs), Jellybean Johnson (drms)*

The Minneapolis music scene was small, but thriving in the late '70s and, under the tutelage of Prince, was about to become a cottage industry. Of the many bands created and deflated during this period, the Time were one of the few who succeeded in holding their own.

Dreamed up by Prince, the Time was initially conceived as a vehicle for singer Morris Day, after he contributed an uncredited track to Prince's *Dirty Mind* album in 1980. The pair had previously played together in the schoolboy band Grand Central, and once reunited in the studio, they quickly pulled a set together and recorded it. Other musi-

cians were then recruited from an earlier Prince project, Flyte Tyme, and the sextet was gigging within weeks.

Prince arranged a deal with Warner Brothers, and Time's eponymous debut album was released in 1981, to instant success. Three singles made the R&B charts, with the band gaining further national exposure as the opening act on Prince's *Controversy* tour that same year.

Favoring retro gangster chic, slicked up in vintage suits and fedoras, the Time made a visual statement that echoed perfectly their interpretation of funk—a bright, tight sound that always checked the mirror before it left the house. In concert, they were unbeatable, turning in sets so energetic that, when they toured with Prince, *he* took to beginning his own set with ballads, simply to calm the audience down.

The Time's second album, 1982's *What Time Is It?*, showcased the group's solid groove, honed during their live sets. Their next single, "777-9311," made #2 on the R&B charts and with a support slot opening for Prince's 1999 outing, the group proved themselves ready for their own headlining tour.

However, a bitter battle was about to commence. While there was no dispute that the Time was essentially a Prince side project, the band members were growing restless. Jimmy Jam and Terry Lewis, in particular, were keen to branch out, choosing to produce the SOS Band's latest album, even though the schedule conflicted with dates on the 1999 tour.

They pulled it off for a time, joining the SOS Band in Atlanta, and flying in and out for shows. One night, however, a snowstorm delayed their flight out, with inevitable results. They missed the gig, and Prince summarily dismissed them; the Time completed the tour with roadie Jerome Benton filling in. (Jam and Lewis continued as producers, founding their own Flyte Tyme Productions and producing Cheryl Lynn, Herb Alpert and New Edition among others. They also oversaw Janet Jackson's *Control*, *Rhythm Nation* and *Janet* albums.)

Returning to Minneapolis, the Time essentially sundered. Monte Moir and Jesse Johnson quit; the latter later returned when Day convened a new Time lineup featuring Benton, the Johnsons, Jerry Hubbard (bs) and Paul Peterson and Mark Cardeas (both kybds). The ensuing *Ice Cream Castle* album became the band's highest charting album yet (#3 R&B, #24 pop), undoubtedly aided by the inclusion of two of the songs, "Jungle Love" and "The Bird," in Prince's 1984 movie *Purple Rain*.

Unfortunately the relationship between Day and Prince soon broke down irreparably, and the singer departed in

1985, to pursue a solo career (in 1988, he reunited with Jam and Lewis, when they produced his "Fishnet"). The remaining Time members disbanded in 1985, leaving Prince with nothing but the name.

A reunion of the original Time lineup in 1990 produced the #1 "Jerk Out" (written by Prince under his Jamie Starr pseudonym) and an accompanying album *Pandemonium*. They also contributed to Prince's latest movie, the underrated *Graffiti Bridge*, before the members returned to their own respective careers.

## THE TIME DISCOGRAPHY
### US CHARTLOG
1981 Get It Up/After High School (WB—#6 R&B)
1981 Cool (Part 1)/(Part II) (WB—#7 R&B/#90 pop)
1982 Girl/The Stick (WB—#49 R&B)
1982 The Stick/Girl (WB)
1982 777–9311/Grace (WB—#2 R&B/#88 pop)
1982 The Walk/Onedayi'mgonnabesomebody (WB—#24 R&B/#104 pop)
1983 Gigolos Get Lonely Too/I Don't Wanna Leave You (WB—#77 R&B)
1984 Ice Cream Castles/Tricky (WB—#11 R&B/#106 pop)
1984 Jungle Love/Oh, Baby (WB—#6 R&B/#20 pop)
1985 The Bird/My Drawers (WB—#33 R&B/#36 pop)
1990 Jerk-Out/Mo' Jerk Out (Paisley Park—#1 R&B/#9 pop)
1990 Chocolate (Paisley Park—#44 R&B)

### LPS
**7** 1981 The Time (WB—#7 R&B/#50 pop)
**9** 1982 What Time Is It? (WB—#2 R&B/#26 pop)
A tight, balanced set gives a smooth ride between ballads and the effervescent funk grooves that the Time do so well. Don't miss out on "onedayi'mgonnabesomebody."
**8** 1984 Ice Cream Castle (WB—#3 R&B/#24 pop)
Fast-paced pop-funk, with the high kicking "Jungle Love" providing the perfect carpet for Morris Day's pimp walk.
**7** 1990 Pandemonium (Paisley Park—#9 R&B/#18 pop)
A triumphant return packed with all the humor, posturing and grooves that made the band a class act. Ferocious rock riffs abound, but the funk is still there, highlighted on "Jerk Out" and "Blondie."

### SELECTED SAMPLES
Gigolos Get Lonely Too — Snoop Doggy Dogg: D.O.G.'s Get Lonely 2 (1998)
777–9311 — 2Pac featuring Danny Boy: What'z Ya Phone # (1996)

## TROUBLE FUNK
**FORMED:** *1978, Washington, D.C.*
**ORIGINAL LINEUP:** *Robert Reed (vcls, gtr), Chester Davis (gtr), Tony Fisher (bs), James Avery (kybds), Emmett Nixon (sax), Dean Harris (sax), David Rudd (sax), Taylor Reed (trum), David Alonzo Robinson (drms), Timothy David (drms), Mack Carey (drms)*

Forming as Trouble in Washington, DC in 1978, with a three drummer lineup guaranteed to grab attention, they were one of the first bands to follow Chuck Brown onto what became the DC go-go scene, while it was still attempting to untangle itself from post Sugarhill hip-hop. Crashing crunching bass lines into half-rapped vocals, then stirring the pot with heavy funk renditions of rerun TV themes (*Andy Griffith*, *Pink Panther* and *The Munsters* were perennial favorites) and old funk classics, their local live shows were legendary before Trouble even cut their first single.

"E Flat Boogie" appeared on "Uncle" Maxx Kidd's Al & the Kidd label, with local sales alone sufficient to push it to the lower reaches of the R&B chart. (Kidd himself cowrote Chuck Brown's "Blow Your Whistle" and, during go-go's mid-'80s peak, was frequently singled out as one of its chief progenitors.)

Changing their name to Trouble Funk, their other early singles (all now compiled onto the *Early Singles* CD) were released on their own TF label and later, the scene-setting DETT, before the group signed to Sylvia Robinson's Sugar Hill label. In 1982 the group finally enjoyed their first major single with "Hey Fellas." The album *Drop the Bomb* followed it chartward, while back home in DC, DETT kept up the pressure with the single "Trouble Funk Express," a dramatic, and idiosyncratic reworking of Kraftwerk's "Trans-Europe Express."

In 1984, the double album *In Times of Trouble* brought go-go to its peak with a monstrous live bass jam. At their best, Trouble Funk could stretch single numbers over 30 minutes; on vinyl, one track was spread across two sides.

A move to Island Records should have seen the group follow through in style, when they were recruited (alongside Chuck Brown and EU) to the go-go heavy soundtrack of the Blaine Novak movie *Good To Go*. It was not to be; while two singles from the soundtrack, "Still Smokin'" and the title theme, made the lower reaches of the R&B chart, the movie itself bombed.

A new album, *Saturday Night: Live! from Washington, DC*, offered up another visceral onstage experience, and Trouble Funk remained on the road in the US and abroad constantly over the next two years. Between September 1986 and October 1987, they played three sold out theater shows in London alone, confirming go-go's importance to the UK. *Say What* was a Top 75 album in 1986; "Woman of Principle" became a minor hit during summer 1987.

However, an attempt to broaden the Trouble Funk sound into melodies rather than moods, was doomed to failure. Another UK hit, 1987's *Trouble Over Here* enjoyed contributions from both ends of the band's stylistic spectrum, Bootsy Collins and Kurtis Blow, but failed to take advantage of either. A less than inspired union with 2 Live Crew, "The Bomb Has Dropped," followed before Trouble Funk faded.

### TROUBLE FUNK
### US CHARTLOG

1980 E Flat Boogie/? (Al & The Kidd—#72 R&B)
1982 Hey Fellas/(remix) (Sugar Hill #63 R&B)
1983 Trouble Funk Express/(instrumental) (D.E.T.T. #77 R&B)
1985 Still Smokin'/(instrumental) (Island #80 R&B)
1986 Good To Go/? (Island #66 R&B)
1989 The Bomb Has Dropped/One and One (Luke Skyywalker #92 R&B)

### LPS

**9** 1982 Drop the Bomb (Sugar Hill—#38 R&B/#121 pop)
Hot debut from the kings of go-go features super tight jams that form the perfect backdrop for the band's verbal riffing. Includes the now classic "Drop the Bomb" and "Pump Me Up."

**8** 1983 In Times of Trouble (D.E.T.T.)

**8** 1985 Live (From Washington DC) (Island)
Excellent live set that showcases the group in their element. The LP exudes an aura of sweaty deep funk, cut with an outrageous energy that's almost as good as being there.

**4** 1987 Trouble over Here Trouble over There (Island)
Sadly soul-less plodding—the one Trouble Funk album that every used record store seems to have, and nobody wants to buy.

### SELECTED COMPILATIONS AND ARCHIVE RELEASES

**6** 1993 Party Classics Vol. 1 (Studio)

**7** 1995 Hittin' Hard Party Classics Vol. 2 (Liason)

**8** 1997 Early Singles (WB)
Must have collection of superb material that includes "Trouble Funk Express"—the band's rendering of the Kraftwerk classic.

**8** 1998 Droppin' Bombs: The Definitive Trouble Funk (Hurt)
Double CD set originally released on three LPS, this collection is packed with the band's best go-go and funk material. Includes "Drop the Bomb," "Freaky Situation," "Pump Me Up" and "I'm Chillin'."

### SELECTED SAMPLES

Good To Go — Beastie Boys: Shadrach (1989)
Grip It — DJ Jazzy Jeff & the Fresh Prince: Trapped on the Dance Floor (1991)

Let's Get Small — Coldcut: Say Kids, What Time Is It? (1987)
Pump Me Up — 2 Live Crew: Megamixx III (1989)
Pump Me Up — EPMD: Funky Piano (1991)
Pump Me Up — Lords of the Underground: What I'm After (1994)
Pump Me Up — M.A.R.R.S.: Pump Up the Volume (1987)
Pump Me Up — Run DMC: Not Just Another Groove (1990)

## 24–7 SPYZ

**FORMED:** *1988, New York, NY*
**ORIGINAL LINEUP:** *Peter Forest (vcls), Jimi Hazel (gtr, vcls), Rick Skatore (bs, vcls), Anthony Johnson (drms)*

Bronx boys all the way, 24–7 Spyz were prime exponents of the mid'80s thrash funk popularized on the West Coast by the Red Hot Chili Peppers and Primus, and on the East Coast by fellow New Yorkers Living Colour. 24–7 Spyz, however, took a harder edged and more low-key route, building a hip, underground fanbase.

With guitarist Jimi Hazel (his name, of course, combining those of his personal heroes, Jimi Hendrix and Eddie Hazel) firmly to the fore, 24–7 Spyz's debut album, 1988's *Harder than You*, was the cue for the group to launch what amounted to a two year US club tour, quickly becoming one of the bands to see.

They followed up with 1990's *Gumbo Millennium*, but even as their momentum continued to build, the lineup fell apart. Peter Forest and Anthony Johnson both quit; Jeff Brodnax and Joel Maitoza replaced them and, acting fast to trounce rumors that the band had, in fact, split, 24–7 Spyz released the EP, *This Is . . . 24–7 Spyz* in 1991.

The group's much-delayed third album, *Strength in Numbers* appeared the following year. And if the US was continuing to prove unreceptive, 24–7 Spyz were taking Europe and Asia by storm—particularly after founders Forest and Johnson returned, and new fans finally discovered for themselves what all the original excitement was about. *Temporarily Disconnected*, their aptly titled next album, was issued in 1995; 6 in 1996. Neither received a US release.

Following a period of late-'90s turmoil and further lineup changes, 24–7 Spyz' most recent release, 1997's *Heavy Metal Soul by the Pound*, was largely conceived by Hazel during the period prior to *Temporarily Disconnected*.

### 24–7 SPYZ DISCOGRAPHY
### LPS

**8** 1988 Harder than You (Relativity)
An excellent LP crash bang packed with a heady brew of rap, funk, rock and metal, all cocooning some fiercely political manifestos. Their amped up version of Kool & the Gang's staple "Jungle Boogie" is an especial treat.

**7** **1990 Gumbo Millennium (Relativity)**

Another solid effort, with just a little less punch than their debut. The social commentary still stands, especially on "Racism" and "We'll Have Power," although "Valdez 27 Million?" is pushing it a little. Another groovy mix of metalfunkajazzyreaggaerap.

**7** **1992 Strength in Numbers (East West)**

Still revolving around their trademark slab of heavy sound, but more cohesive than past efforts, Spyz throw in extra melody for good measure.

**6** **1995 Temporarily Disconnected (Enemy—UK)**

The reunion of the original lineup was a momentous event—the crew's return to the studio, less so. Satisfactory, but not overly inspired.

**5** **1996 6 (Enemy—UK)**

**8** **1996 Heavy Metal Soul by the Pound (What Are Records)**

An introspective, groove-ridden departure, simultaneously one of their best, and one of their most disconcerting.

## BERNIE WORRELL

**BORN:** *4/19/44, Long Branch, NJ*

Worrell was the archetypal musical child prodigy. He began playing piano at three, made his concert debut at four, composed his first concerto at eight, and entered adulthood as a graduate of both the New England Conservatory of Music and Julliard School of Music.

Having already played with a number of local bar bands (including Chubby and the Turnpikes, the future Tavares), Worrell linked with George Clinton and Funkadelic in 1968, shortly before the band recorded their sophomore *Free Your Mind and Your Ass Will Follow* album.

The journey from classical music to funk was not, he told *New Funk Times*, that great a musical leap, rather, "it was just an extension! I never moved from [classical], 'cause if you listen you can hear the influence in whatever I play. I thank God that I had the gift of being able to play more than one type of music . . . 'cause I have perfect pitch, and I can play almost any type of music. And I do the same thing with my music that I do with analog and digital: I mix music."

Worrell's first recording session with Funkadelic produced Rose Williams' "Whatever Make My Baby." Two years later, he scored a monster worldwide smash as pianist on Freda Payne's landmark "Band of Gold" single, following through with session work alongside Ruth Copeland, US, Flo, the Ba-Roz and Chairmen of the Board. The increasing workload of the Parliament/Funkadelic axis, however, curtailed his extracurricular activities over most of the

remainder of the '70s, as Worrell co-wrote and co-produced great swathes of the Parliafunkadelicament canon.

Worrell's greatest contribution to the legend was the keyboard bass sound, which he had recently mastered, that came to define funk into the late '70s. It appeared for the first time on "Flashlight," that oddly unexpected reinvention of dance music that lurked at the end of the *Funkentelechy vs. Tte Placebo Syndrome* album. And, even before Worrell himself had another opportunity to use the effect, it had surfaced in the repertoire of every dance band on the planet. Few, however, played it as well as Worrell.

In 1978, Worrell joined the parade of P-Funk regulars in cutting his first solo album, *All the Woo in the World*. It went nowhere, but Worrell would scratch a minor success in early 1979 with the maddening "Insurance Man for the Funk." The album itself was rushed. Worrell and co-producer Clinton were simultaneously working with the Horny Horns and Parlet, as well as overseeing Funkadelic's continued activities; Worrell subsequently admitted that he really didn't like the record.

Nevertheless, he made no attempt to lighten his workload, even after Parliament/Funkadelic broke up. He visited the UK for a string of gigs in 1981, and was instrumental in the formation of the Edinburgh based dance act The Chimes; members Mike Pedan and James Lockway met when they were recruited into Worrell's backing band.

Work with New York City new wave act Talking Heads, meanwhile, saw Worrell become heavily involved in solo projects by each of the band's core members: David Byrne, Jerry Harrison and the Tina Weymouth/Chris Frantz-led Tom Tom Club—a group, incidentally, that was formed at the suggestion of George Clinton.

Byrne later acknowledged Worrell's impact on the Talking Heads by describing him, simply, as "a genius"; Worrell responded by telling *New Funk Times*, "When they first called me and asked me if I would join them, I didn't even know who they were. So I went and observed one of their rehearsals and listened to some tapes in the studio, and saw that they work the same kinda way that P-Funk does. And I liked the vibes and the music, and I knew what David wanted to put that Black element in there, that funk element. I saw that it could work, and we took it to the top!"

Worrell continued genre-hopping, working with funk heavyweights Mtume, soul acts the Spinners and the O'Jays, rockers Jesse Rae and Fred Schneider (of the B-52s) and reggae legends Black Uhuru and the rhythm masters Sly Dunbar and Robbie Shakespeare. He was also an integral member of producer Bill Laswell's setup, and worked with such rock iconoclasts as Yoko Ono, John Lydon's Public Image Ltd. and Ginger Baker as well. Worrell was one of the first musicians invited to join Rolling Stones guitarist Keith Richards when he launched his solo career in 1987. His keyboards were a featured highlight of Richards' *Talk Is Cheap* solo debut in 1988, prompting the guitarist to later remark, "The rare qualities of intuition and taste—not to mention humor—all come together in Bernie Worrell."

In 1990, Worrell reunited with Bootsy Collins for a series of concerts; that same year, he released his second solo album, *Funk of Ages*, a guest star-studded affair that nevertheless did little. Then 1993 brought *Blacktronic Science*, featuring appearances from Clinton, Fred Wesley, Sly Dunbar, Maceo Parker and Bootsy, and included Clinton's "Dissinfordollars," an alleged reprise of the legendary unreleased P-Funk classic "Niggerish." In between times, Worrell busied himself with Laswell-led projects spread across the producer's Axiom Funk umbrella, including albums by Zillatron, Praxis, Buckethead, Bootsy Collins, the Last Poets and more.

1993 also saw Worrell join Paul Shafer in launching the CBS Orchestra for David Letterman's television series, while continuing to release idiosyncratic solo albums. The keyboardist was inducted (as one of the key members and Musical Director of P-Funk) into the Rock & Roll Hall of Fame on May 6, 1997. Two years later, he and Clinton reunited at Woodstock 99, with Worrell billed as a "special guest" of Clinton's P-Funk All Stars. The pair also toured together in July 2000.

## BERNIE WORRELL DISCOGRAPHY
### SINGLES
1978 Woo Together/Much Thrust (Arista)
1979 Insurance Man for the Funk (part one)/(part two) (Arista—#92 R&B)
1990 BW Jam (club mix)/LP version (Gramavision)
1990 Dub of Doom (Death from Above)/(radio edit) (Gramavision)

### LPs
**6 1978 All the Woo in the World (Arista)**
Co-produced and co-written (six out of seven tracks) with George Clinton, *Woo* opens with a slab of orchestral funk and a duet between Worrell and Junie Morrison, "Woo Together." Morrison takes solo vocals on "I'll Be with You," but elsewhere it's very much Worrell's show, albeit one that is considerably more individual than the usual P-Funk spinoff (and maybe, just a little bit more boring).

**7 1990 Funk of Ages (Gramavision)**
Uniting members P-Funk family with a smattering of the artists Worrell had worked with in the '80s, this likeable, if

eccentric set, is highlighted by the single "BW Jam," the funkiest (if synth-heavy) cut on the album. Elsewhere, reggae and rock take center stage. Keith Richard's appearance on the nearly dubby "Y- Style" is well worth investigation, while a cover of the oldie "Ain't She Sweet" and a reworking of Funkadelic's "At Mos' Spheres" prove Worrell's sense of humor is never far from the surface.

**9 1993 Blacktronic Science (Rhino)**
With Bill Laswell at the helm, Worrell's most successful solo album might be the best post P-Funk album of them all, a devastating hybrid of styles that maintains a funk backing while exploring rap (via contributions from Mike G. and James Sumbi), jazz and the classical undercurrents, which always mark Worrell's most confident work. Elsewhere, ghosts a-plenty chuckle over the hooks and choruses. A masterpiece.

**6 1994 The Other Side**
Recorded with Pieces of Woo (a floating conglomerate that sees Fred Wesley and Bill Laswell, at least, return), *The Other Side* slides off the funk radar altogether as Worrell gets into some heavy ambient territory, then blasts his bass lines and horns straight through it.

**7 1996 Free Agent: A Spaced Odyssey (Woo Music Inc)**
**7 1998 Bernie Worrell & the WOO Warriors Live (Woo Music Inc)**

## ZAPP
**FORMED:** 1978, Dayton, OH
**ORIGINAL LINEUP:** *Roger Troutman (b.11/29/51 d.4/25/99—vcls, gtr), Zapp Troutman (b. Tony Troutman—bs), Lester Troutman (drms), Larry Troutman (d. 4/25/99—perc)*

Beginning in their mid-teens, the four Troutman brothers led a series of high school bands, including Roger & the Veils and Roger & the Human Body, with the latter earning sufficient local, Dayton, acclaim to merit a self-released debut album, *Roger & the Human Body: Introducing Roger*. Vocalist Roger Troutman's solo ambitions were always apparent, although it was bassist Tony (aka Zapp) who was the first to enjoy any success, when his solo single "I Truly Love You" cracked the R&B Top 100 in mid-1975.

Forever experimenting with sound and technology, Roger & the Human Body adopted Zapp's nickname for their own in 1977, around the same time as Roger mastered the vocoder. Gigging constantly, to increasingly impressed audiences, Zapp were finally "discovered" by Bootsy Collins' brother Phelps (Catfish). The Collins were, in fact, long-time friends of the Troutmans. Phelps brought Bootsy down to see the group play; Bootsy in turn invited Roger to Detroit to record at P-Funk's studio base.

Roger appeared on Funkadelic's *Electric Spanking of War Babies* album, while also recording a clutch of his own songs, including the classic "More Bounce to the Ounce." Impressed, George Clinton encouraged him to offer the song to Warner Brothers, using the Zapp band name. The label took the bait and, with Bootsy producing, Zapp—the Troutman brothers, plus Bootsy, keyboardist Greg Jackson and sax player Carl Cowen—began work on the band's debut album.

With "More Bounce to the Ounce" a summertime smash, *Zapp* hit the streets in the fall of 1980. It slammed into both the R&B and pop charts with a sound that was both fully electronic, but also solidly earthy—a dichotomy of style that placed Zapp firmly at the forefront of the still-infant techno-funk movement.

Immediately, Roger began work on a solo album, the aptly titled *The Many Facets of Roger*. Again both his brothers and his favorite electronic tricks accompanied him into the studio, but while the album was a musical success, it ignited a chain reaction that ultimately helped bring down the P-Funk empire. Though the album was financed by Clinton's Uncle Jam label, through CBS, Roger then turned around and sold it to Warner Brothers, negotiating a solo deal separate to Zapp's contract.

It was a duplicitous deed. Quoted in *George Clinton: For the Record*, Roger himself shrugged it off with a flippant ". . . heck gee-willickers, Warner Bros offered me mo' money." But Clinton, in the same book, was furious. "We cut the album. . . . CBS paid for it, I paid for it. I don't like to go into it on the negative side, but it cost about $5 million and a lot of people's jobs and what we consider as the empire falling."

*The Many Facets of Roger* was a monster hit, topping the R&B chart and unleashing a near definitive interpretation of "I Heard It Through the Grapevine," also an R&B chart-topper. However, rather than follow up immediately, Roger reconvened Zapp for their sophomore album, *Zapp II*. Backed with an ever growing retinue of musicians, including Sherman Fleetwood, Jerome Derrickson and Eddie Barber, this set easily proved the equal of its predecessor, along with several attendant hit singles including the massive "Dance Floor," a #1 that summer. (Tony also enjoyed a second hit that year, "Your Man Is Home Tonight.")

Though it reached the Top Ten, and spun off the hit "I Can Make You Dance," Zapp's third album, *Zapp III*, became their first not to go gold. *New Zapp IV U* (1985),

however, placed the band back on course, but the hit ballad "Computer Love" was to spell the group's last success for four years, as Roger turned his attention toward his own studio, Troutman Sound Systems.

There he worked on his own material, cutting another solo album, 1984's Top Ten *The Saga Continues*, and producing sessions for singer Toledo, gospel vocalist Shirley Murdock and the Ohio Players' Leroy "Sugarfoot" Bonner. He reformed the Human Body for a pair of albums, before 1987 brought the audacious *Unlimited*, featuring a Roger-ized version of James Brown's "Papa's Got a Brand New Bag," and another R&B chart-topper, "I Want To Be Your Man." Roger also linked with English soul disciples Scritti Politti for the single "Boom! There She Was."

Zapp were back in 1989 with *Zapp V*, which surprisingly struggled to crack the R&B Top 40; Roger promptly returned to his own career, cutting 1991's *Bridging the Gap* album. But as the '90s continued, his attention again turned toward production. When Warners approached him about a Zapp compilation album, Roger pieced together a new single, "Mega Medley," from both band and solo performances. He also created a new version of "Computer Love," featuring Charlie Wilson and Shirley Murdock; both became hits during 1993–94.

A collaboration with rappers 2Pac and Dr. Dre followed; "California Love" was nominated for a Grammy for Best Rap Song by a Duo or Group in 1996. That same year, Roger also became involved with Curtis Mayfield (the *New World Order* album), Snoop Doggy Dogg (*Doggfather*), H-Town (*Ladies Edition*) and Keith Sweat (*Get Up on It*), and contributed music to the 1996 film *A Thin Line Between Love and Hate*. A new Zapp single, covering Stevie Wonder's "Living for the City," charted in early 1997, while Roger enjoyed further hits alongside Johnny Gill, Nu Flavor and Nastyboy Click.

On April 25, 1999, Roger was shot several times outside his studio. He died in surgery. Brother Larry's body was discovered in a car several blocks away, killed by a single, self-inflicted gunshot wound to the head. A gun on the seat next to him had been used in both shootings. The coroner and police ruled the deaths a murder-suicide. Since the demise of Zapp, Larry had been heading a family-run housing company, Troutman Enterprises, that had just declared Chapter 11, with a delinquent tax bill of $400,000. Serious depression set in, opening the door for the tragedy.

Roger's death sent shockwaves through the R&B community. More than two years later, Internet sites are still appearing, dedicated to his memory; at the time, they were an epidemic. Within weeks of the tragedy, too, a hastily reactivated "Computer Love" single was entering the Top 100, while two of Roger's recent solo recordings, "Nuthin' but a Party" and "Party Time," were placed on Rhino's *United We Funk* compilation that autumn.

## ZAPP DISCOGRAPHY
### US CHARTLOG
#### ZAPP

1980 More Bounce to the Ounce (Part I)/(Part II) (WB—#2 R&B/#86 pop)

1980 Be Alright (Part I)/(Part II) (WB—#26 R&B)

1982 Dance Floor (Part I)/(Part II) (WB—#1 R&B/#101 pop)

1982 Doo Wa Ditty (Blow That Thing)/Come On (WB—#10 R&B/#103 pop)

1983 I Can Make You Dance (Part I)/(Part II) (WB—#4 R&B/#102 pop)

1983 Heartbreaker (Part I)/(Part II) (WB—#15 R&B/#107 pop)

1984 Spend My Whole Life/Play Some Blues (WB—#77 R&B)

1985 It Doesn't Really Matter/Make Me Feel Good (WB—#41 R&B)

1986 Computer Love (Part I)/(Part II) (WB—#8 R&B)

1986 Itchin' for Your Twitchin'/(long) (WB—#81 R&B)

1989 Ooh Baby Baby/(instrumental) (Reprise—#18 R&B)

#### ROGER

1981 I Heard It Through the Grapevine (part one)/(part two) (WB—#1 R&B/#79 pop)

1981 Do It Roger/Blue (WB—#24 R&B)

1984 In the Mix/Bucket of Blood (WB—#10 R&B)

1987 I Want To Be Your Man/I Really Want To Be Your Man (Reprise—#1 R&B/#3 pop)

1988 Thrill Seekers/Composition To Commemorate (Reprise—#27 R&B)

1991 (Everybody) Get Up/A Chunk of Sugar (Reprise—#19 R&B)

1992 Take Me Back/Who-La-Boola (Reprise—#37 R&B)

#### ROGER/THE MIGHTY CLOUDS OF JOY

1984 Midnight Hour (part one)/(part two) (WB—#34 R&B)

#### ROGER/SHIRLEY MURDOCK

1985 Girl, Cut It Out/So Ruff, So Tuff (WB—#79 R&B)

#### ROGER/SCRITTI POLITTI

1988 Boom! There She Was/A World Come Back To Life (WB—#94 R&B/#53 pop)

#### ZAPP & ROGER

1993 Mega Medley/I Want To Be Your Man (Reprise—#30 R&B/#54 pop)

1993 Slow and Easy/A Chunk of Sugar (Reprise—#18 R&B/#43 pop)

1994 Computer Love/Slow and Easy (Reprise—#65 R&B/#108 pop)

1996 Living for the City/(instrumental) (Reprise—#57 R&B/#120 pop)

1999 Computer Love/Slow and Easy (Reprise—#88 R&B)

#### ROGER/2PAC/DR DRE

1996 How Do U Want It (Death Row—#1 R&B)/California Love (#6 pop)

#### ROGER/JOHNNY GILL

1996 It's Your Body/(instrumental) (Motown—#19 R&B/#43 pop)

#### ROGER/NU FLAVOR

1997 Sweet Sexy Thing/(mixes) (Reprise—#93 R&B/#69 pop)

#### ROGER/NASTYBOY KLICK

1997 Down for Yours/Lost in Love (Mercury—#58 R&B/#69 pop)

### LPS
#### ZAPP

**9** 1980 Zapp (WB—#1 R&B/#19 pop)

From "More Bounce to the Ounce" to its companion "Funky Bounce" and onto the excellent "Freedom," Zapp's vocoder is at full crank and the funk is furious. A smashing debut!

**8** 1982 Zapp II (WB—#2 R&B/#25 pop)

Another strong set. The eleven minute-plus "Dance Floor" bleeds perfectly into "Playin' Kind of Rough," while "Come On" lets the horns soar.

**7** 1983 Zapp III (WB—#9 R&B/#39 pop)

With a reprise of *Zapp II*'s "Doo Wah Ditty (Blow That Thing)," added for filler, this set sags in the face of Zapp's stellar success.

**5** 1984 The New Zapp IV U (WB—#8 R&B/#110 pop)

Too gimmicky for its own good, this LP relies heavily on electronic manipulations in place of solid grooves. But it does include an odd cover of "I Only Have Eyes for You," and that's certainly worth experiencing.

**5** 1989 Zapp V (Reprise—#34 R&B/#154 pop)

#### ROGER

**10** 1981 The Many Facets of Roger (WB—#1 R&B/#26 pop)

"Grapevine" is amazing, proof that no song can ever truly be said to be finished with; the remainder of the album is equally inventive, with "Maxx Axe" offering some warped guitar madness to mix with the beats.

**7** 1984 The Saga Continues (WB—#13 R&B/#64 pop)

Less inspired, but don't pass it by.

**6** 1987 Unlimited! (Reprise—#4 R&B/#35 pop)

A little too slick, as Roger settles into his self-appointed role as guardian of the smooth groove, but doesn't seem to have noticed that the talkbox sounds so dated these days.

**4** 1991 Bridging the Gap (Reprise—#45 R&B)

Ooh, mid-tempo, maudlin, and indistinguishable from a thousand other early-'90s R&B smoothies, except they finally dropped the vocoder.

### SELECTED COMPILATIONS AND ARCHIVE RELEASES

**8** 1993 All the Greatest Hits (WB—#9 R&B/#39 pop)

Credited to Zapp and Roger, a nice collection scoops up all the hits, including a live version of "Midnight Hour."

Zapp and Roger again, a great collection picking up the less obvious material.

## SELECTED SAMPLES

Be Alright — Big Daddy Kane: Prince of Darkness (1991)

Be Alright — Keith Murray: Danger (1994)

Be Alright — Poor Righteous Teachers: Shakyila (1990)

Be Alright — South Central Cartel: U Gotta Deal Wit Dis (Gangsta Luv) (1991)

Be Alright — 2Pac: Keep ya Head Up (1998)

Be Alright — Yo-Yo: So Funky (1992)

Coming Home — Professor Griff & the Last Asiatic Disciples: Jail Sale (1991)

Computer Love — Bloods & Crips: Piru Love (1993)

Computer Love — Digital Underground: Digital Lover (1993)

Computer Love — Jodeci: What About Us (1994)

Computer Love — MOP: To the Death (1994)

Computer Love — Notorious BIG: Me & My Bitch (1994)

Computer Love — Redman: Blow Your Mind (1992)

Computer Love — 2Pac: I Get Around (1993)

Computer Love — 2Pac: Temptations (1995)

Computer Love — 2Pac, featuring Jewell, Dramacydall & Storm: Thug Passion (1996)

Computer Love — Zapp, featuring Roger: Slow and Easy (1993)

Dance Floor — Beastie Boys: Hey Ladies (1989)

Dance Floor — Compton's Most Wanted: I Don't Dance (1991)

Dance Floor — EPMD: You Gots To Chill (1988)

Dance Floor — Fu-Shnickens: Breakdown (1994)

Dance Floor — Keith Murray: Danger (1994)

Dance Floor — Redman: Blow Your Mind (1992)

Dance Floor — Threat: Sucka Free (1993)

Dance Floor — Armand Van Helden: Ultrafunkula (1993)

Doo Wa Ditty — Compton's Most Wanted: Hit the Floor (1992)

Doo Wa Ditty — Everlast: Never Missin' a Beat (1990)

Doo Wa Ditty — Kid Sensation: Seatown Ballers (1990)

Heartbreaker — Blacstreet: Booti Call (1994)

Heartbreaker — Fu-Schnickens: Breakdown (1994)

Heartbreaker — Heavy D: Take Your Time (1994)

Heartbreaker — KAM: Neva Again (1993)

Heartbreaker — Threat: Ass Out (1993)

I Can Make You Dance — Compton's Most Wanted: I Don't Dance (1991)

I Can Make You Dance — Das EFX: Brooklyn to T-Neck (1992)

I Can Make You Dance — Erick Sermon: The Ill Shit (1993)

I Can Make You Dance — Redman: Blow Your Mind (1992)

I Can Make You Dance — 2Pac: I Get Around (1993)

More Bounce to the Ounce — A Lighter Shade of Brown: Bouncin' (1992)

More Bounce to the Ounce — Above the Law: Return of the Real Shit (1994)

More Bounce to the Ounce — Bloods & Crips: Shuda Beena B-Dog (1993)

More Bounce to the Ounce — Boss: Comin' To Getcha (1993)

More Bounce to the Ounce — Compton's Most Wanted: Growin' Up in the Hood (remix) (1991)

More Bounce to the Ounce — Compton's Most Wanteda: Hit the Floor (1992)

More Bounce to the Ounce — Coolio: County Line (1994)

More Bounce to the Ounce — Daddy O: Brooklyn Bounce (1993)

More Bounce to the Ounce — DJ Quik: Way 2 Fonky (1992)

More Bounce to the Ounce — Digital Underground: Shake & Bake (1993)

More Bounce to the Ounce — Digital Underground: Sons of the P (1991)

More Bounce to the Ounce — EPMD: You Gots To Chill (1988)

More Bounce to the Ounce — Heavy D: More Bounce (1989)

More Bounce to the Ounce — Ice Cube: Jackin for Beats (1991)

More Bounce to the Ounce — Ice Cube: Look Who's Burnin' (1991)

More Bounce to the Ounce — Ice Cube: What Can I Do? (remix) (1993)

More Bounce to the Ounce — Kriss Kross: It's a Shame (1992)

More Bounce to the Ounce — Low Profile: Pay Ya Dues (1990)

More Bounce to the Ounce — Masta Ace Incorporated: Slaughtahouse (1993)

More Bounce to the Ounce — Notorious BIG: Going Back to Cali (1997)

More Bounce to the Ounce — Paperboy: The Nine Yards (1993)

More Bounce to the Ounce — Professor X: What's Up G? (1991)

More Bounce to the Ounce — Professor X: Close to the Crackhouse (1993)

More Bounce to the Ounce — Public Enemy: Anti-Nigger Machine (1990)

More Bounce to the Ounce — Redman: So Ruff (1992)

More Bounce to the Ounce — Shoop Doggy Dogg: Snoop Bounce (1996)

More Bounce to the Ounce — Threat: 24–7 (1993)

More Bounce to the Ounce — Threat: The Dogs Are Loose (1993)

More Bounce to the Ounce — Wu-Tang Clan: Method man (1993)

More Bounce to the Ounce — X-CLan: Heed the Words of a Brother (1990)

More Bounce to the Ounce — X-Clan: Xodus (1992)

Playin Kinda Ruff — Redman: Time 4 Sum Aksion (1992)

# P-FUNK MEETS THE F-PUNK

For all its later descent into cliche and uniformity, the punk rock movement, which battered the British music scene into submission during 1976–77, was a remarkably egalitarian beast. Performers like Elvis Costello, Sting and Bob Geldof, in modern times so broadly spread across the mainstream musical landscape, all fell as unquestioningly beneath punk's banner as the artists whose names remain locked within that primitive world of safety pins, spit and a barrage of noise: Sid Vicious, Johnny Rotten, Rat Scabies.

There were no barriers. Reggae bands slipped as comfortably into the punk ethic as guitar groups. Jazzman Don Cherry gigged with the noise auteur Slits; and the electronic minimalism of Germany's Kraftwerk encouraged young punks everywhere to invest in synthesizers. Self-appointed punk historian Jon Savage later (*England's Dreaming*, 1992) condemned that, "in denying Black musical forms, punk had got into trouble" and, from the isolated roost from whence he wrote, that might have seemed the case. At ground zero, however, it was a different story entirely.

Roogalator's twisted Amplification of frontman Danny Adler's Cincinatti funk chops notwithstanding, Paul Weller's Jam cut their live teeth on Motown covers, traveling from "Back in My Arms Again" to "War," then throwing Curtis Mayfield's "Move On Up" into the brew as well. The Clash pulled off a remarkably authentic reworking of Booker T's "Time Is Tight," alongside their journeys into dub. The first two singles by Liverpool new wave band Teardrop Explodes were, in band leader Julian Cope's words, "on-the-One precisely."

And no sooner had Johnny Rotten walked out of the Sex Pistols in January 1978, than he was scheming a new band more in tune with his private musical preferences. Public Image Ltd. would never give themselves wholly over to any single style, but the menage in which their best music was made, equal parts funk, dub, jam and jagged experimentation, was unequivocally touched by each all the same.

The yowling defiance of "Public Image," the band's debut (late 1978) single; the apocalyptic "Death Disco"; the unyielding "Fodderstompf"; all were naked slabs of industrial funk, seismic bass lines that carved primeval grooves into the dancefloor. Whether through cosmic symbiosis or simply copycat fervor, it suddenly emerged that Lydon and his bandmates were not the only post-punk pioneers thinking along those lines.

"The name 'James Brown' was whispered," quipped Savage, but in truth it was being shouted, from the northern city of Leeds, where agit-punk art students Gang of 4 were to be found driving out their own brittle, grooving fractures, to the western port of Bristol, where the Pop Group formed around vocalist Mark Stewart's insistence that "punk [had become] a new kind of orthodoxy, and we wanted to experiment" to the new, hip clubs around London, where Light of the World were fusing a ragged approximation of "classic" funk with the electronic disciplines of the synthesizer scene.

Stewart continues, "When I was 14, 15, we were buying New York Dolls albums, but I was also buying really heavy dub, and I was going to Black clubs in Bristol from the age of 12. With the Pop Group, from the word go, I wanted to play funk, really, really heavy funk. I also wanted a funk producer, but [we couldn't get one] so we got in the best English reggae producer, Dennis Bovell." Following in PIL's footsteps (and, before them, early-'70s pioneers Cymande), the ensuing hybrid cut its funk basics with dub techniques. Uniquely, however, the Pop Group then used that basis as a launching pad for further wild experimentation, and two albums that would inform producers as far apart as Bill Laswell and Adrian Sherwood, musicians as disparate as Al Jourgensen and Afrika Bambaataa.

"We couldn't play," Stewart admits. "We were 16-year-old kids, friends from the youth club, mates from school, coming out of punk. We could only play three chords, and we were trying to play funk. Editors from the *New Musical Express* kept coming to the concerts and saying we were like Captain Beefheart. But we never heard of Captain Beefheart! The only reason why we sounded like that is, we couldn't play. In fact, it was quite unlistenable, but amid what was going on at the time, it broke a lot of barriers."

The first time the Pop Group played London . . . the first few times, in fact, the audience was so appalled that the band performed beneath a barrage of cans and abuse. Only slowly did they attract a following that even pretended to enjoy their music (it was a mark of true avant-garde individuality to profess to be a fan); and even more slowly dawned the realization that beneath the cacophony, there really was something worthy going down. Indeed, it took the emergence of the considerably more conventional Gang of 4 as critical darlings in early 1979, to allow many ears to focus on the

Pop Group's convolutions, an event that the Pop Group themselves facilitated by inviting the Gang to open one of their London shows.

Gang of 4 guitarist Andy Gill, reflecting on the band for their *100 Flowers Bloom* box set, explained, "What is special about the Gang of 4 is that they're funky. Most [other] bands weren't." Like PIL and the Pop Group, dub played a major part in the members' musical education; unlike those outfits, however, Gang of 4 did not allow the intruder to obscure their other virtues. "Dub . . . is all about space and things disappearing and coming back. Something's there and then it isn't." The dance music of the future, as he pointed out, would understand that principle fully. In 1978–79, however, it presented an entirely new frontier.

If the Pop Group emerged one of the first genuinely innovative funk bands in British musical history; the Gang of 4 proved one of the most respected. Politically outspoken, musically accessible and commercially successful, Gang of 4 combined the post-punk fascination for kinetic tension with an inherently earthy danceability, angular and stuttering across their *Entertainment* debut album, deep, dark and deliberate across their *Solid Gold* sophomore set.

*Solid Gold* was produced by Jimmy Douglass, best known for his work with Slave; Gang of 4 vocalist Jon King pinpointed his contributions when he remarked in a contemporary interview, "The songs have more feeling in them. We've been too dry before." The arrival of Busta Jones, replacing founder bassist Dave Allen, amplified the band's grasp of the funk experience. Previously instrumental in New York new wavers Talking Heads' own forays into funky territory, Jones imbibed the Gang of 4 with a visceral punch, which would long outlive his own tenure with the group. (He quit to be replaced by Sara Lee before the band's next album.)

"I Love a Man in Uniform," excerpted from 1982's *Songs of the Free* album, gave Gang of 4 their biggest US regional hit, a warmly welcomed second cousin to the electronic dance funk of urban New York. Such success, however, was to spell the end of the band. First drummer Hugo Burnham was dismissed; then, one disappointing album (1984's *Hard*) later, the group itself broke up, with Gill moving into production and discovering—to his own apparent horror—that he was never going to escape the shadow of Gang of 4's legacy.

Newly signed to EMI, the Red Hot Chili Peppers were an unknown Los Angeles funk-rap fusion band with a serious Gang of 4 fixation. Like them, bassist Flea explained, the Peppers' entire trip was based around "being punk rock about funk," and he later told Dave Allen that the first two Gang of 4 albums taught him everything he knew about bass playing. But when he asked Gill about those same records, Flea recalled, "He said he didn't know what he was doing . . . which was disheartening."

The experience went downhill from that revelation. Flea continued, "[We were making] our first record and . . . we weren't about to compromise our sound, which was based on organic bass and drums." Gill, however, folded that exuberance in upon itself, turning in an album that said as much about his own opinions on the state of modern dance music, as it did for the Peppers' own naked attack. "Maybe," Flea reasoned, once the initial disappointment had worn off, "he was too English for us," and, in all fairness to Gill, maybe he was.

For all Gang of 4's American experience—they toured several times, on either side of "Uniform"'s breakthrough—they were nevertheless informed by their homeland's musical upbringing, a land where media coverage of even frontline American funk was confined to the pages of *Black Echoes* magazine, and the only bands you saw on TV were those who made it onto *Top of the Pops*, a half-hour weekly digest of the latest chart hits.

James Brown visited Britain on a semi-regular basis, but Parliament/Funkadelic didn't make it over until 1978, at a time when their high glam-jam reputation was so out-of-step with the mainstream music media's punk-enhanced obsessions that anything even approaching fair coverage was unlikely from the outset. Even as P-Funk's "One Nation Under a Groove" rose into the Top Ten that fall (their first-ever UK hit), funk existed in the shadows, the bad-tempered stepfather of the dreaded disco and so uncool it was literally frozen out of contention. That was why bands like Public Image, the Pop Group and the Gang of 4 made such an impression when they first emerged, proof positive, in a way, that funk could be punk. But even that discovery came replete with pitfalls, the most glaring being, everybody took funk so damned seriously.

Prior to the post-punk explosion, funk was the prized preserve of pop musicologists, people who had long since memorized all of James Brown's King label catalog numbers, and had devised in their own minds generic ground rules so severe, that even the slightest deviation begged instant condemnation.

Now, bands were breaking through for whom those rules and those catalog numbers meant nothing. Andy Gill explained, "[We never] consciously sat down and listened to James Brown, it was really a much deeper assimilation." But that assimilation was weighted, nevertheless, by the need to be seen to be "saying" something worthwhile. George Clinton might, if he'd felt like it, have been able to cover the Gang of 4's "Anthrax." But Gang of 4 could never have tackled Funkadelic's "Flashlight." And when Andy Gill went to work with the Peppers, he found himself surrounded by people who liked "Flashlight."

The essential po-facedness, which marked out British funk rarely cracked. Heatwave, through the end of the decade the country's most visible "traditional" funk band, had long since been dismissed as just another variation on the disco theme. Light of the World had respect, but approached their art with an aloofness that casual listeners found more akin to higher math than R&B. And even amid the London clubs, where lighter spirits simply danced to the classics, the DJ was as likely to spin an underground electro-punk art project as a loose-limbed mover by War or Brass Construction.

Such an environment could not help but prove self-perpetuating. Linx, emergent in mid-1980 with the brittle "You're Lying," were as much a product of this seriousness as synthesized pomp rockers Ultravox. Light of the World spin-offs Beggar and Co. and Incognito were barely less po-faced than Gary Numan or Visage. So when Spandau Ballet and Freeez emerged from the London club circuit, which centered around such portentously named dives as Le Beate Route, the Cabaret Futura and the Club for Heroes (whose regulars, equally portentously, were known to the media as the Cult with No Name), their arrogant stance and art critic ethics were not only expected, they were taken for granted.

Beneath that facade, however, other musical notions were germinating, a realization not only that funk represented the most potent antidote to the facile disco music of the day, but also an acknowledgement of the remarkably well-drawn parallels between the outlaw mentalities that fired both funk and punk.

Freeez would be first to break through with this connection in mind, and the first to make any commercial headway, scoring with the self-released "Keep in Touch" in June 1980. It would be early 1981, however, before their second hit, by which time Spandau Ballet had utterly eclipsed them. Them and every other band on the scene at the time.

Spandau Ballet started life, as guitarist Gary Kemp put it, as five "flash geezers who liked having their picture taken and wearing clothes to be looked at." Forming a band simply gave them more opportunities for both and, over the first months of the group's existence, Spandau deliberately staged shows at the most attention-grabbing venues they could find: aboard the floating HMS *Belfast* naval museum, at singer Toyal Wilcox's Mayhem Studio in Battersea, at the Botanical Gardens in Birmingham.

It was once they got onstage that the preconceptions took a dive, as Spandau leaped headfirst into a heavy funk groove that the *New Musical Express*, in March 1980,—still safe amid those days before the phrase had any other meaning—unhesitatingly described as "soaring Gothic dance that conjures up everything except rock 'n' roll." Concocting solid dance themes lashed into place with the bass sound from hell, Spandau then threw horns (courtesy of the moonlighting Beggar and Co.) into the brew, fashioning a hybrid of almost breathtaking audacity, a European dance with an American soul.

Spandau Ballet made the UK chart with their first single ("To Cut a Long Story Short," in November 1980); consolidated their position with their second and third (the pounding homage "The Freeze" and the slowed-down sinister "Musclebound"); and breathlessly peaked with their fourth, the insistently horn- driven demi-rap "Chant Number One." Then, abruptly, they switched direction, never to aspire to such heights again. But those four singles, spread over the course of one year, represented more than a scintillating starburst of unbridled brilliance. They also unlocked a door in the English musical mind, which many people had not even suspected existed, the realization that funk, homegrown funk, could be fun.

The breakthrough was immediate. Level 42, Imagination, Second Image and more rushed out like so many genies from the suddenly uncorked bottle. Some still approached from a defiantly serious angle (*Melody Maker* once condemned the jazz inflected Level 42 for their "joyless . . . funk-pomp sterility"), but others grasped firmly onto the joie de vivre of funk a la mode.

Queen, long-running hard rockers whose penchant for pomposity was second only to their readiness to put their heads on the block (and their tongues in their cheek), were astonishingly effective frontrunners, hitting the fall 1980 schedules with the near-staccato "Another One Bites the Dust," a dynamic distillation of recent UK developments and more established American formulae. The record not only topped the US pop chart, it also spent three weeks at #2 on the R&B listings, the most successful such import since David Bowie's "Fame" and, alongside that noble predecessor, one of the most frequently sampled white funk records ever. Grandmaster Flash, Kurtis Blow and B-Legit have all drawn from it.

Electro mavens Heaven 17 scored with "Fascist Groove Thang" (1981), a deliberate nod in the direction of Clinton. Producer Trevor Horn inserted at least a ghost of the funk into Frankie Goes to Hollywood's "Relax" (1983); not at all coincidentally, session musicians on that track included members of Chaz Jankel and Ian Dury's Blockheads band. Duran Duran splintered briefly to vent the Power Station, a supergroup of sorts that combined members of Duran Duran and Chic with vocalist Robert Palmer for what bassist John Taylor called "a funky version of T. Rex's 'Bang a Gong.'"

George Clinton enjoyed his first UK hit since "One Nation Under a Groove" in December 1982, when "Loopzilla" went to #57; James Brown his first in just as long when "Rapp Payback" cracked the Top 40. Neither had truly compromised their personal vision during the five year haze of disco supremacy and, in terms of a British profile, both had paid the commercial price. But now those days were over and the land could learn to funk again.

Certainly Earth Wind & Fire mainstays Larry Dunn and Verdine White thought so, tracking down Level 42 in 1983 after hearing one of their earlier recordings played during the intermission at a gig in Germany. "They knew that music from England was really happening," Level 42 drummer and lyricist Phil Gould told *The Face* magazine, and they wanted to find a local band to produce. The ensuing *Standing in the Light* album, Level 42's third, emerged their most relaxed and earthy yet, and became their first UK top ten entry.

Of course, more than one aural hernia would emerge from this sudden explosion of creativity, all the more so once the creativity gave way to just another Top 40 cash cow. Beneath the surface, however, where the mainstream media dared not venture, the action continued. Washington, DC's go-go scene was arguably as big on the UK underground as it ever was in its hometown, with Trouble Funk emerging during 1986–87 as genuine chart contenders on the strength of reputation alone.

Julian Cope, his once righteously on-the-One approach to funk reawakened by Trouble Funk's remix of his "World Shut Your Mouth" single, raced back to the studio to record *My Nation Underground*. Almost every song was back on-the-One and the entire thing was crowned by the title track, "cobbled together [from] many demo riffs." It was, Cope recalled in his *Repossessed* autobiography, "a stomping and overloaded epic . . . recorded live and in chaos." Cope himself claims the finished record was compromised beyond recognition, emerging "an average album which everyone thought was bland enough to be huge." But if that is the case, the original demos must be deadly.

If Cope was spearheading an (albeit limited) drive back toward the hard funk rock of the classic era, other forces were toying with the natural Brit-funk predilection for jazzier sounds and creating what would emerge the final (so far) stage in the domestic genre's development. Acid jazz was a furiously elitist, studiedly cool scene that took its name from the label behind a series of rare groove compilations unleashed during the late '80s, and its attitude from the curious belief that if no one's ever heard of a record, then it must be really good.

Reinventing and invigorating a wealth of hitherto obscure and overlooked '70s jazz and jazz-funk recordings, all prized for their obscurity (but swiftly taking on a new life of their own), the *Totally Wired* compilations proved the cornerstone not only of a new market for old music, but also for a groundswell of new talent.

Jamiroquai, Galliano, the James Taylor Quartet, the Brand New Heavies and Urban Species hit the clubs, while the major labels hit their archives, seeking out their own variations on a theme of *Totally Wired*. By 1990, Britain had not only created its own, wholly individual, scene, it was selling it back to the US as well. Massive hits for Stereo MCs and the Brand New Heavies, the rise of acid-jazz scenes within American cities . . . it might not have been termed the next British Invasion, but for a time, that's what it looked like.

Of course such action blurred the acid jazz boundaries, particularly once the mid-'90s brought the parallel emergence of the so-called Trip Hop movement. Artists like Massive Attack, Portishead and Tricky utilized many of the same jazz-funk rudiments, shot through with smokey loops and sleepy beats, as the acid jazz stable, and therein lies a lovely piece of historical symmetry.

Tricky was discovered and first recorded by the Pop Group's Mark Stewart. Through the convoluted skein of logic, which ties funk to hip-hop and jazz to trip hop and thence, past to present, a process that had begun almost 20 years before, with the unrecognizable thrashings of the Pop Group and the snarling savagery of PIL had finally reached denouement. And, in an odd way, it had come full circle as well.

## RECOMMENDED LISTENING

### Julian Cope: *My Nation Underground* (Island, 1988)

Trouble Funkadelia, middle England style. Cope's unrepentant Anglo enunciation flies like a flag in the mix, but behind him, moogbass, wah-wah, bongos and vibes pound out a truly righteous One-fixated stomp, culminating in the epic seven-minute title track.

### Funkapolitan: *Funkapolitan* (CBS, 1982)

Hastily picking up the baton that Spandau dropped after "Chant," and screaming "early-'80s New Wave!" out of every groove, a solid funk-pop confection well produced by August Darnell.

### Gang of 4: *Damaged Goods* EP (Fast Products, UK 1978)

Fractious, gritty, glacial and lurching; art school funk with politically activated hiccups.

### The Pop Group: *Y* (Radar, UK 1978)

Don't try to dance, don't *try* to listen. But a studiously tuneless wall of noise washes the senses with more soul than is immediately apparent and, deep in the mix, there's the glimmer you're searching for.

### Public Image Ltd: "Death Disco" (12-inch single—Virgin, UK 1979)

No PIL album sits still long enough for inclusion, but two sides of a single are all you really need—"Death Disco" looping Bootsy bass around fragments from Tchaikovsky's "Swan Lake" and "Half Life" boiling their debut album's "Fodderstompf" down to a simple grinding groove.

### Spandau Ballet: "Chant #1 (We Don't Need This Pressure On)" (12-inch single—Chrysalis, 1981)

Any of Spandau's first four singles will do, but this is where everything came together, pounding, punching, ruthlessly moving, and keeping it up for a full six minutes.

# THE BIRTH OF GO-GO

An exuberant collision of primal funk jamming and what was, in the late '70s/early '80s, still the emergent sound of rap, go-go burst onto the Washington, DC club scene as the irresistible soundtrack to underground parties and jam sessions. Anything—up-to-an-hour long percussion—packed grooves were driven by lurid bass, vibrant horns and vocal refrains punched out by musicians and audience alike. Call and response routines ranged from impromptu catchphrases to entire refrains lifted from TV, movies and current hit records; rappers and singers drifted across the stage. At a time when dance music was becoming increasingly reliant on technology, go-go represented an unrepentant return to funk basics, driven by organic energy, primal urgency and inspired instinct.

The scene's founding fathers, Chuck Brown and the Soul Searchers, had been active for a decade by the time the first of the new bands appeared around 1978. The Soul Searchers started out in the late '60s as a Top 40 covers band, then graduated to tightly-sprung political material appropriate to African-American life in the District of Columbia.

Go-go developed on Brown's stage, initially as a means of filling the space between songs, to stop people from leaving their seats. The drummer kept the beat going; Brown picked up the rhythm in words, with dedications to friends, greetings to the audience, and simple conversation wrapped around the pulse. The rest of the band took it from there. Soon, the Soul Searchers were putting on shows without a single natural break, one long, pounding jam within which individual songs became simple refrains and everything became subservient to the groove.

By the time the Soul Searchers scored their biggest hit, 1978's irresistible "Bustin' Loose," the song's key elements had been floating around their set for three years. In finally putting them together, however, Brown created more than a simple hit. He effectively birthed an entire new breed of funk, one that was as individual as George Clinton's in 1971 or James Brown's in 1966, and as exacting as any endurance course. Stamina was a must.

The beat was simple (Brown later admitted it took years for him to find drummers willing to play something so rudimentary) but contagious; the style was deliberately culture conscious. If "Bustin' Loose" is the archetypal go-go recording, Trouble Funk's "Supergrit" (from their *Drop the Bomb* album) is the quintessential one, honking horns and raucous vocals, shot through with distorted snatches of "Hall of the Mountain King." Live, familiar cartoon and TV themes would be added to the potpourri, injecting humor to the proceedings, but also forging a common ground between band and audience.

Trouble Funk keyboard player James Avery told *The Face* magazine, "If I was to meet you in the street for the first time, never knowing anything about you before, I'm gonna try to find out what we have in common. Anything that we are enthused about. The communication between the group and the audience is that both see TV or know certain things. When you reach that apex where both find a communication point like dancing or a certain hookline, that's where the communication starts and it grows from there."

Neither was making go-go music restricted to musicians alone. Audience participation was not simply expected, it was often demanded. Offstage, too, the process continued in an echo of the jugband scene of an earlier age—"junkyard" bands of much younger children, extemporizing their own go-go from cans, bottles, boxes and whatever else they could find to beat upon, reducing the music to its lowest common denominator and then building up from there.

By the mid-'80s, junkyard bands had developed into the second generation of go-go giants, including Ayre Rayde, Shady Groove, Petworth and the Junk Yard Band themselves. *Car Wash* director Joel Schumacher's 1983 movie *Street Fleet*, though taking crippling flak for eschewing go-go music itself, gave fresh impetus to the junkyards through its portrayal of their presence in the city.

The term "go-go" itself was derived from the Yoruba (a Nigerian dialect) word "agogo," a jazz/soul/R&B hybrid popularized in song by Smokey Robinson's 1966 hit "Going to a Go-Go." But more specifically, it was borrowed from an already established DC musical tradition, the Thursday night dance parties staged at the Knights of Columbus Hall on 10th and K. There, too, the need to keep the groove flowing had seen live music eschew the commercial values of the marketplace.

The unique-to-DC social dichotomies, highlighted by Brown's commentaries of the early '70s, remained at the core of go-go, an urban howl played out beneath the very noses of government. Few politicians, however, would even dream of venturing into such south-eastern DC strongholds as the Shelter Room, Cheriys, the Maverick Room and the best known of them all, the Black Hole on South Georgia. In all likelihood, few had even heard of such places, while the neighborhood's own isolation from other points of mainstream cultural contact ensured that go-go (like hip-hop in contemporary New York) would flourish undisturbed even after the success of "Bustin' Loose."

By the early '80s, bands like Trouble Funk, Rare Essence, Experience Unlimited (EU), Little Benny & the Masters, the Mighty Peacemakers and CJ's Uptown Crew had already established themselves at the vanguard of the go-go scene, again without any outside notice. Each brought their own personal influences to the brew, James Brown, the Meters and George Clinton, of course (P-Funk refrains were a frequent feature of early go-go performances), but material was brought in from further afield as well.

EU's Greg "Sugar Bear" Elliott and Tino had previously worked together in a Jimi Hendrix-inspired rock band (the first song the pair ever played was Iron Butterfly's "In a Gadda Da Vida"). Queen and Mothers Finest were both acknowledged influences on go-go's frontal practitioners; so were the Bar-Kays and Mandrill (respectively the creators of "Holy Ghost" and "Fencewalk," non go-go records that nevertheless graced many go-go sound systems). Softer sounds, too, crept in to play; Trouble Funk's debut album included a ballad, "Don't Try To Use Me," which could have stepped out of Philly International.

Reggae, salsa and calypso rhythms twisted around the funk beats; hard rock riffs and synthesizer bombs littered the landscape and, if snatches of contemporary pop music provided the most easily identifiable reference points for listeners, bands were also capable of unveiling some rewarding surprises. One of Trouble Funk's earliest pieces de resistance was a heavily extemporized version of Kraftwerk's "Trans-Europe Express," a throbbing electro monotone that made shocking sense on the dancefloor. The German's original version was a cult hit across the US underground dance scene, but still Trouble Funk's appropriation of it (as "Trouble Funk Express") first shocked, then delighted, unsuspecting out-of-town audiences, many of whom believed that its insistent groove and inate funkiness was their discovery alone.

Such symbiosis could not help but spread the word, first up the coast to New York (Trouble Funk were regulars at the Roxy on West 18th) then across the Atlantic to Britain, where go-go took such a hold that, by 1984, both Chuck Brown and Trouble Funk were established dance club favorites, with their influence percolating even further afield. Julian Cope, arguably one of the quintessential English rock artists of the '80s, was so inspired by their "Parliament non-stop party gig" that he commissioned the band to remix his hit "World Shut Your Mouth," then set about recording an album that would pursue "Trouble Funk Express" to its ultimate destination, combining Kraut Rock with funk.

Maxx Kidd was the first (local) industry entrepreneur to pick up on what was happening on the streets of DC. A former singer, and co-writer of Chuck Brown's 1974 hit "Blow Your Whistle," he was a partner in the DC based Al and the Kidd label when, in 1980, he released the debut single by Trouble (the Funk was added later), "E Flat Boogie."

Other labels followed: Vermack and Inner City (both early homes to EU), Cherry Blossom, and another Kidd enterprise, DETT. But with the flowering, pressures, too, crept in. Redds & the Boys were once offered a deal on the condition that they recorded a song about Loveboat, a local term for the drug PCP. They complied, much to their lasting regret; even with the lyrical safety-net of actually writing about the primetime TV show, the band would forever be tarred with the drug brush.

But still go-go flourished, finally hitting the US mainstream via a trio of dramatic Soul Searchers hits: "Bustin' Loose," 1979's "Game Seven" and 1980's "Sticks and Stones". "E Flat Boogie" followed, scratching the Top 75 almost exclusively on the strength of local sales. The following year Rare Essence were picked up by the Fantasy label, and "Body Moves" became a R&B Top 75 hit in early spring, 1982. Weeks later, Trouble Funk signed with New York's Sugar Hill label and rejoined Rare Essence in the chart with "Hey Fellas."

Despite distilling the go-go essence down to almost inhumanely abbreviated length (seven minutes barely accounted for the track's in concert intro), "Hey Fellas" gave Trouble Funk a spring 1982, hit. "Trouble Funk Express" (the first hit for Maxim Kidd's DETT label) followed in 1983. Brown's "We Need Some Money" reiterated the musical message in summer 1984, when it cracked the R&B Top 30 That same year, a Thanksgiving Day Funk Jam at the Washington Coliseum attracted over 7,000 fans, while a go-go supergroup, Double Agent Rock, formed around members of EU, the Chance band and Ayre Rayde.

The hip-hop scene, too, was paying attention. Kurtis Blow recruited members of EU to back him on 1983's hit "Party Time," then absorbed further go-go magic for 1985's "If I Ruled the World." Doug E. Fresh's "The Show," that same year, paid similar homage to the sound; so did Super Nature (the future Salt-N-Pepa's) "The Show Stopper," an apocalyptic female response to the Fresh hit.

Finally, the industry started to move. Further alerted by Jamaican singer Grace Jones, whose "Slave to the Rhythm" unabashedly employed a deep go-go vibe, Island Records moved for Trouble Funk. Redds & the Boys signed with the same company's 4th & Broadway subsidiary; Rare Essence moved to Capitol; and the Rhythm King label began pumping out a stream of crucial compilations and reissues for the UK market. But the highest hopes of all were sewn when Island convened a solid go-go soundtrack for the 1986 Blaine Novak movie *Good To Go*.

Fifteen years before, Island were behind *The Harder They Come*, the film that almost singlehandedly drew reggae out of the shadows and into the American mainstream. *Good To Go*, as rooted in the DC scene as its predecessor was in its Kingston counterpart, was confidently expected to have a similar effect on go-go and, certainly, its soundtrack left little to the imagination. Trouble Funk, Chuck Brown and the Soul Searchers, EU and Redds & the Boys were all recruited to the score, with Trouble Funk's captivating "Still Smokin'" firing the imminent storm into the R&B chart in late fall 1985.

The media was primed. High profile publicity agency Howard Bloom & Associates were brought in to ensure the widest possible visibility; *Billboard* announced go-go "was ready to go global." But then disaster struck. The movie's release was delayed and, when it did finally open, it was to a flood of poor reviews and weak receipts. Within days, the go-go boom was yesterday's news, and worse, much worse, was to follow.

In April 1987, 11 people were wounded by a gunman firing into the crowd after a Rare Essence show at the Masonic Temple in Washington, DC. The attack made nationwide headlines. Six months later, a fatal stabbing following a show at Celebrity Hall was christened a "Go-Go Slaying" by the *Washington Post*, a label that stuck. After a decade of peaceable concert-going, go-go had suddenly exploded into the headlines as the epitome of violent, drug-fuelled lawlessness. When a "Go-Go Shooting" headline followed in December, the authorities pounced. Legislation aimed at curbing the further growth of DC go-go clubs was enacted. Promoters grew wary; policing and security grew heavier.

But the typically kneejerk response of the authorities was only one of go-go's foes. Media forces, too, were at work, hand in hand with the mass marketplace's inability to deal with more than one "new" musical form at a time. In terms of blunt consumerism, go-go was being eclipsed by the looming political upheaval of rap and hip-hop, with the two musics' once perfect cross fertilization becoming increasingly unbalanced.

Trouble Funk attempted a crossover of sorts, allowing Island to rearrange them in a commercial funk-lite vein redolent of recent Cameo. Unfortunately, it was a move that utterly alienated the group's existing support at home and abroad. The 1987 *Trouble over Here, Trouble over There* album entered the British Top 60 on the strength of the band's live show, then fell out after two weeks, once its contents had been evaluated. A collaboration with 2 Live Crew in 1989, reworking their classic "Drop the Bomb" as "The Bomb Has Dropped," arrived too late to repair the damage.

The Junk Yard Band and EU adapted to the changing times somewhat more successfully. The former showed up in Run DMC's spring 1988, *Tougher than Leather* movie, performing "Sardines" alongside contributions from the Beastie Boys and Slick Rick; the latter simultaneously scoring a R&B chart-topper with "Da' Butt," written by jazz bassist Marcus Miller (ex-Miles Davis) for the soundtrack to Spike Lee's *School Daze* movie. "Da' Butt" was not a go-go track, but in the prevalent musical climate, that worked to its advantage, allowing the band to follow through by teaming with the newly ascendent Salt-N-Pepa for a rap vamp through the Isley Brothers' "It's Your Thing," retitled "Shake Your Thang." EU's future direction was confirmed.

But go-go did not die. Rather, it returned to whence it came, the clubs and dives of DC, where it could continue to dance, drive and develop under its own terms, in its own right. It has changed, mutated and moved on, of course, and the bands that today work under the go-go banner can sometimes seem unrecognizable to ears raised on the classic sounds of the early '80s. But the spirit remains intact and the groove still rules.

**various artists:** *Go-Go Cranking'—Paint the White House Black* **(4th & Broadway)**

From 1985, the first major go-go collection, a statement of defiant intent with liner notes from Maxx Kidd, and contributions from Chuck Brown, Trouble Funk, Slim, EU, Redds & the Boys and Mass Extension.

**various artists:** *Go-Go Posse* **(I Hear Ya!)**

1988 comp featuring DC Scorpio, EU, Little Benny and the Masters, Rare Essence, etc.

**various artists:** *Live at the Capital Center* **(I Hear Ya!)**

1987 in concert comp featuring Chuck Brown & the Soul Searchers, DC Scorpio, EU, Little Benny & The Masters, Rare Essence, etc.

**various artists:** *Paradise a Go-Go* **(Rhythm King—UK)**

1987 comp featuring Code Red, Double Agent Rock, Julia & Co., Milton Smith & Stimulus, Paradise, Rare Essence, etc.

**various artists:** *The Sound of Washington, DC* **(London)**

1985 Redds, Petworth and Shady Groove headline a peak period look at the emergent second wave of go-go.

# RAP: THE SONS OF THE P

In 1991, in the title of their second album, but more significantly across its grooves, Digital Underground proclaimed themselves the Sons of the P. And that was a capital "P" as in Parliment, as the Bay Area rappers laid bare their debt not only to George Clinton, but to all the funk icons whose spirits inhabited the soul of their sound. Sly Stone, Bootsy Collins, Fred Wesley, Jimi Hendrix, they were all in there, haunting the fundamentally heavy, body grooving funk that, whether sampled or played, has always been a crucial element of the Digital Underground sound.

And not theirs alone. As long as rap has been around, it has been inextricably linked to funk. Whether the flashpoint was political, social or nothing more than musical, the two genres share roots that reach back some four decades: through the revivals of the '90s and the electronics of the '80s, the classic swerves of the '70s grooves and the more tentative grooves of the '60s. The Watts Prophets were rappers, though history calls them street poets. Chuck Brown rapped, and birthed what became go-go. James Brown rapped, though posterity says he vamped. The rapid-fire commentary, braggadacio and come-ons, which are at the forefront of rap, have been a vital part of Black music almost as long as there has been music. The difference is, rap made it the most vital part.

Rap and the attendant hip-hop culture have their roots in the break-beat style that evolved in New York in the mid-'70s, and at a time when the hitherto unimpeached domination of James Brown and Sly Stone was being ruthlessly supplanted on radio and the nightclubs by the new sounds of disco.

Funk retreated from the airwaves, but it still held the streets. It was up to block parties and roving DJs to keep the funk flowing: Afrikaa Bambaataa, Kool Herc, Grandmaster Flash, the Cold Crush Brothers, Coke La Rock, Clark Kent . . . the names could fill a book. All bold explorers of sound in the middle of the decade, they created and sustained the earliest hip-hop explorations.

Herc and Flash pioneered the break-beat—the art of finding the break in any disc and prolonging it—to give the audience an extended beat and rapid fire percussion that could keep them dancing for hours. Adding a rhythmic rhyme over the beats—a trick picked up from ex-pat Jamaican toasters, whose own sound systems vied for space in the city—DJ became MC, in control of the flow, of the crowd and the sound.

Hip-hop culture, in its infancy, encompassed so many ideals and ideas. From rival gangs who used complicated rhymes in their never-ending battles of one-upmanship, to the DJs mixing beats at all night block parties, to Bambaataa's militant Zulu Nation, which bridged the gap between both extremes, hip-hop's grasp on the urban underground tightened.

Battles were fought and won over the turntables as the DJs paired with the MCs in a never-ending and good spirited bid for supremecy. It was a tight-knit circle. B-boys and girls, DJs and MCs, it was utterly self-sufficient and absolutely insular.

Short-circuiting the music industry entirely, by mid-1979, DJ rappers the Cold Crush Brothers, the Funky 4+1 and Afrika Bambaataa were regularly releasing live tapes of their own performances. Eazy AD of the Cold Crush Brothers claims sales of 500,000 + tapes long before any rap *records* were ever released. Once the first appeared, however—Fatback Band's "King Tim III" and Sugarhill Gang's "Rapper's Delight"—there was no holding it back.

Both songs hit the R&B and pop charts, and suddenly hip-hop was being called the next big thing. The mainstream public hadn't heard anything like it since the gritty funk at the beginning of the decade; the mainstream industry fell over itself in its haste to feed the audience's hunger. Early critics declared that hip-hop was just another fad, but the proliferation of tiny independent record labels, led by Sugarhill, but pursued by Enjoy, Winley and Sound of New York, bespoke a vitality far removed from the conventions of pop tastemaking.

Afrika Bambaataa is widely hailed as the godfather of hip-hop culture. A self-styled record-collecting fanatic, Bambaataa started DJing in the early '70s, spinning from his own vast collection. A member of the street gang, the Black Spades, Bambaataa's interest in African American studies prompted him to form Zulu Nation in 1976—the gang, the action group, the posse from which he assembled the Soul Sonic Force with whom he would record.

In 1980, Bambaataa brought his history and experience into the recording studio for the first time and, in 1982, he released "Planet Rock"—possibly the single most influential recording in the annals of hip-hop. Using the electronic beats inspired by German band Kraftwerk, "Planet Rock" was groundbreaking in its scope, the birthplace of electro-funk,

**FUNK**

but only the beginning of the artist's experimentation. Constantly exploring the possibilities of drum machines and loops, samples and scratching, Bambaataa opened the doors through which techno, trip-hop, freestyle, drum and bass and so much more would eventually flood.

His association with producer Bill Laswell soon after "Planet Rock"'s release led to the creation of Time Zone, a funk-punk fusion that exploded to worldwide prominence with the Orwellian apocalypse "World Destruction" in 1984. Recorded with Laswell and including Bernie Worrell on keyboards, "Destruction" also featured Public Image frontman John Lydon, and the clash between Bambaataa's urgent warnings and Lydon's lackadaisical sneer was a beauty to behold. "The fact [Lydon] seems not to care while I'm trying to warn the people," Bambaataa mused. "I like that—makes the record more scary."

In 1984, Bambaataa also linked with James Brown, after the pair met during one of Brown's New York performances. The grandmaster of funk and the godfather of hip-hop recorded "Unity," a sprawling, six-part continuation of "World Destruction's dire forebodings, cut through by Bambaataa's love of Brown's past achievements—and Brown's appreciation of Bambaataa's impact on the future.

Bambaataa was never comfortable with the commercialization of hip-hop, a point he continued making throughout the '80s as he eschewed the opportunities for mass acceptance, in favor of pursuing his own hybrid dreams. Working at a furious pace, with an ever-shifting aggregation of friends, musicians and guests, his commentaries shaped the decade's developments, even as he himself snubbed its requirements. That job was left to others. Bambaataa's interest in funk culminated in 1988, when his on-going Family project was expanded to welcome George Clinton, Bootsy Collins, Boy George, Nona Hendryx and Yellowman to the recording of *The Light*—the album that, perhaps more than any other, coalesced the already gestating visions of Digital Underground.

Elsewhere in the decade, however, Grandmaster Flash & the Furious Five, Kurtis Blow, Doug E. Fresh and Eric B. & Rakim, all played their part in pursuing funk through the new brew. The latter not only continued the tradition of utilizing the music to carry a hard-hitting political message (they were fervent adherents of the Nation of Islam), but also made one of the first extensive usages of classic funk samples, across 1987's *Paid in Full* album.

*Paid in Full* was one of the first "provocatively" message-oriented rap albums to cross into the American mainstream. Top Ten on the R&B chart, Top 60 on the pop listings, it publicly announced for the first time something that rap's own audience had known for years (but which white Middle America seemed quite shocked to discover), that rap wasn't simply concerned with penis size and party-going. And if anybody still doubted that fact, the emergence of Public Enemy swiftly pulled the wool from their eyes.

Although they, too, liberally scattered ear-catching samples though their songs, Chuck D. and his crew used rap as a flashpoint for education, teaching lessons through rhyme, and bringing Afrocentric history to life.

As a graphic design student at New York's Adelphi College in the early '80s, Chuck D. worked in college radio with Hank Shocklee and Bill Stephany in addition to MC-ing parties, often alongside DJ Flavor Flav. It was within this group that D. and Flav first recorded "Public Enemy Number One" and, when Stephany took a job at hip-hop maven Rick Rubin's Def Jam label, he offered D. a deal.

Adamant that rap was only worthwhile if the rapper had something to say, D. and Shocklee launched Public Enemy with DJs Professor Griff and Terminator X, abetted by Flavor Flav, an exaggerated b-boy bedecked in his trademark giant clock on a rope, a comedic foil to Chuck D.'s intense MC rap.

Backing themselves on stage and in public with the Black Panther-esque clad members of S1W (Security of the First World), Public Enemy created a storm from the outset, 1987's *Yo! Bum Rush the Show* album. The band's complex arrangement of heavily layered samples and loops created a new blueprint for hip-hop, the funk-laden textures offering vivid slashes of color behind their potent politics.

Public Enemy continued promoting thought and provoking action across five more, increasingly outspoken albums, including the massive hits *It Takes a Nation of Millions To Hold Us Back* (1988) and *Fear of a Black Planet* (1989). In viviparous contrast to the gangsta rappers emerging alongside them at the end of the '80s, Public Enemy's use of history as a reminder of how important militant peacemaking was—and always will be—reshaped the hip-hop landscape. And, while the group itself has since essentially disbanded, their impact on hip-hop and on music in general cannot be disputed.

No matter what camp these different bands came from, they all had one thing in common, and that was sampling. Musicians had been using samples since the early '80s, when electronic music enthusiasts and designers Peter Vogel, Tony Furse and Kim Ryrie, founder of *Electronics Today International* magazine, first began marketing their Fairlight computer to the music community. Since that time, sampling—essentially, the ability to lift sounds from one medium and translate them into another—had become endemic across the musical spectrum.

It had also become a major legal and ethical battleground and, as the end of the '80s hove into view, the inevitable debate over rights, ownership and royalties, was finally moving into the courts. Hip-hop was in the direct line of fire.

It was an emotive issue. Musicians have "borrowed" key elements from one anothers' work for years, centuries even. And in modern rock and R&B, the fair exchange of riffs, chord patterns and grooves was long considered essential—even the essence of—the music's continued development. English jazz funk musician Chaz Jankel remembers his writing partner, Ian Dury, blatantly lifting a bass line from an Ornette Coleman album, then writing to one of the musicians involved, Don Cherry, to ask if he objected. "[Don] sent a card back saying 'this is not my music, you're fine,' meaning that music comes around and goes around and is there to share."

Where matters became more complicated was in the manner in which the sharing occured. Replaying a borrowed riff is one thing. Physically lifting it from an existing performance and grafting it onto your own is another, all the more so since an increasing number of records now seemed to comprise nothing more than a single pilfered sequence, over which the performer would execute his rap.

It was around those instances that the problems arose, particularly those in which the sampled sequence itself was many times more familiar than the artist (Vanilla Ice's "Ice Baby Ice" is possibly a case in point, with its bold simulacre of David Bowie and Queen's "Under Pressure"; MC Hammer's "U Can't Touch This," built around Rick James "Super Freak" another). Who was the performing artist now, the musician whose riff powered the song? Or the guy who conceived the hijack, and then chattered away above it?

But it was an odd divide. Suddenly, all these old school musicians found themselves in the midsts of a revival of their own music, without being even vaguely involved in the process. And for every one who was completely (and, it must be said, rightfully) incensed that not only were they not receiving payment for their work, many weren't even being credited for it, there were others who simply reveled in the exposure.

The Ohio Players' Leroy Bonner fell firmly in the former camp, echoing the anger of many musicians when he explained his frustrations to journalist Maria Granditsky. "What upsets me . . . is that we're letting technology take our jobs. A drum machine is not a human being! And it has taken a lot of people out of their jobs. Now kids can go into the music store and buy [themselves] talent in a box. You can't synthesize life. That's what it's all about. They take a sample of somebody, re-produce it and that's not the way God intended it to be."

Rick James felt the same way. As the demand for live electro-funk faded away, and sample-toting rappers stepped into the spotlight, James was incredibly critical of those bands he perceived to be little more than boys with plug-in toys, stealing music from others for their own ends. But unlike many of his peers, James' view did change—albeit only after he realized that his lawyers had been on the case since the beginning, and ensured he received payment for every sample.

"That was just me going through an ego trip. I didn't want rappers touching my shit . . . [and] a lot of us older musicians felt that way then. But then I saw what kind of money I was making from Hammer and L.L. Cool J. and Will Smith and on and on . . . and I said 'never mind'."

Two well-publicized and closely studied lawsuits finally turned the tide in favor of the sampled musician: '60s hitmakers the Turtles' suit against De La Soul in 1989, and singer-songwriter Gilbert O'Sullivan's battle with Biz Markie three years later. De La Soul settled out of court, postponing the day of legal judgement. Biz Markie, however, went all the way, in a case that finally set the long-awaited legal precedent. All samples had to be cleared with their owners and paid for, and all sampled artists had to be credited as co-composers. The day when the humblest unknown could share a writing credit with George Clinton, James Brown and Prince was upon us.

Samples continue to drive hip-hop as much as the MC's rhymes, with funk—already established as rap's closest living lyrical and emotional relative—by far the most frequently visited catalog. No artists on earth have been sampled as often as James Brown and George Clinton, few as effectively as Rick James ("U Can't Touch This" again) and Sly & the Family Stone (Digital Underground's absorption of "Family Affair" into "Family of the Underground").

But the traffic has never been one way. Indeed, alongside almost any of its other greatest accomplishments, what hip-hop did was to keep the funk alive, not only for the players now being feted by a new wave of musicians, but also for record buyers too young to remember the original days of heavy grooves and thumping bass.

Many old funkers, like George Clinton and Rick James and even the Ohio Players, would turn to the new sounds as they revived their careers in the '90s. Others would simply revive the old, knowing that to the new generation of concert-goers, a familiar riff is a familiar riff, no matter how and where they first heard it.

The funk revival was born.

## RECOMMENDED LISTENING

### Grandmaster Flash & the Furious Five: *The Message* (Sugarhill, 1982)

One of the first, and still one of the best, rap records recorded. The title track is a classic, while "It's Nasty" and "She's Fresh" remind us how cool the old school were.

### Run DMC: *Run-D.M.C* (Profile, 1984)

Although they included their four early singles on this debut album, which was a boon for late arrivals, it was "Rock Box" that stole the show, crossing rap with a full-on frontal metal guitar assault as the searing riffs stacked up around the rap. The "Rock Box" video was the first rap video to receive regular rotation on MTV.

### Afrika Bambaataa: *Planet Rock* (Tommy Boy, 1982)

Outstanding in its scope, both the song and the album were the earliest to combine traditional funk/rap with the electro-techno bells and whistles that would facilitate much electronic music during the late '80s and well into the '90s. "Planet Rock" is unbeatable, but don't forget "Renegades of Funk" and "Looking for a Perfect Beat."

### Beastie Boys: *Licensed To Ill* (Def Jam, 1986)

The first major rap set to cross over to the mainstream. Because of this, and the fact that the band was unconditionally accepted as LEGITIMATE rappers by the Black rap community, doors were opened for other White musicians to explore the genre. On a solid set full of real gems, "Fight for Your Right To Party" set the group on the fast track and catapulted the genre straight into the spotlight. The album remains one of the biggest-selling rap albums ever.

### Salt-N-Pepa: *Hot, Cool and Vicious* (Next Plateau, 1987)

Full of cool raps with hot delivery, Salt-N-Pepa incorporated the essence of go-go style funk, vamping "Push It" and "Twist and Shout" to the limit.

### Eric B. & Rakim: *Paid in Full* (4th & B'Way, 1987)

Full on hip-hop without a disappointment in the bunch, Eric B. & Rakim's groundbreakingly effective use of James Brown samples particularly benefitted "Paid in Full" and "Eric B. Is President"—the latter a masterpiece of complex sonics and (more importantly) lyrics that helped set a standard for the next generation of rappers.

### Public Enemy: *It Takes a Nation of Millions To Hold Us Back* (Def Jam, 1988)

An astounding set, richly textured, intricately layered and pulling in samples from James Brown to David Bowie in a way that few bands have ever emulated. From the manifesto of "Don't Believe the Hype" to the scathing social commentary of "She Watch Channel Zero" this is an important album, and the fact that we can still all go "Cold Lampin with Flavor" proves that it's a fun one as well.

### NWA: *Straight Outta Compton* (Ruthless, 1989)

The first gangsta rap record with major crossover appeal, this set almost singlehandedly brought about the white-hot rise of that particular branch. "Fuck Tha Police" became a smash hip-hop hit and the center of furious controversy, but it also raised some interesting socio-political points along the way.

### De La Soul: *3 Feet and Rising* (Tommy Boy, 1989)

With visual acid-tinged overtones and outrageous sampling creating an unprecedented aural tapestry, De La Soul turned the club scene upside down. Packed with great grooves, the album also kicked out the single and immediate club classic "Me, Myself & I."

# FUNKIN' UP A STORM: ESSENTIAL FUNK COMPILATIONS

The late '90s saw the market for classic funk grooves explode, resulting in a tidal wave of welcome repackagings and reissues. The following notes key various artist compilations from both major and specialist labels, documenting both the familiar hits and the lesser-known obscurities currently available to the discerning funker.

### AMAZING FUNK MASTERS (Soul Patrol—France)

Vintage obscurities, few of which have ever been collected together in the past, and none of which ever seem to turn up in their original vinyl format. Includes: Can You Dig It: Shades of Time/Popcorn '69: Billy Ball & the Upsetters/Never Give Him Up: James Polk & the Brothers/Funky Movement #2: Timothy McNealy/Monkey in a Sack: Lil Buck & the Top Cats

### BACK TO FUNK (BGP/Ace—UK)

Excellent survey of the short-lived Westbound jazz-funk subsidiary Eastbound. Indianapolis three-piece, the 19th Whole's version of War's Slippin' into Darkness is especially worthy of note. Includes: Back to Funk: Robert Love/Hicky Burr: Caesar Frazier/The 19th Whole: Monkey Hips 'n' Rice/Stone Thing (parts one and two): Alvin Cash/Whip! Whop!: Melvin Sparks

### BREAKS: ORIGINAL B BOY STREET FUNK & BLOCK PARTY CLASSICS
(Harmless—UK)

Hot breakbeat-hunters collection, overloaded with unexpected gems. Includes: Scorpio: Dennis Coffey/Funky Mule: Ike Turner/24 Carat Black: 24 Carat Black/Funky Drummer: James Brown/Apache: Incredible Bongo Band/Ashley's Roachclip: Soul Searchers/It's Just Begun: Jimmy Castor/and Let a Woman Be a Woman/Let a Man Be a Man: Dyke & The Blazers

### BREAKS VOL. 2—ORIGINAL B BOY STREET FUNK & BLOCK PARTY CLASSICS (Harmless—UK)

Follow-up unearths another dozen killer cuts, a little less obscure than its predecessor, but still hot. Includes: Chove Chuva: Samba Soul/N.T.: Kool & the Gang/The Revolution Will Not Be Televised: Gil Scott Heron/Assembly Line: The Commodores/I Can't Stop: John Davis/Take Me to the Mardi Gras: Bob James/Memphis Soul Stew: King Curtis/ Melting Pot: Booker T. & the MGs

### CLASSIC FUNK 1 (Mastercuts—UK)

From the early '90s, a stellar collection focuses on a dozen full length, lesser-known grooves by some of the prime movers of '70s dance funk. Includes: NT: Kool & the Gang/Stone to the Bone: James Brown/Pick Up the Pieces: Average White Band/Fencewalk: Mandrill/Who Is He and What Is He to You: Creative Source/Wicki Wacky: Fatback/For the Love of Money: the O'Jays

### DISCO JUICE: THE FUNKY DISCO SOUND OF HARLEM'S P&P RECORDS (Counterpoint—UK)

Patrick Adams and Peter Brown were Harlem-based producers whose disco-funk electro brew never took off on the mainstream, but kept the underground hopping regardless. Includes: Johnson Jumpin: Johnson Products/Dance Freak: Chain Reaction/African Rock: Licky/Feel the Spirit: Foster Jackson/NY Applejack: Scott Davis/Got To Have Your Love: Clyde Alexander/Get Down Boy: Paper Doll.

### FIRST ANNUAL BENEFIT FOR THE CONGRESSIONAL BLACK CAUCUS (Chess)

From the Capitol Centre, Largo, MD in September 1974, an excellent live recording produced by War's Far Out Productions. Includes: Wild and Peaceful: Kool & the Gang/Give Me Your Love: Curtis Mayfield/On and On: Gladys Knight & the Pips/Gypsy Man: War/Goin' Down Slow: Jimmy Witherspoon

### FUNK CLASSICS (MCA Special Products)

Very far-reaching three CD box compilation that, while heavy on the classic period, also peeps into the future with nods toward electro-funk, hip-hop and go-go. Much of the set has also appeared across three separate discs on the Rebound label, as *Funk Classics: The '70s* (two volumes) and *Funk Classics: The '80s*. Includes: Hollywood Swinging: Kool & the Gang/Sex Machine: James Brown/Get the Funk Out Ma Face: The Brothers Johnson/Doing It to Death (part one): Fred Wesley & the J.B.'s/Up for the Down Stroke: Parliament/Shake You Pants: Cameo/Too Hot To Stop: The Bar-Kays/Give

It to Me Baby: Rick James/Cisco Kid: War/I Got My Mind Made Up (You Can Get It . . .): Instant Funk/Shake: Gap Band/Ffun: Con Funk Shun/Brick House: The Commodores/So Fine: Howard Johnson/Push It: Salt-N-Pepa/Doin' Da Butt: E.U.

## THE FUNK BOX (Hip-O)

You want funk? You got it. James Brown, Charles White, Chaka Khan, Jimmy Castor, Curtis Mayfield, Parliament, Graham Central Station, Tower of Power, Brass Construction, Slave, Chuck Brown, Zapp, Cameo.

There's no Sly Stone or Chairman of the Board, which are unforgivable by any standards, and a globule more go-go would have been welcome. And yes, one can also make snippity noises at some of the song selections (why include Bohannon's "Let's Start the Dance" when "Disco Stomp" says the same thing much sweeter?). But get over that and, at the end of the day, *The Funk Box* is just that, four discs/55 slices of more or less primal pounding that opens, of course, with "Sex Machine," closes with "Atomic Dog" and, in between times, ranges in more or less chronological fashion through the highest points of funky creativity.

Of course the early discs are the best, primarily because the featured artists were at their most innovative. War's "Slippin' into Darkness," Billy Preston's "Outa-Space" and New Birth's "I Can Understand It" are disc one highlights in the lead-up to one of the more surprising (but, once you hear it, least shocking) inclusions, Barry White's "I'm Gonna Love You Just a Little More, Baby."

Curtis Mayfield probably could have been better served by something other than "Future Shock," and the Meters definitely deserved more than "Just Kissed My Baby." But Kool's "Hollywood Swinging" sends us careening towards the jazzier spectrum that illuminated great swathes of mid-'70s funk, and Gil Scott Heron's "The Bottle" illuminating the rap-to-come in a manner that readily forgives the absence of the Last Poets and Watts Prophets.

Elsewhere, true believers will insist that Parliament's "Give Up the Funk" cannot hold a candle to the true fount of funkiness that that band represented (what, no "Maggot Brain"? I'm surprised). It did, however, open the doors for all that funk became in the late'70s and into the 80s—the Bar-Kays, Rick James, Fatback, Cameo, "One Nation under a Groove"—and the fact that the box signs off in 1981, with Zapp and the Gap Band fading into Clinton's "Atomic Dog," proves that it shut those doors as well.

Indeed, though another box of equal delight could be culled from the past 20 years worth of funky stuff, in terms of both musical and cultural significance, it really shouldn't be worth the bother. *The Funk Box* is not the be-all and end-all of its subject matter. But it does know where to find it.

## FUNK-DAMENTALS: MIND BLOWIN' FUNK HITS (Right Stuff)

Certainly aimed at the less discerning disco end of the funk audience, *Funkdamentals* nevertheless features enough bona fide funk hits to ensure the mirror ball party will swing all night. Assuming you like that sort of thing. Includes: Atomic Dog: George Clinton/Boogie Wonderland: Earth, Wind & Fire/And the Beat Goes On: The Whispers/Fantastic Voyage: Lakeside/Word Up: Cameo/Fire: The Ohio Players/Movin': Brass Construction

## FUNK ESSENTIALS (Charly)

The title is a misnomer only if you like your funk full-force and traditional. Funkadelic, Maceo and Instant Funk aside, the contents tend toward the fringes, roots and offshoots of the genre, with the pre-Family Stone Sly Stone cut typifying this approach. A strong New Orleans content, however, serves as an admirable primer to the scene, and you can rarely go wrong with the Last Poets. Includes: Move On Up: Curtis Mayfield/The Bottle: Gil Scott Heron/Across 110th Street: Bobby Womack/Funky Miracle: The Meters/I Gotcha: Joe Tex/It's a Trip: The Last Poets/Games: 94 East/The Same Thing: Sly & the Family Stone/Everybody: Roy Ayers

## FUNK ESSENTIALS (Beechwood Music Ltd—UK)

It would be very easy to look at this remorselessly budget-priced four CD box set and think there was something seriously wrong with it. You get what you pay for, after all, and inferior remakes, lousy mastering and substandard live cuts are all par for the cheapo course. Look again. Though a few of the heavy hitters are represented with material that may not necessarily match the music of their prime, and the discs certainly are not stuffed to their 70-plus minute limit, still a heftier dose of primal funk (and more!) would be difficult to imagine at twice the price. Features key cuts from the vaults of Curtom, Salsoul, Alaska and People. Includes: One Nation Under a Groove: Funkadelic/Lucky Fellow: Leroy Hutson/ Summertime: The Ohio Players/Papa Got a Brand New Bag: James Brown/Funky Woman: Maceo & All the Kings

Men/I Got So Much Trouble on My Mind: Sir Joe Quaterman & Free Soul/My Baby Is the Real Thing: Allen Toussaint/Who Gave Birth to the Funk: Joe Tex/You Were Right On Time: Ripple/It's a New Day: Skull Snaps

## FUNK ESSENTIALS (Laserlight)

Competent budget label compilation primarily hampered by the lack of any genuine headline material, and by a strangely familiar title. (The same disc is also available as the second half of a two CD collection, *Funk and Disco Essentials*. Includes: Shake Your Pants: Cameo/Funkin' for Jamaica: Tom Browne/Let It Whip: Dazz Band/For the Love of Money: The O'Jays/Action Speaks Louder than Words: Chocolate Milk/Before I Let Go: Maze/Funk Beyond the Call of Duty: Johnny Guitar Watson

## FUNK FEST (Rivie're International)

An absolutely eccentric (if surprisingly engaging) potpourri that rumages through soul, disco, Philly and funk for a satisfying, but somewhat Mayfield-heavy view of the state of mainstream Black music in the '70s and early '80s. Includes: Bring It On: James Brown/(Jump Up on The) Rhythm & Ride: Kool & the Gang/Car Wash: Rose Royce/Shut Up and Dance: The Commodores/Uptown Festival (part one): Shalamar/I Gotcha: Joe Tex/Kung Fu: Curtis Mayfield/Nutbush City Limits: Ike & Tina Turner/Electric Spanking of War Babies: Funkadelic

## FUNK FU—PSYCHO FUNK VS RARE GROOVES 1970–76 (Fu Music -France)

A late-'60s/early-mid-'70s focus ranges through classic funk to brilliant soul, drawn largely from long-lost 45s. Includes: The Kung Fu: Lords of Percussion/Ba-Feet: Tribe/Ain't Nobody Better Than You: Boobie Knight/Bad Bad Woman: Marie Franklin/Music Makes You Move: Funkhouse Express/Funky Thing II: Larry Ellis & the Black Hammer/So It: Sass/Hippy Skippy Moon Street: The Moon People

## FUNK FUNK: THE BEST OF FUNK ESSENTIAL, VOL. 2 (Polygram)

Deceptively strong (if overly familiar) compilation from the Polygram Funk Essentials collection. Volume one, of course, serves up more of the same. Includes: Aquaboogie: Parliament/Funk Funk: Cameo/Let's Have Some Fun: The Bar-Kays/You Dropped a Bomb on Me: The Gap Band/Get Down Baby: Joe Quarterman/Just a Little More, Baby: Barry White/Confunkshunizeya: Con Funk Shun

## FUNKY 8 CORNERS: ALL PLATINUM CLUB CLASSICS (Sequel—UK)

The All-Platinum was another label most often associated with disco and soul, but was equally capable of thrusting some dynamic funk in your face. This collection cherrypicks a few cool jazz cuts from the label's vast catalog, but it's stone funky too. Includes: Funkanova: Wood Brass & Steel/Cosmic Blues: Eddie Fisher/Dance to the Music: The Whatnauts Band/In the Bottle: Brother to Brother/Funk You: BBP/Hypertension: Calender/Dance Girl: the Rimshots/Tons of Dynamite: Frankie Crocker/Is It Funky Enough?: Communicators & Black Experiences Band/Always There: Wood Brass & Steel

## HIP CITY: TALES FROM THE FUNKY SIDE OF TOWN (Harmless—UK)

Amazing trawl through the rarest roots of funk, the odd over-familiar cut more than outweighed by the sheer wealth of hard-to-find gems. Includes: Cadillac Jack: Andre Williams/How You Gonna Get Respect?: Hank Ballard/Funky Walk (part 2): Dyke & The Blazers/Mashed Potato Popcorn (parts 1 & 2): James Brown/Hip City (parts 1 & 2): Jr. Walker/SOUL: S.O.U.L./The Ali Shuffle: Alvin Cash/Funky Hot Pants: Wee Willie Mason

## HOT, FUNKY, & SWEATY: TEN SUPER RARE ORIGINAL FUNK KILLERS FROM
## THE LATE '60S TO THE EARLY '70S (Soul Patrol—France)

Only ten tracks, but every one's a super-rare, superfunked winner. Includes: Bottom of the Bag: Joe Lee/Super Sweet Girl of Mine: Five Miles Out/No Names Will Be Called: Road Runners/Party: Bird Rollins/Cracker Jack: Richard Marks/Hot Funky & Sweaty: The Soul Lifters/Criss Cross: Harold Young & the Magnificents.

## IN YO FACE (Rhino)

The single most ambitious multi-label funk anthology yet attempted by a mainstream record label, the five volumes in this series hit almost all the essential bases, plus a number of less significant (but no less enjoyable) others. The inclusion of several non-funk acts nevertheless performing enjoyable funk songs adds to the series' appeal.

VOL. 1 includes: I Wanna Know If It's Good to You?: Funkadelic/Think (About It): Lyn Collins/Garbage Man: Ike Turner Presents the Family Vibes/Get Up I Feel Like Being like a Sex Machine (Part 1): James Brown/Thank You

Falettinme Be Mice Elf Agin: Sly and the Family Stone/Express Yourself: Charles Wright and the Watts 103rd Street Rhythm Band.

VOL. 2 includes: What Is Hip?: Tower of Power/Person to Person: AWB/Tell Me Something Good: Rufus/Do It ('Til You're Satisfied): B.T. Express/Sexy Ida (part one): Ike & Tina Turner/Pick Up the Pieces: AWB/Shining Star: Earth Wind & Fire/Shakey Ground: The Temptations

VOL. 3 includes: In Time: Sly & the Family Stone/P. Funk (Wants To Get Funked Up): Parliament/Undisco Kidd: Funkadelic/Jungle Boogie: Kool & the Gang/Papa Don't Take No Mess (part one): James Brown/I Get Lifted: George McCrae/Sophisticated Lady (She's a Different Lady): Natalie Cole/Play That Funky Music: Wild Cherry/Get the Funk Out Ma Face: The Brothers Johnson

VOL. 4 includes: Water: Graham Central Station/Shake Your Rump to the Funk: The Bar-Kays/The Pinocchio Theory: Bootsy's Rubber Band/Got To Give It Up (part one): Marvin Gaye/Slide: Slave/Serpentine Fire: Earth Wind & Fire/Reach For It: George Duke/Take Me to the Next Phase (part one): The Isley Brothers

VOL. 5 includes: Take De Funk Off, Fly: The Ohio Players/I Just Want To Be: Cameo/The Same Thing (Makes You Laugh, Makes You Cry): Sly & the Family Stone/Holy Ghost: The Bar-Kays/Bustin' Loose (part one): Chuck Brown and the Soul Searchers/Shake: The Gap Band/Bustin' Out: Rick James/More Bounce to the Ounce (part one): Zapp

## IN YO FACE 1/2 (Rhino)

A companion to the In Yo Face series, detailing some of the lesser known/documented precursors to the main attraction. Includes: Everything I Do Gohn Be Funky (From Now On): Lee Dorsey/Tramp: Lowell Fulsom/Funky Broadway (part one): Dyke & the Blazers/Boogaloo Down Broadway: The Fantastic Johnny C/Spreadin' Honey: The Watts 103rd St. Rhythm Band/Tighten Up: Archie Bell & the Drells/Cissy Strut: The Meters/Mojo Hanna: Tami Lynn

## INVASION OF THE FUNK MASTERS: 12 SUPER RARE FUNK MONSTERS FROM THE '60S & '70S (Soul Patrol—France)

The early-'70s return across 12 solid gold nuggets, which are harder to find than gold itself. Includes: Sissy Walk: Billy Ball & the Upsetters/The Bottom: Duke Payne/Black Out: Wes & the Airedales/Sagittarius Black: Timothy McNealy/Can We Rap: Carleen & the Groovers/Red Beans & Rice: The Collegiates

## KEB DARGE'S LEGENDARY DEEP FUNK VOL 1 (BBE—UK)

Compiled by UK DJ Keb Darge, a peerless collection of indispensible (not to mention impossible to find) funk 45s. Includes: Quit Jive'in: Pearly Queen/Gimme Some Skin: Frank Penn/Zambezi: The Fun Company/Who Dun It: The Originals Orchestra/The First Thing I Do in the Morning: Joyce Williams

## KURTIS BLOW PRESENTS THE HISTORY OF RAP VOL 1: THE GENESIS (Rhino)

A fabulous assortment based upon the turntable hits of the early hip-hop underground. Includes: Melting Pot: Booker T. & the M.G.'s/Listen To Me: Baby Huey/Scorpio: Dennis Coffey & the Detroit Guitar Band/It's Just Begun: The Jimmy Castor Bunch/Apache: Michael Viner's Incredible Bongo Band/Theme from S.W.A.T. (extended 7 version): Rhythm Heritage/King Tim III (Personality Jock): Fatback

## RIDIN LOW: FUNK JAMS (Right Stuff)

Jam-conscious collection marred by its adhesion to the parent EMI label's funk catalog—such as it was. Includes: Dominoes: Donald Byrd/Atomic Dog: George Clinton/No Parking (On the Dance Floor): Midnight Star/Pumpin' It Up: George Clinton and the P-Funk All-Stars/Body Slam!: Bootsy's Rubber Band/Glide: Pleasure/Get Up: Brass Construction/Dog Talk: K-9 Corp

## THE SOUND OF FUNK (Goldmine/Soul Supply—UK)

With the Goldmine/Soul Supply label catering primarily to the British northern soul scene, *The Sound of Funk* series draws its contents from the vast wealth of utter unknowns who circulated on the American funk scene of the early-mid-'70s, but never collected any of the rewards (many of them didn't even make an album). The music is not always of the highest quality and several of the albums can be infuriatingly hit and miss; unwary fans are recommended to try one or two before diving in for the full ten-volume series. For the more heroic, the following are strongly recommended:

VOL. 1 includes: Damph F'Aint': Herb Johnson Settlement/The Sad Chicken: Leroy & the Drivers/How Long Shall I Wait: James Lewis Fields/Searchin' for Soul: Jake Wade & the Soul Searchers/The Push & Pull: Sons of Slum/Take This Woman Off the Corner: James Spencer/Everything's Gonna Be Alright: Robert Moore/The Tramp (part one): The Showmen Inc/ I'm the Man: Chris Jones/The Whip (part one): Al Brown

VOL. 3 includes: I Got a Thing for You Baby: Mr Perculator/Funky Funky Hot Pants: Wee Willie Mason/JB's Latin: Spittin' Image/The New Bump & Twist: The Kats/Hip Drop: The Explosions/Cambell Lock: Don (Soul Train Cambell)/ Funky Soul Shake: ET White & the Potential Band/Hot Pants (Part 1): 20th Century/Closed Mind: Different Bags

VOL. 4 includes: The Funky Buzzard: Little Oscar/The Funky Fat Man: Burnett Bynum and the Soul Invaders/Keep On Brother Keep On: The Fatback Band, featuring Johnny King/Funky Funk: Big Al & the Star Treks/Funky Moon Meditation: The Moonlighters/Wait a Minute: The Xplosions/Do the Funky Donkey: Otis Turner and the Mighty Kingpins/Funky Line Part 1: The Fabulous Shalimars/Funky Hump: Little Joe Cook and the Thrillers

VOL. 8 includes: Check Your Battery: Johnny Talbot/You Lost Your Thing: Hank Johnson/Movin & Groovin': The Volcanoes/The Funky Donkey: The Illusions/Soul Encyclopedia: Geraldine Jones/Jungle: The Young Senators/Village Sound: The Village Sounds/and Funky Jive: The Soul Crusaders Orchestra

VOL. 9 includes: Akiwawa: Village Crusaders/The Funky Mule: Marvin Holmes & the Uptights/Sock It To Me: Henry Moore/Sound Success: Joe Wallis/Funky Wah Wah: Tony La Mar & EU/Cookies: Brother Soul/Number One Prize: Bare Faxx/Do the Train: The Thrillers/Cool It: Guy Morris

VOL. 10 includes: Quit Jivin: Pearly Queen/Pick & Shovel: The Touch/Super Funky: Thunder/Lightning/& Rain/ Rare Back & Stretch: McKinley Sandifer/Soul Block (Of Rocking People): Len & The PA's/Can You Dig It: the Soul Setters/Allen's Party: Allen Matthews/Down Home Publicity: Apple & the 3 Oranges/Man Hunt: Mitzi Ross/Chicken Peck: The Pronouns

## SPIKE'S CHOICE: DESCO FUNK 45S COLLECTION (Desco)

Exploring the latest generation of funk, Desco have maintained a solid blast of funky 45s and albums through the mid-late-'90s, often limited edition efforts that vanish before you even know you need them; runs of 50 are not uncommon. Gathered up onto one CD, the artefact value might not be so high, but the music's still unimpeachable. Includes: In the Middle: The Daktaris/Toothpick: The Mighty Imperials/Cherry Pickin: Sugarman Three/41st Street Breakdown: Naomi Davis/Waiting for the Juice: The Unstoppable S. Robinson/The Matador: Joseph Henry/and Talking About a Good Thing (parts 1 & 2): Naomi Davis & the Knights!

## TIGHTEN UP TIGHTER—A CHOICE COLLECTION OF FUNK 45S (Pure)

Pioneering funk archaeologists Pure unearth some of the mightiest funk sides you've ever not heard . . . unrelenting obscurity is the name of the game, but after one listen you'll wonder how they ever got away. Includes: Hanging Out: James West/La Turbie Piranhienne: Piranha Sounds/Cold Sweat: Brother William/Countdown to Soul: The Explorers/ In the Pocket: Hindal Butts/Soul Dig part 1: The Soul Diggers/Ghetto Boogie: Ellen Jackson Big Star Band/Loaded to the Gills: Michael Liggins

## TOTALLY WIRED (Acid Jazz Records—UK)

Essential listening for anybody anxious to trace the development of the acid jazz scene from its origins in '70s jazz-funk, through to its early-'90s breakthrough. Of a total of 20 volumes in the first series, the following can be considered especially representative.

VOL 1. includes: Theme from Riot on 103rd Street: Mother Earth/Taurus Woman: Subterraneans/That's How It Is: Grand Oral Disceminator/Machine Shop, part 1: Untouchable Machine Shop/Don't You Care: Alice Clark/Believe in Me: Vibraphonic/Change Had Better Come: Dimmond, Mark

VOL 2. includes: Beads, Things & Flowers: Humble Souls/Trinkets and Trash: Coolbeats/Man Called Adam: Break for Jazz/Nzuri Beat: Steve White & Gary Wallis/Gimme One of Those: Brand New Heavies/Killer: Night Trains/Monkey Drop: New Jersey Kings

VOL 3. includes: Dream Come True: Brand New Heavies/Pound to the Dollar: Marron Town/Real Thing: Children of the Ghetto/Rock Hopper: Hip Joints/Let the Good Times Roll: Quiet Boys/Maniteka: Jazz Renegades

VOL 4. includes: Wah Classic: D-Influence/Party Don't Worry About It: New Jersey Queens/Day at the Seaside: Brand New Heavies/Keep It Up: Milton Wright/Break and What: Ne Krew/Ain't No Sunshine: Beaujolais Band/If I Could Make You (Change Your Mine): Terry Callier

VOL 6. includes: Hercules: Aaron Neville/Lesson One: The Stone Cold Boners/Grounded: Gloria Taylor/The Fifth Quadrant: Mother Earth/Just Dream: The Mac Pac/Got To Be Funky: Dread Flimstone/Retro-Active: Too Darn Hot

VOL 8. includes: Keep It Coming: K Collective/Peace and Love: Janette Sewell/Blow White and the Seven Chords: Izit/Free Man: Southshore Commisssion/Be Someone: B#E* Someone/Waves: Serene/Quiet Dawn: Humble Souls

VOL 9. includes: Mr. Jeckle: Beesley's High Vibes/Warlocks of Pendragon: Mother Earth/Dat's Slammin': Robbie Gordon/I Can't Stand It: Brenda George/Electric Soup: Corduroy/That's It: Grass Snakes/Dreams: Raw

## UNITED WE FUNK (Rhino)

An interesting glimpse into the late-'90s funk revival circuit. All the tracks here are performed by modern-day incarnations of the acts in question; most, thankfully, retain at least some understanding of what made them important to begin with. Includes: Party Time (Tricky Mix): UWF All-Stars featuring Roger Troutman/Girls Night Out: The SOS Band/Shake It Easy: Con Funk Shun/She's My Lady: The Dazz Band/Messin with My Flow: The Gap Band/The Way You Shake: The Bar-Kays/Hello: The System/Table Dance: Rick James

## WATTSTAX: THE LIVING WORD (CONCERT MUSIC FROM THE ORIGINAL MOVIE SOUNDTRACK) (Stax)

Two CD set documenting highlights of the all-day Stax label festival in 1972. Isaac Hayes' role in film and soundtrack alike was abridged following disputes regarding the *Shaft* movie copyright, but 17 minutes of "Ain't No Sunshine" are nothing to sneeze at. Besides, the Bar-Kays ensure that the funk quotient remains high, with their own eight-minute "Son of Shaft" an unforgettable highlight. A second volume rounded up more of the same. Includes: Respect Yourself: Staple Singers/Lay Your Loving on Me: Eddie Floyd/I Like What You're Doing (To Me): Carla Thomas/Do the Funky Penguin: Rufus Thomas/Son of Shaft- Feel It: The Bar-Kays/I'll Play the Blues for You: Albert King/Hearsay: Soul Children/Ain't No Sunshine: Isaac Hayes

## WATTSTAX 2 THE LIVING WORD (Stax)

Includes: Peace Be Still: Emotions/Ain't That Loving You for More Reasons than One: David Porter/Stop Doggin' Me: Johnnie Taylor/Walking the Back Streets and Crying: Little Milton/Niggers: Richard Pryor/Watcha See Is Watcha Get: Dramatics/Rolling Down a Mountainside: Isaac Hayes

# ESSENTIAL FUNK: THE TOP 24

An at-a-glance guide to the 24 ten-star-rated albums in this encyclopedia.

Baby Huey & the Babysitters: **Living Legend** (Curtom, 1971) page 73
Bootsy's Rubber Band: **Ahh . . . The Name Is Bootsy, Baby** (WB, 1977) page 108
James Brown: **Live at the Apollo** (King, 1963) page 18
James Brown: **The Payback** (Polydor, 1974) page 19
Digital Underground: **Sex Packets** (Tommy Boy, 1990) page 301
The Fatback Band: **People Music** (Perception, 1973) page 248
Funkadelic: **Funkadelic** (Westbound, 1970) page 94
Graham Central Station: **Graham Central Station** (WB, 1974) page 128
Herbie Hancock: **Future Shock** (Columbia, 1983) page 131
Isaac Hayes: **Hot Buttered Soul** (Enterprise, 1970) page 138
Rick James: **Street Songs** (Gordy, 1981) page 262
Kool & the Gang: **Spirit of the Boogie** (De-Lite, 1975) page 153
The Last Poets: **Last Poets** (Douglas, 1970) page 42
Curtis Mayfield: **Curtis** (Curtom, 1971) page 162
The Meters: **Rejuvenation** (Reprise, 1974) page 168
Parliament: **Funkentelechy vs. the Placebo System** (Casablanca, 1977) page 96
Prince: **Purple Rain** (WB, 1984) page 322
Roger: **The Many Facets of Roger** (WB, 1981) page 335
Sly & the Family Stone: **There's a Riot Going On** (Epic, 1971) page 51
Undisputed Truth: **Face to Face with** (Gordy, 1972) page 189
War: **All Day Music** (UA, 1971) page 192
Barry White: **Stone Gon'** (20th Century, 1973) page 200
The Watts 103rd St. Rhythm Band: **In the Jungle, Babe** (WB, 1969) page 205

Plus one honorable mention:

Chairmen of the Board: **Skin I'm In** (Invictus, 1974) page 143

# GENERAL BIBLIOGRAPHY

Artist specific material is noted following each entry. The following general works were also consulted.

## PRINTED SOURCES

George, Nelson: *Where Did Our Love Go? The Rise and Fall of the Motown Sound* (St Martin's Press, 1985)

George, Nelson: *The Death of Rhythm & Blues* (Plume, 1988)

*Guinness British Hit Singles*, various editions (Guinness)

*Guinness British Hit Albums*, various editions (Guinness)

Larkin, Colin: *Virgin Encyclopedia of R&B and Soul* (Virgin, 1998)

Neely, Tim: *Goldmine Price Guide to 45 RPM Records*, various editions (Krause)

Rees, Daffyd/Crampton, Luke: *VH1 Rock Stars Encyclopedia* (DK Publishing, 1999)

Smith, Suzanne E.: *Dancing in the Street: Motown & the Cultural Politics of Detroit* (Harvard, 1999)

Stapleton, Chris & May: *African Rock: The Pop Music of a Continent* (Obelisk/Dutton, 1990)

Strong, M.C.: *The Great Rock Discography*, various editions (Canongate)

Vincent, Rickey: *Funk: The Music, the People & the Rhythm of the One* (St Martin's Press, 1996)

Whitburn, Joel: *Top R&B Albums/Top Pop Albums/Top R&B Singles/Top Pop Singles*, various editions (Record Research)

## INTERNET SOURCES

This is a tiny sampling of the many funk resources available on the World Wide Web, concentrating upon those most regularly accessed during the research for this book. All Web addresses were correct at press time.

Dusty Grooves: http://www.dustygroove.com—the greatest Internet source of rare, out-of-print and current funk and soul

Funk: Links Central: http://nettown.com/groove.juicer/flc.phtml—the most comprehensive one-stop source for funk links plus listings for rock, soul and more. An unimpeachable resource for collectors and researchers alike.

Miss Funkyflyy: http://go.to/funkyflyy/—Swedish funk journalist/historian Maria "Miss Funkyflyy" Granditsky's archive of funk/R&B interviews, biographies and information

The Motherpage: http://www.duke.edu/~tmc/pfunk.html—massively detailed George Clinton and related site

S.O.U.L. S.Y.S.T.E.M.: http://www.radio101.it/soul/—Italian site with an enormous sample database

WFNK: The Center of the Funk Universe: http://www.wfnk.com—interviews, news, audio, archives

# PHOTO CREDITS

page 5 Wayne Knight Collection/Chansley Entertainment Archives

page 9 ©Raeburn Flerlage/Chansley Entertainment Archives

page 31 Chansley Entertainment Archives

page 48 ©1969 Joe Sia/Chansley Entertainment Archives

page 70 Wayne Knight Collection/Chansley Entertainment Archives

page 85 ©Henry Diltz/Chansley Entertainment Archives

page 104 ©Anastasia Pantsios/Chansley Entertainment Archives

page 111 ©Joe Sia/Chansley Entertainment Archives

page 119 ©Joe Sia/Chansley Entertainment Archives

page 135 Chansley Entertainment Archives

page 150 ©Anastasia Pantsios/ Chansley Entertainment Archives

page 159 Wayne Knight Collection/Chansley Entertainment Archives

page 165 Mathieu Bitton Inc. Archives/Chansley Entertainment Archives

page 172 Wayne Knight Collection/Chansley Entertainment Archives

page 184 Wayne Knight Collection/Chansley Entertainment Archives

page 190 Wayne Knight Collection/Chansley Entertainment Archives

page 221 Wayne Knight Collection/Chansley Entertainment Archives

page 224 Mathieu Bitton Inc. Archives/Chansley Entertainment Archives

page 232 ©Anastasia Pantsios/Chansley Entertainment Archives

page 240 Mathieu Bitton Inc Archives/Chansley Entertainment Archives

page 246 Mathieu Bitton Inc Archives/Chansley Entertainment Archives

page 251 Wayne Knight Collection/Chansley Entertainment Archives

page 260 Michael Ochs Archives

page 266 ©Joe Sia/Chansley Entertainment Archives

page 273 ©Anastasia Pantsios/Chansley Entertainment Archives

page 280 Mathieu Bitton Inc. Archives/Chansley Entertainment Archives

page 298 ©Paul Harris/Chansley Entertainment Archives

page 303 ©Anastasia Pantsios/Chansley Entertainment Archives

page 309 ©Henry Diltz/Chansley Entertainment Archives

page 317 ©Joe Sia/Chansley Entertainment Archives

page 324 ©Henry Diltz/Chansley Entertainment Archives

# INDEX

## A

Abbott, Pete, 71
ABC Records, 181, 268
Abel, Frank, 156
Above Average Black Band, 145, 146
Abrams, Colonel, 317
Ace Records, 57
Acid Jazz Records, 54, 293-295, 296, 309,
    328, 340
Ackroyd, Dan, 15
Act One, 69
Adam, George, 245–249
Adams, Greg, 184
Adams, Jeff, 276
Adams, Mark, 279–281
Adams, Pepper, 80
Adler, Danny, 5, 29, 103, 326–327, 337
Adu, 295
Aerosmith, 91
Africa 70, 37
Aitkens, Ralph "Love," 250
ALA Records, 53–54
Albright, Gerald, 312
Alexander, Dale, 316
Alexander, Fred, 268–271
Alexander, James, 73–77, 136
Ali, Jerome, 275
Ali, Jimmy, 275
All the King's Men, 177
Allen, Charles, 74
Allen, Dale, 171–176
Allen, Frederick, 106
Allen, Rusty, 50
Allen, Tony, 36, 212
Alpert, Herb, 6, 282, 329
A&M Records, 270, 282, 311
Amboy Dukes, 87
American Breed, 181
Anderson, Carleen, 28
Anderson, George, 327
Anderson, Vicki (Myra Barnes), ix, 1–3, 13,
    27, 28, 103, 109, 145, 146, 179, 194
Anderson, William, 242–243
Angelo, Fred, 71
Animals, The, 62, 75
Antonioni, Michelangelo, 129
Apple Records, 141
Arbus, Allan, 211
Archer, J.W., 10
Archie Bell & The Drells, vii, 3–4, 36, 256,
    257, 353, vii
Arista Records, 173, 276, 320
Arnold, Calvin, 29
Arnold, Joe, 43
Aroyewu, Eddie, 36

Arrival, 149
Asch, Les, 2
Ashford & Simpson, 79, 181
Atkins, Mickey, 86
Atlantic Records, 3, 4, 31, 45, 60, 69, 83,
    112, 196, 227, 279, 284
Aubert, Martin, 299–300
Auger, Brian, 71
Augustin, Nat, 314
Aurra, 219–220, 222, 227, 280
Autumn Records, 2, 47, 48, 60
Austin, Lee, 179
Avenue Records, 50
Average White Band (AWB), 69–73, 70p,
    118, 126, 145, 148, 186, 265, 316, 326,
    350, 353
Avery, James, 330–331, 342
Avery, Margaret, 211
Avery, Val, 210
Aware Records, 115
Axiom Funk, 107, 169, 313
Axton, Estelle, 45
Axton, Packy, 43, 45
Ayers, Roy, 38, 129, 211, 220–222, 227, 351
Ayre Rayde, 342
Azteca, 291

## B

B52s, 79
Babette, Bob, 65, 87
Baby Huey & the Babysitters, 71, 73, 116,
    181, 292, 353
Babyface, 199
Bacharach, Burt, 136
Bailey, Leslyn, 106
Bailey, Philip, 120, 237
Bailey, Richard, 126
Baker, Ginger, 37, 38, 333
Baker, James, 169–171
Ball, Roger, 69–73
Ballard, Hank, 3, 43, 103, 146, 179
Bambaataa, Afrika, 15, 107, 246, 258, 313,
    337, 346–347, 349
Band of Gypsies, 61, 62
Bangles, The, 319
Banks, Bubba, 50
Banks, Harvey, 276
Banks, Richards, 276
Bapiste, David, 295, 314
Baraka, Imamu Amiri, 41
Barber, Eddie, 334
Bar-Kays, The, viii, 45, 73–77, 114, 134,
    135, 231, 235, 343, 350, 351, 352, 353,
    355
Barker, Guy, 256

Barnacle, Gary, 309–310
Barnes, Allan, 80–82
Barnes, Myra. See Anderson, Vicki
Ba-Roz, 332
Barr, Eugene, 124–125
Barres, Michael Des, 316
Bartholomew, Simon, 296, 308–310
Bass, Billy, 86, 87, 88, 89
Bass, Fontella, 118
Bassini, Reubens, 173
Batiste, David Russell, 167
Batlett, David, 185
Battle, Alvin, 29
Bautista, Roland, 120
Baynard, James, 242–243
Beale, Michael, 118–124, 119
Bean, Richard, 157
Beane, Harold, 88, 105
Beastie Boys, The, 93, 344, 349
Beatles, The, 6, 30, 49, 60, 66, 74, 118, 119,
    121, 140, 141, 143, 269
Beau Brummels, The, 2, 47
Beau Dollar & The Dapps, 2–3, 29, 103
Beavers, Norman, 268–271
Beck, Jeff, viii, x, 12, 67, 107, 1117, 126,
    140, 214, 215, 236, 237
Beck, William, 173
Becks, Tex, 36
Bee Gees, The, 6, 160, 181, 289
Beggar and Co., 295–296, 306, 314, 339, ix
Beggars Banquet Records, 304
Beinhorn, Michael, 313, 324
Beket Records, 4
Belfield, Dennis, 181–183
Bell, Archie. See Archie Bell & the Drells
Bell, George, 256–259, 257
Bell, Jerry, 244
Bell, Kelvyn, 299–300
Bell, Robert "Kool," 149–155
Bell, Ronald, 149–155
Bell, William, 6, 45
Bell Biv Devoe, 15
Bello, Ganiyu, 306, 314
Benjamin, Benny, 65, 77
Bennett, Bobby, 10
Benson, George, 79, 125, 129, 237, 254, 284
Benson, Ricci, 277
Benton, Jerome, 329
Beresford, Steve, 326
Berger, Ernest, 245–256
Berry, Chuck, 62, 69, 118
Big Boy Myles, 58
Big Brother & the Holding Company, 59,
    185
Birch, Dyan, 148–149

Bishop, Elvin, 130
Biz Markie, 348
Black Nazty, 77, 124
Blackbyrds, The, 80–82, 208, 282, 293, 308
Blackmon, Larry, 231–234
Blackmore, Ritchie, 140
Blakey, Art, 80, 236
Blazers, The. *See* Dyke and the Blazers
Blockheads, 310–311, 340
Blondie, 79, 134
Bloom, Eric, 73
Blow, Kurtis, 331, 344, 347
Blue, Alan, 329
Blue Flames, The, 126
Blue Note Records, 80, 191
Blue Oyster Cult, 73
Bo, Eddie, 58
Boatman, Wes, 107
Bobby Byrd & Pfunk-ness, 1
Bogan, Ann, 169–171
Bogert, Tim, 128
Bohannon, Hamilton, ix, 77–79, 115
Bonner, Leroy "Sugarfoot," 171–176, 348
Booker, James, 55
Booker T., 56, 111, 118, 134, 268, 337
Booker T. & the MGs, vii, 4–8, 5p, 43, 45,
    59, 65, 69, 73, 118, 134, 164, 185, 214,
    283, 337, 350, 353
Bootsy's Rubber Band, ix, 91, 105, 106, 177,
    353
Boughty, Bob, 259
Bowie, Bryon, 299–300
Bowie, David, viii, ix, x, 89, 116, 216, 255,
    266, 340, 348
Bowie, Joseph, 299–300
Bowles, Thomas, 65
Bowman, William. *See* Beau Dollar
Boxtel, Ben, 170
Boyce, Frankie, 86
Boyce, Richard, 86
Boyer, Boni, 319
Boyer, Greg, 91
Boykins, Gene, 84
Bradshaw, Booker, 211
Brailey, Jerome, 90, 91, 141, 274–275, 313
Bramble, Derek, 255, 315
Brand New Heavies, 293, 296–297, 307, 340
Brass Construction, ix, 223–226, 224p, 230,
    234, 242, 258, 278, 279, 339, 351, 353
Bread, 120
Brecker, Michael, 89, 177
Brecker, Randy, 89, 177
Brecker Brothers, The, 89
Breeders, The, 93
Brewster, Anthony, 302
Brick, 226, 243, 290
Brides of Funkenstein, The, ix, The, 106,
    133, 140, 226–228, 252, 275
Brigham, John, 302
Britt, Johnny, 312

Bronson, Charles, 130
Bronson, Gary, 89
Brooklyn Funk Essentials, 297
Brooks, Greg, 319
Brooks, Ron "Monkey-B," 300–302
Brother to Brother, 79–80
Brothers Johnson, The, 33, 128, 130,
    228–230, 254, 266, 353
Brown, Arthur, 312–313
Brown, Chuck, 297–299, 298p, 330, 342,
    343, 345, 346, 351, 353. *See also*
    Chuck Brown and The Soul Searchers
Brown, Errol, 141–142
Brown, Harold, 189–193
Brown, James, vii, ix, 1, 2, 3, 8–27, 9p, 28,
    29, 30, 36, 37, 45, 47, 49, 55, 56, 59,
    60, 61, 64, 69, 70, 80, 88, 103, 104,
    105, 107, 109, 111, 114, 145–148, 151,
    177, 179, 186, 194, 203, 208, 210, 211,
    214, 216, 259, 275, 277, 287, 289, 291,
    293, 297, 298, 304, 316, 320, 323, 334,
    337, 338, 340, 342, 343, 346, 348, 350,
    351, 352, 353,
    1964-70, 11–13
    1970-75, 13–15
    anthologies, 20–21
    early years, 8–11
    LPs, 18–20
    original releases, 20
    RAPP payback 1980-2000, 15–16
    selected samples, 21–27
    singles/chart log, 16–18
Brown, Jim, 211, 212
Brown, Jocelyn, 307
Brown, Kenji Chiba, 276–278
Brown, Lorenzo, 78
Bruce, Christopher, 308
Bryant, Bobby, 120
Bryant, Jason TC, 282
Bryant, Rusty, 124
B.T. Express, ix, 223, 230–231, 242, 278,
    311, 312, 353
Buchanan, John, 298–299
Buchanan, Roy, 185
Buie, Les, 11
Bull & the Matadors, 29
Burch, Vernon, 74
Burdon, Eric, 31, 32, 62, 63, 190, 191, 214
Burke Family, 116
Burns, Sam, 77
Burrage, Ronnie, 299–300
Burton, Michael, 79
Butler, Huey "Billy," 3
Butler, Jerry, 67, 116, 256, 298
Buttacavoli, Ronnie James, 156
Butterfield, Paul, 59
Byars, Brent, 185
Bykowski, Ron, 133
Bynum, Mark, 74, 75
Byrd, Arthur, 103

Byrd, Bobby, 1, 8, 12, 13, 14, 27–29, 28,
    103, 104, 105, 145, 179, 194, 313
Byrd, Byron, 285
Byrd, Donald, viii, 80-82, 129, 220, 282,
    293, 353. *See also* Blackbirds
Byrd, Tony, 28
Byrne, David, 79, 332
Byrne, Jerry, 58
Byzantium, 311

**C**

Caldwell, Joi, 297
Caldwell, Ronnie, 73, 74
Calhoun, Jimmy, 89
Calibre, 303
Callaghan, Andre, 110, 111, 112
Calloway, Reginald, 272–274
Calloway, Vincent, 272–274
Calvin, Billie, 188–189
Cameo, 173, 194, 231–234, 232p, 344, 351,
    352, 353
Cameron, Rafael, 223, 234–235, 278, ix
Cannon, Vince, 212
Capehart, Art, 249–250
Capicorn Records, 304
Capitol Records, 82, 119, 167, 172, 271,
    279, 344
Carabello, Michael, 60
Carbo, Chuck, 58
Cardeas, Mark, 329
Carey, Mack, 330–331
Carlos, Glenn, 84
Carlton, Carl, 257
Carmichael, James, 256–259, 257
Carnegie, Arthur, 270
Carpenter, John, 137
Carpenters, The, 136, 254
Carter, Clarence, 29
Carter, Raymond, 274–275
Carter, Roy, 258, 315
Casey, Bernie, 210
Casey, Harry Wayne "KC," 262–265
Cash, Alvin, 112
Casper, Jackie, 77
Castanell, Amandee, 235–236
Castillo, Emilio, 28, 183–188
Castillo, Jack, 183–188
Castor, Jimmy, 82–84, 245, 351
Cates, Demetrious "Demo," 115
Cauley, Ben, 73–77
Cave, Nick, 93
Chairmen of the Board, 88, 143, 332, 351
Champagne, 316
Chance, James, 300, ix
Chandler, Chas, 31, 61
Chandler, George, 126
Chapman, Gayle, 318
Charles, Ray, 252, 266
Charles Wright & the Watts 103rd Street
    Rhythm Band, 29, 120, 203-206

Chen, Phil, 126
Chepito, 60
Cherry, Don, 337, 348
Chic, 315, 340
Chimes, The, 332
Chocolate Milk, 55, 167, 235–236, 304
Chong, David Lee, 92, 106
Chopmaster, J., 300–302
Chosen Few, The, 2
Christian, Arlester "Dyke," 29–30
Chuck Brown and the Soul Searchers, 297-299, 330, 342–345, 346
Chuck D., 93, 347
Chung, Phil, 305
Churchill, Tony, 169–171
Chyna, 307
Ciner, Al, 181–183
Cioffi, Charles, 209
CJ's Uptown Crew, 343
Clapton, Eric, 69, 71
Clarke, Kim, 300
Clarke, Stanley, 213, 236–239
Clarke-Duke Project, The, 215, 236–239
Clash, The, 337
Clayton, Curt, 75
Cleaves, Jessica, 120
Cliff, Jimmy, 251
Clinton, Cameron, 302
Clinton, George, viii, ix, x, 8, 14, 42, 47, 50, 57, 59, 62, 66, 77, 84–103, 105, 106, 107, 114, 115, 120, 131, 133, 140, 141, 146, 164, 173, 177, 178, 183, 188, 194, 202, 226, 227, 244, 274, 275, 280, 287, 289, 290, 301, 308, 312, 313, 316, 319, 323, 326, 332, 333, 334, 340, 342, 343, 346, 347, 348, 349, 351, 353
  career of, 84–93, 85p
  discography of, 93–94
  LPs of, 94–96
  selected compilations and archive releases, 96–103
Cobham, Billy, 237, 283
Coffey, Dennis, 65, 87, 223, 353
Cohen, Larry, 14, 210
Cohen, Ted, 249–250
Coke La Rock, 346
Cold Blood, 185
Cold Crush Brothers, 346
Cole, Natalie, 273, 353
Coleman, Lisa, 318
Coleman, Robert, 13, 145, 194
Collins, Avon Troy, 27
Collins, Bootsy (William), 1, 3, 13, 14, 16, 28, 42, 71, 88, 89, 90, 103–108, 104p, 128, 130, 133, 140, 141, 145–148, 177, 194, 223, 227, 244, 272, 308, 313, 326, 331, 333–334, 346, 347. *See also* Bootsy's Rubber Band
  career of, 103–107
  singles/LPs, 107-108

Collins, Catfish (Phelps), 13, 88, 91, 103, 106, 107, 145–148, 177, 194, 333–334
Collins, Frank, 148–149
Collins, Lyn, ix, 1, 13, 109-110, 145, 146, 179, 210
Collins, Mel, 148–149
Collins, Phil, 121
Collins, Troy, 8
Coltrane, John, x, 60, 118
Columbia Records, 60, 120, 186, 230, 302
Commodores, The, 64, 67, 90, 110–114, 111p, 121, 244, 255, 296, 317, 350, 351, 352
Complete Strangers, The, 105, 106
Con Funk Shun, 173, 239-242, 240p, 252, 261, 282, 287, 290, 351, 352, 355
Conley, Arthur, 29
Connick, Harry Jr., 167
Conquest, Junie, 116
Conte, Bruce, 185
Contortions, The, 300
Cook, Peter, 12
Cook, Tony, 14, 146
Cool J., 348
Coolidge, Priscilla, 6
Coolidge, Rita, 6
Cooper, Alice, 74, 257
Cooper, Gary "Mudbone," 38, 92, 105
Cooper, Jeffrey, 272–274
Cooper, Michael, 239–242
Cooper, Wayne, 231–234
Cope, Julian, 337, 340, 341
Copeland, Kenny "Captain Cold," 276–278
Copeland, Ruth, 88, 114–115, 143, 215, 332
Corea, Chick, x, 236, 266
Corley, Albert, 10
Cosby, Bill, 204, 207
Counts, The, 78, 115
Cowan, Bennie, 91
Cowen, Carl, 334
Cox, Billy, 61, 141
Cox, Steve, 244
Craig, Marvin, 268–271
Crawford Hubert, 75
Cray, Robert, 44
Cream, 37
Crichton, Billy, 304
Crimes, Russell, 13, 145, 146, 194
Cropper, Steve, 4, 5, 6, 7, 43–44, 45, 73, 135, 185, 186, 214, 283
Cross, Joe, 3
Crown Heights Affair, 242–243, 278
Crum, Tyrone "Flye," 250
Crusaders, The, 127, x
Crutcher, Rodney, 312
Cunningham, Carl, 73, 74, 134
Cunningham, Roy, 73, 74, 75
Cupples, Peter, 284
Curb Records, 75
Curry, Lige, 308

Curtis, Bill, 245–249
Curtis, King, 86
Curtom Records, 73, 116-117, 158, 160, 194, 210, 212, 265, 351
Cymone, Andre (Anderson, Andre), 316, 318

D
Dabbs, Derek, 75
Dabon, Robert, 235–236
Dade Records, 10
Daniels, Marvin, 274–275
Daniels, Nick, 169
Dave O, 244
Davenport, N'dea, 296
Davies, Cyril, 36
Davies, Roy, 126
Davis, Carl, 78
Davis, Charles, 84
Davis, Chester, 330–331
Davis, JC, 10, 11
Davis, Jimmy, 270
Davis, Joseph, 177
Davis, Larry, 256–259
Davis, Leroy, 312–313
Davis, Martha, 50
Davis, Mary, 282
Davis, Miles, x, 60, 165, 293
Davis, Mose, 78, 115
Davis, Raymond, 85, 89
Davis, Tony, 308
Day, Morris, 329–330
Dazz Band, The, 152, 226, 243–245, 290, 355
De La Soul., 348, 349
Decca Records, 82
DeClouet, Theryl, 304
Dedeaux, Richard, 53–54
Dee, Papa, 297
Dee, Ruby, 6
Deee-Lite, 107
Deep Purple, 92, 120
Def Jam Records, 347
Defunkt, ix, 299-300
Deion, 302
Deliberton, Darryl, 276
De-Lite Records, 150
Dell Graham Trio, 126
Dells, The, 105
DeLopez, Joe, 183–188
DeMudd, Pierre, 243–245
Densmore, John, 126
Derrickson, Jerome, 334
DeSanto, Sugar Pie, 109
DeSario, Teri, 263
Devils, The, 180
Dickerson, Dez, 318
Dickey, Gwen, 276–278
Digital Underground, 300-302, 346, 347, 348

Dixie Flyers, 44
Dixon, Darryl, 274–275, 276
DJ Quik, 252
D.M.C., 349
Dobson, Tamara, 210
Dodson, Larry, 74
Doggett, Bill, 103
Dolphy, Eric, 41
Donable, Ernest "Donny," 156
Donald Byrd and the Blackbyrds. *See*
    Blackbyrds; Byrd, Donald
Doncker, Tomas, 300
DoQui, Robert, 211
Dore Records, 189
Dorsey, Lee, 56, 166
Double Agent Rock, 343, 345
Douglas, Carl, 117-118, 126, 287
Douglas, Gordon, 211
Dow, Gary, 231–234
Dowd, Chris, 302–303
Downs, Bobby, 169–171
Dozier, Tim, 279–281
Dr. Funkenstein. *See* Clinton, George
Dr. John (Rebennack, Mac), 55, 56, 57, 164,
    166, 167, 169, 194, 214, 216
Dramatics, The, 45
Drayton, Leslie, 118–124, 119
Dre, Dr., 93, 301, 334
Dru, 107
Drummond, Patrick, 308
Duke, Calvin "Just Duke," 255
Duke, George, 228, 236–239, 327
Dunbar, Ron, 275
Dunbar, Sly, 333. *See also* Sly and Robbie.
Duncan, Andy, 315
Duncan, Malcolm, 69–73
Dunn, Donald "Duck," 6, 7, 43–44, 135
Dunn, Freddie, 276–278
Dunn, Larry, 120, 340
Dunning, Bonnie, 278–279
Dunning, Delores, 278–279
Dunning, Denise, 278–279
Dupree, Cornell, 283–284
Duram, Eric, 231–234
Duran Duran, 47, 71, 315–316, 340
Dury, Ian, 310–311, 340, 348
DutchBlueFunk Records, 300
Dyke & the Blazers, 29-30, 326
Dylan, Bob, 7, 49, 59, 65, 149
Dynamic Superiors, The, 67
D-Zire, 309–310

**E**

Earl, Raymond, 256–259
Earl, Willie, 29
Earland, Charles, 278
Earth Wind & Fire, viii, ix, 29, 62, 74, 81,
    90, 118-124, 119p, 126, 128, 129, 170,
    188, 204, 208, 240, 243, 244, 285, 290,
    309, 317, 318, 340, 351, 353
East West Label, 3

Eastwood, Clint, 6
Easy AD, 346
Edmunds, Bill, 311
Edwards, Bernard, 315–316
Edwards, Gordon, 283–284
Edwards, Richard, 309–310
Eko, Ray Alan, 256
El, Melvin, 274–275
Elektra Records, 80
Elliott, Greg "Sugar Bear," 343
Ellis, Alfred "Pee Wee," 3, 11, 167, 177, 178,
    194
Ellis, Billy R., 282
Ellman, Ben, 304
EMI Records, 126, 284, 323, 325, 338
Emmanuel, LeRoy, 78, 115
Emotions, The, 45, 121
En Vogue, 15
Ensign Records, 295, 306
Enterprise Records, 77, 124, 135, 209, 212
Epic Records, 49, 50, 181, 264
Eric B. & Rakim, 28, 347, 349
Ernie K, 58
Errico, Greg, 48–53
Etienne, Chris, 314
Eurythmics, The, 107, 252
Evans, Brenda, 188–189
Evans, Gil, 236
Evans, Janice, 275
Eve, Mick, 126
Experience Unlimited (EU), 343, 344, 345
Explosions, The, 58

**F**

Fair, Yvonne, 109, 277
Fame, Georgie, 36
Family, The, 319, 347
Famous Flames, The, 10, 11, 27
Fargas, Antonio, 210
Farmer, Julius, 57
Fat Larry's Band, 249–250
Fatback Band, The, 82, 245–249, 246p, 346,
    351, 353
Fats Domino, 55, 56
Faze-O, 174, 250
Fearman, Eric, 243–245
Fears, Bobby Lee, 171–176
Fennell, Skip, 297–299
Ferrone, Steve, 70, 316
Fiddler, Joseph, 308
Fier, Anton, 313
Fifth Dimension, The, 48, 188
Finch, Richard, 262–265
Fink, Matt, 318, 319
Finney, Albert, 67
First Family, The, ix
Fischer, Andre, 181–183
Fishbone, x, 302-33, 303p
Fisher, Martin, 299–300
Fisher, Phillip "Fish," 302–303
Fisher, Tony, 330–331

Fitz, Greg, 276
5 Stairsteps, The 116
Flames, The, 27, 179
Flavor Flav, 93, 347
Flea, 308, 323–326, 323p, 338
Fleetwood, Sherman, 334
Fleming, LeRoy, 298–299
Flemmons, Wade, 118–124, 119
Flippin, Johnny, 245–249
Floyd, Eddie, 45, 171
Flyte Tyme, 316, 318, 329
Fontana, 1
Ford, Frankie, 56, 57
Forest, Peter, 331
Fortran Five, The, 127
Four Tops, The, 64, 66, 86, 87, 188, 311
Fowler, Bernard, 313
Foxx, Joe, 235–236
Foxxe, Andre, 93, 308, 323
Franklin, Aretha, 65, 79, 127, 184, 296
Franklin, Erma, 105
Franklin, Mallia, 90, 105, 140, 275
Franklin, Melvin, 259
Frazer, Dan, 210
Frazier, Sheila, 210, 212
Fred & the New JBs, 146, 194
Frederick, Kevin, 243–245
Freekbass, 107
Freeman, Bobby, 2, 47
Freeman, Charlie, 43–44, 44
Freez, 303-304, 339
Frehley, Ace, 78
Fresh, Doug E., 347
Friends of Distinction, 120, 252
Frusciante, John, 324–325
Frye, Alan, 169–171
Fugees, 122
Fuller, Bobby, 197
Fuller, Cornelius, 3
Fuller, Karl, 239–242
Fulton, Willie James, 184
Fulwood, Tiki, 115, 133, 140
Funk Brothers, The, 65, 69, 85, 128
Funk Deluxe, 234, 278
Funk Inc., 124-125
Funk Revue, ix, 50, 62, 67, 87, 88–89, 90,
    105, 115, 120, 133, 140, 166, 183, 194,
    195, 202, 215, 227, 290, 297, 323, 332,
    334, 338, 351, 352, 353
Funkenstein, vii
Funkmasters, The, 126
Funky 4 + 1, 346
Funky Meters, the, 304
Funky People, 1
Fuze, DJ, 301
Fuzz, 305

**G**

Gadd, Steve, 283–284
Galactic, 304-305
Gale, Eric, 42, 283–284

Galliano, 42, 293, 340
Gamble & Huff, 66, 136, 256, 289
Gamble, Kenny, 3, 4, 198, ix
Gang of 4, ix, x, 337–339, 341
Gant, Kenneth, 272–274
Gap Band, The, 186, 223, 227, 241, 250-
    254, 251p, 261, 282, 351, 353, 355
Garcia, Arcelio, 157
Gardner, Rick, 91
Garibaldi, David, 184
Garland, Judy, 172
Garner, Henry "Hammer," 276–278
Garrett, Robert, 308
Garrett, Siedah, 266, 296
Gas, The, 117, 126
Gasca, Luis, 157
Gaye, Marvin, x, 32, 64, 65, 66, 67, 78, 113,
    173, 188, 202, 271, 290, 353
Geffen Records, 244
Geisman, Ron, 2
Gelder, Nick Van, 309–310
General American Records, 105
Gentry, Melvin, 272–274
George, Barbara, 56
George Duke Quartet, 236
Gerard, Denny, 259
Gerran, Gregory, 298–299
Get, Janos, 299–300
Getz, Stan, 236
Gibbons, Chris, 326
Gibbs, Charles, 3
Gibbs, Melvin, 299–300
Gibson, Andrew, 115
Gilbert, Michael, 110, 112
Gill, Andy, 338–339, ix
Gillette, Mic, 183–188
Girty, Cynthia, 106
Gladys Knight & the Pips, 143, 160, 202,
    350
Godmoma, 106
Goins, Glen, 89, 90, 91, 274, 276, 313
Goins, Kevin, 276
Golden World, 85
Goliath, 181, 265
Gonzalez, 117, 126, 148, 214, 326
Goodin, Rick, 312–313
Gordon, Alison, 304
Gordon, Dexter, 236
Gordon, Gerald, 211
Gordon, Ronnie, 73, 74
Gordy, Berry, 143, 202
Gorrie, Alan, 69–73
Gould, Phil, 340
Goytisolo, Fermin, 262–265
Graham, Jaki, 315
Graham, Johnny, 120, 170
Graham, Larry, 48–53, 50, 126–129, 145,
    320
Graham Central Station, viii, 50, 127–128,
    185, 229, 300, 320, 351, 353
Grandmaster Flash & the Furious Five, 313,

346, 347, 349
Grant, Darryl, 249–250
Grant, David, 315
Grateful Dead, The, 48, 59, 60
Grease Band, 149
Great Society, The, 2, 48, 60
Green Day, 93
Greenberg, Larry, 278–279
Gregory, Steve, 126
Grier, Pam, 211, 220
Griffin, Johnny, 13, 146, 194
Griffith, Richard, 177, 227
Griggs, Johnny, 146
Groove Collective, 300
Gruber, Markus, 178
Guillerman, John, 209
Guishard, Jeff, 256
Gunn, Moses, 209
Gunnels, Clayton "Chicken," 13, 88, 103,
    145–148
Guy, Sherman, 74, 75

**H**

Haden, Charlie, 311
Hagar, Sammy, 185
Hall, Daryl, 216
Hall, James, 170
Hall, Joe, 80–82
Hall, Willie, 6, 73, 74, 136
Hamilton, Anthony, 53–54
Hamlin, Lewis, 11
Hammer, MC, 15, 122, 261, 348
Hammond, Tim, 12
Hampton, Lionel, 220
Hampton, Michael, 105, 312–313, 313
Hancock, Herbie, viii, x, 8, 93, 107, 123,
    129-131, 146, 167, 220, 254, 293, 313
Handa, Yulo, 297
Hannibal Records, 300
Harada, Kuma, 310–311
Harpe, Lisle, 126
Harrell, Paul, 239–242
Harris, Betty, 166
Harris, Bobby, 243–245
Harris, Dean, 330–331
Harris, James "Jimmy Jam" III, 329–330
Harris, Joe, 171–176, 188–189
Harris, Julius, 210, 211
Harrison, Eddie, 134
Harrison, Jerry, 79, 107, 332
Harrison, Keith "Chop Chop," 244, 250,
    255
Harry, Debbie, 79
Hartley, Keef, 126
Haskins, Fuzzy (Clarence), 85, 89, 90, 133-
    134, 275
Hassan, Umar Bin, 41, 313
Hathaway, Donny, 116, 120
Hayden, Shirley, 275
Hayes, Isaac, viii, 6, 14, 43, 45, 66, 57, 74,
    81, 88, 109, 124, 134-139, 135p, 160,

170, 202, 208, 209, 212, 268, 288, 300,
    355
Hazel, Eddie, 62, 86, 87, 88, 90, 91, 107,
    115, 139-141, 227, 274, 275, 313, 331
Hazel, Jimi, 331
Head Hunters, The, 129
Headhunters, The, 293
Heatwave, 113, 130, 229, 245-256, 258, 288,
    289, 315, 339
Heaven 17, 340
Hedding, Tim, 2
Henderson, Ashley, 284
Henderson, Harvey, 73, 74
Hendrix, Jimi, x, 30, 31, 32, 33, 41, 45, 49,
    53, 59, 61, 62, 63, 67, 74, 77, 86, 117,
    140, 159, 182, 203, 214, 343, 346, 347
Hendry, Gloria, 210, 211
Henning, Doug, 120
Henry, Clarence "Frogman," 56
Herman's Hermits, 56, 141
Hi Tension, 256, 289
Hicks, Joe (Abaci Dream), 49
Hicks, Mark, 279–281
High, Martha, 179
Hill, Jack, 211
Hill, Jessie, 56, 57
Hinds, Peter, 306–307, 314
Hobson, Curtin, 77
Hogue, Liz, 312
Holland, Milt, 181
Hollings, Bill, 10
Holmes, Lenny, 274–275
Hopkin, Mary, 141
Hopkins, Telma, 106
Horny Horns, The, ix, 89, 90, 106, 107,
    177–178, 194, 227, 332
Horton, Tim, 75
Horton, Yogi, 79
Hot Chocolate, 127, 141–142, 289
Hot City Bump Band, 142-143, 284
House Guests, The, 105
Houston, Thelma, 67, ix
Houston, Whitney, 194
Hubbard, Freddie, 129
Hubbard, Jerry, 329
Hubbard, Neil, 148–149
Hudson, Lafayette, 156
Hudson, Ronald, 136
Huey Lewis & the News, 186
Huff, Eric, 256–259
Huff, Leon, ix, 3, 4
Hughes, Cleveland, 259
Hughes, Langston, 41
Human Arts Ensemble, 299–300
Humphrey, Eddie, 300–302
Humpty Hump, 301
Hunt, Cecil, 124–125
Hunt, Marsha, 56
Hunte, Gordon, 126
Hunter, Ivy, 87
Hustlers, 180

Hutch, Willie, 202, 277

**I**

Ice Cube, 93, 164, 227
Ice-T, 160
Imagination, 305-306, 314, 339
Impressions, The, 116, 118, 161, 212, 298
Impromp 2, 312
Incognito, 293, 296, 306-308, 314, 327, 339
Incorporated Thang Band, 308
Ingram, Ashley, 305–306
Ingram, James, 199
Innis, Brad, 87
Insiders, 180
Instant Funk, 4, 90, 256-259, 291, 351
Invictus Records, 105, 114, 143–145, 202
Irons, Jack, 323–324
Irwin, Bobby, 326
Island Records, 313, 344
Isley, Ernie, 31–36, 61, 140
Isley, O'Kelly, 30–36
Isley, Ronald, 30–36, 61, 93
Isley, Rudolph, 30–36
Isley, Vernon, 30–36
Isley Brothers, The, 13, 30-36, 31p, 61, 86,
    140, 175, 257, 284, 290, 291, 344, 353

**J**

J Cool, 93
Jackson, Al, 5, 135
Jackson, Eugene, 276
Jackson, Greg, 334
Jackson, LaToya, 186
Jackson, Michael, 15, 75, 86, 229, 254, 296
Jackson, Robert, 169–171
Jackson, Samuel L., 207
Jackson Five, The, 64, 86, 112, 136, 188,
    282
Jacobs, Alvester, 29
Jacobs, Gregory "Shock G.", 300–302
Jacobs, Laurence-Hilton, 212
Jacobs, Pericles, 80–82
Jagger, Mick, 41, 53, 215, 259
Jaguar Records, 75
Jam, 337
Jamerson, James, 65
James, Etta, 11, 118
James, Larry, 249–250
James, Rick, 241, 252, 258, 259-262, 260p,
    272, 282, 317, 318, 348, 349, 351, 353,
    355
James Taylor Quarter, 340
Jamiroquai, 293, 308–310, 309p, 340
Jamison, Daryl, 13, 104, 145
Jane's Addiction, 47
Jankel, Chaz, 149, 319-311, 340, 348
Jarreau, Al, 327
Jasper, Chris, 32
JB Horns, 1, 194
JBs, 3, 9, 13, 28, 36, 69, 88, 104, 105, 109,

145-148, 170, 177, 178, 179, 187, 194,
    210, 292
Jean, Wyclef, 122
Jefferson Airplane, The, vii, 2, 48, 59, 60
Jeliciano, Felipe, 41
Jenkins, Herbie, 84
Jenkins, Tomi, 231–234
Jenkins, Willie, 312–313
Jennings, Ron, 107
Jerry-O, 29
Jobe, Lequient "Duke," 276–278
Joel, Billy, 44
Johannes, Alan, 324
John, Elton, 185, 216, 217
John, Little Willie, 10, 27
John, Prakash, 88
Johns, Eric, 245–256
Johnson, Anthony, 331
Johnson, Curtis, 297–299
Johnson, George, 228–230
Johnson, Gregory, 231–234
Johnson, Howard, 311
Johnson, Jellybean, 316, 329
Johnson, Jesse, 329–330
Johnson, Jimmy, 110, 111, 112, 283
Johnson, JJ, 210
Johnson, Joel, 106
Johnson, Larry, 75
Johnson, Louis, 228–230
Johnson, Peyton, 146
Johnson, Robert, 106, 262–265, 308
Johnson, Terry, 43–44
Jones, Ben, 75
Jones, Billy, 79
Jones, Booker T. *See* Booker T.
Jones, Busta, 338
Jones, Curt, 219–220
Jones, Doug, 249–250
Jones, Elvin, 118
Jones, Gary, 136
Jones, Grace, 227, 344
Jones, Joe Boogaloo, 125
Jones, Kendall, 302–303
Jones, Marshall, 171–176
Jones, Phalon, 73, 74
Jones, Quincy, 54, 182, 199, 228, 229, 252,
    254, 266, 267, 296, 310, 311
Jones, Uriel, 65
Jones, Williams, 255
Jonnes, James Earl III, 282
Joplin, Janis, 59, 60, 185
Jordan, Louis, 8
Jordan, Steve, 7
Joseph, David, 256
Joseph, Ken, 256
Jourgensen, Al, 337
Judkins, Mike, 77
Junior Walker & the All Stars, vii, 5, 64, 68,
    84, 202, 203
Junk Yard Band, 342, 344

**K**

Kain, Gylan, 41
Kansas, 251
Kaplan, Jonathan, 212
Karikari, Kofi, 309–310
Kash, Frankie, 88
Kashif (Jones, Micheal), 230, 311–312
Kay, Jason, 308–310
KC & the Sunshine Band, 127, 151, 262-
    265, 285, 288
K-Doe, Ernie, 56
Keels, Sylvester, 27
Keene, Bob, 203, 204
Keener, Angel, 308
Keitel, Harvey, 120
Kellum, Alphonso, 177
Kelly, Jim, 212
Kelly, Paula, 212
Kemp, Gary, 339
Kendrick, Nat, 10
Kendricks, Eddie, 120
Kennedy, Errol, 305–306
Kennedy, Hershall, 127
Kenner, Chris, 56
Kenny G, 186, 198, 312
Kent, Clark, 346
Kermode, Richard, 157
Khan, Chaka, 33, 71, 73, 116, 128, 181–182,
    188, 199, 222, 223, 251, 265-268,
    282, 292, 307, 318, 319, 320, 351
Kibby, Walter II, 302–303
Kidd, Maxx, 330, 343
Kiddo, 312-313
Kiedis, Anthony, 93, 308, 323–326, 323p
Kilburns, The, 311
Kilgo, Keith, 80–82
Killebrew, Willie, 282
Kincaid, Jan, 296
King, Albert, 45, 74, 90
King, Anna, 1, 27, 28, 109
King, B.B., 120, 228
King, Ben E., 71
King, Earl, 56
King, Evelyn "Champagne," 257, 311
King, Jimmy, 73, 74
King, Johnny, 245–249
King, Jon, 338
King, Marva, 128
King, William, 110, 111
King Biscuit Boy, 55
King Curtis, 61
King Records, 2, 3, 10, 11, 13, 16, 17, 18,
    19, 20, 27, 109, 145, 149, 179
Kirk, Sidney, 136
KISS, 78, 84, 89, 90
Knight, Curtis, 61, 62
Knight, Gladys, 105, 191, 273
Knox, Nash, 27
Kojima, Ian, 259
Kokomo, 148-149
Kool & the Gang, viii, ix, 42, 122, 149–155,

150p , 178, 191, 219, 235, 241, 244, 269, 279, 282, 287, 290, 291, 314, 331, 350, 351, 352, 353
Kool Herc, 346
Koola Lobitos, 36–41
Korner, Alexis, 36
Kotto, Yaphet, 212
Kraftwerk, 289, 337, 343, 346
Krieger, Robbie, 126
Kronlund, Lati, 297
Kung Fu, The, 352
Kupka, Steve, 183–188
Kuti, Fela Ransome, vii, 13, 36-40, 104, 220, 313
Kwanza, vii
Kynard, Charles, 124–125

**L**

Labelle, Patti, ix, 55, 258, 282, 288
LaBes, Larry, 249–250
Lafayette Afro Rock Band, 156-157
Lakeside, 268-270, 351
Lambers, Mary, 319
Lampkin, Tyrone, 88
Lander, Austin, 169–171
LaPread, Ronald, 112
Larkin, Aya, 329
Larkin, Del, 328
Last Poets, The, 36, 41-43, 53, 293, 313, 333, 351
Last Word, The, ix
Laswell, Bill, 40, 93, 107, 131, 141, 169, 274, 276, 300, 313-314, 332–333, 337, 347
Lawal, Fred, 36
Laws, Ronnie, 120
Leak, Maysa, 307
LeBon, Gerald, 278–279
Led Zeppelin, 12, 214
Lee, Carl, 210
Lee, Jimmy, 249–250
Lee, John, 305–306
Lee, Nat, 274–275
Lee, Peter, 284
Lee, Spike, 158, 208; 344
Leeds, Eric, 319
Leftenent, Arnett, 231–234
Leftenent, Nathan, 231–234
Lennon, John, 56, 141, 305
Level 42, ix, 339, 340
Levy, Andrew, 296
Lewis, Andre, 67
Lewis, Elliot, 71
Lewis, Fred, 268–271
Lewis, Linda, 185
Lewis, Mel, 236
Lewis, Pierre, 316
Lewis, Ramsey, x, 32, 120, 121, 122
Lewis, Smiley, 55, 56
Lewis, Terry, 316, 329
Lewis, Tracey, 308

Life, Theodore, 257
Ligertwood, Alex, 71
Light of the World, 149, 217, 295, 305, 306, 314-315, 327, 337, 339
Linscott, Jody, 148–149
Linx, ix, 149, 314-315, 339, ix
Lipscomp, Belinda, 272–274
Little Benny & the Maters, 343, 345
Little Feat, 164, 185, 215
Little Richard, 10, 30, 55, 61, 86
Little Sister, 50
Lively, Juan, 244
Living Colour, 300, 331
L.L. Cool J., 348
Loadstone Records, 48
Lockett, Tom, 279–281
Lockway, James, 332
Lordan, Bill, 50
Loren, Londee, 169–171
Los Latinos, 298
Louie Bellson Orchestra, 19
Love Unlimited Orchestra, ix
Lover, Ed, 301
Lovett, Skitch, 274–275
LTD, 270-271, 282
Lumpkin, Nimrod, 78
Lunch, Lydia, 300
Lund, Art, 210
Lydon, John, 313, 347
Lymon, Frankie, 82
Lynn, Cheryl, 79, 329

**M**

Maas, Peter, 303–304
Mabry, Lynn, 90, 226
MacGregor, Charles, 210, 212
MacMahon, Ed, 211
Mad Lads, The, 45
Maddox, James, 77
Madison, Jimmy, 12
Madison, Louis, 10
Madonna, 319
Maiden, Tony, 181, 265
Malcolm X, 41, 54
Malo, 57, 130, 157-158, 167, 184, 291
Mandrill, 120
Manero, Tony, 287, 290
Mangrum, Raoul Keith, 115
Mansfield-Allen, Ingrid, 304
Mantese, Mario, 245–256
Manuel, Bobby, 6
Mar-Keys, The, 43–44, 45, 73
Marley, Bob, 54, 126
Marsalis, Wynton, 237
Marshall, Arik, 325
Martin, Cedric, 239–242
Martin, Hearlon, 145, 177, 194
Martin, Kenny, 300
Martin, Peter "Sketch," 315
Martin, Skip III, 243–245
Martindale, Winx, 48

Martinez, Cliff, 308, 323
Martini, Jerry, 48, 320
Masekela, Hugh, 59
Mason, Dave, 67
Massive Attack, 340
Material, 300, 313
Mathis, Johnny, 127
Matthews, Artwell, 77
Matthews, Audrey, 77
Matthews, Dave, 12
Matto, Cibo, 297
Maunick, Jean Paul, 306–307, 314
Mayall, John, 126
Mayfield, Curtis, vii, 14, 66, 73, 116, 117, 126, 134, 136, 142, 159p, 185, 191, 194, 202, 208, 210, 211, 265, 268, 334, 337, 350, 351, 352
    career of, 158–161
    LPs/singles/releases, 161-164
Maze, 33, 271-272, 290, 312, 352
MC Breed, 93
MC5, 84, 87
MCA Records, 191, 212, 213
McCain, Tiemeyer, 268–271
McCall, Louis, 239–242
McCalla, Everton, 314
McCartney, Paul, 55, 71, 166
McClain, Marlon, 244
McClary, Thomas, 110, 111, 113
McConnell, Tommy, 278–279
McCreary, Mary, 251
McCullough, Robert, 13, 88, 103, 145–148
McGee, Harvey, 139
McGee, John, 270
McHugh, Paddy, 148–149
McIntosh, Robbie, 69–73
McIntyre, Onnie, 69–73
McJohn, Goldie, 259
McKay, Al, 29, 120
McKinney, Bill, 210
McKinney, Chuck, 142–143
McKinney, Margaret, 142–143
McKinnon, Russ, 252
McKnight, Blackbyrd, 93, 324
McKnight, John, 302
McKreith, Neville, 295, 314
McLaughlin, John, 41, 236
McLean, Paul, 256
McNally, Sam, 284
McNeil, Dee Dee, 53–54
McNeil, Tiger, 71
McWilliams, Paulette, 181, 265
Mel, Melle, 266, 313
Melvin, Harold, 109
Melvoin, Wendy, 318, 319
Mensah, Paapa, 256
Mercer, Chris, 126
Mercury Records, 55, 74, 252
Mesquite, Skip, 183–188
Messina, Joe, 65
Meters, The, 55, 57, 66, 130, 157, 164–168,

165p, 169, 178, 181, 184, 203, 216, 235, 268, 288, 292, 304, 323, 343, 351, 353
Middlebrooks, Ralph, 171–176
MIDI Rain, 304
Midnight Star, 75, 269, 272-274, 273p, 290
Mighty Peacemakers, 343
Miles, Buddy, 41, 61, 62, 67, 90, 141
Miller, Abraham, 270
Miller, Charles, 257
Miller, Dick, 212
Miller, Floyd, 279–281
Miller, Frankie, 164
Miller, Henry, 270
Miller, Kim, 256–259
Miller, Marcus, 344
Miller, Rufus, 183–188
Miller, Scotty, 256–259
Millet, Lil, 58
Mingus, Charles, 41
Minit Records, 56
Miracles, The, 64
Mitchell, Mitch, 62
Modeliste, Zigaboo (Joseph), 164–169, 313
Mohammed, Sultan, 28
Moir, Monte, 329
Mojo Men, The, 2
Monette, Ray, 87
Monk, Thelonious, vii, 149, 259
Montgomery, Tammi (Tammi Terrill), 11
Montgomery, Wes, 129
Moore, Angelo, 302–303
Moore, Billy, 134
Moore, Dudley, 12
Moore, Melba, 311–312
Moore, Michael, 12, 276–278
Moore, Sam, 27
Moore, Stanton, 304
Morgan, John, 13, 145, 194
Morgan, Meli'sa, 312
Morgan, Paul, 303–304
Morgus & the Three Ghouls, 57
Morrison, Junie, 92
Morrison, Walter "Junie," 91, 173, 275
Morrissey, Dick, 71
Mosson, Cordell "Boogie," 88
Mothers Finest, 343
Motown Records, 45, 63, 67, 84, 169, 202, 211, 256, 259, 261, 277, 283
Moyet, Alison, 15
Mtume, 332
Muddy Waters, 118, 214
Muldaur, Maria, 186
Mulkerin, John, 300
Mullen, Dick, 71
Mullen, Jim, 148–149
Muller, Randy, ix, 223–226, 230, 234, 278, 279
Munford, Jimmy, 124–125
Murdock, Shirley, 334
Muriel, Linda, 296, 307

Murphy, Eddie, 261
Murphy, Kevin, 181–183
Murphy, William, 136
Music Machine Records, 143
Mutiny, 274-275
Myers, Alice, 77
Myles, Carolyn, 106

**N**

Napier, Bruce, 173
Nash, Johynny, 126
Nash, Michael, 277
Nassack, Noel, 212
Navarro, Dave, 325
Neal, Robert Jr. "Bip," 250
Nelson, Billy, 115, 139, 140, 141, 313
Nelson, David, 41–42
Neville, Aaron, 56, 164
Neville, Art, 55, 164–169, 169
Neville, Cyril, 164
Neville Brothers, 55, 164, 169
New Birth, 120, 169-171
New Breed, 145
New Power Generation, The (NPG), 320
New Rubber Band, 107
Newman, Floyd, 136
Newmann, Del, 305
Newmark, Andy, 50
Nice, DJ Jazzy, 297
Nicholas, J. Sonny, 259
Nicholas, James Dean "JD," 113, 255
Nichols, Nichell, 212
Nigeria 70, 37
Nightengale, Glenn, 308–310
Nilaja, 41
Nite Liters, 239
Nix, Don, 43–44
Nix, Victor, 276–278
Nixon, Emmett, 330–331
Nocentelli, Leo, 164–169, 178
Nolen, Jimmy, 11, 14, 146, 177
Northbeach Records, 2
Norwalt, Rose (Dickey, Gwen), 277
NPG Records, 320
Numan, Gary, 327, 339
Nuriddim, Jalal, 41
NWA, 164, 349

**O**

Oates, John, 216
O'Dell, Brian, 212
Odell, Roger, 327
Odum, Bernard, 10, 177
Oglesby, Doyle, 27
Ohio Express, viii
Ohio Players, The, ix, 91, 130, 171–176, 172p, 195–196, 231, 233, 250, 263, 279, 287, 290, 316, 334, 348, 349, 351, 353
O'Jays, The, 29, 86, 112, 146, 231, 256, 257,

350, 352
Okeji, Ojo, 36
Olasugba, Isaac, 36
Olewoye, Abiodun, 41–42
O'Malley, Tony, 148–149
Onderlinde, Johnny, 256–259
103rd Street Band, 29
O'Neal, Ron, 210
Orange, Walter, 112
Osborn, Jeffrey, 127, 270
Osbourne, Ozzy, 92
Osibisa, 37, 143
O'Solomon, Otis, 53–54
Ovid Records, 3

**P**

Pacemakers, The, 88
Pacesetters, The, 3, 13, 104, 105, 145, 177, 194, 326
Padron, David, 184
Page, Jimmy, 33, 140
Paisley Park Records, 319
Palanker, Alan, 244
Palmer, Bruce, 259
Palmer, Earl, 55
Palmer, Robert, 55, 164, 166, 216, 315–316, 340
Palmieri, Eddie, 60
Panna, Larry, 57
Pannell, Steve, 275, 308
Parissi, Robert, 285–286
Parker, Charlie, 59
Parker, Christopher, 283–284
Parker, Gene, 44
Parker, Jimmy, 13, 145
Parker, Kellis, 176–178
Parker, Maceo, 11, 13, 15, 16, 89, 105, 106, 107, 145, 146, 167, 178-179, 194, 227, 297, 300, 304, 313, 323, 333, 351
Parker, Melvin, 11, 176–178
Parker, Roger "Dodger," 250
Parkinson, David, 2
Parks, Gordon Jr., 209, 212
Parks, Gordon Sr., 209
Parlet, ix, 90, 106, 140, 275-276, 332
Parliament, 84–88, 89, 90, 91, 105, 114, 133, 140, 143, 194, 202, 215, 231, 233, 235, 259, 275, 282, 290, 323, 332, 338, 346, 351, 352
Parnell, Willie, 3
Pasternak, Jeff, 326
Patillo, Leon, 89
Patra, 109
Patrick, Roscoe, 10
Patterson, Mark, 77
Payne, Freda, 143, 332
Payne, Mike, 308
Pearl Jam, 324
Pedan, Mike, 332
Peers, Ronnie, 284

Pelligro, DH, 324
Pendergrass, Teddy, 33
People Records, 13, 109, 177, 179-180, 194, 351
Perry, Barney, 80–82
Perry, Hubert, 11
Peters, Brock, 211
Peters, Monica, 276
Peterson, Gilles, 293
Peterson, Paul, 329
Pettus, Kenny, 243–245, 244
Petworth, 342, 345
P-Funk, ix, 33, 38, 42, 50, 67, 74, 77, 89–92, 105, 106, 114, 115, 120, 121, 130, 133, 134, 140, 143, 145, 146, 173, 177, 185, 188, 194, 196, 223, 226, 227, 231, 238, 244, 258, 274, 275, 276, 287, 301, 309, 312, 313, 324, 332, 333, 334, 338, 343, 353
Phillips, Paul, 256
Pickett, Lenny, 185–186
Pickett, Wilson, 29, 171
Pierce, Marvin, 173
Pilate, Felton, 239–242
Piller, Eddie, 293
Pinckney, St. Clair, 11, 145, 177
Pink Rhythm, 304
Pinkney, St. Claire, 194
Pitts, Charles, 136
Platt, Howard, 212
Platters, The, 151
Plytas, Nick, 326–327
Poche, Renard, 169
Poff, Joe, 146
Pointer, Bonnie, 140
Pointer Sisters, 56
Poitier, Sidney, 207
Polydor Records, 13, 14, 15, 16, 17, 18, 19, 20, 21, 109, 113, 137, 179, 210, 211, 220
Polygram Records, 227, 352
Poole, Kenny, 12
Pop Group, ix, 337–338, 341
Porter, David, 45
Porter, George, 164–169, 178
Portishead, 340
Positive Force, 247
Potts, Steve, 7
Power Station, 315-316, 340
Prater, David, 27
Praxis, x, 91, 107, 274, 276, 313
Premiers, The, 134
Prescott, Frankie, 79
Presley, Elvis, 14, 83, 170, 197, 228–230, 259
Prestia, Rocca, 183–188
Prestige Records, 124
Preston, Billy, 47, 228, 251, 351
Price, Lloyd, 55, 65
Primal Scream, 44
Primus, 331

Prince, 15, 50, 92, 93, 127, 128, 178, 233, 240, 244, 259, 266, 267, 301, 305, 326, 329, 348
    career of, 316–321, 317p
    LPs/samplings of, 321–323
Prince Conley, 45
Private Eye Records, 261
Professor Longhair (Byrd, Henry Roeland), 55, 56, 57, 58, 166
Progressors, 180
Pryor, Richard., 207
Public Enemy, x, 93, 164, 347, 349
Public Image Ltd. (PIL), 337–338, 341, 347
Pulliam, Fred, 27
Pure Gold, 310
Purim, Flora, 236
P-Vine Records, 107

**Q**

Queen, 251, 339–340, 343, 348
Quicksilver Messenger Service, 63
Qwest Records, 131

**R**

Ragland, Dean, 308
Raines, Jeff, 304
Rakim, 28
Ramsey, James Thomas. See Baby Huey and the Babysitters
Ramsey Lewis Trio, 118
Raoof, Abdul, 282
Rare Earth, x, 66, 67
Rare Essence, 343, 344, 345
Ravalio, Maurizio, 309–310
Raw Fusion, 301
Ray Charles, 30, 296
RCA Records, 169, 170, 306
Rebennack, Mac, See Dr. John
Red Hot Chili Peppers, The, ix, 92, 93, 130, 164, 308, 323–326, 324p, 331, 338, 339
Redding, Otis, x, 6, 44, 45, 48, 59, 73, 116, 134, 203, 292
Redds & the Boys, 344, 345
Reed, Robert, 330–331
Reed, Taylor, 330–331
Reeves, Martha, 64
Refugee Camp Records, 122
Reid, Bert, 242–243
Reid, David, 256
Reid, Raymond, 242–243
Reid, Vernon, 300
Reprise Records, 166, 167, 261
Revolution, 318–319
Revue, The, 1, 19, 109, 179
Reward, 304
Rhino Records, 191
Rhythm King, 344
Richard, Frank, 235–236
Richards, Dwight, 235–236

Richards, Keith, 33, 107, 169
Richardson, Dennis, 256–259, 257
Richie, Lionel. 110, 111, 111p, 112, 113.
    See also Commodores, The
Riley, Billy Lee, 5
Riley, Jake, 270
Riley, Paul, 326
Ritchie, Lionel, 255
Rivkin, Bobby, 318
Rizzo, Pat, 50
Roach, Bobby, 10
Roach, Max, 41, 80
Roberts, Solomon Jr., 278–279
Roberts, Yinka, 36
Robertson, Robbie, 167
Robinson, Cynthia, 48, 227, 320
Robinson, David Alonzo, 330–331
Robinson, Dutch, 171–176, 172
Robinson, Jay, 212
Robinson, Kay, 103, 145
Robinson, Smokey, 84, 112, 202, 261, 342
Rocca, John, 303–304
Rocco, Alex, 212
Rock, Raymond, 242–243
Rogers, DJ, 251
Rogers, Jerome, 312
Rolling Stones, The, viii, ix, 36, 59, 67, 88, 89, 107, 112, 164, 166, 169, 181, 182, 185, 204, 214, 215, 251
Rollins, Sonny, 80
Ronison, John, 182
Roogalator, 314, 326-327, 337
Rose Royce, x, 188, 202, 203, 208, 223, 276-278, 289, 352
Ross, Diana, ix, 64, 79, 113, 136, 188, 288
Ross, Lucius, 115
Ross, Tawl, 87
Roth, Ed, 259
Rotten, Johnny, 337
Roundtree, Richard, 136, 207, 209
Rouse, Rick, 78
Roy Byrd and His Blues Jumpers, 55
Royer, Peter, 306
Rudd, David, 330–331
Ruffin, Jimmy, 202
Rufus, 33, 73, 181-183, 185, 188, 223, 228, 254, 265, 288, 292, 353
Russell, Leon, 251
Ruth, Ella, 296

**S**

S1W, 347
Safford, Wally, 319
Sakamoto, Ryuichi, 107
Salas, Stevie, ix, 107, 257
Salsoul Records, 278, 279, 351
Salt-N-Pepa, 164, 258, 349, 351
Sam & Dave, 45, 134–135
Sam, Robert, 127
Sam and Dave, 27

Sanders, Pharoah, 42
Sanford, Jerome, 13, 145, 194
Santamaria, Mongo, 60
Santana, 57, 59, 60, 61, 63, 71, 121, 130, 151, 157, 185, 186, 271, vii
Santana, Carlos, 33, 59, 127, 157, 319
Santana, Jorge, 157
Santiel, Terral "Powerpack," 276–278
Satchell, Clarence, 171–176
Satellite Records, 45
Saward, Jill, 327
Scabies, Rat, 337
Schloss, Zander, 325
Schumacher, Joel, 342
Scott, Gloria, 47
Scott, Howard, 189–193
Scott, Ronnie, 62
Scott, Roy, 27
Scott, Sherry, 118–124, 119
Scott, Warwick, 329
Scotton, Johnny, 180
Scram Band and Smokey Johnson,The, 58
Seals & Croft, 284
Searles, Paul, 329
Second Image, 339
Segun, 306
Setser, Eddie, 2
Sex Pistols, The, 107, 315, 337
Shady Groove, 342, 345
Shakatak, ix, 314, 327-328
Sharpe, Allan, 126
Sharpe, Bill, 327
Shaw, Charles "Bobo," 299–300
Sheila E. (Sheila Escovedo), 240, 312, 319
Shelby, Thomas Oliver, 268–271
Shelton, Earl, 245–249
Shepp, Archie, 41
Sherman, Jack, 323
Sherrell, Charles, 11, 145, 146
Shider, Gary, 86, 88, 89, 105
Shider, Georger, 308
Shirley Jean and Relations, 179
Shockley, Steve, 268–271
Shore, Sig, 120, 160
Shorter, Wayne, 129
Shrieve, Michael, 60
Sierra, Anibal Anthony, 278–279
Sigler, Bunny, 4, 160
Silva, Dawn, 90, 226, 252
Silver, Horace, 236
Silver Convention, 288, 289
Simmons, Chris, 329
Simmons, William, 272–274
Simon, Calvin, 85, 87, 89
Simpson, John, 282
Skunkhour, 327-329
Skylark, 170
Skyy, ix, 25, 234, 242, 278-279
Slave, 92, 219, 227, , 279–281, 280p, 290, 308, 338, 351, 353
Slave and Crown Heights Affair, ix

Slick, Grace, 2, 48, 60
Slick Rick, 344
Slovak, Hillel, 308, 323–324
Sly, Slick & Wicked, 179
Sly & the Family Stone, vii, 12, 57, 59, 60, 62, 65, 67, 74, 88, 127, 134, 145, 166, 203, 215, 320, 348, 351, 353. See also Stone, Sly
Sly and Robbie, 311, 313, 332. See also Sly Dunbar
Small, Carl, 106
Smith, Bobby, 109
Smith, Chad, 325–326
Smith, Huey "Piano," 55, 56, 58
Smith, Jerome, 262–265
Smith, Jerry Lee "Smoochy," 43–44,
Smith, Jimmy, 56
Smith, Johnny Hammond, 125
Smith, Kevin, 113
Smith, Larry, 74
Smith, Louis, 304
Smith, Nafloyd, 9
Smith, Toby, 308–310
Smith, Will, 348
Snell, Lester, 136
Snoop Doggy Dogg, 93, 252, 261, 334
Snyder, Bob, 43
Solomon, Dave, 326
S.O.S. Band, 194, 241, 252, 261, 282-283, 318, 329
Soul Believers, 3
Soul Searchers. See Chuck Brown and the Soul Searchers
Soul Sonic Force, 346
Spacey T., 302
Spandau Ballet, 295, 305, 314, 315, 339, 341
Sparks, Willie, 127
Spearmints, The, 2
Specialty Records, 164
Speight, Bruno, 282
Speller, Keno, 156
Spellman, Benny, 56
Spenner, Alan, 148–149
Spinners, The, 88, 105, 332
Spradley, David, 106, 308
Spremich, Richard, 157
Spring, Willow, 43–44
Stallworth, Baby Lloyd, 10
Stannard, Terry, 148–149
Stansfield, Lisa, 199
Staples, Mavis, 319
Staple Singers, The, 45, 74, 116
Starks, John, 104, 145, 177, 194
Starr, Edwin, 64, 66, 67, 188, 202, 211, 276
Starrett, Jack, 210
Stax Records, vii, 5, 6, 43, 45–47, 48, 64, 65, 73, 74, 77, 124, 134, 135, 136, 172, 208, 239, 249, 256, 283. See also Volt Records
Steinberg, Lewis, 5

Stennet, Andy, 303–304
Sterling, Donny, 275, 312–313
Stevens, Rick, 184
Stewart, Dave, 107
Stewart, Freddie, 47, 48
Stewart, James, 118
Stewart, Jim, 45
Stewart, Loretta (Stone), 47–53
Stewart, Mark, 337
Stewart, Rod, ix, 6, 33, 185, 214
Stewart, Rose (Stone), 47–53
Stewart, Vaetta (Stone), 47–53
Stewart, Winston, 74, 75
Stewart Brothers, 47
Stiff Records, 326
Sting, 44, 337
Stockers, Ron, 181–183
Stokes, Otis, 268–271
Stone, Sly (Sylvester Stewart), vii, viii, 2, 8, 32, 36, 47-52, 48p, 53, 59, 60, 61, 66, 75, 81, 87, 92, 112, 115, 120, 127, 129, 140, 142, 183, 188, 202, 223, 227, 229, 251, 271, 288, 289, 299, 304, 313, 323, 346, 351
Stone, Trey, 107
Stooges, The, 84, 87
Stotts, Ritchie, 71
Strong, Ollie, 88
Stroud, Don, 211
Strummer, Joe, 324
Stuart, Hamish, 69–73
Stubblefield, Clyde, 11, 177
Stuff, 195, 283-284
Stylistics, The, 120, 185, 288
Stylus, 284-285
Sugar Ray, 157
Sugarhill Gang, 346
Summer, Donna, 89, 126, 287, 288, 289, ix
Summers, Charles, 2
Sun, 258, 285
Sun Ra, x, 4
Supremes, The,64, 65, 86, 197, 268
Sutherland, Dean, 329
Sutherland, Michael, 329
Sweet Charles, 180
Sydor, Bob, 256
Sykes, Brenda, 210
Szabo, Gabor, 257

**T**

Taj Mahal, 60, 167
Taka Boom (Stevens, Yvonne), 188, 219, 222-223, 265, 277
Talking Heads, 78, 79, 107, 227, 332, 338
Tamla Records, 65
Tapscott, Horace, 54
Taylor, Andy, 315–316
Taylor, Clarice, 299–300
Taylor, Gary, 312, 313
Taylor, Gloria, 105
Taylor, James, 32, 67, 178, 293

Taylor, John, 315–316, 340
Taylor, Johnnie, 45, 89, 112
Team, 306
Tee, Richard, 283–284
Tee, Willie, 57
Teenagers, The, 82
Tellez, Pablo, 157
Temperton, Rod, 245–256
Temprees, The, 74
Temptations, The, 32, 64, 65, 66, 67, 80, 85, 87, 112, 136, 140, 143, 188, 202, 259, 261, 276, 353
Tench, Bobby, 117, 126
Terry, Johnny, 8, 27
Tessari, Duccio, 212
Tex, Joe, 55, 57, x
Thelonious Monster, 324–325
Thirkell, John, 309–310
Thomas, Alex, 118–124, 119
Thomas, Carla, 134
Thomas, Danny, 239–242
Thomas, Eddie, 116
Thomas, Fred, 13, 145, 194
Thomas, Gerry, 83, 245–249
Thomas, Grady, 85, 89
Thomas, Greg, 91
Thomas, Irma, 56
Thomas, Larry, 77
Thomas, Luther, 300
Thomas, Peter, 256
Thomas, Phil, 242–243
Thomas, Rufus, 45, 74, 134
Thomas, Tony, 312
Thomas, Wendell, 316
Thompson, Chester, 185
Thompson, Frank, 74, 75
Thompson, Tony, 315–316
Three Dog Night, 181
Tibbets, Ken, 2
Tillery, Donald, 298–299
Time, The, 50, 219, 316, 318, 319, 320, 329-330
Time Zone, 313, 347
Tino, 343
Tio, Mario, 235–236
TK Records, 15
T-Neck Records, 31–32
Toccoa Band, 9, 10
Toles, Michael, 73, 74
Tommy Boy, 301
Toney, Kevin, 80–82
Tonto's Expanding Headband, 64
Tony Toni Tone, 312
Torkanowsky, David, 169
Toussaint, Allen, 55, 56, 181, 352
Tower of Power, 60, 127, 157, 181, 183-188, 184p, 203, 252, 351, 353
Towns, Clarence, 29
Trammps, 256
Treylewd and Flastic Brain Flam, 308
Tribe Called Quest, A, 93

Tricky, 340–341
Trouble Funk, 299, 330-331, 340, 342–345
Troutman, Larry, 333–336
Troutman, Lester, 333–336
Troutman, Roger, 333–336
Troutman, Zapp (Tony), 174, 333–336
Try Me Records, 11
TSOP label, 4
Tubbs, Hubert, 185, 314
Tuff Gong Records, 54
Turkinton, Earl, 57
Turner, Ike, 61, 193, 251, 284, 350, 352, 353
Turner, Tina, 61, 193, 284, 352, 353
24-7 Spyz
  career of, 331
  LPs of, 331–332
2 Live Crew, 344
2Pac, 334
Tympany Five, 8

U
U2, 44, 107
Ultravox, 339
Uncle Jam Records, 50, 313, 334
Undisputed Truth, 64, 67, 173, 188-189, 202, 203, 223, 276, 277
Urban Species, 340
Uwaifo, 36

V
Van Dyke, Earl, 65, 66, 67–68, 87
Van Hook, Pete, 310–311
Van-Dels, 6
Vandross, Luther, 79, 282
Vanilla Fudge, 86, 128
Vaughan, Stevie Ray, 15
Vega, David, 127
Ventura, Lino, 136, 212
Verdine, White, 119
Vibrettes, The, 58
Vicious, Sid, 337
Vickers, Carle, 270
Vincent, Joyce, 106
Visage, 339
Vogel, Rich, 304
Voice, Roger, 170
Volt Records, 5, 45, 48-47, 73. See also Stax Records
VSOP (Very Special One-time Performance), 130

W
Waddy, Frank, 13, 91, 103, 145–148
Walker, Tony, 106
Wansel, Dexter, 257
War, vii, viii, ix, x, 32, 50, 60, 62, 67, 120, 185, 189-193, 190p, 201, 213, 214, 290, 339, 350, 351
Warner Brothers Records, 50, 119, 127, 130, 170, 185, 186, 203, 204, 210, 317, 319,

320, 324, 329, 334
Warriors, 306
Warwick, Dionne, 186, 312
Washington, Chet, 118–124, 119
Washington, Grover, vii, 122, 277
Washington, Jeanette, 90, 275
Washington, Steve, 93, 279–281, 308
Waterhouse, Ted, 78
Watley, Bobby, 124–125
Watson, Boaz, 272–274
Watson, Bobby, 181
Watson, Johnny "Guitar," 304, 352
Watson, Melvin "Wah Wah Watson," 65
Watts, Charles Wright, 29
Watts, Charlie, 327
Watts, LC, 3
Watts Prophets, The, 53-54, 293, 346
Wave, Mico, 107
Weakley, Steve, 124–125
Weaver, Miko, 319
Webb, Jimmy, 135
Webster, Danny, 279–281
Webster, Greg, 171–176, 172
Weeks, Alan, 212
Wellbanks, Norman, 259
Weller, Paul, 337
Wellington, Canute, 295, 314
Wellman, Ricardo, 298–299
Wesley, Fred, 12, 16, 47, 89, 90, 105, 106, 116, 145, 146, 167, 177, 178, 179, 193-195, 208, 210, 211, 227, 233, 276, 313, 323, 333, 346
Westbound Records, 195-196
Western Toppers Band, 36
Westfield, Ricky, 150
Weston, Azzedin, 173
Weston, David, 146
What Is This?, 323
White, Barry, viii, ix, 66, 135, 137, 204, 312, 351, 352
  career of, 196–199
  LPs/singles of, 199–201
White, Charles, 351
White, Claudia, 308
White, Gary, 290
White, Jeff, 120
White, Lenny, 236
White, Leon Huff, 198
White, Maurice, 118–124, 244, 309
White, Michael, 312
White, Robert, 65
White, Verdine, 118–124, 121, 340
Whitehead, Don, 118–124, 119
Whitfield, Norman, 202-203, 223, 252, 268, 276, 289
Whitfield Records, 277
Whitney, Marva, 1, 13, 27, 103, 109, 179, 216
Whitsett, Carson, 6
Whittens, Jesse, 245–256
Widespread Panic, 304

Wiggins, Dwayne, 312
Wild Cherry, 285-286, 316
Wilder, Jerry, 297–299
Wilder, Johnnie, 245–256
Wilder, Keith, 245–256
Wiley, Isaac, 243–245
Wiley, Michael, 243–245
Wilhoite, Orion, 279–281
Williams, Andre Foxxe. *See* Foxxe, Andre
Williams, Bernard, 29
Williams, Charlie, 262–265
Williams, Deniece, 121
Williams, Eldee, 177
Williams, Erskine, 249–250
Williams, George, 245–249
Williams, James "Diamond," 173
Williams, Lenny, 185–186
Williams, Mason, 32
Williams, Milan, 110
Williams, Paul, 306–307, 314
Williams, Phillard, 118–124, 119
Williams, Rose, 87, 332
Williams, Tony, 129
Williams, Tunde, 36
Williamson, Fred, 136, 210, 211, 212
Willie, Pepe, 316, 317
Willis, Eddie, 65
Wilson, Casey, 252
Wilson, Charles, 250–254,334

Wilson, Ernestro, 275
Wilson, Jackie, 65, 113, 118, 288
Wilson, Leslie, 169–171, 170
Wilson, Melvin, 169–171, 170
Wilson, Muki, 242–243
Wilson, Nancy, 259
Wilson, Robert, 250–254
Wilson, Ronnie, 250–254
Wilson, Tony, 141–142
Winter, Keith, 327
Winters, Shelley, 210
Winwood, Stevie, 15, 266
Wise, James, 3
Witherspoon, Jimmy, 191
Wizard Records, 143
Wolinski, Gary, 181
Womack, Bobby, x, 32, 49, 92, 93, 130, 170,
    189, 204, 261, 351
Wonder, Stevie, viii, x, 30, 32, 54, 64, 67, 68,
    77, 112, 130, 181, 204, 215, 228, 252,
    265, 266, 309, 324
Wood, Mark, 268–271
Wood, Ron, 182, 215
Woods, Ren, 212
Woolfolk, Andrew, 120
Worrell, Bernie, 42, 87, 88, 89, 93, 105, 115,
    131, 133, 140, 141, 194, 227, 274, 313,
    332-333, 347
Wright, Debbie, 90, 275

Wright, Nigel, 327
Wyman, Bill, 185, 215
Wynn, Toby, 270
Wynne, Philippe, 88, 92, 105

**Y**

Yarbrough, Cavin, 252
Young, Arthur, 156
Young, Howard, 242–243
Young, Kenny, 311
Young, Le Ron, 297–299
Young, Neil, 7, 32, 259
Young, Starleana, 219–220
Young Disciples, 293
Youngblood, Lonnie, 61

**Z**

Zapp, 92, 174, 333-335, 351, 353
Zappa, Frank, 48, 67, 90, 236
Zarate, Abel, 157
Zender, Steve, 308–310
Zillatron, 107
Zom, John, 300
Zu Zu Band, 57

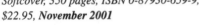